The New York Times

COMPLETE

CIVIL WAR

1861-1865

The New York Times
COMPLETE
CIVIL WAR

1861-1865

EDITED BY
HAROLD HOLZER & CRAIG L. SYMONDS
FOREWORD BY
PRESIDENT BILL CLINTON

BLACK DOG
& LEVENTHAL
PUBLISHERS
NEW YORK

Copyright © 2010 The New York Times

Published by
Black Dog & Leventhal Publishers, Inc.
151 West 19th Street
New York, NY 10011

Distributed by
Workman Publishing Company
225 Varick Street
New York, NY 10014

Manufactured in the USA

Cover and interior design by Sheila Hart Design, Inc.

Cover art: 35 Star West Virginia Statehood Flag, Courtesy Jeff R. Bridgman American Antiques (www.jeffbridgman.com); Colton's new railroad and county map of the United States, 1862, Courtesy of the Library of Congress, Memory Project.

Photo Credits:
All images are courtesy of the Library of Congress, except for the following:
Pages 196, 378, 430, & 435 courtesy of the Louis A. Warren Lincoln Library and Museum, Fort Wayne, Indiana; Page 29 courtesy of the Illinois State Historical Society;
Pages 91, 93, 171, 220, 239, 254, 267, 274, 356, 360, & 390, Frank Leslie's Illustrated Newspaper; Pages 217, 260, 317, 351, & 389, Harper's Weekly.

ISBN-13: 978-1-57912-845-6

hgfedcba

Library of Congress Cataloging-in-Publication Data

The New York times complete Civil War, 1861-1865 / foreword by Bill Clinton ; edited by Harold Holzer and Craig L. Symonds.
    p. cm.
    Includes bibliographical references and index.
    ISBN 978-1-57912-845-6 (alk. paper)
1. United States--History--Civil War, 1861-1865--Sources. 2. United States--History--Civil War, 1861-1865--Personal narratives. 3. United States--History--Civil War, 1861-1865--Press coverage. 4. New York (N.Y.)--History--Civil War, 1861-1865--Press coverage. I. Holzer, Harold. II. Symonds, Craig L. III. New York times.
    E464.N49 2010
    973.7--dc22
                    2010027208

TABLE OF CONTENTS

*Follow The New York Times' coverage of the 150th anniversary of the war, "Disunion: Blogging the Civil War,"
at nytimes.com/opinionator.*

Foreword
BY PRESIDENT BILL CLINTON

This is a book about a war and a newspaper: the Civil War — the bloodiest and most transformative conflict in our history, and The New York Times, which recorded the events of the war and explained them to its vast audience.

In our own age of relentless information and opinion overload from 24-hour television news, talk radio, blogs, Facebook, Twitter, and the World Wide Web, the old-fashioned broadsheet newspaper with its narrow columns and tiny type may seem to be nothing more than a curious antique of limited reach. But such papers managed to elect presidents, propel (or depress) the national economy, sustain wars, and inspire the expansion of human freedom.

During the Civil War era, New York's daily newspapers gave an increasingly diverse population of local readers — native-born New Yorkers, German and Irish immigrants, free African-Americans, and many others — a vivid window into current events and forceful opinions on the most important issues. Their power to inform and persuade also reached well beyond their hometown base, through national editions that reached hundreds of thousands of people from coast to coast, an enormous audience for the period.

This golden age of newspapers did not necessarily guarantee readers greater reliability than the noisy outlets we have today. Unlike today's big urban dailies, nineteenth century papers did not pretend to be neutral and impartial dispensers of information. They were openly and proudly partisan. The New York Herald was the conservative-leaning Democratic paper; The New York Tribune was the paper of the liberal Republicans; and The New York Times was the paper of the establishment Republicans. (Of course, there has been some realignment in the positions of the major parties since Lincoln's time!)

This book vividly reminds us just how strongly the Republican newspapers supported the Union during the Civil War, while the northern Democratic papers questioned and attacked the policies and practices of Lincoln and his administration and those published in the South supported the rebellion and the Confederacy. They were, in effect, the Fox News and MSNBC of their day. The Times, which in modern times has been called the "Gray Lady," was anything but back then.

Even then, however, as this collection shows, The Times pioneered a somewhat different, subtler brand of journalism. Though the paper was unabashedly pro-Republican — its founder, Henry Raymond, had served as the Republican speaker of the State Assembly — The Times promised from the outset of the war to seek truth, avoid extremism, and strive for consensus. At a time when newspapers routinely used the kind of inflammatory language we currently associate with talk radio, this flagship of American dailies all but invented the policy of offering straightforward, temperate, and credible reporting.

Still, its efforts at restraint shouldn't be overstated. Readers who sample this collection — edited by historians Craig Symonds and my friend Harold Holzer — will see that its viewpoint was pro-Union and pro-Lincoln. The Times earnestly supported the war to suppress the Rebellion and, later, cheered the Emancipation Proclamation and the recruitment of African-American soldiers to fight for their own freedom. It condemned weak-kneed Unionism and urged loyalty to the Lincoln administration. Moreover, from the ardor and the emphasis on specific issues evident in the articles, it becomes clear that The Times did more than cheer from the sidelines: it helped spur a sometimes weary North to maintain the struggle to restore the Union and provide the "new birth of freedom" that Abraham Lincoln spoke of so eloquently at Gettysburg. Because there was no live coverage of momentous events, newspapers like The Times gave Americans their only record of the words Lincoln spoke that day. In doing so, it helped create what today we call "the first draft of history."

Presidents of that era held no news conferences or daily briefings. Nor did they employ press and public relations specialists to defend their programs and hone their messages. Instead, they relied on friendly newspapers to print their letters and public statements. Abraham Lincoln made great use of this method of communicating with the American people, thanks in no small measure to The Times.

Times editor Henry Raymond continued running his newspaper even after he assumed the role of chairman of the Republican National Committee and began raising funds for Abraham Lincoln's re-election campaign. There is no modern example of this kind of open political participation by journalists. Imagine the outcry today if the head of one of the major television networks assumed chairmanship of one of the major parties. During the era of the Civil War, such partisanship was not only tolerated, but accepted. Today independent groups issue reports on positive or negative bias in the coverage of candidates and officeholders, while media outlets routinely deny that it exists. Readers of this collection will decide for themselves how effective, responsible, and appropriate the system was then, and whether today's coverage would serve the public better if more media declared their sympathies openly.

For most Americans of the Civil War era, newspapers were the sole source of information — social or political — for a news-hungry population. They were there every morning for a penny or two. Often brilliantly written, they brought the Civil War — with all its terror, grandeur, cruelty, suffering, triumph, and social change — into American homes. They were the eyes and the ears of the people.

The New York Times not only reported these events; it influenced them as well. The first draft of history has never been more passionately presented, nor its role in history more worthy of examination and appreciation.

Introduction

Civilians eagerly reading the latest war news on Broadway in New York City.

THIRTY MILLION AMERICANS lived in the United States during the Civil War. Nearly four million of them began the war as slaves and, by war's end, were free. More than 3.5 million men, black as well as white, served in uniform and fought on the battlefields of that war from Texas to Pennsylvania. For the remaining millions who did not serve, the war ultimately touched nearly every one of them in countless ways. Many had sons, fathers, brothers, cousins, husbands, or sweethearts fighting in the ranks who sent them occasional letters home; some witnessed battles that raged, in a few cases, in their own backyards; Northerners as well as Southerners lost homes and property as cities and towns became military targets. But the vast majority of Northerners experienced the war day to day by reading the country's great newspapers. New York, then as now the publishing center of the nation, boasted more than half a dozen dailies (among some 174 newspapers nationwide), among which three morning papers exerted enormous influence and attracted readers beyond the city's boundaries: James Gordon Bennett's Herald, Horace Greeley's Tribune, and Henry J. Raymond's New York Times.[1] Though newspapers offered the country its principal source of news — the only source for most — editors and reporters in mid-19th century America did not aspire to objective journalism as they do (most of the time) in the 21st century. Papers were expected to maintain a clear and decisive political point of view and reflect it consistently in editorials and news coverage alike. Democrats read Democratic papers, and Republicans read Republican papers, and their respective readers expected no diversity of views in either.

Bennett's Herald was unabashedly Democratic. Bennett himself, who was 61 years old when the war began, was an old Jacksonian who had flirted with the anti-foreigner Know-Nothing movement in the 1850s but returned to "the Democracy" before the war. His paper, with a circulation of 84,000, promoted itself at the time as the most widely read daily in America, a claim The Times once disputed with a rare and savage caricature of Bennett as a horned devil "inflating his well-known, first-class, A-No. 1 Wind-bag Herald." Bennett used his paper to assail Republicans generally, and the administration of President Abraham Lincoln in particular, at nearly every opportunity, though he might dispatch a correspondent to write friendlier stories if they promised to boost readership.

Northern Democrats like Bennett were generally supportive of a war to maintain the Union, but suspicious of any attempt to use the conflict

James Gordon Bennett, founder, editor, and publisher of The New York Herald.

to forward a social agenda, especially if it embraced emancipation, or worse, equal rights for blacks. War for the Union was one thing; war for the black race quite another. As Bennett wrote in 1862: "That the negro should be as free as white men, either at the North or at the South, is out of the question." Bennett was suspicious of Lincoln's emancipationist tendencies, and he was occasionally as vituperative toward the president as the Richmond Enquirer or other Confederate dailies.[2]

On the other side of the political spectrum, Horace Greeley's Tribune had become a liberal Republican paper. That meant that it generally championed the antislavery position, and was often well in advance of Lincoln on the question of emancipation. It was not quite an abolitionist paper like, for example, William Lloyd Garrison's Liberator or Frederick Douglass's Monthly, but when Greeley took Lincoln to task for not being aggressive enough in prosecuting the war or ending slavery, he reached a far larger audience. If Bennett's Herald was the most widely read daily in America, Greeley's Tribune (which reached 200,000 readers nationwide with its weekly edition) may have been the most influential.

The 50-year-old Greeley himself was something of an eccentric who went about New York in every season garbed in a full-length duster and carrying an umbrella. His cheeks were clean-shaven, but he let the white whiskers on his throat grow long and frizzy, giving him the appearance of an old gobbler. A strong supporter of manifest destiny, Greeley had famously urged young Americans to "go west" in 1835. Politically, he generally supported Lincoln and the Republicans, but he also challenged the president on occasion, and aware of Greeley's influence, Lincoln paid attention to what he had to say.

Greeley's politics were somewhat idiosyncratic, however, and occasionally unpredictable. He supported the conservative Edward Bates over the antislavery New York Senator William H. Seward for the 1860 Republican presidential nomination, then tried without success to win Seward's vacant Senate seat for himself after Lincoln made his onetime rival his secretary of state.

It would not be Greeley's only political failure. During the war, he persuaded Lincoln to authorize him to undertake a mission to Niagara Falls to negotiate peace with Confederate emissaries. The adventure proved a debacle. Finally, in 1872, Greeley accepted the Democratic nomination for president to run against the enormously popular President Ulysses S. Grant. Greeley not only lost overwhelmingly, but also became the only candidate in presidential history to die before the electoral votes were officially counted.[3]

In contrast to The Herald and The Tribune (which merged into one paper decades later), The New York Times reflected a centrist position. Its co-owner and editor was Henry Jarvis Raymond (1820–1869), a staunch Republican, who was neither as conservative as Bennett nor

as liberal as Greeley. Born on a farm in the upstate town of Lima, New York (a "poor boy from the country," his obituary stressed), he had graduated from the University of Vermont with high honors at the age of 20 and went to work at once writing for newspapers, including, for a time, Greeley's Tribune. At the tender age of 31, Raymond and a partner, George

Henry Jarvis Raymond, founder and editor of The New York Times.

The first edition of The New York Times was printed on September 18, 1851.

Horace Greeley, founder and editor of The New York Tribune.

Jones, raised $100,000 in pledged capital and formed a new company to establish a third major morning daily in New York. Jones, the largest stockholder, took on the role of publisher and business manager. Raymond, who owned 20 of 89 shares of the paper, became its editor.

Initially the new venture was called The New-York Daily Times, and afterward simply The New-York Times. ("Daily" vanished from the logo in 1857; the hyphen in "New-York" disappeared in 1896.) Founded in 1851 as a pro-Whig paper, but with aspirations to avoid "the advancement of any party, sect, or person," the broadsheet, priced at a penny per issue, or $4 annually by subscription, promised to feature "tales, poetry, biography, the news of the day, editorials upon all subjects of interest, and a variety of interesting and valuable matter." It would be "a family newspaper" committed to "needful reform," yet "conservative." It would try to "allay, rather than excite, agitation," but it would also "inculcate devotion to the Union and the Constitution" and "obedience to law."

The Times's success, however, was by no means automatic. Immediately after Raymond announced its publication, The Tribune threatened local newsdealers that it would cease doing business with them if they dared to carry the new daily. (They defied him.) During the ensuing circulation war, both Greeley and Bennett dispensed rumors that their younger new rival was a dangerous radical.[4]

These harsh responses stemmed not only from the threat of business competition, but of political rivalry as well. Along with many of his fellow editors of the period, Raymond was also an active politician with ambitions not only for his party, but also for himself. Originally an "old Whig of the Seward School," Raymond had served as a New York State Assemblyman — in 1851, the same year he opened The Times, he served as Assembly speaker — and later, from 1855 to 1857, he was New York's "Anti-Nebraska" lieutenant governor (opposed to the controversial Kansas-Nebraska Act, which gave those territories autonomy and the right to decide whether slavery was allowed). For the last-named post he had defeated Greeley himself, ensuring his competitor's lifelong enmity.

Like Lincoln, Raymond abandoned the fading Whig organization to become one of the founding members of his state's new Republican party in the mid-1850s. At the first Republican National Convention in 1856, Raymond was instrumental in writing the new party's founding principles and offered a widely praised speech from the floor. Within only five years, he had thus earned a reputation as both a "great orator" and a "great journalist" who "never absolutely abdicated his real and invisible authority as a writer when he assumed the insignia of a more palpable but a less genuine influence as a politician."[5]

By the dawn of the Civil War, The Times had carved out its own niche in the furiously competitive marketplace for loyal New York readers. Though it still described itself in early 1860 as "the youngest of the daily newspapers of the City," The Times could credibly boast that it had already "become one of the most widely known and most firmly established daily journals of the United States." To be sure, some Republican critics assailed the conservative Raymond for his "thundering orthodoxy"; but others preferred his cautious nature to that of his counterpart at The Tribune. Horace Greeley was perhaps the better natural writer, but he was an inferior editor, for as one admirer wrote, Raymond "did not force, but coaxed, public opinion.... He had the soft answer that turned away wrath." As his associate editor John Swinton recalled, Raymond "was a man of many talents rather than of special genius." Yet this made him "a model editor, a man of mental equipoise, clear-headed, reasonable, ingenious, and genial."[6]

Raymond's Times proved capable of political independence, too — at least at the beginning of the Civil War. Although Raymond had supported Lincoln for president in 1860, he lost patience with the new administration when it failed to act swiftly against secession or to suppress rebellion at once. Less than two weeks after the Confederate attack on Fort Sumter (which The Times, along with most Northerners, including Lincoln, spelled

"Sumpter"), The Times published a scathing editorial that began with the words: "Wanted — a Leader!" Lincoln clipped it along with several similar editorial critiques from the same unsettling period and filed them under the heading "Villainous articles." The president was not pleased.[7]

But relations with the White House improved once Raymond better understood the unprecedented challenges facing the new president (and after he experienced some personal time with the commander-in-chief). After one White House meeting, the editor accepted the president's explanation that he "wished he could get time to attend to the southern question," as Lincoln put it, but for the fact that "the office-seekers demanded all his time." Lincoln, Raymond said, was "like a man so busy in letting rooms in one end of the house, that he can't stop to put out the fire that is burning the other."[8]

Not that Raymond himself did anything to reduce such pressures — quite the opposite. From the beginning of the Lincoln administration, the editor sought to use his political influence to gain jobs for friends and allies. One job-seeker was granted an audience by the State Department simply because, as Lincoln put it, "He has a note from Raymond." Indeed, Raymond asked Lincoln's intervention to secure appointments large and small, both "on public grounds," as he put it in one such plea, and "as a personal favor." Once, when a New York congressman-elect asked Lincoln's help on "a matter of political importance," the president perhaps only half-jokingly urged him to see the editor of The New York Times instead. "Raymond," he said, "is my Lieutenant-General in politics. Whatever he says is right in the premises, shall be done." Those "premises," after all, embraced the largest and wealthiest city in the nation, and Raymond grew in stature, in the words of another newspaper, by sitting "in that editorial chair which has so long swayed the minds of so vast a portion of the mighty multitudes of men that belong to, or are tributary to the heart of the Continent — New York City."[9]

Notwithstanding their common purpose, disputes between Lincoln and Raymond occasionally flared up. When, for example, The Times criticized Lincoln's 1862 proposal for compensated emancipation as too costly, a vexed Lincoln shot off a famous letter to Raymond defending his initiative. "Have you noticed the facts," asked Lincoln, "that less than one half-day's cost of this war would pay for all the slaves in Delaware, at four hundred dollars per head? — that eighty-seven days' cost of this war would pay for all in Delaware, Maryland, District of Columbia,

Wanted—A Leader!

In every great crisis, the human heart demands a leader that incarnates its ideas, its emotions and its aims. Till such a leader appears, everything is disorder, disaster and defeat. The moment he takes the helm, order, promptitude and confidence follow as the necessary result. When we see such results, we know that a hero leads. No such hero at present directs affairs. The experience of our Government for months past has been a series of defeats. It has been one continued retreat. Its path is marked by the wrecks of property destroyed. It has thus far only urged war upon itself. It confidingly enters into compacts with traitors who seek them merely to gain time better to strike a fatal blow. Stung to the quick by the disgraces we have suffered, by the disasters sustained, by the treachery which threatens the annihilation of all order, law, and property, and by the insults heaped upon our National banner, the people have sprung to arms, and demand satisfaction for wounded honor and for violation of laws, which must be vindicated, or we may at once bid farewell to society, to government, and to property, and sink into barbarism.

The spirit evoked within the last fortnight has no parallel since the day of Peter the Hermit. In the last ten days, 100,000 men have sprung to their feet, and, arming and provisioning themselves, are rushing to a contest which can never be quelled till they have triumphed. A holy zeal inspires every loyal heart. To sacrifice comfort, property and life even, is nothing, because if we fail, we must give up these for our children, for humanity, and for ourselves. Where is the leader of this sublime passion? Can the Administration furnish him? We do not question the entire patriotism of every member of it, nor their zeal for the public welfare. The President, in the selection of his Cabinet, very properly regarded the long and efficient services of men in the advocacy of the principles that triumphed in his election. To him the future was seen in the past. But in the few weeks of his official life all past political distinctions have been completely effaced. From a dream of profound peace we awake with our enemy at our throat. Who shall grapple with this foe? Men that can match his activity, quick instincts and physical force. A warrior—not a philosopher; a Cromwell—not a Bacon or a Locke.

Many of the Cabinet, having outlived the hot blood of youth, are vainly attempting to reason with this foe. As well might they oppose a feather to a whirlwind. JEFFERSON DAVIS has surrounded himself with spirits kindred to his own. Think of offering the olive-branch to such men as TOOMBS and WIGFALL. These men are seeking to put a chain about our necks, to secure our humiliation by the destruction of all our national interests, "Our money, or our life, or both."

What are we called upon to defend. The welfare of 19,000,000 of freemen, with everything that render life desirable. Were the selection of the Cabinet to be made to-day, would not the past be entirely forgotten in the present? Would not all party ties be completely effaced?

Is not the Cabinet the representative of the past, instead of the present? Is it not exactly in the frame of mind it was in the day of its appointment? From the first its policy has been purely negative, and cooped up in Washington, surrounded on all sides by a hostile population, it still thinks only of self-defense, and yields to the demands of those seeking its destruction in the measured periods of diplomatic intercourse.

Well may the great heart of the North turn away sickened at such a spectacle. Is this a suitable response to the ardor of youth that rushes to the contest regardless of every consequence, and at the risk of severing every tie that can give grace or charm to life? The hope, and pride, and strength of the country is exposed without plan or forethought for the future, to an able, treacherous and relentless foe. We dread to get the news of the first encounter. We all know how England swayed to and fro under the loss of her best blood in the reckless charge of the light Brigade. How could our more mercurial natures bear up under a similar disaster to the gallant Seventh? It is the duty of the members of the Cabinet to look the thing squarely in the face and conscientiously ask themselves this question: "Are we disqualified from age, from inexperience in Executive action, from constitutional timidity, or from innate reluctance to face the horrors of war, to represent this people and country in this hour of travail?" If not, let them earn the gratitude of the people by giving way courteously to the exigencies of the hour, and laying their ambition on the altar of their country. By a timely act of self-sacrifice they may give relief to the anxious heart of this mighty host of earnest, patriotic men who are unselfishly exposing their lives and fortunes without any other object or motive than their country's honor and welfare,—the relief that follows the knowledge that they are directed by bold, strong and competent men, fitted by sterner natures for this revolutionary epoch of their country's history.

This Times editorial was printed on April 25, 1861.

Kentucky, and Missouri at the same price... Please look at these things, and consider whether there should not be another article in the Times."

Raymond, who had not written the offending editorial himself, quickly saw to the publication of several corrective pieces in the paper. In a personal letter to Lincoln, moreover, he called the compensated emancipation proposal "a master-piece of practical wisdom and sound policy" typical of what he called Lincoln's "plain, self-vindicating, common-sense" approach." Not only did Raymond praise the idea in print as the president requested, he also introduced a resolution in the State Legislature endorsing the idea. For Raymond had returned to the Assembly — and would soon again become Speaker.[10]

Raymond offered further wartime advice after the July 1863 New York City Draft Riots, during which Times shareholder Leonard Walter Jerome (future grandfather of Winston Churchill) took to the roof of the newspaper's headquarters to hold off a mob with a Gatling gun. After order had been restored, and the draft peaceably resumed, Raymond proposed that Lincoln submit the controversial federal conscription law to immediate review by the courts to counter the prevailing impression "that the act is unconstitutional." The editor may well have influenced the prompt — and favorable — judicial review of the nation's new draft laws.[11]

For the most part, Raymond's newspaper remained a consistent champion of the administration and the war. Republican electoral successes and Union battlefield triumphs were invariably headlined as "Glorious News!" Democratic dissent was usually likened to high treason. The editor reliably defended the president from attacks by Bennett on the right and Greeley on the left. Though Greeley regarded Raymond as a "little villain," the Tribune editor later conceded — once Raymond's premature death, just four years after the war, softened the memories of their rivalry — "Abler and stronger men I may have met; a cleverer, readier, more generally efficient journalist, I never saw."[12]

Raymond also grew into a peripatetic personal advocate for the Union and the party. As one example, just two weeks before Lincoln delivered his Gettysburg Address in November 1863, Raymond delivered a pro-war speech of his own in Wilmington, Delaware. In early 1864, a presidential election year, Raymond chaired the New York delegation to the national convention of the newly renamed National Union party, and led the Committee on Resolutions that wrote the party platform calling for a constitutional amendment abolishing slavery. He may have played a role in securing the nomination of conservative Tennessee Senator Andrew Johnson as Abraham Lincoln's vice presidential running mate. Certainly he praised the selection in his editorials. The choice would come back to haunt both the editor and the nation.

By now Raymond had also taken on yet another key political role, the most important of his career: that of chairman of the National Union Executive Committee (the equivalent of today's Republican National Committee). For the 1864 campaign, he also wrote a highly flattering campaign biography titled *History of the Administration of President Lincoln; including His Speeches, Addresses, Letters, Messages and Proclamations; with a Preliminary Sketch of His Life.* Its publisher openly described it as "written with a view to aid President Lincoln's re-nomination," privately confiding: "It cannot fail to have an excellent influence upon everyone who reads it." That publisher, interestingly, referred to his author as "Gov. Raymond," indicating that during the war the editor continued to use the traditional honorific he had earned as the state's antebellum lieutenant governor.[13]

Once the convention chose Lincoln as its nominee in June, Raymond devoted himself, and his paper, to providing "the American people the material for forming an intelligent judgment as to the wisdom of continuing Mr. Lincoln, for four years more, in the Presidential Office." That meant frequent editorials, along with political advice to both his readers and his candidate. When Horace Greeley's Niagara Falls peace initiative collapsed, for instance, Raymond urged the publication of Greeley's correspondence with Lincoln to expose Greeley as a liar for blaming Lincoln for the undertaking's failure. Of course he also no doubt wanted The Times to seize the high ground over The Tribune. Lincoln, however, wanted the letters published only if he could first delete some of Greeley's more incendiary charges about dwindling Northern morale; Greeley refused to authorize the cuts, so Raymond's idea was dropped. "I have concluded that it is better for me to submit, for the time, to the consequences of the false position in which I consider he has placed me," the president explained to Raymond, "than to subject the country to the consequences of publishing these discouraging and injurious parts." Raymond had lost a battle but won a war: he, not Greeley, emerged with the administration's entire confidence.[14]

If Raymond was eager to expose Greeley's willingness to negotiate with the Southern traitors, by the late summer of 1864, he worried that Northern public opinion was turning against the war, and that a clear-cut Union victory was slipping away. In August 1864, he sent the president a brutally frank and politically ominous assessment lamenting Republican prospects in the fast-approaching presidential election, and proposing a peace initiative of his own. Wrote Raymond:

> I am in active correspondence with your staunchest friends in every state and from then all I hear but one report. The tide is turning strongly against us.... Nothing but the most resolute and decided action on the part of the government and its friends, can save the country from falling into hostile hands.... Why would it not be wise, under these circumstances, to appoint a Commissioner, in due form, to make distinct proffers of peace to [Jefferson] Davis, as the head of the rebel armies, on the sole condition of acknowledging the supremacy of the constitution — all other questions to be settled in a convention of the people of all the States?[15]

What Raymond implied, of course, was that in order to get reelected, Lincoln might have to back away from the promise of emancipation. That Lincoln was unwilling to do. He did draft a reply that would have authorized Raymond to seek an armistice under the terms he proposed, but he did so in the conviction that Jefferson Davis and the Confederacy would reject such an overture, and thereby bolster Northern determination. It never came to that. Instead, the cabinet (led by Raymond's particular ally, Secretary of State Seward) urged Lincoln not to make the offer — to Davis *or* to Raymond. Instead, the president met with the entire National Committee at the White House. Arriving "in obvious depression and panic," the party leaders were treated to a briefing and something of a dressing down. Lincoln bluntly told them that "sending a Commission to Richmond would be worse than losing the Presidential contest — it would be ignominiously surrendering it in advance." Though Lincoln had adroitly neutralized Raymond in this instance, the editor and party boss apparently left Washington satisfied, and resumed his active campaigning for the administration in print

— unleashing a stream of pro-Lincoln editorials that masked Raymond's apparent personal yearning for a speedy peace.[16]

The Times's advantages and influence expanded exponentially during the Civil War — and, arguably, because of it. First of all, the paper maintained the strongest connections with the Lincoln administration, which meant its political coverage was authoritative. But it also nurtured a sober style of reporting by a stable of talented and relentless correspondents, plus enviable contacts throughout the country and the world (The Times far outshone its rivals in foreign news). Adding temperate editorializing to its recipe for success, The Times established a major reputation as a source of news and opinion that only grew as the war continued. To some readers, the writing style in this collection will no doubt seem florid and ornamental; but to Civil War–era patrons, it was perhaps the most measured in the field of journalism.

The Times relied on a vast and growing network of sources, including news services it helped create, staff, and manage. During the war, all three New York newspapers also printed official notices provided by the government and public addresses by government officials, but each paper also boasted its own reporters who filed stories from the front — by telegraph if one were available, or by post if necessary. When reporters had access to the military telegraph, they often filed updates on battles as they were in progress. Here, for example, are the reports filed with The New York Times during the Battle of Bull Run, the first engagement of the war, on July 21, 1861, and which appeared in the paper the next day:

11:40. — The fighting is very heavy, and apparently more on our left wing.
11:50. — There is evidently a battle toward our left in the direction of Bull's Run, and a little north. The firing is very rapid and heavy.
1:45. — Heavy guns are heard again, and apparently nearer. The musketry is heavy and nearer.
2 P.M. — The musketry is very heavy and drawing much nearer. There is evidently a movement more to our left.
2:45 P.M — The firing is a little farther off, and apparently in the direction of the Junction. Less heavy guns and more light artillery, as near as I can judge.
3 P.M. — The firing has ceased ten minutes since.[17]

More often, the stories of the fighting at the front reached New York readers in the form of narrative accounts filed by field reporters. Though occasionally it was possible to read these narratives the day after the events took place, a two-day delay often occurred between events at the front in Virginia and the stories that appeared in New York. The delay was greater in the case of events that occurred in the Western Theater — between the Appalachian Mountains and the Mississippi River. The war on the Mississippi was especially remote from New York readers. News about the siege of Vicksburg, for example, had to travel upriver by steamboat to Cairo, Illinois, for several days before it could be sent to New York by telegraph. On one occasion it was further delayed, and rendered almost obsolete, when an assistant of The Times correspondent Franc Wilkie got drunk and allegedly left the reports the correspondent had entrusted to him in a hotel room. Even in the best of circumstances, however, events in "the West" might not be reported in the New York papers for a full week.[18]

Every paper sent reporters into the field. Early in the war, the eager and dedicated Raymond acted as his own correspondent. He accompanied the Union army to Manassas, Virginia, in July 1861 and reported on the battle from there, filing his first dispatch on the pre-battle skirmish that took place along the banks of Bull Run Creek on July 18, 1861. Like most reporters at the time, Raymond described what he observed personally as an eyewitness. He did not interview sources. Generals who tolerated reporters at all were disinclined to grant them interviews. As a result, Raymond's reports were written in the first person, and he often attached himself to a New York regiment, since his readers would want to know what their husbands and sons had done in the battle. The following is representative:

I went out with the centre column. At ten minutes before six we halted about a mile this side of the position of the rebels. The Sixty-ninth and Seventy-ninth Regiments of New-York were thrown to the right, in the woods, and the First and Second Ohio and the Second New-York to the left in advance...."[19]

Like journalists in every era, Raymond and his fellow correspondents worked on tight deadlines. They had to get their stories to the telegraph office in Washington in time to transmit them to the papers in New York for publication early the next morning. As a result, Raymond filed his story on Bull Run early at about 2:15 p.m. on the day of the battle. His dispatch that afternoon read: "I write this at 2 ¼ o'clock, and am compelled to close in order to avail myself of a special messenger to Washington. The fight is still going on with great energy." At that time, the Union was winning the battle, and that was the news that Raymond wired. Alas, 45 minutes after the courier departed, fresh reinforcements from the Confederate army led by Joseph E. Johnston arrived on the field to turn the tide and force a Union retreat, a retreat that soon tuned into an embarrassing rout. Raymond tried to submit an amended report, but it had to wait until he arrived back in the capital. He showed up at the military telegraph office that night "sun-burned, dusty, and hardly recognizable" to file a new story. But the army telegrapher decided that it was not in the national interest to transmit news of a defeat, and would not let him use the army telegraph. Consequently, it was not until July 26, four days later, that The Times carried a full account of the humiliating loss.[20]

Raymond was hardly the only journalist caught short by the events along the banks of Bull Run Creek. All the New York dailies initially reported a Union victory, then had to correct the story later. Raymond decided that his days as a field reporter were over. After that, he sent other men to the front to report the news while he stayed in New York to assemble the paper, which was, after all, the editor's job. But his writers in the field seldom failed him: they wrote quickly, for the most part authoritatively, and almost always evocatively. Their dispatches might offer thrilling accounts of the ebb and flow of distant battles, or features on the everyday life of soldiers: their diets, their frustrations, and their emotional attachment to the Union cause. Raymond supplemented their frontline reporting with editorials that usually ran a day or two after major encounters or political events, assessing each victory or defeat with commentary that not only reflected, but often scripted, the official Republican party line.

The Times could be counted on to reflect administration dissatisfaction with failed commanders, a resolute commitment to the overweening theme of Union and, later, emancipation, hatred of slave owners, the view that Jefferson Davis and other Confederate leaders were traitors, and a deep and abiding hostility to anti-war Democrats. That last category included New York's own Mayor (and later Congressman) Fernando Wood — whose brother owned the anti-Lincoln New York Daily-News, as well as so-called Copperhead activists in other states. There was no pro-secession, pro-Confederate, pro-slavery, or, indeed, anti-Lincoln sentiment to be found on the pages of The Times during the Civil War. Thus, the stories that appear in this collection are undisguisedly, even proudly, biased — just as they would have seemed to the delight of pro-Republican readers of their day.

Raymond's instructions to his correspondents were clear enough: "Don't let anybody croak [lie] in The Times.... Put in as much spice as can be had." And "Uphold Mr. Lincoln always."[21]

Even after he abandoned his brief role as a war correspondent, Raymond did not sequester himself full-time in the paper's lavish, fresco-filled five-story headquarters on New York's "Newspaper Row" — the period name for the cluster of major publishing houses just south of City Hall Park. He still journeyed occasionally to the front or took the train to Washington to see administration officials, including Secretary of State Seward, Secretary of the Treasury Chase and the president himself. It was common understanding that the confidences they shared would not be reported in the paper. Once, Raymond even took on the role of industry lobbyist, traveling to the national capital with other editors to urge the government to repeal or reduce a recently imposed tax on printing paper.[22]

Raymond also traveled to observe the Army of the Potomac on the Virginia Peninsula in mid-1862. And the following January, in response to a sad summons to meet his soldier-brother's corpse in Belle Plain, Virginia, he journeyed down to the remote village on the Potomac Creek. There, to his joy, he found his brother alive and well: the telegraph had garbled the message — the editor had been summoned to visit not his brother's *corpse*, but his *corps*. Happy as he was at this unexpected news, Raymond was horrified at the "state of gloom and discouragement among the officers and soldiers" of Ambrose Burnside's army after its recent defeat at Fredericksburg. The troops had lost confidence in their general, the editor observed, because Burnside "had no confidence in himself." Ever loyal, Raymond confined these observations only to his diary. But he did approach Lincoln at a White House reception a few days later to whisper his concerns about Burnside's rumored successor, Joseph Hooker — whom Raymond and others suspected of harboring dictatorial ambitions. Lincoln reassured him personally. He "put his hand on my shoulders," Raymond later recalled, "and said in my ear, 'Hooker does talk badly; but the trouble is, he is stronger with the country today than any other man.'"[23]

Not even The Times could be everywhere all the time, so occasionally Raymond's newspaper reprinted stories and even editorials from other papers, especially from the West — there was no copyright law then to protect such stories from being copied and reprinted, and most dailies of the time did so routinely. The Times also reprinted stories from some Southern journals. These might present a rare pro-Union or defeatist view from the region, but just as often offer a retrograde defense of slavery or secession, which The Times usually accompanied with an incredulous headline or mocking introductory paragraph. Conversely, stories in The Times were also frequently reprinted in other papers all across the country.

The New York Times building near City Hall was the most elaborate newspaper headquarters in the city.

Most of its original reports came from field correspondents—men (and they were all men) who were embedded (as we would say today) with the army at the front. Some of them became household names, as familiar to readers of The Times as Walter Cronkite became to a later generation of television viewers. There was Lorenzo Livingston Crounse, who reported on the Battles of Chancellorsville and Gettysburg and reveled in pursuing what he called "the single object of getting the news, and getting it first, too," explaining: "In no business in existence is the competition so sharp as between the leading newspapers of New York." There was the "cold-blooded" William Swinton, who once traveled with the army in the company of Raymond, and later covered Gettysburg as well; and George F. Williams, who traveled with Grant's army through the Wilderness and Spotsylvania to Richmond, as well as many others. Sometimes they signed their articles; sometimes they provided only initials (Raymond himself was only "R" or "H. J. R."); and sometimes they employed noms de plume: George H. S. Salter signed his pieces "Jasper"; Franc Banks Wilkie was "Galway," the name of his upstate New York childhood home; and William Conant Church chose the name "Pierrepont." Often their contributions remained entirely unattributed. There was no such thing as an under-the-headline "byline" during the Civil War.[24]

It was not always easy for these reporters to gain the necessary credentials to get to the front lines. Lincoln's personal intervention was required in May 1864 when The Times reporter Edward A. Paul was denied such a pass. "We have had a great deal of difficulty in getting any correspondents into the field for The Times," Raymond huffed, "while special pains seems to have been taken to give the World [an anti-Administration paper], The Herald &c. all possible facilities." Raymond was particularly incensed when Secretary of War Edwin Stanton personally held up Paul's approval (Paul reported that Stanton used "stronger language than is necessary to repeat" to the president), complaining that his "treatment of me in this matter is perfectly inexplicable…. I am not aware of having

ever given him cause for the resentment & hostility he seems to feel towards The Times." Actually, The Times had earlier railed against "the vexatious despotism of the War Department since Mr. Stanton became its chief," and Stanton no doubt held a grudge. History remains unclear about whether Paul ever got his credentials.[25]

But the secretary of war was not the only official in authority to impede the uncensored transmittal of news. The mercurial Union Gen. William T. Sherman made life miserable for nearly every reporter covering his army, and reportedly rejoiced when one of them was captured by Confederates. In September 1864, Maj. Gen. Benjamin F. Butler issued an order to all journalists covering the Army of the James that "there shall be no prognostications, no assertions that you could give news if it were not contraband; no predictions that movements are about to be made that will surprise the enemy or anybody else." Butler perhaps had reason for concern. Earlier that same year, several New York newspapers — though not The Times or The Tribune — had published a bogus presidential proclamation calling for 400,000 fresh Union volunteers. The hoax was designed to enrich Wall Street speculators poised to sell short on the wings of the counterfeit order, but it was quickly exposed. High-speed boats were even successfully sent out from the city's ports to intercept liners carrying the faked news to Europe. One of the reporters responsible for the forgery turned out to be Joseph Howard of The Brooklyn Eagle. Howard had previously worked for The New York Times.[26]

When they could get to the front and do their reporting unobstructed, the lives of wartime correspondents were as adventurous, and occasionally as dangerous, as those of embedded 21st-century reporters in Iraq or Afghanistan. The Tribune reporter Whitelaw Reid recalled an encounter with Crounse of The Times: "A horseman gallops up and hastily dismounts. It is a familiar face — L. L. Crounse, the well-known chief correspondent of the New York Times, with the army of the Potomac. As we exchange hurried salutations, he tells us that he has just returned from a little post-village in Southern Pennsylvania, ten or fifteen miles away; that a fight, of what magnitude he cannot say, is now going on near Gettysburg, between the First corps and some unknown force of the enemy; that Major-General Reynolds is already killed, and that there are rumors of more bad news." Then Crounse and Reid both mounted up to ride toward Gettysburg. Unsurprisingly, perhaps, Crounse had two horses shot from under him during the war.[27]

The "thick-skinned" war correspondent William Swinton (1833–1892) accompanied Grant's army during the decisive Overland Campaign in 1864. He was an indefatigable journalist who often incurred the anger of Union generals who thought him too eager to discover — and to print — stories about the army's movements. After Swinton reported on Burnside's march across the Rappahannock River in January 1863 ("the army was literally stuck in the mud … absolutely helpless"), the general threatened to have him shot. In several of his reports, Swinton kept a running diary

Harper's Weekly illustration from 1864 showing war correspondents interviewing emancipated slaves (left), soldiers (center), and an unidentified man.

recording his impressions hour by hour as the battles in Virginia were being fought, and later relied on that diary to write two acclaimed books: *Twelve Decisive Battles of the War* (1871) and *The History of the Campaigns of the Army of the Potomac* (1882). Henry Ward Beecher said of him, "If any one will know the mechanism and anatomy of battle, let him read our American Napier, William Swinton." It did not hurt that Swinton's brother John was an influential associate editor of The Times. But William more than earned his own reputation (though Herald reporter Henry Villard, for one, thought him a "habitual liar"). Raymond ultimately assigned his star reporter to interview Lincoln himself on his relationship with General McClellan, and to obtain copies of their unpublished correspondence. The editor described William Swinton as "a gentleman of ability & intelligence and fully worthy of any confidence you may place in him." But that did not stop him from leaving the paper by

Times correspondent L. L. Crounse.

1864 for a job with the rival Tribune.[28]

The prototypical Western Theater correspondent Franc Bangs Wilkie beautifully described fresh-faced recruits for whom the war seemed at first "a picnic, a pleasure-trip, a triumphal jaunt through Dixie, with flying banners and beating drums." When Raymond saw one of Wilkie's well-crafted early freelance pieces, The Times hired him for $7.50 per column of type. But Wilkie widened the communications gap between New York and the West by periodically failing to transmit stories (he did not, for instance, file a timely account of the Battle of Wilson's Creek). Raymond nevertheless extravagantly hailed a subsequent contribution as "unparalleled in the history of journalism," and hired him as a full-time correspondent. Wilkie ended up campaigning with Grant for nearly two years. His postwar books included *Pen and Powder* (1888).[29]

Times correspondent Franc Bangs Wilkie.

George Forrester Williams was another daring and intrepid Times reporter. He was so determined to get to the scene of action that during the Battle of the Wilderness in 1864, though he was denied permission by the army's provost marshal to approach the battlefield, he borrowed a horse and rode twelve miles to observe and report on the fighting firsthand. The provost marshal subsequently arrested him and hauled him before General Grant. To the frustration of the provost, Grant declared that the reporter had violated no law, he had merely been resourceful. Then he added: "Your description of the battle, Mr. Williams, was a very good one. I read it with a great deal of interest." After the war Williams wrote *Bullet and Shell: War as the Soldier Saw It* (1884),

Times correspondent Samuel Wilkeson.

though he might have subtitled it: *War as a New York Times Reporter Saw It*.[30]

Arguably no Times reporter endured more danger and sorrow — yet maintained a more professional demeanor — than Samuel Wilkeson, who worked for both The Tribune and The Times, but covered the war's greatest battle, Gettysburg, for the latter paper, knowing that his own son was serving in the ranks of Union forces engaging the Confederate enemy. Once the fighting subsided, he went searching for the boy, only to find him dead. While sitting at his son's grave, Wilkeson wrote the following justly famous lines:

Oh, you dead, who are at Gettysburgh have baptized with your blood the second birth of Freedom in America, how you are to be envied! I rise from a grave whose wet clay I have passionately kissed, and I look up and see Christ spanning this battle-field with his feet and reaching fraternal and lovingly up to heaven. His right hand opens the gates of Paradise — with his left he beckons these mutilated, bloody, swollen forms to ascend.[31]

The articles by these men, and those of many others, form the bulk of this volume. The idea is to allow modern readers to follow the full story of the war as the original readers of the Civil War–era New York Times did from 1861 to 1865. Twenty-five wartime chapters are preceded by a prologue featuring articles covering the major events that led to secession and war; and they are followed by an epilogue containing accounts that carry the story forward through the important postwar period known as Reconstruction. The articles are all reprinted here in the order in which they appeared. For that reason, accounts of the events in the West sometimes appear four, five, or six days after the events themselves. In a few cases, such as during the 1864 Red River campaign in Louisiana, accounts arrived several weeks after the fact.

The emphasis — just as it was in the original editions of the newspaper — remains firmly focused on the military aspect of the Civil War. But the political battles on the home front were seldom far from the lead position of the paper, and they get ample space in this collection, too. Raymond knew that without Republican majorities in Washington and Albany, public and financial support for the Union would evaporate. Consequently, The Times reported avidly on local and national elections alike, not only New York's own, but also assailing Democratic candidates in other states, particularly if they advocated for peace at any price. After Raymond assumed his role as Republican chairman in early 1864, his principal job became defeating Democrats at every level.

On August 27, just days after sending his disobliging letter on the party's prospects and then visiting Lincoln to propose a peace conference, Raymond reiterated to his readers that he was now "deeply impressed with the belief that Mr. Lincoln will be re-elected; and regards the political situation as most hopeful and satisfactory...." To help ensure the victory, he demanded a $500 political contribution from each cabinet secretary. And he proposed assessing the employees of their various departments and tithing workers at the New York Custom House, one of the city's most lucrative patronage mills, to the tune of 3 percent of annual wages. In a letter to government contractors, Raymond blatantly informed them: "I take it for granted you appreciate the necessity of sustaining the government in its contest with rebellion.... Please remit whatever you feel inclined to give in a check, payable to my order as treasurer of the national executive committee. I respectfully ask your immediate attention to this matter, as the need of funds is pressing and the time for using them is short." The dividing line between journalism and politics, if there ever was one, was now totally erased.[32]

By now, Raymond was himself a candidate, too — for the House of Representatives — facing a difficult race of his own in New York's evenly split Eighth Congressional District. Raymond described the candidacies of himself and the president's as representing the conviction that the war must be prosecuted until the "complete and final overthrow of the rebellion." Fundraising was the weapon of choice. Raymond called on Lincoln to sanction active campaigning for money among government workers at the city's post offices and navy yards; Lincoln did nothing to squelch the effort.[33]

Navy Secretary Gideon Welles, for one, resisted Raymond's attempts to pressure employees of his department. Labeling the Times editor "an unscrupulous soldier of fortune," he charged: "He and some of his colleagues are not to be trusted, yet these political vagabonds are the managers of the party." Welles's objections to Raymond's blatant fund-raising were not based entirely on principle. He suspected Raymond at least in part because of the editor's close ties to Welles's cabinet rival William H. Seward. The Navy secretary was convinced that The Times would "attack any and every member of the Cabinet, but Seward." Raymond ultimately journeyed to Washington to plead his case personally to Lincoln at the White House. There, Welles was appalled to find the editor one day speaking "in a low tone of voice" to the president about the lack of party loyalty among the 7,000 employees of the Brooklyn Navy Yard. They should, Raymond brazenly insisted, accept a levy imposed on their wages for the party's use or be fired. Outmaneuvered, Welles reluctantly agreed that the most "obnoxious" foes of the administration at the Brooklyn yard could be dismissed, and shrank away from the meeting, later confiding to his diary: "I am amazed that Raymond could debase himself so far as to submit such a proposition, and more that he expects me to enforce it." To Welles, Raymond's methods represented an "arbitrary and despotic exercise of power." Eventually, some pro-Democratic workers in Brooklyn were indeed fired — but only some 50 of them.[34]

Ultimately, Raymond, like the president, easily won his November election (though Lincoln lost decisively in New York City). Earning 42 percent of the vote in a four-man contest, the editor now became a congressman-elect. Ironically, his victory also hastened his decline; his editorial and political power would never again be so great. By the time Raymond headed to Washington to take his seat in the House in December 1865, his great benefactor Lincoln was dead, and his unpopular successor was splintering the old Republican coalition, while the influential Times languished in the hands of caretaker editors. But then, the great issue of the day — the Civil War — had been settled.

Secretary of the Navy Gideon Welles.

Throughout that war, readers of The New York Times, particularly during election campaigns, were treated to almost daily puff pieces about the Republicans, alongside withering criticisms of the Democrats. But to suggest that The Times featured only war stories and political propaganda would be misleading. Like other broadsheets of the day, it contained reprints of major orations, odd human-interest stories, literary items, business and financial news, reports of public meetings and scientific innovations, crime stories, reviews of art and music, and reports on the comings and goings of the rich and famous — the "early publication of reliable intelligence from both continents," according to its original prospectus. Most of these, the editors have been unable to include in this volume; but we mention them here to give the readers of this book an appreciation of the scope of coverage the paper provided six days a week throughout the war.[35]

It might be added that while The Times and most other newspapers of the period were designed for home-front consumption, the paper also offered soldiers in the field a vital link to the communities they had left behind to fight for the nation. Just as the paper brought news of the war to civilians, it brought civilian news to soldiers as well. In 1864, when The Times and other pro-Republican dailies successfully advocated for the soldiers' right to vote by

Top: A newspaper vendor near a soldier camp in Meade, Virginia, 1863. Bottom: Union General Ambrose E. Burnside reading a newspaper with photographer Mathew B. Brady (nearest tree) at Army of the Potomac headquarters.

absentee ballot if they could not return home on Election Day, the newspaper also became a vital sounding board for campaign politics among the military. Speaking for soldiers and civilians alike, Oliver Wendell Holmes observed early in the war: "If we are rich, we can lay down our carriages, stay away from Newport or Saratoga, and adjourn the trip to Europe *sine die*.... Only *bread and the newspaper* we must have, whatever else we do without."[36]

The American Civil War was the nation's greatest and most traumatic event. Its genesis is covered in a Prologue and its consequences in an Epilogue, but it is the war itself—the bitter, sanguinary conflict that lasted almost exactly four years, from April 1861 to April 1865—that is the centerpiece of this book. To read about it as New Yorkers and other contemporaries did allows a modern reader to gain an entirely new understanding of the complexity of this wrenching conflict. It was not a constant parade of battles, nor was there universal appreciation of the deep channel that the war was carving out for itself. Wars have a tendency to create their own momentum, and the unpredictable and uneven momentum of the Civil War is evident in the pages of The Times.

The national conversation about the relationship of slavery to re-Union, for example, began almost at once and lasted throughout the war and into the Reconstruction era. The understanding of the protocols of war—what today we would call the rules of engagement—changed constantly, too. Lincoln initially declared Confederate privateers to be pirates, and then had to back down from that when Jefferson Davis threatened retaliation. Once Lincoln made the decision to allow black men to serve in the Union Army, Davis asserted that black men under arms would be considered as escaped slaves and would be sold back into slavery, and that their white officers would be treated as guilty of fomenting a slave rebellion and executed on the spot. Other issues, including the treatment of prisoners, the protection of noncombatants, and the legitimacy of targeting factories and farms, emerged as the war progressed. Throughout it all, thoughtful men with various perspectives considered and debated the meaning of these changes in the pages of The New York Times.

The cost of the war, both in dollars and in human lives, astonished everyone. As appalling as the losses in the Battle of First Bull Run in the summer of 1861 seemed at the time, they paled by comparison to the losses at Shiloh in 1862, and those in turn paled in comparison to the killing at Gettysburg. The Overland Campaign in 1864 was a 40-day bloodletting, with no historical antecedent, that foretold the World War I carnage in the trenches of the Western Front from 1915 to 1917. Before the Civil War was over, some 620,000 men lost their lives, and Abraham Lincoln, as The Times reported in detail, became very nearly the last of them.

In editing this volume, the first challenge we faced was selecting from among a truly breathtaking archive—the tens of thousands of stories printed by The Times—those that most accurately revealed the course of events and the shift in attitude provoked by those events. In the end, we chose some 650 articles, editing some of the longer ones down to their central argument. The surgery necessary to do this was painful, but we are convinced that what remains represents the central essence of The Times's reporting of the Civil War. Still, for those who wish to read all the stories in their unedited format, the accompanying disks contain all the raw material. As lengthy as this book is, it could well have been much longer; the enclosed DVD-ROM will allow any interested reader to explore all of the unedited stories in their original format.

To save space, one of the things we were forced to edit was the character of the 19th-century headlines—and Raymond's Times is generally credited with introducing the display headline. During the Civil War, it was common for most important articles to be introduced by as many as a dozen headings and subheadings—"banks" or "decks," as professional journalists call them. In this manner, readers could quickly understand major events as might by glancing at a handbill. As but one daunting example of this tradition, here is the "headline" that led the article printed on July 7, 1863, about the Battle of Gettysburg:

THE GREAT VICTORY.

Gen. Meade's Order of Thanks to the Army.

THE FLIGHT OF THE REBELS.

Lee Reported Fortifying at Newman's Cut, to Protect His Retreat.

The Entire Army of the Potomac in Motion.

Gen. Couch Moving Down from Harrisburgh.

Lee's Retreat Cut Off at the Potomac.

Gen. Meade's Headquarters at Frederick Yesterday.

Rebel Train and Nine Hundred Prisoners Captured by Kilpatrick.

Rather than duplicate all of this, the headline we used in this volume is:

THE GREAT VICTORY.
GEN. MEADE'S ORDER OF THANKS TO THE ARMY.

In the articles themselves, abridged or not, we occasionally indicate the misspelling of a proper name by adding the accurate spelling in brackets. Likewise, the first time an important individual is named in an article, we have had added the first name in brackets. For important historical actors we have provided more detailed information in footnotes at the end of many articles. Otherwise we have retained the original structure and spelling of the articles just as they appeared during the war. The Times spelled Gettysburg and Vicksburg as "Gettysburgh" and "Vicksburgh" and spelled entrenchments as "intrenchments," and we have allowed these to stand, too. Similarly, the paper used capital letters in printing the name of every person it described in print; that practice long ago vanished, but we have retained it here out of respect for the original journalistic convention.

Aside from these minor concessions to modern sensibilities among readers to whom we introduce this material 150 years after the Civil War began, the editors have gratefully allowed The New York Times to speak again for itself. As the following pages will demonstrate, it did so with extraordinary vitality, breadth, and determination.

After Lincoln's death, Raymond wrote a laudatory biography called *The Life and Public Services of Abraham Lincoln* that burnished the martyr's growing legend for an audience beyond even that of The Times. But in his day, Lincoln had expressed similar sentiments about Raymond's newspaper. When Secretary of War Edwin M. Stanton once insisted that he could not issue passes to Times correspondents in advance of those issued to others, Lincoln made clear his undisguised favoritism. "The Times," he wrote, "is always true to the Union, and therefore should be treated at least as well as any other." (See art below.)[37]

The editors hope they have done the same.

NOTES

1. On the eve of war in 1860, the population of the United States was 31,443,321, which included 3,953,760 slaves. Just under 23 million lived in the Union States, and 9.1 million in what would soon become the Confederate States. Of that latter number, more than three million were slaves.

2. The quotation is from The New York Times, December 11, 1861. For Bennett, see Douglas Fermer, *James Gordon Bennett and the New York Herald: A Study of Editorial Opinion in the Civil War Era, 1854–1867* (London: Royal Historical Society, 1986).

3. For Greeley, see Robert C. Williams, *Horace Greeley: Champion of American Freedom* (New York: New York University Press, 2006). Also worthwhile is Greeley's autobiography: *Horace Greeley, Recollections of a Busy Life* (New York: J. B. Ford, 1868).

4. Augustus Maverick, *Henry J. Raymond and the New York Press for Thirty Years* (Hartford, Conn.: A. S. Hale & Co., 1870), 94–95.

5. Obituary of Henry J. Raymond in The New York Times, June 21, 1869; Alexander K. McClure, *Recollections of Half a Century* (Salem, Mass.: The Salem Press, 1902).

6. New York Sun, March 2, 1860; New–York Times, June 21, 1869; John Swinton, "The New York Daily Papers and the Editors," Part 2, *The Independent* (Jan 25, 1900), 237–238.

7. The full article, dated April 25, 1861, is reproduced in Chapter 3 and a facsimile appears on page 10. Historian David Herbert Donald described Lincoln as "wounded" by this and similar editorial attacks. See Donald, "Sixteenth President Wrote His Own Book on Leadership," in David Herbert Donald and Harold Holzer, eds., *Lincoln in the Times: The Life of Abraham Lincoln as Originally Reported in the New York Times* (New York: St. Martin's Press, 2005), 1.

8. Henry J. Raymond, *The Life and Public Services of Abraham Lincoln* (New York: Derby & Miller, 1865), 720.

This endorsement from President Lincoln—and the subsequent comments by Secretary of War Edwin M. Stanton—came after Times correspondent E.A. Paul complained that he had been refused a pass from the War Department to cover General Grant's army in the field. Paul demanded that "The Times be placed on an equal footing with other loyal papers."

The Times I believe is always true to the Union, and therefore should be treated at least as well as any.

A. Lincoln
May 24. 1864

Respectfully returned to the President. The Times is treated by this Department precisely as other papers are treated. No pass is granted by the Department to any paper except upon the permission of General Grant or General Meade. The Repeated application by Mr Forney and by other Editors have been refused on the same ground as the Times until the correspondent is approved by the Commanding General. This is the regulation of all the armies and the Secretary of War declines to do for the Times what is not done for other papers.

Edwin M. Stanton
May 24. 1864

P. S. Since writing the above I perceive a paper purporting to be a pass from Beckwith which I have not before seen. It was shown to Col Hardie who refused to approve it on account of the condition of the army & transportation. I think he did right & that as soon as it is known where the army is a pass may be given if authorised by General Meade or Grant but not without their express or personal authority.

Edwin M. Stanton
Sec of War

9. On the irony of Raymond's efforts to influence the patronage, The Times had insisted that the President "owes a higher duty to the country...than to fritter away the priceless opportunities of the Presidency in listening to the appeals of competing office–hunters" (April 4, 1861). For the endorsement of an office seeker, see Lincoln to William H. Seward, June 8, 1861, in Roy P. Basler, ed., *The Collected Works of Abraham Lincoln*, 8 vols., hereinafter cited as *Collected Works* (New Brunswick, NJ: Rutgers University Press, 1953), 4:397; Raymond to Lincoln, January 16, 1862, Abraham Lincoln Papers, Library of Congress; Francis B. Carpenter, "Anecdotes and Reminiscences," quoted in Raymond, *Life and Public Services of Lincoln*, 758; *Washington Intelligencer* quoted in The New York Times, June 21, 1869.

10. Lincoln to Raymond, March 9, 1862, in *Collected Works*, 5:152–3; Raymond to Lincoln, March 15, 1862, Abraham Lincoln Papers, Library of Congress.

11. Raymond to Lincoln, July 19, 1863, Abraham Lincoln Papers, Library of Congress.

12. The New York Times, June 6, 1869; J. Cutler Andrews, *The North Reports the Civil War* (Pittsburgh: University of Pittsburgh Press, 1985), 11.

13. J. C. Derby to John Nicolay, April 11, May 5, February 24, and March 22, 1864, all in John G. Nicolay Papers, Library of Congress.

14. Raymond, *Life and Public Services of Lincoln*, 5; Lincoln to Raymond, August 15, 1864, *Collected Works*, 7:494.

15. Raymond to Lincoln, August 22, 1864, Abraham Lincoln Papers, Library of Congress.

16. Lincoln's handwritten draft authorization for Raymond's peace mission, dated August 24, 1864, is in *Collected* Works, 8:517. See also, John G. Nicolay and John Hay, *Abraham Lincoln, A History*, 10 vols. (New York: The Century Company, 1890), 9:219

17. See the full entry in chapter 4.

18. Franc Wilkie, *Pen and Powder* (1888), quoted in Louis M. Starr, *The Bohemian Brigade: Civil War Newsmen in Action* (Madison: University of Wisconsin Press, 1954), 239.

19. See the full entry in Chapter 4.

20. Raymond's article, dated July 26, 1861, appears in Chapter 4.

21. Swinton, "The New York Daily Papers, Part II," 238.

22. Henry W. Raymond, "Extracts from the Journal of Henry J. Raymond (Edited by his Son), II," *Scribner's Monthly*, 18 (March 1880): 708. The delegation of publishers lobbying on the paper levy included William Appleton and Fletcher Harper of Harper's Weekly.

23. Nicolay and Hay, *Lincoln*, 6:212; Henry W. Raymond, "Extracts from the Journal of Henry J. Raymond, I," *Scribner's Monthly*, 18 (January 1880): 419–20; Raymond, *Life and Public Services of Lincoln*, 705.

24. "The Army Correspondent," *Harpers New Monthly Magazine* (October, 1863): 627–633; Starr, *The Civil War's Bohemian Brigade*, 232. Sylvanus Cadwallader, *Three Years with Grant*, quoted in James M. Perry, *A Bohemian Brigade: The Civil War Correspondents — Mostly Rough, Sometimes Ready* (New York: John Wiley & Sons, 2000), 254.

25. Henry J. Raymond to Nicolay, E. A. Paul to Lincoln, May 23, May 25, 1864, Abraham Lincoln Papers and John G. Nicolay Papers, Library of Congress. Lincoln's endorsement, May 24, 1864, is in *Collected Works*, 7:360. See also, Starr, *Bohemian Brigade*, 105.

26. Maverick, *Henry J. Raymond*, 257.

27. Frank Moore, ed., *The Rebellion Record: A Diary of American Events* (New York: Putnam, 1864); Andrews, *The North Reports the Civil War*, 419.

28. Beecher's remarks were contained in the Swinton obituary that appeared in The New York Times, December 11, 1892; Raymond to Lincoln, April 4, 1864, Abraham Lincoln Papers, Library of Congress; Henry Villard to John G. Nicolay, June 16, 1863, John G. Nicolay Papers, Library of Congress.

29. Wilkie was praised in an editorial on "one of our special correspondents," in The New York Times, October 3, 1861, reprinted in Andrews, *The North Reports the Civil War*, 128. Wilkie in turn said Raymond "surely was the most appreciative, kindliest, and most courteous of journalists," Perry, *A Bohemian Brigade*, 62.

30. The exchange between Williams and Grant is recorded in Andrews, *The North Reports the Civil War*, 609–10.

31. Wilkeson's full report, dated July 6, 1863, is in Chapter 14. He later became The Times's Washington Bureau chief. See Wilkeson to Nicolay, September 21, 1864, inquiring about President Lincoln's demeanor when visiting the Antietam battlefield (John G. Nicolay Papers, Library of Congress).

32. Francis Brown, *Raymond of the Times* (New York: W. W. Norton, 1951), 224; Henry J. Carman and Reinhard H. Luthin, *Lincoln and the Patronage* (New York: Columbia University Press, 1945), 290–91.

33. Raymond, *Life and Public Services of Lincoln*, 602.

34. Gideon Welles, *The Diary of Gideon Welles, Secretary of the Navy under Lincoln and Johnson*, ed. by Howard K. Beale (New York: W. W. Norton, 1960), 2:87–88, 97–99, 104, 136.

35. Maverick, *Henry J., Raymond*, 93.

36. Oliver Wendell Holmes, "Bread and the Newspaper," *Atlantic Monthly* (September 1861), 346.

37. Lincoln to Edwin Stanton, May 24, 1864, Basler, ed., *Collected Works*, 7:360. Emphasis added.

ACKNOWLEDGMENTS

In assembling this collection we were greatly assisted by our indefatigable and resourceful researcher, Dwight Zimmerman. Without his help, it is fair to say, we could not have created the book as quickly or efficiently as we did. Dwight combed through the voluminous computerized archives of the paper to supply the backbone of this volume, and proceeded to provide, within hours of each endless request, copies of additional articles requested by the editors. We thank him for his energy, skill, and patience. And we are grateful as well to researcher Avi Mowshowitz for his own masterful use of the web to secure elusive materials; and to New York Times executive Ethan Riegelhaupt for sharing books, ideas, and his vast storehouse of knowledge about his newspaper's history.

Thanks, too, go to Mitchel Levitas and Alex Ward of The New York Times, old friends of one of the editors, and new and valued acquaintances of the other, who contributed the full backing of the newspaper they have served so long and so well — along with expert advice on its long and intricate history and traditions. That The Times so strongly believes in consecrating its records from 1861 to 1865 — the true first draft of the history of the Civil War — is a tribute to their expertise and determination.

We have also enjoyed our new relationship with the publishing team at Black Dog & Leventhal. Lisa Tenaglia was a superb line editor and advocate, Nathaniel Marunas was instrumental not only in finding the editors but shaping this colossal book and DVD-ROM package, and J. P. Leventhal who developed a grand vision for this book and expressed lavish, and much-appreciated, confidence in its editors. Thanks, too, to Kraig Smith and Rebecca Schear, who spent some of their valued off hours downloading raw material and printing and copying chapters.

Above all, as always, we are grateful to our wives for their love and active support, particularly when it came to proof–reading and copy editing. For Marylou Symonds and Edith Holzer we are eternally grateful.

"The Question of Freedom or Slavery: The Coming of the Civil War"

1850–1860

Every modern American knows — just as every reader of The New York Times understood at the time — that the Civil War began with the first shots fired at Fort Sumter in April 1861. But there was a dramatic backstory, too: the long-simmering dispute between North and South over the toxic issue of chattel slavery. It had been smoldering anew for nearly a decade, beginning with the passage of the Fugitive Slave Act in 1850. An earlier Fugitive Slave law dating from 1793 had made it unlawful for citizens to harbor runaways or abet their escape from slavery. But this new legislation, passed as part of the Compromise of 1850, went further by making it unlawful for any citizen to refuse to assist authorities in recapturing escaped slaves. In effect, it made every Northerner part of the slave-catching apparatus of the government.

Two years later, author Harriet Beecher Stowe published her explosive novel *Uncle Tom's Cabin; or, Life among the Lowly,* an exposé of the evils of slavery that caused both a literary and political sensation. The book sold 300,000 copies domestically in 1852 alone, and eventually became the biggest best seller of the century. Abraham Lincoln probably did not, as the legend holds, declare on meeting the author for the first time: "So this is the little lady who made this big war." But he might as well have said exactly that.

Politically, the dominant issue of the 1850s was not the continued existence of slavery in the South — only a handful of extremists like William Lloyd Garrison advocated outright abolition, and he was excoriated by the vast majority of Americans, North and South alike. Instead, the issue was the *extension* of slavery into the national territories in the West. Most Americans

Detail from an 1850 editorial cartoon condemning the Fugitive Slave Act.

believed the issue had been settled by two great Congressional compromises: one in 1820 that concerned Missouri, and one in 1850 that concerned the territory that had been gained from Mexico in the Mexican-American War. Then in 1854, Congress passed the Kansas-Nebraska Act. Sponsored by Senator Stephen A. Douglas, an Illinois Democrat, primarily to facilitate the construction of a transcontinental railroad, Southerners refused to support it unless the new territories were opened to slave owners.

To gain Southern support in Congress, Douglas added a codicil declaring that the residents of the new territories could vote on the issue for themselves. This became known as the doctrine of "popular sovereignty." When Southerners protested that it was a false choice because slavery had been banned north of the latitude of 36°30' by the Missouri Compromise, Douglas added another codicil repealing that portion of the 1820 act. In effect, the bill thus opened territories to slavery where it previously had been forbidden. Douglas argued that slavery would never take root in these territories anyway, because the cotton culture was incompatible with the climate in Kansas, but antislavery interests reacted to the legislation with fury, arguing that it threatened to nationalize the "peculiar institution." The legislation hastened the formation of the new Republican Party, which denounced Douglas and mocked his proposal as "squatter sovereignty."

The Nebraska law set the stage for a bloody outbreak in Kansas's territory — in a sense, a violent precursor to the convulsive war yet to come. In a protracted, bitter fight over whether to accept a slave or free constitution for the new territory, sustained fighting broke out between pro-slavery "Border Ruffians" and antislavery Free

Staters, who had poured into the region. They squared off in a series of bloody guerrilla battles that ultimately claimed more than four dozen lives. After pro-slavery zealots burned a hotel in the town of Lawrence, abolitionist John Brown led a band of antislavery zealots into a pro-slavery settlement and killed five men along the banks of Pottawatomie Creek. A few months later, armies of vigilantes on both sides of the explosive issue fought at the so-called Battle of Osawatomie.

At the outset of the Kansas violence, U.S. Senator Charles Sumner of Massachusetts, a champion of abolition and black rights, delivered a speech denouncing the authors of the Kansas-Nebraska Act, describing one of them, Senator Andrew Butler, as a Don Quixote (to Douglas' Sancho Panza). Sumner's three-hour oration featured a devastating impersonation of Butler, who suffered from slurred speech caused by a stroke. The next afternoon, Butler's enraged nephew, South Carolina Congressman Preston Brooks, avenged his uncle by savagely attacking Sumner at his Senate desk, using a heavy cane to beat him into unconsciousness. Sumner nearly died as a result of the assault and, though he ultimately recovered, did not return to Washington for three years. By the end of 1856, Charles Sumner had become a martyr to the cause of antislavery, and Preston Brooks a hero to the champions of Southern chivalry.

The genie was now fully out of the bottle, and bitter debates on the slavery issue roiled Congress, as well as town halls, lyceums, and newspapers nationwide. Two years later, in 1858, Douglas faced a stiff challenge for a third-term from a former Whig Congressman, all but unknown outside of Illinois. Abraham Lincoln, a recent convert to Republicanism, challenged

the incumbent to a series of open-air political debates in Illinois. With newspapers breathlessly reporting the prairies "on fire" with their oratorical dueling, the entire nation focused on this local race as if it would determine the future of popular sovereignty and slavery itself. Douglas won re-election, but Lincoln emerged with a national reputation. Newspaper transcripts of their "joint meetings," followed by publication of a book-length reprint masterminded by Lincoln, immortalized the encounters as the most famous political debates in American history and set the two principals — and the rest of the increasingly divided nation — on a collision course toward the 1860 election.

Until 1857, however, only the legislative and executive branches had weighed in on the growing sectional crisis — with the new President, James Buchanan, feebly (and unsuccessfully) attempting to impose a pro-slavery constitution on Bleeding Kansas. A few days after Buchanan's inauguration, however, the judicial branch was heard from — in thunder tones that shook the very foundation of the country. The Supreme Court's now-infamous Dred Scott decision held that African-Americans could never, in effect, be citizens of the United States, and judged slavery to be permissible anywhere and everywhere. Southerners cheered the ruling as a vindication of their "peculiar institution," while Northerners like Lincoln insisted that the ruling violated the "all men are created equal" spirit of the nation's founding documents.

To some Southerners, outright war became likely, if not inevitable, in May 1859, when John Brown of Kansas fame caused another sensation by leading a raid on the federal arsenal at Harpers Ferry, Virginia — a quixotic, doomed plot designed ☞

to arouse and arm what he hoped would become a massive slave insurrection. Although many Northerners dismissed Brown as a madman, he became a martyr to abolitionists after his trial and execution in December. Antislavery admirers shaved slivers from his wooden coffin. Composers wrote songs in tribute, and artists romanticized his hanging. Brown's martyrdom infuriated and frightened slave owners who worried that their black chattels, more numerous in some Southern states than whites, might one day revolt against them and convulse the region in bloodshed. By the dawn of the critical year 1860, many Southerners were loudly warning that the Union of states would be fatally doomed should any Republican capture the White House later that year. Northerners in turn denounced Southerners for a "rule or ruin" mentality, and insisted that the Union could not be fractured.

In February, at the end of a series of well-publicized audition speeches by Western Republicans in New York, the frontier giant who had captured national attention in his earlier debates with Douglas made his local oratorical debut with an address at Cooper Union. Abraham Lincoln's speech — which ended with the ringing assurance to antislavery men that "right makes might" — set the stage for one of the most rancorous presidential election campaigns in American history. It also triggered the further national convulsions that many Americans, North as well as South, had ample reason to fear would follow.

SOUTHERN SLAVERY.

A GLANCE AT UNCLE TOM'S CABIN.

JUNE 22, 1853

We commence this morning the publication of a somewhat extended notice of "*Uncle Tom's Cabin*," a book which has been more widely read and more generally noticed already than any other ever issued in this country, but which still has a fresh and profound interest for every class of readers, and in every section of the country.[1] The review is written by a Southern gentleman, a lawyer of distinction, an accomplished scholar, and who has filled very high and responsible public stations with honor to himself and credit to the country. It presents naturally enough the opinion of the book generally entertained in the Southern States, where the work has been widely read, and where whatever good it is calculated to effect, will be accomplished. Such a book was scarcely needed to demonstrate to the people of the North the odiousness of many of the features of Southern slavery, and still less to stimulate the hostile intermeddling of officious persons of both sexes in Europe, with evils which, however responsible they may be for their existence, they can now do nothing whatever to remedy, and which their ill-judged action cannot fail to aggravate. But there are many things contained in the book which cannot fail to do good in the South, by directing the attention of those who have it in their power to apply a remedy, to many gross and glaring evils which have grown up in connection with Slavery as it exists in the Southern States. The review referred to, will be read, we think, with general interest.

FIRST PAPER. BY A SOUTHERNER.

The time has come for a calm review of Mrs. HARRIET BEECHER STOWE's[2] book — a book which has attracted so much attention, both at home and abroad. It is quite clear that the review must come from the South.[3] The book cannot be fairly judged anywhere else in all the world; in truth, it cannot be comprehended anywhere else. Its style may be admired the world over, its vivid sketches of the lights and shadows of life, its life-like creation — presenting at one moment the loveliest impersonation of virtue, and at the next the most revolting embodiment of course vice — gives powerful interest to the book, independent of the particular class or race whose wrongs it is intended to depict.

Harriet Beecher Stowe, author of *Uncle Tom's Cabin*, ca. 1880.

The *power* of the book is not to be questioned. Its fidelity, its fairness, its morality we may venture to discuss; but it would be idle to deny that it is a powerful appeal to humanity; that it moves the soul in its very depths; and that it awakens the intensest interest in the fortunes of the humble hero of the story, and of all the personages in any way connected with him. A writer just beginning to be talked about, undertakes to show us that all popular superstitions are founded on some truth. In his argument, which is historical, he overlooks *astrology*, one of the most beautiful, fascinating, and commanding forms of speculative faith which the world has ever acknowledged, since the stars first glittered in the firmament....

There lies the secret power of Mrs. STOWE's sketch of *Life among the Lowly*. It is not merely that it depicts the scenes in the life of a *slave* torn from his happy home, his family, his friends, and subjected to cruel treatment upon a Southern plantation; but it is because the glowing pages exhibit the chequered fortunes of a *man* displaying a character at every step of his eventful history, at once gentle and heroic. Through the darkening shadows of his later years, the beautiful lineaments of the Christian shine out clear, steady and strong; and we do not know whether the soul is most moved by admiration for the lofty courage and sublime faith of the expiring martyr, suffering, bleeding, sinking in the loneliness of a wretched hovel, without an eye to cheer, or a human voice to speak a word of sympathy; or with indignant detestation of the demon-like brutality of a wretch, without a single redeeming quality. Such a picture, drawn anywhere, would move us....

It is quite clear that whatever may be the demerits of the slave system, they are not fairly exhibited in Mrs. STOWE's Book; a book which we do not misconceive or undervalue.

We have already said that it possesses extraordinary attractions. It has fixed in the eyes of the civilized world on the Slaveholding States. Its "still, sad music" has reached the ear of mankind. It is altogether impossible that it should pass away without working great results; indeed we trust that its results will be seen in all the future fortunes of the African race. It ought to be read by every Slaveholder; it is far more important that he should read it, than the Abolitionist of America, or of Europe, should find in its pages fresh fuel for his passions. All this we freely say. But we say something more than this; and it is—that the sympathy of the civilized world has been roused, not by an exhibition of the true relations between master and slave, but by a splendid picture;—an elaborate and successful performance, in which the imagination prevails to so high a degree, that the scene should have been laid in some Oriental region, rather than amidst the sober and commonplace realities of the Plantation States.

Uncle Tom's Cabin stands at the head of that entertaining class of books known as *"Tales Founded on Facts."* WALPOLE. ✸

1. First published in June 1851 as a serial in the abolitionist journal The National Era, the novel *Uncle Tom's Cabin* appeared in book form the following March, creating a national — and ultimately, international — sensation. The book made characters like "Uncle Tom," "Little Eva," and "Simon Legree" pillars of American folklore.

2. Harriet Beecher Stowe (1811–1896) was the daughter of the famous minister Lyman Beecher, and the sister of both minister Henry Ward Beecher and educator Catherine Beecher, with whom she wrote another bestselling book about the American woman's role in the home. It was said that Harriet and her husband, Calvin Stowe, harbored many fugitive slaves in their home as they fled to freedom via the Underground Railroad.

3. This careful and reasoned — but critical — multipart review of the book was anything but typical of Southern reaction to *Uncle Tom's Cabin.* Southern writers also produced some 30 rebuttal books, like Mary Henderson Eastman's *Aunt Phillis's Cabin,* which argued that slavery was a benevolent institution that protected blacks.

THE NEBRASKA BILL.

THE CLOSING SCENES — EFFECT OF THE MEASURE.

MAY 7, 1854

WASHINGTON, THURSDAY, MAY 26, 1854.
1 ½ O'CLOCK A.M.

I have just left the Senate chamber, where the Nebraska iniquity was consummated a few minutes since;[1] and, as I write, the roar of cannon from Capitol Hill is speaking the joy of those who have accomplished it. The work is finished. Tomorrow, doubtless, the bill will receive the President's approval;[2] and by Monday-next, the hireling crew who have betrayed their constituencies for prices stipulated, may walk up and demand the reward of their ignominy. The work of organizing the Territories, and of rewarding those whose consciences would not let them vote the measure until stiffened by Executive promises of a share in the spoils, will probably progress *pari passu*; and it will be an interesting study to analyze the appointments for officers of the new Territories, and ascertain who gives a receipt in full for services rendered, as each commission is filled up by the Executive. The fat jobs and contracts which constitute the price of *some* of those whose votes passed the measure through Congress, will not be available for some time yet; but as they come along in the course of time, I shall hope to have the pleasure of announcing them, and of giving the value of the contract, and the vote which secured it, side by side, as cause and effect.

There is little to be said of tonight's session of the Senate. It was interesting, but not exciting. Mr. [William H.] SEWARD, Mr. [Salmon P.] CHASE,[3] and others, in their speeches distinctly indicated the results which are to flow from the consummation of the Nebraska swindle. Their language was calm, courteous, and forcible. They were replied to by Mr. [Stephen A.] DOUGLAS in a tirade of scurrilous abuse towards themselves, the clergy, and everybody else who does not belong to the Slavery Propaganda, such as he only is capable of; and as he has been practicing this speech and this style before the Senate now for some three or four months, he has become rather perfect in that line, as you may suppose.

The disclosures in the Senate, during the last day or two, in relation to the action of the Southern Whig Senatorial Caucus on the Nebraska bill, presents one fact in a very strong light — to wit: that every man of the Whig party who went for the Nebraska bill, was filled with the conviction that he was going to political death, so far as a *national* political position is concerned. And the same thing is equally true, of nearly every Senator among those who have heretofore claimed the title of Democracy. A more lamentable exhibition of moral cowardice can scarce be imagined, than has been displayed in connection with this bill, from beginning to end. Nobody hardly, except DOUGLAS, has been for it. The men who have spoken for it, and toiled for it with him, have cursed it and him with it, continually, in secret. But they were in his toils, and dared not refuse to do his bidding, lest they should be suspected of being Abolitionists, or of being disloyal to the "Democratic" party. I know this to be true, as does everybody else here, who is at all familiar with political life behind the scenes. It was clear from the first, that there was no sincere, spontaneous support of the bill, from any quarter. And still I saw it must pass, for it had the earmarks of the Administration, which had adopted it, and brought to bear upon it the whole weight and influence of Executive power and patronage — and that, at this day, is irresistible.

It remains now to be seen whether DOUGLAS and Co. can cheat the people into believing that after all it's best to be quiet and "acquiesce" in this new triumph of the Slave Power — whether the arch Demagogue who initiated this scheme, and whose untiring energy and industry this scheme, and whose untiring energy and industry has carried it through, is right when he laughs to scorn all threats of resistance to his plans of Slavery aggression.

The events of last month are considered by all thinking men here to have completely broken down all old party lines. Whigs of the North have no longer any responsibility to or sympathy with the Southern Whigs as such. The line of division is complete. On the other hand a large portion of the Democracy of the North feel that they are thrown out of their old party association, because while they are honest, patriotic *men*, they can never consent to political fellowship with those whose whole end and aim is to strengthen, develop and extend the Slave power, at the sacrifice of all that true ☞

Democracy claims to feel and to inculcate. The old issues by which party lines were marked have been suspended. The question of Freedom or Slavery as the ruling principle, the controlling interest in the Republic, is the *only* issue of any importance now before the people; and it certainly is a far more interesting and vital one than any the country has divided upon since the foundation of the Government. Upon that the country *must* divide. That is inevitably the issue, although the most strenuous efforts will be made to divert public attention from it. The friends of freedom and the public faith must rally under the banner of Democracy, for that *is* the name which expresses the sentiment necessarily embodied in the party of Freedom. Let the organization commence without delay. The enemies of Freedom are untiring, remorseless, sleepless. The true Democracy will need to be ceaselessly vigilant, or the chains, ere long, will have been so firmly riveted upon them that escape will be almost hopeless. It is the time for action. That action has already begun in the hearts of the people. Let the leaders in every hamlet, town and city give it immediate direction and permanent form.

S. ✻

> 1. The controversial Kansas-Nebraska Act, authored by Senator Stephen A. Douglas (1813–1861), Democrat of Illinois, reignited the sectional crisis by repealing part of the Missouri Compromise, which had limited slavery to territory below the 36°30' parallel.
> 2. As predicted, the legislation was signed by Democratic President Franklin Pierce (1804–1869).
> 3. Northern antislavery Senators from New York and Ohio, respectively, who would later serve as Cabinet officers in the Lincoln administration.

RIGHTS OF MINORITIES — A SOUTHERN VIEW OF THE PASSAGE OF THE NEBRASKA BILL.

MAY 31, 1854
FROM THE CHARLESTON (S.C.) MERCURY, MAY 27.

The recent struggle in the House of Representatives over the Nebraska bill will be memorable not only for the pertinacity with which the minority resisted its passage, but also for the extraordinary

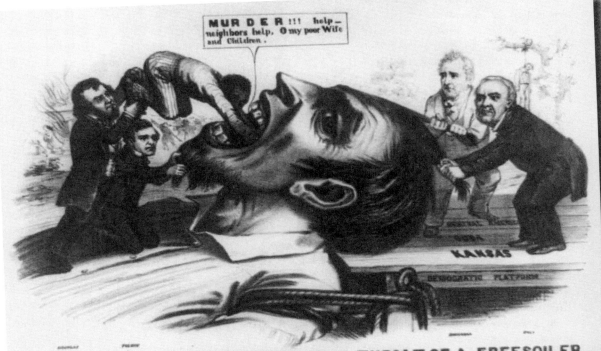

An 1856 poster cartoon attributes the violence in Kansas to proslavery elements.

THE NEBRASKA BILL AGAIN.

JUNE 7, 1854

Popular indignation at the passage of the Nebraska bill finds vent in various projects, some wise and some otherwise. We have all sorts of violent propositions, from all quarters. CASSIUS M. CLAY[1] proposes that every body who voted for the bill shall be treated to a social as well as a political crucifixion — and seeks to prepare the country for a dissolution of the Union. GARRISON, PHILLIPS & Co.[2] are seizing the opportunity to push their project of dissolving the Union and breaking down the Constitution. We hear men a good deal more sensible than any of these, proclaiming their hatred of all compacts which bind us to the Slaveholding interest, and declaring they will keep no faith with those who keep no faith with them. All this effervescence is good so far as it may lead to practical measures. But all measures to be practical, must be rational, judicious and legal. Resisting the law affords no remedy for the wrong we have sustained. Denouncing the Constitution may gratify a temporary indignation, but cooler judgment will not approve it and the great mass of the people will not endorse it. The true remedy is to be sought by the quiet, old-fashioned agency of the *ballot-box*. All we have to do is to elect Congressmen who will make laws favoring *Freedom* instead of *Slavery* — and a President who will not throw the whole power, patronage and influence of that office — as all our Presidents have done hitherto — into the scale of the Slaveholding interest.

The champions of the Nebraska bill know perfectly well that they have acted in direct opposition to the popular will. The originators of the iniquitous measure have for months been as clearly persuaded that the great sense of the country is against this outrageous breach of honor and good faith, as they are of their own existence. Yet they have accomplished it

measures to which the majority resorted at the last to secure their triumph. The amendment offered by Mr. [Alexander H.] STEPHENS[1] in Committee of the Whole, to strike out the enacting clause of the bill, cut off all other amendments, deprived the bill of its vitality, and compelled the Committee to rise and report the bill thus amended to the House. The question then came up in the House upon the adoption of this report. By previous understanding the very majority who had so amended the bill in committee now voted for the rejection of the report.

The effect of this move, then, was to remove the bill from Committee where amendments without limit could impede its passage, and bring it before the House where the call for the previous question to the exclusion of all amendments would force it at once to a direct vote. The tactics were most adroit and as the result showed, entirely successful. Thus after a tedious Parliamentary campaign, which left the question still to be decided by patience and physical endurance, the victory is won by a simple maneuver, as unlooked for as it is unusual. The resort to it is an era in the Parliamentary history of the country. It has closed the door henceforth to the successful resistance on the part of minorities to measure which they deem unconstitutional and oppressive. And the effect of the victory thus won will be to make majorities more intolerant of opposition, and regardless of the claims and arguments of the weaker side. We do not speak of this movement in reference to the Nebraska bill. *We look at it as a question deeply affecting the future history of the country and as such it is worthy of note.*

As Mr. CALHOUN[2] observed, Governments were formed to protect minorities — majorities can take care of themselves. The rules of the House of Representatives constitute a part of the system. The restrictions imposed by them upon hasty or oppressive legislation by placing in the hands of the minority the power to check and defeat it, are among its wisest provisions. They have ever been regarded in England and in this country as necessary to justice and liberty.

We think the late move in the House of Representatives by which the Nebraska bill was carried, subversive of this system and these restrictions. The precedent is established, and majorities in the future need only follow it to perpetrate acts of the grossest injustice. Where now is there any parliamentary protection for minorities. This new system of tactics violates it utterly, and by a single blow deprives them of that power, which, although it may at times be the rallying point of faction, yet in the light of all history is the last strong refuge of justice and freedom. *In the annihilation, therefore, of the power of minorities, in the intolerant spirit which hereafter will actuate majorities, and the consequent wrongful legislation to which they may lead in all these aspects, we regard the precedent established as bad and dangerous.* It is a fearful stride to that fatal evil which ever impends Democratic institutions when minorities, their protests, appeals and rights, are unheeded in the remorseless tread of majorities.

There are some who now congratulate themselves and the country upon the success of Mr. STEPHENS' tactics, who will yet regret and decry their application. *They will yet feel the value of the rights of minorities, when they belong to the weaker side themselves, and will bitterly remember that they first administered the poisoned chalice which evenhanded justice commends to their own lips.* The whole country, and particularly the South, will be made to feel at what cost the passage of the Nebraska bill was bought.

Whatever were the merits of the bill, whatever of wisdom or of justice which may be claimed for it, we place them far below the perpetuity and recognition of those rights which belong to the few against the many.... ✳

1. Georgia Congressman Stephens (1812–1883), floor manager of the Kansas-Nebraska bill in the House of Representatives, called the passage of the bill "the greatest glory of my life."
2. The late Senator John C. Calhoun (1782–1850) of South Carolina was a longtime advocate of the "positive good" of slavery, and ardently believed in the right of a state to secede.

through recreant Northern votes. These Northern traitors prating Democratic cant, have gone deliberately against what they knew to be the mind of the North. The smallest fraction of decent regard to honor and propriety would have led them to put it over, till the sense of the country could be tested by another election. They were chosen to vote on no such question. Its coming up was not dreamed of by the people at large. When it was sprung upon the country, there was but one consentaneous cry of indignation throughout all the Northern land, in which honest and honorable men of all parties joined. Scarcely the slavish officials from Custom-Houses and Post-Offices in small packed meetings, dared peep feebly in its behalf. A large portion of the honest and honorable feeling of the South was against it too. The palpable indecency of driving it through under such circumstances, was doubtless as much a matter of distinct consciousness to the majority that perpetrated it, as to the minority that resisted it, as to the country that cried out against it. They did it because it was in their power to do it — they had the Might and that they knew was all the Right they had. They dreaded to let it go over to another Congress. They feared — they knew, it could not then be passed. Sublime devotion to the Public Will!... ✳

1. Clay (1810–1903) was a onetime Kentucky slave owner who became an abolitionist editor, orator, Mexican War veteran. and founder of the Republican Party. Lincoln would appoint him Minister to Russia.
2. William Lloyd Garrison (1805–1879), editor of The Liberator, and Wendell Phillips, Massachusetts orator, were arguably the nation's best known abolitionists — admired by antislavery Northerners, and reviled in the slaveholding South. It was Garrison who called the Constitutional protection of slavery "a covenant with death and an agreement with hell."

THE COWARDLY ASSAULT ON MR. SUMNER.

MAY 23, 1856

WASHINGTON, FRIDAY, MAY 22

Immediately after the adjournment of Congress, today, PRESTON S. BROOKS, of South Carolina,[1] a member of the Lower House, entered the Senate Chamber, and approaching the seat of Mr. SUMNER,[2] struck him a powerful blow with a cane, at the same time accusing him of libeling South Carolina and his great bearded relative, Senator BUTLER.[3] Mr. SUMNER fell from the effects of the blow, and BROOKS continued beating him. Mr. SUMNER soon recovered sufficiently to call for help, but no one interposed, and BROOKS repeated the blows until Mr. SUMNER was deprived of the power of speech. Some eyewitnesses state that BROOKS struck him as many as fifteen or twenty times. Mr. SUMNER was sitting in an armchair when the assault was made, and had no opportunity to defend himself. After his assailant desisted, he was carried to his room, but the extent of his injuries are not yet ascertained.

Various opinions on the subject are expressed, many applauding and some denouncing the assault as a cowardly attempt to beat down freedom of speech.

Mr. BROOKS has been complained of by Mr. Wm. [name illegible] on whose oath Justice HOLLINGSHEAD required BROOKS to give bail in the sum of [amount illegible] as security for his appearance tomorrow afternoon.

Mr. SUMNER has several severe but not dangerous wounds on his head. The cane used by BROOKS was shattered to pieces by the blows....

Messrs. CRITTENDEN, TOOMBS, MURRAY,[4] and others interfered as soon as they could, and probably prevented further damage. The greatest excitement prevailed. Mr. SUMNER sank perfectly unconscious to the floor, where he lay bloody and dreadfully bruised, till raised by his friends. Mr. Sumner's physicians say his wounds are the most severe flesh ones that they ever saw on a man's head, and deny his friends admission to him. ⊕

Top: Congressman Preston S. Brooks of South Carolina. Bottom: Senator Charles Sumner of Massachusetts, victim of a beating by Rep. Brooks on the Senate floor.

1. Democrat Preston Smith Brooks (1819–1857) was never indicted for attacking Sumner; the House did not even agree on a motion to censure him, but he eventually left Congress on his own. Constituents sent him canes to replace the one he had broken in beating Sumner.
2. A senator since 1851, Charles Sumner (1811–1864) of Massachusetts had declared in his incendiary speech that Senator Butler had a mistress "ugly to others" but "lovely to him.. the harlot, slavery." Sumner did not return to Washington until December 1859, at which time he delivered his first speech on "The Barbarism of Slavery."
3. Andrew Pickens Butler (1796–1857) died shortly after the Sumner attack.
4. John J. Crittenden (1786–1863) of Kentucky, Robert A. Toombs (1810–1885) of Georgia, and possibly Rep. Ambrose S. Murray (1807–1885), a congressman from New York.

THE RUFFIANLY ASSAULT ON SENATOR SUMNER.

SPECIAL CORRESPONDENCE OF THE N.Y. DAILY TIMES.

MAY 24, 1856
WASHINGTON, THURSDAY, MAY 22

I can add but little of fact, in relation to the ruffianly assault upon Mr. SUMNER, to what I have already telegraphed. A well known personal friend of Mr. BROOKS publicly stated, tonight, before a dozen gentlemen, that the assault was premeditated and arranged for at a private conclave, held last evening, at which the individual who made the statement was present. Mr. BROOKS then agreed to do this ruffian work which today he has consummated. Whether the same chivalric Council agreed that the crime thus settled upon should be carried to the extreme of murder, I know not; but the weapon employed, the ferocity of manner with which it was used long after it was apparent that Mr. SUMNER was unconscious, and therefore unable even to raise an arm to ward off the blows, and the fact that the assailant's accomplice exerted himself, cane in hand, to prevent interference with the outrage upon the helpless victim, all tend to produce the conviction in my mind that foul murder *was* the purpose.

The defenders of this outrage (for shame, be it said, it *has* defenders here in creatures bearing the human form) tell us that there was no such purpose — but

STUPIDITY OF THE SOUTH.

MAY 28, 1856

Happily for the world wisdom and wickedness do not often travel together; in fact they are never found in company, and malignity always overreaches itself and neutralizes its bitterness by its own folly. The assault on Senator SUMNER is a notable proof in point, and the most marvelous circumstance about the affair, after all, is the amazing stupidity of BROOKS, and the fatuous blindness of the Southern Senators in their approbation of his conduct. If that chivalric gentleman in his anxiety to defend his uncle's reputation, and uphold the honor of his native State could have

only a design to disgrace the Senator from Massachusetts. Paltry subterfuge! If that were the only purpose, the weapon would have been something far less dangerous to life. Look at the facts. Mr. SUMNER was seated at his desk writing in great haste for the afternoon's mail. Suddenly Mr. BROOKS — who had been sitting in the Chamber during twenty minutes, waiting, apparently, until the object of his malice should be quite alone — suddenly stepped up and addressed him. Mr. S. did not rise from his seat — had not the slightest expectation of being assailed, and had spoken no single word, when he received a blow that deprived him of consciousness. Those who dressed his wounds express their wonder that he was able to move at all after this blow had been inflicted. In the instinct of self-preservation, however, he sprang from his seat, ripping up his desk from the floor in the movement, and overturning it. You will understand that, with his nether limbs under the desk, and his arm chair drawn close up to it, he was, in a manner, pinioned fast. He sprang forward, however, but his strength and consciousness were already lost, and he could do nothing in the way of self-defense....

What will be the end of it all, do you suppose? The proof of the assault without other provocation than words spoken in debate is perfectly conclusive, but a fine of fifty or a hundred dollars will be the extent of the legal punishment visited upon the criminal unless I greatly err; and the

SOUTHERN CHIVALRY — ARGUMENT versus CLUB'S.

An 1856 cartoon laments the caning of Senator Sumner.

chivalric sons of South Carolina who signalize their prowess by first disabling a man whom they take at a disadvantage, and then beating him with perfect safety until taken off, will walk our streets with heads as high as honest men.

I will not trust myself to comment upon the political aspect of this affair. Your readers cannot fail to see in it another exemplification of the arrogance and overbearing insolence by means of which a portion of the champions of the Slave power seek to crush out all liberty of speech or of the Press wherever that privilege is exercised in behalf of Freedom. It is a part of the great plot of fraud and violence and wrong enacting on a larger stage in Kansas. Here it is an Editor or a Senator assassinated

in a manner which should make a coward blush; in Kansas it is a freeman murdered, simply for *declaring* himself a freeman, and another followed by relentless persecutions under the forms of a law which has its basis in fraud, simply because he was a witness of the murder. Where will it end? What is the remedy? *One* remedy of the people have in their hands — and that is a stern rebuke to the time-serving politicians whose attempts to force Slavery into Kansas — by a stupendous scheme of fraud, to be sustained only while freemen live, in violence and blood — have set the example for these no less disgraceful efforts to stop discussion by blackguardism and crime.

S.

foreseen, as in any but a maniac must have done, that for every blow inflicted upon the head of Mr. SUMNER, the cause of Slavery must lose at the least ten thousand votes, he probably would have desisted from his foul and cowardly deed. There never was so good an opportunity offered to the South, before, to make capital for itself, as in this case of the ruffian BROOKS; but, true to their instincts, and blinded by the madness that must lead to their utter defeat, they have chosen to defend the outrageous scoundrelism of their self-appointed champion and have thus made themselves responsible for his acts. In consequence of the notoriety given to Mr. SUMNER's speech it will now have ten readers where it would before have had one; and Mr.

BROOKS may congratulate himself upon having done more to add to the Republican Party, and to give vigor and permanency to the Anti-Slavery sentiment of the North, than all the Free Soilers have done in Congress. Some of the Southern papers have the sagacity to see this; and while they express their admiration of Mr. BROOKS' ruffianism, and pour out their vile abuse upon Mr. SUMNER, they regret the violence of which he was the subject — since it will inevitably strengthen the hands of their opponents. One of the Virginia papers, with unintentional felicity, calls the assault upon Mr. SUMNER a "classical caning." The epithet was well chosen. The brutal act will become classical as the poisoning of SOCRATES and the ostracism of

ARISTIDES are classical; and the speech of the Senator, which might have been forgotten, will become a classic, and be received by future school boys, and be committed to memory and quoted by public orators. We published a supplement, containing this speech, on Saturday, and the call for it has been incessant ever since. It is read more eagerly than a new novel by DICKENS or THACKERAY, and hundreds of thousands will read it now, and treasure up the facts it enumerates, who would never have perused a lie of it but for the stupid brutality of the ruffian BROOKS.

THE SLAVERY QUESTION — THE DECISION OF THE SUPREME COURT.

MARCH 9, 1857

The decision of the Supreme Court in the case of DRED SCOTT completes the nationalization of Slavery. Slavery is no longer a local institution — the creature of local law — dependent for its existence and protection upon State sovereignty and State legislation. It is incorporated into the Constitution of the United States. Its tenure is the tenure of all property, and the Constitution protects and preserves it, to the same extent and upon the same principles, as it protects any other property of any kind whatever. This is the fundamental position which the Supreme Court has just asserted, and upon which all its decisions in this case rest. Congress cannot exclude Slavery from Federal territory, because the *right* to slaves is the right to *property*, and cannot be divested. For the same reason the people of the Territory cannot exclude Slavery from their own domain — and when the time for the next step comes, we shall have it in the logical sequence, that *no State Government has the right to deprive any citizen of property, which the Constitution of the United States protects him in holding.*

It is not too much to say that this decision revolutionizes the Federal Government, and changes entirely the relation which Slavery has hitherto held towards it. Slavery is no longer local: it is national. The Federal Government is no longer held aloof from it, as a thing wholly and exclusively out of its jurisdiction — it is brought directly within its sphere and put immediately under its protection. The doctrine of State Rights, so long its friend, is now its foe.

That this decision is to produce the most profound impression upon the public judgment is certain. Its first effect will be to paralyze and astound the public mind. Familiar as our people have become to the advancement of Slavery towards supremacy in our Government, they have not believed that it could obtain so absolute a seat in the supreme council of the Republic at so early a day. The decision will be accepted and obeyed as law. There will be no wide or loud protest against it. The public peace will not be disturbed — the public ear will not be vexed — by clamorous outcries or noisy denunciations of the court and its decree. But the doctrine it has promulgated will sink deep into the public heart, and germinate there as the seed of discontent and contest and disaster hereafter. They mistake the temper of the men of this Republic, who believe that they will ever accept Slavery as the fixed and permanent law of the American Union. They have trusted to time — to the progress of civilization, to the melioration of legal codes — to climate, to population, to established metes and bounds, to old covenants and compacts and the advancement of Christian principle, for ultimate deliverance. They will strive still to cling to such of these as violence and wrong have left untouched. But this last decision leaves little to hope and everything to fear. And the people will begin to ask why, if Slavery is *national*, the nation should not assume the custody and control of it — why, if its extension is synonymous with its existence, both should not be ended together.

Apparent peace will follow the action of the Supreme Court. The partisans of its conduct and its doctrine will proclaim it to be the end of controversy upon this subject, and the immediate result will seem to confirm their hopes. But it has laid the only solid foundation which has ever yet existed for an Abolition party; and it will do more to stimulate the growth, to build up the power and consolidate the action of such a party, than has been done by any other event since the Declaration of Independence. ⊛

Dred Scott, the most famous slave in America.

POLITICAL CONTEST IN ILLINOIS.

AUGUST 23, 1858

SPECIAL DISPATCH TO THE NEW YORK TIMES
WASHINGTON, SUNDAY, AUG. 22

The city is dull, and there is very little important business transacted by the Cabinet, inasmuch as the Secretary of State, the Attorney-General, and the Secretary of the Navy are all absent in search of a change of air and recruited health.

The engrossing topic of conversation is the fierce contest in Illinois, and how it will end, and the politicians of all sorts are agog to see a report of the encounter between DOUGLAS and LINCOLN, which took place at Ottawa, Ill., yesterday. The friends of the Administration generally seem disposed to occupy a position of armed neutrality between them, taking no especial interest in either, being desirous rather of the election of some reliable Democrat.... ⊛

DOUGLAS AND LINCOLN AT OTTAWA — PERSONAL REMINISCENCES.

AUGUST 26, 1858

Messers. DOUGLAS and LINCOLN had a grand tilt at Ottawa, Ill., last week.[1] Mr. DOUGLAS' speech contained this amusing passage:

In the remarks which I have made upon this platform, and the position of Mr. LINCOLN upon it, I mean nothing personal, disrespectful or unkind to that gentleman. I have known him for nearly twenty-five years. We had many points of sympathy when I first got acquainted with him. We were both comparatively boys — both struggling with poverty in a strange town for our support. I an humble school teacher in the town of Winchester, and he a flourishing grocery keeper in the town of Salem. [Laughter.] He was more successful in his occupation than I, and hence became more fortunate in this world's goods. Mr. LINCOLN is one of those peculiar men that has performed with admirable skill in every occupation that he ever attempted. I made as good a school teacher as I could, and when a cabinet-maker I made the best bedsteads and tables, but my old boss said I succeeded better in bureaus and secretaries than in anything else. [Laughter.] But I believe that Mr. LINCOLN was more successful in his business than I, for his business soon carried him directly into the Legislature. There I met him in a little time, and I had a sympathy for him, because of the up-hill struggle we had in life. [Cheers and laughter.] He was then as good at telling an anecdote as now. He could beat any of the boys at wrestling — could out run them at a foot-race — beat them all pitching quoits and tossing a copper, and could win more liquor than all the boys put together; [laughter and cheers] and the dignity and impartiality with which he presided at a horse-race or a fist-fight were the praise of everybody that was present and participated. [Renewed laughter.] Hence I had a sympathy for him, because he was struggling with misfortune and so was I.

Mr. LINCOLN served with me, or I with him, in the Legislature of 1836, when we parted. He subsided or submerged for some years, and I lost sight of him. In 1846, when WILMOT[2] raised the Wilmot Proviso tornado, Mr. LINCOLN again turned up as a Member of Congress from Sangamon District. I, being in the Senate of the United States, was called to welcome him, then without friend and companion. He then distinguished himself by his opposition to the Mexican war, taking the side of the common enemy, in time of war, against his own country. [Cheers and groans.] When he returned home from that Congress, he

found that the indignation of the people followed him everywhere, until he again retired to private life, and was submerged until he was forgotten again by his friends. He came up again in 1854, in time to make the Abolition Black Republican platform, in company with LOVEJOY, GIDDINGS, CHASE and FRED. DOUGLASS,[3] for the Republican Party to stand upon. TRUMBULL,[4] too, was one of our own contemporaries. He was one born and raised in old Connecticut. Bred a Federalist, he removed to Georgia, and there turned Nullifier, when Nullification was popular. But as soon as he disposed of his clocks and wound up his business, he emigrated to Illinois. When he got here, having turned politician and lawyer, he made his appearance in 1840–41 as a Member of the Legislature, and became noted as the author of a scheme to repudiate a large portion of the

State debt of Illinois, and thus bring infamy and disgrace upon the fair escutcheon of our glorious State. The odium attached to that measure consigned him to oblivion for a time. I walked into the House of Representatives and replied to his repudiation speeches until we carried resolutions over his hear, denouncing repudiation, and asserting the moral and legal obligation of Illinois to pay every dollar of debt she owed — every bond bearing her signature. TRUMBULL's malignity toward me arises out of the fact that I defeated his infamous scheme to repudiate the State debt and State bonds of Illinois. ❋

Painting by Robert Marshall Root of the fourth Lincoln–Douglas debate at Charleston, Illinois. Abraham Lincoln is standing; seated on his right is Senator Stephen A. Douglas.

1. At the first of seven Lincoln-Douglas debates for the U.S. Senate seat from Illinois. The Times barely covered the duel.
2. David Wilmot (1814–1868) was at the time a Congressman from Pennsylvania. In 1846, he had introduced an amendment barring slavery in all territories acquired in the Mexican War. Though it never passed, the so-called Wilmot Proviso was reintroduced countless times over the next few years; Lincoln, as a Congressman, reckoned he voted for its passage more than 40 times in his single term in the House.
3. Abolitionists Owen Lovejoy (1811–1864) of Illinois, Joshua Giddings (1795–1864) of Ohio, Salmon P. Chase (1808–1873), and the African-American leader Frederick Douglass (1817?–1895).
4. Illinois Senator Lyman Trumbull (1813–1896) had won his seat in 1855, defeating Lincoln in a vote of the state legislature.

WHAT DOUGLAS IS, AND WHAT HE HAS DONE.

SEPTEMBER 20, 1858

Senator Stephen A. Douglas, Democrat of Illinois.

FROM THE WASHINGTON UNION.

Mr. DOUGLAS is a self-nominated candidate for reelection to the Senate by the Legislature of Illinois. He asks the Democracy of the State to sustain him and to indorse his opposition last Winter to the President and the Democratic members of the Senate and House of Representatives. He has made that issue. It is not a party contest; it is whether he shall be sustained in his *apostacy*. In other words, Mr. DOUGLAS joined the opposition during the last session of Congress, and he now demands that his conduct, *while fighting in their ranks*, shall be ratified and confirmed, or repudiated, by the people of his State. If the Democracy sustain him, they have a sure thing of it with LINCOLN and DOUGLAS as candidates; for had the former occupied Judge DOUGLAS' seat in the Senate he would doubtless have voted precisely as DOUGLAS did. Would the Democracy of Illinois indorse TRUMBULL on the issue presented? Why express dissatisfaction with TRUMBULL, who voted uniformly with DOUGLAS, and confidence in DOUGLAS, who voted uniformly with TRUMBULL? It must be remembered that the Lecompton issue in Illinois is one of Judge DOUGLAS'

own making. He asks for a special indorsement purely on the strength of his opposition to that measure. Then, why approve DOUGLAS and condemn TRUMBULL? Why fear LINCOLN, who would certainly have acted as DOUGLAS? We oppose LINCOLN because we know he is a Republican, and, had he been in the Senate, would have voted with TRUMBULL and DOUGLAS. We oppose him because he is an Abolition agitator, assailing the decision of the Supreme Court of the United States in order to keep open the Slavery issue. Judge DOUGLAS is doing the same thing. As a representative of the Democracy of the Union, he has forfeited all confidence in his integrity and virtue. He has broken the commandments, derided the faith, set aside the rituals, and violated the moral sense of the whole congregation. He is no longer worthy to be the expounder of our doctrines, the adviser of our people, or their representative in the councils of the nation. *Then let his constituents strip him of the surplice, revoke his commission, disarm him of authority.* That is all we can ask; and we appeal to the Register to modify its indignation, so that, by repentance and well-doing, Mr. DOUGLAS hereafter may associate with the Democracy. ⊛

THE NEGRO INSURRECTION.

ORIGIN AND OBJECTS OF THE PLOT.

CAPT. BROWN, OF KANSAS, ORIGINATOR OF THE DISTURBANCE.

OCTOBER 19, 1859

ORIGIN OF THE CONSPIRACY
FROM THE BALTIMORE AMERICAN, OCT. 18

The principal originator of this short but bloody insurrection was, undoubtedly, Capt. JOHN BROWN, whose connection with scenes of violence in the Border warfare in Kansas then made his name familiarly notorious throughout the whole country. BROWN made his first appearance in Harper's Ferry more than a year ago, accompanied by his two sons — all three of them assuming the name of Smith. He inquired about land in the vicinity, and made investigations as to the probability of finding ores there, and for some time boarded at Sandy Point, a mile east of the Ferry. After an absence of some months the elder BROWN reappeared in the vicinity, and rented or leased a farm on the Maryland side, about four miles from the Ferry. They bought a large number of picks and spades, and this confirmed the belief that they intended to mine for ores. They were

A period woodcut shows federal troops assaulting John Brown's insurgents at Harpers Ferry.

frequently seen in and about Harper's Ferry, but no suspicion seems to have existed that "Bill Smith" was Capt. BROWN, or that he intended embarking in any movement so desperate or extraordinary. Yet the development of the plot leaves no doubt that his visit to the Ferry and his lease of the farm were all parts of his preparation for an insurrection which he supposed would be successful in exterminating Slavery in Maryland and western Virginia.

BROWN's chief aide was JOHN E. COOK, a comparatively young man, who has resided in and near the Ferry some years. He was first employed in tending a lock on the Canal, and afterwards taught school on the Maryland side of the river, and, after a brief residence in Kansas, where, it is supposed, he became acquainted with BROWN, returned to the Ferry, and married there. He was regarded as a man of some intelligence, and known to be Anti-Slavery, but was not so violent in the expression of his opinions as to excite any suspicions.

These two men, with BROWN's two sons, were the only white men connected with the insurrection that had been seen about the Ferry. All were brought by BROWN from a distance, and nearly all had been with him in Kansas.

The first active movement in the insurrection was made at about 10½ o'clock on Sunday night. WILLIAM WILLIAMSON, the watchman at Harper's Ferry Bridge, whilst walking toward the Maryland side, was seized by a number of men who said he was their prisoner and must come with them. He recognized BROWN and COOK among the men, and knowing them, treated the matter as a joke; but, enforcing silence, they conducted him to the Armory, which he found already in their possession. He was detained till after daylight, and discharged. The watchman who was to relieve WILLIAMSON at midnight found the bridge lights all out, and was immediately seized. Supposing it an attempt at robbery, he broke away, and his pursuers, stumbling over him, he escaped. The next appearance of the insurrectionists was at the house of Col. LEWIS WASHINGTON, a large farmer and slave-owner living about four miles from the Ferry. A party, headed by COOK, proceeded thither, and rousing Col. WASHINGTON, told him he was their prisoner. They also seized all the slaves near the house, took a carriage horse and a large wagon with two horses. When Col. WASHINGTON saw COOK he immedi-

ately recognized him as the man who had called upon him some months previous, and to whom he had exhibited some valuable arms in his possession, including an antique sword, presented by FREDERICK THE GREAT to GEORGE WASHINGTON, and a pair of pistols, presented by LAFAYETTE to WASHINGTON, both being heir-looms in the family. Before leaving, COOK wanted Col. WASHINGTON to engage in a trial of skill at shooting, and exhibited considerable skill as a marksman. When he made the visit on Sunday night, he alluded to his previous visit and the courtesy with which he had been treated, and regretted the necessity which made it his duty to arrest Col. WASHINGTON. He, however, took advantage of the knowledge he had obtained by his former visit, to carry off all the valuable collection of arms, which he did not re-obtain till after the final defeat of the insurrection.

From Col. WASHINGTON's he proceeded with him as a prisoner in the carriage, and twelve of his negroes in the wagon, to the house of Mr. ALLSTADT, another large farmer on the same road. Mr. ALLSTADT and his son, a lad of sixteen, were taken prisoners, and all their negroes within reach forced to join the movement. He then returned to the Armory at the Ferry. All these movements seem to have been made without exciting the slightest alarm in town, nor did the detention of Capt. PHELP's train.

It was not until the town was thoroughly waked up and found the bridge guarded by armed men, and a guard stationed at all the avenues, that the people discovered that they were prisoners. A panic appears to have immediately ensued, and the number of insurrectionists at once increased from fifty (which was probably their greatest force, including the slaves who were forced to join) to from five to six hundred. In the meantime a number of workmen, not knowing anything of what had occurred, entered the Armory, and were successively taken prisoners, until at one time they had not less than sixty men confined in the Armory. Among those thus entrapped were ARMISTEAD BALL, Chief Draughtsman of the Armory; BENJAMIN MILLS, Master of the Armory, and J. E. P. DANGERFIELD, Paymaster's Clerk. These three gentlemen were imprisoned in the engine-house, which afterwards became the chief fortress of the insurgents, and were not released until after the final assault. The workmen were imprisoned in a

large building further down the yard, and were rescued by the brilliant Zouave dash made by the Railroad Company's men which came down from Martinsburgh.

THE BATTLE YESTERDAY
BALTIMORE, TUESDAY, OCT. 18 — P.M.

An eyewitness who has returned from Harper's Ferry, describes the scene there as follows:

"The first attack was made by a detachment of the Charlestown Guards, which crossed the Potomac River above Harper's Ferry, and reached a building where the insurgents were posted by the canal on the Maryland side. Smart firing occurred, and the rioters were driven from the bridge. One man was killed here, and another was arrested. A man ran out and tried to escape by swimming the river; a dozen shots were fired after him; he partially fell, but rose again, threw his gun away, and then his pistols, but both snapped; he drew his bowie-knife and cut his heavy accoutrements off and plunged into the river; one of the soldiers was about ten feet behind; the man threw up his hands and said, "Don't shoot;" the soldier fired, and the man fell into the water with his face blown away; his coat-skirts were cut from his person, and in the pockets was found a captain's commission to Capt. E. H. LEEMAN from the Provisional Government. The commission was dated Oct. 15, 1859, and signed by A. W. BROWN, Commander-in-Chief of the Army of the Provisional Government of the United States.

A party of five of the insurgents, armed with Minié rifles, and posted in the rifle armory were expelled by the Charlestown Guards.

They all ran for the river, and one who was unable to swim was drowned. The other four swam out to the rocks in the middle of the Shenandoah, and fired upon the citizens and troops upon both banks. This drew upon them the muskets of between two hundred and three hundred men, and not less than four hundred shots were fired at them from Harper's Ferry, about two hundred yards distant. One was finally shot dead, the second, a negro, attempted to jump over the dam, but fell short, and was not seen afterwards; the third was badly wounded, and the remaining one was taken unharmed. The white insurgent, wounded and captured, died in a few moments after in the arms of our informant. He was shot through the breast and stomach. ☞

He declared that there were only nineteen whites engaged in the insurrection.

For nearly an hour a running and random firing was kept up by the troops against the rioters. Several were shot down, and many managed to limp away wounded. During the firing the women and children ran shrieking in every direction, but when they learned that the soldiers were their protectors, they took courage and did good service in the way of preparing refreshments and attending the wounded."

Our informant, who was on the hill when the firing was going on, says: "All the terrible scenes of a battle passed in reality before his eyes. Soldiers could be seen pursuing singly and in couples, and the crack of a musket or rifle was generally followed by one or more of the insurgents biting the dust. The dead lay in the streets where they fell. The wounded were cared for."... ✸

EXECUTION OF JOHN BROWN.
HIS INTERVIEW WITH HIS WIFE.
SCENES AT THE SCAFFOLD.

Special Dispatch to the New-York Times.
CHARLESTOWN, VA., Friday, Dec. 2,
Half-past 3 o'clock, P.M.

BROWN was executed to-day at a little after 11 o'clock. There was no attempt at rescue, nor any indications of any disposition to interfere with the course of justice in any way. Indeed, there was very little excitement of any kind.

I visited the field in which the gallows had been erected at an early hour this morning. The day was very fine and the air warm. All strangers were excluded from the town. Indeed, no railroad trains were allowed to enter during the entire day.

The gallows was erected at 7½ o'clock, and all preparations for the execution immediately completed. The reporters who had secured the privilege of being present were allowed to enter soon after.

On being summoned, BROWN appeared perfectly calm and collected. He took formal leave of each of his fellow prisoners, and gave each one a quarter of a dollar as a token of remembrance. He remarked to COOK that he did not tell the truth when he said that he had been induced by him to take up arms, and enter upon this project. COOK replied that he did — that BROWN did invite him to the course he had pursued. BROWN replied, "I *did not.*"

As he left the jail COOK bowed to acquaintances outside.

He rode to the scaffold in an open wagon, seated upon his coffin.

At the gallows BROWN was still perfectly cool. He made no remarks. As soon as he had mounted the scaffold the cap was put on and drawn over his face.

He was not standing on the drop. The Sheriff told him to get upon it.

BROWN said, "I cannot see — place me on it, and don't keep me waiting."

DECEMBER 3, 1859

He stood upon the drop nine minutes and a half when it fell. He suffered but little. After three minutes, there were no convulsions, or indications of life. At the end of twenty minutes his body was examined, and he was reported dead.

THE INTERVIEW BETWEEN BROWN AND HIS WIFE — INCIDENTS OF THE EXECUTION.

CHARLESTOWN, Friday, Dec. 2

The interview between BROWN and his wife lasted from 4 o'clock in the afternoon until 8 o'clock in the evening, when Gen. TALIAFERRO[1] informed them that the period allowed had elapsed, and that she must prepare for departure to the Ferry. A carriage was again brought to the door, the military took possession of the square, and with an escort of twenty men, the *cortegé* moved off, Capt. MOORE, of the Montgomery Guard, accompanying her. The interview was, I learn, not a very affecting one — rather of a practical character, with regard to the future of herself and children, and the arrangement and settlement of business affairs. They seemed considerably affected when they first met, and MRS. BROWN was for a few moments quite overcome, but BROWN was as firm as a rock, and she soon recovered her composure. There was an impression that the prisoner might possibly be furnished with a weapon or with strychnine, by his wife, and before the interview her person was searched by the wife of the jailor, and a strict watch kept over them during the time they were together. At the time of separation they both seemed to be fully self-possessed, and the parting, especially on his part, exhibited a composure either feigned or real, that was truly surprising. I learn from Capt. MOORE that she rather repelled all attempt on his part to express sympathy with her under her affliction....

Thomas Hovenden's ca. 1884 painting sympathetically depicted *The Last Moments of John Brown*.

The prisoner said that he contemplated his death with composure and calmness. It would undoubtedly be pleasant to live longer, but as it was the will of God he should close his career, he was content. It was doubtless best that he should be thus legally murdered for the good of the cause, and he was prepared to submit to his fate without a murmur. Mrs. BROWN becoming depressed at these remarks, he bid her cheer up, telling her that his spirit would soon be with her again, and that they would be reunited in heaven.

With regard to his execution, he said, that he desired no religious ceremonies either in the jail or on the scaffold from ministers who consent or approve of the enslavement of their fellow creatures; that he would prefer rather to be accompanied to the scaffold by a dozen slave children and a good old slave mother, with their appeal to God for blessings on his soul than all the eloquence of the whole clergy of the Commonwealth combined. ✸

1. William Booth Taliaferro (1822–1898) was commander of the Virginia state militia at the time of John Brown's raid at Harpers Ferry, and later served in the Confederate Army as a brigadier-general.

REPUBLICANS AT COOPER INSTITUTE.

ADDRESS BY HON. ABRAHAM LINCOLN, OF ILLINOIS.

FEBRUARY 28, 1860

The announcement that Hon. ABRAHAM LINCOLN, of Illinois, would deliver an address in Cooper Institute, last evening, drew thither a large and enthusiastic assemblage. Soon after the appointed hour for commencing the proceedings, DAVID DUDLEY FIELD, Esq., arose and nominated as Chairman of the meeting Mr. WILLIAM CULLEN BRYANT.[1] The nomination was received with prolonged applause, and was unanimously approved.

Mr. BRYANT, after the applause had subsided, said: It is a grateful office that I perform in introducing to you at this time an eminent citizen of the West, whom you know — whom you have known hitherto — only by fame, and who has consented to address a New-York assemblage this evening. The great West, my friends, is a potent auxiliary in the battle we are fighting, for Freedom against Slavery; in behalf of civilization against barbarism; for the occupation of some of the fairest region of our Continent on which the settlers are now building their cabins. I see a higher and wiser agency than that of man in the causes that have filled with hardy people the vast and fertile regions which form the northern part of the valley of the Mississippi — a race of men who are not ashamed to till their acres with their own hands, and who would be ashamed to subsist on the labor of the slave. [Applause.] These children of the West, my friends, form a living bulwark against the advance of Slavery, and from them is recruited the vanguard of the armies of liberty. [Applause.] One of them will appear before you this evening in person — a gallant soldier of the political campaign of 1856 – [applause] — who then rendered good service to the Republican cause, and who has been since the great champion of that cause in the struggle which took place two years later for the supremacy of the Republicans in the Legislature of Illinois; who took the field against Senator DOUGLAS, and would have won in the conflict but for the unjust provisions of the law of the State, which allowed a minority of the people to elect a majority or the Legislature [Applause.] I have only, my friends, to pronounce the name of ABRAHAM LINCOLN of Illinois – [cheers] — I have only to pronounce his name to secure your profoundest attention. [Prolonged applause, and cheers for LINCOLN.]

Mr. LINCOLN advanced to the desk, and smiling graciously upon his audience, complacently awaited the termination of the cheering and then proceeded with his address as follows:

…Some of you admit that no Republican designedly aided or encouraged the Harper's Ferry affair; but still insist that our doctrines and deliberations necessarily lead to such results. We do not believe it. We know we hold to no doctrines, and make no declarations, which were not held to and made by our fathers who framed the Government under which we live. You never dealt fairly by us in relation to this affair. When it occurred, some important State elections were near at hand, and you were in evident glee with the belief that, by charging the blame upon us, you could get an advantage of us in those elections. The elections came, and your expectations were not quite fulfilled. Every Republican man knew that, as to himself at least, your charge was a slander, and he was not much inclined by it to cast his vote in your favor. Republican doctrines and declarations are accompanied with a continual protest against any interference whatever with your slaves, or with you about your slaves. Surely, this does not encourage them to revolt. True, we do in common with our fathers, who framed the Government under which we live, declare our belief that Slavery is wrong; but the slaves do not hear us declare even this. For anything we say or do, the slaves would scarcely know there is a Republican Party. I believe they would not, in fact, generally know it but for your misrepresentations of us in their hearing. In your political contests among yourselves, each faction charges the other with sympathy with Black Republicanism; and then, to give point to the charge, defines Black Republicanism to simply be insurrection, blood and thunder among the slaves.

Slave insurrections are no more common now than they were before the Republican Party was organized. What induced the Southampton insurrection, twenty-eight years ago, in which at least three times as many lives were lost as at Harper's Ferry. You can scarcely stretch your very elastic fancy to the conclusion that Southampton was got up by Black Republicanism. In the

Photograph of Abraham Lincoln the day of the Cooper Union speech, New York 1860.

present state of things in the United States, I do not think a general, or even a very extensive slave insurrection, is possible. The indispensable concert of action cannot be attained. The slaves have no means of rapid communication; nor can incendiary free men, black or white, supply it. The explosive materials are everywhere in parcels; but there neither are, nor can be supplied, the indispensable connecting trains.

Much is said by Southern people about the affection of slaves for their masters and mistresses; and a part of it, at least, is true. A plot for an Uprising could scarcely be devised and communicated to twenty individuals before some one of them, to save the life of a favorite master or mistress, would divulge it. This is the rule; and the slave-revolution in Hayti was not an exception to it, but a case occurring under peculiar circumstances. The gunpowder plot of British history, though not connected with slaves, was more in point. In that case, only about twenty were admitted to the secret; and yet one of them, in his anxiety to save a friend, betrayed the plot to that friend, and, by consequence, averted the calamity. Occasional poisonings from the kitchen, and open or stealthy assassinations in the field, and local revolts extending to a score or so, will continue to occur as the natural results of Slavery; but no general insurrection of slaves, as I think, can happen in this country for a long time. Whoever much fears, or much hopes, for such an event, will be alike disappointed.

In the language of Mr. JEFFERSON, uttered many years ago, "It is still in our ☞

power to direct the process of emancipation, and deportation, peaceably, and in such slow degrees, as that the evil will wear off insensibly; and their places be, pari passu, filled up by free white laborers. If, on the contrary, it is left to force itself on, human nature must shudder at the prospect held up."

Mr. JEFFERSON did not mean to say, nor do I, that the power of emancipation is in the Federal Government. He spoke of Virginia; and, as to the power of emancipation, I speak of the Slaveholding States only.

The Federal Government, however, as we insist, has the power of restraining the extension of the institution — the power, to insure that a slave insurrection shall never occur on any American soil which is now free from Slavery.

JOHN BROWN's effort was peculiar. It was not a slave insurrection. It was an attempt by white men to get up a revolt among slaves, in which the slaves refused to participate. In fact, it was so absurd that the slaves, with all their ignorance, saw plainly enough it could succeed. That affair, in its philosophy, corresponds with the many attempts, related in history, at the assassination of kings and emperors. An enthusiast broods over the oppression of a people, till he fancies himself commissioned by Heaven to liberate them. He ventures the attempt, which ends in little else than his own execution. ORSINI's attempt on LOUIS NAPOLEON, and JOHN BROWN's attempt at Harper's Ferry were, in their philosophy, precisely the same. The eagerness to cast blame on old England in the one case, and on New-England in the other, does not disprove the sameness of the two things.

And how much would it avail you, if you could, by the use of JOHN BROWN, HELPER's book², and the like, break up the Republican organization? Human action can be modified to some extent, but human nature cannot be changed. There is a judgment and a feeling against Slavery in this nation, which cast at least a million and a half of votes. You cannot destroy that judgment and feeling — that sentiment — by breaking up the political organization which rallies around it. You can scarcely scatter and disperse an army which has been formed into order in the face of your heaviest fire, but if you could, how much would you gain by forcing the sentiment which created it out of the peaceful channel of the ballot-box into some other-channel? What would that other channel probably be? Would the number of John Browns be lessened or enlarged by the operation?

But you will break up the Union, rather than submit to a denial of your Constitutional rights.

That has a somewhat reckless sound; but it would be palliated, if not fully justified, were we proposing, by the mere force of numbers, to deprive you of some right, plainly written down in the Constitution. But we are proposing no such thing.

When you make these declarations, you have a specific and well-understood allusion to an assumed Constitutional right of yours, to take slaves into the Federal Territories, and to hold them there as property. But no such right is specifically written in the Constitution. That instrument is literally silent about any such right. We, on the contrary, deny that such a right has any existence in the Constitution, even by implication.

Your purpose, then, plainly stated, is, that you will destroy the Government, unless you be allowed to construe the Constitution as you please, on all points in dispute between you and us. You will rule or ruin in all events.

This, plainly stated, is your language to us. Perhaps you will say the Supreme Court has decided the disputed Constitutional question in your favor. Not quite so. But, waiving the lawyer's distinction between dictum and decision, the Court have decided the question for you in a sort of way. The Court have substantially said, it is your Constitutional right to take Slaves into the Federal Territories, and to hold them there as property.

When I say the decision was made in a sort of way, I mean it was made in a divided Court by a bare majority of the Judges, and they not quite agreeing with one another in the reasons for making it; that it is so made as that its avowed supporters disagree with one another about its meaning; and that it was mainly based upon a mistaken statement of fact — the statement in the opinion that "the right of property in a slave is distinctly and expressly affirmed in the Constitution."

An inspection of the Constitution will show that the right of property in a slave is not distinctly and expressly affirmed in it. Bear in mind the Judges do not pledge their judicial opinion that such right is impliedly affirmed in the Constitution; but they pledge their veracity that it is distinctly and expressly affirmed there — "distinctly" — that is, not mingled with anything else — "expressly" — that is, in words meaning just that, without the aid of any inference, and susceptible of no other meaning.

If they had only pledged their judicial opinion that such right is affirmed in the instrument by implication, it would be open to others to show that neither the word "slave" nor "slavery" is to be found in the Constitution, nor the word "property," even, in any connection with language alluding to the things slave, or slavery, and that wherever in that instrument the slave is alluded to, he is called a "person;" and wherever his master's legal right in relation to him is alluded to, it is spoken of as "service or labor due," as a "debt" payable in service or labor. Also, it would be open to show, by contemporaneous history, that this mode of alluding to slaves and Slavery, instead of speaking of them, was employed on purpose to exclude from the Constitution the idea that there could be property in man.

To show all this is easy and certain.

When this obvious mistake of the Judges shall be brought to their notice, is it not reasonable to expect that they will withdraw the mistaken statement, and reconsider the conclusion based upon it?

And then it is to be remembered that "our fathers, who framed the Government under which we live" — the men who made the Constitution — decided this same constitutional question in our favor, long ago — decided it without a division among themselves, when making the decision; without division among themselves about the meaning of it after it was made, and so far as any evidence is left without basing it upon any mistaken statement of facts.

Under all these circumstances, do you really feel yourselves justified to break up this Government, unless such a Court decision as yours is shall be at once submitted to as a conclusive and final rule of political action?

But you will not abide the election of a Republican President. In that supposed event, you say, you will destroy the Union; and then, you say, the great crime of having destroyed it will be upon us!

That is cool. A highwayman holds a pistol to my ear, and mutters through his teeth, "Stand and deliver, or I shall kill you, and then you will be a murderer!"

To be sure, what the robber demanded of me — my money — was my own; and I had a clear right to keep it; but it was no more my own than my vote is my own; and the threat of death to me, to extort my money, and the threat of destruction to the Union, to extort my vote, can scarcely be distinguished in principle.

A few words now to Republicans. It is exceedingly desirable that all parts of this great Confederacy shall be at peace, and in harmony, one with another. Let us Republicans do our part to have it so. Even though much provoked, let us do nothing through passion and ill temper. Even though the Southern people will not so much as listen to us, let us calmly consider their demands, and yield to them if, in our deliberate view of our duty, we possibly can. Judging by all they say and do, and by the subject and nature of their controversy with us, let us determine, if we can, what will satisfy them.

Will they be satisfied if the Territories be unconditionally surrendered to them? We know they wilt not. In all their present complaints against us, the Territories are scarcely mentioned. Invasions and insurrections are the rage now. Will it satisfy them if, in the future, we have nothing to do with invasions and insurrections? We know it will not. We so know because we know we never had anything to do with invasions and insurrections; and yet this total abstaining does not exempt us from the charge and the denunciation.

The question recurs, what will satisfy them? Simply this: We must not only let them alone, but we must, somehow, convince them that we do let them alone. This, we know by experience, is no easy task. We have been so trying to convince them from the very beginning of our organization, but with no success. In all our platforms and speeches, we have constantly protested our purpose to let them alone; but this has had no tendency to convince them. Alike unavailing to convince them is the fact that they have never detected a man of us in any attempt to disturb them.

These natural and apparently adequate means all failing, what will convince them? This, and this only; cease to call Slavery wrong, and join them in calling it right. All this must be done thoroughly — done in acts as well as in words. Silence will not be tolerated — we must place ourselves avowedly with them DOUGLAS' new sedition law must be enacted and enforced, suppressing all declarations that Slavery is wrong, whether made in politics, in presses, in pulpits, or in private. We must arrest and return their fugitive slaves with greedy pleasure. We must pull down our Free-State Constitutions. The whole atmosphere must be disinfected from the taint of opposition to Slavery, before they will cease to believe that all their troubles proceed from us.

I am quite aware they do not state their case precisely in this way. Most of them would probably say to us, "Let us alone, do nothing with us, and say what you please about Slavery." But we do let them alone — have never disturbed them — so that, after all, it is what we say which dissatisfies them. They will continue to accuse us of doing until we cease saying.

I am also aware they have not, as yet, in terms, demanded the overthrow of our Free-State Constitutions. Yet those Constitutions declare the wrong of Slavery, with more solemn emphasis than do all other sayings against it: and when all these other sayings shall have been silenced, the overthrow of these Constitutions will be demanded, and nothing be left to resist the demand. It is nothing to the contrary that they do not demand the whole of this just now. Demanding what they do, and for the reason they do, they can voluntarily stop nowhere short of this consummation. Holding, as they do, that Slavery is morally right, and socially elevating, they cannot cease to demand a full national recognition of it, as a legal right, and a social blessing.

Nor can we justifiably withhold this on any ground save our conviction that Slavery is wrong. If Slavery is right, all words, acts, laws, and Constitutions against it, are themselves wrong, and should be silenced, and swept away. If it is right, we cannot justly object to its nationality — its universality; if it is wrong, they cannot justly insist upon its extension — its enlargement. All they ask, we could readily grant, if we thought Slavery right; all we ask, they could as readily grant, if they thought it wrong. Their thinking it right, and our thinking it wrong, is the precise fact upon which depends the whole controversy. Thinking it right, as they do, they are not to blame for desiring its full recognition, as being right; but thinking it wrong, as we do, can we yield to them? Can we cast our votes with their view, and against our own? In view of our moral, social, and political responsibilities, can we do this?

Wrong as we think Slavery is, we can yet afford to let it alone where it is, because that much is due to the necessity arising from its actual presence in the nation; but can we, while our votes will prevent it, allow it to spread in the National Territories, and to overrun us here in these Free States?

If our sense of duty forbids this, then let us stand by our duty, fearlessly and effectively. Let us be diverted by none of those sophistical contrivances wherewith we are so industriously plied and belabored — contrivances such as groping for some middle ground between the right and the wrong, vain as the search for a man who should be neither a living man nor a dead man — such as a policy of "don't care" on a question about which all true men do care — such as Union appeals beseeching true Union men to yield to Disunionists, reversing the Divine rule, and calling, not the sinners, but the righteous to repentance — such as invocations of WASHINGTON, imploring men to unsay what WASHINGTON said, and undo what WASHINGTON did.

Neither let us be slandered from our duty by false accusations against us, nor frightened from it by menaces of destruction to the Government, nor of dungeons to ourselves. Let us have faith that right makes might; and in that faith, let us, to the end, dare to do our duty, as we understand it.

When Mr. LINCOLN had concluded his address, during the delivery of which he was frequently applauded, three rousing cheers were given for the orator and the sentiments to which he had given utterance.... ⊛

1. Poet Bryant (1794–1878) was editor of the anti-slavery New York Evening Post.
2. Hinton Rowan Helper (1829–1909), born on a North Carolina plantation, had been denounced in the region as a traitor for writing the 1857 book *The Impending Crisis of the South: How to Meet It*, in which he argued that slavery doomed the South to an inferior economic position in the growing nation.

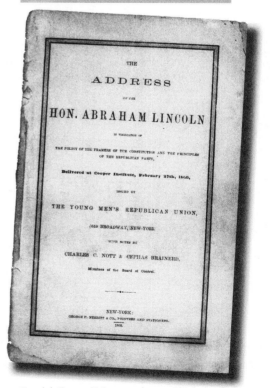

Lincoln's Cooper Union speech was reprinted and sold thousands of copies.

CHAPTER 1

"The Approaching Triumph of Mr. Lincoln"

MAY–NOVEMBER 1860

he unprecedented four-way campaign for President of the United States in 1860 dominated the press and intensified partisan discord during the summer and fall. With a quartet of presidential candidates competing in the race — one representing Northern Democrats, another Southern Democrats, a third reflecting Border State unionism, and a fourth standing for the new antislavery Republicans, Americans split not only along customary party lines, but along rigid sectional lines as well.

For the most part, the nominees themselves, true to the political tradition of the day, stayed home and allowed surrogates, broadsides, banners, pamphlets, cartoons, popular prints, and, of course, newspapers to do the campaigning on their behalf. Abraham Lincoln, the Republican candidate, remained at or close to his hometown of Springfield, Illinois, from May all the way through November, answering letters, advising on strategy, encouraging supporters to work hard on his behalf, and benignly greeting visitors, steadfastly declining to engage in active politics. But Republicans rallied vociferously throughout the Northern states, calling for an end to longtime Southern domination of the executive, legislative, and judicial branches of government.

In Connecticut, eager young Lincoln supporters formed a new organization called the Wide-Awakes, and branches quickly sprung up throughout the North. In city after city, members boisterously marched the streets by night, carrying torchlights atop Lincoln "rails," and garbed in oilskin-glazed capes and caps to protect their clothing from dripping oil and sparks. Their precision demonstrations and slick "uniforms" aroused and entertained Northern

An 1860 photograph of presidential candidate Abraham Lincoln.

voters, but alarmed Southerners. They regarded the Wide-Awakes as a paramilitary organization that might quickly be formed into a conquering antislavery army should Lincoln win the election. Even without taking the stump, the Republican nominee thus aroused virulent opposition among slavery supporters.

But his opponents had little hope of stopping Lincoln at the polls. From the time Democrats split into Northern and Southern factions that year, most observers believed that the Republicans would inevitably win a majority of electoral votes even though Lincoln's name was kept off most presidential ballots in the Deep South. Senator Stephen A. Douglas, once an all-but-inevitable Democratic candidate, proved unacceptable to many slave holders for the same reason he had lost support among most antislavery Northerners: by advocating popular sovereignty. Under its terms, settlers in new western territories could vote on whether or not to allow slavery inside their borders. Northerners believed that the Douglas policy would extend and expand slavery, while Southerners, conversely, feared it would exclude and doom it. Bolting from their party's convention in protest, pro-slavery Southern Democrats regrouped and nominated the nation's sitting vice president, Kentuckian John C. Breckinridge, thus splitting the nation's oldest political party in two. Douglas's subsequent, unusual, and much-criticized personal campaign tour did little to enhance his popularity in the South.

Throughout the roiling 1860 campaign, Democrats aimed at least to block Lincoln from amassing enough electoral votes to win outright victory. Their best chance at stopping him was to win enough states to throw the final decision on the Presidency to the lame-duck House of Represen-

tatives, where the outcome was far less certain and coalescence around a compromise candidate was likely, or at least possible. But the strategy failed, even after Democrats in Pennsylvania abandoned Douglas and unified behind Breckinridge. On Election Day, Lincoln won an enormous victory in the Northern states, amassing 180 electoral votes nationwide, far more than needed for outright victory.

At Cooper Union, Lincoln had predicted that Republicans would win support wherever and whenever Southerners allowed them to contend for office. But Election Day proved him wrong. The final tally gave Lincoln 54 percent of the popular tally in the North and West, but only 2 percent in those Southern States where his name did appear on the ballot. In states like Missouri and Kentucky, where voters could indeed vote for him for President, Lincoln had won almost no support at all, a portent of a dangerous interregnum to come. In the end, Lincoln won the presidency without winning a single electoral vote in the South and less than 40 percent of the overall national popular vote.

The day after the voting, opponents of the so-called Black Republican defiantly unfurled a Palmetto Flag in Charleston, South Carolina. Lincoln was repeatedly hanged in effigy throughout the Deep South. And fire-eater Edmund Ruffin, who had almost diabolically supported Lincoln because he thought a Republican victory would hasten disunion, immediately began leafleting for secession. In a way, the war between the states had already begun.

The national capital received the news of Lincoln's victory with nervousness. The pro-Democratic Washington Constitution, reaching "the lamentable conclusion that Abraham Lincoln has been elected President of the United States," predicted "gloom

and storm and much to chill the heart of every patriot in the land," adding: "We can understand the effect that will be produced in every Southern mind when he reads the news this morning — that he is now called on to decide for himself, his children, and his children's children whether he will submit tamely to the rule of one elected on account of his hostility to him and his, or whether he will make a struggle to defend his rights, his inheritance, and his honor."

It took little time for many Southerners to make that momentous decision. Many in the South pointed to Lincoln's entirely sectional election as the final straw in the long-running battle for political power. Though he had vowed at Cooper Union to leave slavery alone where it already existed, he had also reiterated there his resolve to oppose the spread of the institution into the territories. To the slave holding South, any attempt to use federal authority to bar localities from admitting slavery was tantamount to a declaration of war.

As he had acknowledged at Cooper Union: "Human action can be modified to some extent, but human nature can not be changed." Addressing the South (though there is no evidence his message reached them), he added: "Your purpose, then, plainly stated, is that you will destroy the Government unless you be allowed to construe and enforce the Constitution as you please, on all points in dispute between you and us. You will rule or ruin in all events."

That was one man's opinion. But on November 6, that man was elected President of the soon-to-be-divided United States. "And," as Lincoln would sadly acknowledge four years later, "the war came."

THE DISRUPTION OF THE DEMOCRATIC PARTY.

MAY 4

The Charleston Convention has abandoned the attempt to nominate a Democratic candidate for the Presidency. The failure is due partly to the disorganized condition of the party, and partly to the blind blundering of the Convention itself. The contest between the two sections of the Union has at last penetrated the Democratic Party, and rendered it impossible for the two wings to agree upon a declaration of principles. When the majority adopted its platform the minority seceded. Thereupon the delegates who remained, and who constituted the rightful Convention, resolved that a vote of two-thirds, not of the actual body, but of the whole original number, should be essential to a nomination. In other words, the seceders were still to be counted, and to have all their original weight as members of the Convention! Upon what ground of reason or of common sense, the majority, and especially the delegates from this State, thus put themselves, bound hand and foot, into the power of the seceding minority, it is not easy to conjecture. The result was to give the South the victory. They have controlled the Convention, and prevented the nomination of any candidate. Whether, on reassembling at Baltimore, they will harmonize their differences, remains to be seen.

The disruption itself is a fact of very marked importance, not only in the history of political parties but of the country itself. It seems to sever the last link of nationality in the political affairs of the Union. When all other organizations have been gradually giving way, one after another, to the pressure of sectionalism, timid and conservative men have fallen back upon the national position of the Democratic Party, and felt that so long as this was maintained the Union would be secure. The first effect of this Charleston split will be to alarm this class by the dread of immediate dissolution.

Some of the Republican journals refer to this incident as only another proof of the "irrepressible conflict" between Freedom and Slavery, — and as showing that the contest must go on until one or the other is extirpated. If we believed this to be the true view of the question, we too should despair of the Union. But we do not. We do not believe that the conflict is between Slavery and Freedom, or that the existence of either will be affected by the result. We regard the struggle as one for political power, — and Slavery as playing merely a secondary and subordinate part on either side. Unquestionably, thousands of Northern men seek the overthrow of Slavery, and thousands of Southern men seek its permanence and extension, as the aim of their political contests. But both would be disappointed. Neither class would reap the advantage which it anticipates from victory. The Slave States have substantially controlled the policy of the Federal Gov-

FROM CHICAGO.

ORGANIZATION OF THE REPUBLICAN NATIONAL CONVENTION.

EXTREME EXCITEMENT AND ENTHUSIASM.

MAY 17
SPECIAL DISPATCH TO THE NEW-YORK TIMES.
CHICAGO, WEDNESDAY, MAY 16

The throng of in-pouring multitudes, by rail, by sail and by wagon, has continued without cessation, all the adjacent States sending their innumerable representatives. The Convention met at the hour prefixed, in the great Wigwam, which holds, and today held, ten thousand people, while twenty thousand more surrounded the building. The proceedings, which will be found at length in the general report, were marked with the utmost good feeling and unbounded enthusiasm.

The organization has been completed, GEORGE ASHMUN,[1] the Chairman, is for Mr. SEWARD,[2] and only hesitates to declare himself from fear of the opposition of other States.

Mr. GIDDINGS[3] was greeted with cheers, as was also Mr. GREELEY.[4]

The canvass outside is very animated. Mr. SEWARD would be nominated by acclamation, but for apprehensions of Pennsylvania. The delegates and others opposed to him are unsparing in their efforts to influence New-England and the Southern States. The great difficulty among the opponents of Mr. SEWARD is their inability to unite upon any other candidate. Each State says that its own candidate is the only one who can carry that State, and it is impossible as yet to get any Anti-Seward State to name any man outside its limits who can carry it. This fact leads the friends of Mr. SEWARD to believe that the rest must eventually come to them, from sheer inability to agree upon any one else. Under this conviction they will remain firm. They have been very courteous and conciliatory, but the failure of their opponents to suggest any other candidate strengthens their position. New-York, Michigan, Wisconsin, Minnesota and Iowa will have no second choice in any contingency.

The result is still entirely doubtful. Any attempts to predict the result would be worse than useless. ⊛

Senator William H. Seward of New York.

1. The son of a Senator, Massachusetts ex-Congressman Ashmun (1804–1870) became a railroad executive.
2. New York Senator William H. Seward (1801–1872) entered the convention as the overwhelming favorite for the Republican presidential nomination.
3. Joshua Giddings (1795–1864), Congressman from Pennsylvania, later U.S. minister to the British North American Provinces (Canada).
4. Horace Greeley (1811–1872) was editor of The New York Press & Tribune. The Times's chief rival among Republican readers.

ernment for the last fifty years. Upon all questions — tariff, currency, foreign relations — their views and sentiments have guided the action of the nation. For a long time they held this power by the legitimate tenure of numbers, weight and influence. Then came a period when they held it by alliances with Northern politicians. And for the last few years they have held it by coercion, — by menaces, by appeals to the fears of the timid, the hopes of the ambitious, and the avarice of the corrupt, in the Northern States. The time has come when they must relinquish their grasp. Power is passing into the hands of the majority — into the hands which hold the numbers, the wealth, the energy, the enterprise of the Confederacy. There is no help for it. It is among the inevitable events of political history. It can no more be arrested than the revolution of the earth around the sun, or the rising and falling of the tides of the sea.

Naturally, however, it excites a commotion. All great changes, — especially all restorations of disturbed balances of power, — are attended with more or less of turmoil and alarm. Righting a ship, which has long been so careened as to make it impossible to walk across her deck, throws everything into confusion, and the unaccustomed passenger who has valuables on board, is quite certain she is capsizing. He sees his mistake only when she stands upright, and with full sail makes direct for her destined port.

The South believes sincerely, we doubt not, that the North seeks power in order to crush Slavery. In our opinion it denounces Slavery mainly that it may acquire power. In many respects the policy of the Federal Government in Northern hands would be different from what it has been hitherto. Men would no longer be excluded from office for doubting the wisdom or the justice of the system Slavery. Federal power would not be used to force it upon unwilling communities. We should no longer be represented abroad by active apostles of Slavery, nor would that be held up to the world as the cherished glory of American institutions.

But there would be no interference with Slavery in any Southern State, — no refusal to execute the constitutional provision for the rendition of fugitives, — no attempt to coerce the population of new Territories. A Northern President, — Northern in sentiment as well as geographical position, — would have a degree of influence over his own section, which would disarm the hostility which a Southern sectionalist would be sure to encounter.

One thing is very certain: — the South must make up its mind to lose the sway it has exercised so long. The sceptre is passing from its hands. Its own imprudencies have hastened the departure of its power, but it has always been merely a question of time. The South can either accept it as inevitable and make the best of it, — or plunge the whole country into turmoil, and bring down swift ruin upon its own borders, in the vain contest against national growth and development. ⊛

THE REPUBLICAN TICKET FOR 1860.
ABRAM, LINCOLN, OF ILLINOIS, NOMINATED FOR PRESIDENT.
THE LATE SENATORIAL CONTEST IN ILLINOIS TO BE RE-FOUGHT ON A WIDER FIELD.

MAY 19

SPECIAL DISPATCH TO THE NEW-YORK TIMES.
CHICAGO, FRIDAY, MAY 18

The work of the Convention is ended. The youngster who, with ragged trousers, used barefoot to drive his father's oxen and spend his days in splitting rails, has risen to high eminence, and ABRAM LINCOLN, of Illinois, is declared its candidate for President by the National Republican Party.

This result was effected by the change of votes in the Pennsylvania, New-Jersey, Vermont, and Massachusetts Delegations.

Mr. SEWARD's friends assert indignantly, and with a great deal of feeling, that they were grossly deceived and betrayed. The recusants endeavored to mollify New-York by offering her the Vice-Presidency, and agreeing to support any man she might name, but they declined the position, though they remain firm in the ranks, having moved to make LINCOLN's nomination unanimous. Mr. SEWARD's friends

feel greatly chagrined and disappointed.

Western pride is gratified by this nomination, which plainly indicates the departure of political supremacy from the Atlantic States....

Immense enthusiasm exists, and everything here would seem to indicate a spirited and successful canvass. The city is alive with processions, meetings, music and noisy demonstrations. One hundred guns were fired this evening.

The Convention was the most enthusiastic ever known in the country, and if one were to judge from appearances here, the ticket will sweep the country.

Great inquiry has been made this afternoon into the history of Mr. LINCOLN. The only evidence that he has a history as yet discovered, is that he had a stump canvass with Mr. DOUGLAS, in which he was beaten. He is not very strong at the West, but it is unassailable in his private character.

Many of the delegates went home this evening by the 9 o'clock train. Others leave in the morning.

A grand excursion is planned to Rock Island and Davenport, and another to Milwaukee and Madison, and still another over the Illinois Central, over the prairies. These will detain a great many of the delegates and the editorial fraternity.

The Wigwam is as full as ever — filled now by thousands of original LINCOLN men, who they "always knew" would be nominated, and who first suggested his name, who are shouting themselves hoarse over the nomination. "What was it WEBSTER said when TAYLOR was nominated?" ask the opponents of LINCOLN. "What was the result of the election?" retort LINCOLN's friends.

Thirty-three guns were fired from the top of the Tremont House.[1]

The dinner referred to in Tuesday evening's dispatch was a private one, ☞

and I regret that inaccurate reading of it should have misrepresented the position of the delegation as regards Mr. GREELEY. His right to act as he deemed best politically, was not denied, and consequently there was no defence of his career needed.

Massachusetts delegates, with their brass band, are parading the streets, calling at the various headquarters of the other delegations, serenading and bidding them farewell. "Hurrah for LINCOLN and HAMLIN[2] — Illinois and Maine!" is the universal shout, and sympathy for the bottom dog is the all-pervading sentiment.

The "Wide-Awakes," numbering about two thousand men, accompanied by thousands of citizens, have a grand torch-light procession. The German Republican Club has another. The office of the Press and Tribune is brilliantly illuminated, and has a large transparency over the door, saying, "For President, Honest Old ABE." A bonfire thirty feet in circumference burns in front of the Tremont House, and illumines the city for miles around. The city is one blaze of illumination. Hotels, stores and private residences, shining with hundreds of patriotic dips.

ENOUGH. HOWARD.[3] ⊕

1. Chicago's leading hotel.
2. Maine Senator Hannibal Hamlin (1809–1891) was chosen by the Republicans as their candidate for vice president. It was not lost on readers that the last three letters of Lincoln's given name, plus the first three letters of his family name, spelled out "Hamlin." In the mid-19th century, the conventions chose the presidfential candidate's running mate without consultation or influence.
3. New York Times correspondent Joseph Howard (1833–1908)

Photograph of Abraham Lincoln taken in Springfield two days after he won the Republican party nomination for president. It was engraved for the frontpiece of Lincoln's first campaign biography.

THE BALTIMORE CONVENTION.

JUNE 19

The Baltimore Convention is in full blast. Yesterday was spent mainly in preliminary movements, but some of these were not without significance. The New-York delegation seems to be, as the French say, master of the situation, and it is quite evident that its leading members intend to husband their influence by using it with caution. Nominally they are for DOUGLAS and their votes will probably be cast for him, as decidedly the strongest man whom the party can select for the Northern States. But it is also evident that their devotion to him is by no means of an uncompromising character. Their votes upon questions of order and of form indicate an unmistakable determination not to push their claims or their opinions to any extreme. When they find it impossible to carry DOUGLAS by a two-thirds vote, they will probably present some new name; and it will not be until after every conceivable effort shall have been made to secure the union of the party, that they will consent to the repeal of the two-thirds rule.

The most significant step taken yesterday was the action upon a resolution offered by Lieutenant-Governor CHURCH, of this State, that all the delegates admitted to seats in the Convention should be deemed bound in honor to support its nominees. Nothing could be intrinsically more just than suck a rule. Conventions become a mere farce when they cease to carry any obligation: — and if one portion of their members are held bound by their action, while another portion is entirely free, they become instruments of oppression. But the Southern Delegates refused utterly to assent to any such restriction of their liberty. They declared their determination to secede en masse in advance of any action, if such a rule should be adopted. And nothing can show more clearly the extreme complaisance of the New-York Delegation, than their refusal to second the previous question on this resolution, or to vote for it on its final passage.

It is very clear that every possible concession will be made to the South, consistent with the continued existence of the party in the Northern States. We see, however, no strong reason for believing that these attempts at compromise will prove successful. A large and active portion of the Southern delegates are clearly in favor of having two candidates, and trusting to the chances of an election in the House or by the Senate. The ultra Douglas men are quite willing to accept the issue thus tendered, and will prefer it decidedly to the nomination of any other candidate than the Illinois Senator. The action of the Convention to-day will probably throw more light upon the final result. ✹

A Currier and Ives lithograph of Stephen A. Douglas, Northern Democratic candidate for president.

THE SECESSION MENACE.

HON. LAWRENCE M. KEIST ON THE DUTY OF THE SOUTH UNDER A REPUBLICAN PRESIDENT.

JULY 24

FROM THE CHARLESTON MERCURY.

Under the teachings of the Abolitionists the North is about to be consolidated against the South. It is futile to deny, unless all the signs around us betray, that the Federal Government is about to pass into the hands of the majority section, and that all its power will be used to cripple, and ultimately to destroy, the institution of Slavery as it exists among us. Neither to-morrow, nor the next week, nor the next year, might the dagger be planted in the heart of the South; out, if she submits to the sectional domination which is now threatened against her, this calamity will inevitably befall, unless the whole history of the world be reversed, and the essential principle of humanity be revolutionized. No people can safely commit their rights and civilization to the custody of another and hostile community, and it is idle to deny that the North is to the South a hostile community....

In my judgment, if the Black Republican Party succeeds in the coming election, the Governor should immediately assemble the Legislature, and that body should provide for a State Convention, which should protect the State from the dishonor of submission to Black Republican rule. Before the tribunal of the world, and at the bar of history, we shall stand justified, Freedom lives much more in the spirit of a people than in the forms of a government. We shall receive the plaudits of brave men for preserving freedom, and not reproaches for shattering a despotism. Senator HAMMOND, in his unanswerable and consummate arguments on the admission of Kansas and "Squatter Sovereignty," has exposed the resources and the rights of the South. Upon both we may safely stand. The Union is just as travelers tell us many Eastern habitations are; a palace to look upon; all fair on its outside, and presenting the appearance of a house that should last for generations; but the master puts his walking stick or his boot-heel through the rafters, and he finds that the white ants have eaten all the substance out of the timbers, and that all that he sees about him is a coating of paint, which an intrusive blow may disperse in a cloud of dust. The skirting boards have already perished, the rafters are now ready to tumble in.

We of the South have done everything to preserve the Union. We have yielded almost every thing but our honors. Let us yield that only as an enemy yields his banner. I have the honor to be,

Your obedient servant,

LAWRENCE M. KEITT.
ORANGEBURGH, C.H., JULY 18 ✹

POLITICAL MISCELLANY.
HOW ALABAMA STANDS.

AUGUST 1

Col. CLEMENS, late editor of the Memphis Enquirer, in a letter to that paper, says of the prospects in Alabama, where he is now staying: "Placing no great reliance upon the reports I hear daily from other parts of the State, and judging only from the feeling manifested in this stronghold of Democracy, I tell you with entire confidence that you may set down Alabama as lost to BRECKINRIDGE. He could not carry the State to-day, and will grow weaker from this time until November. The only thing which ever gave the Secession Party any strength in Alabama was its assumption of the name of Democracy, and when that is torn away they will dwindle into a faction too contemptible to excite the fears, or disturb the peace of the country." The Mobile Tribune cannot stop to count the BRECKINRIDGE papers in the State, but numbers sixteen DOUGLAS journals already. It puts it down as certain that Mr. BRECKINRIDGE cannot carry the State.[1].... ✹

1. Notwithstanding this rather biased prediction, on Election Day Breckinridge won Alabama handily.

THE POLITICAL CAMPAIGN.

—

WESTERN POLITICS.

AUGUST 29

We have had a Bell-Everett State Convention in Ohio, and it is worth notice only so far as to say, that it was very small and very unimportant. In fact, this party is now only the fraction of a fragment — the remnant of a tribe that is lost; but, like the poor Indian, — still linger round the graves of their ancestors. FILLMORE had 28,000 votes in this State, and BELL may have 10,000, but, in no case enough to influence, even indirectly, the result. The prominent idea of these gentlemen now seems to be, to defeat Judge BRINKERHOFF — an honest, upright, fearless Judge of the Supreme Court. BRINKERHOFF is rather fervid in his Anti-Slavery sentiment, and may have given rather ultra opinions in the great case of Cotton vs. Freedom. But it seems to me this is hardly a crime, and certainly not enough to feed a political party upon. The Bell-Everetts here are not only an old gentleman's party, but old gentlemen who don't read the papers, and never heard of the great Meteor. But, enough: Let them be treated with respect, while we pass on to livelier topics....

I said in my last that there was a revolution going on in Virginia; and asked, is it impossible for Virginia to vote for BELL? Since that you have had a clear and able article of your own in the TIMES, on that subject, which I read with great interest. But you have only gone part of the way. I will pursue it a little further. For thirty years, Western Virginia has been Anti-Slavery. The people of the West more than once threatened to separate the State, that they might abolish Slavery in the West. In remodeling the Constitution, they would have provided for gradual emancipation, but for the rotten borough system, by which the Eastern slaveholding counties controlled the Conventions. A compromise was made, as you have remarked, by which, the slaveholders control the Senate till 1865, but then their power will pass away. But now, you see they control the politics of the State, and their leaders are from eastern Virginia, and from districts, where light scarcely penetrates, and they are fully capable of believing that SEWARD and CHASE sent JOHN BROWN there to cut their throats and burn their houses....

Senator John Bell of Tennessee, national Union Party candidate for president.

In the coming election, these Anti-Slavery counties must in the main (quoad the Democracy) vote for DOUGLAS, while the Pro-Slavery counties in the main go for BRECKENRIDGE. Hence, the DOUGLAS vote in Virginia will be much larger than any one anticipated at first. Hence, it was the DOUGLAS Staunton Convention bid defiance to the gentlemen assembled at Charlottesville. The delegates assembled at Staunton came from mountains and valleys, where the voice of freedom is still heard. They saw the gathering of the clans, and knew the storm was coming. Hence it is, that the LINCOLN flag flies on the pole at Wheeling, and no man will pull it down. The coming storm will carry WISE, HUNTER, MASON, BRECKINRIDGE, down before it, into a gulf from whence they will never return. The politicians of all parties left the valley of the Ohio out; but they will be awakened with a clap of thunder from a clear sky. The North-west, — Kentucky, Tennessee, Missouri, and Western Virginia, will go together. The vote for LINCOLN, on the north side of the Ohio, and BELL, on the south, will carry everything; and convince the most stupid that the reign of King Cotton is over. The last people to find this out will be your old fogies; — your BROOKS, and HUNT, and DICKERSON, and HALLOCK — et id

omne genus. But they will find it out after a while. It took about twenty years for one of our old Dutchmen, who voted for JACKSON, to find out that JOHN QUINCY ADAMS was not the son of GEORGE III. But he did find it out, and I never despair of teaching anybody. We have a school for idiots in our State, and it is astonishing how much they learn.

I agree fully with you, however, that in New-York, the friends of LINCOLN should work on the supposition that the coalition may accomplish something. I never knew a coalition that did anything; but there may be an exception. Gov. SEWARD used to be a most perfect tactician, and I agree with him, that the LINCOLN majority in New-York will be a very large one. I don't believe the Americans, who vote for DOUGLAS, will be as many as the Democrats who vote for BRECKINRIDGE. New-York will poll 625,000 votes, and 320,000 will be given to LINCOLN, leaving the residue for DOUGLAS, BRECKINRIDGE and BELL.

A VETERAN OBSERVER. ✸

THE PRESIDENTIAL CAMPAIGN.

GRAND WIDE-AWAKE DEMONSTRATION.

OCTOBER 4

Round us a shield and bright as molten silver the moon uprose last evening about 7 o'clock, touching the cupola of the City Hall with right and throwing out into delicate relief the foliage and branches of the Park trees, as your Reporter hastened from the TIMES Office to Broadway, on his way to view the Wide-Awakes.

Even at that early hour, the Park itself and all the sidewalks were densely crowded, the stages and carriages having to slowly crawl up the centre of the street through dense fringes of excited and expectant humanity. Windows and stoops were packed with curious faces; all the corners displayed mass-meetings in embryo — fresh accessions constantly thronging up from the side streets to swell the numbers or supply the places of those lucky ones who had managed to push their way into the main upward-drifts of the palpitating current.

Stepping into a stage and driving up towards Union-square as fast as the many human obstructions would allow us, the scene became more animated and brilliant each moment, as we approached the main centre of attraction. Broadway never more thoroughly displayed its Metropolitan character — all ranks and varieties of men, women and children being collected and merged together behind its curbstone lines on either hand....

Endless seems the procession, fresh and yet fresh companies of the Republican army debouching from side-streets into the Avenue, as room is made for their entrance by the passage downward of those in the van. While waiting for their turn to mix in the march, these regiments of uniformed link-bearers bivouac on the curb-stones or squat complacently on convenient steps. All varieties of military evolutions appear familiar to them — their torches now rapidly forming into hollow square around some decorated wagon filled with ladies in star-spangled robes, or meandering in single file into a curved procession, designed to imitate the waving outline of those fences for which the chief Candidate on their ticket split his immortal rails.

No appurtenance of a military host is lacking here, each third or fourth company having trundled behind it a huge brass howitzer or field-piece, the mouth of which is expected to discourse most eloquent music next Fourth of March, when the patriarchal ABRAHAM of Illinois carries his carpet-bag and portfolio up the shouting steps of the White House. Here are pioneers with ugly hatchets, and it may be observed that all the torch-men carry their illuminating machines as soldiers carry their firelocks. Each captain and other officer is distinguished from his men by appropriate decorations or varieties of uniform — the officers having colored lanterns, with glass shades, while the mere privates bear Britannia-metal lamps, swung on metal forks at the top of each pole. Military bands at the head of every second company discoursed patriotic and thrilling music — fifes and drums predominating, but the ring of brazen instruments also lending vivacity and harmony to the general chorus. These bands, for the most part, are in uniform like the Wide-Awakes, and the incessant peals of their playing must be imagined during every step of our description. ✪

Republican Wide-Awake procession in New York City on the evening of October 3, 1860.

MR. LINCOLN'S CONSERVATISM.

OCTOBER 17

The Journal of Commerce insists, with steadfast earnestness, that the Republican Party is pledged to interfere with the rights and interests of the Slaveholding States. It quotes the oft-repeated and grossly-distorted declarations of Senator SEWARD and Mr. LINCOLN, asserting the fact of a radical hostility between Freedom and Slavery, but lays special stress upon a declaration imputed to Senator WILSON,[1] that he trusted the Republican Party would retain and exercise the powers of the Government "till no man on the continent should hold property in another man." The Journal treats this as conclusive of the radical and revolutionary designs of the Republican Party.

Now, if the Journal adopts this style of argument merely for the purpose of defeating LINCOLN's election, we have nothing special to urge against it. It is quite as legitimate as three-fourths of the partisan logic of the day. But in our judgment it is not likely to prove effectual. The chances are that Mr. LINCOLN will be elected, — and that the control of the Executive Department of the Government will pass into his hands. We are therefore not only curious to know, but interested in knowing, whether the Journal will then insist upon the same views which it now urges upon this subject. In our opinion, the great mass of the members of the Republican Party do not lend the least credit to the representations of their opponents on this point. They do not believe that Mr. LINCOLN has the remotest wish or thought of interfering with Slavery in any Southern State. They do not believe that he will trespass, in the least degree, upon Southern rights, or do anything of which considerate and patriotic Southern men will have the slightest reason to complain. If Senator WILSON, or Mr. SUMNER, or Mr. LOVEJOY, have different expectations, we believe they are destined to be disappointed.

After Mr. LINCOLN shall be elected we think he will very promptly take steps to dispel the fogs that have been thrown around his political position, — and that he will present himself to the country as a Conservative, devoted to the Union, considerate equally of every section and of every State, and resolved faithfully and with firmness to maintain the Constitution in all its parts. We have no doubt that he will proclaim himself opposed to the extension or increase of Slavery, and equally opposed to any interference of Congress, or of the North, with Slavery in the Southern States. He has repeatedly declared himself in favor of an efficient Fugitive Slave Law, and opposed to negro suffrage and the political equality of the negro race. We regard these as eminently conservative views, and if his Administration adheres to them with firmness and fidelity, we believe it will contribute largely to the restoration of the public peace, and fortify the Constitution and the Union still more thoroughly in the affection and confidence of the American people.... ⊛

1. Henry Wilson (1812–1875) of Massachusetts.

HOW TO ELECT A PRESIDENT.

OCTOBER 29

The Journal of Commerce[1] has the following:

"The TIMES is again harping upon its original argument, that people ought to vote for LINCOLN to elect him, to prevent the worse result of his election by the House of Representatives.[2] We believe the TIMES has the exclusive monopoly of this line of argument, — no other paper having stultified itself by following in its footsteps."

This is very peremptory and, probably, very decisive for those who accept partisan assertions for logic. We confess, however, that we remain unconvinced. We don't quite see the absurdity of the point, and shall feel under special obligations to the Journal of Commerce if it will so far condescend to our dullness as to attempt our enlightenment.

We do still insist that, in the existing condition of the country, carrying the election of a President into the House of Representatives, involves much more danger to the peace of the country than the election of LINCOLN by the people. According to all human probability, LINCOLN, BRECKINRIDGE[3] and BELL,[4] will be the three candidates before that body. LINCOLN will start with fifteen States certain, and BRECKINRIDGE with thirteen. Illinois has five Douglas Democrats and four Republicans on her delegation. One of the former, Mr. MORRIS,[5] has pub-

BRECKINRIDGE SMOKED OUT.

OCTOBER 30

We have already published the meagre extracts of a letter from Mr. BRECKINRIDGE to a gentleman in North Carolina, in which he defines his position upon the question of disunion. We have no hesitation in declaring that it places him in a far worse position than he occupied while refusing to answer. His silence was suspicious, and left room for the inference that he might be tinctured with the treasonable sentiments which all the more distinguished leaders of his party own; but his oracular utterance leaves us little room to doubt that he is only for the Union so long as his party holds power.

It will be remembered that the questions put to Mr. [Stephen A.] DOUGLAS at Norfolk, were substantially these:

Do you consider the election of LINCOLN a just cause for breaking up the Union?

Do you believe in the light of peaceable secession without cause?

To these printed interrogatories Mr. DOUGLAS gave answers which did him honor. He not only denied the right of secession, for the cause supposed, but he declared his purpose to sustain Mr. LINCOLN in enforcing the laws. The same questions have been repeatedly addressed to Mr. BRECKINRIDGE, but he has studiously refused to answer, except to one gentleman, Mr. COHOON, the Mayor of Elizabeth City, North Carolina. And what is that question? He says, under date of October 5:

"Yours of the 1st instant has been received. The questions you ask are answered in my inclosed speech. I esteem Mr. YANCEY[1] highly, and have known him long and favorably. * * * Mr. BRECKINRIDGE is not Mr. YANCEY. I love the Union, but the South better. If elected, the Union, under my care, shall never be dismembered."

We substitute "dismembered" for "disseminated," as it originally appeared, and was evidently a typographical or telegraphic error. This is the whole of the letter which has been permitted to see the light, and the inference from it is almost irresistible, that Mr. BRECKINRIDGE will pledge himself to stand by the Union only on the conditions of his own election to the Presidency. If every man in the country stood on this narrow platform, the Union would be rent into some thirty millions of atoms. This is

John C. Breckinridge, Southern Democratic Candidate for President in 1860.

licly declared that he will vote for LINCOLN rather than see BRECKINRIDGE elected, and his vote will decide the vote of his State. Illinois, therefore, may be set down for LINCOLN if it be necessary either to prevent the election of his opponent, or to effect a choice. That leaves LINCOLN lacking but one vote. The seat of the Democratic member from Oregon is contested, and the House, which decides his claim, is against him. The admission of his contestant would give Oregon to LINCOLN, and secure his election.

Now, we put it to the Journal of Commerce, (1), whether it is not probable that LINCOLN would be elected by the House if the choice devolves on that body; (2), whether the South would be any more disposed to submit to his election when thus effected, than when made by the People; and (3), whether the opportunity for making forcible resistance, and for plunging the House and the country into civil strife and commotion, would not be far better and more tempting

than would be afforded by LINCOLN's election on the 6th of November?

These are very simple questions, and they admit of very direct answers. Possibly we are mistaken, but we consider them deserving of a different style of reply from that which the Journal of Commerce has adopted hitherto. We know something of the nature of a sharp sectional contest in the House of Representatives. Two struggles for the Speakership have thrown considerable light upon the measures resorted to by a desperate disunion faction, to avert a threatened defeat. They are not such as encourage us to look with complacency upon the experiment the Journal seems anxious to try. We have great faith in the strength of the Union and the power of the Constitution. We believe both will stand the strain of a popular election, conducted in strict conformity with the laws of the land, whatever may be its result; we have not equal faith in its ability to go through the fearful ordeal which the Journal invites. ◉

> 1. One of New York's pro-Democratic newspapers.
> 2. With Lincoln favored to win by October, desperate foes hoped he would fall short of an electoral majority against his three opponents, forcing the presidential election to the House of Representatives. There, voting would be conducted by delegation, increasing the chances of success by a compromise candidate.
> 3. John C. Breckinridge, Vice President of the United States, was the Southern Democratic candidate for President in 1860.
> 4. John Bell (1796–1869) of Tennessee was Constitutional Union candidate for the presidency in 1860.
> 5. Isaac Newton Morris (1812–1869).

carrying the doctrine of secession to its utmost limits. The question was, whether Mr. BRECKINRIDGE would sustain the Union if Mr. LINCOLN shall be elected President? He answers that he will remain faithful if elected himself, while, in the same breath, he avows an intense degree of sectional feeling. "I love the Union, but the South better." Did ever Presidential candidate avow such a sentiment before? Could YANCEY and KEITT[2] demand more of him?

As we never heard of a President who desired to break up the Union during his own term of office — for even Mr. BUCHANAN[3] cannot agree to that — we are not surprised that Mr. BRECKINRIDGE gives the assurance that he will not rebel against his own Administration. But when this contemptible evasion is given in answer to the direct

question, "will you counsel resistance to Mr. LINCOLN?" it would be an affectation of charity to doubt that he is at heart a Disunionist, or, at any rate, that he has too much respect for the preachers of disunion and treason to take ground against their plans. There can be no two opinions on this matter. The inference is irresistible. ◉

> 1. William Lowndes Yancey (1814–1863) was a fire-eating Democratic Congressman from Alabama.
> 2. Lawrence Massilllon Keitt (1824–1864), Democratic Congressman from South Carolina — would be killed in action in 1864 at Cold Harbor.
> 3. Although not a candidate for re-election, President James Buchanan (1791–1868) remained very much an issue in the campaign to elect his White House successor. A "Doughface" pro-South northerner, Buchanan had favored a pro-slavery Constitution for Kansas and (according to charges by Lincoln) had conspired in the 1857 Dred Scott decision.

REPUDIATION AND DISUNION.

OCTOBER 30

The merchants of our City who are so busy in the Fusion movement,[1] will do well to give some little heed to an article which we copy from the Charleston Mercury. It will probably come home somewhat closely to their "business and bosoms." It discusses the advantages to the South of secession, — and foremost among them it places the Repudiation of all their Northern debts. If they can only get rid of the Federal Constitution, they will obliterate their indebtedness to Northern merchants forever. Disunion is to operate, therefore, as an enormous sponge — to wipe off all their obligations, and release them from the payment of all their dues.

This must be a pleasant prospect for our merchants who have been laboring so zealously in their cause. They have been representing that the South will have cause for dissolving the Union in case the North elects a Republican candidate. LINCOLN is quite certain to be elected, and dissolution involves the repudiation of Southern debts. Are the Messrs. HENRY quite as confident, as they have been hitherto, that the election of LINCOLN will justify secession? Will they think it quite right to lose all their dues, because the people of the Union, in the exercise of their constitutional rights, elect a Republican President? This proposition of the [Charleston] Mercury is the most flagitious scheme to which this disunion madness has given rise. No man, who was not at heart utterly dishonest, would propose to escape the payment of a just debt on the strength of any political differences whatever. No community not dead to all the instincts of commercial honor, would tolerate the suggestion of so base and discreditable a project. The object of throwing it thus shamelessly before the public, is doubtless in part to alarm the North and coerce our people into abandoning their political principles. It takes effect, however, upon those who have already done this in order to secure Southern favor and Southern trade. The whole Fusion movement in this State has been organized, and is sustained, by one or two mercantile establishments who have large transactions with the South, who have large creditors among the Southern merchants, and who are already doing everything in ☞

their power to meet the exacting demands of the Southern States. They are the men, and almost the only men, who would be seriously affected by the wholesale repudiation which the Mercury proposes.

We cannot congratulate the Messrs. HENRY on being very well backed by their Southern friends. Such suggestions as those we quote are rather cold comfort for men in their position. They are really only another turn of the screw, — another blow of the lash, — by which this whole Pro-Slavery movement in our community has been stimulated and pushed into activity. The South are utterly remorseless and relentless in their crusade. They make no appeal to generous sentiments or impulses in support of their cause. They rely solely upon fear. They have coerced our merchants hitherto by threatening to withdraw their trade. Fearing that this will not avail, they now threaten to repudiate their debts. The only consolation our merchants have in the premises is, that they cannot go any further. Their Southern overseers have touched bottom at last. ✺

REPUBLICAN DEMONSTRATION AT LYONS.

SPEECHES OF GOV. SEWARD AND OTHERS — GREAT POPULAR ENTHUSIASM.

OCTOBER 31

SPECIAL DISPATCH TO THE NEW-YORK TIMES.
LYONS, N.Y., TUESDAY, OCT. 30

A very large Republican mass meeting was held here to-day. Over fifteen thousand persons came from Wayne and Cayuga counties expressly to take part in the proceedings.

Gov. SEWARD[1] presided at the meeting and delivered a short opening address, in which he reviewed the history of the country with regard to Slavery, and defined the issues of the present canvass. He said that the early founders of the Government aimed to make all the States free in course of time, and that the present policy was a departure from the policy of the statesmen in the early days of the Republic. Mr. SEWARD's address was quite brief. He was followed by Mr. P. CORBETT and Mr. WM. J. CORNELL.

Mr. H. J. RAYMOND,[2] of New-York, who arrived in the Eastern train, spoke one hour on the issues of the canvass.

The Wide-Awakes are having a very imposing procession to-night. The town is illuminated, and the greatest enthusiasm prevails.

Gov. SEWARD goes to Seneca Falls to-morrow, and will speak in New-York on Friday.

The disunion panic creates great indignation in this section, and will give Republicans thousands of votes. Wayne County will give three thousand majority for LINCOLN. ✺

1. Though greatly disappointed when the Republican Party rejected him and turned to Lincoln as its presidential nominee in May, Seward campaigned loyally for the Lincoln ticket throughout his home state — and elsewhere in the country. A former governor of New York, he was often referred to by that title — even when he became a senator and, later, Lincoln's secretary of state.
2. Henry Jarvis Raymond (1820–1869), editor of the openly pro-Republican New York Times.

THE PRESIDENTIAL CAMPAIGN.

MORE SCHEMES OF THE DISUNIONISTS.

PLAN FOR PRODUCING A GENERAL FINANCIAL CRISIS.

OCTOBER 31

SPECIAL DISPATCH TO THE NEW-YORK TIMES.
WASHINGTON, TUESDAY, OCT. 30

The plan of the Southern Disunionists, as just exposed, is to hold back the Cotton crop, which has already been drawn on, and refuse to let a single bag be shipped to England. The result will be, as they suppose, a drain of specie and a general financial crisis.

Hon. A.R. BOTELER,[1] of Virginia, brings intelligence from New-York to-night that New-Jersey is safe for Fusion, and that the chances are against LINCOLN in New-York.

A letter from Hon. A.H. STEPHENS,[2] declaring that if the Union endures the principles of DOUGLAS will survive, is published in the States this evening.

The secessionists announce their purpose to make Virginia the New-England of the Southern Confederacy, and by stimulating her energies and developing her resources, to increase the value of her slave property. It is not expected that Virginia will join in the secession movement.

O [A REPORTER'S SIGNATURE]. ✺

1. Alexander Robinson Boteler (1815–1892) served a single term in Congress before resigning to join the Confederate army in 1861. He later served as a staff aide to General Thomas J. "Stonewall" Jackson, then entered the Confederate Congress.
2. Alexander Hamilton Stephens (1812–1883) was a veteran Whig congressman from Georgia — and for two years served as a colleague of one-term Representative Abraham Lincoln of Illinois. Though initially opposed to secession, Stephens quit the House when Georgia left the Union, and then became Vice President of the Confederacy.

1. Many New York Democrats advocated that the state's loyal voters should unite behind one of the two Democratic presidential aspirants to increase the party's chances against Lincoln. Most turned to Breckinridge.

THE SOUTH AND THE PRESIDENTIAL ELECTION.

OCTOBER 31

The best informed of our Southern correspondents begin to assure us that the extreme excitement which has for some time past reigned throughout the Southern States, in anticipation of the election of Mr. LINCOLN, already exhibits symptoms of decline. It is more than probable, now, that the State of South Carolina must be regarded as the sole pivot of the Southern revolution, and that the rest of the slaveholding Sovereignties will defer the resumption of their supreme attributes, and the open defiance of the constitutional authorities of the Union, until the Palmetto State shall act in the premises. Whether the Palmetto State will or will not act at all in the premises is another question, upon which we have not yet sufficient grounds for pronouncing a decisive opinion. South Carolina is a very peculiar State, and occupies a quite exceptional position in the Republic. Nowhere else have the ideas of the permanence of Slavery, and of the capacity of the South for independence, struck root so deeply as in the Commonwealth of CALHOUN. Yet, at the same time, it must be remembered that the society of South Carolina is singularly well organized, and therefore essentially conservative, and that the influence of property in that State is more direct and more openly recognized than in any other part of the Confederation.

Meanwhile it may not be out of place or untimely for us to suggest to the more temperate of our Southern fellow-citizens, as well in South Carolina itself as in the other Slaveholding States, one aspect of the approaching triumph of Mr. LINCOLN which well deserves to be gravely pondered by them before they make up their minds to regard that triumph as the signal for a complete severance of the ties which hold together our common country, and give to them and to us our name and place among the nations.

It has been far too generally asserted and far too easily believed that the election of Mr. LINCOLN is to be interpreted as a victory of the North, as such, over the South, as such, and, therefore, as the initial act in the final exclusion of the South from all control in the Federal Government. The overwhelming majorities which are now rallying to the support of the Republican candidate in the only States in

which the antecedents of our political history have unhappily made the Republican Party for the present possible, are the protest of — the nation not only, nor even perhaps chiefly against the extension of Slavery into the National Territories, but also, and in a most important degree, against the intolerable demoralization of an existing Federal Government. No one can doubt that in several States of the North the opponents of Republicanism, as a political party in and by itself, outnumber the supporters of that party. In these States the election of Mr. LINCOLN will be very largely the work of men who act and vote for him simply because the existing Administration has made it impossible for them to act and vote for anybody else. Mr. BUCHANAN, since his advent to power, has surrounded himself with a camarilla of men who have made themselves odious to the country, not because they are Southern men and slaveholders, but because they have prostituted the highest offices of the State to the lowest personal objects. Indeed these men are not by any means exclusively Southern men either in their origin or in their policy. The recklessness of a Pennsylvanian Attorney-General, and the openly shameful Presidential diplomacy of such Northern Senators as Messrs. BRIGHT and FITCH,[1] have done quite as much to make Mr. LINCOLN the coming man, as the Pro-Slavery devices of Messrs. [John] SLIDELL and DAVIS,[2] or the impetuous passions of others of the President's slaveholding champions. The War-Secretary, FLOYD,[3] of Virginia, who has outraged even the not very scrupulous sensibilities of the oldest Washington politicians by his official indecencies, has contributed to the support of Mr. LINCOLN not the impulse of his slaveholding proclivities, but the force of his administrative misconduct. Had Mr. BUCHANAN surrounded himself with Southern men of the honorable and dignified character once identified in the popular mind with the idea of a Southern leader, the course of events in our recent political history might have been gravely modified. The Calhouns, and Haynes, and Pinckneys of the past would never have brought upon the President of their preference that grand consent of public contempt which the Government of Mr. BUCHANAN has

earned for itself, and of which it is now so soon to reap the final harvest.

This is a view of the actual crisis of our current history which neither Fusionists nor confusionists will be very swift to take. But it is a sound and practical view, nevertheless, and as such we commend it to the earnest attention alike of angry Southern patriots and of active Northern panic-makers, in the world of politics or in the world of finance. It will have its value after the 6th of November, and may not be altogether useless before that time. ✸

President James Buchanan.

1. Jesse D. Bright (1812–1875) and Graham Newell Fitch (1809–1892), Democrats from Indiana. Bright was later expelled from the Senate for acknowledging Jefferson Davis as the legitimate President of the Confederacy. Fitch, however, a medical doctor, went on to serve heroically as a colonel in the 46th Regiment of the Indiana Volunteer Infantry.
2. Slidell became even more famous in November 1861 when seized on the high seas en route to a diplomatic assignment representing the Confederacy (see page 124); Jefferson Davis (1808–1809) was then serving as a Democratic Senator from Mississippi.
3. John B. Floyd (1807–1863) of Virginia left the War Department toward the end of the Buchanan Administration. Though he initially opposed secession and favored the re-enforcement of Fort Sumter, he went on to serve in the Confederate army, reaching the rank of brigadier general.

ASTOUNDING TRIUMPH OF REPUBLICANISM.
—
ABRAHAM LINCOLN PROBABLY ELECTED PRESIDENT.

NOVEMBER 7

The canvass for the Presidency of the United States terminated last evening, in all the States of the Union, under the revised regulation of Congress, passed in 1845, and the result, by the vote of New-York, is placed beyond question at once. It elects ABRAHAM LINCOLN of Illinois; President, and HANNIBAL HAMLIN of Maine, Vice-President of the United States, for four years, from the 4th March next, directly by the People: These Republican Candidates having a clear majority of the 309 Electoral votes of the 33 States, over all three of the opposing tickets. They receive, including Mr. LINCOLN's own State, from which the returns have not yet come, in the

New-England States	41
New-York	35
Pennsylvania	27
New-Jersey	7
And the Northwest	61
Total Electoral for LINCOLN	171[1]

Being 19 over the required majority, without wasting the returns from the two Pacific States of Oregon and California.

The election, so far as the City and State of New-York are concerned, will probably stand, hereafter as one of the most remarkable in the political contests of the country; marked, as it is, by far the heaviest popular vote ever cast in the City, and by the sweeping, and almost uniform, Republican majorities in the country.

The State of Pennsylvania, which virtually decided her preference in October, has again thrown an overwhelming majority for the Republican candidates. And New-Jersey, after a sharp contest has, as usual in nearly all the Presidential elections, taken her place on the same side. The New-England majorities run up by tens of thousands.

The Congressional elections which took place yesterday, in this State have probably confirmed the probability of an Anti-Republican preponderance in the next House of Representatives, by displacing several of the present Republican members.

The new House of Assembly for New-York will, as usual, be largely Republican.

Of the reelection of Gov. MORGAN[2] there is little or no question. By the scattering vote thrown for Mr. BRADY in this City, the plurality of Mr. KELLY over Gov. MORGAN is partially reduced, while the heavy Republican majority in the country insures Gov. MORGAN's success.

The rival Presidential candidates against Mr. LINCOLN have probably divided the Southern vote as follows:

FOR MR BELL.

Virginia	15
Tennessee	12
Kentucky	12

FOR MR. BRECKINRIDGE.

South Carolina	8
Florida	3
North Carolina	10
Mississippi	7
Georgia	10
Texas	4
Alabama	9
Arkansas	4

DOUBTFUL.

Missouri	9
Delaware	3
Louisiana	6
Maryland	8[3]

AT THE REPUBLICAN HEAD-QUARTERS GENERAL REJOICING

The Republican rejoicings filled the City last night. They celebrated their triumph in the streets; they gathered in shouting crowds around the newspaper-offices; they inundated the Station-houses, and threw up their hats as the returns were announced; they assembled at the Head-quarters, No. 618 Broadway, in such numbers, that once wedged in one could not turn around to come out again. There Mr. DANIEL D. CONOVER took the Chair, and, with Gen. J. H. HOBART WARD and Mr. CHARLES SPENCER, received the returns, and from time to time computed the probable result. Mr. CONOVER read the figures, and every time he read the people cheered or jeered, according to the complexion of the news. The enthusiasm, which was wild, as soon as it was known how much below the estimate of the Fusionists was the result in the First Ward, increased steadily as the night wore on, and was incontinent at last. Never were there gathered together so many persons in so excellent a humor. While they were waiting for news from some Wards not yet heard from, all were talking and laughing at once; some were giving lusty cheers for LINCOLN and the whole Republican ticket; some were cracking jokes at the expense of the Opposition; those without were endeavoring to elbow their way in, and some within, half suffocated, were trying to force their way out. It was just such a hubbub of hilarity, in short, as you would expect to hear in the Republican Head-quarters on the night of the Republican victory. One, more enthusiastic, was incessantly proposing three cheers for somebody. He proposed three cheers for Gen. WARD; they were given with gusto. He proposed three more for Mr. CONOVER, and three more for Mr. SPENCER; they were given. Then he proposed "Three cheers for me." They were not given. Then, by way of variety, he proposed three cheers for Mr. CONOVER again. Here that gentleman interposed and requested that less noise should be made, and that men would stand still; he did not know how long the floor of the room would support such a mass of enthusiastic people.

A man mounted a chair at the remote end of the room and shouted out the name of a friend, whom he said he wanted to go to a fire that was raging not far off. "There's a fire every where," said Mr. SPENCER, and that brought down the house — almost the floor — again. Loud as the din was during these interludes, as soon as the Chairman announced more returns, quiet was immediately restored — to be lost again amid a storm of cheers as soon as they were read. Thus, till a late hour, they kept it up at No. 618 Broadway.

At the Head-quarters of the various Republican Clubs, too, there were immense throngs. The City Wide-Awakes were at their rendezvous in force, and at Stuyvesant Institute the jam was irrepressible. The interior of the building was choked with people, the entrance was blocked up, and the sidewalk in front was black with Republicans. With the thunders of the thousands there assembled, the vicinity like the rest of the City, was kept thoroughly and wide awake. ◉

1. Final figures gave Lincoln 180 electoral votes.
2. Edwin D. Morgan (1811–1881) was twice elected governor of New York, later serving as a major general of Union volunteers and commander of the Department of New York.
3. Three of these states ultimately fell into Breckinridge's column, too. This table made no mention of Lincoln's Northern Democratic opponent, Stephen A. Douglas, who finished second in the popular vote with 1,376,957 supporters, but won only 12 electoral votes (Missouri and New Jersey).

ELECTION DAY IN THE CITY.

ALL QUIET AND ORDERLY AT THE POLLS.

NOVEMBER 7

The clouds lowered gloomily over the City yesterday morning, when the polls were opened, and very shortly afterward rain began to drizzle, with every prospect of a wet day. Was it an omen, and if so, an ill omen to the Lincoln or Fusion ticket? It did not, at any rate, keep one or the other party from the polls, for never in the history of any political contest in this country, has more enthusiasm been exhibited, and the result has proved that though the "clouds" may have "lowered," the hopes of the Republican Party were not "in the deep bosom of the ocean buried." But of that anon and elsewhere.

People generally were awake — wide awake, in fact[1] — very early yesterday, for they knew they had a duty to perform which could not occur but once in four years, and in the actual shape it assumed, perhaps not more than once in a lifetime. And whether they were Republicans or Fusionists, they went to work with a will. The clouds were dispelled; the sun shone forth as a beneficent sun should shine on such an occasion, and a general good time was the result. In short, although the stake to be played, according to the alarmists, was the continuation or severance of the Union, there was no disturbance, no discordance, no manner of ill-feeling, beyond the impatience produced by the extreme difficulty in getting in "my vote, Sir, my prerogative as an independent citizen, Sir, which I would not barter for my life, Sir."

The vote polled in each Ward, and each District of each Ward, is said to have been the heaviest ever known in this City. At nearly every polling-place — and there were close upon three hundred in all the Wards — voters took their places en queue, and moved on very slowly to their duty as freemen. And wherever we had opportunities of observing them, they did it like men who were fully sensible of the responsibility, whether it came of conscience sake, or was derived from a recollection or a hope of "gilded gain."

Considerable delay was caused at many polls by an indiscriminate challenging process, which occupied so much time that in nearly every Ward at sunset, when the polls closed, some hundreds of voters had not been able to "save the country," and having given the day to that nobly patriotic purpose, they felt, very naturally, slightly irascible thereat.... ⊛

1. A joking reference to the ubiquitous Wide-Awake clubs.

A pro-Republican 1860 presidential campaign cartoon shows the symbol of America ushering Lincoln to the White House.

THE DAY AFTER ELECTION.

THE REPUBLICANS AND THEIR TRIUMPH.

NOVEMBER 8

The Republican pulse continues to beat high. Chanticleer is perched on the back of the American Eagle, and with flapping wings and a sonorous note proclaims his joy at the victory. The return of the First NAPOLEON from Elba did not create a greater excitement than the returns of the present election. All day yesterday the inquiry was in everybody's mouth, "What's the latest news?" Newspapers were in demand. What, with the cries of the urchins who vended them, the demonstrations of the jubilant and the groans of the wounded, the Metropolis of yesterday was to the every-day New-York as Babel to a charnel-house. Every omnibus that carried its dozen of citizens businessward in the morning was a reading room, a political meeting-house and a pseudo stock board, all in one, — e pluribus unum. Some read the papers, some fought the bloodless battle o'er again, bringing their batteries of profound argument to bear upon the proposition that they "knew LINCOLN would be elected;" and some in sarcastic mood bewailed with mock seriousness the heavy losses from depreciated stocks that were sure to follow the dire calamity of the inauguration of the chosen of a majority of the people. In the streets, in the restaurants, in offices and counting-houses — counting certain counting-houses out — such was the tenor of the talk, and the character of the occupations of all to whom a leisure moment came. There were few Fusionists to be found. There was a dearth of Democrats — a scarcity of those who professed and called themselves Bell-Everett men. Republicans everywhere seem wide awake, while "Drowsy tinklings lull the distant fold" of their bell-ringing opponents. Distant, indeed — for this side of Mason and Dixon's line there is hardly a tintinnabulation, where but yesterday the Callithumpians seemed let loose.

We searched in vain for some one that could tell us of the feelings of the defeated. Every one declared himself a Lincoln man, or else said nothing. We visited the Custom-house and studied the triste physiognomies of the Federal office-holders.[1] Some looked blue and sat shivering at their desks; but it was a cold day, — very cold, — much colder than the few that preceded it.

At length passing through Nassau-street we met an acquaintance, — one whom we had heard during the campaign expressing his predilections for DOUGLAS, and his blissful anticipations of Arcadian Winters in office at Washington under the Douglas dynasty. We hailed him; he was in a great hurry and couldn't stop, — bank just closing, — all that sort of thing. We took him by the button; that is the shot across the bows that will always bring one to. He stopped, and, after a moment's attention to our inquiries. "My dear Sir," he said, "I'm a Lincoln man, and always was!" We pursued our investigations in that direction no further. In all seriousness, we heard less about Disunion yesterday than we have heard any day in a month past; we heard quite as many jokes about Dry Goods and Salt River as have come to our ears within the same period; and we learned nothing that would lead us to suppose that the people of the fairly beaten parties will acquiesce now in the expressed, will of the people a whit less gracefully than the Republicans submitted when they were overborne four years ago.

Of course, there will be demonstrations on the part of the Republicans "all the country through." What shall be the nature of them is already a subject of discussion. The Republican State Executive Committee will meet next Tuesday — probably at Albany — and arrange the preliminaries of a grand celebration. The Chairman, Mr. SIMEON DRAPER,[2] in jocose mood, observed yesterday, that for his part, he believed the best way would be to roast a large elephant somewhere in the centre of the State, and invite all the people. A bystander remarked that it would certainly be a "big thing." The Wide-Awakes of the City will have a grand parade some day of this week or the next. Our metropolis just now is one great Rama. Lamentation is in the streets and wailing on the corners. People are weeping for their candidates and will not be comforted, because they are not. Mourners are visible in the parks, and in the "private parlors" of the hotels, and in all other public places. They go about with streaming eyes and red noses, surveying the field of battle, and bursting out with renewed grief when they recognize the fea-

tures of a friend among the slain. Sometimes they become lugubriously jolly, sit down in each other's laps, mingle their woes, clink their glasses together, and become convivial upon tears. These sad scenes are the inevitable result of all great victories. Battlefields are not pleasant for promenades on the day after a battle. The dead tell no tales, but the wounded…cry out pretty loudly. Their cries blend sadly with the shouts of the victors. It is useless to say: "They were rascals and deserved to be killed." The conviction that they were fellow-creatures forces itself upon the most unthinking mind, and it is ever natural to sympathize with suffering humanity. A sensitive spirit would take no delight even in the agonies of an Alderman; and it is questionable whether any man, unless, indeed, he had been brutalized by several years in Congress, would feel any especial pleasure in witnessing the crucifixion of a Common Councilman. We venture to assert that even the most biased Wide-Awake is possessed of a feeling akin to sympathy, if not sorrow, as he meets a discomfited colonel, a disjointed captain, or a scattered sergeant in the late Democratic Army. And his heart would be harder than the nether millstone if he did not.…

The quiet which attended the actual election on Tuesday was only a foreshadowing of the manner in which the result of that election was received yesterday. SHAKESPEARE says that man is a creature who "looks before and after." The "after" of the election, with the "great hereafter" that was predicted by the Southern Press and Northern Fusionists, in case LINCOLN should be elected, was quite mildly treated by the parties which suffered defeat. It is to their credit that, being defeated, they bore it handsomely. Fusionist met Republican amicably at the breakfast table, — amicably in the street, amicably in the store, and, in fact, in an amicable manner, invited him to "just take a little, it won't hurt you."

One of our wandering reporters in a ramble around town, tried to find out some discordant element in the popular sentiment, and to that end visited the chief hotels, especially those which Southerners do most approve; also the restaurants, the public places of resort, and (but it was only as a matter of duty) the drinking saloons. Thus the New-York Hotel, the Lafarge, the Metropolitan and the St. Nicholas were approached with the very best results. Although a large number of Southern gentlemen and families were residing at each of these popular establishments, there were no symptoms of revolt, of dissatisfaction even, or of anything else than a disposition for enjoyment....

In places not so important as these large hotels, those restaurants and saloons, which (in the path of duty only) our wandering reporter visited, everything was equally quiet and congenial. Where, before election, and on the day of election, bands, of men, eight or ten strong, with tumblers in their hands, half filled with some kind of fluid, would impress, with said tumblers on the counter, and with very audible vocal accompaniment, their devotion to the "U-n-i-o-n," there were the same men yesterday, a trifle melancholy, perhaps, "sadder but wiser," quaffing lemonade, or ginger soda, with the very slightest dash of brandy in it, with no tap of tumbler or vocal accompaniment whatever. One thing was on some occasions, but not often, peculiar in their conduct. If, in the street, they espied a Republican friend approaching, something novel in a store window, some architectural ornament in a new building, or an examination of the sky, in anticipation of rain, would so divert their attention, that they allowed their Republican friend to pass. There was also a sheepishness in their countenances which strangely contrasted with their boastful and defiant physiognomy during the last five or six weeks.

Sometimes our Reporter encountered an officeholder — one in the Custom-house, for instance. He was an exception to the general rule of placability and pacificality. He was as ugly as a disturbed snake. Then, on the other hand, making a virtue of necessity, another would say, "Well, after all, perhaps LINCOLN's election will be for the best — may tend to settle things generally, if he is not aggressive, and — do you think there will be a general routing out of us small office-holders?" This shadow of a man, rabid Fusionist on Tuesday, becoming a convert to bread and butter, and roast beef with gravy, devoutly wishes today that he had been a Lincolnite ever since the Chicago Convention.

Our wandering Reporter sums up his experience of yesterday in one comprehensive and satisfactory sentence: LINCOLN's election, acknowledged gloomily and with discontent by his opponents, is, nevertheless, accepted as a fixed fact, without detriment to the Union or to the business relations with the South, but attended with unpleasant results to numerous parties who have to vacate lucrative posts to make way for new-comers.

The Bell-Everett[3] Party gathered, last evening, at their rallying hall in Broadway, though with numbers much reduced, and with greatly chastened enthusiasm as compared with Tuesday night. Some two hundred persons visited the head-quarters during the evening, apparently to pick up such crumbs of comfort as the corrected returns might afford them, and to hear what might be dispensed from the rostrum. There was no formal organization of the meeting, but one of the officers introduced Mr. MORGAN, a gentleman from Tennessee. Mr. MORGAN excused himself from making any lengthy remarks, as he was suffering from a severe hoarseness, contracted by his severe labors during the last few days of the canvass. He had not closed his eyes since yesterday morning, and he had not, therefore, to open them very wide this morning to learn — as he did at a very early hour, by reference to bulletins — that they had been badly beaten. He regretted, as they all did — most deeply regretted — that they had not been victorious; but they would bear their defeat with that equanimity which a consciousness of being in the right inspired. They had now only to wait and see what would come of it, and who were responsible....

A procession of Wide-Awakes, under the lead of Alderman BRADY and Mr. VAN RIPER, visited the residences, first of JOHN KEYSER, in West Twelfth-street, and afterwards of JOHN T. SHAW, in Vandam-street, to congratulate them upon their election. Both gentlemen appeared and made pithy addresses in response to the cheers which called them out, and thanked their friends for the compliment of the visit.

An old man, giving the name of JAMES W. SLOVER, who represented that he had spent the last four weeks in electioneering for the Fusion Party presented himself at the poll of the Eighth election District of the Twenty-second Ward early on Tuesday morning and deposited his ballots without let or hindrance. In the afternoon his enthusiasm had increased to such a pitch that he tried to get in "just one more vote" for the candidates of his choice. To do this he presented himself, shortly before the polls closed, at the same place where he had voted in the morning, and his attempted fraud having been detected, he was taken into custody....

Mr. YANCEY made a speech in New-Orleans after his return from the North, in the course of which he said:

"If New-York is lost to Mr. LINCOLN, then we go into the scramble in the House. But the probabilities are that LINCOLN will get New-York. I traveled through New-York, and the Bell men were working faithfully for the Union ticket, and the Douglas men stood by with folded arms. Although I was using all the influence I possessed in favor of the Union ticket, and in favor of his getting the vote of that ticket in case it would secure the defeat of LINCOLN, yet the Douglas papers flung their Partisan arrows after me, denouncing me with the grossest calumny.

The Bell papers received me with respect, and parted with me with cordiality. The Douglas papers received me with calumny, and parted with me with lies. They used every effort to nullify whatever influence I might have excited in behalf of the Union ticket. What did this mean? It meant, perhaps, as many of our friends feared, that the Douglas party was in secret combination with LINCOLN. I fear, indeed, that this is the case. I wish to God it were not so. Yet if the Union ticket should be elected, and it could elect Mr. DOUGLAS, let its vote be given to him, not for his sake, but for the little good it might do the country." ✱

1. A reference to federally appointed clerks who owed their jobs to Democrats, and now likely to lose their patronage positions.

2. Simeon Draper (1804–1866) was a pro-Republican New York businessman later appointed by Lincoln to the lucrative patronage job of the Collection of Customs for the port of New York.

3. Bell's running mate in 1860 was the distinguished Edward Everett (1794–1865), a former governor, senator, university president, minister to Great Britain, and secretary of state; he is best remembered as the orator who gave the lengthy principal address — now all but forgotten — at the dedication of the Soldiers' National Cemetery at Gettysburg in 1863.

THE PRESIDENT ON THE CRISIS.

DECEMBER 5

The country has now the benefit of Mr. BUCHANAN's advice on the political crisis. The Message is out, and discusses the subject at length. The document will scarcely reward the anxiety which has awaited its appearance. There are many things in it which are true, and some which are new; but its true things are not new, nor are its new things true. It is probably the most elaborate effort Mr. BUCHANAN has ever made to appear bold without taking any risks, and firm without the necessity of proving his firmness. It is possible that it may tranquillize the country, but if so, the disturbance of the public peace is much less serious than has generally been supposed.

True to his partisanship, if true to nothing else, Mr. BUCHANAN attributes the entire responsibility for existing public evils to the Northern States, — and it is they alone who are to make sacrifices of position and principle for their removal. The immediate peril, Mr. BUCHANAN says, arises not from refusals to surrender fugitive slaves, nor the exclusion of Slavery from the Territories, — but from the imminent danger of slave insurrections. There is no longer any feeling of security around the family altar; — and if this goes on much longer, the President; wisely remarks, separation will be unavoidable. We suspect the people of the South will not thank Mr. BUCHANAN for this definition of their dangers. They deny the existence of any such state of things as he describes. Their slaves were never more contented or more loyal, — and they even declare their readiness to put arms in their hands to aid in repelling anticipated inroads of barbarians from the North. The fact, moreover, that all the great slave insurrections which have ever occurred, took place before the agitation of the Slavery question commenced, would indicate some flaw in the President's logic. With still more glaring injustice and want of truth, Mr. BUCHANAN charges the people of the North with seeking to interfere with Slavery in the Southern States, — saying that all the Slave States have ever desired is "to be let alone and permitted to manage their domestic institutions in their own way." It may suit the President's purposes thus to ignore the most conspicuous facts of our recent political history, — but it is scarcely becoming his position, or the character for fairness and truth which that position ought to imply.

The President is quite confident, in spite of all this, that disunion is not likely

An 1861 cartoon likens the seceding states to sheep escaping the control of a shepherdess.

to take place just yet. The election of any man to the Presidency does not, in his judgment, afford any just cause for dissolution, nor should mere apprehensions of a contingent danger arising from his Administration, lead to such a result. The President must, from the very nature of his office, be conservative; nor is it probable in the present instance that Congress will enact any laws impairing the rights of the South in their slaves. Thus far no authority except that of the Territorial Legislature of Kansas has denied to slaveholders the right to take their "property" into the Territories, — and that Act will speedily be set aside by the action of the Supreme Court. The enactment of Personal Liberty bills by several of the States is declared to be a gross invasion of Southern rights; and the President expresses the belief that, "unless the State Legislatures repeal these unconstitutional and obnoxious enactments without unnecessary delay, it is impossible for any human power to save the Union." We regret to find the preservation of the Union made thus absolutely dependent upon what we must consider a very remote contingency. We do not doubt the willingness of all the States concerned to abolish those laws, the moment the Fugitive Slave law shall be divested of those obnoxious and offensive features which provoked their enactment. Upon this view of the case, however, Mr. BUCHANAN does not think it worth his while to bestow the slightest attention. On the contrary, he presently recommends that, instead of being amended, the Fugitive Slave Law be incorporated into the Constitution.

Mr. BUCHANAN next comes to the great question of Secession: — and upon this subject, down to a certain point, his remarks are remarkably sound.

In the first place, he denies utterly the principle that a State has a right to withdraw from the Union at will. Such a position, he says, would render our Confederacy a mere rope of sand, — whereas it is, as he shows by a very clear and conclusive argument, a substantial Government, — perfect in all its forms, invested with all the attributes of sovereignty over the subjects to which its authority extends, and armed with force to execute its laws. The right of secession can only exist as the right of revolution.

In the next place, Mr. BUCHANAN recognizes the duty of the Executive to see to it that the laws are faithfully executed, — and

"from this obligation," he says, "he cannot be absolved by any human power." But if it should become "impracticable" to do this, — through the "resignation of all the officers of the Government," as it is at this moment in South Carolina, — he does not see what he can do about it. He must apply to Congress for more power. And this brings him.

In the third place, to say that he does not think Congress has any right to give him that power! He finds no authority in the Constitution for Congress to "coerce" a State into remaining in the Union. The question fairly stated, he says, is:

"Has the Constitution delegated to Congress the power to coerce a State into submission which is attempting to withdraw, or has actually withdrawn, from the Confederacy? If answered in the affirmative, it must be on the principle that the power has been conferred upon Congress to declare and to make war against a State. After much serious reflection, I have arrived at the conclusion that no such power has been delegated to Congress, or to any other department of the Federal Government."

It seems incredible that any man holding a high official position should put forth such an argument. It is not a question of war at all, — nor is it a question between the State and the Federal Government. It is simply a question of obedience to the laws of Congress, — and the obligation rests upon the individual citizens of the State. It is their duty to obey those laws, and the State has no authority to release them from such obedience, because the Federal Constitution, and the laws made in pursuance thereof, are expressly declared by the Constitution itself to be the supreme law of the land — "anything in the Constitution or laws of any State to the contrary notwithstanding." The Government has

precisely the same power to enforce every law of Congress in South Carolina, that it has to enforce the Fugitive Slave law in Massachusetts. Mr. BUCHANAN does not invoke the war-making power in the one case — why should he in the other?...

The Message, in our judgment, is an incendiary document, and will tend still further to exasperate the sectional differences of the day. It backs up the most extravagant of the demands which have been made by the South, — indorses their menace of Disunion if those demands are not conceded, — and promises the seceding States that the power of the Federal Government shall not be used for their coercion. The entire North will be made doubly indignant by this flagrant dereliction of duty on the part of the Executive of the Nation, while the Disunionists of the South will be stimulated to fresh exertions in the work of ruin upon which they have embarked. The country has to struggle through three months more of this disgraceful imbecility and disloyalty to the Constitution. ✹

Newly bearded President-Elect Lincoln maintained official silence during the secession crisis, practicing what supporters called "masterly inactivity."

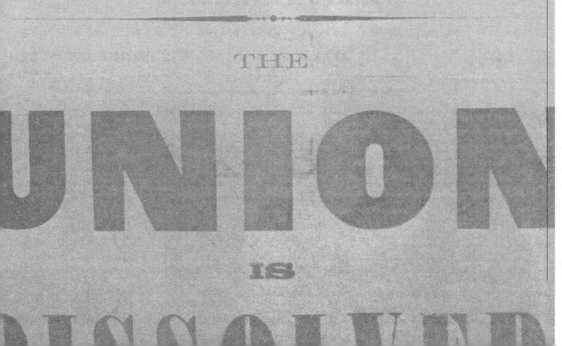

CHAPTER 2

"The Momentous Issue of Civil War"

DECEMBER 1860–MARCH 1861

EXTRA:

passed unanimously at 1.15 o'clock, P. M., December 20th, 1860.

AN ORDINANCE

dissolve the Union between the State of South Carolina and other States united with her under the compact entitled "The Constitution of the United States of America."

The People of the State of South Carolina, in Convention assembled, do declare and ordain, is hereby declared and ordained,

that the Ordinance adopted by us in Convention, on the twenty-third day of May, in our Lord one thousand seven hundred and eighty-eight, whereby the Constitution of States of America was ratified, and also, all Acts and parts of Acts of the General bly of this State, ratifying amendments of the said Constitution, are hereby repea at the union now subsisting between South Carolina and other States, under the nam United States of America," is hereby dissolved.

THE

UNION

IS

DISSOLVED

J ust seven weeks after Abraham Lincoln's election as President — and notwithstanding his effort to avoid coercive language during and after his campaign — South Carolina seceded from the Union, the first Southern state to do so.

Lincoln's sectionally lopsided victory had proved enough to unleash the nation-altering storm. The slave interest was immovably convinced that the so-called Black Republican threatened doom to the institution that kept three million African-Americans in chains.

The New York Times was on the scene at the Charleston secession convention to report on both the unanimous vote and the wild celebrations that erupted thereafter on the city's streets. Yet, in a hopeful editorial, the paper clung to the belief that the move was but an isolated expression of fire-eating radicalism, and that Georgia, scheduled to consider secession next, would never follow South Carolina's lead. In this hope, the paper and many others, including President-Elect Lincoln himself, proved far too optimistic. Southern unionism was fast evaporating.

Lincoln, still at home in distant Springfield, Illinois, and adamantly rejecting suggestions that he speak out to conciliate the South lest he appear to be begging for the right to be inaugurated, remained silent. He continued, however, to make himself available to journalists for the remainder of the four-month-long interregnum that Henry Adams dubbed "the secession winter." While it did not send a correspondent west to report from Springfield, The Times did reprint reports on his activities from other newspapers — a common practice in that time. Editorially, the paper continued to stress and praise Lincoln's moderation.

Poster announcing South Carolina's secession from the United States.

When the train transporting the President-Elect to Washington for his swearing-in reached New York State in mid-February, following stops in Illinois, Indiana, and Ohio, The Times began covering the inaugural journey in depth. Along with other journalists, Times reporter Joseph Howard traveled along with the presidential party. Under the recurring headline, "The Incoming Administrations," readers were treated to exhaustive, and often amusing, accounts of Lincoln's informal, though not particularly reassuring, chats at successive railroad depots, as he moved west from Buffalo to Albany. After delivering a major address to the state legislature, Lincoln and his party steamed south to New York City, where he elicited frosty greetings from the city's Democratic mayor and merchants worried over the prospect of losing profitable commercial ties to the South. By now, six more states had decided to join South Carolina and form a government of their own.

For a time, the newspaper continued to express confidence in the President-Elect, reminding readers that Lincoln had made admirably conciliatory gestures to the South during his preinaugural speeches. But a sense of alarm soon began creeping into its coverage, particularly after Lincoln evaded hostile Baltimore en route to Washington — completing the final leg of his long journey secretly, by night, and, as a Times reporter inaccurately claimed (perhaps angry at being left behind), wearing a disguise. Now The Times began clamoring for Lincoln to unveil his policy plans even before his Inaugural Address. The President-Elect remained unmoved. Though he continued to appear publicly at the Willard Hotel in Washington, and even met with Northern and Southern delegates to a "Peace Convention" that was meeting under the same roof to craft a compromise to head off Civil War, he remained vexingly — some claimed stubbornly — quiet on how he intended to confront what even The New York Times was now calling a "crisis."

Nor did the paper flinch from reporting a portentous irony: the concurrent inaugural journey of another American "president." Jefferson Davis was sworn in February 18 as chief executive of the new Southern Confederacy, prompting William L. Yancey to exult: "The man and the hour have met." The Times reprinted Davis's long inaugural speech in full, but pointed out that his words seemed as bellicose as Lincoln's had been pacific, a bad omen indeed for any prospects for reunion and peace.

The Times proved right. That there were now two separate American governments, facing the long-dreaded prospect of a war over slavery and union, was beyond question.

THE DISUNION CRISIS.
THE FORMAL SECESSION OF SOUTH CAROLINA.

CHARLESTON, THURSDAY, DEC. 20

... The chair announced the appointment of the Committee to draft a summary of the cause of the Secession of South Carolina; also of four standing Committees.

Mr. RHETT's[1] resolutions to appoint a Committee of Thirteen for the purpose of providing for the assemblage of a Convention of the seceding States, and to form a Constitution, was adopted.

Mr. INGLIS[2] made a report from the Committee to prepare and draft an ordinance proper to be adopted by the Convention.

An Ordinance to Dissolve the Union between the State of South Carolina and other States united with her under the compact entitled the Constitution of the United States of America:

We, the people of the State of South Carolina, in Convention assembled, do declare and ordain, and it is hereby declared and ordained, that the ordinance adopted by us in Convention, on the 22d day of May,

DECEMBER 21

in the year of our Lord 1788, whereby the Constitution of the United States of America was ratified, and also all Acts and parts of Acts of the General Assembly of this State ratifying the amendments of the said Constitution are hereby repealed, and that the union now subsisting between South Carolina and other States under the name of the United States of America is hereby dissolved.

The ordinance was taken up and passed by a unanimous vote of 169 members at 1 1/4 o'clock.

As soon as its passage was known without the doors of the Convention, it rapidly spread on the street, a crowd collected, and there was immense cheering.... ✪

1. Robert Barnwell [Smith] Rhett Sr. (1800–1876), former congressman and senator, was a leading South Carolina secessionist and father of the editor of The Charleston Mercury.
2. John A. Inglis (1813–1879) was a Maryland-born politician, jurist, and educator.

A page from Frank Leslie's Illustrated Newspaper showing the secession meeting at Mills House in Charleston, South Carolina. The portraits at the bottom are, from left: Senator James Chesnut Jr. of South Carolina, Senator Robert Toombs of Georgia, and Senator Alexander H. Stephens of Georgia.

THE SECESSION MOVEMENT.

DECEMBER 21

South Carolina passed the ordinance of secession yesterday at 1 o'clock P.M., by the unanimous vote of the Convention; and her action was greeted with a salvo of a hundred guns. As this step was universally anticipated, it will create no special uneasiness. It does not change the relations of South Carolina to the Union in the slightest degree, though it will very possibly be followed by acts that will have that effect. It is not easy to see how she can avoid refusing to pay duties at once, as her continuance in paying, upon her own theory, becomes now an act of gratuitous subjection and tribute to a foreign State. Meantime in other States, and especially in Georgia, the movement is becoming more considerate and dignified, if not less decided. The Cooperationists' seem to have a majority in the Convention, and they may possibly decide not to imitate the hasty and separate action of South Carolina, but to await the cooperation of the other Southern or at least the Cotton-growing States. In various part of the South, moreover, conservative sentiments are beginning to assert themselves. There is no longer that dead monotony of Disunionism which marked the earlier stages of the movement. Very able men in nearly all the States have made very able arguments against rash and injudicious action, and have counseled a resolute attempt to obtain a redress of wrongs within the Union, before absolutely going out of it.

These things naturally encourage the hope of a better result than we have apprehended hitherto. It is thought that time will be gained at all events, and this is a matter of importance.

It will not do, however, to yield too far to these anticipations. Whatever the movement has lost in recklessness and haste, it may have gained in steadiness and strength. There is thus far no Union Party in the South; the only divisions are upon minor points. Some are for seceding now, while others would wait for the cooperation of other States. Some would secede without condition, while others would remain in the Union if their demands should be conceded. What those demands will be we can, of course, conjecture; — and we are bound to add that we see very little prospect that they will be granted.

If the South were in a mood to discuss the subject with candor and fairness, — if they were "open to conviction," or willing even to have their palpable mistakes in matters of fact corrected, we should have little fear of the result. But it is not so, — nor do we see any immediate prospect of their becoming so. ✸

An 1861 sheet music cover illustrates the Union song "Down with the Traitors' Serpent Flag."

1. Delegates to the Peace Convention committed to compromise to prevent secession, even if it meant extending slavery westward and prolonging and protecting its existence indefinitely.

MR. LINCOLN AND NEGRO EQUALITY.

JANUARY 14

We copied some days since from the Albany Atlas and Argus, an extract of a speech said to have been made by Mr. LINCOLN in 1858, in which he denounced those States which withheld from the negro the right of suffrage. We proved that the extract must be a forgery, unless Mr. LINCOLN had directly and distinctly contradicted himself — for we quoted from his speeches the most explicit declarations which language could frame, of hostility to the admission of negroes to the right of suffrage.

The Atlas and Argus has investigated the matter, and arrives at the same conclusion. It states that the extract was from the Nashville Union and American — and that the language attributed to Mr. LINCOLN was really used by Gov. CHASE. It says:

"The speech referred to was made about Sept. 16, 1856, at a banquet at Chicago, and is reported in the Illinois Journal of that date...."

And they were uttered, it is now said, by Gov. CHASE. This may or may not be so. One thing, however, we consider certain: — they could not have been uttered by him on the same occasion as the one on which Mr. LINCOLN spoke, because we know that Gov. CHASE and Mr. LINCOLN have never met, — or had not, up to the date of the last election....

We regard this matter of the alleged speech of LINCOLN as one of considerable importance. It was circulated as genuine throughout the South during the late canvas, — and did very much towards laying the foundation for that utter and complete misapprehension of his sentiments, which is the main cause of our present sectional dissensions. Now that it is known to be a forgery, the Atlas and Argus owes it to its political friends at the South to proclaim that fact distinctly, instead of striving to convey the impression that Mr. LINCOLN actually holds these opinions, in spite of his own disclaimers.[1] ✸

1. In responding to this charge himself, but in the third person, Lincoln had told New York Times editor Henry J. Raymond on December 18, 1860: "Mr. Lincoln is not pledged to the ultimate extinctinction [sic] of slavery; does not hold the black man to be the equal of the white, unqualifiedly...."

ANOTHER INTERVIEW WITH MR. LINCOLN.

JANUARY 14

A correspondent of the Missouri Democrat gives the following particulars of a visit to Mr. LINCOLN:

"We found Mr. LINCOLN in his parlor surrounded by some six or eight gentlemen, who all proved to be temporary visitors like ourselves. Mr. LINCOLN met us with a frank welcome, shaking hands with us, and at once by his words and his manner, making us feel that our call was no intrusion; and on his invitation, we were soon seated with the circle of gentlemen who occupied his parlor. The subject of conversation was politics, and Mr. LINCOLN expressed himself upon every topic which was brought up with entire freedom. He said, at one period in the conversation, 'he hoped gentlemen would bear in mind that he was not speaking as President, or for the President, but only exercising the privilege of talking which belonged to him in common with private citizens.' I chose rather to be a listener than a talker, and paid careful attention both to Mr. LINCOLN's matter and manner, and although he seemed to talk without regard to the fact of his being the President elect, yet it was discoverable that he chose his words and framed his sentences with deliberation, and with a discretion becoming his high position.

He was asked, 'Do you think the Missouri Compromise line ought to be restored?'[1] He replied that although the recent Presidential election was a verdict of the people in favor of freedom upon all the Territories, yet personally he would be willing, for the sake of the Union, to divide the Territory we now own by that line, if in the judgment of the nation it would save the Union and restore harmony. But whether the acquisition of Territory hereafter would not reopen the question and renew the strife, was a question to be thought of and in some way provided against.

He had been inquired of whether he intended to recommend the repeal of the anti-Fugitive Slave laws of the States?[2] He replied that he had never read one of them, but that if they were of the character ascribed to them by Southern men, they certainly ought to be repealed. Whether as President of the United States he ought to interfere with State legislation by Presidential recommendation, required more thought than he had yet given the subject. He had also been asked if he intended to interfere or recommend an interference with Slavery or the right of holding slaves in the dock yards and arsenals of the United States? His reply was. 'Indeed, Sir, the subject has not entered my mind.' He was inquired of whether he intended to recommend the abolition of Slavery in the District of Columbia? to which he replied, 'Upon my word I have not given the subject a thought.'[3] A gentleman present said to him, 'Well, Mr. LINCOLN, suppose these difficulties should not be settled before you are inaugurated, what will you do?' He replied with a smile, 'Well, I suppose I will have to run the machine as I find it.'

In speaking on the subject of a compromise, he said: 'It was some times better for a man to pay a debt he did not owe, or to lose a demand which was a just one, than to go to law about it; but then, in compromising our difficulties, he would regret to see the victors put in the attitude of the vanquished, and the vanquished in the place of the victors.' He would not contribute to any such compromise as that.

It was discernible in the course of Mr. L.'s conversation that he duly appreciates the difficulties which threaten his incoming Administration; also, that he regarded himself as grossly misrepresented and misunderstood at the South; nor did he conceal what was manifestly an invincible conviction of his honest and intelligent mind, that if the South would only give him a fair trial, they would find their constitutional rights as safe under his Administration as they had ever been under the Administration of any President." ⊕

1. Senate and House committees were then considering offering a compromise that would include reviving the old Missouri Compromise line, and extending it to the Pacific.
2. Also called Personal Liberty Laws, these state statutes declared the national Fugitive Slave law invalid within their borders.
3. In fact, years earlier, during his one term in the U.S. House of Representatives, Lincoln had cosponsored a Congressional resolution to bar slavery in the District of Columbia.

INAUGURATION OF JEFFERSON DAVIS AS PRESIDENT OF THE SOUTHERN CONFEDERACY.

HIS INAUGURAL ADDRESS.

FEBRUARY 19

The Inaugural ceremonies, to-day [February 18], were the grandest pageant ever witnessed in the South. There was an immense crowd on Capital Hill, consisting of a great array of the beauty, military and citizens of the different States....

MR. DAVIS' INAGURAL ADDRESS:

Called to the difficult and responsible station of Chief Executive of the Provisional Government which you have instituted, I approach the discharge of the duties assigned me with an humble distrust of my abilities, but with a sustaining confidence in the wisdom of those who are to guide and aid me in the administration of public affairs, and an abiding faith in the virtue and patriotism of the people. Looking forward to the speedy establishment of a permanent Government to take the place of this, and which, by its greater moral and physical power, will be better able to combat with the many difficulties which arise from the conflicting interests of separate nations, I enter upon the duties of the office to which I have been chosen with the hope, that the beginning of our career as a Confederacy may not be obstructed by hostile opposition to our enjoyment of the separate existence and independence ☞

Jefferson Davis, the first and only President of the Confederate States of America.

which we have asserted, and which, with the blessing of Providence, we intend to maintain. Our present condition, achieved in a manner unprecedented in the history of nations, illustrates the American idea that governments rest upon the consent of the governed, and that it is the right for the people to alter and abolish governments whenever they become destructive to the ends for which they were established. The declared compact of the Union from which we have withdrawn was to establish justice, insure domestic tranquillity, provide for the common defence, promote the general welfare, and secure the blessings of liberty to ourselves and our posterity, and when in the judgment of the Sovereign States now composing this Confederacy, it has been perverted from the purposes for which it was ordained, and ceased to answer the ends for which it was established, a peaceful appeal to the ballot-box declared that so far as they were concerned the Government created by that compact should cease to exist. In this they merely asserted the right which the Declaration of Independence of 1776 defined to be inalienable. Of the time and occasion of its exercise, they as sovereigns, were the final judges, each for itself. The impartial, enlightened verdict of mankind will vindicate the rectitude of our conduct, and He who knows the hearts of men will judge of the sincerity with which we labored to preserve the Government of our fathers in its spirit....

As a necessity, not a choice, we have resorted to the remedy of separation, and henceforth our energies must be directed to the conduct of our own affairs and the perpetuity of the Confederacy which we have formed. If a just perception of mutual interest shall permit us peaceably to pursue our separate political career, my most earnest desire will have been fulfilled. But if this be denied us, and the integrity of our territory and jurisdiction be assailed, it will but remain for us with firm resolve to appeal to arms, and invoke the blessing of Providence on a just cause.... ✱

THE INCOMING ADMINISTRATION.
PROGRESS OF THE PRESIDENT ELECT TOWARDS WASHINGTON.

FEBRUARY 19

SPECIAL DISPATCH TO THE NEW-YORK TIMES.
ALBANY, MONDAY, FEB. 18.

The Presidential party were awakened at the early and inconvenient hour of 4 1/2 o'clock this morning. Mr. LINCOLN's general health is good, but the hoarseness of his voice and soreness of his chest do not seem to have been improved by his exertions in Buffalo. The almost entire monopoly of his time by Ex-President [Millard] FILLMORE in Buffalo was by no means objected to by the Republicans of the city. Mr. LINCOLN's ground, most firmly taken, is that he is to be the President of the AMERICAN PEOPLE and not of the Republican Party. Hence he meets and desires to be with men of all parties, and Mr. FILLMORE, though not sympathizing with the principles of the Chicago Platform, is, nevertheless, the leading citizen of the city, and represents the Union-loving sentiment of the place. Therefore, the cordial welcome given by him to Mr. LINCOLN was eminently gratifying. The first 37 miles were made in 30 minutes.

At Batavia, gray as was the light and deep as was the snow, there was a very large gathering of people, who saluted Mr. LINCOLN with cheers and with the firing of cannon. Of course they wanted to hear him speak, but to their calls he replied that he did not appear before them or the country as a talker, nor did be desire to obtain a reputation as such. He thanked them for the kind attention manifested by their rising at so inconvenient an hour, and bade them farewell amidst a burst of genuine enthusiasm. Hardly had the train commenced its career again, when a smell as of burning wood and oil filled the cars, and it was ascertained that one of the journals was heated red. The applying of a proper remedy, however, occupied but a few moments, and all was as it should be. At Rochester, an assemblage estimated by the Mayor to number 30,000 people, thronged the avenues adjoining the depot....

The scene presented by so vast a crowd was truly magnificent. causing Mr. LINCOLN to recall, as he observed to the Mayor, his old campaigning days. The number of ladies present was very great, and from a very fair young source was presented a flo-

ral testimonial of regard for which any one would be grateful—President or citizen....

The Democratic element was well represented by a magnificent locomotive, named Dean Richmond,[1] which drew oddly enough the Presidential cortege from Buffalo to Rochester. This fact created a great deal of amusement among the party, and was productive of much good-natured raillery at the expense of the Republican Party....

The next stoppage was at Clyde, a town of some 3,000 inhabitants. They were all at the station, and brimfull of enthusiasm for the man of their choice. Stepping upon the platform, Mr. LINCOLN said:

"LADIES AND GENTLEMEN: I merely appear before you to say good morning and farewell. I have no time to speak in, and no speech if I had." At this, Mr. PAINE, editor of the local paper, approached Mr. LINCOLN, and said that he had been deputed by the assemblage to shake him by the hand—which shake he would distribute in his next morning's edition. An enterprising artist had placed upon a convenient wood-pile a camera with which he secured pictures of the rear end of the car, of Mr. LINCOLN, Mr. WOOD,[2] a brakeman, and an unlucky reporter....

The announcement was made by telegraph that a very large crowd was waiting for him at Syracuse, who were determined to have a speech. The managers of the train seemed to be in the conspiracy, for the speed was greatly accelerated so as to reach the station several minutes ahead of time.

It was evident, on arrival at the depot, that the report had in no way exaggerated the excitement or the numbers of the crowd. At the intersection of the street with the track, was erected a nicely carpeted platform, on which were the Committee, Rev. Mr. WALDO, and a bald-headed eagle. The immensity of the gathering was equaled only by its absolute order and good behavior. Mr. LINCOLN was urged to go upon the platform, but having declined doing so elsewhere, he felt it his duty to treat all alike, and, therefore, did not go.

Having been welcomed in a rather extended, but cordial speech, by the Mayor, Mr. LINCOLN addressed the assemblage as follows:

LADIES AND GENTLEMEN: I see you have erected a very fine and handsome platform here for me, and I presume you expected me to speak from it. If I should go upon it you would imagine that I was about to deliver you a much longer speech than I am. I wish you to understand that I mean no discourtesy to you by thus declining. I intend discourtesy to no one. But I wish you to understand that though I am unwilling to go upon this platform, you are not at liberty to draw any inferences concerning any other platform with which my name has been or is connected. [Laughter and applause.] I wish you a long life and prosperity individually, and pray that with the perpetuity of those institutions under which we have all so long lived and prospered, our happiness may be secured, our future made brilliant, and the glorious destiny of our country established forever. I bid you a kind farewell.

Rev. Mr. WALDO, who is so infirm as to be scarcely able to totter, but who, nevertheless, voted for WASHINGTON and LINCOLN, was taken from the staging and brought upon the platform of the car, where he shook hands with Mr. LINCOLN, and came very near being pushed off the car by the crowd of people....

At Utica quite a large amount of business was transacted. On a freight-car had been elevated a large platform, the whole of which was rolled up to the rear of Mr. LINCOLN's car. The entire Legislative Committee were on it, and expected to be introduced to Mr. LINCOLN when he should make his appearance, but Mr. WOOD peremptorily forbade it, saying that the time allotted to the citizens of Utica should not be used by the State. There was a tremendous shout when Mr. LINCOLN appeared, and in spite of a heavy fall of snow, the crowd augmented continually, until, as far as the eye could reach, could be seen a pushing, restless tide of humanity, with thousands of faces turned upward toward the future ruler of the nation....

During the entire trip Mr. LINCOLN has worn a shocking bad hat, and a very thin old over-coat. Shortly after leaving Utica, Mrs. LINCOLN gave an order to WILLIAM, the colored servant, and presently he passed through the car with a handsome broadcloth over-coat upon his arm and a new hat-box in his hand. Since then Mr. LINCOLN has looked fifty per cent. better, and if Mrs. LINCOLN's advice is always as near right as it was in this instance, the country may congratulate itself upon the fact that its President elect is a man who does not reject, even in important matters, the advice and counsel of his wife.

To-morrow morning the party will go to Troy, and from thence to New-York. The following is an accurate list of the party proper:

Hon. A. LINCOLN. Mrs. LINCOLN and two children, servant and nurse. ROBERT T. LINCOLN. LOCKWOOD TODD, cousin of Mr. L. Dr. W.S. WALLACE, brother of Mrs. L. JOHN G. NICOLAY, Private Secretary. JOHN M. HAY, Assistant Secretary. Hon. N[orman].B. JUDD, of Illinois. Hon. DAVID DAVIS, of Illinois. Col. E[dwin].V[ose]. SUMNER, U.S.A. Major D[avid]. HUNTER, U.S.A. Capt. GEORGE W. HAZZARD, U.S.A. Capt. JOHN POPE, U.S.A. Col. E[phraim].E[lmer]. ELLSWORTH, of New-York. Col. WARD H. LAMON, of Illinois. J. M. BURGESS, of Wisconsin. GEO. C. LATHAM. W.S. WOOD, General Superintendent. B. FORBES, Assistant. Besides whom are the correspondents of the NEW YORK TIMES, Herald, Tribune and World; of the Chicago Tribune, and of Frank Leslie's Newspaper. A telegraphic operator and the agent of the Associated Press are also of the regular number.

Mr. and Mrs. LINCOLN are highly gratified at the report that apartments are engaged at the Astor House [in New York City]—that being the hotel where personally they feel most at home, and where their friends can have the double pleasure of entertaining them, and benefiting an establishment which stands up for the Union.... ❀

1. Named for Dean Richmond (1804–1866), president of the New York Central Railroad. He was one of the men held responsible for breaking up the Democratic National Convention at Charleston in 1860 by voting that two-thirds of the delegates were needed to select a candidate. His goal was to nominate Horatio Seymour of New York.

2. William D. Wood, of whom little is known, was a railroad man whom Lincoln had named, probably at the suggestion of Albany Republican boss Thurlow Weed, as superintendent of the Lincoln inaugural journey.

A photograph taken of Abraham Lincoln waiting to help raise the flag outside Independence Hall in Philadelphia on February 22, 1861, during his inaugural tour.

THE INAUGURAL OF PRESIDENT DAVIS.

FEBRUARY 19

The last act in the constitution of the Southern American Confederacy was achieved yesterday, by the inauguration of Gen. DAVIS in the Presidential office. The address of the new Chief Magistrate will be found at length elsewhere in this paper. It will be read with profound attention. It is natural, indeed, that the public should hang with intense interest on the utterances of those who are to wield the power and represent the dignities and honors of the State. This interest is heightened, if possible, when the occasion is an era — the severance of old relations or the commencement of a new career. Declarations, at such a time, are taken as the enunciation of the policy, or life, of the new order of things. That of the new Republic, its President tells us, is to be peace in its internal organization, from the homogeneity of its industries and interests. Nothing is to be feared from abroad; because, if war should come, the Southern people must again assert the principles for which their fathers bled in the Revolution. He tells us that the Southern Confederacy will have no complications. Its separation from the old Union is complete. No compromise, no reconstruction can now be entertained.

This speech does not convey much comfort to the Northern sympathizers with the Southern President, nor to the public. For ourselves, we place no very unfavorable construction upon it. If Mr. DAVIS be a man of common judgment or observation he is playing a part not very difficult to be understood. If, on the other hand, he is entirely sincere, then he certainly fails to comprehend the subject on which he speaks. There is a greater want of homogeneity in the Southern States than in almost any other people that can be named. The turning-point of secession is protection to Slavery. Not one-sixth of the people in the South own slaves. When they come to assume the expenditures necessary to be incurred for its maintenance, radical differences will arise. One-half of the area of the whole Southern States is better adapted to Free than Slave labor, and is rapidly becoming the theatre where Free-labor only is used. There is another cause of radical difference, as intense as that which is made the occasion of secession. These differences are to be confronted the moment secession assumes the offensive....

On the whole, we accept Mr. DAVIS' address to be, as most addresses on similar occasions are, nothing more or less than a bit of Southern extravagance, required perhaps by the audience and the occasion. In a speech delivered a few days ago, on his way to the Convention, he tells us that if there are to be hostilities, they must be on the enemy's soil. This is something of a boast

THE STARTING POINT OF THE GREAT WAR BETWEEN THE STATES.
INAUGURATION OF JEFFERSON DAVIS

A postwar lithograph of the Montgomery, Alabama inauguration of Jefferson Davis as President of the Confederacy.

for a people who cannot feed, equip or clothe a regiment without obtaining every article required at the North. We are a nation dealing in hyperbole; but this trait is always more pronounced under a hot than a tempered sun. In genuine gasconade, the people of the extreme South are every way a match for Mexicans. Extravagance of assertions is always in ratio to impotence and execution. So long as the Confederate States cannot build a ship, construct a gun, nor manufacture a pound of gunpowder; can neither clothe nor feed themselves; nor levy war upon us unless we furnish the munitions, fill their commissariat and supply the means of locomotion, we may quietly pursue our avocations. Their internal affairs we do not at present propose to meddle with. We want their trade, and we do not wish to disturb our own, and waste our means at the same time.

There is a very noticeable feature in Mr. DAVIS' speeches, contrasted with those of Mr. LINCOLN. Mr. DAVIS' first idea is to fight; "to baptize his principles in blood." This thought, ever uppermost in the Southern mind, indicates the character of its civilization. Mr. DAVIS, at bay, shows his teeth, and tells us to come on, if we dare. He talks of fighting with entire impunity, and without a breath of censure, North or South. Mr. LINCOLN, at Indianapolis, expressed himself decidedly against coercion, but mildly inquired whether the Government might not proceed to execute the revenue laws. For this a torrent of execration was showered upon him. There is something very curious in the reception which these two men meet with. The President elect, bound by his oath to execute the laws, must not hint at such a proceeding; while entire tolerance is extended to the threats of resistance by parties who are in open rebellion. We would like to have some person cunning in such matters, solve this apparent contradiction. ✸

PRESIDENT LINCOLN AND THE CRISIS.

FEBRUARY 20

Mr. LINCOLN's arrival at Washington is awaited with, eagerness and anxiety. His presence there has become a necessity, — not only to the success of judicious efforts for preserving the Union, but to the peace and harmony of the party which is responsible for the administration of the Government. The Peace Convention is making but little substantial progress. It will have great difficulty in reaching any harmonious conclusion, and still greater in securing for its action, the approval or even the serious attention of Congress. The fact, upon which we have so often insisted, — that the whole responsibility of meeting the crisis devolves upon the incoming Administration, seems now to be gradually recognized: and all parties, and all men, who desire the preservation of the Union, are looking forward with eager anticipation to the day when the policy of that Administration shall be disclosed.

Another fact is becoming painfully prominent — namely, that this policy will depend mainly on the President himself. The Republican Party, as such, has no policy for the crisis, — no settled plan upon which all are united, for carrying the country through the very serious perils which now surround it. Not that its members are indisposed to adopt some plan which shall be at once just and effectual, — nor that they underrate the serious character of the emergency and the necessity of wise and resolute action. With the exception of a small number, who are far more Abolitionists than Republicans, and who look forward to disunion with far more of complacency than of apprehension, the great body of the Republicans in Congress and out of it, are profoundly and sincerely solicitous for some honorable and safe mode of adjusting the sectional differences which threaten our country with the most serious disaster that can befall it. But the great difficulty in the case is the lack of a leader. Mr. LINCOLN has given no indication of the policy which he considers essential, and which he would desire to have adopted. His silence on this subject is unquestionably creditable to his prudence and his modesty, — but it has not been without its embarrassments. It has left the field open for a struggle of factions, and of personal aims at ascendancy, which have largely contributed to the demoralization of the party, and which, unless promptly arrested, must lead to its division and downfall. It has encouraged the vehement attempts which we daily witness to coerce Mr. LINCOLN into a specific and extreme policy, — by waging war upon every man of more moderate councils, by keeping before the public alleged declarations of Mr. LINCOLN, wholly unofficial and even private in their character, by which he is nevertheless to be required to guide his official conduct, and by brandishing over his head the pains and penalties which will follow his departure from the rigid line of policy thus marked out for him; and it has given special scope and opportunity for personal resentments and disappointments to clothe themselves in the garb of political principle and use the patriotism and loyalty of the country as the instruments of their revenge....

We have full faith in the disposition and ability of Mr. LINCOLN to meet the tremendous responsibility which rests upon him. We have no fear that he will either be seduced into fatal concessions of principle, or coerced into a reckless trifling with dangers which are none the less real because they are unreasonable, and which it is his duty to avert, although he is in no degree responsible for their existence. It can never be a matter of indifference, or of secondary moment, to him, whether the Union is destroyed or not, — nor is it possible for him, or for any one in his position, to attach more weight to the mere clamor of selfish and malignant partisans, than to the voice of the country which relies on him for deliverance from the dangers which threaten its existence. But, in common with all who look with concern upon the disturbed state of the country, we are looking forward with eager impatience to the time when he can indicate the policy which, in his judgment, the emergencies of the country require. ✸

MR. LINCOLN IN NEW-YORK.

FEBRUARY 21

Yesterday morning Mr. LINCOLN breakfasted, by invitation of MOSES H. GRINNELL, Esq., together with a number of representatives of the mercantile wealth of the Metropolis. The party included Messrs. ASPINWALL, MINTURN, Capt. MARSHALL, W.M. EVARTS, Mr. WEBB, Ex-Gov. FISH, Mr. TILESTON, and other gentlemen of equal note.[1]

After returning to his hotel, Mr. LINCOLN was called upon by a veteran voter of 94 years of age, who has voted at every Presidential Election, and cast his last ballot for "Honest Abe." The interview was pleasing to both parties.

The morning, up to 11 o'clock, was agreeably occupied in receiving the various distinguished gentlemen who called, and at the hour named the Common Council Committee, headed by Alderman CORNELL, made their appearance to escort the President to the Municipal head-quarters. Two carriages were provided for the Presidential party, who were forthwith hurried through the gaping crowd, amid the most enthusiastic cheering, to the entrance to the City Hall, whence, through the excellence of the Police arrangements of Mr. KENNEDY, an unobstructed passage was afforded to the Governor's Room. The scene on the line of march was but a repetition of that which has characterized Mr. LINCOLN'S every appearance since the commencement of his present journey — only intensified up to the New-York standard.

Meanwhile Mayor WOOD, the Common Council and members of the Press, had been admitted to the Governor's Room,[2] and were eagerly awaiting the arrival which was at length announced by the shouts of the crowd on the stairs, reverberating through the building like a miniature thunder storm.

Escorted by Alderman CORNELL, Mr. LINCOLN entered, hat in hand, and advanced to where Mayor WOOD was posted, behind WASHINGTON'S writing desk, and immediately in front of Gov. SEWARD'S portrait. The bustle of the Aldermanic and Councilmanic rush for good places having in a measure subsided, Mayor WOOD, in a voice that seemed for moment slightly tremulous, spoke as follows:

Mr. LINCOLN: As Mayor of New-York, it becomes my duty to extend to you an official welcome in behalf of the Corporation. In doing so, permit me to say, that this City has never offered hospitality to a man clothed with more exalted powers, or resting under graver responsibilities, than these which circumstances have devolved upon you. Coming into office with a dismembered Government to reconstruct, and a disconnected and hostile people to reconcile, it will require a high patriotism, and an elevated comprehension of the whole country and its varied interests, opinions and prejudices, to so conduct public affairs as to bring it back again to its former harmonious, consolidated and prosperous condition.

If I refer to this topic, Sir, it is because New-York is deeply interested. The present political divisions have sorely afflicted her people. All her material interests are paralyzed. Her commercial greatness is endangered. She is the child of the American Union. She has grown up under its maternal care, and been fostered by its paternal bounty, and we fear that if the Union dies, the present supremacy of New-York may perish with it. To you, therefore, chosen under the forms of the Constitution as the head of the Confederacy, we look for a restoration of fraternal relations between the States — only to be accomplished by peaceful and conciliatory means — aided by the wisdom of Almighty God.

Mr. LINCOLN, who, during the Mayor's speech, had preserved his characteristically thoughtful look, with that sort of dreamy expression of the eye, as if his thoughts were busily engaged, stepped back a few paces, drew up his tall form to its fullest height, brightened his face with a pleasant smile, and spoke as follows:

Mr. MAYOR: It is with feelings of deep gratitude that I make my acknowledgements for the reception that has been given me in the great commercial City of New-York. I cannot but remember that it is done by the people, who do not, by a large majority, agree with me in political sentiment. It is the more grateful to me, because in this I see that for the great principles of our Government the people are pretty nearly or quite unanimous. In regard to the difficulties that confront us at this time, and of which you have seen fit to speak so becomingly, and so justly, as I suppose, I can only say that I agree with the sentiments expressed by the Mayor. In my devotion to the Union, I hope I am behind no man in the nation. As to my wisdom in conducting affairs so as to tend to the preservation of the Union, I fear too great confidence may have been placed in me. I am sure I bring a heart devoted to the work. There is nothing that could ever bring me to consent — willingly to consent — to the destruction of this Union, (in which not only the great City of New-York, but the whole country has acquired its greatness,) unless it would be that thing for which the Union itself was made. I understand that the ship is made for the carrying and preservation of the cargo, and so long as the ship is safe with the cargo it shall not be abandoned. This Union shall never be abandoned unless the possibility of its existence shall cease to exist, without the necessity of throwing passengers and cargo overboard. So long, then, as it is possible that the prosperity and liberties of this people can be preserved within this Union, it shall be my purpose at all times to preserve it. And now, Mr. Mayor, renewing my thanks for this cordial reception, allow me to come to a close. [Applause.]

Mayor WOOD then stepped forward and shook hands with Mr. LINCOLN. The gentlemen of the Common Council, Comptroller HAWES and other distinguished personages, were introduced by Mayor WOOD, and then Mr. LINCOLN was requested to take up his position for the reception of the unterrified. He was first placed where the crowd passed him from right to left, but he did not seem to like that position, and said, pointing to the statue of WASHINGTON, "Let me stand with my back to the old General there," which, with sundry jocular remarks, was acceded to, and the desired position assumed. A line of Police was then formed from one door to the other, so that the crowd could pass by Mr. LINCOLN and into the street rapidly.... ✸

1. Lincoln's meeting with leading New York businessmen — most worried their Southern markets would vanish if Lincoln did not end the secession crisis through conciliation — was not particularly friendly.
2. A suite on the second floor of New York's City Hall.

ARRIVAL AND RECEPTION IN NEW-YORK.

FEBRUARY 20

Punctually at 3 P.M., yesterday, the special train which conveyed the President elect and suite arrived at the new depot of the Hudson River Railroad, on Thirtieth-street, between Ninth and Tenth avenues. The building, which was thrown open for the first time on this occasion, was gaily decorated with flags. None were admitted there but those who had tickets. The Police were stationed in force within, and without, and in Thirtieth-street confined a swaying, compact crowd of men, women and children within the limits of the sidewalks. The carriage-way was kept clear, and there, drawn up near the depot, were thirty-five carriages, provided by Mr. EDWARD VAN RANST, for the accommodation of Mr. LINCOLN and those who were to escort him to his hotel.

Mr. LINCOLN, alighting without delay, passed through the passenger-room, preceded by General-Superintendent KENNEDY, supported by Col. SUMNER and Mr. DAVIS, of Illinois, and followed by his fellow-travelers and the representatives of various Republican organizations who had awaited his arrival in the depot. Amid cheers and the waving of handkerchiefs, he entered his carriage — the same in which the Prince of Wales rode, drawn by six black horses.

A few minutes later the procession started. First came a squad of mounted Policemen; then a carriage drawn by four horses, in which the Reception Committee of the Common Council rode; then the carriage in which the President elect, Col. SUMNER and Alderman CORNELL, Chairman of the Joint Committee....

A strong police force followed the last vehicle, which was an Express wagon, drawn by four plumed steeds, which conveyed the baggage of the party. The route was as follows: Up Thirtieth-street to Ninth-avenue; down Ninth-avenue to Twenty-third-street; up, Twenty-third-street to Fifth avenue; down Fifth-avenue to Fourteenth-street; up Fourteenth-street to Broadway; down Broadway to the Astor House, Mr. LINCOLN's headquarters during his stay in New-York.

The streets were lined with people. Up town their name was legion, and as the carriages proceeded, the crowd became constantly denser.

Everywhere almost flags were flying. All the principal hotels, except the New-York Hotel, displayed the national banner, and from many private houses it was flung to the breeze.

On top of a building on the corner of Eighth-avenue and Twenty-third-street, stood a company of Sixteenth Ward Wide-Awakes in uniform, with their campaign banners flying.

A few doors beyond an American flag was stretched across the street, under which was written "Welcome LINCOLN!"

In the court-yard of a dwelling-house in Twenty-third-street stood a group of little boys, with military caps and uniforms, waving little flags inscribed "LINCOLN and HAMLIN."

Between Seventh and Eighth avenues the procession passed under a banner on which were these words from Genesis:

"Fear not, Abraham, I am thy shield and thy exceeding great reward."

In the window of a store under the New-York Hotel a placard which said: "Welcome, welcome, none too soon!"

From the balcony and windows of this hotel, as elsewhere all along the route, the ladies waved their handkerchiefs, and everywhere the approach of the President elect was greeted with enthusiastic cheering. The front of the Republican Headquarters, No, 618 Broadway, was covered by a large flag and a transparency which bore the inscription: "Welcome to the President elect. Prosperity to his Administration and our Union."

At Putnam, the publisher's, No. 532 Broadway, was hung out a placard with the words originally uttered by Mr. LINCOLN himself, "Right makes might!"[1]

At the corner of White-street and Broadway was another group of Wide-Awakes, in costume, waving American flags.

At the store of ISADOR, BERNHARD & SON, No. 351 Broadway, was a banner with this device: "Welcome, ABRAHAM LINCOLN, we beg for compromise.["]

It was precisely 4 1/2 P.M. when Mr. LINCOLN's carriage reached the Astor House. The crowd at this point was packed, and, almost impenetrable. The Police kept the middle of the street clear with great difficulty and commendable firmness. The Police arrangements throughout were admirable, and only one instance came under our notice in which the guardians of the public peace failed to do their duty calmly, quietly and well; the officer, whose cap is

numbered 1,355, stationed inside the Astor House, was unnecessarily rough and noisy.

Mr. LINCOLN and those who accompanied him alighted without delay and entered the hotel....

MOVEMENTS OF THE PRESIDENT ELECT TODAY.
The official reception of Mr. LINCOLN by the City authorities will take place in the Governor's Room in the City Hall at 11 A.M. this morning, after which the President elect will receive his friends. He has accepted an invitation to visit Barnum's Musseum to-day.[2]

Mrs. ABRAHAM LINCOLN, accompanied by the President elect and suite, will attend the opera to-night, and afford to the citizens of New-York one of the most favorable opportunities of paying polite courtesy and satisfying curiosity without any display of unnecessary or obtrusive rudeness. The opera selected for the occasion is the "Ballo in Maschera," the scene of which, it will be remembered, is laid in Boston, the Cradle of Liberty.[3] The arrangements will be completed in such a way as to prevent an undue crowd, so it will be well for those who would be present on this occasion to secure their seats in time.

The Wide Awake Central Committee will serenade Messrs. LINCOLN and HAMLIN at 12 o'clock to-night. The National Guard Band has been engaged for the occasion.

THE RECEPTION OF THE PRESIDENT-ELECT
If any doubt had previously existed of the steady loyalty and law-abiding temper of this City, it is set at rest by the welcome which yesterday greeted Mr. LINCOLN. An immeasurable outpouring of the people flooded the avenues and streets through which the escort passed; those untold and perhaps fabulous thousands of idle and starving workmen were, doubtless for want of other employment, in curious attendance; and, in fact, New-York may be said to have waited in person upon the coming of the future Chief Magistrate of the nation. And certainly no welcome could have been more cordial or respectful. The harmony of incessant cheers was unbroken by indecent language, or gesture, or act of violence. Along the protracted route the President was encountered everywhere by indications of the most earnest good will and respect for his person, and for his high and momentous vocation; and if there lurked anywhere those feelings of discontent and malignity which a portion of the City Press has been accustomed to dilate upon, they had the rare courtesy to ☞

mask themselves perfectly for this occasion.

There was perhaps some reason to anticipate much less creditable conduct. Mischief-makers have been feverishly busy all Winter in exaggerating the popular suffering, in aggravating the popular temper, and in impressing upon the masses a conviction that the responsibility for their woes rests immediately upon the triumph of the Republican Party, but directly upon Mr. LINCOLN, for not announcing the programme of his Administration, and so giving peace to the country. Acts of outrage and violence have been counseled and justified. Mob-law has had its advocates, and the South has been taught to expect, that the Winter could not pass without an uprising of the many-headed, and the plunder and destruction of the opulent classes. At the very culminating point of the Winter, when such bad dispositions, if they existed, would be wrought to a most mischievous pitch, the man who is marked as the fount and origin of the popular wrongs, comes among the multitude, and is received with every token of respect, satisfaction, and even personal regard. With this crucial test of the general sentiment, we trust the alarmists will feel authorized to rest from their fruitless labors; and take a lesson in loyalty from the impassible mob.... ☺

1. From the peroration of Lincoln's February 27, 1860, speech at New York's Cooper Union.
2. In the end, Lincoln's wife and son visited the celebrated attraction; the President-Elect did not.
3. The new Verdi opera culminated with a political assassination. Lincoln left before the climactic scene.

THE BORDER STATES AND THE UNION.

February 21

We find it not easy to understand why any Republican should resist a policy so thoroughly in harmony with the professions of the party, and so imperatively demanded by the exigencies of The Times. Every Republican is now more than ever interested in preserving the Union and in securing for the Government a successful and satisfactory Administration. We must repeat, therefore, what we said the other day, that none but those who are of heart Abolitionists or Secessionists, or both, will resist every endeavor to retain the Border States in the Union by such acts of friendly conciliation as involve no sacrifice of principle, but only indicate a love of the Union and a desire to preserve it on its original basis. The Union men of the Border States have a right to ask so much at the hands of the North; — and if the Republican Party is stolid enough to reject the proffered friendship, they may rely upon it their opponents will profit by their folly, and speedily expel them from places of power which they were unfit to wield and unable to hold.

An early 1861 cartoon warns of more Southern states joining the new Confederacy.

THE "SECESSION MOVEMENT".

HIGHLY IMPORTANT NEWS.

SECRET DEPARTURE OF THE PRESIDENT ELECT FROM HARRISBURGH.

ALLEGED PLOT FOR HIS ASSASSINATION.

February 25

HARRISBURG, Saturday, Feb. 23 — 8 A.M.

ABRAHAM LINCOLN, the President Elect of the United States, is safe in the capital of the nation. By the admirable arrangement of Gen. SCOTT, the country has been spared the lasting disgrace, which would have been fastened indelibly upon it had Mr. LINCOLN been murdered upon his journey thither, as he would have been had he followed the programme as announced in the papers and gone by the Northern Central Railroad to Baltimore.

On Thursday night after he had retired, Mr. LINCOLN was aroused and informed that a stranger desired to see him on a matter of life and death. He declined to admit him unless he gave his name, which he at once did, and such prestige did the name carry that while Mr. LINCOLN was yet disrobed he granted an interview to the caller.

A prolonged conversation elicited the fact that an organized body of men had determined that Mr. LINCOLN should not be inaugurated, and that he should never leave the City of Baltimore alive, if, indeed, he ever entered it.

The list of the names of the conspirators presented a most astonishing array of persons high in Southern confidence, and some whose fame is not confined to this country alone.

Statesmen laid the plan, Bankers indorsed it, and adventurers were to carry it into effect. As they understood, Mr. LINCOLN was to leave Harrisburgh at 9 o'clock this morning by special train, the idea was, if possible, to throw the cars from the road at some point where they would rush down a steep embankment and destroy in a moment the lives of all on board. In case of the failure of this project, their plan was to surround the carriage on the way from depot to depot in Baltimore, and assassinate him with dagger or pistol shot.

So authentic was the source from which the information was obtained, that Mr.

THE PEACE MOVEMENT.

FEBRUARY 28

The movements at Washington in favor of Peace are drawing to their natural close. The Peace Convention adjourned yesterday sine die, having first adopted the plan reported by Mr. GUTHRIE, as amended by Mr. FRANKLIN, of Pennsylvania. The essential feature of this plan is its restoration of the Missouri Compromise line, with added securities for Slavery in the Southern portion of the Territory thus divided. This action of the Convention was transmitted to the Senate, and ordered to be printed, and referred to a Select Committee, with instructions to report to-day at 1 o'clock.

We do not anticipate the adoption of this plan, — nor do we think it desirable. It is open to very grave and serious objections, — and although the assent of Congress to it would undoubtedly secure the continued loyalty of the Border States, it would be at a greater expense to the country than is required. Still the Peace Conference has been of essential service to the country, — in gaining time for reflection, in discussing the general topics of sectional difference, and in preparing the way for the peaceful opening of the new Administration.

The proper remedy for all existing evils is to be found in the legislative action of Congress; — and the House of Representatives yesterday entered vigorously, and in admirable temper, upon this important task. They first rejected the proposal to call a National Convention to revise and amend the Constitution of the United States, by the decisive vote of 74 to 109. They thus, in our judgment, delivered the country from the most serious of all the dangers which have menaced its existence. They next rejected Mr. KELLOGG's proposition, 33 to 158, — then that of Mr. CLEMENS, 80 to 113, and then adopted, by the decisive vote of 136 to 53, the resolutions reported by Mr. CORWIN's Committee of Thirty-three.

These resolutions will be found at length in our Congressional report. They declare, substantially —

1. That all proper and constitutional remedies for existing discontents, and all guarantees for existing rights, necessary to preserve the Union, should be promptly and cheerfully granted:

2. That all attempts to obstruct the recovery of fugitive slaves are inconsistent with inter-state comity, and dangerous to the peace of the Union:

3. That the several States be requested to revise their statutes and repeal such as may be in conflict with Federal laws on this subject:

4. That Slavery is recognized as existing by usage in fifteen States, and there is no authority outside those States to interfere with it.

5. That the laws on the subject of fugitives from labor should be faithfully executed, and that citizens of each State should be entitled to all the privileges and immunities of citizens in the several States.

6. That there is no cause for a dissolution of this Government, and that it is the duty of Congress to preserve its existence on terms of equality and justice to all the States.

7. That the faithful observance of the Constitution, on the part of the States, is essential to the peace of the country.

8. That each State is requested to revise its statutes, and amend them if necessary, so as to protect citizens of other States who may be traveling therein against violence.

9. That each State be requested to enact laws to punish invasions of other States from its soil.

10. That copies of these resolutions be sent to the Governors and Legislatures of the several States.

11. That as no proposition has been made to abolish Slavery in the District of Columbia or Government dock-yards, or to interfere with the inter-State Slave-trade, no action on these subjects is needed.

The proposition to amend the Constitution, so as to prohibit amendments interfering with Slavery, received 120 votes to 71, — but as there were not two-thirds in its favor it was not passed.

These resolutions cover the whole ground out of which the existing disturbances arise, except that of the Territories. They are so plainly just as to command universal assent, — and yet they provide for all the tangible grounds of complaint that have arisen. If in addition to these resolution, Congress, will take the action proposed by Mr. ADAMS, and pass an enabling act for New-Mexico, they will lay a solid and unexceptionable basis for the adjustment of all our difficulties. We hope they will do so. ✸

LINCOLN, after counselling with his friends, was compelled to make arrangements which would enable him to subvert the plane of his enemies.

Greatly to the annoyance of the thousands who desired to call on him last night, he declined giving a reception. The final council was held at 8 o'clock.

Mr. LINCOLN did not want to yield, and Col. SUMNER actually cried with indignation; but Mrs. LINCOLN, seconded by Mr. JUDD and Mr. LINCOLN'S original informant, insisted upon it, and at nine o'clock Mr. LINCOLN left on a special train. He wore a Scotch plaid cap and a very long military cloak,¹ so that he was entirely unrecognizable. Accompanied by Superintendent LEWIS and one friend, he started, while all the town, with the exception of Mrs. LINCOLN, Col. SUMNER, Mr. JUDD, and two reporters, who were sworn to secresy, supposed him to be asleep.

The telegraph wires were put beyond reach of any one who might desire to use them.

At 1 o'clock the fact was whispered from one to another, and it soon became the theme of most excited conversation. Many thought it a very injudicious move, while others regarded it as a stroke of great merit.

The special train leaves with the original party, including the TIMES correspondent, at 9 o'clock. ✸

The third of a sequence of four cartoons satirizing Lincoln's clandestine passage through Baltimore to Washington, D.C. for his inauguration. The caption read: "He wore a Scotch plaid Cap and a very long Military Cloak, so that he was entirely unrecognizable."

1. Lincoln admitted only that by donning "a soft hat" he was not "recognized by strangers, for I was not the same man." There is no evidence that he wore the elaborate disguise Times correspondent Joseph Howard invented for him in this report. But the calumny took hold, and cartoonists were soon depicting the President-Elect as a coward skulking into Washington in a tam and cloak, or wearing a kilt and dancing "the MacLincoln Harrisburg Highland Fling."

THE NEW ADMINISTRATION.
ABRAHAM LINCOLN PRESIDENT OF THE UNITED STATES.
THE INAUGURATION CEREMONIES.

MARCH 5

The day to which all have looked with so much anxiety and interest has come and passed. ABRAHAM LINCOLN has been inaugurated, and "all's well."

At daylight the clouds were dark and heavy with rain, threatening to dampen the enthusiasm of the occasion with unwelcome showers. A few drops fell occasionally before 8 o'clock, but not enough to lay the dust, which, under the impulse of a strong northwest wind, swept down upon the avenue from the cross streets quite unpleasantly. The weather was cool and bracing, and, on the whole, favorable to the ceremonies of the day.

Mr. LINCOLN rose at 5 o'clock. After an early breakfast, the Inaugural was read aloud to him by his son ROBERT, and the completing touches were added, including the beautiful and impassioned closing paragraph. Mr. LINCOLN then retired from his family circle to his closet, where he prepared himself for the solemn and weighty responsibilities which he was about to assume.

Here he remained until it was time for an audience to Mr. SEWARD. Together these statesmen conversed concerning that paragraph of the Inaugural relating to the policy of forcing obnoxious non-resident officers upon disaffected citizens. When Mr. SEWARD departed, Mr. LINCOLN closed his door upon all visitors, until Mr. BUCHANAN called for him to escort him to the Capitol.

From early daylight the streets were thronged with people, some still carrying carpet-bags in hand, having found no quarters in which to stop.

The busy have of preparation for the parade was soon heard on every side. The New-York delegation; over two hundred strong, formed in procession on Pennsylvania-avenue at 9 o'clock, and proceeded in a body to Mr. SEWARD's residence to pay their respects....

It was nearly noon when Mr. BUCHANAN started from the White House with the Inaugural procession, which halted before Willard's Hotel to receive the President elect. The order of march you will get from other sources, and I will only observe that the carriage containing Mr. BUCHANAN and Mr. LINCOLN, was a simple open brett, surrounded by the President's mounted guard, in close older, as a guard of honor.

The procession, as usual, was behindhand a little, but its order was excellent. Nothing noteworthy occurred on the route. As it ascended the Capitol hill, towards the north gate, the company of United States Cavalry and the President's mounted guard took their positions each side of the carriage-way, and thus guarded the inclosed passage-way by which the President's party entered the north wing of the Capitol to go to the Senate Chamber.

The procession halted until the President and suite entered, and then filed through the troops aforesaid into the grounds.

On the east front, the military took their positions in the grounds in front of the platform, but the United States troops maintained their places outside until the line took up the President and party again after the ceremonies were over, to escort them back to the White House.

The arrangements at the Capitol were admirably designed, and executed so that everybody who was entitled to admission got in, and everybody who could not go in could see from without. The Senate Chamber was the great point of attraction, but only the favored few were admitted upon the floor, while the galleries were reserved for and occupied by a select number of ladies. The scene which transpired there was most memorable, producing a great and solemn impression upon all present. Mr. BRIGHT spent all the morning in talking against time on some Gas Company's bill, greatly to the amusement of Senators, and the ill-concealed annoyance of spectators, who expected to hear some good speaking....

The Senate now waited in silence for the President elect. Gradually those entitled to the floor entered. The Diplomatic Corps, in full court dress, came quite early. The Supreme Court followed, headed by the venerable Chief Justice TANEY, who looked as if he had come down from several generations, and finally the House of Representatives filed in. For at least an hour Mr. HAMLIN was acting President of the United States, but at length, a little after 1 o'clock, the doors opened, and the expected dignitaries were announced.

Mr. BUCHANAN and Mr. LINCOLN entered, arm in arm, the former pale, sad, nervous; the latter's face slightly flushed, with compressed lips. For a few minutes, while the oath was administered to Senator PEARCE, they sat in front of the President's desk. Mr. BUCHANAN sighed audibly, and frequently, but whether from reflection upon the failure of his Administration, I can't say. Mr. LINCOLN was grave and impassive as an Indian martyr.

When all was ready, the party formed, and proceeded to the platform erected in front of the eastern portico. The appearance of the President elect was greeted, as he entered from the door of the rotunda, with immense cheering by the many thousand citizens assembled in the grounds, filling the square and open space, and perching on every tree, fence or stone affording a convenient point from which to see or hear. In a few minutes the portico was also densely crowded with both sexes. On the front of the steps was erected a small wooden canopy, under which were seated Mr. BUCHANAN, Chief-Justice TANEY, Senators CHASE and BAKER, and the President elect, white at the left of the small table on which was placed the Inaugural, stood Col. SELDEN, Marshal of the District, an exponent of the security which existed there for the man and the ceremonies of the hour. At the left of the canopy, sat the entire Diplomatic Corps, dressed in gorgeous attire, evidently deeply impressed with the solemnity of the occasion, and the importance of the simple ceremony about to be performed. Beyond them was the Marine band, which played several patriotic airs before and alter the reading of the address. To the right of the diplomats sat in solemn dignity, in silk gowns and hats, the members of the Supreme Court. Then came Senators, members of the House, distinguished guests and fair ladies by the score, while the immediate right of the canopy was occupied by the son and Private Secretaries of Mr. LINCOLN. Perched up on one side, hanging on by the railing, surrounding the statue of CO-LUMBUS and an Indian girl, was Senator WIGFALL,[1] witnessing the pageant.

Everything being in readiness, Senator BAKER came forward and said:

"FELLOW-CITIZENS: I introduce to you ABRAHAM LINCOLN, the President elect of the United States of America."

Whereupon, Mr. LINCOLN arose, walked deliberately and composedly to the table, and bent low in honor of the repeated and

The inaugural procession of Abraham Lincoln on March 4, 1861. Lincoln rides alongside outgoing President James Buchanan.

probably sleepy and tired, sat looking as straight as he could at the toe of his right boot. Mr. DOUGLAS, who stood by the right of the railing, was apparently satisfied, as he exclaimed, sotto voce, "Good," "That's so," "No coercion," and "Good again."

After the delivery of the address Judge TANEY stood up, and all removed their hats, while he administered the oath to Mr. LINCOLN. Speaking in a low tone the form of the oath, he signified to Mr. LINCOLN, that he should repeat the words, and in a firm but modest voice, the President took the oath as prescribed by the law, while the people, who waited until they saw the final bow, tossed their huts, wiped their eyes, cheered at the top of their voices, hurrahed themselves hoarse, and had the crowd not been so very dense, they would have demonstrated in more lively ways, their joy, satisfaction and delight.

Judge TANEY was the first person who shook hands with Mr. LINCOLN, and was followed by Mr. BUCHANAN, CHASE, DOUGLAS, and a host of minor great men. A Southern gentleman, whose name I did not catch, seized him by the hand, and said, "God bless you, my dear Sir; you will save us." To which Mr. LINCOLN replied, "I am very glad that what I have said causes pleasure to Southerners, because I then know they are pleased with what is right.…"

THE INAUGURATION CEREMONIES

The day was ushered in by a most exciting session of the Senate, that body sitting for twelve hours, from 7 o'clock yesterday evening to 7 o'clock this morning.

As the dial of the clock pointed to 12 o'clock last night, and the Sabbath gave way to Monday, the 4th of March, the Senate Chamber presented a curious and animated appearance. The galleries were crowded to repletion, the ladies' gallery resembling, from the gay dresses of the fair ones there congregated, some gorgeous parterre of flowers, and the gentlemen's gallery seemed one dense black mass 👉

enthusiastic cheering of the countless host before him. Having put on his spectacles, he arranged his manuscript on the small table, keeping the paper thereon by the aid of his cane, and commenced in a clear, ringing voice, that was easily heard by those on the outer limits of the crowd, to read his first address to the people, as President of the United States.

The opening sentence, "Fellow-citizens of the United States," was the signal for prolonged applause, the good Union sentiment thereof striking a tender chord in the popular breast. Again, when, after defining certain actions to be his duty, he said, "And I shall perform it," there was a spontaneous,

and uproarious manifestation of approval, which continued for some moments. Every sentence which indicated firmness in the Presidential chair, and every statement of a conciliatory nature, was cheered to the echo; while his appeal to his "dissatisfied fellow-countrymen," desiring them to reflect calmly, and not hurry into false steps, was welcomed by one and all, most heartily and cordially. The closing sentence "upset the watering pot" of many of his hearers, and at this point alone did the melodious voice of the President elect falter.

Judge TANEY did not remove his eyes from Mr. LINCOLN during the entire delivery, while Mr. BUCHANAN, who was

of surging, heaving masculines, pushing, struggling and almost clambering over each other's backs in order to get a good look at the proceedings....

When the word was given for the members of the House to fall into the line of the procession, a violent rush was made for the door, accompanied by loud outcries, violent pushing and great-disturbance.

After the procession had reached the platform, Senator BAKER,[2] of Oregon, introduced Mr. LINCOLN to the Assembly. On Mr. LINCOLN advancing to the stand, he was cheered, but not very loudly. Unfolding his manuscript, in a loud, clear voice, he read his address, as follows:

THE INAUGURAL ADDRESS.

Fellow-citizens of the United States:

In compliance with a custom as old as the Government itself, I appear before you to address you briefly, and to take in your presence the oath prescribed by the Constitution of the United States to be taken by the President before he enters on the execution of his office.

I do not consider it necessary at present for me to discuss those matters of Administration, about which there is no special anxiety or excitement.

Apprehension seems to exist among the people of the Southern States that, by the accession of a Republican Administration, their property, and their peace and personal security are to be endangered. There has never been any reasonable cause for such apprehension. Indeed, the most ample evidence to the contrary has all the while existed, and been open to their inspection. It is found in nearly all the published speeches of him who now addresses you. I do but quote from one of these speeches. when I declare that "I have no purpose, directly or indirectly, to interfere with the institution of Slavery in the States where it exists. I believe I have no lawful right to do so, and I have no inclination to do so."...

The course here indicated will be followed, unless current events and experience shall show a modification or change to be proper, and in every case and exigency my best discretion will be exercised, according to the circumstances actually existing, and with a view and a hope of a peaceful solution of the national troubles and the restoration of internal sympathies and affections. That there are persons in one section or another who seek to destroy

the Union at all events, and are glad of any pretext to do it, I will neither affirm or deny. But if there be such I need address no word to them. To those, however, who really love the Union, may I not speak. Before entering upon so grave a matter as the destruction of our national fabric with all its benefits, its memories and its hopes, would it not be well to ascertain why we do it. Will you hazard so desperate a step while there is any portion of the ills you fly from have no real existence? Will you, while the certain ills you fly to are greater than all the real ones you fly from?

Will you risk the commission of so fearful a mistake? All profess to be content in the Union, if all Constitutional rights can be maintained. Is it true, then, that any right plainly written in the Constitution has been denied? I think not. Happily the human mind is so constituted that no party can reach to the audacity of doing this. Think, if you can, of a single instance in which a plainly written provision of the Constitution has ever been denied. If, by the mere force of numbers, a majority should deprive a minority of any clearly written constitutional light, it might, in a moral point of view, justify revolution certainly would, of such right were a vital one. But such is not our case....

Physically speaking, we cannot separate — we cannot remove our respective sections from each other, nor build an impassable wall between them. A husband and wife may be divorced, and go out of the presence and beyond the reach of each other — but the different parts of our country cannot do this.

They cannot but remain face to face, and intercourse either amicable or hostile must continue between them. Is it possible then to make that intercourse more advantageous or more satisfactory after separation than before? Can aliens make treaties easier than friends can make laws? Can treaties be more faithfully enforced between aliens than laws can among friends?

Suppose you go to war, you cannot fight always, and when, after much loss on both sides and no gain on either, you cease fighting, the identical questions as to terms of intercourse are again upon you. This country, with its institutions, belongs to the people who inhabit it. Whenever they shall grow weary of the existing Government, they can exercise their Constitutional right of amending or their revolutionary right to dismember or overthrow it. I cannot be

ignorant of the fact that many worthy and patriotic citizens are desirous of having the National Constitution amended. While I make no recommendation of amendment, I fully recognize the full authority of the people over the whole subject to be exercised in either of the modes prescribed in the instrument itself, and I should, under existing circumstances, favor rather than oppose a fair opportunity being afforded the people to act upon it....

My countrymen, one and all, think calmly and well upon this whole subject. Nothing valuable can be lost by taking time.

If there be an object to hurry any of you in hot haste to a step which you would never take deliberately, that object will be frustrated by taking time; but no good object can be frustrated by it. Such of. you as are now dissatisfied still have the old Constitution unimpaired, and on the sensitive point, the laws of your own framing under it, while the new Administration will have no immediate power, if it would, to change either. If it were admitted that you who are dissatisfied hold the right side in the dispute, there still is no single reason for precipitate action.

Intelligence, patriotism, Christianity and a firm reliance on Him who has never yet forsaken this favored land, are still competent to adjust in the best way all our present difficulty.

In your hands, my dissatisfied fellow-countrymen, and not in mine, is the momentous issue of civil war. The Government will not assail you. You can have no conflict without being yourselves the aggressors.

You have no oath registered in Heaven to destroy the Government, while I shall have the most solemn one to "preserve, protect and defend" it.

I am loth to close. We are not enemies but friends. We must not be enemies.

Though passion may have strained, it must not break our bonds of affection. The mystic chords of memory stretching from every battle-field and patriot's grave to every living heart and hearthstone all over this broad land, will yet swell the chorus of the Union, when again touched, as surely they will be, by the better angels of our nature.... ❀

1. Louis T. Wigfall (1816–1874) of Texas resigned from the Senate 19 days after the inaugural, and later served as a Confederate general and member of the Confederate Congress.
2. Edward Dickinson Baker (1811–1861) was an old family friend of the Lincolns'.

THE INAUGURAL.

MARCH 5

Mr. LINCOLN's Inaugural Address must command the cordial approval of the great body of the American people. The intellectual and moral vigor which pervades it will infuse new hope and loyalty into the American heart. The calm firmness with which it asserts the rightful authority of the Federal Government, — the declared purpose which it embodies to preserve, protect and defend the Union and the Constitution, the easy force with which it sweeps away all the cobwebs of secession logic, and vindicates the supreme duty of the Government to defend its own existence, cannot fail to impress even the most determined Secessionist with grave doubts as to the justice of his cause. The characteristic feature of the Address is its profound sincerity, — the earnest determination which it evinces to render equal and exact justice to every State, to every section, to every interest of the Republic, — and to administer the Government in a spirit of the most thorough and impartial equity. To this purpose every other con-

sideration is made to bend. And no one who can understand and appreciate such a character as that of Mr. LINCOLN, will doubt that this spirit will mark every act of his Administration.

In our judgment the Inaugural cannot fail to exert a very happy influence upon public sentiment throughout the country. All men, of all parties, must feel that its sentiments are just and true, — that it sets forth the only basis on which the Government of this country can be maintained, while at the same time it breathes the very spirit of kindness and conciliation, and relies upon justice and reflection, rather than force, for the preservation of the Federal Union....

The Inaugural is equally explicit and emphatic in its proffer of concessions and guarantees to the alarmed interests of the Southern States. The President disavows in the most solemn manner, — and calls the record of his life to witness the justice of the disavowal, — all thought, purpose or inclination to interfere with Slavery in

any State where it exists, — and declares his willingness to assent to an amendment of the Constitution which shall make such interference, on the part of Congress, irrevocably impossible. He declares that the obligation to return fugitive slaves is absolute and unquestionable, and calls for the enactment of laws which shall secure its fulfillment. In regard to differences of opinion as to the Territories, while he asserts the absolute necessity of yielding for the time, and while the decision stands unreversed, to the verdict of the majority and the decisions of the Supreme Court, he also declares his readiness to favor a Convention to amend the Constitution in these or any other particulars. It would scarcely be possible for him, in such an address, to go further towards the conciliation of all discontented interests of the Confederacy.

The Inaugural inspires the strongest and most confident hopes of the wisdom and success of the new Administration. It is marked throughout by consummate ability, a wise and prudent sagacity in the judgment of affairs, a profound appreciation of the difficulties and dangers of the crisis, a calm, self-possessed, unflinching courage adequate to any emergency, a kind and conciliatory temper, and the most earnest, sincere and unswerving devotion to the Union and the Constitution. If the dangers of the hour can be averted and the Union can be saved, this is the basis on which alone it can be accomplished. If the Union cannot be saved on this basis and consistently with these principles, then it is better that it should not be saved at all. ⊛

The inauguration of Abraham Lincoln on March 4, 1861. The scaffolding in the background was being used to erect the new capitol dome.

CHAPTER 3

"The Excitement... Has Been Intense"

APRIL–MAY 1861

For weeks New Yorkers had talked of little else besides the festering crisis in Charleston Harbor, and yet the news of the first shot at Fort Sumter — and especially the news that Major Robert Anderson had surrendered the fort to the secessionists — caught most of them by surprise. Many were loath to believe it. When it was confirmed, it produced a frenzy of patriotic excitement that lasted throughout the rest of April and into May. The Times predicted, accurately as it proved, "The people will respond to this demand with alacrity and exultation." All across the north, from Baltimore to Chicago to Cleveland, the news from Fort Sumter swept aside differences on policy and party.

Soon after the news from Charleston came Lincoln's Proclamation of April 15, which called for 75,000 volunteers "to maintain the honor, the integrity, and the existence of our National Union." As far as the South was concerned, this was coercion, and constituted a declaration of war. It triggered the secession of four more states to join the Confederacy: North Carolina, Tennessee, Arkansas, and, most important, Virginia. With Virginia's secession, the Confederacy moved its capital from Montgomery, Alabama, to Richmond.

On the same day that Virginia seceded (April 17), the Confederate President, Jefferson Davis, announced that his government would begin to issue letters of marque, documents that authorized private citizens to fit out armed vessels to prey on the merchant shipping of the Union. This practice, known as privateering, had been a staple of America's wartime strategy since the Revolution, but it had been declared illegal by the Declaration of Paris in 1856 (though

Fort Sumter, South Carolina, under attack by Confederate forces.

the United States had not signed that protocol). The Times, unsurprisingly, viewed Davis's decision with outrage. Then, two days later, on April 19, came Lincoln's proclamation of a blockade, a decision that had been encouraged by The Times, and which the paper applauded. It did not prove to be the sudden crippling blow promised by its champions, though it did lead in the long term to hardship and war weariness in the South. Embedded in that proclamation, however, was another issue that caused the Lincoln administration much difficulty. Lincoln announced that "any person, under the pretended authority" of the seceded states who attempted to molest the shipping of the country "would be held amenable [accountable] to the laws of the United States for the prevention and punishment of piracy." In the end Lincoln had to back away from that threat for fear of reprisals against Union prisoners of war.

That the war would have far-reaching social and legal consequences became evident that month as well,

when Major General Benjamin Butler, until recently a congressman from Massachusetts and now a major general in charge of Fort Monroe on the Virginia coast, defined escaped slaves as "contraband of war" in order to justify his decision not to return them to their Virginia owners under the Fugitive Slave Law. In addition, The Times reported the arrest in Maryland of a pro-Confederate activist named John Merryman, an event that was made especially newsworthy when Lincoln decided to deny him the right of habeas corpus. That led to a lengthy national discussion about individual rights in wartime.

Lincoln called for Congress to meet on July 4, but that was nearly three months away, and in the meantime, war preparations continued on both sides. Recruiting offices in New York and elsewhere were overwhelmed. Regiments from Massachusetts marching through New York en route to Washington were greeted by an outpouring of enthusiastic, flag-waving patriotism unprecedented

in the Republic. The wildly cheered march of New York's own Seventh Regiment down Broadway symbolized the unity and enthusiasm of the public. These events erased the skepticism of those New Yorkers who had doubted that the crisis would ever escalate into violence, and silenced those who had secretly applauded the boldness of the South's actions. In time, the enthusiasm would fade along with hope for a quick early victory, but the determination and commitment would remain. What was still unclear was, as The Times put it, "How shall the United States Government wage the war?" There was no precedent for such a conflict, and few in the spring of 1861 could foresee the horrible bloodletting to come. Most expected a quick and decisive confrontation. "Whoever has to die," The Times opined, "it is better to die by the guillotine than by a cancer. Then up with the axe, and down with the head, and let the slide fall."

FORT SUMPTER FALLEN.

PARTICULARS OF THE BOMBARDMENT.

APRIL 15

CHARLESTON, SATURDAY, APRIL 13 — EVENING. Major [Robert] ANDERSON[1] has surrendered, after hard fighting, commencing at 4 ½ o'clock yesterday morning, and continuing until five minutes to 1 to-day.

The American flag has given place to the Palmetto of South Carolina....

Major ANDERSON stated that he surrendered his sword to Gen. [P. G. T.] BEAUREGARD[2] as the representative of the Confederate Government. Gen. BEAUREGARD said he would not receive it from so brave a man. He says Major ANDERSON made a staunch fight, and elevated himself in the estimation of every true Carolinian....

The scene in the city after the raising of the flag of truce and the surrender is indescribable; the people were perfectly wild. Men on horseback rode through the

streets proclaiming the news, amid the greatest enthusiasm.

On the arrival of the officers from the fort they were marched through the streets, followed by an immense crowd, hurrahing, shouting and yelling with excitement.... ✪

1. Major Robert Anderson (1805–1871) was a native Kentuckian who commanded the Fort Sumter garrison.
2. Brigadier General Pierre Gustav Toutant Beauregard (1818–1893) was a native of Louisiana and the senior Confederate military officer in Charleston Harbor.

Major Robert Anderson, commander of the federal garrison at Fort Sumter.

THE NEWS IN WASHINGTON.
THE EXCITEMENT AT THE CAPITAL.

APRIL 15

WASHINGTON, SUNDAY, APRIL 14

The excitement here throughout the day has been intense. People gather in groups on the streets and in the hotels, discussing affairs at Charleston and the probabilities of the future.

There is great diversity of opinion relative to the reliability of the news that Major ANDERSON has surrendered. The dispatches to the Associated Press are evidently full of blunders, which cast suspicion on the whole.

The President, nevertheless, has intelligence which satisfies him that the news is too true. Private dispatches from Charleston, signed by trusty men, also confirm it; but as the telegraph is known to have been constantly tampered with by the secession authorities, it is feared that even private dispatches may have been mutilated for the purpose of cutting the Government off from all possible means of correct information....

To-day's excitement has betrayed many secessionists who hold public office, and who could not conceal their joy at the reduction of Fort Sumpter. Several fights occurred, and decided knockdowns. Gen. NYE, among others, has knocked down a couple of secessionists within the last day or two.[1] The fact is, Northern men have got tired of having treason crammed offensively down their throats, and are learning to resent it by force, the only argument the chivalry seems to appreciate....

Everybody here sees that now war has commenced, the question which the Virginia Convention has to decide is simply whether Virginia will declare war against the United States or stand by the Government; whether she will invite the battle upon her soil, to her utter ruin, or aid in bringing the fratricidal strife to a speedy termination by sustaining the Government and Union.

The news from the North of the unanimity of public sentiment in favor of the Government and the strongest policy for the suppression of rebellion gladdens every heart. It is fully believed that all partisan considerations henceforth will be suspended, and that every effort will be directed to saving the country.

You have the President's proclamation, making a requisition for seventy-five thousand volunteers, called from all the adhering States except California and Oregon. That news will thrill like an electric shock throughout the land, and establish the fact that we have a Government at last.

The Cabinet is a unit on these measures, and no man among them was more decided and active in their support than Mr. SEWARD, who urged conciliation and forbearance until the Disunionists were put clearly and thoroughly in the wrong.

The War Department is engaged to-night in calculating the number of troops which each State is entitled to furnish. New-York will be entitled probably to ten regiments. Pennsylvania and Massachusetts to a few less. The estimates are based upon the Federal representation of the States.

This proclamation is the fruit of a prolonged Cabinet meeting held last night.

THE BLOCKADE OF SOUTHERN PORTS.

No policy relative to closing the ports of the Seceding States is yet understood to be settled upon in detail. It is probable, however, that arrangements will be speedily made to cut off all communication with them by sea.[2] There need be no doubt about the power of the Government to do this under its authority to prevent smuggling.

But, independent of that, the occasion justifies the Executive in assuming responsibility. He may well emulate Gen. JACKSON, who, when BOB LETCHER asked him under what law he could bring the Nullifier leaders of South Carolina to Washington for trial and execution, replied that if the Attorney-General could not find a law for it, he would get another Attorney-General who could.[3] Self-preservation is the Government's first duty, and its masters, the people, will justify it in every wise measure addressed to that end.

Gen. SCOTT has been at work all day, with all the energy of the soldier in the prime of life, making calculations for the disposition of the forces to be raised.

The Administration has satisfactory information that the Confederate States have proposed, immediately after reducing Fort Sumpter, to march on Washington with their army of twenty thousand men, for which they will have nothing else to do. Until recently, JEFFERSON DAVIS was disposed to postpone that step until the secession of Virginia and Maryland was effected, but as he despairs of that now, he believes that at the approach of his army those States will immediately unite their forces with his. Men who know those States well say he is in error.

There is one regiment of volunteers now in Baltimore ready to obey the call of the Government immediately, and they will be mustered into service. Virginia also is ready to furnish her quota. The Government designs to bring a force of volunteers to this city not only strong enough to defend it against all comers, but to render an attack on it improbable. Several additional companies of regulars are also ordered here. It is not improbable that this point will be made a grand rendezvous from which troops can readily be sent wherever required.

Congress is called in extra session on the 4th of July — a glorious day for a glorious work! This is essential in order to get the money that will be needed to enable the Government to sustain itself, and to pay as it goes. War is a costly experiment, as the Disunionists will find. It is no longer child's play, and will impoverish them utterly in a few months, if they persist in it, for they must themselves be the aggressors, and transport their troops and supplies long distances. The hopelessness of their unrighteous struggle must speedily force itself upon their minds when they learn how vigorous is the Government in its present hands, and how unanimous the people are in sustaining it.

The President had not at nine o'clock to-night determined upon putting Washington under martial law. But there is little doubt that it will be done within a day or two. If so, it is hoped that possession will be taken of the telegraph office to prevent its employment by Disunionists for treasonable purposes.... ◉

1. Republican James W. Nye (1815–1876) had until 1859 been the police commissioner of New York City. In 1861, Lincoln appointed him to be the first governor of Nevada.

2. Lincoln announced a blockade of southern ports on April 19.

3. President Andrew Jackson believed it was essential to pass what was called the Force Bill in 1832 before Congress agreed to modify the tariff that had prompted South Carolina's revolt. Robert Letcher was a congressman from Kentucky and Henry Clay's chief lieutenant in the House of Representatives.

THE GREAT REBELLION — THE BEGINNING OF THE END.

APRIL 15

The curtain has fallen upon the first act of the great tragedy of the age. Fort Sumpter has been surrendered, and the Stars and Stripes of the American Republic give place to the felon flag of the Southern Confederates. The defence of the fortress did honor to the gallant commander by whom it was held, and vindicated the Government under which he served....

The Government of the United States is prepared to meet this great emergency with the energy and courage which the occasion requires, and which the sentiment of the nation demands. The PRESIDENT issues his proclamation to-day, convening Congress for the 4th of July, and calling for SEVENTY-FIVE THOUSAND volunteers for the defence of the Union, and the protection of the rights and the liberties of the American people.[1] The people will respond to this demand with alacrity and exultation. They ask nothing better than to be allowed to fight for the Constitution which their fathers framed. Whatever may have been their political differences, there has never been a moment when they were not ready to sink them all in devotion to their common country, and in defence of their common flag. The President's Proclamation will be hailed with an enthusiasm which no event of the last twenty years has called forth, — with a high-hearted determination to exterminate treason, which will carry terror into the hearts of the Confederates, who have conspired for the destruction of the freest and best Government the world has ever seen.

We repeat what we have had occasion to say more than once already, that the history of the world affords no instance of so utterly groundless a war, as that which the Southern Confederates have commenced upon the United States. The future historian will grope in vain for any adequate causes for such a movement. In no solitary instance have their rights been infringed, their liberties abridged, or their interests invaded by the Government of the United States. On the contrary, they have known that Government only by the blessings it has conferred upon them. It has fought their battles, enlarged their area, paid for their postal service, augmented their power and consideration abroad, and shielded their peculiar institution from the hatred and hostility of the civilized world. But for the Union, and the protection which it has afforded them, they would long since have sunk under the weight of their own evils, or been crushed by the enmity of hostile powers. During the whole period of their connection with the Union, they cannot point to a single instance of hostile or unfriendly action on the part of the United States. Not a single law has ever been passed interfering with Slavery in the slightest degree, while scores have been passed and enforced for its protection. Their fugitive slaves have been remanded in almost every instance where they have been claimed, and more than once the Army and Navy of the Federal Government have been used for that purpose. But the States which have commenced this horrid rebellion, have lost scarcely any fugitive slaves, while those States which have a right to complain of losses on this score, are still loyal to the Union and the Constitution. The John Brown invasion, the only instance of aggressive action from the North upon Slavery, during the whole history of the Government, was the act of a band of fanatics for which no considerable portion of the community was in the least responsible, and was suppressed by the Government of the United States itself. In no solitary instance have the rebel States had the slightest reason to complain of oppression or injustice at the hands of the Federal Government.

Indeed they have, themselves, more than once confessed that the question of Slavery had nothing to do with their rebellion. In the Convention which declared South Carolina to be out of the Union, it was openly avowed that Secession was merely the consummation of a purpose which had been pursued for the last thirty years. The same declaration has been made in other quarters. The fact is, the present movement is the result of as clear and deliberate a conspiracy as blackens the page of history. It was concocted and has been prosecuted by a few leading men in the Southern States, who have, year after year, made it their special business to inflame the public mind in the Southern States against the North, — by the most flagrant falsehoods and misrepresentations, — and to prepare the Southern people upon some favorable contingency, to be precipitated into revolution. They have accomplished their purpose. They have so debauched the minds of the great body of the people in seven of the States of the Union, that they have led them into open and flagrant armed rebellion against the Government of the United States. ◉

Reaction in the North over the attack on Fort Sumter.

1. Lincoln's proclamation is in Roy P. Basler, ed., *The Collected Works of Abraham Lincoln*, 8 vols. (New Brunswick, NJ: Rutgers University Press. 1953–55), 4:331–2.

HENRY WARD BEECHER ON THE CRISIS.

APRIL 15

The good people of Brooklyn have shared with us all the anxiety, the excitement and the fears of the past week. Sunday is with them a day of rest, of moral culture, and of religious instruction, and one on which, for the better development of those attainments, they visit, one and all, the house of the Lord, and particularly that one of which Mr. BEECHER is the shepherd.[1] Yesterday was no exception to the rule, only in that there was, if possible, a more dense mass of human beings packed within the walls of that sanctuary, and a more than ordinary curiosity on the part of strangers and a more than customary solemnity pervading the congregation. It was manifestly the belief of all there that the pastor would not fail to improve the occasion by preaching to the people of this age upon the necessities and the duties of the present trying hour, and that he would deal with so grand a subject in a manner befitting its character, its importance, and its universal occupation of the American mind.

The services began at 7 1/2 o'clock, and ... the paucity of space compels us to reduce the report....

"The horrors of war, and the horrors of civil war especially, are easy to paint. I will yield no whit in keen appreciation of the dreadful calamities attendant upon such a sad condition — but with a fail realization and an entire conception of all the horrible possibilities of war, I say that I for one would...rather let there be war ten thousand times over than that slavery, with silent corruptions should be permitted longer to fester in our body politic. War is as resurrection, and though bad, very bad, is surpassed in evil by the results which flow from other sources. In our case, it will not be an unmixed evil. Eighty years of unexampled prosperity has hardened us, we have gone recklessly onward, doing this that and the other, as it might best advance our mutual interests. Our standard of morals has been commercial, and from a commercial stand point we have taken our observations. Should it please God to plunge this casualty into war, it will benefit us, in that we will be called upon at last, not only to talk, but to suffer for our faith, to bear for it and to endure for it....

Let this matter be settled now. Let it never come up again. If war must come, let us meet in; it's better to brave it thoroughly now; to brave, if necessary, a protracted war, so that it is a final one, than for twenty years to come be troubled with an intermittent breaking out at every period. It has got to be settled one way or the other, The North has the population, the means and the courage — for there is no such breath of courage at the South as there is at the North."

Mr. BEECHER appeared about six inches taller than usual, and his eye flashed fire as he looked upon the enthusiasm of his charges. ✸

1. The abolitionist preacher Henry Ward Beecher (1813–1887) was the son of Lyman Beecher, brother of Harriet Beecher Stowe (author of *Uncle Tom's Cabin*), and the minister at the Plymouth Congregationalist Church in Brooklyn.

Reverend Henry Ward Beecher.

IMPORTANT FROM VIRGINIA.

DEBATE IN CONVENTION ON THE PRESIDENT'S PROCLAMATION.

APRIL 18

FROM OUR SPECIAL CORRESPONDENT,
RICHMOND, VA., MONDAY MORNING, APRIL 15

The public mind of old Virginia is to-day boiling like one of the ocean's great whirlpools; or rather, I should say, rushing like the Gulf Stream's torrent; for it has ceased to meet in jarring conflict, resulting in a round of policy without progress, but is dashing onward to action — decided, open and irrevocable. What that action is, I need not repeat; I have already signified it clearly enough in the TIMES.

A man may live fifty years and see no such period of excitement as has prevailed in Virginia since the insurgent guns opened on Fort Sumter. When the news came that the "Stars and Stripes," that never fell before in the face of an enemy, had been lowered to the flag of the Confederate States, a delirium of joy seized the Disunionists of Richmond. They turned out by thousands, paraded the streets in companies, shouting the war cries of secession, were addressed at different points, as they passed through the city, by revolutionary orators, and finally proceeded to a State armory, and took without leave a number of field-pieces, with which they fired from Capitol Hill one hundred guns in honor of Sumter's surrender. Not satisfied with this, a passion seized them to exalt the secession flag over the State House, and a band instantly proceeded to execute the purpose. The State flag, renowned and honored in the old Commonwealth for its brave motto, "Sic semper tyrannis," was hauled down, and the banner of strange device — that of the seven Cotton States — dominated the haughty old State of Virginia! And many thousands of her sons and daughters shouted hosannas of submission!

Torchlight processions and illuminations at night succeeded the demonstrations of the day, and shouting, speech-making and revelry extended into the Sabbath morning.... ✸

THE WAR FEELING IN BROOKLYN.

APRIL 18

The war feeling in Brooklyn, and in fact throughout Long Island, is rapidly reaching that point when something must be done; in a word, the people are spoiling for a fight. Recruiting offices have been opened at different points, and those in charge expect to be able to fill up a Regiment at an early day. The regular State militia are drilling constantly in the State and City armory, and also evenings in the streets. The Regiments are rapidly filling up.

At about 9 o'clock last evening a party of about 1,500 men went to the offices of the Brooklyn Eagle and Daily News — Democratic papers — and requested the proprietors to raise the Stars and Stripes. The demand was speedily complied with, when the party moved on, and after giving three cheers for the Star, dispersed…. ✷

ENLISTMENT FOR THE WAR.

APRIL 19

The patriotic enthusiasm that has swept this City with a whirlwind of Union demonstrations, continued unabated yesterday. The universal display of the American colors in every available locality; the parading of the Boston troops through the streets, on their way to Washington; the busy preparations of the Seventh Regiment; the flocking of crowds to the numerous recruiting stations; the arrival of Major ANDERSON and the veterans of Fort Sumter; the running to and fro of military men; the resonance of martial music; the reception and discussion of the war bulletins from the South, made the occasion one of the most exciting in the annals of New-York City. Below we give succinct details of the various demonstrations:

Among the most prominent incidents connected with the Military movements of the City yesterday, was the arrival, by the early morning train from Boston, of the Sixth Regiment, Massachusetts Militia, en route for Washington…. The Bunker Hill boys were not without a reception, however, for early in the morning, and long before the train arrived, a throng of citizens, numbering 5,000 or over, had congregated about the New-Haven depot, at the corner of Twenty-seventh street, and when the cars came, the Regiment was greeted with long, loud and repeated cheers for the "Bay State Boys," the "Boston boys," the "Bunker Hill boys," and various other titles indicative of the State from which they came. Capt. [Francis C.] SPEIGHT, of the Metropolitan Police, with 30 men, was present to preserve order, and to escort the regiment to their quarters at the various hotels which had been selected for their accommodation. After receiving the congratulations of the crowd the regiment formed in line and marched down Twenty-seventh-street to Fifth-avenue, thence up Broadway to Union-square, around the Square and down Broadway to the Metropolitan Hotel…Flags were displayed at all the hotels on the route, and waving handkerchiefs from the balconies and windows signified the warm greetings of the fair sex to the brave Bay State soldiers. Opposite the New-York Hotel a gray-haired old man mounted a stoop and addressing the soldiers and the people, said that he had fought under the Stars and Stripes in the War of 1812 against a foreign Power, and now that flag was dishonored and spit upon by those who should be its defenders. He closed his remarks by a "God bless our flag," and left the crowd with the tears streaming down his wrinkled cheeks…. ✷

VOLUNTEERS FOR THE UNION.

APRIL 19

The patriotism of the loyal States is at last aroused, our people gradually realizing that an attack on the National Government is no longer confined to the bombast of Southern speeches, but has become an active and embodied principle, dominant in seven of the extreme Southern States, and struggling for impious ascendency in all. Naturally, and as a tribute of honest respect to our late brethren, we were slow to suspect them of deliberate treason — reluctant to let the idea get lodgment in our minds, that any considerable portion of American citizens could be brought to unite in so foul and causeless a conspiracy. Great latitude was allowed in estimating the fiery expressions of Cotton State stump eloquence, — the loyal States feeling conscious of their strength, and reposing in complacent, and even amused, security, while listening to the bluster and braggadocio in which certain blatant captains of the "Gulf Squadron" have lived and moved and had their being for the past ten or a dozen years.

But, with the first shot fired against Fort Sumter, all these cherished illusions have vanished. The veil raised by our confiding affection is rudely torn aside, and we stand face to face with masses of armed and furious rebels, seeking our lives with weapons stolen from the national armories of the country by one of their own number, whom we had loaded with honors and ☞

Departure of the New York Seventh Regiment, known as the "Silk Stocking" regiment.

invested with the solemnities of official trust. In the blackened and dented walls of Sumter — its terraces desolated by fire, its guns dismounted or unmanageable, its roof strewn with broken shells and flattened shot, its weaker parapets in ruins, and its magazines swept clear of the last pound of moldering biscuit on which the gallant handfull of its defenders had subsisted and defied the power of seven thousand assailants, until compelled by hunger to succumb, — in this sad scene of ruin, and raising our eyes to the snake-wreathed Palmetto emblem now floating from the staff which held aloft, through two days of fire, the banner of the Union, — we of the loyal States dismiss the generous illusions that have beset and betrayed us, acknowledging the rugged fact of rebellion, and casting aside all former considerations, while we prepare rapidly, though still with reluctance, for the bloody arbitration of civil war.

The rebels of the Cotton States, in our days of peace, have taunted the North with lack of physical courage. The brawlers of Cotton State tap-rooms, and the desperadoes of the Mississippi gaming-table, have been unable to account otherwise for the concerted refusal of many Northern representatives to violate the laws, both of God and man, by engaging in duels, whenever challenged, with adversaries who have reduced this species of private slaughter to a cruel and deliberate art. The challengers grew vain of the cheap glory thus purchased — their blunted intelligence or long habits of violence not allowing them to comprehend that moral repugnance and not physical fear — respect for law and not apprehension of death — the manifest inequality of the combat and not any unwillingness to engage in fair fight for a sufficient cause — lay behind the refusal of our Northern Congressmen and Senators, to adjourn debate from the floor of the house to an open field near Bladensburgh, and to exchange the weapons of logic and fact for the much briefer arguments invented by Cols. COLT and BOWIE.[1]

But in the aroused enthusiasm which now fills every street and highway with thronging cohorts of volunteers, — hundreds and thousands pouring out from every Ward, and District, and hamlet, and eager to be employed in defence of the Union, where only dozens or scores can be accepted; — in the elate and joyous military spirit, now flashing from every house-top in waving banners, filling every avenue and thoroughfare with files of glittering steel, and causing the air to vibrate, as fresh and yet fresh accessions of ardent Volunteers sweep onward, keeping time to martial music, in these first rudimentary demonstrations of the response to be made by the loyal States to Mr. LINCOLN's call, those Fire-Eaters who have flattered themselves that we are not "a military people," encounter their first rebuke, — to be bitterly emphasized hereafter whenever the shock of arms is reached.... ✹

1. A reference to Samuel Colt and James Bowie and the famous weapons they invented. The implication is that Southerners were accustomed to resorting quickly to weapons of violence rather than reasoned argument.

STARTLING FROM BALTIMORE.

THE NORTHERN TROOPS MOBBED AND FIRED UPON.

APRIL 20

There was a horrible scene on Pratt-street, to-day. The railroad track was taken up and the troops attempted to march through. They were attacked by a mob with bricks and stones, and were fired upon. The fire was returned. Two of the Seventh Regiment of Pennsylvania were killed and several wounded.

It is impossible to say what portion of the troops have been attacked. They bore a white flag as they marched up Pratt-street and were greeted with showers of paving-stones. The Mayor of the city [George William Brown] went ahead of them with the police. An immense crowd blocked up the streets. The soldiers finally turned and fired on the mob. Several of the wounded have just gone up the street in carts.

At the Washington depot, an immense crowd assembled. The rioters attacked the solders, who fired into the mob. Several were wounded, and some fatally. It is said that four rioters and four of the military are killed.[1] The city is in great excitement. Martial law has been proclaimed. The military are rushing to the armories.... ✹

1. Four soldiers (Corporal Sumner Needham, and Privates Luther C. Ladd, Charles Taylor, and Addison Whitney) and twelve civilians were killed in the riot. Some 36 other solders were wounded and left behind. It is uncertain how many additional civilians were injured.

The Sixth Massachusetts Volunteer Regiment firing into a mob of Southern sympathizers on the streets of Baltimore.

THE GREAT CONFLICT.

The secession of Virginia has cleared the skies.[1] A treacherous enemy has deserted our ranks, who, while she remained, was incessant in her efforts to encourage the rebellion, to shield its outrages, and to arm the traitors, with an assurance that she would join them at the right moment in overthrowing a Government which she has been embarrassing to the utmost of her power by a feigned loyalty. She has now elected to make her soil the battle field. She could not have done us a better service.

If secession was incomplete without Virginia, we can crush it in its great leader, who brings it directly within reach of our blows. In dictating terms to Virginia, we can do it to the whole Union. We can dictate these at Richmond in sixty days, if we will. We can now make the war a short one. It should be ended in one campaign. A column of 25,000 men should, at the earliest moment possible, march from Washington on Richmond. Another, equally strong, should proceed from James River to Fort Monroe. Resistance to two well-appointed armies would be impossible. Once at Richmond, we should hold 500,000 slaves, rated in Virginia to be worth $400,000,000, as hostages for the good conduct of the enemy. Should we be forced to extreme measures, all the other States would take warning by the example made of their great leader. If Mr. LINCOLN does not now strike an effectual blow, upon him will rest the responsibility of a prolonged and cruel war. If Mr. BUCHANAN had, at the right moment, seized and hung a half dozen of the traitors, treason would have been quelled, and thousands of innocent lives, and the waste of hundreds of millions of property, would have been saved. Let Mr. LINCOLN take warning by the criminal neglect of his predecessor, and learn that in a great emergency, prompt action, which may involve 10,000 lives, will be the certain means of saving ten-fold that number, and the horrors of a prolonged civil war.

In Virginia, as the head and front of secession, we have a position the most vulnerable to attack. We hold complete control of all her outlets to the seas. With Maryland remaining loyal, we command her on every side but one. From Fort Monroe expeditions can penetrate by water far into her interior. Washington will soon be an immense fortified camp. Expeditions can penetrate the State from Pennsylvania, at numerous points on the North, and on the West from the Ohio, should not that section prove loyal, as we firmly believe and hope it will. Threatened on every side, she can concentrate no large bodies of troops, if she had them. If she had such, she could not keep them in the field, for want of means. She has no money in her treasury. She cannot borrow a dollar, nor can she raise any considerable sums by taxation.

At the very moment we are striking a blow at Virginia, we should fit out a large naval and military force to operate against the Cotton States. Both Charleston and Savannah might be threatened and captured by a force landed at Port Royal, a deep estuary about equi-distant from these two cities. The capture of the City of Mobile, which is almost entirely unprotected, would be an easy matter. New-Orleans might be threatened or assailed at the same time. Such an expedition would keep President DAVIS and all the forces he could raise at home, and constantly on the look-out for his winged enemy, which, beyond reach of attack, could select its own time and place to deal a decisive blow. Such a force would compel Virginia to fight out her own battles single-handed, and with probably half of her people loyal, against the overwhelming force of the United States.

In this contest two issues of the deepest moment are involved; the supremacy of the laws, and the moral and political superiority of the North. We cannot admit the right of secession, because we cannot admit a proposition that involves our own destruction. If the will of a particular community, or individual, is paramount, then we accept anarchy as our necessary condition. We will never admit such a proposition. We will fight to the last man and the last musket first. Neither will we admit Slavery to be equally desirable as freedom. We will live up to our compact, and protect it as property in every loyal State, as we have done without complaint for seventy years. But when Slavery assumes a hostile attitude, and is fighting to put a chain round our necks, we will put forth all our power to confine it within its present area, and if no other resort is left us, we will proclaim freedom in its place. Mr. DAVIS has taken the initiative, and invites pirates and privateers to prey upon our private property. We will show him that we can retaliate with thousand-fold force, and remove from our system an element which, has brought upon us our present misfortunes, which has always been a source of discord, and which must always continue to he so while it exists.

Another point of great strategical importance is Cairo, at the confluence of the Ohio and Mississippi Rivers. This commands completely the States of Missouri and Kentucky, and a portion of Tennessee, and would be an admirable base of operations for a force, sent down the Mississippi. Upon this point a large force should be immediately concentrated, amply supplied with materials and munitions of war.

Now that we are in for a fight, let us finish it at a blow. The first thing is to know where we stand, to learn who are our friends, and who our foes. We want no relations that can embarrass the unity of our purposes or plans. We are infinitely stronger with Virginia an open enemy, than a treacherous ally. If Kentucky, or Maryland, or Tennessee, are not heartily with us, let them follow the example of Virginia. We want no friends who will be holding one of our hands while we are striking with the other. We not only want to have the issue squarely presented, but we want the battle fought with the antagonists ranged under the appropriate banners. ✸

1. Virginia formally seceded from the Union on April 17.

THE PIRATE FLAG.

APRIL 20

Mr. JEFFERSON DAVIS, in his proclamation inviting applications for letters of marque and reprisal against Northern commerce, has hung out the true flag of the Confederates. Nothing more was needed to secure for the Southern movement the scorn and indignation of the civilized world. If there had been any doubt before of the attitude of commercial men in this country and of the commercial interest throughout the world towards the new Confederacy, this proclamation would have ended it. Under any circumstances, privateering has become an odious, indeed an infamous weapon of warfare. The whole tendency of modern civilization has been towards an amelioration of the laws of war. It is universally felt that the destruction of private property, in case of war, is a relic of barbarism, and that hostilities ought to be restricted to the public forces of the hostile powers. And although this principle has not yet secured recognition as part of the code of international law, the practice of nations has been towards its adoption. During the Crimean war each nation prohibited its subjects from accepting letters of marque, and privateering was formally discarded by Great Britain as a weapon of war.

The United States have recognized the salutary character of this principle more than once in their legislation. An act of Congress still stands upon the statute book, by which all American citizens are prohibited from fitting out privateers against friendly powers; and all the other nations of the world have enacted similar laws. Indeed, we have at the present time, treaties with France, Holland, Sweden, Prussia, Great Britain, Spain, and other Powers, by which it is agreed that no subject or citizen of either shall accept a commission or letter-of-marque to assist an enemy in hostilities against the other, under pain of being treated as a pirate. These treaties put an extinguisher at once upon any hope which JEFF. DAVIS may entertain of enlisting in his service privateers from any of the Powers of Europe, — or of securing the toleration of any European nation for his letters of marque and reprisal. Suppose that vessels were to be captured under authority of his letters: — into what port on the face of the earth could they be taken with the slightest hope of being recognized as lawful prize? Even if JEFF. DAVIS' kingdom were a legitimate nation, duly recognized by the world as an established and independent power, the treaties to which we have already alluded would shut him out from all the ports of the civilized nations of Europe. There is not one in which he would not instantly be condemned as a pirate. And if any man, in this country or any other, permits himself to be enticed into accepting one of these letters and acting upon it, he may rely upon meeting the fate which his crimes deserve. Privateering, under the most favorable circumstances, is but one degree removed from piracy. It is only the positive law and usage of nations that establishes any difference. And in this case international law, treaty stipulations, and every consideration which nations hold sacred in their dealings with each other, brand the proclamation of JEFF. DAVIS as a formal sanction of piracy.... ✺

WANTED — A LEADER!

APRIL 25[1]

In every great crisis, the human heart demands a leader that incarnates its ideas, its emotions and its aims. Till such a leader appears, everything is disorder, disaster and defeat. The moment he takes the helm, order, promptitude and confidence follow as the necessary result. When we see such results, we know that a hero leads. No such hero at present directs affairs. The experience of our Government for months past has been a series of defeats. It has been one continued retreat. Its path is marked by the wrecks of property destroyed. It has thus far only urged war upon itself. It confidingly enters into compacts with traitors who seek them merely to gain time better to strike a fatal blow. Stung to the quick by the disgraces we have suffered, by the disasters sustained, by the treachery which threatens the annihilation of all order, law, and property, and by the insults heaped upon our National banner, the people have sprung to arms, and demand satisfaction for wounded honor and for violation of laws, which must be vindicated, or we may at once bid farewell to society, to government, and to property, and sink into barbarism.

The spirit evoked within the last fortnight has no parallel since the day of Peter the Hermit.[2] In the last ten days, 100,000 men have sprung to their feet, and, arming and provisioning themselves, are rushing to a contest which can never be quelled till they have triumphed. A holy zeal inspires every loyal heart. To sacrifice comfort, property and life even, is nothing, because if we fail, we must give up these for our children, for humanity, and for ourselves. Where is the leader of this sublime passion? Can the Administration furnish him? We do not question the entire patriotism of every member of it, nor their zeal for the public welfare. The President, in the selection of his Cabinet, very properly regarded the long and efficient services of men in the advocacy of the principles that triumphed in his election. To him the future was seen in the past. But in the few weeks of his official life all past political distinctions have been completely effaced. From a dream of profound peace we awake with our enemy at our throat. Who shall grapple with this foe? Men that can match his activity, quick instincts and physical force. A warrior — not a philosopher; a Cromwell — not a Bacon or a Locke.

Many of the Cabinet, having outlived the hot blood of youth, are vainly attempting to reason with this foe. As well might they oppose a feather to a whirlwind. JEFFERSON DAVIS has surrounded himself with spirits kindred to his own. Think of offering the olive-branch to such men as [Robert] TOOMBS and [Louis] WIGFALL. These men are seeking to put a chain about our necks, to secure our humiliation by the destruction of all our national interests, "Our money, or our life, or both."

What are we called upon to defend. The welfare of 19,000,000 of freemen, with everything that render life desirable. Were the selection of the Cabinet to be made to-day, would not the past be entirely forgotten in the present? Would not all party ties be completely effaced? Is not the Cabinet the representative of the past, instead of the present?

Is it not exactly in the frame of mind it was in the day of its appointment? From the first its policy has been purely nega-

LATEST FROM THE SEAT OF WAR.

APRIL 27

PHILADELPHIA, FRIDAY, APRIL 26

I have just arrived from Annapolis, which place I left at 8 o'clock last evening. Most of the middies at the Naval Academy have been sent to New-York in the Constitution, which sailed for New-York last night. Their quarters are occupied by the troops.[1]

The grounds of the Academy are now a military camp. Gen. BUTLER is in a command for which he is eminently qualified, as his conduct has already proved. He has seized upon the railroad between Annapolis and Washington, and it is guarded with troops. The track has been relaid, and communication is now open with the Capital.

Owing to the blockade of the Port and the seizure of the railroad, no provisions can be brought into Annapolis, and the inhabitants apprehend famine. The leading hotel was unable, yesterday morning, to furnish breakfast for myself and a friend, and we were obliged to scout around town for a meal. Flour has been sold at $20 per barrel. The troops have provisions in plenty,

and this irritates the inhabitants. Not a Union flag is to be seen, nor did I hear one loyal sentiment uttered in the City. They blame the North for all their troubles, and express intense hatred towards the troops.

The troops arriving are moved on as fast as possible. The New-York Seventh Regiment, at last accounts, was en route for Washington, with several other Regiments. It was reported that the Secessionists would give them a running fight on the march, but this is not probable....

C. H. W.[2] ✺

1. The U.S. Naval Academy was moved from its home in Annapolis to the Atlantic Hotel in Newport, Rhode Island, for the duration of the war. The frigate *Constitution* (Old Ironsides) had been used as a training ship at the Academy and carried the midshipmen to Newport.
2. These are the initials of Charles Henry Webb, a New York Times reporter.

tive, and cooped up in Washington, surrounded on all sides by a hostile population, it still thinks only of self-defense, and yields to the demands of those seeking its destruction in the measured periods of diplomatic intercourse.

Well may the great heart of the North turn away sickened at such a spectacle. Is this a suitable response to the ardor of youth that rushes to the contest regardless of every consequence, and at the risk of severing every tie that can give grace or charm to life? The hope, and pride, and strength of the country is exposed without plan or forethought for the future, to an able, treacherous and relentless foe. We read to get the news of the first encounter. We all know how England swayed to and fro under the loss of her best blood in the reckless charge of the light Brigade. How could our more mercurial natures bear up under a similar disaster to the gallant Seventh?[3] It is the duty of the members of the Cabinet to look the thing squarely in the face and conscientiously ask themselves this question: "Are we disqualified from age, from inexperience in Executive action, from constitutional timidity, or from innate reluctance to face the horrors

of war, to represent this people and country in this hour of travail?" If not, let them earn the gratitude of the people by giving way courteously to the exigencies of the hour, and laying their ambition on the alter of their country. By a timely act of self-sacrifice they may give relief to the anxious heart of this mighty host of earnest, patriotic men who are unselfishly exposing their lives and fortunes without any other object or motive than their country's honor and welfare — the relief that follows the knowledge that they are directed by bold, strong and competent men, fitted by sterner natures for this revolutionary epoch of their country's history. ✺

1. Lincoln clipped this article along with other editorial critiques and filed it under the heading "Villainous articles."
2. Peter the Hermit was a poorly dressed and poorly equipped pauper-priest who helped instigate and then participated in the First Crusade (1095–1099).
3. Like the British Light Brigade, the New York Seventh Regiment was a socially elite unit. Called a "silk stocking" regiment by some, it included men from some of the best families in New York.

WHAT THE ABOLITIONISTS THINK OF THE WAR.

DISCOURSE OF WENDELL PHILLIPS[1] AT BOSTON.

APRIL 28

All Winter long, I have acted with that party which cried for peace. The anti-slavery enterprise to which I belong, started with peace written on its banner. We imagined that the age of bullets was over; that the age of ideas had come; that thirty millions of people were able to take a great question, and decide it by the conflict of opinions; and without letting the ship of

Wendell Phillips.

State founder, lift four millions of men into Liberty and Justice. We thought that if your statesmen would throw away personal ambition and party watchwords, and devote themselves to the great issue, this might be accomplished. To a certain extent, it has been. The North has answered to the call. Year alter year, event by event, has indicated the rising education of the people, — the readiness for a higher moral life, the patience that waits a neighbor's conversion. The North has responded to the call of that peaceful, moral, intellectual agitation which the anti-slavery idea has initiated. Our mistake, if any, has been that we counted too much on the in- ☞

telligence of the masses, on the honesty and wisdom of statesmen as a class....

Our struggle, therefore, is no struggle between different ideas, but between barbarism and civilization. Such can only be settled by arms. [Prolonged cheering.] The Government has waited until its best friends almost suspected its courage or its integrity; but the cannon shot against Fort Sumter has opened the only door out of this hour. There were but two. One was Compromise; the other was Battle. The integrity of the North closed the first; the generous forbearance of nineteen States closed the other. The South opened this with cannon shot, and LINCOLN shows himself at the door. [Prolonged and enthusiastic cheering] The war, then, is not aggressive, but in self-defence, and Washington has become the Thermopylae of Liberty and Justice. [Applause.] Rather that surrender it, cover every square foot of it with a living body, [loud cheers;] crowd it with a million of men, and empty every bank vault at the North to pay the cost. [Renewed cheering] Teach the world once for all, that North America belongs to the Stars and Stripes, and under them no man shall wear a chain. [Enthusiastic cheering.]....

The noise and dust of the conflict may hide the real question at issue. Europe may think — some of us may — that we are lighting for forms and parchments, for sovereignty and a flag. But really, the war is one of opinions; it is Civilization against Barbarism — it is Freedom against Slavery. The cannon shots against Fort Sumter was the yell of pirates against the DECLARATION OF INDEPENDENCE: the war-cry of the North is its echo. The South, defying Christianity, clutches in victim. The North offers its wealth and blood in glad atonement for the selfishness of seventy years. The result is as sure as the Throne of God. I believe in the possibility of Justice, in the certainty of Union. Years hence, when the smoke of this conflict clears away, the world will see under our banner all tongues, all creeds, all races—one brotherhood; and on the banks of the Potomac, the Genius of Liberty, robed in light, four-and-thirty stars for her diadem, broken chains under feet, and an olive branch in her right hand. [Great applause.]

1. Wendell Phillips (1811–1884) was a leading abolitionist.

FROM KENTUCKY.

JOHN C. BRECKINRIDGE[1] IN LOUISVILLE.

APRIL 28

LOUISVILLE, SATURDAY, APRIL 20

Mr. BRECKINRIDGE for an hour and a half addressed a large audience here this afternoon, with his customary fluency, graceful delivery, and melodious utterance. He was listened to with marked respect, but with little show of enthusiasm, and no general applause. The majority of his audience was evidently by no means prepared to indorse him. The staple of his speech was laudation of the South and abuse of the North. The South has always in its every act done right, and stood on the defensive! The North and the Republican Party have done all the wrong and committed all the aggression, and history will so declare! He casts upon the Republican Party and Administration all the blame for the tragic scenes now enacting! No seceded State has done anything meriting his censure. South Carolina did right when she bombarded Sumter! The President's Proclamation of the 14th inst. was infamous — it was the declaration of a deliberate sectional war, deliberately inaugurated by a sectional President. His attempted blockade of Southern ports is illegal and unjustifiable.

Mr. BRECKINRIDGE advises Kentucky to put herself immediately in a post on of self-defence, so as to be prepared, in all events, to take care of herself. An armed neutrality may do as a temporary contrivance, but not as a permanent policy.[2] It is utterly impossible for her long to maintain it. To hold a perfect neutrality, Kentucky should furnish not a man nor a dollar to either Government. If she did, she would cut off her communications with both. She don't hold such a position now. While in the Union, she pays revenue, and helps to furnish Mr. LINCOLN with the sinews of war, for the conquest and subjugation of the South. This will not do. Kentucky must play her part to prevent civil war, and must throw her moral power and whole weigh against Mr. LINCOLN'S atrocious policy. She should have a State Convention before the 4th of July, and counsel with every slave State in the Union for opposition to an attempted solution of the controversy by arms. If Kentucky and her Southern sisters fail to avert civil war, no earthly power can keep her out of that war, and she will have to take a large part in it. The united protest and the united front of fifteen States and thirteen millions of people against the folly of Mr. LINCOLN'S war appeal, can keep the public peace and save the Union,

HOW THE WAR SHALL BE WAGED.

MAY 1

The gauge of war having been offered by the Confederate States, and promptly accepted by the United States Government, it only remains to end the contest by the most desperate and fatal agencies of destruction that the respective parties can command. It is one of the triumphs of art and civilization, that, while they have not the power to change the nature of man and eradicate his passions, they give to his passions such formidable instruments of destruction that wars cannot be lingering.

We are now at war with the Confederate States. They have seized the Federal property; they have defied the Federal laws; they have attacked the National forts; pillaged the arsenals and treasuries; insulted the Nation's flag; stoned and murdered its soldiers, and are now seeking to capture the Federal Capital and depose the constitutionally elected officers of the Government. Not stopping at attacks on Federal property, they have set the example of the seizure and confiscation of private properly, under circumstances of wrong not recognized by rules of honorable war, for no proclamation of hostilities preceded the seizure and confiscation. And as the crowning act of injury, the persons in revolt against government and society have seized and now hold as prisoners citizens of the United States, and next propose to arm lawless corsairs, and turn them out upon the high seas to plunder and kill as only pirates do.

So far, the United States Government have been submissive and apologetic only. They have carried the mails for those who rifled them at will. They have paid salaries to those who were seeking the Government's overthrow. They have parleyed

if it can be saved. While he (BRECKIN-RIDGE) has never uttered a word or entertained a thought hostile to the Constitution and the Union, his loyalty to his noble Commonwealth is paramount. Whatever her position, whether in accordance with his judgment or not, he will stand by her. Kentucky must be a unit, and allow no party rancor or intestine strife. Her action should be prompt and quick. A State Convention of her people before the meeting of Congress should be held, and take ground for a peaceful solution and a reconstruction of the Union, But if, as Mr. B. says he greatly fears, the Union is past recovery and the separation of the seceded States is permanent, then, in his judgment, every consideration of geography, of commerce, of self-interest and self preservation, carries Kentucky entirely with the South! ⊛

1. John C. Breckinridge (1821–1875) of Kentucky had been Vice President of the United States under James Buchanan, and the Southern Democratic candidate for President in 1860. Siding with the Confederacy after hostilities began, he subsequently became a major general in the Confederate Army and eventually Davis's secretary of war.

2. Unwilling to cast its lot with either side, Kentucky initially declared its neutrality in the war. As Breckinridge warned, however, such a stance proved too precarious to maintain, and eventually it became a battleground with Kentucky regiments fighting on both sides. Because it did not secede, it remained a Union state, though one with mixed loyalties.

and expostulated with rebels in arms, and shunned the national highway with their troops, marching under the nation's ensign, as if it were a pirate's bunting or a helot's disgraceful rag, that needed to hide itself in the corners and by-ways of the land.

But now, with God's help, the tables will be turned, and war must become a game for two to play at. How shall the United States Government wage the war? In mercy, both to winner and loser, let it be short. If it is to cost one or two hundred millions of dollars, let every dollar be spent in ninety days. Whoever has to die, it is better to die by the guillotine than by a cancer. Then up with the axe, and down with the head, and let the slide fall.... ⊛

NOT A WAR AGAINST THE SOUTH.

MAY 10

It is a great mistake to suppose that the war, which is now being initiated, is a war "against the South," or against Southern institutions. It is true that geographically the North occupies one side of the controversy and the South the other, but this is simply owing to the fact that the treason which renders the war inevitable, originated and prevails only at the South, while loyalty to the Union is the universal sentiment of the Northern people. On the part of the South the war was begun, and is being prosecuted, for the overthrow of the Government, to pull down and destroy this free Republic, that for more than three-quarters of a century has been the astonishment and the admiration of the world. There never was a war so utterly, causeless forced upon a peaceful people. No right of any citizen has been invaded, no privileges withheld or interfered with. No right of any State has been invaded, no attribute of State Sovereignty interfered with. There is no pretence on the part of the seceding States that the rights of the citizen or the security of the State will be enhanced by successful revolution.

The Constitution of the Federal Government in all its essential features has been adopted as the organic law of the new Confederacy, while the Constitutions of the States themselves remain unchanged. Their relations to the central Government differ in no material respect from their relations to the Government at Washington. Still the people of the South, with a madness that is unaccountable, rush into rebellion as if the overthrow of government and the initiation of a bloody civil war were no crime.

The North have from the beginning acted only upon the defensive. The Federal property has been plundered or destroyed by the seceding States, and the North stood still. It was not until treason assumed such gigantic proportions as to threaten the destruction of the Union, that the loyal people of the Free States were roused from their dream of security and their hope of peace. That they are aroused the signs of the times abundantly testify, and that this war forced upon them is to be fought out to the bitter end is one of the things in regard to which no doubt need be entertained.

But it is not a war against the South. The loyal people of the Free States are engaged in no sectional struggle. In this conflict they know no North, no South, no East, no West. What they do know and feel is that the Constitution is imperiled; the Union in danger; that treason is mining beneath their foundation, and rebellion hewing at the pillars which sustain them; and knowing this, they are arming and will march and fight to the death against the traitors who would destroy these free and cherished institutions. They do not ask whether those traitors come from the South or the North. They do not inquire whether the conspiracy against the Republic is of Northern or Southern growth. Their sword would as readily seek a Northern heart that was false to the country as a Southern bosom, and the halter would be as readily fitted to the neck of a Northern as a Southern traitor. They make war in defence of the free institutions of the country; and if the march of their armies shall be southward it will only be because in that direction lies the treason that is to be crushed. The loyal man of Virginia or of South Carolina will be met as warmly, and embraced as cordially and earnestly, as if he were from New-York or Ohio. His greeting will be the more fraternal because it is the highest proof of integrity to resist the temptations of association, and remain faithful among the faithless.... ⊛

HIGHLY IMPORTANT FROM MISSOURI.

MAY 13

ST. LOUIS, SUNDAY, MAY 12

The city was the scene of another terrible tragedy last night. About 6 o'clock a large body of the Home Guards entered the city, through Fifth-street, from the Arsenal, where they had been enlisted during the day, and furnished with arms. On reaching Walnut-street, the troops turned westward, a large crowd lining the pavement to witness their progress.

At the corner of Fifth-street ladies among the spectators began hooting, hissing, and otherwise abusing the companies as they passed, and a boy about fourteen years old discharged a pistol into their ranks. Part of the rear company immediately hurried and fired upon the crowd, and the whole column was instantly in confusion, breaking their ranks, and discharging their muskets down their own line and among the people on the sidewalks. The shower of balls for a few minutes was terrible, the bullets flying in every direction, entering the doors and windows of private residences, breaking railings, and even smashing bricks in the third stories.[1]

The utmost confusion and consternation prevailed, spectators fleeing in all directions, and but for the random firing of the troops, scores of people must have been killed. As most of the firing was directed down their own ranks, the troops suffered most severely, four of their number being instantly killed, and several wounded.... ❋

Above: Detail of a period engraving of the Battle of Wilson's Creek.

1. On May 10 Nathaniel Lyon forced the surrender of the Confederate militia in St. Louis. As Lyon marched the prisoners through the city, a crowd gathered. Exactly what provoked the shooting remains unclear, but the most common explanation is that a drunkard stumbled into the path of the marching soldiers and fired a pistol into their ranks, fatally wounding one German soldier, Captain Blandowski. The volunteers, in retaliation, fired into the crowd, killing some 20 people, some of whom were women and children, and wounding as many as 50 more.

COLONEL ELMER E. ELLSWORTH[1]

MAY 25

We are again called upon to record the death of the commanding officer of a New-York Regiment. The flags which, half masted, expressed to all beholders the sympathy extended by our citizens to the family of Col. VOSBURGH[2] had but just flung forth from staff top their Stars and Stripes, when again they were lowered in token of bereavement.

Without a doubt, the name of Col. ELLS-WORTH is more familiar to the ears of New-Yorkers than that of any other officer who has left this City during the present emergency. He was not a resident here, but the peculiar introduction afforded him by the exhibitions of his Chicago Zouave corps,[3] his subsequent participation in the Presidential tour from Springfield to Washington, and finally the deep interest felt in the Fire Brigade by all ranks and conditions of citizens, have combined to render him popularly famous and deserving of more than ordinary notice. To these is added a last but unanswerable argument in support of his fame — for we learn by reliable dispatches from Washington, that while on Virginia soil, in performance of an honorable duty, he was shot and infamously murdered....

He has been assassinated! His murder was fearfully and speedily revenged. He has lived a brief but an eventful, a public and an honorable life. His memory will be revered, his name respected, and long after the rebellion shall have become a matter of history, his death will be regarded as a martyrdom, and his name will be enrolled upon the list of our country's patriots. ❋

SLAVES CONTRABAND OF WAR.

MAY 27

Gen. [Benjamin] BUTLER[1] appears to be turning his legal education, to good account, in the construction of the law in reference to articles that are contraband of war. Three negroes, having escaped into Fort Monroe, he set them at work on the fortifications, and when demanded by an F. F. V.[2] he replied that they were contraband of war, for the reason that they might be employed by the enemy, for the service to which he had assigned them. We believe the General did so far modify his refusal, as to offer to give up the negroes, providing their

A Currier and Ives print depicting the death of Colonel Ellsworth.

1. Colonel Elmer Ellsworth (1837–1861) was killed by a Southern partisan while removing a Confederate flag from atop an Alexandria hotel. His death was notable not only for the circumstances and the fact that it was still very early in the war, but also because of his friendship with President Lincoln. After his death, his body lay in state in the East Room of the White House for a day before being sent on to New York for burial.

2. Colonel Abram S. Vosburgh, commanding officer of the 71st Regiment New York Militia, died in Washington of a heart attack on May 20. His body was returned to New York for a public funeral on May 23.

3. The 11th New York Regiment that Ellsworth commanded had been recruited from New York City's fire departments. It was also a Zouave regiment, which meant that the men wore colorful uniforms (inspired by the French North African soldiers) consisting of baggy red trousers, short blue jackets, and caps with a tassel. For these reasons, the 11th New York was generally referred to as the "Fire Zouaves."

owner would take the oath to support the Constitution of the United states! All this, upon the Sacred Soil of Virginia! We think the people of the State will find the General a match for them in more ways than one. ✹

1. Benjamin F. Butler (1818–1893) was a Massachusetts lawyer and politician who served several terms in the House of Representatives. A War Democrat with a state militia rank, Lincoln made him a brigadier general upon the outbreak of war, and he commanded troops at Fort Monroe on the Virginia Peninsula in May of 1861.

2. F.F.V. is an abbreviation for First Families of Virginia — a mocking reference to the aristocratic pretensions of Virginians.

THE ERROR IN THE FOREIGN VIEW OF THE CONTEST.

MAY 27

One of the most remarkable features of the present crisis in our national affairs are the crude and inadequate views taken of it by foreigners, particularly Englishmen. They appear to think the tie that holds the States together is a mere rope of sand, to be severed at will; that there is no good reason why the country should not be broken into two, three, or four Confederacies, instead of constituting one. They say that if the present Union combines elements that are uncongenial, or that have a mutual repulsion, why not leave them to their natural tendencies, instead of holding them together by force? The same idea was prevalent among a portion of our people at the North till the rupture actually occurred, when the alternative instantly presented itself to each section — the triumph over the whole country of its own ideas, institutions and industries, or subjection of all these to the other.

One of the parties must be now prepared to submit to this inevitable result. …We now can have no peace till one of the two civilizations triumphs. We lived together for a long time in harmony, upon the assumption that we constituted one nationality. This the seceding States deny, and seek to embody their own in a new Government, and by new laws and institutions. If a peaceful separation could have been effected in the outset, the antipathy that would instantly have sprung up would have been full of future wars. England and Scotland were always embroiled till they were united under one Government. The short cut to peace in this country is a reunion of the States, though this may cost us a great war. The weaker party must take and forever keep the subordinate place…. ✹

THE PROCLAMATION OF THE BRITISH GOVERNMENT.

MAY 28

We place, this morning, before our readers the Proclamation of the British Government in reference to the rebellion existing in certain States against the Government of the United States, forbidding its subjects to take any part in the contest, or to interfere with the blockade that may be established by either party, or to transport officers, soldiers, dispatches, arms, military stores or materials, and enjoining strict neutrality toward the belligerents, and placing both upon exactly the same footing.[1]

This proclamation cannot fail to be highly offensive to the United States, as it is a virtual recognition of the Confederate States; or, should this be disclaimed, as a direct encouragement, by a great nation, of a purely domestic quarrel — of an armed resistance to legally-constituted authorities, which is already assuming all the horrors of a civil war. Such an act is unexampled in the history of diplomatic intercourse. There is no more reason why England should take the position she has in reference to our controversy with the rebels, than with the Mormons….

Here is the policy that governs the United States in its intercourse with other nations. Will that Government use similar language to one of its subjects proposing to go to South Carolina to join the rebels? Will it proclaim the soil of that State to be still a part of our own Confederacy? We treated the outbreak in Canada as if it was a resistance to constituted authorities, to be put down by the local police, aided if necessary by the military arm. We did not speak of the contending parties then as standing in the same relation to us, nor extend to a rebellion the same consequence and dignity as to the Government seeking to put it down. ✹

1. The British proclamation, dated May 13, 1861, ordered British citizens to respect a strict neutrality between the United States and "certain states styling themselves the Confederate States of America." Despite protests by Union sympathizers (like The Times), it worked to the benefit of the Union cause since, among other things, it prevented Confederate raiders from using British ports for supply or refit.

AFFAIRS IN BALTIMORE.
HABEAS CORPUS CASE.

MAY 29

BALTIMORE, MONDAY, MAY 27

At 11 o'clock A.M., to-day, the United States Marshal made his return to the writ of habeas corpus issued by Chief Justice TANEY in the case of JOHN MERRYMAN, of the Hayfields.

The writ was returned served.

At the same time appeared in Court Major BELGER, one of Gen. CADWALADER's Staff, and with permission of the Court read a communication from the latter officer, stating that Mr. MERRYMAN was held in arrest at Fort McHenry, on the charge of treason, and that he, Gen. CADWALADER, had received instructions from the President to suspend within the limits of his command the writ of habeas corpus.

The body of Mr. MERRYMAN not having been brought into Court in obedience to the writ, the Chief Justice ordered an attachment against Gen. CADWALADER, returnable to-morrow, Tuesday, at 12 o'clock P.M.

Great interest is felt in this case; one of the most important in its connection with the powers of the Executive, and the rights and liberties of the citizen, that has arisen since the formation of the Government.

Mr. MERRYMAN is a man of family, and a gentleman of property and position, President, also, of the Maryland State Agricultural Society, and widely known and respected. He was arrested on a general order, issued for the apprehension of "The Captain of a Secession Company in Baltimore County." The order did not set forth any name or offence, and was executed at night by a detachment of the First Regiment Pennsylvania Volunteers, under a Capt. YOE. Mr. MERRYMAN is not the Captain of any company, but is a Lieutenant in a company of cavalry, commanded by Mr. CHARLES RIDGELEY, of Hampton.

The State of Maryland is still a member of the Union, and in her political character has taken no steps hostile to the Government. The

DECISION OF CHIEF JUSTICE TANEY ON THE JOHN MERRIMAN HABEAS CORPUS CASE.

MAY 29

BALTIMORE, TUESDAY, MAY 28

St. Paul's-street, fronting the United States Court house, was densely crowded, as was, also, the court-room, at noon to-day, to learn the proceedings in the habeas corpus case of JOHN MERRIMAN [sic].[1]

Gen. CADWALLADER[2] having, as stated yesterday, declined acceding to the demand until he could hear from Washington, a writ of attachment was issued against him, to day, for contempt of court. The Marshal reported that, on going to Fort McHenry to serve the writ he was refused admittance. Chief-Justice TANEY[3] then read the following statement:

"I ordered the attachment, yesterday, because upon the face of the return the detention of the prisoner was unlawful, upon two grounds.

First — The President, under the Constitution and laws of the United States cannot suspend the privilege of the writ of habeas corpus, nor authorize any military officer to do so.

Second — A military officer has no right to arrest and detain a person, nor subject him to the rules and articles of war for an offence against the laws of the United States, except in aid of the judicial authority, and subject to its control, and if the party is arrested by the military, it is the duty of the officer to deliver him over immediately to the civil authority, to be dealt with according to law.

I forebore yesterday to state orally the provisions of the Constitution of the

Roger B. Taney, chief justice of the Supreme Court.

United States Courts are here in full and free
discharge of their functions, and the United
States Marshal can execute processes without the slightest danger of obstruction in all
parts of the territory occupied by her citizens.
The Administration, in ordering these military arrests, and in suspending the privilege
of the writ of habeas corpus, is not regarded
here as being in any way justified by that salus
populi which is supposed sometimes to overrule the Constitution.[1] ⊛

1. Roughly translated, this means: "The welfare of
the people shall be the supreme law."

United States which make these principles
the fundamental law of the Union, because
an oral statement might be misunderstood
in some portions of it, and I shall therefore
put my opinion in writing and file it in the
office of the Clerk of the Circuit Court, in
the course of this week."

The Judge added that the military authority was always subordinate to civil.
That, under ordinary circumstances, it
would be the duty of the Marshal to proceed with posse comitatus and bring the
party named in the writ into Court; but
from the notoriously superior force that
he would encounter, this would be impossible. He said the Marshal had done all in
his power to discharge his duty.

During the week he should prepare his
opinion in the premises, and forward it
to the President, calling upon him to perform his constitutional duty, and see that
the laws be faithfully executed, and enforce the decrees of this Court. ⊛

1. John Merryman (1824–1881) was a Maryland citizen arrested for burning bridges in his state to prevent the passage of Union troops to Washington.
2. Major General George Cadwalader (1806–1879)
commanded the troops that arrested Merryman. He
denied Taney's writ upon orders from Lincoln.
3. Roger Brooke Taney (1777–1864) was chief justice
of the U.S. Supreme Court and author of the notorious majority opinion in the Dred Scott case (1857). In
the Merryman case, acting as a circuit court judge,
he ruled that only Congress could suspend the writ
of habeas corpus. Lincoln ignored Taney's decision
and defended his actions before Congress, asking
rhetorically: "Are all the laws, but one, to go unexecuted, and the government itself go to pieces, lest
that one be violated?" In 1863 Congress formally
suspended the writ.

CHAPTER 4

"The Greatest Battle Ever Fought on This Continent"

JUNE–JULY 1861

 s the number of Union soldiers in and around Washington swelled, anxiety that the rebel forces might seize the capital gradually gave way to demands that the Union should initiate an offensive of its own. Horace Greeley, editor of the rival New York Tribune, ran the banner headline "On To Richmond" above the paper's masthead. Feeling the pressure of public expectations, Lincoln encouraged General Winfield Scott to authorize an offensive. Elderly and in fragile health, the 74-year-old Scott was aware that he could not lead the army in person, and he chose as the army's commander 42-year-old Irvin McDowell, who was promoted from major to major general in one step. Lincoln then urged McDowell to take the offensive, and when the young general protested that his soldiers were "green," Lincoln famously replied: "You are green, it is true. But they are green also. You are all green alike."

There were four field armies in the Virginia theater in June of 1861. One was McDowell's own force of about 30,000 men near Alexandria, just across the Potomac River from Washington. Some twenty miles to the south was a Confederate army of about 22,000 under Major General P. G. T. Beauregard, who had commanded the batteries that had fired on Fort Sumter. Beauregard's army was encamped in the vicinity of Manassas Junction, where the Manassas Gap Railroad met the Orange and Alexandria Railroad, just south of Bull Run Creek. West of these two armies were two more: a Union force of 18,000 or so under Major General Robert Patterson at Harpers Ferry, where the northward-flowing Shenandoah River ran into the Potomac, and a Confederate force of about 12,000 men under General

Union General Irvin McDowell and some members of his staff at Arlington House in 1862.

Joseph E. Johnston just to the south. Each Federal army outnumbered its Confederate counterpart, but if the two Southern armies could combine against one of the Union armies, it would more than even the odds, and that is what happened.

McDowell set out from Fairfax in northern Virginia on Tuesday morning, July 16, 1861. That same day, Robert Patterson cautiously probed southward from Harpers Ferry with the objective of pinning Johnston's army in place. But Patterson's feint was unconvincing, and almost at once, Johnston put his small army in motion marching toward Ashby's Gap in the Blue Ridge Mountains, and from there to the Manassas Gap Railroad to join Beauregard.

The first contact between the armies came on July 18, when skirmishers from McDowell's force encountered Beauregard's army behind Bull Run Creek south of Centerville. Henry J. Raymond, the 41-year-old owner and editor of The Times, had accompanied the Union army to Centerville, and he filed a lengthy story of the skirmish. This early in the war, the confrontation seemed of great importance and deserving of extended treatment. His report is a personal narrative, written in the first person, and with little effort to maintain detachment.

Two days later, McDowell sent the bulk of his army on a long predawn flank march around the rebel left. This move began early on July 21 and achieved initial success, driving the rebel defenders off Matthews Hill, and across Youngs Branch to Henry House Hill — so named because the home of the widow Judith Henry was there. For several hours the two armies slugged it out on that broad plateau where "Stonewall" Jackson earned his nickname.

Once again, Raymond was a witness. In order to get his story back to New York as quickly as possible, he filed it at two o'clock on the afternoon of the battle while the armies were still engaged. Like all early reports from the front, Raymond's announced a Union victory. But only about an hour after Raymond filed his story, late arriving reinforcements from Johnston's army turned the tide, and it was the Federal army that began to retreat, a retreat that soon turned into a rout. When Raymond appeared at the army telegraph office — "sun-burned, dusty, and hardly recognizable" — to file an updated report, the army telegraph officer was reluctant to let him do so. Consequently the true account of the debacle at Bull Run did not appear in the pages of The Times until July 24.

Raymond filed an even longer story the next day (July 22) that appeared in the July 26 issue. Like his earlier reports, it was a personal account that focused particularly on the exploits of the 11th New York Regiment, called the Fire Zouaves — Elmer Ellsworth's old regiment. At Bull Run, the Fire Zouaves were commanded by Colonel Noah Farnham, affectionately called "Pony" by the men because of his short stature (5'4"). Farnham was mortally wounded in the fighting that day, one of 35 killed from the regiment. This tale, a moving and detailed description of one unit's fight, is a paean to the New Yorkers who fought and fell in the first great battle of the war.

A Currier and Ives lithograph of a Fire Zouave.

THE BATTLE AT GREAT BETHEL.

JUNE 14

FORTRESS MONROE, VA., JUNE 11

Old Point Comfort, Fortress Monroe and parts adjacent, have been full of all sorts of rumors since last evening, respecting the preliminary engagement between the United States troops and the secession forces which took place, yesterday, at a place called "Bethel."[1]

The first part of the work was well done, between 11 o'clock at night and daylight in the morning, by a detachment of the Naval Brigade. The manner in which they handled their boats, receiving and landing the regiments committed to their care, elicited the warm personal commendation of Gen. BUTLER, who was soon on the ground. From this point of landing, the troops marched toward Yorktown, suffering some detention and annoyance from the well-directed but mistaken fire of the Steuben rifles. These German soldiers are among our best, and at the proper time and place will be found powerful in defence of the Union.[2]

The regiments detailed were soon marched, one by one, into the open and marshy field in front of the secession works at Bethel. Here, under a raking fire, they behaved with great bravery. Many instances of valor occurred worthy of honorable mention. Among others, Col. [Frederick] TOWNSEND, of the Albany Regiment, dashed on horseback to within a few feet of the battery, in the midst of a shower of bullets, to ascertain the extent of the works and the best manner of assailing them. For hours together our men withstood the deadly fire of these intrenchments, behind which was a superior body of secession troops, entirely protected, wielding several large guns, among them rifled cannon, and commanded by experienced officers who had recently deserted from the United States Army. At the close of two hours' hard fighting the Union forces withdrew in good order, to recruit, reinforce, arm with large ordnance, and renew the attack.... ⊛

---

1. The Battle of Big Bethel (June 10, 1861) is often held to be the first battle of the war. Union troops venturing westward out of Fort Monroe ran into a Confederate defensive line behind Brick Kiln Creek near Big Bethel Church. After some desultory firing, the Union withdrew, though not (as the article states) "in good order."
2. The Steuben Rifles was a New York infantry unit composed of men of German ancestry.

WESTERN VIRGINIA TO FORM A NEW STATE.

JUNE 19

The Convention now in session at Wheeling, in which are represented about forty counties of Western Virginia, have, by a formal and unanimous vote, resolved to cut loose from the Old Dominion and form for themselves a new and independent State.[1] What name they will give to their new Commonwealth is not yet discussed. It may be ALLEGHANY. But whatever the name, the fact will be the same. The great State of Virginia is to be dismembered by the voluntary act of over a half million of her late citizens; and a new State formed from the Western part of her territory will claim a place in the Union....

The regret felt by a portion of the public at this action, arises from the fear that it may occasion embarrassment in failing to meet the approbation of Congress. If the Federal Government refuse to acknowledge the secession of a State, it cannot well recognize, in attempted secession, a cause for the dismemberment of a State by its loyal inhabitants, as a remedy for the evils with which they are threatened.

Then there are other questions touching the existence of Slavery in the new Commonwealth — for it would contain a considerable number of slaves — and the consequent increase of slave representation in the United States Senate would not fail

WHERE WILL THE INSURGENT ARMY OFFER BATTLE?

JUNE 19

Our readers will not have forgotten our attempt to demonstrate, some weeks since, that the insurgent army was distributed over so large an area that its communications could not be maintained, and that, consequently, some of its isolated divisions must either retreat or be cut off. Gen. JOHNSON's [Joseph E. Johnston's] command at Harper's Ferry, we ventured to suggest, was posted in a position utterly untenable — a very trap, whence it would be compelled either to retreat or surrender. A few days since, we began to receive news of the destruction of the bridges across the Potomac; then, of breaking up the boats on the Chesapeake and Ohio Canal; next, that the insurgents were tearing down the locks; and, finally, that they were destroying the dams on that costly work — together with accounts of much other of that preliminary devastation which usually marks the beginning, and too often the progress, of a retiring army.[1]

The question now naturally arises for speculation and solution — What is to be the line of the retreat, and the strategical movements which will necessarily result from it; and, finally, the point which the rebel army is likely to select as the place where it may stake the existence of the insurrectionary Government on the result of a battle?

Public opinion has very generally fixed upon Manassas Junction as the chosen field of the approaching conflict; but we cannot suppose — although we do not hold a very exalted opinion of Mr. President DAVIS, or, indeed, of either of his traitor Generals, all of whom, as leaders of armies, have yet their first spurs to win — that the insurgents will be imprudent enough to risk the fate of the rebellion on that ground. It is true that, after first hastily occupying, they have since been industriously strengthening, that position — which possesses in itself no peculiar natural advantages for defence — and have already assembled a very formidable force there. But we look upon that force as merely intended to cover the retreat of Gen. JOHNSON's [Johnston's] command, and the intrenchments which have been formed there as only the customary prudent precaution against an unexpected attack.[2]

General Joseph E. Johnston, C.S.A.

to excite more or less jealousy in certain parts of the Union.

But these difficulties are rather technical than substantial. The division of a State and the creation of a new one out of a part of its territory is, under certain circumstances, feasible under the Federal Constitution. Virginia is a very large State, and very susceptible of division. It is not homogeneous in any respect. The Eastern part differs from the West in climate, soil and productions — in customs, political sentiments and institutions. The trade of the two divisions of the State falls into different channels and reaches the market by routes that require wholly different systems of internal improvements. And herein lies one cause for the deep feeling of alienation in Western Virginia from the Eastern portion of the State: — that the latter has, by an unfair basis of representation in the Legislature, founded on Slavery, controlled the internal improvement system of the State, and run up an enormous debt of near fifty millions of dollars which rests like an incubus on the people, for the advantage and development of the Eastern counties; while the West has received practically no share of the improvements they are taxed to pay for.

In the facts of their physical relation and political condition, there is abundant reason for Eastern and Western Virginia forming two separate and distinct Commonwealths; and apart from the connection of the present movement for dismemberment with secessionism, and the quasi acknowledgment of this modern, political heresy that is supposed to be involved, the erection of a new State in Western Virginia might well be advocated as a wise and necessary measure.... ✹

1. The first Wheeling convention met May 13–15, 1861, and voted to separate 39 counties from Virginia to form the new state of Kanawha, or West Virginia. In a disputed election, voters ratified the decision on May 23. A second convention held June 11–25 also voted to secede from Virginia. A pro-Union Virginia government in exile headed by Francis H. Pierpont approved the separation, but the difficulty was the existence of slavery. In the end, West Virginia was not admitted as a separate state until June 20, 1863, and only on the condition that a provision for the gradual abolition of slavery be inserted in its constitution.

As a question of political strategy on the part of the insurgents, the position now occupied by their army at Manassas Junction should certainly be maintained, in order to avoid the discouragement which a retreat always sheds over the spirit of a rebellion. But, viewed in a purely military aspect, there can be no doubt that the rebel army should retire upon Richmond — where, resting on James River, the surrounding hills and valleys, properly intrenched, would enable them to make a formidable and prolonged resistance.

In our view, this problem will be solved — though doubtless with much reluctance — in a council of war, with reference mainly to military prudence; and Manassas Junction, like Harper's Ferry, is therefore, we think, destined to be speedily abandoned; while the force which has already retired from the Potomac, will retreat up the Valley of Virginia upon Staunton, leaving only the needful detachments temporarily to guard the passes of the Blue Ridge, and follow on as the rear guard of the retreating army.... ✹

1. General Joseph E. Johnston (1807–1891) was the senior ranking officer in the Confederacy at the time. Johnston himself argued that his position at Harpers Ferry was untenable, but Jefferson Davis urged him to hold it anyway. When Johnston withdrew nonetheless, it marked the beginning of a disagreement between them that would eventually poison their relationship.
2. In this, of course, The Times was in error. Beauregard preferred to defend his position at Manassas and Johnston brought his army from the Shenandoah Valley to reinforce him.

THE PRESIDENT'S MESSAGE.

JULY 6

It is common to herald a President's Message to the world as an important document. And often it is so. But never was a Message less important than the one transmitted yesterday to Congress by President LINCOLN, of which a report will be found in the TIMES to-day, although the occasion is the most extraordinary that ever occurred in our country for the writing of a Message.[1] The telegraph, or some strange fate that presided in the transmission and reprint of the document, has apparently coincided in this view of its value, for never before have we had a more painful jumble from which to extract the pith and meaning, the statement and sequence of a State paper.

We have at the outset what perhaps is in the original document, a faithful narrative of events in the progress of secession down to the bombardment of Fort Sumter. And there is a careful effort to establish the fact that the Seceding States had become the aggressors in their struggle against the Union by the act of bombarding that fort. And the enormity of this assault on Fort Sumter is particularly dwelt upon in view of the circumstance that the Government only intended to "send bread to a few brave and hungry men," on the occasion when the assault to repel or prevent was made by South Carolina.

To our minds, the people of the United States attach little consequence, to the event, here magnified as the justifying cause for war. That was only the culminating act, the last, but not the worst, of a long series of insults, wrongs and robberies against the National Government, any one of which would have fully justified the steps for repressing rebellion that have since been taken.

The firing on the Star of the West was as much the beginning of the war as the bombardment of Fort Sumter.[2] The erection of a hostile battery, without a gun fired, was an equal act of war and demanded chastisement. Long before the assault on Fort Sumter, the act of treason in South Carolina was complete; the Flag of the Nation had been hauled down from every Government building, and insulted, the property of the Government had been seized, and its officers forcibly withheld from the discharge of National duties. Let the case of Sumter go, and the pitiable question of a supposed armistice with South Carolina rebel rulers at the time. They have very little to do with the righteousness of this war.... ✹

1. Lincoln's Message to Congress, presented on July 4, and containing the memorable rallying cry "this is a people's contest," can be found in Basler, ed., The Collected Works of Abraham Lincoln, 4:421–41.
2. In January 1861, President James Buchanan had sent the chartered steamer Star of the West to Charleston with supplies for Major Anderson's beleaguered garrison. On January 9, it was fired on as it attempted to enter the harbor. Arguably, those shots, and not the ones three months later, were the first of the Civil War.

THE FIGHT AT BULL'S RUN.

A RECONNAISSANCE IN FORCE — THE TROOPS ENGAGED AND HOW THEY BEHAVED.

JULY 21

CENTREVILLE, VA., THURSDAY EVENING, JULY 18

This has been an eventful day for the Army of Advance, and the result will unquestionably be represented as a great victory on the part of the rebels.[1] In a word, the affair was a reconnaissance in force of a wood at Bull's Run, whose contents were unknown. It proved to be a masked battery, behind which some 5,000 of the rebels had entrenched themselves, and our five regiments, which were sent against it, were repulsed with considerable loss — a loss, the extent of which I cannot state with any accuracy, but which probably amounted to not far from in 150 killed and wounded.[2] On our side, [William T.] SHERMAN's battery, under Capt. [Romeyn Beck] AYRES, was the only one engaged. It behaved with great gallantry, but the extent of damage inflicted cannot be known, as it fired constantly into dense woods. Our forces were all withdrawn to the rear, the most of them as far back as Centreville, four miles from Bull's Run, which is itself about the same distance from Manassas Junction. The attack will unquestionably be renewed in the morning, not only upon this masked battery but upon the entire rebel force at Manassas — with what result I shall probably be able to tell you to-morrow.

So much for the general result — now for the details of the affair, so far as they came under my personal observation.

I left Fairfax Court-house at a later hour than I intended, and reached Centreville at about 11 o'clock. The rebels here had thrown up intrenchments on a high hill, overlooking the road as it debouches from a fine wood, and a large open field, admirably fitted for defence. They had abandoned them, however — and this confirmed the general impression that they did not mean to fight. The troops which had been brought forward — comprising only a portion of Gen. [Daniel] TYLER's brigade, were here halted for rest, and remained three or four hours. My carriage had become entangled in the baggage-train, and was some two miles in the rear. I began the tour of Centreville in search of food, as I had had no breakfast, and was nearly famished. While swallowing a cup of very poor coffee, which I persuaded the

servants of a deserted mansion to sell me, I heard the sound of cannon in the direction of Manassas. I immediately pushed forward on foot, under a blazing sun, and after a brisk walk of three miles — during which the only refreshment I could procure was a little vinegar and water — I came to a wood through which the road leads over a high rise of ground, with an oatfield on the right, and on the left a meadow, in which is placed a small house, with an adjoining shed. In the oatfield, on the right, were stationed two of the Parrot guns, under Lieut. [Samuel N.] BENJAMIN. As you pass the crest of the hill, your eye falls upon a gentle slope of meadow on the left of the road — bordered on the lower side by a thick growth of low trees, and rising, after passing a ravine, to high ground on the other side. At the right of the wood was an open plain — with a house and barn some fifteen or twenty rods from the wood. As I approached the first hill, I saw SHERMAN's battery drawn up on the left, behind the crest, and the First Massachusetts Regiment, in line of battle, some twenty paces behind, in a hollow, to be out of reach of the rebel batteries.

At about 1 o'clock, as the head of our column rose over the crest of the hill, it was saluted by a shot from the rebel battery quite across the ravine — which fired eight or ten rounds from two guns, and was briskly answered by Capt. AYRES. After about ten minutes, their firing ceased, and it was supposed that the rebels had retreated. They had fired no rifled cannon, and it was believed they had none.

Skirmishers were at once thrown out from the whole brigade, which was commanded by Col. [Israel] RICHARDSON, and consisted of five regiments, into the woods on the left — while the First Massachusetts was drawn up in line of battle immediately in front of the woods, and the Twelfth New-York, Col. WALWORTH [actually Colonel Ezra Walrath], just at their right. The Second and Third Michigan Regiments were sent to the extreme right, and marched in a right line from the road, towards the wood, and drew up in line of battle. The skirmishers pushed into the wood and were permitted to penetrate to some distance, without being

fired on. Soon a few scattering shots were fired at them — and then the First Massachusetts Regiment and the Twelfth New-York were pushed in together. I had gone into the field bordering the wood, about one-third of the way to the wood, and watched them enter. They had been gone perhaps five or ten minutes when a full, round volley was fired directly in their faces from a breastwork in the, ravine, behind which the whole rebel force had been drawn up. They could not see their assailants, — they scarcely fired a single shot at them, but were shattered by the deadly fire thus suddenly opened upon them. At intervals of perhaps a minute this volley was repeated five or six times — the rebels accompanying each fire with tremendous shouts. Two howitzers, belonging to SHERMAN's battery, were sent past me through the field into the wood, and opened fire, which was returned by the same vollies. After a few minutes a rebel battery of cannon, planted upon a small cleared space in the wood, which I could see very distinctly with my glass, opened fire, first upon the howitzers in their vicinity. But after two or three shots they sent half-a-dozen balls into the field where I stood, and over my head into the group of officers and soldiers gathered about the house to watch the firing. One shot struck some 20 feet from me, — another went through the shanty adjoining the house, and a shell exploded in the field some 20 rods from where I stood, without doing any damage.

At 2 1/2 o'clock a company of cavalry, Texas Rangers, belonging to the regular force, had crossed the field and taken possession, the men dismounting, armed with carbines, immediately in front of the wood. While stationed on the hill during the first firing, one of the rebel shots had fallen in their midst and severely wounded one of them who had been carried back into the wood. After the firing from cannon and musketry which I have mentioned had been continued some twenty minutes — many of the musket shots reaching the point where I stood — I saw the Twelfth New-York Regiment rush pell-mell out of the wood, followed by the Massachusetts men, marching in good order. Their appearance was the signal for a general

Preliminary movements by federal troops at Bull Run.

retreat of the forces in that neighborhood. The regular cavalry wheeled and ran their horses up the hill at the top of their speed — putting those of us who were on the hill side in greater peril of life and limb than we had been before during the day. Two companies of the New-York Twelfth kept their ground well and came off in good order. The rest made good time in leaving a position which it could not be expected for a moment that they could hold. The Michigan regiments, on the right, kept their position for a time, but soon drew off with the rest.

It was clear that the rebels were intrenched in great force in the wood, and that they had a powerful battery there, some of the guns being clearly rifled cannon from the noise the balls made as they passed over our heads. Clouds of dust, coming towards the front from the hills in the rear, indicated that they were bringing up reinforcements. The withdrawal of our troops was in pursuance of a purpose to change the plan of attack. Orders were sent back for reinforcements. SHERMAN's whole battery was ordered into the garden on the left of the road, just in front of the house; two guns were planted in the oatfield on the opposite side, and at 3 1/2

o'clock, a shot from the rebels flying over my head, followed by two from the Parrott guns in the oatfield rushing in the opposite direction; satisfied me that the safest place during an engagement was not between two hostile batteries. We fell back, therefore, behind the crest of the hill. The firing on both sides grew very brisk, and the shot from the rebels nearly all passed overhead, crashing among the trees of the wood beyond, and wounding several of the great number of persons, troops and others, who had collected there for shelter. Just then the Sixty-ninth New-York Regiment came up through the wood — the ears of its men being constantly saluted by these whistling balls — and was ordered to form in the field behind the house. It was soon followed by the Seventy-ninth, who did not, however, go out of the wood. The firing which had commenced at 3 1/2 o'clock ceased on both sides at five minutes before four, and our entire force was ordered to withdraw on Centreville.

This is the whole of it — and I have no time to add comments, as this hasty letter must be sent at once by a special messenger, who may reach Washington in time for the 4 1/2 o'clock mail to-morrow morn-

ing. Gen. MCDOWELL, who had been to visit the other column, came up just as the engagement was over. I believe he says the existence of this battery was well known, and that the men ought not to have been sent against it. Gen. TYLER, formerly of the U.S. Army is an officer of merit and experience. He displayed great coolness throughout the whole affair. I met a son of Gen. [Henry] LEAVENWORTH coming off the field, a lad of 17, who had staid in the wood to bathe his feet, after the Twelfth, to which he belonged, was driven out, and who says he was surprised to find he was not half as much scared as he had expected to be. While on the side-hill, being half famished with thirst, I asked a swallow from the canteen of a portly gentleman who was passing. He gave it to me, and I found it was Hon. Mr. LOVEJOY, of Illinois.[3] There were half-a-dozen private gentlemen present as spectators.

The criticism which will be made on this mishap will be that men should not have been thus thrust upon a masked battery — that it is a repetition of the old Big Bethel and Vienna affairs. Gen. TYLER, however, says that it was only a reconnaissance in force — that the object he had in view was to determine what force and batteries the enemy had at that point — and that he now understands this perfectly. Undoubtedly, this is so; the only question is, whether the knowledge was not purchased at too dear a cost. Upon one thing you may rely. This misfortune will not delay the attack on Manassas. On the contrary, it will hasten it. But I think that, instead of leading troops directly against batteries, whether masked or not, Gen. MCDOWELL will turn their entire position. The movement of troops, to-night; indicates a purpose to throw the troops upon the north side of the intrenched camp, from this point, while other columns will approach it from other directions. The result will vindicate the movements.

H. J. R.[4] ❀

1. This article refers to the skirmish on July 18 at Blackburn's Ford, and not the much larger general engagement three days later.
2. The estimate is quite accurate. Union losses were 85, and Confederate losses 66, for a total of 151.
3. Owen Lovejoy (1811–1864) was a Republican congressman from Illinois and the brother of Elijah P. Lovejoy, who had been murdered in 1837 for running an abolitionist newspaper.
4. Henry J. Raymond.

WILL GEN. SCOTT LEAD THE ARMY — GEN. MCCLELLAN — A CHANCE FOR SPECULATION.

JULY 21

WASHINGTON, FRIDAY, JULY 19

It is not known whether Gen. SCOTT intends to take the field in person. Some think he will; but it is probable that his age and feeble health may interpose barriers to an active participation in the fight. At any rate he will receive the glory of having planned the campaign, when success… crowns it, and his laurels will not be sullied by his remaining quietly at Washington. He may follow the Army and direct its movements, but it cannot be expected of a man 75 years of age, that he should lead the advancing columns which he has organized and assigned to their respective duties. If Gen. SCOTT shall, for the reasons here assigned, remain in Washington, there is ground to hope that he will call [George B.] MCCLELLAN[1] to the command of the centre, putting him over the divisions of PATTERSON and MCDOWELL, and of the whole Army when its several parts shall converge together. The achievements of Gen. MCCLELLAN in Western Virginia have fully sustained the high expectations of his friends, and they now think that he should be placed in the more responsible command of leading the Grand Army to Richmond. He has already achieved all the glory that remains for him in the West, for if he expects to overtake [Henry A.] WISE,[2] I predict that he will be sadly disappointed. Unless Gen. SCOTT in person shall take the field, and there is reason to apprehend that his health will not be equal to the task, — there is no man in the country in whom the people and the Army would repose so much confidence as in MCCLELLAN. His capture of the enemy's camp, baggage, artillery and provisions, and an embarrassing number of prisoners, with a loss of less than fifteen killed, shows a power of combination and strategy from which we may expect the grandest achievements if he shall be placed in the right position. It must be remembered that Gen. MCCLELLAN's Army is made up — with the exception of two companies — entirely of volunteers, and is indifferently provided with auxiliaries for prosecuting a successful campaign. The troops opposed to him were commanded by a distinguished Virginia officer, formerly of our Army, and the names of several others among the killed and prisoners may be found upon the Army Register for January, 1861.

The TIMES is unjust to the Virginians in its criticism upon the speed displayed by them in Western Virginia. There must have been some great natural impediments in their way — high-walled mountain barriers, or unfordable streams — to explain their ill-luck in getting out of the way of MCCLELLAN's troops. At any rate, they have retrieved themselves by their expedition at Fairfax Court-House,[3] and have well earned the new reading which some wag has given to the cabalistic letters, F.F.V. — viz., fast-footed Virginians.

It is due to the produce-dealers of New-York, and especially those of the West, to know that the Government is now paying $2.50 per bushel for beans. I understand from a Buffalo man that they can now be bought in that city for $1.37 1/2 to $1.50, and that the expense of transporting them to Washington is 20 cents — viz., to New-York 16 cents, and from thence to this city 4 cents. Here, then, is a chance for somebody to make money, and for the Government to save it. When the new crop comes in, it is said that beans will be sold for $1.25 in Buffalo. Peas, which are a good substitute for beans, sell for 75 cents at Buffalo, and may be had here at 95. These facts are sufficient to demonstrate that we have a liberal commissariat, and those who have provisions to sell should not stand back. ⊛

An editorial cartoon tribute shows General Winfield Scott slaying the Confederate states, represented by the mythological hydra.

THE HERCULES OF THE UNION,
SLAYING THE GREAT DRAGON OF SECESSION.

1. George B. McClellan (1826–1885) won several small engagements in western Virginia in the summer of 1861, including the battles of Rich Mountain (July 11) and Corrick's Ford (July 13), that established his reputation as a successful general.
2. Henry A. Wise (1806–1876), a former governor of Virginia, led a contingent of Confederate forces in this campaign. He soon quarreled with another Confederate political general, John B. Floyd, and the rift led to confusion and retreat. Indeed, McClellan's early success in this campaign can be attributed in large part to the poor quality of these opposing generals.
3. A skirmish at Fairfax Courthouse on June 1, 1861, resulted in a small Confederate victory.

DISPATCH TO THE ASSOCIATED PRESS.

JULY 22

WASHINGTON, SUNDAY, JULY 21

The Secretary of War has received a dispatch that the fighting was renewed at Bull's Run this morning. Our troops engaged the enemy with a large force, silenced their batteries, and drove the Secessionists to the Junction.

The city is wild with joy.

Firing was heard in this city to-day from the direction of Bull's Run, from 11 till about 3. There was a cessation till nearly 5, and at 7 this evening the reverberation of cannon was again audible.

A gentleman who arrived to-night says at 3 o'clock this afternoon the Second and Third New-Jersey Regiments were ordered to march forward from Vienna, the First sending their baggage back to Camp Trenton. Other troops were hurrying forward to the scene of hostilities, and there is much military excitement and bustle in the direction of all the camps....

It is not doubted in military quarters that Gen. JOHNSTON was enabled to effect a junction with the Confederates some time during yesterday.

Official dispatches were sent to Gen. MCDOWELL at 2 o'clock this morning.

The New-York Thirty-seventh Regiment passed over into Virginia this morning, the band playing "Dixie," amid the cheers of the soldiers and citizens.[1]... ⊛

1. The song "Dixie" debuted in a minstrel show in New York in 1859. During the 1860 election, Lincoln's supporters used it in their rallies. During the war, Southerners changed the lyrics and declared it a regional anthem, though it continued to be played by both sides.

PREPARATIONS FOR THE BATTLE.

JULY 22

CENTREVILLE, SUNDAY, JULY 21, VIA FAIRFAX COURT HOUSE, SUNDAY, JULY 21

We have successfully outflanked the enemy. At 2 1/2 o'clock this morning the various regiments about Centreville were formed for march, and at 3 o'clock they were in motion in the direction of Perryville, leaving Bull's Run to the left. At 6 o'clock the first gun was fired by a thirty-pound rifled cannon, sent ahead to batter the masked batteries that might be encountered on the road. There was no reply from the enemy, and the advance moved on.

At Gen. MCDOWELL's head-quarters, three miles beyond Centreville, the greater part of the army moved to the right, to avoid a bridge some distance beyond, said to have been undermined. They will pass over upon pontoons prepared by Capt. ALEXANDER, of the Engineer Corps, and who has inspected the country minutely in a previous reconnaissance, and to whom, in a great measure, the plan of the campaign is due.

A general battle is expected to-day or to-morrow, and which will probably decide the fate of the whole campaign.

If Gen. JOHNSON [Johnston] has not yet formed a junction with Gen. BEAUREGARD, he will be entirely cut off by this manoeuvre. Thrown back upon the mountains, his army will become utterly demoralized, and probably fall into the hands of Gen. MCCLELLAN, who is advancing beyond the Blue Ridge. And if he has formed a junction with Gen. BEAUREGARD, it opens our communication with Gen. PATTERSON's column; and thus reinforced, the National army can crush out opposition.

If we are driven back the army can retreat upon Centreville, and keep open the communication with Washington. If Gen. BEAUREGARD remains where he is, his communications in the rear are endangered, and Manassas Junction being situated in the apex of a triangle formed by railroads, a movement in his rear would destroy his communications with Richmond.

The only danger the National troops run by this flank march would be by a sudden advance of Gen. BEAUREGARD upon Centreville, interrupting communications and cutting off our supplies. But this manoeuvre would be desperate, as cutting himself off from supplies, and placing himself in an exhausted country, and between the National troops and the Potomac. The Sixty-ninth New-York Regiment[1] was assigned the post of honor in advance. The members of this regiment have agreed unanimously to serve, although their time is now out.

All the New-York regiments will follow this example.

For five hours one steady column of troops passed through Centreville.

The morale of the soldiers is excellent. All are anxious for a battle, and when informed of the purpose to advance, the enthusiasm was beyond all description.

It is supposed that Gen. BEAUREGARD's forces are larger than ours.

A battle is imminent at any moment, but it may not take place till to-morrow night.... ✪

1. Recruited in New York City and known as the "Fighting 69th," this regiment was composed largely of men of Irish descent and is the origin of the now famous "fighting Irish."

A Frank Leslie's Illustrated Newspaper woodcut depicting the First Battle of Bull Run.

THE GREATEST BATTLE EVER FOUGHT ON THIS CONTINENT.

JULY 22

BULL'S RUN, SUNDAY, JULY 21 — 2 P.M.

The great battle occurred to-day, and the result is not certain at the moment I write. Both sides have fought with terrible tenacity. The battle has been hot and steady for three hours, and the loss must be very heavy — certainly not under one thousand on each side.[1]

The Union Army advanced from Centreville in three columns at 3 o'clock this morning. Col. [Israel B.] RICHARDSON commanded the column by the road to Bull's Run, where the action of Thursday took place, and Col. [Dixon] MILES lay on the road and at Centreville to support him.

Gen. [Daniel] TYLER commanded the centre division, which took the Warrenton Road — Gens. [Robert C.] SCHENCK and Col. [William T.] SHERMAN being in advance. He had the three Connecticut Regiments, two from Michigan, two from Wisconsin, and the Sixty-ninth and Seventy-ninth, from New-York. Gen. MC-DOWELL, with Col. HUNTER and a very powerful division, went out on this road, which leads directly forward to Manassas, crossing Bull's Run by a stone bridge, which had been mined.

The attack by these two points was intended mainly as a feint. The real attack was by [David] HUNTER, who took a narrow road two miles out leading to the right, having [Henry] HUNT's and the Rhode Island batteries, and leaving Col. [Erasmus] KEYES on the centre at the crossing of the roads as a reserve. His orders were to proceed high up the stream, cut himself a path through the woods, cross over, and turn the position of the rebels on the north.

I went out with the centre column. At ten minutes before six we halted about a mile this side of the position of the rebels. The Sixty-ninth and Seventy-ninth Regiments of New-York were thrown to the right, in the woods, and the First and Second Ohio and the Second New-York to the left in advance....

At about ten o'clock heavy clouds of dust showed that reinforcements were coming up to the rebels from Manassas, and was continued through the next three or four hours.

At 11 o'clock [Captain Romeyn B.] AYERS' [actually Ayres] Battery went to the front; the Sixty-ninth, New-York, was or-

dered to deploy into the field in front, and firing was heard from HUNTER's Division, on the extreme right, far in advance.

The Ohio regiments were pushed forward with the Second New-York, and ran upon a masked battery of four guns, which killed and wounded quite a number of both. Of the latter, MICHAEL MCCARTY, Sergeant of Company H, was wounded, and afterwards was reported dead. Lieut. DEMSEY received a slight wound. Some twenty or thirty of the Ohio regiment broke and run, but the rest stood firm, as did the Second New-York.

[Captain John H.] CARLISLE's Battery was brought to the front on the right, and soon drove the rebels out of the masked battery.

It was now 11 1/2 o'clock, when HUNTER's column appeared across the Run, advancing on the flank of the rebels, and the engagement soon became very active in his position. He kept steadily advancing, pouring in a steady fire of artillery and musketry.

The whole Brigade under TYLER was ordered forward to his support. The Sixty-ninth and Seventy-ninth New-York, the First, Second, and Third Connecticut, and the Second Wisconsin were sent in. A con-

stant roll of musketry marked HUNTER's advance, and the artillery from our column played incessantly on the flank of the rebels. So far as I could see, the latter were pushed backward a considerable distance to the road directly in front of where I stood, across which they charged twice with the bayonet upon our troops, but were repulsed each time. Our men crossed the road and poured in upon them a terrible fire of artillery and musketry.

I write this at 2 1/4 o'clock, and am compelled to close in order to avail myself of a special messenger to Washington. The fight is still going on with great energy. The rebel batteries have again commenced firing upon us, and their balls and shells fall thick upon the road and in the field which I had selected as my observatory.

Gen. SCHENCK and two batteries are ordered up to repulse an attempt of cavalry to outflank us. I shall try to send the result in a later dispatch.

H. J. R.

1. Actual casualties were: Union – 460 killed, 1,124 wounded, 1,312 missing; Confederate – 377 killed, 1,582 wounded, and 13 missing.

Caring for the wounded after the battle.

BULLETINS OF THE BATTLE.

JULY 22
WASHINGTON, SUNDAY, JULY 21

The following bulletins were received in official quarters, during the progress of the battle from the telegraph station about four miles from Bull's Run:

FAIRFAX COURT-HOUSE, SUNDAY, JULY 21 — 11 A.M

There is rapid firing from heavy guns and frequent discharges of musketry.

11:40. — The fighting is very heavy, and apparently more on our left wing.

11:50. — There is evidently a battle toward our left in the direction of Bull's Run, and a little north. The firing is very rapid and heavy.

1:45. — Heavy guns are heard again, and apparently nearer. The musketry is heavy and nearer.

2 P.M. — The musketry is very heavy and drawing much nearer. There is evidently a movement more to our left.

2:45 P.M. — The firing is a little farther off, and apparently in the direction of the Junction. Less heavy guns and more light artillery, as near as can judge.

3 P.M. — The firing has ceased ten minutes since.

3:35 P.M. — The firing has almost entirely ceased, and can only be heard with difficulty. I shall telegraph no more unless there should be a renewal of the battle, which has been so gloriously fought for the old Stars and Stripes, and from all indications here our troops have at least stood their ground.

FAIRFAX COURT-HOUSE, SUNDAY, JULY 21 — 3:50 P.M.

Our courier has not yet returned. Quartermaster BARTON, of the Second Regiment of Michigan, has just passed, and says that the officers, men, and citizens at Centreville say a general engagement of the whole line had taken place, three and a half miles this side of Manassas, and that our troops had driven and forced the Secessionist lines back to Manassas. We expect a courier now every moment.

CENTREVILLE, SUNDAY, JULY 21 — 4 P.M.

Gen. MCDOWELL has ordered the reserves now here under Col. MILES to advance to the Bridge over Bull's Run, on the Warrenton road, having driven the enemy before him. Col. MILES is now three or four miles from here, directing operations near Blackburn's ford.

Colonel Ambrose Burnside's brigade fighting at the First Battle of Bull Run.

FAIRFAX COURT-HOUSE — 4:45 P.M.

Two of our couriers have returned, but are unable to communicate in person with Gen. MCDOWELL. One of the couriers was on the field of battle. He says our troops have taken three masked batteries, and forced the enemy to fall back and retire. He says the battle was general on Bull's Run for some distance. One of the batteries taken was in a wheat field, and the other some distance from it, and the third still further on.

5:20 P.M. — Another dispatch says that the Nationals have won the day. The loss on both sides is heavy, but the rout of the rebels is complete. The batteries at Bull's Run are silenced, and two or three others taken.

5:45 P.M. — The firing has ceased. We shall send another courier there in a few minutes. The Colonel went at 4 o'clock and will be back soon. A still later report, not official, but from apparently reliable source, says that the column under Col. HEINTZELMAN has followed the rebels to Manassas Junction, and has opened fire on their entrenched camp, and was then shelling them.

The cannonading can occasionally be heard in Washington from Georgetown Heights.

The head-quarters of the Army is inaccessible to-night, the President and Cabinet being privately with Gen. SCOTT and Staff, and other distinguished gentlemen. ✴

EFFECTS OF THE BATTLE IN WASHINGTON.

JULY 22
WASHINGTON, SUNDAY, JULY, 21

The most intense excitement is everywhere existing to hear further from the field of battle. Every returning spectator of the event is immediately surrounded to relate his observations.

The demand for intelligence is insatiable, and unauthenticated rumors prevails, which serve to confuse the truth.

The smoke from the battle could be seen from the eminences in Washington.

A number of members of Congress, and even ladies, went to the neighborhood of Bull's Run, to witness the battle. One of them reports Col. [David] HUNTER, of the Third Cavalry, acting as Major-General, was seriously, if not mortally, wounded.[1]

It is stated with confidence in all quarters that Col. [J. C.] CAMERON, of the Seventy-ninth Regiment, and brother of the Secretary of War [Simon Cameron], and Col. SLOCUM, of the Second Rhode Island Regiment, were killed.[2] ✴

1. Brigadier General David Hunter (1802–1886) was wounded in the neck and cheek, but not seriously.
2. Colonel J.C. Cameron of the 79th New York and Colonel John S. Slocum of the 2nd Rhode Island were both mortally wounded.

VICTORY AT BULL'S RUN — SUMTER AVENGED.

JULY 22

The news from the seat of war must thrill every loyal American heart with deep emotion. The trust reposed by the country in its heroic Army has not been misplaced. After a battle of unparalleled severity, in which our soldiers fought against great odds in regard to position, and against forces not much inferior, if at all, in point of numbers to their own, they have come off more than conquerors — not only driving the enemy from their formidable positions, but seizing all their guns and equipments, and pausing only when the sheltered ranks of the rebels found safety, after retreat, in other and equally strong defences.

The intrenchments of the enemy at Bull's Run were believed to be quite as impregnable as those at Manassas. The distance between the places is only a few miles, and after the repulse of our reconnoitering regiments, on Thursday, it is known that large reinforcements were sent forward by the rebels, and that they were exultant with the belief that their lines could not be forced. They had two days in which to make their defences complete, and BEAUREGARD's entire Army, if not actually present, close behind them, from which to draw all of actual, and all of strategetic aid that their selected field was fitted to

receive. That the rebels had chosen Bull's Run as a position they would maintain, would seem to be evident both from its fitness, according to all descriptions for military defence, and from their reluctance to leave it. The fighting was terrific, we are told; the enemy contested every inch.; they did not cease to wield their guns until every battery was taken; and when they were finally expelled, it must have been in all cases at the point of the bayonet, for "all their guns and equipments" were left in the hands of the victorious Union Army. It was a bloody expulsion from their breastworks and guns, and not a retreat from a field that could no longer be contested.

We are aware that the public will have no care for editorial comments on this grand event. The occasion is too solemn, and the emotion it calls up too deep for expression in any language that we can command. We can only bow in heartfelt gratitude to the God of battles that he has seconded our noble Army, and caused victory to rest with the eagles of the Union. The glorious flag that fell at Sumter is now fully avenged. The folds that hid its bright stars when it was lowered in Charleston harbor, under BEAUREGARD's guns, as a conquered ensign, flamed out again in

the smoke and fire of the Bull's Run batteries, and sent dismay to the hearts of the ingrates that had shouted impiously over its former brief humiliation.

The repulse of the enemy at Bull's Run, we must believe is but the prelude to his greater and perhaps final overthrow at Manassas or Richmond. We now know that our gallant and laurel-crowned Army is equal to any work that rebel genius and rebel arms can give it; and in this hope we await events. But we cannot dismiss the subject without a word of consolation and of cheer to the many thousands whose hearts will bleed, even while they may shed tears of joy over this great victory. The list of the dead will soon be coming along, for such a victory is only bought at a fearful price, coined from the heart's blood of fathers, husbands, brothers, sons. To those who are to be agonized by the terrible record, we can only say, no higher fame can be enjoyed, than to have perished in order to make liberty safe. ⊛

GEN. MCCLELLAN ASSIGNED TO THE COMMAND OF THE POTOMAC.

JULY 23

WASHINGTON, MONDAY, JULY 22

Gen. MCCLELLAN has been summoned by the Government from Western Virginia to repair to Washington to take command of the Army of the Potomac.

Gen. ROSENCRANZ takes his place in command of the Army of Western Virginia.[1]

The Corps d'Armee at Washington is to be instantly reorganized and increased. The orders have already been given. Offers of regiments already raised and being made, will be accepted with such rapidity as to insure that this will be accomplished in a few days. Large reinforcements from various districts are already on the way hither, orders having been telegraphed for them yesterday, while the battle was in progress. ⊛

1. Major General William S. Rosecrans (1819–1898).

WHO WON THE VICTORY?

JULY 24

Exaggeration played its usual trick with the news of Sunday's battle. In the light of more detailed and authentic advices, it may fairly be considered doubtful whether either party has gained a victory; for while, panic-stricken, our exposed forces left the field, it is clear that the enemy never quitted their entrenchments to occupy it; in fact, they appear to have been so much intimidated by the encounter, as to pretermit the opportunity they undoubtedly possessed to cut to pieces our retiring troops. This omission may be explained in two ways. In the fighting throughout the day the National troops had exhibited every superiority of strength, tact, and courage, uniformly driving before them the enemy when he ventured beyond his defences, and even capturing three of his batteries in succession. Such exploits could not fail to fill the insurgent ranks with dread of the

equal terms upon which they must stand were they to quit their lines; and, indeed, after the prodigies of valor our fellows had displayed, they had every reason to believe the backward movement was a feint to decoy them from their almost impregnable works, to ground where the conditions of the contest should be equalized.

There is much reason, also, to believe that the enemy suffered in killed and wounded far more severely than did the National forces. Testimony from a dozen independent sources is to this effect. They were thus probably in as bad a condition to pursue as our shattered columns were to fight; for by such arguments only can we account for the omission to follow the retreating Army into Washington itself; and for the ability of our people to retrace their steps, as they subsequently did, and recover guns and baggage, which had

NOTES OF THE GREAT BATTLE.

HOW THE AFFAIR WAS REGARDED IN WASHINGTON AND ELSEWHERE — FACTS AND INCIDENCES — CAUSES OF THE DISASTER.

JULY 26

CORRESPONDENCE OF THE NEW-YORK TIMES.
WASHINGTON, MONDAY, JULY 22 —
MIDNIGHT.

There can be no possible use in bemoaning the present state of things in this city, at the seat of war or elsewhere. One can best forget himself and his feelings by plunging at once in medias res' as they are, and that I propose to do. On Sunday, our earlier dispatches gave most cheering accounts of the gallantry of our soldiers, of the rout of the rebels, and of the undoubted success of the United States troops, and well aware of the eager anxiety of all the citizens of the great metropolis concerning the events of the day, we promptly and regularly forwarded the news as obtained at headquarters. The scenes which took place at every public resort, at the corners of the streets and throughout the entire city indicated the hearty gratification and great enthusiasm of the people. So soon as a dispatch was received at the War Department or by some fortunate newspaper man, it was copied, put upon the bulletins, and read to the assembled hundreds, who joyfully greeted each and every word with rousing, sympathetic cheers, and as accessions were made to the surging crowd, the word of glad tidings was read and reread until the reader became hoarse, though the hearers called for more. The President in his Cabinet received the same news that so electrified New-York; Gen. SCOTT, in his little back office, heard with satisfaction the same bulletins that so excited the noisy crowds; and no one dreamed for a moment that while these spontaneous tributes of thankfulness to God, and of honor to our brave men, were bursting forth from eye, from lip, from heart, those very men were being mowed down upon the field of battle like grass upon the meadow.

Towards 10 o'clock at night there were rumors of trouble, stories of repulse, and narratives indicating disaster, but they were not credited. Gen. [Joseph K.] MANSFIELD stated distinctly at the hotel that the guns and equipments of the enemy were in the hands of our troops, and an official courier from Gen. MCDOWELL to the Commander-in-Chief telegraphed that a "great battle had been fought, and victory won," and that he was on his way to this city with details. That for the time being settled the matter, and it was not until Mr. [Henry J.] RAYMOND, sunburned, dusty, and hardly recognizable, entered the telegraph office at midnight, that the news of our rout was even credibly suggested. It was then too late to countermand the dispatches already sent, and the telegraphic censor, undoubtedly thinking Mr. RAYMOND's dispatch contained too much truth, struck it from the "all right" file, and the TIMES was compelled, as were its contemporaries, to go forth to its readers, with an incorrect statement of the day's result.

This morning, at first slowly and by twos and threes, came the stragglers into town with melancholy faces, dirt-begrimed and weary, with corroborative accounts of the disaster. Many of them were wild with excitement. Men who, on ordinary occasions, are calm, cool, and sensible, seemed beside themselves, and gave utterance to the wildest, most incoherent and senseless statements concerning the light, the subsequent stampede, and the latest situation of affairs. It was apparently impossible to obtain anything approximating a truthful resume, or one which it would be safe to transmit to the thousands of loving ones at home, who wait on the telegraphic word as they would on the report from head-quarters. After a little, others, more composed, arrived, and we then hoped to get at something worthy of belief, but, after patient hearing and careful comparison, it was evident that if a thousand men, having seen the battle, should publish each an account, there would be exactly one thousand conflicting stories.

The rain poured down in torrents. Like the thick, heavy drops of an August thundershower, has been the fall of rain all day long. From early morning until now, the cumbersome baggage-wagons have jolted over the stones of our roughly-cobbled streets, bringing the wounded and the dying to the hospitals and the infirmaries. So, too, have the easier riding ambulances, all of which were filled with our disabled and suffering soldiers. Very many of the soldiers, having received discharges from their companies, sought the way to Gen. MANSFIELD's head-quarters, that they might receive the necessary signature of some official therewith connected. I had occasion to go at an early hour to the office, and truly the scene there was a sorrowful one.

Gen. MANSFIELD occupies a house on the corner fronting the War Department.

been abandoned in the flight, and which an enemy, assured of victory, would have hastened to gather up. From this review of the business we can only derive the impression that but for the reasonless panic which was communicated to our men, and the influence of which was favored by the broken and woody peculiarities of the country, which prevented any one regiment from knowing what had befallen its neighbor, the victory would have been ours, much more certainly than it can now be attributed to the enemy.

Later information illustrates another important point. In this conflict the rebels exerted and perhaps exhausted all the military energies at their command. Their Army, which was recruited by conscriptions and impressments, represents perhaps as large a force as they could, without the prestige of success, bring to the field; while it was directed by the only commanders upon whose skill they are willing to stake their fortunes. President DAVIS was in charge of the main body, while BEAUREGARD and JOHNSTON commanded the wings.' Thus we have encountered all the strength and skill they can muster with a tithe of our strength, and without the employment of any of the military talent upon which our soldiers have learned to rely, because approved by military successes; and it is for this reason, in connection with the excessive numbers and better position of the enemy, that we have come out of the conflict with no better result. The reflection is at once encouraging and instructive. ✸

This is inaccurate. Davis arrived at Bull Run just as the battle was ending and played no significant role in the management of the fighting. Johnston was the senior Confederate officer present, but since he arrived on the eve of the battle, he left the tactical management of the fight to Beauregard.

In the second story are his offices. Passing the sentry at the foot of the stairs, I entered the front room, which is his private office. It is uncarpeted. In the centre of the room was a large table covered with papers; at the further corner was a little box desk, at which sat the pale-faced, grief-stricken General, and at the opposite corner was another desk, on which leaned, fast asleep, the worn-out Secretary, Capt. DRAKE DEKAY. In the connecting room, waiting in turn to speak with Maj. TALBOT or Gen. MANSFIELD, was a group of men whose appearance I can never forget. One poor fellow, apparently about twenty-five years old, seemed to be in the last stage of consumption. He was, oh! how thin and pale, and when the sharp, curt voice of the peremptory official called his name, it was with the greatest difficulty he could tremblingly stagger to the desk. His head was covered with a handkerchief; his eyes fairly stood out from their bony sockets; his beard was half-grown, and his moustache but just starting; his pale lips were parted; his neck seemed unnaturally long, and his scanty uniform hung upon him like a sack. Unfortunately an informality in his papers made it necessary for him to go back to Alexandria, that an additional signature might be obtained; and when, after some ineffectual argument, he found it was useless to urge his illness as an excuse, he turned away with a look so full of weariness and so pitiful in expression, that I could not refrain from inwardly cursing the infernal system of routine and tape which so annoys and perplexes our entire military action. I handed the man a glass of water, at which he seemed surprised, but thanking me, gulped it down, and then asked permission to sit upon a bench in the hall until he could be somewhat restored. I left him asleep.

The others are in various stages of disability. Some had no shoes, others no hat; some fell asleep standing in their turn, others sat upon the floor and snored with exhaustion. All, however, were unprovided with decent clothing, and each man seemed an object of pity and of charity. But while I was waiting with them, a loud cheering was heard in the vicinity of the White House, and going thither, I met a company of Fire Zouaves, numbering one hundred and twenty-five, under command of First Lieut. EDWARD B. KNOX, who was formerly of the Chicago Zouaves, and is one of the ten first lieutenants selected from that corps by ELLSWORTH for the Fire Brigade. The company had halted near the White House,

and instantly the men were surrounded by hundreds of people, each and all eager to talk with them concerning the events of the day. I tell you they were a sight to behold. All of them wore the red skull cap, the red shirt and regulation pants, and each carried his gun. Their heads are shaven close, so close that an attempt to part the hair would be absurd, and so close that to rumple it would be impossible. Their eyes were keen and clear, their faces almost black from exposure to the sun, their hands like marble, and their arms and limbs like iron. They were proud, boastful, full of excited and colored narrative, jolly, good-natured, and ready for more work. But they were only kept up by that nature which has so often kept them up after hours of self-sacrificing labor at a fire, and by the exciting cheers and huzzahs given them by the admiring crowd which thronged about them. Presently they took up their march for MANSFIELD's Headquarters, before which they halted, while Lieut. KNOX went in to report. I went in with him, and was present at the meeting between the veteran and the younger officer.

Gen. MANSFIELD — Well, Sir. Who and what are you? Who are these men?

Lieut. KNOX — I am Lieut. KNOX, of the Fire Zouaves. These men, with a few others, are what is left of our regiment, and I want quarters for them.

Gen. MANSFIELD — Why you are only about a hundred. Is it possible (and here the tears came to his eyes, for he doubtless remembered the time when he thanked the twelve hundred for their courage at the fire) that you have sustained such a loss?

Lieut. KNOX — Yes, Sir. We had pretty lively work. There are about 400 of us left, out of the regiment. We have marched all the way from Fairfax, to-day, and we would like to get into quarters.

After this and some other conversation, the General, with great feeling, promised to find them a place at once, and sent DE KAY out for that purpose. While he was gone, I went out, that I might hear what the fire boys said.

One little short fellow, with a bright black eye, having his red skull-cap pushed on the back of his head, his arms akimbo, and his cheek dilated with the weed, was holding forth to a knot of admiring men and boys, somewhat in this fashion: "Fight! Oh, no. We didn't fight — perhaps we didn't. Just see here. After we'd been a standing three hours…in the grass, up come a long-legged cuss, and says he, follow me. We went, we did — first short, and then double-quick. All

Lieutenant General Winfield Scott, U.S.A.

of a sudden pop, bang, bang, bang went the bloody guns on our left, that God only knew was there, for we didn't, and the boys fell down like sheep. And then the way we took them batteries. Well, you ought to have seen it — that's all. We saw our men drove away from their guns, and we made up our minds to get 'em, and we charged, yelling like bloody h--l, drove the seceshes back a deuced sight quicker than they come, and popped 'em down at every shot. But when we'd got the guns the fellers didn't come to hold 'em, and of course we couldn't work 'em, and we left. But the charge of those d--d Black Horse "Calvary" was the best thing. I say, Bill, those fellers weren't no darned persimmons — no, Sir-ee — they did well, they did; but they don't brag much where they are now. Well, Sir, they came a riding down on to us like the very devil, and we just come the three-rank arrangement on 'em — one rank was down there, the second just above their shoulders, and the third fellers stood up straight. On they came — sword and pistol in hand, and the horses galloping like d--n. Don't fire till they get way up, says Pony — and we didn't.[2] The cusses didn't know what to make of it, but we soon informed 'em. Pop went the first rank, and the poor devils fell out of their saddles like dead sheep. Bang went number two, and down come another batch, and I'll be d--d if I believe there was a third of 'em left when they turned tail and scud away, as if all h--l was after 'em." The boys were very tired and hungry and thirsty, and the timely present of a lunch of bread and butter, sent by a lady in the vicinity, was cheerfully and gratefully received. For about half an hour they remained there, telling wonderful stories of personal adventure and regimental prowess, winding up invariably with a good round cursing of the General in command, and an earnest desire to have another chance at the "bloody seceshers." Knowing that anything connected with the New-York Fire Brigade would prove interesting to the mass of the readers of the TIMES, I procured the following statement of Lieut. KNOX, of Company A, in that regiment:

The regiment was encamped on Saturday night at a place about a mile this side of Centreville. At 2 o'clock on Sunday morning, the men were aroused, and remained under arms until 7 o'clock, at which time they started forward. There were 950 men, all told, with "Pony" FARNHAM at their head.[2] With cheers they moved briskly forward through the woods, singing and laughing and eager for the fight. They had marched about 14 miles, and were within three miles of the battlefield, when they heard the guns and saw the smoke from an eminence. This excited the men wonderfully, and at double-quick step they pressed on, with the intention of joining Col. [Orlando] WILCOX, who, with the Michigan regiment was a short way ahead. Halting at a pool of dirty water, they refreshed themselves, and went on until they came to a church three-quarters of a mile this side of the battle-field, where they left their overcoats and haversacks, and having formed by companies, again went on at double-quick step. As they passed a bit of woods they were fired at by some cavalry who were concealed there, but stopping only to return the fire, they moved on until they reached a fair halting ground. While there, the enemy succeeded in taking from the United States regulars a battery which was stationed in the woods at the right of the Zouaves, who were at once impressed with the idea that they had a mission, and that mission was to retake those guns. Whereupon with a wild, wild yell, three cheers and a loud, fierce cry of "Remember ELLSWORTH," they dashed across the intervening space, rushed in the face of a murderous discharge from the cannon on the hill, and with loud whoops and hurrahs drove some away, killed the rest, occupied the position, and attempted to use the guns. The regulars did not return to receive at their hands the recaptured battery, and it was useless in their hands. While in possession of this battery a body of infantry who were in the woods in their right rear, fired with considerable effect several vollies into their midst, and the Colonel gave the order to leave

the battery and dislodge the enemy. This they did effectually, and compelled the rebels to flee from the wrath behind. Unfortunately the Zouaves were not aware of the state of affairs on the other side of the woods, and with hot haste, and in considerable disorder, they rushed out only to find themselves the target for another body of infantry beyond, while the Black Horse Cavalry were seen charging full upon them. Things looked badly, when, fortunately, the infantry were engaged by another regiment, thus giving the Zouaves time to prepare for the charge from the horsemen. They formed hastily in line, kneeling, semi-kneeling and standing, that, ELLSWORTH fashion, they might receive their enemies with successive volleys. On came the Horse — a full regiment of brave men splendidly mounted, and as ready for mischief at those on whom they hoped to fall. To an early discharge from the cavalry the Zouaves made no response, although several of the men were killed, but waited patiently until the enemy was almost upon them, when, in quick succession, the three ranks fired, each man doing his best for the good cause. The shock to the rebels was great, but they rallied, behaving splendidly, and attempted a renewal of the charge, for which, however, the excited firemen were prepared, and for which the Black Horse Cavalry paid most dearly. They were completely shattered, broken up and swept away. Not more than a hundred of them rode off, and as they went, their rebellious ears were saluted with "One, two, three, four, five, six, seven, tigah, Zouave," and such a "tiger repeat" as one can only appreciate when he has heard it. What happened after that, it is hard to detail. Grape and canister were poured in upon them thick and fast. Down on their faces till the shot passed on fell every man, and then "up and at 'em" till the next volley, was the cry of them all. This continued for a long time, during which squad after squad was used up, man after man fell dead, or receiving a shot while on the ground, failed to rise at the next command. Then came the order to retreat, which slowly and gradually was obeyed. The regiment broke ranks — some of the men walked slowly off; others went into the woods and fought from behind the trees on their own hook; others falling in with different regiments, joined forces against, the common enemy, and other climbed the trees to see "what was up." While in the woods the slaughter amongst the men was very great, and the cross fire to which they were there exposed did them more damage than all else beside. The retreat with them was as with all

the regiments — not particularly an orderly one, but rather a free and easy retrograde movement, which, if not a stampede or a rout, was at least a very unmilitary operation.

From the above outline of Mr. KNOX's very interesting statement, it will be seen that the firemen did then, as ever, their duty. They receive from all sides the most flattering commendation, and it is gratifying to know that immediate steps will be taken to recruit men enough to fill up the sadly broken ranks. New-York may well be proud of her representatives in this regiment, and it is only to be regretted that all did not do as well. They had a good breakfast at Willard's, have been lions all day long, and are now quartered in the old homestead of the New-York Twelfth.

But I find that I am forgetting my notebook. In that I have noted many incidents which ought to be told, but it is now nearly 12 o'clock, at which hour the mail closes. I regret to say that the enemy to-day have proved themselves most brutal. I have the authority of one of the first artists of the country, who has just left my room, and also of a well-known army officer, for stating that the rebels shelled the Hospital Church, in which were our wounded men; that they fired repeated volleys at our ambulances, which were crowded with sick and dying soldiers; that they cut off the heads of men on the field, and absolutely kicked them from one to another; that they have bayoneted many of our men who lay wounded on the field of battle; that thievish knaves were on the ground early this morning, pilfering and pillaging, and that scenes of horror such as no imagination can suggest, or imagery convoy, have been of frequent occurrence since the disastrous termination of the engagement.

I have not time to quote opinions or suggest criticisms, but will say that the most thorough and immediate investigation of the affair is to be had, and no stone will be left unturned that the censure of the nation may be cast heavily upon the proper person. The enemy at noon to-day were not aware of the extent of our rout; by this time they are, and I violate no confidence when I state that, in high military quarters great fear is entertained concerning the possible developments of the next forty-eight hours. ✪

1. In the middle of things.
2. Colonel Noah Farnham (1829–1861) succeeded to the command of the Fire Zouaves after Elmer Ellsworth's murder. He was called "pony" because of his height — five feet four inches. He was wounded by a musket ball to the head at Bull Run, and died on August 14.

CHAPTER 5
"What We Are Fighting For"
AUGUST–OCTOBER 1861

After the debacle of Bull Run, Lincoln brought 34-year-old Major General George B. McClellan to Washington to command the army. But "Little Mac," as he was known, wanted to ensure that the army was ready. Consequently, as late summer turned to fall, McClellan's growing army did little more than drill and train. Some observers grew impatient at this perceived delay and criticized the army's new commander for indolence; others, including The Times, defended him on the grounds that he had inherited an army that was falling apart. At this point in the war, Lincoln was willing to grant his new general whatever time he needed — though that would change.

Meanwhile, the readers of The Times followed the emerging national conversation about the conduct — and ultimately the meaning — of the war. Some argued that rebels should not be treated as prisoners of war because it would legitimize their claim to nationhood. Lincoln had previously declared that rebel privateers would be treated as pirates; now, at least one reader thought that rebel soldiers deserved no better. More central to the national debate, however, was the inescapable issue of slavery. It was generally understood that slavery had caused the war, and more than a few New Yorkers began to wonder why the national government should continue to honor slaveholders' rights in the rebellious states. To circumvent the Fugitive Slave Law (enacted in 1850), Major General Benjamin F. Butler had argued that escaped slaves were "contraband" and did not need to be returned to their disloyal masters. His clever legal stratagem worked, and for the rest of the war, escaped slaves

Detail of an etching of the Battle of Ball's Bluff.

were known as "contrabands." But when Major General John C. Fremont in Missouri declared martial law in his theater, and announced that all the slaves of disloyal masters were now free, it was a direct blow at the "peculiar institution" and undisguised by any legal subterfuge. Unsurprisingly, it provoked both a public outcry (as well as some applause), and a rebuke from the President. Fremont sent his wife, Jesse Benton Fremont, to Washington to plead his case with the President, but the interview did not go well, and Lincoln removed Fremont from his position. Meanwhile, McClellan's habit of returning escaped slaves to their masters brought complaints from other quarters.

In October, what was intended as a reconnaissance across the Potomac River at Edward's Ferry led to the Battle of Ball's Bluff (October 21, 1861). Though like the Battle at Bull Run it was first reported as a Union victory, it was a badly bungled affair that resulted in an ignominious Union retreat

back across the river. Details of the battle were provided by Times reporter Elias Smith who was "embedded" (as we would say today) in Company H of the 15th Massachusetts infantry. His lengthy report is a vivid firsthand account from the ground level.

Among those killed at Ball's Bluff was Colonel Edward D. Baker, the commander of the 71st Pennsylvania Volunteers (known as the California regiment since many of the soldiers were from the West Coast). Baker was not only a popular commander, he was also a sitting senator from Oregon and a personal friend of President Lincoln, who had named his second son for him. When Lincoln received the news, it struck him like a blow; witnesses saw the President stagger and nearly fall, and many saw the tears in his eyes.

In addition, reports of the battle in other papers (especially Horace Greeley's Tribune) suggested that Brigadier General Charles P. Stone, a West Point graduate, was jealous of volunteer officers like Baker and had deliber-

ately put him in an impossible position. Congress demanded an investigation, with not a few hinting darkly that treason was at work. McClellan, with his tolerant attitude toward slavery, was their real target, but it was Stone who took the fall. He was arrested and held without charges for six months. Though he served briefly in the Red River campaign in 1864 and the siege of Petersburg in 1865, his reputation never recovered. To conduct their investigation, Congress formed a new standing committee — the Committee on the Conduct of the War — that spent the rest of the war looking over Lincoln's shoulder, second-guessing his decisions, and keeping a sharp eye out for any officer who failed their test of loyalty.

Throughout the early fall of 1861, many of the New York Times articles evince a people struggling to understand the meaning and impact of the war, and experimenting with new and increasingly radical notions of freedom and liberty.

ABOUT PRISONERS OF WAR, PRIVATEERS, &C.

AUGUST 7

To the Editor of the New-York Times:

In your paper of last Thursday you seem to have some hesitancy as to the proper way of treating prisoners of war, pirates and others found in arms against the Government and people of the United States. Do not accuse me of egotism if I assert that there is no need of any halting (but there is need of a vast amount of haltering) in the matter. What are the facts? A part of the people have attempted to subvert the Government by force of arms. The Government (the centralized and legal embodiment of the people) in maintaining its authority, also resorts to arms. Collisions and battles occur. Both sides take prisoners. Now comes the question, "What shall be done with these men?" I admit the question is one of vast importance, not only as regards the proper way of dealing with the rebellion, but also as to

the personal rights and privileges, pains and penalties of the captured men. The Government should not treat its captured rebels as prisoners of war. Neither should it do that other and much worse thing, discharge them on their parole. To do the first is a virtual admission that the rebels are a lawful enemy. This must not be admitted. If it is, ground is laid for their recognition by foreign nations. The Government must do all in its power to place the rebels outside of law, and not allow them to claim or exercise any legal privileges whatever.

They are rebels, and should be treated as such. When taken in arms against the Government, they should be disarmed, and compelled to aid the Government in maintaining itself against the rebels. They should never be treated as prisoners of war, neither should the Government ever recognize a flag of truce from rebels. Every man bearing such a flag should be arrested as a rebel, the bearing the flag being prima facie evidence of his being a rebel; for if there were no rebels there

could be no rebellion, and if there was no rebellion, there would be no war or collision needing the intercession of a flag of truce. Every bearer of one should be locked up as a rebel. No treating with them as lawful enemies. No discharging or swearing allegiance. Men that forswear their natural inherited allegiance, by engaging in a rebellion against a Government like ours, cannot be trusted on their oath, especially an oath taken under such circumstances. Never trust a rebel's oath.

So much for land rebels. Now about rebels and pirates afloat. They should be hung at the yard-arm of the National vessel capturing them, without ever being brought ashore to be tried and sympathized with, and kept at the public expense. The summary hanging of a few would scare the rest and drive them from the ocean....

SINCLAIR TOUSEY.[1] ⊛

1. Sinclair Tousey (1815–1887) was a New York newspaperman and later the founder of the American News Company.

INDIRECT BENEFITS OF WAR.

AUGUST 8

Hard as the war we are now engaged in may bear upon individual interests, and calamitous as it doubtless is, for the time, to the commerce and trade of the country, yet it has its elements of good as well as of evil. The American people, in their fierce pursuit of those vast material enterprises, of the success of which we boast so much, were in danger of forgetting the necessity of providing for the possible contingencies of the future. More than three-quarters of a century of internal repose, and, with the exception of three or four years, of peace with all the world, afforded an opportunity of developing the natural resources of the country, of changing continental forests to farms and fields, of building up cities and towns; of creating for ourselves a world-wide commerce, and of advancement in a career of progress that carried us to a high position in the scale of nations. But this long period of peace made us negligent of preparing for the accident of war. In our prosperity we overlooked the teachings of history. The fallacy that the future would be as the past, that the Union would never be disturbed by internal revolt, because it never had been, that the people and the States would always be loyal to the Constitution, because they had never been otherwise, came to be with us an article of political faith, upon the assumed truth of which the policy of our Government was based. We kept no standing Army, because we had no martial neighbors whose enmity we feared, or whose power we had occasion to dread. Even the militia of the States came to be contemned as a useless pageant, and was fast falling into disrepute under the ridicule it attracted by its broad caricature of war. Thus, while all our energies were directed towards the accomplishment of physical enterprises, the martial spirit, so essential to the maintenance of the power and strength of a great nation, was fast dying out. We were warned of possible insurrection — of collision between the State and National Governments. We laughed at the folly of the admonition. We refused to listen to the roar of the cataract, even when its sound was in our ears, until in sight of the rapids down which the inevitable drift lay. We started at last from our dream of security, to see treason organized into open revolt, without a preparation in advance to meet it. We had no Army, no arms, no munitions of war; and for the time, the Government was at the mercy of a rebellion whose conspiracies had been ripening for years. Up to this time we had scarcely thought of country or of home. We had given no consideration to the idea that we might one day be required to preserve the power inherent in a united people by compelling national unity. Our pros-

POPULAR IDEAS OF THE REBELLION.
THE WAR AND SLAVERY.

AUGUST 9

WESTPORT, CONN., THURSDAY, AUG. 8

To the Editor of the New-York Times:

You say truly that this war in which we are engaged has for its object simply to put down the rebellion against our nationality. This is the object and the whole of it.

But how are we to accomplish this object? Many say, "Gather an immense Army, pay hundreds of millions of money, and go on from battle-field to battle-field, till the treason is stamped out; meanwhile, scrupulously respecting the institution of Slavery. In case it shall be found impossible to succeed in this way, then, as a last resort, decree emancipation." The plan is to do all we can toward crushing out the rebellion without harming the peculiar institution; and if, after an immense outlay of money and life, we find that either the Republic or Slavery must die, then Slavery must take the death. It is assumed, and with reason, that a decree of emancipation by the war power would make short work with the rebellion. It is capable of demonstration that, with it and ten thousand men properly applied, a single month would suffice to revolutionize the larger part of the South into submission — and that with a less amount of suffering and outrage than ordinarily follows in the track of war.

Now, gentlemen, I have never been an ul- traist; but I cannot help asking, why not adopt this conclusive measure at the outset? What is this Slavery? What has it done that it should be treated so tenderly, and be marked as the last thing to be thrown overboard in the endeavor to save the laboring ship? Here we are, proposing to sacrifice great commercial and manufacturing interests, hundreds of millions of ready money in the shape of taxes, and tens of thousands of precious lives in an experiment to get along without harming the institution of Slavery by this war. What have these rebels and traitors done that we should be so much more chary of their property than of our own — so much more tender of their investment in human flesh and blood than of the lives of our own sons and brothers? What is there so very precious about this very peculiar institution of our deadly enemies that we should shield it from harm with our own fortunes and bodies up to the last possible minute; that we should dare and sacrifice to the last extremity before consenting to have it perish? One would think Slavery to be the Kohinoor[1] of the country, instead of the nation's shame, the by-word of Christendom, the incorrigible fire-brand and disintegrator of our nationality, the mother of treason and rebellion. Was not this rebellion got up in the interests of Slavery? Are not these men who are stabbing at the public heart, slaveholders, and is it not because they are slaveholders that they are so stabbing? Is not Slavery at this moment the right arm with which treason is working against us? Who plant the masked batteries, who make the intrenchments, who drag and manipulate the munitions of war, who furnish the food to support the armies of our enemies, who raise the cotton from which, if at all, our foes must get the sinews of war — who but slaves? The system of American Slavery does not deserve the forbearance and sacrifices we are practising in its favor. On my conscience, I believe we are acting like fools in this whole matter.

To you, merchants and tax-payers — to you, citizens, whose brothers and sons are taking daily risks at the cannon's mouth, it is not merely a question how this rebellion may be suppressed, but how it may be suppressed in the most speedy, economical, and effectual manner. If you fail to say "Yes" to this with all your hearts — then let me tell you that after all your sacrifices you will still have the great thing to do. All your costly make-shifts to spare your enemies and the assassins of your country will come to nothing. Slavery or the Republic must die. Let the people understand it — Slavery or the Republic must die. The sooner the lesson is learned the better. God Almighty will crowd us with reverses on reverses and almost kill us with mortification and blood-shedding, till we are ready to part with the monster that defies alike God and man. ✸

1. This refers to the Kohinoor diamond, the most famous jewel in the world. It was said that whoever owned it could rule the world.

perity was our boast and our idol, and in our folly we did not admit, even to ourselves, the possibility of its interruption. We had come to measure everything, even the Union itself, by the standard of commercial value.

If our boastful spirit, in reference to our national prosperity, excited the ridicule of Europe, the promptness with which the Northern States have risen to the level of the emergency will now command its respect. The energy displayed by them in defence of the Constitution, and in sustaining the Union, will serve to demonstrate that our patriotism has not been destroyed by our lust of gain, and that the martial spirit of the nation was not dead, but sleeping.

This war, melancholy as its presence may be, will educate our people in the science of arms, will revive and invigorate that martial spirit which is essential to a great nation, but which was in danger of becoming extinct in the welling prosperity of long-continued peace. While it will demonstrate the power, it will strengthen the bands of the Union, and give increased stability to Republican institutions. The teachings of the present will make us wise in the future. While our material prosperity will not be neglected, there will be a careful watch set against treason, and if it shall ever again venture into the daylight, a strong and mailed hand will be ready to strike it down. The experience in arms gained in this war by intelligent citizens from every part of the country, will keep alive military organizations that will be able to send into the field an Army respectable both in numbers and discipline, whenever, the exigencies of the times shall demand it.

Aside from these considerations, the business prosperity of the country will by no means suffer to the extent that the fears of some have led them to apprehend. The necessity for a foreign loan will add some two hundred millions or more in coin to the available capital of the nation. The expenses of the war are to be paid out at home. The millions thus expended will permeate all the channels of circulation. The daily average of half a million of expenditure will drift for a long while on the currents of trade before falling into the great reservoirs of capital. The genius of the American people is already accommodating itself to the new order of things. We can feel that we have already touched bottom in reference to the commercial evils of this war. And that, whether its duration shall be long or short, the course of trade will hereafter be upward. The business of the country, though to some extent changed, will revive, and if our business men will give heed to the lessons of economy inculcated by the occasion, they will enjoy a season of prosperity, as the result of the war, very different from that which their fears predicted. ✹

A BENEFIT OF DIRECT TAXATION.

AUGUST 9

There is one advantage that the nation will derive from the system of direct taxation soon to be inaugurated,[1] that should go far to reconcile all good citizens to its inconveniences and its burdens. That is, the economy it will in the end, insure in the expenditures, and the honesty in the disbursements of the Government.

We cannot shut our eyes to the fact, that corruption and profligacy of the most alarming character and extent have, for many years past, disgraced the legislation of the country and the administration of our State and National Governments. This evil has increased with a rapidity that was frightful, and not a few of our most thoughtful Republicans have been learning to dread lest public virtue should, in a few years, be so thoroughly overthrown, that the continuance of the Government in form and vigor would be impossible. The fear was, not that the Government would be overthrown, but that it would rot down.

The chief cause of the public corruption and official degeneracy was undoubtedly the great prosperity of the people, the cheapness of our Government, and the consequent indifference of the people to the riotings and plunderings of their public servants. The National Government has been collecting and expending annually for nearly twenty years an average of say seventy millions of dollars a year. Scarcely a dollar of this vast sum could be said to be drawn directly from the pockets of the people.[2] When, therefore, Texas Indemnity bills, and Gardner frauds, and Fort Snelling swindles were perpetrated,[3] and the Government mulcted of perhaps ten millions a year, or nearly one-sixth of the whole amount of revenue yearly raised through the downright villainy of Congressional and Governmental agents, there was no citizen that felt sufficiently personally aggrieved to demand the punishment of the offenders and to prosecute with the interest and earnestness necessary to procure conviction.

The public feeling will become different now. The burdens of Government will begin to be felt, which has never been the case before. When every man in the community — every man in the United States — finds he must put his hands into his pocket and draw out a portion of his hard-earned gold and silver to deliver to a Government agent, he will not be indifferent any longer as to how that money goes. If it is stolen by the Collector, or squandered by Congress through lobby legislation, or sequestered by Cabinet officers through nepotism in contracts, the people who have paid will know it, and they will know how to punish.

It is remarkable, the contrast that exists between the punishment of public defaulters in England and France, or any Government in Europe, and in the United States. In any of the former, the convicted defaulters (and all defaulters are convicted if caught) go to the dungeons, chains and prison-hulks for life, and draw ignominy on themselves and families. In the United States no defaulter is convicted. Distinguished friends screen him in fashionable hotels, and dismiss him to Cuba, or some other foreign land. Or if his stealings be large enough, he may safely stay at home, buy his discharge through a flaw in the law, as [John B.] FLOYD[4] did; and ☞

1. In July 1861, Congress passed an act that levied a tax of 3 percent on all incomes over $800 per year. It was the first income tax in American history.
2. Virtually all federal revenues before the Civil War derived from duties levied on imports. Since the tariffs were intended to protect domestic industry rather than to generate revenue, the income often exceeded what the government could easily spend. Hence The Times's argument that this led to corruption.
3. These all refer to scandals involving government funds in the antebellum years.
4. John B. Floyd (1806–1863) had been President Buchanan's secretary of war. In December 1860, on ascertaining that Floyd had paid out large sums to government contractors in anticipation of their earnings, Buchanan requested his resignation. Floyd was indicted for malfeasance in office, but the indictment was overturned on technical grounds.

then he feted and feasted in the capitals of the country, as among the first gentlemen of the times. Defaulting is not stealing in the estimation of American society. It will be different when the money stolen is first taken directly out of the people's pockets. And the correction of the standard of morality in this regard will be worth many millions of dollars yearly to the public Treasury, and more than can be expressed in dollars to the general cause of honesty and virtue; for it is notorious that the pernicious example of unpunished political embezzlements has affected and greatly impaired the safety of all commercial transactions in the United States. ✷

THE ADMINISTRATION AND THE FUGITIVE SLAVE LAW.

SEPTEMBER 2

Some time since Marshal MCDOWELL (U.S. Marshal for Kansas,) addressed a letter to the U.S. Attorney General, stating that he did not deem it his duty to return fugitives to Missouri, until she became more loyal, and asking for advice on the subject. The following reply we find in the Leavenworth Times:

ATTORNEY-GENERAL's OFFICE, JULY 23, 1861.
J. L. McDowell, U.S. Marshal, Kansas:
SIR: Your letter of the 11th of July, received 19th, (under the frank of Senator [Joseph] LANE, of Kansas,) asks advice upon the question whether or no you should give your official services in the execution of the Fugitive Slave law.

It is the President's constitutional duty to "take care that the laws be faithfully executed." That means all the laws. He has no right to discriminate — no right to execute the laws he likes, and leave unexecuted those he dislikes. And, of course you and I, his subordinates, can have no wider latitude of discretion than he has. Missouri is a State in the Union. The insurrectionary disorder in Missouri are but individual crimes, and do not change the legal status of the State, nor change its rights and obligations as a member of the Union.

A refusal, by a ministerial officer, to execute any law, which properly belongs to his office, is official misdemeanor, of which I do not doubt the President would take notice. Very respectfully,

EDWARD BATES[1] ✷

1. Edward Bates of Missouri (1793–1869) was Lincoln's attorney general.

IMPORTANT FROM MISSOURI.
PROCLAMATION OF GEN. FREMONT

ST. LOUIS, SATURDAY, AUG. 31

The following proclamation was issued this morning:

HEAD-QUARTERS OF THE WESTERN DEPARTMENT, ST. LOUIS, AUG. 31
Circumstances, in my judgment, of sufficient urgency, render it necessary that the Commanding General of this Department should assume the administrative powers of the State. Its disorganized condition, the helplessness of the civil authority, the total insecurity of life, and the devastation of property by bands of murderers and marauders, who infest nearly every county in the State, and avail themselves of the public misfortunes and the vicinity of a hostile force to gratify private and neighborhood vengeance, and who find an enemy wherever they find plunder, finally demand the severest measures to repress the daily increasing crimes and outrages which are driving off the inhabitants and ruining the State.

In this condition the public safety and the success of our arms require unity of purpose, without let or hindrance, to the prompt administration of affairs.

In order, therefore, to suppress disorders, to maintain, as far as now practicable, the public peace, and to give security and protection to the persons and property of loyal citizens, I do hereby extend and declare established martial law through-

Major General John C. Frémont, U.S.A.

SEPTEMBER 2

out the State of Missouri. The lines of the Army of occupation in this State are for the present declared to extend from Leavenworth, by way of the posts of Jefferson City, Rolla, and Ironton, to Cape Girardeau, on the Mississippi River. All persons who shall be taken with arms in their hands, within these lines, shall be tried by Court Martial, and, if found guilty, will be shot. The property, real and personal, of all persons in the State of Missouri, who shall take up arms against the United States, or who shall be directly proven to have taken active part with their enemies in the field, is declared to be confiscated to the public use, and their slaves, if any they have, are hereby declared free men.

All persons who shall be proven to have destroyed, after the publication of this order, railroad tracks, bridges or telegraphs, shall suffer the extreme penalty of the law.

All persons engaged in treasonable correspondence, in giving or procuring aid to the enemies of the United States, in disturbing the public tranquillity by creating and circulating false reports or incendiary documents, are in their own interest warned that they are exposing themselves.

All persons who have been led away from their allegiance are required to return to their homes forthwith; any such absence without sufficient cause will be held to be presumptive evidence against them.

The object of this declaration is to place in the hands of the military authorities the power to give instantaneous effect to existing laws, and to supply such deficiencies as the conditions of war demand. But it is not intended to suspend the ordinary tribunals of the country, where the law will be administered by the civil officers in the usual manner and with their customary authority, while the same can be peaceably exercised.

The Commanding-General will labor vigilantly for the public welfare, and in his efforts for their safety hopes to obtain not only the acquiescence, but the active support of the people of the country.

(SIGNED) J.C. FREMONT,
MAJOR-GENERAL COMMANDING. ✷

SLAVERY AND THE WAR —
A BLOW THAT WILL BE FELT.

SEPTEMBER 2

There is no victory so complete as that which solves a great political dilemma, which has rested like a pall upon the public mind, destroying all life and spirit, paralyzing all enterprise and action, and producing all the consequences of a disastrous defeat. It is a happy stroke of genius that can overstep the bounds of tradition, or conventional rule, and show a clear path in a direction supposed to be set with insuperable difficulties. Such is the service rendered the nation by Gen. FREMONT's proclamation, placing Missouri under martial law and visiting upon traitors, the penalties due to treason, with all the celerity of military dispatch. The traitor is to be divested of property, as well as life; and further, a blow is struck where it has long been seen it might fall, upon the institution which is both the cause and support of the rebellion. Self-preservation renders no other course as longer possible. If we would save ourselves, we must take from treason every weapon by which it can strike the deadly blow. We must maintain the rights of loyal men intact, but take from those in arms against us the means of keeping them in the field.

It has long been the boast of the South, in contrasting its strength with that of the North, that its whole white population could be made available for the war, for the reason that all its industries were carried on by the slaves, in peace as well as war; while those of the North rested upon the very men, who in case of hostilities must be sent into the field. For the North, consequently, to fight, would be the destruction of all its material interests; for the South, only a pleasant pastime for hundreds of thousands of men, who, without war, would have no occupation. The South was another Sparta, the Helots of which, a degraded caste, performed all the useful labor, leaving to the privileged one only the honorable occupation of arms. The vast host which the South has put into the field, has, to a great extent, made good these words. With the enemy at our throat, we must strike from under him the prop upon which his strength rests. It is our duty to save every life, and every dollar of expense in our power. By seeking to put down the rebellion only by meeting the enemy in the open field, is uselessly to sac-

rifice hundreds of thousands of lives, and hundreds, if not thousands of millions of money, and perhaps, after all, accept a disastrous defeat as the result.

In this crisis Gen. FREMONT has sounded the key-note of the campaign that will be echoed wherever we have a soldier in arms. He has taken a step which cannot fail to produce a very marked effect throughout the South. He has declared that every slave who may be employed or permitted by his master to aid in the rebellion against the United States, shall be free. This, it will be seen, is no general act of emancipation. It has nothing to do with that general crusade against Slavery which many have urged as the proper means of carrying on the war. It simply confiscates the property of rebels employed against the Government. It does not touch the slaves of loyal citizens, nor affect the institution in any way, except as those responsible for it may choose to identify its fate with that of the rebellion itself. But just so far as Slavery actively supports the rebellion must it become the object of attack. Up to the present time nothing can be more marked than the forbearance of the Government towards Slavery. While it has from the beginning seemed certain that, if the South persist in war, Slavery must inevitably perish in its progress, the Government has carefully avoided everything which looked towards hostility against the institution itself. The constitutional rights of the slaveholder have been as scrupulously regarded, and as carefully protected, as if he had not repudiated the Constitution, and was not making war

upon the Government which gives him this protection.

This course of things is to be changed. Hereafter Slavery will not be allowed to stand in the way of a vigorous prosecution of the war. If slaves are employed against the Government, their masters will thereby lose all claim to their services. The fact of their being so employed will suffice to set them free.

It is impossible to avoid seeing that this proclamation of Gen. FREMONT, carrying into effect the law of Congress, will be understood at the South to have a much broader application. The rebels will denounce it as an act of wholesale emancipation, and the slaves will thus be taught to regard it in the same light. FREMONT's name, it will be remembered, was widely connected in their minds, in 1856, with the expectation of immediate freedom,[1] and this act will revive all the passions and aspirations which were then aroused. It is useless to speculate upon the tremendous results to which such an impression may give rise. But it is very clear that FREMONT's proclamation is, up to this time, by far the most important event of the war. ✪

1. John C. Fremont (1813–1890) had been the Republican candidate for President in 1856 on a platform that advocated the eventual eradication of slavery.

SPECIAL DISPATCH FROM WASHINGTON.

SEPTEMBER 13

WASHINGTON, THURSDAY, SEPT. 12

There is much feeling here among leading men, caused by the action of Gen. McCLELLAN in ordering the return of fugitive slaves, or, rather, their arrest in camps and imprisonment in jail to await the claim of their masters. This is in contravention of the spirit of the letter addressed by the Secretary of War to Gen.

BUTLER, for it constitutes our troops but an army of negro catchers. It is directly in contradiction to the letter of FREMONT's proclamation, which has been unanimously accepted by the people of the loyal States as the true interpretation of our relation to the slaveholders in rebellion against the Government.... ✪

RUMOR THAT GENERAL FREMONT IS TO BE SUPERSEDED.

SEPTEMBER 14

We learn that a rumor was prevalent in Washington yesterday that Gen. FREMONT is to be superseded in his command and that Quartermaster-General [Montgomery] MEIGS is to take his place.

We have also what we deem good authority for saying that this rumor, unlike many others, is founded in fact; and that Mr. [Francis P.] BLAIR, at whose earnest recommendation Gen. FREMONT was placed where he is, accompanied Gen. MEIGS, in order to explain to Gen. FREMONT the reasons and the necessity for the step.

These reasons, we think it will be found, are that Gen. FREMONT exceeded his authority by the proclamations he issued — that being the main reason — and that he has in other respects acted in important matters not only without consulting the Government, but in contravention of its orders and practice.

(Notwithstanding the apparent positiveness of this statement we are informed, by telegraph from Washington, that Mrs. FREMONT left there yesterday morning for St. Louis with assurances that the General should not be interfered with. — ED. TIMES.)[1] ✳

1. Jesse Benton Fremont (1824–1902) traveled to Washington and met with President Lincoln to urge him to support her husband. The meeting was a disaster and Mrs. Fremont succeeded only in angering the President — something that was not easy to do. Lincoln's decision to remove Fremont stood.

LINCOLN—"I'm sorry to have to drop you, Sambo, but this concern won't carry us both!"

A period cartoon criticizes President Lincoln's decision to revoke Frémont's emancipation order.

WHAT WE ARE FIGHTING FOR.

SEPTEMBER 17

In his appeal to the people for means to carry on this war, Secretary CHASE[1] declares that "the National Government, compelled by a guilty conspiracy culminating in a causeless insurrection, is engaged in a war for the security of liberty, for the supremacy of the law, for the defence of the Union and for the maintenance of popular institutions."

This is a broad and sweeping statement. If true to its full extent, it affords a full and complete justification of the war. Let us look at the particulars of it a little.

"Compelled by a guilty conspiracy." Is not that true? How long the Government bore with those who would overthrow it! How earnestly it sought to do nothing which should be any excuse for passion's usurping the sway over reason, choosing in repeated instances to risk the greatest injury, and to allow its enemies the greatest advantage, in order that its good intentions might be known! But all forbearance was but the incentive to further aggression, until the guns of Charleston harbor — which, like that famous shot on Concord Green, will be "heard round the world," but with how different a voice — until the marshaling of troops and the boastful threat of burning Washington "compelled" the Government to defend itself. That this was the result of a conspiracy all know — a conspiracy the growth of years, as has been openly avowed by the conspirators, and carried on by fraud, theft, desertion, perjury and treachery, the conspirators' weapons. And if the purpose of the war is as stated by Mr. CHASE, who can estimate the guilt of the conspirators who, for such purposes, have desolated so many homes, destroyed so many lives, brought upon our land such wide-spread devastation, and upon the hearts and hopes of all friends of humanity everywhere, such chilling fear and anxious doubt?

Was the insurrection in which that conspiracy culminated "causeless?" Their own leaders bearing witness, it was so. There was no oppression at the hands of the Government which they sought to overthrow. Its dealings with them were only beneficent. We hear them claim that they are but sustaining the right of the people to self-government. But if they succeed, they will only be where they were before. They had always governed themselves as much as is possible, where the rule that the majority shall govern is carried out. If they succeed in their attempt, they can do no more than that, and will in all human probability do far less. For if there are any lessons to be drawn from history, it is plainly to be seen that the tendencies of the Southern States are not towards self-government but towards a despotism.

And, if it is said that the insurrection was necessary for the protection of Slavery, let the increasing numbers of "contrabands" at Fortress Munroe, and the sound of FRE-MONT's Proclamation, as it echoes through Missouri and through Kentucky, and thence downward to the Gulf, answer that the insurrection is Slavery's death-blow. "Causeless!" must be the verdict of history upon this insurrection; as causeless as the inroad of any burglar into an unprotected house, whose servants have given him, by their aid, his only chances of success; causeless as any scheme which the ambition of man, set on fire of hell, has ever embarked in.

And the purposes of the war. Is it a war "for the security of liberty?" How can it but be such, when we fight to sustain a Constitution whose purpose is "to secure the blessings of liberty;" while the rebels fight to establish one, of which, as they themselves have said, Slavery is the corner-stone. We have believed as our fathers believed, that liberty was best secured by placing the Government in the hands of rulers chosen by the people. Their ruler has been appointed by a few delegates from conventions, chosen for no such object. We believe that the extension of the right of suffrage to all is one of the safeguards of liberty. They loudly advocate its restriction. We believe that the right of the majority to govern is essential. They scoff at the idea of being governed by a "vulgar Yankee majority," and boldly advance the right of the minority to rule. Yes! Mr. SEWARD was right when he declared that Liberty is always in the Union, and clear though it was to his farseeing mind when he stated it, that it was so, he could hardly have anticipated that so short a time would bring so many proofs of its truth as the present state of facts, and the tendencies of the future throughout the rebellious States now plainly exhibit.

We fight "for the supremacy of the law." If ever there was a violation of all law, of

Secretary of the Treasury Salmon P. Chase.

statute law and common law, of the laws of honesty and common sense, this insurrection is such an one. And if there were no other reason for putting it down, we, who claim to be a law-abiding people, should be earnest to put it down so thoroughly, and with so stern a punishment, that all men should learn, as they never learned before, that law is supreme, and that that very voice which calls upon us not to yield obedience to a human law which would compel us to wrong doing, calls upon us as loudly, and with as terrible sanctions, to yield to it implicit obedience in every other case.

We fight "for the defence of the Union" — that Union with which all our national associations are entwined — which has protected us from foreign foes upon our own soil, and when we went abroad — whose name and flag have been the symbol of hope to the oppressed nationalities of the world — whose overthrow would send a throb of grief to the heart of every friend of human progress, and bring a shout of triumph from the lips of every tool of despotism, the world over — that Union whose destruction is the overthrow of peace among us, and brings us to a period of standing armies and large navies, and incessant preparation for only another war with the same States, after we have allowed them to strengthen themselves by sea and land, at home and abroad; for that

Union we are called upon to give our means. And if we gave them all, the sacrifice would be little, so that our children, for whom we love to labor and to save, should be spared from such long-enduring trouble and terror.

And, lastly, we seek "the maintenance of popular institutions." We have always claimed that such institutions were the best for man; that they furnished more liberty, more scope for individual, and thus for national development and strength, than any others. But if they have no self-sustaining power — if they must yield to the first attack of an internal enemy — if they furnish us a Government only so long as we allow a selfish and ambitious privileged class to carry it on, then is their name but a delusion and a snare, and the sooner we give them up, and return to that which answered for the darker ages of the world, the better. See how earnestly our struggle is watched by those who have always hated us because of these claims of ours, and because we could point to our own growth as proof of their justice. See how quick they are to point out our weaknesses and to rejoice over our calamities, and to use our present disturbed state, which is the result, not of our popular institutions, but of that element which was not popular in them, as an argument against those who strive for liberty elsewhere. Fancy their malignant joy, if the insurrection is successful, and the United States, instead of being at liberty to lend a helping hand to the oppressed abroad, is thenceforth incessantly watched and worried by a malignant foe at her own door. Fancy their terror an dismay, and the joy of the friends of liberty, when our flag shall again in triumph "float o'er the free from the Gulf to the main," and insurrection and treason shall have met with their deserved punishment.

If there were no other inducement for us, it would call forth our utmost exertions to give those friends that joy, and to deprive those foes of that triumphant "I told you so."

Yes! Mr. CHASE has well characterized the war; and every day's experience shows that his call upon the people will be answered as it deserves. ⊛

1. Salmon P. Chase (1808–1873) was secretary of the treasury in Lincoln's cabinet and a strong anti-slavery Republican.

GENERAL FREMONT'S COLUMN.

ARREST OF FRANK BLAIR — PROCLAMATION BY GENERAL FREMONT.

SEPTEMBER 18

Col. F. P. BLAIR. Jr.,[1] was ordered yesterday, by the Provost-Marshal, to report himself under arrest on a general charge of using disrespectful language, when attending superior officers. With reference to the removal of Gen. FREMONT, the Democrat, this morning, holds the following language:

"The removal of Gen. FREMONT, we do not think, has been seriously considered by the Administration. Complaints have undoubtedly been made against him, and possibly charges preferred, which of course will be duly and properly investigated, but those proceedings we are now satisfied have never looked to a result so serious as his removal from this Department. His extraordinary energy and efficiency are too highly appreciated by the Government, and the man and his measures are too deeply seated in the affections of the people of the loyal States to admit the probabilities of any such event."

The Republican learns that Col. [Humphrey] MARSHALL, when at Lexington, a few days ago, took possession of a quantity of property belonging to the State, including the books, papers and great seal of the State, which CLAIBORNE JACKSON took from Jefferson City.[2] After the defeat of the State forces at Booneville by Gen. [Nathaniel] LYON, JACKSON publicly announced his intention to establish the capital at Lexington, claiming that he had full authority to do so. It may be that this programme has not been relinquished, and the present movement of [Confederate] Gen. [Sterling] PRICE,[3] who doubtless is now in possession of Lexington, is with the view of planting the seat of Government there.

Whether the deposed Legislature, which adjourned in May last, to meet again to-day, will be ready to proceed to business, cannot be now ascertained.

Postmaster-General BLAIR and Quartermaster-General MEIGS left for Washington this morning.

It is understood that the precise charge on which Col. BLAIR was arrested is insubordination in communicating, while a military officer, with the authorities at Washington; making complaints against and using disrespectful language towards Gen. FREMONT, with a view of effecting his removal. It is stated that letters written by Col. BLAIR are now in possession of Gen. FREMONT…. ◉

1. Francis P. (Frank) Blair, Jr. (1821–1875) was a former member of Congress from Missouri and the brother of Montgomery Blair, Lincoln's postmaster general. Fremont and Blair were political rivals, and Fremont blamed Blair for contributing to the ill feeling toward him in Washington.
2. Claiborne Jackson (1806–1862) was governor of Missouri. Siding with the Confederacy, he was in effect a governor in exile after the Union occupied the state.
3. Sterling Price (1809–1867) had opposed secession in Missouri, but was outraged when Union forces seized Camp Jackson in St. Louis, and he threw in his lot with the Confederacy. Claiborne Jackson made him a major general of volunteers.

Francis P. Blair, photographed when he was a major general.

GEN. McCLELLAN AND THE ARMY OF THE POTOMAC.

OCTOBER 22
WASHINGTON, FRIDAY, OCT. 18
CORRESPONDENCE OF THE NEW-YORK TIMES.

No man ever rose more suddenly into the front rank of eminent public characters than the young Commander of the Army of the Potomac. Six months ago, the name of McCLELLAN was only known to army officers, or to the men of business with whom he had been brought in contact, as President of a Western Railroad. To-day all eyes are turned toward him, either expressive of hope and confidence in his genius, courage and conduct, or of envy and ill-boding prophecy. When there seemed to be no especial need for his services to the country, he retired from the profession of arms, to which he had been educated, and in which, before he was thirty years of age, he had scarcely a peer, as regards accomplishments. But when the tocsin of rebellion was sounded, he was among the first to tender his services to the Government, which at once recognized his merit by placing him in a high command. His bold and brilliant achievements in Western Virginia justified the confidence reposed in him; and, after the mortifying defeat at Bull Run, he was called, as much by the acclamations of the people as by the Administration, to take the command of the Army of the Potomac. It need not be repeated here how thoroughly that army was disorganized, how totally disqualified it was for offensive operations, and how barely adequate it was to a defence of the Capital against a bold and vigorous assault of the rebel enemy. The great majority of the troops had been called into service for three months, and their term of service had nearly expired. The whole business of organization and training had therefore to be gone over again, and, in a word, a new army, composed of fresh volunteers, had to be substituted for that which had been repulsed and routed in July. To do this requires time. It cannot be done in a week or a month. It required several weeks to raise the troops and bring them here, and certainly two weeks are not too long to accustom farmers and mechanics to use the weapons of war with dexterity, to move in masses, on foot or on horseback, at the word of command; to acquire the habit of mind which enables the soldier to feel strong in the consciousness that he is only a part of a great engine, and that fidelity to his duty is his best guaranty of safety.

A correspondent of the TIMES alluded the other day to the public impatience with the cautious policy pursued by Gen. MCCLELLAN, and to the blame which begins to be laid to his door. His enemies are taking advantage of these complaints, and it begins to be whispered about Washington that a conspiracy has been formed against him, looking to his displacement and supercedure. It is true that the conspirators are not the men to bring forward a charge of inaction, or aversion to offensive operations against the enemy—because it so happens that the "rascally virtue," prudence, is a distinguishing characteristic of MCCLELLAN's enemies. But they nevertheless foster the spirit of complaint, and throw in the ingredients of fault-finding with the personnel of his military household. It is proper to notice some of these insinuations.... ✦

THAT'S WHAT'S THE TROUBLE WITH JOHN C.

MRS. COLUMBIA. "Tell me, DOCTOR, what is the *matter* with him? Do you think his Brain is affected?"

DOCTOR JONATHAN. "Oh! no, my dear MADAM; it's only a rather aggravated case of *Sore Head!*"

Political cartoon shows General Fremont as a child clutching an African-American doll, but encumbered by the unseen "Sore Head" President.

WHY THE WAR SHOULD BE AT ONCE ENDED.

OCTOBER 23

So long as the insurrection of the South seemed a spiteful rebellion against the results of a particular election we were compelled to regard it as utterly unjustifiable. If it meant only, as has been asserted, "bullet" against "ballot," we should look upon it as a wicked and treasonable act; for never could the North be charged, notwithstanding its commercial bias, with a want of consideration for the institutions of the South. If, again, the question could be argued on pure grounds of expediency, we should here also, though not so decidedly, pronounce against the resolution taken by the South to divorce itself from the North. But the actual case is very different. The last twelve months have shown that Northerners and Southerners are as irreconcilable as Greeks and Turks, or Germans and Magyars. This war will but intensify and perpetuate animosities which the very nature of things had long ago created. "Sectional" antipathies have proved as stubborn as national antipathies. They could not be assuaged by compromise, and they will assuredly not

be abolished by conquest. The armies of the North may overpower the armies of the South, but South and North can never be expected to amalgamate again. It is for this reason, and because territories so prodigious as those of the Southern States can never be retained by armed occupation, that we think the policy of the Federal Government wrong. If the whole case of the war is to be analyzed, we must needs say the Northerners have the right on their side, for the Southerners have destroyed, without provocation, a mighty political fabric, and have impaired the glory and strength of the great American Republic. But, as they have chosen to do this, as they have shown themselves hitherto no less powerful than their antagonists, as the decision of so large a population cannot be contemned, and as we cannot persuade ourselves that a genuine peace is likely to spring from protracted war, we should rejoice to see the pacification of America promoted by other means. ✦

THE FREMONT TROUBLE.

OCTOBER 25

The Washington correspondent of the Philadelphia Press writes under date of Oct. 20:

"It seems to be an established fact that Gen. FREMONT is really to be removed. The charges against him were forwarded to the President by the friends of Mr. [Francis] BLAIR [Jr.]. It is reported that he has involved the Government in unnecessary expenditures to the amount of nearly ten millions of dollars; that he gave to his California friends contracts for fabulous sums without requiring any security whatever; that he denied the Government officers interviews with him, unless it particularly suited him; that he assumed supreme powers which were not delegated to him; that he did not obey the instructions of the Government unless they met his views. The friends of Gen. FREMONT here say, in unmistakable language, that he has been unfairly dealt with; that he has been villainously persecuted, because some members of the Cabinet are jealous of his popularity; and that, when an investigation takes place, he will make these things manifest, and show a cleaner record than any other officer of his rank in the service." ✦

THE BATTLE AT EDWARDS' FERRY.
FULL DESCRIPTION OF THE ENGAGEMENT.
REPULSE OF THE UNION FORCES.

FROM OUR SPECIAL CORRESPONDENT.
EDWARDS' FERRY[1] SUNDAY — 6 P.M, OCTOBER 20

OCTOBER 25

The Union troops have commenced shelling the rebels on the Virginia shore across the river, whether merely to drive them out or as preliminary to an advance, we shall probably known in the morning. As I intend to make my letter, as far as possible, a journal from hour to hour of what actually takes place under my own observation, I shall not attempt to anticipate movements, but only record what I see and hear. The firing commenced at 4:35 this afternoon, from VAN ALLEN's Battery of two Parrott guns — 12-pounders — the shells going well over to the Virginia side, to the north of Goose Creek. Their explosion is very distinctly heard. Seven shells have been thrown within ten minutes, without eliciting any response from our friends across the water. Gen. [Charles] STONE is directing the movement. The tenth and eleventh shells fired were long range, the explosion not being heard for ten seconds. The next two exploded in five. The direction given to the shells is varied so as if possible to find out the location of the rebels, who are supposed to be concealed in a thick wood to the southwest, on the hill, and apparently a mile from the mouth of Goose Creek. The fourteenth founded like a solid shot, and the three following shells, which made a loud explosion, brought no answering shot from the rebels.

At five minutes to 5 P.M. the battery in charge of Lieut. FRINK, situated in a field to the southeast and some quarter of a mile from the Ferry, also opened with shell, the two batteries keeping up the fire with rapidity, each missile exploding beautifully. Just as the sun is going down, the First Minnesota and Second New-York came down over the hill, and take the road to the Ferry. The sun sets gloriously, reflecting his rays from the thousands of bayonets which line the road. The firing is renewed again from both VAN ALLEN's and FRINK's Batteries. The troops are marching to the river with the intention either of crossing or of working a feint to do so, with a view of trying what effect the movement may have upon the enemy.

The air is perfectly still, and the close of this pleasant Sabbath is impressively calm and beautiful. The view of the Virginia hills from where I stand, near the battery, is almost enchanting. The echo of each report of our guns is heard from the opposite hills as distinctly as the report itself, and the explosion of each shell makes the third distinct report caused by each discharge. Something which resembles the sound of a drum-corps is distinctly heard from the Virginia side. The troops are drawn up along the bank in open order, and the order is now again passed along the lines to "Fall in." There goes a boat-load of troops across the river, which looks like a real movement.

The two companies, after landing, were recalled, but at 12 o'clock three regiments crossed over, encamping on the Virginia side. This was evidently designed as the opening of the campaign in Upper Virginia, and to-morrow, no doubt, the whole force encamped near here will be thrown over. There is every prospect of lively, I hope not of disastrous, times. The rebels will not do anything we wish them to. I now proceed to the camp near the Monocacy, to observe movements.

MONDAY MORNING.

The engagement has been renewed this morning. At daylight, portions of the Massachusetts Twentieth, Col. [William R.] LEE, and the Massachusetts Fifteenth, Col. [Charles P.] DEVENS, not over 300 in all, crossed over three-quarters of a mile below Conrad's Ferry. They crossed the island [Harrison's Island], which at this point is about 150 yards wide, and three miles in its extreme length. These two companies — viz., I and D, commanded respectively by Captains BARTLETT and CROWINGSHIELD — met with no opposition on landing, and pushed on until they had reached the open space. This company (H, of the Fifteenth Regiment) went ahead as skirmishers, and were met in an open field by a company of 70 rebels, who fired the first volley, wounding ten and taking two prisoners. The company charged on them, and drove them back, but were in return driven back by a large cavalry force, besides a Mississippi rifle company.

This ended the contest for the morning;

but a straggling fire was kept up on both sides until 1:30 P.M. when the rebels renewed the engagement with great fury. They attacked in front and on the right flank. At this time Gen. [Edward D.] BAKER's Brigade was arriving. They consisted chiefly of the Philadelphia Zouaves, under command of Col. [De Witt Clinton] BAXTER.

Col. [actually Captain Thomas] VAUGHAN, of the Rhode Island [Battery B], had also arrived, and, with the greatest difficulty, succeeded in getting one of his six-pounder guns up the ascent, being obliged first to dismount the gun. This piece, with the two mountain howitzers belonging to the Twentieth Massachusetts, were all the heavy guns on the field. The fire was kept up from the right flank and front with great activity, the rebels raining a perfect storm of balls upon the Union forces. The Twentieth, although mostly raw recruits, stood the enemy's fire like veterans. They ran up to the brow of the hill, delivered their fire, and only fell back to reload and repeat. This continued until 5 1/2 P.M., the Union forces maintaining their position steadily against the deadly, ranking cross-fire from the front and left of the woods.

At this juncture Gen. BAKER, who had dismounted from his horse, and was advancing at the head of his command, coolly, but, resolutely encouraging his men, received a ball through his head, killing him instantly.[3] The General's blood but pattered Capt. CROWNINGSHIELD, who stood beside him at the moment. He never spoke. His body was immediately taken to the rear by his men, who freely wept at their loss. He was placed in a scow, and transported to the island, and thence to the Maryland shore. His remains were sent to Edward's Ferry, and thence to Poolsville, is horse, which had been left standing, was after wards shot. A small canvas satchell, containing his papers, I saw in the hands of a young man to whom they were delivered shortly before he fell.

This was the turning point of the battle. The rebels were five to one of the Union force, and the latter were finally ordered to leave the field. The retreat was made after the Bull Run pattern, with slight improvements, the men rolling, sliding, and almost turning summersaults down hill, to escape the galling fire which now assailed them from all points. The rebels were constantly reinforced, screaming like furies at each onset. Before retreating they threw the six-pounder down the hill into the river. The howitzers were left on the field, and fell into the enemy's hands.

An Illustrated London News woodcut depicting a scene from the Battle of Ball's Bluff.

The Fifteenth and Twentieth Massachusetts Regiments suffered very severely, losing a large part of their numbers in killed and wounded.

The Tammany Regiment[4] covered itself with glory. Capt. [Timothy] O'MEARA often rallied his command, throwing defiance into the very teeth of the enemy, and showing the rebels that he could scream equal to the worst of them. Capt. O'MEARA took charge of the landing, and refused to let any but wounded men enter the boat, ordering the sound troops to go back and pepper the rebels. His conduct was very gallant throughout, evincing a true and lofty courage. Lieut. [Nathaniel] MESSER took command of the scow, and continued to ferry over the wounded, who poured down the hill. Several times the rebels fired upon him as he was crossing with the wounded men. The fourth boat-load was capsized, by the men rushing into it in too great numbers, and the whole party, about fifty in number, well and wounded, were precipitated into the stream. Ten of the party, at least, were drowned. A great many tried to swim the river, and sank from exhaustion. One half of those who are missing were drowned in this manner. It is

not yet known how many of our men have fallen into their hands. The destruction of life has been far greater, in proportion to the numbers engaged, than at Bull Run....

I arrived at the ferry, and crossed over shortly after 3 o'clock P.M. Only three scows were in use, carrying say fifty men each, and occupying at least thirty minutes in getting each load over! I met wounded men returning in their comrades' arms, and bleeding from feet, legs, chest, head, arms, and every other description of wounds. I assisted in conveying them to a comfortable place in a large shed near the river, and proceeded toward the scene of action. Soon I reached an old farm-house, which was being used us an hospital. Groups of soldiers and persons not in uniform were crouching behind a corn-crib, built of logs, to shelter themselves from the bullets, which were now singing fearful music over our heads. The aim appeared to be at the house containing our wounded. In the yard, and covering its whole space, lay the wounded, dead and dying, in every stage of mutilation. The house contained two rooms, which were also full to repletion. Not a square foot of space remained unoccupied by the bleed-

ing, wounded congregation. I took off my coat, and for half an hour rendered such assistance as an amateur surgeon could render. There was, as usual, a plentiful lack of surgical assistance, twenty poor fellows calling for aid, where only one or two could be attended to.

It was dark before the conflict closed, and I then recrossed the river and worked until this hour, (7 A.M. Tuesday morning,) in transporting the wounded in boats and litters to places of safety. I took my horse and rode to Edwards' Ferry, where I obtained a canal boat, in which a large quantity of hay was placed for the, comfort of the wounded. I reached the Ferry, and by 2 o'clock this morning we had about forty poor wounded soldiers on board, and quietly proceeding to the Ferry. Some fifty wounded were taken to a barn half a mile from the line of the canal. A large number who could not be removed remained at the farm-house on the island, and multitudes were left dead and dying on the bank of the Old Dominion, their groans waking mournful echoes from the hills and woods. The officers have suffered severely. There is no way of ascertaining the actual number of casualties.[5] ☞

STATEMENT OF LIEUT. MESSER.

Lieut. MESSER, of Company D, Twentieth Massachusetts Regiment, who was among the first to gain a position on the Virginia side, about 4 o'clock A.M., gives me the following description of the localities. The landing, which was made in a batteau carrying only 28 men at a time, was upon a steep, clayey bank, ten feet high, very slippery. Having gained the top of this muddy bank, they struck a path which they followed to the left for about one hundred yards, when they filed right, went up over the hill, at an angle of 45 degrees, the top of which was some 100 feet above the river level. Here they came to an open space 150 yards wide and 300 long, which was surrounded on the right, left and front with a dense forest, in which the enemy were strongly posted, but entirely protected from view. In the rear was he steep hill which they had ascended. On the centre of the opening was a gully, and at the left a cowpath; thus, with the river behind them, the troops fought desperately. To think of retreat was equivalent to death by bullet, by drowning, or of torture and imprisonment among the rebels. The fact that Gen. STONE was known to have crossed at Edwards' Ferry, with a strong force, (it was between three and four thousand men,) with the intention of attacking the rebels in the rear, gave them great courage. How dreadful must have been the suspense waiting — waiting with such fearful odds against them — fighting in momentary expectation that they should hear the roar of friendly cannon in the enemy's rear. The reason why the reinforcements did not arrive in time to co-operate is not yet explained. A story prevails here (at Edwards' Ferry, where I am now writing,) that our force yesterday lost four out of six pieces of artillery after crossing into Virginia. It not generally credited here.

Gen. STONE sent an order late last evening to hold the island at any cost. The artillery and Harris Cavalry, in consequence, remained on the Canal line. It was generally believed that the rebels would shell us out of the island in the morning, if possible.

As I write, (7.30 A.M., Tuesday,) the rebels are firing from their side of the river. Possibly an engagement is now going on. The Sixteenth Indiana and Sixth Pennsylvania have just passed to cross the river. The firing increases, and affairs look like a general engagement to-day. We are where the rebels could reach us easily with shells. There is another camp of the Twentieth Massachusetts just arrived — Capt. JOHN SAUNDERS, of Salem. The space surrounding the ferry is now compact with men and horses....

The wounded were mostly sent down to Edwards' Ferry by canal boats, and were carried thence in ambulances to Poolesville.

A heavy northeast rain-storm has been prevailing for 18 hours, and the Potomac is rapidly rising. The difficulty of crossing will soon be greatly increased.

Half of the Fifteenth Massachusetts are reported to be killed, wounded, or missing. The Twentieth is nearly as badly broken up. I saw a member of the Twentieth Massachusetts to-day who had been over to the Virginia shore to look after our comrades. He was fired on, and compelled to leave. The condition of the wounded who came down to Edwards' Ferry this morning by a leaky canal-boat — the rain having wet many of them to the skin — was pitiable indeed. They are by this time safely in hospital....

I have no time for further details.

E. S.[6]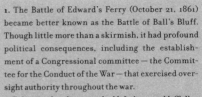

1. The Battle of Edward's Ferry (October 21, 1861) became better known as the Battle of Ball's Bluff. Though little more than a skirmish, it had profound political consequences, including the establishment of a Congressional committee — the Committee for the Conduct of the War — that exercised oversight authority throughout the war.

2. Believing that the enemy had left the area, McClellan ordered Brig. Gen. Charles P. Stone (1824–1887) to conduct what McClellan called "a slight demonstration" in order to see how the Confederates might react.

3. Colonel Edward Dickenson Baker (1811–1861), though English-born, was a veteran of the Mexican war, and a sitting U.S. senator from Oregon. He remains the only sitting U.S. Senator ever killed in battle. His popularity in the Senate was very likely a factor in making Stone a scapegoat.

4. The Tammany regiment was the 42nd New York Infantry. It had been organized by the Tammany Society and the Union Defense Committee from New York City.

5. Precise casualties remain difficult to determine, but best estimates show about a thousand Union casualties (449 killed or wounded, plus another 553 captured). Confederate losses were significantly less: 36 killed, 117 wounded, and 2 missing.

6. The initials of Elias Smith, a Times reporter.

Brigadier General Charles P. Stone and his daughter, Hettie.

THE REBELS STATING THEIR OWN CASE.

OCTOBER 25

It is not often that we get so complete a statement of the case of an enemy, as that published by us yesterday, copied from the Richmond Whig. "Unless," says that paper, "we are prepared to conquer peace upon the enemy's soil, the sooner we propose terms of submission the better. The enemy has command of the sea, and a defensive policy is simply to place ourselves at his mercy." This confession, uttered in the Capital of Rebeldom, and directly under the noses of the despots that rule there, is the most notable thing that has yet come to us from the seceding States. It is evidence that the actual condition of the rebels is rapidly being understood by themselves. They do not act upon the offensive because they cannot. A defensive policy is nothing less than destruction, because it allows the North to take away from the South every attribute of independence, if not the very means of existence. What is the condition of a people who depend, for almost every luxury and necessity, upon other nations, and are completely cut off from intercourse with all others? For one whose productions and social organization are like those of the South, it is subjection in its harshest and most odious form. Suppose the Government should not proceed a step further, except to rigidly enforce the blockade, and protect the loyal States, can the rebels put forth a single claim to have their assumed nationality respected? The final result is no less certain than if we could instantly overwhelm them in the field with a resistless force.

We hear a great deal in England about the ability of the rebels to achieve their independence. What is the independence of a nation? Is it not the ability, in the face of the enemy, to exercise those functions necessary to a proper development of the material interests of its people? Is Virginia independent, throttled as she is by Fortress Monroe? Is Louisiana, that cannot send a bale of cotton out of the Mississippi, and that dares not allow one to reach New-Orleans? Is the South independent, when she is so effectually besieged that her reduction, with the force now employed, is a mere question of time? She cannot put forth the least effort to raise the siege. No matter if it take five years to reduce her to submission. We have a right to select our own mode of carrying on hostilities. The inconvenience

to foreign nations is no cause of complaint. It is enough for us that our blockade is effectively maintained. It has one object — to starve the rebels to submission. So far, it is most effectual. Not a bale of cotton comes in sight of tide-water, much less to sea....

The truth is, that the very act of secession was the only thing necessary to demonstrate the utter impotence of the South. The rebels always denied that war could be caused by rebellion. England and France would never allow the North to resort to arms. The North itself could not afford to accept any alternative but submission. Hostile relations to the South, it was affirmed and believed, would bankrupt every Northern State. Upon this hypothesis the rebellion proceeded. The North is not only an unit in opinion, resolute in the prosecution of the war, but was never richer or stronger for offensive operations. With such a state of things assumed, the rebels themselves would have pronounced their attempt not only impossible of success, but the veriest piece of madness ever thought of. With all their frenzy they cannot help slowly coming to such a conviction. The universal want and distress prevailing at the South is certainly not proof of victories or strength. Without the sight of an enemy or of a ship, or of the power that causes a change from plenty to poverty, they cannot help asking the cause.

Is this likely to be removed? Not by any power the rebels can put forth. Will they not in time become wearied of a bootless contest, that inflicts no injury upon their enemies, but destroys themselves? In the outset they may, as the Richmond Whig does, throw the blame upon the military leaders. These are not in any degree in fault. They have, with the means at command, accomplished wonders. But they are leading a people who number only one to five of the North, and who, in all the means of warfare, are inferior in a vastly greater ratio. The trouble with the South is that they cannot reverse natural laws and make the weaker the stronger. Unless they can do this they must accept defeat as the inevitable alternative. Anywhere "to be weak is to be miserable." ✷

AFFAIRS ON THE UPPER POTOMAC.

THE LATE DISASTER.

OCTOBER 31
FROM OUR SPECIAL CORRESPONDENT.
POOLESVILLE, TUESDAY, OCT. 29

It is now a week since the battle took place between the opposing forces which met this side of Leesburgh [Ball's Bluff]. During that time many versions of the affair have been given, all more or loss incorrect, and the country has been balancing between the blame which certain correspondents insist should fall upon Gen. STONE and the unbounded praise which the same parties lavish upon the late Col. BAKER.[1] I have prepared, from official documents — the same from which Gen. STONE has made up his report — the following statement, which embraces every movement, every order and every result up to the time when Gen. BANKS assumed the command and the general retreat was ordered. Before giving that statement, I will remark that the order said to have been found upon the person of Col. BAKER, signed STONE, and ordering him to go on to Leesburgh, is a forgery. Gen. STONE is not NAPOLEON and does not sign his dispatches STONE, nor does he address Colonels as Generals, nor does he write ungrammatical orders. I have his word for it, that the document is a forgery.

It seems that on the 20th instant, Gen. STONE, having been advised of the movement of Gen. MCCALL to Darnestown, determined to make a demonstration to draw out the intentions of the enemy at Leesburgh. Consequently he proceeded, at 1 P.M., to Edwards' Ferry, from this point, with GORMAN's Brigade, the Seventh Michigan Volunteers, two troops of the [James H.] Van Alen Cavalry and the Putnam Rangers, sending at the same time to Harrison's Island and vicinity four companies of the Fifteenth Massachusetts Volunteers, under Col. DEVENS, (who had already one company on the island,) and Col. LEE, with a battalion of the Twentieth Massachusetts ....

The movement of Gen. MCCALL, on the day previous, seems to have attracted the attention of the enemy, as just previous to the arrival of Gen. STONE at Edwards' Ferry, a regiment of infantry had appeared from the direction of Leesburgh, and taken shelter behind a wooded ☞

A Currier and Ives lithograph depicting the death of Colonel Edward D. Baker at the Battle of Ball's Bluff.

hill near Goose Creek, 1 3/4 miles from the position of the Union troops at the ferry. Gen. STONE ordered Gen. GORMAN to display his forces in view of the enemy, which was done, without inducing any movement on their part, and then ordered three flat boats to be passed from the canal into the river, at the same time throwing shell and spherical shot into and beyond the wood where the enemy were concealed, and into all cover from which fire could be opened on boats crossing the river, to produce an impression that a crossing was to be made. Orders were also sent to Col. DEVENS, at Harrison's Island, some four miles up the river to detach Capt. PHILBRICK and twenty men to cross from the island and explore by a path through woods little used, in the direction of Leesburgh, to see if he could find anything concerning the enemy's position in that direction; but to retire and report on discovering any of the enemy. The launching of the boats and shelling at Edwards' Ferry caused a rapid retiring

of the force which had been seen there, and Gen. STONE caused the embarkation of three boat-loads of thirty-five men each, from the First Minnesota, who, under cover of the shelling, crossed and recrossed the river, the boats consuming in crossing from three to seven minutes. The spirit displayed by officers and men at the thought of crossing the river was most cheering, and satisfied the General that they could be depended on for most gallant service, whenever more than demonstration night be required of them.

As darkness came on Gen. STONE ordered GORMAN's Brigade and the Seventh Michigan to fall back to their respective camps, but retained the Tammany Regiment, the companies of the Fifteenth Massachusetts and artillery near Conrad's Ferry, in their position, waiting the result of Capt. PHILBRICK's scout, he (STONE) remaining with his Staff at Edwards' Ferry. About 4 P.M., Lieut. HOWE, Quartermaster of the Fifteenth Massachusetts, reported to Gen. STONE that Capt. PHIL-

BRICK had returned to the island after proceeding unmolested to within a mile and a half of Leesburgh, and that he had there discovered, in the edge of a wood, an encampment of about thirty tents, which he approached to within twenty-five rods without being challenged, the camp having no pickets out any distance in the direction of the river. Gen. STONE at once sent orders to Col. DEVENS to cross four companies of his regiment to the Virginia shore, and march silently, under the cover of night, to the position of the camp referred to, to attack and destroy it at daybreak, pursue the enemy lodged there as far as would be prudent with the small force, and return rapidly to the island, his return to be covered by a company of the Massachusetts Twentieth, which was directed to be posted on a bluff directly over the landing place. Col. DEVENS was ordered to use this opportunity to observe the approaches to Leesburgh and the position and force of the enemy in the vicinity, and in case he found no enemy, or found

DIAGRAM OF THE BATTLE OF BALL'S BLUFF.

A map published in The New York Times showing troop dispositions at the Battle of Ball's Bluff.

him only weak and in a position where he could observe well and be secure until his party could be strengthened sufficiently to make a valuable reconnaissance, which should safely ascertain the position and force of the enemy, to hold on and report. Orders were dispatched to Col. BAKER to send the First California Regiment to Conrad's Ferry, to arrive there at sunrise, and to have the remainder of his brigade in a state of readiness to move after an early breakfast. Also to Lieut.-Col. WARD, of the Fifteenth Massachusetts, to move with a battalion of a regiment to the river bank opposite Harrison's Island, to arrive there by daybreak. Col. DEVENS, in pursuance of his orders, crossed the river and proceeded to a point indicated by a scouting party, Col. LEE remaining on the bluff with 100 men to cover his return. ●

1. Witnesses to the Congressional committee declared that Stone secretly communicated with Southerners and that he returned runaway slaves to their owners. Secretary of War Edwin Stanton ordered Stone's arrest on February 8, 1862, and he was imprisoned, though no charges were ever filed. He spent ten months in prison without a trial and was released in August, still with no explanation. Very likely, The New York Times played a role in his reinstatement. It editorialized: "General Stone has sustained a most flagrant wrong — a wrong which will probably stand as the very worst blot on the National side in the history of the war." Stone got a second chance in 1864, when Nathaniel Banks selected him as his chief of staff for the Red River campaign. See Chapter 18.

CHAPTER 6

"The Darkest and Gloomiest Year"

NOVEMBER 1861–JANUARY 1862

After the demoralizing Union defeat at Manassas, the Lincoln administration entered the fall of 1861 determined to save the federal capital and reorganize the army — and not altogether certain it could accomplish either goal.

Inertia followed on the heels of humiliation. The Times likened the Union's new commanding general's vast army to that of Louis XIV. But it was to another Frenchman that George B. McClellan would more often be compared: he was breathlessly greeted as the "Young Napoleon."

Unlike the original, however, "Little Mac" showed no immediate determination to invade. However frustrated, as The Times reported, Lincoln would not yet entertain the notion of deploying one major weapon at his disposal: emancipation. A move to liberate would score points with Northern progressives, but Lincoln believed it would anger pro-war Democrats, particularly in the loyal border states of the South, who were willing to fight to restore the Union, but not to free slaves. Lincoln would do nothing yet to upset his fragile coalition. The Times both reported and supported this wait-and-see position.

Of immediate concern, the President concluded he must strengthen Union command in the west. Though enormously popular with liberal politicians, General John C. Frémont, the Republican Party's first presidential candidate (in 1856) was proving himself ineffective in the field. Defying a vocal pro-Frémont claque, Lincoln replaced him with Major General David Hunter in early November, stirring much controversy. The administration was not averse to using either so-called political generals like Frémont, or ethnic generals like Franz Sigel (who was even more inept in battle). The Times could be critical of such commis-

Detail of the cover of sheet music devoted to Major General George B. McClellan.

sions, but not, of course, when New York's own Irish brigade marched off to war under the command of Colonel Thomas Francis Meagher. Then the paper all but burst with pride.

Desperate for victories, even small ones, the Union celebrated minor successes on the sea as well as on land. In November, a federal flotilla bombarded Confederate forts around Hilton Head Island, South Carolina, after which Union troops occupied Port Royal, an important anchorage between Charleston and Savannah. The Times reprinted the blunt warnings issued to South Carolina by General Sherman — not the more famous one, but Thomas W. Sherman, one of the heroes of the federal invasion force. Out west, a little-known brigadier general named Ulysses S. Grant captured the river town of Belmont, Missouri. This news was enough to invite cautious optimism in the North.

There was a cost attached to these minor successes. The wide circulation of paper currency and the suspension of specie payments worried fiscally conservative Northerners. And to the horror of many, early in the year Congress began debate on a 3 percent income tax (5 percent for incomes greater than $10,000) to pay for the war. Not until 1863 would a desperate Confederacy violate its own principles of state rights and limited government and impose an income tax levy, too.

The year 1861 ended with a diplomatic crisis that nearly catapulted the Union to the brink of a potentially catastrophic war with England. It began in November, as The Times reported, when the USS *San Jacinto*, commanded by the mercurial Charles Wilkes, confronted the British mail packet *Trent* in the Old Bahama Channel, seizing two Confederate emissaries headed to London and Paris, respectively: James M. Mason and John Slidell. Arousing an instant international uproar, the "Trent Affair" dominated the press for the next two months, as Richmond and London alike charged the Lincoln administration with violating international law. Parliament lobbed threats of retaliation against Washington. Seeing no way to end the crisis without capitulating, the President ordered the diplomats' release in late December. By then, much of the public enthusiasm for Wilkes had dissipated, though administration enemies nevertheless cited the capitulation to Britain as a national humiliation.

APPOINTMENT OF GENERAL MCCLELLAN AS COMMANDER-IN-CHIEF.

NOVEMBER 8

GEORGE B. McCLELLAN is Commander-in-Chief of the Armies of the United States! This important step was taken, to-day, in Cabinet Council. The young General finds himself at the head of a force as numerous as that of Rome in her palmiest days, and not since equaled except by a monarch of the last century — LOUIS XIV — until we descend to the wars of NAPOLEON. What changes have nine centuries introduced in the mode of warfare. How different our weapons from those of the Legions who fought under CAESAR, or defended the throne of the Antonies. The open helmet, the lofty crest, the breast-plate of mail, the greaves for the legs and the buckler for the arms, would be useless defences to the modern soldier; while, for aggressive warfare, the pilum and sword bear no comparison to the cannon and rifle, in death dealing properties. With such an army Rome extended and maintained her sway from the Western Ocean to the Euphrates, embracing the fairest portion of the earth, and peopled by one hundred millions of souls. Our own army, inspired with valor, improved by discipline and commanded by officers of education, will be found adequate to suppress domestic treason, as well as to repel foreign invasion. May they never lay down their arms until the Government is restored in all of its purity and integrity. May our young General prove a fit leader for such an army. Amid disheartening incapacity, may he be alive to his own glory and the regeneration of his country. Modest and simple in his habits, he has thus far yielded, through a spirit of discipline, to those superior in station, whose counsels might become fatal to the Republic. Six months ago a private citizen, to day he finds himself vested with almost supreme power. May he use that power with moderation, and with a single view to his country's good. Above all, may he not become ensnared in political intrigues, or inspired with political ambition.

Gen. [Winfield] SCOTT this day retires with the best wishes of his countrymen. Two generations have been witnesses of the services which have made his name illustrious. It was to his firmness and that of the little band that surrounded him on the 4th of March last, that we owe the preservation of the Capital. Since then, incessant labor has pressed heavily upon his declining frame, and he himself has felt that that power which he has wielded so long and so well, must be transferred to a successor, so soon as one worthy of it could be found. To-morrow he will be escorted by his own staff and by Gen. MCCLELLAN and staff to the cars, on his way to New-York, where a cordial reception will await him. Peace to his declining years. ⊛

Major General George B. McClellan, U.S.A.

MOVEMENTS OF THE ARMY.

NOVEMBER 8

To the Editor of the New-York Times:

In your paper of to-day you manifest impatience in regard to the movement of the army of the Potomac, and you cannot brook the idea of going into Winter quarters without a decisive battle with the enemy. As a constant reader of the TIMES, and one who has generally approved its course, I cannot but regret this feeling on your part. It may do wrong in two ways — first, by giving erroneous views to your numerous readers; secondly, by its tendency to urge the army into conflict before it is ready. From the commencement of this war I have urged upon the powers at Washington not to move against the enemy until they had a well-disciplined and overwhelming force. Had such counsels prevailed, we should never have heard of the disastrous result at Bull Run, but, in due time, our arms would have been crowned with victory. The urgency of editors and the clamor of politicians overruled the judgment of military men, and the consequences followed as they anticipated. The injurious effect, both at home and abroad, we have all seen and felt. We are just beginning to recover from it. But now an effort is again being made to supersede the judgment of military commanders, and substitute for it the feelings, and wishes, and anxieties of those who are incapable of judging, because they have not the information from which to draw proper conclusions. After the Bull Run affair it seemed to be conced-

ed that, in future, military matters should be left to military men. There I am content to leave them. Individuals may make suggestions, but the decision must be left to those to whom it properly belongs.

In the recent affair at Ball's Bluff, there was either a misapprehension or a military blunder. We are again defeated by a superior force. This is generally the case. Why is this? Why are the rebels permitted to have this advantage over us? If we cannot outnumber them, we should, at least, be equal to them. It is true, our men behave gallantly and fight bravely, But the enemy has the prestige of victory! If the enemy will meet us in the open field, man to man, I will guarantee a victory to our aims in any conflict in which he may see fit to engage. But the rebel will not, and dare not, do this. They always retire before an equal or superior force, and wait till their own force is overwhelming. Fas est, et ab hoste doceri,[1] is an old maxim, and it is not too late for us to act upon it. The recent disaster, for aught I know, may have been occasioned by an outside pressure — a desire to satisfy supposed public expectation, without being prepared for each an emergency....

N.P. TALLMADGE.
CORNWALL, N.Y. ✸

---

1. Latin: "It is right to be taught, even by an enemy."

MITTENS FOR SOLDIERS.

NOVEMBER 8

To the Editor of the New-York Times:

As you recommend the employment of "nimble patriotic fingers" in making mittens or gloves for the army, I would suggest that the mittens be made with a first finger as well as thumb. It is quite difficult to pull a trigger with a mitten of the usual shape, and the finger could be used or not as required. Mittens are much warmer than gloves, for the same reason that four children would be warmer in one bed than sleeping alone.

VERY RESPECTFULLY, A PHYSICIAN. ✸

IMPORTANT IF TRUE.

NOVEMBER 8

The Independent of this week has the following paragraph:

"Just as we are going to press, we receive a most important piece of information from a reliable source. It is nothing less than the expressed conviction of Mr. Seward that the Government cannot succeed in this war; that the Confederacy will probably be recognized by the European Powers; and that peace will be the result in sixty days. In view of this, Mr. THURLOW WEED[1] has been sent to England, and if he shall find the British Ministry determined to recognize the Confederacy, the Administration here will prepare at once for peace."

THE SLAVERY QUESTION — NECESSITY FOR SOME UNIFORM POLICY

NOVEMBER 9

How to deal with slaves in the Southern States must speedily become a practical question, and the sooner the better. Hitherto it has been mainly a theme for speculation. Every man has had his theory about it, and has been urgent for its immediate adoption. The Government has shown a disposition, very natural and proper, to postpone the subject as long as possible, and especially to leave it to the control of Congress. The landing of troops upon the Southern coast, however, in the very midst of the densest slave population, and in the heart of the Cotton region, where the treatment of slaves is the most severe, and their desire to escape the strongest, will compel prompt and decisive action on the subject.

Beaufort District, at the head of Port Royal harbor, contains 38,805 inhabitants, of whom 32,279 are slaves, the slaves thus outnumbering the whites in the proportion of more than five to one. They are mainly employed upon large cotton plantations, are severely worked, given to insurrectionary schemes, and more intelligent than the corresponding class in Alabama and Mississippi. There can be no doubt that thousands of them will flock into the National camp, with the expectation of protection under the National flag.

It has been stated that in certain parts of Tennessee the slaves are drilled and equipped as soldiers for service in the field. In South Carolina, where they so largely outnumber the whites, no such rash experiment will be hazarded. The masters there will be very careful

The fact that Mr. SEWARD has selected the Independent as the special organ of the State Department, for the publication of the laws of the United States, may give this paragraph more apparent importance than it deserves. We do not believe there is a particle of truth in it, or the slightest foundation for it. Mr. SEWARD expresses uniformly in conversation, and in all his communications with the public, precisely the opposite conviction from that which he is here said to entertain. He believes that the Government can succeed in the present war, and that its prospects of speedy and decided success were never brighter than at this moment. He has no fear, moreover, that the Confederacy will be recognized by any leading foreign Power, nor would such a rec-

about putting arms in their hands. If any such step should be taken — if our troops should meet regiments of slaves in the field against them, or employed in any way in actively aiding the rebellion — our commander would be perfectly justified in offering them freedom on condition of surrender. As a military act, he certainly would have quite as much right to free them as to kill them, and it would be for him to decide which of the two would best promote the success of his military operations. But it is not likely that the question will be presented to him in any such shape. The slaves are not likely to be employed as rebel soldiers. They will either remain on their plantations, or come into camp in search of freedom. If they are entirely passive, Gen. SHERMAN will probably not interfere with their condition. He could scarcely appeal to them to rise against their masters, or offer them freedom as an inducement to come into our camps. His instructions on this subject, issued by Secretary CAMERON, state that he is to "avail himself of the services of any persons, whether fugitives from labor or not, who may offer than to the National Government;" assuring the loyal masters "that Congress will provide just compensation to them for the loss of the services of the persons so employed." This limits his action to the specific cases of those who may offer their services to the Government; — though the mere fact of coming into camp will doubtless be regarded as such an offer. What is to be done with them afterwards, whether they are to be returned to their masters, compensation being merely for their services while thus employed, — or whether they are to be set free and paid for in full, the letter of instructions does not state. If they belong to rebel masters, the

manner of dealing with them, beyond setting them to work, is not specified.

A paragraph in one of our exchanges, a few days since, stated that in Western Virginia many fugitives were arriving in the camp of Gen. KELLEY,[1] who put them in confinement, "awaiting the claim of their masters." By what authority Gen. KELLEY pursues this course we arc not aware. He has no commission, we presume, to act as slave-catcher for Southern slaveholders, nor to imprison any man whom he may suffer to enter his camp, on suspicion of belonging to somebody else. It is no part of his duty to enforce the local laws of the States he may invade, — nor to arrest and detain persons whom he may suspect of trying to escape from their operation. He may refuse to permit a slave to come within his lines, — but if he does permit it, he must treat him as a person simply, — and precisely as he would treat any other person to whom he may accord a similar privilege. He has no means of knowing whether he "owes service or labor," — any more than whether he owes money, to any other person or not: — nor has he any more right to inquire. That is a matter which belongs wholly to the local, civil tribunals of the State: and it should be left solely and exclusively to their jurisdiction. If they are suspended or nullified by the rebellion, so much the worse for the rebels; — but it is their own act, and they must hear both the penalty and the responsibility.

Gen. LANE,[2] of Kansas, gave a clearer definition of the duty of the Government in this matter than we have met elsewhere. He said it was to "put down rebellion, and let Slavery take care of itself." This is the simplest solution of the whole problem — at least in the

present stage of the war. Our Generals have nothing to do with Slavery; they are under no necessity of recognizing its existence. If men, black or white, anywhere tender their services, let them be employed, if needed, if not, let them go their way. If they choose to travel Northward, no General has any right to interrupt them. If they wish to remain in camp, it is for the General to decide whether they can be accommodated or not, and to act accordingly. But he has no right to return them, or to detain them, as fugitives. If he can make them prisoners at all, it can only be as prisoners of war, or as suspected spies, or as persons who have come improperly within his lines. And any man who comes to claim them at his slaves is equally liable to the same arrest, and upon precisely the same grounds.

We have been and still are opposed to the adoption by the Government, under existing circumstances, of any general policy of emancipation, — either as the object of this war, or as a means of carrying it on. We do not believe such a policy either necessary, wise or feasible in the present condition of affairs. But the Government should adopt some general rule in regard to the action of our Commanders in their several Departments. That action ought to be uniform and explicitly understood. And whatever else may be done or left undone, our camps should not be degraded into slave-pens, nor our armies sent South to act as constables for the seizure of fugitive slaves. ❁

1. Benjamin Franklin Kelley (1807–1883).
2. James H. Lane (1814–1866, a suicide), a Republican senator who raised a Kansas regiment in anticipation of a Confederate invasion from Missouri.

ognition change in the least the determination of the Government to crush the rebellion. The Independent has been very grossly misled into making a very serious imputation upon the Secretary of State. We venture to predict that when his correspondence with our Minister in England shall come to be published, it will indicate anything but a purpose of being governed by the action of Great Britain in the course to be pursued by our Government. If England were to recognize the Southern Confederacy to-morrow, the war would be not an hour nearer its end than it is now. ❁

1. Thurlow Weed (1797–1882), an Albany, New York, publisher (Albany Evening Journal) and Republican political leader, was Seward's chief political advisor.

STORY OF AN EXCHANGED PRISONER.

FROM THE LOUISVILLE JOURNAL, NOV. 5.
We have had an interview with Mr. P. H. LIPPERT, of the Twenty-fourth Illinois Regiment, who was taken prisoner some months ago, about twenty miles from Centerville, Mo., while acting as a messenger bearing dispatches. He was arrested by rebel Missourians and placed under charge of Gen. HARDEE's[1] command in the southeastern part of the State, where he was exposed to great privations and sufferings. In company with twenty other Union prisoners he was lodged in a horse-

NOVEMBER 10
thief jail at Bloomfield, for nearly a month. This place was an apartment 16 by 18 feet in dimensions, and 7 feet high, with two air holes on two sides. In this cage the twenty were cooped during the hottest weather, without any effort being made to remove their excrement, which of course produced the foulest stench. Their food was dough and water, and even that in insufficient quantities, and they were never once taken into the fresh air, which produced great sickness. While there three Union men were hung, and five shot, because ☞

they refused to take the oath. These villainies were committed by Capt. [Robert M.] WHITE and his Texan Rangers. From Bloomfield, Mr. LAPPERT was taken to New-Madrid for a few days, during which he received no food at all, and was nearly starved; thence he was transferred to Columbus, with seven prisoners from Cape Girardeau, and placed at work on the fortifications; and they were so engaged, being driven to the works in gangs, like slaves, at the time of the engagement between the batteries and the Union gunboats, exposed to all the fire and bursting shells, but providentially none were injured. They were by this time greatly in need of clothes and blankets, and their wants were contumeliously neglected.... ✱

1. Confederate General William J. Hardee (1815-1873), a native of Georgia.

DYING STRUGGLES OF THE SLAVE TRADE.

NOVEMBER 11

The vigorous measures set on foot by the new Administration, for the suppression of the slave-trade, have already succeeded in reducing that infamous traffic to its last extremity. It was one of the first points to which Mr. LINCOLN and Mr. SEWARD gave their attention, and they have followed it up with vigor and success. The meeting of the United States Marshals, some weeks since, did a great deal to infuse vigor and harmony into their action, and the conviction last week of Captain GORDON,[1] will satisfy the parties who have hitherto grown rich on the profits of this nefarious trade, that the law is no longer to be a dead letter.

We believe there is now not a single port in the United States from which a slaver can be fated out. The attempt has been made at nearly every port from Bangor to Baltimore, and in every instance the design has been detected and defeated. One or two vessels have recently left this port for Portuguese ports with legitimate cargoes, but with the well-understood purpose of refitting there and going to the coast of Africa. Through the vigilance of Marshal MURRAY, however, our Government has made full representations to our Consuls at the ports in question, and the vessels will he sharply watched from the moment of their arrival. Secretary SEWARD has also informed the British Government that, since the slavers have been driven out of the United States, some of them have resorted to Liverpool for the purpose of securing outfits. He has sent full descriptions of the vessels implicated, and so pressed the matter upon the attention of the British authorities that they cannot avoid prompt and effective action. Within a few days a person resident in this City, extensively engaged in the traffic, becoming alarmed at the vigor with which these prosecutions are pressed, has fled to Canada. Some others will probably find it expedient ere long to follow his example. ✱

1. Captain Nathaniel Gordon (1826–1862) was convicted as a slave trader in November 1860 and sentenced to death. Lincoln refused to stay his execution.

GENERAL MCCLELLAN'S PROGRAMME.

NOVEMBER 10

CORRESPONDENCE OF
THE PHILADELPHIA PRESS.
WASHINGTON, WEDNESDAY, NOV. 6, 1861.

Gen. MCCLELLAN heartily approves the proposition for an exchange of prisoners. This has been his sentiment from the start and I believe the majority of the Cabinet have always taken the same side. Gen. McCLELLAN'S views are sustained by his confidential friend, the distinguished Ex-Attorney-General, EDWIN M. STANTON, who, notwithstanding his connection with the Buchanan Administration, now maintains, as during his association with that Administration, the most decided and uncompromising Union doctrines. He declares that "the principle of an exchange of prisoners is demanded by the highest considerations of policy and humanity." I have, therefore, no doubt that some arrangement will be made, in a very short time, by which our absent and beloved fellow-citezens in the Southern prisons may be restored to their families and friends. The reasons for refusing such an arrangement have passed away. The highest considerations require that the health and lives of our captured fellow-soldiers should alone be taken into view. Etiquette and diplomatic forms have too long impeded the consummation of this important arrangement.

So much has, been said of the safety of Washington, and many complaints have come from the Western Department, that a sufficient number of troops had been, concentrated at this point, that a few words upon the probable programme of Gen. MCCLELLAN may not be inopportune. Now that he is clothed with supreme power, and a thousand ardent expectations are indulged that he may win a conclusive victory, it is well to state that he has never faltered in the belief that it was his first duty to see that the National capital was put in a position of impregnable defence, and that no movement should be made until this was entirely settled. Previous to the ill-fated reconnoissance at Bell's Bluff, a large number of troops were taken from his military district, and sent to other points, Had that reconnoissance been crowned by the seizure of Leesburgh—had MCCALL been enabled to effect a junction with STONE and BAKER — vast advantage would have been secured, and the facilities for a forward movement immeasurably increased. The failure of that reconnoissance has necessitated new delays.

You will perceive that the Secessionists in Maryland are held down only by the strong hand. The proclamation of Gen. DIX,[1] admonishing all persons of seces-

RETIREMENT OF GENERAL FREMONT.

NOVEMBER 11

SPRINGFIELD, MO., MONDAY, NOV. 4, 1861.

We have had stirring times here yesterday and today. Late on Saturday night, one of three messengers sent forward by Col. LEONARD SWETT,[1] from St. Louis, succeeded in eluding the vigilance of the guards stationed to prevent access to Gen. FREMONT'S[2] Headquarters, and served on the General personally the orders from Washington turning over the command of the Western Department to Maj.-Gen. DAVID HUNTER.[3]

Upon this there was, of course, unutterable consternation and commotion in and around headquarters, and it appeared doubtful for several hours what course Gen. FREMONT would pursue. Many of his leading personal adherents, chiefly of the Teutonic stripe, were in favor of disregarding the removal and refusing to recognize Gen. HUNTER's appointment — a course which, if they had persisted in it, (and it was not wholly abandoned until late last evening,) would have caused a very considerable row — for Gen. HUNTER is not the sort of man it would be safe to trifle with.

In the end, however, wiser counsels prevailed, — Gens. SIGEL and ASBOTH[4] both refusing to countenance or be concerned in the mutiny; and Gen. FREMONT, it must be said,

either not knowing anything of the contemplated movements, or opposing them, as in duty bound, with all his force. On this point, however, we are in the dark. Certain only it is that a council now known as the "Council of Insubordination" was held last evening only a few hours before Gen. HUNTER's arrival; that regular invitations to it had been issued, and that the affair looked very threatening until suppressed by the emphatic course of Gen. SIGEL. Early yesterday morning, therefore, Gen. FREMONT issued his farewell address to the "Soldiers of the Mississippi Army,"—though to say why "Mississippi Army" and not "Western Department," might well puzzle a Philadelphia lawyer to explain. Here is the document, neatly printed as you see and placed in the hands of all the soldiers in the army.... ✪

1. "Of all living men," a contemporary once asserted, "Leonard Swett [1825–1899] was the one most trusted by Abraham Lincoln. Swett had been his legal colleague in Illinois for years, and carried the title of "colonel" from his Mexican War service.
2. Major General John C. Frémont (1813–1890).
3. David Hunter (1802–886) had been corresponding with then President-elect Lincoln since the fall of 1860 and rose quickly in the ranks once war broke out.
4. German-born Franz Sigel (1824–1902) and Hungarian native Alexander Asboth (1810–1868) were among the many "ethnic generals" commissioned by the Union early in the war to rally support from foreign-born Northerners. After the war, Sigel became a journalist and politician, Asboth a diplomat.

---

sion proclivities against interfering with, or exercising the right of suffrage at the election to-day, show the absolute necessity of maintaining a large force of United States soldiers in Maryland, and proves, also, the persevering purpose of the traitors now in Virginia to take possession of this Capital if they can. Within the last ten days Gen. MCCLELLAN's column has been greatly augmented by accessions from the reserves of the different States, but it must be recollected that a large force has been thrown — some estimate the number at twenty thousand — opposite the rebel batteries on the Potomac, and that the late offensive demonstrations in Maryland will compel an increase of the forces under Gen. DIX in that quarter. Gen. MCCLELLAN cannot, therefore, advance until every position in his rear is thoroughly and impregnably fortified, nor should he attempt to attack without such a force as will render defeat impossible. Meanwhile the late news from Western

Virginia indicates that our armies are triumphant, and unless the removal of Gen. FREMONT has entirely demoralized the army of Missouri, we ought to expect a victory in that State.

I recur to these points to show that the programme of Gen. MCCLELLAN has been wise from the first, and especially to convince that large class of critics who have been complaining that too much attention has been given to the protection of the Capital that all their censures have been unjust. On or about the 10th of November you may look for a forward movement. I am sure that if it is made, unless the rebels retreat before our advancing troops, there will be a complete and annihilating victory. ✪

1. John Adams Dix (1798–1879)

MILITARY CRITICISMS OF THE NEWSPAPER PRESS.

NOVEMBER 12

It has been the fashion of very foolish people to speak disrespectfully of the military suggestions of newspapers. It has rather come to be considered the thing to warn the Government against listening to the mere wild and unskillful speculation of writers, whose knowledge must necessarily spring from other sources than the lessons of experience; and invite it to throw itself wholly upon that sounder understanding of martial affairs, which comes from active and successful action on flood and field. Clamor of this description, which, unhappily, had an apparent warrant in the disaster upon which undue precipitancy urged the army on the 21st of July, has served to silence a criticism, which might at all times have proved wholesome, and to suppress suggestions dictated by practical common sense — in the present instance a better adviser than an experience which has no application to the anomalies of civil war, and an attachment to routine, slow to abandon the inadequate machinery of a peace establishment.

We indulge these remarks because in the supposed success of the expedition to Port Royal, there is an ample vindication of the rectitude of the judgment the Press has most generally exercised in such matters. In the TIMES, of April 23, the following passage occurred in an editorial discussion of the plan upon which the war, not yet fairly begun, should be conducted:

FROM THE NEW-YORK TIMES, APRIL 23.

"At the very moment we are striking a blow at Virginia, we should fit out a large naval and military force to operate against the Cotton States. Both Charleston and Savannah might be threatened and captured by a force landed at Port Royal, a deep estuary about equidistant between these two cities. The capture of the City of Mobile, which is almost entirely unprotected, would be an easy matter. New-Orleans might be threatened or assailed at the same time. Such an expedition would keep President DAVIS, and all this forces he could raise, at home, and constantly on the look-out for his winged enemy, which, beyond reach of attack, could select his own time and place to deal a decisive blow."

This was written during the seven days following the fall of Fort Sumter; at the moment when the nation had just awakened to a consciousness that ☞

war had begun; while the Administration and the country were in a mad panic in regard to the safety of the Capital; and before the first outline of a campaign had been conceived of by those in command of the National army. Advice thus calmly given was at that period of general trepidation lost upon the Government. But it was not thrown away. We have reason to believe, that strongly impressed with the wisdom of the suggestion, Maj.-Gen. WOOL, from his retirement at Watertown, addressed an able letter to the War Department, ad-

vocating its early adoption, especially so far as it related to Port Royal and Beaufort. This letter was submitted to Gen. SCOTT, who at once acquiesced in the ultimate propriety of the measure; but believed that the Summer was too far advanced to render the expedition safe in a sanitary point of view. The TIMES repeatedly recurred to the importance of the immediate execution of the plan; showed what seemed to have escaped the attention of the authorities at Washington, that Beaufort was entirely exempt from the prevalent

unwholesomeness of the Southern coast at Mid-summer; and pointed to the alarm the landing of a large National force in that very heart and centre of the slave region would communicate to the entire population of the rebel States.

Now, it is quite possible the arguments of this paper are not the immediate, motives which at last prompted the action of the Government. We are not, indeed, participants in the counsels which regulate such matters at Washington; and are certainly without the very common ambi-

GENERAL SHERMAN'S PROCLAMATION TO THE PEOPLE OF THE SOUTH CAROLINA.

NOVEMBER 14

After landing and taking possession of the forts, Gen. SHERMAN[1] issued the following proclamation:

To the People of South Carolina: In obedience to the orders of the President of these United States of America, I have landed on your shores with a small force of National troops. The dictates of a duty, which, under the Constitution, I owe to a great sovereign State, and to a proud and hospitable people, among whom I have passed some of the pleasantest days of my life, prompt me to proclaim that we have come amongst you with no feelings of personal animosity; no desire to harm your citizens, destroy your property, or interfere with any of your lawful laws, rights, or your social and local institutions, beyond what the causes herein briefly alluded to may render unavoidable.

CITIZENS OF SOUTH CAROLINA: The civilized world stands appalled at the course you are pursuing! Appalled at the crime you are committing against your own mother, the best, the most enlightened, and heretofore the most prosperous of nations. You are in a state of active rebellion against the laws of your country. You have lawlessly seized upon the forts, arsenals and other property belonging to our common country, and within your borders with this property you are in arms, and

waging a ruthless war against your Constitutional Government, and thus threatening the existence of a Government which you are bound by the terms of the solemn compact to live under and faithfully support. In doing this you are not only undermining and preparing the way for totally ignoring your own political and social existence, but you are threatening the civilized world with the odious sentiment that self-government is impossible with civilized man....

T. W. SHERMAN, BRIG.-GEN. COMMANDING,
HEADQUARTERS, G.C., PORT ROYAL, S.C.,
Nov. 8, 1861. ✪

1. General Thomas West "Tim" Sherman (1813–1879) was a Rhode Island–born, West Point–trained career army officer, and no relation to William T. Sherman, who became famous later and with whom he is often confused.

Brigadier General Thomas W. Sherman, U.S.A.

IRISH BRIGADE OFF TO THE WAR.

NOVEMBER 14, 1861

The First and Fourth Regiments of the Irish Brigade proceed to Washington on Monday next. It has been so determined by the Governor of the State, in accordance with the earnest desire of the President and Secretary of War. Gen. MCCLELLAN also has expressed an ardent wish to have the soldiers of the Irish Brigade in his command as soon as possible. Nothing, therefore, will prevent the regiments above mentioned from marching on Monday, the 18th. The regiments will leave Fort Schuyler at 7 o'clock, on board one of the largest river steamers. Disembarking at the foot of Thirty-fourth-street, the troops will proceed to Madison-avenue, and halt in front of Archbishop HUGHES' residence. They will here be presented with their colors. After which, marching through Fifth-avenue, and thence into Broadway by Fourteenth-street, they will proceed to the Jersey ferry, en route for the Philadelphia cars.

On Saturday, at 2 o'clock P.M., there will be an inspection and review of the brigade, by the Acting Brigadier, Col. THOMAS FRANCIS MEAGHER.[1] Every private and officer will have to appear in complete marching trim. No visitors will be permitted to the fort on that day. To-day and to-morrow, however, all who desire to see their friends will have free access to the brigade. But on Saturday and Sunday there will be a peremptory exclusion of all strangers. Parties wishing to visit Fort Schuyler to-day and to-morrow will have to apply for passes at the headquarters of the brigade, No. 595 Broadway.

The colors of the brigade are now on exhibition at TIFFANY's, Broadway, at which establishment they were manufactured. They are of the costliest material, splendid design and the most artistic workmanship. The

tion to be considered the prime motors of all there is sensible and energetic in the conduct of public affairs. But it is due to the Press to show that its opinions, even in professional and purely strategic questions, are not without claim to careful and respectful consideration; and that, when put in action, they sometimes result in positive success. And the success in the present instance, if it be not exaggerated in transmission, or lost through inadequate support, is certainly the most brilliant of the war. ✸

---

motto of the brigade, a line from the grand old Celtic Homer, OSSIAN — "They shall never retreat from the charge of lances" — is worked in gold, in ancient Irish characters, on the emerald field, whilst the symbolic harp of Erin appears amid all the splendor and glory of the famous sunburst, the war-signal of the Irish in their fierce battles with the Danes.... ✸

1. Onetime revolutionary leader of the "Young Irelanders," Irish-born Meagher (1823–1867) formed Company K of the 69th New York Regiment following the attack on Fort Sumter—the regiment that earned fame as the "Fighting Irish."

THE NAVAL VICTORY AT PORT ROYAL.

NOVEMBER 14

We print a brilliant chapter of history this morning. In other columns will be found the official dispatches of Commodore DUPONT[1] and Gen. SHERMAN, with proclamations, general orders, and the exhaustive rehearsal of our special correspondent, who gives a complete view of the entire affair. The detailed official account of Commodore DUPONT is not yet issued indeed; but the ample materials we publish leave little to be desired.

The dead under the smoking ruins of the forts that flank Port Royal, the troops of rebel planters flying in dismay before the avenging oriflamme of the Union, and the swarms of slaves flocking to our ships and our lines for deliverance and protection, are the flaming initials with which the Book of Retribution — just retribution, if ever such were! — opens in South Carolina. Twenty millions of loyal freemen are shut up in measureless content at the tidings. Now, indeed, Sumter begins to be avenged!

Few naval expeditions of a large scale — none of the proportions of this — have been successful. We trembled for its safety; we exult at its success. If not a victory which takes its lustre from the accomplishment of an end by disproportioned means, it is a success, the result of a plan admirably conceived and carried out with skill, with energy and with pluck. "I think my plan was clever," remarks Flag-Officer DUPONT, in an unofficial letter to the Assistant Secretary of the Navy.[2] The whole country will answer YES, in capital letters. Neither will the country forget the gallant marines and seamen who so finely sustained the glorious traditions handed down by American sailors of an earlier age.

The general outlines of the bombardment have already been anticipated. The leading plan of the manoeuvre was as masterly as it was novel, and was executed with splendid success. The seventeen men-of-war, forming in double line of battle, performed three magnificent intersecting circles, delivering raking broadsides from their starboard and port sides successively, and bringing the forts on either sides in range by turns. Five gunboats formed a flanking division, and did excellent service. "In truth," says Commodore DUPONT, "I never conceived such a fire as that on the second turn." This triple circle, pouring its showers of shot and shell on the forts, occupied three hours. When preparing for the fourth round of "damnable iteration," the fortifications surrendered! It was a hotly contested fight. The South Carolina journals, in declaiming on the imbecility of the artillerists that manned the batteries, have done them great injustice. All our accounts concur in testifying that the rebels fought bravely and well. But our broadsides were overwhelming. The masterly manoeuvre of Commodore DUPONT, in causing the fleet to describe a series of intersecting circles, had at once the effect to destroy the range of the rebel guns, and to greatly diminish the exposure of our ships to the rebel ☞

Lithograph depicting the bombardment of Port Royal, South Carolina, on November 7, 1861.

fire, and when the action was over, nothing had befallen our fleet that could have prevented its paying its respects to Charleston or Savannah the next morning.... Such is the brilliant chapter of History made on that beautiful Autumnal morning, under the splendid Southern sky. The drama was not without spectators. Numerous steamers, with excursion parties on board from Charleston, Savannah, and other neighboring towns, stood off, at safe distances, to view the combat. The denouement was not exactly that of Fort Sumter, witnessed by a like assemblage! It is stated that on board some of these craft were the consular agents of France and England: they probably found suggestive materials for dispatches!

It is impossible to over-estimate the importance of this successful lodgment of Union forces on the soil of South Carolina. Securely intrenched on Hilton Head Island, the whole entourage of which is commanded by our fleet, there is a point d'appui for indefinite future operations. Henceforth the rebels cannot but know that any point upon their extended coast is equally untenable in the presence of the overwhelming naval power of the loyal States. The inland water-way which the rebels have hitherto so effectually used, is now wholly cut off and in our possession. There are also some illusions dispelled. There is an end to some old assumptions of South Carolina courage. The nonsense of the readiness of the slaves to fight for their masters is also for ever ended. Some were dragged away by force, others, refusing, were shot down like dogs, while a black tide poured towards the Union forces for protection....

We cannot see but that this success is the prologue to the swelling act of the imperial theme of Union triumph and rebel discomfiture; and the national salute booming from the Navy-yards of the States at noon to-day will awaken such echoes of high hopes as nothing in the war has yet inspired. ⊛

"Vandalia."   The Prize "Arthur Middleton."   "Roanoke,"

THE BLOCKADE OF CHARLESTON.

Three Union blockade ships at Charleston harbor.

THE CAPTURE OF SLIDELL AND MASON.

NOVEMBER 17

We do not believe the American heart ever thrilled with more genuine delight than it did yesterday, at the intelligence of the capture of Messrs. SLIDELL and MASON,[1] recently of the Senate of the United States, the most prominent and influential actors in the rebellion, and on their way to England and France, to represent the rebels at the Courts of these countries. The capture of Beaufort [Port Royal] may have created a deeper and more lasting impression, from a consciousness of the important results accomplished, but really no satisfaction is equal to that experienced when base and treacherous knaves meet their deserts. If we were to search the whole of Rebeldom, no persons so justly obnoxious to the North, could have been found as those just caught.

DAVIS himself has some redeeming qualities; MASON and SLIDELL, none ... .

Both are sworn enemies of order and law — of constitutional Government — of free labor — of human progress. They belong to an age in which the basest of passions and motives bore sway. For seeking to restore such an age they fled their country, and are now happily the prisoners of the very Government they sought to overthrow.

These are the men whom we have just caught and who are now safely caged. All thanks to Capt. WILKES,[2] who, consulting the dictates of common sense alone, marched straight to his object, unmindful of protests, convinced that an act which every honest heart must approve, could not be contrary to usage and law. In this he was perfectly cor-

EARL RUSSELL TO LORD LYONS.[1]

FOREIGN OFFICE, Nov. 30

... Her Majesty's Government having in mind the friendly relations which have long subsisted between Great Britain and the United States, are willing to believe that the United States naval officer who committed the aggression was not acting in compliance with any authority from his Government, or that it he conceived himself to be so authorized, he greatly misunderstood the instructions which he had received. For the Government of the

DECEMBER 29

United States must be fully aware that the British Government could not allow such an affront to the National honor to pass without full reparation, and Her Majesty's Government are unwilling to believe that it could be the deliberate intention of the Government of the United States unnecessarily to force into discussion between the two Governments a question of so grave a character, and with regard to which the whole British nation would be sure to entertain such unanimity of feel-

1. Samuel Francis Du Pont (1803–1865) received a special commendation from Congress for securing southern coastal waters in this engagement.
2. Assistant Secretary of the Navy Gustavus Vasa Fox (1821–1883)

rect. The only mistake he committed was in not seizing the ship from which he dragged the traitors.[3] England fully recognizes the right of belligerents to search, on the high seas, the vessels of neutrals for articles contraband of war. We do the same, as a pact of the laws of nations. About this right there is no dispute. If the English steamer had been captured, she would been condemned in any English Court of Admiralty, the proclamation of the Queen at the outbreak of the rebellion, forbidding her subjects to take any part in the war, or to transport arms or munitions for either belligerent, even dispatches of their Governments, was only a reiteration of the laws of nations, applicable to the position she assumed. Her subjects were told that the violation of these laws would be at their own peril. The steamer in question was the bearer of articles contraband of war, and was liable to seizure and confiscation. This, however, would have been a small matter after we had taken out the freight. We have not the slightest idea that England will even remonstrate. On the contrary, she will applaud the gallant act of Lieut. WILKES, so full of spirit and good sense, and such an exact imitation of the policy she has always stoutly defended, and invariably pursued.

There is, consequently, no drawback whatever to our jubilations. The universal Yankee Nation is getting decidedly awake. Its naval arm begins to tell. It is not only all powerful, but will soon be omnipotent at sea. The cordon we have thrown around the rebels is being drawn tighter and tighter. It will not be long before they will find their quarters very circumscribed and very uncomfortable. For a long time they jeered at the turfs we were throwing at them. They

are beginning to feel something much denser, although we have not fired the train that would overwhelm them in an instant. Every day we are addressing ourselves more earnestly to our work, and persistence much longer in the rebellion will lead to the extremest of measures, perfectly justifiable from the outset, but which we have thus far waived, on the ground, very probably, of mistaken humanity.

As for Commodore WILKES and his command, let the handsome thing be done. Consecrate another Fourth of July to him. Load him down with services of plate and swords of the cunningest and costliest art. Let us encourage the happy inspiration that achieved such a victory. In this contest it is safe to adopt the Irishman's advice to his son on leaving for a fair: "When the music opens, whenever you see a (rebel) head, hit it!" A clear instinct is always in harmony with law.[4] ✪

1. Former U.S. Senators James Murray Mason (1798–1871) of Virginia and John Slidell (1793–1871) of Louisiana were named as Confederate envoys in 1861. They would assume their posts in early 1862, following resolution of the Trent Affair.
2. Navy Captain Charles Wilkes (1798–1877) of the USS *San Jacinto* ordered the seizure of Mason and Slidell from the British mail packet *Trent* on November 8, 1861.
3. Indeed, this omission was the key to British objections. According to the laws of war at sea, Wilkes should have taken the *Trent* as a British prize and carried it to a port for adjudication by a Prize Court. By removing four men (Mason, Slidell, and their two male secretaries) and letting the ship continue on its way, he played the role of both captor and prize court judge.
4. The North did indeed lionize Wilkes; he was feted in both Boston and New York for his actions.

FINANCIAL CONDITION OF THE COUNTRY.

DECEMBER 10

We present this morning the Report of the Secretary of the Treasury, which has been awaited with an interest quite as great as that felt in reference to the Message of the President. No matter what may be the magnitude of the task in hand, the crushing of the rebellion, or what may be our relations with other countries, the public will clearly see its way out of all our difficulties, provided everything is sound in the department of "ways and means." In the predicament we are in, abundance of money is always success. So far there has been no lack, and with a vigorous and successful prosecution of the war, and a wise administration of the National finances, there need be no apprehension for the future....

The report of the Secretary has many things to commend it. It is lucid and frank in its statements; and as far as it proposes any plans for the future, it is without arrogance or assumption. His suggestions are timely, as bases for discussions in Congress, where they will be considered in the same liberal and candid spirit with which they are made. Mr. CHASE's present wants are so well supplied that ample time can be taken for deliberation. The means of the country, as experience has shown, are sufficient for all the wants of the Government. We need have no fear on this score, if we only make the right use of them. It is a matter in which the Government and the people have a common interest, and we have no doubt it is one in which they will work to a common purpose. ✪

ing. Her Majesty's Government, therefore, trust that when this matter shall have been brought under the consideration of the Government of the United States, that Government will, of its own accord, offer to the British Government such redress as alone could satisfy the British Nation, namely: The liberation of the four gentlemen, and their, delivery to your Lordship, in order that they may again be placed under British protection, and a suitable apology for the aggression which has been committed.... ✪

1. British Prime Minister Lord John Russell (1792–1878) sent this harsh letter to his ambassador to the United States, Lord Richard B. P. Lyons (1817–1887), for delivery to Secretary of State William H. Seward.

James M. Mason.

MR. SEWARD TO LORD LYONS.

DECEMBER 29

...This dispatch has been submitted to the President....

The question before us is, whether this proceeding was authorized by, and conducted according to, the law of nations. It involves the following inquiries:

Lord Lyons.

1. Were the persons named, and their supposed dispatches, contraband of war?

2. Might Capt. WILKES lawfully stop and search the Trent for these contraband persons and dispatches?

3. Did he exercise that right in a lawful and proper manner?

4. Having found the contraband persons on board and in presumed possession of the contraband dispatches, had he a right to capture the persons?

5. Did he exercise that right of capture in the manner allowed and recognized by the law of nations?

If all these inquiries shall be resolved in the affirmative, the British Government will have no claim for reparation....

In the present case Capt. WILKES, after capturing the contraband persons, and making prize of the Trent in what seems to us a perfectly lawful manner, instead of sending her into port, released her from the capture, and permitted her to proceed with her whole cargo upon her voyage. He thus effectually prevented the judicial examination which might otherwise have occurred. If now the capture of the contraband persons, and the capture of the contraband vessel, are to be regarded, not as two separable or distinct transactions under the law of nations, but as one transaction, one capture only then it follows that the capture in this case was left unfinished or was abandoned. Whether the United States have a right to retain the chief public benefits of it, namely, the custody of the captured persons, on proving them to he contraband, will depend upon the preliminary question whether the leaving of the transaction unfinished was necessary, or whether it was unnecessary, and, therefore, voluntary. If it was necessary, Great Britain, as we suppose, must of course waive the defect, and the consequent failure of the judicial remedy. On the other hand, it is not seen how the United States can insist upon her waiver of that judicial remedy, if the defect of the capture resulted from an act of Capt. WILKES, which would be a fault on their own side....

The four persons in question are now held in military custody at Fort Warren, in the State of Massachusetts. They will be cheerfully liberated. Your Lordship will please indicate a time and place for receiving them.

I avail myself of this occasion to other to your Lordship a renewed assurance of my very high consideration.

WILLIAM H. SEWARD. ✽

INTERNATIONAL LAW AND THE CASE OF THE TRENT.

DECEMBER 31

Several momentous questions of maritime law have been raised in the discussion of the Trent case, which will, it is hoped, by the action of an International Congress, or by special treaties with the various Powers of Europe, be set at rest forever. Should this result be achieved, it will be of immense value to this country, and the peaceful negotiations of 1862 will contribute even more than the war of 1812 to the growth of our commerce and the development of our national prosperity. Prominent among the questions which invite such international action as we have suggested, is that of contraband of war. No better proof is needed of the obscurity which has hitherto surrounded this question, than may be obtained from the dispatches of Messrs. SEWARD and THOUVENEL,[1] which appeared side by side in our columns yesterday. From a comparison of those documents it will be seen that while the American and British authorities attach a contraband character, under special circumstances, to civilians, the French Government assumes that the civil servants of a belligerent Power are never contraband, though the military officers and forces of such a Power are so. Now, as the precise conditions under which persons, whether civil or military, acquire a contraband character are thus seen to be uncertain, and as different nations hold conflicting views on this important subject, it is obviously desirable, for the prevention of future complications, that an exact definition should be mutually agreed upon, and should be embodied in treaties or protocols under the authority of the Governments of this country and of Europe.

Besides the question of contraband as applied to persons and to merchandise, there are other equally important points which claim attention. There is, for instance, the belligerent right of visit and search, which has always been a fruitful source of international trouble, and needs to be regulated by new and more satisfactory rules. Connected with this is the obligation to take every captured vessel into port for adjudication, which has not always been insisted on, though our Government, as Mr. SEWARD properly claims, has always contended that it is indispensable to the legality of the capture. This rule, we believe, has never been authoritatively affirmed, and it is certain that in searching our vessels and impressing our sailors, Great Britain formerly violated it most flagrantly and in very numerous instances. Another point requiring attention is the privilege of refitting belligerent vessels in neutral ports. France and some other nations have established by law certain municipal regulations, which place this privilege under a certain degree of control. But in England and elsewhere there is

SUSPENSION OF SPECIE PAYMENTS.

December 31
BOSTON, Monday, Dec. 30

The Presidents and Directors of the Banks of this city held a meeting this morning and resolved to suspend specie payments forthwith.

PHILADELPHIA, Monday, Dec. 30

The Banks of this city have resolved to suspend specie payments in consequence of the suspension in New-York.[1]

ALBANY, Monday, Dec. 30

In consequence of the action of the New-York Banks, the Banks of this city suspended specie payments to-day. The suspension occasions no excitement.

PITTSBURGH, Penn., Monday, Dec. 30

The news of the suspension by the Eastern Banks was not wholly unexpected here, and created little or no alarm. Our banks have not generally suspended. Three of them, it is understood, have suspended, but four are still paying specie, viz.: The Old Bank, of Pittsburgh, the Mechanics', Citizens' and Iron City.

CLEVELAND, Monday, Dec. 30

The Cleveland Banks suspended specie payment this morning. ⊛

1. With controversial new government-supported greenbacks increasing in circulation, the traditional right of exchanging paper currency for gold or silver was suspended. The suspension lasted for another 17 years.

John Slidell.

NEW-YEAR'S DAY.

The darkest and gloomiest year in our country's history has passed away. It opened with a portentous cloud in the Southern sky, then not bigger than a man's hand; but which has since overspread and wrapped as in a pall the whole nation. Last New-Year's Day, only South Carolina had committed herself to dis-union; and almost every one then thought and hoped that the process of disintegration would not go any further; but that the conservative element in the South, and the conciliatory element in the North, would speedily devise some way by which the old fraternal Union would he peacefully maintained, and the Ship of State, compact and strong though storm-beaten, would again pursue her course in placid seas. But before the first mouth had passed away, seven States were in the hands of the mutineers, and it seemed for a time almost as though the whole National fabric would tumble to pieces. The second month of the year shaped and compacted the revolt, by giving it a Confederated legislature and an Army, and by placing at its head the adroitest of the conspirators. In April the war — henceforth to become a war of sections and systems — opened in Charleston Harbor. Then followed the formation of the

no such established and permanent rule. It could not be a difficult matter for all the Great Powers to agree upon some definite united action on these and other points, in which all commercial nations are so deeply interested. We do not wish, however, to discuss these several questions in this place. We would only suggest the propriety of holding an international Congress or of concluding special treaties with the various Powers of Europe, in which the uncertain and vexed claims of maritime law may be so completely settled as to prevent, if possible, the danger of any misunderstanding between ourselves and those Powers of Europe with whom it is both our highest interest and our established policy to live on terms of perfect friendship and national comity. ⊛

1. Edouard Antoine de Thouvenel (1818–1866) was French minister of foreign affairs.

January 1

two great armies — by this time thirteen rebel States contributing their troops to the one, while twenty-three Union States furnished the soldiers for the other. Since then, for nine dreary months past, the progress of the National arms has been fitful and uncertain — reverse and victory checquering the record of each week. But at the close of the year of rebellion, we can at least say that the military forces of the nation; on land and sea, have been brought together, and are, apparently, ready to descend effectively upon the nation's foes.

The opening of the year found South Carolina assailant and defiant, with her clutch upon the nation's throat; its close finds her assailed, confused and desperate, with the sword of the nation planted well in her vitals. The opening of the year found a cowardly old fool and a Cabinet of knaves ruling in Washington, while the nation was doubtful even of its capital: now we have upright and courageous rulers, and half a million Republican bayonets to do their bidding. January found the nation struggling in the dark, and not knowing what to do; December leaves it with a clear purpose and a fixed aim. The outlook, too, has appeared gloomy enough all the year; but it seems now as though light was almost ready to break forth, all round the horizon, upon our arms and our cause.

It is to be hoped that the old year carries with it too the final solution of the trouble lately threatening us from across the seas. It carries a message and a pledge of peace from us to England; and if England does not desire to thwart this nation's purposes and destiny, (which it is not, indeed, in her power to accomplish,) she will accept our pledge of peace in the spirit of conciliation in which it is offered....

We begin the new year with hope, and with a consciousness of National strength which contrasts wonderfully with the dubious feeling of a year ago. And we believe that many of the weeks of the year will not pass away before light and victory will break forth over the whole country, and that, before its close, the full fruition of the nation's hopes will he realized. In this consciousness, we wish to our brave soldiers in their tents, to our gallant sailors in their ships, and to all true men the world over. A Happy New Year. ⊛

THE CONVICTION OF GORDON, THE SLAVE TRADER.

JANUARY 4

FROM THE LONDON HERALD.

As to the law of the United States upon the subject there is no doubt. Since the year 1819 it has been a capital offence for American citizens to engage in the African Slave-trade; and had this law been duly enforced, there would have been an end of the traffic long ago. But it is notorious that this has not been the case. The continued refusal of America to allow the right of search under any circumstances in time of peace has hitherto proved fatal to every attempt upon our part and upon the part of other nations to put down the Slave-trade. It is notorious that that trade has of late years been carried on principally by means of American capital, and under the American flag, which could alone protect it. Vessels were built and fitted out at New-York and Baltimore expressly for the purpose, and they could pursue their lawless traffic without the risk of interruption from any cruiser except those of the Union. There is no doubt that for some time past joint-stock companies have been established expressly for the purpose of carrying it on. It may be said, in short, that American enterprise and avarice has for years past supplied Cuba with slaves. What effect is this recent conviction at New-York likely to have upon this disgraceful state of

THE IRON-PLATED GUNBOATS.

JANUARY 7

People addicted to naval matters have become suddenly awakened to the importance of iron-clad vessels of war. It is generally the case, where we have been criminally apathetic upon a subject of National importance, and have finally come to give it attention, we go at once to the opposite extreme. So, in this instance, we delayed too long the construction of iron-clad vessels, of which every great Power should possess a few, and when we tardily determine upon providing ourselves with this class of war-engines, we pour out our ten or twelve million dollars like so much water, to build twenty vessels upon entirely novel plans, designed by people who have never seen such ships, or even the detailed designs of any of the considerable number which have been built in Europe.

The extra session of Congress last year acted very judiciously in directing the construction of one or more such vessels, and appropriating one and a half million dollars for the purpose; the bill directing that the talent of the country should be called, forth by the issue of advertisements for plans, and that these should be submitted to a Board of competent officers for approval and selection. This was done; three plans were adopted, and one vessel directed to be constructed upon each, one of which is now nearly completed in this City, and will be ready for service before this month is out.[1] With the commencement of this session, however, the Navy Department asked for the immediate construction of twenty more, and pending the decision of Congress upon the subject, the officials in the Bureau of Construction have completed a design upon which they propose to build them, and have invited to Washington and been in consultation with representatives of all the principal builders in our Atlantic cities. The House of Representatives has passed the bill appropriating ten millions for the purpose, but it has not yet been acted upon by the Senate.

In the designs we, allude to, the vessel just described as nearly completed is followed in many of its important features, and its imitators intended to carry precisely the same armament, namely, two guns of the largest calibre used in the navy. If, therefore, the vessel now building is successful, and can place her two guns in position to destroy our enemies, and can maintain them there until such destruction is completed, it is clear that every additional dollar which vessels carrying the same armament shall cost is thrown away, even if we were certain that the more costly vessels would be entirely successful. The batteries, designed by the officials in Washington, are expected to cost at least ten million dollars; whereas we have reason to believe that twenty like the one now nearly completed could be built in less time for five millions.

It is true that this Naval Board affects to believe that the one they have partially followed will not be successful, but would not any prudent and disinterested man consider it much the wiser course to unit a few weeks, and ascertain, beyond the possibility of a doubt, whether it was necessary to go to this additional expense of five or more millions to attain the desired end?

The subject, we repeat, is still before the Senate. We trust the Committee on Naval Affairs in that body has not overlooked the considerations we have hinted at; so may it give the navy far more efficiency, and leave the Treasury millions the richer. ◉

1. This is the vessel that became the USS *Monitor*.

HOW THE EXPENSES OF THE WAR ARE TO BE MET.

A PROPOSED TAX OF ONE HUNDRED AND FIFTY MILLIONS.

JANUARY 8

WASHINGTON, TUESDAY, JAN. 7

The Committee of Ways and Means have concluded to provide by taxation for a hundred and fifty millions during the current year.

The Committee of Ways and Means should not fail to impose a monthly tax on those who perform the office of sutlers to our armies.[1] It is an exclusive privilege and a very valuable one. Merchants in civil life always pay a license. Those who sell in the camps should do likewise, and the funds go into the Government treasury. The average value of a sutlership to a regiment is said to be $6,000 a year. If we have 600 regiments in service, the furnishing of sutler's goods to them yields a profit of nearly four millions annually. Why should not a fair per cent. of this sum go to the Government, that furnishes the customers and the money they buy with?

Senator HALE's[2] bill to protect the Government Treasury from swindling contracts comes none too soon. Its introduction to-day was marked by a severe speech from that Senator. ◉

1. "Sutlers" were civilians who set up huts in army camps to sell approved items such as newspapers, tobacco, and cutlery to the troops. Throughout the war, these businessmen were accused of inflating prices and profiteering from the soldiers' deprivation.
2. John P. Hale (1806–1873) of New Hampshire.

things? Let us hope, whether the extreme penalty of the law is inflicted or not, that it will prove salutary. It is the capitalists of the North, not the slaveowners of the South, who now encourage the African traffic. We shall soon know whether President LINCOLN is true to his professions in this important matter, or whether he has adopted them for personal and party purposes. ✹

REBEL TESTIMONY TO THE EFFICIENCY OF THE BLOCKADE.

JANUARY 9

It is very curious that while the British journals tell us a great deal about the utter inefficiency of the blockade, the Southern journals, on the contrary, are constantly testifying to its rigor. We have repeatedly quoted testimony to this effect from Richmond Charleston and New-Orleans papers. The latest we copy this morning from the Richmond Examiner, of the 30th December. It contains this emphatic statement:

"The only effective weapon of assault that the public enemy have yet wielded against us, is the weapon of blockade; and, so far, neither Southern ingenuity, statesmanship, nor pride has been able to provide a single measure for its counteraction."

This is evidence which the journals of secessionist proclivities, on the other side of the water will hardly attempt to rebut, however indiscreet they may consider their rebel friends in blazoning forth to the world the proofs of the extraordinary perfection of our blockade, and thus spoiling the efforts they have been making to convince Europe that it is of no account. ✹

INACTIVITY OF THE AMERICAN ARMY.
—
EXTRACTS FROM THE SPECIAL CORRESPONDENCE OF THE LONDON TIMES.

WASHINGTON, DEC. 9

There is little probability of anything occurring to disturb the march of events, which are the only things that march at Washington, and which have got into a humdrum sort of parade and review order, making one day as like the other as can be. There is, to be sure, always the confidential assurance that "there will be a move soon," and perhaps there may; but hitherto Gen. McClellan has succeeded in averting the danger which is presented to him of making an attack on a desperate and brave enemy with an ill-disciplined army. He may, however, at any moment be led to order an advance, and his army is certainly better prepared to make it now than it has been at any previous time. It would be amusing to took back to the Northern journals, and see how much of the pompous programme of "our Fall campaign" has been fulfilled. New-Orleans was to have been seized, Charleston laid waste, Memphis, Savannah, Richmond, and Nashville occupied, and the seceding States held in subjection till the loyal men could be induced to come out and vote themselves back into the Union. The good public is presented with a strip of sand at Hatteras, and an inlet at Port Royal, and so far it is thankful for the results of these conquests. The "Rat-hole squadrons" are at their work, and the task of the blockading vessels will soon be light enough. In fact, the weather is such on the Southern coast during January, February, and March that it would not be

JANUARY 9, 1862

possible to maintain a force of observation off the harbors; hence most of them will be blocked up, and the others can be watched from time to time by vessels running out of Port Royal. Another great expedition, the naval part to be commanded by a very dashing officer, Capt. DAVID PORTER, is to be prepared immediately, and Gen. BURNSIDE's Corps is now ready to start from Annapolis. The utmost exertions are made by Government to procure mortars of the largest size, but these are not to be made in a day. Nothing indicates any expedition of the first class — one intended to operate against Charleston or New-Orleans, which are the favorite objects of the Northerners.

To the earnest, self-sacrificing thousands who regard this war as the holiest and best in which man ever drew a sword, the conduct of affairs must be most discouraging and irritating. There are myriads of people who literally worship the Union, and who would gladly lay down their lives for that political "idea." But they have no opportunity. They have left professions, trades, and pleasant homes to go out and fight, and as they stand in front of the battle, they feel the ground for which they are striving crumbling under their feet. There are hundreds of men in the Northern armies, like JAMES WADSWORTH, Gen. SPRAGUE and Gen. BUTTERFIELD, who have abandoned ease and comfort to set an example in person of devotion to — well, not their country so much as to — the Union, or,

as Earl RUSSEL styled it, "Power." And the Union was assuredly power. It was power for the slaveholder, power for Slavery, power for democratic institutions to affront the world. Without the Union, the Northern States would be cabined and confined within the Canadian lakes and Virginia, and no reasonable human being can object to their refusal to submit to such a fate. To be deprived of the Mississippi would be to have the main artery torn from the heart. Are they not justified in striking for life at the hand which is stretched out for the purpose? But it is beyond conception that, all this being so, the war is carried on as if it were intended to irritate to madness rather than induce "surrender to force of arms." God and Nature may not, indeed, have put the Black into the hands of the Northerners any more than the Indian was placed at our disposal by the same Power in the American war. But here are all the horrors without any of the results of war. Conquest over the South may mean great ruin to the North, but at least it would be a proof of strength given in the achieving of the result; now all the cost of armaments, prodigious and profuse, is endured without any actual operation in esse to realize the Northern idea. That it may at last be attained I cannot hesitate to admit, but the realization will be terrible to victor and vanquished alike. The question of the fate of that which is not yet in the power of the North already distracts and convulses the country before the battle has been fought at all. It is not, indeed, unlikely that Gen. MCCLELLAN may be averse to a great battle, on the mere grounds of aversion to bloodshed, and the hope of success by milder means; and the smaller operations of war may encourage him to resist the suggestions which are to my ☞

knowledge made to him for an attack upon the enemy. Magnificent weather is lost, and no sign of an advance is visible. There are impatient Senators and angry Congressmen, but no one dares open his lips who remembers the result of the "On to Richmond!" cry of June and July last. The expeditions, and the news of others about to be, amuse the people for the time, but the pressure of taxation will soon render them irritable in their clamors for peace or victory. As yet the war has not pressed hardly on the bulk of the people. Six hundred thousand of the people are amply paid and well fed, and to them are joined hundreds of thousands who are employed in civil work about the army. The noble army of contractors and sutlers is making a fortune, and the theory that the country cannot be losing anything because all the money is spent in it, finds universal acceptance. There are large frauds understood to have been detected in commissariat transactions recently. No doubt greater may be undiscovered. Many persons have already made large fortunes very honestly. Fraud seems somewhat superfluous where prices are so rumunerative and examiners so lenient. "All is quiet along our lines." The river blockade still continues. No men-of-war except a tiny gunboat has passed up or down in front of

the enemy for weeks. Mr. SICKLES is still at work on board the Pensacola, which lies motionless off Alexandria. Reviews go on daily, and for the most part satisfactory in all that relates to the marching of the men, but I never chance to see a decent battalion drill, or any formations, except of the most rudimentary kind, and I much doubt if there are half a dozen regiments here which could form square with steadiness and rapidity against a charge of cavalry. ⊕

Brigadier General Ulysses S. Grant, U.S.A.

ARMY OF THE POTOMAC.

JANUARY 10
CORRESPONDENCE OF
THE RICHMOND EXAMINER.

MANASSAS....

To-day our whole army is engaged in building log houses for Winter quarters, or in moving to sites already selected. Several brigades will remain where they now are, near the fortifications in Centreville, and the remainder will fall back a mile or two upon Bull Run....

In case of an attack by the Yankees, it will take about two hours to get the main strength of the army across to Bull Run. Information of an approach would be given at least two hours before an enemy could come up, and in that time we could be well prepared to resist any force that can be brought up. This is about the situation of affairs for the Winter, and it remains to be seen whether our men are to have an opportunity of a brush with the Yankees, or whether they will be allowed to enjoy their new houses in quietness. ⊕

IMPORTANT FROM THE WEST.

—

THE ADVANCE OF GEN. GRANT'S FORCES DOWN THE MISSISSIPPI.

JANUARY 18
CAIRO, SUNDAY, JAN. 12, 1862.

In common with everybody else, your correspondent was electrified by the announcement on Friday last, that the long-expected "advance" was about to take place — in fact, was already begun. I hastened here as fast as steam could whirl me; found crowds at every station, who fought, crowded, struggled to gain admittance to the train in order to be in time to hang on the skirts of the grand forward movement; heard every hour, as I neared this notorious town, exciting rumors of a fight already commenced

WHO INVENTED "CONTRABAND?"

An enterprising antiquarian has discovered that the happy epithet of "contraband," which Gen. BUTLER applied to the slaves of rebels, and which was at once universally recognized as both a pun and a stroke of genius, is not so much the impromptu inspiration it was thought to be. It seems the original author of the term is our present excellent Mayor, GEORGE OPDYKE.[1] Ten years ago he published a treatise on Political Economy — a book whose merit has never received adequate appreciation — in one chapter of which, treating of Slavery, the following passage occurs: "Slaves are not often furnished, as they formerly were, by African traders, at the cheap rates of stolen goods — the article being now contraband with us," etc. Now, it is not improbable that BUTLER's happy hit was a reminiscence of this, though it is not impossible — for such coincidences do occur — that similar reasonings brought out similar results. If

JANUARY 20
BUTLER has been pilfering, one would like to know it. So good a thing should have its proper paternity. We venture to suggest the matter as a proper subject for inquiry by the V.W.C.I.C — i.e., the Van Wyck Congressional Investigating Committee.[2] ⊕

1. Millionaire clothing manufacturer George Opdyke (1805–1880) served as mayor of New York from 1862 to 1863.
2. New York Congressman Charles Van Wyck (1824–1895) chaired House committees on Mileage and Revolutionary Pensions.

at Columbus, of day-long cannonades heard in the direction of Cairo; rushed from the train the instant it was consistent with safety; "broke" for a livery stable to overtake the advance by land, and when I made known my wishes, was — laughed at!

Forward movement! Troops embarked! Gen. GRANT and Staff en route for the Tennessee River! Gunboats, tugs and transports all left this morning! Such was the telegraph news which went over the wires the day before. The levee was alive with tugs and steamboats — out upon the river, like huge black whales sleeping on the Pacific, lay the gunboats. I visited the headquarters and found a quiet-looking man in a farmer's dress, lazily smoking a meerschaum, and he was the departed General. His Staff was there too — one was smoking with an air of placid contentment — another was brewing a small fight between a couple of specks of children — a third was lazily reviewing the dispatches of a telegraphic reporter for a St. Louis journal — in short, the Staff were just as far from Columbus, and looking just as little like going, as their chieftain.

The troops were not "all embarked" either — across the Ohio the white tents and broad shanties of the usual force gleamed clear against the dark background, formed by the leafless woods of Kentucky — over the Mississippi could be seen the huge encampment, whose occupants guard the fortifications of Bird's Point, while on this side the black muzzles of the Columbiads still looked grimly over the parapet of Fort Cairo; sentinels paced around its walls, naval and military uniforms thronged the streets or lounged in the hotels without number; from the long lines of barracks arose the smoke of a thousand fires.

After taking in all these points, I became satisfied that the "forward movement" had not taken place, and that some unblushing liar had "sold" the public most unmercifully. Upon inquiry, I find that the dispatches announcing the movement are said to have been written by some Government official, handed by him to the agents of the St. Louis and Chicago papers, and, of course, forwarded by them under the supposition that they were reliable. The thing has excited a good deal of angry discussion, particularly among the classes "sold" by the operation; while ingenuity is exhausted in trying to find a reason, ever so slight, for making such an announcement. Even the St. Louis papers seem to have been a party to the thing, for, in the dispatch from this point to them, it was stated that 25,000 troops had left St. Louis for Cairo, and although they must have known its falsity, they did not contradict it. It is asserted that Gen. HALLECK originated the canard, but this I do not believe, as he is at once too much of a gentleman and a soldier to perpetrate a huge lie upon the public, even under the pressure of a military or any other necessity.

A few ill-natured ones argue that the whole thing was done by way of a sop to a public, ravenous for an advance; but even this is too shallow a trick for any one above an idiot, because the reaction of the public feeling, as any one would know, would produce a state much worse than before.

That there was a small movement is true. Five thousand infantry and one thousand cavalry, under [John A.] MCCLERNAND, went down the Mississippi a distance of seven miles, to a point upon which once stood an old Indian fort, and named Fort Jefferson. Here they rested, and went into camp. Being on the east side of the river, on the Kentucky shore, it may be used as a base of operations for excursions into the interior, in the direction of and to the rear of Columbus; and possibly it may be a link in the chain of events intended for direct operations upon that town. ✺

An escaped slave, a "contraband of war," greeting Union soldiers.

CHAPTER 7

"The Iron Gunboats Have Settled the Question"

FEBRUARY—MARCH 1862

Though it remained all quiet along the Potomac during the winter of 1861–62, that season marked a period of active operations in what was called the Western Theater — the area between the Appalachian Mountains and the Mississippi River. There the control of the major river systems was a key factor in all military operations. In February, the Union naval squadron of Flag Officer Andrew Hull Foote, and a Union army commanded by a little-known brigadier general named Ulysses S. Grant, captured two key forts in a campaign that smashed the Confederate defensive line in Tennessee.

As The Times correctly noted, the capture of Fort Henry on the Tennessee River on February 6, and Fort Donelson on the Cumberland River on February 15, were the most important strategic successes of the war to date, and led directly to the capture of Nashville, the first state capital to be reclaimed by the Union. An important factor in these riverine victories was Foote's squadron of iron-armored warships that had been built under the supervision of James B. Eads. The Union's ability to produce such specialized vessels in quantity gave it an unquestioned advantage in the western war. On February 17, The Times boasted that the success of the armored river gunboats demonstrated "the ingenuity, mechanical skill, perseverance and calm courage of a Northern free people over the ardor and impulse, and want of thoroughness, of a Southern and slaveholding population." The ironclads, plus another novel weapon, huge 13-inch mortars on rafts, also proved useful in the investment of Island Number Ten on the Mississippi River, though it held out until April.

Iron armor proved newsworthy in the Eastern Theater as well when,

Detail of the battle between the USS *Monitor* and the CSS *Virginia* at Hampton Roads on March 9, 1862.

on March 9, the USS *Monitor*, built in only 93 days by John Ericsson in Brooklyn, arrived in Hampton Roads, Virginia, literally in the nick of time to thwart the ambitions of the Confederate ironclad *Virginia* (which The Times, like everyone else in the North, called the *Merrimac*). The conversion of the wooden-hulled steam frigate USS *Merrimac* into the iron-armored CSS *Virginia* was no secret, for its transformation had been chronicled in the Southern newspapers. The Times exalted when a Southern newspaper called it "an abortion," though its subsequent success in the destruction of the sailing frigates USS *Cumberland* and USS *Congress* on March 8 was sobering until the arrival of the little *Monitor* that very night neutralized its offensive power.

Even as New Yorkers followed the course of the new armored warfare both on the western rivers and along the Atlantic coast, reports of these events were interlaced with speculations about the future of slavery. The progress of the war was the main story to be sure, but the backstory — the future role of the slaves in a postwar America or, alternatively, the role of free blacks — remained a constant counterpoint to the stories of battles and leaders, victories and defeats. Northerners, including many New Yorkers, wondered in print what would happen to the former slaves if the institution of slavery itself were to be abolished. In a speech at the Cooper Union (then called the Cooper Institute), Frederick Douglass, who as much as anyone was a spokesman for the black race, assumed that the war would result in black emancipation, and suggested that "after the slaves were emancipated to let them alone, do nothing with them…. Let them take care of themselves as others do." But others were not so sure. One article in The Times written by the

Maryland reformer Anna Ella Carroll suggested that the solution was relocation: "a settlement beyond the limits of our own territory." Clearly, despite the Lincoln administration's

official policy that the war was being fought only to reunify the country, the public was already engaged in a discussion about what a post-slavery America would look like.

THE ABOLITION OF SLAVERY IN DELAWARE

FEBRUARY 5

A bill will be introduced in the Legislature providing that every slave 35 years of age and upwards, shall be free within 90 days after its passage; and all slaves under 35 shall become free as they reach that age; and that from and after the 1st day of January, 1872, there shall not be Slavery or involuntary servitude, except as a punishment for crime.[1] Males born of a slave mother after the passage of the act, shall be held as indentured servants until the age of 21, and females until they are 18. The above provisions are based upon the condition that Congress will … engage to pay to the State of Delaware, in bonds of the United States, bearing interest at the rate of six per centum per annum, the sum of $900,000, in ten annual installments, $90,000 to be payable on some day before the first day of September, 1862, to establish a fund for securing full and complete compensation to the owners of slaves who shall have been divested of their property by force of the act in question. The bill provides for the appointment of an assessor in

each county, who shall estimate the value of the slaves, and fix the price which shall be paid for them. The salary of the State Treasurer shall be raised when the act goes into operation from $500 to $1,000, on account of his increased responsibilities and duties in making payment to the owners for their slaves. If Congress will make the appropriation of $900,000 for this purpose, we think every man in the State will esteem the act calculated to promote the interests of our people. Many of the slaveholders would gladly exchange their slaves for money, which they could use in payment for their lands and contemplated improvements. We are informed that many of the largest slaveholders favor the measure. ⊛

> 1. Though officially a slave state, Delaware had only about 1,800 slaves in 1861. That fall, Lincoln proposed to Delaware Congressman George P. Fisher a plan to compensate Delaware's remaining slaveholders with federal funds if they would free their slaves. The proposal was never implemented, and Delaware's slaves were not liberated until the ratification of the Thirteenth Amendment in late 1865.

OUR FIRST VICTORY IN TENNESSEE.

FEBRUARY 8

We have cheering news this morning from Tennessee. The United States soldiers and sailors have at last attained a foothold in that State, after a brilliant naval engagement, a foothold at a point, too, most important for operations, which will now very soon be begun, against Nashville, Memphis, and the whole of the rebel region of the Southwest. As Gen. HALLECK[1] says in his brief bulletin of victory: "The flag of the Union is reestablished on the soil of Tennessee. It will never be removed." It must henceforth be borne steadily southward to the Gulf of Mexico.

Our late military operations in the West have been remarkable for one thing; they have uniformly achieved the purpose for

which they have been undertaken. We have had several considerable actions in, and on the line of Kentucky, and we have not there yet suffered one defeat. This augurs well for our success in the two decisive engagements which must yet be fought there ere the rebel hordes are finally expelled from the soil of that proud and loyal State. The battle and the victory at Fort Henry, on the Tennessee River, which this morning we record, and the subsequent seizure of an important strategic point on the line of the Memphis and Ohio Railroad, are, in their bearings on the pending general advance of our troops from Kentucky, by far the most important events that have taken place in that section since the war began. Not on account of the greatness of the rebel force defeated — for it was not very great — nor on account of the deeds of valor wrought by our brave troops — though ☞

we doubt not they have earned laurels as gay as ever decked a soldier's brow; but because the points gained give us the control of the direct line of railroad which connects the great rebel force at Columbus with that at Bowling Green — and because, also, it clears away another, and perhaps the last, of the obstacles which have heretofore prevented the southward advance of the grand Western army under Gen. Don CARLOS BUELL.[2] There is another and stronger rebel fort on the Cumberland, a few miles eastward of the scene of our present victory; but considering the fact that our troops are now in the rear of that fort, and learning, as we do, from the West, the movement that is on the tapis to bring it down as suddenly as Fort Henry has been brought down, we look upon the victory we have gained as being full and complete, as regards the object in view. Look at the map at that part of Tennessee where Fort Henry is located, and at that point of the Memphis and Ohio Railroad which our troops now hold, and see how far we have penetrated in the rear of Bowling Green — see how far in the rear of Columbus — how convenient we are for sweeping down on the railroad to Memphis — see how near we now are to Nashville — and how Nashville is related to the whole State of Tennessee, and that again to the whole of the rebel States of the Southwest, and some idea will be had of the value of the present advance and victory.

From our telegrams, and the official dispatch of Commodore FOOTE,[3] it appears that this victory was entirely a naval one — the troops of the expedition not having come up to the scene of action until the rebels had surrendered. The gunboats engaged are a part of those strong iron-clad river boats, or turtles, which were built, within the last few months, at St. Louis, Carondelet, and other points, and which were originally destined for the expedition down the Mississippi....

The boats are built very wide, in proportion to their length, giving them almost the same steadiness in action that a stationary land battery would possess. They are constructed upon the same principle as the famous iron battery at Charleston,[4] the sides sloping both upward and downward from the water line, at an angle of 45 degrees. The bow battery on each boat consists of solid oak timber 26 inches in thickness, plated on the exterior surface with iron 2 1/2 inches thick. The side and stern batteries are somewhat thinner, but have the same thickness of iron over that portion covering the machinery. The boats are not plated on the roof, which consists of a 2 1/2 plank. Of course a shot falling upon

Bombardment of Island Number Ten by federal Flag Officer Andrew H. Foote's fleet.

this deck, even at an acute angle, would go through, and a heavy shell so entering would blow up the boat; but the chances of this occurring are not as one in a thousand.

The boats are intended, in action, to be kept "bow on;" hence the superior strength of the bow battery. Broadsides can be delivered with terrible effect while shifting position. To facilitate movements in action, the engines and machinery are of the most powerful kind. The boilers are five in number, constructed to work in connection with or independently of each other. In case of damage done to any one or more of them, a valve closes the connection between the damaged and undamaged boilers, and the latter operate as if nothing had happened.

The most dreadfully savage contrivance upon these boats is that to prevent boarding. Each boat is supplied with a number of large hose-pipes for throwing hot water from the boilers, with a force of 200 pounds pressure to the square inch. Any human being who shall encounter this terrible stream of hot water will be boiled in an instant. Fort Henry, situated in Tennessee, upon the Tennessee River, and a short distance from the northern boundary of the State, was constructed last Summer by the rebels. It is an earthwork, and stands in the river bottom, about the high water mark, just below a bend in the river, and at the head of a straight stretch of about two miles. It, therefore, commands the river for that distance down stream, and very little else. The land around it is a little higher than the fort, and a portion of it is covered with heavy timber. On the opposite side of the river are three hills commanding the fort completely. The armament of the fort,

according to Commodore FOOTE's report, was twenty guns and seventeen mortars. It consisted, we understand, of two 64-pounders, eight 32-pounders, four 12-pounders, and the rest 6-pounders, most of them smooth-bore. It was also supported by a battery of two guns planted on the commanding hills on the opposite side of the river, but of whose capture we have no record. A small creek setting into the Tennessee just at the south of the fort admits back water into the low lands behind the fort, forming a pond of marsh. Across this a bridge or causeway has been constructed, giving communication by means of a military road . . . recently cut directly back to Fort Donelson, at Dover, on the Cumberland River. From a point on this road back of the pond another road has been cut, leading around under the bluffs back of the bottom land to the Pine Bluff landing, six miles below the fort. The chart of the fort, which we give, will furnish an idea of the position of the guns of the battery on the west side of the Tennessee, and of the relation of Fort Henry to Fort Donelson, which at latest accounts, was still unreduced.

Until lately, the garrison of the place was but one regiment, the Tenth Tennessee, 900 strong, and composed mostly of Irishmen; but since the fort was menaced, reinforcements of two Mississippi and one Louisiana regiments, have been sent, and likely also some additional Tennessee troops. The Memphis Appeal of the 12th of January said that the rebel authorities had taken into consideration the critical condition of Fort Henry, and that vigorous and energetic preparations had been made, by land and river, to meet our advance. The whole force was placed under command of Gen. LLOYD TILGHMAN, of Kentucky, a graduate of West Point, and reported an able commander.[5] He is now a prisoner in our hands, and this most important and strategical position is in possession of United States troops.

Commodore ANDREW H. FOOTE, who so gallantly led the gunboats in the action at Fort Henry, is a native of Connecticut, and entered the service from that State in 1822. Since that time he has been continually in service, making the whole time of his naval career extend over forty years. He is still, however, full of the fire and vim of youth, and is one of the best specimens of the old sea dogs in America. Over twenty years of his time he has been on ocean service, cruising in almost every sea; ten years he has been on shore duty, and twenty years of his time has been what is designated as unemployed. He received his commission as commander in 1852, and was last at sea in 1858. Since that time he has been on service in the Brooklyn Navy-yard; but about eight months ago was assigned to the duty of superintending the putting up of the great Mississippi flotilla. Commodore FOOTE is known in the navy as one of its most efficient officers, and distinguished himself greatly in China by the bombardment and breaching of a Chinese fort, the fort, in all respect, a superior work of masonry. The feat called forth the praise of all foreign naval officers on that coast. Commodore FOOTE is an affable gentleman, and, as will be seen by his reply to the rebel TILGHMAM, never surrenders.

Capt. PORTER,[6] of the gunboat Essex, who is reported as badly scalded by the bursting of his boat's boiler, is a native of Louisiana, but entered the navy from Massachusetts in 1823. He is a son of the renowned Commodore PORTER, who figured so prominently in the war of 1812. He has been thirty-eight years in the service, and has seen twelve years sea duty, five years shore duty, and the rest of the time unemployed. He was last at sea in 1850, and was then and has been since until recently in command of the sloop St. Marys. His commission as naval commander dates only since 1855. When the Mississippi flotilla was projected, he was detailed to the command of a gunboat. The Captain christened his boat the Essex, after his father's renowned vessel, and judging from precedent, Capt. PORTER is the "bull-dog," or fighting man of this expedition. He has Dahlgren guns for his armament, and delights in "shelling." He worked prodigiously getting his boat ready, and since then he has been cruising round, stirring up the rebels wherever he could find them.

It was the boast of Commodore PERRY that he built some of his vessels on Lake Erie in twenty-six days. Capt. PORTER took the ferry-boat New Era, completely stripped her of everything but the framework of her hull, and entirely remodeled, rebuilt, and planked her, strengthened her with additional timbers and knees, caulked her, put in bulkheads, built strong and ample gun-decks, cased her hull with iron plates, in fact, constructed a new vessel, carrying nine heavy guns, and floated her out of her dock in fourteen days. The mechanics tell with considerable zest how, on the fourteenth day, Capt. PORTER, who had been crowding the work night and day, without giving notice, opened the ☞

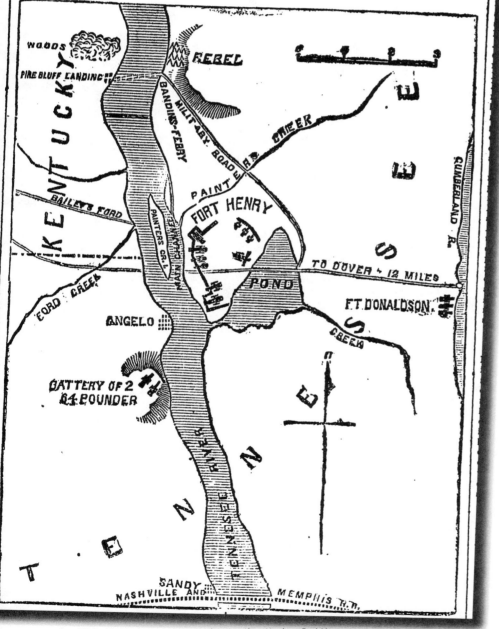

A map published in The New York Times showing the attack on Fort Henry.

gates of the floating dock, let on the water, and, to the astonishment of the industrious artisans aboard, the craft was in her element.

It is earnestly to be hoped that the gallant Captain will speedily recover, and be ready once more for active duty on his loved element.

The rebel commander of Fort Henry [Tilghman], who was so gallantly captured by our navy boys, is a native of Maryland; entered West Point as a cadet in 1831; was made brevet Second Lieutenant in the First Dragoons in 1836, but shortly after resigned, and became division engineer on the Baltimore and Susquehanna Railroad, and afterward on the Baltimore and Ohio Railroad. In the Mexican war he reentered the service as volunteer Aid-de-Camp to Col. [David] TWIGGS, and was present at the battles of Palo Alto and Resaca de la Palma. He commanded a Volunteer till October, 1846, and in January, 1847, was made Superintendent of the defences of Matamoras; finally he acted as Captain of Volunteer Artillery in [George W.] HUGHES' regiment from August, 1847, till July, 1848. At the close of the war he again entered civil life, and was chosen principal Assistant Engineer in the Panama Isthmus Railroad. On the breaking out of the war he was acting as railroad engineer, but joined the rebels, and was appointed to command at Fort Henry, where he has been ingloriously captured. ✸

1. Major General Henry Wager Halleck (1815–1872) was the Union theater commander in the West.

2. The Times reporter showed great strategic insight in this analysis, for cutting the Memphis and Ohio Railroad just below Fort Henry did indeed compel Albert Sidney Johnston to abandon Bowling Green and retreat southward (see below). Major General Don Carlos Buell (1818–898) commanded the Army of the Ohio.

3. Flag Officer Andrew Hull Foote (1806–1863) commanded the Union naval squadron in the West.

4. This is a reference to the floating Iron Battery anchored off Morris Island during the bombardment of Fort Sumter in April 1861. That battery had an iron shield placed at an angle atop a wooden raft.

5. Lloyd Tilghman (1816–1863) was a former railroad engineer from Maryland. He was later killed at the Battle of Champion Hill in Mississippi.

6. William D. Porter (1809–1864) was the son of Navy Commodore David Porter and the older brother of David Dixon Porter. He was known as "Dirty Bill" for his financial irregularities, for which he was court-martialed in 1855. He was restored to active duty in 1859.

THE TENNESSEE VICTORY AND ITS FRUIT

FEBRUARY 9

The victories of Mill Spring[1] and Fort Henry, followed as they have doubtless been by the reduction of Fort Donelson, have cleared both flanks of Gen. BUELL'S army of opposing enemies. The former success, preceded by the dissolution of Humphrey Marshall's corps, compelled the rebels to evacuate Eastern Kentucky, leaving all the approaches into Eastern Tennessee open to the Unionists. The capture of Fort Henry, if supplemented by the capture of Fort Donelson, exposes both Nashville and Memphis to attack; and will doubtless compel the retirement of [Albert Sidney] JOHNSTON, and the evacuation of Columbus. Indeed, the movements of Gen. GRANT and Flg. Offr. FOOTE are so very energetic, that at any moment we may receive, without astonishment, news that the capital of Tennessee has fallen into their hands. A gunboat squadron is known to have entered the Cumberland, where the water is at the high stage of the Winter months. There is nothing to interrupt its voyage to Nashville. If the land forces could move with equal celerity, the movement would be the work of a day.

The importance of the plans which this portion of Gen. HALLECK's command is realizing, as subsidiary to the task assigned Gen. BUELL, is not to be overrated. Already the Memphis and Clarksville Railroad is in the possession of our forces. Over this route the army of Gen. JOHNSTON has received the bulk of its supplies and reinforcements since the destruction of the bridge over the Cumberland at Nashville. Merely to have lost this communication would of itself be the worst conceivable omen to the rebel army at Bowling Green; but when the advantage thus secured by the National force is followed up actively by land and water, there will be reason for the utmost consternation in the rebel lines. We may be assured that the first move backwards, or the first attempt to detach a force to cut off the advance of GRANT, will be the signal for a grand attack, before which the insurgent army is in no condition to stand. ✸

Above: Major General Henry W. Halleck, U.S.A.; Right: Flag Officer Andrew H. Foote, U.S. navy.

1. The Battle of Mill Springs, in Kentucky, also known as the Battle of Fishing Creek (January 19, 1862), was a Union victory. Confederate Brigadier General Felix Zollicoffer (1812–1862) was killed in the battle, the first Confederate general officer to die in the Western Theater.

THE MERRIMAC AS A TYPE OF THE REBELLION

FEBRUARY 9

The rebel iron-sheathed annihilator, the Merrimac, is reported a total failure. We might suppose that this was given out as a rebel ruse, with the design to throw our naval force on the Potomac off its guard, had not various facts come out in the course of its construction that made it pretty evident it would be a failure. Months ago, on trying the iron-sheathing with columbiads it proved to be almost worthless. It now appears that an enormous error in the calculation of displacement, amounting to two hundred tons, was discovered when the ship was floated off lately, and that she "hogs" and "logs" and is a botch generally. The Norfolk Day Book, while censuring certain Richmond journals for letting out the fact of the Merrimac's failure, declares it is "an abortion." Horrors — an abortion! But it is very much such "an abortion" as the rebellion, of which it is a very good type, is beginning to prove. Both have been put forth with the most blustering claims of what they would do — both have been gigantic blunders in construction — and the fizzle of the one is a sure harbinger of the failure of the other. ✸

BURNSIDE AT ROANOKE ISLAND — NORFOLK THREATENED

FEBRUARY 12

We have now news enough from Southern sources to infer that BURNSIDE[1] has achieved a complete success, and that the rebels have suffered a severe defeat by land and by water. With Norfolk in a panic, as is reported from Fortress Monroe, we can hardly expect to receive a composed or consistent account of the affair, even if there were the disposition to give it, and we shall probably have to await a dispatch-boat by way of Hatteras for detailed intelligence. For the information that we have, we, in common with other journals, are indebted to the enterprise of the Fortress Monroe correspondent of the Philadelphia Inquirer, and it establishes, beyond a doubt, that Roanoke Island is in the possession of our forces, after a three days' combat, naval and military, which brilliantly illustrated the resources, the pluck and the valor of both arms of the National service. For, in this victory, the cooperation of the land and sea forces seems to have attained a completeness not reached in any of our former expeditions. Port Royal and Hatteras were exclusively naval victories, but Roanoke called forth and combined the effective qualities of both arms of the service. We have as yet no details of the work done on the island after landing, and only know it was triumphantly done, and that the National Standard was planted over the enemy's fortifications. But the naval bulletin is certainly as brilliant as one could well desire.... ✱

1. Brigadier General Ambrose E. Burnside (1824–1872) led a combined army-navy expedition into the sounds of North Carolina. Though he successfully seized Roanoke Island, a lack of available support prevented his campaign from achieving an important strategic success.

FORT DONELSON ATTACKED.

DESPERATE FIGHTING FOR AN ENTIRE DAY.

FEBRUARY 15
CHICAGO, FRIDAY, FEBRUARY 14

Fort Donelson is invested by our troops. Our lines are formed from right to left and from north to south, nearly surrounding the fort. A heavy cannonading and skirmishing have been going on since 7 o'clock this morning, but, owing to the extent of our line of action, but little can be learned of the result.... ✱

FRED. DOUGLASS ON THE WAR.

AN INTERESTING MEETING AT THE COOPER INSTITUTE.

FEBRUARY 13

A very large audience assembled at the Cooper Institute last evening, on the occasion of the lecture of FRED. DOUGLASS[1] on "The War." A somewhat unusually large number of policemen were visible in all portions of the house, although the necessity for their presence was not apparent....

Mr. DOUGLASS, in commencing, said that at the time he proposed to speak, the victories of Fort Henry and Roanoke Island had not been fought, and even those victories had not removed the somewhat sombre view which he took of the war. This war had developed our patience. (Laughter.) He was not here to find fault with the Government; that was dangerous. (Laughter.) Such as it was, it was our only bulwark, and he was for standing by the Government. (Applause.) He would not find fault with Bull Run, Ball's Bluff or Big Bethel, but he meant to call attention to the uncertainty, and vascillation and hesitation in grappling with the great question of the war — Slavery. The great question was, "What shall be done with the slaves after they are emancipated?" He appeared as one who had studied Slavery on both sides of Mason and Dixon's line. He considered himself an American citizen. He was born on the most sacred part of the soil. (Laughter and applause.) There was nothing in the behavior of the colored race in the United States in this crisis, that should prevent him from being proud of being a colored citizen of the United States. (Applause.) They had traitors of all other nations in Fort Lafayette as cold as Stone — (laughter) — but they had no black man charged with disloyalty during this war. Yet, black men were good enough to fight by the side of WASHINGTON and JACKSON, and were not good enough to fight beside MCCLELLAN and HALLECK. (Laughter.) But, he would not complain — he only threw out these hints. (Laughter.) The question was simply whether free institutions and liberty should stand or fall. Any peace without emancipation would be a hollow peace. Even that rhinoceros-hided place, Washington, had by a species of adumbration, come to realize this truth. (Laughter.) What had Slavery done for us, that it had any claim upon us that we should spare it? Tens of thousands of American citizens were now taking their first lessons in Anti-Slavery. He held up in a ludicrous vein the tenderness of many who, like the New-York Herald, would hang a rebel and confiscate all his property — except his slaves. Slavery had kept our army quiet for seven months, and displaced good and loyal men by incompetent and disloyal ones. The question was, What shall be done with the 4,000,000 slaves if emancipated? He might ask what shall be done with the 350,000 slaveholders? His plan was, after the slaves were emancipated to let them alone, do nothing with them. (Laughter.) Let them take care of themselves as others do. (Applause).... ✱

1. Frederick Douglass (1818–1895) was born a slave in Maryland, escaped to freedom, and became editor of Douglass' Monthly and an acclaimed orator in support of abolitionism and black rights.

Frederick Douglass.

FORT DONELSON.

ITS POSITION, ARMAMENT AND STRATEGIC VALUE.

FEBRUARY 17

The news of the capture of Fort Donelson — or at least its virtual capture by the taking of the redoubt commanding the rebel positions that still held out on Saturday — which is announced by telegraph this morning, and the still more important news of the rebel evacuation of Bowling Green, will attract undivided attention to the great military operations now being carried out in the Southwest. To render more clear to everybody the value of these victories, we give the above map, showing not only the important positions which have of late been the scenes of Union triumphs, such as Fort Henry on the Tennessee, Fort Donelson on the Cumberland, Bowling Green on the Big Barren, Mill Springs on the Eastern waters of the Cumberland, and other strategic localities, but showing also the bearing of these points on Columbus and Memphis, on Clarksville and Nashville, on Cumberland Gap and Knoxville, still in rebel hands; and exhibiting, too, the relation of the several places captured, and of those on which our army is now rapidly advancing, to the rebel States immediately south and east of Tennessee, to the Gulf States of Mississippi and Alabama, and to Georgia, North and South Carolina. If the reader will give a few minutes' study to this little reference-map, to its topography, railroads, rivers and mountains, he will gain a more accurate knowledge of our present military situation in the Southwest, and of the directions and places whence our banners will next be borne, than could possibly be given by verbal descriptions. As the scene of our main operations for some time to come is likely to be within the territory included in this map, those who wish to follow them up intelligently will find it convenient to clip out and preserve for reference.

Fort Donelson, as will be seen, is situated at Dover, Tennessee, on the west bank of the Cumberland River, a few miles south of the northern boundary of the State, and was built last Summer, about the same time as Fort Henry. It is located at a point where the river washes an obtuse angle in its northward course. It is twelve miles southeast of Fort Henry, which was captured just nine days before the present victory. The main object of the fort was to stand as a rear de-

fence to Bowling Green, and also as a defence against our approach to Nashville by the Cumberland River. It was believed by the rebels that it would block up effectually our passage into Tennessee in this direction. Some seven or eight post roads here intersect each other, and the railroad from Bowling Green to Memphis passes but four miles south of it. This same railroad, it will be remembered, was cut a short distance west, at the Tennessee River, by our gunboats, immediately after the fall of Fort Henry, and is now again destroyed at the crossing of the Cumberland. Fort Donelson controls the river as far up as Clarksville, where the rebels may perhaps again make a stand as we advance onward to Nashville. At Clarksville they have fortifications and a pretty strong armament, and lately they had there also a considerable body of troops.

The enemy are supposed to have had three batteries at Fort Donelson — one near the river's edge, one fifty feet above this, on the high ground, and a third fifty feet above the second; this upper one mounted four 18-pounder guns. Our gunboats first

attacked the water battery, but the rebels held back the fire of their upper and strongest work until Commodore FOOTE, with his usual daring, had brought his boats within 400 yards of the fort. He still advanced, however, until he got within 100 yards of it. At 4 o'clock on Saturday this upper redoubt, constituting the right wing of the enemy's fortification, and which commands the remainder of the rebel works, was taken by our troops, and from it the old flag was flung to the breeze. Of the exact armament of these various works we have not information, but, at the latest date to which our knowledge extends there were mounted some 20 heavy guns, 18, 32, and 64-pounders. It is not to be wondered, placed as these were, that they should have done considerable damage to even such strong boats as compose our iron-plated Western river fleet. And there is no doubt that large additions to the number were within a week made from Bowling Green — as Commodore FOOTE says, in his official dispatch, that in the upper and lower redoubts alone there were mounted 20 guns.

The number of rebels manning the fortifications was estimated, last Thursday, by our commanders on the field, in the dispatch published last Saturday, as high as 15,000. No further reinforcements could have been thrown in after that time, as

A postwar Kurz and Allison chromolithograph of the Battle of Fort Donelson.

our forces then had invested the fort. If Gen. HALLECK's statement was correct that FLOYD (the thief) was then inside the fort, it is likely that he had taken the division with which he left Bowling Green last Monday, along with him, instead of having taken it to East Tennessee to fight Gen. THOMAS, as was supposed. That division consists of three brigades, one of which was immediately commanded by FLOYD himself, another by HARDEE, and a third by SIMON BOLIVAR BUCKNER. The regiments were from Arkansas, Mississippi, Tennessee, Virginia and Kentucky, and were the flower of the rebel army in the Southwest. The four regiments also which fled from Fort Henry on its capture by Commodore FOOTE, had probably also taken refuge in Fort Donelson. The rebel troops at Clarksville too, could have been easily thrown forward after the fall of Fort Henry. There is no doubt that all the rebel forces that could possibly be spared were there. Up to the 20th of last month, the fort was occupied by only a few companies of Tennesseeans, and so strongly were the rebels there posted that they did not believe we would dare to assail even them. But give the rebels all the reinforcements and the largest number claimed, and there was still an immense preponderance of men on our side — the Union force investing the fort being stated by Gen. HALLECK to be fifty thousand strong. Considering the location of the fort, its defences, and the force manning it, and it will be seen that the rebels could make a severe fight. There are other things beside superior numbers to be taken into consideration in estimating the chances of a battle. The rebels succeeded, too, in disabling the most efficient of our gunboats. But as at the latest hour, the mortar boats were nearly ready to open fire on the positions the rebels still held, in connection with the guns from the commanding position we had captured, and as our brave troops were breast to breast with the rebels, we may at any hour anticipate news of the complete reduction of Fort Donelson. ⊛

1. The loss of Forts Henry and Donelson allowed Union forces to cut the Memphis and Ohio Railroad that connected Bowling Green (where the Confederate theater commander, Albert Sidney Johnston, made his headquarters) with Memphis. This prompted Johnston to evacuate Bowling Green and fall back, through Nashville, all the way into northern Alabama.
2. A shot from Fort Henry punctured the steam drum on the ironclad USS *Essex*, scalding ten men and putting her out of the fight.

THE MEANING OF THE IRON GUNBOATS.

FEBRUARY 17

It is not becoming in us, as yet, to be too confident, but we think it may now be fairly said that the iron gunboats have settled the question where the Mississippi River shall belong. Whatever fortune betide the Virginia army, or the rebel States on the Atlantic, the Valley of the Mississippi has now passed over to the control of those to whom, in the natural course, it must belong — the ingenious and hardy population of the West and Northwest. The iron gunboats are merely an exponent of those qualities which have gained the victory — the ingenuity, mechanical skill, perseverance and calm courage of a Northern free people over the ardor and impulse, and want of thoroughness, of a Southern and slaveholding population.

If half a dozen of these gunboats could reduce a strong fort, with 20 guns, in an hour and a quarter, there is certainly nothing from Cairo to the Balize[1] which could long withstand thirty of them, with the enormous Pittsburgh mortars, and a hundred thousand men following in transports.

For it must be remembered that in modern days the great difference between the armies of civilized nations is not so much in personal courage as in equipment and discipline. Accordingly, numbers, with artillery and under good drill, must prevail. There is scarcely such a thing in modern warfare as a small army beating, in a long campaign, a large army.... War among civilized peoples, equal in number, is a contest of Science and Wealth. It is true, that in the beginning a people like ours, composed

so largely of those engaged in agricultural and mechanical employments, and unaccustomed both to the implements and the passions of war, may receive severe checks from a population much lower in intelligence, but used to weapons, and in the habit of giving loose rein to resentment and passion. But this is a mere matter of loss in the opening of a war. Such a people as ours, hardy, ingenious and naturally bold, as they become accustomed to martial operations and dangers, make the best kind of soldiery. Their invention is incessantly at work; the genius which has won such successes in the arts of peace is now applied constantly to the formation of implements of destruction, or to the combinations of strategy. We are to have enormous floating batteries of iron, which no existing fortifications can resist; mortars throwing their tremendous projectiles, weighing, it is said, thirty tons, for six or eight miles; new weapons will be invented, and all the energy of our untiring and ingenious national improvement will be turned to the shortest and most terrible methods of destruction.

...The iron gunboats which are now deciding the fate of the Valley of the Mississippi, are merely an index of the power which must now henceforth bear down overwhelmingly from the North upon the South. If they had not been invented, something else would have been. The old, steady and patient courage which in all ages has given a Northern people victory over a Southern, is now winning our battles.... ⊛

1. Balize (or La Balise) was the first French settlement in Louisiana (1699) and was at the very mouth of the Mississippi River.

THE FALL OF FORT DONELSON.
FIFTEEN THOUSAND ... PRISONERS

FEBRUARY 18

The following brief telegrams announcing the surrender of Fort Donelson to the land forces under Gen. GRANT, were received in this City, yesterday and appeared in "Extras" and in the afternoon papers.

...Dispatches from Gen. GRANT to Gen. HALLECK announce the surrender of Fort Donelson, with 15,000 prisoners, including Gens. JOHNSTON, BUCKNER and PILLOW.[1]

Further official advices from Fort Donelson, say that Gen. FLOYD escaped during the night,

and the rebels in the fort denounced him as a black-hearted traitor and coward.... ⊛

1. Though Confederate Brigadier General Simon Bolivar Buckner was captured along with nearly 15,000 Confederate soldiers at Fort Donelson, neither Albert Sidney Johnston nor Gideon Pillow were. Johnston remained at his headquarters in Bowling Green, and Pillow escaped along with John B. Floyd, who handed command of Fort Donelson and most of its garrison to Buckner before taking the last steamboat out of the surrounded fort. The next day, Buckner asked Grant for terms.

CHIVALRY.

FEBRUARY 19

Gen. Buckner, when told by Gen. GRANT that no terms but absolute and immediate surrender would be accepted, replied that, "notwithstanding the brilliant success of the Confederate arms," he was obliged to "accept the ungenerous and unchivalrous terms" which were proposed. We are ready to make all reasonable allowance for a man who two days before had boasted of the impregnability of his position, and who found himself suffering severe punishment and disastrous defeat; but we must say that this reply of Gen. BUCKNER's was one of the silliest sentences ever written. Why, the absolute and immediate surrender of that post, and the punishment of those who held it, was the very object of the expedition under Gen. GRANT's command. It was to attain that end that he planned, and that the brave fellows with him fought, and bled, and died. And when by skill, courage, endurance, suffering and death their prize was within their grasp, what absurdity to expect that they would forego one jot or tittle of it!

And then this talk of chivalry! Good people at the South, understand us plainly, we had enough of this, long ago, and we are now heartily sick of it. Chivalry had its place in the world once, when common sense, and common honesty, and the spirit

of Christianity, were more prevalent than they are now. And even now there is in gallantry an element of accomplished manhood which is akin to chivalry. But chivalry has done its work in the world, and is dead and buried. There stalks about a mouthing sham which assumes its name, but it is mostly given to the oppression of the miserable, to getting drunk in the morning, to elaborate and inordinate profanity, to belching tobacco-juice, flourishing bowie-knives, and to shooting "on sight" people with whom it has a misunderstanding....

Finally, let the insurgents understand that we are not sacrificing our brothers by thousands and our money by millions for the sake of having knightly passages at arms with them. We go out to fight them because they are banded together to destroy a beneficent Government, to resist laws which they have helped to make, to set at naught a Constitution which the people whom they assume to represent voluntarily accepted. The President read the riot act to these men last April; and now we are the officers of the law who are putting that act into effect. In so doing, we take the risk of suffering ourselves; but neither reason, nor generosity, nor gallantry lays upon us the obligation of staying our hand short of the absolute submission of the culprits. ✦

SECRETARY STANTON ON THE WAR AND THE CREDIT OF OUR VICTORIES.

FEBRUARY 21

To the Editor of the New-York Tribune:

SIR: I cannot suffer undue merit to be ascribed to my official action. The glory of our recent victories belongs to the gallant officers and soldiers that fought the battles. No share of it belongs to me.

Much has recently been said of military combinations and organizing victory. I hear such phrases with apprehension. They commenced in infidel France with the Italian campaign, and resulted in Waterloo. Who can organize victory? Who can combine the elements of success on the battle-field? We owe our recent victories to the spirit of the Lord, that moved our soldiers to rush into battle, and filled the hearts of our enemies with terror and dismay. The inspiration that conquered in battle was in the hearts of the soldiers and from on high; and wherever

there is the same inspiration there will be the same results. Patriotic spirit, with resolute courage in officers and men, is a military combination that never failed.

We may well rejoice at the recent victories, for they teach us that battles are to be won now and by us in the same and only manner that they were ever won by any people, or in any age, since the days of Joshua, by boldly pursuing and striking the foe. What, under the blessings of Providence, I conceive to be the free organization of victory and military combination to end this war, was declared in a few words by Gen. GRANT's message to Gen. BUCKNER — "I propose to move immediately on your works!"

YOURS, TRULY, EDWIN M. STANTON. ✦

THE NEWS OF THE CAPTURE OF NASHVILLE CONFIRMED.

FEBRUARY 26

Gen. MCCLELLAN received a dispatch an hour since, from the West, confirming the report that Nashville, Tenn., is taken by Gen. Buell's army, and stating that the rebels have fallen back on Murfreesboro, about thirty miles from Nashville.[1] ✦

1. Albert Sidney Johnston and his army abandoned Nashville on February 23. Union Major General Don Carlos Buell did not so much capture Nashville as occupy it after the Confederates evacuated.

THE SUPPRESSION OF WAR NEWS.

FEBRUARY 28

The order of the War Department suspending the publication of news of military movements, naturally provokes the comment of the Press. The Press is the ear of the people. It collects and transmits to the popular sensorium all the passing events of the hour. When the newspaper is bidden to silence, the people. . . is bidden to be deaf, and its censure to be dumb. The public has, therefore, its incontestible right to question this curtailment of its privileges of hearing and judging the doings of its servants. The same right belongs to the Press, that immediate servant of the people. The journals, which are looked to as the most prompt and trustworthy reporters of intelligence, maintain their repute for promptitude and accuracy, by untiring enterprise and the lavish outlay of money. At great conjoint expense, they support a system of telegraphic communication which reaches over the entire surface of the loyal section, from ocean to ocean. The NEW-YORK TIMES has its special telegraphic reporters at every point of interest, its correspondents with every division of the army. Our readers are able to judge the results of this extended enterprise. The columns of this paper have furnished the earliest and fullest intelligence of those brilliant actions which, during the last six weeks, have done imperishable honor to the soldiers of the Union, as well as to those who planned and directed their movements, and to those who gave to those movements

THE REBELLION.

FEBRUARY 26

The Secretary of War has issued an order announcing: 1. That from and after to-day, the President takes military possession of all telegraph lines; 2. All telegrams relating to military operations, excepting those from the Department and the Generals commanding, are prohibited transmission; 3. Journals publishing military news, unauthorized, are to be punished; 4. Appoints a military supervisor of messages, and a military superintendent of telegraph offices; 5. This order not to interfere with the ordinary operations of said companies.... ❋

a necessary impulse. With the entire system, which at a cost hardly less than would suffice to sustain an army, has produced results so satisfactory to the public, the order of the War Department is in conflict, and if correctly interpreted as a permanent war measure, must be fatal to newspaper enterprise. Journals whose arrangements are of the same comprehensive and elaborate character as our own, are, therefore, warranted in scrutinizing this step of the Administration with jealous eyes, and only surrendering their well-ascertained privileges upon thorough conviction that the public is best served by misinformation, and that the duty of the Press is to reverse its mission, and propagate ignorance. The Secretary of War, we doubt not, has given due weight to considerations like these. He has not taken the step unadvisedly. We are impelled to believe that the restriction is a necessary protection to the movements of the utmost importance now making by a portion of the army, which has so long stood inactive; and that its duration will only extend to the time, which may be reached at any moment, when those movements have been crowned with victory. In this light, the order may be submitted to patiently, and even hailed as an omen of that triumph which has been so long awaited, and which is now hopefully expected. In any other light, the very general expression of discontent with which the public has received the regulation, would be well grounded, and would presently require its abrogation. ❋

THE WESTERN SANITARY COMMISSION.

This body has issued its report for the month of January, 1862, under date of St. Louis, Feb. 10. It has distributed 15,589 different articles, consisting, among other things, of 696 bed comforts, 1,507 towels, 2,328 pairs of socks, etc. The total number of articles distributed to Feb. 1 was 34,604, and since its establishment the Commission has received 525 boxes and barrels of goods from different States and cities, and the sum of $2,276[.] 45 has been received in money, two-thirds of which has been expended. The Commission calls for additional contributions, and asks that all boxes of goods may be directed to JAMES

MARCH 2

E. YEATMAN, President Western Sanitary Commission, St. Louis, Mo., as heretofore, and the names of the parties sending, and of the place sent from, should be plainly marked on the boxes, that their receipt may be more readily acknowledged.[1] ❋

1. The Sanitary Commission was founded in 1861 by the Women's Central Relief Association of New York. A forerunner of the Red Cross, its purpose was to promote clean and healthy conditions in the Union army camps. The Western Sanitary Commission, founded in St. Louis, was independent of the national organization.

ABANDONMENT OF MURFREESBORO BY THE REBELS.

OFFICIAL ANNOUNCEMENT BY GEN. BUELL.

WASHINGTON, SUNDAY, MARCH 2

Gen. BUELL telegraphed to Gen. McCLELLAN last night that the rebels have abandoned Murfreesboro, and are in full retreat towards the Tennessee River. Crossing this river will place them in Ala-

MARCH 3

bama, and free Middle Tennessee of every armed rebel force. Inasmuch as the enemy retreat along a railroad line, tearing up the rails as they pass, it will be difficult for Gen. BUELL to catch them .... ❋

NEWS FROM THE REBEL PAPERS.

ST. LOUIS, MONDAY, MARCH 3

The Memphis Appeal[1] of the 28th ult., has the following:

We have information from Nashville up to noon of Wednesday. Gen. BUELL and Commodore FOOTE arrived and occupied the place. The United States [flag] was raised over the dome of the Capitol, and floats there now. But one Federal flag was exhibited, and that from the shop of a Yankee jeweler, who had long been suspected of disloyalty.

The feeling in Nashville is strongly southern. A deep gloom seemed to cover the community. Citizens avoid intercourse of any kind with the invaders. Two British flags have been raised by the prop-

MARCH 4

erty holders, thus evincing their intention to claim the protection of that Government.... ❋

1. The pro-Confederate Memphis Appeal had a curious history during the Civil War. On June 6, 1862, with Union forces closing in on Memphis, the presses and plates were loaded into a boxcar and moved to Grenada, Mississippi. The Appeal later journeyed to Jackson and then Meridian in Mississippi, to Atlanta, and finally to Montgomery, Alabama, where the plates were destroyed on April 6, 1865.

THE FREEDMEN OF THE SOUTH — WHAT SHALL BE DONE WITH THEM?

MARCH 6

Hundreds of thousands of this unfortunate people, and among them many of the most advanced intelligence, in the South, can now be colonized and made free and independent, without any other action on the part of the National Government than the gift of a settlement beyond the limits of our own territory. This can be done now. Hereafter it will be too late, when the Union is restored and the rights of all will stand again on the basis of the Constitution.

To provide a settlement and government for the African race on this Continent, is a duty, which, if promptly performed on the part of the Government, will secure an inestimable blessing to the future of our own country as well as to the cause of humanity and civilization; while it would be an impossible bar to future litigation in the Courts, which will otherwise occupy the attention of the next generation.

To provide a government for the colored population within the limits of any State of this Union is too palpable an infraction of the Constitution to admit of any controversy, whatsoever.

There is no territory belonging to the United States adapted by soil or climate to the African people, and even if this were not the case, the very purpose would be defeated for which the colony would be initiated — the object being to secure freedom forever for these Africans, by putting them beyond the power of molestation by the rebels who have held them as slaves.

Liberia is too remote to meet the exigency of the case, and beside the enormous expense which it would cost the Government, these people would never remove there without compulsion.

Hayti is wholly under European influences, which are intensely hostile to the United States, and will forever remain so, unless at some future day this Government shall extend its jurisdiction over the West India Islands.

The policy of colonizing our African people would be to place them under an influence friendly to this Government, and favorable to their political and social advancement.

Central America presents this field. Its climate soil, and wealth in natural products, preeminently, adapt it to the African — whilst there he would at once be placed upon an entire social and political equality with the native or other resident.[1]

It must be plain to every statesman that, upon the restoration of the Union, Central America and Mexico will become more and more under the influence of the United States; while England and France, hitherto so potential, will be constantly diminishing in influence over these Powers.

Thus the United States Government is destined to become really the guardian and protector of both Central America and Mexico.

Could we look into the vista of the future, it might be clearly seen that, by the necessary operations of social and natural law, the negro race of this Continent will be the predominating and governing race of all tropical America; and this Government, in settling a colony there to-day, will be but laying the foundation for a vast colored empire....

Thousands of slaveholders in the South would joyfully emancipate their slaves, were a settlement in Central America provided, as it would impose on the owners no further obligation than the actual cost of their transportation.

ANNA ELLA CARROLL[2] ⊛

1. Abraham Lincoln supported the notion of establishing a colony in Central American (in present-day Nicaragua) for emancipated slaves. His notion was that such a colony would provide a safety valve for emancipated slaves who found life in the post-war South intolerable.
2. Anna Ella Carroll (1815–1893) was a Maryland reformer and author who became an unofficial advisor to President Lincoln. Her support of a Central American colony for emancipated slaves may have triggered Lincoln's effort to establish such a colony.

THE BATTLE OF HAMPTON ROADS.

MARCH 10

For a Sea-piece, that fulfills all the conditions of dramatic art as completely as it is possible for a real event to do, commend us to the recital of the battle of Hampton Roads, which we publish to-day.[1] ARISTOTLE himself could not ask a nicer observance of the unities than it displays; and it needs no aid from the playwright's craft to throw the series of naval actions that took place off Newport's News, on Saturday, between noon and night, into the form of a dramatic composition, perfect in design and execution, with its beginning, middle and end, and its moral lesson all included.

The scene opens with the sudden appearance in Hampton Roads of that mysterious marine monster, the Merrimac, and two attendant rebel war-dogs. Down they come, belching fire and destruction, and heading straight towards the National fleet that lay at anchor in the Roads. Imagine the thrill of terror that ran through their wooden walls as the terrible mailed monster made his appearance. Such as had steam to aid their flight, hastily rushed, like herring chased by a shark, for the protecting guns of Fortress Monroe; but alas for those that had not! Two fine old sailing frigates lay at anchor off Newport's News — the Congress and the Cumberland. Into the latter the iron-clad steamer plunged her steel plow, crashing through the frigate's bow, sinking her instantly, and it is said, carrying down half her crew of five hundred souls. Later accounts diminish this tragic catastrophe to one hundred men. Let us trust that further reports will show this to be still an exaggerated number.[2] The other frigate, the Congress, was next attacked in turn, and after pouring in a shower of shot, which rained like pebbles on the mailed sides of the Merrimac, she surrendered. The events which immediately succeed are but obscurely reported in the telegraphic dispatches; but we catch glimpses of a scene that is painfully dark and disastrous.[3] The National steamers that had taken to flight on the approach of the Merrimac appear all to have grounded on the way between Newport's News and Fortress Monroe; and it seems inevitable that the iron-sheathed annihilator shall go on destroying each in turn, and make her way out to

The USS *Monitor*, left, attacking the CSS *Virginia*.

out on the rampage, she would play the butt in the crockery-shop with our wooden block-aders; and it is difficult to see what would have prevented her going down the coast like a destroying angel and anni-hilating our whole fleet. The London Times not long ago threatened to lay the Warrior broadsides of New-York and Hoboken; what was there to hinder the Merrimac's realizing the threat? One can imagine how the rebel chiefs at Richmond will gnash their teeth over this fatal delay that has dashed their hopes of success on the sea, and put an end for-ever to their navy.

If the Battery had not arrived in time! — one trembles to look along the line of this contingency. Suffice it to say that it did arrive in time, and that the National cause has had an escape and a triumph whose romantic form stirs the mind with min-gled wonder and joy. ❁

sea, to descend in a new destroying avatar on the blockading fleet along the coast.

In the midst of this gloomy scene the ex-clamation which spontaneously leaps to the lips is, "Where is the Ericsson Battery?" It alone is able to cope with this destructive monster. Sudden as the realizations of a fairy tale the Battery makes her appear-ance.[4] A deus ex machina! one may well exclaim. Here, indeed, is a knight in mail fit to cope with Sir Merrimac. At this most critical and interesting "situation" the telegraph becomes tantalizingly brief; but we learn that the Battery made its appear-ance late in the evening and put her iron sides between our vessels and the enemy. Yesterday morning the fight began, and the Battery, after engaging the Merrimac and the two rebel gunboats, in a five hours' ac-tion, put them all to flight, the Merrimac slinking off "in a sinking condition."[5] The timing of the action is really so nice that it sounds like a romance, and one might well be incredulous, were not our tidings official, and were it not known that the Er-icsson Battery sailed from New-York last week for Fortress Monroe, with the express purpose of going up to Norfolk and beard-ing the monster in his den. Her arrival was certainly in the very nick of time, and the result one which does honor not only to the

officers and men, but to the ingenious in-ventor who shaped the victorious creation of naval art.

And this reminds us that we must not, in the contemplation of the merely aes-thetic aspects of the battle of Hampton Roads, lose sight of the practical import of this brilliant affair. The Merrimac is undoubtedly a most formidable engine of war, and previously to the construc-tion of Ericsson's iron-clad Battery, we had nothing in our navy that could begin to stand before her. The stories of her in-efficiency and failure, that the Richmond journals have published at various times, were probably in great measure intended as a mask; the work on her has been done by Northern mechanics, and is no doubt well done. The rebels have thrown their whole resources into her, and, in despair of obtaining a navy of their own, thought to send out an engine of war that would utterly destroy ours. The vision was not altogether baseless. If they had been only a month earlier with the Merrimac, it is hard to set limits to what the might have done. That she would have been able to de-stroy every vessel in the Roads, brave the batteries of Fortress Monroe and the Rip Raps, and make her way out to sea may now be considered a demonstrated fact. Once

1. Often labeled the Battle between the *Monitor* and *Merrimac*, this engagement in Hampton Roads, Vir-ginia, on March 9 was the first-ever contest between armored warships. The Southern ironclad *Virginia* was built on the hull of the former USS *Merrimack*, which is why Northern papers continued to refer to it as the *Merrimac* (often spelled without the terminal "k").
2. Of the *Cumberland*'s crew of 376, 111 were killed.
3. Despite the surrender of the *Congress*, soldiers on shore (part of McClellan's army) continued to fire, which meant the Confederate could not take posses-sion of their prize. In consequence, the Confederate commander Captain Franklin Buchanan ordered the *Congress* burned by firing hot shot into it.
4. The USS *Monitor* arrived the same night after the *Virginia/Merrimac* sank the *Cumberland* and *Congress*.
5. The *Monitor* actually retired from the fight first after commanding officer, John Worden, was wounded. The *Merrimac* retired after the *Monitor* returned to the fight, but it was in a sinking condi-tion; it retired because (1) it was running low on both coal and powder, and (2) the resulting loss in weight threatened to expose its wooden lower hull.

THE BATTLES IN HAMPTON ROADS.
SPECIAL DISPATCH FROM WASHINGTON.

WASHINGTON, MONDAY, MARCH 10

A gentleman who witnessed the naval engagement in Hampton Roads, on Saturday and Sunday, says that only one man was killed by the shelling of Newport News. The fire of our ships had no effect on the Merrimac until the arrival of the Monitor. The Merrimac can do no damage to a vessel or fort, unless within a half mile, on account of the lowness of her guns, which are barely above the level of the water; in a gale she would be powerless.

The report of the Monitor's guns was much heavier than those of the Merrimac's.[1] Not a man was to be seen on either ship — all being housed.

MARCH 11

Top: Franklin Buchanan, C.S. navy.
Above: John L. Worden, U.S. navy.

Our informant says the Merrimac is a "devil," but the Monitor a little more so: and that unless a gun explodes on the Monitor, she would have the advantage over her adversary....

The Government has no uneasiness about the Merrimac. The Monitor is considered, by naval men to have clearly established her superiority in the conflict of Sunday. The Merrimac cannot escape.

Lieut. [John L.] WORDEN, who handled the Monitor so splendidly, and who was the only man wounded in the engagement, arrived in Washington to-day, and reported to the Navy Department in person. WORDEN is injured about the eyes, which are closely bandaged and he has to be led from place to place. He gives many interesting incidents of the fight, and is quite sure that three of his heavy shot penetrated the Merrimac.[2]

When the news was received in Washington of the Merrimac's advance, and the havoc she was committing among our war-vessels, there was a burst of indignation against the Navy Department for not having been prepared to meet her. It was for the moment forgotten that Congress had made no appropriation to enable Secretary [Gideon] WELLES to build iron-plated ships, although he had urged it three months ago, and, if Congress had acted, the iron-plated ships might now be in service. ✹

1. The *Monitor* carried 11-inch guns whereas the largest gun on the *Virginia* (*Merrimac*) was a 9-inch smoothbore.
2. After hearing a firsthand account of the *Monitor-Virginia* fight from Henry A. Wise, Lincoln declared his desire to go see Worden. He made his way across Lafayette Square to Wise's home, where the temporarily blinded Worden was recuperating and, with tears in his eyes, told Worden that he was being promoted to captain. Worden's account was incorrect in that no shots from the *Monitor* actually penetrated the casemate of the *Virginia/Merrimac*.

THE FUTURE OF SLAVERY.

MARCH 17

What is to be the effect of the war upon Slavery? is a question more easily asked than answered, but one which presents itself continually before the mind of almost every one. And naturally enough. The Slavery question has been so much before the people of late years that not only those who have made a specially of it, but every one at the North has had something to say upon it, and has come to recognize it as the greatest question of all which were devolved upon the American people to settle. And now when from the same quarter of the land whence in past years have arisen political controversies based upon this question, there has come up this tempest of rebellion, having the same source, it would be most extraordinary if we did not

THE FIGHT AT ISLAND TEN.
A DISPATCH FROM COMMODORE FOOTE.

MARCH 21
WASHINGTON, THURSDAY, MARCH 20

An official dispatch from Commodore FOOTE, received at 12 o'clock last night at Cairo, and telegraphed hither to-day, says:

"Island No. 10 is harder to conquer than Columbus as the island shores are lined with forts, each fort commanding the one above it. I am gradually approaching the island, but still do not hope for much until the occurrence of certain events, which promise success." Commodore FOOTE adds:

"We are firing day and night on the rebels, and we gain on them. We are having some of the most beautiful rifle practice ever witnessed. The mortar shells have done fine execution. One shell was landed on their floating battery, and cleared the concern in short metre."

WASHINGTON, THURSDAY, MARCH 20

The following dispatch has been received here, dated St. Louis, March 20:

"The enemy's flotilla, which is hemmed in between Commodore FOOTE and Gen. POPE,[1] has made another attempt to escape down the river. Their gunboats engaged Gen. POPE's batteries on the 18th for

ask ourselves what was to be the effect of the war upon its cause; no one can tell this as yet, because it is not yet settled what steps are to be taken against Slavery in the prosecution of the war. If it is long enough and embittered enough by defeats on both sides, to lead our generals to declare the slaves free as a military measure, then, of course, the war will be the utter destruction of the system, bringing it to a sudden and violent end. And there are those who are impatient to have that course pursued, because they earnestly desire the overthrow of the systems and believe that such a sudden and violent destruction is the only way to reach the evil. And there are those, too, who argue, that we shall never establish a firmly cemented Union again, unless Slavery is first utterly overthrown.

But let us suppose that no such measure is adopted; that the rebellion is subdued before it has developed enough latent heat to bring out the force necessary for its adoption, and that without the passage of any act of Congress declaring all slaves of rebels free, without the issuing of any proclamation by any one of our Generals giving freedom to all within his Department, the armed traitors are quelled, and their leaders scattered in flight or in prison, and the authority of the Constitution and laws of the United States again recognized as before throughout rebeldom. Is it not perfectly clear that even in that case, the ruin of Slavery, though not so speedy, is no less certain? What would be the condition of the system if the rebellion were to be overthrown to-day? Over wide tracts of country, which but a few months ago were tilled by slaves alone, now no master's authority is recognized, no overseer's lash is authorized by the law. The South has lost more slaves in this one year of rebellion than in any ten years that preceded it. But the loss in those that have run away is as nothing in its effects upon the system compared with the effects of the recognition by the Government as free men of those who remain behind in the Port Royal District and around Fortress Monroe when their rebel masters fled, of the schools set up for these freedmen by Government authority, and the teachers and missionaries provided for them at Government expense. These things cannot be limited in their effect to the districts immediately around them. They will be felt throughout the utmost bounds of Slavery. They will lessen the value, as a slave, of everyone upon whom the yoke of servitude rests. They will lessen the gulf which now for each one of them yawns between a chattel and a man…. ✦

an hour and a half, but were driven back, with a severe loss. One gunboat was sunk, and several badly damaged. They are completely hemmed in, and can escape only by fighting their way out."

Between 5 and 6 o'clock P.M., the fleet appeared in sight, and rounding to, landed at Hickman, Ky. The reception was not very cordial, however, although a number of Union ladies appeared at the doors and windows of their dwellings and waved their handkerchiefs, while the men cheered the old flag. The town had been partially deserted. A detachment of rebel cavalry were seen leaving the place as we approached — a portion being visible from the tops of the bluffs. The telegraphic operator "departed" for Union City, on a fiery charger, (taking along his instrument,) but before leaving, took the precaution to notify all Secessia that our fleet had arrived. A portion of his instrument, and a number of dispatches and other papers, left in his office, were appropriated by the soldiers as trophies. It was a grand and thrilling spectacle to see our infantry land and quietly march through Hickman, with the old banner flourish proudly to the breeze, the field band playing "Yankee Doodle," "Dixie," and other patriotic airs….

We conversed with a number of citizens, both loyal and rebel. One old gentleman, Mr. FREELEY, introduced to us by Capt. MCMILLAN, of the [ship] Silver Wave, was almost overcome with joy. He hailed the old flag with tremulous and tearful emotion. "Ah!" he says, "you don't know — can't imagine — how and what we've suffered. But, thank God, there's the old flag! I knew it would come; yes, I knew it would come!"

The Secessionists were bitter and determined in their denunciation of Lincolnites, yet argued the point mildly. One portly, red-faced, Wigfallish-looking[2] institution, asked us, "Which way is your gunboats bound?" "For Memphis and New-Orleans," was the reply. "When do you expect to get to Memphis?" "Well, I don't exactly know: some time next week, I suppose." He replied, "Next week! I'll just bet you ten dollars (putting his hand in his pocket, and hauling out a Confederate shinplaster) that you don't get to Memphis for six months! Don't you know Island 10's fortified?" "No," we replied, "Well, I think you'll find out soon enough to your sorrow." The majority of the Union people appear to have been badly used, but are in high glee now, and take pains to post Flag-Officer FOOTE relative to the strength of the enemy, and location of rebel batteries. Between Columbus and Hickman many of the people came to the doors of their farm-houses, and out on the river bank, and waved their hats, bonnets and handkerchiefs, as the fleet passed down. While at Hickman, the transport Dan Pollard, from Cairo, joined us, laden with stores for the army and gunboats.

Before leaving Hickman, a bearer a despatches from Cairo brought the intelligence that the rebels had evacuated New-Madrid. Gen. POPE was to have erected a battery of twenty-three 24-pounders at a formidable point below New-Madrid, for the purpose, we suppose, of cutting off the rebels in their retreat, by boats, down the Mississippi.

ISLAND NO. 10.

On Saturday, the 15th inst., at 6 A.M., the expedition left Hickman for Island No. 10 — the weather being cold, and raining, with high winds. Just below the foot of Island No. 8, (twelve miles below Hickman,) the rebel gunboat Grampus, observing our fleet approaching, rounded down from the Kentucky shore in a hurry, being some two miles ahead of the flagship Benton — the latter sending a couple of rifled 42-pounders after her both shots falling short. In the meantime the Grampus scudded off down the river at her best speed, her steam whistle shrieking and screaming incessantly, in order to warn the rebel batteries below of our approach. At 8 A.M. we were signaled to follow the movements of the flag-ship, when all the gunboats dropped down stern foremost, to a point within one mile of the head of No. 10. Being formed in a line across the river, all headed up stream — the flag-ship several hundred yards in advance, and the furthest down. The fleet dropped ☞

A Currier and Ives lithograph portrays the bombardment of Confederate-held Island Number Ten by Flag Officer Andrew H. Foote's fleet.

down slowly to within half a mile of the Missouri Point above the Island, which by an air line, is 2 1/2 miles distant, while by the river owing to the head, it is four miles from the head of the Island.

While in this position the flag-ship opened fire on the Kentucky shore, two and a half miles above No. 10, discovering an unknown rebel battery — gave it three 70-pound rifled shells, which fell short of the battery half a mile. They responded promptly, their shots not touching to within one mile of us. At 12 M., weather raw and chilly, still floating around in the stream; the flag-ship again tried her guns, but was at too great a distance to reach the enemy. Our decks were all cleared for action. At 2:40 P.M. a couple of mortar-boats[3] were got into position on the Missouri shore, half a mile above the Point, when they commenced throwing across or over the point on Island No. 10. Owing to the intervening woods the effect produced was not learned. After throwing three or four shells in that direction, they turned their attention to the rebel battery previously shelled by the Benton. The first two shells falling short, were immediately replied to from the batteries, when, at our next shot — having got the proper elevation — some eight or nine

of our shells appeared to land and explode directly amidst and over the enemy's works. There was not a single gun afterward fired, indicating that their battery was effectually silenced. The distance was fully two miles. With the aid of the glass, several of the mortar shells were seen to explode — one, in particular, striking their earthwork, sending up a column of dirt as high as the tall cottonwood tree-tops.

This battery being silenced, the mortars again turned their attention to Island No. 10, which they continued to shell until dark, but with what success we could not learn.

The Kentucky shore is lined with tents for two miles at the head of Island No. 10. A glimpse of the head of the Island is all that was perceptible through the timber. Seven or eight transports, including the Ohio Belle and John Simonds could be seen occasionally crossing to and from the Island to the Kentucky shore. ⊛

1. Brigadier General John Pope (1822–1892) was the commander of the Union Army of the Mississippi. He captured New Madrid, Missouri, on March 14, but needed the support of Foote's squadron to get across the river and encircle the Confederate defenders of Island Number Ten.

2. This is a reference to Texas Congressman Louis T. Wigfall, a portly and bewhiskered Southern politician and volunteer general.

3. These were essentially rafts each bearing a heavy 13-inch mortar that fired shells on a high arcing trajectory to targets beyond the range of conventional artillery.

OUR NEW IRON-CLAD NAVY — SUGGESTIONS AND CAUTIONS.

MARCH 21

SIDNEY SMITH[1] used to say that if needed a surgical operation to get a joke into a Scotchman's skull; and, in like wise, it required the terrible surgery of Hampton Roads to arouse the Naval Committee of Congress to the importance of armored ships of war. If, however, our legislators were, previous to the combat between the Merrimac and the Monitor, chargeable with remissness in this respect, we are bound to give them credit for promptly acting on the light which that wonderful and epoch-making event has let into their minds. Senator HALE,[2] as Chairman of the Senate Committee on Naval Affairs, has reported a bill appropriating fifteen million dollars for the commencement of an iron-clad navy. The terms of the bill are comprehensive and judicious, and provide for the construction of a steam-ram of five or six thousand tons burden, at a cost of a million of dollars or under, and appropriate $13,000,000 for the building of iron-clad gunboats, $783,000 for the completion of STEVENS' Battery,[3] and $500,000 for extending the facilities of the Washington Navy-yard, so as to roll and forge plates for the armored ships. We trust the bill may pass without any further delay than is necessary to secure the most judicious investment of the money appropriated.[4] There is no provision of the bill more important than that contemplating the construction of a mail-clad steam, battering-ram, and this arm of our new navy should receive the very first attention of the Department. The country will never feel secure while the Merrimac and the four other shot-proof batteries which the rebels have nearly ready, (two on the Lower Mississippi and two at Mobile) menace our navy and our seaboard cities with destruction. Now the Steam-Ram is the only engine of naval warfare capable of sinking these vessels with absolute certainty. Admirably as the Monitor behaved, and perfectly as it realized all the ends of its design, its slowness forbids its utilizing the tremendous force of momentum by hurling its weight against the enemy and if it succeeds in sinking the Merrimac and her mates, it will be by picking out the weak places in the hull below the armor, of by the impact of the still untried wrought-iron shot. Not a moment, therefore, should be loss in providing the country with at least one of these tremendous engines, the direct shock of which the hull of no iron-plated vessel can resist.

We are glad to see that the Senate, in proposing for the construction of a ram, has borne in min the two great elements of weight and speed. It is to be "of not lost than 5,000 or 6,000 tons burden, and of great swiftness and strength," and if constructed in accordance with these conditions, it will undoubtedly be an engine of warfare against which no iron-plated vessel, battery, or ram in the world, either built or being built, can cope. The British steam-ram, the Defence, which, like the Warrior, may be considered the pioneer of her class, and which has just made her official trial of speed at Portsmouth, England, is only of 3,668 tons, which is not much over half the burden of our proposed ram. Moreover, her mean speed was but a fraction over eleven knots per hour; whereas the Stevens Battery will make more than nineteen knots per hour: so that either the ram or the battery would be able to sink the Defence itself, if Iron should meet Iron in the shock of war.

If we once had provision made for our present safety and for the destruction of the rebel iron-plated floating batteries — which we should consider done were the Pain, a brace of Monitors, and the three iron-clad gunboats now in process of construction, completed -we could almost wish that we should pause awhile before going any further — at least that we should await the results of the experiments that will be made with these, before spending many more millions. It is our National temperament to "put things through," and rush to an extreme, and there is just a danger that the mania for iron-clad vessels may cost us dearly.[5] We shall consider, for example, that every dollar expended in the construction of such plated eggshells as the Galena (built at Mystic, Conn., and now being completed at Greenpoint,) is so much money thrown away. The action of the Monitor and Merrimac has already taught us a great deal, of which we shall avail ourselves, and impending naval developments will no doubt touch us a great deal more. It may, further, be mentioned that a series of experiments with regard to the backing and joining of the plates has just been initiated at Shearness, England, which will, in a large measure, determine the future of iron-plated vessels.

Of course the first thing is to provide for our immediate needs; and all questions of form, material or structure, however important in themselves, are, and should be, subordinate to the supreme question of putting afloat, at the earliest moment, armed engines of naval warfare enough to send to the bottom all the devices of the enemy. But that done, let us bear in mind that we have large and prospective needs as well as present demands; and that it is the plain dictate of prudence to avail ourselves of all the experiments, on both sides of the Atlantic, that tend to throw light on these novel and still obscure, though overwhelmingly important questions. One thing is certain, we are bound to have an iron-clad navy that will defy those of the most powerful European nations. Already, at one leap, we have taught the world more than all it before knew respecting this new warlike enginery. The country is opulent with creative genius and engineering skill. This genius and skill will now largely take the direction of iron-clad vessels. Let us, therefore, not sink money in building structures which the rapid strides in the science may soon render obsolete. ⊛

1. A reference to British Admiral Sir Sidney Smith (1764–1840), a dashing hero of the Napoleonic wars.
2. New Hampshire Senator John P. Hale (1806–1873) chaired the Senate Naval Affairs Committee. He was a critic of Gideon Welles, with whom he quarreled for most of the war.
3. The Stevens Battery had been laid down in the 1840s as an iron-armored warship, but was never completed. By the time of the Civil War, technology had advanced so far as to make its design obsolete. Though the navy ended up spending a half million dollars on it, it was never commissioned as a warship.
4. Despite The Times' enthusiasm for it, it proved an expensive failure.
5. The Times was correct. A so-called "Monitor fever" swept the north leading to appropriations for no fewer than 64 Monitor type ironclads before the war was over.

CHAPTER 8

"Operations Seem Everywhere to Have Come Almost to a Dead Halt"

APRIL–MAY 1862

hroughout the winter, even as his army drilled and paraded, McClellan had made no move against the enemy. The country grew impatient, and sensing that, Lincoln attempted to prod and encourage his young general. When McClellan fell ill with typhoid fever in January, Lincoln held a council of war with his leading subordinates. Jealous of his command authority, McClellan got out of his sickbed and appeared at the next meeting. When Lincoln asked him if he had a plan of operations, he replied that he did, but that he could not reveal it because people in the White House could not be trusted to keep it secret. Despite this implied disparagement of the President, Lincoln agreed that he would not press McClellan for details. The plan, when it was revealed, turned out to be a massive turning movement by sea: the entire Army of the Potomac would be sent by transports to the Virginia coast and advance on Richmond from there.

The move took place during the last two weeks of March 1862, as 389 ships carried more than 120,000 men, 15,000 animals, and 1,200 wagons to Fort Monroe at the tip of the peninsula of land formed by the York and James rivers. It was a remarkable demonstration of the North's material superiority and impressive sealift capability, as well as McClellan's logistical skills. Once there, however, McClellan behaved as if he expected that the rebels now might as well simply give up. The Times thought so too. An article that appeared on April 7 suggested that "the rebels are preparing to flee from Virginia altogether." They were not. Instead, McClellan spent all of April and part of May besieging the Confederate defensive lines at Yorktown on the site of the old Revolutionary War

Detail of a drawing of the Battle of Shiloh.

battlefield. Once again, critics in the North grew impatient.

At the same time, Confederate Major General Thomas J. "Stonewall" Jackson inaugurated a campaign in the Shenandoah Valley that was destined to become a model of effective small-unit warfare. It began poorly. On March 23, 1862, Jackson launched an attack on a Federal force at Kernstown that was stronger than he thought. He was driven off with heavy losses, and The Times crowed that "we will not be likely to hear any more of this audacious rebel in this quarter." Seldom has a prediction been more wrong. By the end of May, Jackson had chased his Federal foe, Major General Nathaniel P. Banks, all the way back across the Potomac and disrupted McClellan's plans as well. Once again The Times came to the defense of a much-criticized general proclaiming that Banks's ability to retreat "so far in the face of an enemy so overwhelming," and to get his men safely across the Potomac was "proof of the highest generalship."

Great events were taking place to the west as well. In Tennessee, Albert Sidney Johnston tried to recoup his prolonged retreat by attacking Grant's army at Pittsburg Landing near Shiloh Church on April 6. The surprise attack drove Grant's men to the bank of the Tennessee River on the first day of fighting, but a reinforced Grant counterattacked the next day and regained all the lost ground. With a total of 24,000 casualties on both sides — five times the losses at Bull Run — Shiloh was the first battle of the war that presaged just how costly the conflict was likely to be.

Two weeks after that, the naval squadron of Flag Officer David G. Farragut fought its way past the forts guarding New Orleans to capture the South's largest and most important commercial city.

The conversation about slavery and its future continued. Congress abolished slavery in the District of Columbia on April 16, though this did not mark the onset of a general movement toward emancipation. When on May 9 Major General David Hunter, commanding the Department of the South, declared that slavery was abolished within the area of his command (Florida, Georgia, and South Carolina), Lincoln felt compelled to repudiate Hunter's action, saying as he did so, "Whether it be competent for me, as Commander-in-Chief of the army and navy, to declare the slaves of any State or States free; and whether at any time, or in any ease, it shall have become a necessity indispensable to the maintenance of the Government to exercise such supposed power, are questions which, under my responsibility, I reserve to myself."

JACKSON'S CAMPAIGN IN NORTHERN VIRGINIA.

APRIL 1

The column of the rebel Gen. JACKSON, which has just been routed at Winchester, chased from Strasburgh, and is now probably plodding its weary, way through the mountains, and up the Shenandoah Valley for Stanton, was, as Gen. [James] SHIELDS says, considered the bravest and best-disciplined corps in the rebel army. It was composed of men who had been in the very hardest service ever since the war opened; and, for its supposed invincible qualities was known as the "Stone Wall Brigade." The rebel papers have given it credit, too, for a continuous series of quite wonderful victories. At the beginning of last Winter, JACKSON was put in command of Northern Virginia, and he was ordered to drive the National troops from that part of Virginia between Harper's Ferry and the western line of Maryland, and to destroy whatever had been rebuilt of the Baltimore and Ohio Railroad, which was then guarded by the troops of Gen. [Nathaniel] BANKS. With a force estimated at 6,000 strong, JACKSON set out from Strasburgh last December, advanced rapidly to Winchester, and thence toward Martinsburgh, destroying the Baltimore and Ohio Road, tearing up the rails and using them to finish the line between Winchester and Strasburgh. In the beginning of January he advanced toward Bath, in Morgan County, where were two National regiments and a force of cavalry and artillery, supported by two other regiments at Hancock, ten miles north. Our troops at Bath were driven across the Potomac, and a number of them taken prisoners. He then advanced to Hancock, sent notice to the Mayor that he intended to cross at that point, and began shelling the town. He next moved upon Romney, and our troops stationed there retreated north to Cumberland. Having thus cleared that entire section of the National forces, he returned to Strasburgh, but in February again occupied Romney, from which he was driven by Gen. LANDER. From Strasburgh he advanced once more to Winchester, and of late has been flitting between these two points, and occasionally approaching well

Thomas "Stonewall" Jackson, as he appeared after he became a lieutenant general.

up to the Potomac. When he saw his best line of retreat cut off by our occupancy of Manassas, and found Gen. BANKS' corps d'armee advancing in force against him, he began to move up the Shenandoah Valley; but, imagining that BANKS' army ☞

had nearly all gone to Manassas, he again came up a fortnight ago to his old ground at Winchester, where his forces were suddenly attacked and routed by Gen. SHIELDS, on the 23d ult., and subsequently chased up to and beyond Strasburgh. The official reports indicate that his original force had been more than doubled by reinforcements from the main rebel body. As his column seems to have been terribly cut up, and the remnant has retreated from Northern Virginia, we will not be likely to hear any more of this audacious rebel in this quarter. Gen. JACKSON is a Virginian and a West Point soldier, and his troops are mostly Virginia mountaineers, with regiments from the far Southern States. He has been a terrible scourge to the section over which JEFF. DAVIS gave him command; but his defeat and retreat clears the mountain region of armed rebels. ✪

1. This refers to the Battle of Kernstown (March 23, 1862), in which the army of Thomas J. "Stonewall" Jackson attacked a larger Union force near Winchester and was repulsed. Despite that, Lincoln decided to reinforce Union armies in the Valley and divert units that had been intended for McClellan's army.

QUAKER GUNS.

APRIL 3

Certain Quaker guns which were found in position at Centreville, after its evacuation by the rebels, and which are held up as proof-positive of the cowardice or inefficiency of Gen. MCCLELLAN.[1] This view can be honestly taken only on the assumption that the works at Centreville were never mounted with any other than Quaker guns — a conclusion which could be arrived at only by those who are entirely ignorant of the arts and practices of war. For this device of Quaker guns is one constantly and successfully used by commanders who intend to retreat from forts or entrenchments. Next to his men, an officer's first care is his artillery. But to remove his guns in sight of the enemy would be to notify him in the quickest and most unmistakable manner of the intended evacuation. So his pickets are strengthened, and even pushed forward, as if for an advance, then in the night the guns are removed, and wooden ones of similar size and appearance, so like as to make detection even with a glass impossible, are substituted for the real Simon Pures.

Daylight manifests no change in the apparent strength of the works; the bulk of the troops move off by daylight; and when the next night comes, the pickets withdraw suddenly, and run for it. There is obviously no protection against this trick, except a nightly driving in of pickets, and reconnaissance in force in the dark, which is generally more harrassing to those who undertake it than to the enemy, and is rarely productive of much good. The supposition that, because the rebels left only Quaker guns behind them, they took none of "the world's" guns with them, makes it plain that they did not use up all the wood in the world in making sham artillery. ✪

1. Believing that his force was too exposed at Manassas, Confederate army commander Joseph E. Johnston withdrew his army southward behind the Rappahannock River on March 8–9. When Union forces moved forward to occupy the now-abandoned rebel camp, they found that several of the cannon frowning from the Confederate defensive lines were so-called "Quaker guns" — carved logs painted black to resemble artillery. McClellan's critics seized on this to prove that Little Mac should have attacked Manassas before the rebels decamped. In this article, The Times comes to McClellan's defense.

Federal troops at a Confederate fort on the heights of Centreville, Virginia, armed with Quaker guns.

EMANCIPATION IN THE DISTRICT.

APRIL 4

The bill for abolishing Slavery in the District of Columbia was passed yesterday in the Senate. The vote was sufficiently decisive. Only fourteen names are recorded as opposed to it, while for it there were twenty-nine. But of the twenty-nine, several Senators had taken occasion to express objections to leading provisions of the bill. Some deprecated its effect upon the Border States. Others would have had the subject referred to a vote of the whites in the District. Others still would have made the emancipation gradual and provided for the removal of the blacks from the country. But the adherence of the majority to the bill as reported from the Committee, was too steadfast to be shaken. The only modification accepted was one appropriating $100,000 for the colonization of the liberated negroes.[1] There was no other alternative, therefore, for those who were friendly to the measure on general principles, but who objected to various of its provisions, than to vote for or against it directly. It therefore received their voices.

The bill goes to the House of Representatives. A generation has passed since a simple petition for such a measure threw that body into convulsions, procured the establishment of a more arbitrary code of rules and gag-laws than ever disgraced a chapter of the Inquisition, and placed an Ex-President at the bar of the House for trial, as if guilty of treason.[2] The change is the natural product of that very tyranny. Elated by their triumph, and assured of the servile support of the Northern National Democracy, the Slavery party gave way to suicidal arrogance and presumption. They demanded uninterrupted and despotic control of the National Government. Its patronage and its legislation were alike in their hands. And to such a pitch was this petulant selfishness carried, that a threatened suspension of its rule for the four years through which we are now struggling, was made the pretence of a revolution the most gratuitous of any recounted in history. But — so surely does time bring about its revenges — this revolution has rendered it possible to complete the labor of expelling Slavery from the National Capital — a task beneath which JOHN QUINCY ADAMS sunk into his grave.

The House of Representatives will, we trust, amend the Senate bill in several particulars. The appropriation for removing the negroes from the country, wise in itself, becomes folly in the presence of immediate emancipation ... . The transformation of domestic servants, accustomed life-long to none but indoor employments, into tamers of tropical forests and successful cultivators of new and unaccustomed regions, may be effected in a long course of years; but not without some little preparation and some skill in the arts of self-support. The substitution of the provision for gradual emancipation for the peremptory method of the bill, can alone save its framers from the charge of disguising heartless cruelty under mask of eager philanthropy. The measure we believe to be ill-timed; let it not also be ill-contrived and mischievous in practice. ◉

1. In fact, an amendment to the bill that would have required compulsory emigration of all blacks from the District failed only when Vice President Hannibal Hamlin broke a 19–19 tie.
2. This refers to the repeated efforts by Congressman and former President John Quincy Adams to present petitions to the House regarding slavery in the District. Weary of his constant efforts, the House passed a so-called "gag rule" that no petition concerning slavery would be allowed. When Adams tried to present one anyway, he was held in contempt.

THE PENDING BATTLES.

APRIL 7

The two great National armies the Army of the East and the Army of the West are now in the situation promised by Gen. McCLELLAN in his address to the soldiers of the Potomac "face to face with the rebels;" and it is evident that it cannot be long before they meet the rebellious foe "on the decisive battlefield." In the East, the late Army of the Potomac — a host greater than that of either of the belligerents at Waterloo — and under commanders of approved loyalty, skill and courage, — is moving upon the strong places and key positions of the audacious enemy who, for over a year, has stood before the Capital defying the National power and insulting the flag of the Union. At any hour the telegraphic wire may tremble with news grander and more momentous than it has ever yet borne since lightning was used as an agency for transmitting thought. When it photographs before us the scenes of the great day and the be great field — a day and a field upon which will be decided the fate of this Satanic revolt — we shall see not merely legions of men, and miles of steel, and an hundred parks of artillery in collision, but principles and ideas greater and more enduring than these, contending for the supremacy. Our army is strong, not merely in numbers and equipment, but in courage, and in having a just quarrel. The enemy is inspired only by the lust of Slavery, and stimulated by desperation. We have met him this year already on twenty fields; we have fought him, with the odds in his favor, at Newbern, and at Winchester, and at Pea Ridge; we have conquered him behind intrenchments at Donelson and at Roanoke. In no instance has he stood the onset of our columns, or the contact of the bayonet. In every case he has given way before the invincible men of the North and the great flag of the Republic. With this prestige on our side, our troops now advance to meet him in general battle; and, if he dare to face us at all on either of the lines, East or West, on which he is now showing fight, like results must inevitably, under Providence, crown our arms. There are rumors, however, and they are likely enough to be correct, that, as our various Eastern corps d'armee advance southward, the rebels are preparing to flee from Virginia altogether. They see, not only that their late boasts of conquering the North, are false and futile, but that they are unable, even with all their forces concentrated and planted behind intrenchments, to make a successful resistance to our army. They think that by retiring Westward and Southward, our army will be unable to follow them among the mountains of the West, and into the alligator swamps and under the hot Summer sun of the Gulf States. In making this confession, and in acting upon it, they virtually give up the whole contest; for, with our army advanced to the line of the warm States, and with our seaboard navy and army acting on the coasts of North and South Carolina, Georgia, Florida, Mississippi, and Louisiana, and our river navy and our Western army acting on their lines, a residence for the rebels in the everglades and alligator swamps would be as fatal as for us. If, moreover, they really mean to leave Virginia without giving battle, it would be well for them to be in haste. ◉

THE NEW ORDER OF THE SECRETARY OF WAR.

APRIL 7

The enemies of Gen. MCCLELLAN are at a loss for the material of warfare. For the lack of anything better offering just now, they seize upon the creation of a new military district for MCDOWELL, and a new department for BANKS, as evidence that the Commander of the Army of the Potomac is in disfavor with the President, who thus seeks to curtail his authority. The truth is, the new arrangement is simply an affirmation of the obvious fact that it is impossible for Gen. MCCLELLAN to be in three places at once. Should his advance carry him to Richmond, there are palpable reasons why he should be unable to control the operations in front of Washington, much less the movements of Gen. BANKS beyond the Blue Ridge. The President merely consults public necessity in making the change. The fact has no personal significance whatever.[1] ✪

1. Lincoln held back McDowell's corps from the army that McClellan took to the Virginia peninsula because he learned that McClellan had left too few units behind to ensure the security of the national capital. Lincoln's designation of McDowell's force as a separate command did, therefore, have some "political significance."

IMPORTANT WAR NEWS.
GEN. McCLELLAN BEFORE YORKTOWN WITH THE NATIONAL ARMY.

APRIL 8

WASHINGTON, MONDAY, APRIL 7

The following is a summary of the intelligence received by the War Department up to 10 o'clock to-night:

Yesterday, the enemy's works were carefully examined by Gen. MCCLELLAN, and were found to be very strong and the approaches difficult. The enemy was in force and the water batteries at Yorktown and Gloucester said to be much increased. There was sharp firing on the right, but no harm was done. Our forces were receiving supplies from Ship Point, repairing roads and getting up large trains.

It seemed plain that mortars and siege-trains must be used before assaulting.

Another dispatch received at 10 1/2 A.M. states that Yorktown will fall, but not without a siege of two or three days.[1] Some of the outer works were taken....

There were no signs of the Merrimac. A rebel tug was seen making a reconnaissance off Sewall's Point, on the afternoon of Tuesday.

WASHINGTON, MONDAY, MARCH 7

On the afternoon of Sunday, Ship Point Battery had been taken, and our gunboats had shelled out the water batteries.

There was considerable delay caused in crossing Deep Creek, at Warwick Court-house, and resistance was made by the rebels, during which several casualties occurred on our side.

All the fortified places of importance before Yorktown had been taken at every point. The greatest enthusiasm prevailed among our troops. ✪

1. The siege actually lasted nearly a month, from April 5 to May 4, 1862.

A federal mortar unit at Yorktown.

THE BATTLE OF PITTSBURGH.
IMPORTANT PARTICULARS OF THE TERRIBLE STRUGGLE.

APRIL 10

CAIRO, WEDNESDAY, APRIL 9

Further advices from Pittsburgh Landing[1] give the following about the battle:

The [Confederate] attack was successful, and our entire force was driven back to the river, where the advance of the enemy was checked by the fire of the gunboats.

Our force was then increased by the arrival of Gen. GRANT, with the troops from Savanna, and inspirited by reports of the arrival of two divisions of Gen. BUELL's army.

Our loss this day was heavy, and, besides the killed and wounded, embraced our camp equipage and 36 field guns.

The next morning our forces, now amounting to 80,000, assumed the offen-

The Battle of Pittsburgh Landing, also known as the Battle of Shiloh.

sive, and by 2 o'clock P.M. had retaken our camp and batteries, together with some 40 of the enemy's guns and a number of prisoners, and the enemy were in full retreat, pursued by our victorious forces.... ✪

1. Better known today as the Battle of Shiloh for the small church nearby.

THE REBEL GENERAL KILLED.
GEN. ALBERT SIDNEY JOHNSTON.

APRIL 10

Gen. JOHNSTON, the bogus report of whose capture at Fort Donelson gave him a biographical fame two months ago, is now certainly disposed of at last, as his dead body is in our hands. He was one of the five rebel "Generals," the other four being BEAUREGARD, LEE, [Samuel] COOPER and JOE JOHNSTON. He was for half a year commander of the rebel Department of Kentucky, with his headquarters at Bowling Green, which famous stronghold he evacuated six weeks ago. He is 50 years of age, a native of Kentucky, and graduated at West Point in 1826. He was engaged in the Black Hawk war, in the Texan war of independence, in the Mexican war, and in the war against the Mormons. He was Brigade-General in command of the Military District of Utah, and at the opening of this rebellion, was in command of the Department of the Pacific. Shortly after the rebellion got under way, his loyalty was suspected, and Gen. SUMNER was sent out to supersede him. Before Gen. SUMNER reached California, JOHNSTON had left to join the rebels. For fear of being caught, he took the overland route, with three or four companions, on males, and passed through Arizona and Texas, and thence to Richmond. At first he was appointed to a rebel command on the Potomac; but upon the great importance of the Western Department being seen by JEFF. DAVIS, he was appointed to take chief command at Bowling Green. He did everything to strengthen that position, and bring as large a force as could be got for its defence. But, on being outflanked by our advance up the Cumberland, he incontinently deserted his stronghold, fled to Nashville, from thence to Decatur, and from thence to Corinth, and now has fallen — a traitor to his native State and to his country. JOHNSTON was a little over six feet high, of a large, bony, sinewy frame, with a grave, gaunt and thoughtful face; of quiet, unassuming manners — forming, in all, a soldier of very imposing appearance. He was considered by military men the ablest General, for command, in the rebel service, and his loss will be a severe blow to the tottering rebellion. ✹

IMPORTANT FROM WASHINGTON.
THE ABOLITION OF SLAVERY IN THE DISTRICT OF COLUMBIA.

APRIL 17

Fellow-citizens of the Senate and House of Representatives:

The act entitled "An act for the release of certain persons held to service or labor in the District of Columbia," has this day been approved and signed.

I have never doubted the constitutional authority of Congress to abolish Slavery in this District, and I have ever desired to see the National Capital freed from the institution in some satisfactory way. Hence there has never been in my mind any question upon the subject except the one of expediency, arising in view of all the circumstances. If there be matters within and about this act which might have taken a course or shape more satisfactory to my judgment, I do not attempt to specify them. I am gratified that the two principles of compensation and colonization are both recognized and practically applied in the act.

In the matter of compensation it is provided that claims may be presented within ninety days from the passage of the act, but not thereafter, and there is no saving for minors, femmes coverts, insane or absent persons. I presume this is an omission by mere oversight, and I recommend that it be supplied by an amendatory or supplemental act.

(SIGNED) ABRAHAM LINCOLN.
WASHINGTON, APRIL 16, 1862. ✹

END OF SLAVERY IN THE DISTRICT OF COLUMBIA.

APRIL 17

The act of the President, in signing a bill to put an end to Slavery in the District of Columbia, places the Government of this country in its proper position, in reference to the subject of human bondage. It is a declaration that its sympathies and its action, as far as they can be constitutionally exerted, are henceforth to be in favor of freedom, as better in a moral point of view, and more economic in a material one, than Slavery. Such is the genius of the age, as well as Christianity. This act of Government is but the record of a progress in this country in liberal ideas, common to the whole civilized world. In the United States, the comparative economic value of freedom and Slavery have had a double test. At the adoption of the Constitution, the two sections exactly divided the population between them, but Slavery claimed by far the fairer portion of the country. Seventy years have elapsed, and the Free States, with equal area, number nearly twice the population of the Slave, and ten times their wealth and material strength, to say nothing of the infinitely superior type of civilization of the former. The Slave States denied this superiority, and demanded the arbitrament of the sword. The last decision has been conclusive in favor of freedom. We cannot avoid the effect of the moral if we would, while the action of the slaveholding section has fully warranted Government in affirming a judgment irresistibly sustained by results, and at the same time by the general sense of mankind. Henceforth it will stand as the representative of freedom and progress, although the members of what it is composed may, for an indefinite period, maintain Slavery, which must, for the future, as it should, look to local law for its support. The Constitution of the United States cannot be directed to its overthrow in the States composing the Confederacy, but it must not be used as the instrument of its extension.

Upon these fundamental principles there will be little difference of opinion. We have objected to the manner in which emancipation in the District is to be accomplished, as unwise and impolitic, both for those to be manumitted as well as the public generally. Change in the social structure of society should, as far as possible, have all ☞

the attributes of growth. By allowing ample time, those to be affected will adapt themselves to the new order of things, without suffering in any respect in their condition. In all radical changes the only way to proceed safely is to proceed slowly, in which case experience will supply guides to our conduct as we move along. But, while objecting to the mode, we emphatically approve the principles which lay at the foundation of this new declaration of human rights, which cannot fail in the end, by eliminating, through the working of natural laws, and by peaceful modes, the only real cause of discord, to render us a perfectly harmonious and united people. ⊛

MR. BLAIR ON EMANCIPATION AND COLONIZATION.

APRIL 17

In other columns of the TIMES is given a report of a speech on the President's view of Slavery, delivered in the House of Representatives by Mr. [Francis P.] BLAIR [Jr.], of Missouri. Mr. BLAIR is the author of an admirable, if practicable, plan of removing the African race from this to some other American territory. As long ago as 1858, he commenced the public discussion of his project, securing, among other converts, the actual President, who, having always held that emancipation and colonization should go hand in hand, cheerfully accepted the idea of a Central American home for the deported race. The accord of Mr. LINCOLN's opinions with those of Mr. BLAIR is understood to be perfect upon the entire subject. Both believe that Slavery is only indirectly chargeable with the war; that the real groundwork of Southern aversion from the North is a belief that negro freedom is to carry with it negro equality; and that nothing will so surely extirpate the opposition to emancipation as a knowledge that the two races are to be forever separated. Mr. BLAIR discusses these propositions with his usual ability and earnestness; and will be listened to by the public with the greater attention because he reflects the policy which the Government proposes to follow. ⊛

THE GREAT NEWS OF THE DAY.

APRIL 28

NEW-ORLEANS is repossessed! The mortar and gunboat fleet of Capt. PORTER is in front of the City.[1] The rebels have fled in consternation, after destroying, by military order, all the cotton in the presses and warehouses of the place, and burning all the steam craft at the wharves, except such as were required to carry off the munitions and supplies of the army, for which they would seem to have no use at home. The news comes through rebel sources, and on the point of resistance, after PORTER had successfully passed Forts Jackson and St. Philip, the dispatches are somewhat blind. But the plain inference is that more thought was taken as to how the rebel forces should make their own exit than of the way to resist PORTER's entrance. The telegraphic operator, after announcing the appearance of the fleet, the consternation of the city, the wanton destruction of property under martial rule, took his own hasty leave, and in this probably followed, rather than anticipated, the example of the rebel army of defence. We shall, no doubt, have fuller accounts in a few days. Meanwhile let the loyal heart of the Nation rejoice that the Stars and Stripes again float over the Crescent City of the Southwest. ⊛

1. In fact, it was the squadron of David G. Farragut, and not the mortar squadron of his foster brother David Dixon Porter, that ran past the river forts and compelled the surrender of New Orleans. Porter's squadron and Butler's army both remained below the river forts for several more days. Porter, however, had a talent for self-promotion and managed to get his version of events out first.

A lithograph depicting the Battle of New Orleans.

THE CAPTURE OF NEW-ORLEANS.

APRIL 28

The news of the capture of New-Orleans which we received from the South at a late hour last night, clears up gloriously the mystery which for some time has hung around the movements of our navy and army upon the Lower Mississippi. We had already had intelligence that our bomb ketches[1] had opened fire upon Fort Jackson, 60 miles below the city, and yesterday morning we published news derived from the rebels that one of our gunboats had run past that work. But the defenders of the fort, it was said, had sent word to their friends that they were confident of their strength, and were able to endure the shelling as long as our fleet was able to keep it up. That news was up to Tuesday last. It appears certain that, notwithstanding the rebel bombast, Fort Jackson, and probably, also, Fort St. Philip, on the opposite side of the river, were reduced that very day;[2] for by the gray dawn of Wednesday morning, our armada had steamed past the fortifications, and by noon it appeared, with power and terror, before the Crescent City. At this point the telegram stops short, and leaves us completely in the dark as to what has been done during the past four days. Whether Gen. BUTLER, as is probable, sent in a demand for the capitulation of the city,[3] and what may have followed — a compliance with, or refusal of the terms of the demand — we do not yet know. But it is altogether unlikely that any serious attempt was made to defend the city itself. Indeed, New-Orleans was utterly incapable of defence, when once our fleet got in front of it.[4] With a hundred gun and mortarboats riding high above the city, ready to pour down upon it a torrent of fire and iron, it would be madness for the rebels to dream of any other terms than unconditional surrender. It has been thought that the land force accompanying the expedition was too small to repossess a city, which must still count somewhat like a hundred and fifty thousand inhabitants. And so it would be if the military contingent had to act alone. But the fact is, that the naval arm when once raised over the city, was of itself sufficient to hold it in complete subjection. And the only work for the troops would be to seize and garrison some few important positions in the city, raise the Stars and Stripes over the United States property and other public places, and act as a repressive police force. The rebels will be disarmed; the Union element, which is known to be strong in New-Orleans, will be organized; and Gen. BUTLER, from his headquarters in the St. Charles Hotel, will put in force whatever other measures are necessary for the securing of public order.

The seizure of this, the greatest city of the Jeff. Davis Confederacy, will be a terrible disheartenment for the rebels, and is in itself almost equivalent to a defeat of BEAUREGARD's army at Corinth, if that army has not yet been destroyed by the forces of Gen. HALLECK. At all events, it will compel the rebels of the Southwest to fight their last battle on their present line of operation. BEAUREGARD is pressed, if not already assailed, by HALLECK in front; Gen. [Ormsby] MITCHEL will prevent his retreat toward Mobile; BUTLER forbids his approach to New-Orleans; and our gunboats can pass up the Mississippi and attack Memphis in front — acting in conjunction with Commodore FOOTE above. The way is also opened for the gunboats to pass up the Red River and across the entire State of Louisiana to Shreveport; to pass up the Arkansas River and through the entire State of Arkansas to Fort Smith; and to pass up the Yazoo River and through a great part of the State of Mississippi. In fact, it opens up a passage through more than a half of the remnant of a Confederacy still nominally held by the rebel rulers. Thus, by this splendid stroke of our river navy, we see not only the fall of the Southern Metropolis, but also a moral and territorial gain for the National cause, which far overshadows in importance even this. If the news be allowed to reach the rebel army at Corinth — and it certainly cannot be kept from it for more than a day or two — it must complete its demoralization; for it will demonstrate beyond a peradventure that the cause in which it fights is hopeless. There can be no prospect to the rebels of recapturing the city; for the railroad leading to it will be destroyed, and a descent by the river is impossible. The whole of Southern Louisiana is a vast plain, and in no event can the rebels make a stand anywhere near the city.

New-Orleans is the great commercial and financial emporium of the South. It is to the Gulf coast what New-York is to the Atlantic coast. Its fall will be to the South a worse blow even than the capture of New-York by an enemy would be to the North. Through it more than half of the cotton crop of the entire South passes to the world, while its exports of sugar, molasses, tobacco and corn exceed those of any other Southern city. There is probably not much cotton there now, but the fact that we also virtually possess a great part of the cotton-growing territory, will secure its speedy export with or without the will of the planters.

It is nearly half a century since an enemy appeared before New-Orleans. That enemy was repulsed with a slaughter which renders memorable the plains of Chalmette. But this time an army captures the City almost without loss of blood — though it has doubled its population many times since then. Such are the advances made by science; and such are the irresistible powers which the Nation now brings into the field against its enemies.

The Mississippi is now virtually opened throughout its entire length.[5] That was the work which the men of the Northwest laid out for themselves a year ago. The West has done a good share of the work; but it has been left to the men of the East to complete it. ✸

Major General Benjamin F. Butler, U.S.A.

1. These were seagoing vessels under the command of Commander David Dixon Porter that carried large heavy mortars that fired 13-inch projectiles on a high arcing trajectory to bombard targets at extreme range. The shells from these mortars were called "bombs."

2. The forts were not reduced, but Farragut ran past them anyway on the night of April 24.

3. It was not Butler who demanded the surrender of the city, for his troops were still on transports below the fort. Farragut sent Navy Captain Theodorus Bailey to raise the U.S. flag above the customhouse.

4. New Orleans had been stripped of its defenses in order to reinforce Albert Sidney Johnston on the eve of the Battle at Shiloh.

5. Not quite. Though Farragut took his squadron upriver to Vicksburg, he could not capture the city without a land force. Vicksburg would hold out until July of 1863. See Chapter 14.

THE FLIGHT AND FIGHT IN THE PENINSULA.

MAY 7

It is almost bewildering to attempt to follow the campaign in the Virginia peninsula, as reported in the rapid throng of telegrams. Not one, but half-a-dozen centres of action attract the eye in the complex though converging scheme of operations in front and flank and rear, adopted by Gen. MCCLELLAN for the capture of the enemy. If anything could be unlike the unity of action that has characterized the siege of Yorktown for the past month, it is the exciting and shifting spectacle now presented by the rebel force in mingled fight and flight, pressed and pursued by the Army of the Union.

What were the plans and hopes of the rebel commanders when, to save themselves from certain destruction, they resolved to abandon their stronghold at Yorktown?[1] To form a new defensive line this side of Richmond? We can hardly think so; and neither the abandonment of that powerful position, on whose defences ten months' labor was spent, nor the form of the retreat — leaving behind them vast supplies of cannon, stores and equipments, indispensable in forming a new line of defence — encourages the surmise that they had any such hope. What, in all likelihood, they did and do hope, is to protract the advance of the National force so as to cover the retreat of the rebel "Government" from Richmond, and such of their military force as can be withdrawn. With this view they have established a series of works, extending back the whole line to the rebel capital, and on these works hundreds and thousands of negroes have for months been employed. These will form so many stepping-stones, as it were, where they may make successive stands, and both delay and cripple the advancing Union army. Whether their demoralized force is the stuff with which to carry out this programme, remains to be seen. But it is obviously the plan of the chiefs, and Gen. MCCLELLAN, in his latest dispatch, mentions it as the unanimous testimony of the prisoners taken, that the rebels will "dispute every step to Richmond."

The first of these stopping-places is Williamsburgh, and here the rear of the enemy, in strong force, has taken up its position, under Gen. JOE JOHNSTON. Indeed, so strong is the enemy at this point, that Gen. MCCLELLAN, who hurried up thither on Monday, found his progress barred by a force a "good deal superior" to his own.[2] When, however, the Commander states that his entire army is considerably inferior to that of the rebels, we must, of course, understand thereby the force before Williamsburgh, exclusive of the division of FRANKLIN, then on its way up York River, and the reserves left behind at Yorktown. Our details of the engagement which took place at Williamsburgh on Monday, are yet very imperfect, but it seems to have been a severe encounter, in which our troops displayed all their wonted bravery and vigor, and gained some positive advantages. Gen. MCCLELLAN modestly confines his present in-

GEN. McCLELLAN AND THE POLITICIANS.

A LETTER FROM SENATOR WILSON.

MAY 16

Senator [Henry] WILSON [of Massachusetts][1] has fully answered certain charges which have been preferred against him by political opponents, in the following letter:

**SENATE CHAMBER, WASHINGTON,
MAY 9, 1862.**

DEAR SIR: I have this day received your note, in which you say that it is reported by some persons that the Secretary of War [Edwin Stanton], Mr. [Charles] SUMNER, myself and others are interfering with Gen. MCCLELLAN's military plans. I am sure Mr. SUMNER in no way, directly or indirectly, has interfered or attempted to interfere with any of Gen. MCCLELLAN's military plans, or with the plans of any other General in the field. Mr. STANTON entered the War Office at a time of anxiety and gloom, when the most thoughtful men of the country were oppressed with solicitude concerning the condition of the country, foreign and domestic. Mr. STANTON carried into the War Office industry, zeal and an iron will, actuated by an intense and vehement de-

sire to promptly crush out this rebellion. He pressed upon all, in both the military and civil service, the importance of prompt and decisive action. He may have committed some errors, but I am sure he has done intentional injustice to none. I do not know that he has ever interfered with any of the plans of Gen. MCCLELLAN, but I do know that he has labored with unflagging zeal to place all the resources of the Government at the disposal of Gen. MCCLELLAN and other military commanders. I believe that EDWIN M. STANTON deserves, not the censure, but the gratitude of all men who would promptly suppress this unhallowed rebellion.

I have never interfered, either directly or indirectly, with the plans of Gen. MCCLELLAN, or an other of our military Commanders, nor has the Military Committee or any of the members of that Committee so interfered. The Military Committee, composed of four Republicans and three Democrats, is now, and has been, a unit in regard to military affairs. The members of the Committee may have their opinions in regard to men and operations in the field, and as individuals they may have canvassed the acts of military men with that freedom with which American citizens and legislators may canvass the acts of public men in civil and military life, but they have not in Committee, or in the Senate, or else-

where, attempted in any way to interfere with the plans of military commanders, or to advise Congress or the Government to interfere with those plans. The members of the Committee have never been actuated by partisan feelings in regard to military appointments or operations. Since the war commenced, nearly 2,500 names have been before the Committee to be canvassed and passed upon; of this number nearly 250 were Generals. I have never been actuated by political considerations in any of these nominations, and I am sure I can say the same for each of the other members of the Committee. I have aided in securing the appointment in the army of nearly one hundred citizens of Massachusetts. I am sure that at least half of them are men who are politically opposed to me, and some of them, or their relatives and friends, have been the most active of my political enemies....

I have believed, and I have acted upon the belief, that it was my duty, as a member of the Senate, and Chairman of the Military Committee, to support Gen. MCCLELLAN and other military commanders, and to place at the disposal of the War Department the resources of the country, and to leave the responsibility of action with the Executive Department and the military commanders. The other members of the Committee, and I think I may

tentions to "holding them in check," but this is qualified by the significant phrase, "while I resume my original plan."

What does this expression signify? Obviously it means the plan indicated in Gen. MCCLELLAN's first dispatch of Sunday, sent on the heels of the retreat of the rebels. In this he says: "I move FRANKLIN's Division and as much more as I can transport by water up to West Point to-day." It appears, however, that the movement was not executed that day; but the gunboats alone were sent up on a reconnaissance, with intent that the transports should follow if the report proved favorable. We have already intelligence that the gunboats have reached West Point, capturing or destroying many rebel transports on their way, and subsequently landed a force and destroyed a bridge on the railroad leading to Richmond. We may therefore suppose that Gen. MCCLELLAN's plan was promptly carried out. If so, twenty-five thousand men are now at the neck of the peninsula, a dozen miles in the rear of JOHNSTON's force, barring its escape to Richmond.[3]

The entire rebel army is thus confined in a cul-de-sac, with outlet nowhere, and the two Union forces pressing upon it from opposite sides. Whether they fight with the passion of beasts driven to bay and goaded to desperation, or, as they have done on so many other occasions, quietly resign themselves to inevitable fate, their ultimate capture can hardly be escaped. It would be impossible to imagine a more intensely exciting situation than that presented by the campaign in the peninsula, whither all eyes are now directed. ✪

1. Joseph E. Johnston's Confederate army evacuated its position on the Yorktown line on the night of May 3 and fell back toward Williamsburg. This changed the campaign from one of a static siege to a pursuit.
2. McClellan's army significantly outnumbered Confederate forces throughout the campaign. At the Battle of Williamsburg (May 5, 1862), Union forces of some 41,000 fought rebel forces of about 32,000.
3. McClellan successfully put a force ashore at Eltham's Landing at the head of the York River on May 7, 1862, but that force was pushed back by a division under John Bell Hood and did not manage to get behind Johnston's army.

say that nearly all, if not all, the members of the Senate, concur in this opinion. Gens. SCOTT, MCCLELLAN, FREMONT, MCDOWELL, BANKS, BUTLER, BURNSIDE, and other leading Generals, can bear ample testimony to this statement, in regard to the operations in the field, as in civil affairs, I form my opinions from the facts that come within my knowledge, and, as is my habit, have expressed these opinions freely, perhaps too freely, but I am not the partisan or the enemy of any of our military commanders. I go as far as he who goes the farthest in applauding the successful efforts of any and all of our military men. I regret to see that we have a class of men who are swift to censure and arraign others, both in the civil and military service, who are striving to impress the country with the conviction that there is in Congress a party disposed to interfere with the plans of Gen. MCCLELLAN. To accomplish their objects, some of these people do not scruple to misquote or misrepresent the feelings, words and acts of the men the seem desirous of placing in a false position, but such conduct can only harm themselves.

VERY TRULY YOURS, HENRY WILSON. ✪

1. Senator Henry S. Wilson of Massachusetts (1812–1875) was a staunch Republican and antislavery activist who was chairman of the influential Senate Military Affairs Committee. He subsequently became Vice President of the United States during Grant's second term.

Senator Henry Wilson of Massachusetts.

NEWS FROM WASHINGTON
THE PROCLAMATION OF GEN. HUNTER.
HIS IMMEDIATE RECALL PROBABLE.

MAY 18

The more that is known of Gen. HUNTER's instructions from his Government, the more indefensible and insubordinate does his conduct appear.[1] It is conceded now that the President not only did not authorize his foolish proclamation, freeing the slaves of three States, but he actually forbade him to issue any proclamation whatever. There was deep regret in Washington when Gen. SHERMAN, who had done all the hard work in South Carolina and Georgia, was superseded, and HUNTER sent to reap the laurels of Pulaski's reduction. HUNTER lately abandoned the while Unionists at Jacksonville, Fla., to unnamed cruelties from the rebels, because, as he alleged, he had nut forces enough in his Department to protect them, But while not able to free loyal whites from oppression, he undertakes the liberation of a million blacks. His removal from command is a foregone conclusion. The President to-day said to a Senator that he was waiting for authentic information, and that if Gen. HUNTER had either given free papers to negroes or issued the proclamation attributed to him, he would immediately suspend him from his command.... ✪

1. On May 9, Major General David Hunter (1802–1886), in command of the Department of the South, declared all slaves within his command area to be free.

IMPORTANT FROM WASHINGTON.

GEN. HUNTER'S ORDER REPUDIATED BY THE PRESIDENT.

MAY 20

Whereas, There appears in the public prints what purports to be a proclamation of Major-Gen. HUNTER, in the words and figures following, to wit:

HEADQUARTERS DEPARTMENT OF THE SOUTH, HILTON HEAD, S.C., MAY 9, 1862. GENERAL ORDERS, NO 11. — The three States of Georgia, Florida and South Carolina, comprising the Military Department of the South, having deliberately declared themselves no longer under the protection of the United States of America, and having taken up arms against the said United States, it becomes a military necessity to declare them under martial law. This was accordingly done on the 25th day of April, 1862. Slavery and martial law in a free country are altogether incompatible. The persons in these three States, (Georgia. Florida and South Carolina,) heretofore held as slaves, are therefore, declared forever free. [Official,] DAVID HUNTER,

MAJOR-GENERAL COMMANDING.

ED. W. SMITH, ACTING ASST.-ADJT.-GEN.

And whereas, The same is producing some excitement and misunderstanding;

Therefore, I ABRAHAM LINCOLN, President of the United States, proclaim and declare, that the Government of the United States had no knowledge or belief of an intention on the part of Gen. HUNTER to issue such a proclamation, nor has it yet any authentic information that the document is genuine; and, further, that neither Gen. HUNTER, nor any other Commander or person, has been authorized by the Government of the United States to make proclamation declaring the slaves of any State free, and that the supposed proclamation now in question, whether genuine or false, is altogether void, so far as respects such declaration. I further make known, that whether it be competent for me, as Commander-in-Chief of the army and navy, to declare the slaves of any State or States free; and whether at any time, or in any ease, it shall have become a necessity indispensable to the maintenance of the Government to exercise such supposed power, are questions which, under my responsibility, I reserve to myself, and which I cannot feel justified in leaving to the decision of commanders in the field. These are totally different questions from those of police regulations in armies and camps.

On the 6th day of March last, by a special message, I recommended to Congress, the adoption of a joint resolution, to be substantially as follows:

Resolved, That the United States ought to cooperate with any State which may adopt a gradual abolishment of Slavery, giving to such State in its discretion to compensate for the inconveniences, public and private, produced by such change of system.

The resolution, in the language above quoted, was adopted by large majorities in both branches of Congress, and now stands an authentic, definite and solemn proposal of the nation to the States, and people most immediately interested in the subject matter. To the people of these States I now earnestly appeal — I do not argue, I beseech you to make the arguments for yourselves. You cannot, if you would, be blind to the signs of the times. I beg of you a calm and enlarged consideration of them, ranging, If it may be, far above personal and partisan politics. This proposal makes common cause for a common object, casting no reproaches upon any. It acts not the Pharisee. The change it contemplates would come gently as the dews of Heaven, not receding or wrecking anything. Will you not embrace it? So much good has not been done by one effort in all past time, as in the Providence of God it is now your high privilege to do. May the vast future not have to lament that you have neglected it.

In witness whereof I have hereunto set my hand and caused the seal of the United States to be affixed.

Done at the City of Washington this 19th day of May, in the year of our Lord one thousand eight hundred and sixty-two, and of the Independence of the United States the eighty-sixth.

ABRAHAM LINCOLN. ⊛

THE PRESIDENT AND GEN. HUNTER.

MAY 20

No one can be surprised by the announcement that Gen. HUNTER'S military order, emancipating all the slaves in South Carolina, Georgia and Florida, on the absurd pretext that "martial law and Slavery are incompatible in a free country," is repudiated by President LINCOLN. Gen. HUNTER will be largely indebted to the President's forbearance if he is not recalled. His order involved a very gross departure from his official duty, was utterly unjustifiable in itself, and was calculated very greatly to embarrass the General Government in its great task of dealing with the rebellion.

From the very beginning of this rebellion, President LINCOLN has been perfectly clear and decided on the subject of Slavery. He has refused to make this war one of emancipation, and has steadily treated it as designed to restore the integrity of the Union and the supremacy of the Constitution. He has not yielded one iota to the fierce and relentless pressure brought to bear upon him in favor of a sweeping abolition policy. He required Gen. FREMONT to modify his proclamation of freedom to the slaves of rebels, so as to conform strictly to the law of Congress. He has more than once declared himself hostile to any scheme of emancipation which was not gradual in its operation, which did not compensate the owners and which did not provide for colonizing the enfranchised slaves. He is not likely, to change these views merely to accommodate Gen. HUNTER. This country has had no President for years who has shown greater tenacity of purpose — a more fixed and immovable adherence to a line of policy — than President LINCOLN. He has his own views of the public exigency and of the way to meet it. He knows the objects to be accomplished and how to reach them. He has evinced all the firmness of JACKSON without his violence, and enjoys all his popularity without its drawbacks. He commands to-day the confidence of the American people to a degree unsurpassed by any of his predecessors. Such a man is not likely to surrender his own opinions or to abandon his own policy, without better reasons than those assigned by Gen. HUNTER. It is urged in defence of the General's act, that the yellow fever season is approaching, and that he needs acclimated negroes to work upon his fortifications. He gives no such reason for his decree. He bases his action on no such ground. Besides, the yellow fever is not to be averted by a military order, nor can laborers be commanded by such a process. If he needs slaves for work, let him seize them for military purposes; his powers are ample for so doing. But proclaiming their freedom neither swells the numbers of his workmen, nor gives him command of their labor. So far as practical results are concerned, it is brutum fulmen. If it takes effect and actually frees the slaves, it plunges those States into an abyss of blood and terror which might glut the most wolfish hatred, but which could not contribute in the least toward the peace and union which the war professes to seek.

We have very little doubt that Slavery is to receive its death-blow at the hands of this rebellion. That its political power is already destroyed no sensible man can doubt. The day has gone by forever when Slavery could dictate the policy of the General Government — control the action of nominating Conventions, terrify Congress into the enactment of laws for its special benefit, or ostracise those who refuse to believe in its divinity as unfit for public office in a free Republic. If the rebellion were to end today, and every Southern State were to return to the Union, the slaveholding interest would hold forever hereafter only a secondary and subordinate position in the Government of the country. That the leaders of the rebellion will consent that it should hold such a place without a further struggle for the maintenance of its supremacy, is not probable. They will fight on its behalf to the end. But the contest now is with the political power of Slavery. The point to be decided is, which of the two, Slavery or the Constitution, is strongest in the control of the Government.

We believe that Slavery will be beaten in the battle, and that the supremacy of the Constitution will be maintained. We hope that its supremacy will be restored over every State and every part of our common country, without any such violent rupture of their local institutions as shall plunge them into social chaos. The political power of Slavery will be forever destroyed. Its supreme dictatorship over thought and speech and freedom of action, will be annihilated. If this result can be

accomplished now, all the rest will follow in due time. Slavery, as a form of labor, as a social institution, cannot long survive its downfall as a political power. And its extinction will be most safely reached, if it shall thus come gradually, as a result of the working of social laws, with due preparation, and accompanied by just guiding and restraining influences.

When the military power of the rebellion has been broken, we shall be able to judge of the possibility of such an issue. If the Southern people shall then insist on peace, and accept it on terms honorable to themselves, and safe for the Union, we may hope for a return of our former mate-

rial prosperity, with a healthier and better development of our political principles. If they refuse peace, and still insist on war, — if after their armies have been defeated, and their resources exhausted, they persist in gratifying their blind and baseless hatred of the Government of the Union, they must be prepared for such a form of war as the emergency may require. They will then have no right to complain if their whole land should be swept with the besom of destruction, and its social forms and usages replaced by others more in conformity with the civilization of the age and the principles of the Government under which we live. ⊛

Major General David Hunter, U.S.A.

THE RETREAT OF GEN. BANKS.

HIS WHOLE FORCE AND TRAINS ACROSS THE POTOMAC IN SAFETY.

MAY 27

WASHINGTON, MONDAY, MAY, 26

The following was received at the War Department, at 11 P.M.:

WILLIAMSPORT, MONDAY, MAY 26 — 4 P.M.

To the President:

I have the honor to report the safe arrival of my command at this place last evening at 10 o'clock, and the passage of the Fifth Corps across the river to-day, with comparatively but little loss. The loss of men in killed, wounded, and missing in the different combats in which my command has participated since the march from Strasburgh on the morning of the 24th inst., I am unable now to report; but I have great satisfaction in being able to represent that, although serious, it is much less than might have been anticipated, considering the very great disparity of forces engaged, and the long-matured plans of the enemy, which aimed at nothing less than the entire capture of our force. A detailed statement will be forwarded as soon as possible. My command encountered the enemy in a constant succession of attacks, and in well contested engagements at Strasburgh, Middletown, Newton, at a point also between these places, and at Winchester. The force of the enemy was estimated at from 15,000 to 20,000 men, with very strong artillery and cavalry supports.

My own force consisted of two brigades, less than 4,000 strong, all told, 1,500 cavalry, ten Parrot guns, and six smooth-bores. The substantial preservation of the entire supply is a source of gratification. It numbered about five hundred wagons, on a forced march of fifty-three miles, thirty-five of which were performed in one day, subject to constant attack in front, rear, and flank, according to its position, by the enemy in full force....

Our troops are in good spirits, and occupy both sides of the river.

N.P. BANKS,

MAJOR-GENERAL COMMANDING. ✸

WHAT IS THOUGHT IN WASHINGTON.

MAY 27

WASHINGTON, MONDAY, MAY 26

The repulse of Gen. BANKS from the Shenandoah Valley excited the greatest surprise because the country was kept so ignorant of his force. It turns out that, instead of having a corps d'armee and "a large force," as you state in Sunday's TIMES, and as the country generally has believed, he had not more than a full brigade left to him when he was attacked by the enemy. BANKS repeatedly and earnestly protested against bring stripped of his command; and many of his friends advised him to resign, but this he bravely refused to do. There is felt to be a heavy responsibility on somebody in this matter, and it is not just to put it all on Secretary STANTON. The President magnanimously "takes the responsibility," but it is well known he only "permitted to be done" that which his own judgment disapproved.

The enemy's raid is at an end, and has fallen far short of his expectations, and the country may yet have reason to rejoice in what has occurred, if it shall result, as every one hopes, in the President's throwing off the dangerous counsels he sometimes yields to, and trusts more to his own clear head and honest heart.

There is no need for a moment's anxiety about Washington, and Gov. ANDREW's Proclamation No. 2 excites a general smile.' Gen. JACKSON's rebel army is probably nearer to Staunton, Virginia, at this reading, than he is to Washington, and much more anxious to reach the former place than the latter.

The events of the two past days have wonderfully stimulated our Government, and there is now a "movement along the whole line." Dress parades at Fredericksburgh, it is supposed, will cease, and Cabinet visits to that point be suspended till the war is over. On the whole, the martial aspect of affairs is more encouraging since the escapade of Gen. JACKSON than before.

There is universal sympathy felt and expressed here [Washington] for Gen. BANKS, and the hope of all is that he may be furnished an army suitable to his rank,

WHAT STONEWALL JACKSON HAS DONE FOR THE UNION.

MAY 30

The raid of the rebel JACKSON down the Shenandoah Valley, has not been without its most salutary fruits. In this case, as in so many others during the progress of the unholy rebellion against our Government, our reverses have seemed designed by Providence to strengthen and glorify our cause....

The Union is stronger for this sudden attack upon a weak point. It has awakened the country to an appreciation of Major.-Gen. N. P. BANKS, one of the ablest and most useful of our chieftains and statesmen. It has drawn out, in the most unexpected manner, new and gratifying evidence of the inexhaustible patriotism and resources of the Union — rendering it sure that our Government is more than equal to any possible strain that may come upon it. So much has the raid of JACKSON done for the Government per se.

On the other hand, the result cannot but be most disheartening to the enemy. They have boasted always of their ability to bring the war into the loyal States; and they threaten often to do so. They have professed to believe that Maryland is enslaved, and that on the first appearance of a rebel army on her borders, her people would break out in irrepressible revolt against the Government at Washington. The raid of JACKSON extinguishes both delusions. They find how signally a distinguished General has failed, under circumstances more favorable than will ever occur again, to put a single rebel soldier on the soil of a loyal State. And they find how Maryland, instead of springing to arms to hail their coming as that of deliverers, is set a-surging with loyal indignation at their approach, bringing speedy and fierce punishment on every manifestation of sympathy with the rebel cause....

For all these blessings that we have enumerated, and for many more that we could easily call attention to, have we not reason to thank STONEWALL JACKSON, and him only? No man on our own side, animated by the best intent, could have done so much in a single campaign for the strengthening of the Union cause as he has done. ✸

and allowed to become his own avenger… and the fact that he retreated so far in the face of an enemy so overwhelming, and crossed his men in good order and good spirits, is taken as proof of the highest generalship. No other course could have kept JACKSON from crossing into Maryland.

The dispatch this morning received from Gen. BANKS, dated at Williamsport, Md., and announcing the belief that his whole force, trains and all, would cross the Potomac in safety, was hailed with the liveliest satisfaction. The dispatch from the Secretary of War which Gen. BANKS refers to as having read to his troops amid the liveliest cheers, is understood to have contained the thanks of the President and Secretary, for his excellent conduct of the retreat. High military authority pronounces it one of the most masterly movements of the war, and regular officers here, who have been slow to acknowledge the generalship of Gen. BANKS, now accord to him great tact and ability as a commander. The fact that at Winchester, with a small force of less than five thousand men,

he stubbornly held his ground, and resisted the enemy's force of three times his own, and afterwards retreated in order, is taken as evidence of superior generalship.

There are no details of the fight at Winchester.[2] The allusion to it in the dispatch of Gen. BANKS creates anxiety among the friends of troops in his command. It is feared that many of the wounded were of necessity left to the mercy of the enemy.

A report was circulated this afternoon — probably founded on an intimation in the dispatch of BANKS to the effect that JACKSON has drawn back his advanced force, and was not likely to attempt to get possession of the Baltimore and Ohio Railroad, although he swore an oath when routed by [James] SHIELDS, to seize that thoroughfare at an early day. He may again have to make good his escape from the gallant Irish Brigadier.

The steps taken to regain the lost ground would, if known to the public, establish the vigilance of the President; but for prudent reasons they must not be developed at this time.[3] It is enough to say that they are considered all sufficient to insure not only the

safety of the capital, but also to prevent the further advance of the enemy in the direction of the Potomac, and probably to insure the capture, bag and baggage, of JACKSON's entire force. Should the well devised plans be carried out, as there is every reason to suppose they will be, what yesterday seemed a serious disaster to our cause may be made to result in a very decided and important triumph over the enemy. ✺

1. On March 11, 1862, Governor John A. Andrew (1818–1867) of Massachusetts issued a proclamation calling for "Thursday, the third day of April next, to be observed throughout this Commonwealth, as a day of public HUMILIATION, FASTING, AND PRAYER."
2. At the Battle of Winchester (May 25, 1862), 16,000 soldiers under Jackson attacked and routed a force of 6,500 under Banks. Union forces suffered 2,000 casualties to the Confederates' 400.
3. President Lincoln determined to trap Jackson in the lower valley by directing Fremont from western Virginia, and James Shields' division of McDowell's Corps, to move into the valley. Jackson managed to avoid the trap by hard marching.

An Edwin Forbes sketch of the Battle of Cross Keys during Jackson's Shenandoah Valley Campaign.

THE PROGRESS OF THE CAMPAIGN.

MAY 30

To the public, at the present moment, military and naval operations seem everywhere to have come almost to a dead halt. The main body of our Eastern Army is, and has been since the early part of the month, in front of the rebel Capital, and of the main body of the Eastern rebel army; but nothing more decisive than a few skirmishes have yet taken place. The main body of the Army of the West has been planted before Corinth ever since the battle of Pittsburgh [Shiloh]; a period of now three months; but of its doings we know nothing excepting the fact that it has not yet fought a battle or moved upon the enemy's works. These two mighty armies — jointly numbering over two hundred thousand men — have certainly not been inactive during their respective brief periods of pause; but neither have they dazzled the public with any of those grand actions which have been by it daily expected.

So also it is and has been for some length of time, with the minor divisions of the army. Gen. MCDOWELL has been between one and two mouths on the Rappahannock, and his column has lain there peacefully since the beginning, and in tranquility remains there still. Gen. FREMONT has been in the mountains of Western Virginia, with a very respectable force, for some time; but excepting one or two engagements of small detachments of his army, he has done nothing. Gen. BURNSIDE has been quiescent for a month; Gen. HUNTER for a still longer period; and our troops in Florida do not take possession of that easily captured State. Our iron-clad gunboats are stuck just below Richmond; our flotilla is stuck just above Fort Pillow; and there being no rebels on the sea now to fight, our navy is everywhere at its ease.

This state of things contrasts strongly with the extraordinary activity all along the line, in the two months preceding the one just passing away. Then all around rebeldom was daily and ceaselessly heard the thunderings of war. Great battles fought; great armies driven back; great cities captured and states repossessed; forts falling daily; strategic positions occupied; and both our navy and army furnishing, through each morning's newspaper, some new illustration of their prowess and activity.

All these things stood out largely before the public eye, and fully satisfied the demand that our army should do something. These victories have greatly altered the aspect of the rebellion, and, it must be remembered, have necessarily altered somewhat the look of the campaign's progress. We cannot continue to take forts every day; they are nearly all taken now. We cannot enjoy a captured city with our breakfast every morning; there are only two or three more rebel cities worth capturing. We cannot expect to see the rebel army of the West fall back from Corinth as it fell back from Bowling Green; for where now shall it fall back to? We can hardly hope to see the rebel army of the East fly as suddenly from Richmond as it previously fled from Manassas and from Yorktown; for to give up the rebel Capital is virtually to give up the rebel cause. All this great but

WHAT ARE OUR IRON-CLADS DOING?

MAY 30

It seems, as matters now stand, that our fleet of iron-clad gunboats on the James River is destined to have no part in the operations against Richmond. Ever since their repulse from Fort Darling, a fortnight ago, they have been, and are still, lying idle, fifteen or twenty miles below City Point.[1]

We cannot but think this is a great mistake. Their cooperation would secure the immediate capture of Richmond, and would also secure important results attainable by no other means. Whether the rebel army in front of Richmond is beaten there or concludes to evacuate the city, its retreat in either case must be by a line that can be completely commanded by our gunboats. Let them either destroy or hold the railroad bridge of the Danville line across the James River at the Capital, while they do the same by the line of communication over the Appomattox at Petersburgh, (within easy striking distance of our fleet from where it now is,) and the only two routes of retreat southward will be effectually cut off. This omitted and the best strategy of MCCLELLAN will be unavailing — the rebels will make good their flight.

We fear there is no evidence that the Navy Department proposes pursuing this course. The inference is either that it regards the task as impracticable, or the end to be gained as not worth the effort. We can hardly suppose that even the Navy Department will be so blind as to take the latter view; we must, therefore, conclude that it regards the obstructions and defences between Fort Darling and the rebel Capital as too formidable to repeat the attempt. We have no precise information as to the nature of these obstructions; but it is well known that they are of recent adoption, and it is also well known that no obstructions can be placed in the channel of a river that cannot be cleared away or blown up in a few days. All our previous naval expeditions have found their course arrested by similar devices, and notably in the approach to New-Orleans every form of obstruction that rebel ingenuity could devise — sunken vessels, chains, torpedoes, fire-ships and what not — were placed to retard the passage of our fleet, which, mark well, were not iron-clads, but wooden gunboats. But engineering skill made short work with these impedimenta. The same skill and energy would speedily send our fleet to Richmond. At least we should like to see it tried, in place of that inertia that keeps our iron-clad vessels lying idle for a fortnight. ✸

1. A squadron of navy warships, including the partially armored USS *Galena* and the ironclad USS *Monitor*, attacked Confederate defenses at Drewry's Bluff just seven miles downriver from Richmond on May 15, 1862. The attack was driven off, and the *Galena* in particular suffered severe damage.

still minor work is now done; and there needs only the defeat or dispersion of the two great rebel armies at Corinth and Richmond before the whole rebellion is brought to a close. An assault on these two points, and on these two armies, is a thing not at all similar to any of the previous and preparatory operations.

Before Richmond and Corinth, the whole strength of the South is arrayed. To suffer a repulse at either place would be to incur a fearful risk. Our military leaders, therefore, are wise in being cautious of prematurely beginning assaults, and in making such preparations as will enable them to throw against the enemy all the force that can possibly be rendered available. This, the daily chronicle of events and movements shows they are doing. And, though the impatient public may not be gratified every day with a new and glittering victory, it can see that, from these preparations, the consummation of victory will speedily be realized. ❂

Federal ironclad gunboat *Galena* patrols the James River.

CHAPTER 9
"In Front of Richmond"

JUNE–JULY 1862

he dominant news story in the summer of 1862 was the progress — or lack of progress — of George McClellan's Peninsular Campaign in Virginia. Then on the last day of May, the rebel army under Joseph E. Johnston struck at McClellan's army outside Richmond. The Battle of Fair Oaks, also called the battle of Seven Pines, was not strategically decisive, but it did have two important results: first, Johnston himself fell wounded and had to give up command to Robert E. Lee, who proved far more aggressive than his predecessor; and second, McClellan was so appalled by the heavy losses that he became even more cautious. In effect, the initiative in the campaign passed from the Federals to the Confederates.

Unsurprisingly, these circumstances increased the number of McClellan's public critics, including several Northern newspapers that called for McClellan to be replaced. The Times continued its support, but that support had its limits. After Lee launched a series of headlong counterattacks against McClellan's army in late June, in a campaign known to history as the Seven Days Battles (June 26–July 1, 1862), even The Times had to acknowledge that "the public faith in his ability to lead an army in the field to victory, has been greatly shaken." In late July, Lincoln summoned Major General Henry W. Halleck from the Western Theater to assume command as general-in-chief, a title once held by McClellan.

As the summer marked McClellan's fall, it also marked the rise of Robert E. Lee. Previously the military advisor to Jefferson Davis, Lee made the army his own, and even though the Seven Days Battles were more costly to the rebels than to the Union, Lee succeeded in driving off the approach-

General McClellan's headquarters near Yorktown, Virginia.

ing foe, and Richmond celebrated its deliverance and its new savior. The other Southern hero that summer was Thomas "Stonewall" Jackson, whose rampage through the Shenandoah Valley, followed by a quick movement to Richmond to join Lee during the Seven Days, made him as exalted a Southern icon as Lee himself. Though The Times initially disparaged both Jackson and his campaign, dubbing him "that old rebel hypocrite and knave," by July The Times was wondering if there was a "danger of his taking a column, and with it marching suddenly in the direction of Washington?"

There was news from the West, too. In Louisiana, Major General Benjamin Butler earned the criticism of Southerners and Unionists alike in his role as the occupier of New Orleans. Annoyed that the women of the city were making disparaging remarks whenever they passed a Union officer on the sidewalks, he issued an order declaring that "whatever woman, lady or mistress, gentle or simple, who, by gesture, look or word, insults, shows contempt for, thus attracting to herself the notice of my officers and soldiers, will be deemed to act as becomes her vocation as a common woman." Such aspersions on Southern womanhood enraged the local population. But Butler also earned the opprobrium of Unionists when, after encouraging runaway slaves to come within the Union lines, he issued an order to "to turn out all [blacks] not employed by the officers."

Upriver from New Orleans, the fighting continued at Vicksburg (which The Times spelled "Vicksburgh") where the Union gunboat squadron of Charles Henry Davis coming from the north, and the ocean-going squadron of David Glasgow Farragut coming from the south, joined to assail the Confederate bastion. Despite a severe bombardment, it soon became evident that Vicksburg could not be taken without troops.

Finally, the character of the war itself continued to evolve. The Second Confiscation Act, signed into law on July 17, 1862, declared that "every person who shall hereafter commit the crime of treason against the United States" would lose his property, including "all his slaves" who would "be declared and made free." Many in the North did not see this as progress. A bitter and poisonous unsigned editorial printed on June 14 was a reminder that racism remained a powerful sentiment in the North as well as in the South. At the same time, however, Congress debated the wisdom of arming slaves for combat. The war for Union was already becoming a social revolution.

McCLELLAN VINDICATED BY HALLECK.

JUNE 1

The evacuation of Manassas by the rebels was the signal for an outcry against Gen. MCCLELLAN, because he had not prevented it. And when Yorktown was evacuated, the same outcry was repeated. And men asked why he had not attacked the rebels, why he had not prevented their retreat, why he had not known of it before, and there were not wanting those who intimated that MCCLELLAN could not do anything except build fortifications, and that if we expected to have anything done on the east of our line, in the way of fighting, we should have to send for Gen. HALLECK to take the chief command.

We look with some interest to see how the gentry who thus howled after MCCLELLAN will look upon the recent evacuation of Corinth.[1] They cannot treat it as an evidence that HALLECK is not a fighting General, because their mouths will be stopped by their own statements made heretofore, that he was the man, and that all the fighting took place in his Department. They will either have to give up HALLECK, too, or else to admit that victories are won sometimes by the trench and the battery, as well as by the sword and bayonet. Whatever conclusion they come to, however, the country will recognize the fact that these three evacuations have been three of the greatest victories ☞

The Battle of Fair Oaks.

of the war. The Richmond papers so recognize them. One of these papers, in an article upon the subject, quotes very appositely the answer of MARIUS to SILA — "If thou art a great general, MARIUS, come down and fight." "If thou art a great general, SILA, make me come down and fight."[2] The fact was that MARIUS was a great general, and, though we doubt not that at the time he was scoffed at by those who stayed at home in Rome for staying behind his intrenchments, he could afford to wait for time to do him justice. And so will it be with our leader. He will not fight till he is ready, unless, indeed, the rebels have some greater general, who can make

him fight, which has not yet been shown. And, when the time does come, we doubt not he will show himself as good a fighter as MARIUS ever was. ✹

1. After the Battle of Shiloh, Beauregard retreated to the railroad crossroads of Corinth, Mississippi. Halleck, with a vastly superior army, followed and slowly began to encircle the position. On May 30, Beauregard quietly decamped, leaving Halleck the prize but without an engagement. The Times notes that this was similar to what happened to McClellan at Manassas. Yet while McClellan was excoriated for being too cautious, Halleck was praised for his strategy.

2. Gaius Marius and Lucius Cornelius Sulla (not Sila) fought in the Roman Civil War of the first century B.C.

OUR NAVY AT NEW-ORLEANS.

JUNE 3

For some inscrutable reason, the Navy Department has thus far withheld from the public the official reports of the naval officers engaged in the memorable action which led to the capture of New-Orleans. We are thus compelled to rely for our knowledge of what was done upon such newspaper correspondence as the authorities permit to see the light, and upon private letters to friends at home. One of the latter, which has been handed to us, contains some interesting memoranda concerning the participation in the fight of the Brooklyn, Capt. [Thomas T.] CRAVEN. The Press has made the fact pretty widely known already, that this ship bore the brunt of the fight, and

that her commander behaved in the most gallant manner. But the following paragraph, from the private letter referred to, gives still further testimony on this point. The writer says: "After the battle Flag-Officer FARRAGUT took Capt. CRAVEN by both hands, and said publicly, 'You and your noble ship have been the salvation of my squadron. You were in a complete blaze of fire, so much so that I supposed your ship was burning up. I never saw such rapid and precise firing. It never was surpassed, and probably was never equaled.' " This is high praise and from a high quarter, but all the reports thus far received show that it was deserved. ✹

GEN. McCLELLAN TO HIS SOLDIERS.

JUNE 6

McCLELLAN'S HEADQUARTERS,
TUESDAY EVENING, JUNE 3

The following address was read to the army this evening at dress parade, and was received with an outburst of vociferous cheering from every regiment:

**HEADQUARTERS ARMY OF THE POTOMAC,
CAMP NEAR NEW-BRIDGE, VA., JUNE 2, 1862.**
SOLDIERS OF THE ARMY OF THE POTOMAC:

I have fulfilled at least a part of my promise to you. You are now face to face with the rebels, who are held at bay in front of the Capital. The final and decisive battle is at hand. Unless you belie your past history, the result cannot be for a moment doubtful. If the troops who labored so faithfully, and fought so gallantly, at Yorktown, and who so bravely won the hard fights at Williamsburgh, West Point, Hanover Court-house and Fair Oaks, now prove worthy of their antecedents, the victory is surely ours.

The events of every day prove your superiority. Wherever you have met the enemy you have beaten him. Wherever you have used the bayonet, he has given way in panic and disorder.

I ask of you now one last crowning effort. The enemy has staked his all on the issue of the coming battle. Let us meet him and crush him here, in the very centre of the rebellion.

EMANCIPATING THE SLAVES OF REBELS.

JUNE 5

[The] House yesterday voted to reconsider the slaves of rebels confiscation bill,[1] which was rejected by a very close vote a fortnight ago. The majority for reconsideration was 21, the total vote being; for, 84; against, 65. It is not likely that the rejected bill will pass the House or become a law in its original form; but the necessity of some action in the premises is admitted on all hands. Probably not less than a hundred thousand slaves have been directly engaged in forwarding this rebellion; and leaving out altogether Slavery as the ultimate inducing cause of the revolt, it is very doubtful whether, in a military point of view, it could have attained anything like its present proportions with-

out the labor and the aid of Southern slaves. It cannot be that this rebel live stock shall be protected and preserved for the future use of the rebels. It cannot be that we should neglect to inflict a just punishment upon the slaveholding traitors and usurpers who have plunged the country into this bloody war. Still, hasty action on a subject of such vast and enduring import is dangerous to all parties: and while justice should be inexorably administered, it should also be administered discreetly, and in such a manner as not to reflect unjustly upon those who may be innocent. There is no doubt of the correctness of the oft-made assertion, that a large part of the Southern people was forced into this rebellion. As things went, it was a virtual impossibility for them to resist it. When, then, the question of confiscation assumes a practical shape, these

men should have an opportunity of proving their virtual innocence. Neither their civil rights nor their estates should be interfered with, without trial; and it is to be hoped that the bill which may pass Congress will make ample provision for this. It must not be forgotten that while the people of the South had a duty of fealty to the Government, the Government also had a duty of protection to them; and that the Government is morally as culpable for failing in its imperative duty as the loyal men of the South were for failing to do their whole duty. We do not say that when the protection due the Southern loyalists was for so long a time withheld, the latter were inexcusable for succumbing to the de facto powers. We only say that there was a joint culpability of citizen and Government. And as soon as the Government, by suppressing the rebellion, sets

Soldiers, I will be with you in this battle, and share its dangers with you. Our confidence in each other is now founded upon the past. Let us strike the blow which is to restore peace and union to this distracted land. Upon your valor, discipline and mutual confidence the result depends.

(SIGNED,) GEO. B. MCCLELLAN,
MAJOR-GENERAL COMMANDING. ⊛

A Currier and Ives lithograph of Brigadier General Thomas Meagher commanding troops at the Battle of Fair Oaks.

A Sanitary Commission lodge at Alexandria, Virginia.

itself right toward the Southern people, the latter also should have an opportunity to set themselves right toward the Government. For convicted traitors — for those who have willingly furnished slaves to aid the rebel cause, there should be punishment and confiscation severe and exemplary; but, as we already said, in providing for this, care should be taken that the innocent do not suffer with the guilty. We are glad to learn that the feeling of Congress is in favor only of judicious legislation on the question. ⊛

1. The First Confiscation Act of August 6, 1861, had authorized the confiscation of slaves who worked for the Confederate military. The act under debate here became the Second Confiscation Act, and freed the slaves of any Confederate official, military or civilian, who did not surrender within 60 days of the act's passage.

THE REBEL GEN. JO. JOHNSTON REPORTED TO BE MORTALLY WOUNDED.

MCCLELLAN'S HEADQUARTERS, JUNE 6

Two deserters, who came in this morning, state that Gen. Jo. Johnston was seriously, if not mortally wounded, through the groin, by a Minie ball, during the late battle. Gen. G.W. SMITH is now in command. Other information received goes to corroborate the report.[1]

These deserters state that the rebel loss is estimated at ten thousand in killed, wounded and missing.[2]

No material change has taken place in the position of the enemy.

JUNE 7

A contraband has arrived who left Richmond yesterday. He represents things there as in a terrible state of confusion and uncertainty. No troops are in the city excepting those doing guard duty and attending to the sick and wounded, all being compelled to remain outside.

There were no signs of evacuation; but, on the contrary, everything goes to show a determined resistance on the part of the rebels.... ⊛

1. Joseph E. Johnston was wounded twice on May 31: hit in the shoulder by a musket ball, and struck in the chest and thigh by fragments from an artillery shell. Though it was feared he had been killed, he survived the battle and, later in the war, he commanded Confederate armies in the West. Gustavus Woodson Smith (1821–1896) superseded him temporarily until Davis appointed Robert E. Lee to command.
2. Confederate losses were about half that: 6,134 in all, as compared to just over 5,000 Federal casualties.

MORE WORK FOR WOMEN — THE WOUNDED SOLDIERS.

JUNE 8

The wounded from the battle-field of Fair Oaks, and other Virginia fields, are now arriving here daily. Six hundred came in last evening, and were sent to the different places previously chosen for the purpose in this City. These wounded and sick men will all be taken care of by the Government, aided by the Sanitary Commission, and by the efforts of professional and other benevolent persons in the City. Still there is much that private beneficence and attention can do for them. They need comforts, delicacies, attentions, underclothing, and a thousand other things. Any one who has had sickness in the house, and knows those things that the sick and suffering need, can do daily a little work that will relieve much suffering. Any woman, any lady, with a little leisure, a needle, and a kind heart, can make herself of service. If she has no other time, let her work for the suffering soldiers on Sundays. It is no harm, but rather a positive virtue, to ply the needle or kindle the fire on the holy day for such a purpose. Most of these private benefactions had better reach the soldiers through the Sanitary Commission, which is in need of constant renewals of labor, supplies, and money. It depends upon private contributions for the means of carrying on its great work. The public have well supported it hitherto; but it needs much more at present, when such large numbers of sick and wounded are daily thrown upon its care. Let no woman waste any time while this war lasts. The sex cannot fight, (not in regiments, we mean,) but they can serve their country equally effectively, otherwise.

The benevolent also should have an eye upon the families of those of the soldiers who need aid. Many of them are in want, and no man who has offered his life for his country should ever be allowed to suffer, either in his person or his family, because he has done so. ⊛

AFFAIRS BEFORE RICHMOND — DELAY OF THE MOVEMENT OF THE ARMY.

JUNE 9

There is an ominous pause in the movements of our Army in front of Richmond. It is now a week since the rebel attempt, with an overwhelming force, to break our lines was repulsed and punished with dreadful slaughter, but also, it must be remembered, at very serious cost to ourselves. Gen. MCCLELLAN's order, issued immediately after that sharp engagement, indicated a purpose on his part to push forward speedily, and force his way into Richmond. The terrible storm of Wednesday last so swelled the streams he has to cross as to delay the movement for four or five days, — and it may be that this is the only reason why that movement is delayed.

It is not impossible, however, that other causes may have something to do with it. Gen. MCCLELLAN has said nothing, so far as the public are informed, of the relative strength of the opposing armies, or of his ability, without additional aid, to cope with the rebel hosts that have gathered from every quarter for the defence of Richmond. The Government at Washington cannot be misinformed as to the number of effective troops whom he could lead to such an encounter; — though it may be ignorant or incredulous, of the strength of the forces with which MCCLELLAN is required to contend.[1] An error on one point would be as fatal as on the other. We have reason to believe that MCCLELLAN rates the rebel army in front of him at a higher figure than the War Department; whether his information is likely to be more, or less, accurate, the public can judge. Hitherto, it may be well to remember, he has not been at fault in this respect. His delay before Yorktown, while it incurred the censure of the ignorant and impulsive, proved to be the salvation of his army and of the cause.

We understand that Rev. Dr. STYLES, whose ministrations at the Mercer-street Church in this City must be well remembered, and who has for the last year resided in Richmond, states in a private letter recently received by a friend in New-Haven, that the Confederate army there numbers 200,000, and that it is well disciplined, and determined to make a desperate fight in defence of the city. One or two rebel officers who have been taken prisoners, are reported to have made statements to the same effect; and so far as we are aware,

the whole weight of testimony entitled to credit, favors the belief that the rebel army approximates, if it does not actually reach, that high figure. It is always safe to look upon the worst side of such a question, and it is wiser, as well as safer, to overrate than to underrate the strength of an enemy. There is no reason why Gen. MCCLELLAN, or the Government, in the present aspect of affairs, should run any risk whatever of a defeat or even of a half victory in front of Richmond. It is the last stronghold of the rebels. At every other point their power has been broken and their armies scattered. A decisive victory here ends the campaign, if not the war. We can take our own time — and can make victory absolutely certain. Indeed, it is our duty to do so before we venture upon a fight. If the general contest were undecided, if our armies were needed elsewhere, if delay involved loss to us and augmented strength to the enemy, or if our cause needed the prestige of victory, or of a desperate attempt to secure it, there would be reason for taking risks, and for trusting to superior valor and endurance, without regard to numbers. But to do so now would be a crime — one which, if the attempt were not crowned by success, would incur the swift and lasting reprobation of the people upon the authority, whether military or civil, who should prove to have been responsible for it. We do not believe that either Gen. MCCLELLAN or President LINCOLN will take any such risk, or put the Union cause in any such needless jeopardy.

In one of the recent dispatches from Gen. MCCLELLAN's headquarters, it is stated that a reconnaissance had shown that the enemy had no troops between the Rappahannock and the army under Gen. McClellan's command. This establishes the fact that MCDOWELL can effect a junction with MCCLELLAN, and bring to his aid the forty thousand men under his command in two days' march, and without encountering any obstacles.[2] It may possibly intimate, also, the desirableness of such a junction preparatory to an attack upon Richmond. Of its wisdom and prudence, provided Washington would not be left unduly exposed, there cannot be a moment's doubt. Indeed, we find it somewhat difficult to understand how the President should consent to an attack, while there

is even a probability that the rebel force outnumbers MCCLELLAN's, without the active aid and cooperation of MCDOWELL's corps.[3] The force now under BANKS and FREMONT seems to have been strong enough to chase JACKSON back through the valley of the Shenandoah, if not swift enough to overtake him. It does not seem, therefore, as if it could be extra-hazardous to rely upon that force for the protection of the capital, while MCDOWELL goes to aid in the capture of Richmond. We see, by the telegraph, that MCDOWELL and his Staff were in Washington on Saturday. We hope it was to arrange for some speedy movement in that direction.

It is not unlikely that we may hear of an assault upon Richmond at any moment. When we do we shall have the utmost confidence in its success: for we do not believe that MCCLELLAN will incur for himself, his army, the Government and the Union, the enormous risks of an assault for which he cannot predict an absolute and nearly certain success — unless, indeed, he should be ordered peremptorily from Washington to make it: and we have too much reliance on the President's prudence to believe that any such order will issue. If, on the other hand, the movement is not made at once, we shall find a full justification for the delay in the necessity of providing for the cooperation of other forces, in order to secure that certainly of success to which, in the present condition of affairs, the country is entitled. ✪

1. McClellan insisted that he was badly outnumbered by the rebel army, claiming at one point that the enemy had over 200,000 soldiers. In fact, McClellan's army outnumbered the Confederate forces throughout the campaign. After Seven Pines, McClellan had approximately 105,000 to Smith's (formerly Johnston's) 60,000.

2. When Lincoln learned how few troops McClellan had left behind for the defense of the capital, he ordered that Irvin McDowell's corps, the last to embark, be instead retained at Washington. Subsequently, he allowed McDowell to begin moving southward to join McClellan, but only if McDowell remained in between the rebel army and Washington.

3. This was McClellan's argument, but it was palpably false. Even without McDowell, McClellan significantly outnumbered his Confederate foe.

THE SHENANDOAH CAMPAIGN.

JUNE 10

OPERATIONS IN SOUTHWESTERN VIRGINIA. — FREMONT has now reached Harrisonburgh, the furthest point up the Shenandoah Valley that was reached by Gen. BANKS; and Stonewall JACKSON has retreated as steadily before him as he did before BANKS, and a good deal more hastily.[1] It seems utterly impossible to overtake that old rebel hypocrite and knave. He was within a few miles of Staunton last Saturday, and has probably reached that place by this time, and from there he most likely has taken the railroad to some point east of the Blue Ridge. Harrisonburgh, where our forces were last Saturday, is but twenty miles from Staunton. FREMONT was get-ting minor and indecisive fights out of JACKSON, and was expecting hourly that the latter would make a grand stand. Judging from his antecedents, however, it is unlikely that he will do anything of the sort.

But when all the Generals and troops pursuing the rebels up the Shenandoah Valley — FREMONT, BANKS, SIGEL, and SHIELDS — shall reach Staunton — what then? Turn around and march back again, for want of anything more to do? We hope not. There are two things that may be done. Leave a force at Staunton strong enough to hold it, and let the rest of our troops go and reinforce somebody in the field who needs troops. Or let the whole of the force in the Valley push through from Staunton to Charlottesville, seize the East Tennessee and Virginia Railroad, capture Lynchburgh, and preoccupy that Southwestern section of Virginia, where, JEFF. DAVIS says, if driven from Richmond, he will carry on the campaign for twenty years. The thirty or forty thousand troops in pursuit of JACKSON could easily, by a rapid move across the mountains, block any such game as this before JEFF. DAVIS begins it. ✸

1. After Jackson drove north to the Potomac in May, Lincoln ordered the reinforcement of Union armies in the valley, sending Fremont and the division of James Shields (of McDowell's corps) there. McClellan later claimed that this was a principal cause of his failure on the Virginia Peninsula. Jackson fell back southward, while Federal forces tried to catch him. A skirmish at Harrisonburg (June 6) cost the South the life of Brigadier General Turner Ashby. But on June 8 and 9, in the battles of Cross Keys and Port Republic, Jackson turned on his pursuers, defeated both Fremont and Shields, and still managed to get to Richmond in time to join Lee for the big counteroffensive.

THE MYSTERY OF NEGROPHILISM.

JUNE 14

Of all topics now engaging the thoughts of gods and men, the American negro is unquestionably the chief. From the lowest place in the scale of human existence, he has reached the highest; and even yet the interest in him seems unabated. To what new honors he is reserved — to what remarkable career he is predestined — it would be a rash prophet that would attempt to foretell. But the evidences are abundant that he is the central figure of the nations — the unit of existence around which "the rest of mankind" parade themselves as mere cyphers.

It would be hard to tell whence this extraordinary interest in the negro has come. It does not arise from his beauty, for no writer on aesthetics has ever pretended to find either beauty or grace in the shambling African. It cannot be because of his illustrious or romantic history, as a race or as a nation; for classic literature is extremely barren of the records of orators, statesmen, philosophers or warriors of negro origin. It cannot be because of any physical affinity between the white race and the black, for the black has always been declared unsavory, and naturally beset by laziness and vermin. And lastly, it cannot be because of the sympathy of the whites with a weak, down-trodden and enslaved race; for the negro of Africa (from which the American negro was taken,) is weaker to-day, and more oppressed, and nearer a barbarian and cannibal, than his American cousin has ever been. And yet no Anglican Duchess, nor American Greeley, is ever heard wailing over the sorrows of the sons of Ashantee.

The passion for the American negro must be considered, therefore, entirely abnormal — a phenomenon, which was defined once by a Western pioneer as "something that never had happened before, and never would happen again." The African in America is an exotic — he is a hot-house plant, and, like all exotics, he is valued just in proportion to the care required in his cultivation — the intrinsic value of the plant never being considered at all.

The American Government about a year ago sent an amateur attache of the Patent-office to Europe to buy seeds, with a view to improve the American botany. He saw a stylish, if not gaudy, annual blooming profusely along the highways abroad, and he caused the ripened seeds to be gathered carefully and shipped in a box to Washington, to be distributed by thoughtful Congressmen among their constituents throughout the Union. A shrewd farmer paid a visit to the Department, caught a sight of the treasure, and pronounced it the seeds of one of the most pestiferous kinds of thistle that ever beset the labors of husbandman!

The American negro is an exotic, and our people nurse him in their hot-house as though Africa was not teeming with millions like him — like him, truly, but with a thousand attractive variations; negroes that hunt negroes, that buy negroes, that sell negroes, that kill negroes, and that eat negroes; negroes that go naked through life, and negroes that clothe their shame with beads on their necks and rings on their fingers. Three hundred years ago we got our Africans from that unfortunate continent which, Mr. SEWARD once very aptly said, "Nature had fortified against civilization." We took them naked into our land, and lo! they have come in the end to clothe the whole world.

MALTHUS[1] wrote a book on political economy which was calculated to discourage marriage, on the ground that the human family was increasing faster than the production of food necessary for their subsistence. If celibacy did not stop the breed, he was afraid that famine would. The odious philosopher died amid the execrations of the female world.

But there is something, after all, in the theory. Population will increase in any country almost in the exact ratio of the increase of clothing and food, cheaply available to the masses. There is no ability to calculate how much the naked African that was brought to America has contributed to the white population of the world by furnishing them cheap cotton for shirts and gowns. All civilized nations feel the importance of our African, and all have become profoundly interested in his future. He has not ☞

only multiplied and replenished himself, but he has caused the civilized world to prosper and multiply. A genuine black diamond he is, and every country is holding out its arms to receive him. WENDELL PHILLIPS bids him flee from the South and head for the North Star. Hayti sends Commissioners here, and begs him fly to that sea-girt isle and get a free home. Liberia calls aloud that Africa has become proud of her American lineage, now that they walk erect, and wear broadcloth, and begs them to return to a doting mother, and flourish in the reformed Court of Dahomey. Even Denmark, far up in northern latitudes, has heard of our tropical contraband, and directs her representative at Washington to say to Mr. LINCOLN that she will be glad of all the specimens we can spare, to plant in her West India possessions.[2]

With such a rush for our American negro, who can deny that he is the world's pet and favorite? Is it surprising that our Southern States wish to keep what other countries deem so valuable, and are trying so hard to get? Has not the South taught the world the value of African labor, and is not mankind better off to-day than if this discovery had never been made?

These speculations, however, are profitless. What is it about our American negro that recommends him to the absorbing and passionate attention of the world? Why are many thousands fanatics about him, and more thousands fools about him? Is it possible that black is the primeval and regal color of the race — that Adam was a black man, as well as Cain and Abel; and that Cain turned white only when caught in crime and driven out to be a vagabond on the earth? This we know is the faith of the dusky gospellers of the South, and, doubtless, they are rejoicing to see the day returning when Heaven's favor will triumph over the white man's crime, and the black man will again gather fruits in tropical Edens, untroubled by visions of shovel or hoe. ✹

1. A reference to Thomas Malthus (1766–1834) author of *An Essay on the Principle of Population* (1798).
2. During the discussion about the colonization of emancipated blacks outside the United States, the Danish Island of St. Croix in the West Indies indicated a willingness to receive some former slaves.

GEN. BUTLER AND THE WOMEN.

The [New Orleans Daily] Delta publishes a carefully prepared sketch of the manner in which Gen. BUTLER has dealt with the rebels in New-Orleans, and introduces the following letter, which was sent to Mayor MONROE during the controversy about the famous "women of the town" order:

GEN. BUTLER HOLDING THE MOB IN CHECK AT NEW ORLEANS.

JUNE 15

HEADQUARTERS DEPARTMENT OF THE GULF, NEW-ORLEANS, MAY 16

SIR: There can be, there has been, no room for misunderstanding of General Order No. 28.

No lady will take any notice of a strange gentleman, and a fortiori of a stranger, simply in such form as to attract attention. Common women do.

Therefore, whatever woman, lady or mistress, gentle or simple, who, by gesture, look or word, insults, shows contempt for, thus attracting to herself the notice of my officers and soldiers, will be deemed to act as becomes her vocation as a common woman, and will be liable to be treated accordingly. This was most fully explained to you at my office.

I shall not, as I have not, abated a single word of that older; it was well considered; if obeyed, will protect the true and modest women from all possible insult. The others will take care of themselves.

You can publish your letter, if you publish this note, and your apology.

RESPECTFULLY,
BENJ. F. BUTLER, MAJOR-GENERAL COMMANDING. ✹

Print depicting New Orleans citizens' angry reaction to General Butler's rule.

IN FRONT OF RICHMOND.

JUNE 26

We suppose that, by an attentive perusal of our daily budget of correspondence and telegrams from our army in front of Richmond, the reader will obtain as correct an idea of the situation and prospects there as it is in the power of words to give. It is briefly this: — that affairs are in an exceedingly critical condition; that any hour may bring on a conflict which will rage along the entire line, and that that conflict is very likely to decide the fate of Richmond; that our army is in fine condition, morally, physically, and militarily, for the battle; that it is prepared, and quite ready for it; that it has been largely reinforced; that daily, though slowly yet surely, it is planting itself in more favorable positions, and making headway, ceaselessly, toward the rebel capital.... ✹

POPE AGAINST JACKSON — FLANK MOVEMENT UPON RICHMOND.

JUNE 27

The country will be rejoiced this morning to learn that President LINCOLN has at last, by a word, brought order and unity out of the confused and discreditable condition of army affairs that has so long existed in the Valley of the Shenandoah and on the Rappahannock. The forces under FREMONT and BANKS in the Valley, and those under MCDOWELL at Fredericksburgh and elsewhere, are consolidated into one army, divided into three corps, and the whole of them put under the command of Gen. POPE. The first work of the new Commander will of course be to take in hand that audacious rebel marauder, Stonewall JACKSON, (and in this business of rebel catching, he has had more experience than any man in the field,) and drive him finally out of the region which he has so long ravaged — or, what would be still better, and more accordant with POPE's antecedents, "bag" or destroy him and his entire command.[1] ✳

1. McClellan considered the formation of this Army of Virginia a direct attack on his own authority. He resented the implication that two generals were needed to manage affairs in Virginia, and believed that in any case all available troops should be sent to his army on the peninsula.

AFFAIRS BEFORE RICHMOND.
ATTACK OF THE REBELS UNDER JACKSON
UPON OUR RIGHT WING.

JULY 1

CAMP BEFORE RICHMOND,
SATURDAY, JUNE 28

The Army of the Potomac has no longer need to complain of inactivity, for the comparative quiet of the past month has given place to three days of as desperate, determined and bloody work as the fiercest clamorer for active movements could desire. Though the contest is not yet decided, the result thus far, in its bearings on the general plan of operations, is all that could be desired. We have no great victory to report, no long list of trophies to record, and the movements of an army may present the indications of a reverse, but to those who have been familiar with the position of things here, and the plan of operations they necessitated, matters are assuming a new and more hopeful aspect, for an apparent retreat has really brought us practically nearer to Richmond than we have been at any time before. A military manoeuvre, among the most difficult of any when performed in face of an enemy, has been successfully accomplished, and, with forces concentrated upon a new base we are prepared to operate more efficiently than ever against an enemy divided and in the wild pursuit of an imaginary success. He has been tempted to his ruin; and if I read the signs of the times, his joy will be turned into mourning, and that ere many days. It is vain to be temperate, and I may seem over-hopeful in the midst of apparent disaster, but ... MCCLELLAN appears more completely the master of his position than at any time before.[1]

It was soon apparent, after Fair Oaks, that the rebel attack upon our left wing had induced a change of programme, and what the new plan has been I think to-day is showing. Up to that time our left wing was the weak point, and to that the chief efforts of the enemy were directed, but with the withdrawal of our main body to the south side of the Chickahominy, the right wing, with its exposed line of communication between the river and White House, has been ... inviting attack, and though the rebels have apparently been chiefly concerned with efforts against our left wing, there have not been wanting signs and evidence that their real purpose was directed against the right, whose exposed situation must have been fully revealed to them by the bold dash of [J. E. B.] STUART's Cavalry across our rear.... ☞

FROM GEN. M'CLELLAN'S ARMY.

THE STEP IN ADVANCE TOWARD RICHMOND.

JUNE 27

JUNE 25 — EVENING.

Gen. HOOKER, at 9 o'clock this morning, advanced his Division with the view of occupying a new position. The result was that his troops met with a most determined resistance from the enemy, which lasted until four o'clock in the afternoon, but the rebels were forced to give way before the invincible courage of our men....[1] ✳

1. This was the Battle of Oak Grove (June 25, 1862), the first of the "Seven Days." McClellan sought to push his front line to within siege-gun range of Richmond, but Union forces advanced only about 600 yards at a cost of about a thousand casualties. It was the last Union initiative of the campaign.

The Battle of Gaines's Mill.

On Thursday [June 26] they came ... Crossing the river in strong force, under cover of a heavy fire from their batteries on the opposite side, the enemy pressed down the road against the position of Gen. [George A.] MCCALL, first attacking his First Brigade, consisting of the Bucktails, and the Fifth, Eighth, Ninth and Tenth Pennsylvania Regiments. These troops were soon reinforced by the six regiments forming the other two brigades of the division, and from their strong position behind the swampy ravine of Beaver Dam Creek, held the greatly superior force of the enemy at bay from the time of attack until the going down of the sun, at near 9 o'clock....[2]

That night an order came from Gen. MC-CLELLAN for Gen. PORTER to withdraw his forces gradually to a point near Meadow's Bridge. After a few hours' sleep upon their arms, our troops were aroused, and, in accordance with the plan of operations, Gen. MCCALL, at 3 o'clock, opened a fire of artillery on the enemy who vigorously responded, until our forces began gradually to retire before them as if retreating, but maintaining their ranks in good order, crossing a bridge over a creek on the way, destroying it behind them, compelling the enemy to wait the slow construction of a new passage-way in the fire of our opposing artillery and heavy musketry fire from the Ninth Massachusetts....

It was now near noon, and our troops had taken fresh courage for effort from the hour or two for rest and refreshment which they had enjoyed. Then the enemy were reported to be again advancing; they opened fire on our men from the woods skirting the plain in which the latter were posted.[3]

First commencing with the usual picket skirmishing, and then swelling into the roar of the artillery duel, the struggle opened between the advanced guard of the two armies, until by 3 or 4 o'clock in the afternoon the battle raged fiercely all along the lines, until within an hour or two of sunset, when the storm lulled for a time, and then the rebels, who had been meanwhile reinforced, came on with fresh vigor to the assault... Not until after 9 o'clock did the men find rest, which, we may be sure, came not unwelcomed to such of the men as had passed through the struggle, commencing early in the afternoon of the previous day....

And so the sun went down upon that battle-field strewn with the bruised and mangled forms of what have once been men, of what were still men, though shorn of their full proportions, and bidden to go maimed and halting through life.... And who can estimate our loss, when none but an Omnipotent eye can, in the confusion of the first hours that follow the engagement, search out the fate of all who appear not with their comrades as they gather with their regiments at night?[4] It will surely exceed a thousand, and I hope not pass the 1,500; but a few days more will tell, while, meanwhile, the list must swell greatly, for the battle is not yet fully ended. Strategy or no strategy, there must still be desperate fighting.... ✺

1. The Times reporter was hopelessly overoptimistic. To be sure, the attempted turning movement was extremely costly to the Confederate attackers, and MClellan did indeed manage to extricate his right wing from north of the Chickahominy River, but he had lost control of events and for the rest of the campaign would focus on trying to fend off relentless rebel attacks.
2. This was the Battle of Beaver Dam Creek (June 26, 1862), as A. P. Hill's Confederate division assailed the position of Union Major General Fitz John Porter. "Stonewall" Jackson was supposed to have led the assault, but he was late in arriving and the Confederates attacked without him. It was a Union tactical victory in that Confederate losses were far heavier, but the fury of the assault convinced McClellan to order Porter to fall back.
3. This was the Battle of Gaines' Mill (June 27).
4. Union losses in the two battles totaled 7,201; Confederate losses were 9,477.

The Battle of Malvern Hill.

THE NEW CALL FOR TROOPS.

MILITARY FEELING IN THE CITY.

JULY 3

The important position held by the Empire State in its relations to the country at large is indicated by the fact that its quota of the three hundred thousand fresh troops called for by the President will be fifty thousand, or one-sixth of the whole number.[1]

These fifty thousand, from present indications, will not be slow in forthcoming. The mere supposition of peril to the cause of the Union, consequent on Gen. MC-CLELLAN being in insufficient force to fall at once on the rebel capital, has created an excitement in the city that could only have been surpassed by the certain knowledge of defeat and the responsibilities which that knowledge would have entailed.... ◉

1. On July 1, Lincoln called for an additional 300,000 soldiers, "chiefly of infantry," and quotas were assigned to the various states.

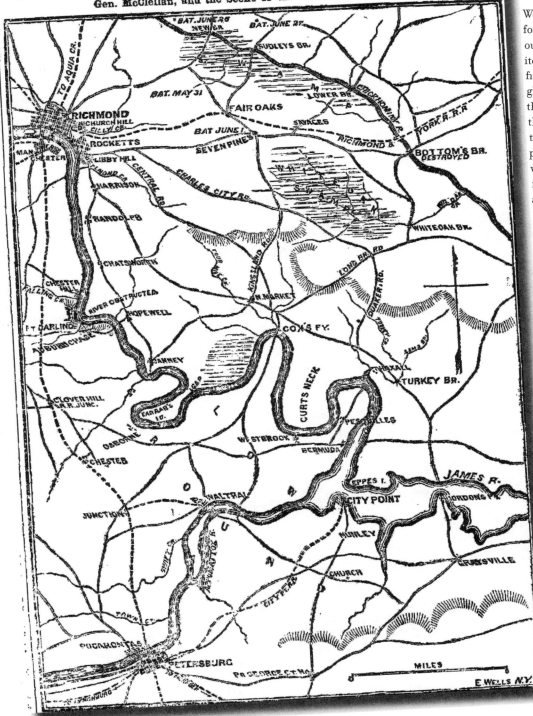

THE RECENT GREAT BATTLES.

Map Showing Richmond, Fort Darling, the Line of the James River, the Present Location of Gen. McClellan, and the Scene of the Recent Great Battles.

THE LINES BEFORE RICHMOND.

JULY 2

We are still without any specific information as to the present status of our army on the James; but all the items of news that trickle from official and unofficial sources, the gleanings from persons who left the lines as late as Sunday, and from the bearings of movements known to have been successfully accomplished, the inference is that the work which Gen. MCCLELLAN has in hand is progressing to a favorable result....

What Gen. MCCLELLAN's programme of action now may be will very soon develop itself. Army correspondents are busy predicting that he will be in the rebel Capital by the Fourth of July, and some papers have published the news that he is already there. He is, doubtless, as anxious to get there as any body can be, knowing what a destructive effect such a movement would have upon the rebellion and the rebel army. Things are evidently in that peculiar condition at present when any hour may flash over the wires the news that he is there, and that the rebel army is in a worse place. In the meantime, he needs that every soldier that can possibly be spared be pushed on to reinforce him, that so, when he does strike, he may make of his stroke a sure thing. ◉

Map published in The New York Times of the region where General McClellan conducted his Peninsula Campaign.

THE NEWS FROM RICHMOND — THE NEW CALL FOR VOLUNTEERS.

JULY 3

We have at last full reports of recent movements in front of Richmond. We are sorry to say that they do not fully sustain the encouraging interpretation which the public sought to put upon the brief announcement, that our right wing had been attacked and had withdrawn to the other side of the Chickahominy. We have now no room to doubt that our army has met with a very serious reverse, and that it is in a condition of peril, which, if not imminent, at least calls for the instant and energetic efforts of the Government and the country.

Two of the regular corps of the TIMES Reporters left Gen. MCCLELLAN's headquarters, which are now on the James River, on Monday afternoon, and reached this City last evening. They were spectators of the events which they describe, and although their reports are of necessity written in haste, and may, therefore, err in matters of detail, there is no reason whatever to doubt the entire accuracy of the narrative they give of the principal movements of the opposing forces.

It seems from their statement, that the right wing of our army, numbering about 20,000 men, was attacked on Friday by an overwhelming rebel force of not less than 50,000, and that after a hot and protracted fight, sustained with the greatest gallantry by our troops, they effected their retreat across the Chickahominy. This leading fact was known before. But it now for the first time appears that they did not wait to destroy the bridges across the swamp so effectually as to prevent the passage of the rebels, — that our forces on the left, for some reason or other, did not dispute the passage, although they had planted batteries for the purpose of doing so, but decided to abandon their position, — and that accordingly, on Saturday night and Sunday, the whole left wing, comprising the main body of the army, under [Samuel P.] HEINTZELMAN, [Erasmus D.] KEYES and [Edwin V. "Bull"] SUMNER, fell back along the line of the railroad and the Williamsburgh Road, turned the foot of the White Oak Swamp, which approaches the Chickahominy, and marched to the James River, a distance of from ten to fifteen miles .... .

Our whole army, therefore, now lies upon the James River, at a point called Turkey Bend, within reach, and under cover of our gunboats. Supplies will speedily reach it from Fortress Monroe, and it seems, indeed, to have withdrawn its stores in good order and without serious loss.

Beyond all question, this intelligence will fall with heavy weight upon the public heart. It is entirely unexpected, and shatters the high hope which the whole country has of late indulged, that, with the fall of Richmond, the end of the rebellion was close at hand. But this depressing effect will be temporary. A day's reflection will rouse the whole country to the necessity of another effort to crush the rebellion.... ✳

A federal field hospital at Savage Station, Virginia.

BUTLER AND THE CONTRABANDS.

EQUIVOCAL CONDUCT OF THE GENERAL — FATE OF NEGROES EMPLOYED WITHIN OUR LINES.

JULY 3

To the Editor of the New-York Times:

The Thirteenth Connecticut Regiment took up quarters on May 15th in the New-Orleans Customhouse. Within a few days after our arrival, 200 negroes had crossed our lines. Families came with their luggage, having heard that the Yankees were to make them free; boys with market baskets, saying that they were "going home;" women, wearing iron neck-yokes, and bearing various marks of cruelty.

Both Gen. BUTLER and the Colonel of the Thirteenth, were importuned to grant the privilege of looking after these refugees. Several attempted seizures were prevented by the Colonel and other officers. Animated discussions were frequent between Secessionists and soldiers. Soldiers cheered when slaves refused to go back to their kind masters. The unsuspecting negroes laughed at the imagined advantage which the American Flag gave them.

GEN. BUTLER'S ORDER.

Next in the sequence of events to this search for slaves, came the order to turn out all not employed by the officers.

Inasmuch as the flocking of negroes to our protection must have been foreseen, why did not the General prohibit their admission, rather than receive and then turn them out?

The day before the order was carried into effect, boys and girls, men and women, went from room to room with solicitations for work. Said a mother, "take my children, if I must go back to suffer." Well nigh one hundred were kept as cooks, waiters, Company laundresses, hospital nurses and laborers about the Custom-house. Those for whom no place could be found, plead with us to rescue them — depicting the revenge they must suffer for confiding in the Yankees, and telling us that we ought not to have taken them at first, and then to send them back. At the fixed time all the negroes were collected in the open area of the Custom-house. Dread, sorrow, despair could be seen on many faces. Women who had fled miles from a hated despotism, mothers with their infants, families of children, the old and decrepit, were there. One by one, such as had not tickets of employment, moved away, attended by guards. Tearful entreaties were in vain. Children often preferred to stay, even if their parents must go. Bitterly disappointed and hopeless they lingered in the basement, still imagining that their friends, the Yankees, would help them. Puzzling questions rained like shot from this despairing group. A few stayed till midnight before venturing to leave....

The duty of the Government need not be equivocal, as to the condition of the slaves to whom the double pledge has been given of reception within our camps, and taking into our employment. It should be taken out of the power of any General to return or to countenance the return of men and women who have done hard work in the service of our armies, and who must suffer bitter revenge as the penalty of their confidence and their labor. Such negroes, and all giving information to our Government, should have free papers. How can any other policy look the North, or Christian civilization anywhere in the face?

A CHAPLAIN. ✱

IS WASHINGTON SAFE?

JULY 7

If "Stonewall" JACKSON be not dead — and there is now a doubt thrown over the statement that he was veritably and actually killed in the late battles — is there no danger of his taking a column, and with it marching suddenly in the direction of Washington? The movements of this daring rebel, during the last two months, have been as rapid and successful as they have been extraordinary in other respects. It is but a few weeks since he pounced upon and defeated the forces of [Robert H.] MILROY and [Robert C.] SCHENCK, in the Shenandoah Valley. From that work he entered upon the pursuit of Gen. BANKS, drove him to Winchester, defeated him there, pursued him a distance of seventy or eighty miles up to the Potomac; then retired, and during his retreat defeated FREMONT and SHIELDS; then swept over the Blue Ridge and across Eastern Virginia to the Chickahominy, and attacked the right wing of our main army ten days ago — with what success is known to our readers — having in this brief space of time fought four battles at distant points, and traversed a distance of four or five hundred miles. In each of the instances his movement was more or less of a surprise, and each of them would have been declared by most men quite impossible before it was actually done. It would undoubtedly be a difficult thing for JACKSON, whether he be or be not dead, to take twenty thousand rebels and move north to Fredericksburgh, thence to Manassas, thence eastward to the Potomac; and it is not likely he will try. We believe, moreover, that our troops now at Washington and the points named are fully prepared to resist such a movement. At least we hope so. And we also hope, that now that it is known that JACKSON's forces are at Richmond, our troops in the Shenandoah Valley and elsewhere in Eastern Virginia, will be so disposed of as to effectually prevent any other northward movements of this rebel, if he be alive, or of his ghost, if he be dead. ✱

SENATE DEBATE ON ARMING SLAVES.

JULY 10

The question of employing negroes as soldiers or as military laborers was again up in the Senate yesterday, and the debate upon it was very interesting.... The question was treated entirely in its practical bearings; and with a view to legislation for filling up the new requisition of troops called for by the President. The speakers were very serious; and their views were evidently greatly affected by the recent rebel doings on the Peninsula. There was strong opposition to what was called the "white-kid-gloved," "rose-water" mode of conducting the war; and Mr. SHERMAN[1] argued that we "could not fight against savages unless we became part savage ourselves," and that "rather than that the Union should be destroyed, he would organize a great army of black men, and desolate every Southern State." Other speakers were not behind this in strength of expression or in determination to ☞

adopt any and every means to put down the rebellion. To the proposition of the Senators from New-York and Kentucky, there certainly can be no reasonable objection. There is a vast amount of military labor on which the slaves in the districts occupied by our army might be employed, and the doing of which by our troops has in some places terribly affected their health and general sanitary condition, and quite unfitted whole regiments for the proper duties of the field. The lines upon lines of prodigious earthworks, constructed before Corinth by our gallant Western soldiers, and the hard labor of which sent thousands of them to their graves in those dismal swamps, should all have been built by the slaves of the insolent rebels of West Tennessee, who were within easy reach, but who, by HALLECK's Order No. 3, were excluded from the lines.[2] So in South Carolina, so in New-Orleans, on the Mississippi, in the Valley of Virginia, and elsewhere. There is enough military work, other than fighting to be done, to employ all the rebel slaves we now have, or are likely to catch for some time. We believe that, just now, it would be better to employ them in this work than to use them as soldiers, for which plenty of far more efficient men can be found. This would be a good point to begin with, and to stop at, at present. And to use them in this way our military commanders should be promptly authorized and ordered. ✹

1. John Sherman (1823–1900) was a United States senator from Ohio and the brother of William T. Sherman.
2. On November 20, 1861, Halleck had ordered that escaped slaves would no longer be "admitted within our lines."

Operations Against Vicksburgh.

JULY 14

OPPOSITE VICKSBURGH, Wednesday, July 2

Last Thursday, the mortar vessels, sloops of war and gunboats of Flag-Officer FARAGUT'S fleet arrived below here.

Lying below the city now before us, our officers saw its strength, but resolved nevertheless on an immediate attack. It was necessary there should be a cooperating naval fleet above the town, and Flag-Officer [Charles H.] DAVIS' fleet had not arrived. Early next morning it was resolved a portion of the vessels should run by.... Instantly as they came in range the batteries opened. Rifle and round shot whistled among the masts, and often "hulled" the vessels with rapid and terrible broadsides. Our fleet answered, and the immense improvements recently made in war vessels' ordnance became manifest. So accurate was the return fire, that every battery was speedily enveloped in clouds of dust, and the gunners again and again driven from their posts, only to be forced back by bayonets in the rear.

Just below, the splendid mortar fleet of Commodore PORTER had commenced playing, and a shower of missiles fell into and around the doomed city. Buildings were scattered, and soldiers and citizens fled hastily away. The morning air drove down upon stream and city the dense smoke of conflict, and one of the most terrible cannonades of the war went on, each combatant hidden from the other's view....

Vicksburgh cannot be taken by the navy, although it may be destroyed, and we will have to patiently wait until a land force arrives. Determined that they should have little rest, Commodore PORTER improved the position of his mortar vessels, and at short intervals threw shell. The rebels from their batteries thought our fleet lay at the bend, and that troops were being landed. It was, apparently, a tempting opportunity for "boarding," throwing overwhelming bodies on the two or three thousand soldiers that might be opposed to them, and by one grand coup de main gaining success. Doubtless VAN DORN was in ecstacies over the sudden idea, and his evil genius prompted him to make one of the boldest, and as it proved, most unsuccessful dashes yet undertaken. Cautiously marching 6,000 troops out from their camps, far behind the bluffs, he skirted the woods, passed unseen below the vessels on that side of the river, and cautiously approached his intended victims. Hidden in dense timber, he deployed his troops with the rare military skill of a veteran, and when two hundred yards from the river ordered a charge. Uttering an exceedingly terrifying yell, the butternut multitude rushed forward, and so quickly, that they were surprised themselves at arriving so soon upon the open bank, and still more at being greeted by a terrible discharge of grape. Quicker than the approach was the retreat, and a headlong flight ensued. Some hundreds were for a few moments seen struggling waist deep through a swamp, while other regiments were ordered near to prevent any attack upon the miring warriors. Three were captured, but the number killed and wounded is unknown. The prisoners stated that VAN DORN and BRECKINRIDGE were at Vicksburgh, and would endeavor, at every cost, to hold it. They belonged to regiments, one of which numbered two hundred, the other a hundred and fifty men. Gen. DUNCAN and three Captains, with thirty privates, according to them, were killed during the fleet's passage.

Finding that Vicksburgh would hold-out, Flag-Officer FARRAGUT determined to open the Mississippi in another way, namely; by cutting a canal across the bend, and leaving Vicksburgh far to one side.[1] Instantly the work commenced. Negroes were gathered from every plantation around, and three or four hundred of them set to work. The canal is already partly finished, and in a week will be completed. The bed is to be sunk eight feet below water level. Naval officers are confident of its success. Were the river rising instead of falling there would be little doubt but that the work might be brought to a successful issue. As it is, the probabilities are of its failing. No rebel forces are upon the bank opposite Vicksburgh, and from there it is easy to view the city, and the position of the batteries and fleets. Yesterday I visited Commodore PORTER's mortar fleet. It is composed of seven steamers and twenty schooners, commanded by DAVID D. PORTER, probably the best naval officer in the United States service[2]....

These vessels are none of them shotproof, and had it not been for the following precautions, numerous casualties must have happened: Masts and sides are completely draped with branches, and lying, as they do, close to the bank, it is impossible to see them at any distance. They seem a part of the surrounding forests, and hostile shot have to be directed by guesswork. ✹

1. The canal was actually Grant's idea, not Farragut's.
2. Porter was a ferocious self-promoter who played up to reporters precisely so he could get newspaper mentions like this one.

THE PRESIDENT AND THE CONFISCATION BILL.

JULY 18

Whatever doubts have rested upon the President's views of confiscation, are quieted by the message sent to Congress yesterday. The measure, as amended, meets with his entire approval.[1]

Congress, with great promptness, modified the bill in deference to the scruples of the President in regard to some of its provisions....

The Confiscation bill, as originally passed, authorized the President to seize the property of persons engaged in the rebellion and convert it to the uses of the Government. This would be depriving not only the persons actually guilty of treason, but their children and descendants to the remotest generation, of their property. The President deemed this clause to be in violation of the Constitution. Even if he should sign it, therefore, which he could not do if that was his opinion, the law would be utterly inoperative, because its validity must depend in the last resort upon the decision of our Courts, and they will necessarily be governed by the provisions of the Constitution. Congress has very wisely cured this defect by limiting the penalty for treason so as to conform to the requirements of the Constitution.

The Confiscation bill cannot fail to have a marked effect upon the conduct of the war. It fixes definite and severe legal penalties to the crime of rebellion, and adds to the actual perils of war the certain and severe punishments of courts of law. In the absence of such a law the rebels had a very great advantage over us. They were not restrained by the Constitution, or anything else, from inflicting whatever severities they chose upon Union men. We meet them now upon their own ground. We are clothed by law with all the powers they have usurped in the conduct of the war. We invade the South as we would invade Mexico or Canada, under the laws of civilized warfare, but determined to use every weapon which the country offers.... ✹

1. Lincoln signed the Second Confiscation Act on July 17.

TWO IMPORTANT POINTS OF MILITARY POLICY SETTLED.

JULY 23

The President, through the Secretary of War, has just issued a very important order, which will settle, for the remainder of this war, two points of military policy, regarding which there has been wide discussion, and for lack of which there has been much embittered feeling. The first provision of the order is, in brief, that military commanders within the rebel States shall seize any property which may be needed for supplies or other military purposes; and the second provision is that commanders shall employ as laborers so many slaves as are needed for military or naval purposes. Both of these measures are strictly within the established rules provided for an army when operating in an enemy's country.... ✹

THE WORK OF GEN. HALLECK

JULY 24

Gen. HALLECK's new position and duties are at length authentically and officially defined. He is to take "command of the whole [of the] land forces of the United States, as General-in-Chief," with his headquarters at Washington. This is the third or perhaps the fourth, functionary of that grade which we have had since the opening of the war—SCOTT, MCCLELLAN, and STANTON, or rather the President, having preceded HALLECK. It is just a year ago that Gen. MCCLELLAN was assigned to the position; and he performed its arduous duties for about nine months. The events that have taken place over the country since he entered upon active field work, show the imperative necessity for some strong, clear-headed military man to guide the movements of all our armies.

Gen. HALLECK enters upon his great duties at a moment and under circumstances requiring the exercise of the most comprehensive and skillful genius. The work before him is tremendous. But he has a magnificent army with which to accomplish it; and a great nation at his side to strengthen and encourage him. The tools to operate with are at his hands, and anything that he may need, which the nation has, will be given to him. He enters upon his duties with a large amount of popular confidence and respect, which it is the duty of every man and journal now to encourage, and to increase, as his actions will warrant. If he

A romanticized Currier and Ives lithograph of Major General Henry W. Halleck.

achieves the same amount of success in the East that he has had in the West, within the past year—if he causes the rebel host at Richmond to dissolve or fly as the rebel armies at Bowling Green, Columbus and Corinth have dissolved or fled—it will not be many months before the enemy's forces now at Richmond will be reduced to roving guerrillas, scouring through the States of the far South. The country looks to him and will wait upon him with assured confidence. ✹

GEN. McCLELLAN AND THE TIMES.

JULY 25

We feel greatly obliged to those journals which have complimented the TIMES by attaching so much importance to its assumed "change of tone" in regard to Gen. MCCLELLAN. Even the Evening Post, which is nothing if not bilious, is fairly entitled to a share of our gratitude.

But we need scarcely remind our neighbors that they very grossly exaggerate the matter in question. We have nothing to retract of any opinions we have expressed of Gen. MCCLELLAN, least of all, have we indicated any concurrence in the damaging denunciations in which many of our contemporaries have seen fit to indulge. We repeat what we have said hitherto, that in the great work of organizing an army he has proved his possession of the highest ability; — that his siege of Yorktown (whether it might have been avoided or not) was a masterpiece of successful soldiership; — that his preparations for an advance upon Richmond were complete and perfect; — that he has the rare quality of inspiring confidence and thorough respect among his troops, — and that his conduct of the retreat to the James River was a most masterly execution of one of the most difficult and dangerous movements which an army is ever compelled to make.

To all this we still adhere. But it does not in the least affect the truth of what we have also said, that the public faith in his ability to lead an army in the field to victory, has been greatly shaken. That the fact is so, no man of common sense can doubt, and no man of common honesty would think of denying. Whether public confidence in him is justly shaken or not, is another question. If what is said on his behalf, that he was never allowed the means he deemed requisite to carry out his plans, is true, then the

THE PRESIDENT'S PROCLAMATION — SOVEREIGN AND BELLIGERENT RIGHTS OF THE GOVERNMENT

JULY 28

The President has just issued a Proclamation which forms another step in the grand process against the giant crime of Rebellion. By this Proclamation, made in pursuance of the sixth section of the act of Congress, entitled "An Act to suppress insurrection, to punish treason and rebellion, to seize and confiscate the property of rebels, and for other purposes," approved July 17, 1862, he warns "all persons within the contemplation of said sixth section, to cease participating in, aiding, countenancing or abetting the existing rebellion, or any rebellion against the Government of the United States, and to return to their proper allegiance to the United States, on pain of the forfeitures and seizures as within and by said sixth section provided."

The historian who shall record the progress of the present war will have no trouble in determining the theory on which it was conducted by the United States. Vast though the proportions were which the revolt assumed from the very start, the Government had no difficulty in at once making the diagnosis of the disease in the body politic as an insurrection, a rebellion. The acts of hostility against the Government had, perhaps, assumed such formidable proportions as to be appropriately designated as war; but it was a war of persons owing allegiance to the General or National Government, and not a war of Governments. As Prof. [Joel] PARKER [of Harvard Law School] has well said, those acts were not more than acts of treason because millions were engaged in them, and they were not less than treason because of the assumed titles, military and civil, or of the assumption of State or Confederate authority, under color of which they were committed. Gigantic though the proportions are which the rebellion has since grown to, and complicated though the relations which we hold to the revolted States have become, the complexion of the Southern treason remains, in the eyes of the Government, unchanged. No lapse of time, no change of circumstance, has produced any alteration in the mode of treatment of the "so-called Confederacy" by the United States. The rebels who opened their batteries on Sumter are rebels still, not "belligerents." The Proclamation which the President issues to-day is the same in theory as that which he made fifteen months ago. In his proclamation of the 15th April, 1861, he called on the persons forming treasonable combinations to "disperse and retire peaceably to their respective abodes, within twenty days from this date." He now addresses the same combinations, commanding them within sixty days to "cease participating in, aiding, countenancing or abetting the existing rebellion." It is probable enough that the last Proclamation will be heeded no more than was the first. But with that fact we are not now dealing.

In a superficial aspect, it may seem inconsistent with this theory, that not only has the Government repeatedly entered into various transactions of a quasi-international character, such as flags of truce, exchanges, & e.g., with the Confederates; but that it has just concluded with the rebel authorities a general cartel for the exchange of prisoners, based on the cartel of 1812. The Richmond journals, it will have been noticed from the extracts we have given, are jubilant over this procedure as an acknowledgment of the "quasi-nationality" of the Confederates. "This cartel," says the [Richmond] Enquirer, "marks an important era in the war. We are by it made belligerents, and the Government of the United Slates treats with the Government of the Confederate States through Commissioners." The rebels are welcome to whatever comfort or encouragement they can extract from this transaction. But the journal mentioned is entirely off the mark, in claiming that it inaugurates any "new era" in the war. It is needless, at this late day, to recur to the principles and precedents that govern the exchange of prisoners between parties holding to each other the relations that obtain between the United States and the rebels. The whole matter is summed up in the one principle that, in a civil war such as ours, the Sovereign has all the

public verdict is unjust. We stated all this very fully in the very article from which our critics quote: but they find it convenient to omit mention of it altogether.

We are very glad that President LINCOLN has seen fit to leave Gen. MCCLELLAN in command of the Army of the Potomac, and to intrust to him still the task of taking Richmond. Certainly no other General could take command of that army now, with half as good a prospect of leading it successfully against the rebel capital. It cannot be denied that Gen. MCCLELLAN's abilities as a leader in the field are still to be proved. But we believe that, with proper support, he will vindicate the claims which have been put forward in his behalf. ❂

rights of a belligerent in addition to those of Sovereign. This doctrine, though held by the masters of international law, from SUAREZ[1] downwards, we have, it must be confessed, been somewhat slow to understand and take advantage of. And this jealousy of our sovereignty, and the attendant unwillingness to do aught that might seem to recognize the rebels even by implication — a spirit shared to some extent by the Government as well as by the people — have proved no inconsiderable drawback to an efficient conduct of the war. But the potent education of events has not been without avail. Henceforth woe put forth all our strength unweakened by any such pedantic legal limitations. Whatever belligerent rights it may be conducive to the great end of the war to employ, them we may freely put forth. The rights of sovereignty meanwhile reside in the United States, where they have been from the beginning and where they shall continue to be. And while in our sovereign capacity we may show toward those misguided men who have lifted up their hands against their country all needed forbearance — while we make the war what Mr. SEWARD at its outbreak announced in his diplomatic correspondence that it should be, "An example of moderation and generosity such as history does not show the like of;" it is our own fault if we do not call out all the means that can give unity, energy and success to the work of putting down utterly the rebellion. ❂

1. Probably a reference to Francisco Suarez (1548–1617), a Jesuit and a pioneer in international law.

NEWS FROM WASHINGTON.

IMPORTANT PROCLAMATION OF THE PRESIDENT.

THE CONFISCATION ACT.

JULY 28

A PROCLAMATION.

In pursuance of the sixth section of the Act of Congress entitled "An Act to suppress insurrection, to punish treason and rebellion, to seize and confiscate the property of rebels, and for other purposes," approved July 17, 1862, and which Act, and the joint resolution explanatory thereof, are herewith published, I, ABRABAM (sic) LINCOLN, President of the United States, do hereby proclaim to and warn all persons within the contemplation of said sixth section to cease participating in, aiding, countenancing, or abetting the existing rebellion, or any rebellion, against the Government of the United States, and to return to their proper allegiance to the United States, on pain of the forfeitures and seizures as within and by said sixth section provided.

In testimony whereof I have hereunto set my hand and caused the seal of the United States to be affixed.

Done at the City of Washington, this twenty-fifth day of July, in the year of our Lord one thousand eight hundred and sixty-two, and of the Independence of the United States the eighty-seventh.

ABRAHAM LINCOLN. ❂

CHAPTER 10
"Removing That Dreadful Evil"

AUGUST–OCTOBER 1862

It was the second autumn of this unexpectedly long war — but perhaps first among all its seasons in terms of historical importance, because it brought nothing less than a new cause for the Northern war effort: black freedom.

Between August and October of 1862, as armies engaged in furious battles in both Eastern and Western theaters, public agitation built for both emancipation and colonization, while home-front and volunteer charity activities reached new levels of participation, replenishing troops and engaging women in the war effort as never before.

It was a season of military engagements on both new and old ground alike. As McClellan withdrew from the Virginia Peninsula, Northerners were stunned to learn that Union forces under the command of General John Pope, and Confederate forces now led by Robert E. Lee (a veteran officer once dismissed as "Granny"), met again at Manassas (Bull Run), Virginia, for the second time in thirteen months. The reporting from the front proved much the same, too: optimistic early dispatches, later modified by subsequent acknowledgment of a Confederate rally, but never quite confirming the true nature of the Federal disaster.

The defeat the Second Battle of Bull Run left Lincoln both disconsolate and "outspoken," at least behind the closed doors of the White House, about the reigning belief that "McClellan wanted [Second Bull Run Commander John] Pope defeated." But the President was not yet ready to dismiss "Little Mac" from overall command. Instead, he defended him publicly, and spent hours privately imploring the general to restore cohesiveness to the army.

General Robert E. Lee, C.S.A., an 1864 photograph by J. Vannerson of Richmond.

Readers of The Times would also learn about fresh fields of glory in such distant places as Corinth, Mississippi, and Perryville, Kentucky. The results there were largely inconclusive, but as the coverage suggested, the war was inexorably widening. Meanwhile a growing "fire in the rear" — Northern antiwar copperheadism, threatened to sap crucial support for the Union cause. In the end, other momentous revolutions — one social, the other technological — left the most lasting impressions on the nation.

In the wake of the latest Bull Run defeat, Lincoln prepared to play what he believed would be his last hand: an order emancipating slaves in the rebellious states. After drafting a proclamation and reading it to his Cabinet in July, the President had bowed to his ministers' insistence that he table the decree until a Union battlefield victory allowed the administration to issue it from a position of strength, rather than desperation. Otherwise, as Secretary William H. Seward advised, it might be seen as a "last shriek, on the retreat." In the meantime, Lincoln offered a series of public feints intended to prepare a white voting public he feared would punish the administration for acting in behalf of the slaves. His activities — belying no immediate intent to proclaim freedom, coupled with an insensitivity toward the plight of both enslaved and free African-Americans (indeed, he declared for the record that free blacks ought to cheerfully relocate in Africa or the Caribbean) were meant to remind anxious Northern whites that the Administration considered emancipation a military, not a philanthropic, option. The lingering result was to taint Lincoln as insensitive to the slaves themselves — the roots of a historical debate that continues to this day.

The opportunity for the President to act came after General Lee, seeking a victory that would altogether destroy Northern morale, audaciously marched his forces into Maryland. McClellan repaid Lincoln's patience at last with a victory in the bloodiest single day's fighting in the entire Civil War — indeed, in all of American combat history — at Antietam on September 17. Though dismayed that McClellan failed to pursue the Confederates back into Virginia (even The Times was soon complaining again about the general's chronic inertia), the triumph was enough to justify Lincoln's pact with his Cabinet, himself, and, he said, with God. On September 22, he announced the preliminary Emancipation Proclamation, giving the Confederacy one hundred days' notice to end its rebellion or lose its slave property forever. Of course, the society-altering story dominated the press for weeks. The war for the Union now became a war for expanded liberty as well, as evidenced in the new virulence of the campaign for New York governor.

Another revolution — a subtler one, but carrying enormous consequences — occurred around the same time. In a New York gallery, Mathew Brady put on public view his shocking photographs of the Antietam battlefield — littered with bloated corpses. Military art had long focused on heroes who fought and, even if they fell, died bloodlessly in comrades' arms. Such photography — instantly made, quickly developed, and brutally realistic — abruptly changed the romantic sensibility about warfare. Civilians now saw for themselves the horrifying human consequences of the fighting — and recoiled at the sight. War would never again be fought in a vacuum.

THE UNION PRESCRIBED FOR BY DR. VALLANDIGHAM.

AUGUST 4

Mr. VALLANDIGHAM[1] has hopes that the Union will be restored, and has so informed his constituents in a recent speech. We are sure our readers will rejoice and take courage. But Mr. VALLANDIGHAM is not too sanguine. He sees that it will take some time and some labor, that something has got to be done before that goal is reached. And what do our readers suppose it is that must be done to attain that end? Fill up the last call for volunteers? Take Richmond? Destroy Stonewall JACKSON? Take Vicksburgh [sic] and town? Hang JEFF. DAVIS? Overrun all the Gulf States? Break down the military despotism which now rules over them? Emancipate the negroes? Carry out the confiscation act? Adopt a more stringent military policy or a more lenient one? None of all these things are necessary in the view of the Ohio patriot. The one thing needful is far different. It is not anything to be done in the military way. Labor and money spent in raising armies and training soldiers and preparing munitions of war are all thrown away, he thinks. Nor is it anything to be done in rebeldom. Things are all right there, you see. There is nothing there which interferes with the restoration of the Union. Take Mr. VALLANDIGHAM's word for that. We all who desire that restoration, must cease at once all these mistaken efforts which we are making, and, following the advice of this wise and honest statesman, turn our attention to "annihilating the Northern Abolition Party," for this he assures us is the only way to a restoration of the Union....

No doubt if our people want to be trodden under foot by these barbarian slavedrivers — if they wish to see JEFF. DAVIS in the White House, and those who have cherished and held dear the principles of our Fathers, and the rights of man, driven out of the land, or given over to imprisonment and death — if they wish to see such a restoration of the Union as that, then they will do well to follow the advice of Mr. VALLANDIGHAM. We doubt whether even his constituents wish such a restoration, or would follow such advice. Anywhere else such a suggestion could only lead those who heard it to the unanimous expression of the opinion that the worst kind of gammon is Vallandi-gammon.[2]

✸

1. Clement Laird Vallandigham (1820–1871), Democratic Congressman from Ohio, was a leader of the antiwar, anti-Lincoln "copperheads."
2. A whimsical reference to the board game, backgammon, and perhaps a play on words — since "gammon" is a certain cut of ham.

UNION FOR THE SAKE OF THE UNION.

AUGUST 8

President LINCOLN did an honor to himself in doing justice to Secretary STANTON, in the brief speech he delivered at the war meeting in Washington, on Wednesday afternoon.[1] He declared that the Secretary of War had, at no time, withheld anything from Gen. MCCLELLAN that it was in the President's power to give him. And he further asserted that the supposed quarrel between STANTON and MCCLELLAN had less existence between them than between some of those presuming to be their friends. Secretary STANTON has suffered very much in public estimation, because of his supposed refusal to reinforce Gen. MCCLELLAN for the great battles before Richmond. It is now found that he suffered wrongly, and that the President acted justly in refusing to dismiss him in order merely to appease a popular clamor. But the President fails to indicate where lies the blame for the inability to reinforce Gen. MCCLELLAN. The latter was in the enemy's country, in front of his capital, and opposed by an immense army, daily increasing in numbers....

Perhaps the War Department is not to blame for not knowing how many soldiers it had in the field, and for stopping enlistments at the very time when the organization of a reserve was so necessary. We are glad to find the President giving so hearty an indorsement to the War Secretary; for it is better to have the people confide in all their officers than distrust any, seeing that they will be retained in their places by the President. And whatever errors or omissions may have marked the past, we may safely accept the President's statement of human philosophy, that, "in the selfishness of their natures," our leaders must all desire success; and, desiring it, they will work for it all the more zealously and effectively, perhaps, for having made some mistakes, and seen the unhappy results flowing from them. Let us have, then, the good old motto again, "Union, for the sake of the Union." ✸

President Abraham Lincoln and George McClellan confer in General McClellan's tent near Antietam on October 3, 1862.

1. Aware that McClellan had circulated rumors that Stanton had sabotaged his recent Peninsula campaign by ordering troops transferred to the defense of Washington, Lincoln made a rare public appearance to defend his Secretary of War on August 6. Lincoln magnanimously praised both Stanton and McClellan, and insisted, "justice requires me...to take [blame] upon myself"

THE END OF THE REBEL RAM ARKANSAS.

AUGUST 11

The rebel ram Arkansas,[1] which made so brilliant a debut on the Mississippi a few weeks ago, has closed its career in precisely the same manner as the Merrimac did — namely, by an act of suicide.[2] Rebel rams seem to have an inherent predisposition to felo de se,[3] for the two chief representatives of that type of marine creature have adopted this method of taking off. Each signalized its advent in the most spirited style, each seemed for a while to have things all its own way, and both have finally been hedged around with so many obstructions that a desperate making away with themselves was the only outlet left them.

The distant theatre on which the Arkansas played its part, has perhaps caused its career to be followed with less interest than attended that of the Merrimac; but no one can be blind to the immense stake for which it played, and how near it came to winning it. The successful manner in which it made its advent by the raid on our gunboats at Vicksburgh, proved its powerful fighting qualities, and showed that we had nothing on the Mississippi fit to cope with it. What wonder, then, if a wild, ambitious dream possessed the minds of its commander and the Richmond usurpers — if they saw in it — who knows? — perhaps the mistress of the Mississippi, and the means whereby New-Orleans itself might be won back and the whole river reclaimed to rebel rule?

It appears, according to the Richmond Dispatch, that the Arkansas had started on this mission and was on its way to cooperate in the attack on Baton Rouge, when its machinery became disabled, and whilst attempting to adjust it, was set upon by the National gunboats, and so entrapped that nothing was left for the rebels but to blow it up.... ✸

1. The Arkansas, laid down at Memphis and completed with much effort up the Yazoo River, was one of two large ironclads designed by the Confederates to defend the Mississippi River. The Louisiana was destroyed when Farragut captured New Orleans, the Arkansas as noted here.

2. Though Navy Captain William "Dirty Bill" Porter, brother of David Dixon Porter and captain of the ironclad Essex, claimed to have disabled the Arkansas by cannon fire, the fact was that the engines of the Arkansas failed and she was driven ashore and set on fire by her crew.

3. Latin for "suicide."

THE PRESIDENT AND COLONIZATION.
INTERESTING INTERVIEW WITH A COMMITTEE OF COLORED MEN.

AUGUST 15

WASHINGTON, THURSDAY, AUGUST 14

This afternoon the President of the United States gave audience to a Committee of colored men at the White House.[1] They were introduced by Rev. J. MITCHELL, Commissioner of Emigration. E. M. THOMAS,[2] the Chairman, remarked that they were there by invitation, to hear what the Executive had to say to them.

Having all been seated, the President, after a few preliminary observations, informed them that a sum of money had been appropriated by Congress, and placed at his disposition, for the purpose of aiding the colonization in some country of the people, or a portion of them, of African descent, thereby making it his duty, as it had for a long time been his inclination, to favor that cause; and why, he asked, should the people of your race be colonized, and where? Why should they leave this country? This is, perhaps, the first question for proper consideration. You and we are different races. We have between us a broader difference than exists between almost any other two races. Whether it is right or wrong I need not discuss; but this physical difference is a great disadvantage to us both, as I think. Your race suffer very greatly, many of them, by living among us, while ours suffer from your presence. In a word, we suffer on each side. If this is admitted, it affords a reason, at least, why we should be separated. You, here, are freemen, I suppose.

A VOICE—Yes, Sir.

The PRESDENT [sic]—Perhaps you have long been free, or all your lives. Your race are suffering, in my judgment, the greatest wrong inflicted on any people. But even when you cease to be slaves you are yet far removed from being placed on an equality with the white race. You are cut off from many of the advantages which the other race enjoys. The aspiration of men is to enjoy equality with the best when free, but on this broad continent not a single man of your race is made the equal of a single man of ours. Go where you are treated the best, and the ban is still upon you. I do not propose to discuss this, but to present it as a fact, with which we have to deal. I cannot alter it if I would. It is a fact about which we all think and feel alike, I and you. We look to our condition. Owing to the existence of the two races on this continent, I need not recount to you the effects upon white men, growing out of the institution of Slavery. I believe in its general evil effects on the white race. See our present condition — the country engaged in war! our white men cutting one another's throats — none knowing how far it will extend — and then consider what we know to be the truth. But for your race among us there could not be war, although many men engaged on either side, do not care for you one way or the other. Nevertheless, I repeat, without the institution of Slavery, and the colored race as a basis, the war could not have an existence. It is better for us both, therefore, to be separated. I know that there are free men among you who, even if they could better their condition, are not as much inclined to go out of the country as those who, being slaves, could obtain their freedom on this condition. I suppose one of the principal difficulties in the way of colonization is that the free colored man cannot see that his comfort would be advanced by it. You may believe that you can live in Washington, or elsewhere in the United States, the remainder of your life; perhaps more so than you can in any foreign country, and hence you may come to the conclusion that you have nothing to do with the idea of going to a foreign country. This is (I speak in no unkind sense) an extremely selfish view of the case. But you ought to do something to help those who are not so fortunate as yourselves. There is an unwillingness on the part of our people, harsh as it may be, for you free colored people to remain with us.... ✸

An unidentified African-American who participated in the American Colonization Society's program.

MR. LINCOLN TO MR. GREELEY.

AUGUST 24

The President's response to Mr. GREE-LEY's[1] public letter, addressed to him last week, is explicit enough, and settles one or two disputed points as to Mr. LIN-COLN's opinions and policy. His one and paramount object in the war is "to save the Union" — to save it with or without Slavery, under one set of circumstances or another, or by one agency or another, but at all events to save it somehow. His simple platform is "The salvation of the Union." To this end his whole policy looks, and whatever he does or fails to do is with reference to its bearings upon this one great point. He could not have said anything more satisfactory to the country in general.

The letter, like all Mr. LINCOLN's lit-erary attempts, exhibits the peculiarities of his mind and style; but the logical sequence and precision, and the grammatical accuracy of this, is greatly in advance of any previous effort. It is in infinitely better taste, too, than the rude epistle to which it is an answer.

EXECUTIVE MANSION, WASHINGTON, AUG. 22

Hon. Horace Greeley:

DEAR SIR:

I have just read yours of the 19th, addressed to myself through the New-York Tribune. If there be in it any statements or assumptions of fact which I may know to be erroneous, I do not now and here contro-vert them. If there be in it any inferences which I may believe to be falsely drawn, I do not now and here argue against them. If there be perceptible in it an impatient and dictatorial tone, I waive it in, deference to an old friend, whose heart I have always supposed to be right.

As to the policy I "seem to be pursuing," as you say, I have not meant to leave any one in doubt.

I would save the Union. I would save it the shortest way under the Constitution. The sooner the national author-ity can be restored the nearer the Union will be "the Union as it was." If there be those who would not save the Union un-less they could at the same time save Slavery, I do not agree with them. If there be those who would not save the Union unless they could at the same time de-

THE SECOND BATTLE OF BULL RUN.

AUGUST 31

In the closing week of June last, the so-called Confederate President, JEFF. DA-VIS, from his chamber at Richmond, listened to the thunder of the cannon of hostile armies battling before his capital. In the closing week of August, President LINCOLN, from the White House, heard the deep peals of the artillery of the con-tending hosts which, having now changed location, are struggling for supremacy be-fore the National Capital. The geographi-cal change of position does not indicate that Richmond is any the less likely to fall, or that Washington is any the less safe now than it was then. In truth, the fact rather is, that if we have any one General with sense and pluck enough to take advantage of the palpable opportunity the rebels have given us, we may be said to he much nearer to Richmond now when the battle-field for its possession is a hundred miles away from, it than we were two months ago, when our fevered and shrunken army had shoveled its way up to within seven miles of its outskirts.

The accounts of the sanguinary battles of the last four days fought in the rear of Gen. POPE's[1] army, have been very meagre and contradictory. They have been con-fined to POPE's two very brief official re-ports, dated the 28th and 30th, and to such information as could be picked up by an active corps of correspondents stationed at Washington, Alexandria, and other points outside of the army lines from which they have not yet been expelled. Many of these statements are rumors brought by fugi-tive soldiers, fleeing Unionists, women and negroes, and from their evident want of truthfulness, many of those which we have received have been excluded from our columns. Gen. POPE's official dispatches give us no details....

Of Friday's battle, which was fought on the identical battle-field of Bull Run, he reports: "We fought a terrific battle with the combined forces of the enemy, which lasted with continuous fury from daylight until after dark, by which time the enemy was driven from the field, which we now occupy." And he further states our loss on that day as being "not less than eight thou-sand men, killed and wounded," while the enemy's loss he puts down as at least "two to our one."[2] Of the battle of yesterday we have as yet nothing official; but the tele-graph from Washington reports that one was actually raging, and that the cannon-ading could be heard in that city....

All these engagements seem to have been to the last degree indecisive.[3] Up to The rebels have, within the week, exhibit-ed an audacity, if not a desperation, that is extraordinary; and now, in falling back to Centreville, and in throwing detachments of their army to Vienna, to Leesburgh, and even, it is said, to the line of the Potomac, they show that they are making the grand struggle for life or death. If this Richmond rebel army, which has thus pierced almost to our Capital, be permitted to retire again into Central Virginia, there will be plenty of future fighting for us on fields infinitely less advantageous than that they have now challenged us to combat upon. They have given us an opportunity to destroy them never equaled in the history of this war, and seldom offered by an army to its ad-versary in any war. With our far superior numbers and position, there will be ter-rible culpability somewhere if the chance be not taken advantage of. ✸

1. Major General John Pope (1822–1892) was brought east at Stanton's urging, after the fall of Island No. 10. Stanton, who was no friend of McClellan, wanted to establish a rival to "Little Mac" in Virginia.
2. Union losses in this battle were 1,724 killed and 8,372 wounded, plus another 5,958 missing; Con-federate losses were 1,481 killed and 7,627 wounded.
3. In fact, the Union suffered a major defeat at the Second Battle of Bull Run (August 28–30, 1862), leaving victorious Confederate armies again dan-gerously close to Washington. Union forces lost 10,000 killed and wounded, plus another 6,000 missing, while Confederate losses totaled 8,300.

stroy Slavery, I do not agree with them. My paramount object in this struggle is to save the Union, and is not either to save or destroy Slavery. If I could save the Union without freeing any slave. I would do it, and if I could save it by freeing all the slaves, I would do it, and if I could save it by freeing some and leaving others alone, I would also do that. What I do about Slavery and the colored race, I do because I believe it helps to save this Union, and what I forbear, I forbear because I do not believe it would help to save the Union. I shall do less whenever I shall believe what I am doing hurts the cause, and I shall do more whenever I shall believe doing more will help the cause. I shall try to correct errors when shown to be errors; and I shall adopt new views so fast as they shall appear to be true views. I have here stated my purpose accord-ing to my view of official duty, and I intend no modification of my oft-expressed personal wish that all men, everywhere, could be free. Yours,

A. LINCOLN. ✇

1. Horace Greeley, editor of The New York Tribune, had published "The Prayer of Twenty Millions" on August 20, charging Lincoln was "strangely and disastrously remiss" for not ordering emancipation. Again keeping his intentions secret, the President wrote a brilliant reply to assure the country that whatever he decided about slavery would be for union-saving reasons. He then made sure The Times and other rival papers had access to his letter. Of course he was being disingenuous, having already decided to issue a proclamation as soon as Union armies own a victory.

THE REBEL INVASION OF THE LOYAL STATES.

SEPTEMBER 9

It seems to be settled that a force of at least 40,000 rebels has crossed the Potomac and taken position at Frederick, in Maryland, about sixty miles west of Baltimore, and about forty north from Washington. They have been permitted by the Government to cross without resistance. Telegraphic reports from the Capital would almost lead us to believe that they had been invited there, — for we are assured that the Government is perfectly satisfied with their position, and that none of them will ever return. We hope this may prove to be true; — but we would rather see it proved than give full credence to it in advance. As we remarked yesterday, we have too many of these official assurances already on hand unredeemed, to be especially eager for more.... ✇

A woodcut depicting the second day of fighting in the Second Battle of Bull Run.

THE GREAT BATTLE OF THE WAR.

SEPTEMBER 18

At last our Generals in the field seem to have risen to the grandeur of the National crisis. The desperate attempt of the rebel leaders to force their way into the heart of the North, has been fairly met with the whole strength of the National armies before Washington, and before the sun goes down upon this day we shall learn the issue of the greatest battle ever fought upon American soil — a battle which, in the numbers of the troops engaged, in the fierce energy with which the prize of victory has been contested, and in the tremendous importance of that prize itself, must take its place among the grand decisive conflicts of history.

In the absence of anything approaching to full and coherent details of the scene and scope of this great contest, it is impossible for us to attempt any systematic view of the movements by which the action was brought on; but thus much it is, we think, safe to say, that by noon of yesterday the National army under Gen. MCCLELLAN, numbering 100,000 men, had become engaged along its whole line with the combined and concentrated rebel forces of Gens. LEE and JACKSON, in numbers certainly not inferior to our own.[1]

The battle, raging apparently from a point near Sharpsburgh to the vicinity of Harper's Ferry, was under circumstances and in a position which make it next to impossible that the result of the conflict should be anything less than decisive of the fate of one or other of the opposing hosts. The fortunes of the fight, though wavering and uncertain through the earlier portion of the day, were steadily inclining to the National advantage, and down to 2 o'clock P.M., (the hour of our latest authentic intelligence at this present writing from the immediate scene of action,) the hope of victory was plainly with our army. Should this hope resolve itself into glorious certainty, the direct fruits of our triumph cannot easily be overestimated.... ✸

1. In fact, McClellan's army of 87,000 significantly outnumbered Lee's army of 41,000. McClellan lost some 12,400 casualties to Lee's 10,000.

A GLORIOUS VICTORY.

THE LATEST REPORTS BY WAY OF HARRISBURGH.

DREADFUL CARNAGE ON BOTH SIDES.

SEPTEMBER 18

HARRISBURGH, WEDNESDAY, SEPT. 17 — 10 P.M.

Gen. MCCLELLAN has achieved a glorious victory[1]....

REPORTS FROM THE PRESS CORRESPONDENT.
HARRISBURGH, WEDNESDAY, SEPT. 17

A great battle has been fought, and we are victorious.

The carnage on both sides was awful.

Gen. LONGSTREET was wounded and taken prisoner.

HARRISBURGH, WEDNESDAY, SEPT. 17 — 10 P.M.

Dispatches just received at headquarters from Hagerstown say: "We have achieved a glorious victory."

LONGSTREET is not killed, but is wounded and a prisoner. Gen. HOOKER was wounded in the foot.[2] No particulars are received. ✸

1. At the Battle of Antietam (Sharpsburg).
2. Confederate Major General James Longstreet was neither wounded nor captured; Union Major General Joseph Hooker was wounded in the foot during the morning attack and had to leave the field.

Top: A Kurz and Allison lithograph of the Battle of Antietam. Above: The New York Times map showing troop positions during the Battle of Harper's Ferry, part of the Antietam campaign.

A PROCLAMATION BY THE PRESIDENT OF THE UNITED STATES.

A DECREE OF EMANCIPATION.

WASHINGTON, MONDAY, SEPT. 22

By the President of the United States of America:

A PROCLAMATION.

I, ABRAHAM LINCOLN, President of the United States of America, and Commander-in-Chief of the Army and Navy thereof, do hereby proclaim and declare, that hereafter, as heretofore, the war will be prosecuted for the object of practically restoring the constitutional relation between the United States and the people thereof in which States that relation is, or may be suspended or disturbed; that it is my purpose, upon the next meeting of Congress, to again recommend the adoption of a practical measure tendering pecuniary aid to the free acceptance or rejection of all the Slave States so called, the people whereof may not then be in rebellion against the United States, and which States may then have voluntarily adopted, or thereafter may voluntarily adopt, the immediate or gradual abolishment of Slavery within their respective limits; and that the efforts to colonize persons of African descent with their consent, upon the Continent or elsewhere, with the previously obtained consent of the governments existing there, will be continued.

That on the first day of January, in the year of our Lord one thousand eight hundred and sixty-three, all persons held as slaves within any State, or any designated part of a State, the people whereof shall then be in rebellion against the United States shall be then, thenceforward, and forever, free; and the Executive Government of the United States, including the military and naval authority thereof, will recognize and maintain the freedom of such persons, and will do no act or acts to repress such persons, or any of them, in any efforts they may make for their actual freedom.

That the Executive will, on the first day of January aforesaid, by proclamation, designate the States and parts of States, if any, in which the people thereof, respectively, shall then be in rebellion against the United States; and the fact that any State, or the people thereof, shall on that day be in good faith represented in the

SEPTEMBER 23

Congress of the United States by members chosen thereto at elections wherein a majority of the qualified voters of such State shall have participated, shall, in the absence of strong countervailing testimony, be deemed conclusive evidence that such State and the people thereof have not been in rebellion against the United States.

That attention is hereby called to an act of Congress entitled "An act to make an additional article of war," approved March 13, 1862, and which act is in the words and figure following:

Be it enacted by the Senate and House of Representatives of the United States of America in Congress assembled, That hereafter the following shall be promulgated as an additional article of war for the government of the army of the United States, and shall be obeyed and observed as such.

ARTICLE — . All officers or persons in the military or naval service of the United States are prohibited from employing any of the forces under their respective commands for the purpose of returning fugitives from service or labor who may have escaped from any person to whom such service or labor is claimed to be due, and any officer who shall be found guilty by a court-martial of violating this article shall be dismissed from the service.

SECTION 2. And be it further erected, that this as shall take effect from and after its passage. Also to the ninth and tenth sections of an act entitled "An act to suppress insurrection, to punish treason and rebellion, to seize and confiscate property of rebels, and for other purposes," approved July 17, 1862, and which sections are in the words and figures following:

SEC. 9. And be it further enacted, That all slaves of persons who shall hereafter be engaged in rebellion against the Government of the United States, or who shall, in any way give aid or comfort thereto, escaping from such persons and taking refuge within the lines of the army; and all slaves captured from such persons or deserted by them and coming under the control of the Government of the United States, and all slaves of such persons found on (or) being within any place occupied by rebel forces

and afterwards occupied by the forces of the United States, shall be deemed captives of war, and shall be forever free of their servitude and not held again as slaves.

SEC. 10. And be it further enacted, That no slaves escaping into any State, Territory or the District of Columbia, from any of the States, shall be delivered up, or in any way impeded or hindered of his liberty, except for crime or some offence against the laws, unless the person claiming said fugitive shall first make oath that the person to whom the labor or service of such fugitive is alleged to be due, is his lawful owner, and has not been in arms against the United States in the present rebellion, nor in any way given aid and comfort thereto, and no person engaged in the military or naval service of the United States shall, under any pretence whatever, assume to decide on the validity of the claim of any person to the service or labor of any other person, or surrender up any such person to the claimant, on pain of being dismissed from the service.

And I do hereby enjoin upon and order all persons engaged in the military and naval service of the United States, to observe, obey and enforce, within their respective spheres of service, the act and sections above recited.

And the Executive will in due time recommend that all citizens of the United States who shall have remained loyal thereto throughout the rebellion, shall (upon the restoration of the constitutional relation between the United States and their respective States and people, if the relation shall have been suspended or disturbed,) be compensated for all losses by acts of the United States, including the loss of slaves.

In witness whereof, I have hereunto set my hand, and caused the seal of the United States to be affixed.

Done at the City of Washington, this Twenty-second day of September, in the year of our Lord one thousand eight hundred and sixty-two, and of the Independence of the United States the eighty-seventh.

ABRAHAM LINCOLN.
BY THE PRESIDENT. WILLIAM H. SEWARD,
SECRETARY OF STATE. ⊛

THE PRESIDENT'S PROCLAMATION.

SEPTEMBER 23

There has been no more important and far reaching document ever issued since the foundation of this Government than the proclamation of President LINCOLN concerning Slavery and slaves, published this morning....

The wisdom of the step taken — we refer at present to that clause in the document which declares free the slaves of rebel States after the 1st of January — is unquestionable; its necessity, indisputable. It has been declared time and again by President LINCOLN that as soon as this step became a necessity, he should adopt it. Its adoption now is not a confession that the military means of suppressing the great rebellion have proved a failure; but simply that there is a point at which any other legitimate appliances that can be called in, shall also be availed of. Slavery is an element of strength to the rebels if left untouched; it will assuredly prove an element of weakness — it may be of total destruction — to them and their cause, when we make such use of it and its victims as lies in our power.

From now till the 1st of January — the day when this proclamation will take effect — is little over three months. What may happen between now and then, in the progress of the war, it is hard to say. We earnestly hope, however, that by that time, the rebellion will be put down by the military hand, and that the terrible element of slave-insurrection may not be invoked. If, by that day, the rebel army be overthrown, and their Capital captured; and, if the slaveholding rebels still prove malignant, irrepressible, and, as in the Southwest, disorganizers and marauders, then let that which Vice-President STEPHENS called the corner-stone of the Southern Confederacy be knocked from under it, and see whether the whole fabric of rebellion will not necessarily tumble to the ground. ✹

A POLICY AT LAST.

SEPTEMBER 26

The President's proclamation, suspending the writ of habeas corpus in certain cases,[1] excites quite as much disgust in the minds of the opponents of the Administration as did the Proclamation of Emancipation. The latter was pronounced objectionable because immediately impracticable, and as tending to provoke the augmented animosity of the South. The former is represented to be a return of the Administration to the policy of restricted speech and summary imprisonment, which excited so much popular discontent last Winter.

Both papers, however, are free from the defects complained of, while they possess others for which the entire country has been clamorous. The Government has lacked a determined policy. It has assumed no fixed relation to the Slavery difficulty. And whatever may be the view taken of the expediency of the emancipation measure at the present moment, it certainly has the merit of placing the Administration in an intelligible and entirely definite position before the country, so that the standing charge of indecision ceases to be applicable. So with the proclamation touching arrests. Heretofore they have been made without regard to any fixed principle. Sentiments and acts which were in one locality indulged with perfect impunity, in another involved a prompt consignment to Fort Lafayette. And while the bench generally declined to interpose the habeas corpus to discharge the prisoner, judges were found always ready to issue that great prerogative writ. It is not, therefore, to introduce a new system of espionage and arrest, that the recent declaration is issued; but to restrain and define and mitigate the operation of a system which is already in active use.... ✹

1. Lincoln issued his proclamation two days after the Emancipation Proclamation, September 24, 1862.

THE EMANCIPATION EDICT.

SEPTEMBER 30

Our secession scribes deal very gingerly with the President's proclamation. They say much less terrible things about it than they threatened in advance. It is not to be supposed that they have experienced any change of heart in regard to Slavery; but they evidently consider it somewhat more dangerous than it used to be to praise and glorify the peculiar institution. They croak a little, it is true, about making this a war for abolition, but they do it faintly and with evident misgivings. Like Macbeth's amen, it "sticks in their throats."

The proclamation is simply a weapon of warfare — perfectly legitimate and perfectly proper. From the very moment when the slaveholding aristocracy raised the banner of rebellion against the Government, it has been perfectly competent for the Government to resort to emancipation as a means of crushing their hostility. We had just as much right to free their slaves, as we had to take their horses, to seize their ships or destroy their lives. It was ridiculous and absurd to say that we might wage war against them, — that we could bombard their towns, kill their troops, confiscate their goods, occupy their lands, forfeit their cattle, their crops, and everything else that they possessed, — but that we could not strip them of their slaves. What gave such supreme sanctity to this specific form of property or of labor? Not the Constitution — for it does not even, in explicit terms, mention its existence. What was there that thus consecrated, beyond

President Lincoln reading the Emancipation Proclamation to his cabinet in July 1862, painted two years later by New York artist Francis B. Carpenter.

all reach of punishment, the very root and cause of this gigantic crime?

The whole question of dealing with Slavery has, from the very beginning, been one of expediency. We had a perfect right to decree its abolition — to strike a fatal blow at its existence, — whenever it could be done with advantage to the Union cause. It was to be decided, like any other movement of the war, like the planning of a campaign or the direction of an army, purely by considerations of public expediency. Whenever it would produce more good than harm, it was to be done. Until then, it would have been impolitic and therefore unwise.

The Proclamation has done great good already. It has had a good effect upon the public mind in the Northern States. It has carried the conviction everywhere that the Government is in earnest in its contest with rebellion — and that it has at last a policy, a clear and distinct system of conduct, by which it seeks to crush it. It has met a strong and fervid aspiration of the Northern heart, and given new life and vigor to the determined purpose of the Northern mind. It increases the motives for perseverance in this gigantic contest. It holds out the hope that besides restoring the Union, we shall extinguish forever that dire curse which poisoned the very fountain of liberty, and detracted infinitely from the value of the Union itself. It holds out the promise of re-establishing the Constitution in all its old supremacy, and at the same time of removing that dreadful evil which has weakened its authority and prevented it from securing the blessings it was intended to confer on ourselves and our posterity.

One thing only now remains: — let us push forward our armies, clothed as they are with this new and terrible power. Let us carry them into the very heart of the slaveholding States, that they may there give full and complete effect to this edict of emancipation. Let us crush the military power which is the only bulwark of Slavery at the present moment, and at the same time put an end to the rebellion itself. Henceforth they must stand or fall together. ❀

THE STATE CANVASS — THE SEYMOUR PARTY AND THE REBELLION.

OCTOBER 6

The Seymourites make very wry faces when forced to swallow a little of their own medicine. Ever since the war began they have been calling the Republicans and other Anti-Slavery men traitors; they have been denouncing them most vehemently as enemies of the Government — as haters of the Constitution and the Union, and as seeking the overthrow of both. They have charged them with conspiring against our Generals in the field; with seeking to cripple the operations of our armies, and to give victory and conquest to the rebels. And they have been calling very lustily for their arrest and imprisonment, — for the suppression of their Presses and the confinement of their persons in Fort Lafayette.

This was very fine fun, while they had it all to themselves. But when they are compelled to swallow a little of the same mixture themselves, they take a very different view of the subject. They are shocked at the bad manners of their opponents. The absurdity of calling men traitors, merely because they differ from you in opinion, strikes them with much more force than it did a month ago. They always supposed this to be a free country, — where every man had a right to his own judgment on public affairs; and it seems to them exceedingly unkind to stigmatize them as disloyal, because their judgment does not agree with ours. This is very good doctrine, but they are new converts to it. While they could amuse themselves by pelting the Abolitionists with stones of this sort, it never struck them as particularly objectionable; but between the boys and the frogs in such a game they have suddenly discovered there is quite a difference.

We congratulate our political opponents on the theoretical improvement in their manners. We have no disposition to call names or bandy epithets. Nor have we anything to do with the personal motives which prompt their political action and give it character; that is a matter for which they must give account elsewhere. But we have a right to hold them responsible for the tendency and effect of their political action, and we intend to exercise it. We have never said that Gov. SEYMOUR[1] was a rebel or a traitor: we do not believe he is. We have never said that any of his supporters were personally rebels or traitors, though we believe

that at heart many of them are both. But we have said, and we repeat, that the election of SEYMOUR to be Governor of this State, under the present circumstances of the country and the canvass, will give substantial aid and comfort to the rebellion. It will be a heavy blow and great discouragement to the Government in its contest for self-preservation. It will do more to encourage the rebels to persevere in their war upon the Constitution and the Union, than could possibly be done within this State in any other way. And there is not a man living who would have more reason to rejoice over such a result, or to whom it would carry more solid comfort and encouragement, than the President of the rebel Confederacy.

Every man knows this to be so. Mr. SEYMOUR himself knows it. The Atlas and Argus[2] knows it. The party have put forward so clearly, the real spirit and animus of the movement, in the speech of Mr. SEYMOUR which they adopted as their platform, that in spite of their faint protestations of loyalty and patriotism, it is impossible for any man to doubt the real drift and tenor of the action they propose to take. Whatever ulterior object, may lie behind the movement, — whether they design to surrender the Government to JEFF. DAVIS, and thus preserve the Union, or to "let the South go," and thus destroy it, — one thing is very clear; — they mean to encourage the rebels to persevere in the war, and to cripple the Government in its efforts to push it to a victorious end. If they don't mean — this, what do they mean? They have organized their movement on the specific and exclusive ground of opposition to the Government. They denounce its action against the rebellion; they brand as illegal and tyrannical its efforts to protect itself against spies and traitors at home; they magnify its faults and vilify its motives, and do everything in — their power to make it odious and offensive in the eyes of the world; — and then they put forward Mr. SEYMOUR as the representative of this hostility to the Government, and, as such, ask the people of the State to elect him Governor. Is not this giving aid and comfort to the rebellion? If not, what would be?

Now we don't imitate the example our opponents have set us in calling ☞

them traitors, and invoking the penalties of treason against them. We have not asked that Mr. SEYMOUR should be sent to Fort Lafayette,[3] or that the editors of the Atlas and Argus should be hanged, drawn and quartered, for the aid they are proposing to give the rebel Confederacy. We appeal to the PEOPLE. We ask them to squelch this attempt to hamstring the Government while engaged in a life and death struggle with its foes. We ask them to say whether the political weight of the Empire State shall thus be cast into the scale of rebellion against the Government. The friends of SEYMOUR appeal to them to end the war. But how? By its vigorous prosecution? By striking the rebels as quick, as hard, and as often as possible? By making them feel the full evils of the war they have invoked, as a penalty for the crimes they have committed? By stripping them of the means of waging war? By seizing their agents and preventing them from giving them aid and comfort?

This is Gen. WADSWORTH's[4] method, not Gov. SEYMOUR's. This is precisely the method on which Gov. SEYMOUR and the party at his back are making war. It is precisely the method they are trying to stop. They are for ending the war by compromise, — by concessions to the South, — in a single word, by a surrender. We appeal to the People to judge between them, and we have not the slightest apprehension as to the verdict they will give. ✸

1. Horatio Seymour (1810–1886) was the Democratic candidate for governor of New York.
2. A pro-Democratic newspaper in Albany, the state capital.
3. A prison in New York.
4. James S. Wadsworth (1807–1864) left his command to serve as military governor of Washington from March to September 1862. He was Seymour's opponent for governor of New York at this time. After losing the election, he returned to active command, and fought at Chancellorsville and Gettysburg, dying in action at the Wilderness.

EMANCIPATION AND FREE NEGROES.

OCTOBER 7

Thousands of well-meaning persons have been alarmed at the prospective emancipation of the slaves, from a belief that they would flood the North and bring their labor into direct and disastrous competition with our own. This has been a favorite argument with Pro-Slavery Democrats, who have used it very vigorously, first in opposition to the war and now in support of SEYMOUR's election. They aim especially to alarm the Irish laborers, who are naturally sensitive on a point which threatens to affect so nearly their own interests....

It is common, we know, to say that the whites and negroes cannot exist together at the South except in the relation of masters and slaves, — and that if the latter are set free they must be colonized, either to the North or to some foreign country. We do not believe this. The prejudices of the present class of Southern whites, especially slaveholders, are doubtless very strong — perhaps unconquerable. But in the long run the laws of political economy are more powerful than social or personal prejudices, — and sooner or later they will overcome them. When it shall once be decided that Slavery is to end, — that this form of labor can no longer exist in the Southern States, the question will instantly arise, What shall be substituted for it? It may be a system of apprenticeship — it may be the system of hired wages — or it may be a modification of one or the other, or a combination of both. But one thing is clear: — negro labor will always be more needed and more valuable in the Southern States than anywhere else; — and therefore it will always remain there. The staple productions of that region are better adapted to negro culture: the climate is better suited to the negro constitution, — and the interests, material and moral, of the whole world, require that negro labor should continue to cultivate the Southern soil; and so long as this is the case, there it will stay.... ✸

HOW GOVERNOR SEYMOUR CENSURES THE REBELLION.

OCTOBER 7

We have already more than once urged the fact that Gov. SEYMOUR devotes ten times as much space and labor to the condemnation of our own Government as he does to that of the rebellion. "But he does condemn the rebellion, nevertheless," say his supporters, — "and that is all you have any right to ask." Perhaps it is — and perhaps not. But let us see how he condemns the rebellion. "We charge," says Mr. SEYMOUR, "that this rebellion is most wicked, because it is against the best Government that ever existed." That starts off very well. It seems explicit and emphatic. But Gov. SEYMOUR proceeds to enlarge upon the point. "Rebellion," he says, "is not necessarily a wrong; it may be an act of the highest virtue." Possibly, then, there may be some extenuation for this rebellion. "To resist a bad government is patriotism, — to resist a good one is the greatest guilt." Here, then, is the test which Mr. SEYMOUR proposes to apply. If our Government, in its actual and practical workings when the rebellion broke out, was a good one, then the rebellion was wicked. If not — not. Now what has Gov. SEYMOUR to say on this point? "Our Government and its admin- istration are different things; — but in the eyes of the civilized world, abuses, weakness or folly in the conduct of affairs go far to JUSTIFY RESISTANCE." And then Gov. SEYMOUR comes back to the main staple of his speech, and proceeds to show that "abuses, weakness and folly in the conduct of affairs" have characterized our Government since its administration passed into Republican hands.

Gov. SEYMOUR is very chary in his use of language. He picks his way over this delicate ground as tenderly as if he were treading on eggs. But he leaves no room to doubt that his real drift was to excuse the rebellion, while he seemed to condemn it. Not that he would have started it himself, — not that he is personally and at heart a rebel or a traitor; but he sees extenuating circumstances in the case. While "legal tribunals can only regard resistance to laws as a crime," he sees very many things in the action of the Government, — very many of those "abuses, weaknesses and follies in the conduct of affairs," — which "go far to justify resistance." We are to be very tender of the Southern rebels. We must think twice before we confiscate

PROGRESS OF THE SEYMOUR CAMPAIGN.

OCTOBER 8

Our Seymour friends are not having quite as good a time with their canvass as they anticipated. They have encountered several unexpected obstacles. The changed condition of the country, and especially the altered aspects of the war, cause them considerable embarrassment. The fact is, they jumped into their partisan movement against the Government at a moment of disaster and discouragement. Reverses had overtaken our arms. Our armies had been driven back in their advance upon the rebel capital, and had been beaten in their attempt to defend our own. Discord prevailed among our Generals, — hesitation and weakness seemed to characterize our Executive councils, — and a feeling of profound despondency had seized upon the public mind.

This was the moment chosen by the Pro-Slavery Democracy to rally their forces for a combined and vigorous assault upon the Government. Every man who had sympathized with the rebellion seized the opportunity offered by the public calamities to stab the Government which was contending against it. They gathered from every quarter of the State, men who had been imprisoned for disloyal practices, men whose sympathies with rebels had been more prudent, but none the less active; men whose reverence for Slavery was greater than their love for the Constitution; men who from the very beginning of the war had done everything they dared to check its progress and diminish its results, — met for the express purpose of raising the standard of discontent and hostility to the Administration, upon which alone depended the hope of the country for the conquest of the rebellion. Unquestionably they derived strength from the circumstances of the country. Thousands, whose hearts were depressed by the reverses of the war, were ready for the moment to seek a remedy in any quarter....

But the state of things has changed essentially since this movement was set on foot.

The prospects of the war have brightened. Our armies have achieved brilliant victories, which have removed from the public heart its weight of despondency. And the Government has taken steps which indicate greater vigor in the prosecution of the war, and a clearer perception of the tendencies and necessary results of the rebellion. The public confidence in the Administration rises just as its energy increases; and now the universal demand is, that the Government shall be sustained, thoroughly and heartily, in its contest with the rebellion. The people are becoming impatient therefore of the Seymour movement, which seeks its overthrow; and unless we are greatly mistaken in the tendencies of public opinion, Gov. SEYMOUR will have serious reason to regret, by the time the election is over, that he ever intrusted, his political fortunes to so desperate a venture as that of crippling the Government of his country in the midst of a desperate war. ✪

their property, or set free their slaves, or disturb their peace. They have had great provocations. The Government, in its practical administration, has not been a very good one. It has been a very bad one — and "to resist a bad Government," says Gov. SEYMOUR, "is patriotism."

Now are we very far out of the way when we say that to elect Mr. SEYMOUR Governor of New-York, on the strength of such sentiments, — on this speech as a platform, — in the very midst of the war waged by these rebels on the Government, while they are threatening the North with invasion, and the Constitution and the Union with utter overthrow, — would be to give them aid and comfort?... ✪

THE VICTORY AT CORINTH.
DESPERATE ASSAULT UPON THE PLACE BY FIFTY THOUSAND REBELS.

OCTOBER 9

CORINTH, MISS., SUNDAY, OCT. 5

The correspondent of the St. Louis Democrat has the following details of the battle at Corinth:

"On the morning of the 3d, our outposts were attacked by the enemy in force, about six miles northeast of Corinth, and before 9 o'clock the engagement became general

end fierce, and a sanguinary battle was fought.[1]

Our men under ROSECRANS stood up manfully, and fought with great coolness and bravery; but regiment after regiment, and brigade after brigade poured in upon us, and we were forced slowly backward, fighting desperately. The rebels pushed forward with determined obstinacy, and held every foot of their advantage ground.

They outflanked our inferior force and were forming in the rear, and we were obliged to fall back still further to prevent this movement from being accomplished. The enemy were now inside our breastworks pushing us backward toward the town when darkness put an end to fighting that day.

During the day's fight our loss was heavy, but that of the enemy must have largely exceeded ours.

Three pieces of the First Missouri Battery were captured after having stood for hours before the enemy's fire. ☞

A Currier and Ives lithograph of the Battle of Corinth.

Brig.-Gen. [Pleasant A.] HACKLEMAN fell mortally wounded at the head of his men, and died the same evening. Gen. [Richard James "Uncle Dick"] OGLESBY was shot in the breast.

About 4 o'clock A.M. of the 4th, the enemy opened on the town with shot and shell. Our batteries replied, and for an hour or more a heavy cannonading was kept up. At the expiration of that time, two rebel guns had been disabled, and, shortly after-daylight, their battery of seven guns was captured.

A portentous quiet soon occurred, and it was evident that some movement was being made by the enemy. The Western Sharpshooters, under Col. [Patrick E.] BURKE, were ordered forward as skirmishers, to feel the enemy. At 9 1/2 they met him three-quarters of a mile in advance of our line of battle, advancing rapidly in heavy columns upon the town. Immediately a murderous fire was opened on this heavy line by our skirmishers, who slowly began to retire, returning the fire of the enemy with effect.

The woods seemed alive with rebels, and it appeared impossible for this gallant regiment to escape destruction in their retreat over the three-quarters of a mile of open ground which intervened between them and our temporary works of defence.

In a few moments the engagement became general; our batteries opened a destructive fire on the exposed ranks of the rebels, mowing them down like grass. Their slaughter was frightful, but with unparalleled daring and recklessness they pushed impetuously forward.

They charged our works desperately, broke our lines of infantry, and captured a small fortification, in which a battery of the First Missouri was planted. All seemed lost, and a temporary panic seized our men, and the rebels once more marched into the streets of Corinth; but new batteries opened on them, and our men, under the direction of a few courageous officers, and stimulated by their example fought desperately, and the advance of the enemy was checked.

They wavered, and then fell back. Our lost battery was regained, and once more it hurled destruction into their ranks. The day was saved, and the enemy was in full retreat . . . ." ⊕

1. However inconclusive, the Battle of Corinth, Mississippi (October 3–4), showed that the Union's western armies could defend key railroad lines against the Confederates. The Union suffered 2,800 casualties at the battle, the Confederates 5,986.

THE BATTLE AT PERRYVILLE, KY.
THE ENEMY IS EVERYWHERE REPULSED.

OCTOBER 12

GEN. BUELL'S REPORT. PERRYVILLE, KY., VIA BARDSTOWN, OCT. 10

To Maj.-Gen. Halleck, General-in-Chief:

I have already advised you of the movements of the army under my command from Louisville.¹ More or less skirmishing has occurred daily with the enemy's cavalry. Since then it was supposed the enemy would give battle at Bardstown. My troops reached that point on the 4th inst., driving out the enemy's rear guard of cavalry and artillery. The main body retired toward Springfield. whither the pursuit was continued.

The centre corps, under [Major] Gen. [Charles] GILBERT, moved on the direct road from Springfield to Perryville, and arrived on the 7th instant within two miles of the town, where the enemy was found to be in force.

The left column, under [Major] Gen. [Alexander] MCCOOK,² came upon the Nashville road about 1 o'clock yesterday, the 8th instant. It was ordered into position to attack, and a strong reconnaissance directed.

At 4 o'clock I received a request from Gen. MCCOOK for reinforcements, and learned that the left had been severely engaged for several hours, and that the right and left of that corps were being turned and severely pressed. Reinforcements were immediately sent forward from the centre.

Orders were also sent to the right column, under [Major] Gen. [Thomas] CRITTENDEN, which was advancing by the Lebanon road, to push forward and attack the enemy's left, but it was impossible for it to get in position in time to procure any decisive result.

The action continued until dark. Some fighting also occurred on the centre. The enemy were everywhere repulsed, but not without some momentary advantage on the left.

The several corps were put in position

THE OHIO ELECTION.
DEFEAT OF VALLANDIGHAM!

OCTOBER 15

CINCINNATI, TUESDAY, OCT. 14 — MIDNIGHT.
The election passed off very quietly. The Democrats have elected the entire county ticket. PENDLETON, Dem., in the First District, and the present member, is reelected.

In the Second District, LONG, Dem., probably beats GURLEY, Rep.

Returns from the other counties come in slowly. VALLANDIGHAM, in the Third District, is probably beaten.

THE ELECTIONS YESTERDAY; Overwhelming Triumph of the Union Ticket in Pennsylvania.

PHILADELPHIA, TUESDAY, OCT. 14.
The following is a special to the Press:

HARRISBURGH, TUESDAY, OCT. 14.
Glorious news from all parts of the State. BLAIR, BAILEY and MCPHERSON are elected by heavy majorities, Gen. MCCALL is shelved. It is thought here we will carry the State by 50,000. THAD. STEVENS goes back to Congress.

WHY THE ARMY WAITS.

OCTOBER 20

It was about this time last year that the public were comforted by the story that Gen. MCCLELLAN's army was waiting for the leaves to fall, so that our men might be able to see the enemy upon whom they were to bring to bear their musketry, artillery and bayonets. The story was a capital one, and relieved the popular impatience until such time as the leaves fell, which, in turn, was followed by that period of moral and material mud, in which the nation and the army stuck so long. We have not heard anything of the Virginia leaves falling this year yet as an excuse for delay; but a Washington telegram the other day solemnly announced that our army was waiting for shoes before it attempted to advance. That yarn is not near as good as the one of last year; for last year's left the time indefinite, inasmuch as it depended upon a slow natural phenomenon: but we suppose it car be demonstrated that, Lynn and Boston could shoe all MCCLELLAN's troops in three or four days, at the end of which time a bran new excuse will have to be invented. While the army, however, is waiting for new brogans, we suggest that Government exam-

during the night, and moved to the attack at 6 o'clock this morning. Some skirmishing occurred with the enemy's rear guard. The main body had fallen back in the direction of Harrodsburgh.

I have no accurate report of our loss yet. It is probably pretty heavy, including valuable officers.[3]

Gens. [James Streshly] JACKSON and [William Rufus] TERRILL, I regret to say, are among the killed.

D.C. BUELL, MAJOR-GENERAL COMMANDING.
⊛

1. This battle proved the apogee of General Braxton Bragg's invasion of Kentucky (August–September 1862). He made a fatal error by not attacking Union forces quickly, preferring to head into Bluegrass country, where he believed he could attract additional recruits.
2. A member of the astonishing military family known as the "Fighting McCooks."
3. Union losses in the Battle of Perryville were 845 Union soldiers killed and 2,851 wounded; Confederate losses were 510 killed and 2,635 wounded.

PATRIOTIC WORK FOR WOMEN.

OCTOBER 12

The women of the United States have done nobly since the war opened, in working for the soldiers. They began by making havelocks,[1] scraping lint, putting up delicacies and comforts for the sick and the well: they have volunteered for nurses, and for hospital service, and in every way conceivable they have served those who were suffering for their country. This work is still actively kept up all over the land; and to each appeal of the army medical authorities, or the Sanitary Commission[2] for aid of any kind, a prompt response has always been made. Cold weather is now coming on in Virginia as well as here; and the Sanitary Commission makes a request that the energies of the patriotic ladies of the land be now turned to the knitting of socks and the making of underclothes for the soldiers. Of lint there is enormous quantities on hand, and havelocks have long been discarded. Warm socks, warm undershirts, and warm drawers, are the things that are now wanted. Let every fine lady, young and old, let every mother who has a son, every sister who has a brother, every maiden who has, or expects to have a beau in the army, let every woman in the country and in the city, who has days or hours or minutes to spare, and who loves her country, devote their spare time to this patriotic work.... ⊛

1. Named for a British officer, havelocks were white linen or cotton cap covers designed to cover soldiers' necks and protect them from the sun. Many disdained them, and used them for coffee strainers.
2. The U.S. Sanitary Commission promoted cleanliness, health, education, and nourishment in Union camps. Founded in 1861, the commission was directed by Frederick Law Olmsted, best known as the landscape architect of New York's Central Park.

ine, and see that each man of it is supplied with pantaloons; for the weather will soon be so cold, that if it is discovered they are without that article of clothing, it will be impossible for a single regiment to advance — except, of course, the gallant Seventy-ninth New-York Highlanders, who go into battle without breeches. Let all these matters be attended to at once, and quickly; and then, let our army, with its new shoes, kick the rebels southward till they are beyond the furthest limits of the Confederacy. ⊛

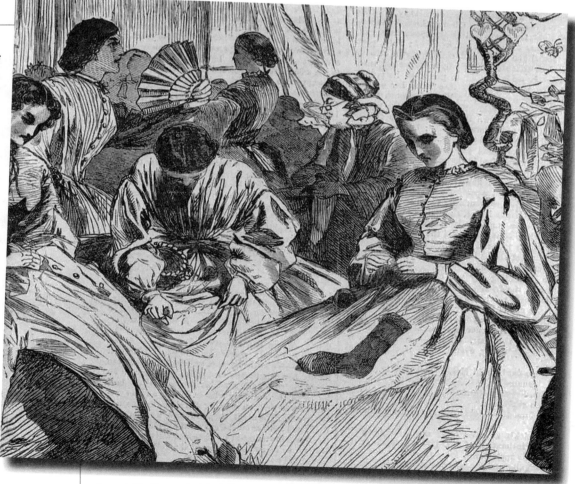

Harper's Weekly woodcut depicting women sewing clothes and darning socks for troops.

BRADY'S PHOTOGRAPHS.

PICTURES OF THE DEAD AT ANTIETAM.

OCTOBER 20

The living that throng Broadway care little perhaps for the Dead at Antietam, but we fancy they would jostle less carelessly down the great thoroughfare, saunter less at their ease, were a few dripping bodies, fresh from the field, laid along the pavement. There would be a gathering up of skirts and a careful picking of way; conversation would be less lively, and the general air of pedestrians more subdued. As it is, the dead of the battle-field come up to us very rarely, even in dreams. We see the list in the morning paper at breakfast, but dismiss its recollection with the coffee. There is a confused mass of names, but they are all strangers; we forget the horrible significance that dwells amid the jumble of type. The roll we read is being called over in Eternity, and pale, trembling lips are answering to it. Shadowy fingers point from the page to a field where even imagination is loath to follow. Each of these little names that the printer struck off so lightly last night, whistling over his work, and that we speak with a clip of the tongue, represents a bleeding, mangled corpse. It is a thunderbolt that will crash into some brain —a dull, dead, remorseless weight that will full upon some heart, straining it to breaking. There is nothing very terrible to us, however, in the list, though our sensations might be different if the newspaper carrier left the names on the battle-field and the bodies at our doors instead.

We recognize the battle-field as a reality, but it stands as a remote one. It is like a funeral next door. The crape on the bell-pull tells there is death in the house, and in the close carriage that rolls away with muffled wheels you know there rides a woman to whom the world is very dark now. But you only see the mourners in the last of the long line of carriages — they ride very jollily and at their case, smoking cigars in a furtive and discursive manner, perhaps, and, were it not for the black gloves they wear, which the deceased was wise and liberal enough to furnish, it might be a wedding for all the world would know. It attracts your attention, but does not enlist your sympathy. But it is very different when the hearse stops at your own door, and the corpse is carried out over your own threshold — you know whether it is a wedding or a funeral then, without looking at the color of gloves worn. Those who lose friends in battle know what battle-fields are, and our Marylanders, with their door-yards strewed with the dead and dying, and their houses turned into hospitals for the wounded, know what battle-fields are.

Mr. BRADY has done something to bring home to us the terrible reality and earnestness of war. If he has not brought bodies and laid them in our dooryards and along the streets, he has done something very like it. At the door of his gallery hangs a little placard, "The Dead of Antietam." Crowds of people are constantly going up the stairs; follow them, and you find them bending over photographic views of that fearful battle-field, taken immediately after the action. Of all objects of horror one would think the battle-field should stand pre-eminent, that it should bear away the palm of repulsiveness. But, on the contrary, there is a terrible fascination about it that draws one near these pictures, and makes him loath to leave them. You will see hushed, reverend groups standing around these weird copies of carnage, bending down to look in the pale faces of the dead, chained by the strange spell that dwells in dead men's eyes. It seems somewhat singular that the same sun that looked down on the faces of the slain, blistering them, blotting out from the bodies all semblance to humanity, and hastening corruption, should have thus caught their features upon canvas, and given them perpetuity for ever. But so it is.... ✸

Top and Above: Photographs taken of Confederate dead from the Louisiana regiment at Antietam attributed to Mathew Brady.

SEYMOURISM AS CONSERVATISM.

OCTOBER 21

The Seymourites of this State love to style themselves Conservatives. They are somewhat chary of the old appellation of Democrats. Seeing that the leading portion of the old party of that name are now in armed rebellion, and that its best portion are now staunch supporters of the Government in distinction from themselves, and mindful too of the prejudices of their old foes, and present allies, the Know-Nothings, they rather shun a designation so unpleasantly suggestive, and take to one of a little more attractive east. They fancy that they gain a point in adopting a name usually connected with respectability.

But what do these politicians mean by it? Does it involve any idea appropriate to the period? Every man, of course, knows what conservatism implies in the "piping times of peace." We can all understand, and in some sort admire too, the disposition to walk in the good old ways, and to cultivate the virtues of contentment, mod-eration, and prudence. In ordinary times, the conservative policy is simply the policy of keeping things quiet, and maintaining the status quo. But we are not living in ordinary times. We are in the midst of the most dreadful civil war this globe has ever known. Death is now the only quiet, and rivers of blood the only status quo. Is it the conservation of these things the Seymourites mean? We suppose not. They are said to have a particular aversion to all such sights and experiences.

Well, then, is it the conservation of the Constitution and the Union they are after? It is precisely this which Gen. WADSWORTH seeks, and every man in the State who intends to vote for him. It is precisely this which President LINCOLN, and all his constitutional advisers, and all his Generals, are trying to accomplish. The sole object of the war is to save the Constitution and the Union. It was so declared in the beginning, and will be so followed to the end. In this sense, those who support the war are conservatives, and the only conservatives. The rebels who struggle to break up the Constitution and the Union, and they who give them aid and comfort, are the true and only destructives....

The difference between the Administration and its enemies lies here exactly. While the former holds everything subordinate to the salvation of the Constitution, which it has sworn to protect without condition, the latter holds everything subordinate to the security of Slavery, which they have never failed to serve without limit. While the former works for and looks for no end of the war, but in the complete restoration and vindication of Federal authority, the latter seeks and anticipates a peace short of that — a peace which shall be a compromise, and, by new concessions, reconcile Slavery to the present Government; or, that failing, a peace which shall be a surrender, and remit Slavery to a distinct and independent Government. In short, while the former would destroy Slavery, if need be, to save the Nation, the latter would destroy the nation, if need be, to save Slavery. So much for the conservatism of the Seymourites. ⊛

SEYMOURITE EXPEDIENTS

OCTOBER 31

THEIR SPIRIT AND EFFECT. — Denounce the Proclamation as a usurpation, and declare Slavery inviolable — and encourage the rebels.

Abuse the President, if he attempt to stimulate the Generals to a forward movement, as a civilian ignoramus and an impertinent intermeddler — and encourage the rebels.

Magnify the public debt, discredit the National currency, hold out the bugbear of foreign intervention, concoct false reports about the conclaves of Governors, threaten riots in the street, mutinies in the camp, violence upon Congress, and a deposition of the President — and encourage the rebels.

Restore the old party lines, regear the old party machinery, revive the old party catchwords, and spare no means to divide the North — and encourage the rebels.

Select candidates of notorious peace antecedents and proclivities, support them with speakers who heap curses upon the Abolitionists as the cause of the war, and who name occasions and contingencies for leaving the Confederacy to itself — and encourage the rebels. Vote against JAMES S. WADSWORTH, Col. MCLEOD MURPHY, ELLIOTT C. COWDIN, and the other nominees of their spirit, and for HORATIO SEYMOUR, FERNANDO WOOD, BENJAMIN WOOD, and the others of that stripe — and encourage the rebels. ⊛

CHAPTER 11

"A People Suffering Fearfully"

NOVEMBER 1862–JANUARY 1863

I n November 1862, voters throughout the Union at last had their official say — about the war, the Lincoln administration, and emancipation. Their verdict did not cheer the President or the Republican Party. Democrats made strong gains in the House and Senate in these bellwether off-year elections and won crucial statewide contests throughout the North. In New York, notwithstanding dire editorial warnings from The Times and other pro-Republican papers, a gubernatorial candidate vigorously opposed by The Times, Horatio Seymour, took the state house for the Democratic Party. The Times quickly concluded that a politically wounded Lincoln would have no option but to compromise and seek peace. Instead, the very morning after Election Day, the President boldly dismissed General McClellan and replaced him with Ambrose E. Burnside.

But things did not improve. In December, Burnside began an offensive against Robert E. Lee's Confederate army, hoping to get across the Rappahannock River at Fredericksburg, Virginia, before Lee could react. But the delivery of Union bridging equipment was delayed, and by the time the pontoons were in place, Lee had entrenched on the high ground behind the city. Burnside attacked anyway, and the result was an overwhelming catastrophe for Union forces, thousands of whom were all but massacred as they charged up Marye's Heights into the blazing guns of impregnable Confederate defenders. The defeat triggered a wave of second-guessing and Congressional investigations, and Times readers were invited to speculate whether Burnside was incompetent or had been ordered by ignorant superiors into an attack he opposed.

Lincoln's image emerges in high relief over the words of the Emancipation Proclamation.

For the Union, the news from the west was only marginally better. In Tennessee, Major General William S. Rosecrans advanced cautiously against the rebel army under Braxton Bragg along the banks of Stones River near Murfreesboro. Bragg, however, decided to preempt things by attacking first. In a battle that spanned the observation of the new year (December 31, 1862, to January 2, 1863), the two armies fought a bloody engagement that ended indecisively. As usual, details of the fighting in the west were "extremely meager and unsatisfactory," but afterward, Bragg retreated, making it officially a Union victory even though Rosecrans's army suffered some 13,000 casualties to Bragg's 10,000.

Things went from bad to worse for Lincoln's beleaguered government when senators from his own party attempted to force moderate Secretary of State William H. Seward out of the Cabinet. Senate Radicals considered Seward an obstacle to the vigorous prosecution of the war and emancipation. With characteristic political deftness, Lincoln outfoxed his challengers to keep his Cabinet intact. But as Secretary of the Navy Gideon Welles, a sad witness to the attempted coup d'état, observed at the close of the year: "It is not to be denied ... that the national ailment seems more chronic. The disease is deep-seated. Energetic measures are necessary, and I hope we may have them."

One hoped-for cure was at hand. After reminding Congress in his December annual message that "we cannot escape history," Lincoln and the nation braced for the most revolutionary change in American life since the Revolutionary War itself: the final Emancipation Proclamation, scheduled for presidential approval on New Year's Day, January 1, 1863. New York Times editor Henry J. Raymond wrote Lincoln in late

November to propose that the final Proclamation be crafted as a "Military order" so it would not "revolt the Border States," "make triumphant the opposition," and "destroy the Union." Lincoln promised the editor: "I shall consider it," then proceeded exactly as the editor had counseled.

On December 31, 1862, Raymond wired the White House to ask that the Proclamation be telegraphed to the Associated Press by day's end, so it might be published quickly without "robbing it of its New Year's character" (no papers would be published the day after the holiday). Lincoln did not comply. Still working to rewrite his momentous order, he did not issue his document until late in the day January 1, forcing exactly the kind of two-day news lag about which Raymond had warned.

On New Year's Day, white and black citizens gathered at rallies and in churches throughout the North to await definite word that Lincoln had signed the document as promised — some doubting until the last moment that he would actually do so. In Washington, Lincoln in fact waited until he could leave a White House New Year's Day reception, then delayed signing until the circulation returned to a right hand "numb" from hours of handshaking. Only then did he affix his name to the "engrossed" document. "If my name ever goes into history," he told the tiny knot of witnesses gathered in his office, "it will be for this act, and my whole heart is in it."

The New York Times agreed, heralding 1863 as a new "era in the history, not only of this war, but of this country and the world."

New York Governor Horatio Seymour.

1. Horatio Seymour (1810–1886), the antiwar, pro-Compromise Democratic candidate for governor of New York.

LET THE PRESIDENT STAND FIRM.

NOVEMBER 8

Nobody who knows the vaulting audacity of the man FERNANDO WOOD, can doubt, now that he is elected, that he will make good his promise to his liegemen, to "go to the President and tell him that without we have a change of measures, so help me God! we will make a change of men." The President may as well make up his mind at once to be soon bullied and brow-beaten in a style that he has never before seen or heard of; — that is to say, if he does not "put his foot down" at the first rampant word. Of course FER-NANDO does not intend to operate slope. He will choose unto himself seven other spirits as presumptuous as himself, and with them he will assume to speak in the name of the triumphant Democratic Party. Not entirely

without reason, either. Every reader of history understands that in revolutionary times. It is almost invariably the oldest and the most violent who lead; and really if the Democratic Party, as revived, is to have any leadership in Washington, we know of nobody so likely to succeed to it as FERNANDO WOOD. At all events, whatever the power behind him, this man will attempt to use against the President all the airs of authority and all the arts of intimidation, of which his long discipline in the democratic politics of this city — the most mephistophilian school extant — has made him the complete master.

With bald impertinence, if it he offered, of course the President will know how to deal. But FERNANDO has acquired some knowledge of the usages of society, and will probably take care to phrase himself in a manner that shall secure him from being shown the door. Notwithstanding the

coarseness of his manifesto here, he will, most likely, when it comes to the ease in hand, make a special effort to pitch his dictation in as respectful a key as possible. We trust, however, that the President will abide dictation from FERNANDO WOOD in no way. He should meet the very first approach to it peremptorily, with the same spirit as that with which his predecessor. Old ZACH-ARY TAYLOR, silenced a correspondent, and, in many respects, a counterpart of this same WOOD, ROBERT TOOMBS,[1] when engaged on a similar errand. Of course, it is fit for the President to receive suggestions, and even advice, from any intelligent citizen, whether in or out of public life. But he degrades himself and his high office, if he endures the first word of either behest or menace, from any quarter whatsoever.

Unquestionably, in consequence of the late elections, every influence, proper and

THE ELECTION

NOVEMBER 8

FROM THE ALBANY EVENING JOURNAL.

The returns received, although imperfect, indicate the election of the Democratic ticket by a few thousand majority. The result is none the less mortifying because it was not altogether unexpected. In the present terrible crisis of the country, New-York should occupy no equivocal position. That she now does, will embarrass the Government and give heart to its enemies....

The result is what we feared at the time, but which we hoped might be averted by hard work and general organization. Besides this fundamental error, other causes aided to effect this result. The Democratic orators and Press availed themselves of every salient point in the legislative, financial and military departments of the Government, to warp the judgment, prejudice the minds, and arouse the passions of the people. Every error of Congress, the unavoidable derangement of the currency, all the mishaps of the army, the oppression of conscription, the burdens of taxation, and the prolongation of the war, were all charged upon the Republican Party. Falsehood, perversion and misrepresentation were never more freely employed, and the public mind was never so ready to absorb whatever was persistently pressed upon it. Starting in the contest at a disadvantage voluntarily assumed, it was impossible — felt to be so at every stage of the campaign

— to regain ground then lost, or to counteract, by simple truth and unimpassioned argument, the effect of these persistent and unpatriotic perversions, and the blind passions they excited. We will not venture to predict the effects of the election of Mr. SEYMOUR upon the future. While we have looked upon its happening with apprehension, we have not permitted ourselves to believe that it would ultimate in unmitigated disaster. We have unwavering faith in the patriotism of the great body of the people; and, however disposed, no man in any responsible position would dare to initiate or suggest any measure designed to thwart the loyal purpose of the Administration to call into requisition the concentrated power of the Government to crush out the rebellion and to restore the Republic. The Democratic Party, by its recent success, is given an opportunity seldom vouchsafed to any political organization to demonstrate its loyalty, and to attach to itself the gratitude and confidence of the people. Whether the leaders of that party have the wisdom and patriotism to achieve such results, remains to be seen. We hope for the best, and shall rejoice if our expressed fears, and the apprehensions of those who labored to avert these successes, shall be proved unjust and unfounded. ✸

THE DEMOCRATS AND THE ELECTION.

NOVEMBER 9

Throughout the whole of the late political campaign we recognized the fact that the votes to be cast for Mr. SEYMOUR would come from two entirely opposite classes of voters; that every one who opposed the war and was in favor of peace, immediate and on any terms, would be found voting for him, and that many would also vote for him who were earnestly and honestly in favor of prosecuting the war vigorously till the rebellion was suppressed. We recognize this fact now. The Tribune declares that it found no supporter of SEYMOUR, who did not support him "as the Peace candidate." Our own experience is different. We found many who supported him claiming that he would push on the war heartily. They seemed to us under a very strange hallucination, and we warned them repeatedly that they were going in bad company, and were in danger of being cheated upon this very point, which seemed to us a vital one. They did not give heed to our warnings, and the election of Mr. SEYMOUR is the result.

The election has not done away with the fact of which we have spoken. It has rather brought Mr. SEYMOUR and his supporters face to face with it. It is still true that men have voted for him believing that his election would tend to help the rebels in successfully maintaining their position, and that others have voted for him believ-

improper will be brought to bear upon President LINCOLN to obtain his committal to some compromising policy. Let him see to it that he stands firm. The determination he has so often expressed to uphold the Federal authority in all its breadth must be kept to unflinchingly. Nothing is so demoralizing as vacillation. Of all forms of weakness, this is the most mischievous — the one most sure to invite disasters and contempt. Human nature looks with involuntary respect, and a certain fear, upon those who choose their course with clear and deliberate foresight, and pursue it, when chosen, with unswerving resolution; who form their decisions cautiously and considerately, but refuse to reconsider them in difficult conjunctures, or to abandon them before unforeseen obstacles. There is an instinctive feeling that such men have within them the qualities which command success. They

challenge confidence and support in advance. The President has been crossed in a way he hardly looked for — has experienced a defection that may well occasion anxiety; but there must be no irresolution that sways backward and forward with the fortunes of the day; no undervaluing for a moment of the great cause of the Constitution to which he has, committed himself; no misgiving lest right, if he sustains it faithfully, should, in the end, not triumph. The President has no alternative but to go straight on, consistently and persistently, to the end. It was long ago decided that the rebels, of their own motive, had cut short all forbearance and blocked up all accommodation. The whole guilt of this conflict rests with them; and not for an instant can the Government falter until its authority is vindicated, and the submission complete.

The legitimate influence of the late elec-

tions is directly the reverse of what the FERNANDO WOOD[2] type of politicians will endeavor to make it. Instead of encouraging conciliation, it urges intenser hostility. It is not the olive branch the people mean, but the more trenchant sword. The loyal States are more impatient this day than ever for swift, sweeping war — the summary extermination of the rebellion by terrific battle. If President LINCOLN will only see that this cry is answered, the great-souled people will stand by him more devotedly than ever; and the insolent pack which now threatens him will make haste to hide their heads. ✸

1. Robert A. Toombs (1810–1885), a Georgia senator who resigned to vie for the presidency of the Confederacy, and thereafter served in the Confederate army while serving simultaneously in its Congress.
2. Wood, former mayor of New York City, had won election to the 38th Congress in 1862 as an antiwar Democrat.

ing that his election would speed on the war to the overthrow of the rebellion; and both parties, now that the result which they hoped for is attained, are outspoken in their views of it. We know of one instance, and we doubt not there have been many, in which it has been openly declared by Mr. SEYMOUR's supporters since the election that they would now proceed and carry out their original programme of bringing the two sections together under the Montgomery Constitution, and then by Convention, or some other means, excluding New-England from the new nation; and in our opinion the call now made in some quarters for an immediate meeting of the new Congress, which cannot by law meet till a year from next December, unless convened by the President, points in this direction.

And therefore we warn the loyal portion of Mr. SEYMOUR's supporters, as we have warned them before, that there is danger in this direction. It cannot be denied that the result of the late elections has been to place in positions of power and influence some men whose sympathies are not with us, but with the rebels — men to whom the rebels look with hope for help, and whom they consider to bear the same relation to the body of loyal men at the North as "the five just men in Sodom" did to their besotted fellow-citizens. It remains to be seen whether these men shall be able to wield the power which has been placed in their hands for the overthrow of the nation before the people can interfere. The voice

of the people cannot be uttered again in a popular election for a year. We know well that if the efforts of these men to destroy the nation shall be made, and shall not be successful before that time comes round, there will be another political revolution which will throw them out of power with more speed than they have now been put in.

We shall do all in our power to prevent their success; and we call upon the loyal supporters of Mr. SEYMOUR to watch them and work against them, for the preservation of the country; assuring them that in such a work they will find themselves seconded and supported by the great body of the loyal men of the land. ✸

SUSPENSION OF THE DRAFT.

NOVEMBER 9

A dispatch from Adjutant-General HILLHOUSE still further postpones, and this time indefinitely, the long talked-of and much dreaded draft. The reason assigned is, the difficulty of procuring correct returns of the persons who have enlisted in all the counties, so as to apportion rightly among the counties the number to be drafted from each.

The practical operation of the effort of the Government to get soldiers into its service by draft, is far from satisfactory. There must be a glaring defect somewhere in the laws, and it is the duty of Congress at its next session to find where the trouble is and remedy it. In midsummer, the President of the United States deeming the Republic in imminent danger, ordered a draft of 300,000 men to its immediate support in the field. More than three months have passed, and yet not a man has been obtained from the great State of New-York under the President's order for a draft. Nor is it possible to tell when the first conscript will be had. If in this mode the Government is to be preserved when in great danger, then is its continued existence extremely precarious.

We cannot for a moment think that the authorities of New-York State have purposely obstructed the draft; though we must not shut out the fact that other States — Connecticut, Pennsylvania and Ohio, for instance — have long since complied with the ☞

requisition of the General Government, and enforced the conscription. We have subjected the Republicans and Unionists in New-York State, who were the earnest supporters of the Government, to all the injuries and losses politically of the draft, in the late canvass. We had thorough searching enrollments; ostentatious parade of the voluminous lists under the protection of soldiers to the place of sacred deposit; formal and protracted sessions of Commissioners and Surgeons, for the purpose of relieving from the draft all who were rightfully exempt. All this was in progress in the heat and excitement of the State canvass, and it was doubtless the means of much disaffection to the Government among the electors. And now, when all the harm possible has been done, and after the Government is defeated before the country, we are told that the draft cannot take place as soon as expected, and it is postponed till further orders.

All this delay and confusion must be attributed to the original, cardinal mistake, of allowing credits to counties for volunteers furnished previously to the draft. This rests on no sound principle. A volunteer goes to the war because he is willing and prepared, and chooses to go. He does not put himself in the hands of his county in order that it may trade on him, and make aught by his going or staying. Reject this mischievous mistake of attempting to equalize — the source of endless and fatal delay and confusion — and any draft ordered by Government could be filled in ten days. ✪

THE REMOVAL OF GEN. McCLELLAN

NOVEMBER 10

Gen. McCLELLAN has been removed from the command of the Army of the Potomac and Gen. BURNSIDE[1] appointed in his place. The immediate cause of this removal has been Gen. McCLELLAN's refusal to advance against the enemy, even under the most peremptory orders of the General-in-Chief [Halleck]. It will be seen, by a letter from Gen. HALLECK to the Secretary of War, which we publish in another column, that on the 1st of October Gen. MC-CLELLAN was urged by Gen. HALLECK to cross the Potomac and give battle to the enemy, — being at the same time reminded of the disadvantages of delaying until the Potomac should be swollen, and the roads impaired, by the autumnal rains. Finding that this produced no effect, Gen. MC-CLELLAN was "peremptorily ordered" by Gen. HALLECK, on the 6th of October, to "cross the Potomac and give battle to the enemy or drive him South." For three weeks this order was not obeyed, and the only excuse given for not obeying it, so far as appears, — the want of supplies, is shown by the letter of Gen. HALLECK to have been utterly without foundation. The disclosures of that letter, concerning Gen. MCCLELLAN's constant and reiterated complaints of lack of supplies, are very remarkable and deserve special attention.

We presume that this particular instance of disobedience of orders, though the immediate occasion, is not the whole cause of Gen. MCCLELLAN's removal. It is pretty generally understood that this is only the culmination of a systematic disregard of orders, of a steady and obstinate tardiness in the conduct of the campaign against the rebels, and of a consequent inefficiency in command, which would long ago have secured his dismissal under any Administration less timid than that which has now possession of power. The fifteen months during which he has had virtual control of the war have been utterly barren of results to the cause he has professed to serve. Few commanders in history have had such splendid opportunities, and fewer still have so ostentatiously thrown them away. With an army capable of the most heroic achievements, powerful in numbers, unrivaled in discipline and equipment, eager always for active and onward movement, he has accomplished absolutely nothing but successful retreats from inferior forces, and the defence of the Capital at Washington, which he should have left no foe capable of menacing. The rebel armies have grown up in his presence, and by his toleration. Through all his long career he has made but one attack and won but a single victory: and that became absolutely fruitless through his failure to follow it up.

We have no theory on which to explain this most extraordinary failure of Gen. MCCLELLAN as a commander, or the still

---

GOV. SEYMOUR ON THE ELECTION.

NOVEMBER 10

Gov. SEYMOUR made a speech at Utica on Thursday night, to a large crowd that came to congratulate him on the result of the election. We find no report of his speech, and only a meagre reference to it in the Utica papers. We do not see that he threw much light on the specific manner in which his election is to restore the Union, though he was profuse in declarations that it would have that effect. "The success of the Democracy," he said, "would bring back the country to the position of years ago, when the Constitution was the supreme law, and the laws were impartially administered. Henceforth the laws were to be obeyed, and constitutional authority respected." We can understand how all this may happen in the North, — but not

how Mr. SEYMOUR's election is to restore that happy time to the Southern States. He says that "from this time henceforth it would seem there is a great Union party all through the South, who desire to cooperate with a party they know to be ready to welcome them back into the Union." This may be so — but as yet we don't see it.

Mr. SEYMOUR talks as if there had been a rebellion in the North, which the Democracy had succeeded in putting down. He says not one word about the Southern rebellion, nothing about aiding the Government to crush it out and thus restore the Union. He denies that the Democrats are disloyal, and says that they intend to sustain the Government "in all its Constitutional acts." He did not specify, however, what these are, so that we are left to a wide field of conjecture as to the exceptions which Gov. SEYMOUR would feel inclined to make. ✪

THE PRESIDENT'S MESSAGE.[1]

DECEMBER 2
WASHINGTON. DEC. 1

["...]The proposed emancipation would shorten the war, perpetuate peace, insure this increase of population, and proportionately the wealth of the country. With this we should pay all the emancipation would cost, together with our other debts, easier than we should pay our other debts without it. If we had allowed our old National debt to run at six per cent. per annum, simple interest, from the end of our Revolutionary struggle till to-day, without paying anything on either principal or interest, each man of us would owe less upon that debt now than each man owed upon it then; and this because our increase of men through the whole period has been greater than 6 per cent., and has run faster than the interest upon the debt. Thus, time alone re-

more extraordinary persistence of the President in committing the fortunes of the war to his hands. Gen. MCCLELLAN has shown too many of the qualities of an accomplished soldier to attribute his failure to simple incapacity. That he is absolutely disloyal to the Government we have never permitted ourselves to believe. Yet we think it quite probable that his heart has never been in the war, — that through it all he has had hopes of a compromise which should end it, and that he has feared the effect upon such a compromise of a stern and relentless prosecution of hostilities....

In this view of the case, Gen. MCCLELLAN has been encouraged by the political partisans who, at an early stage in the war, made him their prospective candidate for the Presidency, and came thus to have an interest in putting him in opposition to the Administration which he professed to serve. They defended his errors, and made themselves the special champions of his worst mistakes. They had unquestionable provocation and some excuse for much of this in the intemperate zeal with which he was assailed; but they betrayed him into an undue reliance on the support of a party, and a ruinous subserviency to their wishes and views. We know not how else to account for the steady and systematic disregard he has shown of the wishes and orders of the Government, and for his adherence to a deliberate and methodical inactivity, which has brought the cause of the Union to the very verge of ruin....

Gen. BURNSIDE has been three times offered the command of the Army of the Potomac. He declined it twice, partly from a strong feeling of personal affection for Gen. MCCLELLAN, and partly from thorough confidence in his military capacity, and his devotion to the Union cause. This confidence, we suspect, was somewhat shaken during and after the battle of Antietam; while the treatment he has since received for having remonstrated against the General's causeless suspension of the fight, has probably released him from the personal obligations on which he was previously inclined to lay such controlling stress. We presume, therefore, that he will now accept the command. He has shown thus far during the war great military ability, and a thorough, unqualified, unquestioning devotion to the cause he serves.... ✻

1. Ambrose E. Burnside (1824–1881).

Major General Ambrose E. Burnside, U.S.A.

lieves a debtor nation so long as its population increases faster than unpaid interest accumulates on its debt. This fact would be no excuse for delaying the payment of what is justly due; but it shows the great importance of time, in this connection, the great advantage of a policy by which we shall not have to pay until we number a hundred millions, what, by a different policy, we could have to pay now when the number is but thirty-one millions. In a word, it shows that a dollar will be much harder to pay for the year than will be a dollar for emancipation on the proposed plan. And then the latter will cost no blood, no precious life. It will be a saving of both....

I cannot make it better known than it already is, that I strongly favor colonization; and yet I wish to say, there is an objection urged against the colored persons remaining in the country, which is largely imaginary if not sometimes malicious. It is insisted that their presence would injure and displace white labor and white laborers. If there ever could be a proper time for mere arguments, that time surely is not now. In times like the present men should utter nothing for which they would not willingly be responsible through time and eternity.

Is it true, then, that colored people can displace any more white labor by being free than remaining slaves? If they stay in their old places they jostle no white laborers. If they leave their old places, they leave them open to white laborers. Logically there is neither more or less of it. Emancipation, even without deportation, would probably enhance the wages of white labor, and very surely would not reduce them. Thus the customary amount of labor would still have to be performed. The freed people would surely not do more than their old proportion of it, and very probably, for a time, would do less, leaving an increased part to white laborers, bringing their labor into greater demand, and, consequently, enhancing the wages of it. With deportation, even to a limited extent, enhancing wages to white labor, is mathematically certain. Labor is like any other commodity in the market; increase the demand for it, and you increase the price of it. Reduce the supply of black labor, by colonizing the black laborer out of the country, and by precisely so much you increase the demand for and the wages of white labor. But it is decided that the freed people will swarm forth, and cover the whole land. Are they not already in the land? Will liberation make them any more numerous? Equally distributed among the whites of the whole country, and there would be but one colored to seven whites. Could the one in anyway greatly disturb the seven? There are many communities now having more than one free colored person to seven whites, and this without any apparent con- ☞

sciousness of evil from it. The District of Columbia and the States of Maryland and Delaware are all in this condition. The District has more than one free colored to six whites. Yet, in its frequent petitions to Congress, I believe it has never presented the presence of free colored persons as one of its grievances. But why should Emancipation South send the freed people North? People of any color seldom run unless there be something to run from. Heretofore, colored people, to some extent, have fled North from bondage, and now, perhaps, from both — bondage and destitution; but if gradual Emancipation and deportation be adopted, they will have neither to flee from. Their old masters will give them wages, at least, until new laborers can be procured; and the freed men, in turn, will gladly give their labor for the wages till new homes can be found for them in congenial climes, and with people of their own blood and race....

I do not forget the gravity which should characterize a paper addressed to the Congress of the nation, by the Chief Magistrate of the nation, nor do I forget that some of you are my seniors, nor that many of you have more experience than I in the conduct of public affairs; yet I trust that in view of the great responsibility resting upon me, you will perceive no want of respect to yourselves in any undue earnestness I may seems to display. Is it doubted, then, that the plan I propose, if adopted, would shorten the war, and thus lessen its expenditure of money and of blood? It is doubted that it would restore the national authority and national prosperity, and perpetuate both indefinitely? Is it doubted that we here, Congress and Executive, can secure its adoption? Will not the good people respond to a united and earnest appeal from us? Can we, can they, by any other means, so certainly or so speedily assure these vital objects? We can succeed only by concert. It is not "Can any of us imagine better?" but "Can we all do better?" Object whatsoever is possible, still the question recurs, "Can we do better?" The dogmas of the quiet past are inadequate to the stormy present. The occasion is piled high with difficulty, and we must rise with the occasion. As our case is new, so we trust think anew, and act anew. We must disenthrall ourselves, and then we shall save our country.

Fellow Citizens — We cannot escape history. We, of this Congress, will be remembered in spite of ourselves.

No personal significance, or insignificance, can spare one or another of us.

The fiery trial through which we pass, will light us down in honor or dishonor to the latest generation.

We say that we are for the Union. The world will not forget that while we say this, we do know how to save the Union. The world knows we do know how to save it. We, even we here, hold the power and hear the responsibility.

In giving freedom to the slave, we assure freedom to the free, honorable alike in what we give and what we preserve.

We shall nobly save or meanly lose the last best hope of the earth.

Other means may succeed. This could fail.

The way is plain — peaceful, generous, just — a way which, if followed, the world even applaud and God must forever bless.["]

ABRAHAM LINCOLN.

The Message of President LINCOLN ... is a concise, clear and perspicuous document. It will of course be read by every one able to read in this country, and by every person in Europe and over the world, who takes an interest in the military and civil affairs of this Government and people....

What the President has to say of prospective emancipation, and of the colonization of the enfranchised slaves, will not command universal assent, and we deem it very doubtful whether Congress will enact the laws necessary to carry his recommendations into effect.[2] But no one can doubt that the President has made them from the most patriotic motives, and with a sincere desire to contribute all in his power to the permanent settlement of the most important question of the age. ✪

1. As was customary, The Times published the President's annual message to Congress — precursor of the State of the Union message — in full, and added editorial comments.

2. Lincoln laid out a complex, conservative plan for compensated emancipation in the loyal states and colonization of freed blacks. And yet he ended the message with ringing rhetoric, declaring, "The fiery trial through which we pass, will light us down, in honor or dishonor to the latest generation." For the full text, see Basler, The Collected Works of Abraham Lincoln, 5:518–537.

OUR FOREIGN RELATIONS.

THE CORRESPONDENCE BETWEEN THE STATE DEPARTMENT AND HON. C. F. ADAMS, OUR REPRESENTATIVE AT LONDON.

DECEMBER 8

The correspondence between the State Department and the American Representatives abroad has reached us in advance of its submission to Congress. The publication is of the highest importance. It tells in the most authentic form the story of our intercourse with foreign nations during the most difficult stage of the National career; how faithfully and ably the justice and progress of our cause have been presented to the Governments of Europe, and why the various difficulties necessarily incident to a contest such as ours have been prevented from becoming the provocations of an external war by the conciliatory weapons of diplomacy. It will be seen that the labors of Secretary SEWARD have been as heavy as they have been successful; and have embraced the discussion of a large number of questions, the chief of which is evidently the Relations of Europe to the War.

The efforts of the Secretary of State have been mainly directed to the neutralizing,

THE EFFICIENCY OF THE BLOCKADE

DECEMBER 10

Five hundred and forty-three vessels seized by the blockading squadrons, worth, with their cargoes, forty millions of dollars! Verily this is a splendid record, and yet it but faintly tells the story of the actual amount of service rendered to the good cause by this ceaseless, noiseless agency.

In casting the fortunes of the war, we are too apt to look exclusively to the battle-field. We measure progress, or the contrary, by bulletins. We must have sounding events, or nothing, we fancy, is doing. This is a mistake. The silent agencies of this war are quite as serviceable in bringing it to a favorable end as gunpowder. We believe, in fact, they are worth more. Of the two we could better afford to give up campaigning than to give up the blockade. The former is at best but of uncertain progress; what is gained to-day may be lost to-morrow, and it is possible that all may end in disasters. The

as far as practicable, the effect of European recognition of the Southern insurgents as belligerents, to prevent any measure looking to the recognition of their independence, or lending direct and moral aid to the cause of rebellion. To communicate constantly to our foreign agents the events of the war, glozed with such commentaries as should go to satisfy the Governments to which they were accredited that those events were rapidly conducing the struggle to a close, has been a material portion of the Secretary's task, and one into which he has thrown all his skill as a dialectician, and all the confidence of a sanguine temperament. We propose for the present to confine our extracts to the correspondence with Mr. CHARLES FRANCIS ADAMS, the Minister to England.

DEPARTMENT OF STATE, WASHINGTON, NOV. 10

SIR:

It is probable that the ground which the enemies of the Union in Europe will next assume, in prosecuting their war against it, will be an alleged defection of popular support of the Government at the elections recently held in the loyal States. The reports of the results of these elections in the forms adopted by the Press are calculated, though not designed, to give plausibility to this position. I observe that these reports classify the members of Congress chosen as Union and Democratic,

or Union and opposition. Such classifications, though unfortunate, do less harm here, where all the circumstances of the case are known, than abroad, where names are understood to mean what they express. Last year, when the war began, the Republicans, who were a plurality of the electors, gave up their party name, and joining with loyal Democrats, put in nomination candidates of either party under the designation of a Union party. The Democratic Party made but a spiritless resistance in the canvass. From whatever cause it has happened, political debates during the present year have resumed, in a considerable degree, their normal character, and while loyal Republicans have adhered to the new banner of the Union party, the Democratic Party has rallied end made a vigorous canvass with a view to the recovery of its former political ascendency. Loyal Democrats in considerable number retaining the name of Democracy from habit, and not because they oppose the Union, are classified by the other party as "opposition." It is not necessary for the information, of our representatives abroad that I should descend into any examination of the relative principles or policies of the two parties. It will suffice to say that while there may be men of doubtful political wisdom and virtue in each party, and while there may be differences of opinion between the two parties as to the measures best

calculated to preserve the Union and restore its authority, yet it is not to be inferred that either party or any considerable portion of the people of the loyal States, is disposed to accept disunion under any circumstances, or upon any terms. It is rather to be understood that the people have become so confident of the stability of the Union that partisan combinations are resuming their sway here, as they do in such cases in all tree countries. In this country, especially, it is a habit not only entirely consistent with the Constitution, but even essential to its stability, to regard the administration at any time existing as distinct and separable from the Government itself, and to canvass the proceedings of the one without the thought of disloyalty to the other. We might possibly have had quicker success in suppressing the insurrection if this habit could have rested a little longer in abeyance; but, on the other hand, we arc under obligations to save not only the integrity or unity of the country, but also its irrestimable and precious Constitution. No one can safely say that the resumption of the previous popular habit, does not tend to this last and most important consummation, if at the same time, as we confidently expect, the Union it sell shall be saved.

I am, Sir, your obedient servant,

WILLIAM H. SEWARD.

CHARLES FRANCIS ADAMS, &c., LONDON. ☻

---

latter knows no vicissitudes, and, if long enough maintained, can possibly have but one result — and that favorable to the belligerent that employs it. What ends a war, where both adversaries are alike courageous, is the exhaustion of one of them. It is of little consequence how that exhaustion is produced — whether by blows or by stilling — so that it be brought about. Three years of strict blockade, without aggressive fighting, we believe, would reduce the South to greater weakness than three years of such fighting, without a blockade. But we have it in our power to use both means; and through both we expect to subdue this rebellion in less time than three years. In estimating the progress of the war, we should, then, avoid the common error of paying regard only to deeds of arms.

Our fighting has not as yet evoked any such cry of distress as the blockade constantly occasions. The stern, relentless exclusion from all the markets of the world, comes home with sharp effect to every man, woman and child in the Confederacy. It has not only thus wrought great personal distress,

but has dragged the rebel Government itself into hopeless bankruptcy, by destroying the value of the Southern staples, upon which it was calculated that public credit could be secured abroad. The cotton-planters have not been able to sell their cotton, because it could not leave the country, and without such sale, they have had only the scantiest means of supporting themselves and their slaves. Those of them who were induced to pledge their cotton to the Government, as a basis for its credit, got nothing in return — the Government expressly refusing to give its notes or bonds for what was of no present value to it. The cotton pledged, it was found, did not add a dime's worth to the Government's credit across the water; and, of course, the Government could not afford to give any of its own credit, poor enough at best, in return. The cotton has proved alike worthless to the planter and to the Government. It was thought to be gold; under the blockade it has turned out to be rubbish.

Of all the countless delusions of the rebels, the most stupendous and the most fatal one was the taking it for granted that the

blockade would not be long permitted by Europe — that the necessities of the Old World for the raw material from which millions find work, would perforce override our national rights. It is now settled that our national rights will not be interfered with. Providence has secured this by interposing a greater necessity for the wheat of the North than could possibly exist for the cotton of the South. It is doubtful whether the European Powers, in any event, would have violated our blockade; but, as matters now stand, it is impossible. Peace with the North is the supreme consideration. The blockade will continue unmolested until we choose to end it — in other words, until rebellion yields. And its silent, ceaseless pressure must tell with constantly increasing effect upon the South — paralyzing trade, industry, currency, credit, every thing which in these modern times gives strength and resource to a people. The rebellion, under any circumstances, could not long endure it; least of all, when called to such desperate exertions such as our invading armies must henceforth compel. ☻

IMPORTANT FROM VIRGINIA.

THE GREAT BATTLE FOUGHT ON SATURDAY AT FREDERICKSBURGH.

DECEMBER 15

SATURDAY, DEC. 13
IN THE FIELD — 11 O'CLOCK, A.M.

The great battle, so long anticipated between the two contending armies, is now progressing.

The morning opened with a dense fog, which has not entirely disappeared.

Gen. REYNOLDS'[1] Corps, on the left, advanced at an early hour, and at 9:15 A.M., engaged the enemy's infantry. Seven minutes-afterward the rebels opened a heavy fire of artillery, which has continued so far without intermission.

Their artillery fire must be at random, as the fog obstructs all view of almost everything.

Our heavy guns are answering them rapidly.

At this writing, no results are known.

HEADQUARTERS OF THE ARMY
OF THE POTOMAC,
SATURDAY DEC. 13 — 11 P.M.

The fog began to disappear early in the forenoon, affording an unobstructed view of our own and the rebel positions....

The troops advanced to their work at ten minutes before 12 o'clock at a brisk run, the enemy's guns opening upon them a very rapid fire. When within musket range, at the base of the ridge, our troops were met by a terrible fire from the rebel infantry, who were posted behind a stone wall and some houses on the right of the line. This checked the advance of our men, and they fell back to a small ravine, but not out of musket range.

At this time another body of troops moved to their assistance in splendid style, notwithstanding large gaps were made in their ranks by the rebel artillery. When our troops arrived at the first line of the rebel defences, they "double quicked," and with "fixed bayonets" endeavored to dislodge the rebels from their hiding places. The concentrated fire of the rebel artillery and

infantry, which our men were forced to face, was too much for them, and the centre gave way in disorder, but afterwards they were rallied and brought back.

From that time the fire was spiritedly carried on, and never ceased until after dark....

Our troops sleep to-night where they fought to-day. The dead and wounded are being carried from the field.

...It is impossible to form an accurate idea of the loss on either side, as the firing is still going on, rendering it extremely difficult to remove the killed and wounded.

The city suffered terribly from the enemy's artillery, and is crowded with our troops, the front extending but a short distance beyond.

The balloon has been up all day.[2] During the morning but little could be seen, owing to the dense fog; but the afternoon was remarkably clear.

This evening the rebels have been shelling Fredericksburgh, endeavoring to drive our troops out of the place, but without success.[3] ✽

---

1. Major General John F. Reynolds (1820–1863), commanded the Union I Corps at Fredericksburg and was killed in action seven months later at Gettysburg.
2. Undoubtedly a reconnaissance balloon, of limited use on a battlefield shrouded in smoke and fog.
3. The Union suffered 12,653 killed, wounded, and missing at Fredericksburg; the Confederate total was 5,309.

A Kurz and Allison lithograph of the Battle of Fredericksburg.

THE FACTS CONCERNING FREDERICKSBURGH CALLED FOR.

DECEMBER 19

The country will be gratified to learn that the Congressional Committee on the Conduct of the War were yesterday "directed to inquire into the facts relative to the recent battle at Fredericksburgh, Virginia, and particularly as to what officer or officers are responsible for the assault which was made upon the enemy's works, and also for the delay which occurred in preparing to meet the enemy." We trust the committee will push this matter through with a promptitude equal to that with which they have performed other essential services to the country, and let the facts be known to the people at once, so that swift

THE RESIGNATION OF SECRETARY SEWARD.

A CAUCUS OF REPUBLICAN SENATORS REQUESTS HIS WITHDRAWAL

DECEMBER 21

The following is the statement of the Washington Star, regarding the resignation of Secretary SEWARD,[1] which was briefly referred to in our morning edition of yesterday:

"A majority of the Senate, in caucus, on the 17th inst., adopted a resolution which, as first prepared, declared a want of confidence on their part, in the Secretary of State, but which was modified so as to express to the President a unanimous recommendation of a partial reconstruction of the Cabinet. A committee was appointed to wait upon the President, and communicate their action. On being informed of the fact, the Secretary of State on the same day sent to the President his resignation, and requested that it might be immediately accepted. The Assistant Secretary of State sent in his resignation at the same time and in the same manner. The Secretary and Assistant Secretary still remain at their desks, awaiting the appointment of their successors." ✽

---

1. Following the Union defeat at Fredericksburg, a caucus of Republican senators pressed Lincoln to reshuffle his Cabinet. The President outmaneuvered the delegation by inviting them to confront Seward face-to-face; they quickly backed down and Lincoln refused his secretary of state's offer to quit, along with that of his treasury secretary, Salmon P. Chase, thus averting a major government crisis.

punishment may follow upon the crime. The feelings of the country are terribly strong upon this subject, and instead of decreasing, are daily becoming more intense. We assure those in authority that it will be dangerous to trifle with them.

...Congress must drag forth the guilty party, that he may receive the maledictions and the justice of the country. Fifteen thousand heroes killed and wounded in vain (ah! not in vain!) demand it. A hundred and fifty thousand brave souls, who for a long day breasted the iron storm of the rebel artillery, demand it. A country and a people suffering fearfully, will compel it. Neither the heroes dead nor the heroes living, nor the country in general, would begrudge the blood necessary to save the Union. But it must not be forever shed in vain. ⊛

Photomechanical print showing Confederate troops fighting at the Battle of Fredericksburg.

THE CABINET CRISIS.

A FULL EXPOSITION OF THE CAUSES WHICH LED TO IT.

WASHINGTON, SATURDAY, DEC. 20

The political crisis which has been impending so long, was precipitated by the military disaster of Saturday last. Not even the most reckless politicians affect to regard it with indifference, and the universal feeling is one of gloom and apprehension....

The occasion for the extraordinary demonstration on the part of the Senate, which has led to this political crisis, was the repulse of the Army of the Potomac, in its attempt upon the rebel lines at Fredericksburgh. It was evident that the country would be roused by that disaster to the highest pitch of indignation, and men who had political ends to serve were quick to appreciate the opportunity thus afforded of directing public sentiment against the objects of their resentment. Naturally enough Mr. SEWARD was the spe-

DECEMBER 22

cial victim first selected....

I do not, therefore, believe that the authorities at Washington can, in any just sense, be held responsible for the result of that specific action. But I am inclined to think that Gen. BURNSIDE has reason to complain that the Government did not fulfill the conditions which he had laid down as absolutely essential to the success of his movement upon Fredericksburgh, when he first proposed that movement the day after receiving his command, and to which the President and Gen. HALLECK gave their explicit assent. But my letter is already too long to permit me to state the facts on which I base this opinion. Yours,

&C., R[AYMOND]. ⊛

Major General William S. Rosencrans, U.S.A.

A TERRIBLE BATTLE.

ATTACK UPON THE REBELS AT MURFREESBORO BY GEN. ROSECRANS.

NEAR MURFREESBORO, WEDNESDAY, DEC. 31

The following has just been received by telegraph from Cincinnati, dated Murfreesboro, Jan. 1, 1863:

A terrible battle was fought yesterday. The latest from the field is up to noon. The rebel centre had been broken, and things looked favorable. The losses are reported to be enormous. STANLY, ROUSSEAU and PALMER are wounded, and the rebels CHEATHAM and RAINS are killed.[1]

JANUARY 3

Gen. ROSECRANS[2] occupies Murfreesboro.

(SIGNED,) J.T. BOYLE, BRIGADIER-GENERAL. ⊛

1. David S. Stanley (1828–1902); Lovell Harrison Rousseau (1818–1869); John McC. Palmer (1817–1900); Confederate General James E. Rains (1833–1863) was indeed killed at Murfreesboro (Stone's River), but Benjamin Franklin Cheatham (1820–1885) was not. Union casualties for the two-day engagement totaled 12,966; Confederate, 11,739.
2. Major General William S. Rosecrans (1819–1902)

EMANCIPATION. PRESIDENT LINCOLN'S PROCLAMATION.
THE NEGROES TO BE RECEIVED INTO THE ARMED SERVICE OF THE UNITED STATES.

WASHINGTON, THURSDAY, JAN. 1

Whereas, on the twenty-second day of September, in the year of our Lord one thousand eight hundred and sixty-two, a Proclamation was issued by the President of the United States containing among other things the following, to wit:

By the President of the United States of America — a Proclamation:

"That on the first day of January, in the year of our Lord, one thousand eight hundred and sixty-three, all persons held as slaves within any State or designated part of a State, the people whereof shall there be in rebellion against the United States, shall be then, thenceforth, and forever free; and the Executive Government of the United States, including the Military and Naval authority thereof will recognize and maintain the freedom of such persons, and will do no act or acts to repress such persons or any of them in any effort they may make for their actual freedom.

"That the Executive will, on the first day of January aforesaid, by Proclamation, designate the States and parts of States, if any, in which the people therein, respectively, shall then be in rebellion against the United States, and the fact that any State or the people thereof, shall on that day be in good faith, represented in the Congress of the United States by Members chosen thereto at elections wherein a majority of the qualified voters of such States shall have participated, shall in the absence of strong countervailing testimony, be deemed conclusive evidence that such State and the people thereof, are not then in rebellion against the United States."

Now, therefore, I, ABRAHAM LINCOLN, President of the United States, by virtue of the power in me vested, as Commander-in-Chief of the Army and Navy of the United States, in time of actual armed rebellion against the authority and Government of the United States, and as a fit and necessary war measure for suppressing said rebellion, do, on this first day of January, in the year of our Lord one thousand eight hundred and sixty-three, and in accordance with my purpose so to do, publicly proclaimed for the full period of one hundred days from the day of the first above-mentioned, order and designate as the States and parts of

JANUARY 3

States wherein the people thereof respectively, are this day in rebellion against the United States, the following, to wit:

ARKANSAS, TEXAS, LOUISIANA—except the Parishes of St. Bernard, Plaquemines, Jefferson, St. Johns, St. Charles, St. James, Ascension Assumption, Terrebonne, Lafourche, St. Mary, St. Martin, and Orleans, including the City of New-Orleans — MISSISSIPPI, ALABAMA FLORIDA, GEORGIA, SOUTH CAROLINA, NORTH CAROLINA and VIRGINIA — except the forty-eight counties designated as West Virginia, and also the counties of Berkley, Accomac, Northampton, Elizabeth City, York, Princess Ann and Norfolk, including the cities of Norfolk and Portsmouth, and which excepted parts, are for the present, left precisely as if this proclamation were not issued.

And, by virtue of the power, and for the purpose aforesaid, I do aver and declare that all persons held as slaves within said designated States and parts of States are, and henceforward, shall be FREE, and that the Executive Government of the United States, including the military and naval authorities thereof, will recognize and maintain the freedom of said persons.

And I hereby enjoin upon the people so declared to be free, to abstain from all violence unless in necessary self-defence, and I recommend to them that in all cases, when allowed, they labor faithfully for reasonable wages.

And I further declare and make known that such persons of suitable condition, will be received into the armed service of the United States, to garrison forts, positions, stations, and other places, and to man vessels of all sorts in said service.

And, upon this — sincerely believed to be an act of justice, warranted by the Constitution — upon military necessity — I invoke the considerate judgment of mankind and the gracious favor of Almighty God.

In witness whereof I have hereunto set my hand and caused the seal of the United States to be affixed.

Done at the City of Washington, this first day of January, in the year of Our Lord one thousand eight hundred and sixty-three, and of the Independence of the United States of America the eighty-seven.

ABRAHAM LINCOLN.
BY THE PRESIDENT,
WM.H. SEWARD,
SECRETARY OF
STATE. ⊛

A postwar lithograph shows President Abraham Lincoln holding the Emancipation Proclamation that he had just signed.

THE PRESIDENT'S PROCLAMATION

JANUARY 3

President LINCOLN's proclamation, which we publish this morning, marks an era in the history, not only of this war, but of this country and the world. It is not necessary to assume that it will set free instantly the enslaved blacks of the South, in order to ascribe to it the greatest and most permanent importance. Whatever may be its immediate results, it changes entirely the relations of the National Government to the institution of Slavery. Hitherto Slavery has been under the protection of the Government; henceforth it is under its ban. The power of the Army and Navy, hitherto employed in hunting and returning to bondage the fugitive from service, are to be employed in maintaining his freedom whenever and wherever he may choose to assert it. This change of attitude is itself a revolution.

President LINCOLN takes care, by great precision in his language, to define the basis on which this action rests. He issues the Proclamation "as a fit and necessary war measure for suppressing the rebellion." While he sincerely believes it to be an "act of justice warranted by the Constitution," he issues it "upon military necessity." In our judgment it is only upon that ground and for that purpose that he has any right to issue it at all. In his civil capacity as President, he has not the faintest shadow of authority to decree the emancipation of a single slave, either as an "act of justice" or for any other purpose whatever. As Commander-in-Chief of the army he has undoubtedly the right to deprive the rebels of the aid of their slaves — just as he has the right to take their horses, and to arrest all persons who may be giving them aid and comfort, — "as a war measure" and upon grounds of military necessity.

It may seem at first sight a matter of small importance in what capacity the act is done. But its validity may, in the end, depend upon that very point. Sooner or later his action in this matter will come up for review before the Supreme Court; and it is a matter of the utmost importance to the President, to the slaves, and to the country, that it should come in a form to be sustained. It must be a legal and a constitutional act, in form as well as in substance. We wish that for this reason the President had given it the form of a Military Order, — addressed to his subordinate Generals, enjoining upon them specific acts in the performance of their military duties, — instead of a Proclamation addressed to the world at large, and embodying declarations and averments instead of commands.

What effect the Proclamation will have remains to be seen. We do not think that it will at once set free any considerable number of slaves beyond the actual and effective jurisdiction of our armies. It will lead to no immediate insurrections, and involve no massacres, except such as the rebels in the blindness of their wrath may themselves set on foot. The slaves have no arms, are without organization, and in dread of the armed and watchful whites. Besides, they evince no disposition to fight for themselves so long as they see that we are fighting for them. They understand, beyond all question, that the tendency of this war is to give them freedom, and that the Union armies, whatever may be their motive, are actually and practically fighting for their liberty. If the war should suddenly end, — if they should see the fighting stop, and the Constitution which protects Slavery restored to full vigor in the Slave States, their disappointment would vent itself in the wrathful explosion of insurrection and violence. But so long as the war continues, we look for nothing of that kind. Whenever our armies reach their immediate vicinity, they will doubtless assert their freedom, and call upon us to "recognize and maintain" it. Until then, they will work for their masters and wait for deliverance.... ✦

An allegorical portrait of Abraham Lincoln created from the text of the Emancipation Proclamation.

THE BATTLE IN TENNESSEE

JANUARY 3

The last day of the old year went out in quiet all over the great theatre of military operations excepting in Middle Tennessee. But there, on that day, one of the greatest, and we judge it will prove to be the very greatest battle yet known in the Southwest, was fought. The only other Southwestern battle that equals it in the magnitude of the forces engaged, was the battle of Pittsburgh Landing — and that only on the second day, after the arrival of BUELL's[1] column. The army of Gen. ROSECRANS comprises the greater part of the magnificent force so long drilled and manoeuvred by Gen. BUELL in Kentucky and Tennessee, and which was transferred to Gen. ROSECRANS after BUELL had failed, in Northern Kentucky, to destroy with it the same rebel army which it has now again met near Murfreesboro. The opposing rebel force is, next to the army at Fredericksburgh, the largest rebel army in the South. It was recently reviewed by JEFF. DAVIS; and in the account of the review published in the Chattanooga Rebel, the columns of Polk, Bragg, Hardee, Breckinridge, Cheatham and others were mentioned as being present. The whole, we believe, was under the immediate command of Gen. BRAGG, who handled the same army during the campaign in Kentucky. For, although Gen. JOSEPH JOHNSTON is the Commander of the Department, it was said when he took command that he was only to be a sort of closet strategist or Generalissimo, and not to lead in the field. We judge it would be a fair estimate to put each of the armies at least eighty thousand men....

Concerning the engagement of that day, we have a dispatch from Gen. BOYLE,[2] which comes from Murfreesboro on New-Year's Day, asserting that the battle had been a terrible one, and that the losses were reported to be enormous, but that things looked favorable for us at noon. Another dispatch, dated on the afternoon of the battle, said that the enemy had been driven a mile, that his intrenchments were in our hands, and that we were then advancing our whole line. But the reports are as yet extremely meagre and unsatisfactory, and for what we know of the further progress of operations, we shall have to refer our readers to the telegraphic columns, where will be found everything received up to the moment of going to press. ❊

1. Don Carlos Buell (1818–1898) had been replaced as a commander by Rosecrans before the Battle of Murfreesboro.
2. Jeremiah T. Boyle (1818–1871), commander of Union forces in Kentucky.

ARRIVAL OF GENERAL BUTLER AND STAFF.
HIS VIEWS ON THE CONDUCT OF THE WAR

JANUARY 3

The arrival of Gen. BUTLER this evening, accompanied by Col. SHAEFER and other members of his Staff, caused a very decided sensation, and his rooms at the National Hotel were immediately besieged by numbers of people anxious to see and hear the man who succored Washington, captured Baltimore, and evangelized New-Orleans. He was visible to very few, however, as his duty called him early in the evening to wait on President LINCOLN at the White-House. Gen. BUTLER seems in excellent health, and is apparently all the better for the severe labors of his late command. He is entirely uninformed of the intentions of the Government as regards himself, but says that, on the arrival of Gen. BANKS at New-Orleans as his successor, he was convinced that he was not wanted there, and he thought he would come to Washington. It is needless to say that he is ready and anxious to serve his country, in whatever way his labors can be made most useful.

The intimations which have reached the public occasionally, in regard to the Anti-Slavery convictions of Gen. BUTLER, have done him no injustice. He is satisfied, he says, that in this war the whole property of the South is against the Government; that it is a revolt of the upper classes against the people; that so long as these upper classes retain their property, it will be used to aid the rebellion. It is a war of three hundred thousand property holders against the Union, or even less than this number, for they are not all fools. In depriving these class rebels of their property in slaves, they, of course, are weakened. The rich slaveholders must be extinguished as a class. He does not say "exterminated," but "extinguished." Their property must change owners. This done, they may go to Mexico, or to Cuba, or stay here, as they choose, for they will then be harmless. His expressions are equally strong in affirming the sincere loyalty of the poorer classes. Entertaining these opinions, he confesses to some chagrin on reading Gen. BANKS' disclaimer, in his proclamation, of any designs against Slavery; and had almost feared that in giving frank expression to his own views in his farewell address, he had gone counter to the policy of the rulers from whose counsels Gen. BANKS had so lately come.

Gen. BUTLER's interview with the President was prolonged till a late hour, and took place in the presence of Secretary SEWARD and Senator BROWNING, the former being sent for on the General's arrival.

THE TENNESSEE BATTLE.

The city is filled with rumors in regard to the late battle in Tennessee — some favorable and some adverse. The latest dispatches known to the President, at 8 o'clock, were an indication of the success of ROSECRANS and his gallant army.

WEST VIRGINIA A STATE.

The President signed the West Virginia bill yesterday morning. It has still to be ratified by a Convention of the new State before being put in force. In case it shall be thus ratified, it is not yet known what will be the effect upon the present State Government of Virginia, — whether the State officers and Senators will resign their positions, or whether the Governor and members of the Legislature resident outside the new State, only seven in number, will remove to Alexandria and continue their functions. ❊

EXECUTION OF THE INDIANS IN MINNESOTA.

THEIR CONFESSIONS OF GUILT — DESCRIPTIONS OF THE PARTING SCENES.

JANUARY 4

The St. Paul (Minn.) Press of Saturday last brings us details of the execution of the thirty-nine Indians whose death sentence was sanctioned by President LINCOLN....[1]

The prisoners received their sentence very coolly. At the close of the first paragraph they gave the usual grunt of approval; but as the second was being interpreted to them, they evidently discovered the drift of the matter, and their approval was less general and with but little unction. Several Indians smoked their pipes composedly during the reading; and we observed one in particular who, when the time of execution was designated, quietly knocked the ashes from his pipe and filled it afresh with his favorite kinnekinnick....[2]

Late on Thursday night, in company with Lieut.-Col. MARSHALL, the report of the Press proceeds, we visited the building occupied by the doomed Indians. They were quartered on the ground floor of the three-story stone building erected by the late Gen. LEECH.

They were all fastened to the floor by chains, two by two. Some were sitting up, smoking and conversing, while others were reclining, covered with blankets and apparently asleep. The three half-breeds and one or two others only, were dressed in citizens' clothes. The rest all wore the breech-clout, leggings and blankets, and not a few were adorned with paint. The majority of them are young men, though several are quite old and gray-headed, ranging perhaps towards seventy. One is quite a youth, not over sixteen. They all appeared cheerful and contented, and scarcely to reflect on the certain doom which awaited them....

At precisely 10 o'clock the condemned were marshaled in a procession, and headed by Capt. REDFIELD, marched out into the street, and directly across through files of soldiers to the scaffold, which had been erected in front.... They went eagerly and cheerfully, even crowding and jostling each other to be ahead, just like a lot of hungry boarders rushing to dinner in a hotel. The soldiers who were on guard in their quarters stacked arms and followed them, and they in turn were followed by the clergy, reporters &c.

As they commenced the ascent of the scaffold, the death-song was again started, and when they had all got up, the noise they made was truly hideous. It seemed as if pandemonium had broken loose. It had a wonderful effect in keeping up their courage. One voting fellow, who had been given a cigar by one of the reporters, just before marching from their quarters, was smoking it on the stand, puffing away very coolly during the intervals of the hideous "Hi-yi-yi," "Hi-yi-yi," and even after the cap was drawn over his face, he managed to get it up over his mouth and smoke. Another was smoking his pipe. The noose having been promptly adjusted over the necks of each, by Capt. LIBBY, all was ready for the fatal signal.

The scene at this juncture was one of awful interest. A painful and breathless suspense held the vast crowd which had assembled from all quarters to witness the execution.

Three slow, measured and distinct beats on the drum by Major Brown, who had been announced as signal officer, and the rope was cut by Mr. Duly, the scaffold fell, and thirty-seven lifeless bodies were left dangling between heaven and earth. ✹

1. A military commission had sentenced 303 Sioux to death after an August 1862 uprising in Minnesota. Although the state's white population overwhelmingly favored retribution, Lincoln insisted on reviewing the case records personally. He pardoned all but 39 of the Indians, who were executed in Mankato on December 26. The mass hangings, however tempered, created a sensation.
2. Traditional Indian tobacco mixture that included leaves and bark.

A lithograph depicting the public execution by hanging of the thirty-eight convicted Sioux warriors.

COLORED JUBILEE IN BROOKLYN.

JANUARY 4

The colored people of Brooklyn held a grand jubilee on Friday evening in the Bridge-street African Methodist Church, in honor of the President's Proclamation of freedom. A platform was erected in front of the pulpit for the use of the officers of the meeting, over which was extended a banner bearing the inscriptions: "Wilberforce." "Our Country and the Day we Celebrate," "Clarkson," "Emancipation in 1827, New-York State," "Emancipation in 1834, British West Indies." This banner also represented three slaves with broken fetters under the folds of the British flag. Immediately opposite the platform, at the other extremity of the church were hung pendant from the choir gallery, the inscriptions: "Inasmuch as ye do it unto the least of these little ones, ye do it unto me;"

"The Glory of a United People." At 8 o'clock the church was very comfortably filled, not a few of the audience being whites, among whom were numerous ladies. The meeting was called to order by the nomination of Rev. J.H. GLOSTER (colored) as President, and a number of Vice-Presidents and Secretaries. Rev. Mr. KING (colored) opened the proceedings with prayer, after which the audience joined in singing "Blow ye the trumpet, blow."

The President then addressed the meeting. We lived, he said, in the midst of great events. We now saw thirty millions of professedly free and eminently civilized people engaged in a most desolating war, out of which had grown the principle of liberty for all mankind. He then went on to show that Slavery was the bane of any nation that incorporated that institution in its governmental system, instancing Egypt in the time of Pharaoh, Rome under the Caesars, and following the course of

history down to our own times. Rome sacrificed liberty in the millions of her slaves and this caused her ruin. This would be the destiny of all Governments that followed her example. From the position of mistress of the world, Rome sank to nothingness, because of Slavery. In our country God had sanctified holy liberty — it was a spirit inborn in the first settlers in America, for the old Puritans combined the principles of liberty and religion in their earliest acts. He then alluded to the proclamation — rejoiced at it as a precious boon of freedom, but regretted that it did not extend to all who are held in Southern bondage. The only hope of rescue from the perils that environed us was by conforming to the moral of the proclamation. Providence was working in that proclamation for the benefit of the black man. The establishment of freedom throughout all our broad domain was, he thought, only a work of time.... ✸

OUR GREAT BATTLES: THEIR FEWNESS AND INDECISIVENESS.

JANUARY 17

It is extraordinary that, though it is now over a year since the National and the rebel forces under arms have each comprised many hundreds of thousands, the number of firstclass battles by which we mean battles wherein at least fifty thousand are engaged on each side have not exceeded four all told. These are Shiloh, Antietam, Fredericksburgh, and Murfreesboro. There was severe fighting on the Peninsula, during the memorable seven days; but at no time was there what could rightly be called a general engagement. At Gaines' Mills, the heaviest action of all, only 35,000 of our forces were engaged. No other example can be found in modern history of such great armies, with so few great collisions. Of minor fights there has been no lack. They number scores. It is of the great effective conflicts alone that the list is so strangely meagre.

But even our four large battles will not bear impartial examination. Not one of them is entitled to rank among our best-

fought battles. In not one of them was the best use made — or anything like it — of the material in hand .... We refer to the actual destruction suffered and inflicted. With scarcely an exception all the ablest and most telling battles in history have been the bloodiest. Our sensibilities shrink from this, but it is useless to hide it. It is one of the grim conditions of war. ✸

GEN. GRANT AND THE JEWS.

JANUARY 18

One of the deepest sensations of the war is that produced among the Israelites of this country, by the recent order of Gen. GRANT, excluding them, as a class, from his Military Department. The order, to be sure, was promptly set aside by the President, but the affront to the Israelites, conveyed by its issue, was not so easily effaced. It continues to rankle, and is leading to sharp controversies and bitter feuds in the ranks of the Faithful. It seems that a committee of Jews, in this City, took it upon themselves to thank the authorities at Washington for so promptly annulling the odious order of GRANT. Against the conduct of this committee the bulk of the Jews vehemently protest. They say they have no thanks for an act of simple and imperative justice — but grounds for deep and just complaint against the Government, that Gen. GRANT has not been dismissed from the service on account of his unrighteous act. The matter has been made to assume an importance that requires a mention of it in our columns, as constituting an exciting chapter in our current history.[1]

THE CHANGE OF COMMANDERS.

JANUARY 27

The Army of the Potomac, during the less than two years of its existence, has had a larger number of Generals at its head than has fallen to the lot of any great army of modern times during an equal period. From the days when it was organized by Gen. SCOTT, to the time when it was led to the fatal field of Manassas by Gen. MCDOWELL, — and after that during the period of its reorganization by Gen. MCCLELLAN and its campaign on the Peninsula, — subsequently during its operations under Gen. POPE, and its Maryland campaign after the reinstatement of MCCLELLAN — down to the appointment of Gen. BURNSIDE and the campaign of the Rappahannock, — it has been without a leader capable of handling it so as to produce by it those victorious results which the nation deemed it capable of achieving.

Its last commander, Gen. BURNSIDE, who now in turn gives place to a General from whom, the country hopes much, held his position for just eleven weeks and three days. He assumed the command at a time when the whole country was thoroughly tired out by the successive and interminable delays of Gen. McCLELLAN. He had a reputation for activity, courage, skill, hearty devotion to the cause, and honest greatness, excelled by no man in the army. Above all, he had the prestige of success.... And, notwithstanding the failure at Fredericksburgh, and the want of success in his projected movement last week,[1] he leaves his command without having lost the esteem and admiration of the country.... Unfortunately, there were matters and men working against him in the circle of his own Generals, in the condition and circumstances of his army, and in the events of fortune; and, feeling himself powerless against these, Gen. BURNSIDE has laid down his command.

His successor, Gen. HOOKER, brings with him an excellent reputation. He, too, has been tried in the field, and in high command; and, taking his career from the beginning, he has perhaps been the most uniformly successful of all our officers in his work. He will have a better support from his subordinate Generals than fell to the lot of his predecessor, and with the mass of the soldiers he will be equally popular. While he remains in command, we shall do all that lies in our power to sustain him, for the sake of the great cause for which he leads our army. Of his party predilections we know and care nothing. But he is entitled to public confidence, and it is all-important to the army and the country that he should have it. ◉

1. A horrendous "mud march" through boggy roads near Fredericksburg.

As to the odious principle of Gen. GRANT's order, there can be no doubt whatever. To condemn any religious body, as a class, and by wholesale, is contrary to common sense and common justice — contrary to Republicanism and Christianity. Gen. GRANT may have been harassed by hangers-on of his army, who were swindlers and extortionists. It was desirable that he should be rid of such. But will he say that all the swindlers that beset him are Jews? We are of opinion that there are degrees of rascality developed by the war that might put the most accomplished Shylocks to the blush. We have native talent that can literally "beat the Jews." Gen. GRANT's order has the demerit of stigmatizing a class, without signalising the criminals. All swindlers are not Jews. All Jews are not swindlers ... and it is a humiliating reflection that after the progress of liberal ideas even in the most despotic countries has restored the Jews to civil and social rights, as members of a common humanity, it remained for the freest Government on earth to witness a momentary revival of the spirit of the medieval ages....

But, rejecting all such considerations, we rely on the general principles of republican right and justice for the utter reprobation of GRANT's order. Men cannot be condemned and punished as a class, without gross violence to our free institutions. The immediate and peremptory abrogation of GRANT's order by the President saved the Government from a blot, and redeemed us from the disgrace of a military assault upon a people whose equal rights and immunities are as sacred under the Constitution as those of any other sect, class or race. ◉

1. Grant's "General Order No. 11," issued December 17, barred "Jews, as a class" from Grant's military department for allegedly "violating every regulation of trade." After receiving letters and delegations protesting the ill-advised order, Lincoln ordered it revoked, avoiding a public rebuke that would embarrass one of his most promising generals.

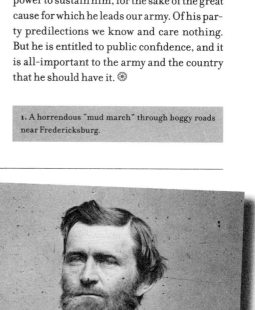

Major General Ulysses S. Grant, U.S.A.

CHAPTER 12

"If We Win a Battle"

FEBRUARY–APRIL 1863

The second winter of the Civil War heated up considerably in the early months of 1863, as Americans extended their ongoing debate over the long-term consequences of emancipation. Supporters giddily compared Lincoln's edict to a second declaration of independence — even a second Sermon on the Mount. But unanswered questions troubled many others. Would African-Americans really now serve in uniform? Could they be trusted to carry weapons? Would their recruitment lead to social equality? (The Times trusted not.)

Certainly the basic rights of the common soldier — white as well as black — were very much in the news as spring approached. Legislatures at the time debated the novel idea of granting men in uniform the right to vote — even from distant campsites — a basic right Americans only later came to take for granted. The initiative meant much to the future of both the Union war effort and the Lincoln administration. Though some wondered if the soldier vote might not hurt the administration's cause, the President was convinced that the soldier vote would tilt the final counts in the Republicans' favor in the following year's national elections, in which he had every intention of seeking a second White House term.

Men on the march needed nutrition, as well as the franchise, and The Times openly worried that hardtack was too often being substituted for bread in military diets, threatening the health of the troops on campaign. Ironically, during this same period, on March 2, Richmond's starving women erupted in a so-called Bread Riot — which President Jefferson Davis himself put down first by turning out his pockets, and then with a speech ordering the mob

Watch, waiting for midnight, January 1, 1863, when the Emancipation Proclamation was scheduled to take effect.

to disperse at risk of being shot. The home front was changing drastically — with more and more women, North as well as South, now often bearing sole responsibility for their own destinies as well as those of their families, and ready to demand jobs and food from governments they believed were indifferent to their deprivation.

The political alignment of the states was shifting, too. Notwithstanding shaky constitutional arguments — after all, how could *part* of a state secede from a state, if an entire state could not secede from the Federal Union? — West Virginia statehood became a reality, complete with a constitution that called for gradual emancipation. The Lincoln administration would now have two new Republican senators to swell its shaky majority in Washington and a reliable political toehold south of the Mason-Dixon Line. Further south, in Louisiana, The Times noted a groundswell for abolition as additional territory came under Union control. Though most Northern-occupied parishes of the state had been excluded from the requirements of the Emancipation Proclamation precisely because they no longer fell under Confederate jurisdiction, Lincoln was now encouraging local leaders to move on their own to widen the promise of freedom.

As spring approached, Union forces began major actions — trying again, for example, to move land and naval forces against the well-protected citadel on the Mississippi at Vicksburg. Just before midnight on April 16, Admiral David Dixon Porter successfully ran a squadron of ships past Confederate batteries firing from the bluffs, a public relations triumph for the North that also set the stage for subsequent attacks on the city.

It remained quiet for these three months in the Eastern Theater — but observers sensed a spring awakening and predicted a major battle in Virginia. Lincoln chose a new commander for the Army of the Potomac, Joseph Hooker, known in the press as "Fighting Joe." Eager to encourage him, Lincoln even allowed Hooker to bypass customary military protocol and report directly to him. But the President seemed concerned about the general's boastfulness, and on January 26 wrote him an extraordinary letter. "I believe you to be a brave and skilful soldier, which, of course, I like," said Lincoln. But he was suspicious of Hooker's boastfulness, and had "heard, in such a way to believe it, of your recently saying that both the Army and the Government needed a Dictator. Of course it was not *for* this, but in spite of it, that I have given you the command. Only those generals who gain successes, can set up dictatorships. What I now ask of you is military success, and I will risk the dictatorship."

The letter remained private. Unaware of Lincoln's concerns, The Times remained certain not only that there would be a major battlefield test, but also a vindication of the President's public faith in his new commanding general. Not for the first time, these hopes for an easy, early triumph were destined to be dashed.

EMANCIPATION IN LOUISIANA.
THE EFFECT OF THE PRESIDENT'S PROCLAMATION.

FEBRUARY 2
FROM OUR OWN CORRESPONDENT.
DEPARTMENT OF THE GULF,
NEW-ORLEANS, MONDAY, JAN. 19

The first of January, 1863, is past, and the President's Proclamation, declaring Slavery abolished in the United States of America, has been given to the world; — it is an accomplished fact; it is history, and what is most, it is an irrevocable decree against human bondage ever again existing under the flag of the Union. It is astonishing to me, when I think of the vast consequences to follow to my own county and to the world, that a document so wonderful in its character could be issued without some attending miracle — some strange yet cheering natural phenomenon. So important, indeed, do I deem this proclamation of Mr. LINCOLN, that I consider it surpassed in the magnitude of its humanity only by the inspiration of the Sermon on the Mount, and it will, in my opinion, for all time be pointed at as an instrument the most wonderful in consequences and benign in influence that was ever given to the world by human agency. It was proper and right that the first enthusiastic and practical recognition of this proclamation should come from Louisiana. This State, swindled out of its allegiance to the Union against the wishes of its people, sacrificed by one of the most unprincipled sets of politicians that ever disgraced humanity, is the first to spring forward to greet the only remedy that will enable its oppressed people to once more take their place among the honored and prosperous sons of this great Government....

If anything can take place that will shame the Secessionists of the Free States into decency and patriotism, this resolution, and the circumstances under which it was heralded to the world, should do it.... ☻

Freed African-Americans enter Union lines at Newbern, North Carolina.

FRED. DOUGLASS ON THE PROCLAMATION.

HE PRONOUNCES IT A MIGHTY EVENT FOR THE COLORED RACE, THE NATION AND THE WORLD.

FEBRUARY 7

A large and respectable audience collected at Cooper Institute to hear FREDERICK DOUGLASS' views on the Proclamation.

Mr. DOUGLASS was introduced by Rev. H. H. GARNETT, and spoke substantially as follows: He had come to talk to them of the greatest event of the century — of our whole history. That event was the fact that since the first day of January there had not been a slave in any State recognized as in rebellion against the Government, and that any slave had now the right to defend himself against the slaveholder as against a common robber. [Applause.] Assuming that the Proclamation of the President would be made good, it was impossible to conceive of a greater overturning by any nation, than would be occasioned. He hailed the Proclamation with joy, notwithstanding all that could be said against it. Our Star Spangled Banner now has a meaning. It affords shelter to all nations and all colors. He stood here not only as a colored man, a colored American, but as a colored citizen. The Attorney-General had announced that color is no disqualification of citizenship in the United States. [Applause.] We are all liberated — the black and the white — and the army is authorized to strike with all its might, even if it does hurt somebody. [Laughter and applause.] Mr. LINCOLN has dared to apply the old truth of human liberty to this time. He has dared to declare the truth of the Declaration of Independence. If adhered to, that truth will carry us through the struggle through which we are passing. [Applause.] As one who had been a slave, and bore upon his person the marks of Slavery, it was but natural that he should look at the Proclamation as a colored man.... Though wrung out by the stern dictates of military necessity, it was in reality a moral necessity. We had been fighting the rebels with our soft white hands, and kept back our iron black hands [Applause]....

The black man could not be expected to go into the army as he had heretofore gone through the community — but, he must fight under the same protection and guarantees as the white soldier. He wanted the Government, to compel the same guarantees for the safety of black prisoners as well as of white prisoners [applause.] He was with the Government so soon as the recruiting office was thrown open, and the right hand of fellowship extended. [Applause.] Stop calling us niggers, and call us soldiers, and, in such a war, we will fight with a will. [Applause.] The most delicate lady can be near a negro when he is a servant. The only objection to him is when he appears as a gentleman. [Laughter.] The negro fought the British, under [Andrew] JACKSON. Why not fight the rebels under HOOKER? [Applause.] He believed the negro would yet have his opportunity to be a soldier. He had faith in the virtue of the North, but none in the villainy of the South. [Laughter and applause.] JEFF. DAVIS would set us the example of employing negro soldiers.

For himself, he had felt whiter, and had combed his hair more easily since the 1st of January. [Laughter.] Mr. DOUGLASS detailed with much humor the proceedings of the Boston meeting, and the reception of the President's Proclamation. Concluding with a hopeful prognostication for the future. The proceedings closed with the singing of the new John Brown song. ✸

WHAT COMPROMISE WITH THE REBELS MEANS.

FEBRUARY 9

The agents of secession who are now laboring at the North for compromise and peace, profess to be working in the interest of the Union, and with what FERNANDO WOOD would call "a single eye" to its restoration. But we would once more warn those whom they are bout to supply with their "political information," that compromise or peace upon any other terms than the naked, unconditional submission of the South, would be just as fatal to the Union as if we acknowledged the independence of the Confederacy to-morrow. This is a fact which some simple people, bewildered by he bombastic effusions of "the Conservatives" about liberty and the Constitution, are beginning to forget, but if we all forget it, we do so at the risk of destruction as utter and complete as ever overtook any nation.... ✸

PEACE MOVEMENTS.

FEBRUARY 12

The Copperheads are fast getting into line. They of Indiana briskly follow those of New-Jersey and Illinois. In fact, they take the track with a little more fierceness. The others have as yet only asked for an armistice; these demand one, and threaten independent State action unless the Government complies. If the present Congress will not authorize a Convention of all the States, they present as an alternative that Indiana, by her delegates, will meet as many of the States, both Confederate and National, as will send delegates to Nashville, and proceed to make peace on their own responsibility.

We hail these movements with satisfaction, because they show unmistakably the essentially disloyal character of all opposition to the war. The strength of faction hitherto has been in its avoidance of all definite action and plans. It has devoted itself to general and indiscriminate fault-finding about the conduct of the war, rather than labored directly for its cessation. It has found its account in taking advantage of the popular feeling — unhappily too well founded — that the war has not been carried on with proper vigor and sound judgment. By continued clamor and intrigue, and the careful concealment of their real designs, they succeeded in securing anti-administration majorities in many of the Legislatures, which were elected in the Fall. Safe for the present, from the reach of the people they have betrayed, they lose no time, after the Legislatures have met, to bring out and push forward their reserved schemes. This has been done already in the three Legislatures which are deemed most manageable. The measures submitted vary just enough to avoid the appearance of their having been prepared in concert, while they all tend exactly to the same end — a suspension of hostilities and a peace with the rebels on any terms. This object is now made so patent that nobody can longer mistake it.

The revolutionary shape given by the Indiana resolutions is simply a little fuller development of the work in hand. It is a necessity; for it is certain that there can be no peace at present without a revolution. The Executive at Washington has neither the disposition nor the power to make peace. It is sworn to maintain the Constitution and the laws, and can have no other dealings with the rebels than to fight them, or receive their unconditional submission. Congress has as little discretion. It can make laws under the Constitution, but aside from that it is powerless, so far as all definitive action is concerned. It can, indeed, if two-thirds of both Houses agree, propose amendments to the Constitution. But two-thirds will not agree to do any such thing; and even if they would, three-fourths of the States can never be brought to ratify its proposed amendments, which, under the Constitution, would be necessary to give them any force. Even were a convention called, the latter necessity would in like manner exist. Under the Constitution, there is no possible method of changing a syllable of it without the express acceptance and confirmation of three-fourths of the States. This concurrence cannot be gained. Even if the "Confederate States" would put their proclaimed independence in abeyance long enough to go into such a Convention, they would consent to no arrangement that did not confirm that independence; and it is just as certain that the Northern States generally would not peaceably grant such independence, or anything approaching it. As from the beginning of the rebellion, so now — war alone can settle it.

These plotters, if they would go on at all, have no alternative but to override all constitutional barriers, and trust entirely to independent State action, which, of course, must be irregular and revolutionary. It is thus that the leaders in Indiana propose to put their State in direct relations with the rebellion. Could they, in conjunction with their fellow-workers in Illinois, carry their measures, they undoubtedly might subject the National Government to great embarrassment....

We are in no dread of these legislative movements. It, in fact, rather gives us satisfaction to see them. While they can never succeed, they are yet palpable proofs of the treacherous spirit and treasonable intent of the politicians who have been so busy in stimulating disaffection. The people need just such evidences that this disaffection was only meant to be preparative for revolution. Everybody, in fact, may now understand better than before that the only safety is in adhering faithfully to the war policy; and in laboring rather to incite the Administration to redoubled effort than to weaken its arm, or chill its spirit. The near affinity of Faction with Treason is made plainer than ever. ✹

THE USE OF NEGROES AS SOLDIERS.

FEBRUARY 16

Whether negroes shall or shall not be employed as soldiers, seems to us purely a question of expediency, and to be solved satisfactorily only by experiment. As to our right so to employ them, it seems absurd to question it for a moment. The most bigoted and inveterate stickler for the absolute divinity of Slavery in the southern States, would scarcely insist that, as a matter of right, either constitutional or moral, we could not employ negroes as soldiers in the army. Whether they are, or are not, by nature, by law, or by usage, the equals of the white man, makes not the slightest difference in this respect. Even those at the North who are so terribly shocked at the prospect of their being thus employed, confine their objections to grounds of expediency. They urge:

1. That the negroes will not fight. This, if true, is conclusive against their being used as soldiers. But we see no way of testing the question except by trying the experiment. It will take but a very short time and but very few battles to determine whether they have courage, steadiness, subjection to military discipline, and the other qualities essential to good soldiership or not. If they have, this objection will fall; if not, then beyond all question they will cease to be employed.

2. It is said that whites will not fight with them, — that the prejudice against them is so strong that our own citizens will not enlist, or will quit the service, if compelled to fight by their side, — and that we shall thus lose two white soldiers for every black one that we gain. If this is true, they ought ☞

A Union officer teaches African-American soldiers how to use their firearms.

not to be employed. The object of using them is to strengthen our military force; and if the project does not accomplish this, it is a failure. The question, moreover, is one of fact, not of theory. It matters nothing to say that it ought not to have this effect — that the prejudice is absurd and should not he consulted. The point is, not what men ought to do, but what they will do. We have to deal with human nature, with prejudice, with passion, with habits of thought and of feeling, as well as with reason and sober judgment and the moral sense. Possibly the Government may have made a mistake in its estimate of the effect of this measure on the public mind. The use of negroes as soldiers may have a worse effect on the army and on the people than they have supposed. But this is a matter of opinion, on which men have differed. Very prominent and influential persons, Governors of States, Senators, popular Editors and others have predicted the best results from such a measure, while others have anticipated the worst. The President has resolved to try the experiment. If it works well, the country will be the gainer. If not, we have no doubt it will be abandoned. If the effect of using negroes as soldiers, upon the army and the country, proves to be depressing and demoralizing, so as to weaken rather than strengthen our military operations, they will cease to be employed. The President is a practical man, not at all disposed to sacrifice practical results to abstract theories.

3. It is said we shall get no negroes — or not enough to prove of any service. In the Free States very few will volunteer; and in the Slave States we can get but few, because the rebels will push them Southward as fast as we advance upon them. This may prove to be so. We confess we share, with many others, the opinion that it will. But we may as well wait patiently the short time required

to settle the point. When we hear more definitely from Gov. SPRAGUE's black battalions and Gov. ANDREW's negro brigades,[1] we shall know more accurately what to think of the measure as one for the Free States; and when we hear further of the success of Gen. BANKS and Gen. SAXTON[2] in enlisting them at the South, we can form a better judgment of the movement there. If we get very few or even none, the worst that can be said will be that the project is a failure; and the demonstration that it is so will have dissipated another of the many delusions which dreamy people have cherished about this war.

4. The use of negroes will exasperate the South: and some of our Peace Democrats make that an objection to the measure. We presume it will; but so will any other scheme we may adopt which is warlike and effective in its character and results. If that consideration is to govern us, we must follow Mr. VALLANDIGHAM's advice and stop the war entirely.... We are not quite ready for that yet.

The very best thing that can be done under existing circumstances, in our judgment, is to possess our souls in patience while the experiment is tried. The problem will speedily solve itself — much more speedily than heated discussion or harsh criminations can solve it. If it proves a success, we should all be glad to adopt the policy. If it proves a failure, none will be more interested in dropping it than the Government. ⊛

1. References to two New England governors who favored black recruitment: William Sprague (1830–1915) of Rhode Island and John A. Andrew (1818–1867) of Massachusetts.
2. General Rufus Saxton (1824–1908) served as military governor of the Georgia–South Carolina coastal islands, and executed the War Department's first orders to recruit "colored" troops.

THE CONSTITUTION OF WESTERN VIRGINIA.

WHEELING, TUESDAY, FEB. 17

FEBRUARY 18

The amendment known as the "Willey Amendment," inserted by Congress in the new Constitution of the new State of Western Virginia, was unanimously ratified to-day by the Constitutional Convention.[1] It will be submitted to the people on the 26th of March. There is no doubt that it will be over-whelmingly ratified. The amend-

ment provides for gradual emancipation, commencing July 4, next. ⊛

1. Weary of the precedents involved in granting statehood to the western counties of Virginia, Lincoln insisted that their new constitution include gradual abolition. He would make his feeling known in a proclamation issued on April 20. West Virginia achieved statehood on June 20.

IMPORTANT FROM VICKSBURGH.

THE GUNBOAT INDIANOLA RUNS BY THE REBEL BATTERIES.

FEBRUARY 19
CHICAGO, WEDNESDAY, FEB. 18

A special dispatch from Memphis, dated the 17th inst., says:

"The new Monitor gunboat Indianola ran the blockade of Vicksburgh on Friday night. In spite of the rebel precautions, the Indianola obtained a full view of the rebel batteries, all of which vied with each other to sink her. She passed all the rebel batteries safely."

CORRESPONDENCE OF THE MISSOURI DEMOCRAT.
MOON LAKE, MISS., SATURDAY, FEB. 7

To-day I have had the pleasure of making a trip on the mosquito gunboat Forest Rose, Capt. BROWN, master, through the Yazoo

MUTINY OF NEWSBOYS.

FEBRUARY 21

The newsboys in the army are in a state of insubordination. They are evidently "demoralized." The telegraph advises us that they have refused to do duty, unless Gen. HOOKER rescinds the order restricting their numbers to one to each division. This is quite in keeping with the general course of things in the army, so far as a portion of its officers and men are concerned. We are not at all surprised that the newsboys should have come to the conclusion that they had as good a right to command the army as Gen. HOOKER. He ought to get in the habit of submitting his orders for their approval, before issuing them. We shall probably have a strike of the sutlers next, then of the persons employed in the Quartermaster's Department, and we should not be at all surprised to find the example finally infect the Generals of Divisions.

Gen. HOOKER merits the thanks of the country for bringing the sale of newspapers, and the conduct of army correspondence, within some systematic regulations. He is the first of our Generals who has made any serious attempt to remedy the gross abuses which have obtained in these Departments. We hope he will make the reform thorough and effective, and that when he has once laid down a rule, he will insist upon rigid observance of it. ⊛

Pass into Moon Lake, which at present is swollen to a size even beyond the Mississippi River. The expedition is an exploring one, under the direction of Gen. GORMAN[1] and Lieut.-Col. WILSON,[2] of Gen. GRANT's staff, who are endeavoring to find a navigable road into the Yazoo River.

We entered the pass about 10 o'clock this morning, passed through the channel which was made a few days ago in the levee, and after passing through a narrow and swift current for about a mile, we came out into Moon Lake. This lake is several miles long, and twenty feet deep in the shallowest place, It is at least half a mile in width. We entered the pass again after sailing through the lake, but were soon arrested in our progress by fallen trees which have been cut down on both sides of the narrow bayou, and in some cases making a complete lock....It may be slow work, yet I am satisfied that within ten days small boats may easily pass from the Mississippi River at the Delta to the Yazoo. There is no additional news from Vicksburgh. Our troops are threatened with being drowned out, and Gen. GRANT consequently may have to withdraw his forces temporarily....

Admiral Porter's fleet at the mouth of the Yazoo River.

SPECIAL DISPATCH TO THE CHICAGO TRIBUNE.
MEMPHIS, MONDAY, FEB. 16 — 10 P.M.

Advices from Vicksburgh to Friday, says the Queen of the West has been supplied with coal, and had gone on another expedition down the river.[3] It is believed that a grand movement is to be commenced, shortly, which will put Vicksburgh in our possession. The movement is so formidable in character that it is certain of success. It is feared the enemy may evacuate before it is fully brought to bear. The nature of the movement is contraband. ✹

1. Willis A. Gorman (1816–1876) played only a small role in the Vicksburg campaign.
2. James H. Wilson (1837–1925), one of the youngest of the war's Union generals.
3. The Union ram *Queen of the West* ran past the Vicksburg fortifications on February 2 and quickly destroyed four rebel steamers. But Confederates captured the vessel and added it to their fleet. Ironically, it was the Union navy that destroyed its onetime prize ship on April 14.

EPITHETS AND NICKNAMES A STUDY FOR THE TIMES.

FEBRUARY 22

Men betake themselves so naturally to the use of epithets, as a weapon, in any contest, that the study of the epithets in use during any given period is often a very necessary preparation for the history of it. This is likely to be a more or less important part of history in proportion to the intensity of public feeling at the time. The fluctuations of feeling, and the different directions which it has taken, may be pretty accurately traced in the epithets applied at the different stages of the progress of events. The past two years have formed no exception to this rule. Let us look a little at their history from this point of view.

Among the rebels we notice rather a paucity of the epithets which characterize. Their poverty of invention exhibits itself clearly here. They have called us Abolitionists; probably, because that was the worst thing they could think of, and they had become habituated to using it against their adversaries in previous political and even personal contest. They have also called us Unionists, and Lincolnites; but here their inventive powers were pretty much exhausted, and they have had to fall back upon ordinary billingsgate and call us thieves, savages, brutes, hyenas, fiends, and the like.

At the North, too, there have been in constant use from the first, epithets expressing the aspect which the rebellion has borne to us. We have called our opponents generally Rebels, and this very epithet of ours has been a source of strength to us. It carried moral weight with it. Not but that there have been brave and true men in history, who were rebels. But history has not given them that epithet permanently. She has generally applied it not to her favorites, but to those whose company good men would avoid.

The epithet Secessionist has also been in constant use. This, too, was a characterization. It touched one of the important points in the controversy, and we have applied it not only to the rebels, but with equal pertinency to their Northern sympathizers. In fact, it has been chiefly against these that the fire of epithets has been directed. At the outset they were sometimes designated as conditional Unionists. This name marked the early stage of the contest, before the lines were drawn, when yet policies were undefined and the conflict had not assumed its present vast proportions. That term has pretty nearly passed out of use. It marked a period of transition, and with that period it in great measure passed away.

Then the epithet of Skedaddlers arose. It came from the far West, but had its popular application in the early struggle in Virginia, before the rebels had fought themselves into steadiness, and their frequent retreats won them this contemptuous title. But when questions arose among ourselves as to the draft, we transferred it almost entirely to that set of poltroons who tried to evade their country's call, who became afflicted with all sorts of diseases and "pangs unfelt before," who all at once found important business abroad, or intimate friends in Canada. And along the Northern line, after one stout young fellow was caught trying to get away in his sister's crinoline, these parties were divided into skedaddlers and she-daddlers. These epithets, too, have pretty much passed into history. They mark the period of the draft.

Copperhead is the term which characterizes the present period. Its use shows the increased intensity of the struggle. The sly and slimy courses which the rebel sympathizers have adopted to assail the cause of the Union — the venomous zeal with which they have lost no opportunity to strike their fangs into Government credit and Government treasures — these are fitly embraced in the term, and it has been the very aptness of the epithet which has given ☞

it existence, and will make it through future history an epithet which will cast light upon the feelings and passions which pervade this present hour.

It is a chance if this term does not shortly undergo a modification. It is from among the Copperheads that the recent demonstrations toward peace have arisen, for which reason they have also been called Peace-Secesh — Peace-at-any-price-men, & c.; and when

in the New-Jersey Legislature one of them introduced resolutions appointing three Copperheads, or peace commissioners to Richmond, some loyal man, a shipbuilder evidently, disgusted with such poltroonery, and in view of the probable reception of such commissioners at Richmond, suggested an appropriation to have them soppered-bottomed before they went. The change would not be a great one from Copperheads

to Copper-bottoms, and the term would certainly be quite appropriate to those in whom subserviency to party and to Slavery, has so killed out the manly feelings and impulses that they cannot be kicked into hostility to their former masters, but are never so well content as when groveling before them, and begging to be ruled over.

These terms, Conditional Unionist, Skedaddler, Copperhead, express the positive, comparative and superlative degrees of the same thing, viz: a sympathy with the rebellion, and they have shown themselves so nearly related, that it was almost certain that any one who began with the positive degree should come out with the superlative. What further new degrees of comparison may be required, only the progress of events can show; but whatever may be that progress, there will be no loss for an epithet to characterize it. These epithets, in the future as in the past, will mark the varying changes of the times. ❀

Alfred Waud's sketch of Skedaddlers Hall, Harrison's Landing, Virginia.

AN UNDISCRIMINATING WAR.

FEBRUARY 24

We have an announcement now and then from the West that the gunboats or National forces have destroyed this or that town or landing on the Mississippi River, "in retaliation for the firing of guerrillas on steamboats from the place." This sort of news is more or less gratifying to the public, because it conveys the idea of prompt punishment for a very foolish and cruel style of warfare frequently adopted by the rebels.

We are in possession of information, however, which places these transactions in a less favorable light, and leads us to doubt the justice or the chivalry of the mode of revenge adopted for these river annoyances. The supposition that the inhabitants of the little towns on the river bank harbor and encourage the bandits that occasionally come in to assail passing steamboats, is contrary to reason, as we are assured it is to fact. These resident people feel and know themselves to be entirely unprotected and at the mercy of the gunboats that are constantly patroling the river in their front. To provoke the National forces by so silly an act as firing on a passing

boat, is but to bring down utter ruin on their homes from the next gunboat that comes by. The fact is, that the people resident on the western river banks are disposed to be on the best terms with the National forces, and desire to have the navigation of the river free and harmless. They institute, whenever and wherever they can, a petty trade with the boats and with the country back of them, and they profit largely wherever they are permitted to do so. They know the guerrillas, by their predatory invasions to the river side, as their deadliest enemies, and dread their coming as an event threatening them with calamity.

It may be said that the residents of the villages and landings on the river should organize and keep the guerillas away. But this suggestion comes from ignorance of facts. The truth is that people in the Southwestern seceded States were at the beginning of the war wholly disarmed by the rebels, on the pretence of arming the Confederate soldiers in the field. But the arms so gathered up were not used in the field, we know. The intention was merely to take them from the

hands of the masses, whose fidelity to treason was distrusted. It is because the people are unarmed that very small guerilla squads can enter western villages with impunity, and put the lives and property of hundreds of noncombatants in peril.

Another fact serves to strengthen the view of the case we are taking. The guerrillas that depredate in the Southwest are rarely citizens of the locality where their evil deeds are committed. Their acts are those of unrestrained brigandage, and those who follow the lawless pursuit find it easier to prey on strangers than upon the people with whom they have ties of acquaintance and consanguinity. Hence the guerrilla bands are generally not citizens of the county that is cursed by their presence, and care nothing for the "retaliation" that follows their acts; and to burn a town because guerrillas have been found lurking and depredating in it, is merely to crush a people by national wrath whom internal enemies have signalized by their unwelcome and disastrous presence. We have unquestionable information that much cruel wrong has been done to wholly innocent communities by the thoughtless destruction of their homes, in consequence of guerrilla parties being found in the vicin-

IMPORTANT FROM WASHINGTON.

PASSAGE OF THE CONSCRIPTION BILL BY THE HOUSE.

WASHINGTON, WEDNESDAY, FEB. 25

The strong affirmative vote to-day in the House on the Conscription bill surprised even its friends, and is a hopeful sign of renewed determination to prosecute the war with vigor. Out of the thirty Southern members, twelve voted for the bill, and several were absent.

PROPOSED REORGANIZATION OF THE ARMY.

Gen. MCDOWELL has submitted to the Military Committee of the two Houses a plan for consolidating the regiments in the field, or for filling them up to the maximum, and keeping them full, from troops to be raised under the new Conscript law. The plan does away with the present anomalous state of affairs, in which a wasted regiment, perhaps hardly counting a hundred and fifty muskets, has the full complement of

FEBRUARY 26

staff, line and field officers for a thousand men. It proposes to make such a change as will consolidate parts of regiments in whole ones, thereby disposing of supernumerary officers; then forming them into brigades, with a Brigadier for each, and then into divisions with a Major-General to command. It gives the President power to muster out of the service officers whom the consolidation may leave without commands, always discriminating in favor of those oldest in the field and most noted for services and ability. Gen. MCDOWELL appeared in person before the Committee and explained his plan at length. The Committee were very forcibly impressed with his views, and will endeavor to carry them out before Congress adjourns. The chance of the passage of a bill based on Gen. MCDOWELL's suggestions at

this stage of the session are not, however, first-class. Both the General and the Committee are of the opinion that the army as at present organized must be very inefficient.

GEN. M'CLELLAN.

It is understood that Gen. MCCLELLAN has obeyed the summons of the Committee on the Conduct of the War, and has appeared to testify again on matters touching which he has before given evidence. Some curiosity is felt to ascertain whether any member of that Committee will deny the fact on the floor of the House.

GEN. HOOKER'S DISCIPLINE.

Gen. HOOKER has arrested thirty deserters, had them tried by Court-martial and sentenced to be shot. It is believed he will inexorably enforce the sentence. The case is noteworthy, as almost the first where the rule against desertion has seemed likely to be executed, and as illustrative of the vigorous means by which Gen. HOOKER is raising the efficiency of the Army of the Potomac. ❁

---

ity. This is a cheap mode of earning military fame; and Western Commanders should see to it that more discrimination is observed, in future, in trying to punish guerillas. If the miscreants cannot be followed and chastised, in propria persona, it is a poor satisfaction to burn houses that shelter women and children; which houses, perhaps, the guerrillas have plundered before leaving, numbers, a quarter of a million of dollars, and the receipts three-quarters of a million; and there is now in the hands, of the Assistant Treasurer at New-York, a half million of dollars saved through these operations, which, says Mr. CHASE, belongs more rightfully to the laborers who planted, cultivated and gathered the cotton, than to any other possible claimant. The management of the negroes and the cultivation of the soil has, since the time up to which this report comes, been transferred from the Treasury to the War Department; but we have no doubt that Secretary STANTON, at the close of next year, will be able to make an equally favorable exhibit.

We have already had an inkling of this report by telegraph, but it is well worthy of reading and study. The negroes have enough sins, including their black skins, to bear, without having to endure all the false assertions of their malignant foes in the North. ❁

GEN. W. T. SHERMAN AND THE PRESS

Gen. W[illiam].T. SHERMAN has addressed the following card to the editor of the Memphis Bulletin:[1]

CAMP BEFORE VICKSBURGH, FEB. 6, 1863.

SIR: Whilst intensely interested and engaged in obeying the laws of our Government and the constituted authorities, far to my rear in the North, for whose cause I thought I was fighting, I find myself universally denounced as the inveterate enemy of the Press. You published your paper under my rule in Memphis for several months, and know the simple order I prescribed. There were no anonymous publications; anything worth printing was with the real name of the author. No publication of the movements of troops, arrivals and disposition of regiments, or anything the knowledge of which would enable the enemy to guess at our purpose. No comments upon the motives and conduct of officers calculated to encourage jealousies and discord among the people or our troops. These are about all the restrictions I ever placed on the Press. You also know that while I suffered the efforts of the enemy to learn our plans and intentions, I was minutely informed of all the enemy did or could do.

MARCH 1

You have heard me again and again say it publicly that all men must forego their private opinions and personal wishes and obey the law; not because the law was of their liking or disliking, but because it was the law, which all good citizens and soldiers must obey, to secure unity of action. Without such implicit obedience, there could be no Government. Now, what is the law of the land? See act of Congress, approved April 10, 1806....

People at a great distance, in their quiet homes, cannot measure the difficulties here, and cannot judge of acts and events so remote. I can well afford to wait and see others do better. No amount of detraction or defamation will change what I conceive to be the only hope of restoring our proud nation to its proper station among the nations of the earth, viz.: a cheerful, willing and intelligent submission to the laws of our country and the constituted authorities of the Government.

W.T. SHERMAN, MAJ.-GENERAL. ❁

1. General William Tecumseh Sherman probably hated journalists as much as he hated rebels — particularly after reporters claimed he had suffered a nervous breakdown early in the war. Sherman at one time banned the press entirely from his army.

WHAT THE SOLDIERS THINK.

MARCH 1

The following is an extract from a letter of an officer of the Ninth Army Corps, who has borne an important part in nearly every battle of the Army of the Potomac. It is dated HAMPTON, Va., Sunday, Feb. 15, 1863.

The chimneys of the burnt dwellings, the blackened walls of the church, bear witness that the storm of war has swept over this plain. Here and there an earth-work, weather-beaten and weed-grown, shows where the picket skirmishes took place in the early part of the war. Nearly a week ago we landed at the same wharves and encamped near the same place. Nothing here has changed — the same level brown fields, scarred with old furrows; the same dark pine woods and dreary marshes, crossed by low sandy roads full of large mud-holes and quick-sands. The place is the same; but where are the thousands that gathered here, full of pride and patriotism, less than one short year ago? Yorktown,

Williamsburgh, Seven Pines, Fair Oaks, Mechanicsville, Hanover Court-house, Chickahominy, Beaver Dam, Gaines' Mill, Peach Orchard, Golding's, Garnett's, Savage Station, White Oak Swamp, New-Market, Turkey Bend, Malvern Hill, Malvern, Bristow, Groveton, Bull Run, Chantilly, South Mountain, Antietam, Fredericksburgh, the hundred skirmishes, the deadly camp diseases. How many they have taken from us. Divisions now are smaller than brigades were then; and the people say we have done nothing.

We have done much, and will do more, but we want help and not weak complaining.

Can the North falter, and make unavailing the treasure, suffering and blood which we have given to redeem our Union? We must go on and win, or lose all. No half-way measures or half countries.

Union or annihilation. ❋

FRESH BREAD VS. "HARD TACK."

MARCH 4

We are glad to hear of the success of the system inaugurated by Gen. HOOKER for supplying his army regularly with fresh bread. If we may judge of the style of ovens used by the pictures of them given in the illustrated papers they are simple and well contrived, and ought to turn out a good loaf or biscuit. There are professional bakers enough in every brigade of the army to work the matter, as well as the dough, properly. As each soldier is entitled to a pound loaf every other day, we suppose between sixty and seventy thousand loaves will be consumed per diem by the infantry, artillery and horse-marines under command of Gen. JOE HOOKER.

DE QUINCEY¹ says that one can form some conception of the vast mass of human beings who dwell in London by observing the prodigious droves of cattle that march into it daily, never to march out again, but to be devoured by the Cockneys; and on the same principle, some

A typical long-term Union army camp. Note the chimneys and log walls with the tents. In the background, a sentry is marching on a wooden breastwork erected to protect the camp.

conception can be formed of the magnitude of Gen. HOOKER's army by pondering upon the prodigious pyramid of bread (not to speak of cattle) that it makes away with daily. Sixty thousand pound loaves, if put together end-wise, would stretch from the Battery to Seventieth-street; if piled on top of each other, would reach — not quite to the Dog-Star; if they were used for a breastwork, with a hungry army to defend them, all the rebels in the South, with JEFF. DAVIS at their head, could not capture it.

We hope that as Gen. HOOKER has introduced the fresh bread ration into his army, he will look around occasionally to see that the bakers furnish a good, light, digestible article. There is nothing worse for the stomach and pluck of the troops than damp, heavy, half-cooked bread. A single meal of it, on the eve of a battle, would almost certainly insure defeat. We are no special admirers of the bran-bread school of philosophers; but in favor of bran-bread itself, as an article of diet, there are excel-lent arguments, which would have more than ordinary force in the army. Everybody knows that there are some quite valuable elements of the flour lost in the super-refining process; and many a dyspeptic can testify to the value of the invention of Rev. Mr. GRAHAM. Corn bread or "dodgers," also, would form an excellent article for the army — cheap, nutritious and whole-some. All the Western troops would far prefer it to the flour bread, and their preference would be justified by chemistry, physiology and experience. The rebel soldiers, it is true, live on this article to a great extent; but we do not see that that furnishes any argument why our gallant boys should live on an article which is in every way its inferior. Corn bread and bacon; corn bread and coffee! They're dishes fit for a sovereign, or an army of sovereigns, such as Gen. JOE HOOKER commands. ✸

1. Of course, English author Thomas De Quincey (1785–1859) had also advocated consuming opium.

THE COPPERHEADS AND THE CONSCRIPTION BILL.

MARCH 10

VALLANDIGHAM, in his speech before the Copperhead Association of this City, again threatened "resistance" to the conscription.[1] The word resistance, in any connection, from the lips of such a notorious dastard, naturally produces contempt simply. Of course these factious speech-makers have no idea of committing themselves personally to an armed fight against the Government. There never yet, from Cleon down, was a creature of that sort whose bite was like his bark. Courage is a high quality, and it is never found associated with the base elements that make up the demagogue.

Yet it does not do simply to despise these men. Impotent as they are in action, and every way contemptible in spirit, they yet are very pernicious. CARLYLE hit off the species exactly when he says: "Consider that little spouting wretch. Within the paltry skin of him, it is too probable, he holds few virtues beyond those essential for digesting victuals; envious, cowardly, vain, a splenetic, hungry soul—what heroism in word or thought or action will you ever get from the like of him?" And yet it is a mistake, he observes, to deem them harmless or insignificant. They are "ugly and perilous." The mischief is that their rant may mislead the unreflecting. It may inflame bolder tempers. It may instigate impetuous men to lawless acts, who are a thousand times more honest at heart. Though VAL-LANDIGHAM, himself, is incapable of lifting a finger in the "resistance" he prates about, his language may excite others to such resistance. His words, notwithstanding his disclaimer in another column, were studiously adapted to re-vive, on a yet wider field, the violence which was raised against the last draft in certain localities in Pennsylvania and Wisconsin....

We trust that the Government will meet these sedition-mongers promptly, the first instant they trench upon the law. VAL-LANDIGHAM and his associates have given notice that the conscription shall be resisted. They have thrown out unqualified defiance. Very well; let it be tested which is the stronger — they or the lawful authorities of the United States. A new draft, in accordance with the late act of Congress, cannot be far distant....

The Government will find no difficulty in joining clear issue with Mr. VALLAN-DIGHAM, at the very first word he utters against the draft after the order for it is issued. Let there be no lingering until the resistance actually takes shape; but let the blow fall at once upon the caitiffs who instigate it, and yet dare not commit themselves personally to its perils. Theirs is the greatest guilt; and they should be the first to feel the penalty. ✸

1. Lincoln signed the Federal Conscription Act on March 3, 1863. The law imposed compulsory military service on all males between 25 and 45, but allowed for exemptions for certain disabilities and circumstances, and also for the hiring of a "substitute" at $300.

COMPENSATED EMANCIPATION — THE CONDITION OF MISSOURI

MARCH 5

While so much has been done by Congress to sustain the Administration in its measures of national policy, there will be a regret felt by many that the bills providing for compensated emancipation of slaves in the States of Maryland and Missouri failed to become laws. No part of the President's policy for conducting the present war to an issue consistent with the interests of freedom and humanity has had a more prominent place, or, in all his messages, a more extended and earnest advocacy, than this scheme for ridding the Border States of Slavery[1]....

The answer of those who have permitted the bills before Congress to fail is, that the Democrats opposed them, and would have "filibustered" them to death if they had been pressed. And, besides, that they would have excited prejudices among the people against the Administration on account of the resulting tax, if the bills had been passed. These can hardly be reckoned good reasons for abandoning any policy believed to be right and promotive of human freedom. And it is doubtful if the loss to the cause of emancipation by reason of this abandonment of a plan so cordially adopted, and acted on by one State, at least — Missouri — in good faith, will not counterbalance all the gain expected from the possible exemption from Copperhead abuse. Every other measure of the Administration was passed, despite the filibustering of the Democrats. Why should this very important one be abandoned to such an unpatriotic enemy? ✸

1. Lincoln was consistently frustrated in his efforts to promote gradual, compensated emancipation in the border slaveholding states.

VICKSBURGH AND THE YAZOO.

MARCH 17

There seems now to be no doubt that our fleet which made its way through the Yazoo Pass and down the Cold water to the Yazoo River has at least met with its first success. A dispatch from Vicksburgh says that it had captured twenty-six rebel steamboats, eighteen of which were destroyed, and our gunboats had arrived at Haines' Bluff, which forms the outer defence of Vicksburgh on the Yazoo. An official dispatch from Admiral PORTER, under date of the 7th inst., confirms the statement of our fleet's having arrived in the Yazoo. He heard the signal of nine minute guns and three guns afterward in quick succession, which were agreed upon to be fired by the Commander of the expedition on his reaching that point.

We suppose we may now expect daily and hourly to hear of the combined attack on Vicksburgh; for it will be impossible for Gen. GRANT to leave the men and vessels of the Yazoo expedition where they now are. The signal was probably a signal for him to get ready to cross with his army and navy and cooperate in the attack. We shall not speculate either on prospects or results, for a few days are likely to give us the accomplished facts.

We learn also from New-Orleans that Gen. BANKS about the same time that this signal was fired on the Yazoo, had his army and navy all ready at Baton Rouge for an advance upon Port Hudson. It was probably intended that all these movements should be simultaneous. If so, the problem of the rebellion in the Valley of the Mississippi is likely to be solved before the close of the first quarter of 1863. ◉

THE PORT HUDSON REPORT.

MARCH 19

WASHINGTON, WEDNESDAY, MARCH 18

Gen. DIX, at Fortress Monroe, reports that the Richmond papers of the 16th inst, give an account of an attack on Port Hudson by Admiral FARRAGUT, on the 15th inst., in which he was repulsed. One vessel, the steam frigate Mississippi, is said to have been sunk, and another vessel, name not given, is reported to have successfully passed the bat-

teries, and is now between Port Hudson and Vicksburgh. The report is not fully credited here.[1] ◉

> 1. In fact, Farragut had bombarded this strategic point on the Mississippi River on March 14; the Union lost a ship named the USS *Mississippi*. Union attacks continued until July.

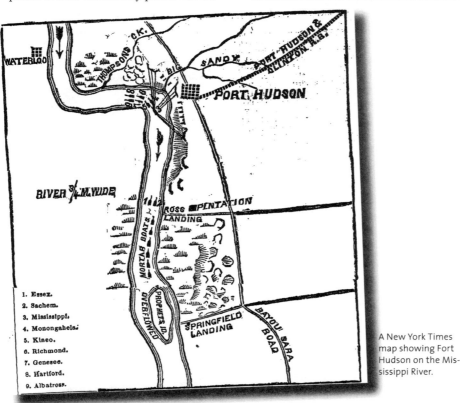

A New York Times map showing Fort Hudson on the Mississippi River.

THE COPPERHEADS AND FUTURE HISTORY.

MARCH 18

…Our people generally find it very difficult to bring home to themselves the fact that they are living in the most momentous days of the age. On a little reflection, they will allow it, and yet too many of them conduct themselves after their old political habits, as if the war were nothing more than one of the old political struggles in a new shape. They do not appreciate that their present public conduct has got to be judged more severely than ever before, and by altogether new standards. That which divides Americans now relates not to measures of mere expediency, but to practical acts involving national life or national death. The difference lies not between Whiggism and Democracy, or

THE CONSCRIPT LAW AND THE POOR MEN.

MARCH 26

The Peace Democrats have commenced an attack on the Conscription law of Congress, because, as they allege, it makes a distinction between the rich and poor. The Mozart Hall[1] Democrats, led by FERNANDO WOOD, have proclaimed hostility to the act on this ground, — one of their resolutions, passed formally at headquarters on Tuesday night, declaring that

"The people everywhere should be awakened to the infamous distinction which it [the Conscription law] makes between rich and poor, whereby the former is allowed to buy his freedom for the sum of three hundred dollars, while the latter, unable to command that sum, is to be torn away from his employment, his home and his family, and forced, at the point of the bayonet, into the ranks of the army."

The tableau of the reluctant conscript pricked away from home by bayonets is calculated to be effective, and if the objection to the law, as thus presented, were well taken, its moral force would be greatly impaired. But the fact is otherwise. The complaint made of the law is wholly unjust, and the attempt to create prejudice against it must fail. The law does not fix three hundred dollars as the sum that any one must pay in order to obtain exemption from the draft. It gives to the Secretary of War discretionary power to fix the sum which shall

between Democracy and Republicanism, all of which were compatible with the most thorough loyalty; but it lies essentially between loyalty and disloyalty — between faithfulness to the Republic in its hour of peril, and defection. Posterity will so see it, and will judge in that light exclusively.

When this tremendous scene shall have passed — and it cannot last long at longest — every actor in it will receive honor or dishonor. Every American, high or low, is an actor in it. He can't escape it if he would, for neutrality is in itself defection and disloyalty. It will be known and remembered how every man bore himself in this crisis of the nation's life — every man from ocean to ocean. With men in general it will not be written on the page of history, but it will be written on a tablet yet more distinct, the living memory. Ten, twenty, thirty, fifty years hence it will be inquired about, and it will be known how every living American who was on the stage in the Great Rebellion then acted — whether he took sides for or against the Government; and every man, woman and child in the parish will understand it. The honor or dishonor of it will cleave not only to the individual himself, but to his children.

There are those living who remember the odium which, after the Revolution, clung to every Tory to his latest breath. No intellectual accomplishment, nor any moral worth, could exempt from it. But more than that, it was transmitted to his children and his children's children. Even to this day, the American whose ancestor at that time was known as a Tory, hears of it with burning shame. Similar contempt was entailed upon the blue-light Federalists of the last war. So far as regards the private character of its members, the Hartford Convention of 1814 was probably equal to any political assembly ever held in this country; but after the war closed, every man of them to his dying day was held in dishonor. He could no more obtain a public office than if he had been positively disqualified by law. The ban of public opinion was upon him. Though it was very clearly shown in subsequent years that the majority of the Convention had no such treasonable intentions as were imputed to it, yet it is enough that it was a peace assemblage, calculated to embarrass the Government. To this day the Hartford Convention is a by-word. There were Federalists who did not approve of the Convention, and yet even they do not escape. It is still everywhere a reproach to have been at that time an opponent of the Administration at all.... ⊛

buy exemption in each individual case, but in no case shall over three hundred dollars be demanded. The Secretary may require of a rich man $300 for exemption, and he may let a poor man off — one who deserves exemption for reasons of sickness and helplessness of his family — for the sum of $3, if he will, intended to relieve poor families from too large a share of its burdens....

With such exemptions as these, which are of manifest propriety, and which preclude, as far as law can, the possibility of aged and infirm parents or orphaned children suffering — and with the discretion which is given to the Secretary of War to fix the sum of exemption money, in every case, as low as the condition and necessities of the drafted person may render proper — it cannot occur that any, the slightest, injustice can happen under its enforcement. It was intended to bear equally on all classes, according to their condition, and it does, in its letter and spirit, treat the poor as justly as the rich.

Mozart Hall imagines, no doubt, that it has started out on a very promising tack in originating this impeachment of the Conscription act; but so soon as the people, having their attention drawn to the subject, learn how wise and benign in its provisions the law really is, they will have a stronger reason than ever to distrust, as utterly false and disloyal, the opposition of the Copperheads to the necessary war measures of the nation. ⊛

1. A Manhattan Democratic political club.

Democratic Congressman Fernando Wood of New York.

ELECTION IN WESTERN VIRGINIA.

MARCH 27

WHEELING, W.V., THURSDAY, MARCH 26.

An election was held to-day for ratifying the Willey amendment and Constitution of the new State of Virginia. This city gives 1,375 for the amendment to 3 against. The county will vote in like proportion. Returns from the State show an almost unanimous vote in favor of the amendment. ✸

SHALL THE SOLDIERS BE DISFRANCHISED?

APRIL 1

In another column may be found a Bill, now before the Legislature of New-York, providing that every qualified and duly registered voter of the State, now in the military or naval service, shall be entitled to vote at every general State election hereafter held in the election district where he has a residence. It is very carefully guarded against all chance for fraud or other abuse, and is adapted to the sole purpose of enabling our gallant fellow-citizens, who are engaged in defending the integrity of the Republic, to exercise the most sacred right which the Republic guarantees. The Republican majority of the Committee have reported in favor of the bill; the Demo-cratic minority have reported against it.

We trust that the measure will be brought to a test vote in both branches at as early a day as possible. The army and the people are alike anxious to see what record the two great parties of this State will make on this question.

Of course the ground on which the opponents of the measure rest their objections is that of pretended unconstitutionality — their favorite ground from the outset in respect to all measures unfavorable to the peace policy. All the resources of special pleading are exhausted to make out that no vote can be valid under any circumstances unless cast within the geographical limits

NEGRO EQUALITY AND SLAVERY.

MARCH 29

That any portion of the Republican party or any but a very small and insignificant portion of the people of the North believe the negro race to be the equal of the white race, or that any such doctrine is to be found in the speeches or writings of any but a half dozen of the extreme Abolitionists, we totally deny. Moreover, we cannot help thinking that these Disusionists are just as well aware of this fact as we are. It is not about negro inequality we differ with the South or with the Democrats. There is nothing within our knowledge so well established, as that some races are inferior to others, morally, intellectually and physically. One might as well deny that some men were more eloquent, or more clever, or handsomer, or stronger than others, as to deny this. Where we part company with the Stephenses and the Morses[1] is in drawing the inferences from this patent truth. They hold that where a body of weak, ill-favored, stupid men are dwelling alongside a stronger, better-looking, abler and more energetic ones, it is the right of the latter to rob, beat and sell the former. This is the great "truth" on which the Confederacy is founded. It is, too, the great "truth" on which the social organization of all the Slave States rests. As long as it is confined in its operation to those States, we cannot constitutionally, perhaps, overthrow its application. But we object, and shall always object, to its extension to territories in which it does not now exist, and which are under our

protection, and for whose future we are legally and morally responsible; and we object to the use of our Courts, or armies, or ambassadors for its dissemination or support.

We do so, because we not only believe it to be fatal to the material and moral welfare of every community which adopts it, but because we hold that the sound republican theory of human rights and human duties makes physical weakness and mental or moral deficiency titles to pity and protection, and not invitations to fraud and violence; that the more helpless and inferior a man is by nature, the more carefully should the laws of a democratic commonwealth enforce his claim to his wages, his wife, his children, and his own body. We do not advocate, because we do not believe in, negro equality. We would not, if we could, give negroes a share in the Government. But we heartily indorse Mr. BATES' doctrine that they are entitled to protection, not only none the less but all the more because they are inferior; and they are entitled to it in an especial manner at our hands, because we have, more than any people in the world, preached the doctrine of the inherent dignity and value of humanity in its humblest, most helpless and most degraded condition. ✸

1. A professor who had published a racist rant in the pro-Democratic New York World.

BREAD RIOT IN RICHMOND.

—

THREE THOUSAND HUNGRY WOMEN RAGING IN THE STREETS.

APRIL 8

BALTIMORE, TUESDAY, APRIL 7.

Col. STEWART, of the Second Indiana Regiment, one of the fourteen United States of-

Richmond women rioting in front of a bakery.

of the election district by the very hand of the voter. No attempt is made to show the justice or the fairness of denying the absent soldier his most valued franchise; the disposition is simply that of Shylock when he cried, "I stand here for law.... "

We cannot comprehend either the mind or the heart of any really loyal man who interposes these wretched quibbles and cavils to prevent his neighbor, who has answered his country's call, from exercising the same civil rights he himself enjoys, though he has not answered it. We should suppose the mere thought would overwhelm him with shame. Are not those officers and soldiers the very bravest, noblest, best patriots in the land? Do they not sacrifice immeasurably more than any other of our people for the common good?

Have they not as much at stake in the policy of the Government? Is not their property as much subjected to taxation, their liberty and their life as much exposed to peril? Are not their opinions as intelligently formed and as honestly entertained? The man does not live who dares deny any of these things. And yet men who call themselves respectable, have the hardihood to try to torture the Constitution into some construction that shall reduce these citizen-soldiers from the rank of freemen to the condition of voiceless, voteless myrmidons. Even the rebel chiefs — soulless traitors as they are — have soul enough to leave their soldiers the right to vote. That right is exercised by every regiment in the Confederacy. It is only here we see the political depravity that would rob the soldier

of his birthright....

Does facing the enemy forfeit the franchise? That is the question. Get these peace-plotters on the record. We much mistake the character of the two hundred thousand New-York soldiers now in the field, and of the honest, patriotic body of the people who, though at home, are still for sustaining the Government, if the time does not come when every man in this Legislature who shall vote against a measure so distinctly dictated by every consideration of justice and equality, will not feel like fleeing to the clefts of the rocks. We repeat — Give the soldier his franchise, and fix his home enemies on the record. ❧

---

ficers just released by the rebels, and who has just arrived here, makes the following statement: On Thursday last he saw from his prison window in Richmond a great bread riot, in which about three thousand women were engaged, armed with clubs, guns and stones. They broke open the Government stores and took bread, clothing and whatever else they wanted. The militia were ordered out to check the riot, but failed to do so. JEFF. DAVIS and other high officials then made speeches to the infuriated women, and told them they should have what they needed. They then became calm, and order was once more restored. All the other released Union officers confirmed this statement. ❧

THE ADVANCE OF GEN. LONGSTREET.

CORRESPONDENCE OF
THE BALTIMORE AMERICAN:
SUFFOLK, VA., SUNDAY, APRIL 12

The some-time expected advance of the rebel Gen. LONGSTREET [1] upon this place occurred yesterday. He made a forced march from beyond the Blackwater with a force of not less that thirty thousand men, evidently intending to surprise the post. But we had been well informed of his movements, our pickets were strengthened, and though he was within three miles of us at dark last night, he has made no attack up to this hour — 8 o'clock in the morning. We have taken quite a number of prisoners from Gen. HOOD's Texas

APRIL 16

brigade, which held the advance, and are well informed of the strength and movements of the enemy. You may look for stirring news from here in my next if LONGSTREET should not, as I fear he will, fall back. We are fully prepared for him, even if his force is doubled. ❧

[1]. Because Lee dispatched James Longstreet and his corps to re-capture the city of Suffolk, Longstreet was not present at the Battle of Chancellorsville.

WAR MOVEMENTS IN THE WEST.

The absorbing interest felt by the country in the fight at Charleston [1] led to an undue magnification of the value of the struggle there. A few days have elapsed, and confidence with calmness has returned to the public mind. Attention is now again directed to the great armies in the field under HOOKER, ROSECRANS and GRANT. There is hope for the Republic in these armies. Their leaders are a gallant trio — much alike in many of the high qualities of soldiers — hopeful in spirit, fervid in patriotism, bold in emprise

APRIL 16

and execution. In brief time the armies of these three leaders will be in motion, seeking the face of the enemy.

The dispatches from the West to-day will attract attention as indicating, perhaps, a rapid flank movement of GRANT to the aid of ROSECRANS, by passing from Memphis toward the Tennessee River. The Memphis and Charleston railroad furnishes convenient facilities for this movement, leading direct to Huntsville, quite in the rear of the rebel army in Tennessee....

No season could be more favorable for

active operations of ROSECRANS and GRANT's armies in the West than the mild and cheerful Spring now at hand, and we shall be mistaken greatly if those zealous leaders do not improve their opportunity, and give the nation substantial cause for joy and triumph. ❧

[1]. Union naval forces were determined to retake Charleston, where the war had begun two years earlier, even if it meant leveling the bastion they had once tried to protect: Fort Sumter.

SCARCITY IN THE SOUTH — THE TESTIMONY OF JEFF. DAVIS.

APRIL 17

The Copperhead journals, whose general policy it always is to darken, so far as they can, every prospect of subduing the rebellion, have taken particular pains to argue down, or, in lack of argument, to sneer down, the likelihood that it must soon suffer serious straits from the want of food. Calculations based upon the figures of the last census tables — conclusions drawn from the known agricultural resources of the region now within the command of the rebels — accounts of great scarcity, which from every direction have been constantly finding their way across the lines — and the prices current of the great staples of food as given in the principal Southern papers, have done nothing to diminish the assurance of these rebel-sympathizing prints that there is and always would be plenty of provisions in Dixie. Even the Proclamation of Gov. [Zebulon B.] VANCE, of North Carolina, last month, invoking the attention of his people to this great "danger," had no effect upon these "never-can-conquer" dogmatists. They have flouted straight on.

But these people have much faith in JEFF. DAVIS. We therefore commend to them the address of the arch-traitor to the people of the Confederate States, to be found in another column. It was issued from the "Executive Office," in Richmond, just one week ago to-day, and has all the advantage of freshness. After depicting in high colors the remarkable success of the "young Confederacy" thus far, he declares that there is "one danger" which he "regards with apprehension." He makes free to say that unless there is a special effort made to produce "grain and live stock and other articles necessary for the subsistence of the people and army, the consequences may prove serious, if not disastrous." Even at the present time, he says, "the supply of meat for the army is deficient," and "the ration is now reduced to one-half the usual quantity in some of our armies." We take it this is conclusive testimony. Determined as our Copperhead organs are to believe nothing to the disadvantage of the rebellion, we presume they will now accept the fact that it is hardly as full-fed as they have pretended.

The truth is that this difficulty in obtaining the necessaries of life is doing more to break down the Confederacy than all other causes combined. ✸

GEN. HOOKER'S MOVEMENTS — PRECAUTIONS IN ADVANCE.

APRIL 30

If we are rightly informed, our army on the Potomac is once more on the move, and we may expect, within the next few days, a good deal of successful or unsuccessful fighting. We entertain confidence in Gen. HOOKER; first of all, because he has shown himself, in a subordinate position, to be a man of ability; and, secondly, because he has that confidence in himself without which ability is useless. We are satisfied that he will fight and march with the expectation of winning uppermost in his mind, and will not pass the most momentous hours of great conflicts in making preparations for disastrous retreat. But we do most earnestly, for the sake of the nation as well as for his, beg of politicians and strategists, of all sects and parties, to let him severely alone for the next half year at least. If he achieves a great military reputation inside that period, he will have accomplished a very extraordinary feat, but there is not the smallest probability that one week less than that time will suffice for any such purpose.

Consequently, even if he should win a battle within the month of May, it will still be premature to announce that the "back of the rebellion is broken," and it will be in the highest degree rash to pronounce him either a young or a middle-aged Napoleon....

GALLANT WORK AT VICKSBURGH.

APRIL 22

The feeling of disappointment that has, for some time, existed over the supposed failure of our army and gunboats before Vicksburgh, was suddenly removed yesterday by the news from the Southwest. It is announced that on the night of Thursday last, the gunboats Tuscumbia, Lafayette, Benton, Pittsburgh, Carondelet and Gen. Price, with three transports, ran the rebel batteries at Vicksburgh, and all went out safely below except one transport, which was burned.

In this list of gunboats will be recognized some of the very best iron-plated vessels we have on the Western waters. The Lafayette and Tuscumbia, in particular, are vast iron-clad floating batteries, which are now seeing about their first service on the Mississippi, and which we expect will give an excellent account of themselves on whatever work they are sent. The other four boats mentioned are of a highly serviceable, but much inferior class, partly clad with cotton and partly with iron, and two of them, at least, will be remembered as historically and honorably associated with the reduction of Forts Donelson and Henry, Island Ten, Fort Pillow and Memphis. The passage of this formidable fleet below Vicksburgh puts an end to all doubt as to the mastery of the Red River, and of the Mississippi between Vicksburgh and Port Hudson. It settles beyond quibble the question of the absolute supremacy of the National Government over every mile of the navigable waters of the Mississippi, save immediately in front of the batteries of Vicksburgh and Port Hudson.

But it is not the control over the navigation of the Mississippi alone, and the consequent severance of the rebel Confederacy from its dependencies west of that river, that gives, at this moment, this gunboat movement its most salient significance. The communications across the Mississippi had already been seriously disturbed and almost broken up by Admiral FARRAGUT's presence between the two great rebel positions. All the gunboats that have passed Vicksburgh were not needed to patrol the river and destroy the vagrant rebel craft still left on its waters. They are intended to play an immediate and important part in the reduction of Port Hudson. And this work being accomplished, Vicksburgh will be flanked on the south and forced to yield to the National power.

If we win a battle in the month of May, it will doubtless furnish strong reason for believing that we have at last got the right man in the right place, but it will not prove it. The whole campaign will prove it, and nothing less. And the public may rely on it that it will take a whole campaign, and perhaps two, to reduce the South to subjection. Nothing can be more inconvenient, and nothing can be more ridiculous, therefore, than to crown Generals with laurels, and dub them saviors of the nation, and worthy of its highest civil honors, in the month of May, and then have them uneasily "changing their base," and proposing to burn their baggage in order to save themselves from destruction in the month of July. We are far past the happy time when all that we needed in a President was that he should be unknown, or harmless and good-natured. Our great public rewards must be, henceforward, won in the old-fashioned way, by hard work, by brilliant achievements, by unquestioned ability and victorious and undisputed success. So that common policy, as well as justice, demands that Gen. HOOKER should have a fair field and no favor; that all factions should keep their hands off of him, and let him do his duty. One of them cannot adopt him as its champion without setting the others to bark at him; and no man can do his work well with two packs of this kind barking mingled applause and censure at his heels. ❁

In connection with this news of events at Vicksburgh, we learn also that Admiral FARRAGUT is communicating easily with his fleet below Port Hudson. And from New-Orleans we have intimations that a new combination, almost assuring success, is making against Port Hudson. Putting all these developments together, and interpreting them by the aid of our knowledge of Admiral FARRAGUT's splendid qualities as a leader who seeks victory through the fiercest flames of battle, we cannot but derive confidence and hope that the tedious struggle for the possession of the two strongholds on the east bank of the Mississippi is about to be brought to a speedy close, and that our late misgivings are to be changed to the realization of complete and unexpected victory. ❁

CHAPTER 13

"A Terrific Crash of Musketry"

MAY–JUNE 1863

May marked the traditional onset of the campaigning season, and Joseph Hooker was eager to put his splendid army into action. Since Fredericksburg, the Rappahannock-Rapidan river line had become the de facto military boundary between the opposing armies in Virginia, and Hooker led his army across that boundary on April 26 to inaugurate what history would record as the Chancellorsville Campaign. With that army went Lorenzo Livingston Crounse, the chief field correspondent for The New York Times. Communications between the front lines and the major cities of the North had improved tremendously since 1862, and for the next two months Crounse's reports offered readers of The Times a detailed and often vivid narrative of the fighting. His lengthy report on the Battle of Chancellorsville, which appeared on May 5, is an eyewitness account (though of only one side) that stands up to the best modern narratives. The outcome of the battle — another Confederate victory — was crushing to the hopes of the North. When he heard the news, President Lincoln paced the White House hallways in anguish asking, "My God, my God, what will the country say?"

These months also witnessed the slow unfolding (too slow, it seemed to some) of the Vicksburg Campaign in the west. There, Ulysses S. Grant tried several stratagems to work his way around behind the Confederate citadel until his successful effort in May. After landing at Bruinsburg on the east bank of the river on April 30 (four days after Hooker crossed the Rapidan), he moved inland to Jackson, the Mississippi state capital, which fell on May 14. He then turned westward

Detail of a postwar woodcut showing General Grant's troop transports running the Confederate defensive batteries during the siege of Vicksburg.

and defeated the army of Confederate Major General John C. Pemberton in the Battle of Champion Hill, or the battle of Big Black River, two days later. By the third week of May, he had clamped a siege around Vicksburg, and by the end of June the beleaguered defenders inside the city were running desperately short of food.

One hundred and twenty miles south of Vicksburg (as the crow flies), Nathaniel Banks was besieging Port Hudson, Louisiana. There, the politically sensitive issue of using black soldiers to fight for the Union cause received a boost from the performance of two black regiments in an attack on Port Hudson on May 27. Two regiments of Louisiana militia called the Louisiana Native Guards had initially paraded (though not fought) under Confederate colors until the fall of New Orleans,

then they changed sides and became part of the Union army. Port Hudson was their first trial by combat. In a report printed by The Times, Banks wrote, "No troops could be more determined or more daring. They made, during the day, three charges upon the batteries of the enemy, suffering very heavy losses, and holding their position at nightfall with the other troops on the right of our lines."

In addition, the politically sensitive question of what constituted disloyalty in wartime came to the fore with the arrest of former Congressman Clement L. Vallandigham, a bitter critic of the administration and the war. Arrested for disloyalty by Burnside, his case was resolved by sending him southward into Confederate lines. Denying that he was disloyal, Vallandigham later made his way

out of the Confederacy to Canada, and then back into the United States, where the government left him alone.

Meanwhile, in the aftermath of his victory at Chancellorsville, Lee began a move westward into the Shenandoah Valley in June, and then northward, down the Valley, and across the Potomac. As cavalry forces skirmished along the slopes of the Blue Ridge, Lincoln called for more volunteers and called up the Pennsylvania militia. The object of Lee's advance was unclear. Was it the Pennsylvania state capital at Harrisburg? Or was it Philadelphia, Baltimore, or Washington itself? The Army of the Potomac, still under the command of Joe Hooker, moved northward, too, under a hot summer sun, as the two armies headed for a clash of monumental proportions.

DETAILS OF THE CROSSING ABOVE FREDERICKSBURGH.

The Rappahannock is again crossed by the Army of the Potomac, and this time without the shedding of a drop of blood, or the firing of a single gun.

The great movement which we have been so long anticipating began in earnest at daylight on Monday morning [April 27], by the movement of a very heavy force up the Rappahannock. The Eleventh Army Corps, Gen. [Oliver Otis] HOWARD,[1] had the advance on the march, and still has it. At this hour it is hardly prudent to enter into the minute details of the force and the march, as they have undoubtedly a great deal of work yet before them.

The weather on Monday was remarkably fine — even sultry, and the men found marching in over-coats too fatiguing. They threw them away in large numbers, and the track of the column can be traced by the abandoned clothing.

Tuesday morning we had a cloudy sky, and before 9 o'clock a drizzling rain began falling. But our column kept steadily moving, and by 1 o'clock Gen. HOWARD's advance arrived at Mount Holly Church, one mile from Kelly's Ford, having marched sixteen miles

MAY 2

since daylight. The rain continued until the middle of the afternoon, when it ceased, it having at no time been very severe, but just enough to make marching heavy, and to stall one or two of our very small number of wagons in some of the chronic mud-holes. Otherwise, the move prospered. The arrival of the troops in the vicinity of the Ford was well masked by Col. BUSHBECK's brigade, of the Eleventh Corps, who had been guarding the post for two weeks.

The troops marched rapidly and in fine spirits. [Henry W.] SLOCUM camped last night near Hartwood Church, and MEADE just east of it — all were well up by 4 P.M. to-day.

At 8 this morning Gen. HOOKER left his headquarters, and accompanied by his personal Staff, rode straight to Morrisville, 20 miles distance, and but six miles to the Ford. His passage through various columns of troops was marked for miles by tumultuous cheer, enthusiastically genuine.

At Morrisville he makes his headquarters for the day and night. A consultation of corps commanders, including [Cavalry commander] Gen. [George] STONEMAN, who had come from Warrenton Junction,

was at once held, and then and there Gen. HOOKER first revealed to these, his principal subordinates, a portion of the plan and nature of the present movement. Beyond what has been already developed, none but these officers know anything, Yet there is reason to believe that it is startling in the magnitude of what it contemplates, and general officers remarked this afternoon that if officers and men did one-half their duty, it could not fail of success.

HOWARD rested his men four hours, and they were then got under arms ready to support the operations at the ford. The pontoon train for the bridges arrived with great promptness, having come from Bealeton Station, being transported thither by a railroad from Alexandria. They are the usual wooden boat, save being smaller in size than those formerly used. The pontoons and timber were all unloaded on the bank of Marsh Creek, near its mouth, and the boats launched before dark.

These operations, be it known, were conducted in plain sight of the enemy, who appeared only in small force — a few straggling pickets, who seemed to be there as lookouts only. They kept a sharp watch, but not a shot was fired. The work went rapidly on. The pontoons were at once shoved from the mouth of Marsh Creek into the Rap- ☞

pahannock. Seventeen boatloads of men from Col. [Adolphus] BUSHBECK's brigade were thrown over at once, followed by a reinforcement of as many more.

The bridge-laying began at 8 o'clock, and proceeded vigorously, under the direction of Capt. COMSTOCK, Engineer Officer on Gen. HOOKER's Staff. By 9 1/2 P.M., one bridge was completed, and another under way. HOWARD's corps was put under motion for crossing, BUSHBECK's brigade leading, followed by [Carl] SCHURZ's division, then by [Charles] DEVEN's, the balance of [Adolph] VON STEINWEHR bringing up the rear. This force was disposed on the south bank, for the night, doing picket duty on the different roads. Just before our forces landed a small body of cavalry, numbering twenty, perhaps, dashed down nearly to the river, and halting for a short time, leisurely surveyed our operations and then retired.

That there was no resistance at the Ford caused much surprise. Not a single shot was fired. The enemy had rifle pits, but did not use them. We took no prisoners.

There is the best reason for believing that up to noon to-day the enemy had not discovered this movement. Every citizen on the line of march was put and will be kept under close guard until they can do no damage. We speculate freely on the events of the morrow ere we reach our destination, which is Culpepper on the one hand, and Ely's Ford, on the Rapidan, on the other. We shall undoubtedly meet the enemy before we reach either place, though each are less than a day's march distant. STUART's cavalry have not shown themselves to any extent, and FITZHUGH LEE is reported absent, sick.

We are certain of one or more things. There are no heavy fortifications in front of us, there are no very strong positions which can be defended. The enemy must have as great a force as ours to beat us back.

Bridges will undoubtedly be laid at other fords, further down the river, for the benefit of our transportation, which is in a safe place. Once well across here, we can protect the laying of bridges at any of the fords below.

The sun set clear and red to-night, and gave promise of a fair day to-morrow. But the night is thick with mist, and the moon is "eating fog," which sailors say is a sure sign of a coming storm.

Before to-morrow night there will undoubtedly be some blood-letting. Our commander looks and feels as though he was in his element.

There are other important movements on foot by other portions of the army.

A correspondent of the Herald, named [J. H.] VOSBURG [Vosburgh], was captured yesterday, by three dismounted rebels, who crossed the river below Ellis' Ford, and stole him away, horse and all, while he was enjoying a secesh breakfast. He had foolishly gone outside the lines to get greater comforts than the camps afford — hence his grief. His host, who is a rebel parson, named MCMURRAY, betrayed him. This parson lives on property owned by P. W. ENGS, of New-York. His reverence was gobbled in return, and from a host will become a hostage.

I am in bivouac to-night with Lieut.-Col. [Duncan] McVICAR, Sixth New-York cavalry, an intrepid officer, who pickets the line in the immediate front of our operations.

Gen. PLEASANTON's cavalry division will take the advance in the morning....

L. L. C. ✸

> 1. Oliver Otis Howard (1830–1909) was a regular army officer who had graduated fourth in the class of 1854. He replaced German-born Franz Sigel as commander of the mostly German XI Corps, which bred some resentment by the rank and file. Howard had received the Medal of Honor for his service at the Battle of Fair Oaks (Seven Pines) on the Peninsula in 1862, where he also lost an arm.

Major General Olivier Otis Howard, U.S.A.

MAY 3

The opening of the month of May shows an almost universal activity in our armies, great and small. Everywhere we are acting on the offensive, with the trifling exceptions of the affairs in Missouri and in Western Virginia. Gen. HOOKER's movements are, of course, those which most profoundly excite the interest and stir the heart of the nation, for they are more important than any other — we may say than all others put together. His army is the grand army of the nation, and his work is to strike the fatal blow at the rebellion's head. In the inception of the movement which commenced on Monday last, he certainly appears to have shown consummate skill. He moved both of the wings of his army rapidly and cleanly; and so well were his purposes and aims covered, that the rebels at each point seem to have been taken entirely unawares. The laying of the pontoons and the crossing of the river were admirably performed, and in less than two days from the time his movement commenced the main body of his army had made a march of twenty miles, crossed a difficult river, and was ready for action on the other side. It would appear that it was by far the larger part of his army which marched north from Falmouth, and crossed the Rappahannock at Kelly's and adjacent fords. Judging by our letters, it is the lower movement that is a feint; but what is to be the real mode of action on the upper line cannot yet be told. What last week opened, however, this week will undoubtedly develop; and we prefer waiting for events to indulging in useless speculations. The movement which seems most obvious and likely to the non-military observer will probably be the movement which Gen. HOOKER will not make.

The army of Gen. GRANT seems at about the same moment to have commenced an important movement. On Sunday evening last, according to a dispatch of yesterday, nearly the whole of the army stationed at Milliken's Bend (18 miles above Vicksburgh, on the right bank of the river) was in motion, with six days' rations. …The point of destination is not given; but latterly GRANT has been planting his forces at New-Carthage, 25 miles below his old quarters opposite Vicksburgh; and it is generally believed that his purpose is to throw his troops quickly over on to the high ground on this side of the river, from which they will be able to make a land attack on Vicksburgh with greater advantages than have ever heretofore fallen to their lot. We shall watch the denouement of this great scheme with an interest only second to that with which we watch the manoeuvres of Gen. HOOKER.

The only one of our great armies that gives no sign of movement is the army of Gen. ROSECRANS. Several times it has appeared as if he was about again to attack the rebels; but the signs have failed, and to-day he seems solidly planted at Murfreesboro. It is very probable that he is waiting for the result of combinations and movements which have only lately been commenced.

It looks as if we should have a very active Summer. Before it passes away, each of our chief armies will have fought great battles, the result of which, we devoutly hope, will be the complete quelling of the rebellion. ✪

FROM THE ARMY OF THE POTOMAC.

TWO MILES BELOW FREDERICKSBURGH,
THURSDAY, APRIL 30 — 11 O'CLOCK A.M.

The following inspiring address is being read to the various troops, amid tremendous cheering and other demonstrations of delight:

HEADQUARTERS ARMY OF THE POTOMAC, NEAR FALMOUTH, VA., APRIL 30

It is with heartfelt satisfaction that the General Commanding announces to the army that the operations of the last three days have determined that our enemy must ingloriously fly, or come out from behind their defences and give us battle on our own ground, where certain destruction awaits him. The operations of the Fifth,

MAY 3

Eleventh and Twelfth Corps have been a series of splendid successes.

BY COMMAND OF MAJ.-GEN. HOOKER.[1] ✪

1. Joseph Hooker (1814–1879) had commanded the III Corps and was elevated to command of the Army of the Potomac by Lincoln on January 26, 1863. Lincoln was aware that Hooker had declared that the Union could win only with a military dictator in charge. In his letter of appointment, Lincoln wrote him: "I have heard, in such way as to believe it, of your recently saying that both the Army and the Government needed a Dictator. Of course it was not for this, but in spite of it, that I have given you the command. Only those generals who gain success can set up dictators. What I now ask of you is military success, and I will risk the dictatorship."

Major General Joseph Hooker, U.S.A.

THE GREAT BATTLE OF SUNDAY.

MAY 5

Another bloody day has been added to the calendar of this rebellion. Another terrible battle has been fought, and more fields crimsoned with human blood. [A] Few more such days as this will find no armies left on either side to fight battles.

My last letter brought up the situation to Saturday morning [May 2]. It was then certainly expected that the enemy would begin the attack as soon as it was day, and our dispositions were made accordingly. But the attack did not begin. Events proved that the enemy did design to attack, but he chose to make that attack in a manner and at a point different from what was generally anticipated by us on Saturday morning. Daylight grew broader and yet no guns. Finally, about 6 o'clock, a brass Napoleon, looking down the plank road in front of the Chancellor House, saw a regiment come into the road in column and attempt to deploy. One or two doses of canister caused them to deploy rather irregularly, and more like skirmishers on the retreat.

Soon after, Gen. HOOKER and Staff began an inspection of our lines, which occupied full two hours. Every portion was visited, and the work of the night was closely inspected. On the extreme left new lines were chosen, and the engineer officers soon marked out the line and character of the defences to be erected. When,

the inspection closed, the intrenchments were pronounced to be of the very best character, especially those on the right, where the columns of [Henry W.] SLOCUM and [Oliver O.] HOWARD were posted.

There had been only slight disturbances during the night, as both forces had been busy with their axes rather than their muskets. From Gen. HOWARD's front came a report that the enemy was engaged all night in cutting a road past his picket line to the right. How much attention was paid to this fact at the time I do not know, but subsequent events proved that it was very significant.

The day continued to pass in a very dull manner for a day of battle, and only here and there was there anything more even than desultory skirmishing and picket firing.

About 3 o'clock the pickets on the right of Gen. SLOCUM's front reported that from a certain position wagons had been seen moving in a westerly direction nearly all day. It was at once surmised that this might be a retreat, but subsequent events proved that it was a part of an affair of altogether another nature. To ascertain, however, what it really was, Gen. [Daniel] SICKLES, who was still in reserve, was ordered to make a reconnaissance in heavy force in that direction. This was done with great promptness, and the di-

visions of Gens. [David] BIRNEY and [Amiel] WHIPPLE, with Gen. [Francis C.] BARLOW's brigade, from HOWARD's corps, were pushed out to the front, BERDAN's brigade of sharpshooters' having the advance, and supporting [George E.] RANDOLPH's battery. Our troops moved rapidly and soon became more or less engaged, especially with the artillery and the sharpshooters as skirmishers. BERDAN soon sent in some sixty prisoners, belonging to the Twenty-third Georgia, including one Major, two Captains and three Lieutenants. Being upon the ground, I examined these prisoners, and soon found that the "wagon train" which we had seen moving during the day was composed mainly of ordnance wagons and ambulances, and that Stonewall JACKSON and Staff were at the head of a column of troops which the wagons followed.

Nothing more was needed to convince us that this daring opponent was executing another of his sudden movements, and it was at once resolved to checkmate him. Gen. SICKLES was ordered to push on, and Gen. [Alpheus S.] WILLIAMS' division of SLOCUM's column was ordered to cooperate. BIRNEY pushed ahead with great vigor, and with RANDOLPH's battery soon sent to the rear as prisoners of war the entire remnant of the Twenty-third Georgia regiment, numbering over four hundred officers and men. The column of the enemy which had been moving up this road was now literally cut in two, and Gen. WILLIAMS had commenced a flank movement on the enemy's right, which promised the most auspicious results.

But at 5 o'clock a terrific crash of musketry on our extreme right, announced that JACKSON had commenced his operations. This had been anticipated, but it was supposed that after his column was cut, the corps of Gen. HOWARD, (formerly Gen. SIGEL's,) with its supports, would be sufficient to resist his approach, and finding that

The Battle of Chancellorsville.

he was himself assailed in the rear, he would turn about and retreat to escape capture.

But to the disgrace of the Eleventh Corps be it said, that the division of Gen. [Carl] SCHURZ, which was the first assailed, almost instantly gave way. Threats, entreaties and orders of commanders were of no avail. Thousands of these cowards threw down their guns and soon streamed down the road toward headquarters. The enemy pressed his advantage. Gen. [Charles] DEVENS' division, disaffected by the demoralization of the forces in front of him, soon followed suit, and the brave General was for the second time severely wounded in the foot, while endeavoring to rally his men. Gen. HOWARD, with all his daring and resolution and vigor, could not stem the tide of the retreating and cowardly poltroons. The brigades of Cols. [Adolphus] BUSHBECK and [Nathaniel] MCLEAN only remained fighting, and maintained themselves nobly as long as possible. But they too, gave way, though in good order, before vastly superior numbers.

Gen. HOOKER now sent to the aid of Gen. HOWARD the choicest division of his army, the creation of his own hand — the famous Second Division of the Third Corps, commanded by Major-Gen. [Hiram G.] BERRY. Capt. [Clermont] BEST soon moved his batteries on a ridge running across the road, and after a short, but sanguinary contest the further advance of the enemy was stayed.

Of course this disaster compelled the recall of SICKLES and SLOCUM, who had been pursuing their work with remarkable vigor. Gen. WILLIAMS' division returned only to find a portion of their works filled with the enemy. SICKLES' division could not communicate with the rest of the army at all by the way they advanced, and only at great risk by any other route.

This was the position at dark, and it did not look very promising. But our energetic commander was more than equal to the emergency. New dispositions to repair this disaster were at once resolved upon. Communication was at once had with Gens. [David] BIRNEY and WHIPPLE, and a night attack ordered, to restore the connection of the lines. Gen. [Hobart] WARD's brigade, of Gen. BIRNEY's division, made the attack at 11 at night, aided by Capt. [Clermont] BEST's guns, massed on the ridge in front of the enemy. BIRNEY's position was on the extreme left of this new line of battle, but WARD's terrific attack was entirely suc-

cessful, communication was restored, and in a charge made by the brigade, a portion of the artillery lost by HOWARD was gallantly retaken by Gen. HOBART WARD.

This night attack was the most grand and terrific thing of the war. The moon shone bright, and an enemy could be seen at good musket range. The air was very still, and the roar and reverberation of the musketry and artillery past all conception. Malvern Hill was a skirmish compared with this, save in the degree of slaughter. But it was successful — the enemy were driven back nearly half a mile, and our tired men once more slept on their arms. That night's work was ended.[2]

Now I come to Sunday [May 3]. It was perfectly evident, from the position of affairs on Saturday night, that there must be a change of our lines, which would throw the enemy out of our rear and into our front again. It will be seen by what skillful generalship the enemy was fought and checked on front, and flank, and rear, while this was being done.

Gen. REYNOLDS' First Army Corps arrived at United States Ford on Saturday afternoon. It was immediately put into position on our right, which was withdrawn from the plank road to the Ely's Ford turnpike. This line was immediately formed by Gens. REYNOLDS and MEADE, the latter's position, on the left, having been relieved by Gen. HOWARD's Eleventh Corps, which, notwithstanding its disorganized condition was so far reorganized during the night as to be fit for duty again this morning. They were assigned the position on the left, where it was probable there would be little or no fighting, and were protected by the strong works built the day before by Gen. MEADE's corps. Our new line now assumed the shape of a triangle, prolonged at the apex, the right of the line being somewhat longer than the left. As the portion of the line on the right was new, time was necessary to fortify and intrench it, and the work was carried on vigorously by the Fifth and First army corps.

It was very evident at daylight this morning that the day would bring forth a terrific battle. We knew that the enemy had been re-enforcing his line all night, at the expense, undoubtedly of the strength of his force on our left. His intention was, evidently, to fight for the possession of the plank road, which it was perfectly apparent he must have, as that portion of it which we then held, was subject to the en-

emy's assaults in front and on both flanks.

But the possession of this road was not obtained by the enemy save at our own time, at his severest cost, and after one of the most desperate, tenacious and bloody conflicts, for its short duration, of the whole war. At 5 o'clock A.M. the rebels could be plainly seen up the plank road, about a mile and a half from the Chancellor House, which Gen. HOOKER still retained as his headquarters, though a shell had gone through it the evening before, and another had cut down a tree directly in front of it.

Our line of battle was formed with Gen. BERRY's gallant division on the right. Gen. BIRNEY next on the left, Gen. WHIPPLE and Gen. WILLIAMS supporting. At 5 1/2 A.M. the advance became engaged in the ravine, just beyond the ridge where Capt. BEST's guns had made their terrific onslaught the night before, and where they still frowned upon the enemy and threatened his destruction.

The rattle of musketry soon became a long continued crash, and in a few moments, as battalion after battalion became engaged, the roar surpassed all conception, and indicated that the fight would be one of the most terrible nature. Gen. BERRY's division, which had checked the enemy's advance the night before, engaged him again, and if it were possible for them to add more laurels to their fame, then they did it thrice over again. The enemy advanced his infantry in overwhelming numbers, and seemed determined to crush our forces. But the brave men of SICKLES and SLOCUM, who fought their columns with desperate gallantry, held the rebels in check, and inflicted dreadful slaughter among them. Gen. [William H.] FRENCH's division was sent in on the right flank of our line at about 7 A.M., and in a short time a horde of ragged, streaming rebels running down the road, indicated that that portion of the enemy's line had been crushed. At 8 o'clock A.M., Gen. FRENCH sent his compliments to Gen. HOOKER, with the information that he had charged the enemy and was driving him before him.

SICKLES maintained the attack upon his line with great endurance. The enemy seemed determined to crush him with the immensity of his forces, and, as subsequently shown from the statements of prisoners, five whole divisions of the rebel army were precipitated upon this portion of the line, for from these five divisions ☞

we took during the day an aggregate of over two thousand prisoners.

The exploits of our gallant troops in those dark, tangled, gloomy woods may never be brought to light; but they would fill a hundred volumes. It was a deliberate, desperate hand-to-hand conflict, and the carnage was perfectly frightful. Cool officers say that the dead and wounded of the enemy covered the ground in heaps, and that the rebels seemed utterly regardless of their lives, and literally threw themselves upon the muzzles of our guns. Many desperate charges were made during the fight, particularly by BERRY's division. [Gershorn] MOTT's brigade made fifteen distinct charges, and captured seven stands of colors, the Seventh New-Jersey, Col. FRANCINE, alone capturing four stands of colors and five hundred prisoners.

Gen. [Darius] COUCH's Second Army Corps, though only in part present, did excellent work. It was Gen. FRENCH who charged and drove the enemy on the flank, and it was the indomitable HANCOCK who gallantly went to the relief of the hard-pressed SICKLES.

The engagement lasted without the slightest intermission from 5 1/2 A.M. to 8:45 A.M., when there was a temporary cessation on our part, occasioned by getting out of ammunition. We held our position for nearly an hour with the bayonet, and then, being resupplied, an order was given to fall back to the vicinity of the Chancellor House, which we did in good order. Here the contest was maintained for an hour or more, not so severely as before, but with great havoc to the enemy, and considerable loss to ourselves.

The vicinity of the Chancellor House was now the theatre of the fight, and my visits to that spot became less frequent. Gen. HOOKER maintained his headquarters there until 10 A.M., when it was set on fire by the enemy's shels, and is now in ruins. Chancellorsville is no longer in existence, having perished with the flame, but Chancellorsville is in history, never to be effaced.

Our new line was now so far established as to render it safe to withdraw all our forces on that front, which was accordingly done, and at 11:30 A.M. the musketry firing ceased.

The engagement had lasted six hours, but had been the most terrific of the war. Our artillery had literally slaughtered the enemy, and many of the companies had lost heavily in men themselves, but the

guns were all saved.

The enemy was now no longer in our rear, but had been shoved down directly in our front, and is now directly between us and our forces in Fredericksburgh, and we were again in an entrenched and formidably fortified position. The enemy has gained some ground, it is true, but at the sacrifice of the flower of his force, five of his seven divisions having been cut to pieces in the effort, and over 2,000 of them have fallen into our hands.

Our right wing, under Gens. REYNOLDS and MEADE was not engaged, save the division of Gen. HUMPHREYS, which went into the woods on the enemy's left flank, and fought valiantly under their brilliant leader, until their ammunition was exhausted.

During the afternoon the enemy has made several attempts to force our lines, particularly at the apex of our position, near the Chancellor House, but Capt. WEED has massed a large quantity of artillery in such a position as to repulse with great loss everything placed within its range. The enemy tried several batteries and regiments at that point at different times during the afternoon, and they were literally destroyed by the fire of our terrible guns. Nothing can live within their range.

Our present position is impregnable if our troops continue to fight as they have to-day. Gen. LEE, the prisoners say, has issued an order that our lines must be broken at all hazards. Let them try it again, with what they have left. They can, and perhaps will destroy themselves by attacks upon this position.

Our troops are perfectly cool and confident. They have fought with great spirit and enthusiasm and will continue to do so.

L. L. CROUNSE. ◉

1. Colonel Hiram Berdan (1824–1893) led two regiments of sharpshooters that acted as scouts for the Army of the Potomac.

2. Crounse does not mention the most important event of that evening because it took place on the Confederate side of the field. While returning to his own lines after an evening reconnaissance, Thomas "Stonewall" Jackson was mortally wounded by fire from his own soldiers.

FROM HOOKER'S ARMY.

FURTHER DETAILS OF THE GREAT BATTLES.

MAY 6
HEADQUARTERS IN THE FIELD,
NEAR CHANCELLORSVILLE, SUNDAY EVENING,
MAY 6

At this hour of writing, it is impossible to estimate the loss in to-day's battle on either side.[1] We know that ours is heavy — heavier than ever before in a battle of so short duration. We further know that the loss of the enemy is admitted by themselves to be perfectly frightful. We had the advantage in artillery, and our shells and canister tore and mangled their ranks fearfully. The prisoners are silent as to the loss of prominent officers, but some of the Alabamians in A.P. HILL's division say that he was killed early in the day, and that Gen. RAYNOR is now in command of the division.[2]

Probably no battle was ever fought upon ground more unfavorable for the maneuvering and deploying of troops. Nearly the whole country in this vicinity is covered with dense forest, much of it being of the same character as "The Wilderness," lying only a short distance west of this point. The timber is mostly dead, and still very dense; then, to make the forest still more impenetrable, there is a denser growth of dead underbrush, so that it is hardly passable for man — certainly not for beast — and the worst place conceivable for handling troops. Yet a very great part of to-day's terrible battle was fought in this almost impenetrable jungle, and many dead and wounded on both sides still lie there, concealed in the gloomy depths of "The Wilderness." The only open ground upon which the battle was fought, was the plain on the south side of the plank-road, near Chancellorsville, half a mile long, and perhaps three hundred yards wide. The only open ground in our present position is a semi-circular crest, extending from the left of Gen. SYKES' position to the right of Gen. HOWARD's. Immediately in front of this are dense woods, concealing our skirmishers and those of the enemy. This crest is our artillery position, and here guns enough are massed to blow to atoms the armies of a dozen Southern Confederacies. The enemy seem to have a proper appreciation of the courtesies in waiting for them from this position. Twice to-day they have essayed out of the woods toward our guns, and twice have those guns sent to their earthly doom untold numbers of desperate wretches. The artillery at this point is in charge of Capt. WEED, Chief of Artillery of the Fifth Army Corps.

The exact count of prisoners thus far taken, during the battle of Sunday, is not yet known, but it must be, all told, nearly, if not quite, two thousand. They were brought in singly, in squads, in companies and by regiments; and our men say that they could have taken many more, "but for the trouble of bothering with them on the field of battle." They would rather shoot than capture. Two regiments were taken entire — the Twenty-third Georgia and the Fourth Alabama — the former yesterday and the latter to-day. Then there are detachments from fifty or sixty other regiments, including many North and South Carolina, Virginia, Mississippi and Louisiana regiments. The enemy has undoubtedly taken several hundred of our men, mostly wounded, with some from the Eleventh Corps, who couldn't run fast enough to get away.

The unaccountable and inexcusable conduct of a large portion of this corps, was the means of turning to ashes a grand victory almost within our grasp, while the position was only retrieved by the superb generalship of the Commanding General. A portion of the troops, the brigades of Cols. BUSHBECK and MCLEAN, stood their ground manfully until overpowered by vastly superior numbers. Gen. BARLOW's brigade was absent with Gen. SICKLES.

The manner in which Gen. HOOKER proposed to checkmate the rear attack of JAKSON strikingly illustrates the bold and daring character of our commander. Finding that JACKSON was marching by the old Catharpin road post our right front, Gen. HOOKER promptly ordered Gen. SICKLES to attack that impudent column on the flank. This was not more quickly conceived than vigorously executed. In one hour and a half from the time the movement began the head of Gen. BIRNEY's division was engaging the enemy, and our force and vigorous attack were so great that the enemy's left flank was speedily turned, his columns doubled back one upon the other, and his men seized with demoralization and panic. WILLIAMS' division ably assisted this dashing movement, while Gen. GEARY attacked sharply on our centre front, and the prospects were cheering indeed. The Eleventh Corps was strongly intrenched. Its position ought to have been held, and somebody is to blame

for this disgraceful affair which smote us so sorely, just as we were about to reap rich fruits from the boldest move yet projected since we crossed the river. And to remedy the effect of this disaster, we have spent this day in fighting which only puts us in our former condition, and the enemy once more in our front. Albeit we have inflicted on LEE a murderous loss, and so shattered his columns that he must have time and reinforcements to enable him to fight again as savagely as he fought to-day. Beside, his position is now such that he must inevitably attack our strong position, or retreat. Retreat in his case, with our swift-marching army after him, is most surely disastrous. He may precipitate his whole force upon SEDGWICK, who can retire to the Heights of Fredericksburgh, and wait for HOOKER to follow up in his rear. Two or three times Gen. HOOKER has said that he would compel the rebels to come out of their fortications and attack him on his own ground. It is brilliant generalship, indeed, that has so faithfully fulfilled this promise. To-day the enemy literally leaves his fortifications, and stands before our intrenched camp, essaying its capture.

The question of supplies must now be of great moment to the enemy. His communication by rail, if not totally severed by our cavalry, must be seriously interrupted by the presence of our forces in the vicinity of Hamilton's Crossing, five miles below Fredericksburgh, which has been the rebel supply depot during the Winter. The prisoners taken to-day had nothing to eat, and some of them say no rations had been issued to them for three days.

Our men never behaved more magnificently. Cool, confident and brave, they fought with splendid valor, and were even complimented by the prisoners who fell into our hands. The demoralization of the Eleventh Corps did not affect the rest of the army in the least. Some how or other they looked upon it as a matter of course. Gen. HOOKER's appearance on the field, under severe fire, created tumultuous enthusiasm among the men, and he was cheered to the echo time and again. When it became known that he had been struck by a piece of spent shell, (although uninjured,) the cheers grew louder still.

To the indefatigable efforts of Major-Gen. HOWARD, commanding the Eleventh Corps, is due the fact that before daylight this morning this corps was so far reorganized as to be placed on duty again in an

important position. Gen. HOWARD is one of our bravest and best officers. His emotions at the conduct of some of the brigades cannot be described. Had he been longer in command of these men, undoubtedly this stampede would not have occurred....

The headquarters of the Army of the Potomac in the field are to-night under a large tree, just in the rear of our front line of rifle-pits and abattis. Gen. HOOKER has just dined on hard tack and cold ham. The gentlemen of the Staff are looking for their "pack mule."

L. L. CROUNSE. ✸

1. Officially, Union casualties at Chancellorsville were 17,197 (a number that includes nearly 6,000 missing), and Confederate casualties were 13,303 (including 2,000 missing). Significantly, as a percentage of the forces engaged, the Union lost 12 percent while the Confederacy lost 21 percent.

2. When Jackson was wounded, Hill took over his corps while Brigadier General Harry Heth took command of Hill's division. When Hill was himself wounded, Lee assigned his cavalry chief J. E. B. Stuart to corps command. Crounse's mention of a "General Raynor" may refer to Dorsey Pender, who took over Hill's division after Heth was wounded.

THE CONTEST ON THE RAPPAHANNOCK.

MAY 7

The telegraph last night was altogether dumb in regard to military movements on the Rappahannock; and the few items of news that reached us by mail and otherwise during the day and evening did not bring us down beyond Monday. The extensive operations of Sunday were not renewed on Monday, and there was, on that day, no general battle between the armies. In the afternoon one division had a fight for half an hour with a rebel column, but beyond that nothing was done by HOOKER or LEE, except to prepare with all their might for the renewal of the action, which each knew could not be postponed.... ✸

THE DISCOMFITURE OF GEN. HOOKER

MAY 8

The retrograde movement of Gen. HOOKER to this side of the Rappahannock has been to the people one of the very sharpest of their many disappointments. They had counted with peculiar confidence on a triumphant issue. The superb condition and splendid spirit of the army, the personal prestige of its chief, who had never fought but to conquer, the remarkable ability with which the new campaign was planned, and the signal success with which its first stage was consummated, to all appearance justifying the bulletin of the commander that "the enemy must ingloriously fly, or come out from behind their defences and give us battle on our own ground, where certain destruction awaits him" — all combined to raise the public expectations to the highest pitch. When next came the tidings that the army was hastening back over the river, with all its material, there could not but be a most painful revulsion of feeling. Every loyal man is in truth smitten to the very soul, and with reason.... ✦

FROM HOOKER'S ARMY.
ABANDONMENT OF THE SOUTH SIDE OF THE RAPPAHANNOCK.

MAY 8

Our intelligence this morning puts beyond doubt the fact that Gen. HOOKER'S army has again retired to the north side of the Rappahannock. From various sources we collect the following facts in regard to the movement.

There was no fighting on Tuesday [May 5] of any consequence, and the rumors to that effect were founded on a misapprehension.

The sharpshooters were quite active, and the artillery opened occasionally, but results were unimportant. The enemy had evidently massed his army on our right.

About 5 o'clock in the morning it commenced raining. The water fell in torrents over an hour, deluging the roads, tearing up the corduroys, sweeping away bridges, and threatening the destruction of the pontoons. The river rose with great rapidity, and soon overflowed the ends of the pontoons, rendering crossing impracticable. The upper pontoon [bridge] was taken up, and used in lengthening out the others, and after several hours of very hard labor the bridges were once more ready. It was soon evident that Gen. HOOKER, seeing his position was rendered temporarily untenable by the storm, had determined to cross over again to this [side] of the Rappahannock. On Tuesday the order was given to retreat. New roads were cut. The trains and reserve artillery were sent back, and the evacuation was commenced.

Pine boughs were spread upon the pontoons to prevent the noise of crossing, and at 10 o'clock Tuesday night the troops commenced falling back.... ✦

OFFICIAL DISPATCH FROM GEN. GRANT.

MAY 10
GRAND GULF, MAY 3,
VIA MEMPHIS, TENN., MAY 7

Maj.-Gen. Halleck, General-in-Chief:

We landed at Bruinsburgh, April 3oth, moved immediately on Port Gibson, met the enemy, 11,000 strong, four miles south of Port Gibson, at 2 A.M. on the 1st inst., and engaged him all day, entirely routing him with the loss of many killed, and about 500 prisoners, besides the wounded. Our loss is about 100 killed and 500 wounded.

The enemy retreated toward Vicksburgh, destroying the bridges over the two forks of the Bayou Pierre. These were rebuilt, and the pursuit has continued until the present time.

Besides the heavy artillery at this place, four field pieces were captured and some stores, and the enemy were driven to destroy many more.

The country is the most broken and difficult to operate in I ever saw.

Our victory has been most complete, and the enemy are thoroughly demoralized. Very respectfully.

U.S. GRANT, MAJOR-GENERAL COMMANDING. ✦

LATEST FROM THE ARMY.
DEATH OF STONEWALL JACKSON.

MAY 13

HEADQUARTERS ARMY OF THE POTOMAC,
TUESDAY, MAY 12

The Richmond papers of yesterday announce the death of Stonewall JACKSON, on Sunday afternoon, from the effects of his recent amputation and pneumonia. His burial was fixed for to-day. The military band in Fredericksburgh had been performing dirges a greater portion of the afternoon.... ✦

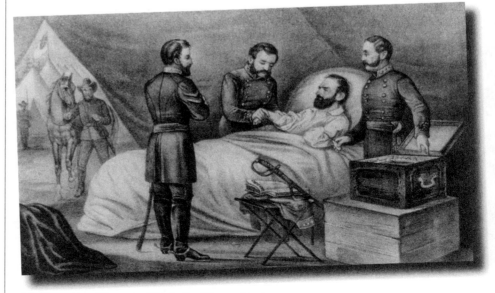

A Currier and Ives lithograph of the death of Stonewall Jackson.

WHERE SHALL VALLANDIGHAM GO?

MAY 13

We published on Monday morning the charges upon which Mr. VALLANDIGHAM[1] was recently tried by Court-martial in Cincinnati. We have no doubt that the evidence offered was sufficient to establish their truth. There remains the question, what sentence the Court will pass upon him. If we could have our choice in the matter, it should be that he be sent South beyond our lines. Taking his life might seem too hard, imprisonment would quite likely make a martyr of him, but every one will recognize the fitness of sending him to Dixie, to join that noble company of traitors whose praises he has sounded so loudly, and to receive from them in person that meed of praise which they have so steadily bestowed upon him at a distance.

It is quite time that he should appear upon another stage. He has appeared before our Northern people in the character of a pacificator quite often enough. He has inculcated, everywhere he has gone, the doctrine that nothing could be gained by war. Let him go now and try what he can do in that line on the other side. Let him urge upon the rebels the manifold evils of the war which they are waging, and the utter impossibility of accomplishing anything by battle. He has lifted up a testimony among us against the dangers of military power. Let him have the chance to lay open the same matter before the rebels, for they are, to say the least of it, in as much danger as we in this direction. He has dilated to us upon the glories of the Union, and its benefits to us all in the years that are past. Let him see what he can accomplish by portraying them before those who have assailed it. He has been earnest in setting before our people the horrors of abolition. Let him go and suggest to the slaveholding rebels how much rebellion has done for abolition. He has exhausted his resources for opprobrious terms for those who would put arms in the negroes' hands, who would fight by their side, or consent to receive a helping hand from them. Let him go and pour out the vials of his condemnation upon those at the South who would conscript the slaves into the rebel army, as Gen. BANKS found was about to be done in Louisiana.

It would be very interesting, perhaps instructive, to see what reception he would meet with. Will the rebels clothe him in robes of honor, and send him upon a triumphal procession, as one whom they delight to honor? We rather incline to think that they will let him alone severely. While he was among us he might do them some good. When he has crossed our lines he is to them but one more mouth to feed, unless indeed he should don the butternut uniform and shoulder a rebel musket. He may, perhaps, avoid being conscripted, if he strongly maintains that he is a citizen of the United States, as we see that an act providing for the conscription of such citizens "sojourning in the Confederate States," which passed the rebel Congress, failed to become a law by JEFF. DAVIS not signing it, and we all know that the rebels would never force a man into the army, except with the fullest warrant of law.

On the whole, we are inclined to think that sending him South now would do more good to our cause, than his presence has done us harm heretofore. Not that he will say anything to help us — not that anything he could say would have the slightest influence upon the rebel leaders, for as soon as he crosses their lines, he is a squeezed orange. But the fact of our ejecting him will be one which must be widely spread, and it will speak most convincingly to every one who hears it of the determination of the North, which is hardening from flint to adamant, to suppress this rebellion, and to grind to powder all those who would sustain it; — and so, if we could reach the ear of the powers that have it in charge, we should urge upon them to send him across our lines, treating him as tenderly, but as inflexibly, as IZAK WALTON would have the angler treat the frog.[2] ⊛

1. Clement L. Vallandigham (1820–1871) was an anti-war Democrat from Ohio. He publicly denounced "King Lincoln," and called for Lincoln's removal from the presidency. On May 5 he was arrested on orders from General Burnside for violating General Order No. 38. This was an embarrassment for Lincoln, who would have preferred that Burnside ignore Vallandigham altogether. The question posed here is: What to do with him now?
2. Izaak Walton, in his famous book *The Compleat Angler* (1653), wrote that the fisherman should use the frog "as though you loved him, that is, harm him as little as you may possibly, that he may live the longer."

Clement L. Vallandigham.

VALLANDIGHAM IN DIXIE.

HIS TRANSFER TO THE REBEL LINES.

MAY 26

MURFREESBORO, MONDAY, MAY 25

VALLANDIGHAM arrived here on a special train under a strong escort, at 10 o'clock last evening, having left Louisville this morning, and passed through Nashville without stopping.

He was quietly taken in a carriage to the quarters of Maj. MILES. Provost-Marshal-General, where he was received by Gen. [William S.] ROSECRANS and a number of other officers. He appeared to be fully composed, and abstained from the expression of any disagreeable sentiments.

At 2 P.M., his southward journey commenced. Major MILES, with a mounted escort, started down to take him below our lines in Shelbyville. The prisoner was very cheerful, and discussed his situation indifferently, but on approaching the nearest rebel picket, commanded by Col. WEBB, of the Eighth Alabama, some eight miles out, he became perceptibly affected.

Upon taking leave of his companions, he said in substance: "I am a citizen of the United States, and loyal to them. I want you to understand that you have brought a prisoner to the Confederate authorities."

To Col. WEBB he made similar remarks. The former received him with a remark that he had read his speeches, but did not like him; that he could not receive him within the Confederate lines, but he would permit him to remain at his post until he had ascertained the pleasure of the authorities.

The flag of truce party then left VALLANDIGHAM and returned. ⊛

GRANT AND JOHNSTON.

JUNE 1

It is now fifteen days since the battle of Big Black Bridge [Big Black River or Champion Hill], and fourteen since the investment of Vicksburgh. With the first of these events, Gen. JOHNSTON saw the desperateness of the rebel situation at Vicksburgh, and the necessity of the utmost energy in concentrating all possible troops to flank GRANT, and, if possible, to raise the siege. We have had no special information as to his success during these fifteen days in bringing up reinforcements — though the dispatch said to have been sent by him to PEMBERTON assured the latter that in fifteen days he would aid him with a hundred thousand men. His facilities for bringing forward men are not very great, as the railroads are few, ricketty and much damaged by our raids, and the places from which reinforcements can be obtained are very distant. We have the evidence of eye-witnesses that troops have been brought from Charleston, which is distant from Jackson 767 miles; and if they have been brought from Charleston, they have doubtless also been brought from Savannah, Mobile, and all the garrisoned positions in the Gulf States, if not from North Carolina. We have also had numerous rumors that reinforcements were being got from [Braxton] BRAGG's army....

GRANT, however, with his right on the Mississippi River, above Vicksburgh, is in far better position to receive reinforcements than JOHNSTON, and the War Department is, doubtless, fully advised of his necessities.... ⊛

RAILROADS AND THE WAR.

JUNE 8

Never has the old adage, "it is an ill wind that blows nobody good," been more completely verified than in the effect the present war has produced on the railroad interests of the loyal States. At the time of the breaking out of the rebellion, and for a number of years previously, the majority of the great railroads of the Middle and Western States, were financial failures. They were dragging out a weak and crippled existence — staggering under Floating Debts, Preferred Stock, First, Second, Third, and even Fourth and Fifth, Mortgage Bonds. The ownership of railroad Shares was considered almost a premonitory symptom of bankruptcy, and Bankers had learned to fear a connexion with railroad enterprises as something fatal to their credit.

There were a few exceptions to this general condition of great leading railroads. The New-York Central persevered in paying dividends, though it was sometimes doubted whether they were fairly earned. The Michigan Central kept itself in pretty good fame. The Cleveland, Columbus and Cincinnati line was a notable exception of a profitable railroad. The Galena and Chicago, and the Chicago and Rock Island Roads, though having once enjoyed an apparently solid prosperity, had gone far down in popular estimation, and stockholders had begun to be familiar with the necessity of "passing dividends." These railroads, with a number of local and less important roads in Ohio and Indiana, were all that stood with even tolerably hopeful character at the time of the breaking out of the war. As to the rest, they were in the main admitted and gigantic failures. Stockholders, though still clinging to their shares, had ceased to think of dividends, and almost ceased to hope for any change that would give real value to their property....

Two years and a half of war have passed, and a magical change is observed. The business of every road has been enormously increased, and this increase has been so steadily maintained that munificent revenues are flowing into once exhausted treasuries. These incomes have been sufficient in many cases to retrieve the fortunes of the roads entirely; by wiping out floating debts, perfecting roads, increasing rolling stock, and inducing lately inexorable creditors to enter into reasonable arrangements for adjusting their claims, and permitting the roads to continue in the hands of stockholders. In some cases where receivers had been appointed, the revenues of the roads have so outrun all calculation, that roads have been surrendered back again to their owners, and are now earning handsome dividends on the stock that was so lately valueless and in actual process of legal extinguishment.... ⊛

NEGRO SOLDIERS — THE QUESTION SETTLED.

JUNE 11

We have from the outset avoided all discussion of the question of employing negro soldiers, because we have regarded it as a purely military question, which it was the province of the military authorities alone to settle. The political bearings of the policy we have steadily refused to recognize. The efficiency of our armies has been our paramount concern; for on that alone depends the suppression of the rebellion, and without that suppression the nation is ruined, and all politics are worthless.

The military inquiries to be determined were four: Whether the negroes were able and willing to fight at all? Whether their nature could be kept under such constraint that they would fight in accordance with the laws of civilized warfare? Whether the white soldiers would not become so much disaffected and demoralized by the enlistment of blacks as to more than countervail any possible advantage that could be gained by

it And whether white soldiers could not of themselves speedily close the war?

…But at last we have an official report from Major-Gen. BANKS himself, which describes the part taken by the colored regiment in the battle of Port Hudson, whose terrible nature tested the fighting qualities of all, white and black, to the utmost. Gen. BANKS says:

"On the extreme right of our line I posted the First and Third regiments of negro troops. The First regiment of Louisiana Engineers, composed exclusively of colored men, excepting the officers, was also engaged in the operations of the day. The position occupied by these troops was one of importance, and called for the utmost steadiness and bravery in those to whom it was confided.

"It gives me pleasure to report that they answered every expectation. In many respects their conduct was heroic. No troops could be more determined or more daring. They made, during the day, three charges upon the batteries of the enemy, suffering very heavy losses, and holding their position at nightfall with the other troops on the right of our lines. The highest commenda-

tion is bestowed upon them by all the officers in command on the right.

"Whatever doubt may have existed heretofore as to the efficiency of organizations of this character, the history of this day proves conclusively to those who were in condition to observe the conduct of these regiments, that the Government will find in this class of troops effective supporters and defenders. The severe test to which they were subjected, and the determined manner in which they encountered the enemy, leaves upon my mind no doubt of their ultimate success.

"They require only good officers, commands of limited numbers, and careful discipline, to make them excellent soldiers."[1]
◉

1. At the Battle of Port Hudson (May 27, 1863), the all black 1st and 3rd regiments of the Louisiana Native Guards participated in the Union attack. These units, initially formed as part of the Louisiana State Militia, had paraded under Confederate colors until the fall of New Orleans, then they changed sides and became part of the Union army. Port Hudson was their first trial by combat.

The Battle of Port Hudson.

THE REBEL INVASION.

JUNE 16

The excitement that was produced in the City yesterday by the publication in the TIMES of the news that LEE'S rebel army had crossed the Rappahannock and was marching northward, and that HOOKER'S army had also left camp to take up a new line of operation, will be greatly increased to-day by the news of the battles in the Shenandoah Valley on Saturday and Sunday — the rebel advance into Pennsylvania — and the call of the Government for 120,000 more troops — 20,000 of whom are to be from this State. It may be thought passing strange that we were not permitted to hear of these important battles two days ago. They were known in Baltimore and Washington on Sunday, and details of them were published in the Baltimore papers of yesterday morning. It is the withholding of the news of rebel movements, that does more than anything else to precipitate the country into demoralizing excitements. We were assured last week, up to its very last day, that the rebel army was still at Fredericksburgh — while the fact is, that they must have begun their march with the week, for on Friday they appeared before Winchester, in the Shenandoah Valley, with 18,000 men, and another force as high up as Martinsburgh, on the line of the Baltimore and Ohio Railroad. The people of Pennsylvania were in as great darkness as ourselves, and the rebel army, by a forced march might actually have filed into Philadelphia while its shad-bellied citizens were reading in their morning papers that all was quiet on the Rappahannock. Now, as a matter of course, on learning the facts, they are in an unparalleled condition of excitement; and even the Copperheads, who were preparing to hold their great Peace meeting in Independence-square, may first have to fight two or three battles with the rebels for its possession.... ⊛

LEE'S NEW CAMPAIGN — THE OPPORTUNITY IT OFFERS US.

JUNE 17

The Northward movement of the rebel army is certainly very audacious, though we are not yet able to divine its precise course, nor the special object it may have in view. We do not even yet know whether it has crossed the mountains or is still on the upper waters of the Rappahannock. Some think that LEE will offer HOOKER battle on the present ground now held by our army, near the old Bull Run battlefields; others hold that he is going to march his whole army into Pennsylvania by the Shenandoah Valley, and attempt a short campaign in the North; while others think his object is an attack on Washington from the rear. A short time must develop the truth in the matter. His plan and course are doubtless clearly enough marked out in his own mind. But their execution will depend very much upon us. We have already an army in the field near Washington far superior in numbers to his; and twice a hundred thousand volunteers are rushing to arms in the five States nearest to the theatre of operations. If we have energy and vigor in our movements; if we have intelligence and unity in our plan; if we have skill and sagacity in our leadership, there is no reason under Heaven why LEE's new campaign should not prove as disastrous as it is daring.... ⊛

THE CAVALRY FIGHT AT ALDIE.

FULL PARTICULARS BY OUR SPECIAL CORRESPONDENT.

JUNE 20
ALDIE, WEDNESDAY, JUNE 17

The advance of Gen. [David M.] GREGG's cavalry command reached this place at about 2 o'clock this afternoon, where two brigades of the enemy, commanded by Gen. STUART in person, were found in possession. After three hours' hard fighting they were forced to retire. The fight, while it lasted, was one of the sharpest that has occurred during the war, and as a consequence the loss of officers and men on both sides is very heavy.[1]

The enemy's pickets were first encountered a little east of the village by Companies H and M, of the Second New-York (Harris Light) cavalry, under the command of Lieut. DAN. WHITTAKER, and were by them driven through the town back to a ridge of hills half a mile to the west, extending across from the Middleburgh and Snicker's Gap Road, where the rebel force was in position ready for action. The advance brigade, under Gen. [Judson] KILPATRICK, immediately moved through to the westerly edge of the town. The First Maine, Col. [Calvin] DOUTY, was sent off to a point half a mile to the left, and the Fourth New-York, Col. CESNOLA,[2] to the right, to support a section of ANDREWS' battery placed on a rise of ground north of the Snicker's Gap road. The enemy at this

THE REBEL INVASION.

THE REBELS REPORTED MOVING ON HARRISBURGH.

HARRISBURGH, PENN.,
TUESDAY, JUNE 16 — 1 A.M.

Everything looks very gloomy here.

The indications are that the rebels will be within sight of Harrisburgh to-morrow, and in the absence of troops to stop the advance of the rebels, the destruction of all the bridges along the Susquehanna is inevitable.

The troops, as fast as they reach this city and report for duty, are sent to the different fords on the river, where works are being constructed to prevent the crossing of the rebels.

The hills on the opposite side of the river

JUNE 17

are illuminated by the fires of the working parties engaged in throwing up intrenchments. The attempts to get troops from Washington have failed, and all the energies of the State must be directed toward arresting the progress of the rebels.

The rebels must not be allowed to cross the Susquehanna River. The country south of the river there is no hope of saving from devastation and pillage. ⊛

time occupied the hill, as before stated, where they had four guns in position; a line of their skirmishers occupied a fence on the eastern slope, and a long ditch, just in front off which were half a dozen stacks of hay — thus commanding both Middleburgh and Snicker's Gap roads. A stronger position could not well have been selected.

When the exact position of the enemy had been ascertained by drawing; their fire, Gen. KILPATRICK rode up to the Second New-York (Harris' Light.) and said then was the time for them to wipe out the reflection cast upon them for their alleged misconduct in the fight of last week, at Brandy Station, He ordered them to charge into the valley and secure the hay-stacks — the ditch or ravine at the rear of this position had not then been discovered. Companies H and M. accompanied by Lieuts. WHITTAKER, RAYMOND, MARTINSON, HOMAN and STUART, moved off down the Middleburgh road, the fence to the right was quickly thrown down, and with a dash, this forlorn hope rushed up to the hay-stacks. For the first time their fire was opened from the ditch little to the rear of the hay-stacks. This was filled with rebel cavalry — many of them armed with rifles. Capt. GRINTAR, with Lieuts. MATTISON and SHAEER, and Company K, dashed up immediately to the support of these companies, F, I, D and G, went to the light up the Snicker's Gap road a piece, turned

to the left, crossed the field, and reached the scene of conflict in time to take an active part. The contest for twenty minutes at this point was about as spirited a scene as is often witnessed on a battle-field. The Sixth Ohio, Maj. [William] STEADMAN, was sent up the road to the left to support the Harris Light, when the whole command, with the Major at its head, dashed into the fight just in time to decide the unequal contest. The rebels were forced to abandon their position, and all who were not killed or captured fled precipitately up the hill. They made a short stand behind the fence, when a dash from a battalion of the Fourth New-York, called in from its position behind the battery, together with the other regiments already named, drove them pell mell over the hill. The First Maine, at about this time, was called in from the left, and with the First Massachusetts, stationed on the Snicker's Gap road, to a position held by the Second battalion of the Fourth New-York. The rebels, at this time, charged down the same road and drove before them a squadron, when Gen. KILPATRICK ordered the First Maine, Col. DOUTY, First Massachusetts, Lieut. Col. [Sylvanus] CURTIS, and a battalion of the Fourth New-York, under Col. CESNOLA, to charge up the road. There was a little hesitancy at first, when Gen. KILPATRICK, accompanied by Col. DOUTY of the First Maine, and Capt. COSTAR of Gen. PLEASANTON's Staff, went

to the front and called upon the troops to follow. There was no hesitancy then. The Maine boys gave three cheers for Gen. KILPATRICK, and the whole column made a dash up the road in the face of a terrible fire from carbines, rifles and cannon, sweeping everything before them. This virtually ended the fight. The rebels, after a little more skirmishing, fell back, and our forces to-night occupy their position.

More than 100 prisoners were captured — members, principally, of the First, Third, Fourth and Fifth Virginia cavalry. They say they were under the command of Gen. STUART. Among the prisoners is one Colonel, three Majors and a lot of line officers. The Major and sixty men, who were stationed behind the hay-stacks, were nearly all captured. The Major considered his position impregnable, not believing that any cavalry would dare make a charge upon the place, swept as the whole field was by three lines of guns....

E. A. PAUL[2] ✹

1. In the Battle of Aldie (June 17, 1863), a column of about 2,200 Union cavalry under Brigadier General Judson Kilpatrick attempted to force its way through a screening force of 1,500 Confederate troopers under Brigadier General Thomas Rosser. Despite furious fighting at close range, the Union cavalry was forced back. Union losses (300) were about three times those of the Confederates.

2. Luigi Palma di Cesnola (1832–1904) was an Italian-American adventurer who was wounded and taken prisoner in this battle. For his actions, he was subsequently awarded the Medal of Honor.

3. Edward A. Paul was the cavalry correspondent of The Times.

Edwin Forbes's sketch of the Battle of Aldie.

THE ARMY OF THE POTOMAC.
THE WHOLE ARMY PUSHING FORWARD WITH GREAT RAPIDITY.

FROM OUR SPECIAL CORRESPONDENT.
ON THE MARCH, VIRGINIA,
WEDNESDAY, JUNE 17

The Army of the Potomac progresses with huge strides toward the supposed position of the enemy. A fearful collision cannot be avoided many days longer. The weather is terribly hot, the roads, fields, the very air filled with interminable clouds of dust, and the brave men suffer, but they march with a velocity such as never before has been known on this continent. Twenty to twenty-three miles per day in such weather is something unheard of heretofore. One day has been spent since Saturday to let all the corps get up well in hand, and the whole army is now pushing forward with great rapidity. Further particulars concerning our march it would be imprudent to give now, but I venture to say that when all the facts are known, it will be acceded that this march has no parallel....

Everything is reduced to the very lightest marching order. Trains are cut down, wagons and baggage are being reduced to a smaller limit than ever before. Yesterday Gen. HOOKER ordered his Staff, and the members of all the Staff Departments at headquarters, to dispense with all their

JUNE 20

baggage, including valises, carpet bags, &c., and they were sent to the rear to-day. All they take is a change of under-clothing, rolled in their blankets, or put in their saddle-bags or pockets, wherever most convenient. Headquarters goes in lighter orders than anything else.

Notwithstanding the intense heat, there is very little straggling. A strong Provost-Guard of cavalry brings up the rear of each corps, and everything moves with great vigor.

The direction of our march may be spoken of probably, in a day or two, when it will have become apparent to the public.

A curious fact connected with the late cavalry fight I must not forget to relate before the recollection of the fight has died away. A couple of days after the fight Gen. [Alfred A.] PLEASANTON's command made a requisition for twenty grindstones with which to grind up their sabres. This is a positive fact, and illustrates very pointedly the nature of the contest. Hand-to-hand it was in earnest.

L.L. CROUNSE. ⊛

GEN. HOOKER AND HIS DETRACTORS.

JUNE 22

There seems to be in certain quarters a determination that Gen. HOOKER shall not succeed. Nothing has been left unsaid or undone to weaken the confidence of his soldiers in his leadership, and to prepare the people for his being overmatched and overwhelmed. Flippant criticism, jaunty raillery, bitter sneers, high dudgeon, rueful repinings and hysterical despair — all the resorts that could excite contempt for the commander and alarm for the country — have been exhausted. Gen. HOOKER still retains command, and will to the end of the campaign.[1] The Government trusts him, the soldiers follow him, the people believe in him. But if the spirit that has been shown against him be any index, it may well be doubted whether his triumph over LEE would excite more disappointment and grief among the rebels than among the Copperheads....

The Army of the Potomac, though considerably reduced in numbers, was never in so effective a condition as it is to-day; and there is no good reason for doubting that the same skill which has so shaped it, will be equally competent to handle it. If this turns out otherwise, sincerely as we may regret it, we shall not seek to evade the truth. But we protest against a condemnation before trial. It can spring from no worthy motive. It can secure no good end. It is unjust to Gen. HOOKER, it is injurious to the army, and in every sense it is a public scandal. ⊛

> 1. Six days after this article appeared, on June 28, George G. Meade replaced Hooker in command of the Army of the Potomac. That was not the end of Hooker's service, however. He led two corps (15,000 men) to the Western Theater in 1863 and fought well in the Battles for Chattanooga (see Chapter 16).

THE SIEGE OF VICKSBURGH.

JUNE 27

It is now forty days since the siege of Vicksburgh was commenced. It was on the 18th of May — the day after that on which was fought the last of the five victorious battles which illustrated GRANT's march, that the investment of the city was effected. The three corps of the army moved up to the siege work after their field struggles with irresistible determination and unflinching valor — [William T.] SHERMAN's corps on the right, [James B.] MCPHERSON's in the centre and [John A.] MCCLERNAND's on the left. During these forty days, the hard labors of the siege have been prosecuted steadily and unintermittingly. By day and by night, the great siege guns have flung their tremendous projectiles into the doomed city; while several times in the day and night, the bells of the clocks of Vicksburgh gave the signal to our mortar-boats in the river to open their fires and throw their death-laden bombs among the rebels. Latterly we have been informed that Gen. GRANT was about to use red-hot shot in his bombardment, which would probably have the effect of at least destroying the town; but as its people are all said to have taken refuge in caves dug in the hill-sides, they might escape any serious inconvenience from this cause. Since the general

REMOVAL OF GEN. HOOKER — APPOINTMENT OF GEN. MEADE.

JUNE 29

The country will be astounded by the news from Washington this morning that Gen. HOOKER has been relieved from the command of the Army of the Potomac, and Gen. Meade appointed as his successor. We have had no hint hat a change was anticipated; and probably it has not been anticipated long. No reasons for the change are given; but it is doubtless owning to the fact that the Government has at last come too entertain the feeling so widely prevalent in the country, of a want of that perfect confidence in Gen, HOOKER, which is so essential at a crisis like this. During the recent and present movements of the rebel army against Washington, the manouevers of Gen. HOOKER were, to a great extent, incomprehensible to the general public; but we had daily assurances from

A Kurz and Allison lithograph presents an unusual perspective on the siege of Vicksburg.

assault made upon the rebel works, four days after investment, nothing farther of the kind has been attempted — though Gen. GRANT's action in dismissing from command Gen. MCCLERNAND, who was mainly blamed for the failure of that attack, indicates that GRANT did not consider the failure to take the works by storm to be owing to their impregnability to direct assault[1].... ✸

1. John A. McClernand (1812–1900) was a former Democratic congressman from Illinois and therefore a so-called "political general." Lincoln had agreed to allow him to raise an army in the Midwest to clear the Mississippi River, and McClernand was subsequently disappointed to find himself subordinate to Grant. His battlefield performance was adequate, but what turned Grant against him was his proclivity to issue public statements inflating the contributions of his own corps to the detriment of others. The politically sensitive Grant checked with Lincoln first, and when the president did not object, he dismissed McClernand from his command.

Washington that our army was being so handled and placed as to insure the circumvention of LEE in his designs. Those of us who knew what HOOKER's movements had been for the past fortnight, found in them some things that were admirable and others that were inexplicable. But we could only wait patiently for results, devoutly hoping that those who had the Government of the country and the ordering of the army in their hands, and who were thoroughly informed concerning much that was dark to mere observers, were working for the public salvation to the best of their knowledge and ability. If so it be that Gen. HOOKER has been removed for good cause, the country will cheerfully acquiesce in the removal.

We have, to the best of our ability, sustained Gen. HOOKER in his efforts as commander of the Army of the Potomac from the day he took command until now. We know the necessity of upholding the confidence of the people, and of the army in its leader, as long as he is retained in that position. Whenever we have not been able to applaud, we have remained silent, publishing only the news of events and the details of movements and actions, and permitting every intelligent man to form his own conclusions....

Gen. MEADE takes command of the army at a very critical moment, and while it is placed in a critical position. As already indicated, the main body is on this side of the river, and north of Washington, but we cannot give any further details. The whole country will unite in devoutly hoping fro him the greatest success. And we earnestly trust that, after so many changes, we have at last, in this hour, fallen upon an officer capable of leading the nation and its gallant army to victory. ✸

CHAPTER 14

"An Action of Gigantic Magnitude"

JULY 1863

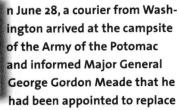

On June 28, a courier from Washington arrived at the campsite of the Army of the Potomac and informed Major General George Gordon Meade that he had been appointed to replace Joseph Hooker in command of the Union army. Hooker had insisted that the garrison at Harpers Ferry be added to his field army and, when the government disagreed, he submitted his resignation expecting to shock the civil leaders into compliance. Instead Lincoln accepted it. Meade was the obvious alternative but, in addition, Lincoln hoped that as a Pennsylvanian, he would fight well, as the President said, "on his own dunghill." Three days later, on the rolling farmland south of Gettysburg (which The Times spelled Gettysburgh), the Union Army of the Potomac and the Confederate army of Northern Virginia fought the bloodiest battle in the history of the Western Hemisphere.

News of the battle trickled into New York bit by bit in telegraphic reports from the front, almost like radio bulletins. Though, as usual, the reporters from the field put a hopeful face of their accounts of the fighting, not until July 6 was it clear that Meade's army had won an unquestioned victory. The New York Times of that date was virtually filled with articles about the victory and Lee's retreat. Six of the articles from that date are reproduced here. Once again, The Times's Lorenzo Crounse provided day-by-day — almost hour-by-hour — reports. But other Times reporters were there, too. Samuel Wilkeson arrived in Gettysburg on the night of July 1, only to learn that his son, Lieutenant Bayard Wilkeson of Battery G, Fourth U.S. Artillery, had been mortally wounded that afternoon by an artillery shell. Taken to a poor-

Detail of an illustration of the fighting at Devil's Den during the Battle of Gettysburg.

house that was being used as a field hospital, young Wilkeson had been left behind when the Union army fell back through town to Cemetery Hill, and he died that night. His father's field report, which appeared in the July 6 issue of The Times, is especially poignant for its cri de coeur at the outset: "Who can write the history of a battle whose eyes are immovably fastened upon a central figure of transcendently absorbing interest — the dead body of an oldest born, crashed by a shell in a position where a battery should never have been sent, and abandoned to death in a building where surgeons dared not to stay?"

News of the victory triggered celebrations all across the North, including in New York City. Then, only days later, came news of the capitulation of Vicksburg in far-off Mississippi, and the surrender of its garrison — an entire Confederate army. When Gideon Welles brought the news to Lincoln, the President threw his arm around his secretary of the navy and proclaimed, "I cannot in words tell you my joy over this result. It is great, Mr. Welles, it is great!" Indeed, the capture of Vicksburg was even more strategically important than the defeat of Lee's army, and led Northerners — and some Northern newspapers — to begin talking about a swift end to the war. Alas, despite the importance of these events as a turning point, it is noteworthy that more American soldiers — on both sides — died in the twenty-two months of war after Gettysburg and Vicksburg than in the twenty-seven months of war that preceded them.

For New Yorkers, celebration of the twin victories turned to horror when, only days later, the city erupted in five days of bloody rioting on the streets of Manhattan. Labeled the "New York City Draft Riots" by historians, the five-day rampage was initially triggered by opposition to the draft, but was fed by complex social, ethnic, and economic issues, including a fear within the poor white working class (especially the Irish) that free blacks would take their jobs. Eventually the protests morphed into a horrific race riot. The police crackdown provoked its own opposition, and the fighting became a war of the white working poor against the symbols of authority. Before it was over, 105 citizens were dead.

The Times took a hard line toward the rioters, insisting that the perpetrators constituted "the lowest and most ruffianly mob which ever disgraced our City," and it called for the mayor to put his foot down. "The duties of the executive officers of this State and City are not to debate, or negotiate, or supplicate," The Times opined, "but to execute the laws." The solution to quelling the riots, the paper declared, was for the authorities to "Give them grape, and plenty of it." And that is what happened. On July 16 and 17, five regiments of the Union army arrived in New York, including several batteries of artillery. Only then did the riots end.

THE REBEL INVASION.
HIGHLY IMPORTANT FROM THE ARMY OF THE POTOMAC.

JULY 2

SPECIAL DISPATCH TO THE NEW-YORK TIMES.
HEADQUARTERS ARMY OF THE POTOMAC,
TUESDAY EVENING — 8 P.M.

I am just in from the front, and send by a messenger to Frederick a brief dispatch of the occurrences of yesterday and to-day. The rebel force which made the raid on the Baltimore and Ohio Railroad consisted of STUART'S whole force, with eight pieces of artillery.[1] On Monday night they arrived at Westminster and interrupted the Western Maryland Railroad. They threw out strong pickets, and shot two citizens who attempted to escape and give us information. Early this morning, Gen. [David M.] GREGG attacked STUART and drove him all the way from Westminster to Hanover, Pennsylvania — a distance of eighteen miles. During the forenoon Gens. [Judson] KILPATRICK and [George A.] CUSTER drove STUART out of Hanover after a splendid fight, and they are still pursuing him; part of his force going toward Gettysburgh and part toward York.

During the day Gen. [John] BUFORD drove a regiment of rebel infantry out of Gettysburgh, who also retired in a north-easterly direction.

You may expect to hear of brilliant news. The whole army is in splendid spirits. ✸

1. As his infantry marched northward down the Shenandoah Valley, Lee assigned J. E. B. Stuart with three of the army's five cavalry brigades to screen the advance. Stuart decided he could do that best by riding around the Federal army (as he had done twice before). On June 29, his troopers broke the B&O Railroad north of Cooksville, and that afternoon they rode through Westminster, Maryland. At Hanover, Pennsylvania, an attack by Kilpatrick and Custer caught Stuart by surprise and he was nearly taken prisoner, escaping only by jumping his prized mare over a deep gulley.

THE WAR IN PENNSYLVANIA.

JULY 3

The people of New-York and the country generally, as well as the Government at Washington, were in hourly expectation of the news of a battle in Southern Pennsylvania yesterday, when they learned by the special and exclusive dispatch from Gettysburgh to the NEW-YORK TIMES that one had actually been fought on Wednesday [July 1] at that place. The dispatch was brief, but up to 2 o'clock this morning no material facts had been added to it.

We had known previously, and we announced on Wednesday, that the columns of the rebel army, which had been scattered over a wide region in Pennsylvania, were being drawn in toward Chambersburgh, and had also taken up their march in a southeasterly direction — it appears now, in a direct line for Gettysburgh. We knew also that the Army of the Potomac under Gen. MEADE was advancing northward in the same direction, and we ☞

had published a letter from the army, dated at Middleburgh, Md., which is only fifteen miles south of Gettysburgh. Those who observed these facts were prepared for early news of a collision in that vicinity.

The battle raged for nine hours — beginning at nine in the morning, and ending at four in the afternoon. We had but two corps engaged, out of the seven into which the Army of the Potomac is divided — or probably not much over thirty thousand men. Opposed to these were the forces of [James] LONGSTREET [actually Richard S. Ewell] and [A. P.] HILL — or probably about two-thirds of the rebel army. In the day's fight nothing decisive was achieved by either side, though casualties are reported as heavy; and in the death of that splendid soldier, Gen. [John F.] REYNOLDS, and also of Gen. [Gabriel] PAUL, we have suffered irreparable losses.[1] In the afternoon, two other corps of our army had arrived on the ground, and at the close of the evening, the whole Army of the Potomac had reached the field, and its different corps had been strongly posted by Gen. MEADE for a renewal of the mortal struggle yesterday morning.

The rebels, we suppose, on learning the news of Wednesday's battle, also hastened to the field their columns outlying on the line of the Cumberland Valley Railroad, and, if there were a collision yesterday, it was doubtless between the two armies in force.

"The Army of the Potomac is in fine condition and very enthusiastic," says the dispatch of to-day. It would seem that, being well posted, well concentrated, and in good spirits, all it needs to insure victory is skillful handling. To Gen. MEADE the whole country anxiously looks for that. ✸

Lieutenant General James Longstreet, C.S.A.

Major General George G. Meade, U.S.A.

1. Major General John F. Reynolds (1820–1863), commander of the Union First Corps, was killed while directing his men into the fight atop McPherson's Ridge on July 1. Brigadier General Gabriel Rene Paul (1811–1886) was shot in the head and severely wounded but survived, though his military career was effectively ended.

JULY 1863

247

DETAILS OF WEDNESDAY'S BATTLE.
—
BATTLE-FIELD NEAR GETTYSBURGH.

JULY 6
THURSDAY, JULY 2 — 12 P.M.

The engagement yesterday [July 1] was very sharp, and one of the bloodiest, for its duration, yet encountered by the Army of the Potomac. It was entirely between our Advance Guard, the First corps, supported subsequently by the Eleventh, and the combined forces of the rebel Generals HILL and EWELL.

[James S.] WADSWORTH'S Division, which encamped Tuesday night at Marsh Creek, five miles south of Gettysburgh, moved forward in the morning, and at 10 A.M., were at Gettysburgh. Half a mile beyond the town they met the rebels in force, who were advancing rapidly, Gen. REYNOLDS, apparently under the impression that the force was not more than equal to his, immediately attacked the enemy with great vigor, and drove them back, capturing 400 prisoners, including one Brigadier-General ([James J.] ARCHER) on the spot. It was just before this, while forming the line of battle, that Gen. REYNOLDS was killed by a rebel sharpshooter, concealed near by, who shot him through the head. The enemy had taken a position which was very strong, but our men, with fixed bayonets, drove them from it. WADSWORTH, with two brigades, now became hotly engaged, and held the position fuller an hour unsupported. The second division, under Gen. [James S.] ROBINSON, then became engaged, and also one brigade of Gen. [Abner] DOUBLEDAY's command, his division being commanded by Col. [Thomas A.] ROWLEY after Gen. REYNOLDS was killed, DOUBLEDAY being assigned to the corps. About half-past one o'clock, the Eleventh corps arrived on the field from Emmetsburgh, and formed on the right of the First corps, but did not get engaged until 3 P.M. The fighting on the left now became very heavy, the enemy pouring in large masses of troops on both flanks. But our men stood their ground with great tenacity, especially the First corps. WADSWORTH's and ROBINSON's divisions, aided in the most gallant manner by Col. ROY STONE's brigade, of Gen. DOUBLEDAY's division.

Two lines of the enemy, who advanced against WADSWORTH's division, were literally crushed, nearly every man being killed or wounded, so accurate was the aim of our men — especially of Gen. SOL. MEREDITH's brigade of Western men [the Iron Brigade].

At length the enemy displayed a strong force on each bank, and compelled our men to fall back, they having no supports within reach. This they did in good order, passing through the town to just the southern and eastern edge of it where a new position was taken on a range of high hills circling around the town from north to south [Cemetery Hill and Cemetery Ridge].

The Eleventh corps in action was commanded by Gen. [Carl] SCHURZ. His division was on the right of WADSWORTH's, and Gen. BARLOW's on the right of SCHURZ's, with [Adolph] STEINWEHR's in reserve. The conduct of the corps partially redeemed the reputation lost at Chancellorsville, though in coming through the town, in retiring, there was considerable confusion, an a great many stragglers were lost. There way very little artillery in the early part of the fight. [James] HALL's Second Maine battery distinguished itself, as also did STUART's Battery B, Fourth artillery, who mowed the rebels down by hundreds.

We lost no artillery, and by 6 o'clock Gen. HANCOCK, who had been ordered up to take command on the field, arrived, and, with Gen. HOWARD's assistance, soon formed new lines to the east and south of the town. We still occupied a portion of the place, but the enemy held the most, of it and with it many of our wounded, who were brought there during the fight.[1]

The principal portion of the fight took place near the Pennsylvania College, which building is now used by the enemy as a hospital.

By dark the Twelfth, Third and Second corps had arrived as reinforcements, and Gen. [Henry W.] SLOCUM was temporarily in command.

Gen. MEADE arrived about 9 o'clock P.M., and immediately began making the dispositions to give or receive battle.

I send a duplicate list of such casualties among officers as I have thus far obtained — one to go by telegraph. The losses on both sides were very heavy. In MEREDITH's brigade, the loss reported this morning is 728 killed and wounded, out of 1,850 who went into the fight, and 400 more are yet unaccounted for.[2]

Col. ROY STONE, of the Pennsylvania Bucktails, behaved with great gallantry, and was severely wounded. His brigade—the first time under fire — behaved like veterans.

There is no cause whatever for discour-

agement at the result of yesterday's fight. It was simply an advance of two corps engaged with, two whole corps (two-thirds) of the rebel army.

Our forces are now all up, and dispositions are making for a grand attack. All the morning both armies have been deploying their columns, preparatory to a great contest. We occupy and hold the Baltimore pike, Taneytown road, and Emmettsburgh Pike, all leading south and east to Baltimore and Washington.

The country is generally open and rolling, affording great opportunities for the use of artillery. There is not much timber, and the rebels have fewer advantages than heretofore. Our losses cannot at present be estimated. They are already among the thousands and number some of our best hundreds.

Gens. REYNOLDS and, PAUL are killed, the latter having died of his wounds this morning.[3] Gen. [Francis] BARLOW is severely wounded, and in Gettysburgh — a prisoner. Gen. [Alexander] SCHIMMELFENNIG is a prisoner, but not hurt.[4] Col. LUCIUS FAIRCHILD of the Second Wisconsin, has lost his left arm, and is a prisoner, but be sent me word, last night, that he was doing well and in glorious spirits.

I have no time to send further particulars. The enemy are now feeling our line, preparatory, apparently, to making an attack. He may receive one before he can give one. Large misses of artillery are arriving and being pat in position, there being many fine opportunities for its use.

The great fight will probably begin this afternoon, and continue through to-morrow.

L.L. CROUNSE. ✖

1. There was some initial confusion when Hancock arrived. After learning of Reynolds's death, Meade sent Hancock galloping ahead of his corps to take command of the forces on the field. But Howard, who was already on the field, ranked Hancock by date of rank, and he was somewhat offended to be superseded by a junior. He nevertheless accepted Hancock's authority and worked with him to establish the new defense line.
2. The Iron Brigade lost 1,153 men out of 1,885 engaged, a loss of 61 percent.
3. Paul survived, dying in 1886.
4. Francis Barlow (1834–1896) was wounded north of Gettysburg atop the knoll that now bears his name and very near where Samuel Wilkeson's son fell wounded. Brigadier General Alexander Schimmelfennig (1824–1865) suffered the ignominy of being discovered by Confederates and captured after hiding in a back yard pig sty during the Union army's retreat through the town.

SPECIAL DISPATCHES TO THE NEW-YORK TIMES.

BATTLE-FIELD NEAR GETTYSBURGH.

THURSDAY JULY 2 4:30 P.M.
VIA BALTIMORE, FRIDAY A.M.

The day has been quiet up to the present moment. The enemy are now massing a heavy force on our left, and have just began the attack with artillery. The probability is that a severe battle will be fought before dark. The rebel sharpshooters have been annoying our batteries and men all day from the steeples of the churches in Gettysburgh. We hold the Emmettsburgh and Baltimore roads.

L. L. CROUNSE.

BATTLE-FIELD NEAR GETTYSBURGH.
FRIDAY MORNING JULY 3, — THREE A.M. VIA
BALTIMORE, ONE P.M.

At the close of my last dispatch at 4 1/2 P.M. yesterday, the enemy had just opened a heavy attack by artillery on our left and centre. The tactics of the enemy were soon apparent — a massing of their main strength on our left flank, which covered the Frederick road, with the determination to crush it. So intent were the enemy on this purpose, that every other part of the lines was left alone.

JULY 4

The fighting was of the most desperate description on both sides. Our gallant men fought as they never fought before. We had against this great onslaught of the enemy three corps — the Second, Third and Fifth. The Third and Fifth joined hands, and fought heroically. The Second ably supported them, and at the same time held its own position. One division of the First was also engaged.

The fighting was so furious that neither party took many prisoners. We captured about 600 in one or two charges.

The losses, considering the duration of the conflict, are more than usually heavy on both sides. Many of our most gallant officers have fallen. Gen. [Daniel] SICKLES' right leg was shot off below the knee. Amputation has been performed, and he is doing well.

Late in the evening, Gen. MEADE called a council of his corps commanders, and it was re-solved to continue the fight so long as there was any one left to fight.

L. L. CROUNSE. ✸

NEWS OF THE DAY.

THE REBELLION.

JULY 6

Our news from the great battlefield of Gettysburgh this morning is of the most cheering and satisfactory character. The great battle of Friday — the third in the series — proves to have been by far the most desperate one of the war, and to have resulted in the complete discomfiture of the enemy. At daylight LEE's right-wing batteries opened upon our left, and shortly afterward those of his centre followed, but little damage being done by his fire. Soon afterward an impetuous infantry attack was made upon our right, which was repulsed after a sharp struggle — the enemy leaving a considerable number of prisoners in our hands. There was then a lull of several hours, and at 10 o'clock LEE, having massed about 80 pieces of artillery, opened a terrific cannonade upon our centre, but their range being imperfect, it did comparatively little damage to us, and was replied to by our artillery with the best effect. Under cover of this fire, LEE advanced his columns of infantry, and made several desperate attempts to carry our lines by assault, but each successive charge was repulsed with terrific havoc in the rebel

Peter F. Rothermel's colossal 1872 painting, as engraved by John Sartain, showed the Union repulse of Pickett's Charge on the final day of the Battle of Gettysburg—the so-called "high water mark" of the Confederacy.

ranks. About 4 1/2 o'clock P.M., the fire of the enemy's artillery slackened, and at 5 it had entirely ceased, and their infantry had withdrawn to cover. During the latter we captured upwards of 3,000 prisoners, and lost but very few. LONGSTREET is very positively stated to have been mortally wounded, and to have fallen into our hands. Gen. MILL is said by prisoners to have been killed outright during the battle.

The official dispatches from Gen. MEADE to the War Department are brief but, corroborates the statements made by our correspondents regarding the events of the battle. At the close of the engagement, he says, the movements of the enemy induced him to believe a retreat was intended. He accordingly pushed forward a strong reconnaissance, which found the enemy in force. On the morning of Saturday, the Fourth, however, it was found that the enemy had withdrawn from the position occupied by him on the day previous, abandoning a large number of killed and wounded on the field. Gen. MEADE's latest dispatch is dated 8 1/2 o'clock A.M. yesterday.

News was received in Baltimore yesterday afternoon that the rebels were in full retreat. ✸

THE GREAT BATTLE OF FRIDAY.
OUR SPECIAL TELEGRAMS FROM THE BATTLE-FIELD.

JULY 6

Another great battle was fought yesterday afternoon [July 3], resulting in a magnificent success to the National arms.

At 2 o'clock P.M., LONGSTREET's whole corps advanced from the rebel centre against our centre. The enemy's forces were hurled upon our position by columns in mass, and also in lines of battle. Our centre was held by Gen. [Winfield S.] HANCOCK, with the noble old Second army corps, sided by Gen. DOUBLEDAY's division of the First corps.

The rebels first opened a terrific artillery bombardment to demoralize our men, and then moved their forces with great impetuosity upon our position. HANCOCK received the attack with great firmness, and after a furious battle, lasting until 6 o'clock, the enemy were driven from the field, LONGSTREET's corps being almost annihilated.

The battle was a most magnificent spectacle. It was fought on an open plain, just south of Gettysburgh, with not a tree to interrupt the view. The courage of our men was perfectly sublime.

At 5 P.M. what was left of the enemy retreated in utter confusion, leaving dozens of flags, and Gen. HANCOCK estimated at least five thousand killed and wounded on the field.

The battle was fought by Gen. HANCOCK with splendid valor. He won imperishable honor, and Gen. MEADE thanked him in the name of the army and the country. He was wounded in the thigh, but remained on-the field .... .

The conduct of our veterans was perfectly magnificent. More than twenty battle flags were taken by our troops. Nearly every regiment has one. The Nineteenth Massachusetts captured four. The repulse was so disastrous to the enemy, that LONGSTREET's corps is perfectly used up. Gen. [John] GIBBON was wounded in the shoulder. Gen. [Alexander] WEBB was wounded and remained on the field. Col. [John S.] HAMMELL, of the Sixty-sixth New-York, was wounded in the arm.

At 7 o'clock last evening. Gen. MEADE ordered the Third corps, supported by the Sixth, to attack the enemy's right, which was done, and the battle lasted until dark, when a good deal of ground had been gained.

During the day EWELL's corps kept up a desultory attack upon SLOCUM on the right, but was repulsed.

Our cavalry is to-day playing savagely upon the enemy's flank and rear.

L. L. CROUNSE ✸

GETTYSBURGH.

JULY 6

The Army of the Potomac, under its new leader, has won its greatest victory. The tremendous actions of the first three days of the month of July at Gettysburgh have been followed by the complete discomfiture of the entire rebel army, which so audaciously and exultingly crossed the Potomac, and planted itself on Pennsylvania soil less than a fortnight ago. Entertaining not a doubt of triumph, it advanced with flying banners, defiant shouts, and steady tread. From the Rappahannock to the Blue Ridge, from the mountains to the Potomac, from the Potomac to the Susquehanna, they swept unmolested over a distance of two hundred miles; and at the beginning of last week, were just preparing to consummate their triumphant campaign. They condemned the Army of the Potomac, sneered at its late leader, and

boasted that they could kick him and his army around the continent. Their commander had already led them in five great campaigns, two of them in their inception offensive, two defensive, and one what JOMINI[1] styles offensive-defensive; and all of them they regarded as victorious. There were but three things more needed to insure their final success, and these were — to rout the Army of the Potomac, capture Washington, and hold their army on our soil until they could dictate terms of peace and enforce the recognition of the Southern Confederacy. By the seizure of Philadelphia and Baltimore, they could also thoroughly humiliate us, and after the fashion they established at York, could fill the coffers of the Confederacy, and gratify their army with plunder.[2] Their task was simple and their assurance unbounded.

So at least it appeared last Monday. So it appeared on the first day of the month of July.

But their lately exultant and defiant army of invasion — where is it, and what is it now?

Defeated in the very opening of the campaign, Defeated in three great battles in which their whole force of infantry, cavalry and artillery was engaged. Defeated by the Army of the Potomac, Defeated by Gen. MEADE, who then fought his first battle at the head of the army, Defeated with tremendous loss in killed and wounded, in prisoners and in artillery; and defeated when defeat was destruction. Defeated after struggling for three days with a fury more than mortal and an energy madder than that of despair.... ✸

1. Baron Antoine-Henri Jomini (1779–1869) was a French general and military theorist who wrote several books on the theory of war, including *The Art of War* (1838) which was used as a text at the U.S. Military Academy.
2. At York and elsewhere in Pennsylvania, Confederate forces coerced a payment from the townspeople on threat of having their city put to the torch.

DETAILS FROM OUR SPECIAL CORRESPONDENT.

HEADQUARTERS ARMY OF POTOMAC,
SATURDAY NIGHT, JULY 4

Who can write the history of a battle whose eyes are immovably fastened upon a central figure of transcendently absorbing interest — the dead body of an oldest born, crashed by a shell in a position where a battery should never have been sent, and abandoned to death in a building where surgeons dared not to stay?[1]

The battle of Gettysburgh, I am told that it commenced, on the 1st of July, a mile north of the town, between two weak brigades of infantry and some doomed artillery and the whole force of the rebel army. Among other costs of this error was the death of REYNOLDS. Its value was priceless; however, though priceless was the young and the old blood with which it was bought. The error put us on the defensive, and gave us the choice of position. From the moment that our artillery and infantry rolled back through the main street of Gettysburgh and rolled out of the town to

JULY 6

the circle of eminences south of it. We were not to attack but to be attacked. The risks, the difficulties and the disadvantages of the coming battle were the enemy's. Ours were the heights for artillery; ours the short, inside lines for maneuvering and reinforcing; ours the cover of stonewalls, fences and the crests of hills. The ground upon which we were driven to accept battle was wonderfully favorable to us. A popular description of it would be to say that it was in form an elongated and somewhat sharpened horseshoe, with the toe to Gettysburgh and the heel to the south.[2]

LEE's plan of battle was simple. He massed

An Alexander Gardner photograph shows Confederate dead at Devil's Den.

his troops upon the east side of this shoe of position, and thundered on it obstinately to break it. The shelling of our batteries from the nearest overlooking hill, and the unflinching courage and complete discipline of the army of the Potomac repelled the attack. It was renewed at the point of the shoe [Cemetery Hill] — renewed desperately at the southwest heel [Little Round Top] — renewed on the western side with an effort consecrated to success by [Richard S.] EWELL's earnest oaths, and on which the fate of the invasion of Pennsylvania was fully put at stake. Only a perfect infantry and an artillery educated in the midst of charges of hostile brigades could possibly have sustained this assault. [Winfield Scott] HANCOCK's corps did sustain it, and has covered itself with immortal honors by its constancy and courage. The total wreck of [Alonzo] CUSHING's battery — the list of its killed and wounded — the losses of officers, men and horses [Andrew] COWEN sustained — and the marvellous outspread upon the board of death of dead soldiers and dead animals — of dead soldiers in blue, and dead soldiers in gray — more marvellous to me than anything I have ever seen in war — are a ghastly and shocking testimony to the terrible fight of the Second corps that none will gainsay. That corps will ever have the distinction of breaking the pride and power of the rebel invasion.

For such details as I have the heart for. The battle commenced at day light, on the side of the horse-shoe position, exactly opposite to that which EWELL had sworn to crush through. Musketry preceded the rising of the sun. A thick wood veiled this fight, but out of its leafy darkness arose the smoke and the surging and swelling of the fire, front intermittent to continuous, and crushing, told of the wise tactics of the rebels of attacking in force and changing their troops. Seemingly this attack of the day was to be made through that wood. The demonstration was protracted — it was absolutely preparative; but there was no artillery fire accompanying the musketry and shrewd officers in our western front mentioned, with the gravity due to the fact, that the rebels had felled trees at intervals upon the edge of the wood they occupied in face of our position. These were breastworks for the protection of artillery men.

Suddenly, and about 10 to the forenoon, the firing on the east side, and every where about our lines, ceased. A silence as of deep sleep fell upon the field of battle. Our army cooked, ate and slumbered. The reb-

el army moved 120 guns to the west, and massed there LONGSTREET's corps and HILL's corps, to hurl them upon the really weakest point of our entire position.

Eleven o'clock — twelve o'clock — one o'clock. In the shadow cast by the tiny farm; house 16 by 20, which Gen. MEADE had made his Headquarters, lay wearied Staff officers and tired reporters. There was not wanting to the peacefulness of the scene the singing of a bird, which had a nest in a peach tree within the tiny yard of the whitewashed cottage. In the midst of its warbling, a shell screamed over the house, instantly followed by another, and another, and in a moment the air was full of the most complete artillery prelude to an infantry battle that was ever exhibited. Every size and form of shell known to British and to American gunnery shrieked, whirled, moaned, whistled and wrathfully fluttered over our ground. As many as six in a second, constantly two in a second, burning and screaming over and around the headquarters, made a very hell of fire that amazed the oldest officers. They burst in the yard-burst next to the fence on both sides, garnished as usual with the hitched horses of aids and orderlies. The fastened animals reared and plunged with terror. Then one fell, then another — sixteen laid dead and mangled before the fire ceased, still fastened by their baiters, which gave the expression of being wickedly tied up to die painfully. These brute victims of a cruel war touched all hearts: Through the midst of the storm of screaming and exploding shells, an ambulance, driven by its frenzied conductor at full speed, presented to all of us the marvelous spectacle of a horse going rapidly on three legs. A hinder one had been shot off at the hock.... During this fire ... soldiers in Federal blue were torn to pieces in the road and died with the peculiar yells that blend the extorted cry of pain with horror and despair....

Then there was a lull, and we knew that the rebel Infantry was charging. And splendidly they did this work — the highest and severest test of the stuff that soldiers are made of. HILL's division, in line of battle, came first on the double quick. Their muskets at the "right-shoulder-shift." LONGSTREET's came as the support, at the usual distance, with war cries and a savage insolence as yet untutored by defeat. They rushed in perfect order across the open field up to the very muzzles of the guns, which tore lanes through them as

they came. But they met men who were their equals in spirit, and their superiors in tenacity. There never was better fighting since Thermopylae than was done yesterday by our infantry and artillery. The rebels were over our defences. They had cleaned cannoniers and horses from one of the guns, and were whirling it around to use upon us. The bayonet drove them back ...So terrible was our musketry and artillery fire, that when [Lewis] ARMISTEAD's brigade was checked[3] in its charge, and stood reeling, all of its men dropped their muskets and crawled on their hands and knees underneath the stream of shot till close to our troops, where they made signs of surrendering. They passed through our ranks scarcely noticed, and slowly went down the slope to the road in the rear....

What remains to say of the fight?... My pen is heavy. Oh, you dead, who at Gettysburgh have baptised with your blood the second birth of Freedom in America, how you are envied! I rise from a grave whose wet clay I have passionately kissed, and I look up and see Christ spanning this battle-field with his feet and reaching fraternal and lovingly up to heaven. His right hand opens the gates of Paradise — with his left he beckons these mutilated, bloody, swollen corpses to ascend.

S. WILKESON ✦

1. Samuel Wilkeson's reference here is his son, First Lieutenant Bayard Wilkeson, commander of Battery G, Fourth U.S. Artillery, who was mortally wounded on Barlow's Knoll on July 1. Wilkeson's right leg was shattered by a Confederate cannonball and was hanging only by a shred of skin. Tradition has it that young Wilkeson cut off the leg with his own knife. Samuel Wilkeson supposedly wrote this report while gazing on his son's body.
2. Other writers have suggested that the Union's position resembled a fishhook.
3. Brigadier General Lewis Armistead (1817–1863) led one of the three brigades in George Pickett's division, and was the only general officer to pierce the Union line on July 3, leading the charge with his hat on his sword point, up to the very muzzles of a Union artillery battery commanded by Alonzo Cushing. The spot where Armistead fell mortally wounded is generally considered to be the Confederate "high water mark" at Gettysburg.

THE GREAT BATTLES.

SPLENDID TRIUMPH
OF THE ARMY OF THE POTOMAC.

ROUT OF LEE'S FORCES ON FRIDAY

HEADQUARTERS ARMY OF POTOMAC, NEAR
GETTYSBURGH, FRIDAY, JULY 3 — 8 1/2 P.M.

The following has just been received:
Major-Gen. Halleck, General-in-Chief:

The enemy opened at 1 P.M., from about one
hundred and fifty guns, concentrated upon
my left centre, continuing without intermission for about three hours, at the expiration of
which time, he assaulted my left centre twice,
being, upon both occasions, handsomely repulsed, with severe loss to him, leaving in our
hands nearly three thousand prisoners.

Among the prisoners is Brig.-Gen.
ARMISTEAD and many Colonels and officers of lesser rank.

The enemy left many dead upon the field,
and a large number of wounded in our hands.

The loss upon our side has been considerable. Maj.-Gen. HANCOCK and Brig.-
Gen. [John] GIBBON were wounded.[1]

JULY 6

After the repelling of the assaults, indications leading to the belief that the enemy
might be withdrawing, a reconnaissance
was pushed forward from the left and the
enemy found to be in force.

At the present hour all is quiet....

The army is in fine spirits.

GEORGE G. MEADE, MAJ.-GEN. COMMANDING.

✳

> 1. Winfield Scott Hancock (1824–1886) was a con-
> spicuous target on horseback during the charge. He
> was severely wounded when a bullet struck the pom-
> mel of his saddle and entered his inner right thigh
> carrying wood fragments and a large bent nail. He
> survived his wound and seventeen years later, in
> 1880, he was the Democratic candidate for Presi-
> dent. John Gibbon (1827–1896) was wounded by a
> minie ball through the left shoulder.

THE PRESIDENT TO
THE COUNTRY.

JULY 6
WASHINGTON, D.C, JULY 4 — 10:30 A.M.

The President announces to the country
that news from the Army of the Potomac,
up to 10 P.M. of the 3d, is such as to cover that army with the highest honor; to
promise a great success to the cause of
the Union, and to claim the condolence
of all for the many gallant fallen; and that
for this, he especially desires that on this
day He, whose will, not ours, should ever
be done, be everywhere remembered and
reverenced with profoundest gratitude.

(SIGNED) LINCOLN. ✳

THE REBELS REPORTED
IN FULL RETREAT.

JULY 6
BALTIMORE, SUNDAY, JULY 5

The [Baltimore] American has just put
upon its bulletin the important announcement that the rebel army it in full retreat,
which was commenced on Friday night.
Many thousand prisoners — and a large
number of cannon are captured. ✳

Edwin Forbes's sketch of federal troops pursuing Lee's army during a rainstorm
after the Battle of Gettysburg.

THE GREAT VICTORY.

GEN. MEADE'S ORDER OF THANKS TO THE ARMY.

JULY 7

HEADQUARTERS ARMY OF POTOMAC, NEAR GETTYSBURGH, JULY 4.
GENERAL ORDERS NO. 68.

The Commanding General, in behalf of the country, thanks the Army of the Potomac for the glorious result of the recent operations. Our enemy, superior in numbers, and flushed with the pride of a successful invasion, attempted to overcome or destroy this army. Baffled and defeated he has now withdrawn from the contest. The privations and fatigues the army has endured, and the heroic courage and gallantry it displayed, will be matters of history to be ever remembered.

Our task is not yet accomplished, and the Commanding General looks to the army for greater efforts to drive from our soil every vestige of the presence of the invader.

It is right and proper that we should, on suitable occasions, return our grateful thanks to the Almighty Disposer of events, that, in the goodness of His providence He has thought at to give victory to the cause of the just.

By command of

(SIGNED) MAJ.-GEN. MEADE[1] ✸

1. When he read Meade's directive "to drive from our soil every vestige of the presence of the invader," Lincoln blurted out. "Drive the invaders from our soil! My God! Is that all?" In his view, all of the country was "our soil," and the object was not to drive the rebels out but to restore the Union. The President indulged himself to the extent of writing a critical letter to Meade about this and other things, but then, thinking better of it, he consigned the letter to a drawer and instead sent Meade a letter of congratulations.

TROUBLE AMONG IRISH AND COLORED STEVEVEDORES [SIC].

JULY 8

BUFFALO, MONDAY, JULY 6

There was a difficulty between the Irish stevedores and negroes, this afternoon, in consequence of the former trying to prevent the negroes from unloading propellers [that is, propeller-driven ships]. One negro shot an Irishman, it is said, in self-defence, which was the signal for a general onslaught on all the negroes, several of whom are reported killed, and a number severely wounded. To-night all is quiet, but the longshoremen and stevedores are determined to prevent the negroes from working on the docks. ✸

THE PURSUIT OF LEE.

OUR SPECIAL TELEGRAMS FROM THE ARMY OF THE POTOMAC.

JULY 7

GETTYSBURGH, PENN., MONDAY, JULY 6

The reports from the extreme front are very cheering. Our cavalry, supported by infantry, are close upon the heels of the enemy, and important results are likely to occur before night....

GETTYSBURGH, PENN., VIA HANOVER, MONDAY, JULY 6 — 8 P.M.

The latest Intelligence from the front is to the effect that the enemy is making all possible speed toward the Potomac. I have just come in from the front, and have learned that the lead of the rebel retreating column commenced to pass through Greenwood, twelve miles northwest of Hagerstown, yesterday morning at 10 o'clock....

The rebels are reported to have a trestle bridge just built across the Potomac above Williamsport. If so, I fear their main force may escape.

L. L. CROUNSE. ✸

THE SURRENDER OF VICKSBURGH.

JULY 8

The State of Mississippi passed its ordinance of secession on the 9th day of January, 1861. Four days afterward the Governor of the State ordered artillery to Vicksburg, "to hail and question passing boats on the Mississippi River." From that time until the Fourth of July, 1863 — a period of nearly two years and a half — there has been no passing of that point on the great river, except by the sovereign pleasure of the rebels, or under a tempest of fire that threatened annihilation. For the last four days the passage has again been free to the American flag, without batteries opened, or questions asked, and so it will remain until the end of time.

We may now, in fact, consider the entire Mississippi substantially open. Though Port Hudson still held out against Gen. BANKS at the latest advices, its fall was daily expected. The surrender of Vicksburgh forthwith settles its fate.[1] When the stronghold succumbs, the outworks have no alternative. The desperate defence which the rebels have made, both at Vicksburgh and the smaller post, is the best proof of the transcendant importance which they attached to the command of the river. They have fought as if the very life of the Confederacy turned upon the issue there; and it was the foreboding that this issue must go against them that excited that desperation which impelled the reckless dash of LEE into Pennsylvania. No man has understood better than JEFF. DAVIS, whose own home is on the banks of the Mississippi,[2] that the power which holds that "inland sea," as Mr. [John C.] CALHOUN termed it, rules the continent; and that this lost — even if all else were won — the independence of the Confederacy would be but a name. He has done his best, both by proclamations and through Congressional resolutions, to propitiate the Northwest into some sort of an acquiescence in his possession, by promises of a joint free navigation of the river. What cajolery failed to do, he has done his best to make good by defiance. There has never been a fortification on the continent — if Quebec, perhaps, be excepted — at all to be compared in strength with that which has so long and so marvellously withstood the National armies and navies on the Mississippi. Every resource of the most consummate engineering skill was expended to make the work absolutely impregnable. And in fact it is still doubtful whether even GRANT's army, than whom there are no better soldiers in the world, could have taken it by any series of assaults, ☞

however often repeated. Deficiency in supplies, if we are to judge from our present information, alone compelled the garrison to capitulate — the same agency upon which all investing armies have to rely when all other means fail. The Confederate Government perhaps may find some little solace for their pride, that Vicksburgh at last yielded to the necessities of physical nature, rather than to the overwhelming rush of serried battalions. But the surrender is to them none the less fatal, while to us there is the exceeding gratification of reflecting that this substantial result was secured at comparatively little sacrifice of life.

This is a proud day for Gen. GRANT. It may well, too, be a proud day for President LINCOLN, who has so firmly stood by him through good report and evil report. There has been no such indomitable resolution, since this war, as that exercised by GRANT in his long work of reducing this rebel Sebastopol. Nothing like it. There is not a man in a million who would not have been disheartened by the long succession of failures. Every conceivable expedient

had been thoroughly exhausted, except the last one, which was so desperate on its face, that even the stoutest-hearted might well have been appalled by it. We look in vain through all history, for another instances of such a passage of vessels in the face of miles of the heaviest batteries, as that by which Gen. GRANT's transports were taken below Vicksburgh. And we hardly remember another such instance of an army launching, itself with but two or three days' rations, into an enemy's country, with too small numbers to make even the attempt to keep its communications in the rear open, without any definite knowledge of the topography of the country, or of the location of its adversaries, or of the fortified works it might find in its path, certain only that the region somewhere contained hostile forces far outnumbering its own. Such an inland enterprise would heretofore have been deemed quite as rash as the other one on the water. And yet the result of all this terrible daring has been a success which overtops every other that the war has presented, or, indeed, can

present, for it is decisive of the fate of the war. GRANT, for the last year, at least, has as completely ignored the word impossible as NAPOLEON boasted that he did through his whole career. If he should lay down his sword to-morrow, he would already have earned an imperishable name in American history. But no sword can be reckoned upon with more confidence than his to the end of the war; and, unless we grandly mistake, it will make many a notable mark yet. ✸

1. Port Hudson surrendered on July 9.

2. Jefferson Davis's plantation, Brierfield, was on a bend in the Mississippi River just south of Vicksburg.

Some of the shelters constructed by the citizens of Vicksburg during the siege.

THE NEWS IN WASHINGTON.

GREAT JUBILATION.

JULY 8

SPECIAL DISPATCH TO THE NEW-YORK TIMES.
WASHINGTON, TUESDAY, JULY 7

The Cabinet was in regular session to-day Admiral PORTER'S Vicksburgh dispatch was received by Secretary WELLES, and read to the President. The news immediately spread throughout the city, creating intense and joyous excitement. Flags were displayed from all the Departments, and crowds assembled with cheers. Secretary STANTON issued an order for a salute of one hundred guns.

The fall of Vicksburgh, conjointly with the Gettysburg successes, is regarded as the turning point in the war. The President and high officials express a determination that the campaign shall not slacken off in consequence, but be carried on with renewed vigor . . . .

At 8 P.M., a crowd assembled in front of the National Hotel, and marched up Pennsylvania-avenue, headed by the Marine Band, to the executive Mansion, serenaded, and enthusiastically cheered the President, with repeated cheers for Gens. GRANT, MEADE, ROSECRANS, the Armies of the Union, etc. The President appeared at the window, amid loud cheers, and said:

"FELLOW-CITIZENS: I am very glad indeed to see you to-night, and yet I will not say I thank you for this call but I do most sincerely thank Almighty God for the occasion on which you have called. (Cheers.) How long ago is it? Eighty odd years since on the Fourth of July for the first time in the history of the world a nation, by its representatives, assembled and declared as a self-evident truth, 'that all men are created equal.' (Cheers.) That was the birthday of the United States of America. Since then the Fourth of July has had several very peculiar recognitions. The two most distinguished men in the framing and the support of the Declaration were THOMAS JEFFERSON and JOHN ADAMS — the one having penned it, and the other sustained it the most forcibly in debate — the only two of the fifty-five who sustained it being elected president of the United States. Precisely fifty years after they put their hands to the paper, it pleased Almighty God to take both from this stage of action. This was indeed an extraordinary and remarkable event in our history. Another President, five years after, was called from this stage of existence on the same day and month of the year; and now in this last 4th of July, just passed. When we have a gigantic rebellion at the bottom of which is an effort to overthrow the principle that all men were created equal, we have the surrender of a most powerful position and army on that very day, (Cheers,) and not only so, but in a succession of battles in Pennsylvania, near to us. Through three days, so rapidly fought that they might be called one great battle on the first, second and third of the month of July: and on the 4th the cohorts of those who opposed the Declaration that all men are created equal, "turned tail" and run. (Long continued cheers.) Gentlemen, this is a glorious theme, and the occasion for a speech, prepared to make one worthy of the occasion. I would like to speak in terms of praise due to the many brave officers and soldiers who have fought in the cause of the Union and liberties of their country from the beginning of the war. These are trying occasions, not only in success, but for the want of success. I dislike to mention the name of one single officer, lest I might do wrong to those I might forget. Recent events bring up glorious names, and particularly prominent ones; but these I will not mention. Having said this much, I will now take the music." [1]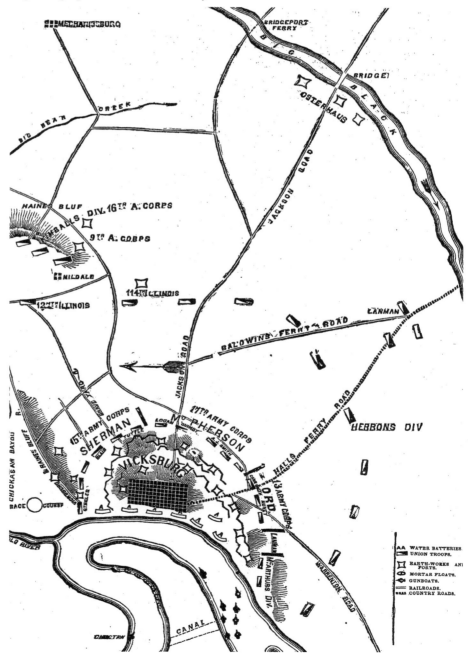

1. Several scholars have noted the similarity between this extemporaneous speech and Lincoln's subsequent Gettysburg Address delivered in November.

A New York Times map showing federal troop dispositions during the Siege of Vicksburg.

THE CONSCRIPTION AND THE WAR.

JULY 10

The Administration is acting wisely in ordering the immediate enforcement of the draft.[1] We have just achieved two great victories which it seems should paralyze the war power of the rebellion. We have beaten its greatest army, and captured its most powerful stronghold. Upon LEE's army the eastern half of the Confederacy depended for protection. Upon Vicksburgh the western half depended for safety. After LEE's defeat and Vicksburgh's fall, it might seem that the rebellion would come to a speedy end, and without further effort on the part of the North. We shall soon know the effect of these losses on the rebel States; but we are prepared to hear that no signs of submission appear, and that redoubled bitterness and frenzy rule the Southern heart.

The rebels have had great losses, heretofore, and they have met them patiently and stoutly. Their losses of Forts Henry and Donelson, of Forts Philip and Jackson, and of the Cities of New-Orleans and Norfolk, were great calamities, but they did not destroy their spirit or purpose. The obstinacy of the rebels has been sufficiently proved by their action in the past. They have evinced a recuperative power after mishaps, and given evidence of a fertility of resource, and an ingenuity in creating the appliances of war, for which they had never before had credit. We see no reason to believe that their spirits will now, all at once, give way, that their obstinacy will be broken, or their aptness for war will fail. With all the harm we have just done them, their power is yet immense. And no cause so desperate as theirs is likely to be abandoned until the last moment, and when there is no longer a leader or an army to stand in its defence.

Granting that we utterly disable Gen. LEE, and that we drive the rebel arms from the Mississippi River, we must still have the work of invasion and conquest to prosecute. And this is harder than the work of expelling from our soil an invader, or capturing a stronghold to which we advance with such a line of communication as the Mississippi River opens to our army. How much harder it is to invade successfully than to beat back an invader, let two years' history in Virginia tell — let us recall events from Bull Run to Chancellorsville. We have an instructive lesson, also, in the State of Tennessee. With a railroad and river behind it, our army has, for half

a year, been held fast bound in sight of the hills and steeples of the City of Nashville. Gen. ROSECRANS lay half a year at Murfreesboro, after a great victory over the enemy. He durst not pursue; because every mile of advance, penetrating inland into the enemy's country, weakened his army, exposed him to annoyances and attacks on flank and rear, and endangered his communications with his depots of supplies at Nashville and Murfreesboro. Such dangers will always beset an invading army.

We have captured many points around the edges of the Confederacy — Norfolk, Suffolk, Roanoke Island, Newbern (N.C.,) Port Royal, (S.C.,) San Augustine and Pensacola, Fla., Ship Island, New Orleans, and at one time, Galveston, Texas.[2] But we have done nothing but hold those places. Every attempt to penetrate inland from them has been baffled. It is only when we have controlled deep navigable waters that our armies have been able to invade and hold their own in the rebel States. Armies as large as those that have hitherto made the attempt to penetrate Virginia must renew that attempt. Armies greater than Gen. ROSECRANS now leads may be required to capture Chattanooga, and go into Georgia. Gen. GRANT, with all his reinforcements, may not be able to protect the Mississippi River from the depredations of PRICE on the West, hold Vicksburgh and Jackson, and pursue Gen. JOE JOHNSTON's new army to the interior of Alabama, with the hope of getting a safe fight out of him.

Therefore, the conscription is necessary. Even after the late great victories, a new army of 300,000 men must be got ready to move upon the Confederacy. Let the rebel States see that not only are they beaten now, by the forces at present in the field, but that in the Fall they must meet the same veteran armies, recruited, and 300,000 stronger. And then, if they mean to stop short of annihilation, they will certainly see the propriety and necessity of yielding. ✸

1. Congress passed the first Conscription Act on March 3, 1863. The Confederacy had passed a Conscription Act almost a year earlier, on April 16, 1862.
2. Federal forces captured Galveston, Texas, in October 1862, but it was retaken by Confederate forces in January 1863

THE CONSCRIPTION A GREAT NATIONAL BENEFIT.

JULY 13

The National Enrollment Act, the enforcement of which was commenced in this City on Saturday, will be carried into execution until the quota of the State of New-York and of every State in the Union shall be raised and in the field. It may not be necessary that a man of those drafted shall ever go into line

THE RIOTS YESTERDAY.

JULY 14

The outrages upon law and public order yesterday, in this metropolis, will revive the heart of every rebel, and of every hater of our institutions the world over. The assiduous fanning of every malignant passion by a portion of our public Press, and by platform demagogues, has at last resulted in an open outbreak, and for hours a mob, embracing thousands, raged at its full bent through an extended section of our City, with arson and bloody violence. The absence of nearly our entire military force, in their great patriotic work of aiding to beat back the invaders of Northern soil, gave these public enemies a rare opportunity for carrying things with a high hand. The law was not only defied but was successfully resisted. For the first time within the memory of this generation, it could not command means for its protection. It stood paralyzed, helpless, humbled. It was a spectacle that may well crimson the check of every true American with shame. Yet, if that were all, there might be some resignation, for public humiliations have been no rarity in New-York. But, unfortunately, there is danger in it, as well as disgrace. There is something portentous in this lawlessness at this juncture.

It has long been declared by the rebel journals, and also by the European journals in the interest of the rebels, that the Conscription act could not be enforced, and that this would compel a discontinuance of the war. The anti-war journals here in the North, while they in general have not ventured to recommend violent resistance to the Conscription, have yet studied to excite against it every unreasoning passion and prejudice. Malignants, too, of the Vallandigham type, have for months been doing their best, by artful harangues, to foment a spirit of resistance. These men understood

of battle during this war. Yet it is a national blessing that the Conscription has been imposed. It is a matter of prime concern that it should now be settled, once for all, whether this Government is or is not strong enough to compel military service in its defence....

For a time after the act was passed, the chiefs of faction were free in their threats that any attempt to carry it out should be resisted by force and arms. In some few localities they succeeded in working up popular passion against its first processes, even to a fighting pitch; but it was very quickly made apparent that the people at large would never sustain any such resort to violence, and that it was worse than idle to contend thus with the Government. Since then, the talk of these factionists on the platform and in their newspaper organs has been that the appeal shall be carried to the ballot-box. They flatter themselves that, by working diligently upon the basest motives and meanest prejudices, they can secure popular majorities that will force a repeal of the measure, or at least deter the Government from carrying it out to its complete execution.

Well, let them do their worst. We want it determined whether the majority of the American people can be induced by any such influences to abandon the cause of their country. So far as the Government itself is concerned, we have no fear that it will fail to do its duty.... ✺

their work thoroughly. Their business was to bring about violence, and at the same time keep themselves personally uncommitted to violence; and [Marc] ANTONY himself never managed that business more skillfully. Every discerning man saw what it would end in — the mob in the street taking upon themselves all the risks, these gentry in their closets rejoicing in the fray in which they dared not mingle. The Government could not blind itself to this flagitious course of action. It made some effort to defeat it; but it was found that this only armed these public enemies with new power, for they turned it to their advantage by pretending that it was now a question of freedom of speech, and gained new influence by setting themselves up as its champions. Thus the dangerous element has been continually growing. It has spread more or less through every part of the North. It has reached all the baser portions of society everywhere, and made them restless, and ready for almost any violence. In most communities this spirit is effectually kept under by superior public opinion. But there are localities where this public sentiment has no such force. This has been shown in the rural districts by the outbreaks which have already occurred in Ohio and Indiana. It is now being shown amid a city population, where the passions of men are far more inflammable, and where the facilities for effective organization are far greater. What its real strength is no man can yet measure; but yesterday's demonstrations sufficiently attest that it is quite strong enough to be formidable and dangerous.

The practical question now is, how this spirit of resistance is to be met. Is it to be done by discussing the merits and the necessities of the Conscription act? Decidedly No! It will be a fatal mistake for the friends of the Government to suspend their action on the turn of any such question. No man who is at heart for the war, by which alone the Government can be sustained, has a serious doubt about either the constitutionality, or the justice, or the propriety, or the necessity of this resort for replenishing the national armies....

The issue is not between Conscription and no-Conscription, but between order and anarchy. The question is not whether this particular law shall stand, but whether law itself shall be trampled under foot. Is this City to be at the mercy of a mob? Have the statutes of the land to await the approval of all the Jack Cades of society before they can attain any binding force? Nobody ever imagined that this conscription act would suit either rebels in the South, or rebel-sympathizers in the North. No valuable law is ever passed that has the favor of the evil-minded. Yield to them the ratification of our public legislation, and you will speedily be reduced to the condition of being without any law whatever. There is not a man's life in this City that is safe, nor a dollar's worth of property, if the spirit which dominated this City yesterday is to be left to its own working. It is as fatal to our whole civil and social organization as the plague is to the physical constitution of man. To give way before it is simply to invoke destruction. Our authorities, we perfectly understand, have been taken at a great disadvantage. These riots have been precipitated upon them at the very time when they were least able to meet them with promptitude. It has proved to have been a great mistake to suffer our city to be so completely stripped of its military defenders. But it is idle now to repine over this. There are yet available means enough, if seasonably and properly taken in hand, to crush, before another twenty-four hours, this twin hydra of the rebellion utterly, beyond all possibility of its ever writhing again. But it will require boldness, decision, nerve of no ordinary character. The responsibility is practically with Gov. SEYMOUR and Mayor OPDYKE. Men in their positions never were confronted with more stupendous duties. ✺

SHALL RUFFIANS RULE US?

JULY 14

The mob yesterday was unquestionably started on the basis of resistance to the draft. But that was a very small part of the spirit which really prompted and kept it in motion. It was, probably, in point of character the lowest and most ruffianly mob which ever disgraced our City. Arson, theft and cowardly ferocity seemed to be the animating impulse of a very large portion of the mass that composed it. We have never witnessed a more disgusting or more humiliating sight than was offered in every street which these gangs of outlaws tramped through with their hideous uproar. A large portion of them were mere boys, and their special delight seemed to be to hunt negroes. One would have supposed that every colored man, woman and child must be a wild beast — to judge from the savage and eager delight with which they were chased and beaten and stoned by these wretched brutes in human form. It seems inconceivable that so much of pure, unadulterated ferocity — so much of that clear, undiluted cruelty which feels a keen and ecstatic relish in the infliction of torture upon others for its own sake, can dwell in the human heart. But such hideous outbreaks as that of yesterday draw aside the curtain and show us how much of the wild beast, in spite of our better qualities, really belongs to the baser elements of our social life.

There is but one way to deal with this coarse brutality. It is idle to reason with it, — worse than idle to tamper with it; it must be crushed. Nothing but force can deal with its open manifestations.... ✺

THE MOB IN NEW-YORK.

RESISTANCE TO THE DRAFT — RIOTING AND BLOODSHED.

JULY 14

The initiation of the draft on Saturday in the Ninth Congressional District was characterized by so much order and good feeling as to well-nigh dispel the forebodings of tumult and violence which many entertained in connection with the enforcement of the conscription in this City. Very few, then, were prepared for the riotous demonstrations which yesterday, from 10 in the morning until late at night, prevailed almost unchecked in our streets. The authorities had counted upon more or less resistance to this measure of the Government after the draft was completed, and the conscripts were repaired to take their place in the ranks, and at that time they would have been fully prepared to meet it; but no one anticipated resistance at so early a stage in the execution of the law, and, consequently, both the City and National authorities were totally unprepared to meet it. The abettors of the riot knew this, and in it they saw their opportunity. We say abettors of the riot, for

it is abundantly manifest that the whole affair was concocted on Sunday last by a few wire-pullers, who, after they saw the ball fairly in motion yesterday morning prudently kept in the back ground. Proof of this is found in the fact that as early as 9 o'clock, some laborers employed by two or three railroad companies, and in the iron foundries a the eastern side of the City, formed in procession in the Twenty-second Ward, and visited the different workshops in the upper wards, where large numbers were employed, and compelled them, by threats in some instances, to cease their work. As the crowd augmented, their shouts and disorderly demonstrations became more formidable. The number of men who thus started out in their career of violence and blood, did not probably at first exceed threescore. Scarcely had two dozen names been called, when a crowd, numbering perhaps 500, suddenly made an irruption in front of the building, (corner of Third-avenue and Forty-sixth-

street,) attacking it with clubs, stones, brickbats and other missiles. The upper part of the building was occupied by families, who were terrified beyond measure at the smashing, of the windows, doors and furniture. Following these missiles, the mob rushed furiously into the office on the first floor, where the draft was going on, seizing the books, papers, records, lists, &c. all of which they destroyed, except those contained in a large iron safe. The drafting officers were set upon with stones and clubs, and, with the reporters for the Press and others, had to make a hasty exit through the rear. They did not escape scatheless, however, as one of the enrolling officers was struck a savage blow with a stone, which will probably result fatally, and several others were injured.

SCENES BY AN EYE-WITNESS

At 11 A.M. word reached the Park Barracks of the disturbance, and Lieut. RIED and a detachment of the Invalid corps immediately repaired to the scene of the riot. They

The burning of the Fifth Avenue Orphan Asylum for Colored Children by rioters in New York.

went by the Third avenue route, the party occupying one car. On the way up, crowds of men, women and children gathered at the street corners, hissed and jeered them, and some even went so far as to pick up stones, which they defiantly threatened to throw at the car. When near the scene of disturbance, Lieut. RIED and command alighted, and formed in company line, in which order they marched up to the mob. Facing the rioters the men were ordered to fire, which many of them did, the shots being blank cartridges, but the smoke had scarce cleared away when the company (which did not number more than fifty men, if as many.) were attacked and completely demoralized by the mob, who were armed with clubs, sticks, swords and other implements. The soldiers had their baronets taken away, and they themselves were compelled seek refuge in the side streets, but in attempting to flee thither several, it is said, were killed, while those that escaped, did so only to be hunted like dogs, but in a more inhuman and brutal manner. They were chased by the mob, who divided themselves into squads, and frequently a single soldier would be caught in a side street, with each end blocked up by the rioters. The houses and stores were all closed (excepting a few liquor shops, which had their shutters up, but kept the back door open,) no retreat was, therefore, open for him, and the poor fellow would be beaten almost to death, when the mob becoming satiated and disgusted with their foul work, be would be left sweltering in blood, unable to help himself.

Elated with success, the mob, which by this time bad been largely reinforced, next formed themselves into marauding parties, and paraded through the neighboring streets, looking more like so many infuriated demons, the men being more or less intoxicated, dirty and half clothed. Some shouted," Now for the Fifth-avenue Hotel — there's where the Union Leaguers meet!" Others clamored among themselves for the muskets which they had taken from the soldiers. The streets were thronged with women and children, many of whom instigated the men to further work of blood, while the injured men left the crowd, and found seats up the street corners....

By this time the Fire Department of the District arrived on the ground, and were preparing to work on the fire; but were prevented from doing so by the mob, who threatened them with instant death if their orders were disobeyed. The ears were stopped from running either way; the horses in several instances were killed, and the cars broken to pieces; the drivers were threatened with violence if they attempted to move on, as by this means the City authorities would hear of the outbreak.

The fire, which had now consumed the wheelwright's shop, had extended to the Provost-Marshal's office, which was soon enveloped in flames, from which issued a large and dark volume of smoke.

The rioters meantime danced with fiendish delight before the burning building, while the small boys and "Rocks" and "Softs" sent showers of stones, against the office, smashing in the doors and windows, the fire seeming to do the work too tardily to suit them. The murky atmosphere and the heavy black clouds which lined the horizon, formed a strange, weird spectacle, which was made the more complete by the demoniac yells of the mob.

It new became evident to the firemen that if the flames were not subdued the whole block would be consumed; and, accordingly, several attempts to operate on the fire were made, but without success, as their apparatus was seized by the mob, and the firemen themselves were severely beaten. At this stage of the proceedings. Chief-Engineer DECKER, or some other high official of the Fire Department, appeared amongst the crowd, and, after much persuasion and talking, finally succeeded in quieting the rioters. The military, however, soon appeared on the ground, which aroused the ire of the mob, who renewed their violence with increased numbers....

The Orphan Asylum for Colored Children was visited by the mob about 4 o'clock. This Institution is situated on Fifth-avenue, and the building, with the grounds and gardens adjoining, extended from Forty- third to Forty-fourth-street. Hundreds, and perhaps thousands of the rioters, the majority of whom were women and children, entered the premises, and in the most excited and violent manner they ransacked and plundered the building from cellar to garret. The building was located in the most pleasant and healthy portion of the City. It was purely a charitable institution. In it there are on an average 600 or 800 homeless colored orphans. The building was a large four-story one, with two wings of three stories each.

Among the most cowardly features of the riot, and one which indicated its political animus and the cunningly-devised cue that had been given to the rioters by the instigators of the outbreak, was the causeless and inhuman treatment of the negroes of the City. It seemed to be an understood thing throughout the City that the negroes should be attacked wherever found, whether then offered any provocation or not. As soon as one of these unfortunate people was spied, whether on a cart, a railroad car, or in the street, he was immediately set upon by a crowd of men and boys, and unless some man of pluck came to his rescue, or he was fortunate enough to escape into a building he was inhumanly beaten and perhaps killed. There were probably not less than a dozen negroes beaten to death in different parts of the City during the day. Among the most diabolical of these outrages that have come to our knowledge is that of a negro cartman living in Carmine-street. About 8 o'clock in the evening as he was coming out of the stable, after having put up his horses, he was attacked by a crowd of about 400 men and boys, who beat him with clubs and paving-stones till he was lifeless, and then hung him to a tree opposite the burying-ground. Not being yet satisfied with their devilish work, they set fire to his clothes and danced and yelled and swore their horrid oaths around his burning corpse. The charred body of the poor victim was still hanging upon the tree at a late hour last evening.... ✪

THE RIOT IN SECOND AVENUE.

EIGHTEEN PERSONS REPORTED KILLED, SEVERAL FATALLY INJURED.

JULY 15

Between 12 and 1 o'clock yesterday, the rioters commenced their attack upon the Union Steam Works, situated on the corner of Twenty-second street and Second-avenue. The guns taken from the armory on Monday were stored in this building, and the most active efforts were made by the insurgents to secure them.

The rioters turned out in large force, numbering from 4,000 to 5,000 people — including children. The shops and stores for half a mile around were closed, and the streets were filled with crowds of excited men, women and children.

At 2 P.M. three hundred Policemen, under the command of one of the Inspectors, arrived upon the ground. The rioters had in the meantime taken possession of the building, and, when the officials made their appearance, they attempted to escape by the rear windows; but too late to escape the notice of the Police. Finding themselves caught in a tight place, they made an attack on the Police. This assault the Officers met by a volley from their revolvers, and five of the mob were shot.

About twenty rioters remained in the building; there was but one way for them to make their exit. The police filled the door, and each had, in addition to his usual weapons, a loaded revolver. The mob became desperate and made a deadly assault upon the police; they in turn used their weapons so effectually that fourteen of the mob were almost instantly killed. A scene, which defies all powers of description then followed. Men, women and children rushed through the streets in the most frantic state of mind, and as the dead and wounded were borne from the place, the wild howlings of the bereaved, were truly sad to hear....

At about 8 1/2 o'clock yesterday morning a telegraphic dispatch was received that a large crowd of rioters were gathering all along the Second-avenue, in the neighborhood of Thirty-fourth-street, threatening all the houses along that thoroughfare. A strong force of police, about 300, were immediately detailed under Inspector [Daniel C.] CARPENTER to break up the crowd.... On arriving at Thirty-second-street, the railroad track was found obstructed, and

the police then formed in a solid column and marched down to the Second-avenue. They were met by the assembled mob with silence. When the whole force had got in the block between Thirty-fourth and Thirty-fifth streets, they were closed in upon by the mob and assailed by a thick shower of bricks and stones, which rained from the houses and windows in the neighborhood. For some moments the men wavered and the peril was imminent, when the reassuring voices of the officers in command recalled them, who then returned the shower of stones with their revolvers. The order was then given to charge, and a most furious onset was made on the rioters, driving them into the houses, the officers chasing them all over the buildings and driving them into the street, where they were scattered by a most vigorous application of clubs. All the side streets were then cleared, and the police marched over the battle-ground victorious.... ❁

Police fight rioters in front of the New York Tribune office.

THE RAGING RIOT — ITS CHARACTER, AND THE TRUE ATTITUDE TOWARD IT.

JULY 15

The mob in our City is still rampant. Though the increasing display of armed force has done something to check its more flagrant outrages, it is yet wild with fury, and panting for fresh havoc. The very fact of its being withstood seems only to give it, for the time, new malignity; just as the wild beast never heaves with darker rage than when he begins to see that his way is barred. The monster grows more dangerous as he grows desperate....

This mob is not the people, nor does it belong to the people. It is for the most part made up of the very vilest elements of the City. It has not even the poor merit of being what mobs usually are — the product of mere ignorance and passion. They talk, or rather did talk at first, of the oppressiveness of the Conscription law; but three-fourths of those who have been actively engaged in violence have been boys and young men under twenty years of age, and not at all subject to the Conscription....

It doubtless is true that the Conscription, or rather its preliminary process, furnished the occasion for the outbreak. This was so, simply because it was the most plausible pretext for commencing open defiance. But it will be a fatal mistake to assume that this pretext has but to be removed to restore quiet and contentment. Even if it be allowed that this might have been true at the outset, it is completely false now. A mob, even though it may start on a single incentive, never sustains itself for any time whatever on any one stimulant. With every hour it lives, it gathers new passions, and dashes after new objects. If you undertake to negotiate with it, you find that what it raved for yesterday, it has no concern for to-day. It is as inconstant as it is headstrong....

You may as well reason with the wolves of the forest as with these men in their present mood. It is quixotic and suicidal to attempt it. The duties of the executive officers of this State and City are not to debate, or negotiate, or supplicate, but to execute the laws. To execute means to enforce by authority. This is their only official business. Let it be promptly and sternly entered upon with all the means now available, and it cannot fail of being carried through to an overwhelming triumph of public order. It may cost blood — much of it perhaps; but it will be a lesson to the public enemies, whom we always have and must have in our midst, that will last for a generation. Justice and mercy, this time, unite in the same behest: Give them grape, and plenty of it. ✷

AN EVENING RIOT IN THE FIRST AVENUE.

THE RABBLE IN CONFLICT WITH CITIZEN-VOLUNTEERS — THIRTY OR FORTY PERSONS KILLED.

JULY 16

A messenger brought information to the Seventh regiment Armory, at 6 o'clock last evening, that the mob was in great strength in the First-avenue, between Eighteenth and Nineteenth streets, apparently organizing, preparatory to moving upon a marauding expedition. Col. [Cleveland] WINSLOW, of the [New York] Fifth regiment, (Duryea Zouaves,) then in command at the Armory, immediately ordered a detachment of volunteers under arms, consisting of three companies, comprising an aggregate of 150 men, and a battery of two howitzers. Placing himself at the head of this force, ... Col. WINSLOW led his command at the double quick to the scene of the disturbance. Passing down Nineteenth-street, the howitzers were brought into position, promptly unlimbered, and trained up and down the First-avenue, while the infantry formed in line to support them. The locality abounds in tenement-houses, where the class of persons live of which the mob is composed, and into these buildings the mass of the rioters took refuge on the appearance of the soldiers. From the roof and windows of every house the mob at once opened an attack, delivering a brisk and persistent fire upon the military of musketry and pistols, as well as a volley of bricks and other missiles. To this assault the soldiers replied, and the howitzers raked the avenue up and down with canister, of which ten rounds were discharged. It is estimated that this fire killed as many as thirty persons, and the effect was a partial dispersion of the rioters, although some of the more bold among them lurked behind the corners of the buildings, whence they would sally out, discharge their guns, and again go to cover....

About 11 o'clock the riot in Nineteenth-street and First-avenue was renewed. Capt. PUTNAM and Capt. SHELBY, of the United States army, with two field pieces and 150 men, repaired to the scene. They were assaulted with stones and brickbats from the tops of houses and from windows. They fired upon the mob and cleared the streets. The brickbats came so thick from the houses that it became necessary to give the order to turn the fire on the buildings. Five rounds of grapeshot were fired, with destructive effect. It is impossible at this late hour to give the number killed.[1] The troops remained on the ground until 12 1/2 o'clock, at which time perfect quiet reigned in the neighborhood. ✷

---

1. A total of 105 New Yorkers were killed in the rioting.

CHAPTER 15

"A Desperate Engagement"

AUGUST–SEPTEMBER 1863

s Lee's veterans had streamed back across the field at Gettysburg after the failure of Pickett's Charge, a subordinate officer turned to General Meade and asked permission to salute him as the next President of the United States. Meade scoffed at the notion, but there was a short-lived boomlet for Meade's candidacy that summer, though it was complicated by the fact that he had been born in Cadiz, Spain, which some argued made him constitutionally ineligible. Once it became clear that the twin victories at Gettysburg and Vicksburg were not going to result in a swift end to the war, the interest faded.

As July turned into August, the gravitational center of the war shifted away from the battlefields in the east and moved west to Tennessee, where Union Major General William S. Rosecrans attempted to outflank the army of Confederate General Braxton Bragg at Chattanooga. Commanding a bend in the Tennessee River as well as being the nexus of several railroads, Chattanooga was the gateway to the South. Initially there was much impatience with Rosecrans in the North for his apparent caution. With Meade defeating Lee in Pennsylvania, and Grant taking Vicksburg, it seemed to many that Rosecrans was insufficiently bold in his maneuvers. The Times defended him as vociferously as it had defended McClellan, Burnside, and Hooker, insisting that Rosecrans was forced to operate in "an Alpine region, which presents every imaginable obstacle to military operations or military movements, where there are few or no roads, while such as there are scarcely passable." Its support was justified when Rosecrans, in a series of deft moves, flanked the Confederates out of their defensive positions in middle Tennessee, crossed the Tennessee River, and forced Bragg

Detail from a Kurz and Allison lithograph of the Battle of Chickamauga.

to evacuate his stronghold and fall back into Georgia. Rosecrans occupied Chattanooga on September 9.

The campaign was not over, however; Bragg had retreated, but he was not in flight. He received reinforcements from across the South, adding 9,000 men under Simon Bolivar Buckner and smaller elements of Joe Johnston's army from Mississippi. Most important, Davis and Lee acceded to the pleas of James Longstreet (himself a Georgian) to send two divisions from the Army of Northern Virginia to the west by rail. The divisions of John Bell Hood and Lafayette McLaws, veterans of the Wheatfield and Peach Orchard at Gettysburg, arrived at Ringgold, Georgia, on September 18, and the very next day Bragg turned on Rosecrans and assailed him. The Battle of Chickamauga (September 19–20, 1863) was a bloody and confusing engagement that ranks second only to Gettysburg in terms of total casualties.

As usual, the first reports to reach New York from the battlefield spoke of great courage in the Union ranks and predicted a Federal victory. The reality was much grimmer. Longstreet's veterans charged through a gap in the Federal defensive line and put Rosecrans's army to flight — all but one corps, that is. The men of George H. Thomas's XIV Corps stood their ground on Snodgrass Hill, a stand that allowed the rest of the army to escape back to Chattanooga, earning for the Virginia-born Thomas his sobriquet as the "Rock of Chickamauga." Even after it became clear that the battle had gone against the Union, The Times wrote not of defeat, but of hope. "There is little cheer on the surface of the dispatch," it acknowledged, "but we think there is ground for encouragement. The fact that ROSECRANS held his ground for two days is a very favorable sign."

That may have seemed to be grasping at straws, but in fact, The Times accurately (if somewhat cold-bloodedly) put its finger on a key factor in the war, and that was that in winning its victory, the rebel army had suffered more losses than it could afford. Nearly 35,000 men fell in the battle, and because the Confederates had assumed the burden of the tactical offensive, the majority of them wore butternut and gray. Bragg lost 18,454 men out of an army that numbered 65,000 — twenty-one percent of his entire command, the same as the percentage that Lee's army had suffered at Chancellorsville. As The Times pointed out, the South could not afford such victories, for "every battle thins the ranks of the faithful few." The terrible arithmetic of war was unarguable: "Whether they win or lose, as long as fighting makes gaps in their columns which they cannot fill, the only result of their struggles is to defer for a short time the doom of the Confederacy."

GEN. MEADE'S CITIZENSHIP.

AUGUST 1

To the Editor of the New-York Times:

You published in the TIMES, Sunday, July 26, a note from "J.C.," in response to the question — "Is Gen. MEADE eligible to the office of President?" Your correspondent, arguing from a clause in the Constitution, (Art. 2, sec. 1, cl. 4.) dogmatically answers this question in the negative.[1] He summarily disposes of the act of Congress of April 14, 1802, commonly known as the Naturalization Act, by an indirect denial of its constitutionality. He very sagely asserts:

"The law of Congress cannot override the Constitution. It cannot make a foreign born a natural born person of the United States any more than it can make a dead man a live man. If it can, it can make the Prince of Wales a natural born citizen of the United States, and make him eligible to the office of President. Congress cannot change the place of a man's birth. A man excluded by the Constitution cannot be made eligible by act of Congress."

Several newspaper editors have also expressed opinions adverse to the eligibility of Gen. MEADE, in view of the constitutional provision that no person except a natural born citizen, or a citizen of the United States at the time of the adoption of the Constitution, shall be eligible to the office of President. I remember reading an article in the TIMES to this effect; also one in the Chicago Tribune, obviously based upon that in your journal.

I beg leave to differ with these writers, and to explain why I do so....

In his edition of Blackstone's Commentaries, CHITTY[2] says: "Natural born subjects are persons born within the allegiance, power or protection of the Crown of England, which terms embrace not only persons born within the domination of His Majesty, or of his homagers, and the children of subjects in the service of the King abroad, and the King's children, and the heirs of the Crown, all of whom are natural-born subjects, by the Common Law, but also under various statutes, all persons, though born abroad, whose father and grandfather by the father's side were native-born subjects at common law." (Book 1, chap. 10. note 1.)

Adopting as our guiding rule — what cannot be reasonably objected to — this exposition of English law, as that law was understand and interpreted antecedent to the American Revolution, both in the British Islands and their dependences, we may justly conclude that the eminent men who framed our Constitution really mean: by the phrase "a natural burn citizen," not only a person born within the United States, but also any person, though born abroad, whose father was a natural born citizen of, and owed allegiance to the United States. It would not be very complimentary to the memory of the founders of the Republic to say that they were less liberal in dealing with their own citizens than had been the British monarchy in its treatment of its subjects....

Very truly yours,

MICHAEL HENNESSY. No, 54 SUMMIT-STREET, BROOKLYN, JULY 30, 1863. ⊕

1. Meade had been born in Cadiz, Spain, the son of Richard Worsam Meade, a wealthy Philadelphia merchant serving in Spain as a naval agent for the U.S. government.
2. This is a reference to the volume of Blackstone's *Commentaries on the Law* edited by J. Chitty and published in 1826.

A VISIT TO THE FIELD OF GETTYSBURGH.

AUGUST 2

A correspondent of the Philadelphia Press writes from Gettysburgh:

"We took our start from Cemetery Hill, and passed over all our lines on the first day. Shells, solid shot and bullets are still lying around, one would think as thick as ever, although a great many persons have, ever since the battle, made it their business to hunt bullets and sell them by the pound. Many thousand pounds have been gathered and disposed of in this way. Nearly every stranger returns from the field with his pockets filled with lead. Government has forbidden any of the relics to be removed, so whatever visitors can conceal about their persons they are most likely to take with them. All who come from a distance naturally desire to return home with some trophy of war. On account of this propensity, some very amusing scenes are sometimes enacted. Quite a number of those who come in from the country are not aware, that these broken implements are 'contraband of war,' so in their innocence, they pick up a handful of bayonets, or sometimes they think it would be a capital idea to take along a good Enfield rifle; they shoulder arms, walk off coolly and exulting over their fortune, when all at once they are arrested in their triumphant march, and deprived of their plunder...." ✪

THE LAWS OF WAR.

AUGUST 3

We have the text of the Proclamation of the President concerning retaliation upon the rebels for the maltreatment of the black troops in our army.[1] By this document, it is ordered "that for every soldier of the United States killed in violation of the laws of war, a rebel soldier shall be executed, and for every one enslaved by the enemy or sold into slavery, a rebel soldier shall be placed at hard labor on the public works." We suppose no man can deny the validity of this principle, its absolute justice, or its conformity to the laws of war. There are probably, altogether, not less than twenty thousand colored soldiers now in the National service, and since they have been in numerous battles lately, and some of them were, of course, taken prisoners of war, it was necessary that some rule should be established to counteract the atrocious proclamation of JEFF. DAVIS, which threatened all captured soldiers of this class and all white officers commanding them, with summary execution. Having entered upon war, the rebels are bound by, and must be compelled to abide by, its laws. ✪

> 1. Lincoln's executive order was dated July 30 and can be found in Basler, ed., *The Collected Works of Abraham Lincoln*, 6:357.

PROCLAMATION BY GOV. SEYMOUR.

A WARNING AGAINST RESISTANCE TO THE DRAFT.

ALBANY, MONDAY, AUG. 17

AUGUST 18

Gov. SEYMOUR[1] has prepared a proclamation, warning all citizens against any disorderly conduct when the draft is made in New-York and Brooklyn.

The feeling in regard to the draft, which takes place in the Sixth District to-morrow, is somewhat equivocal, but the preponderance of indications among the disaffected is that no opposition will be attempted. Certain it is, sure as fate, that any violent demonstrations against it will be met with instant and exemplary punishment. Gen. [John A.] DIX[2] is not a man who will for one moment hesitate in the discharge of a duty. When he was queried as to what to do with any one who, in the early days of New-Orleans disloyalty should attempt to haul down the Stars and Stripes, his response, "Shoot him on the spot!" rang in clarion tones throughout the land. Let those who would forcibly dispute the sovereignty of the Government, and so attempt to prevent the enactment of its laws, have a care. Let

THE SIGNIFICANCE OF THE KENTUCKY ELECTION.

AUGUST 7

The strongest argument of the Copperheads,[1] from their first origin, has been the necessity of conciliating the Border States and keeping them well-affected. In itself it was a fair argument. No intelligent man could deny that it was a matter of great moment that Maryland, Kentucky, and Missouri, which originally held back from the Confederacy, should still be retained on the side of the Union. This was important physically, for their combined population was over three millions; and still more important morally, for they were all Slave States, and their interests were identical with those for the defence of which the rebellion had been originally undertaken.

The fault was not in the argument that the object was an important one, but in the assumption that it could never be effected except by Copperhead methods. There was what was called a "Border State policy," which, it was claimed, must be particularly favored by the Government. The distinctive features of this policy were such a conduct of the war that Slavery should suffer in the least degree possible, and the procurement of peace at the earliest day, by overtures and a liberal compromise. The Administration was denounced by the Copperheads in the most unmeasured terms for refusing that policy. The confiscation bills, and the President's Emancipation Proclamation, and the stand taken that loyalty was to be unconditional, were

An election-year broadside castigates antiwar Democrats.

THE COPPERHEAD PARTY.——IN FAVOR OF *A VIGOROUS PROSECUTION OF PEACE!*

A cartoon showing Columbia, representing the United States, defending herself against traitorous Copperheads.

declared to be expressly calculated to drive the Border States into the arms of the Confederacy; and there were no maledictions strong enough to be vented against the Government for its blindness and its treachery. The abuse which these Copperheads have kept up against the Administration in behalf of the wronged Border States has been what they lived on — their meat and their drink — ever since they were spawned into life.

Well, isn't it extraordinary that, after all this peculiar concern for their feelings and their interests, these same Border States should spurn the Copperheads with greater vehemence than any other part of the country? Kentucky, which has been the special object of solicitude, has rejected WICK-

LIFFE, the very paragon of Copperheads, by a majority almost unexampled in the political history of the State — and that, too, though his opponent boldly espoused the entire general policy of the Government.[2] No Northern State, during the last year, has pronounced so emphatically for the continuance of the war without reserve or qualification as Kentucky has just done…. ✦

> 1. The term "copperheads" refers to a group of antiwar Democrats who called for immediate negotiations to end the conflict. The term was applied to them by their opponents (like The New York Times) who likened them to the poisonous snake of the same name.
> 2. Former governor Charles A. Wickliffe (1788–1869) ran for governor in 1863 as a Peace Democrat. He lost to Thomas E. Bramlette (1817–1875) in a landslide.

them take the measure of the man to whom the protection of that sovereignty is, in this Department, intrusted….

In regard to the character of the preparations made by the authorities, nothing is known in detail; that they are abundant, there is no question, and that they will, if occasion requires their use, be effective, there is not a particle of doubt.

We hear of one jolly party of Democrats and Republicans in the Sixteenth Ward, who have agreed, if any of them are drawn, to have a grand "powwow" and a masquerade procession; the first man drawn is to be King, and on the night of the procession the most absolute homage is to be paid him; the largest liberty and the greatest

amount of fun are to be his perquisites. It is just such sensible, good-natured views as this indicates, which will rob the draft of the especial horrors and hardships with which it has interestedly been surrounded. ✦

> 1. Horatio Seymour (1810–1886) served as New York governor in 1853–54 and again in 1863–64. A Democrat, he opposed many of Lincoln's policies, including the draft, which he believed violated the Constitution. Nonetheless, he did not believe the answer was in street violence and he supported the crackdown.
> 2. John A. Dix (1798–1879) was a former Democratic senator from New York and a "political general." Considered too old for field command, he had several administrative commands during the war. In August 1863, he commanded the Department of the East.

PROCLAMATION BY GOV. SEYMOUR.

AUGUST 19
EXECUTIVE CHAMBER, AUG. 18

I have received information that the draft is about to be made in the Cities of New-York and Brooklyn, and I understand that there is danger of disorderly and riotous attacks upon those who are engaged in executing the law of Congress.[1]

I cannot believe that any considerable number of citizens are disposed to renew the shameful and sad scenes of the past month, in which the lives of so many, as well of the innocent as of the guilty, were destroyed.

Our Courts are now consigning to severe punishment many of those who were then guilty of acts destructive of the lives and property of their fellow-citizens. These events should teach all that real or imaginary wrongs cannot be corrected by unlawful violence. The liberties of our country and the rights of our citizens can only be preserved by a just regard for legal obligations, and an acquiescence in the decision of judicial tribunals….

I hereby admonish all judicial and executive officers, whose duty it is to inforce the law and preserve public order, that they take vigorous and effective measures to put down any riotous or unlawful assemblages; and if they find their power insufficient for that purpose, to call upon the military in the manner pointed out by the Statutes of the State. If these measures should prove insufficient, I shall then exert the full power of the State, in order that the public order may be preserved and the persons and property of the citizens be fully protected.

HORATIO SEYMOUR. ✦

> 1. During the Civil War, New York and Brooklyn were separate cities. New York was the largest city in the country by population, and Brooklyn was the third largest.

THE ARMY OF THE CUMBERLAND.

The report we had a few days ago of a movement by the Army of the Cumberland, in two columns, on Chattanooga, has not been confirmed, and was not in itself very probable. The fact is, the further progress of the army of Gen. [William S.] ROSECRANS is not conditioned so much on the movements of the enemy in front, for we believe it is able to whip [Braxton] BRAGG at any time, but on circumstances of another nature, of which people generally take small cognizance. Glance at the position of his army from Tullahoma to Bridgeport, on the Tennessee, and then run the eye northward, to Louisville and Cincinnati, on the Ohio, and consider that every pound of food for man and beast has to be transported over the intervening distance, through a country infested by guerrillas and exposed to constant cavalry raids, and some idea may be formed of the enormous task Gen. ROSECRANS has in keeping up his line of communications.

A front of operations removed three hundred miles from the base of supplies — which is Gen. ROSECRANS' situation — presents a combination of difficulties of which few are able to form any conception, and which it must absorb the best energies of any commander to overcome. In such circumstances the course which military prudence dictates is the formation of what are styled "secondary or eventual bases," enabling the commander to cut loose from his primary base, and thus shorten his line of communications. Readers of NAPOLEON's campaigns will remember what care that great master of the military art took to form these secondary bases, whenever his operations conducted him to inconvenient distances from his starting point. Of course in warfare in this country, where there are no depots of supplies, and few or no resources from which an invading army can draw, the necessity becomes a hundred-fold greater.

It is now no secret that Gen. ROSE-CRANS is engaged in the important task of transferring his base. The completion of the fortifications at Nashville, which when done will render that place another Gibraltar, will enable him to remove his base of supplies from the Ohio to the Cumberland, thus shortening his line of communication by the whole intervening distance. The completion of the works at

AUGUST 20

Murfreesboro will also give him a powerfully fortified intermediate depot. Every energy is now being bent to these tasks, and their consummation is, we trust, only a matter of a few weeks more labor. When this is done it is evident that he can advance with some degree of safety and confidence, and he will not be under the necessity of frittering away half of his force in guarding his line. Until this is done his present position can be only provisional. A movement by BRAGG by way of East Tennessee threatening his communications, must make him about-face instanter, as it did BUELL, under the same circumstances and in almost the same situation, last Summer.

We have no doubt that Gen. ROSECRANS will find it easy to give his army all the employment it needs; but we conceive that military operations on a grand scale in the West will be conditioned on such things as we have indicated, and especially the completion of the fortifications of Nashville and the construction of the military railroad route toward Cumberland Gap and

Major General William S. Rosecrans, U.S.A.

East Tennessee. By this time, too, we hope, the situation will be such as to authorize the junction of several of our non-isolated forces in the West. The campaign against Chattanooga should not be undertaken without a great army, for its possession will change the whole character and complexion of military operations both East and West. ❂

ROSECRANS ON THE WAR-PATH.

AUGUST 22

We have private advices from the Army of the Cumberland that make it positively certain that ROSECRANS is again on the war-path. It might not be prudent, at this moment, to mention such details as we have; but this much we may say, that the advance is under such circumstances and with such combinations as look toward the most important results.

We need not say that the operations in Tennessee will be followed with the liveliest interest by the whole nation. ROSE-CRANS is on a line of operations where every step he takes has a momentous bearing, not merely with reference to the special rebel force he may encounter, but with re-

gard to the whole theatre of war. If he takes Chattanooga as his "objective" — and we need not say that he aims at nothing short of this — we will have seized a point whose possession by us will radically change the whole aspect of warlike operations. Chattanooga is a natural citadel in the heart of the Confederacy, and on the salient angle of the great rebel line of communications between the East and the West. This seized, we shall hold interior lines and force the rebels to operate on exterior lines, thus completely turning the tables on them.... ❂

MARKET PRICE OF SLAVES.

AUGUST 22

Slaves command a higher price in Kentucky, taking gold as the standard of value, than in any other of the Southern States. In Missouri they are sold at from forty dollars to four hundred, according to age, quality, and especially according to place. In Tennessee they cannot be said to be sold at all. In Maryland the negroes upon an estate were lately sold, and fetched an average price of $18 a head. In the farther States of the Southern Confederacy we frequently see reports of negro sales, and we occasionally see boasts from rebel newspapers as to the high prices the slaves bring, notwithstanding the war and the collapse of Southern industry. We notice in the Savannah Republican of the 5th, a report of a negro sale in that city, at which, we are told, high prices prevailed, and at which two girls of 18 years of age were sold for about $2,500 apiece, two matured boys for about the same price, a man of 45 for $1,850, and at woman of 23, with her child of 5, for $3,950. Twenty-five hundred dollars, then, may be taken as the standard price of first-class slaves in the Confederacy; but when it is remembered that this is in Confederate money, which is worth less than one-twelfth its face in gold, it will be seen that the real price, by this standard, is only about $200. In Kentucky, on the other hand, though there is but little buying or selling of slave stock going on, we understand that negroes are still held at from seven to twelve hundred dollars apiece. ✹

FROM ROSECRANS' ARMY
HIGHLY IMPORTANT AND GRATIFYING NEWS.

AUGUST 25

STEVENSON, ALA., SUNDAY, AUG. 23
The advance of the Army of the Cumberland appeared in front of Chattanooga on the 21st inst., and opened fire on the city at 10 A.M.

The enemy replied from nineteen guns, mostly small ones, which did little damage; but also with one 83-pounder, which swept the opposite shore, and one fire from which killed a horse and took off the leg of A. B. MCCOOK, of LILLY's battery.[1]

Our fire was very destructive, and every battery which opened on us was disabled.

LILLY's battery threw shells with great precision into the embrasures of the enemy.

The works of the enemy on the river are reported to be very strong, the parapets of which are not less than fifteen feet wide. Several water batteries on a level with the river have also been discovered. Moored at the wharf are two steamers, and opposite the city is a pontoon bridge of forty-seven boats.

The largest of the steamers was sunk by our fire and the smaller one disabled.

An attempt to destroy the pontoon bridge was frustrated by the sharp fire of the rebel sharpshooters.

Forty prisoners were taken. Two rebels were killed and several wounded....

Important events must soon transpire in the vicinity of Chattanooga and Harrison. ✹

1. Lilly's Battery was organized and commanded by Eli Lilly (1838–1898) who, after the war, founded the firm of Eli Lilly and Company.

The Union Army of the Cumberland on the march.

THE PROGRESS OF GEN. ROSECRANS' CAMPAIGN.

AUGUST 31

The dispatches which have been reaching us with regard to the advance of the Army of the Cumberland, have been of a nature to cause public anticipation to outrun the actuality of operations, and even the possibility of operations. The bombardment of Chattanooga, of which we had intelligence a week ago, turns out to have been no more than a few shell thrown across the river by Col. [John T.] WILDER, whose light-moving column of mounted infantry and battery of horse-artillery had made a flying visit to the neighborhood of Chattanooga. But the movements of the adventurous leader of the flying brigade, who has no heed for supplies, roads, trains or communications, are no criterion for the movements of the main body of the army which is strictly dependent on these conditions. Gen. ROSECRANS is now operating in a region of country the difficulties of which are almost inconceivable. The front of operations which he gained in his last advance, when he turned the rebel position at Tullahoma, and compelled BRAGG's retreat to Chattanooga, brought him just to the base of the mountains. Thence to Chattanooga, eighty or a hundred miles, is through an Alpine region, which presents every imaginable obstacle to military operations or military movements, where

there are few or no roads, while such as there are scarcely passable. To those who glibly talk of "throwing" troops here, or "throwing" troops there, a fortnight or three weeks will doubtless seem an unpardonably long period to occupy in a journey of three or four score miles; but should they go to ROSECRANS' field of operations and find that roads had to be made before they could "throw" even themselves, they would probably acquire and beget a little of that "temperance" that would give them "patience." It is in this arduous but indispensable work that Gen. ROSECRANS has been engaged for the past fifteen or twenty days. Details of whole divisions have been out road-making, hauling trains, &c.; and the result is that he has at length succeeded in transferring his whole army across the Tennessee River.

The crossing of the Tennessee is announced as having taken place yesterday at four different points, though the points themselves are not designated, and we are thus left in the dark as to the nature of ROSECRANS' designs. His strategy will, of course, have to consult the position and movements of the enemy. Now, there are a good many indications that BRAGG, fearing another flank movement on the part of Gen. ROSECRANS, that would cut him off

and leave him in the mountains, has withdrawn into the open country below, simply observing Chattanooga and the Tennessee line with a small force. It, as at present appears probable, he is holding the line from Dalton to Rome, his design would seem to be to cover that line of railroad, and be ready to fall on ROSECRANS at any point where he may attempt to debouch from the mountains.

It is not unlikely, therefore, that Gen. ROSECRANS will now cease to make Chattanooga his objective point, (though he will, of course, swing his left round in that direction, and occupy it on account of its commanding importance as a as a strategic point of manoeuvre,) but will make directly for the rebel army. There is certainly nothing the Army of the Cumberland desires so much as a fair stand-up fight with a foe that has never met it but to run. Still, from the extreme difficulties that hedge and hamper the march of Gen. ROSECRANS, we have no right to expect active work for a good many days to come. ✱

WILL THE REBELS ARM THEIR SLAVES?

AUGUST 31

The report that JEFF. DAVIS has decided to organize five hundred thousand black troops, with a promise of land and freedom, is not entitled to credit. Undoubtedly there is rebel authority for it, as is stated; but that is nothing in its favor. Sensation-mongers ride their high horse in Dixie, as well as in all other parts of the land. There are conclusive reasons, extrinsic and intrinsic, for disbelieving it....

We may set it down as absolutely certain that whenever the alternative of arming the negroes or submitting to the national rule once definitely takes shape before the Southern mind, there will not be a moment's hesitation which of the two to choose. Humiliating as an acknowledgment of defeat, and a return to the old

Government, may be, it will be accounted a thousand times preferable to the converting of half a million of slaves into trained soldiers, and thereby fitting them to become masters of the land. The rebel chiefs will never have the temerity even to propose the measure for public consideration. Infinitely less would they dare attempt, as this report represents, to impose it by their own arbitrary will, without regard to the popular feeling, or any pre-announcement of their intention. They could not keep their seats twenty-four hours after such an act. They would find a doom from their own people worse even than any that awaits them from the unchecked progress of the National arms. It is possible some of them may get clemency from the National

Government by timely submission; but they might better meet the three Furies than confront their own people after their declaration of a purpose like that ascribed to them by this report.[1] ✱

---

1. The Times was correct. When in January of 1864, Confederate Major General Patrick Cleburne proposed that the Confederacy should free and arm its slaves, his proposal was not only rejected—Jefferson Davis ordered that it must never be spoken of again. In February of 1865, in the last days of the war, when Robert E. Lee urged arming slaves, the rebel Congress passed an act authorizing it, though the war ended before any armed slaves took part in the war. See Chapter 24.

THE PRESIDENT AND GEN. GRANT.

TO WHOM BELONGS THE CREDIT OF THE VICKSBURGH CAMPAIGN.

SEPTEMBER 2

When it was officially known that Vicksburgh had surrendered to the victorious legions of GRANT, the President wrote the General the following private letter of acknowledgment and thanks for the "inestimable service" he had rendered the country.

EXECUTIVE MANSION, WASHINGTON, JULY 13

Major-General Grant:

MY DEAR GENERAL:

I do not remember that you and I ever met personally. I write this now as a grateful acknowledgment for the almost inestimable service you have done the country. I wish to say a word further. When you first reached the vicinity of Vicksburgh, I thought you should do what you finally did — march the troops across the neck, run the batteries with the transports, and thus go below, and I never had any faith except a general hope that you knew better than I, that the Yazoo Pass expedition and the like could succeed. When you got below and took Port Gibson, Grand Gulf and vicinity, I thought you should go down the river and join Gen. BANKS; and when you turned northward, east of the Big Black, I feared it was a mistake. I now wish to make the personal acknowledgment that you were right and I was wrong.

Yours, very truly,

(SIGNED) A. LINCOLN.

GEN. ROSECRANS' ADVANCE.

THE ARMY WELL ACROSS THE TENNESSEE.

SEPTEMBER 7

A dispatch dated "four miles South of Bridgeport, Sept. 3," says:

The army is well across the Tennessee, and occupies a strong position several miles south of the river. No resistance was made to the crossing.

Reconnaissances have been made to Trenton, Georgia, without finding the enemy in force. He is said to be intrenched east of Chattanooga.

The trestle bridge at Bridgeport, just completed this morning, gave way this afternoon, while the train of the Fourth Michigan battery was crossing. One mule only was drowned, the water not being over four feet deep. Several brigades of infantry and batteries had just preceded the train. The bridge will be replaced by to-morrow. There are several more at different points. Gen. ROSECRANS and Staff crossed this afternoon.

An Alfred Waud sketch of the Battle of Chickamauga.

THE RIGHT MAN IN THE RIGHT PLACE.

SEPTEMBER 7

The President's letter to the Springfield Convention receives the unqualified admiration of loyal men throughout the breadth of the land.[1] Various as have been their sentiments on some of its topics, it is yet their universal testimony that nothing could have been more true or more apt. Its hard sense, its sharp outlines, its noble temper, defy malice. Even the Copperhead gnaws upon it as vainly as did the viper upon the file.

Men talk about a courtly felicity of speech, and term it a rare accomplishment. So indeed it is. Nothing but high culture and the most patient practice confers it. Here is a felicity of speech far surpassing it, yet decidedly uncourtly. The most consummate rhetorician never used language more apt to the purpose; and still there is not a word in the letter not familiar to the plainest plowman. But what is still better than even felicity of expression, is felicity of thought. Not only the President's language is the aptest expression of his ideas, but there is a similar fitness of his ideas to the occasion. He has a singular faculty of discovering the real relations of things, and shaping his thoughts strictly upon them, without external bias.

In his own independent, and perhaps we might say very peculiar way, he invariably gets at the needed truth of the time. When he writes, it is always said that "he hits the nail upon the head," and so he does; but the beauty of it is that the nail which he hits is sure to be the very nail of all others which needs driving....

It is almost fearful to contemplate what might have been the consequences had we an Executive of different mould. We have had Presidents of a headstrong temper, who, when hard pressed, would listen to no counsel, but rush on self-willed; others of a feebleness of spirit that made them the mere playthings of circumstances, or the passive tools of other men's arts. We have had Presidents who would have found it almost impossible, in any exigency, to rise above a party level; others who, though they might detach themselves from party,

would do so only to seek the swift popular current that should bear them on to a second term. Had we a man now at the head of affairs belonging to any of these classes, the national ruin would be almost inevitable. There could have been hardly a hope of escaping wreck, in this dreadful storm, under such pilotage. The very knowledge that we had so unreliable a hand at the helm would have almost paralyzed effort. There would have been no such collected energy as we have seen, no such steady confidence in the great popular heart. All would have been uncertainty, dissension and confusion. We have had many reasons to be thankful to heaven for its orderings in aid of our rightly acquitting ourselves toward this wicked rebellion; but for no one thing have we so great cause for gratitude as for the possession of a ruler who is so peculiarly adapted to the needs of

the time as clear-headed, dispassionate, discreet, steadfast, honest ABRAHAM LINCOLN. ⊛

1. This is a reference to a public letter that Lincoln sent to James C. Conkling on August 26, 1863, in which he answered the complaints of those who had been angered by his Emancipation Proclamation. "You say you will not fight to free negroes," the President wrote. "Some of them seem willing to fight for you; but no matter. Fight you, then, exclusively to save the Union." Perhaps the most famous passage in this letter was this one: "There will be some black men who remember that with silent tongue, and clenched teeth, and steady eye and well-poised bayonet, they have helped mankind on to this great consummation; while, I fear, there will be some white ones, unable to forget that, with malignant heart, and deceitful speech, they have strove to hinder it." The letter can be found in Basler, ed., *The Collected Works of Abraham Lincoln*, 6:406-10.

MOVEMENTS IN EAST TENNESSEE OCCUPATION OF KNOXVILLE BY GENERAL BURNSIDE.

SEPTEMBER 10

On Sunday intelligence was received in this city from Gen. BURNSIDE that a portion of his army had entered and taken possession of Knoxville, the principal military position and city of East Tennessee, and that the Star-Spangled Banner, in all its brilliancy, was again floating over that late rebel stronghold. Gen. BUCKNER, with a strong rebel force, upon learning of the arrival of Gen. BURNSIDE at Kingston, concluded to retire toward Chattanooga, which he did successfully. Gen. BURNSIDE went with a portion of his army and took possession of Knoxville, while the remaining portion crossed from Kingston over the railway, which had been torn up, and, taking the pike, went in pursuit. The main portion of Gen. Burnside's army is pushing on to reinforce Rosecrans, and no doubt exists but that the advance has already reached the army of the Cumberland BUCKNER has reinforced BRAGG, and reports are current, and believed at the headquarters of ROSECRANS, that a portion of JOHNSTON's army from the extreme South has also arrived and reinforced "a little more grape, Capt. BRAGG."[1]

Gen. ROSECRANS at an early hour yesterday morning was in front of the rebel works at Chattanooga, and his army in

position for a battle. As an evidence that the General had decided to give the enemy battle yesterday is the fact that he telegraphed yesterday morning early the Archbishop in this city a request that all the Catholic Churches be opened during the day, and that masses be held for the success of the Federal arms this day, (yesterday,) as he had fully determined to attack the rebel works. In obedience to this request, the churches were thrown open, and masses held as desired.[2] Stirring intelligence from that army may confidently be expected, as there is, no doubt, a severe and hotly-contested battle now progressing, or will immediately take place at that point. ⊛

General Braxton Bragg, C.S.A.

1. Bragg earned his first national reputation in the Battle of Buena Vista (February 23, 1847) during the Mexican-American War. There, when General Zachary Taylor's army was under great pressure from charging Mexican infantry, he is reputed to have told Bragg, then a captain, "A little more grape, Captain Bragg." An illustration of this event by Currier became a popular print of the 1850s.
2. Rosecrans was born a Methodist, but converted to Catholicism while serving as an instructor at West Point and remained a devout Catholic until he died.

CAPTURE OF CHATTANOOGA.

SEPTEMBER 10

We have the news that on Tuesday last the rebel army evacuated Chattanooga, and yesterday Gen. ROSECRANS' army marched in and took possession of the great Western mountain stronghold. The rebels are reported to have fled southward into Georgia; but sure it is that if they could not hold their unsurpassed natural fortress at Chattanooga, they can hold no point from the mountains to the seaboard.

The manoeuvres of Gen. ROSECRANS show that he expected to force BRAGG's army to a fight, and he had advanced a column to Trenton, twenty miles southwest of Chattanooga, but the rebels had an easy line of retreat which he had not yet been able to cut, and thus they escaped down the Western Georgia Railroad. It would have been better had ROSECRANS achieved his object, and thus at once brought the war in the Southwest to a finality; but it seems to be reaching a finality very rapidly as it is. ☻

THE MAIN REBEL ARMY.
THE REPORTS OF ITS RETREAT TO RICHMOND.

SEPTEMBER 14

From the best information that can be obtained, it is now rendered certain that the inactivity of the rebel army [in Virginia] is at last broken by an important movement — not an offensive movement against this army, but a movement rendered necessary by the cooperate condition of their affairs in the Southwest, and by which they hope to check, if not retrieve, the tide of disaster which has been steadily rushing on them for the last year. It is believed that one corps of LEE's army, or about one-third of it, under LONGSTREET, is now moving to Richmond, there to be transferred, two divisions of it to the Southwest, and one to Charleston. And if LONGSTREET, whose ability as a leading subordinate commander is unquestioned, should soon appear in principal command on either of these fields, it will not be surprising, — not at least to this army....

The weakening of the rebel army in front of us would seem to indicate that the rebels in Virginia will remain entirely upon the defensive for the coming campaign. They count upon the presumed weakness of this army; rendering two-thirds of their army, acting strictly upon the defensive, able to resist our advance; at any rate, if not able to do it this side of Richmond, they are confident of their ability to do it there. And as long as they hold Richmond they hold Virginia, even if they do surrender a considerable portion of its territory.... ☻

GEN. LEE STUMPING IN THE NORTH.

SEPTEMBER 17

It would appear from the Richmond Enquirer, that fraternal feeling has so far revived at the South that Southern politicians are anxious to act once more with their old allies, the Northern Democrats, at the approaching election. We have always doubted the statements made by FERNANDO WOOD[1] and others of his way of thinking, as to the willingness of any considerable portion of the Secessionists to cooperate with their old associates in winning victories at the polls, but the article to which we have referred so strongly confirms the view of the matter taken by these gentlemen, that we cannot permit ourselves to doubt any longer. The Enquirer expresses the greatest anxiety for the success of the "Northern Democratic party," which it appears is already so nearly on a par with its antagonist, that "the least advantage thrown in its favor will insure its success." The mode in which the writer proposes that the South should lend its aid in the matter, will probably be pronounced by some captious persons somewhat irregular; and there is no denying that it does seem a little singular. But the eccentricity can easily be accounted for by ascribing it to the warmth of the Southern temperament, and the extreme violence which has of late characterized the proceedings of the Abolitionists. The Enquirer suggests, in short, that the South should aid the Democratic party by deputing LEE "to advance once more on MEADE." "Let him," says it, "drive MEADE into Washington, and he will again raise the spirits of the Democrats, confirm their timid, and give confidence to their wavering." And it adds:

"It matters not whether the advance be made for purposes of permanent occupation, or simply for a grand raid, it will demonstrate that in the third year of the war they are so far from the subjugation of the Confederate States that the defence of Maryland and Pennsylvania has not yet been secured. A Fall campaign into Pennsylvania, with the hands of our soldiers untied — not for indiscriminate plunder, demoralizing and undisciplining the army, but a campaign for systematic and organized retaliation and punishment — would arouse the popular mind to the uncertainty and insecurity of Pennsylvania. This would react upon the representatives in Congress, strengthening the Democrats, and mollifying even Hardshell fanaticism itself."

We have no doubt that some of the zealots who now urge "a vigorous prosecution of the war," for the filling of their own pockets, regardless of the blood and desolation with which it covers the land, will with fiendish ingenuity, endeavor to twist these words into a declaration of hostile intent and try to persuade the public that the Enquirer advocates an armed invasion of the North, and really believes that this would help the Democratic party. Those who are familiar with Southern language, however, as well as with Southern feeling, will not be the victims of any such imposition. The whole paragraph which we have quoted is the aphorical — a style of composition to which Southern writers are much addicted, and in which they greatly excel. We all know the extent to which it has been used of late years by politicians even at the North, and that they draw most of their similes from military life. The preparation for an election is said to be "a campaign." The leader of a party is called its "standard bearer." The party, when bringing its strength to bear at the polls, ☞

is said "to wheel into line." Its divisions are called "its wings," and it spends most of its time "marching shoulder to shoulder." Occasionally a politician is "left out in the cold," or compelled "to take a back seat in the rear car," but generally he is supposed to pass his time in the army.

We have only to mention this practice to make it clear to all candid minds that the "advance on MEADE," which the Enquirer recommends, is simply a figurative mode of advising the Southern population to go to the polls at the approaching elections — that MEADE is "to be driven into Washington" means simply that the Republican party is to be driven out of Washington, by dint of majorities at the polls, just as we constantly talk of inflicting on our adversaries at elections "a Waterloo defeat," or "outing them horse, foot and dragoons." When a Northern newspaper uses these phrases, no one supposes the writer to mean that a bodily conflict is to take place, in which one party is to be sabred and bayoneted and shot till it retires; and why should we impute such meaning to South-

ern editors?. When the Enquirer talks of the hands of our soldiers being "untied" during "a Fall campaign in Pennsylvania," and "inflicting systematic and organized retaliation and punishment," it is simply a strong way of stating the old Democratic proposition, "to the victors belong the spoils." The plunder referred to is neither more nor less than the wresting the spoils of office from Republican hands, through the aid of Southern stump orators, or "soldiers," as the Enquirer chooses to call them; and when it says their "hands are to be untied," it means their tongues. If there were any doubt about this elucidation, the context would remove it, for one or two lines before the passage we have extracted, the writer says plainly and explicitly: "Gen. LEE must turn politician as well as warrior, and we believe he will prove the most successful politician the Confederacy has ever produced." Nothing can be plainer than this. LEE, with a number of other Southern speakers, or "soldiers," is to stump Pennsylvania this Fall in the interest of the Democratic party.

This interpretation ought not to be necessary and would not be necessary, but for the malignity with which, alas! party warfare is now carried on. In no way is it displayed with such persistence as in insinuations and often direct charges from various quarters; that the Democratic party seeks or desires help from the public enemy. Some malicious people will have it that the success of the rebellion not only aids it, but is desired by it; and others go so far as to ascribe the interviews of the Democratic leaders with Lord Lyons, last year, to their anxiety to degrade the nation by inviting foreign interference in our domestic affairs. No reputation is safe from slanderous tongues. ❀

1. Fernando Wood (1812–1881) served as mayor of New York 1854–1857, and again 1860–62. He was openly sympathetic to the Confederacy and in 1861 had suggested that New York should secede from the Union and become a free city in order to maintain commercial ties with the Confederacy. In 1863 he was elected to Congress.

HIGHLY IMPORTANT.
GEN. ROSECRANS' ARMY.
A BATTLE IMMINENT.

SEPTEMBER 19
HEADQUARTERS IN THE FIELD, TEN MILES NORTHEAST OF LAFAYETTE, GA., WEDNESDAY, SEPT. 16

On evacuating Chattanooga the enemy retired to Lafayette and massed a force at that place, taking possession of the gaps of the Pigeon Mountain directly in front of Gen. THOMAS' column. The rebel force had been made formidable by new additions from [Joseph E.] JOHNSTON, [Thomas] HINDMAN, [Simon] BUCKNER AND [Dabney] MAURY.

Deserters report the enemy now superior in numbers to the army they had at the battle of Murfreesboro ... in all, thirty-five brigades of infantry, not less than 65,000 men.

Thus formidable in numbers and position, ROSECRANS was compelled to concentrate his forces, necessarily much scattered in crossing the Lookout Mountains. The lines of the opposing armies may now be represented as a crescent, shaped by the Pigeon Mountains, which extend like the arc of a circle around

Lafayette. The rebels hold the interior and we the exterior lines.

The two forces are within a few miles of each other, but are effectually separated by the range of mountains. The rebel position can only be approached by the Cattlet's, Wing and Blue-Bird Gaps, which are well guarded. This position of the rebels covers excellent lines of retreat on Rome and Cal-

houn, where they will probably make a new line should they be defeated here. There are rumors that they have been retiring for a day or two; but they are considered unreliable.

Gen. ROSECRANS left Chattanooga on Sunday, and is now engaged in making dispositions for a new situation. He has been ill, but is in fine spirits. ❀

Frank Leslie's Illustrated Newspaper woodcut depicting the Battle of Chickamauga.

COMMUNISM IN DIXIE.

SEPTEMBER 20

One of the ablest citizens of Louisiana has put forth his views through the South Carolinian — the organ of the present State Government of South Carolina — on the proper policy for the rebel Government to adopt in this crisis. His scheme is altogether a nice one.

"The war," he says, "can no longer be conducted as it has been. Our currency is so depreciated that it will soon cease to be available. I see but one remedy. Let no more paper money be issued. Let the whole Confederacy be divided into two classes — the combatants and the producers. As long as this war shall last, every one of us must be satisfied with shelter, food and clothing, and nothing else. The soldiers and officers, from the highest to the lowest, must fight without pay. Why should they need money, when provided with necessaries, and their families taken care of?

Let all the resources and productions of every farmer or planter be put at the disposal of the Government, without pay. Let every woman and every child, old enough for the purpose, be made to work without pay. Let the President and every civil officer or employe have no pay. In fact, let it be a penal offence to buy or sell anything; but let food, raiment, shelter and medicine be secured to every one under a parish or county organization, controlled or supervised by the General Government."

This would be the most gigantic scheme of practical socialism that the world ever saw. All the resources and productions of every Southern farmer and planter is to be placed at the disposal of the rebel Government without pay; it is to be a penal offence to buy or sell anything; labor is to be universal and compulsory — every woman, even, and every child, being forced to work without pay; and the rebel Government, from the stores thus placed at its disposal, is to furnish every man, woman and child — of both colors, we

suppose — in the Confederacy with all needed food, raiment and shelter. It is as wild a scheme of socialism as ever was conceived in the brain of man. There would be perfect equality as regards property, perfect equality as regards labor, and perfect equality as regards compensation.

We know the immense and despotic power of the rebel Government over the Southern people; but we should think it beyond even its power to force every human being of both sexes in the Confederacy to work — to force all workers and property-holders to turn over the fruits of their labor and their property into a common fund — to force all soldiers and officers to fight without pay — to force every civil officer or employee to labor without pay. But if "one of the ablest citizens of Louisiana" favors the scheme, we do not see why JEFF. DAVIS should not try it. ✪

THE IMPENDING FIGHT IN GEORGIA.

SEPTEMBER 20

We are in expectation of stirring news from the Department of Gen. ROSECRANS. The combined and rapid advance of this chief and Gen. BURNSIDE evidently took Gen. BRAGG by surprise, and compelled the abandonment of Chattanooga. The evacuation of this place was not intended by the Confederates. Since the first of this year they have been at work upon it, steadily increasing its fortifications, and trying to make it impregnable. They meant to hold it to the last, and were sure they could do so. But, as in the case of Columbus, Fort Pillow, Memphis, Corinth, Vicksburgh and Port Hudson, they only spent their labor for the benefit of Nationals. As soon as their work was done at Chattanooga, they quietly gave up the place to Gen. ROSECRANS.

The prompt reinforcement of Gen. BRAGG by LONGSTREET and detachments from JOE JOHNSTON's army, shows what the intentions of the rebel Government were. They did not intend to retreat, and BRAGG is enabled to stop his flight and turn upon his pursuers, almost in sight of his late stronghold. He is said to be stronger in men now than Gen. ROSECRANS. The two armies confront each other, and a battle is momentarily expected.

The immense importance of the impending contest must be admitted. If ROSECRANS should be worsted, the effect would be very bad in Tennessee. Much of the State would be again overrun by guerrillas, and the loyal population of the State, now just prepared to return to the Union, would be frightened and deterred from their contemplated action. If the Confederate army should be beaten, the rebellion would be instantly lost. Alabama and Georgia would be open to the advance of the Union troops, and thus the heart of the Confederacy be pierced. The result would be quickly fatal. Into these two States are now gathered the major part of the property and chiefs of the rebellion. The bulk of the slaves of Virginia, Tennessee, Mississippi and Eastern Louisiana have been gradually withdrawn before the march of our armies, and have found refuge, along with their masters, in Alabama and Georgia. The influx of this class of persons from Mississippi, at the time of GRANT's occupation of Jackson, was so great, it will be remembered, that the Governor of Alabama was obliged to take steps to stop it. He feared the effect on the food supplies of his State.

The accumulation of slaves in the States of Georgia and Alabama must, at the present time, be enormous. It is not unlikely that half the remaining slave wealth of the Southern States is compacted within their borders. And the effect of the Union army's advance among them would be disastrous. A spark might be as safely admitted into a powder magazine. The rebels appreciate this perilous state of things, and hence they are preparing, no doubt, to make a superhuman effort to check and drive back Gen. ROSECRANS. We trust this brave General, backed now by BURNSIDE, will be equal to the shock coming against him. It would be gratifying to know that Gen. GRANT was hard by, with part of his veteran army, to take part in the grand and final contest for the possession of the citadel of the enemy's strength. But there is no reason to hope for this. Gen. ROSECRANS must rely on his unaided strength to fight one of the most critical and important battles of the war. As a lover of honorable fame, this is, perhaps, the very thing he would desire, for he is confident of victory, and the glory of success will be exclusively his own. ✪

HIGHLY IMPORTANT.
A GREAT BATTLE FOUGHT NEAR CHATTANOOGA.

HEADQUARTERS OF THE ARMY OF THE
CUMBERLAND, CRAWFISH SPRINGS, GA.,
SEPT. 19

A desperate engagement commenced this morning at 11 o'clock. The rebels made a heavy attack on the corps of Gen. THOMAS, forming the left wing of our army, and at the same time they attacked the right wing, which was thought to be a feint.

Gen. [Alexander] MCCOOK's and Gen. [Thomas] CRITTENDEN's troops were thrown into the engagement as convenience offered, the main portions of their forces being on the march at the time.

The fight on the left was of a very desperate character. The enemy were repulsed, but, on being reinforced, regained their position, from which they were subsequently driven, after a severe engagement of an hour and a half.

Gen. [George H.] THOMAS' forces then charged the rebels for nearly a mile and a half, punishing them badly.

About two o'clock in the afternoon the rebels made a fierce dash on our centre, composed of the divisions of Gens. [Horatio] VAN CLEVE and [Joseph] REYNOLDS.

Gen. VAN CLEVE's forces were struck on the right flank, and being vigorously pushed by the rebels fell back, until Gen. CARTER's line was broken and the troops became much scattered.[1]

Gen. THOMAS on the left, and Gen. [Jefferson C.] DAVIS on the right, then pushed forward their forces vigorously toward the gap, and, after a hard fight, recovered the ground which had been lost on the extreme right.

The fight disclosed the intention of the rebels, which evidently was to get between us and Chattanooga.

The general engagement, which commenced at 11 A.M., ended about 6 P.M....

The battle is not yet over. It will probably be renewed to-morrow.

Rebel prisoners taken represent that the corps of Gens. [Daniel H.] HILL, [Leonidas] POLK, JOHNSTON and LONGSTREET, were in the engagement.[2]

Our men are in the best of spirits, and eager to begin anew.

SEPTEMBER 21
SPECIAL DISPATCH TO THE NEW-YORK TIMES
WASHINGTON, SUNDAY, SEPT. 20

ROSECRANS, in a dispatch to HALLECK, says:

"In the early part of the fight the rebels drove us some distance, capturing seven guns. Later in the action however, we drove the enemy, reoccupying all our lost ground and capturing ten pieces of artillery. A number of prisoners, representing forty-five regiments, were captured by our forces." The battle was probably renewed yesterday morning. ✦

---

1. There was no General Carter at Chickamauga. Almost certainly, this is a reference to Colonel Charles G. Harker, who commanded the Third Brigade, First Division, in Crittenden's Corps.
2. This is mostly correct. Daniel Harvey Hill was present with his command, though Ambrose Powell Hill's Corps remained in Virginia. Also, while there were elements of Joe Johnston's army present, Johnston himself remained in Mississippi.

POSTSCRIPT.
BAD NEWS FROM ROSECRANS.
DEFEAT OF OUR ARMY IN GEORGIA.

SEPTEMBER 21
MONDAY, 4 O'CLOCK A.M.

We have the following brief and very painful news from Gen. ROSECRANS' army. The occupation of the telegraph lines for military purposes prevents, for the present, the transmission of details:

LOUISVILLE, MONDAY, SEPT. 21 — 12:45 A.M.
Our army under Gen. ROSECRANS has been badly beaten, and compelled to retreat to Chattanooga, by BRAGG, with heavy reinforcements from LEE, BEAUREGARD and JOE JOHNSTON. ✦

Repulse of a Confederate attack by federal troops at Crawfish Creek during the Battle of Chickamauga.

THE BATTLE IN GEORGIA.

SEPTEMBER 21

Gen. ROSECRANS has again met the enemy, whom he fought and defeated at the opening of the year, and whom he has been pursuing for the past three months, for the purpose of fetching to the test of battle. It has been an unaccountable mystery why Gen. BRAGG should have executed such a series of retreats as he has carried his army through since it occupied Murfreesboro — why he should have evacuated in succession points of such vast natural and artificial strength as Shelbyville, Tullahoma, and especially Chattanooga? The reason, however, was probably simply because, though his positions were very strong, his army was not of sufficient magnitude and courage to cope with the well-trained Western legions that Gen. ROSECRANS marched upon him. Had ROSECRANS attacked him in front of any of the positions named, BRAGG, with his advantages, might have had a show of success; but the flanking movement so skillfully executed by Gen. ROSECRANS in each instance, necessitated that BRAGG should come forth from his stronghold and give battle on ground where his acquired advantages availed him nothing.

At last, however, in the evacuation of Chattanooga, BRAGG had got to a point in his retreats when further backward movement was destruction. To have retreated from Rome or Atlanta would have been to give up Alabama, Mississippi and Upper Georgia, and would have given us a pass to the important parts of the Carolinas sloping from the Alleghanies. BRAGG and all his army knew this — JEFF. DAVIS and the whole Confederacy knew it. Hence, as a matter of necessity, BRAGG halted his columns but a short distance south of Chattanooga, and DAVIS made haste to reinforce him from West and East. The army of JOE JOHNSTON, which, since its defeat at the capital of Mississippi, had been unable to subserve any military purpose, and had wandered from one point to another, was brought up to Georgia from its latest camping ground on the Tombigbee, and attached to BRAGG's force. The corps of LONGSTREET, or, if not exclusively his corps, a large force from the army of Gen. LEE, was hastened westward from Virginia, and combined with BRAGG's and JOHNSTON's armies. The considerable force under BUCKNER, which retreated from East Tennessee, before Gen. BURNSIDE, was consolidated with the rest, and doubtless all the other detachments of infantry and cavalry that have been roaming and operating throughout the Southwest, were hastened forward at the critical moment to the critical point. With all these bodies and reinforcements, a very large and formidable army was mustered to confront the Army of the Cumberland.

The rebels began the attack on ROSECRANS' army, the lines of which were established along Chicamauga Creek, a short distance south of Chattanooga, shortly before noon on Saturday. They adopted the style of tactics which they have so often practiced with success — massing their troops, and attacking with fury, in succession, the different corps of our army, forcing its wings and centre. In each attack they seem to have been temporarily successful, but only temporarily, for, at nightfall, our lines were reestablished as they had been before the battle began, and Gen. ROSECRANS held his ground, having severely punished the rebels. Gen. ROSECRANS has telegraphed to Washington that he anticipated that the battle would be renewed yesterday, and another dispatch represents our men as in the best of spirits and eager to begin the fight anew. The rebels, undoubtedly, attacked on Saturday with the whole of their force, as this is the policy which they have universally pursued, when they had the initiative in the action, and their failure in the first day augurs ill for their success yesterday. There has been no instance in the war in which the rebels, foiled in the first day of the battle, retrieved their fortunes on the day succeeding. And they were even less likely than usual to succeed on this occasion against the hero who, at Murfreesboro, wrenched victory from the very jaws of defeat. ⊛

THE BATTLE IN GEORGIA.

SEPTEMBER 22

As was anticipated by Gen. ROSECRANS, the great battle which opened on Saturday forenoon, and raged till after nightfall, was reopened on Sunday morning, and continued throughout the day. The aspect of the battle of Sunday is no better than was that of Saturday. On Saturday, the rebels first massed their troops on our right, then on our centre, then on our left, attacking each in succession, and gaining important advantages, and though at evening our army occupied the same ground as when the action commenced, it would appear that Gen. ROSECRANS suffered severely. On Sunday the enemy again advanced in force; but the only details of the battle given are, that it raged fiercely all day — that two of ROSECRANS' divisions gave way in panic, but were subsequently rallied, while the remainder of the army stood its ground, and it is reported that at night we were driving back the rebel advance. The casualties were very heavy — the dispatch asserting that the killed and wounded on both sides will not fall short of thirty thousand.

There is little cheer on the surface of the dispatch, or in the details as given, but we think there is ground for encouragement. The fact that ROSECRANS held his ground for two days is a very favorable sign. In their desperate and overwhelming assaults of Saturday and Sunday, the rebels failed to drive him back, or at least failed to keep him back. On Saturday ROSECRANS was unable to bring his artillery favorably into action, and this was probably also the case on Sunday, as the ground of the battle was the same on both clays. If he has subsequently succeeded in getting it into good position, we do not fear for the result.... ⊛

THE MILITARY BEARINGS OF THE GEORGIA BATTLE.

SEPTEMBER 23

Whatever may prove to have been the facts and results of the late battle in the north-western corner of Georgia, we may all find comfort in the reflection that although our winning a great battle just now might bring the Confederacy to the verge of dis-solution, our losing one can do but little for its salvation. We are long past that stage of the war in which a single defeat can stay our progress. The fact, for fact it seems to be, that the rebel army of Virginia has been largely drawn upon to supply BRAGG with the means of striking the blow under which ROSECRANS is now reeling, proves that the surmise which gave them but one army remaining of the various hosts which they possessed, a year ago, is well founded. They have no longer an army of the East and an army of the West, an army in Vir-ginia and an army in Tennessee. When they seek to accomplish great things at any one point, it has to be by forces drawn from all others. This is unquestionably a game in which great skill and judgment, celerity and audacity, may be displayed, and it would be childish to refuse the reb-els the credit of displaying every one of these qualities. But, then, it is a desperate game — a game which Generals play rather to save their honor than to retrieve their fortunes. It was probably never played so magnificently, and may never he played so magnificently, as in that brilliant cam-paign by which NAPOLEON sought to save Paris after the fatal field of Leipsic. There was something awful in the genius with which, during that terrible month, he shot small masses of raw levies up and down the chord of the arc, in the vain effort to stem the great tide which was gradually hemming him in. and under which he soon after sunk in the court-yard of Fontainebleau. But for-tune was still on the side of the big battal-ions, and proved, for perhaps the hundredth time, that no amount of either energy or ability can, at the close of long wars, make up for the exhaustion of the supply of men.

It is from this that the South is now suf-fering. Its losses on the battle-field have been enormous ever since the beginning of the war, and its reverses have every month diminished the area of its recruit-ing ground, so that a levy en masse would produce very different results, even now, from those which it would have produced two years ago. At that time it would, if JEFF. DAVIS had ordered it, have brought almost the whole armsbearing population south of Mason and Dixon's line into the field. To-day it could not, supposing it to be obeyed, bring more than that of five States. But it will not be obeyed even in these; and when matters come to such straits as this with any Power, the ability to raise men by force diminishes in the precise ratio of its need of them. We have the confessions of the warmest Southern partisans that the mar-tial ardor of the people has so far declined, that not only do those not already on the rolls not rush to arms, but half those who are on them skulk at home with the con-nivance of their friends and neighbors.

So that every battle, whatever its nomi-nal result may be, is a defeat for the South, simply because every battle thins the ranks of the faithful few who still keep the

THE GREAT BATTLES.
IMPORTANT DETAILS.

SEPTEMBER 23
SPECIAL DISPATCH TO THE NEW-YORK TIMES
WASHINGTON, TUESDAY, SEPT. 22

Shortly after noon to-day a dispatch was received here from an officer in com-mand at Chattanooga, speaking in most encouraging terms of the general result of the actions of Saturday and Sunday last, wherein, according to his representations, the Union army achieved a substantial suc-cess instead of being beaten — the enemy being more damaged in killed, wounded, &c. On Sunday night Gen. ROSECRANS changed the position of his army to points near Chattanooga, with Gen. THOMAS' command still occupying the front, which shows how much less that officer's corps was crippled than the first newspaper ac-counts alleged. Our total loss in prisoners was but 2,000, while 1,300 rebel prisoners had been sent to the rear when the dispatch in question left Chattanooga, and more were being expected in from the front. The army is in excellent spirits, and the bright-est anticipations are entertained. ❊

FROM ROSECRANS' ARMY.
NO FIGHTING YESTERDAY.

SEPTEMBER 25
WASHINGTON, THURSDAY, SEPT. 24

A dispatch from Gen. ROSECRANS, dated at his headquarters last night, says:

"I cannot be dislodged from my present position."

Another dispatch from one of Gen. ROSECRANS' Staff, written at forty min-utes past 11 o'clock last night, says:

"No fighting to-day, the 23d." ❊

MAJ.-GEN. THOMAS.

SEPTEMBER 26

The full accounts that are reaching us from the hard-contested field near Chickam-auga Creek do justice to the services of one of the ablest and most successful Generals in the Union army — Maj.-Gen. THOMAS. It appears that this gallant soldier bore the brunt of the rebel attack unharmed, on both days of the fight, though the onset in each case was impetuous and overwhelm-ing. It is no discredit to the corps of Gens. MCCOOK and CRITTENDEN that they were broken by the outnumbering hosts of the enemy. The metal of these men had been tried before, and they are known and approved as among the bravest of our Union soldiers. But if a part of the gallant army of ROSECRANS could be driven back without disgrace, it must not be denied that unusual credit and renown are due to that portion which withstood every shock, and dealt horrible slaughter upon a foe so numerous as to be deemed invincible. This is the signal merit of the corps of Gen. THOMAS in the sanguinary battle in Northern Georgia. The stubborn fighting of this portion of the army is all that saved

field, — doubtless the choice spirits of the Confederacy. Whether they win or lose, as long as fighting makes gaps in their columns which they cannot fill, the only result of their struggles is to defer for a short time the doom of the Confederacy. If they utterly destroyed the armies of ROSECRANS and BURNSIDE tomorrow, it could only be by the sacrifice of three-fourths of that of BRAGG, and there would still remain those of BANKS and GRANT — of [Frederick] STEELE, [Stephen A.] HURLBUT and [Grenville] DODGE, and behind all, the millions of the North. The fact is the game is, for all practical purposes, over. It has been well played, and what we now witness is but the frantic maneuvering of a solitary king, to avoid checkmate on a board crowded with adverse pieces. Every fight which occurs after this is simple butchery, which, though it may gratify the hate or ambition of the rebel leaders, can have no real influence upon the fortunes of the fabric which they have cemented with so much blood and so many tears. ✹

the fortunes of the day, as we understand the contest at this distance; and if the enemy fails to follow up his supposed advantages, it will be mainly because of the damaging blows inflicted by this heroic General.

Gen. THOMAS is a Southerner, a native-born Virginian, and will be remembered as the leader of the Union forces in that first fortunate and decisive battle in Kentucky, Mill Spring, in which Gen. ZOLLICOFFER lost his life, and the rebel Gen. CRITTENDEN was driven across the Cumberland and out of the State in such confusion and rout. He has the prestige of success, and richly deserves the gratitude of the nation. ✹

WHAT BRAGG MAY DO.

Some of our Western exchanges took a gloomy view of the results that might follow a "bad defeat" of ROSECRANS near Chattanooga. They anticipated, in that case, a flank movement by BRAGG that would bring him immediately northward again through Tennessee into Kentucky. And ROSECRANS, if beaten in battle, would not be able to follow and head him off, as Gen. BUELL did so successfully on the former occasion....

On the whole, it does not appear that BRAGG can reenact the campaign he performed last year, fruitless as that remarkable episode was. If ROSECRANS is too much crippled to pursue, BRAGG is unquestionably too much exhausted to march, as he would have to march before entering Kentucky. The audacious enterprise could hardly be put on foot before overwhelming masses could be thrown in the way, and the enemy met nearer to Chattanooga than to Chaplin Hills.

The danger in Tennessee is not that BRAGG will flank ROSECRANS as he did BUELL, and march North, but that he will send cavalry raids to the rear and break the communications of ROSECRANS with Nashville. Such a movement would compel ROSECRANS to weaken his front to protect his rear, and the great extent of line to be guarded, though threatened by only a small portion of the foe, might so weaken his garrison at Chattanooga as to render its hold of that place doubtful. Let the Government see to it that communications are kept open between ROSECRANS and Nashville, and BRAGG will remain in Georgia. ✹

Major General George H. Thomas, U.S.A., the "Rock of Chickamauga."

CHAPTER 16
"The Shock of Battle"

OCTOBER–NOVEMBER 1863

fter his headlong flight from the battlefield at Chickamauga in September, Rosecrans fell back to Chattanooga and prepared for a Confederate assault. Bragg followed cautiously but, instead of assaulting the enemy, placed his army on the high ground south of the city to inaugurate a kind of siege that would sever Union supply lines and starve Rosecrans out of the city.

In Washington, Lincoln and General-in-Chief Halleck decided not to wait for such an eventuality, and they made two decisions: first, to re-inforce Rosecrans by sending Joseph Hooker with two corps from the Army of the Potomac to Chattanooga by rail; and second, to send Ulysses S. Grant there to take overall command. Grant's orders gave him the authority to relieve Rosecrans if he thought it advisable (Lincoln believed Rosecrans had lost his "spirit and nerve"), and Grant decided not to wait, sending orders ahead by telegraph for George H. Thomas to take his place.

Grant arrived in Chattanooga on October 23 and dealt first with the problem of dwindling provisions. He opened a line of supply over the Tennessee River at Brown's Ferry, es-tablishing what the soldiers called the "cracker line." After that, Grant turned his attention to the challenge of driv-ing off Bragg's besieging army. With Hooker's 16,000 men and 20,000 more on their way under William T. Sherman, Grant could now begin to think of-fensively. The Times obligingly treated its readers to a detailed appreciation of Grant, elaborately comparing his achievements in the war to date to no less than the fabled Hercules.

Meanwhile, the Lincoln adminis-tration had reason to celebrate after learning of glorious results at the polls in mid-October. In Pennsylvania,

Detail of an illustration depicting President Abraham Lincoln delivering his Gettysburg Address.

pro-Lincoln Governor Andrew Curtin easily won a second term. Republican gubernatorial candidates were victorious as well in Iowa and Indiana. The President could take special consolation from the results in Ohio, where his nemesis, former Congressman Clement Laird Vallandigham, went down to a stunning defeat in his attempt at a political comeback. "Valiant Val," as his copperhead supporters dubbed him, was badly defeated for governor by Republican John Brough. The Times joined other pro-war journals in exulting at the Democratic embarrassment. Not only had Vallandigham lost, he had been compelled — as a convicted traitor — to campaign from exile in Canada.

Amid much heartening news, Lincoln decided to accept an invitation to make a rare visit to a battlefield in November — in this case the sacred ground of Gettysburg, for the dedication of a new Soldiers' Cemetery to accommodate the thousands of corpses left unattended after the July conflagration there. Organizers asked the President, almost reluctantly, to give but "a few appropriate remarks" at a ceremony to which the nation's foremost public speaker, Edward Everett, had been asked to deliver the principal address.

Lincoln had scant time to prepare for his appearance exhaustively, but wrote at least one draft of his brief comments at the White House before departing for Pennsylvania. The Times reported that he was greeted enthusiastically when he arrived in Gettysburg on November 18, after which he retired to his room to edit his manuscript further.

When Lincoln rose the next day to deliver his 271-word speech, few on the scene expected anything like the masterpiece he delivered — not only an eloquent justification for the sacrifices Union troops had made at that battlefield, but also an extraordinary hymn to use the war to complete the "unfinished work" proposed by the founders. To the legalistic "prose" of the Emancipation Proclamation, this master writer had at last provided the explicatory "poetry" that consecrated the fight to save the Union and eradicate slavery.

Within the next few days, The Times obligingly reprinted the President's brief text without comment, reserving its most lavish praise for Everett's purple stem-winder. Everett himself knew better. Writing to Lincoln the day after their joint appearance at Gettysburg, the old orator graciously admitted: "I should be glad, if I could flatter myself that I came as near to the central idea of the occasion, in two hours, as you did in two minutes."

Lincoln must have been gratified, but as he had said a year earlier, "breath alone kills no Rebels." By month's end, the President and the readers of The Times received the news they were waiting for: stirring reports of unqualified Union triumphs at Chattanooga on Lookout Mountain and Missionary Ridge.

A LATEST FROM CHATTANOOGA.
STORIES FROM OVER THE REBEL LINES.

OCTOBER 17

CHATTANOOGA, SATURDAY, OCT. 10

Since the 7th, no hostile demonstrations have been made by the enemy upon our front. Their batteries on the northeastern slope of the Lookout Mountain have undoubtedly been withdrawn, while those on the left have remained silent.

Yesterday and the day before our guns on the left and right opened, and compelled Gen. BRAGG to remove his headquarters from Missionary Ridge, and drove away the whole signal corps on Lookout Mountain.

Up to noon to-day both sides have been quiet.

Day before yesterday, a rebel picket, composed of a Sergeant and six men of the Third Kentucky, deserted to us. They report that the mysterious engagement within the rebel lines, observed from our left on the 6th, was a fight between a brigade of Georgia militia and the regular troops. The former refused to cross the State line, and their refusal brought on the collision. Strange as the story is, it is credited at headquarters. That a fight took place is confirmed by hundreds of eye-witnesses on our side.... ⊛

An 1886 Louis Prang chromolithograph showing General Grant and other senior staff observing the Battle of Chattanooga.

OUR SPECIAL ARMY CORRESPONDENCE.

OCTOBER 18
ARMY OF THE POTOMAC,
THURSDAY, OCT. 15

Another day has been devoted to the by-play or the strategic efforts of the commandants of the two great armies now moving in parallel lines, each endeavoring to secure the advantage of situation — movements that always precede a general engagement. Nothing but skirmishing, (and only little of that,) moving of trains and immense columns of troops has been done to-day, but the shock of battle is imminent, and no one can tell what an hour may bring forth. Both armies are seemingly in readiness, and, apparently at least, eager for the fray. No men ever fought with more determination than that portion of the gallant and battle-stained Second corps, engaged yesterday at Bristow's [sic] Station,[1] under the accomplished and energetic WARREN.[2] With the enemy there was an unmistakable difference. While their officers fought as only desperate men can fight in a failing cause, their men did not seem to be imbued with the same spirit, and fled or surrendered themselves as prisoners of war, more readily than has been their wont in previous trials of strength. I have good authority for reporting this state of things, but as obvious facts are more potent with the reader, I will cite in evidence of this want of spirit, that in one single division of HILL's corps, (so say the prisoners,) one Colonel was killed, and three other Colonels and one General were wounded, 470 of the 700 prisoners reported captured, I have seen; I have also seen and examined five of the six pieces of artillery captured, the sixth piece haring been left behind owing to the want of means to bring it from the field; moreover, forty-seven of the prisoners say they are tired of fighting Yankees, and have signified a wish to take the oath of allegiance. These men say they know many others now in the rebel ranks who are only awaiting an opportunity to come within our lines and give themselves up....

Everything thus remains; the army is ready for any new scheme of LEE's, or, if he decides to retreat, to follow him up again. It is evident that MEADE has foiled the rebel General, and left him somewhat doubtful what to do next.

J. ✱

1. The Battle of Bristoe Station on October 14, not far from the familiar terrain of Manassas, Virginia, proved little more than a large, inconclusive skirmish.
2. General Gouverneur Kemble Warren (1830–1882).

THE NEGRO SOLDIER QUESTION.

OCTOBER 18

The opposition which was made at first to the employment of negroes in our armies, has all but passed away, as indeed it could not fail to do, for it was founded in great part upon erroneous views as to their capacity, which have been entirely dissipated by a little experience. But that there should have been such opposition at all, will always be one of the singular features of the history of the rebellion. One would have thought the employment of negroes in the army during the Revolution and the war of 1812, and their constant employment in the navy, would have prevented the rise of any such feeling.

There is another feature about the matter which is also notable. It has been found easiest to make use of the negroes by forming them into separate regiments and companies. It would not be possible to employ them if they were to be introduced into the ranks of our armies indiscriminately. But in the Revolution it was just the reverse. There were numbers of negro soldiers who stood in the ranks with their white fellow citizens on many a hard fought field, beginning with the battle of Bunker Hill, where PETER SALEM, the colored man, spoken of by Mr. EVERETT in his address on the inauguration of the statue, of Gen. WARREN,

FROM OHIO.

VALLANDINGHAM'S DEFEAT[1] — THE GHOST OF THE COPPERHEADS

OCTOBER 18

CINCINNATI, OHIO, FRIDAY, OCT. 16

Did you hear the clap of thunder from Ohio? Was it not a startling Alpine peal, leaping from crag to crag across the continent, and warning our own and other nations that a frightful bolt had struck somewhere. It was here it struck — here in this stretch of "Northwestern territory," lying between the Ohio River and Lake Erie; the first soil consecrated to Freedom by National act on this continent — here the bolt struck on Tuesday last, paralyzing every arm that would raise again the black banner of Human Slavery, and sealing, as it were, by Divine wrath, the work long since decreed by Divine goodness. "The voice of the people is the voice of God," and never was that voice uttered with more emphasis and effect than in the late election. Defeated partisans, lately raging with fury, stand appalled and abashed by the visitation, and meekly admit the irreversible and overwhelming judgment against them. But I will leave it to the "Veteran Observer" to philosophize for you on the extraordinary phenomenon of the Ohio election.

Six weeks ago I passed through this broad State, from west to east, somewhat leisurely — and I told you, as the result of my observations, that VALLANDIGHAM would be beaten by 100,000 majority. No one else seemed to think so — least of all the people of Ohio. When I came back here — reentering the State on the day of the election, and passing through it all day long, while the ballots like snow-flakes were falling — I found the Union men working for dear life at the polls. They gathered in the voters anxiously and hastily, as a farmer gathers in his hay-cocks when a dark storm is brewing. I met sons of Ohio who had come all the way from Memphis to cast a ballot. Chicago and New-York sent home their contributions, and even the eminent Minister of Finance, Secretary CHASE, drooped for a brief time his national reckonings, and returned hither to vote the Union ticket! Loyal Ohio was terribly excited, if not alarmed, and dealt on Tuesday last her most tremendous blow. She struck as if for existence as well as honor, and the wires have told you the result. I think the 100,000 majority will be more than realized. The majority of the home vote will approach 70,000, and the soldiers' vote will swell that to almost its own extent, for few soldiers vote for VALLANDIGHAM. It is well the majority in the home vote is so vast. If VALLANDIGHAM had received a majority of these, and the

shot Maj. PITCAIRN, of the British marines; and there never seems to have been any opposition to it at all. But there was very heavy opposition to the formation of separate bodies of negro troops, and in many of the States, as Col. LAURENS, who went to South Carolina with a project for raising such battalions, wrote to Gen. WASHINGTON, "the single voice of reason was drowned by the howlings of a triple-headed monster, in which prejudice, avarice and pusillanimity were united."

Still, such regiments were formed and did good service — as witness the Rhode Island regiment of blacks — but the instances were few; while in almost all, if not in every one of the States, colored soldiers, not only of the free men, but of those who had been slaves, were received into the ranks of their white regiments without objection. It is possible that one reason for this latter fact maybe found in that absence of personal repugnance for the negro, which the Southerners have always claimed, and which they have often pointed to as a proof of the excellence of the "institution." Most of the States during the Revolution being Slave States, might be subject to the same influences as our Slave States now, and freed from prejudices to which these also claim that they are not exposed; and the history of this war will prove, we have no doubt, that from the first there have been cases of negroes fighting in the ranks of the rebellion. Not, however, in any such numbers, as the muster rolls of the Revolution would show. And the reason of this is manifest. Our fathers fought in the Revolution for freedom. That was the sign by which they must conquer. That was emblazoned amid the glories of the banner under which they fought. And feeling this great truth pulsating in their every heart-beat, they could not but look kindly upon the effort of any slave to make himself a freeman among freemen, by offering his life as readily as they were offering theirs for their common country.

But with the rebels it is the reverse. They have set Slavery as the foundation-stone of their Government. They have plunged into rebellion and crime of all sorts in defence of Slavery. The liberty which they claim to be fighting for is a liberty to enslave others. They declare their Confederacy to be "a God-sent missionary" to teach "Slavery, Subordination and Government." We, on the other hand, fight on different conditions. All the logic of the struggle leads us more and more toward universal freedom. Every dollar spent, every drop of blood shed, is an argument in this direction, and leaves behind an influence which leads us to take a bolder stand and more decided measures for freedom to each and to all. The bravery of the black man has already silenced the opposition to these regiments. ✷

An African-American volunteer soldier as imagined in a period lithograph.

votes of the army had overcome that majority, we should have had no end here, or in the great rebel organ in England, of lamentations over the fatal advances of "military despotism" in America.

Now that the affair is over, there is something almost ludicrous in the condition of "copperheadism." It seems that there was nothing of strength or danger in it. It was like one of the ghosts of your theatres — sepulchral in aspect, dark in its haunts and sulphurous in smell — but when robust loyalty dashed forward to grapple with it, it vanished into thin air, and sought its fit infernal shades. It never had even "the ghost of a chance" of success. ✷

ROSECRANS RELIEVED BY GRANT.

OCTOBER 21

We have this morning the news that Gen. ROSECRANS has been relieved from the command of the Army of the Cumberland; and that Major-General ULYSSES S. GRANT takes command of that Department and of the Army of the Tennessee, (GRANT's old army,) the Army of the Cumberland, (ROSECRANS' late army,) and the Army of Kentucky (BURNSIDE's.) Gen. THOMAS, who fought so splendidly at Chickamauga takes the immediate command vacated by Gen. ROSECRANS.

It now remains to the great and unconquerable hero of the Mississippi Valley — who has defeated more armies, reduced more strongholds, and conquered more territory than all our other Generals put together, or than any General since the days of NAPOLEON the First — it remains for Major-Gen. GRANT to overcome the rebels now intrenched among the mountains of the West, as he has already routed them through the length and breadth of the great River of the West. ✷

THE VOTE OF THE SOLDIERS AGAINST THE COPPERHEADS.

OCTOBER 21

Will some Anti-Administration man, who is wont to protest that his party is very sharp-set against the rebellion, have the goodness to tell us why the vote of the soldiers, when they have the chance to vote, goes so overwhelmingly against its candidates? Don't the soldiers know what good, stiff loyalty is? Don't they go for it when they see it? Either they must be very dull in apprehension, or very deficient in public spirit — or there must be some screw loose in Copperhead patriotism. Now, how is it? Are the soldiers fools? Or are they renegades? Will some Copperhead tell us which? If they are neither, what then are we to think of their judgment of the Copperheads?

Possibly it may be intimated that the officers are all for the Administration because they hope for promotion, and the soldiers because they fear the officers. We doubt, however, whether any responsible man of the opposition will seriously aver this, however much he may hint it. It would be a very bold act. Even could it be plausibly made out that the officers were all a pack of sordid adventurers, caring everything for self and nothing for country, it would be pretty tough business to maintain that the half million of American citizens in the rank and file are subject to their political orders — that they have ceased to be freemen and become mere liegemen and vassals. Copperhead audacity we know is great; but it is not quite equal to that. It is too well es-

tablished that Americans don't yield their manhood in any such fashion....

Wherever the soldiers have the power to vote, they invariably use that power with trenchant effect upon the enemies of the Administration. They don't strike the rebels with the sword one whit more resolutely than they do the Copperheads with the franchise....

This staunch, consistent, thoroughgoing loyalty of the army is a mighty political fact. Its influence in bracing the hearts of loyal civilians all over the land, and nerving the arms of those who officially direct the war, is beyond measure valuable. In fact it may, we believe, be truly said that the National cause would be utterly, hopelessly lost, if the army should imbibe the spirit or become partial to the policy of the enemies of the Administration. The war would inevitably languish and die under such a military feeling. Thank heaven, it is not in the human nature to lapse in any such way as that. Every day's perils encountered for his flag only make the soldier all the more devoted to it; and he worships it the most, when most rent by the battle's rage. The war is one constant school of patriotic training to all engaged in it. The army has, from the beginning, hated all factionists and malcontents, and that hatred will deepen to the end. The soldiers will retain that feeling when they return to civil life; and we may be sure that in their day, at least, copperheadism in any form will never dare lift itself above the dust. ⊕

THE REMOVAL OF GEN. ROSECRANS.

OCTOBER 22

As we are not of the number of those who think that the President ought to take the vote of the people and of the army before removing or appointing a General, we have no fault to find with the dismissal of Gen. ROSECRANS from his command in Tennessee. We are bound, at least in courtesy, to suppose that there are good reasons for a step in many respects so grave, and that in this, as in other things, the President has been guided, in the exercise of an undoubted prerogative, by a sense of duty, and by nothing else. What these reasons are it would be idle now to inquire. It would be just neither to Gen. ROSECRANS nor to

the Government to discuss seriously the dozen rumors which are flying from lip to lip touching the General's alleged mistakes, or shortcomings, or misfortunes. We may be sure that we shall know in due time whatever he considers it necessary for the vindication of his own fame that we should know, and until that time comes we may well be spared the task of investigating the probability or improbability of every bit of camp gossip that is offered to us in explanation of one of the most untoward incidents of the war. ⊕

THE ARMIES IN THE WEST — THEIR NEW CHIEF.

OCTOBER 23

As, at the fall of Vicksburgh in July last, the three great armies which the rebels had long maintained were reduced to two — those of BRAGG and LEE — so now, the three firstclass armies which we have maintained for nearly two years have been reduced to two — those of GRANT and MEADE. That splendid army, eighty thousand strong, which in the first months of the year was planted in front of Vicksburgh, and in May, June and July last lay in its rear, exists no more as a unit. Part of it has gone down the Mississippi to Gen. BANKS, part has gone up the Arkansas to Little Rock, part is in East Tennessee, a large part has gone to join the army of Chattanooga, and many detachments are scattered at the various military posts along the line of the Mississippi River. But nearly, if not quite all of these troops are in the new Military Division or Department of Gen. GRANT, and to the old army under his command is now added the late army of Gen. ROSECRANS. This will give Gen. GRANT a very large army — at least twice as large as that under Gen. MEADE, and six times as large as that under any other General in the country.

The first work of Gen. GRANT will doubtless be to combine these armies, as far as possible, into one active body; and in those cases in which incorporation is impossible or undesirable, he will so place and operate the various bodies as to produce essential unity of purpose and object. The lack of this has of late been the greatest drawback to success in the Southwest. Gen. BURNSIDE has had an independent command in East Tennessee; and though, weeks ago, we had the assertion that his army was in conjunction and cooperation with that of ROSECRANS, there was in reality no communication between the two departments beyond the scout of an occasional small body of cavalry. Going west a hundred miles from BURNSIDE's headquarters at Knoxville, we had the army of ROSECRANS at Chattanooga. West of the latter, some forty miles, we had the army under Gen. HOOKER, which the latter also claimed to be an independent command; and as HOOKER ranked ROSECRANS, it is said he declined obeying his orders. Still further West, we had a large body of troops under

Gen. DODGE at Corinth, and here began the forces of Gen. GRANT, which were scattered from Memphis northward through West Tennessee, and down the Mississippi as far as Vicksburgh, and beyond. At these various points and along these various lines, we have probably at this moment not far short of two hundred thousand troops. This army, massed and properly handled (if there be any living man, or if there ever were a man, who could properly handle it on the field,) or, if not concentrated in mass, were it wielded and directed by one strong hand, guided by a broad brain, could trample out any Southern army, or march to any point, or achieve any object in the Confederacy. But, under four independent commanders, hundreds of miles apart, without communication with each other, each "working at his own job," little or big — each and all, it may be, working laboriously and conscientiously, but disjointedly and lacking mutual purpose — how could we expect the highest results — particularly when it was evident that since the opening of the Mississippi, the great object of the campaign in the West was one and simple? The appointment of Gen. GRANT to the chief commandership of the military division of the Mississippi (its limits as yet unknown to us) and the armies therein, unifies all operations, and he will doubtless bend all his powers and forces to the achievement of a common result. This army, massed and properly handled (if there be any living man, or if there ever were a man, who could properly handle it on the field,) or, if not concentrated in mass, were it wielded and directed by one strong hand, guided by a broad brain, could trample out any Southern army, or march to any point, or achieve any object in the Confederacy. But, under four independent commanders, hundreds of miles apart, without communication with each other, each "working at his own job," little or big — each and all, it may be, working laboriously and conscientiously, but disjointedly and lacking mutual purpose — how could we expect the highest results — particularly when it was evident that since the opening of the Mississippi, the great object of the campaign in the West was one and simple? The appointment of Gen. GRANT to the chief commandership of the military division of the Mississippi (its limits as yet unknown to us) and the armies therein, unifies all operations, and he will doubtless bend all his powers and forces to the achievement of a common result.

Lieutenant General Ulysses S. Grant, U.S.A., in a William Sartain engraving based on a painting by Christian Shussele.

Gen. GRANT we believe to be just the man for the post. Having been granted plenary powers in his Department, he will doubtless make short work with any officer of any grade who will not cordially cooperate in carrying out his plans; and to all such, the example made of MCCLERNAND by Gen. GRANT last Summer, will stand as a solemn warning. In many respects, GRANT's new field of action is more difficult than his former one. But having already performed his other Herculean labors with such consummate success — having fought the Nemean lion at Donelson, and sent its carcass to Chicago — having burned the heads of the Lernaean hydra at Shiloh — having captured the Arcadian stag at Vicksburgh — having hunted the Erymanthian boar till it was captured at Arkansas Post — having destroyed the swarm of Stymphalian guerrillas who haunted the Mississippi, feeding upon human flesh — having cleansed the Agean stables throughout his Department — and having performed other and sundry of the labors of the great Greek, it now only remains that he seize the rebel dog Cerberus' that guards the gates of the Confederacy in Northern Georgia, and force him back howling to Hades. ☉

1. An elaborate reference to the mythological Labors of Hercules, including: clubbing and strangling the Nemean lion to death; killing the multiheaded Hydra snake in the Lernaean swamps; snaring the sacred hind of Artemis; capturing the Erymanthian beast that roamed the mountains between Arcadia and Achaia; destroying the man-eating Stymphalian birds; and cleansing King Augeas' stables at Elis. Now, The Times continued, Grant was ready for the 11th labor, confronting the three-headed dog Cerberus that guarded the gates of Hell.

THE WAR IN VIRGINIA — THE LATE CAMPAIGN.

OCTOBER 24

The Fall campaign of Gen. LEE, which has, been in progress for nearly a fortnight past, and about which we have known so very little and speculated so much, is probably already closed. His army crossed to the northern bank of the Rapidan with cooked rations for fourteen days, on the 9th inst., and it recrossed the river on Wednesday of this week, and returned to the point from which it had started — having been gone almost the precise length of time for which provision had been made. During that time they made a march which, by the line they took, could not have been short of sixty miles, had a number of heavy skirmishes, and fought an action in which one-half of their force was engaged.

The object of the campaign certainly does not appear on the face of it. We are accordingly left to speculation, to such deductions as may be made from their movements, and to such evidences of their design as the rebels may have left behind them. The fact that they made two efforts to flank MEADE, and a desperate effort to get in his rear at Centreville before he should be able to get to that position, indicates that their army was formidable; and of this fact, indeed, we have positive proof from the details given by the rebels themselves. But their efforts at flanking were failures, and they retreated without having had a general engagement and without having attempted any of the great things which some Northern writers had marked out for them....

Now that the late campaign may be supposed to be closed, the new question is, What next? It is credited at headquarters that another of LEE's corps (A. P. HILL's) has now rushed westward to Georgia, to strike a quick blow at the army of Gen. THOMAS at Chattanooga. We believe that the latter army, under its new direction, and with the cooperation of the forces heretofore acting independently, will be able to endure even this. ✹

FROM THE REBEL STATES.

ADDRESS OF JEFF. DAVIS TO BRAGG'S ARMY.

OCTOBER 25
HEADQUARTERS ARMY OF TENNESSEE,
OCT. 14

SOLDIERS: A grateful country recognizes your arduous services, and rejoices over your glorious victory on the field of Chickamauga. When your countrymen shall more fully learn the adverse circumstances under which you attacked the enemy, though they cannot be more thankful, they may admire more the gallantry and patriotic devotion which secured your success. Representatives of every State of the Confederacy, your steps have been followed up with affectionate solicitude by friends in every portion of the country. Defenders of the heart of our territory, your movements have been an object of interest, anxiety, and hope.

Our cause depends on you, and happy it is that all can reply upon your achieving whatever, under the blessing of Providence, human power can effect.

Though you have done much, very much remains to be done. Behind you is a people providing for your support, and depending upon your protection. Before you is a country devastated by your ruthless invaders, where gentle women, feeble age and helpless infancy have been subjected to outrages without parallel in the warfare of civilized nations.

With eager eye they watch for your coming to their deliverance, and homeless refugees pine for the hour when your victorious arms shall restore their family shelters from which they have been driven and forced to take up arms to vindicate their political rights, freedom, equality and state sovereignty, which were a heritage purchased by the blood of your Revolutionary sires.

You have but the alternative of being slaves of submission to a despotic usurpation or of independence, which a vigorous, united and persistent effort will secure.

All which fires a manly breast, moves a patriot, or exalts a hero, is present to stimulate and sustain you. Nobly have you redeemed your pledges, given in the name of freedom, to the memory of your ancestors and the rights of your posterity.

That you may complete the mission to which you have devoted yourselves, will require of you such exertions in the future as you have made in the past, and the continuous self-denial which rejects every consideration at variance with the public service, as unworthy of the holy cause in which you are engaged.

When the war shall be ended the highest need of praise will be due, and probably be given, to him who has claimed the least for himself in proportion to the service he has rendered. And the bitterest self-reproach which may hereafter haunt the memory of any one will be to him who has allowed selfish aspiration to prevail over his desire for the public good.

United as we are in a common destiny, obedience and cordial cooperation are essential. There is no higher duty than that which requires one to exert and render to all what is due to their station. He who sows the seeds of discontent and distrust prepares for a harvest of slaughter and defeat.

To your gallantry, energy and fortitude you crown this harmony with due subordination and cheerful support of lawful authority.

I fervently hope that this ferocious war, so unjustly waged against our country, may soon end, and that, with the blessing of peace, you may be restored to your homes and useful pursuits, and I pray our Heavenly Father may cover you with the shield of His protection in your battle, and endow you with the virtues which will close your trials in victory complete.

JEFFERSON DAVIS. ✹

ORATIONS OF EVERETT AND BEECHER.

NOVEMBER 20

We devote a broadside of this morning's TIMES to the publication of two orations which we are sure will command the attention of the day. And not of this day only. Elaborate and finished discourses from two such men as EDWARD EVERETT and HENRY WARD BEECHER, upon topics of such great National interest as those they discuss, will not lightly be passed over, much less ignored altogether, by any intelligent citizen. Mr. EVERETT's theme is the "Battle of Gettysburgh," and the occasion is the dedication of that historic field as a National Cemetery[1]....

Mr. EVERETT's oration is, of course, classical and ornate in its diction, felicitous

THE HEROES OF JULY.

A SOLEMN AND IMPOSING EVENT.

DEDICATION OF THE NATIONAL CEMETERY AT GETTYSBURGH.

NOVEMBER 20

The ceremonies attending the dedication of the National Cemetery commenced this morning by a grand military and civic display, under command of Maj.-Gen. COUCH. The line of march was taken up at 10 o'clock, and the procession marched through the principal streets to the Cemetery, where the military formed in line and saluted the President. At 11 the head of the procession arrived at the main stand. The President and members of the Cabinet, together with the chief military and civic dignitaries, took position on the stand. The President seated himself between Mr. SEWARD and Mr. EVERETT after a reception marked with the respect and perfect silence due to the solemnity of the occasion, every man in the immense gathering uncovering on his appearance.

The military were formed in line extending around the stand, the area between the stand and military being occupied by civilians, comprising about 15,000 people and including men, women and children. The attendance of ladies was quite large. The military escort comprised one squadron of cavalry, two batteries of artillery and a regiment of infantry, which constitutes the regular funeral escort of honor for the highest officer in the service.

After the performance of a funeral dirge, by BIRGFIELD, by the band, an eloquent prayer was delivered by Rev. Mr. STOCKTON....

PRESIDENT LINCOLN's ADDRESS.

The President then delivered the following dedicatory speech:

Fourscore and seven years ago our Fathers brought forth upon this Continent a new nation, conceived in liberty and dedicated to the proposition that all men are created equal. [Applause.] Now we are engaged in a great civil war, testing whether that nation, or any nation so conceived and so dedicated, can long endure. We are met on a great battle-field of that war. We are met to dedicate a portion of it as the final resting-place of those who here gave their lives that that nation might live. It is altogether fitting and proper that we should do this. But in a larger sense we cannot dedicate. We cannot consecrate, we cannot hallow this ground. The brave men, living and dead, who struggled here have consecrated it far above our power to add or detract. [Applause.] The world will little note nor long remember, what we say here, but it can never forget what they did here. [Applause.] It is for us, the living, rather to be dedicated here to the refinished work that they have thus so far nobly carried on. [Applause.] It is rather for us to be here dedicated to the great task remaining before us that from these hon-ored dead we take increased devotion to that cause for which they here gave the last full measure of devotion; that we here highly resolve that the dead shall not have died in vain; [applause] that the Nation shall under God have a new birth of freedom, and that Governments of the people, by the people and for the people, shall not perish from the earth, [Long continued applause.]

Three cheers were then given for the President and the Governors of the States.

After the delivery of the addresses, the dirge and the benediction closed the exercises, and the immense assemblage separated at about 4 o'clock.

About 3 o'clock in the afternoon, the Fifth New York regiment of heavy artillery, Col. MURRAY, was marched to the temporary residence of Gov. SEYMOUR, where they passed in review before the Governor, presenting a handsome spectacle. Upon the conclusion of this ceremony, which attracted quite a crowd of sight-seers. Gov. SEYMOUR presented a handsome silk regimental standard to the regiment, accompanying the gift with the following speech:

GOV. SEYMOUR'S SPEECH.

SOLDIERS OF NEW-YORK: We love our whole country, without reservation. But while we do so, it is not inconsistent with that perfect and generous loyalty to love and to be proud of our own State. This day, when I took part in the celebration that was to consecrate yonder battle-field, while I felt as an American citizen, proud of my own country, and proud of the gallant services of her citizens, in every State, nevertheless my eye did involuntarily wander to that field where lie the glorious dead of our good and great State, and when I returned, to see marching before me your manly and sturdy columns, not knowing you belonged to New-York, my heart did quicken and my pulse tingle, to learn that you were acting commissions issued by myself; I am most proud and most happy that I have had this opportunity, on behalf of the merchants of the great commercial City of New-York; to present to you this glorious banner, which has been sent as a token of their confidence is your loyalty and your courage, and your fidelity in the hour of danger. Sergeant, I place these colors in your hands in the firm confidence that they will be borne through every field of triumph, of toil and of danger, in a way that will do honor to yourselves, to the great State which you represent, and the still greater country, to which we all belong. My God bless you as you serve your ☞

in illustration, well-wrought and strong in its logic, correct and explicit in its statement; in a word, it is eloquent, in the best sense of that much-abused term. His exordium is of great beauty; and his peroration is splendid. If we might offer a single point of criticism on the oration, it would be upon that part of it, constituting one-half of its body, which gives a narrative of the marches, manoeuvres, skirmishes and strategy of Gens. HOOKER and LEE, Gens. PLEASON-TON and STUART, from the time at which the two armies left the opposite banks of the Rappahannock until they confronted each other on this side of the Potomac, and also the detailed account of the preliminaries of the battle, and of the action itself. Mr. EVERETT enters into a very minute statement of these things; and the elaborateness of the details, the large number of names, places and circumstances he has occasion to recall, will tend to confuse and repel those who are less familiar with the events than himself, and crowd out those "glittering generalities" which he or any other great orator might be expected mainly to deal in on such an occasion. It may be said that these things were dwelt upon, as the oration is intended and expected to be enduring and historical; but so also will be the reports of Gens. MEADE and LEE, from which the facts are largely drawn. After he gets through with this, however, Mr. EVERETT does justice to his subject and himself. ✺

1. The Times thus published and praised Everett's now-forgotten oration a full day before reprinting the elegiac little speech that Lincoln had delivered afterward.

country in the distant field of danger. We find in those glorious fields you left behind you are not indifferent to this conflict; are not indifferent to the welfare of the whole Union. I do not doubt, therefore, that when you shall return from your dangerous fields of duty, you shall bring back this standard to place among the archives of our State with honorable mention of the services her sons have performed. I do not doubt that though it may perhaps be returned torn and stained, yet it will be still more glorious, and with glorious recollections clustering around it. In concluding these remarks, I ask in return of the men of New-York, to give three cheers for the Union of our country, and three cheers for the flag of our land.

Gen. SCHENCK followed in a short speech.

A subscription of $280 was made by the Marshals attending these ceremonies, to he devoted to the relief of the Richmond prisoners.

In the afternoon, the Lieutenant-Governor elect of Ohio, Col. ANDERSON, delivered an oration at the Presbyterian Church.

The President and party returned to Washington at 6 o'clock this evening, followed by the Governors' trains. Thousands of persons were gathered at the depot, anxiously awaiting transportation to their homes; but they will probably be confined to the meagre accommodations of Gettysburgh till tomorrow. ⊛

THE GETTYSBURGH CELEBRATION.

FROM OUR SPECIAL CORRESPONDENT.

NOVEMBER 21
GETTYSBURGH, PENN.,
THURSDAY EVENING, NOV. 19.

All the noteworthy incidents of the celebration here to-day have already been sent off to you by telegraph, and it would have gratified your correspondent exceedingly if he could also have got off, but fate, combined with the miserable railroad arrangements, has ordained that he should spend another night in this over-crowded village. The only train that has been permitted to leave here, to-day, was the special train bearing the President and his party, which left at 6 o'clock this evening. Even the mail train, which should have left at 8 o'clock this morning, was detained for fear it would come in collision with some of the numerous trains that have been following each other in rapid succession from Hanover Junction, bringing visitors to the Dedication. How they are all to sleep here to-night it is difficult to imagine. All the hotels as well as the private houses were filled to overflowing last night. Every housekeeper in Gettysburgh has opened a temporary hotel, and extends unbounded hospitality to strangers — for a consideration. People from all parts of the country seem to have taken this opportunity to pay a visit to the battle-fields which are hereafter to make the name of Gettysburgh

immortal. The Dedication ceremonies were apparently a minor consideration, for even while Mr. EVERETT was delivering his splendid oration, there were as many people wandering about the fields, made memorable by the fierce struggles of July, as stood around the stand listening to his eloquent periods. They seem to have considered, with President LINCOLN, that it was not what was said here, but what was done here, that deserved their attention. During the last three days, the scenes of the late battles have been visited by thousands of persons from every loyal State in the Union, and there is probably not a foot of the grounds that has not been trodden over and over again by reverential feet. But little over four months have passed away since the champions of Slavery and Freedom met here in deadly strife, and already the name of Gettysburgh has become historical, and its soil is classic ground. This, too, while the contest is yet undecided, and the camp-fires of the contending armies still illumine the Southern sky. If the people of the North can thus forestall history, it is because the manifest justice of their cause enables them to see the future in the present, and to behold in the fresh made graves of their fallen sons the shining monuments of their glory in ages to come.

The National Cemetery which has been consecrated to-day by such imposing ceremonies is located in the very midst of the fierce strife of those terrible July days, and many of the Union heroes fell on the ground comprised within its inclosure. It is little over half a mile to the south of the Gettysburgh Court-house, in the outskirts of the town, on what is called Prospect Hill, which is but a continuation of the elevated ridge known as Cemetery Hill. This hill, it will be recollected, formed the northernmost line of the Union armies during the last two days of the battle, and was several times stormed by the rebel infantry without success. The new cemetery is contiguous to the town cemetery of Gettysburgh and comprises 17 1/4 acres. It was purchased by the State of Pennsylvania at something like $25,000, and is to be devoted exclusively to the loyal dead who fell in the three days' battles. The present appearance of the cemetery is not very inviting, but the plan on which it is laid out is excellent, and when it is finished and covered with green sward, it will be one of the most beautiful burial-grounds in the country. The graves will form semicir-

President Lincoln on the speaker's platform at Gettysburg, November 19, 1863—the only photograph of the President on the day he delivered his most famous speech.

cular rows, one within another, the whole presenting an appearance similar to the Senate Chamber or House of Representatives at Albany. Sections of the semicircle are allotted to the various States whose soldiers fell at the Gettysburgh battle, the different sections being divided from each other by a foot-walk. The number of States represented is eighteen, and at either end of the semicircle is a section devoted to the "unknown" dead, or those whose identity cannot be established. This class, however, is fortunately not so large as one would naturally be led to suppose. I am told that nearly all who fell in the last two days of the battle can be easily identified by the temporary head-boards placed ever their graves by their comrades. Out of 1,300 who have thus far been exhumed from the various battle-fields and buried in the new cemetery, there are not more than one hundred whose identity is not used. The work of exhuming the bodies and reburying them in the National Cemetery is to be done by the various States individually, or at least at their expense. It is proposed to erect a large monument near the base of the semicircle, to which all the States will contribute, and leave each State to erect such other monuments in its own section as it may see fit. All the bodies exhumed from the battle-fields are placed in most substantial coffins, and buried two feet apart in trenches from four to five feet deep. At the head of the coffins will be built a continuous stone wall 1 1/2 feet in thicknesss and extending from the bottom of the trench to the surface of the ground. On the top of this wall a smooth granite or marble railing will be erected 1 1/2 feet in height and one foot thick, on which will be inscribed the names of the dead, with the regiment and State to which each belonged.

The position of the new cemetery is very fine, and commands a view of the whole country for miles around, including the entire ground covered by the Union and rebel lines. It is less than a quarter of a mile from the house occupied by Gen. MEADE as his headquarters, about half a mile from Culp's Hill, where the hardest fighting occurred on the 3d of July, and about two miles from Round Top, which was occupied by the extreme left of the Union lines, and was the scene of the hand-to-hand fight of the 2d.

In wandering around these battle-fields, one is astonished and indignant to find at almost every step of his progress the carcasses of dead horses, which the negligence, or laziness or stupidity of the people of Gettysburgh have permitted to remain above ground since the battle, and which still breed pestilence in the atmosphere of this whole region. I am told that more than a score of deaths have resulted from this neglect in the village of Gettysburgh, during the past Summer; and in the house in which I was compelled to seek lodgings there are now two boys sick with typhoid fever, attributed to this cause. Within a stone's throw of the whitewashed hut occupied as the headquarters of Gen. MEADE I counted yesterday no less than ten carcasses of dead horses, lying on the ground where they were struck by the shells of the enemy.

The ceremonies of the Dedication to-day, of which you have already read a full account, passed off without accident, and nearly in accordance with the programme previously published. There was not, however, so large a military display as was anticipated, and the procession was unexpectedly slim, for the reason that most of the guests who were expected to join it were either off viewing the battle-fields, or hurried up to the cemetery before the procession started. The opening prayer, by Rev. Mr. STOCKTON, was touching and beautiful, and produced quite as much effect upon the audience as the classic sentences of the orator of the day. President LINCOLN's brief address was delivered in a clear, loud tone of voice, which could be distinctly heard at the extreme limits of the large assemblage. It was delivered (or rather read from a sheet of paper which the speaker held in his hand) in a very deliberate manner, with strong emphasis, and with a most business-like air. Previous to the President's address, the following ode, by Maj. B. B. FRENCH,[1] was sung by a vocal Club from Philadelphia, in a dirge by J.C. PERCIVAL, which was to have been sung: "Tis holy ground — This spot, where, in their graves, We place our country's braves, Who Fell in Freedom's holy cause Fighting for Liberty and Laws — Let tears abound. Here let them rest — And Summer's heat and Winter's cold, Shall glow and freeze above this mold — A thousand years shall pass away — A nation shall still mourn this clay, Which now is blest. Here, where they fell, Oft shall the widow's tear be shed, Oft shall fond parents mourn their dead, The orphan here shall kneel and weep, And maidens, where their lovers sleep, Their

woes shall tell. Great God in Heaven! Shall all this sacred blood be shed — Shall we thus mourn our glorious dead; Oh, shall the end be wrath and woe, The knell of Freedom's overthrow — A country riven? It will not be! We trust, oh God! Thy gracious power To aid us in our darkest hour. This be our prayer: "Oh Father! save A people's freedom from its grave — All praise to Thee!" After the dedication ceremonies were over, the President returned to the residence of Mr. WILLS, whose guest he has been since he arrived here, and from thence walked to the church on Baltimore-street, to listen to an oration by Lieut.-Gov. ANDERSON, of Ohio. He walked up to the church arm in arm with the famous TOM BURNS, the only man in Gettysburgh who had patriotism or pluck enough to take a gun on his shoulder and help the Union army defend his town. Soon after the arrival of the President at Gettysburgh last evening, he was serenaded by a Baltimore band, and after numerous calls for "the President," "Old ABE," "Uncle ABE," "Father ABRAHAM," "the next President," &c., &c., was induced to make his appearance at the door. He said he was fired, and old not feel like speaking, and as a man who did not feel like talking was apt to say foolish things, he begged to be excused from making a speech. The audience cheered the sentiment, and the President, taking it for granted he was excused, retired to his room. The crowd then called on Secretary SEWARD, who was stopping near by with Mr. HARPER, editor of a paper printed here, and were more successful. After two or three airs by the band, mingled in the calls for the Secretary, Mr. SEWARD made his appearance, and spoke as follows:

MR. SEWARD'S SPEECH. FELLOW-CITIZENS: I am now sixty years old and upward; I have been in public life practically forty years of that time, and yet this is the first time that ever any people or community so near to the borders of Maryland was found willing to listen to my voice; and the reason was that I said forty years ago that Slavery was opening before this people a grave-yard that was to be filled with brothers falling in mutual political combat. I knew that the cause that was hurrying the Union into this dreadful strife was Slavery, and when I did elevate my voice it was to warn the people to remove that cause when they could by constitutional means, and so avert the catastrophe of civil war that now unhappily ☞

Abraham Lincoln a few days before leaving for Gettysburg, photographed in Washington by Alexander Gardner.

has fallen upon the nation, deluging it in blood. That crisis came, and we see the result. I am thankful that you are willing to hear me at last. I thank my God that I believe this strife is going to end in the removal of that evil which ought to have been removed by peaceful means and deliberate councils. [Good.] I thank my God for the hope that this is the last fratricidal war which will fall upon the country — a country vouchsafed by Heaven — the richest, the broadest, the most beautiful, most magnificent and capacious ever yet bestowed upon a people, that has ever been given to any part of the human race. [Applause.] And I thank God for the hope that when that cause is removed, simply by the

operation of abolishing it, as the origin of the great treason that is without justification and without parallel, we shall thenceforth be united, be only one country, having only one hope, one ambition and one destiny. [Applause.] Then we shall know that we are not enemies, but that we are friends and brothers, that that this Union is a reality, and we shall mourn together for the evil wrought by this rebellion. We are now near the graves of the misguided, whom we have consigned to their last resting place with pity for their errors and with the same heartful of grief with which we mourn over the brother by whose hand, raised in defence of his Government, that misguided brother perished. When we

THE GEN. GRANT'S DEPARTMENT.

THE ARMY AT CHATTANOOGA — THE QUESTION OF SUPPLIES.

NOVEMBER 23
CHATTANOOGA, SUNDAY, NOV. 15

The operations of this army for the present, and for some time to come, will relate to supplies and recuperation. When Gen. THOMAS succeeded Gen. ROSECRANS its condition was extremely critical. The time has not yet arrived for relating how really we were besieged, and how nearly we were to the point of retreat for the want of subsistence; how much less than even half rations were for days served to the men, and even less to the animals, hundreds and thousands of which have died of starvation and excessive work. This vital question of subsistence was the first to which Gen. THOMAS gave his attention; and in the briefest time possible it was happily solved by the skillful movement conceived and executed by Gen. W. F. SMITH,[1] Chief of the Engineers, by which Brown's Ferry was snatched from the enemy, though carefully guarded by LONGSTREET, the river opened to Bridgeport, and the wagon-hauling reduced from sixty-five miles in distance, over a route perfectly indescribable for its difficulties — an average of ten days each way in time — to two miles at the shortest and seven miles at the longest, over a comparatively good route. This movement, which the enemy has pronounced "masterly," relieved this army from a difficulty

under which it could not for a week longer have rested, and since that hour there has been no question of its ability to meet the expectations of the country.

But the country should take into consideration that much time is absolutely required to furnish and recuperate an army like this — not only its present wants, but to supply this point as a depot for future operations. Practically, its base is at Cincinnati and Louisville, a distance wholly unprecedented in the history of army movements. All the supplies, all the clothing, all the ordnance — everything the army needs — must be brought over that long reach of railway. To increase the difficulty, the road from Nashville to Bridgeport (we hope it will be open to Chattanooga before long) is to nearly worn out, had so poorly equipped, that it can perform scarcely a quarter service, and is in daily danger of breaking down entirely. The Louisville and Nashville road is some better, but is so wretchedly managed that hardly one-half the service is got out of it that should be. Both roads are liable to raids from rebel guerrillas and bushwhackers. There are other difficulties to which it is unnecessary to allude — all of which, taken together, render supplying the army a task of peculiar character. Nevertheless, the chief obstacle having been removed, there is no ground for apprehension, and all doubts are at an end. We are under the clearest, brightest sky imaginable, compared with what our condition was before the taking of Brown's Ferry, a name and a position that every man in this army will remember with the liveliest feelings. Let the country be pa-

tient. This army will do its work in good time, and it will do it well.

Little or nothing is known of the plans of the rebels, beyond the expedition dispatched against BURNSIDE, which, though it may obtain some successes, they will be but temporary, and of little or no account in deciding in favor of the rebels the great struggle to take place in this immediate locality. BRAGG's line stretches from Lookout Mountain, below which, contrary to what seems to be the general impression, he still holds ground to Missionary Ridge and the river above Chattanooga, nearly or quite the whole distance of the semicircle being in full view of our line of defences. All thought or expectation of his ever attempting to operate directly against those defences has ceased to be entertained. There are not men enough in the Confederacy to make an impression on them. What, therefore, BRAGG intends to do, can only be conjectured, but not easily. His flanks are by no means as secure as our own. With him the question of supplies is a far more difficult one than with us. His army, it is settled, is not in the heart that ours is; and the next three months — should that length of time be passed in inactivity — will bring upon him new embarrassments, certainly bring him no better prospects, while it will give to us that condition always a necessary precedent to vigorous action and heavy blows.

Gen. GRANT, whose headquarters are now here, but will be in the saddle, or wherever else his great duty calls, is not idle; nor will he commit any grave mistake; we all feel confident of that. The energies of the army will not be flittered away on pur-

part to-morrow night, let us remember that we owe it to our country and to mankind that this war shall have for its conclusion the establishing of the principle of Democratic Government — the simple principle that whatever party, whatever portion of the Union prevails by constitutional suffrage in an election, that party is to be respected and maintained in power until it shall give place, on another trial and another verdict, to a different portion of the people, [Good.] If you do not do that, you are drifting at once and irresistibly to the very verge of the destruction of your Government. But with that principle this Government of ours — the freest, the best, the wisest and the happiest in the world —

must be, and, so far as we are concerned practically will be, immortal. [Applause.]
※

1. Benjamin Brown French (1800–1870) was U.S. commissioner of public buildings during and after the Civil War, during which time he served as well as grand master of the Knights Templar of the United States. French wrote what he called "some rhymes for the celebration" after arriving in Gettysburg on November 14. He later confided: "I never was so flattered at any production of my own, in relation to that same Hymn. All who heard it seemed to consider it most appropriate, and most happily conceived." See Benjamin Brown French, *Witness to the Young Republic: A Yankee's Journal, 1828–1870*, ed. Donald B. Cole and John J. McDonough, Hanover: University Press of New England, 1989, 432–435.)

---

poseless undertakings, on nothing that will not make for the great end in view, — the complete success of our arms. Like a great player, he will make no move on board for the mere purpose of causing his antagonist to make another without some certain prospect of deciding the game in favor of the Union cause. Something like the game of Vicksburgh may be repeated here, for which time, resources and skill are absolute requisites. But no time will be lost. The country may make sure of that, too.

Beyond the fact that Gen. SHERMAN, with a considerable force, is soon to arrive, there are certain things — movements, doings, and so on — that should not be more particularly referred to, which indicate purpose, skill, will and capacity equal to the great work.

Of the stern, grim fact of scarcity of every description of food, not only in the rebel army, but more especially with the home population, of even their ordinarily plentiful part of the South, we have abundant assurance. Word now and then comes back surreptitiously from those who fled from this place when BRAGG retreated, to friends and relatives left behind, to the effect that they have gone to a hard lot and worse fare. Tennesseeans are not treated with favor by their Georgia brethren, who affect to despise them because they did not keep back the "Yankee invaders." Georgians say, furthermore, that Tennesseeans should have remained where there ought to be plenty of "hog and hominy," and not have fled to the State that was already supporting a million of extra consumers.

Great pains are taken by BRAGG to pre-

vent Tennesseeans in his army to indulge their favorite disposition to desert to our lines. It is known that special care is taken to put none but reliable men, those who are proof against desertion, on guard. Notwithstanding this precaution, many desert; and within the last few days the number has become greater than ever before. What reason there is for this I am unable to say. Those who came in yesterday reported that our cavalry had got in the rear of BRAGG, and burnt five railroad bridges between him and Atlanta. Of the truth of this, there is no corroborating testimony; nor is there, I believe, anything known at headquarters calculated in prove or disprove the report. The deserters say, also, that rations are scarce in BRAGG's army, and that that is the reason they deserted. They say that thousands of others would do the same thing had they the opportunity of making the attempt with a reasonable chance of success. Many of those who came in yesterday were fired on by the rebel pickets, but none of them were hit.

Of our situation, let there be no uneasiness. At the same time let not too much be expected in too short a time.

RODERICK. ※

1. William F. "Baldy" Smith

IMPORTANT FROM CHATTANOOGA.

GENERAL GRANT MOVING ON THE ENEMY'S WORKS.

OUR FORCES HOLDING ALL THE HIGH GROUND IN FRONT OF MISSIONARY RIDGE.

NOVEMBER 25
SPECIAL DISPATCH TO THE N.Y. TIMES.
WASHINGTON, TUESDAY, NOV. 24

The latest news, up to 10:40 this evening, from GRANT is of a most satisfactory character. Gens. THOMAS and SHERMAN have got well ahead.

The fighting in our immediate front has lasted all day long. At every point along the line we have forced the rebels backward. There is joy in the War Department.

CINCINNATI, TUESDAY, NOV. 24
The Commercial of this city has a special dispatch dated Chattanooga, the 23d instant, which says:

"Deserters last night reported that the rebels were falling back of Chickamauga Station.

Their artillery has been withdrawn from our front.

The whole rebel army is apparently in retreat. A reconnaissance this afternoon reveals that the enemy apparently are in force between us and Missionary Ridge.

Gen. WOOD,[1] in charging up Orchard Ridge, carried the rifle-pits under a severe musketry and artillery fire, taking 200 rebel prisoners.

We now hold all the high ground this side of Missionary Ridge.

Our troops are in line of battle, and will lie on their arms to-night.

Hard fighting is inevitable to-morrow, unless the rebels withdraw to-night.["]

WASHINGTON, TUESDAY, NOV. 24
The Star of this afternoon contains the following account of a brilliant preliminary movement by Major-Gen. THOMAS: ☞

The Battle of Missionary Ridge near Chattanooga.

CHATTANOOGA, TENN., MONDAY, NOV. 23
The reconnaissance in force made by Major-Gen. THOMAS has been completed in the most brilliant and successful manner.

The troops employed were the divisions of Gens. WOOD and SHERIDAN, of the Fourth army corps, under the immediate direction of Gen. GRANGER.[2]

The object of the movement was not only to ascertain the strength of the enemy, but to occupy two bold knolls in front of our left, half way between our lines and Missionary Ridge.

The principal attack was made by Gen. HAZEN's brigade, commanded by that General, supported on the left by Gen. WILLICH's brigade, and on the right by the whole division of Gen. SHERIDAN.[3]

The entire field was distinctly visible from Fort Wood, in front of which Gen. HAZEN's[4] line of battle was formed, and as the whole army was under arms, with Gen. HOWARD's[5] corps formed in a solid column, as a reserve to the attacking force, the spectacle was one of magnificence.

The field being commanded by the heavy guns of the fort, only one field-battery was taken into action. This was planted on an elevated knoll, in the centre of which Gen. SHERIDAN's line of battle was formed before the order, to advance was given.

The troops moved out of their position just before 1 o'clock in the afternoon, and

A Kurz and Allison lithograph of the Battle of Missionary Ridge.

remained in line for three-quarters of an hour in full view of the enemy.

At last, everything being ready, Gen. GRANGER gave the order to advance, and Gen. HAZEN and Gen. WILLICH pushed out simultaneously.

The first shot was fired at 2 o'clock in the afternoon, and in five minutes the lines of Gen. HAZEN were hotly engaged while the artillery of Fort Wood and Gen. THOMAS were opened upon the rebel rifle-pits and

the camps behind the line of fighting.

The practice of our gunners was splendid, the camp and batteries of the enemy being about a mile and three-quarters distant; but our fire elicited no reply, and it was soon evident that the rebels had no heavy artillery in that part of their intrenchments at least.

Our troops rapidly advancing, as if on parade, occupied the knolls, upon which they were directed at 2:20 o'clock.

GLORIOUS VICTORY!

GEN. GRANT'S GREAT SUCCESS.

GEN. HOOKER ASSAULTS LOOKOUT MOUNTAIN.

NOVEMBER 26
DISPATCHES TO THE ASSOCIATED PRESS.
CHATTANOOGA, WEDNESDAY, NOV. 25

We are completely victorious. The enemy is totally routed and driven from every position. Our loss is very small and the enemy's is heavy in prisoners. Finding Gen. HOOKER so successful in his movements against Lookout Mountain, the enemy evacuated that position during the night.

Gen. HOOKER took possession early this morning. The enemy moved south and got on Missionary Ridge on the battle-field somewhere near Chickamauga. He is expected to

intercept the flying foe. Gen. HOOKER is said to have captured 2,000 prisoners in his magnificent assault of Lookout Mountain.

Gen. SHERMAN being all prepared to begin an assault at 8 A.M. to-day, upon the strong position of the enemy at the north end of Missionary Ridge. He had the day before taken a hill near the position of the enemy, but commanded by their artillery. He had to descend into a valley, and he then made another ascent to the position held by the enemy. Two unsuccessful assaults were made by Gen. SHERMAN, but, with the cooperation of the centre, he ultimately gained the position, and completed the great victory.

The brigade of Gen. CARSE, with a portion of Gen. LIGHTPEWS brigade, composed the storming party in the first assault. They were repulsed with quite a heavy loss after an attack persisted in for an hour; but being reinforced they were

enabled to hold a part of the hills. In this attack Gen. CARSE was wounded quite severely in the thigh. The Thirty-seventh Ohio and Sixth Iowa and One Hundred and Third Illinois regiments were in the attack. A second assault was made at 3 1/2 o'clock, in which MATHIAS' [sic][1], LOOMIS' and RAUL'S brigades were engaged. The force reached within twenty yards of the summit of the hill and the works of the enemy, when they were flanked and broke, retiring to their reserves.

In this assault Gen. MATHIAS was wounded and Col. PUTNAM, of the Ninety-third Ohio, killed, their persistent efforts compelled the enemy to mass heavily on his right in order to hold the position of so much importance to him. About 3 o'clock Gen. GRANT started two columns against the weakened centre, and in an hour desperate fighting, succeeded in breaking the centre,

Ten minutes later Gen. WILLICH, driving across an open field, carried the rifle-pits in his front, whose occupants fled as they fired their last volley; and Gen. SHERIDAN, moving through the forest that stretched before him, drove in the enemy's pickets and halted his advance in obedience to orders on reaching the rifle-pits, where the rebel force was awaiting for his attack.

No such attack was made, however, the design being to recover the heights on our left, but not to assault the rebel works.

We have taken about 200 prisoners, captured mostly from Alabama troops, and have gained a position of great importance, should the rebels still attempt to hold the Chattanooga Valley, as with these heights in our possession, a column moving to turn Missionary Ridge is secure from flank artillery.

The rebels fired their small cannon only during the affair. ⊛

1. Thomas J. Wood (1823–1906), who was criticized for his actions at this battle for failing to move rapidly when ordered to close a gap in Union lines.
2. Gordon Granger (1822–1876), whose decisiveness and bravery helped save Rosecran's army at Chickamauga.
3. William B. Hazen (1830–1887); August von Willich (1810–1878); and Philip H. Sheridan (1831-1888).
4. General William B. Hazen (1830–1887).
5. O. O. Howard (1830–1909).

OFFICIAL REPORTS FROM GEN. THOMAS AND GEN. GRANT.

NOVEMBER 26
WASHINGTON, WEDNESDAY, NOV. 25

The following official dispatch from Maj.-Gen. GRANT has been received at the headquarters of the army here:

CHATTANOOGA, TENN.,
TUESDAY, NOV. 24 — 12 M.

Major-Gen. H.W. Halleck, General-in-Chief:

Yesterday, at 12 1/2 o'clock, Gen. GRANGER's and Gen. PALMER's[1] corps, supported by Gen. HOWARD's, were advanced directly in front of our fortifications, drove in the enemy's pickets, and carried his first line of rifle-pits between Chattanooga and Citer's Creek.

We captured nine commissioned officers and about 100 enlisted men.

Our loss is about 111.

To-day Gen. HOOKER, in command of Gen. GEARY's[2] division, Twelfth corps; Gen. OSTERHAUS'[3] division, Fifteenth corps, and two brigades, Fourteenth corps, carried the north slope of Lookout Mountain, with small loss on our side, and a loss to the enemy of 500 or 600 prisoners; killed and wounded not reported.

There has been continuous fighting from 12 o'clock until after night; but our troops gallantly repulsed every attempt to take the position.

Gen. SHERMAN crossed the Tennessee River before daylight this morning, at the mouth of the South Chickamauga, with three divisions of the Fifteenth corps and one division of the Fourteenth corps, and carried the northern extremity of Missionary ridge.

Our success so far has been complete and the behavior of the troops admirable.

GEORGE H. THOMAS, MAJOR GENERAL.

SECOND DISPATCH.
CHATTANOOGA, TUESDAY, NOV. 24 — 6 P.M.

Maj.-Gen. Halleck, General-in-Chief, Washington:

The fighting to-day progressed favorably.

Gen. SHERMAN carried the end of Missionary Ridge, and his right is now at the Tunnel, and his left at Chickamauga Creek.

The troops from Lookout Valley carried the point of the mountain, and now hold the eastern slope and point high up.

I cannot yet tell the amount of casualties, but our loss is not heavy.

Gen. HOOKER reports 2,000 prisoners taken, besides which a small number have fallen into our hands from Missionary Ridge.

U.S. GRANT, MAJOR-GENERAL. ⊛

1. John McCauley Palmer (1817–1900) had been a legal associate and political supporter of Lincoln in Illinois, and later served as his state's governor.
2. John W. Geary (1819–1873) later served as governor of Pennsylvania.
3. Peter J. Osterhaus (1823–1905) led the drive against Braxton Bragg.

and gaining possession of the ridge in which the enemy was posted, the main force was driven northward toward Gen. SHERMAN, who opened on them, and they were forced to break, and seek safety in disordered flight down the western slope of the Ridge, and across the western ridge of the Chickamauga. We have taken not less than 5,000 prisoners and perhaps 10,000. Gen. HOOKER will probably intercept the flying enemy in the vicinity of Rossville and the region east of it.

There are reports that we have taken a whole corps.

Among the casualties are Lieut.-Col. ESPY, of the Sixty-eighth Indiana regiment; Major MCCAWLEY, of the Tenth Iowa; Col. OMARS, of the Ninetieth Illinois; Lieut.-Col. STUART, of the Ninetieth Illinois; Major WALKER, of the Tenth Missouri; Major WELSE, of the Fifty-sixth Illinois; Major INNISS, of the Sixth Iowa, wounded; Major

IRWIN, of the Sixth Iowa, killed.

Full reports of the killed and wounded cannot be attained, as most of the killed were in Gen. SHERMAN's corps, and remained at dark in the hands of the enemy. The list will be telegraphed to-morrow. The prisoners say that BRAGG was on the Ridge just before they were taken.

The successful storming parties consisted of WOOD's and BAIRD's divisions on the left centre and JOHNSTON's and SHERIDAN's on the right centre. Some of our wounded were left in the hands of the enemy after Gen. SHERMAN's unsuccessful assault, but were ultimately recovered.

CHATTANOOGA, WEDNESDAY, NOV. 25 —
10 P.M.

The captured artillery is reported at about forty pieces. Gen. HOOKER captured five boxes of new muskets on Lookout Mountain.

We are in entire possession of the field. We have control over the railway and river to Bridgeport. Two boats came through this morning. Our loss will not amount to more than 300 killed and 250 wounded in the three days operations. The success has been most brilliant.

The enemy is reported to be bivouacking two miles beyond Missionary Ridge. Col. PHELPS, of the Thirty-eighth Ohio, and Major GLASS, of the Thirty-second Indiana, are killed. Gen. JOHN E. SMITH[2] is reported wounded. Col. AVERY, of the One Hundred and Second New-York, lost a leg, and Major ELLIOTT is the same as dead. ⊛

1. Charles (Karl) L. Matthies (1824–1868).
2. John Eugene Smith (1816–1897) survived his wounds and went on to join Sherman on the "March to the Sea."

CHAPTER 17

"By Renouncing Their Treason"

Another winter of unresolved war opened in frustration over ongoing stalemates east and west. The Federal assault on Charleston continued unabated — but with no signs of easy triumph and few signs of progress. The Confederate siege of Knoxville proceeded as well — punishing both the armies and the city. Once again, The Times wondered what the hunkered-down troops would do when spring finally arrived.

In December, all eyes turned to America's two Presidents, Abraham Lincoln and Jefferson Davis, as they offered annual messages to their respective Congresses. Davis's to the fourth session of the First Confederate Congress was frank, bellicose, and resentful. Conceding that the South had suffered "grave reverses" on the battlefield the previous summer, Davis blamed the Lincoln administration's "savage ferocity" and its refusal to continue exchanging prisoners of war. That policy shift was harsh but strategically logical: Confederate soldiers were far scarcer than Union soldiers, and the more Confederates that remained in prison, the greater the proportional impact on the strength of its depleted army. However heartless the policy, the keeping and feeding Union prisoners under Southern confinement strained the Confederate home front, which was having difficulty feeding its civilian population.

Lincoln endeavored to judge the human consequences of the new policy firsthand. On December 27, he journeyed with Secretary of War Stanton to visit the newly established prisoner-of-war camp at Point Lookout, Maryland. Its commanding officer, General Gilman Marston, told the President

Detail of a print showing the Point Lookout prisoner of war camp in Maryland. Approximately 50,000 Confederate enlisted men were contained within the walls of the camp between 1863 and 1863.

exactly what he wanted to hear: that there was a "strong feeling of attachment to the Union" and "disgust for the rebellion...among his prisoners."

In his own annual message to the 38th Congress on December 8, Lincoln supplied his usual rousing eloquence — reminding the legislative branch that a secure Union would set an example for the rest of the world. He also offered a new policy that looked past the fighting to the eventual restoration of the Union. Lincoln's Proclamation for Amnesty and Reconstruction proposed to re-establish state governments in the rebellious states upon approval of only 10 percent of all voters who had participated in the 1860 election. And it offered to pardon all rebels who took an oath of loyalty to the Union. But Lincoln's magnanimity went only so far. The proclamation specifically excluded high-ranking Confederate military and naval officers, "officers or agents of the so-called confederate government" (small "c" intentional), and "all who have engaged in any way in treating colored persons or white persons...

unlawfully as prisoners of war."

Lincoln brought the controversial issue full cycle on January 2, ordering General Benjamin Butler to discharge any prisoner at Point Lookout who was ready to take the oath prescribed in his order. The released prisoners could either enlist in the Union military or go home in peace, but only if their homes lay "safely within our military lines." On February 18 Lincoln ordered a relaxation of the three-year-old blockade on those Southern ports now controlled by the Union. But to be certain his army would be manned for as long as it took to win the long conflict, Lincoln also ordered a draft of 500,000 men on February 1 to serve for three to four years or until the war ended.

That month, while the armies in the east remained stalled in their winter camps, William T. Sherman conducted a campaign into the heart of Mississippi aimed at the town of Meridian, an important railroad center that was home to a Confederate arsenal, hospital, and prisoner-of-war

camp. Sherman set out on February 3 with a main force of 20,000 infantry, plus a cooperating cavalry force of 7,000 under Brigadier General William Sooy Smith. Union forces reached Meridian on February 14, and Sherman ordered his troops "to wipe the appointed meeting place off the map" by destroying the railroads and burning much of the town to the ground. Afterward, Sherman is reported to have said: "Meridian with its depots, store-houses, arsenal, hospitals, offices, hotels, and cantonments no longer exists." It was a harbinger of the hardening war, and a portent of things to come.

Yet if President Lincoln was coming to the belief that such actions might bring victory closer, he was soon enough reminded otherwise. On February 20, Confederate forces prevailed at the Battle of Olustee, the only major Civil War engagement fought in Florida. The Union casualty figure was 1,861: an almost surreal reminder of the year this long war had started.

GEN. GRANT'S OPERATIONS — WHAT NEXT?

DECEMBER 1

Those who fancy that Gen. GRANT will pursue BRAGG from the hills of Georgia down to its plains, or down to the seaboard, will most likely find themselves mistaken. It is a painful necessity of our Western heroes that each hero of them requires his "pound of flesh" every day, not to speak of an equal weight of "hard tack;" and those who will for a moment reflect on the amount of solid victual required to sustain the hearts of fifty or sixty thousand men for a week, will at once see the difficulty of sending them on a campaign, which, at its best, would occupy them for months, through a region bare of food, and into which it is impossible for Gen. GRANT to convey supplies. We do not think it would be feasible to maintain the army of Gen. GRANT even at Atlanta during the Winter; for, though the forces of BRAGG may be pretty thoroughly demolished or dis-

persed, there would still be bodies of them left to roam through the country, who would operate on our lines after the style of MOSBY in Virginia, and with a hundred-fold the effect. We doubt whether, even if the rebels had but ten thousand men in Northern Georgia, against ten times that number on the Union side, it would be possible for GRANT to plant his army fifty miles south of Chattanooga and maintain his communications with it. On this account, we do not entertain the idea that Gen. GRANT will, at this time, push on his victorious columns, as many seem to imagine he must do. There is an operation secondary to the route of BRAGG, which would be in keeping, and in which, there is reason to believe, Gen. GRANT is at present engaged. We refer to the cutting off and defeat of LONGSTREET's column in East Tennessee. In his official dispatch ☞

Lieutenant General James Longstreet, C.S.A.

of Friday morning last, and in his operations of Thursday, GRANT gave us ground to believe that this was the matter next in hand — that is, to intercept LONGSTREET in his attempt to join himself to BRAGG. Even if he had the idea of pushing down into Georgia after the flying rebels, it would be necessary to attend to this first; for he could not allow a column of eighteen or twenty thousand men to exist and operate in his rear, to threaten his lines and threaten Chattanooga itself. It will not be until we have determinate operations bearing upon LONGSTREET, that the next movement of Gen. GRANT will unfold itself.

As it is preposterous to conceive of Gen. GRANT extending his lines down into Georgia, we think it altogether likely that his next movement will be to contract his lines around Chattanooga. The aim and end of the late campaign was to push the menacing rebels from his front — to effectually raise the siege of Chattanooga, if the rebel attempt at investment may be called a siege. This has been done in the most perfect and conclusive manner; and as nothing whatever would be gained by forcing his advance southward, until such time as he is ready to begin the grand advance that shall change his base to the Atlantic seaboard, we have no idea that such unmilitary step will be taken. If, therefore, it should soon be announced that GRANT's army has fallen back to Chattanooga, there need be no dreadful disappointment expressed. The view of the case and of the campaign just set forth is confirmed by a telegram just received from Chattanooga as we write, which announces that "there has been no fighting for two days," and that "the campaign in Northern Georgia is probably ended."

GRANT's grand campaign, in the direction of Augusta, the final campaign of the war in the Southwest, commences properly with the incoming Spring. A great depot, or base, will by that time have been established at Chattanooga — the army will have recruited from its prodigious labors of the last few months, and it will take up the final march under its great leader, well assured of a final success. ⊛

THE PRESIDENT'S PLAN OF RECONSTRUCTION.

DECEMBER 11

We long ago took decided ground against all schemes of provincializing the rebel States — maintaining that they were radically wrong in principle, and would prove calamitous in result. The President's plan of restoring our Federal system to its normal operation, therefore, finds us already thoroughly committed to it in every essential particular.[1] But, apart from our own foregone conclusions, we cannot help feeling the convincing power of the mere enunciation of the President's programme. Feasibility, justice, consistency, and security, are so patently met by it, in the fullest measure, that it challenges at once the acquiescence of all truly loyal men. Of course Faction will bark at it. It is the very nature of Faction to fly at any public good. But this manifestation of instinct will only be corroborative of the intrinsic excellence of the plan. There has not been a great efficacious measure in this war whose first appearance was not assailed thus. Could this prove an exception, we should at once surmise there must be something wrong about it.

What is the problem to be solved? It is — How to restore truly and safely the part of the Union which revolted.

The scheme to provincialize the rebel States does not meet it, for it would not be a true restoration. It would be, on the other hand, a destruction. Our Federal system is composed of States. The Federal Constitution is the basis on which States agreed to establish a common Power. It has its name — Federal — from that fact solely. Otherwise it would be purely national. The fact that the General Government is the paramount Government, to which the people of the States are directly responsible in certain relations, don't in the least affect its Federal character. There may be disputes about the measure of State rights — that is to say, about the extent to which the States accorded or reserved powers — but there never has been a dispute, and never can be, that the Union was originally and essentially one of States, and that the nation itself has no existence but as THE UNITED STATES. The transformation of a State into a province — supposing any power, military or other, could do it — would

PRESIDENT'S LINCOLN'S PLAN OF RECONSTRUCTION.
— VIEWS FROM WASHINGTON.

DECEMBER 13

The conflicting theories and speculations which have been afloat for a twelvemonth past in regard to the mode of restoring the rebellious portions of the South to their allegiance, and to the enjoyment of peace and protection under the Constitution have been happily blended into a practical measure by the President's Proclamation and Message.[1] Those who maintained that the States in rebellion had ceased to be States, and that they should be treated as unorganized territories; and those who advocated the contrary theory, will find in the Proclamation that practically the President has secured all that either had in view. The great object of one class of persons was to secure the abolition of Slavery, and of the other, to maintain the ancient landmarks, and in some sort, the continued existence of the States. Both these ideas are embodied in the plan of the President.

There are those who think that any plan of reconciliation and restoration is premature at present; but it is only necessary to recur to the actual condition of things in Arkansas, Tennessee and Louisiana, to remove all doubt as to the propriety of the President's course. In each of these States the rebel power is completely broken, and their populations are practically without any regular governments. The rebel State functionaries have run away, and there remains only the military control of the General Government. This is very necessary to prevent the inroads of the enemy, and to crush the latent disloyalty which would otherwise break forth; but there still is lacking the machinery of Civil Government, Courts of Justice, and a constabulary force for the preservation of order.

The plan, suggested by the President, is admirably fitted to supply this want. In the

be to just that extent a retrenchment of the Union, an elimination of the nationality. Georgia, as a province, would be no more a part of the Union than Canada. It might be, indeed, a territorial appendage of the Union, an external possession of it; but, in no legitimate sense, a part of it. Therefore, those who talk of restoring the Union by provincializing any of the States advance a self-contradiction. There can be no true restoration except by conserving the integrity of all the parts to be restored.

But again, on the other hand, they who advocate a restoration without any Federal action whatever — a restoration which shall be simply an emergence from the war, and resumption of the old status without any new limitations or conditions — fail to meet the other requirement of the problem, safety. What endangers this Union, is not the rebellious spirit in itself, as a passive thing, but the rebellious spirit in outward act — not the feeling cherished, but the power exerted. The object of the war is not to convert traitorous into loyal sentiments, but to protect itself from the military power of those sentiments. So the object of the whole policy of the Government must be to protect itself from the power of the rebel spirit, however

exerted. It is certain that the rebel spirit, for a time, at least, will survive the war which crushes its military power. Deprived of its war-weapons, it will seek other; means of hostile action; particularly the ballot, which, in the hands of enemies, is perhaps more formidable to any Government, than any other. There will be a necessity, therefore, for the Government of the Union to protect itself from this rebel power of hampering, and crippling, and destroying it by voting. Self-preservation just as much forbids it to tolerate enemies in its Senate-house as enemies in the field. To insure security, traitors must be stripped of their civil power, as absolutely as of their military power, and must remain so disabled until they cease to be traitors, by renouncing their treason. This is the only safeguard. We don't remember yet to have seen the plain, distinct avowal that the rebel civil power of a State shall remain intact after its rebel military power is crushed, for everybody would feel it almost treason to sustain a principle assuming just that shape. Yet this is simply the full, consistent development of the doctrine of restoration by non-interference. No man, not an outright supporter of the rebellion, can deny that the safety of the Govern-

ment requires it to put its hand on the rebel civil machinery at some point. It is only those who don't value, or who don't stop to regard the safety of the Government at all, that deny or ignore this. But if it be allowed that the civil machinery of the rebels is to be touched at any point, the whole principle of non-interference collapses.

The President's plan avoids all incongruities, and fulfills each cardinal requirement. By preserving the integrity of the States, it secures a Federal restoration, true alike in name and fact. By necessitating an oath of loyalty as a condition precedent to amnesty and pardon and the renewal of civil rights, it deprives unrepentant traitors of the malign use of any civil power, and thus makes the Federal restoration safe. The plan, in principle and application, is perfectly adapted to the exigency, and will be approved by the loyal people. ✸

1. Citing his broad "power to grant reprieves and pardons for offences against the United States," President Lincoln issued his Proclamation of Amnesty and Reconstruction on December 8, 1863, the same day he submitted his third annual message to Congress. For text, see Basler, ed., *The Collected Works of Lincoln*, 7:53–56..

total disruption of Southern society, which the rebellion has caused; in the waste and dispersion of the male inhabitants of mature age, it would be absurd to expect that half of the voting population could now be rallied, or even found within the limits of the State. If, therefore, one-tenth of those who voted in 1860, can now be found ready to take the oath of allegiance presented, the General Government will be well warranted in recognizing them as "the people" with authority to reconstruct the machinery of State Governments, upon the conditions stipulated. I regard the appearance of the Proclamation as most opportune....

OBSERVER ✸

1. Lincoln's annual message to Congress focused on what he called "the new reckoning." Lincoln optimistically declared: "The crisis which threatened to divide the friends of the Union is past." And he warmly saluted Union troops, "to whom, more than to others, the world must stand indebted for the home of freedom disenthralled, regenerated, enlarged, and perpetuated." For the text, see Basler, ed., *The Collected Works of Lincoln*, 36–53.

A Mathew Brady studio photograph of President Abraham Lincoln taken on February 9, 1864.

THE NATIONAL AUTHORITY — A TEST VOTE IN CONGRESS.

DECEMBER 20

Well, the House has taken a test vote on the really vital principle of the war. It has long been plain to discerning minds that behind all this talk about habeas corpus, emancipation, State rights, and other questions which mere party men have sought to keep in the foreground, there has been a controlling influence quite distinct from anything that appeared in the controversy. It was something that shaped and colored the opinions of men, and predisposed them in advance to approve or denounce — something that was "the master light of all their seeing." Between the supporters and opponents of the Administration there has been a higher issue, not so palpable as the others, because abstract, and yet that dominated all the others. The leaders of the Opposition have in general tried to keep it from view, and to this mainly they are indebted for the little success they have ever achieved.

This superlative issue is, whether authority is a necessity of this Federal Government or not. Mr. CALHOUN, JEFF. DAVIS, and all the rebel crew have maintained that the Federal Government had no authority at all. They held that a portion

Congressman Green Clay Smith of Kentucky.

of the people, through the State organizations, might nullify it or secede from it, which was equivalent to holding that the Federal Government had no authority. Power, resting on permission, is not authority. Authority involves coercive right. Mr. BUCHANAN committed himself to the same doctrine in his last annual message, wherein he denied any Federal right to coerce States, or the people of a State acting through the State Government. Gov. SEYMOUR of Connecticut took the same ground in the gubernatorial canvass of that State last Spring.

But the leaders of the Opposition generally do not believe in, or if they do, they do not dare to take this extreme ground that there is no such thing as Federal authority. They may or may not allow its existence, but if it does exist, they do not consider it at all a necessity. According to them, it can be dispensed with just as convenience or transient expediency may prompt. Up to a certain mark they have no particular objection to it, but beyond that they are disposed to treat it as an intrusion and a nuisance. Of course they don't say so, exactly. This would hardly answer, for the people have still some remnant of the old-fashioned prejudice about the supremacy of law and the inviolable sanctions of Government. But the language and acts of their leaders for the last two years have indicated their disbelief in the necessity of maintaining authority. They have manifested it indirectly, but none the less unmistakably.

The war against the rebellion was undertaken to vindicate and enforce Federal authority. The first Proclamation of President LINCOLN — that of the 15th of April, 1861, calling for 75,000 militia — set forth that the object was to "cause the laws of the United States to be duly executed." That is the end, the sole end, and nothing but the end of the war. On that principle the President stands, and ever has stood. His language from the beginning has been that the men in rebellion could have peace by obeying the laws and submitting to the authority of the United States, and in no other way whatever. His opponents have never confronted him squarely on that ground, but they have sought to deprive him of the means of prosecuting the war effectually upon it. They undertook to take from him the right of suspending habeas corpus, though its suspension in case of rebellion is expressly recognized by the Constitution as a necessity. They undertook to break down the National Enrollment Act, which was necessary to supply the armies in the field against the rebellion. They undertook to put the war under an interdict against touching Slavery, when it was not a human possibility to carry on the war with any effect without touching Slavery. They have in this way constantly operated against the methods used by the President to maintain the national authority, and have used every variety of pretext to do it without rousing the people to the fact that they really did not believe in maintaining the national authority. It was high time that this matter should be exactly understood.

Mr. GREEN CLAY SMITH,[1] of Kentucky, submitted to the House of Representatives the following resolution:

"Resolved, That as our country and the very existence of the best Government ever instituted by man, is imperiled by the most causeless and wicked rebellion that the world has ever seen, and believing as we do that the only hope of saving the country and preserving this Government is by the power of the sword, we are for the most vigorous prosecution of the war until the Constitution and laws shall be enforced and obeyed in all parts of the United States, and to that end we oppose any armistice, or intervention, or mediation, or proposition for peace from any quarter, so long as there shall be found a rebel in arms against the Government; and we ignore all party names, lines and issues, and recognize but two parties in this war, patriots and traitors."

That resolution struck directly at the heart of all this difference between the Administration and its opponents. It was an assertion of the right and the necessity of an unyielding maintenance of authority by the National Government. It was a recognition that this nation lives in law, and not in chance, or individual pleasure; and that when this vital principle is assailed, it cannot be surrendered, in whole or in part, but must be protected and preserved in its absolute integrity. A court of justice has judicial authority, conferred by law; but if that authority is used to negotiate with criminals, it ceases to be authority, and becomes a mere parleying between equals. Law is maintained not by negotiation, but by judgment. If clemency is to come in at all, it comes after the law has asserted itself, and not before. Just so if clemency is to extend to the rebels, if concession in any shape is to be given them, it must be done after the lawful authority of the United States has vindicated itself. That resolution presented this vital principle distinctly. What was the vote upon it? Ninety-three members of the body said yes to it; Sixty-four said no. Every man of these sixty-four is an opponent of the Administration of President LINCOLN.

This settles the matter. The animus which will prompt the future votes of these men against the measures of the Administration is now put beyond all further doubt. They oppose not because the measures are inexpedient as means, but because they are calculated to promote an end which they do not believe in — enforcement of law on one hand, unconditional submission on the other. They occupy a position between loyalty and rebellion — but nearer the latter than the former, for while they may agree with the one that authority exists as an abstraction, they agree with the other in the much more practical thing that there is nothing in it that ought to be exercised. They may accord with the loyal men so far as regards the form, but they actually do accord with rebels so far as relates to the substance — with the one in the theory, the other in the practice.

The division of this resolution supplies a classification long needed. It puts a distinctive mark on our Representatives, that is the only really essential one. The principle it involves will hereafter assume a yet bolder form, and, in all probability, will make the main issue in the great elections of the coming year. ✹

1. Green Clay Smith (1826–1895) was a congressman from Kentucky who had resigned as brigadier general of volunteers to take his seat as an Unconditional Unionist.

HOW THE AMNESTY PROCLAMATION WORKS.

It is not yet three weeks since that Amnesty Proclamation was issued. Of course no sensible man ever imagined that it would have any speedy effect within the rebel lines. It would require time for it to be brought to the knowledge of the people. And, again, after a right understanding of it had been gained, it would take a yet longer time for definite resolutions to be formed upon it, and definite lines of action to be adopted. In fact, under the despotism which presses everywhere in the Confederacy, any popular demonstration in response to the President's offer was extremely improbable. The chief value of that offer, so far as relates to those parts of the South yet unreached by our arms, was simply moral. It was calculated not so much to excite a counter-revolution, as to predispose the common people of the South to a prompt and cheerful submission, when our armies shall advance. It was adapted to wean the people from the desperation into which the rebel leaders, had sought to plunge them by the representation that there was no such thing as yielding but at the cost of perpetual vassalage. We must, therefore, expect that the results of the Proclamation will only gradually reveal themselves, and must await them in patience. That they will come in due time, and in a very valuable shape, we have not a doubt.

The rebel Congress affects to treat the Proclamation with sovereign contempt. Of course it does; and for two reasons. First, there is not a man of them who is not expressly excluded from the benefit of its provisions, by being "civil officers of the so-called Confederate Government." And again, there is probably not a man of them who is not a slaveholder, and the oath to support the Emancipation Proclamation, until declared null by the Supreme Court, must be to all slaveholders like holy water to the Evil One.

The Proclamation of course was not designed to appease and win over the Slave Power. The man is a fool who at this day believes in this possibility, under any device short of a complete and absolute surrender of this Government to that power. It made the rebellion; it staked its all on the rebellion, and whatever the attitude of the Government, it will adhere to the rebellion to the last gasp. But the Slave Power and the Southern people are not identical. The one is only a small part of the other, though it has hitherto been the supremely controlling part. There is nothing inherent to prevent their being dissociated. On the contrary, there long has been the strongest reason why the Slave Power should be repelled by the common people of the South; for it is an undeniable truth that it always kept them in ignorance, poverty and degradation, and, through its instrumentality alone, they have for the last two years been subjected to the most terrible woes that have befallen any people. By virtue of every right feeling and sound principle, there certainly ought to be a break between the slaveholders and the poor whites. It is just and wise in President LINCOLN to labor to produce it. If once effected, the rebellion would speedily sink, and the complete reconciliation of the vast majority of the South would follow with little delay or trouble. The Amnesty Proclamation takes away all inducement to follow the Slave Power to "the last ditch," and die with it there. By proffering reinstatement every right and privilege valuable to an American citizen; it, in fact, makes all each desperation morally impossible. Arbitrary power, which is still wielded exclusively by those to whom Slavery is the supreme concern, will for the present hold the people to the fight. But it will be able to push the people to no such extremity as it once believed it could do, if the necessity were upon it. There may be, and probably will be, good stiff fighting yet up to a certain point; but, before being pressed beyond that point, there will be general escape through the wide and safe gate which this Amnesty Proclamation will always keep open. ✹

GEN. GRANT'S WINTER OPERATIONS.

JANUARY 13

Whatever may take place in any other department, the public attention naturally centres, even at this quiet season, upon the great central department, the operations in which must again bisect the Confederacy and eventually end the rebellion. We presume no one expects any grand military operations to be undertaken in that region at present. But there is much to do — indeed, there is much being done — which is all-important and highly essential to future operations. Spring opens next month in the latitude of Chattanooga, and the month of March may admit of a movement.

But the extent of Gen. GRANT's Department is so vast, and the character of his operations so vital, that it is eminently necessary that the preparations now making should be entirely and permanently complete, before another step in advance is taken. Hitherto, operations in that immediate vicinity have been attended with unparalleled difficulties as to supplies and transportation. Actual experience is necessary to convey a truthful and adequate idea of the obstacles overcome, and the sufferings endured by the armies under ROSECRANS, THOMAS, GRANT and BURNSIDE, during the past ten months. To permanently remove these obstacles — to render it certain that no

step backward shall be taken on any account, is Gen. GRANT's present work. One line of railroad is no longer sufficient as a means of communication and supplies; two must be had, and with the Tennessee River, possibly three lines between Chattanooga and Nashville, or any other secondary base, may be kept up. Nashville was fortified, and by the accumulation of immense supplies, rendered the great secondary base of the army in the Middle Department, before the advance through Tennessee could be commenced. And so with Chattanooga. Its strategic relations to the remaining part of the Confederacy indicate it as another point for a great secondary base of supplies; the point from which the last onward movement in that quarter, and probably the final movement in the suppression of the rebellion, is to be made. Considering, then, the magnitude of the force which must be concentrated for this work, it is easy to see that Gen. GRANT's winter operations, though they are not resounding with the clash of arms, nor stirring us with bulletins of victory, are of a character not less important than the vital movements which are dependent upon them.

Information reaches us now and then from the Department of the Mississippi, going to show what is being done in the

matter of opening and establishing lines of railroad and water communication. The line of the Nashville and Chattanooga Railroad, now about being opened to Chattanooga for the first time, has long been inadequate to the proper supplying of even a small army. It is full of heavy grades, has poor rails, and miserable rolling stock. But it is employed to its fullest capacity. Within the past ten days the great bridge over the Tennessee, at Bridgeport, has been completed; also, that over Running Water Creek, near Chattanooga, 25 feet high and 800 feet long. This brings the cars into Chattanooga, from whence they can run to Atlanta or Augusta, to Knoxville or Richmond, whenever the condition of affairs shall permit. Another line of railroad will soon be, if it is not already, in full operation between Nashville and Bridgeport, (or Stevenson) Alabama. This is the Tennessee and Alabama Railroad, which intersects the Memphis and Charleston Railroad at Huntsville, the latter forming a junction with the Nashville and Chattanooga Railroad at Stevenson — thence over the track of the latter, or by river from Bridgeport, to Chattanooga. This gives Gen. GRANT substantially two routes of rail communication with his first secondary base. By next month, through the means of a railroad from Nashville to the Tennessee River, he will have two reliable railroad lines, and

HOW SOON WILL THE WAR END?

JANUARY 21

This question is asked, in public and private, a hundred times a day, and but few of the answers are ever based upon any sound reasoning or reliable facts. It is in small, almost insignificant occurrences and expressions that the true condition of the rebellion, and that of the people of the South, is most truly indicated. A Richmond paper of a recent date announces with extreme gratification the arrival of one hundred live fat hogs in the neighboring city of Petersburgh, styles it a "very pleasant kind of invasion," much more agreeable than to be "invaded by a hundred lean, slab-sided Yankee prisoners," coming to eat pork instead of producing it. Another article recommends a plan by which every portion of the cattle and hogs slaughtered for the use of individuals and the army may be made available, and significantly adds that in

"many portions of the States the supply of these animals is exhausted." Thus, day after day, these little irrefutable indications of the condition of the rebellion manifest themselves in a plain, unprejudiced manner, and are worthy, therefore, of general credence. Let those who study the progress of the war carefully note these certain developments, and they can obtain an idea of how soon the war will end, which will be far more reliable than if based on almost any other reasoning or hypothesis. The people of the South are so despotically ruled, that their demands for peace will be stifled so long as there are bayonets at the command of the rulers. But as the progress of our armies narrows still more closely the country on which they depend for food, actual starvation, now threatened, will become an inevitable fact, unless submission

to the rightful Government is promptly accorded. So long as the lines of the armies of the rebellion covered the States of Kentucky, Tennessee, Arkansas and Texas, the weapon of starvation was one on which we could place no dependence. But the condition of affairs now justifies the public in placing some dependence on the indubitable evidences of a speedy dissolution which appear from time to time in the rebel journals, and which they cannot repress if they would. ❊

one water line available a portion of the year, (the Cumberland River), with his primary base, the Ohio River....

That indomitable Western energy which carries all before it will prevail, and though the next movement in the Southwest may not be in February, nor perhaps even in March, yet when it does take place, there will be no backward steps, and no such word as fail. With Spring-time comes vegetation, and the subsistence of animals will be less difficult, and as the army advances it will, as it has heretofore, inevitably find a considerable quantity of supplies that has escaped the rebel fighting-man. So let the Government not fail to see to it that Gen. GRANT has an army in numbers sufficient for his work; all other armies are of secondary account; the last fatal blow to the rebellion is to be struck by Gen. GRANT; the rebels appreciate this, and such efforts to avert it as they are capable of they are making. It would be a shame if any pains, or labor, or material, or men should be withheld, which, if furnished, might speedily give us a crowning and final success. ✹

THE RESTORATION OF LOUISIANA.

JANUARY 21

The wheels have started. The work of bringing back the "Confederate" States has begun. Maj.-Gen. BANKS, under the authority of the President, has issued a proclamation to the loyal citizens of Louisiana, providing for an election of Governor and other State officers on the 22d of February next, and the installment of such officers on the 4th of March; also, for an election of delegates, on the first Monday of April, to a Convention for the revision of the Constitution. He has taken this step on the assurance that more than one-tenth of the population desire the speedy reinauguration of civil rule on the basis of the Amnesty Proclamation of the President, and that the movement will be carried through in absolute good faith to the National Government.

The experiment will be watched with great interest. Its success, which is confidently anticipated, will demonstrate the complete efficiency of the plan of the President, as applicable to every "Confederate" State. Louisiana was driven into the "Confederacy" more reluctantly, perhaps, than some of the other States; but, after a brief period, it yielded to the dazzling promise that New-Orleans should be the great emporium of the new slave empire, and became as fanatical as any in its devotion to the treason. No part of the "Confederacy" that we have yet regained has exhibited such intensity of hate to the old flag, as was shown by both sexes and all classes in New-Orleans on its first occupation by Gen. BUTLER, a year ago last May. So far as appearances indicated, it was not possible that rebels could be more irreclaimable. And yet, under a regimen at first severe and then relaxing, the rebel spirit has been gradually giving way to loyal sentiment, and it is believed that there is now enough of the latter to control the State, if trusted with civil powers. If the programme of Maj.-Gen. BANKS is carried out, within two months Louisiana will be as literally and completely a loyal State in the Union — with a loyal State Government and loyal representatives in both branches of Congress — as New-York itself.

What will be more notable yet, Louisiana, within three months, will have a Constitution as thoroughly purged of negro Slavery as our own[1]....

If this method of restoring Louisiana succeeds — and it is almost impossible to doubt that it will — all further concern for the fate of Slavery anywhere will be entirely useless. By the simple re-establishment of loyal State power, the whole question of Slavery is decided in fact, if not in form. This ought to content all rational men. ✹

Major General Nathaniel P. Banks, U.S.A.

1. Lincoln moreover urged the state's new governor, Michael Hahn, to include negro suffrage in its new constitution—for "the very intelligent, and specially those who have fought gallantly in our ranks"—the first time an American President ever endorsed the right of African-Americans to vote. "They would probably help," Lincoln said, "to keep the jewel of liberty within the family of freedom." See Basler, ed., *The Collected Works of Lincoln*, 243.

JOHNSTON'S RETREAT — MOVEMENT OF THE REBEL ARMY.

JANUARY 29

A dispatch wearing all the appearance of authenticity reaches us with the important intelligence of the rebel Gen. JOHNSTON's withdrawal from the front which he has lately held at Dalton. The news, up to the hour of writing, lacks official confirmation; but it comes in a circumstantial and veracious form. This is the most important military event that has happened since the battles in front of Chattanooga, though it is still a text that does not add it of a perfectly satisfactory interpretation.

If the whole of JOHNSTON's force has withdrawn toward Atlanta, as would seem to be the inference from the dispatch, (since the advanced pickets were found no further north than Kingston, Ga., forty miles south of Dalton,) the ultimate purpose of the movement must remain a military enigma until further developments of the rebel intentions are made. But it is not impossible that while all that was left of JOHNSTON's force retired in the direction of Atlanta, a strong column may have previously passed up the valley for the purpose of furnishing LONGSTREET with the reinforcements necessary to enable him to make his long-meditated attack on Knoxville. It would seem difficult that such a movement could have taken place without its becoming known to the Commander at Chattanooga, for we have occupied a position en echelon to bar the head of the valley, and it has been understood that a force of observation has held a position at Cleveland, which, if the case, would make it difficult for any body of troops to pass, unbeknown, into the valley; but indeed the movement of the whole rebel army appears to have been conducted with such marvelous secrecy that the withdrawal does not seem to have been known to the Union Commander till a flag of truce, sent into the rebel lines, came back after having gone forty-five miles South without finding the enemy! With this tact before us, there is no great unlikelihood that a column may have passed up by a circuitous route to form a junction with LONGSTREET.

The supreme strategic value to the rebels of the position LONGSTREET holds in the great valley of East Tennessee, and the facility it presents for a movement through the debouches of the mountains on GRANT's communications, were indicated in this journal a few days ago, when we also pointed out the probability of LONGSTREET's being reinforced from JOHNSTON in precisely the manner here supposed. Of course, if additional rebel forces have passed up into the valley, it can only be with a view to immediate action, for the body already occupying that position were too numerous for the scanty supplies of the country, from which they have been compelled to live. There is very great probability, therefore; that we shall speedily hear that the garrison at Knoxville has been assailed by a force greatly superior in point of strength to that under command of Gen. FOSTER.[1] But we presume there is little doubt that Gen. GRANT will see to it that all the strengthening needed at that point is added.

We are pushed to this interpretation of the scantily-reported fact of the rebel retrograde movement, from the utter absence of any other adequate rationale of the withdrawal. The rebels had lately taken up a very strong line, not precisely at Dalton, but along the Coosawattee, an affluent of the Coosa, about midway between Dalton and Rome. Here they had a position as technically strong as that of LEE on the Rapidan, and strategically stronger, from the fact that, owing to the mountain walls that hem the only approach, it was not susceptible of being turned. Military men at Chattanooga have indulged the full belief that JOHNSTON would lie posted there for the winter, awaiting the approach of our army in the Spring. The present reported movement upturns this calculation, and raises other contingencies. It leaves us mentally somewhat in doubt as to the precise turn events are likely to take, but it does not disturb a whit the confidence with which the country can look forward to any military event that may happen in that region. ☉

1. John Gray Foster (1823–1874) gave up his command a few weeks later when his horse fell on him. After recovering from his injuries, he commanded the Department of the South.

FEBRUARY 1

An Executive order, published to-day, fixes the long-delayed draft for the 10th of March.[1] It also carries the number for which the drawing will be made from three hundred thousand men, which was the number called for last October, up to Half a Million. Against this number, however, will be credited all who may have enlisted or been drafted prior to the 1st of March and have not been credited to other calls. We have no data regarding the number that is thus to be subtracted from the 500,000, and can, of course, form no precise estimate how many may enlist during the month of grace yet remaining. We are thus left in doubt as to the exact number that will need to be drafted; but as volunteering has been quite brisk and gives

RECONSTRUCTION IN TENNESSEE.
—
PROCLAMATION BY GOV. JOHNSON.[1]

FEBRUARY 1
NASHVILLE, JAN. 26

Whereas, in consequence of the disloyalty of a large majority of the persons filling the offices established by the Constitution and laws of Tennessee, and of the majority people of the of the State, and as part of the legitimate fruits of secession and rebellion against the Government of the United States the people of Tennessee have been deprived for nearly three years of all free, regular and legitimate civil government, and they are now without a Governor chosen in the ordinary way, Legislature, representation in the Congress of the United States and without courts, judges, chancellors and the various legitimately authorized county officers; and Whereas, it is believed that a majority of the people of the State are ready and desire to return to their allegiance to the Government of the United States, and to reorganize and restore the State Government to the exercise of its rightful functions, as a State of the American Union, under the Constitution of the United States, and as an initiatory step in such reorganization and restoration, it is determined to open and hold an election on the first Saturday in March next, in the

promise of being so, a very handsome subtrahend should appear. There is reason to believe that the number needed will not go over three hundred thousand men.

We are to conclude from the ordering of this draft that the Administration, taking into account the needs of the country, and the comparative availability of the two methods of raising troops, has adopted it as a measure of necessity. The Government can have no predilections for the draft so strong that it should prefer it as a system to volunteering. Were there any well grounded certainty that the armies of the Republic would be within a reasonable time filled up by volunteer recruits, we have no doubt the Administration would gladly put aside the severe regimen of the conscription. But there is no such certainty, while there is the present and imperative certainty that if the rebellion is to be put down, our armies must be increased to do it. It is therefore as

the country shall elect: if the men needed are not forthcoming it must be accepted as a verdict in favor of the draft.

In attempting to estimate the efficiency of the coming draft to accomplish the object proposed, it is impossible to go beyond general conjecture, for the provisions under which it will be made have not yet been elaborated by Congress. The bill, passed by the Senate, is to come up for discussion in the House to-day, and will, doubtless, be completed and become a law in the course of the week. Those who have followed the history of this bill through the Senate debates are aware that it will be much more rigid in its provisions than the act of last year. The price of commutation is raised from $300 to $400. Besides, persons furnishing substitutes from any source but the class not liable to draft (as aliens, persons under twenty years of age, etc.,) become themselves subject to draft, on the ex

haustion of the enrollment. This measure was adopted as an indispensable means of avoiding such an abuse of commutation as would presently have exhausted the military basis itself.

To all those who, on theoretical or practical grounds, dislike the conscription, there now remains but one course — to volunteer themselves, or to encourage volunteering. There is a month during which the stimulus of the large bounties offered by the Government, as well as State and local bounties, can operate, and after that they cease. The more we do now, the less onerous the draft will be on the ides of March. ❀

1. Lincoln's order called for half a million men "to serve for three years or during the war" (Basler, ed., *The Collected Works of Lincoln*, 7: 164).

---

various precincts, districts, or wherever it is practicable so to do, in the respective counties of the State, as prescribed by the laws and Constitution of the State, to wit: Justices of the Peace, Sheriffs, Constables, Trustees, Circuit and County Court Clerks, Registers and Tax Collectors.

Now, therefore, in virtue of the authority vested in me, and for the purpose of bringing the State of Tennessee within the provisions of the Constitution of the United States, which guarantees to each State a republican form of government, I do order said elections to be held in the various counties on the first Saturday in March next, for the officers aforesaid and none other.[2]

But, inasmuch as these elections are ordered in the State of Tennessee, as a State of the Union under the Federal Constitution, it is not expected that the enemies of the United States will propose to vote, nor is it intended that they be permitted to vote, or hold office.

And in the midst of so much disloyalty and hostility as have existed among the people of this State, towards the Government of the United States, and in order to secure the votes of its friends, and exclude those of its enemies, I have deemed it proper to make known the requisite qualifications of the electors at said elections. To entitle any person to the privilege of voting, he must be a free white man, of the age of twenty-one years, being a citizen of the United States,

and a citizen of the county where he may offer his vote, six months preceding the day of election, and a competent witness in any Court of Justice of the State, by the laws thereof, against a white man, and not having been convicted of bribery, or the offer to bribe, of larceny, or any other offence declared infamous by the laws of the State, unless he has been restored to citizenship in the mode pointed out by law. And he must take and subscribe, before the Judges of the Election, the following oath:

"I solemnly swear that I will henceforth support the Constitution of the United States, and defend it against the assaults of all its enemies; that I will hereafter be, and conduct myself as, a citizen of the United States, freely and voluntarily claiming to be subject to all the duties and obligations, and entitled to all the rights and privileges of such citizenship; that I ardently desire the suppression of the present insurrection and rebellion against the Government of the United States, the success of its armies and the defeat of all those who oppose them; and that the Constitution of the United States, and all laws and proclamations made in pursuance thereof, may be speedily and permanently established and enforced over all the people, States and Territories thereof; and further, that I will hereafter heartily aid and assist

all loyal people in the accomplishment of these results. So help me God."…

By the Governor: ANDREW JOHNSON. ❀

1. Andrew Johnson (1808–1875) had been the only Southern senator to remain in Congress after secession. He became war governor of Tennessee, and later, Vice President of the United States, succeeding Lincoln after his assassination in 1865.
2. Pro-Union Tennesseans had met on January 21 to propose a new constitutional convention to abolish slavery.

Senator Andrew Johnson of Tennessee.

COAST EXPEDITIONS — WASTE OF STRENGTH AND TIME.

FEBRUARY 4

We hear rumors — we know not how well founded — of another Burnside coast expedition as in preparation. Much as we respect the brave officer who is reported to be about to lead it, we sincerely trust that no men will be raised for another coast attack. It is apparent now to the dullest eye that the grand mistake of our strategy in the whole war has been our want of concentration. It may be doubted whether a single one of our coast expeditions, with the grand exception of the attack on New-Orleans, has tended to the successful closing of the war.

The strength of the rebellion, as we have repeated over and over again, is in its organized armies, and while these exist, we may capture every port and every large city, and still not have touched the life of the rebellion. In the Revolutionary War, the British took and occupied some of our largest cities and best harbors without in the slightest degree affecting the result of the struggle. The rebel papers say truly that they have now reached that point of the war in which they are best defended by the immense extent of territory, so that our armies, after guarding their communications, will not be able to penetrate to the heart of the country with forces larger than their own.

This redoubles the importance of largely reinforcing the two great armies of the Republic, Gen. GRANT's and Gen. MEADE's. Any troops withdrawn from them, for however brilliant side-attacks, will only delay our final victory....

Let us have no more coast expeditions, however brilliantly executed and bravely born. Let us fritter away no more gallant lives and sums of treasure. Every nerve should be strained to fill up the ranks of the two great armies so that when the Spring campaign opens, decisive blows may be struck, which shall tell directly toward the crushing of the rebellion. Time hastens, and it is too late now for anything but the most effective strokes. ⊛

GEN. GRANT AND THE LIEUTENANT-GENERALSHIP.

FEBRUARY 6

The proposition to revive the military grade of Lieutenant-General, with the view of conferring the title on Gen. GRANT, commands the hearty approval of the country[1]; and if the purpose of the resolution which has passed the House of Representatives was simply to confer a great honor on one who has greatly served his country, few would question its entire propriety. We do not think much of the argument of some of the members opposed to the resolution, that, as the war is not yet over, it would be better to wait till the finale and see whose head towers above all others, and then give him the crown. The services of Gen. GRANT have already been so signal as to merit a signal honor; and we should be willing to see it become a law that any General, who shall take a hundred thousand prisoners and four hundred pieces of artillery, shall thereby be entitled to the rank of Lieutenant-General. We have always held that our military hierarchy is entirely too restricted; it was arranged for the cadre of the insignificant army we have hitherto kept on foot; and we should be glad to see. not only the revival of the grade of Lieutenant-General, but the creation of the still higher grade of General, as prizes held out to the laudable ambition of commanders, and as a proper extension of the military hierarchy, to meet the vast proportions of our military organism. ⊛

1. Congress had begun to consider awarding Grant a military rank no officer had held since George Washington. The Times soon came out against the initiative, pointing out that the President alone had such power, and worrying that a promotion might take the Union's most successful general out of action.

VALLANDIGHAM IN THE SUPREME COURT.

FEBRUARY 16

The United States Supreme Court has decided against the application of VALLANDIGHAM to annul the sentence passed upon him by the military court. It pronounces that it has no jurisdiction over the case. In other words, that the military authority for the common defence, in time of war, inheres in the Commander-in-Chief to the exclusion of the civil authority.

This is a hard blow upon the Copperheads. There has been no end to the vituperation they have vented against Gen. BURNSIDE and President LINCOLN for usurping judicial authority over VALLADIGHAM, which belonged only to civil tribunals. Neither

Clement L. Vallandigham, Ohio Democrat.

did they hesitate when Judge LEAVITT, the District Judge in Ohio, refused the application for a writ of habeas corpus, to pour upon him, even though a Democrat, their foulest venom. He was the miserable tool of a tyrant, a puppet, a minion, a creature destitute of respect for either himself or his station, a perjured betrayer of his trust. The World, the Cincinnati Enquirer, and all the Copperhead organs, fairly reeked for months with the virus excited by the case; and it was emitted with the most indiscriminate spite upon every official who had connection there with, whether military or civil. We are rather curious to see what will be their demeanor towards the Supreme Court. The majority of that court hitherto, alone of all the functionaries of the Government, have been spared their abuse. This has been owing, we suppose, to an inference, from certain antecedents of the court, that it had proclivities in their favor. But no warrant for this has been found in any utterance of the court since the beginning of the rebellion. In no single instance has its opinion been at variance with the executive action of the President. But in this case the Copperheads did hope for something favorable to their factious ends. The decision will be a sharp disappointment. Will they dare to give their malignity, here too, full play? ⊛

THE REBEL CONSCRIPTION AND ITS EFFECTS.

FEBRUARY 19

As the end of the rebellion draws nearer, and its condition becomes more desperate, the oppression under which the Southern people labor is made to bear more heavily upon them, and there begin to be symptoms of a speedy resistance on their part. The newspapers, which have been and are heartily in the service of the leaders, indicate it by the violence with which they speak of the shifts and schemes employed by the people to escape from the tyranny which is burdening them. And it is indicated more plainly by the notes of hostility and defiance which rise, and grow louder and louder, in those parts of the Confederacy where the people have not wholly thrown away their care for their own freedom in the intensity of the struggle the past three years. In North Carolina especially, do we find these developments.[1] Public meetings are held, whose resolutions attack the Conscription Act, denounce the despotism of the Confederate Government, and call upon Gov. VANCE[2] to convoke a convention, and newspapers declare that "North Carolina cannot and will not submit to have every able-bodied man conscripted, and the whole State turned into a military camp."

Nothing seems to have excited this spirit of resistance more than the determination to force into the ranks the men who had furnished substitutes, and thus became exempt from military service under the former conscription. And no wonder. No Government in the world could afford to commit such a breach of faith, unless under the plea of the most stringent necessity. Thus, its adoption is the clearest proof of the desperate condition of their cause, a proof which must come home with tenfold vividness to every one who is the victim of it.

That very sense of the desperate state of affairs must have in its turn the effect upon these men, who are thus dragged into the service, of making them feel that this great crime is committed upon them to no purpose. From men forced into the ranks with such feelings what can be expected? The streams of deserters which now flow steadily toward our lines from every place where rebel soldiers are collected, will gather increased volume as soon as these victims of treachery begin to be brought out to fill the thinning ranks....

A more terrible oppression never ground a people more uselessly. Even the rebel leaders themselves feel that they are straining the patience and faith of their dupes to the uttermost. Their speakers declared that these measures were worse than "the ruthless conscription which NAPOLEON inflicted on France." They pronounced the act a "desperate measure." It was "breaking up the farms and reducing the agricultural interests of the country to about naught;" it was "breaking down and crippling resources that were left to carry on the war. But the plea of necessity prevailed, and the measures were adopted.

In view of such facts and statements, the words of the Salem Press, that "every day convinces us more and more that we are on the eve of events which are pregnant with the fate of the Confederacy," and those of the Montgomery Mail, that "there is a movement on foot which will create more consternation at Richmond than anything that has occurred during the war," become very suggestive. ☉

1. Protests had broken out in North Carolina against the new Confederate draft law, enacted December 28, 1863, abolishing the provision allowing substitutes.
2. Zebulon B. Vance (1830–1894), was elected governor of North Carolina in 1862 following service in the Confederate Army during the Seven Days campaign near Richmond earlier that year.

PROGRESS OF SHERMAN'S OPERATIONS — THE CAMPAIGN IN THE SOUTHWEST.

FEBRUARY 20

If we may put faith in the reports of SHERMAN's advance which reach us through rebel sources, and which have every evidence of authenticity, the march of that General has been one of the most rapid and brilliant in military annals. His column, or at least the vanguard of it, has already tapped the communications of Mobile by striking the Mobile and Ohio Railroad in the vicinity of Meridian.

In discussing, a few days ago, the probable line of march of SHERMAN's force, we assigned it Meridian and the Mobile and Ohio Railroad as a primary objective, and said he would do well if he made the point aimed at in three weeks or a month. It has taken that vigorous and energetic commander less even than the shorter of these periods to make good the prime object.

SHERMAN's column left Vickburgh on the 3d inst.; on the 5th it crossed the Big Black; on the 7th it is reported to have occupied Jackson; and the intelligence we publish to-day reports a fight at Enterprise, which is located on the railroad line running northward from Mobile, somewhat over a hundred miles north of that city, and about twenty miles south of Meridian. This report comes through rebel sources, and it receives confirmation by tidings from Chattanooga, announcing that SHERMAN has destroyed the bridges over the Mobile and Ohio Railroad.

The progress of Gen. SHERMAN's advance, the line of march he has taken up, and the points embraced in the scope of his operations, add the authority of fact to the theory of his advance put forward by this journal as a simple matter of speculation. It is obviously the purpose of this portion of Gen. GRANT's army to preoccupy the strategic lines of the Tombigbee and the Alabama, and to seize the great region of productive territory covered and commanded by these lines. The importance of this conquest is comparable as a strategic stroke, and in the weight it must have in determining the issue of the war, only to the longitudinal bisection of the Southern territory by the opening of the Mississippi, and to its lateral bisection by the possession of Chattanooga. This conquest once fairly consolidated by the opening up of the two rivers just named, will give us command of the great water-shed between the Mississippi and the western boundary of Alabama. It will, in fact, "corral" the rebel forces within the restricted parallelogram of the Atlantic States.

It would be folly to conceal, however, that this great result can only be obtained by a protracted and difficult campaign; for the country to be occupied is of vast extent, and though it is not believed that the rebels have at present in that region a force sufficiently large to be a very formidable barrier to SHERMAN's progress, yet it is scarcely credible they should give it up without a blow. ☉

THE PAY OF COLORED SOLDIERS.

FEBRUARY 21

HEADQUARTERS FIRST SOUTH CAROLINA VOLUNTEERS, BEAUFORT, S.C., SUNDAY, FEB. 14

To the Editor of the New-York Times:

May I venture to call your attention to the great and cruel injustice which is impending over the brave men of this regiment?

They have been in military service for more than a year, having volunteered, every man, without a cent of bounty, on the written pledge of the War Department, that they should receive the same pay and rations with white soldiers.

This pledge is contained in the written instructions of Brig.-Gen. SAXTON,[1] Military Governor, dated Aug. 25, 1862. Mr. Solicitor WHITING,[2] having examined those instructions, admits to me that "the faith of the Government was thereby pledged to every officer and soldier under that call."

Surely if this fact were understood, every man in the nation would see that the Government is degraded by using for a year the services of the brave soldiers, and then repudiating the contract by which they were enlisted. Yet this is what will be done should Mr. WILSON's bill,[3] legalizing the back pay of the army, be defeated.

We presume too much on the supposed ignorance of these men. I have never yet found a man in my regiment so stupid as not to know when he was cheated. If the fraud proceeds from Government itself, so much the worse, for this strikes at the foundation of all rectitude, all honor, all obligation.

Mr. Senator FESSENDEN[4] said, in the debate on Mr. WILSON's bill, Jan 4, that the Government was not bound by the unauthorized promises of irresponsible recruiting officers. But is the Government itself an irresponsible recruiting officer? and it men have volunteered in good faith on the written assurances of the Secretary of War, is not Congress bound, in all decency, either to fulfill those pledges or to disband the regiments?

Mr. Senator DOOLITTLE[5] argued in the same debate that white soldiers should receive higher pay than black ones, because the families of the latter were often supported by Government. What an astounding statement of fact is this! In the white regiment in which I was formerly an officer (the Massachusetts Fifty-fourth) nine-tenths of the soldiers' families, in addition to the pay and bounties, drew regularly their "State aid." Among my black soldiers, with half pay and no bounty, not a family receives any aid. Is there to be no limit, no end, to the injustice we heap upon this unfortunate people? Cannot even the fact of their being in arms for the nation, liable to die any day in its defence, secure them ordinary justice? Is the nation so poor, and

SHERMAN'S SPLENDID ADVANCE — MOBILE THREATENED.

FEBRUARY 21

Although the grand objects of SHERMAN'S advance have been from the start evident to every one capable of looking at the map with a military eye, yet we have, ever since he crossed the Big Black, been left in tantalizing obscurity as to his progress. This state of things has been the necessary consequence of the manner in which Gen. SHERMAN has made his march. Having gone forward to stay, and expecting to open up a new base on the Gulf, he cut himself entirely loose from his base on the Mississippi, abandoned his line of communications, tore up the railroad and bridges in his rear, and thus severed all communication with the world that is behind and awaits with eagerness the reports of his progress. In this condition of things it was plain enough that we should have to depend on the rebels for our current history of this important movement.

They give us to-day a chapter that must be as sombre and saddening to them as it is bright and inspiring to us. The raising of the curtain reveals that far-off theatre of war all astir with advancing hosts — SHERMAN, with his column in the heart of Mississippi; FARRAGUT, with his fleet in the immediate neighborhood of Mobile. All that we have been predicting for this expedition is now fully justified; and the bold and brilliant campaign, revealed in its magnificent ensemble, is already half accomplished at a stroke.

An official dispatch to the rebel War Department at Richmond, under date of the 18th inst., announces Gen. SHERMAN's arrival at Quitman, on the Mobile and Ohio Railroad. Quitman is about twenty-five miles south of Meridian, and being thus taken in reverse, that important strategic point — the point of intersection of the Mobile and Ohio and Southern Mississippi Railroads — was evacuated by the rebels on the 14th inst. Considering that this march of a hundred and fifty miles has been accomplished in ten days, the rebels do not overestimate it when they characterize it as "without comparison, the boldest movement of the war." We ventured to speak of it ourselves in similar terms on Saturday last.

The point at which Gen. SHERMAN has tapped the communications of Mobile would seem to indicate his intention to push forward one of his columns on the rear of that place. The rebels there are anticipating as much, and declare he will not be allowed to take Mobile "without a desperate battle." If this determination has the effect to keep the rebels there till he gets in position to bag them, we sincerely hope it will be persevered in. From Quitman to Mobile he has a march due south of a little better than a hundred miles. The entire distance from Meridian to within five miles of Mobile is unfortified, and has been up to a very late period unprotected by rebel troops. In the rear of Mobile, and as much as five miles from the city, are three heavy lines of earthworks. The first line is on the southeast side of the city. The second is on the east side of the river, opposite the termination of St. Michael-street. Down the river to the left is the landing of the Mobile and Ohio Railroad. Here is located Spanish Battery, consisting of three rifled 32-pound guns and one 10-inch gun. Further down the bay, to the left, is Pinto's Battery. Between this and Fort Morgan are Batteries Choctaw, Cedar Plain, Grand Spell and Lighthouse Battery — in all six — consisting each of six 32-pound rifled cannon. This fortified region is, however, described as low and flat, and not capable of defence, even when thus fortified — the lay of the land being an effectual barrier to such defence.

to utterly demoralized by its pauperism, that after it has had the lives of these men, it must turn round to filch six dollars of the monthly pay which the Secretary of War promised to their widows? It is even so, if the excuses of Mr. FESSENDEN and Mr. DOOLITTLE are to be accepted by Congress and by the people.[6]

Very respectfully, Your obedient servant,
T.W. HIGGINSON, COLONEL COMMANDING 1ST S.C. VOLUNTEERS. ✹

1. Rufus Saxton (1824–1908) was assigned to the recruitment of ex-slaves into the Federal army.
2. William Whiting (1813–1873) was solicitor of the War Department, whose opinions on presidential war powers had helped Lincoln conclude that he could issue the Emancipation Proclamation; later served briefly as a congressman from Massachusetts.
3. Senator Henry Wilson (1812–1875) of Massachusetts.
4. Senator William Pitt Fessenden (1806–1869) of Maine.
5. Senator James R. Doolittle (1815–1897) of Wisconsin.
6. Not until 1865 did black soldiers receive pay equal to their white counterparts.

But if it be Gen. SHERMAN's purpose to make a march on the rear of Mobile, he will not be left alone: he will have the powerful cooperation of FARRAGUT's fleet, and the land force from New-Orleans. From the somewhat obscure rebel dispatches, we gather that FARRAGUT had already made an attack on the works at Grant's Pass, at the entrance of Mobile Bay; but contrary weather had somewhat delayed operations. There is little fear, however, of his being behindhand in any part of the work intrusted to him. ✹

GEN. GRANT AND THE LIEUTENANT-GENERALSHIP.

FEBRUARY 26

The Senate deserves public thanks for its decisive vote, striking out Gen. GRANT's name from the joint resolution reviving the grade of Lieutenant-General. The attempt of the House to prescribe, as it virtually did, that one particular man, and no other, should receive that rank, was unconstitutional, unseemly, unsafe. But for so many other odd performances of the House, it would have excited astonishment.

The Constitution makes the President the sole executive head of the nation, and devolves upon him the entire executive responsibility. In consistency therewith, it gives him the sole appointing power, subject only to the approval of the Senate. The House has no more constitutional right to say that Gen. GRANT shall be Lieutenant-General than it has to say that some other popular General shall be Secretary of War, and some other one yet Minister to England. The fact that the office to be filled is military instead of civil, makes not the slightest difference. The Constitution makes no distinction. The President has the same appointing power to all offices, military and civil alike. There never was a clearer unconstitutional assumption than in that resolution. Nothing is made by saying that the President was only "recommended" to make that appointment. The House has no voice in the matter whatever — either to request or to dictate. It has as little right to trammel the Executive judgment as to control it. The Constitution expressly gives the President the power to recommend measures to Congress, but it gives no authority to Congress to make recommendations of men to the President. It intends that the House of Representatives shall confine itself to its own legislative business....

But Gen. GRANT is about to commence a grand and, as he believes, a decisive campaign, and he deems that he can best serve his country in his present work. He considers himself better qualified for the field than for the closet. The President so judges him, and so do the people.[1] Why should the House, then, take it upon itself to say that he shall be transferred to a different sphere? How can they reconcile it with the public interests that this great Spring campaign, just in its incipient stage, should be hazarded by the withdrawal of him who conceived it, and who, more than any other man, has the executive ability to consum-

mate it? It is preposterous to maintain that Gen. GRANT can conduct that Southwestern campaign in Washington as well as he can at the seat of war. With all his genius, he is not superior to NAPOLEON; and NAPOLEON, during his great campaigns, was never in Paris, but always with his army.

If the majority of the House wish well to Gen. GRANT, they will let him alone. One of his crowning virtues, thus far, has been his steady determination to know nothing of politics, and to attend exclusively to his business as a soldier. All solicitations to lend his name to party schemes he has repelled with a firmness that has proved him every inch a man. Had Gen. MCCLELLAN shown any such elevation of spirit, he never would have sunk to his present discredit. Of course, there will be, and ever must be, a breed of pigmy politicians, who are always on the spring to be the first to mount to the shoulders of rising greatness, it being their only way to make themselves conspicuous. Gen. GRANT shakes them off with a sovereign contempt it is refreshing to behold. If they have any regard for his comfort or for their own appearance before the country, they will now stop infesting him, and leave him free to do his own chosen work, in his own chosen way.

There is not the slightest danger that Gen. GRANT will fail of being properly honored and rewarded by his country at the appropriate time. He himself has no concern about this. He finds his complete content in the consciousness of grand duties grandly performed. He can but know that he is making a name for history, in the light of which all the distinctions which Congress, or which even the people can bestow, pale into insignificance. But, notwithstanding that, the people will insist, and ought to insist, when his work is done, upon conferring on him every mark of their admiration, and gratitude. This will surely come in its due season, and by a spontaneous, irrepressible impulse of the popular heart, immeasurably more gratifying to the recipient than any of these equivocal demonstrations of eager politicians. The House will do well to study and, if possible, emulate the wise composure of Gen. GRANT and of the people. ✹

1. Lincoln appointed general-in-chief with the three stars of a lieutenant general the following month.

THE SEVERE REVERSE TO THE FLORIDA EXPEDITION. [1]

—

OUR FORCES OVERPOWERED BY NUMBERS AND COMPELLED TO RETREAT

FEBRUARY 27

The steamship Fulton, Capt. WOTTON, from Port Royal on Wednesday last, arrived here at a late hour last night, bringing information of a sad reverse to our expedition, under Gen. SEYMOUR,[2] in Florida.

We are unable to give details, because after the Fulton had put out into the bay, she was boarded by the provost-Marshal and Quartermaster, with orders from Gen. GILLMORE[2] to deprive the passengers of all private letters in their possession. Thus, the letter of the correspondent of the TIMES, who had returned from Jacksonville, on purpose to send full particulars, and who had inclosed a partial list of the killed and wounded, amounting to five hundred names, was seized and retained until the next mail — a week hence. The cruelty of this short-sighted proceeding, considering the anxiety of relatives and friends, is evident. Gen. GILLMORE's dispatches were sent on, and will doubtless soon be made public.

To a passenger by the Fulton we are indebted for the following main facts of the battle:

On the afternoon of the 20th, our troops, under Gen. SEYMOUR, met the enemy, 15,000 strong, fifty-five miles beyond Jacksonville and eight miles beyond Sanderson, on the line of the Jacksonville and Tallahassee Railroad. The battle was desperately fought during three hours, and at sunset our forces, overpowered by numbers, retired to Sanderson, taking with them the greater part of the wounded.

The Seventh Connecticut, Seventh New-Hampshire, Fortieth Massachusetts, Forty-eighth and One Hundred and Fiftieth New-York and Eighth United States were engaged. Col. FRIBLEY, of the Eighth United States, was left dead on the field. Col. REED, a Hungarian officer, was mortally wounded.

All the officers of HAMILTON'S Battery were wounded. Capt. HAMILTON (wounded in the arm) and Lieut. MYRICK (wounded in the foot) are at Gen. GILLMORE'S headquarters at Hilton Head.

Col. GUY HENRY, of the Fortieth Massachusetts, had three horses shot under him, but escaped hurt.

The Cosmopolitan arrived at Beaufort, on Monday evening, with 240 of the wounded; Col. REED among them who was living when the Fulton left, on Wednesday.

The enemy's loss is not known. They captured five guns.

It is supposed that the troops were from BRAGG'S army. Gen. HARDEE himself was on the field, having come to Florida on a visit to his family, and also to form a second marriage.

Our loss is variously estimated at from 500 to 1300 Seventy-eight rebel prisoners brought by the Fulton. The Fulton's passage was remarkably short and pleasant; a striking contrast to the previous one.

We understand that the Purser of the Fulton has a list of the killed and wounded, which he will show, but will not allow it to be copied. ⊛

1. Later known as the Battle of Olustee, on February 20, 1864, notable for the engagement—and near slaughter—of the Eighth U.S. Colored Troops. The Union lost more than a third of its forces.
2. Truman Seymour (1824–1891) was relieved after this failed invasion of Florida.

THE REAL MILITARY IMPORTANCE OF FLORIDA.

FEBRUARY 28

The rebels certainly have a faculty of turning up where they are not expected; and the late blow they have delivered — namely, at our force in Florida — is the most unexpected of all. Everybody agrees that Florida has no strategic value, either to ourselves or the rebels. It is quite removed from the great lines of operation; and as a military possession seems hardly worth while being made a serious bone of contention. But the rebels appear to have discovered in it some kind of value, and that, too, of sufficient moment to have made it worth their while sending a powerful force to oppose and punish the Union expedition that has lately made that peninsula the theatre of its operations. For an adequate explanation of this we are driven to fall back on the consideration of the material value of Florida to the rebels, in the point of view of the question of its supplies of beef cattle, respecting which

A Kurz and Allison lithograph of the Battle of Olustee.

important developments were lately made.

The very important circular of the rebel Chief Commissary of Florida, received from our special correspondent and published in the TIMES a few days since, gives a new turn to our notions of the military value of that State. While it remains perfectly true that Florida possesses no strategic relations of sufficient importance to authorize the detachment of a force strong enough to insure its permanent occupation, yet the disclosures of its material value to the rebel cause, made in the document referred to, prove conclusively that Gen. GILLMORE's[1] expedition is a most timely blow in the very spot in which the rebels are now most sensitive. Operations that aim at cutting off the rebel armies from their supplies, and depriving them of extensive areas of productive territory are, at the present stage of the war, secondary in importance only to the destruction of their armed forces in the field — if, indeed, they are not equal in substantial value. It was this fact that gave its immense importance to the stroke that severed the rebel

communications with the Trans-Mississippi region; and it is the prospective results in the same direction that add a double value to the operations of SHERMAN in Mississippi and Alabama. The occupation of Florida shares this characteristic with the conquests just mentioned. The circular of the rebel Commissary shows that both JOHNSTON's army in Georgia and the army of BEAUREGARD at Charleston, have for sometime been dependent mainly on Florida for their supplies of beef cattle. This is made manifest by citations in the circular from the letters of commissaries of both these armies....

Now, crediting part of the urgency of these statements to the pressure which these officials would naturally use in order to stimulate exertion in those addressed, these representations nevertheless show very clearly how exceedingly straitened the rebels are for supplies, and the importance attached to Florida in this particular. As some attempts have been made by the Copperhead presses to deny the authenticity of this document, (which has

every internal evidence in its favor, and was found by our correspondent among the private papers of the rebel writer,) we may add, that the wealth of Florida in beef cattle has long been known to our old army officers, who have campaigned in that State. The prairies afford excellent pasture; cattle require little care from their owners and no housing in Winter; and, in most parts of the State, hogs fatten without any other support than that which they derive from the roots and mast of the forest. It was intended that the Union force, which has planted itself in Florida, should keep up constant and extensive raids, and cut off the rebels from their beef-supplies. We trust that, despite the ill luck that has met the opening of the Florida campaign, the work may still be kept up, if its results should promise to be really as important as is surmised. ✹

1. Quincy Adams Gillmore (1825–1888) was in charge of the campaign to reduce Fort Pulaski, which guarded the sea approach to Savannah, Georgia.

RECONSTRUCTION.

CONVENTION OF LOYAL PEOPLE IN WEST TENNESSEE.

CARIO, ILL., FRIDAY, FEB. 20

The following particulars of the Convention of Loyal People of West Tennessee, are taken from the Memphis Bulletin:

"The adjourned meeting of the Convention of Loyal People of West Tennessee, which met in this City, on the evening of the 23d instant, was a large and enthusiastic affair.

A loyal and eloquent address was made by Dr. BUTLER, of Arkansas.

The following resolutions, in substance, were unanimously adopted:

First — Disavowal of further participation in and responsibility for the rebellion, and providing that proper measures be immediately adopted for reorganizing the State Government on the basis of absolute loyalty to the Union and the Constitution.

Second — All acts passed by the Legislature, dissolving the relation of the State of Tennessee to the United States are declared to be without authority and null and void. Third — Declares for the resumption of Federal relations in the Union, with such reforms in the State Constitu-

tion as will make future rebellion and secession impossible.

Fourth — The importance is recognized of making the State Constitution republican in fact as well as in name, by guaranteeing the natural and inherent rights of all persons in the State; also providing that Slavery shall henceforth cease and be forever prohibited; also denying the elective franchise to all persons who have been engaged in the rebellion, who fail satisfactorily to establish their fidelity to the National Government and its laws.

Fifth — That immediate steps be taken to reorganize the State under the Constitution and laws of the United States, and to that end all the loyal people are invited to take the oath of allegiance to the United States, prescribed by Gov. ANDREW JOHNSON.

Seventh — Requests Gov. ANDREW JOHNSON to issue a proclamation for the election of delegates to a convention to amend the State Constitution, so as to confirm the fact of emancipation already accomplished by the rebellion and the war.

Eighth — Requests the Loyal Union State

FEBRUARY 28

Executive Committee for West Tennessee to lay these resolutions before Gov. ANDREW JOHNSON, and to confer with him as to the accomplishment of the facts therein set forth.

Ninth — The acts of President LINCOLN and his Administration in suppressing the rebellion are indorsed, and they pledge their support to sustain and complete the work."...
✹

CHAPTER 18

"Grant and Staff Arrived Here To-day"

MARCH–APRIL 1864

In the early spring of 1864, prior to the traditional onset of the military campaigning season in May, the dominant topic of conversation in New York and elsewhere was the impact that newly promoted Lieutenant General Ulysses S. Grant was likely to have on the course of the war in the east. After he arrived in Washington on March 8, Grant reorganized the Army of the Potomac and, after some delay, confirmed Meade as its commander. Grant planned to travel with Meade's army and direct its strategic movements, but Meade would remain responsible for its day-to-day management. Grant also assigned William T. Sherman as the commander of the three western armies, and he found employment for three of the Union's most prominent "political generals": the German-born Franz Sigel in the Shenandoah Valley, Benjamin Butler with the Army of the James at Fort Monroe on the Virginia coast, and Nathaniel P. Banks with the Army of the Gulf in Louisiana. Grant wanted Banks to seize Mobile, Alabama, but Lincoln's eagerness to complete the restoration of Louisiana, and Seward's concern for French adventurism in Mexico, led Banks instead to launch an offensive up the Red River toward Shreveport in partnership with Rear Admiral David Dixon Porter. It proved an ill-fated campaign with near-disastrous consequences both for Banks and for the Union cause — though not for Porter who, as usual, managed to avoid recrimination.

As the redirection of Banks's operations demonstrated, politics were never very far away during the war. There was already talk about the fall presidential elections. The strongly pro-Lincoln Times was more annoyed than surprised by the short-lived challenge

Lieutenant General Ulysses S. Grant, U.S.A.

to Lincoln's renomination from Treasury Secretary Salmon P. Chase. One of the reasons Chase sought to challenge the President (beyond mere ambition) was his eagerness for a more progressive policy toward the emancipated former slaves. Lincoln's emerging reconstruction policy, evident in his management of the readmission of Louisiana and Arkansas, was moderate and incremental. He insisted on emancipation, but he did not demand that the reconstructed state constitutions grant either black citizenship or black suffrage rights. To Chase and some others, this moderate progressivism was not enough. But when a public letter circulated by Kansas Senator Samuel C. Pomeroy, criticizing Lincoln and praising Chase, failed to generate any support and instead provoked an angry backlash, Chase formally withdrew from the contest.

The issue of black rights asserted itself on the battlefield as well. Though Lincoln had declared that any mistreatment of black Union soldiers as prisoners would initiate a reciprocal treatment of white Confederate prisoners, it did not save the Union garrison at Fort Pillow. A division of 2,500 men under Confederate cavalry leader Nathan Bedford Forrest attacked Fort Pillow, forty miles north of Memphis, on April 12, 1864. Half of the 600-man Union garrison was made up of black soldiers. Most of them were former slaves who feared that if they were captured, they would be treated not as prisoners of war but as escaped slaves and very likely be sold back into slavery. The fort's commander, Major Lionel Booth, rejected Forrest's demand for Fort Pillow's surrender, so when Forrest's men swept over the barricades and into the fort, they refused to accept the surrender of the black troops, slaughtering them where they stood, and even pursuing them out of the fort and down to the riverbank. Of the 262 black soldiers in the fort, only 62 survived. This episode has gone down in history as the Fort Pillow Massacre and generated the Union rallying cry to "Remember Fort Pillow." It was one more example of how the increasingly bitter war was bending the rules of combat.

SLAVERY AND THE NEGRO.
NEGRO EQUALITY BEFORE THE LAW.

WASHINGTON, WEDNESDAY, MARCH 2

The report made by Senator [Charles] SUMNER[1] to-day, from the Committee on Slavery and Freedmen, in the bill to secure equality before the law in the courts of the United States, reviews the history of our jurisprudence in respect to the exclusion of colored testimony in the courts, and examines the laws in the several States relative to this subject. South Carolina, it appears, has never had a law excluding such testimony, yet practices exclusion. In concluding this review the report says: "It is difficult to read the provisions in a single State without impatience, but the recurrence of this injustice, expressed with such particularity in no less than fifteen States, makes injustice swell into indignation, especially when it is considered that in every State this injustice is adopted and enforced by the courts of the United States." It further appears that in no State can a slave testify against a white person, excepting that in Maryland he may testify against a white person who is not a Christian. Only under certain circumstances in Delaware and Louisiana can a free negro testify against a white person. The eccentricities of judicial decisions illustrating this branch are numerously cited — among

MARCH 5

the consequences of exclusion are mentioned the maltreatment or murder of slaves, with impunity, and the perpetration of crimes against white men, in the presence of colored persons, with the same immunity from punishment. The report traces this proscription to the barbarous ages, and makes it the offspring of Slavery originating in ignorance and prejudice. Among the ancient Greeks, a slave's testimony was not believed upon his oath, but was admissible under torture. The Romans adopted similar legal practices. In England, under the common law, this proscription was again recognized. The grounds for such injustice are examined at length, and the report concludes as follows: "It is for Congress to determine whether the proscription shall continue to be maintained." ✪

1. Senator Charles Sumner of Massachusetts (1811–1874) was the leader of antislavery forces in the Senate.

Senator Charles Sumner, Republican of Massachusetts.

THE LOUISIANA ELECTION — SECESSIONISM AND COPPERHEADISM SPURNED.

MARCH 5

The first application of the President's plan of restoring the Union has been grandly successful. Through it Louisiana has been brought completely back; and that State is to-day under a civil rule as loyal as that of New-York itself, and many would say even more so. The State officers, which have been elected by a large majority, are most earnest supporters not only of the Government, but of the administration of the Government, and can be implicitly relied upon, whatever be the effort or the sacrifice demanded.

We confess ourselves surprised, both at the magnitude of the vote, and the comparatively small number received by Mr. [J. Q. A.] FELLOWS, the Copperhead candidate for Governor.[1] Before the "secession," the vote usually polled in the elections of Louisiana was from thirty-five to forty thousand; never, we believe, beyond forty-five thousand. Considering the large numbers (almost all voters) who went at an early day into the rebel army, and also the fact that there are extensive districts in the State which are still under rebel duress, it is surprising that nearly eleven thousand ballots, or more than one-fourth of the regular vote of the State,

have been cast on this occasion — and all by citizens who have taken a very stringent oath of allegiance. This election, it must be borne in mind, was confined exclusively to residents, who had the franchise under the State laws. The extent of the response is remarkable; but more remarkable yet is its character.

Of the entire number of votes given, less than one-fifth were received by the Copperhead candidate. No loyal Northern State can show any such preponderance on the side of staunch Unionism. It is particularly gratifying, too, to note in the returns that between New-Orleans and the country parishes there is no essential difference in this respect. If anything, the planting population has polled a stronger vote, comparatively, against FELLOWS, than the city population. This indicates an extraordinary readiness in those who have the most at stake to accept the new order of things; for it was universally understood that the election of [Michael] HAHN would be equivalent to the conversion of Louisiana into a Free State. He had identified himself completely with the Free-State movement, and one of his first official duties will be to make arrangements for the convention to be held in April, to frame a Free-State Constitution[2]....

This result in Louisiana will soon be followed by similar ones in Tennessee and Arkansas. All accounts betoken that the Unionism which is reasserting itself in

those States is of the same sterling cast. It will give no aid or comfort to Copperheadism of any type. It has formally seen and felt the infernal malignity of the rebellion, and, in putting its heel upon that, it cannot by any moral possibility, embrace anything in sympathy therewith.

As it is preposterous to conceive of Gen. GRANT extending his lines down into Georgia, we think it altogether likely that his next movement will be to contract his lines around Chattanooga. The aim and end of the late campaign was to push the menacing rebels from his front — to effectually raise the siege of Chattanooga, if the rebel attempt at investment may be called a siege. This has been done in the most perfect and conclusive manner; and as nothing whatever would be gained by forcing his advance southward, until such time as he is ready to begin the grand advance that shall change his base to the Atlantic seaboard, we have no idea that such unmilitary step will be taken. If, therefore, it should soon be announced that GRANT's army has fallen back to Chattanooga, there need be no dreadful disappointment expressed. The view of the case and of the campaign just set forth is confirmed by a telegram just received from Chattanooga as we write, which announces that "there has been no fighting for two days," and that "the campaign in Northern Georgia is probably ended."

GRANT's grand campaign, in the direction of Augusta, the final campaign of the war in the Southwest, commences properly with the incoming Spring. A great depot, or base, will by that time have been established at Chattanooga — the army will have recruited from its prodigious labors of the last few months, and it will take up the final march under its great leader, well assured of a final success. ◉

1. Louisiana was the first Confederate state to be reconstructed. In an election supervised by Union Major General Nathaniel Banks, a moderate Republican candidate, Michael Hahn, defeated the conservative John Quincy Adams 54 percent to 26 percent, with Radical Republican Franklin Flanders receiving 20 percent. Hahn was sworn in as Louisiana's governor on March 4.
2. Louisiana's new constitution abolished slavery and authorized free public schools for children ages six to eighteen without regard to race. It did not, however, grant voting rights to blacks, despite Lincoln's suggestion to Hahn that it should consider offering the franchise to black veterans at least. Worse (to progressives), when the first legislature was elected, it barred blacks from the new public schools.

The inauguration of Michael Hahn, sworn in as governor of Louisiana under Lincoln's Reconstruction program.

THE BUREAU OF FREEDMAN'S AFFAIRS.

MARCH 5

The bill which has passed the House to establish a bureau of freedmen's affairs creates that office in the War Department.[1] It is to be placed in charge of a Commissioner, at an annual salary of $4,000, to whom is to be referred the adjustment and determination of all questions arising under any laws not existing or hereafter to be enacted concerning persons of African descent, and persons who are, or shall become free, by virtue, of any proclamation, law, or military order, issued, enacted, or promulgated during the present rebellion, or by virtue of any act of emancipation which shall be enacted by any State for the freedom of such persons held to service or labor within such State, or who shall be otherwise entitled to their freedom.

The Commissioner is also charged with the execution of all laws providing for the colonization of freedmen, and with the delivery of any bonds of the United States, or any indemnity to any State which shall become entitled by reason of the emancipation of slaves within such State, and of any act of Congress authorizing the issue of such bonds or payment of such indemnity. The bill, among other things, provides for the appointment of Assistant-Commissioners and other officers, who are to permit persons of African descent, and persons who are, or shall become, free, to occupy, cultivate and improve all lands lying within the districts now or heretofore in rebellion, which lands may have been, or may hereafter be abandoned by their former owners, and all real estate to which the United States shall have acquired title, and to advise and aid them when needful, to organize and direct their labor, adjust with them their wages, and receive all returns arising therefrom, which shall be duly accounted for to the Commissioner, and all balances, if any there be, after defraying the charges and expenses of the bureau, are to be annually paid into the Treasury of the United States. ✵

1. The bill authorizing this bureau, renamed the Bureau of Refugees, Freedmen, and Abandoned Lands, triggered heated debate. The House wanted to establish it in the War Department, the Senate in the Treasury Department. The bill was not passed by both houses of the Congress until March 3, 1865, only a month before Appomattox.

FROM CHICAGO.

MR. LINCOLN'S RENOMINATION.

CORRESPONDENCE OF THE NEW-YORK TIMES.
CHICAGO, MONDAY, FEB. 29

The recent development of an active opposition to the renomination of Mr. LINCOLN, with extensive ramifications, has created no little surprise and excitement in this quarter. People had generally settled down into the conviction that the choice of the Union men would fall unanimously upon the present incumbent, at least so nearly so that there would be no organized opposition. Consequently, the "Chase Circular," which made its appearance at the Louisville Convention, and which has since turned up in all parts of the country under the franks of leading Republican members of Congress, fell like a bombshell among us.[1] The most commonly expressed feeling is indignation that such underhanded means should be resorted to in assailing the Administration. But Mr. CHASE is relieved of any complicity in the scheme, for all hold him to be too high-minded and honorable to be engaged in such intrigues, while holding his present relation to the President.

These men may as well be informed, first as last, that their intrigues will be of no avail. Mr. LINCOLN will as surely be the Union candidate,[2] if he is alive when

MARCH 6

the Nominating Convention meets, as the sun will rise on that day. The signs of the times — the action of State Legislatures and State Conventions — ought to be sufficient to convince any sane man that all factious opposition will be unavailing, and that it will recoil upon those engaged in it. The West, whose voice is somewhat potent in the Union, as it is, knows no other man in connection with the Union nomination for the Presidency but ABRAHAM LINCOLN, and those gentlemen had better "stand from under" who carry their opposition to an undue and unwarrantable extent. ✵

1. Often called the Pomeroy Circular after Kansas Senator Samuel C. Pomeroy, who initiated it, this was a public letter that criticized the Lincoln presidency and openly advocated replacing him with Treasury Secretary Salmon P. Chase. As a "trial balloon," it backfired and discredited Chase as a rival to Lincoln. 2. In 1864, the Republican Party redesignated itself as the National Union Party to attract War Democrats.

THE SINKING OF THE HOUSATONIC.

ORDER BY ADMIRAL DAHLGREN.

MARCH 6
PORT ROYAL HARBOR, S.C., FEB. 10

ORDER No. 50. — The Housatonic has just been torpedoed by a rebel David, and sunk almost instantly.[1]

It was at night, and the water smooth.

The success of this undertaking will, no doubt, lead to similar attempts along the whole line of blockade.

If vessels on blockade are at anchor, they are not safe, particularly in smooth water, without outriggers and hawsers, stretched around with rope netting, dropped in the water.

Vessels on inside blockade had better take post outside at night, and keep underweigh,

until these preparations are completed.

All the boats must be on the patrol when the vessel is not in movement.

The commanders of vessels are required to use their utmost vigilance — nothing less will serve. I intend to recommend to the Navy Department the assignment of a large reward, as prize money, to crews or vessels who shall capture or, beyond doubt, destroy one of these torpedo boats.

JOHN A. DAHLGREN, REAR ADMIRAL, COMMANDING SOUTH ATLANTIC BLOCKADING SQUADRON. ✵

1. "David boats" were small steam-propelled vessels that ran on the surface and employed spar torpedoes in an effort to sink blockading ships. The vessel that sunk the Housatonic on February 17, 1864, however, was not a David boat, but the submarine H. L. Hunley.

THE ARMY OF THE POTOMAC. ARRIVAL OF GEN. GRANT.

MARCH 11

HEADQUARTERS ARMY OF THE POTOMAC,
THURSDAY, MARCH 10

Gen. GRANT and staff arrived here to-day, at 3 o'clock P.M. Gen. MEADE being slightly indisposed, Gens. [Andrew A.] HUMPHREY[S] and [Rufus] INGALLS met him at Brandy Station, whence the party proceeded to headquarters in carriages.

On their arrival in camp, the band of the One Hundred and Fourteenth Pennsylvania Regiment struck up "Hail to the Chief!" with other patriotic airs.[1]

It was raining very fast at the time, which prevented such a demonstration as would otherwise have been made.

The Lieutenant-General dined with Gen. MEADE, and the evening was spent in social converse. It is understood that the visit of Gen. GRANT will be extended over three or four days.

A letter from the Army of the Potomac says that an order has been issued directing that all ladies within the lines shall leave as early as practicable, and that no more passes shall be granted to such visitors[2].... ✣

1. Though commonly used to greet the President, this tune was not established as the formal Presidential march until 1954. The use of it here was not intended as a challenge to Lincoln's leadership.

2. During the winter months, it was not uncommon for friends, relatives, and entrepreneurs of all types to visit the army camp. When spring arrived and the campaigning began again, these visitors were expelled.

THE DECLINATION OF MR. CHASE.

MARCH 12

Secretary CHASE has done himself new honor in refusing to let his name be longer used in connection with the Presidential nomination. His letter to the member of the Ohio Senate is very timely, and in all respects very appropriate. He defers gracefully to the almost unanimous decision of the Union members of the Legislature of his own State in favor of the reelection of President LINCOLN; and thus, without unduly sacrificing any honorable ambition, prevents all use of his popularity for any purpose calculated to generate discord among loyal men.

We say loyal men, and not Union party, for we agree with Mr. CHASE that "persons and even parties are nothing in comparison with the great work to be accomplished." The term Union party is really a misnomer. Strictly speaking there is no such organization. For a party is political, and has to deal with politics. But the saving of the nation from the rebellion that has threatened to destroy it is not a matter of politics, any more than the saving of a man's life is to him a matter of business. A party has to do with the mere administration of a government, not with the vital concern of its life or death. The Union party, so called, is in fact nothing more than the great loyal body of the Northern people, who are opposed to the rebellion, and are loyally sustaining the Government in its efforts to put the rebellion down. It is made up of men of all the former parties; and they still have different opinions in regard to the scanty remnants of the old party issues which the war has now swept out of sight forever. The so-called party lives only in the war which is rescuing the nation; and it will come to an end whenever the war comes to an end. It acts for the emergency only. When that is over, and the Republic is once more safe, political parties will again form themselves, and contend, as in former time, for certain political principles on which the Government shall be administered. It is grossly wrong to speak of the Union men of the country as constituting a party, in the sense ordinarily attached to the term. They have an infinitely higher purpose and aim than any which either party spirit or party principle can prompt. They work not that the Government should be managed in this way or that, but that we may have a Government to be managed at all.

Mr. CHASE delivers himself in his letter as a statesman and a patriot, who appreciates the difference between the public duties of this day and the mere political duties of ordinary times. Recognizing that the hearts of the great mass of the loyal people are set upon the retention of ABRAHAM LINCOLN at the head of affairs, and that the persistent efforts of a handfull of politicians to put forward his own name, with an adverse political bearing, were engendering dissension where there ought to be completest harmony, he makes an end of every chance of difficulty by this distinct refusal to be longer considered a Presidential candidate. The magnanimous patriotism will be well noted and remembered by all good loyal men; for there never was a time when the public were more keenly appreciative of genuine public devotion.

This act of Secretary CHASE is all the more to be hailed because it insures his continuance in the position whose extremely responsible duties he is discharging with masterly ability. Though there has not yet been the slightest misunderstanding, or coolness, between him and the President, in consequence of the fact that their names were, of late, so frequently arrayed against each other in connection with the Baltimore nomination, yet there is no denying that a new relation was thus springing up between the two, which might have become so delicate and embarrassing before the meeting of the convention three months hence, as would have been almost intolerable to the sensitive nature of Mr. CHASE, and have constrained him to resign his present place, even against the most urgent remonstrances of the President. No two men, even though of the very highest disinterestedness and singleness of purpose, and most cordial mutual friendship, would willingly be kept in such intimate official connection, when others were scheming to make them rivals and competitors. Even if the two should understand and trust each other thoroughly, there would inevitably be constant misconstruction by the public at large, which no high-souled public man will endure, if there is a way to avoid it. Mr. CHASE, we are very sure, would have found that way by resignation. The withdrawal of his name from all association with the Baltimore nomination relieves the country of all danger of its losing the services of the man who, of all others, is best qualified to manage its finances. He is comparatively young yet — only fifty-six — and the nation will have ample opportunity hereafter, if he lives, to advance him to its highest position.

Much importance has been attached by some of the special adherents of Mr. CHASE to the supposition that he would be more thorough, or as they like to call it, more radical in his public policy than Mr. LINCOLN. The simple truth is, that all this talk of conservatism and radicalism has very little to justify it. It is supported by no essential distinction. The difference, so far as there is any at all, is but a difference in time. President LINCOLN, perhaps, has not been so rapid in his striking at the roots of the rebellion as some other men would have been. He has been circumspect when others, perhaps, would have gone in at a venture on the instant. But nothing has been lost by this prudence, and much gained. The work against Slavery is just as effectually and thoroughly accomplished, and yet public opinion has had time to enlighten and establish itself. Thus the extirpation of Slavery has gone on without any danger of reaction in its favor. The radical end is practically realized, alike whether the Executive Chair is filled by Mr. LINCOLN or by Mr. CHASE, or by some one who has the name of being even more radical than either. Moreover, the mere current of the war has far more to do with the shaping of public policy than have the preconceived theories of any man, or school of men. It is the war itself that has been our greatest schoolmaster — not moral text-books, nor political creeds. All men who have committed themselves to the war, that is to say, all men who are truly loyal, have found themselves borne along, almost whether they would or no, to the same conclusions in respect to all the great questions of the day. The loyal man who distrusted the propriety of the preliminary Emancipation Proclamation eighteen months ago, has long ago accepted its wisdom; and so in respect to every other Anti-Slavery measure of the Government. The whole course of the war, from the outset, has been to bring all true war men, sooner or later, to the same position. For the friends of the war to quarrel about their relative rates of progress is as absurd as it is mischievous. ⊛

THE COMMAND OF THE ARMIES — IMPORTANT CHANGES.

MARCH 15

We publish to-day a highly important military order dated on Saturday last, at the War Department. The main provision of the order, and the only one which is of national scope and importance, is that which relieves Gen. HALLECK from the position of General-in-Chief of the Army, and assigns Lieut.-Gen. GRANT to the "command of the armies of the United States." We presume this order confers upon the new Lieutenant-General plenary powers as acting Chief of the National forces, subject, of course, to the approval of the President. If so it be, we are confident that it will give great and general satisfaction throughout the country.

As a corollary, we suppose, to this order, changes in the command of one, and in the organization of the other, of our two great armies have been made or are in progress. The Army of the Potomac, we learn unofficially, is being reorganized into three corps, which shall be commanded respectively by Gens. [Gouverneur] WARREN, [John] SEDGWICK and [Winfield S.] HANCOCK.[1] The late command of Lieut.-Gen. GRANT, designated as the "Military Division of the Mississippi and the armies therein," has been assigned to Gen. SHERMAN, (W. T.) and it has been enlarged by the addition of Arkansas to its former limits. Still greater unity of action would be secured were it extended southward to the Gulf of Mexico.

The country will look anxiously for speedy and happy results as the consequence of these fundamental changes in command. ⊛

1. The Times was correct. Hancock commanded the II Corps, Warren the V Corps, and Sedgwick the VI Corps. Ambrose Burnside commanded the IX Corps, which was technically separate from the Army of the Potomac because Burnside was senior to Meade by date of rank. After the campaign began, Burnside agreed to relinquish his seniority so that his corps could serve under Meade.

THE FREED NEGROES OF LOUISIANA.

HAPPY CONDITION OF THE NEGROES — SUCCESS OF THE NEW LABOR REGULATIONS.

MARCH 21

CORRESPONDENCE OF THE NEW-YORK TIMES.
NEW-ORLEANS, THURSDAY, MARCH 10

Here, in Louisiana, wonders have been wrought. A few months ago, to find a negro who could read was a wonder; to find one who could write was a greater wonder, and to find one who understood arithmetic was a greater wonder still. Fortunately, a good Providence has seen fit to ordain better things, and now here, in this sin-cursed city, nineteen hundred colored children are reading and writing in the day schools which they attend.

One year ago, Col. HANKS[1] was feeding from the Government Commissariat more than twenty thousand negroes. Beside this number, there were quite fifteen thousand who hung around the camps and elsewhere, obtaining their living partly by cooking, washing, fishing and stealing; yet these were, to a large extent, an incubus upon the Government.

Now all the negroes have been placed in a condition of profit to the Government and to themselves. Not only does the labor system furnish employment to those within the limits of this department, but had we ten thousand more they could all be employed without expense, but rather with great benefit to the Government.

The benefits that will return to the Government this year, resulting from the operations of this system of labor, will more than pay all the expense that the refugee negroes have been to it since the occupation of the State by our forces.

Facts furnish the best proof of the success of any system; and, when we compare the condition of fifty thousand negroes in this State last year with their condition now, we need hardly allude to a thousand particulars.... ⊛

1. Colonel George H. Hanks was the superintendent of freedmen's affairs in Louisiana.

THE RESTORATION OF ARKANSAS.

MARCH 21

Arkansas has given a larger vote for the Union than even Louisiana, and is also ahead of her in the adoption of a Free State Constitution.[1] Though the latest reduced "Confederate" State, it is yet the first of any to reconstitute itself on a Free State basis. It has been admirably prompt both in deciding and executing. Undoubtedly the chief cause of this superior promptitude over Louisiana and Tennessee is the fact that the slave population of the State has been at no time more than one third as large. On account of the comparative newness of the country, the large slaveholders were comparatively very few, and the great majority of the people had no slaves at all. It was only by the most villainous chicanery that the Secession Convention was elected which professed to take Arkansas out of the Union. Slavery did not supply the same stimulus in that State that it did in some of the others. It is not at all strange that when brought back by force, she so much more readily accepts the result, and adapts her social system to the new order of things.

There has been some apprehension that a disagreement which has existed to some extent between the Military Commander, Gen. [Frederick] STEELE, and some of the leading citizens, respecting the best plan of restoration, would delay, if not absolutely frustrate, the movement. But the largeness of the vote given, and the decisiveness of the majority, evince that these dissensions were brought happily to an end; and the path now seems to be perfectly clear to the early and complete fulfillment of the will of the people just expressed. The Legislature will meet next month to elect Senators to Congress; the election has already taken place for Representatives to the House. The whole machinery of the State Government will soon be in operation throughout all parts of the State which have been reclaimed from rebel control, now amounting to nearly four-fifths. The rebel authorities are not blind to the fact that Arkansas is about to pass forever from their grasp, and have again put Gen. [Stirling] PRICE in the supreme command of the department, in order to make one last desperate effort for its recovery. We have no belief, however, that the demonstration will be pushed to any great length. It is too palpably impracticable for even rebel insanity to entertain seriously for any long period. PRICE, who has so often failed before in his operations upon that region, will find himself, after such a development and organization of Union feeling, baffled worse than ever.

The vote of Louisiana upon a Free State Constitution takes place next month, as does also that of Maryland. Tennessee will also pass upon the same question before the end of May. We may confidently reckon that before the Spring closes four Slave States will have become transformed by organic law into Free States, leaving but nine still under the thrall of the institution. Kentucky alone of the loyal States will enjoy the unenviable distinction of adhering to a relic of barbarism which is uniformly spurned by every regenerated rebel State, as incompatible with true devotion to the Union. As our arms advance, and the remaining rebel States successively yield to the old flag, beyond all doubt a Free State Government will be adopted in each. This result will be brought about with less difficulty in some than in others, but it is sure to come, sooner or later, to all alike. It will come not simply by the military effect of the President's Proclamation. It will obtain a more important sanction yet from the direct political action of the people. Arkansas was included in the Emancipation Proclamation; and, so far as that momentous document could avail, the freedom of the slave was already secured. Yet that did not hinder the people of Arkansas from ratifying, with the President's own approval, this extinction of Slavery in the State. Just such a popular ratification will be given in every other reclaimed State — destroying the last chance for cavilling against the legal effect of the proclamation, which the enemies of the

---

THE RED RIVER EXPEDITION.
SUCCESSFUL OPERATIONS ON THE ATCHAFALYA.
A BRILLIANT PIECE OF 'YANKEE' STRATEGY.

MARCH 25

CINCINNATI, THURSDAY, MARCH 24
A dispatch from Cairo says: "We have good news from the Red River expedition, which comes from undoubted authority.

Gen. A. J. SMITH landed his forces from transports a few miles below Fort De Russey. The rebel Gen. DICK TAYLOR[1] promptly marched against him with his whole force, and attacked him in his rear.

Gen. SMITH, instead of attempting to keep up communication with the river, proceeded by forced marches toward the fort.

When TAYLOR saw the trick, he started for the same destination, and for a time the race seemed doubtful. But finally the Yankees came in about three hours ahead, capturing the fort and eleven guns, four of them Parrotts, one an eleven inch and several thirty-two pounders, and also 300 prisoners.

This gives Gen. SMITH a strong foothold in the country, and will enable Admiral PORTER to proceed to Alexandria with his gunboats without opposition."[2] ❧

1. Confederate Major General Richard Taylor (1826–1879) was the youngest major general in the rebel army and the son of former president Zachary Taylor.
2. Rear Admiral David D. Porter called Smith's capture of Fort DeRussy "one of the best military moves made [in] this war." It was, however, the last good news to come from Louisiana. For the next month there was almost no news at all, since information had to travel down the Red River, then up the Mississippi to Cairo, then by telegraph to New York, or else downriver to New Orleans and then to New York by steamboat. Not until the last week of April did readers of learn the fate of this expedition. See articles dated April 24 and April 30.

President have denounced with such bitterness.

The President's method of reconstruction may now be considered to be "in the full tide of successful experiment." It is progressing with every promise of complete success. Every new application of it only furnishes new evidence of its wisdom. It will soon, we believe, be universally recognized to be the only true way — the way at once perfectly safe and perfectly effective. ✸

1. The new constitution of Arkansas was written in accordance with Lincoln's so-called Ten Percent Plan: Whenever ten percent of the voting population of any state agreed to denounce secession and ban slavery, delegates could be selected to write a new state constitution. A new Arkansas constitution was ratified under U.S. army oversight on March 4, 1864. It abolished slavery but (like Louisiana's) it did not define the rights of former slaves. It lasted until 1868, when it was replaced by a more "radical" document that granted civil rights to blacks. That document was replaced in 1874, when conservatives came back into power. The 1874 constitution is still in effect.

Rear Admiral David Dixon Porter, U.S. navy.

PRESIDENTIAL PROCLAMATION.
THE AMNESTY PROCLAMATION DEFINED.

BY THE PRESIDENT OF
THE UNITED STATES OF AMERICA:
WASHINGTON, MARCH 26

A PROCLAMATION.

Whereas, it has become necessary to define the cases in which insurgent enemies are entitled to the benefits of the Proclamation of the President of the United States, which was made on the 8th day of December, 1863, and the manner in which they shall proceed to avail themselves of these benefits; and whereas the objects of that proclamation were to suppress the insurrection and to restore the authority of the United States; and whereas the amnesty therein proposed by the President was offered with reference to these objects alone.

Now, therefore, I, ABRAHAM LINCOLN, President of the United States, do hereby proclaim and declare that the said Proclamation does not apply to the cases of persons who, at the time when they seek to obtain the benefits thereof by taking the oath thereby prescribed, are in military, naval or civil confinement or custody, or under bonds, or on parole of the civil, military or naval authorities, or agents of the United States, as prisoners of war, or person detained for offences of any kind, either before or after conviction, and that on the contrary, it does apply only to those persons who, being yet at large, and free from any arrest, confinement or duress, shall voluntarily come forward and take the said oath, with the purpose of restoring peace and establishing the national authority.

MARCH 28

Persons excluded from the amnesty offered in the said Proclamation may apply to the President for clemency, like all other offenders, and their application will receive due consideration.

I do further declare and proclaim that the oath presented in the aforesaid Proclamation of the 8th of December, 1863, may be taken and subscribed before any commissioned officer, civil, military or naval, in the service of the United States, or any civil or military officer of a State or Territory, not in insurrection, who by the laws thereof, may be qualified for administering oaths.

All officers who receive such oaths are hereby authorized to give certificates thereon, the persons respectively by whom they are made, and such officers are hereby required to transmit the original records of such oaths at as early a day as may be convenient, to the Department of State, where they will be deposited and remain in the archives of the Government.

The Secretary of State will keep a registry thereof, and will on application, in proper cases, issue certificates of such records in the customary form of official certificates.

In testimony whereof I have hereunto set my hand and caused the Seal of the United States to be affixed. Done at the City of Washington [L.S.] the 26th day of March, in the year of our Lord 1864, and of the Independence of the United States the Eighty-eighth.

BY THE PRESIDENT, ABRAHAM LINCOLN. ✸

MR. LINCOLN'S RE-ELECTION AND REBEL
DISCOURAGEMENT.

APRIL 1

In a speech just delivered in Portland, Gen. NEAL DOW,[1] who for nine months has been a prisoner at Richmond and other points, detailing his personal observations, made the statement that "at present the rebels are looking anxiously at movements at the North in relation to the next Presidential election, and their hope is that some other man than Mr. LINCOLN may be nominated and elected." He testified that they would regard the election of any other person as a sure indication that the loyal North tires of the war and means

to change its policy. This special spite of the rebel press against President LINCOLN, has long indicated the same thing. His "tyranny," as it is termed, is uniformly treated as the special motive power of the war. Their fixed idea is, that if an end could somehow be made of that, the war itself would speedily come to an end. This idea, doubtless, springs quite as much from blind feeling as from sober thought. When a man is hard pressed, he is apt to fancy that a change of any sort would bring relief. So long as a change is in ☞

prospect, even though there may be nothing promising in it, he yet is very sure to keep up his hope by imagining that somehow it may turn to his advantage. This is as true of a whole people as of an individual. It is human nature. There has never been a people so unimaginative and unimpassioned that it did not have some influence over them. It always operates, more or less, even though reason is dead against it.

But in this case reason is not dead against it. Just the contrary. If ABRAHAM LINCOLN shall be superseded by the nominee of the Democratic party, there would almost surely be an abatement of the war, and a resort to negotiation. The rebels would understand that this negotiation, once begun, would result, sooner or later, in securing their independence. It might take a long while to clear the way for this consummation, but it would in all probability be reached before the Copperhead Presidency ended. The war once suspended would never be resumed....

The reelection of President LINCOLN by the unanimous vote of all the vast loyal majority of the North, would do more than anything else to shut off the last hope of the rebels. His war policy, developed through three years, and thoroughly tested, needs only the complete ratification of the people to stand as an adamantine barrier against all possibility of "Confederate" independence. It would confront the rebels like doom itself. Though yet only foreshadowed, the rebels even now shrink from it. The political event which, of all others, they most deprecate, is the election of ABRAHAM LINCOLN to a second term of office. As it is with them, so is it with their Northern sympathizers. ✪

FORREST'S RAID. THE CAPTURE OF UNION CITY — THE REPULSE AT PADUCAH.

APRIL 1

CORRESPONDENCE OF THE CHICAGO TIMES.
CAIRO, SUNDAY, MARCH 27,

The rebel Gen. [Nathan Bedford] FORREST is again on the rampage through Western Kentucky and Tennessee, plundering, burning, killing and doing whatever other damage he can to the rebel cause. Last Wednesday afternoon, about 3 o'clock, Gen. [Mason] BRAYMAN, Commander of the District of Cairo, received information from Col. [Isaac R.] HAWKINS, of the Seventh Tennessee Cavalry, in command at Union City, that FORREST was reported to be advancing with seven thousand men. Gen. BRAYMAN advised the Colonel to hold his position, if attacked; that he would join him in the course of twenty-four hours, if necessary, with two thousand men....

The expedition went within six miles of Union City, where the General was informed that Col. HAWKINS had surrendered his whole force, amounting to four hundred, at eleven o'clock A.M., and had been carried off in the direction of Paducah.

Deeming it useless to proceed any further, the General and his men returned. A negro who escaped reported that the Seventh Tennessee, who were within fortifications, repulsed the enemy, who numbered about one thousand mounted men, twice, when they came up with a flag of truce, saying, if the Federals would not surrender, they would open on them with artillery. No reliable information concerning the capitulation has been received....

By some, Col. HAWKINS is very much censured for not maintaining the fight longer, but it must be remembered that the enemy greatly outnumbered him. He was captured once before by FORREST, but, then, as in this instance, he could not contend against such great odds.[1]

Last Friday night information reached us that FORREST had made his appearance at Paducah at 2 P.M. with 2,000 men, and had begun an attack on that city. Col. [Stephen G.] HICKS, commander of the post, withdrew all his men, some 800, into the fort [Fort Anderson], and sent the citizens across the river to the Illinois side. The telegraph operator at Mound City said he could see a great light in the direction of Paducah, and supposed the city was in flames.[2]... ✪

Major General Nathan Bedford Forrest, C.S.A.

1. Brigadier General Neal Dow (1804–1897) was wounded during the Union assault on Port Hudson on May 27, 1863. Sent to a nearby plantation to convalesce, he was captured there by Confederates in early July. He was imprisoned for eight months in Richmond, and exchanged for Confederate General William H. Fitzhugh Lee, son of Robert E. Lee, on February 25, 1864.

1. Colonel Hawkins's unit was composed of 272 Tennessee Unionists. They were captured by a force variously estimated at from 2,500 to 6,000. Perhaps because Forrest's men considered them traitors to Tennessee, they were harshly treated, robbed of their personal possessions, and forced to march to Alabama with little food.

2. Forrest took several hundred horses, but he did not burn the town.

WILL THE EMANCIPATED NEGROES INTERFERE WITH NORTHERN LABOR?

APRIL 3

To the Editor of the New-York Times:

No more effectual outcry against the abolition of Slavery has been raised among our laboring population, than the one that the slaves, if emancipated, would come to the North, and would reduce the rate of wages. It was in vain that Democrats were assured of the improbability of such a result. The politician disregarded the facts, that the South was the natural home of the negro, that the slave sought the North only that he might escape from bondage, and that his labor would still be required in his native regions, when they should be brought under a system of freedom. At present laborers are greatly needed in the Northern States, and attempts have been made to procure help from the parts of the South that are occupied by our troops. Allow me to present you with an extract from a letter, written by a teacher of the American Missionary Association, and dated from Fortress Monroe. It effectually answers the objection to which I have referred. I am,

WM. HAMILTON,
AGENT OF THE A. M. ASSOCIATION.

"I should have replied to yours before; but I hoped that by delaying I might be able to say I had found some of the young men inquired for. On two successive Sabbaths I have publicly mentioned the main subject of your letter, and of others similar in character, requesting that if any young men would like to go North for good wages and with the assurance of receiving kind treatment, they should report themselves to me on Monday or early in the week; but, up to the present time, not one has appeared to confer with me on the subject.

"Our people here are adverse to going North. They feel that the South is their home; and they suppose that at the North they would be regarded as nothing the better for their color. Besides, the male part of our population have employment hereabouts. So many are in the army or otherwise engaged in Government service, that to find men or boys ready and willing to work for us, even in Hampton, is not generally a very easy matter." ✹

THE BLACK FLAG.

HORRIBLE MASSACRES BY THE REBELS.

APRIL 16
CAIRO, THURSDAY, APRIL 14

On Tuesday morning the rebel Gen. FORREST attacked Fort Pillow. Soon after the attack FORREST sent a flag of truce demanding the surrender of the fort and garrison, meanwhile disposing of his force so as to gain the advantage. Our forces were under command of Major [Lionel F.] BOOTH, of the Thirteenth Tennessee (U.S.) Heavy Artillery, formerly of the First Alabama Cavalry.

The flag of truce was refused, and fighting resumed. Afterward a second flag came in, which was also refused.

Both flags gave the rebels advantage of gaining new positions. The battle was kept up until 3 P.M., when Major BOOTH was killed, and Major [William F.] BRADFORD took command.

The rebels now came in swarms over our troops, compelling them to surrender.

Immediately upon the surrender ensued a scene which utterly baffles description. Up to that time, comparatively few of our men had been killed; but, insatiate as fiends, bloodthirsty as devils incarnate, the Confederates commenced an indiscriminate butchery of the whites and blacks, including those of both colors who had been previously wounded.[1]

The black soldiers, becoming demoralized, rushed to the rear, the white officers having thrown down their arms.

Both white and black were bayoneted, shot or sabred; even dead bodies were horribly mutilated, and children of seven and eight years and several negro women killed in cold blood. Soldiers unable to speak from wounds were shot dead, and their bodies rolled down the banks into the river. The dead and wounded negroes were piled in heaps and burned, and several citizens who had joined our forces for protection were killed or wounded.

Out of the garrison of six hundred, only two hundred remained alive....

The steamer Platte Valley came up at about half-past 3 o'clock, and was hailed by the rebels under a flag of truce. Men were sent ashore to bury the dead, and take aboard such of the wounded as the enemy had allowed to live. Fifty-seven were taken aboard, including seven or eight colored. Eight died on the way up. The steamer arrived here this evening, and was immediately sent to the Mound City Hospital, to discharge her suffering cargo....

LATER: CAIRO, THURSDAY, APRIL 15

Two negro soldiers, wounded at Fort Pillow, were buried by the rebels, but afterward worked themselves out of their graves. They were among those brought up in the Platte Valley, and are now in hospital at Mound City.

The officers of the [steamship] Platte Valley receive great credit from the military authorities for landing at Fort Pillow, at eminent risk, and taking our wounded on board, and for their kind attentions on the way up. ✹

1. The Union garrison at Fort Pillow consisted of 557 soldiers: 295 white and 262 black.

An artist's recreation of the Fort Pillow Massacre.

THE MASSACRE AT FORT PILLOW.

OFFICIAL CONFIRMATION OF THE REPORT.

APRIL 18

WASHINGTON, D.C., SATURDAY, APRIL 16

Yesterday afternoon, about 5 o'clock, dispatches were received here from Gen. SHERMAN, confirming the surrender of Fort Pillow, and the brutal conduct of the rebels immediately afterward, which bids fair to be amply retaliated in that quarter in due time.

The Star says:

"According to Gen. SHERMAN, our loss was fifty-three white troops killed, and one hundred wounded, and three hundred black troops murdered in cold blood after the surrender. Fort Pillow is an isolated post, of no value whatever to the defence of Columbus, and utterly untenable by the rebels, who have no doubt left that vicinity ere this, having been disappointed, with considerable loss, in the object of their raid thither, which was the capture of Columbus, whence they were promptly and severely repulsed with no loss to us. We are satisfied that due investigation will show that the loss of Fort Pillow was simply the result of a mistake of the local commander, who occupied it against direct orders a contingency incident to all wars."

"The rebels, according to official dispatches, received here last evening, effected nothing at Paducah, losing a soldier killed or wounded, for every horse they succeeded in stealing, and doing us no other damage than by a few thefts."

It is believed that FORREST's raiders will next appear in the vicinity of Memphis, where they can effect no more than at Columbus and Paducah, and stand a very fair chance, indeed, of finding themselves surrounded by overwhelming superior forces. ⊛

THE RED RIVER EXPEDITION. DETAILS OF THE RECENT BATTLES.

APRIL 24

CORRESPONDENCE OF THE NEW-YORK TIMES:
DEPARTMENT OF THE GULF,
NEW-ORLEANS, SATURDAY, APRIL 16

The history of the rebellion has had another fearful page added to its record. The gallant soldiers of the East and the West have, side by side, emulated each other in devotion to their country's cause; they have fallen side by side as they have together triumphed over the common enemy, and throughout all time the fire-side stories of the homes of those who live in the Upper Mississippi Valley will be details of how their fathers fought shoulder to shoulder for freedom along with their brothers of New-England homes.

No information has reached this city, of an official character, but there are continual arrivals of wounded, of prisoners, and intelligent persons attached to the steamers in the Red River trade. From all these witnesses have been gathered such particulars as we have of the battles of the 7th, 8th and 9th.[1] The account published in the New-Orleans Era, of the 14th inst., from my most intimate acquaintance with the country where the battles took place, seems to be justly entitled to precedence, and from that source I am almost entirely indebted for the details of the battles.

The country lying between Grand Ecore, which is the river landing of Nactchedotches and Shreveport, one hundred miles in extent, is not alluvial but level land, broken by slightly elevated ridges, bisected in places by bayous, which empty into Red River. The distance between the Shreveport road and the river varies from five to ten miles, which intervening land is almost entirely composed of impenetrable swamp. It is therefore perceivable that the gunboats are useless to the army after it leaves Grand Ecore. The whole distance from Nactchedotches to Shreveport is more or less a low sandy ridge, broken by straggling forests of pine and scrub oaks. Crump's Mills consists of one or two miserable houses, and there are no settlements, the plantations that once existed having been long abandoned, until you get to Pleasant Hill, which is a little village situated on a low ridge, containing in place times probably 300 inhabitants. Just beyond the town are still the marks of the track of a hurricane that, some two years ago, nearly destroyed every house in the place. This drift is lower than the ridge on which the town is built; it is very dense, the road having been cut through the fallen timber and the sandhills, which were thrown up by the roots of the trees. On the left of Pleasant Hill, and on the right, up to the edge of the "drift," are abandoned plantations, here and there covered with groups of low, second growth pine. Passing on, you come to WILSON's plantation — a place of cleared land on each side of the road, surrounded by dense woods. Just beyond are Bayou de Paul and the old Sabine Road, which make the place by nature a strong military position. Two miles beyond WILSON's is Mansfield, the shire town of De Soto Parish, a very pretty place, containing 800 inhabitants.

Our army broke up its encampment on the 6th inst., and marched along the Shreveport Road twenty-one miles, the cavalry in advance, resting at Crump's Mills, the supporting infantry some four miles in the rear, on a pleasant bayou, famous for affording good spring water in its vicinity. On the morning of the next day, the 7th, at daylight, the cavalry started, and ere it had gone two miles, commenced heavy skirmishing with the enemy. This running fight was kept up for fourteen miles, until our cavalry passed through the drift above Pleasant Hill, and reached the open fields, known as WILSON's plantation. Here was a heavy body of rebel infantry, 2,500 strong, deployed along the edges of the woods, by which disposition our men were, to avoid them, compelled to charge over the abandoned fields. The only Union soldiers that had advanced far enough to take part in the fight, which was inevitable, was the cavalry brigade of [Albert L.] LEE's corps, commanded by Col. HARAI ROBINSON. As he had either to attack or be attacked, he decided to take the initiative, and he led his men in with such a dash and vigor, that at last the enemy was completely whipped and driven from the field. This engagement lasted two hours and a half, and our losses amounted to about forty killed and wounded, the enemy's being at least as many. Col. ROBINSON pursued the retreating rebels as far as Bayou de Paul, where he found they had received heavy reinforcements, including four pieces of artillery, and were again in line of battle waiting attack. As it was nearly dark, and the risk was too great in again attacking with his small force, he placed his men in the most advantageous position available, and awaited the progress of events.

Early on the following morning, the 8th, the cavalry, supported by a brigade of infantry, under Col. [William J.] LANDRUM, resumed its march. The enemy was discovered to be on the alert, and a battle almost instantly commenced. Col. LANDRUM's infantry brigade was on the right of the road, and Col. [Thomas] LUCAS' cavalry brigade on the left. The skirmishing was very fierce, and every foot of ground won from the enemy had to be taken by hard knocks, but at two o'clock in the afternoon our forces had compelled the enemy to retreat beyond Pleasant Hill. Our loss, as well as the enemy's, was very severe during this time. Lieut.-Col. WEBB, of the Seventy-seventh Illinois, shot through the head and instantly killed, and Capt. BREESE, commanding Sixth Missouri Cavalry, severely wounded in the arm, being among the casualties on our side.

From the constantly increasing severity of the fighting, it was evident that a large force of the enemy was near, as it was subsequently ascertained that Gens. DICK TAYLOR, [Alfred] MOUTON, [Tom] GREEN, and [Sterling] PRICE were present with a command of not less than 18,000 men, while our force by comparison was nothing.[2]

The rebels occupied a strong position in the vicinity of Sabine Cross Roads, concealed in the edge of a dense wood, with an open field in front, the Shreveport road passing through their lines. Gen. [T. E. G.] RANSOM, arriving on the field with his command, formed his line as well as circumstances would permit, after reconnoitering and feeling the rebel position. Col. [Frank] EMERSON's brigade, of the Thirteenth Corps, was Stationed on the left of the line, with [Ormand] NIM's Massachusetts Battery. Col. LANDRUM's forces, parts at two brigades on the right and centre, with RAWLE's Battery G, Fifth Regulars, and a battery of the First Indiana Artillery in rear of his right and centre. Col. [N.A.M.] DUDLEY's brigade of cavalry, of LEE's corps, supported the left and held itself in readiness to repel any attempt to flank; while LUCAS protected the right flank. Col. ROBINSON, with his brigade, was in rear of the centre, protecting the wagon train which was on the Shreveport road.

Gen. BANKS and Staff rode upon the field by the time this disposition of our forces was effected, and word was sent back to Gen. [William B.] FRANKLIN to make all speed for the scene of the momentarily expected battle. It was the design of Gen. BANKS to remain quiet until the remainder of his army came up, and then open the battle himself; but [Confederate General Edmund] KIRBY SMITH, knowing his own superiority of numbers, began the conflict before they could arrive.

About 5 o'clock the firing between the skirmishers become very hot, and in a short time our skirmish line was driven back upon the main body by an overwhelming force. The whole strength of the enemy was then advanced and heavy and repeated volleys were discharged and replied to on our right and centre. Soon this portion of our line became heavily engaged, and all our available strength was required to prevent their being crushed by the masses of the enemy. Our left, which was now, also, hotly fighting, was necessarily much weakened, and it was observed that a strong body of the enemy was massing in a dense piece of woods, preparatory to dashing down and flanking this end of our line. The danger was plain and imminent, but there was no remedy. Gen. [Charles P.] STONE[3] ordered Gen. LEE to have NIM's battery withdrawn, although it was doing great execution, in order that it might not become a prize to the enemy, and Gen. LEE sent his Aid-de-Camp, Col. J. S. BRISBIN, to withdraw the battery. On reaching the point, its removal was found impossible, nearly every one of the horses having been killed. In a few moments more a solid mass of the rebels, under command of Gen. MOUTON, swept down upon the spot and four of the guns were taken, the other two being dragged from the field by hand. The havoc made in the ranks of the enemy at this point of the action is represented as appalling, the whole six guns belching forth double charges of grape and canister; and some five or six rounds were fired between the time the rebels left the woods until the artillerymen were forced from their pieces. As the rebels were in mass, the execution such a shower of missiles caused can be easily imagined. MOUTON fell mortally wounded. The two senior officers of NIMS' battery were wounded, Lieut. SNOW mortally, he having since died.

The fighting on all parts of our line was now at short range, and to use the expression of one of the participants, "we were holding on by the skin of our teeth only." It was known that FRANKLIN's troops had been sent for, and anxious and wistful were the glances cast to the rear. Gen. [Robert] CAMERON, with his brigade came up, and going at once into action on the right, where the battle again waxed hottest, created the impression that the veterans of the Nineteenth had arrived, and a glad and exultant shout went up from our wearied and desperately situated little band. This belief was strengthened by the arrival of Gen. FRANKLIN, who dashed boldly into the thickest of the fray, cap in hand and cheering on the men. Gen. BANKS, too, seemed ubiquitous, riding wherever the men wavered, and by personal example inciting them to renewed deeds of daring and reckless valor. Cols. [John S.] CLARK and [James] WILSON, with other members of the staff, sabre in hand, mixed with the soldiers on foot and horseback, and cheered and encouraged them to continue the unequal fight.

But human beings could not longer withstand such fierce and overpowering onslaughts as our men were bearing up against, and our line finally gave way at all points, and the men fell back fiercely contesting the ground they yielded. Unfortunately a sad mishap befell them at this time. The large and cumbersome wagon train blocked up the way; the frightened horses dashed through the infantry lines, entangled themselves with the artillery, and created a momentary but unfortunate confusion. This gave the rebels, who were rapidly pressing us, possession of several pieces of artillery.

The enemy followed our men step by step for three and a half miles but he was advancing to meet a fearful retribution. The Nineteenth Army Corps had been ordered to stop and form its line of battle — the retreating Union troops passed through this line and formed in the rear. The rebels thinking they had repulsed our whole army, dashed impetuously on, and thought the line, but half visible in the woods before them, was another feeble but desperate stand of a few men.

Gen. EMORY commanded this force, consisting of two full brigades, and he ordered the fire to be reserved until the rebels were within short range, when from both infantry and the artillery posted thickly along his line, a storm of iron and lead was hurled upon the foe that literally mowed them down. The rebels halted in amazement, but still they fought and bravely. Volley after volley was discharged from each side full into ☞

the ranks of their opponents, but neither gave signs of yielding, and night charitably threw her mantle over the ghastly scene, and enforced a cessation of hostilities.

The two divisions, under command of Gen. A.J. SMITH, belonging to the Sixteenth and Seventeenth Army Corps, had reached Pleasant Hill, and were there halted. Gen. BANKS determined to withdraw his army to that point, for the sake of the advantageous position which he could there occupy, knowing that the enemy would follow what they supposed to be a demoralized army. In accordance with this plan of operations, all our men were quietly withdrawn from the enemy's front, and the line of march taken up for Pleasant Hill. This conjunction of his forces was satisfactorily effected, and the result confidently awaited. So well was the movement conducted that although the first body started at 10 o'clock, and the remainder were not under way until

Major General Nathaniel P. Banks, U.S.A.

nearly day, the rebels had not the slightest suspicion of what was going on.

Gen. FRANKLIN was conspicuous during this part of the day, rallying his men, and two horses were killed under him; Capt. CHAPMAN, of his staff, had both feet taken off by a round shot, and the horse of Capt. FRANKLIN was killed at the same time.

THE THIRD DAY'S FIGHT
[BATTLE OF PLEASANT HILL, APRIL 9]

At 7 o'clock on Saturday morning our forces were all at Pleasant Hill, and the rebels were advancing, cavalry in front, endeavoring to discover our position. Col. O. P. GOODING, with his brigade of LEE's cavalry corps, was sent out on the Shreveport road, to meet the enemy and draw him on. He had gone about a mile, when he came upon the rebel advance. Skirmishing immediately ensued, and according to the plan he slowly fell back. The fight was very sharp between these cavalry bodies, and GOODING lost nearly forty men killed and wounded, inflicting, however, as much damage as he received. Among his casualties are Capt. BECKER and Lieut. HALL, of the Second New-York Veteran Cavalry. Lieut. HALL has since died of his wounds, Col. GOODING made a narrow escape, a ball passing through and tearing out the crown of his hat, and grazing the skin. The brigade behaved very gallantly, covering Gen. [William] EMORY's front until his line was formed.

The battle-field of Pleasant Hill, as we have already described, is a large, open field, which had once been cultivated, but is now overgrown with weeds and bushes. The slightly-elevated centre of the field, from which the name Pleasant Hill is taken, is nothing more than a long mound, hardly worthy the name of hill. A semicircular belt of timber runs around the field on the Shreveport side. Gen. EMORY formed his line of battle on the side facing these woods, Gen. [James] MCMILLAN's brigade being posted on the right, Gen. [William] DWIGHT's on the centre, and Col. [Lewis] BENEDICT's on the left. TAYLOR's Battery, L. First Regulars, had four guns in rear of the left wing, on the left of the Shreveport road, and two on the road in rear of Gen. DWIGHT's line, HIBBERD's Vermont battery was on the right. In the rear of EMORY, and concealed by the rising ground were Gen. SMITH's tried troops, formed in two lines of battle fifty yards apart. All his

artillery was in the front line, a piece, section or battery being on the flank of each regiment, the infantry lying between them. The Thirteenth Corps was in reserve in the rear under Gen. CAMERON — Gen. RANSOM having been wounded the day before. Gen. SMITH was Commander-in-Chief of the two lines back of the crest, while Gen. MOWER was the immediate Commander of the men. The Commander of the right brigade in Gen. SMITH's first line was Col. LYNCH; the left brigade was Col. [William] SHAW's. The second line also consisted of two brigades — the right under control of Col. ____, and the left commanded by Col. HILL. CRAWFORD's Third Indiana Battery was posted on the right of the Eighty-ninth Indiana Infantry, and the Ninth Indiana Battery on the right of the line of battle. The Missouri Iron Sun Battery, and others whose names and numbers we could not ascertain, were also in this section of the battle.

The skirmishing was kept up with considerable vigor until about 5 o'clock in the afternoon, when the rebels had completed their arrangements for the attack. At about this hour Gen. EMORY's skirmish line was driven in on the right by the rebels, who appeared in large force, coming through the timber above-mentioned. They soon reached the open ground, and moved on to the attack in three lines of battle. Our batteries and infantry opened with terrible effect, doing great slaughter with grape and canister, while the enemy's artillery, being in the woods and in bad position, did scarcely any damage.

Col. BENEDICT's brigade on the left was first engaged, soon followed by DWIGHT's and MCMILLAN's. The fighting was terrific — old soldiers say it never was surpassed for desperation. Notwithstanding the terrible havoc in their ranks, the enemy pressed fiercely on, slowly pushing the men of the Nineteenth Corps back, up the hill, but not breaking their line of battle. A sudden and bold dash of the rebels on the right, gave them possession of TAYLOR's Battery, and forced our line still further back.

Now came the grand coup de main. The Nineteenth, on arriving at the top of the hill, suddenly filed off over the hill, and passed through the lines of Gen. SMITH. We must here mention that the rebels were now in but two lines of battle, the first having been almost annihilated by Gen. EMORY, what remained being forced back into the second line. But these two lines came on exultant, and sure of victory.

The first passed over the knoll, and all heedless of the long line of cannons and crouching forms of as brave men as ever trod mother earth, pressed on. The second line appeared on the crest, and the death signal was sounded. Words cannot describe the awful effect of this discharge. Seven thousand rifles, and several batteries of artillery, each gun with an extra load of grape and canister, were fired simultaneously, and the whole center of the rebel line was crushed down as a field of ripe wheat through which a tornado had passed. It is estimated that one thousand men were hurried into eternity or frightfully mangled by this one discharge.

No time was given them to recover their good order, but Gen. SMITH ordered a charge, and his men dashed rapidly forward, the boys of the Nineteenth joining in. The rebels fought boldly and desperately back to the timber, on reaching which a large portion, broke and fled, fully two thousand throwing aside their arms. In this charge TAYLOR's Battery was retaken, as were also two of the guns of NIM's Battery, the Parrott gun taken from us at Carrion Crow last Fall, and one or two others belonging to the rebels, one of which was considerably shattered, besides, 700 prisoners. A pursuit and desultory fight was kept up for three miles, when our men returned to the field of battle.

The accounts from all quarters agree in stating that Gen. BANKS, during the entire contest, showed the greatest possible daring and valor, as did Gen. FRANKLIN, and the staffs of each. They will reap their reward in the grateful hearts and prayers of the American people, and in the increased devotion and love of their soldiers.

Gen. RANSOM, when wounded, was directing the firing of the Chicago Battery, standing among the men, and he had scarcely been removed when the rebels were in possession of the spot on which he fell. This gallant officer, the youngest of his rank in the army, has been, I believe, now three times wounded. He is one of the men chosen by Gen. GRANT to give his celebrated unconditional surrender order. He now lies at the St. Charles Hotel, shot through the leg with a musket ball. He will most certainly recover.

Col. BRISBIN, of Gen. LEE's Staff, had his horse's head blown off while riding across the field, by a shell, and would have been taken had not some of the men pulled him out. He succeeded in capturing a rebel horse and leaving the field on his back. Col. BRISBIN lost in his trunk, in the baggage train, the sash taken from Gen. [William] BARKSDALE on the field at Gettysburgh, which had been made a present to him, and Gen. VILLEPIGUE's sabre, taken from him in Virginia.[4]

Col. ROBINSON, while defending the wagon train on the first day, was shot in the hip, but refused to leave the field for two hours after. It was supposed he would lose his leg in consequence, but the surgeons now think it can be saved. Among the most regretted of the slain is Col. BENEDICT of the One Hundred and Sixty-fifth New-York. ✸

1. The two principal confrontations were the Battles of Mansfield or Sabine Crossroads (April 8) a Confederate victory and Pleasant Hill (April 9), a tactical Union victory, but a strategic defeat since Banks decided to continue his retreat.
2. The Confederate army probably numbered no more than 7,000. Counting Franklin's corps, the Union army actually had superior numbers (around 12,000), but Franklin's men, in the rear of the column, did not get to the battlefield in time.
3. Charles P. Stone was Banks's chief of staff. It was his first active duty after his arrest following the Battle of Ball's Bluff (see Chapter 5). On April 4, 1864, Stanton rescinded Stone's volunteer commission as a brigadier general and he reverted to his rank of colonel. He served briefly as a brigade commander during the siege of Petersburg, but resigned from the army on September 13, 1864.
4. Brigadier General William Barksdale was mortally wounded on the battlefield at Gettysburg; Brigadier General John B. Villepigue of South Carolina died of pneumonia after the Battle of Corinth.

NAVAL OPERATIONS ON RED RIVER.
ADMIRAL PORTER'S OFFICIAL REPORT.

APRIL 30
MISSISSIPPI SQUADRON, FLAG-SHIP CRICKET, OFF GRAND ECORE, LA., APRIL 14

SIR:

I had the honor of reporting to you the movements of the squadron as far as Alexandria, and the intentions of Gen. BANKS to move on at once to Shreveport. He deemed the cooperation of the gunboats so essential to success, that I had to run some risks, and made unusual exertions to get them over the falls. The army started on the appointed day, and I pushed up the gunboats to cover them (if there should be need) as fast as they got over the falls. The vessels arrived at Grand Ecore without accident, and had good water, the river apparently about to reach its usual stage at this season.

The Cricket, Eastport, Mound City, Chillicothe, Carondolet, Pittsburgh, Ozark, Neosho, Osage, Lexington, Fort Hindman and Louisville were the vessels sent up, and a fleet of thirty transports followed them.

Grand Ecore was occupied by our forces without opposition — the works deserted. Lieut.-Commander [Seth Ledyard] PHELPS captured one 33-pounder on the river below Grand Ecore, which he destroyed, making twenty-two guns captured from the enemy since we entered the river. The army had arrived at Natchitoches, near Grand Ecore, when I got up here, and were preparing for an immediate march. As the river was rising very slowly, I would not risk the larger vessels by taking them higher up, but started on the 7th of April for Shreveport with the Cricket, Fort Hindman, Lexington, Osage, Neosho and Chillicothe, with the hope of getting the rest of the vessels along when the usual rise came. Twenty transports were sent along filled with army stores, and with a portion of Gen. A.J. SMITH's Division on board. It was intended that the fleet should reach Springfield Landing on the third day, and then communicate with the army, a portion of which expected to be at Springfield at that time.

I found the difficulties of navigation very great, but we reached the point specified within an hour of the time appointed. At this point we were brought to a stop; the enemy had sunk a very large steamer, the New Falls City, right across the river, her ends resting on each bank, and her hull broken ☞

in the middle, resting on the bottom. This was a serious obstruction, but I went to work to remove it. Before I commenced operations, however, a courier came in from Gen. BANKS, bringing the unpleasant and most unexpected news that "our army had met with a reverse," and was falling back to Pleasant Hill, some sixty miles in our rear. Orders also came to Gen. [Thomas] KILBY SMITH[1] to return to Grand Ecore with the transports and the troops he had with him. Here was an end to our expedition for the present, and we reluctantly turned back, after having nearly reached the object we were aiming at.

The information we received was of a very unsatisfactory kind, and we did not know really what was the exact state of affairs, no letters having been sent by post courier.

It would be very difficult to describe the return passage of the fleet through this narrow and shaggy river. As long as our army could advance triumphantly it was not so bad, but we had every reason to suppose that our return would be interrupted in every way and at every point by the enemy's land forces, and we were not disappointed. They commenced on us from the high banks of a place called Coushatta, and kept up a fire of musketry whenever an opportunity was offered them. By a proper distribution of the gunboats I had no trouble in driving them away, though from the high banks they could fire on our decks almost with impunity. As we proceeded down the river they increased in numbers, and as we only made thirty miles a day they could cross from point to point and be ready to

meet us on our arrival below. . . .

On the evening of the 12th instant we were attacked from the right bank of the river by a detachment of men of quite another character. They were a part of the army which two or three days previous had gained success over our army, and flushed with victory, or under the excitement of liquor, they appeared suddenly upon the right bank, and fearlessly opened fire on the Osage, Lieut.-Commander T. O. SELFRIDGE, (iron-clad,) she being hard aground at the time, with a transport (the Black Hawk) alongside of her, towing her off. The rebels opened with 2,000 muskets, and soon drove every one out of the Black Hawk to the safe casemates of the monitor. Lieut. [George] BACHE had just come from his vessel, (the Lexington,) and fortunately was enabled to pull up to her again, keeping close under the bank, while the Osage opened a destructive fire on these poor deluded wretches, who, maddened by liquor, and led on by their officers, were vainly attempting to capture an iron vessel. I am told that their hootings and actions baffle description. Force after force seemed to be brought up to the edge of the bank, where they confronted the guns of the iron vessel only to be mowed down by grapeshot and canister. In the mean time Lieut. BACHE had reached his vessel, and widening the distance between him and the Osage, he opened a cross-fire on the infuriated rebels, who fought with such desperation and courage against certain destruction that it could only be accounted for in one way. Our opinions were verified on inspection of some

of the bodies of the slain, the men actually smelling of Louisiana rum. The affair lasted nearly two hours before the rebels fled. They brought off two pieces of artillery, one of which was quickly knocked over by the Lexington's guns, the other they managed to carry off. The cross fire of the Lexington finally decided this curious affair of a fight between infantry and gunboats. The rebels were mowed down by her canister, and finally retreated in as quick haste as they had come to the attack, leaving the space of a mile covered with dead and wounded, and knapsacks. A dying rebel informed our men that Gen. GREEN had his head blown off, which I do not vouch for as true; if true, it is a serious loss to the rebels. Night coming on, we had no means of ascertaining the damage done to the rebels. We are troubled no more from the right bank of the river, and a party of five hundred men, who were marching to cut us off, were persuaded to change their mind after hearing of the unfortunate termination of the first expedition. That same night I ordered the transports to proceed, having placed the gunboats at a point where the rebels had a battery. All the transports were passed safely, the rebels not firing a shot in return to the many that were bursting over the bills.

The next morning, the 13th inst., I followed down myself, and finding at Canette, six miles from Grand, Ecore, by land, that they had got aground, and would be sometime getting through. I proceeded down in this vessel to Grand Ecore, and got Gen. BANKS to send up troops enough to keep tie

Admiral Porter's fleet crossing the dam at Alexandria during the Red River Campaign.

guerrillas away from the river. We were fired on as usual after we started down, but when I had the troops sent up, the transports came along without any trouble. This has been an expedition where a great deal of labor has been expended, a great deal of individual bravery shown, and on which occasions the Commander-in-Chief is apt to find out the metal of which his officers are made, and on future occasions it will enable him to select those who will not likely fall in the time offered. To Lieut.-Commander T.O. SEL-FRIDGE, commanding Osage, and Lieut. GEO. M. BACHE, commanding Lexington, I am particularly indebted for the gallant manner in which they defended their vessels, and for their management during the expedition, always anticipating and intelligently carrying out my wishes and orders.

I found the fleet at Grand Ecore somewhat in an unpleasant situation, two of them being above the bar and not likely to get away again this season, unless there is a rise of a foot. I could not provide against this when over a hundred miles up the river. If nature, does not change her laws, there will no doubt be a rise of water, but there was one year, 1846, when there was no rise in the Red River, and it may happen again. The rebels are cutting off the supply, by diverting different sources of water into other channels, all of which would have been stopped had our army arrived as far as Shreveport. I have done my best (and so have the officers and men under my command) to make this expedition a success throughout, and do not know that we have failed in anything we have undertaken. Had we not heard of the retreat of the army, I should have gone on to the end. A wise Providence, which rules and directs all things, has thought proper to stay our progress, and throw impediments in the way, for some good reason. We have nothing left but to try it again, and hold on to this country with all the force we can raise. It is just as valuable to us and important to the cause as any other portion of the Union. Those who have interests here, and are faithful to the Government, have a right to our protection, and when this point of Louisiana is conquered, we hold Arkansas and all the right bank of the Mississippi, without firing another gun.

There is a class of men who have during this war shown a good deal of bravery and patriotism, and who have seldom met with any notice from those whose duty it is to report such matters. I speak of the pilots on the Western waters. Without any hope of future reward through fame, or in a pecuniary way, they enter into the business of piloting the transports through dangers that would make a faint-hearted man quail. Occupying the most exposed position, a fair mark for a sharpshooter, they are continually fired at, and often hit, without so much as a mention being made of their gallantry. On this expedition they have been much exposed, and have shown great gallantry in managing their vessels while under fire, in this, to them, unknown river.

I beg leave to pay this small tribute to their bravery, and must say, as a class, I never knew a braver set of men. I beg leave to mention favorably Acting Master H. H. GARRINGE, commanding this vessel. He has shown great zeal, courage and ability during this expedition, serving his guns rapidly and well, at his post night and day, ready for anything, and assisting materially in getting the transports by dangerous points; mounting one of his two 10-pound howitzers on his upper deck, he was enabled to sweep the bank in all directions, and one or two fires had the desired effect. He was of great service to me throughout the expedition; was slightly wounded, but nothing of consequence, (owing to his exposing himself so much.) I have the honor to be, very respectfully, your obedient servant,

DAVID D. PORTER, REAR-ADMIRAL. ✪

1. Thomas Kilby Smith (1820–1887) commanded a division in Smith's corps. He should not be confused with Lieutenant General Edmund Kirby Smith (1824–1893), who commanded the Confederate Trans-Mississippi Department.

CHAPTER 19

"We Are Going on to Richmond, Depend Upon It"

MAY 1864

May of 1864 was the bloodiest month of the American Civil War. On May 4, the Army of the Potomac, officially under George Meade but supervised by Ulysses S. Grant, crossed the Rapidan River to inaugurate what has gone down in history as the "overland campaign." Lee's Army of Northern Virginia assailed it almost at once in the tangle of undergrowth south of the Rapidan called the Wilderness. For more than a month, the two armies slugged it out across the northern Virginia countryside, enduring combined casualties of nearly 100,000 men. At the same time, reports from the west showed that William T. Sherman had inaugurated his campaign in north Georgia, and from Louisiana came news of the denouement of Nathaniel Banks's expedition up the Red River. For readers of The Times, it was like a three-ring circus as Union armies seemed everywhere on the march.

It was all part of a deliberate strategy. Lincoln had been urging just such a coordinated offensive since the spring of 1862, but Grant was the first of his generals to achieve it. The principle worked particularly well in Virginia for on the same day that Meade's army crossed the Rapidan, General Franz Sigel in the Shenandoah Valley and General Ben Butler on the Virginia Peninsula moved forward as well. The idea was to compel Robert E. Lee to choose which of these thrusts to oppose. If he focused on one, the others could advance. As Lincoln famously put it: "Those not skinning can hold a leg."

In the end, Lee was able to focus on the Army of the Potomac because of missteps by both Sigel and Butler that blunted their offensives. Sigel was defeated in the Shenandoah Valley by a scratch force at the Battle of New Market (May 15, 1864), and Butler became bottled up in the cul-de-sac

A dead Confederate soldier after the Battle of Spotsylvania.

of the Bermuda Hundred near Petersburg, Virginia. As a result, the heaviest fighting — indeed the fiercest fighting of the war — took place between Grant and Lee. Nearly every day came reports of another engagement and more slaughter. From the Wilderness, to Spotsylvania, the North Anna River crossing, and at Cold Harbor, the furious battles blended together in a near-continuous maelstrom of bloodletting. To follow the campaign, readers of The Times relied on the stories sent in by William Swinton (1833–1892), a Scottish-born academic and reporter who was so dedicated to digging out the news that Grant accused him of eavesdropping on his conversations with Meade. Henry Ward Beecher called Swinton "our American Napier," comparing him to the seventeenth-century mathematician and philosopher John Napier. William C. DeWitt declared his work "the finest contribution which America has ever made to the war literature of the world." After the war, Swinton became a professor at the University of California and a well-known writer of histories and textbooks, some of which are still in print. In several of his reports from the front, Swinton kept a running diary recording his impressions hour by hour as the battle was being fought.

Reports from the west arrived later and were sketchier. Sherman commanded three armies — what in the twentieth century would be called an "army group." The bloodshed in northern Georgia was significantly less than in Virginia largely because the opposing generals — Sherman and Confederate General Joseph E. Johnston — relied more on maneuver than direct assault. Sherman flanked his rebel opponent out of Dalton, Resaca, and Cassville, and tried to do so again at New Hope Church, though this time Johnston got in front of

him and forced a series of battles in the last week of the month. Despite these different strategies, the result was the same: both Union armies moved inexorably southward, forcing the smaller rebel armies back toward the cities they defended: Richmond in Virginia, and Atlanta in Georgia. This time the undeniable progress of the Union armies was evident to all, and readers of The Times

began to hope, once again, that the end might be near. The Times owner and editor, Henry Raymond, who was also chairman of the Republican Party, credited President Lincoln for this success. "Every right-minded man," he wrote, "sees in these magnificent successes the crowning glory of President LINCOLN's administration."

A GIGANTIC COOPERATIVE MOVEMENT.
ADVANCE OF THE ARMY OF THE POTOMAC.

MAY 5

The Army of the Potomac began its forward march on Monday. The crossing of the Rapidan was effected without opposition on Tuesday and Wednesday [May 3-4] at Culpepper, Jacobs', Germanna and Ely's Fords. No rebels were seen, except a few pickets, who retired as we advanced. If LEE intends to make a stand this side of Richmond, it is possible he may be met near the old battleground of Chancellorsville, but it is the general impression that he has fallen back from his position on the Rapidan to Richmond, in order to protect that City from the formidable force now marching upon it from the rear [Butler's Army of the James], and which is as likely to strike on one side of the James River as the other.

Culpepper is being strongly fortified, and will be used as a depot for stores.

It is reported here to-day that a strong column of troops under Gens. [Darius] COUCH and [Franz] SIGEL are marching

from Winchester up the Shenandoah Valley as a cooperating column, destined eventually to cut the Virginia and Tennessee Railroad, while BUTLER's force, or a part of it, strikes the other railroad at or near Petersburgh, thus severing all railroad communications between Richmond and the South.

Gen. BUTLER took the field in person at the head of the army on the Peninsula yesterday, and his host is marshaled by such leaders as W. F. SMITH, [Quincy Adams] GILLMORE, [Alfred H.] TERRY, and GODFREY WEITZEL.

The movement assumes an expeditionary character. An immense fleet of transports, and a strong squadron of monitors and gunboats will convoy it up one of those broad rivers to the gates or to the back door of Richmond, and perhaps the iron-clads may once more try the strength of the rebel batteries and line the James, the Pamunkey, and the Rappanhannock.

The feeling prevails that there is desperate work before this army. But there is nerve and strength for it. The iron-clads lie in the still waters off Newport News, and the fleet of gunboats are in communication with them. All the auguries are favorable. ✹

Alfred Waud's sketch of General Grant writing a dispatch reporting that the Army of the Potomac has crossed the Rapidan River.

THE CAMPAIGN OPENED.

MAY 6

Lieut.-Gen. GRANT has spoken the word, and the long-anticipated "forward march" of our great armies has begun. On the first secular day of the current month, the soldiers struck their tents by the Rapidan, and probably also by the Tennessee; and, with rifle and knapsack, with the enthusiasm of volunteers and the stern spirit of veterans, advanced to the struggle with the rebellion.

The movements of our armies are not very well defined to the vision from this point. Of the army of the Potomac it is known that, taking up its advance from its camping ground near Culpepper, it had effected the crossing of the Rapidan by Wednesday morning. Of the cooperating army on the Peninsula [Butler's], it is reported that a portion advanced to and occupied West Point, at the head of York River, on Monday. From the West, it is reported that on the same day the army at Chattanooga [Sherman's] was to move forward in three columns; but the report of this movement is rendered dubious by the latest advices. Now, if any one can deduce the plan of the Virginia campaign from the telegraphic statement that MEADE's troops crossed the Rapidan at Jacob's, Culpepper, Germanna and Ely's Fords, and from the additional statement that a body of BUTLER's troops ascended the York River to West Point, he is free to attempt it. The Lieutenant-General in command of all the forces, evidently has de-termined that the campaign shall soon reach a crisis, for a telegram has been received from him in Washington, dated Wednesday, which says that forty-eight hours would determine whether he was to have a battle on the line of the Rapidan or under the works around Richmond. So that this day is the day of decision. This style of operation is characteristic of GRANT. He prepares for a movement deliberately and carefully, but when once ready for it, his blows fall with tremendous rapidity and vigor. Witness his November battles in front of Chattanooga; witness his marches and battles in the rear of Vicksburgh this month last year; witness his early operations on the Cumberland and Tennessee Rivers.

Of the movements and strategy of the rebel armies, we are no better informed than in the case of our own. LEE, it would seem, has fallen back from his defensive line on the south bank of the Rapidan; but the speculations of the Washington scribe as to his position and plans are not worth much. If we might judge of LEE by his antecedents, we should think he might manoeuvre his army very adroitly and deceivingly, and try to strike our forces piecemeal. If there is any detached body operating at a distance from the main army, and beyond the possibility of immediate support, it would not be unlikely that he would rush at it, and try to destroy it, expecting thus at once to effect this lesser object, and disarrange GRANT's entire plan of campaign. But we shall know in a few days what his mode of action is, as well as what is his success in carrying it out.... ✸

GEN. MEADE'S ADDRESS TO HIS ARMY.

MAY 6

HEADQUARTERS ARMY OF THE POTOMAC,
WEDNESDAY, MAY 4

SOLDIERS:

Again you are called upon to advance on the enemies of your country. The time and the occasion are deemed opportune by your Commanding General to address you a few words of confidence and caution. You have been reorganized, strengthened and fully equipped in every respect. You form a part of the several armies of your country—the whole under the direction of an able and distinguished General, who enjoys the confidence of the Government, the people and the army. Your movement being in cooperation with others, it is of the utmost importance that no effort should be left unspared to make it successful.

Soldiers, the eyes of the whole country are looking with anxious hope to the blow you are about to strike in the most sacred cause that ever called men to arms. Remember your homes, your wives and children, and bear in mind that the sooner your enemies are overcome the sooner you will be returned to enjoy the benefits and blessings of peace. Bear with patience the hardships and sacrifices you will be called upon to endure. Have confidence in your officers and in each other. Keep your ranks on the march and on the battle-field, and let each man earnestly implore God's blessing, and endeavor by his thoughts and actions to render himself worthy of the favor he seeks.

With clear consciences and strong arms, actuated by a high sense of duty, fighting to preserve the Government and the institutions handed down to us by our forefathers, if true to ourselves, victory, under God's blessing, must and will attend our efforts.

GEORGE G. MEADE, MAJ.-GEN. COMMANDING. ✸

FROM THE RED RIVER.

GEN. BANKS AT ALEXANDRIA — GUNBOATS ABOVE THE FALLS.

MAY 7
ALEXANDRIA, LA., SATURDAY, APRIL 23, VIA
CAIRO, TUESDAY, MAY 3

The Red River expedition, as far as an offensive campaign against the rebels is concerned, is for the present at an end. Gen BANKS and army are now falling back upon this place, the advance of the baggage trains having arrived last night. The whole army will be here in a day or two.

The gunboats and transports have nearly all arrived at a point just above the falls, two miles above Alexandria. Some of the transports are aground up the river, but will all probably be able to get to the falls. The majority have dropped over the falls empty. There is only about three feet of water on the shoals. The iron-clads above, some six or eight, all draw over six feet and cannot be brought over. It is rumored that Admiral PORTER has declared that his men shall remain on their boats if the land forces leave the river, and await a rise.[1]

It is impossible at present to determine whether Gen. BANKS will hold Alexandria or not. It is believed that the low stage of water in the river will force him to fall back to the Mississippi River — to what point will be determined by circumstances.

Rebels in the country back of and below this place came in yesterday within thirteen miles, and burned 2,000 bales of cotton belonging to [loyalist] Lieut.-Gov. [James Madison] WELLS.

Yesterday the steamer Superior, was fired into, 25 miles below here, with cannon and musketry. Three men were killed and eleven wounded. They were soldiers belonging to the Third Rhode Island Cavalry. A gunboat came to the relief of the Superior, and shelled the woods for miles. Soldiers went ashore and fired some buildings in retaliation.

Lieut.-Col. PARKER, Third Rhode Island Cavalry, gave orders to his men, on the Superior, to fire on every white man, woman or child seen on the shore as the boat came up. The order was executed. Two or three unarmed citizens, riding along on shore about fifteen miles below here, waved their hats to the boat as a friendly recognition, but were fired upon, and fell from their horses. They were doubtless Union men, as all rebel citizens have left that part of the parish. Houses were shelled along the river. The banks of Red River are steep and the river narrow. The high levee protects guerrillas with a complete breastwork. Transports hereafter will go accompanied by gunboats.

The Superior was also fired into with cannon at Tunica Landing, on the east side of the Mississippi River, fifteen miles below the mouth of Red River. Eleven shells were thrown at her. Three struck and went diagonally through her cabin. One shell went through the pilothouse. The Superior was very roughly handled. Five cannon shots and shells struck her on the way up here, and a hundred musket balls.

Hot work may be expected between here and the mouth of the river, and the scenes that have taken place on the Mississippi may be reenacted on Red River. Plantations will doubtless be destroyed indiscriminately, and the torch and cannon be applied to the innocent and guilty alike.... ✹

Confederate troops attack Union gunboats on the Red River.

> 1. In the event, most of the navy gunboats were saved thanks to an ingenious dam built by Colonel Joseph Bailey that raised the level of the water in the river and allowed the ships to slip through.

THE RED RIVER EXPEDITION.

THE GUNBOAT EASTPORT BLOWN UP.

MAY 7

CAIRO, FRIDAY, MAY 6

A gunboat from the Red River brings information that finding it impossible to get the Eastport off and being attacked by the enemy while endeavoring to lighten her, Admiral PORTER ordered her to be destroyed to prevent her falling into hands of the enemy.... ✹

THE BATTLE.

IMPORTANT NEWS FROM VIRGINIA.

A GREAT BATTLE BEGUN ON THURSDAY.

MAY 8

WASHINGTON, SATURDAY, MAY 7

The statements which were received here today, and which are entitled to belief, are that Gen. LEE made a tremendous and violent attack to pierce our centre, hoping thereby to divide our forces and to secure a victory; but Gen. [Ethan Allen] HITCHCOCK's corps came to the relief, and, amid a murderous fire, formed in line of battle, and thwarted the designs of the rebels. The loss was heavy on both sides.[1]

Gen. [Philip] SHERIDAN was profitably engaged in another part of the field, and sent the Chief in command a message that he had routed STUART's cavalry.[2]

The attack of LEE was on our advancing columns, who doubtless anticipated a victory by his onslaught, before the main body could advance to the field of battle.

The appearances on Thursday were that the hostilities would be renewed on Friday. ✹

A Currier and Ives lithograph of the Battle of the Wilderness.

> 1. The Battle of the Wilderness began on May 5 and lasted until May 7. Union losses over the three days totaled 17,600 while Confederate casualties totaled 11,125. Once again, however, Confederate losses were heavier when expressed as a percentage.
>
> 2. Sheridan's troopers fought a series of cavalry engagements with Stuart's men from May 5 to May 8. They did not, however, rout Stuart's forces, which got the better of each engagement. When Meade reprimanded Sheridan for not effectively performing his duties of screening and reconnaissance, Sheridan went to Grant and asked to be released for independent raiding missions. Grant agreed.

THE EXPEDITION UP THE JAMES.

MAY 9

STEAMER GRAYHOUND, OFF FORT POWHATAN.

JAMES RIVER, VA., THURSDAY, MAY 5

The movement of the Union army in this direction, which, for weeks past, has been vaguely expected, commenced this morning. The obligation to keep silence respecting the hostile preparations, which for prudential reasons was imposed, is now removed; and here, under the shadow of the commanding fortification, erected by the rebels in 1862, for the purpose of interrupting McClellan's water communications after his reverses before the rebel Capital, known as Fort Powhatan, I commence the record of the campaign. Premising that up to this point every circumstance has been auspicious, and that not the slightest symptom of resistance on the part of the enemy to our advance in the direction of Richmond has been encountered, either from guerillas, torpedoes or any other source, I shall go back a few weeks, and briefly trace from its conception the enterprise which, to the present point, in all its details, has been a wonderful success.

THE PLAN

To Major-Gen. BUTLER, I am told, is exclusively due whatever credit shall result from the inception and execution of the plan. When, four weeks since, Lieut.-Gen. GRANT, the actual commander of the armies of the United States, visited Fortress Monroe, it was for the purpose of ascertaining the views of Gen. BUTLER respecting an advance upon the rebels by way of the Peninsula, to be carried out in cooperation with the Grand Army of the Potomac. Gen. GRANT had considered the various plans proposed with this object in view, but had committed himself to none, and was inclined, therefore, to listen attentively to what Gen. BUTLER might suggest. The sequel proves that the proposition of Gen. BUTLER fully commended itself to the judgment and acquiescence of the Commanding General, and measures were taken at once to put it in execution.

Briefly the project was to advance upon Richmond by the James River; get a foothold as near the city as possible, on the south bank of the stream; seriously interrupt the communications of the rebel Capital southward, and eventually compel the evacuation of LEE's army of their strongly fortified position on the Rapidan, thus forcing the rebels to give GRANT battle, or press rapidly rearward to the walls of their Capital. This plan will be generally admitted to be both bold and comprehensive, while the arrangement of its preliminaries has been marked by the rarest shrewdness and military sagacity....

THE ADVANCE OF THE MAIN FORCE

As on every occasion when a large piece of machinery is put in operation, there is certain to be more or less friction of the parts, so this complex machine of a gallant and mighty army did not move smoothly according to the programme. The Eighteenth Corps (Gen. Smith's) having the advance, was promptly up to time, dawn finding all the steamers used for its transportation steaming by Newport News into the mouth of the James river. But the steamers of the Tenth (Gen. Gillmore's) Corps were still quietly at anchor off Fortress Monroe. Here was an unsuspected source of detention. Gen. BUTLER had every reason to suppose that the sailing orders were perfectly understood, and would be implicitly followed by his Corps Commanders. It was easy to perceive that he was both distressed and annoyed at the delay. He had hoped to reach his intended port of debarkation (City Point, fifteen miles below Richmond) at three o'clock in the afternoon. This he expected to accomplish, even in the case that the possession of two points on the way up the river, viz., Wilson's Wharf and Fort Powhatan, should be contested by the enemy, as it was very likely would be done. There was nothing for it, then but to learn the cause of this dilatoriness of the Tenth Corps, and to hasten the vessels forward. This was done....

The scene in the hazy light of the beautiful Spring morning was picturesque and animated. Crowded steamboats labored heavily through the still water, pontoon trains and lumbering canal barges, to be used in disembarking, were in tow of the swifter transports. The long, low lines and wedge-like shapes of those naval nondescripts, the monitors, with their high cylindrical turrets amidships, gave variety to the scene ... "Give her all the steam you can, Captain," shouts the General, with upraised cap, and as the crowds of blue-coats recognize him, they burst out vociferously in cheers. The scene as we pass up the river, is charming in the extreme. The high wooded banks of the stream present us every variety of delicate foliage with which the Spring delights to clothe the earth in vernal beauty.... ⊛

GLORIOUS NEWS.
DEFEAT AND RETREAT OF LEE'S ARMY.

MAY 9

TO GEN. JOHN A. DIX, NEW YORK

WASHINGTON, SUNDAY, MAY 8 – 9 A.M.

We have no official reports from the front, but the Medical Director had notified the Surgeon-General that our wounded were being sent to Washington and will number from six to eight thousand.

The Chief Quartermaster of the Army of the Potomac has made requisition for seven days' grain, and for railroad construction trains, and states the enemy is reported to be retiring.

This indicates Gen. Grant's advance, and affords an inference of material success on our part....

You may give such publicity to the information transmitted as you deem proper.

It is designed to give accurate official statements of what is known to the department in this great crisis, and to withhold nothing from the public.

EDWIN M. STANTON, SECRETARY OF WAR ⊛

A SPEECH FROM THE PRESIDENT — GEN. GRANT NOT JOSTLED FROM HIS PLANS.

MAY 10

WASHINGTON, MONDAY, MARCH 9

A large number of persons, on short notice, assembled in front of the Executive mansion to-night, and, with the band of the Twenty-seventh Ohio Volunteers, now on their way to the field, complimented the President with a serenade.

The President appeared on the portico and made a brief speech, in which he said the honor extended was not so much, perhaps, to him, as to Gen. GRANT and the gallant officers and soldiers under his command. He was exceedingly gratified to know that Gen. GRANT had not been jostled from his plans, but was now on the line of movement according to the original design. While, however, we might rejoice at what had already been accomplished, much more remained to be done.

The proceedings, which were of short continuance, terminated with repeated cheers for the President, Gen. GRANT, and the army.... ⊛

THE RESULT OF FRIDAY'S FIGHTING VERY ADVANTAGEOUS — LEE FALLING BACK.

MAY 10

WASHINGTON, MONDAY, MAY 9

The extra Star says:

"Reports from the front, not official, by parties that left there on Saturday, are to the effect that the result of the fighting on Friday [May 6] was yet more advantageous to the Union cause than that of Thursday, resulting in LEE's falling back, according to some reports, twelve miles, leaving his dead and wounded in our hands.

GRANT, according to the same report, has a field full of prisoners, and had advanced to Spottsylvania Court-house.

A verbal message received at Gen. HALLECK's headquarters, by a messenger from the Army of the Potomac, is to the effect that the battle closed on Friday, the enemy having fallen back about twelve miles, leaving his dead and wounded on the field.

On Saturday, at 3 o'clock, LEE's army was in full retreat through Spottsylvania, and when the messenger left, Gen. HANCOCK was entering the place in pursuit.[1]

We have captured many prisoners, but the number is not known.

Gen. WADSWORTH is reported killed, and Gen. WEBB wounded.[2]

Gen. BUTLER is reported to be within ten miles of Richmond. This information comes by a boat from Alexandria [Virginia], passengers from there reporting the arrival of parties from GRANT's army with news to that effect.

Parties in Alexandria County yesterday heard firing, as from heavy siege guns, in the direction of Spottsylvania Courthouse, from 11 A.M. until 1 P.M. The distance is over sixty miles, but the day was quiet and the wind from the southwest, making it not improbable that the firing was from the battle going on yesterday between GRANT and LEE.... ✶

1. The report is not quite accurate. Lee's army had much of the better fighting in the Wilderness, but Grant nevertheless moved his army southward toward Spotsylvania Court House on the night of May 7. Lee scrambled to get there ahead of him, which he did by a matter of minutes.

2. James S. Wadsworth was mortally wounded in the fighting on May 6; Alexander S. Webb was shot through the head, but survived.

The battlefield after the fighting at the Wilderness. Note the gathered skeletons of slain soldiers in the foreground.

GRANT'S ADVANCE.

OFFICIAL DISPATCHES TO SUNDAY NOON.

THE REBELS MAKE A STAND AT SPOTTSYLVANIA.

WASHINGTON, TUESDAY, MAY 10

To Maj.-Gen Dix:

Dispatches have been received this evening from Lieut.-Gen. GRANT dated at 1 o'clock yesterday.

The enemy have made a stand at Spottsylvania Court-house. There had been some hard fighting, but no general battle had taken place....

The army is represented to be in excellent condition, and with ample supplies.

Gen. [John C.] ROBINSON and Gen. [William H.] MORRIS are wounded. No other casualties to general officers are reported ....

Gen. GRANT did not design to renew the attack to-day, being engaged in replenishing from the supply train, so as to advance without it.

EDWIN M. STANTON, SECRETARY OF WAR.
(SIGNED,) BENJ. F. BUTLER, MAJOR-GEN.

WASHINGTON, TUESDAY, MAY 10 — 7 A.M.

Maj.-Gen Dix:

A dispatch from Gen. SHERMAN, received at midnight, states that we are fighting for the possession of Rocky Face Ridge, and I have

MAY 11

knowledge that [James B.] MCPHERSON took the Snake Creek Gap and was within seven miles of Resaca this morning.[1]

You will remember that on Saturday the rebels were forced from Tunnel Hill by Gen. [George H.] THOMAS and took position at Buzzard Roost, in a bend at Mill Creek, just north of Dalton.

This is represented to be a very strong position, which Gen. THOMAS was unable to drive the enemy from on a former occasion, when he advanced on Dalton; but Resaca is a position on the railroad, about fifteen miles south of Dalton, and this will place MCPHERSON, with a strong corps of veteran troops in the rear of the enemy, while THOMAS advances upon the front and [John] SCHOFIELD closes in on the flank from Cleveland....

EDWIN M. STANTON, SECRETARY OF WAR. ⊛

> 1. This was the first of Sherman's several flanking movements in northern Georgia. Pinning Joseph E. Johnston's Confederate army in place with two of his armies, he sent James McPherson's Army of the Tennessee around Johnston's left through Snake Creek Gap. Johnston hurried back to Resaca to block him, but he had to give up his defensive position at Rocky Face Ridge to do so.

NEWS OF THE DAY.

THE REBELLION.

MAY 11

The latest news from Gen. GRANT's army in Virginia is up to Monday [May 9] at noon, at which time Gen. GRANT sent a dispatch to Secretary STANTON that the rebels were making a stand at Spottsylvania Court-House, and that though there had been some hard fighting, no general engagement had been fought. Gen. SEDGWICK was killed in a skirmish by a ball through the head from a sharpshooter. Gen. GRANT wrote that he was replenishing the provisions of his army from the supply train, so he could advance with out it. The wounded were being received and cared for at Fredericksburgh.

The news from Gen. BUTLER's army is highly important. He fought a severe battle with BEAUREGARD's forces on Monday, drove them three miles, occupied the railroad and captured many prisoners.[1]

Gen. [August] KAUTZ's cavalry expedition had cut the railroad at Stony Creek, south of Petersburgh, and BEAUREGARD's force had thus been cut in two. Gen. BUTLER's telegraphs that his position is impregnable, and that Gen. Grant need not fear that LEE can be reinforced by BEAUREGARD.[2]

Advices also come from Gen. SHERMAN's army, indicating that the corps under THOMAS and HOOKER are attacking JOE JOHNSTON's position near Dalton in front, while SCHOFIELD attacks on the flank, and McPHERSON is operating in the rear. All the very latest advices everything was going well. ⊛

> 1. This was the Battle of Swift Creek (May 9, 1864), in which Butler made a thrust toward Petersburg, but did not follow up. After skirmishing, Butler seemed content to tear up the railroad tracks and did not press further.
> 2. This was certainly putting the best face on it. Butler's assignment was to act offensively; to report that his position was "impregnable" communicated to Grant that he had instead gone over to the defense. In fact, Butler's decision to entrench in the Bermuda Hundred effectively took him and his army out of the campaign.

THE RED RIVER EXPEDITION.

THE ARMY RETURNED TO ALEXANDRIA.

MAY 12

ALEXANDRIA, LA., WEDNESDAY, APRIL 27

All day yesterday and to-day the army has been reentering this place, returning from the disastrous expedition toward Shreveport. Gens. BANKS, [William B.] FRANKLIN and A.J. SMITH are now here, together with their respective commands. Alexandria begins to assume the appearance it wore four weeks ago, when the army, with high hopes and full of life, took up its march for Shreveport. Crowds of officers, soldiers and citizens are everywhere to be seen. The levee is lined with steamers, and the tents of a large army surround the place.

Gen. FRANKLIN and Gen. A. J. SMITH held a consultation at Grand Ecore last week, and agreed upon a programme by which they could bring the army successfully back to Alexandria. FRANKLIN laid this plan before Gen. BANKS, and told him that he (FRANKLIN) had held a consultation with Gen. SMITH, and that they had agreed upon the plan, and that he would undertake to conduct the retreat, if he (BANKS) would not interfere.

THE BATTLE OF SUNDAY, MAY 8.

MAY 13

NEAR SPOTTSYLVANIA COURT-HOUSE, VA.,
MONDAY, MAY 9 — 2 P.M.

I [William Swinton] have this morning returned from our advanced line of battle, which lies within two and a half miles of Spottsylvania Court-house, the enemy confronting in force. Our army reached this position yesterday morning, WARREN's corps having the advance, and heavy fighting took place during the day. It was hoped that we could have reached Spottsylvania before the enemy would be able to make that point but in the foot race which the two armies ran on Saturday night, from the battle ground of the Wilderness, the rebels beat us. LONGSTREET, it appears, started at 11 P.M. of Saturday; our advance left at 10 P.M. The two columns marched by parallel roads, but LONGSTREET's corps had time to arrive and form line of battle, and

Artillery duel between Confederate land forces and federal ships on the Red River.

Gen. BANKS assented, and thus virtually turned the command over to Gen. FRANKLIN. Gen. BANKS must have felt humiliated at this proposition, but he submitted. He took a cavalry escort and came on to Alexandria, arriving here a day or so in advance of the main army....

Admiral PORTER is now about sixty miles above here, trying to save the iron-clad gunboat Eastport. This boat got aground, sprung a leak and sunk near Grand Ecore, but was subsequently raised. She came on down a few miles, when she again met with a similar misfortune. The Admiral is now endeavoring to save her.... ⊕

---

when our force was thrown out to feel the enemy this morning, he was found in position. Our first attack was made by [Joseph J.] BARTLETT's brigade of [Charles] GRIFFIN's division, on the right of the road, with [John C.] ROBINSON's division on his left. BARTLETT had been ordered by Gen. WARREN to attack in column, under the belief that only rebel cavalry would be found. Instead of this, however, he ran on the whole of LONGSTREET's corps, and his brigade, already reduced by the fearful losses of the three days' battle of the Wilderness, was frightfully cut up. One of his regiments, the First Michigan, went in a hundred strong and came out with but twenty-five, having lost three-fourths of its numbers in fifteen minutes. ROBINSON's division, which held the left, was also roughly handled, and broke in disorder. Seeing this, Gen. WARREN seized the division flag and rallied the men in person. Fresh troops were thrown in, and after fighting from 8 A.M. till 12 M.,

our troops had gained the object sought — an open space up to the woods in which the rebel line was formed. In this engagement Gen. ROBINSON was severely wounded in the leg, and will have to lose his limb.[1]

At 6 P.M., two fresh divisions, namely, those of [Samuel] CRAWFORD, (Fifth Corps,) and [George Washington] GETTY, (Sixth Corps,) were thrown in, and after a severe engagement lasting for an hour and a half, CRAWFORD carried the rebel position, took their first line of breastworks and captured over a hundred prisoners. This ended the action of yesterday. For the numbers engaged our losses were extremely severe, and will count up to 1,000.

This morning found our line established two and a half miles this side of Spottsylvania Courthouse, and securely intrenched. LONGSTREET has also been strengthened by the arrival of EWELL's corps. The rebel line lies on a ridge a mile in front of the Court-house, and it will be a position

somewhat difficult to carry, should it be decided to make a direct attack.

It will be observed on the map that our present position carries us many miles south and in the rear of Fredericksburgh, whose famous fortified heights are in our possession without the need of firing a shot. It will be used as a depot and for hospitals, and several thousand of our wounded were, yesterday, sent there. A small army of 2,500 greybacks have also just been marched by headquarters en route to the same point. They are generally hearty-looking fellows, and rather better clad and shod than I have before seen them.

Everything thus far has gone on satisfactorily, although it would doubtless have been better had we been able to find an opportunity of fighting a decisive battle.

The Army of the Potomac is in superb condition and spirits — in fact, was never before in any such condition. We are going on to Richmond, depend upon it; at least, some ☞

more formidable obstacle than has yet appeared will have to present itself to stop us....

P.S.—We have this moment been shocked by the announcement that Gen. [John] SEDGWICK, Commander of the Sixth Army Corps, has just been killed by a shot through the head. He was standing up with his staff in his advanced line of breastworks, and was picked off by a rebel sharpshooter, perched in a tree. The ball entered the face a little below the eye, and came out at the back of his neck. He lived for half an hour after being struck, and then expired. His body has just passed headquarters in an ambulance. It will be embalmed and sent North.[2] The profoundest grief is felt at the death of the lionhearted chieftain, and

it is felt that we could better afford to lose a whole division of the army than one whose valor, illustrated on so many fields, we can ill spare at this time. He never fought so well as in the arduous three days' fight in the "Wilderness," and it was a matter of general remark how splendidly SEDGWICK had been doing. It is presumed that Gen. [Horatio] WRIGHT will take the vacant command of the Sixth Corps. ✹

1. John C. Robinson (1817–1894) received a bullet through the knee in this attack and his left leg was amputated. It ended his military career.
2. Toward the latter part of the war, it was not uncommon in the Union armies to embalm bodies, especially those of officers, on the battlefield.

THE COMBINED MOVEMENTS IN VIRGINIA.

Map Showing the Lines of Operation on the Rapidan, the North Anna and the James Rivers, where Grant and Butler, Lee and Beauregard are Manœuvering; and their Relations to Richmond.

A New York Times map of Richmond and the surrounding area, the scene of the last great campaign in Virginia.

THE BATTLE OF TUESDAY, MAY 10.

MAY 13
WASHINGTON, THURSDAY, MAY 12

The following dispatch has just come to hand:

HEADQUARTERS ARMY OF THE POTOMAC, NEAR SPOTTSYLVANIA C.H., WEDNESDAY, MAY 11

Yesterday's operations now assumed the character of the most bitter and perhaps the most bloody of the series of battles which have been fought since we crossed the Rapidan. Knowing as we do, that our cavalry force has been working havoc with LEE's communications, that his supplies are almost exhausted, that the lines of investment are being drawn around Richmond, and that echoes of disaster reach his ear from afar off Tennessee, and presage the downfall of the fabric of the rebellion, we are left to infer that the attack of yesterday[1] was a desperate, and, let us hope, final attempt to retrieve the rebel fortunes by dealing a crushing blow at this army. It is enough to say that it failed, and though he inflicted a severe loss of life upon us, he suffered not less himself, and we still hold a position against which the rebel fury may dash itself in vain. It would seem to have been the policy of LEE in the series of battles which he has delivered during the past week, to contest the advance to Richmond at every available point, to wear us away by degrees, and then, perhaps, to fall upon the Union forces under BUTLER, and endeavor to annihilate them. This plan he has carried into execution with a masterly skill, inspired by a fury perfectly diabolical.

FROM SHERMAN'S ARMY.

PROSPECTS OF THE CAMPAIGN IN GEORGIA.

MAY 13

The Indianapolis State Journal says:

"Capt. WILLIAM C. McGONIGAL, of our Second Cavalry, but recently of Gen. THOMAS's Staff as Inspector of Railroads, arrived in the city early yesterday morning, with about ninety men of his regiment, who long ago reenlisted as veterans but have only just now found an opportunity to get home. He left Chattanooga on

A painting by artist Thure De Thulstrup depicting the Battle of Spotsylvania.

We are steadily pressing the rebels southward. The enemy have been greatly favored by the nature of this country, in whose dense woods and tangled chapparal the lithe and wary are much more at home. Fortunately, if we once carry the position which they now hold in front of Spottsylvania Court-house, we shall be out of the "Wilderness" and reach open country.[2]...

The losses of the army up to this time exceed anything that any previous battle has cost us.[3] Nothing has been developed up to this hour respecting the enemy's position or intentions for the day, and there is nothing to indicate whether they will retreat, remain on the defensive, or assault.

W. SWINTON.

> 1. This was an attack by the division of Harry Heth against the division of Francis Barlow on the afternoon of May 10.
> 2. When Union troops finally reached the open ground south of the Wilderness, several of the units began singing an old gospel song: "Ain't we glad to be out of the Wilderness..."
> 3. Grant's total losses from the crossing of the Rapidan to May 14 totaled 33,000 men; Lee's losses in the same period totaled 23,000.

Saturday and therefore brings us as late news as the telegraph, and more of it. He says SHERMAN's force is greatly superior to JOHNSTON's, how much it would not be proper to state, and that it is thought by no means improbable that the latter will make no stand this side of Atlanta....

SHERMAN is advancing by way of Dalton, toward Atlanta or the rebel army, whichever gets in his way first, and Gen. MCPHERSON, with the Fifteenth and Sixteenth Corps, is advancing toward Rome, and in that direction cooperating with SHERMAN. JOHNSTON's force is estimated to be about 30,000 men, or but little over, and if LEE is kept busy by GRANT but few reinforcements can be added to it.[1]

The chances of success certainly seem to be good in this central spot of rebeldom. The railroads, Capt. MAGONIGLE says, are able to supply the whole army of the department and accumulate about thirty-seven per cent. of each day's transportation, so that the rebels are not likely to make much by our inability to keep going when we start."

> 1. Once he was reinforced by the army of Leonidas Polk, Johnston's force numbered almost twice as many as estimated here (Johnston reported his strength as 60,564 in June), though that was still just over half the number available to Sherman.

THE GREAT CAMPAIGN.

GEN GRANT'S DECISIVE BATTLE.

MAY 14

WASHINGTON, FRIDAY, MAY 13 — 5.30 A.M.

Maj.-Gen. Dix:

Official dispatches just received by this Department dated yesterday, 8 A.M. at the battle-field, near Spottsylvania Court-House. They state that during the night, Gen. HANCOCK marched from his previous position on our right and occupied the ground between Gens. WRIGHT and BURNSIDE; at daylight he attacked with his accustomed impetuosity, forcing the first and then the second line of the enemy's works, capturing the whole of Gen. EDWARD JOHNSON's Division and part of EARLY's, together with Maj.-Gen. JOHNSON, Gen. GEO. H. STUART, and from thirty to forty cannon.[1]...

> 1. This attack on a rebel salient, called "the mule shoe," achieved initial success because Lee had been planning to abandon the position to shorten his line. He had removed the artillery but not the infantry when Hancock struck.

LEE'S ARMY.

MAY 14

The terrible series of battles which, during the last ten days, have tried the mettle of our army, and the remarkable succession of victorious bulletins which have thrilled the nerves of the nation, seem to be reaching their consummation. The great army of the rebellion, which has held its ground against the power of the United States for three long years, which has fought more great battles than any army that has existed in the world for the last half century, which has twice crossed to this side of the Potomac, and four times driven back mighty armies led by four Generals in succession — the veteran army of ROBERT E. LEE is breaking up. Or rather, it is being defeated, demolished, crushed and annihilated by the courage of our soldiers and the masterly generalship of their Commander....

SPECIAL DISPATCHES TO THE N. Y. TIMES.
FULL DETAILS OF THE GREAT BATTLE.

MAY 14

The four hours that have passed since the date of my last dispatch have been occupied with vigorous hammer-and-tongs work that does not appear to have greatly advanced the upshot of the contest, save in the destruction of life to the enemy that may have been accomplished. The resistance of the rebels is most stubborn, and it seems from present appearances that we shall be thrown over till to-morrow, when we shall have a continuation of the same, unless indeed the enemy be so harassed in his communications as to compel him to retreat.

But whatever may be the determination of the enemy, there will be no change nor let up in the resolve of this army, of its Commander and of the head of the armies of the United States. That resolve is to put the matter through, cost what it may. In doing this we shall add to the already appalling list of losses we have experienced in this unparalleled battle of eight day's duration, but we shall end by crushing the enemy to powder .... .

Gen. MEADE's fame rises every day from the masterly manner in which he handled this army. He enjoys the highest confidence and respect of Gen. GRANT.

It is now certain that the struggle is over for the day. It has been a good day's work. The sun is setting and we hold two miles more ground than we had when it rose, besides the captures already mentioned.

THURSDAY, MAY 12

Let the twelfth day of May be written in the calendar as one of the fasts of the Republic, for it marks the date of one of the deadliest and most decisive victories of the war. Knowing the ebbs and flows of battle, I refrain from attempting to anticipate what the after hours of to-day may bring forth; but if victory continues to smile on this army as it has up to this hour — 2 P.M. — tonight will see the greatest army of the rebellion not merely beaten, but destroyed.

HANCOCK this morning, by a splendid assault, turned the enemy's right flank, carried both their lines of breastworks, captured forty-two pieces of artillery, and from 5,000 to 7,000 prisoners, and is now rolling up their line.[1] The other corps have joined in and engaged in furious battle, which continues at the hour of writing. In the impossibility of at present obtaining accurate details, and desirous of sending the outlines of the battle at the earliest moment, I transmit the rough jotting of my note-book, which must stand until a full recital can be written out.

SIX O'CLOCK A.M. — At midnight last night HANCOCK with his corps changed from his position on the extreme right, and went in on the left of the line between the Sixth Corps and BURNSIDE's, where there had been a gap. At 5 o'clock this morning he assaulted the enemy's position, carried their second line of breastworks, and turned the right flank of the rebels. It was a complete surprise, favored by a mist, which concealed our movements. He has taken 3,000 prisoners and three Generals, namely, Gen. STUART [actually George H. Steuart], commanding a brigade in Gen. [Edward] JOHNSON's division of EWELL's corps; Major-Gen. JOHNSON, Commander, and another Gen. JOHNSON, commanding a brigade. This is entirely reliable, as I have heard the dispatch conveying the joyfull intelligence read aloud by the Chief-of-Staff.

Everybody is in the best of spirits....

SEVEN A.M. — A most interesting scene is now before us at headquarters. Maj.-Gen. ED. JOHNSON, who, with his whole division. was captured this morning, has just been brought up, under charge of an officer, to headquarters in the woods, where Gens. GRANT and MEADE and their staffs are seated around a bivouac fire. Gen. MEADE, who had been an old friend of Gen. JOHNSON, shook hands with him and introduced him to Gen. GRANT ... Almost all the staff appear to have been old friends and acquaintances of JOHNSON, and numerous mutual inquiries in regard to old army comrades are being made. Gen. HUNT, Chief of Artillery, when he met him, had a mind to make a set speech, but the old familiar formula, "Ed, I'm glad to see you," came out in a salutation, to which JOHNSON replied: "Well, HUNT, under the circumstance, I am not glad to see you."

An Aid who has just come in from Gen. HANCOCK's headquarters says that when the captured Gen. STUART — G.H. — was brought in, HANCOCK extended his hand, but the high-born captive drew back, saying that "his feelings would not allow him to shake hands" — an incident which has just created a merry laugh at headquarters .... .

TEN A.M. — The whole line is now engaged, including the Corps of WARREN's Fifth, of WRIGHT's Sixth, of HANCOCK's Second, and of BURNSIDE's Ninth. From the present position of headquarters, which is near enough to be under fire, we can distinguish BURNSIDE's and HANCOCK's line of battle in our front, and WRIGHT and WARREN stretched off to the right. It is too densely wooded to see the manoeuvres, or even the line of battle, but we mark the line by the margins of smoke rising up above the trees, and the flashes of artillery.

ELEVEN O'CLOCK — There is a lull along the line, with the exception of a vigorous cannonading, which continues. The rebels have been fighting with an obstinacy that challenges the name of sublime, and LEE has been putting forth his best powers. The situation at this hour leaves our line holding all the ground they have gained; but they are not now advancing. The men are excessively fatigued, and it is now somewhat doubtful whether the issue can be decided in to-day's battle.

TWELVE M. — The rain has ceased and the sun has just burst forth. May it be another sun of Austerlitz.[2] BURNSIDE, who has hitherto had but one division (POTTER's) of his corps engaged, is ordered to make an attack with his whole force. The left has been the cardinal point ever since HANCOCK's turning movement.

TWO P.M. — It has been impossible yet to dislodge the rebels, who hold their position most stubbornly. LEE has repaired his left on a strong position, and his line is covered all along by breastworks. A tremendous cannonade is now being made for the purpose on the enemy's position. Though victory now appears highly probable, you must not be surprised if the final result is not achieved to-day. The rebels will fight to the last, and have already, in the wonderful eight-days Battle of the Wilderness — of which this is but a continuation — made good all the boasts ever made of their prowess. They will really die in the last ditch, and only then. They are, however, now out of supplies, their rations having, according to the statements of prisoners, been exhausted last night, and if SHERIDAN's destruction of their communications has been as complete as is believed at headquarters, they will be able to get no more. Quite a number of deserters have come in from all the corps, and they say if there is a chance many more may be expected to-night.

Of our losses thus far during this day's severe battle it is impossible to form anything like an accurate estimate; but they must be extremely heavy. The losses of officers is also very great, but I forbear to mention names until the facts are placed beyond dispute. Gen. WRIGHT, commanding the Sixth Corps, was this morning wounded in the soft part of the leg, but still continued to command.

W. SWINTON ⊛

LEE'S RETREAT BECOMING A ROUT.

WASHINGTON, FRIDAY, MAY 13 — 10 O'CLOCK P.M.

Dispatches just received from one of your correspondents at the front, dated Headquarters, eight o'clock last night, say that the rebels are in full retreat to North Anna

MAY 14

River, with fresh troops in hot pursuit.[1] ⊛

1. This conclusion was premature. Lee held his position at Spotsylvania until Grant began another flanking maneuver around his right on May 20.

Alfred Waud's sketch of the action during the Battle of Spotsylvania.

1. Grant's predawn assault on May 12 against "the mule shoe" was initially a complete success. Hancock's corps took 4,000 prisoners in part because many of the Confederates suffered from wet powder in their rifled muskets due to rainfall the night before. Both Ed "Allegheny" Johnson and George H. Steuart (not Stuart) were captured. then the fighting bogged down, in part because Grant had not properly prepared a second wave to take advantage of the success. The two armies also suffered some 17,000 casualties (9,000 Union; 8,000 Confederate).
2. In the Battle of Austerlitz (December 2, 1805), Napoleon ordered a unit to storm Pratzen Heights. As the men began to climb, the heavy mist that had obscured the field cleared, and the sun shone forth. The defenders of the Pratzen Heights were astonished by the sight of their attackers and broke.

LATEST FROM THE BATTLE-FIELD

HEADQUARTERS ARMY OF THE POTOMAC, NEAR SPOTTSYLVANIA COURT-HOUSE, FRIDAY, MAY 13

The terrible pounding which the rebels received yesterday, has compelled them again to fall back, which they did during the night. Reconnaissances this morning develop nothing but a skirmish line on their front. The operations of yesterday brought our lines so closely up to theirs, that they could hardly have hoped to hold their position to-day. It is not expected that they will fall back far, but

MAY 14

will make another stand at the first defensible position. Should they not find such until they come to the North Anna, they will undoubtedly dispute the passage of that stream.[1]

This army holds them with the grasp of a bull-dog, and will never let go while life remains.

WILLIAM SWINTON. ⊛

1. Lee fell back only to another line he had prepared across the base of the "mule shoe."

THE PRESIDENT AND THE WAR.

MAY 16

It was quite fashionable two or three weeks ago for the Copperhead press to sneer at the idea that President LINCOLN would permit any decisive fighting to be done until the Presidential nomination had been made. His chances, they assumed, depended on the prolongation of the war; and although scarcely willing to impute openly to him the infamously selfish design of sacrificing the country to his personal ambition, they were not ashamed to imply that he was governed by such a motive.

The recent campaign in Virginia has very effectually silenced that calumny; for one of its most conspicuous features has been the zealous cooperation of every department of the Government and every branch of the public service, in the great and complicated movement by which it has been marked. The plan of the campaign and the supervision of its details undoubtedly belong to Gen. GRANT; but he has had, at every stage of its execution, the zealous, vigorous and effective support of the supreme authorities at Washington. President LINCOLN has done everything in his power to insure success; and Secretary STANTON has, in the same manner, devoted all the energy and impulsive enthusiasm of his nature to the prompt supply of everything essential to the perfect execution of the plans and purposes of the Lieutenant-General. Nothing in the history of the war is more remarkable than the perfect accuracy and harmony with which the gigantic machinery of this movement has been worked. It was by far the most complicated plan of campaign which has been attempted; yet every man at every point seems to have "come to time," and to have done, thoroughly, at the date appointed, the precise task to which he was assigned....

With equal energy and promptness the Government has been sending forward supplies and reinforcements. The moment it was seen that LEE was repulsed, and that Washington was no longer in danger, the troops collected and held there in reserve were pushed forward to repair the losses of the heroic Army under MEADE, and by this time the Army of the Potomac must have at least as many effective men as it had when the campaign opened.[1] This fact of itself is decisive of the result. LEE cannot be reinforced. JOHNSTON's Army cannot come to him for SHERMAN not only holds it fast, but threatens it with destruction. BEAUREGARD cannot aid him, for BUTLER holds him in check, and even if both were free, the destruction of their railroad lines would so retard their progress that they could not reach LEE in season to arrest the coming catastrophe.

The country may rely, with unfaltering trust, upon the supreme devotion of the President to the defence of the Government and the suppression of the rebellion. He has never, in a single instance, given the slightest ground for the imputation of being governed by personal ambition, or by any other motive than devotion to the public good. Most certainly he has in this instance given the most decisive rebuke to those who, in the recklessness of party zeal, charged him with delaying the war for his own promotion. ◉

1. Though Grant's army lost more men than Lee's in these battles, Grant was able to replace his losses. In mid-May, Grant asked Lincoln to "rake and scrape" all the reinforcements he could, and by May 25, Lincoln had sent him 33,000 more men, almost exactly the number he had lost since crossing the Rapidan.

A woodcut of the Battle of Resaca.

GEN. SHERMAN'S ARMY.

THE REBELS ABANDON RESACA.

MAY 17

WASHINGTON, MONDAY, MAY 16

Official advices received here, to-day, from Gen. SHERMAN, announce that he had forced JOHNSTON out of his formidable position at Resaca, the latter evacuating the position during last night, SHERMAN would pursue vigorously. Atlanta is the point now aimed for by both armies. ◉

GEN. SIGEL'S REPULSE — ITS LESSON.

MAY 19

We have one more victim of "superior forces" to add to the long list which already adorns our military annals. Gen. [Franz] SIGEL on Sunday last, "fought the forces of [John] ECHOLS and [John D.] IMBODEN under BRECKINRIDGE, at New-Market," and in consequence of the enemy's forces being superior in number, "he gradually withdrew from the battle-field, having lost five pieces of artillery and six hundred killed and wounded." Translated into simpler English, this means that he was well beaten, though not routed.[1]

One does not need to be a professional soldier to arrive at the conclusion, from what has happened in the course of this war, that fighting "superior forces" of the enemy is a losing business. Some of our Generals are constantly doing it, and whenever they do it they are defeated. It seems to us, that this ought to settle the question of its propriety, or rather of its impropriety. Does it not seem, after all that has happened, that it would be well to let the enemy alone, whenever he is found numerically stronger than the attacking force? A battle is not a prize-fight. Its object is not to test either the pluck or endurance of the combatants, but to secure possession of certain positions. And when an enemy is in such force that attacking him is not likely to result in driving him from his position, it is great cruelty to attempt it. When a General, therefore, coolly informs us — and how many Generals have done so! — that he voluntarily, and with the choice of staying quiet or retreating open to him, assails a much heavier force than his own, and gets badly thrashed, it is simply a euphemistic mode of informing us that he is either a very stupid or a very inhuman person.... ❂

> 1. Major General Franz Sigel's Army of the Shenandoah, numbering 6,275, was routed by a force of 4,000 Confederates (including 257 cadets from VMI) under Confederate Major General John C. Breckinridge in the Battle of New Market on May 15, 1864. The tone of The Times report here carries with it a hint of sarcasm.

REOPENING OF THE GREAT STRUGGLE IN VIRGINIA.

MAY 19

We have a special dispatch from our correspondent at Lieut.-Gen. GRANT's headquarters, under date of yesterday morning, 5 o'clock, in these words: "The struggle has this moment begun with skirmishing on our extreme right. We fully expect a great, a bloody, and, we trust, a decisive battle to-day."[1] The progress and result of the day's work — whether the skirmishing swelled into a general battle — whether the two Commanders spent the hours in a game of strategy — whether the issue was for or against the Union arms — we do not yet know.

But this preliminary work gives sufficient proof — if we had not abundant other evidence — that the Lieutenant-General means to indulge in no long period of inaction, and that no obstacles that can possibly be overcome will be allowed to retard the progress of his campaign. In him is embodied the earnestness, the persistency, the endurance, the quickness, the valor, of the American people. He feels all the impatience with treason which is felt by the nation. And not a soldier in the army nor a loyal citizen in the whole land, has more of a single-hearted determination to expend every energy, faculty, and power, in the imperative work of crushing out the rebellion.

We know the great losses his army has already suffered; we hear privately and otherwise of the fearful mud of Virginia; we learn that the soldiers are greatly exhausted with their recent fighting and marching. But we have seen also, under GRANT's management in the West and in the East, what can be accomplished by able generalship.

There is proof that LEE has succeeded in getting some reinforcements as well as Gen. GRANT, and our correspondent yesterday stated that the rebel General had not abandoned his works on the River Po. It is possible that the contest is yet for Spottsylvania Court-house. ❂

> 1. Rather than mark the prelude to another battle, the skirmishing on May 18 presaged another of Grant's maneuvers around Lee's right flank. The Union army left its lines on May 20 and raced for the North Anna River. Once again, Lee matched this move, setting up a defensive line behind the river.

GEN. GRANT'S SUCCESSES AND PRESIDENT LINCOLN.

MAY 20

The Copperhead journals have at last found how to extract some comfort from GRANT's success. They are discovering that this success is just the thing to defeat the renomination of President LINCOLN! They feel quite certain that the Baltimore Convention, in view of these victories, will adjourn until September, and then select a more available candidate.[1]

Now we would not have the heart to say one word tending to deprive these people of their one poor little solitary consolation, were there a particle of reason in it. But it is better to be rationally unhappy than to live in a fool's paradise. Of course, we appreciate the frame of mind superinduced upon both classes of Copperheads by the achievements in Virginia. To the straight-out "Peace Democrat" they come as gall and wormwood, because they are fast making an end of his favorite assumption that the rebels cannot be conquered. They aggrieve the partisans of MCCLELLAN, because they are proving conclusively, before the eyes of all living men, that the reasons assigned by President LINCOLN, in his memorable correspondence with MCCLELLAN, for the overland, in preference to the Peninsular, campaign against Richmond, were sound reasons, and that MCCLELLAN's objections and fears were absurd. But, in common decency, the enemies of the Administration ought to submit to all this in silence, if they do not choose to recant. They only make themselves ridiculous by pretending to find in these achievements a cause for the repudiation of President LINCOLN by the people.

Every right-minded man sees in these magnificent successes the crowning glory of President LINCOLN's administration. If there is a man in the National army who, from the beginning, has been more tenaciously adhered to, through good report and through ill report, by President LINCOLN, than any other, it is ULYSSES S. GRANT. Had his constancy been less, Gen. GRANT long since would have been thrust aside through the influence of his detractors. All the splendid generalship he has revealed during the last year has only justified the early confidence in him which President LINCOLN so notably manifested, by promotion after promotion. ☞

The unqualified trust, too, with which the entire planning of the present campaign was committed to Gen. GRANT, and the tremendous energy with which everything needful was supplied, reflects most signal credit upon the Government at Washington. It passes comprehension that any man in his senses should imagine that Gen. GRANT's success is President LINCOLN's condemnation. President LINCOLN is to-day more implicitly confided in by the great loyal mass of the people than ever, and his renomination, which two months age was almost morally certain, is now as fixed as any earthly event can be. We say this not because we assume to know the special intentions of the majority of the Baltimore Convention, but because it is certain that no delegates of the people will or can disregard a popular feeling so decided.... ⊛

1. The political convention held in Baltimore on June 7–8 did nominate Lincoln for a second term. It titled itself the National Union convention, rather than the Republican convention, in order to attract the support of War Democrats.

ANTI-SLAVERY PRINCIPLES AND PRESIDENT LINCOLN.

May 21

The Union Convention of Vermont, which has just adjourned, unanimously adopted a resolution declaring ABRAHAM LINCOLN the first choice of the people of that State for the next Presidential term. This is another proof of the falsity of the pretense that Mr. LINCOLN has not the confidence of the earnest Anti-Slavery men of the country. No State in the Union has so steadily and so emphatically testified its abhorrence of human chattelism as Vermont. In its very earliest history, one of its judges refused to recognize an affidavit of the ownership of a fugitive slave, saying that he "would take no evidence short of a bill of sale from the Almighty;" and that has ever been the spirit of the State in every line of its public action. Its mountains have not been firmer than its Anti-Slavery principles.... ⊛

GRANT'S FLANKING OPERATIONS.

May 30

The official dispatches from the War Office, as well as our own dispatches from army headquarters, furnish accounts of the new flanking operation which the Lieutenant-General has under way. Ten days ago, GRANT having previously tried hard to force the lines of Spottsylvania, began his march on their right flank, and instantly LEE was compelled to retreat. He fell back, however, but a few miles, and again assumed battle-front on the north side of the South Anna, a line which they had long been preparing, and meant to defend to the last. To compel a retreat from this position, the new flanking movement was begun on Thursday night last [May 26]. The army recrossed the North Anna, whose lines it had forced a few days before, struck a short distance east, and then south for the Pamunky, at the Hanovertown crossing of which it arrived on Friday. The full effect of this march on the army of LEE yet remains to be developed. But that development cannot be long delayed. From GRANT's position on the Pamunky, it is only about fifteen miles to the immediate defences of Richmond, which is a shorter distance than LEE has to travel from the South Anna to reach them.

People who do not study the movements intelligently are making anxious inquiries about GRANT's base. GRANT's base is all right. After he had left his lines on the Rapidan, at the opening of the month, he very soon found a new base at Fredericksburgh; subsequently, as he progressed, he abandoned the latter in turn, and made a base at Port Royal. This also, we fancy, he will now abandon; but there is another excellent base all ready for him, not far from his present lines on the Pamunky. When GRANT does not carry his base along with him, as he has done on several occasions, he always finds one very handy. He thus not only outwits LEE, but also [Confederate cavalry raider John S.] MOSBY.

The remarkable series of flanking operations which GRANT began on the Rapidan, and has carried on upon the Po, the Anna, and down as far as the Pamunky — the marvelous skill with which he has manoeuvred the army, and the great success which he has achieved, are deserving of profound admiration. Mainly by force of arms it was that he drove LEE's army from the Rapidan, but chiefly by force of intellect he has driven LEE from the all but impregnable positions that he had prepared on the road to Richmond.

There has been a popular impression,

A federal pontoon bridge over the North Anna River near Jericho Mills, Virginia.

springing, perhaps, from the character of the first great battle of our present Lieutenant-General at Fort Donelson, that GRANT, as a soldier, was merely a hard fighter — that his style was simply that of concentrating great masses of men, hurling them upon the enemy or his works, and achieving success, by what is called "pounding," or "Stanton's strategy." The operations in the rear of Vicksburgh, one year ago, showed that this conception was erroneous; for although there never was harder fighting than at the battle of Champion Hills, yet even the grandeur of the fighting seemed obscured by the splendor of the strategy. At the November victory at Chattanooga, again, we heard much of the heroic achievements of the different divisions of the army, and all that ever was said on this point, and much more, was well deserved; but no one who has read the greatest of all military documents, GRANT's Chattanooga report, and observed the maze of strategical and tactical combinations from which victory was brought forth, can have failed to perceive that the intellectual part of the battle — the mode in which GRANT wielded the forces of his brain — lent lustre even to the sublime valor of the simple men of the sword. The impression of his military character, however, to which we at first referred had not died out when the Lieutenant-General, three months since, transferred his headquarters to Virginia, and very many were greatly afraid that the wily and practised LEE would prove more than a match for the muscular Western Hercules. The idea that he was merely a fighter was greatly confirmed in the public mind by the reports of the first two days' battle in the Wilderness; for we heard only of ceaseless, desperate and deadly struggles between huge masses of men, and could discern little or nothing of the soldierly skill that presided over the movements of these masses. Since, however, the course of events and our correspondents have revealed somewhat of the strategy that GRANT has pursued during this memorable month of May — since we have been able to gain glimpses, not only of the movements, but of their mode and their aim, we have been enabled very clearly to discover, not only the blaze of musketry and the march of columns, but the flashing of genius and the triumphs of intellect.

What would it not have cost GRANT to "move directly upon the enemy's works" at Spottsylvania with his whole army? Our intelligent correspondent at headquarters confesses that the position could not thus have been taken, or, in other words, that GRANT might have dashed his whole army against the works in vain. What might we not have paid for the line of the North Anna had GRANT done nothing there but pounding? What streams of bloody currency we might have given for the line of the Little River, of the South Anna, and others, had it not been for the skill of this Commander? The present moment is a critical and a perilous one for him, for the army, and for the country; but we devoutly hope that these intellectual gifts, on which, along with the courage of our soldiers, our hopes are now based, may enable him to continue in his course of victory until the land is free from rebellion. ⊛

SHERMAN'S GREAT FORWARD MOVEMENT.

SPECIAL CORRESPONDENCE OF THE CHICAGO EVENING JOURNAL.
NASHVILLE, WEDNESDAY, MAY 25, 1864

I am under the impression that Gen. SHERMAN resumed his forward movement from Kingston, Ga., last Monday morning; but up to this time, I have seen no official confirmation of the fact. If he did advance then, you will doubtless have heard of a battle or a foot race ere this reaches you.[1] Altoona, on the Etowah River, is nineteen miles beyond SHERMAN's front on Sunday last, and the only possible place for a stand north of Atlanta. JOHNSTON must either fight there, or fall back to the latter place, which is much weaker. Therefore, why should he retreat?

[Leonidas] POLK's army, and all the Mobile garrison, except two or three companies of heavy artillery, are with JOHNSTON; he has as many men now as he could have a week or a month hence. Altoona is among mountain fastnesses; Atlanta is on a broad plain; and the question now is, if he does not fight at the former place, will he at the latter?

After all, I have one query to ask the reader to reflect upon, and it is this: is not JOHNSTON too weak to fight SHERMAN? and is he not falling back to make the distance between GRANT and SHERMAN greater, by railroad, while that between JOHNSTON and LEE, by the same method of travel, is constantly diminishing? and is JOHNSTON not gradually reinforcing LEE? and when overtaken, will there be any of his army left? I am not prepared to solve this problem; perhaps its solution may come before this letter reaches you, though I think not that soon.[2]

Suppose brigade after brigade were transferred to BEAUREGARD, at Petersburgh, thus making his army sufficiently strong to annihilate BUTLER, or compel him to retreat; what then? I hope and believe both GRANT and SHERMAN are providing against such a possible contingency. The result of such a concentration of the rebel forces, would be to enable us to defeat them easier than at present, provided we could concentrate as readily as they; but if we failed to do this, then disaster would follow. A junction between BEAUREGARD, LEE and JOHNSTON, would leave but a single force to fight and follow; but suppose they were to unite before those of BUTLER, GRANT and SHERMAN?

I never saw more delightful weather. Vegetation springs up as if by magic. Green peas and ripe strawberries are luxuries in which our people can indulge, to their heart's content.

LATEST.

Since the above was written, I have learned positively, from official dispatches, that SHERMAN moved on Tuesday morning [May 24] by way of Dallas, completely flanking Altoona. He has with him thirty days' provisions of all kinds, and finds plenty of green pasture for his cavalry horses. Other supplies are being sent forward to Kingston without delay, as the railroad is completely repaired to that place. The rebels retreat in such haste that they do little damage to the bridges. ⊛

MAY 30

1. Sherman's three armies left Kingston, Georgia, on May 23 seeking to get around Johnston's left flank. Johnston scurried southward to interpose himself in front of Sherman at New Hope Church where a series of fierce battles were fought May 25–28.
2. Though Johnston had begun the campaign with a determination to fight Sherman in northern Georgia and then launch a counteroffensive, by now he was beginning to make the argument presented here: that a deliberate retreat into the Confederate heartland was actually a good strategy, for it lengthened Sherman's supply lines and shortened his own. He was not, however, sending any reinforcements to Lee in Virginia.

CHAPTER 20
"Fighting has been Going on Nearly All Day"
JUNE–JULY 1864

O n the last day of May, Grant executed another crab-like shift to the left from the banks of Totopotomoy Creek to Cold Harbor, a small crossroads only about a mile west of the site of the 1862 Battle of Gaines' Mill. In effect, Grant had returned to the same battlefields over which the armies had fought more than two years before. The difference was not only that Grant had done so by moving overland — keeping the Army of the Potomac between Washington and the enemy — but also that the two intervening years had dramatically depleted the manpower of the Confederacy. Now, after making four flanking marches to get around Lee's right, Grant decided that he would try again to punch through Lee's center. On June 3, he ordered a general assault on the rebel lines at Cold Harbor. Though historians have often cited this as the epitome of the kind of butchery that characterized the entire Overland Campaign, to Times readers it was simply one more bloody battle among many others. Grant reported the assault to Secretary of War Stanton, and put "the number of our killed and wounded at about three thousand," acknowledging that it did not gain any "decisive advantage."

After that, Grant maneuvered again around Lee's right, this time crossing to the south side of the James River and assailing Petersburg. Lee was dependent on Petersburg because the railroad lines connecting Richmond with the rest of the Confederacy all passed though that city. Though a quick Union dash into Petersburg might have captured it, Confederate forces arrived there in time to prevent it, and the campaign in Virginia settled into a lengthy siege of Richmond and Petersburg. After the high expectations of late May and

Detail of a Kurz and Allison lithograph of the Battle of Cold Harbor.

early June, the public again became impatient. On June 22, The Times ran an article entitled "Public Impatience About Military Movements."

On the political front, Lincoln's re-election hopes were threatened by John C. Fremont, the 1856 Republican candidate, who resigned his commission as a major general in order to accept the nomination of a splinter group of progressive Republicans. The move threatened to split the vote of Republicans, and to prevent that, Lincoln accommodated Fremont by asking for the resignation of Fremont's rival, Montgomery Blair, as postmaster general. Thus assuaged, Fremont agreed not to run. Lincoln won the nomination, but he did not run as a Republican. The party restyled itself as the National Union Party in order to attract War Democrats, and in pursuit of that, the party dropped Hannibal Hamlin, the dour incumbent from Maine, in favor of Andrew Johnson, a Tennessee Democrat. As The Times noted, this demonstrated "the thoroughly unsectional character of the Union party."

Another political problem was Chase. Though Chase had formally withdrawn as a presidential candidate, he continued to cause Lincoln political difficulties and occasional embarrassment. When Lincoln expressed dissatisfaction with Chase's intervention in an issue of political patronage in New York, Chase offered his resignation. To Chase's surprise, Lincoln accepted it. "Of all I have said in commendation of your ability," Lincoln wrote to him, "I have nothing to unsay, and yet you and I have reached a point of mutual embarrassment in our official relations which it seems can not be overcome, or longer sustained."

In the west, William T. Sherman continued his adroit maneuvering against Joe Johnston's Army of Tennessee. Jefferson Davis had

watched with growing alarm as Sherman drove deeper and deeper into Georgia. As The Times noted, Johnston did not strike at Sherman, and instead "simply tried to retard our advance at such commanding positions as were found along the line of the railroad." Like Grant at Cold Harbor, Sherman made one attempt to smash through Joe Johnston's Confederate defenses before resuming his campaign of flank marches. At Kennesaw Mountain on June 27, he found that the rebel army was still too tough to crack. So he moved eastward again, and crossed the Chattahoochee River on July 16. For Davis, that was the last straw, and he removed Johnston from his command on July 17, replacing him with John Bell Hood. Knowing what was expected of him, Hood immediately unleashed a series of furious offensives against Sherman at Peachtree Creek (July 20) and the Battle of Atlanta (July 22). Alas, for Southern hopes, those battles not only failed to slow Union progress, they also seriously depleted Hood's own army. By the end of July, Hood, with barely 35,000 men, retreated back into the city, and Sherman began to envelop it. As July turned into August, Hood's position became increasingly precarious and the war itself had coalesced around two poles: Grant's siege of Richmond and Petersburg, and Sherman's siege of Atlanta.

As The Times noted, the auguries were good, but the paper also reminded its readers not to be impatient. "It is highly desirable," the paper declared in June, "both for our own comfort and for the sake of the country and the cause, that we should all try and acquire a calmer and more critical temper in talking and thinking of the war."

Sketch depicting the death of Colonel John McMahon, commander of 164th New York State Volunteers, at Cold Harbor.

IN FRONT OF RICHMOND.

STUBBORN VALOR OF THE NATIONAL TROOPS.

JUNE 6

HEADQUARTERS OF THE ARMY OF THE POTOMAC, FRIDAY, JUNE 3 — 9 P.M.

Fighting has been going on nearly all day along the line, principally with artillery. The casualties have been quite large.

When [Francis] BARLOW's division charged the enemy's works [at Cold Harbor] early this morning he succeeded in getting possession of 17 guns and taking 250 prisoners. But not being supported he was exposed to an enfilading fire, and was compelled to evacuate the works which he had so gallantly captured, and also had to abandon the guns....

The Eighteenth Corps [William F. "Baldy" Smith] were engaged skirmishing most of the day, and made a charge on a line in their front but were unable to hold it. They fell back to their former position.

The Sixth corps [Horatio G. Wright], on the left of the Eighteenth, have been engaged more or less all day and have suffered a great deal the past two days.

An attack on the left centre of the Second Corps [Winfield S. Hancock], supposed for the purpose of feeling our left, was made an hour ago, but the enemy were soon driven off. The loss is not known....

Our losses in the past two days, at Cold Harbor, will number nearly five thousand killed and wounded, while the enemy's loss will be nearly the same.[1]

The change in position to-day has been very little, our advance being about a mile beyond Cold Harbor.... ⊕

1. On June 3, Grant ordered an assault by three corps against the Confederate lines at Cold Harbor. Only Francis Barlow's division of Hancock's corps managed to break the enemy line, and it was soon driven out. The Union lost between 3,000 and 7,000 men to the defenders' 1,500. After the war, Grant wrote, "I have always regretted that the last assault at Cold Harbor was ever made."

THE ACCEPTANCE OF FREMONT.

JUNE 6

Of course FREMONT accepts. He laid the plot on purpose to accept. His griefs would run to seed if he did not accept. His "whole charge of ancients, corporals, lieutenants, gentlemen of companies, discarded unjust serving men, revolted tapsters," would all go to the dogs if he didn't accept. It is plainly enough now but an ill venture; yet, being in so far, there was no alternative but to stand to it.

It was needful not only to accept, but to give reasons. FREMONT has given them, in the letter we published yesterday. They are very vague. Words lie so thick about them that it is not easy to make them out. But we gather that his acceptance is necessary because Mr. LINCOLN has violated personal liberty, and the liberty of the press, and especially the right of asylum; because his foreign policy has been feeble and without principle; and because the war has been managed with incapacity and selfishness, with all "the abuses of military dictation, without its unity of action and vigor of execution." These, every one sees at once, are Copperhead reasons, pure and simple....

Gen. FREMONT by this letter breaks definitively with the Union party. We are sorry for it. Not for the party's sake, but for his own. The party is sure to prevail. It will not feel his loss. But it is not pleasant to reflect that a name which was once peculiarily associated with a grand struggle against the slave power in the political field should now be connected with a movement tending only to encourage that power, when in flagrant rebellion. The wish of Gen. FREMONT is to draw off a portion of the Union party to his own support — in other words to divide it. No extensive division could take place without neutralizing its power, and giving the next Presidency to the party which is opposed to the war, and in favor of negotiating with JEFF. DAVIS — the party for whose success the rebels have a special solicitude. The spirit must come either from hostility to the aims and objects of the Union party, or from a personal feeling against Mr. LINCOLN. If the former, JOHN C. FREMONT is ex animo a Copperhead. If the latter, he is a man who permits his personal spites to overrule his public duties. The special anti-Lincoln tone of his letter, his expressed willingness to support any other nominee of the Baltimore Convention, indicates that the latter branch of the alternative is the correct one. This conclusion finds an additional support in the fact that he has once proved himself capable of this same littleness of action. When Gen. POPE was transferred to the Department of Northern Virginia, Gen. FREMONT, though in the face of the enemy, refused to retain his command in the Mountain Department, for the avowed reasons that his personal relations with Gen. POPE were such that he could not acknowledge the latter as his military superior. It was a display of personal spleen of which a true soldier would be incapable. A similar grudge against President LINCOLN seems to be his ruling motive now. But whether it be this or a new-born hatred of the Union cause that impels him, he is alike dishonored. The impotence of his effort does not make it a whit the less odious. ❀

A Currier and Ives poster for the short-lived presidential candidacy of John C. Fremont.

THE CLEVELAND CONVENTION.
LETTER OF ACCEPTANCE OF FREMONT.

JUNE 6
NEW-YORK, SATURDAY, JUNE 4.

GENTLEMEN:

In answer to the letter which I have had the honor to receive from you, on the part of the representatives of the people assembled at Cleveland on the 31st of May, I desire to express my thanks for the confidence which led them to offer me the honorable and difficult position of their candidate in the approaching presidential election....

My own decided preference is...not to be myself a candidate; but, if Mr. LINCOLN be renominated, as I believe it would be fatal to the country to endorse a policy and renew a power which has cost us the lives of thousands of men and needlessly put the country on the road to bankruptcy, there will remain no alternative but to organize against him every element of conscientious opposition, with the view to prevent the misfortune of his reelection.

In this contingency, I accept the nomination at Cleveland, and as a preliminary step, I have resigned my commission in the army. This was a sacrifice it gave me pain to make. But I had for a long time faithfully endeavored to obtain service. I make this sacrifice now only to regain liberty of speech and to leave nothing in the way of discharging to my utmost ability the task you have set for me.

With my earnest and sincere thanks for your expressions of confidence and regard, and for the many honorable terms in which yon acquaint me with the actions of the committee, I am, gentlemen,

Very respectfully and truly yours,

J. C. FREMONT. ❀

THE PLATFORM OF THE UNION PARTY.

The Union party, now for the first time meeting in National Convention, for the first time gives its combined sanction, and an authoritative form, to its tenets. Its series of resolutions embrace nothing novel; they are but the reassertion of principles which have already shaped the character and policy of the Administration; and yet their clear and systematic statement, accredited by the unanimous assent of the party in convention assembled, is an important act, which will pass into history.

The prime characteristic of the resolutions is their thoroughness. Never before was this exhibited in any national convention of any great party. Democratic, Whig, American, Republican — they all, in greater or less degree, were subject to the necessity of dealing largely in carefully qualified and restricted language. In respect to the great question of Slavery, the difference between them was only a difference where the limitation should be made. The Republican platform, in which the line against Slavery was drawn the farthest, yet exhibited special solicitude in its framers to preserve intact the inviolability of Slavery in the States. In fact, the shaping of a political platform, so as to supply a party with a distinctive and peculiar foothold, and at the same time not disturb the conservative and compromising spirit of the people, has always been a work of high art, requiring consummate political experience and skill. Among the political debris of the past can be found specimens of party platform joinery, so exactly set and fitted, that the mosaics turned up from Pompeii are but mere botchwork in comparison. As you go back to look at them, you are almost lost in wonder that political craft could have ever attained such nicety of measurement. The present platform shows nothing of the kind. Without a curve or an indentation, or a dovetail, or any balancing or adjusting method of any sort, it stands out in simple square outlines, every plank and every line running straight through from one end to the other, without break or deviation.

Upon the matter of the rebellion, a resolution sets forth an unqualified determination to accept of nothing short of unconditional surrender. Upon the manner of prosecuting the war, a resolution declares for the utmost possible vigor.

Abraham Lincoln 1864 presidential campaign badge.

Upon Slavery, a resolution demands its utter and complete extirpation from the soil of the Republic. Upon the policy of employing negro soldiers, a resolution declares its absolute approval. Upon the question of protecting these soldiers, a resolution calls for the full protection of the laws of war. Upon the paramount authority of the Constitution and laws of the United States, and the necessity of bringing rebels and traitors to due punishment, none but positive terms are employed. Upon the Monroe doctrine, the encouragement of foreign immigration, the maintenance of the national credit and currency, the speedy construction of the Pacific Railroad, and every other important point, the doctrine is thorough, and the language explicit.

The great Union party is fortunate in being thus able to plant itself upon a basis so completely consistent with every loyal obligation and every principle of justice and truth. It has been enabled, by the irresistible course of events, to get clear of the old compromising and temporising necessities. It has reached the fullness of time where political expediency and moral right completely coincide, and where matured public opinion is prepared to meet

and steadily support it. It can now set forth its great principles with the strongest emphasis, and keep, rigidly to their extreme logical consequences, without danger of estranging from the war any portion of the people who have any heart in it at all. The very radicalism of these resolutions, which two years ago would have been a fatal reproach against them, is now their most potent recommendation.

The Copperheads will have a very different task of it when they come to frame their platform. Instead of a few consistent, solid, stable principles, they have got to join together the most diverse and incongruous dogmas and policies. Every sort of opinion respecting the right of making war upon rebellion, respecting the expediency of continuing the war, respecting the policy of offering terms to the rebels, and the kind of terms that should be offered, respecting the future treatment of Slavery, will have its exponents in the Chicago Convention. To assimilate these opinions will be impossible. There will be no alternative but either to make a platform without any definite principles and policy, or to make such a one as cannot be sustained by more than a fraction of the party, and thus be a cause of party division instead of party union. We don't doubt that a vast deal of ingenuity will be exercised to contrive a basis on which all can make shift to stand, and quite likely it may be accomplished. A common hatred is always a strong stimulant to cooperation, and all these varieties of Copperheads, if they agree in nothing else, most certainly are of one feeling against President LINCOLN. Perhaps they will all consent to resolutions of any conceivable shape, that may afford a chance, or something they can imagine to be a chance, of defeating their common enemy. We await with a good deal of curiosity their action in this matter. But it is curiosity unmingled with the slightest apprehension. Whether they unite or divide, make one platform or a dozen, is all the same. No earthly device can prevent the vast majority of the people from pronouncing resolutely and decisively in favor of the principles and the nominations just put forth by the great loyal convention at Baltimore. That ratification by the people is as sure as their national spirit is indestructible. ⊛

THE BALTIMORE PLATFORM AND THE QUESTION OF RECONSTRUCTION.

JUNE 11

The Copperheads, who are nothing if not querulous, complain of the Union platform for not touching upon the question of reconstruction. They say that the supporters of the Administration have different opinions on this cardinal point, and that it was pusillanimously avoided in order to escape discord. They try to make it appear that the seeming unanimity of the Convention was secured only by concealment and evasion.

Now we do not grudge the Copperheads any comfort they can find in this view of the case. They need comfort badly enough, considering their broken fortunes and ruined prospects. They are quite welcome to the fact that loyal men do hold very different opinions on this question of reconstruction, and also to the fancy that the Baltimore Convention was afraid to make an attempt to settle it. It is no discredit to be afraid to do a foolish thing.

The simple truth is that the time has not yet come for a fixed conclusion upon the best mode of reconstruction. Such a decision now by the Union party would be premature, unsafe, and unwise. The prime element in the problem is as yet indeterminable — we mean the disposition of the Southern people after the overthrow of their armies. This, in the very nature of the case, cannot be known except by practical experience after that overthrow takes place. We may speculate about what it will be, ever so confidently, and yet it is nothing but speculation — the stuff that dreams are made of....

First subdue the rebels. When that is done, and not before, can it be known what the Southern temper toward the Government will be, and what course of action that temper will make practicable and expedient. We must trust the President and Congress, and, if need be, the loyal States, with their Constitution-amending powers, to settle that, when the time comes, in the light of actual facts. It would be sheer folly to seek to do the thing now. ✸

OLD ABE'S CHOICE.

JUNE 13

A gentleman in conversation remarked to President LINCOLN on Friday that nothing could defeat him but GRANT's capture of Richmond, to be followed by his nomination at Chicago and acceptance. "Well," said the President, "I feel very much like the man who said he didn't want to die particularly, but if he had got to die, that was precisely the disease he would like to die of." ✸

JAMES RIVER.

GEN. GRANT ON THE SOUTH SIDE.

JUNE 16

WASHINGTON, JUNE 15 — 7 A.M.

To Major-Gen. Dix:

The movement of the Army of the Potomac to the south side of Richmond, across the Chickahominy River and James River, has progressed far enough to admit the publication of some general facts, without danger of premature disclosure.

After several days' preliminary preparations, the movement commenced on Sunday night [June 12]. The Eighteenth Army Corps, under command of Gen. [William F. "Baldy"] SMITH, marched to White House and there embarked on transports for Bermuda Landing. Gen. [Horatio] WRIGHT's corps and BURNSIDE's moved to James Bridge, when they crossed the Chickahominy and marched thence to Charles City, on the James River. Gens. HANCOCK's and [Gouverneur] WARREN's corps crossed the Chickahominy at Long Bridge, and marched thence to Wilcox's, on the James River....

A dispatch from Gen. SHERMAN's headquarters, dated at 3 o'clock yesterday afternoon, near Kenesaw, states that the General is in front, advancing his lines on Kenesaw. Another unofficial dispatch, dated at 9 o'clock last night, reports some advance to-day; that Gen. THOMAS has gained ground, and that one rebel brigade is nearly surrounded. It further reports that the rebel Gen. POLK was killed to-day, and his body sent to Marietta.[1]...

EDWIN M. STANTON, SECRETARY OF WAR. ✸

1. Lieutenant General Leonidas Polk (1806–1864) was both an Episcopal bishop and a general in the Confederate army. He was killed by a Union artillery shell while standing with several other officers atop Pine Mountain on June 14, 1864.

THE ENGAGEMENTS BEFORE WASHINGTON AS VIEWED BY A SOLDIER.

JULY 18

SPECIAL CORRESPONDENCE OF THE NEW-YORK TIMES.

...Washington has been in serious danger.[1] At the time of the appearance of the first Butternut at Rockville, Md., the capital city had not force enough to man four rifle-pits. It was uncertain at which point of the thirty odd miles the columns of [John C.] BRECKINRIDGE and [Jubal] EARLY might be hurled. And when it was learned at midnight of Sunday, the 10th instant, that the enemy were massing their columns against Fort Stevens, with the knowledge of our weakest point of defence — which was the most alarming feature of the whole affair — the terror of the citizens amounted almost to paralysis....

The report Sunday night, that the enemy were at Rockville, eighteen miles distant, brought all the reserves from the Alexandria side.

As your correspondent and the sunlight passed up Fourteenth-street, the thunder of the guns of Fort Reno, which were bellowing under the frantic practice of the militia, was swaying the people to and fro with excitement. A broad grin was very hideously perceptible on the secession mouth, and many an anxious face looked out from behind a waving flag, and many a hearty "God bless you," came from a loyal heart as we marched up the road.

Arriving at Fort Stevens, in the suburbs of the city, we found a few regiments scattered around. In that lazy indifference which is evinced only by the veteran at such an hour. The rifle-pits were sparely occupied, and troops slowly coming in, comprised only of dismounted cavalry and convalescents from hospital.

We were ordered three miles to the left to Fort Reno, and stationed there in the rifle-pits; but until one o'clock the grumbling of the men under the intolerable heat in that shadeless plain "was all the sound we heard." After resting a few moments, we were ordered back again. On our arrival one-third of the regiment and fire commissioned officers had bean stricken down with heat and sun-stroke.

By two o'clock the rebel skirmishers were appearing and disappearing, in that snake-in-the-grass style so becoming to their status, near the residence of Hon. FRANK BLAIR [in Silver Spring]. By three o'clock their skirmish line had worked its insidious way within pistol shot of the gunners at the fort, and matters were becoming decidedly interesting, sufficiently so to beguile the President, the Secretary of State and his son, many of the foreign Legations, and all the military notabilities of the capital, to the scene.

So close were they that one of the gazers from Fort Stevens was shot on the parapet, and the whistle of a bullet was heard close beside the President's carriage, which, at this stage of the proceedings, was in a position enabling its distinguished occupant to crack a joke in response to the crack of the rebel rifle.[2]

Whether it was this last outrage that determined the officers in charge or not we do not know; but about this time proceedings were being taken to put an end to this rebel recreation.

A line of skirmishers, composed of the Veteran Reserves, some dismounted cavalry and hundred-day men, were deployed in front, and steadily drove back for a short distance the whole rebel line....

A vast audience with hushed voices and earnest gaze were looking out upon the scene, and there, in sight of the greatest men of the day, with honest ABRAHAM on one side of the rifle-pits and dishonest JOHN C. BRECKINRIDGE on the other.... ✪

THE ARMY.
PROGRESS OF THE ASSAULT ON PETERSBURGH.

JUNE 20
WAR DEPARTMENT,
WASHINGTON, JUNE 19 — 9:45 P.M.

To Major Gen. Dix:

This evening a dispatch from City Point, dated at 9 o'clock this morning, reached the Department. It reports that our forces advanced yesterday to within about a mile in front of Petersburgh, where they found the enemy occupying a new line of intrenchments, which after successive assaults we failed to carry, but hold and have intrenched our advanced position. From the forces of the enemy within their new line it is inferred that BEAUREGARD has been reinforced from LEE's army.[1]... ✪

Alfred Waud's sketch of federal sharpshooters at Petersburg.

1. As Lee had done at Spotsylvania, Beauregard constructed a shorter defensive line closer to the city and retreated into it June 15. Three days later, part of A. P. Hill's Corps from Lee's army marched into Petersburg to support Beauregard.

THE SIEGE OF PETERSBURGH.

JUNE 22

CORRESPONDENCE OF
THE PHILADELPHIA INQUIRER.
BEFORE PETERSBURGH, SATURDAY, JUNE 18 — 10 P.M.

Reviewing the operations of to-day, I may safely write that affairs are progressing favorably. Standing on the heights occupied by the rebel line of fortifications captured by the Eighteenth Corps on the evening of the 15th, I could distinctly see the extreme right of our front line of battle resting on the Appomattox River not more than half a mile from Petersburgh. This was near sunset to-night. From the point where I stood, a broad, flat plain extends toward the Appomattox on the right, and toward Petersburgh in front, and looking across these flats to the right of the line, at a distance of more than two miles, it appears close to the suburbs of the city.

It has swung around since early this morning a distance of two and a half miles, and is now that much nearer Petersburgh. This morning the front of the right wing ran obliquely to the river, and was much extended, two divisions covering more than two miles of ground; but in sweeping up the river its length has been shortened one-half. On the left we have been equally successful, for although there has not been so great an advance there as on the extreme right, the movement was less of the nature of swinging on a pivot, and the average distance gained is nearly equal. At all events we have gained on the left not less than a mile since four A.M., and this gain was sufficient to throw our line across the Petersburgh and Norfolk Railroad. This places us in possession of two of the several branches that diverge east, southeast, south and southwest from Petersburgh.[1]

The next is the Petersburgh and Roanoke Railroad [also called the Weldon Railroad], the main artery of the rebel Confederacy, and the only direct line of communication between Richmond and the seaboard and Gulf States. It is on this that the strategic value of Petersburgh mainly depends. The centre has not advanced so far beyond its former position as the two wings; but up to last night it was considerably nearer Petersburgh than the right or left, and a greater advance of the two latter portions of our lines was necessary. On an average our present position is probably a mile in advance of the one held this morning. This advance has been made without any severe fighting. The way had been paved for it by the assaults of yesterday, in which ☞

1. In an effort to loosen Grant's grip on Richmond and Petersburg, Lee sent Major General Jubal Early northward through the Shenandoah Valley to invade the North. Early crossed the Potomac and turned east toward Washington arriving in Silver Spring on the outskirts of the capital on July 11.

2. President Lincoln went out to Fort Stevens north of the city to watch the fighting. While standing atop the parapet of the fort, a physician near him was shot in the thigh. According to tradition, a young officer (reputed to be Oliver Wendell Holmes) then told the President to "Get down, you fool," though no contemporary source confirms it.

the enemy had lost portions of their lines of intrenchments.

In my last I mentioned the assault by the Third Division of the Ninth Corps [Willcox's], at 3 P.M. yesterday, which was unsuccessful. The charge was made on the line of breastworks opposite our left, and running across a cornfield front of and parallel with a track of pine woods. The Third Division advanced from their own position across a ravine running parallel with the breastworks, and over the crest of its further declivity into the open fields before the works. Then, under a heavy fire, they advanced across the field nearly to the rifle-pits before them; but their having to cross a slight hollow, which afforded shelter from the shower of bullets that had been pelting them, they stopped and did not advance further. At 6 P.M. Gen. [James H.] LEDLIE's division of the First [actually Ninth] Corps was ordered to renew the attempt.

Gen. LEDLIE formed his attacking column under cover of the ravine above mentioned, in three lines — the First Brigade, Col. [Jacob P.] GOULD; Second Brigade, Col. [Ebenezer W.] PIERCE, and Third Brigade, Col. [Elisha G.] MARSHALL, succeeding each other in the order named. Reaching the open field at the top of the slope, and emerging, they started on a run for the intrenchments, with fixed bayonets, and without stopping to fire a gun. Two batteries to the left and one to the right poured a heavy enfilading fire of grape and canister into them as they advanced, while another was firing at extremely short range

directly in front, combined with musketry. It was a terrible tempest of deadly missiles to pass through, and many a good man fell on the way, but the work was nevertheless accomplished in gallant style.

The enemy displayed the utmost pertinacity, and in the rifle-pits the fight was waged hand to hand, and large numbers of dead rebels were left in them, mingled with our own men. After being driven from the main line, the enemy rallied at the second and smaller line, not more than one hundred yards in the rear, from which also they were driven, but rallying, again retook them, but again were compelled to retreat. Still they returned to the charge four separate times, rushing from the woods in our front with a determination that seemed inexhaustible; and after dark, when the firing had somewhat subsided, their skirmishers crawled forward and scooped out in the light sand soil their little rifle-pits, as close as possible to our lines. During the night, however, they withdrew to a position further back.

The Second Maine Battery, Capt. THOMAS, and Fourteenth Massachusetts, Capt. WRIGHT, posted in the rear of the ravine above-mentioned, did splendid service in this assault. A caisson belonging to the rebel battery in front was blown up by one of their shells. The woods just in its rear bore evidence of tremendous shelling, and on the space where the fire had been concentrated a considerable number of dead were found, killed by shot and shell. On this space I was shown a re-

markable spectacle. At a distance of two or three rods apart, and in line with each other, were three dead rebels, each killed in precisely the same way, the top of the skull being taken completely off and the brains of each lying near him. From their relative positions it seems that all three had been killed by the same round shot.

The severity of the fighting in this assault is attested by the losses sustained, which are estimated at nearly one thousand. Major HEDGES, of the Fourteenth New-York Heavy Artillery, was killed while leading his men in a charge. Col. MARSHALL, of the same regiment, received a contusion of the thigh. Lieut. MCKIBBEN, Fourth United States Infantry, A.D.C. to Gen. LEDLIE, was wounded in the neck. That the rebels suffered severely was evident from the number of dead left on the ground. In the intrenchments they lay, in some places, three or four deep, while the ground between the intrenchments and the woods was thickly strewn with them. Muskets lay scattered around by scores, and the evidences of the hot work that had taken place, were visible everywhere.

Beside their losses in killed and wounded, the enemy left in our hands, at this point, a considerable number of prisoners and one stand of colors, captured by LEDLIE's division. Those portions of the rebel lines continuous with the section whose capture is above narrated, and not already in our hands, were occupied by us in the first advance this morning at 4 A.M., on the broad flats near the Appomattox, on the right of

Alfred Waud's sketch of federal artillery at Petersburg.

the Second Division of the Sixth Corps, and even [John H.] MARTINDALE's division of the Eighteenth Corps gained the rebel line of works in their front in the first charge.

At this part of the lines our further advance was delayed for some time by the rebel sharpshooters, who occupied a house near by, and whose fire was especially troublesome. Battery H, First Ohio, Capt. DORSEY, getting the range of the house, quickly dislodged them. Three successive advances were made during the day along the whole line, to a greater or less extent, the first occurring at four A.M., the second about noon, and the last between three and four P.M., each succeeding with but little difficulty, except the afternoon attack by portions of the Second Corps in the centre or right centre, where the enemy showed a more spirited resistance, and inflicted on us a partial repulse. The fact is, there has been no very severe fighting on any part of the line to-day, and our advantages have been gained at comparatively small cost.

It is evident that a deep game of strategy is being played by the Commanders of the opposing armies, in which, of course, the object of each is to learn as much as possible of the designs and dispositions of the other while keeping his own concealed; and under such circumstances too much care cannot be exercised to guard against improper disclosures.

Among the casualties of the day are Col. [Joshua L.] CHAMBERLAIN, commanding the First Brigade, First Division, Fifth Corps, wounded.[2]

It appears to be the opinion now that only a portion of LEE's force is opposed to us here, and it is apprehended that he will concentrate, against BUTLER at Bermuda Hundred. No uneasiness, however, is felt on this score, as we are prepared at that point for any attack that may be made. I refrain from giving any statement of our forces at this point, or even the exact information of our line of battle, as in the present peculiar state of affairs the publication of such information might be injurious. 🌐

1. The railroads connecting Petersburg to the rest of the Confederacy were crucial, for if Grant could break them, Lee would be unable to sustain his army in Richmond. After breaking the Norfolk & Richmond, only two railroads remained: the Weldon Railroad southward, and the South Side Railroad to the west.

2. This is the same Colonel Chamberlain who won fame on Little Round Top on July 2, 1863, at Gettysburg while in command of the 20th Maine.

OUR CANDIDATE FOR THE VICE-PRESIDENCY.

JUNE 22

The thoroughly unsectional character of the Union party is strikingly evinced in the ardent satisfaction with which the nomination of ANDREW JOHNSON for the Vice-Presidency is hailed by the party throughout the North. We have yet to hear of the slightest murmur. Neither in the Middle nor in the Eastern States is there any complaint that both candidates on the ticket come from the States west of the Alleghanies. All local jealousy is swallowed up in the general sense of the propriety of making special recognition of the peculiar desert of Southern loyalty.

This display of feeling is of much more significance than a superficial glance would discover. Every one who has been in the habit of reading the extracts copied from the Southern newspapers, has seen that the constant effort of the leaders of the rebellion has been to fill the popular heart with rancor against the North, as a geographical division. The term "Yankee" is made the epitome of everything that is odious, and is applied indiscriminately to all who dwell north of Mason and Dixon's line. When Northern parties are spoken of, a certain difference is made between the epithets applied to each. The supporters of the Administration usually get the benefit of the adjectives that express pure hate; while its opponents are more apt to be favored with those that imply contempt. But whatever discrimination there may be in the language used, there is one constant object — and that is the surcharging the Southern heart with the intensest aversion to the Northern people. As the Carthagenian was taught to regard the Roman, as the Frenchman, a half century ago, was taught to regard the Englishman, as his natural enemy, so the Southern man has every influence brought to bear upon him to make him inveterately hostile to the Northern man. This is just what might be expected. The supreme object of the rebellion is separation from the North; and, of course, the more complete the moral separation, the easier becomes the material.

On the other hand, the supreme object of the Union party is to prevent separation and promote union. They are not for fighting the South at all, as a geographical division. They do not even allow the fact that the rebellion is exclusively seated in the South, and that the great majority of the Southern people have given their adhesion to it, to induce upon them anything like an anti-Southern feeling. It is the rebellion alone that they hate. A Southern man who opposes the rebellion, who stands firmly by the old flag, instead of suffering any distrust or prejudice on account of his nativity, in fact is admired and applauded all the more because of his nativity. ANDREW JOHNSON to-day has a far stronger hold upon the great popular heart of the North than he could have had if he had been born in the North. He is no more loyal than hundreds of thousands of others. But the peculiar glory of his loyalty is that it is Southern loyalty; and it is because the people are particularly desirous to recognize and honor that loyalty that his nomination to the second office in the gift of the people affords such particular satisfaction. This manifestation is conclusive evidence of the genuine national spirit of the Union party. It is a new proof that the party is truly entitled to the grand name it bears, — a yet further pledge that the party, in its work of restoring the Union, will know no such thing as sectional antipathy.

This nomination for the Vice-Presidency receives peculiar favor for another excellent reason. It not only attests the true Union feeling, but it vindicates the genuine free-labor principle. It completes the thoroughly representative character of the ticket. The New-York World, with a maladroitness as laughable as the spirit was contemptible, sneered at the ticket as made up of "a rail-splitting buffoon and a boorish tailor, both from the backwoods, both growing up in uncouth ignorance" — ending its period with an allusion too obscene to be republished. In like manner the Richmond Examiner announces the ticket as "a renomination for President of ABRAHAM LINCOLN, the Illinois rail-splitter, and for Vice-President, ANDREW JOHNSON, known in the West as the Tennessee tailor, one of the meanest of that craft." The idea of both the Copperhead and the rebel is the same — namely, that LINCOLN and JOHNSON are unworthy of honor because they once lived by manual labor. It is an idea inseparable from a friendship for Slavery. That institution, every body knows, rests solely on the assumption that manual labor should be the lot of an inferior caste only. In every slave-holding country, that manner of work is always accounted a degradation. Nothing ☞

is more natural than that the upholder of Slavery should taunt the Union party for naming candidates who were at one period of their lives plain working men. Nothing is more fit than that the Union party which has declared that Slavery must be exterminated from the land, should have selected two just such candidates. It is precisely in keeping with the character of a free-labor party. It presents palpably to the people the question whether labor is or is not worthy of honor. It is believed by the Union party that the majority of the people esteem work; and that the public men of the country who have risen from the hardest and the humblest work to high positions by native force of character and by self-education, are the very men who are most to be commended, and who best illustrate both the power and the beauty of American institutions. This certainly was the prevailing feeling in the early days of the republic. It is well to test whether it yet survives or not. We reckon that it will unmistakably manifest itself in November, in spite of all the malign influences of Slavery upon the public mind during these latter years. We think that the fling at the former employments of the candidates of the Union party will be proved a very stupid thing — of all acts the one least calculated to impair their good name or injure their popularity. ◉

PUBLIC IMPATIENCE ABOUT MILITARY MOVEMENTS.

JUNE 22

Since the successful passage of the James River, and the advance on Petersburgh, many people have begun once more to fix a day on which Richmond is to be in our possession. The more sanguine spirits have, as might have been expected, fixed upon the Fourth of July, while others refuse to defer the realization of their hopes for more than one week more at the outside. The speedy capture of the place is looked forward to by a still larger number, who refrain from meddling with dates, but expect the news of it every week. All this, we need hardly say, is but a repetition of what we have been witnessing ever since the war began. After the commencement of every new movement, if it should be attended with the smallest success, a portion of the public has at once rushed to the conclusion that "the back of the rebellion was broken;" that the rebel army was demoralized, and incapable of further resistance. We witnessed this after Mill Spring, after Roanoke, after Fort Donelson, after the fall of New-Orleans, and after that of Vicksburgh. No amount of experience of the risks and uncertainty of war, and of the desperation with which the enemy is fighting, seems sufficient to counteract this most unfortunate tendency to ex-

aggeration. More recently, we have witnessed it after the battle of the Wilderness. GRANT's successful advance threw the public into its usual fever, and they looked for nothing less than his unbroken progress and immediate entry into Richmond.

This would all be, perhaps, a harmless amusement, if it were not that each of these fits of exaltation is followed by great despondency, a general disposition to abuse the Government, to doubt the General-in-Chief, and, of course, also by an upward tendency in prices. We had a week or two of the deepest dejection after it was discovered that the battle of Spottsylvania had not caused LEE's army to dissolve in thin air; and we fully expect that we shall have another week or two of despair as soon as it is discovered, as it will be, probably, in a few days, that the capture of Petersburgh Heights has not rendered Richmond untenable, or reduced the Confederate forces in Virginia to inaction.

It is highly desirable, both for our own comfort and for the sake of the country and the cause, that we should all try and acquire a calmer and more critical temper in talking and thinking of the war, and that we should, as far as possible, prevent our desires from clouding our judgment . . . . ◉

THE PRESIDENT'S VISIT TO THE ARMY.

JUNE 26

HEADQUARTERS DEPARTMENT OF VIRGINIA AND NORTH CAROLINA, IN THE FIELD, THURSDAY, JUNE 23, 1864

Gen. BUTLER's army was honored yesterday by a visit from President LINCOLN. As if they had regard for his presence and safety, the rebels retrained from firing a shot all day, and His Excellency examined the whole length of the line of intrenchments without interruption. He also made a trip up the James River, visiting Admiral [Samuel Phillips] LEE's squadron, going directly to the place where, on Tuesday, the missiles of the enemy plumped and hissed down into the murky waters of the stream,' and no salute from the shotted guns at the rebel rams were fired to do him honor. I am inclined to think that "our

Southern friends" must have been ignorant of the proximity of so distinguished a guest, or their hospitality would have been shown in their own peculiar manner. This is the only explanation of a silence which otherwise must be construed into contempt, and that quality which JEFF. DAVIS and his colleagues cannot afford to exhibit toward Mr. LINCOLN.

The particulars of the President's tour of observation may be written briefly, as they were not marked by any striking incidents. As early as eight o'clock A.M. Gen. BUTLER, accompanied by only a few members of his Staff, rode down to the Point of Rocks Landing, on the Appomattox River, and embarked on the fine steamer Greyhound, Capt. MARTIN, which took them to Bermuda Hundred. Here they were joined by the President, Messrs. [Gustavus] Fox and [Charles H.] DANA, Assistant Secretaries, Col. [Adam] BADEAU, and other officers of Gen. GRANT's Staff, when the trip

Andrew Johnson 1864 vice presidential campaign button.

THE ABOLISHMENT OF SLAVERY IN MARYLAND.

JUNE 25

BALTIMORE, FRIDAY, JUNE 24

The Constitutional Convention of Maryland, in session at Annapolis, passed, to-day, by a vote of 53 yeas against 27 nays, the following article of the Bill of Rights: "Hereafter, in this State, there shall be neither slavery nor involuntary servitude, except in punishment of crime, whereof the party shall have been duly convicted; and all persons held to service or labor as slaves are hereby declared free." ⊛

THE PRESIDENCY.

ACCEPTANCE OF MR. LINCOLN.

JUNE 29

NEW-YORK, JUNE 14

HON. ABRAHAM LINCOLN — Sir, The National Union Convention, which assembled in Baltimore on June 7, 1864, has instructed us to inform you that you were nominated with enthusiastic unanimity for the Presidency of the United States for four years from the 4th of March next....

We are, Sir, very respectfully, your friends and fellow-citizens,

WM. DENNISON, Ohio, Chairman.

was resumed up the river. Arriving at the flag-ship of Admiral LEE, that officer and Fleet-Captain [John S.] BARNES joined the party, and the Greyhound went on until she came to the fleet of monitors at Farrar's Island, which on Wednesday were the targets of the rebel battery on the heights just beyond. Here the President, Gen. BUTLER and some of the more distinguished officials left the Greyhound, and visited the double-turreted monitor Onondaga and machinery and construction were examined apparently with great interest, this being the first opportunity Mr. LINCOLN has had to personally inspect the iron-clads of the Onondaga's class.

Having remained on board the iron-clad a sufficient period to see all the novelties about her, the party landed at Crow Nest, on the south side of the river, where horses were in waiting for their use. Thence a brilliant cavalcade set out to inspect the line of works which are stretched along

REPLY OF MR. LINCOLN.

JUNE 29

EXECUTIVE MANSION, WASHINGTON, JUNE 27

Hon. William Dennison and others, a Committee of the Union National Convention. GENTLEMEN:

Your letter of the 14th inst., formally notifying me that I have been nominated by the convention you represent for the Presidency of the United States for four years from the 4th of March next, has been received. The nomination is gratefully accepted, as the resolutions of the convention — called the platform — are heartily approved.

While the resolution in regard to the supplanting of Republican Government upon the Western Continent is fully concurred in, there might be misunderstanding were I not to say that the position of the Government in relation to the action of France in Mexico, as assumed through the State Department and indorsed by the convention, among the measures and acts of the Executive, will be faithfully maintained so long as the state of facts shall leave that position pertinent and applicable.

I am especially gratified that the soldier and the seaman were not forgotten by the convention, as they forever must and will be remembered by the grateful country for whose salvation they devote their lives.

Thanking you for the kind and complimentary terms in which you have communicated the nomination and other proceedings of the convention, I subscribe myself,

YOUR OBEDIENT SERVANT,
ABRAHAM LINCOLN. ⊛

Members of General Grant's staff at City Point, Virginia.

our position at Bermuda Hundred. Mr. LINCOLN and Gen. BUTLER rode in advance, the latter to the left, Admiral LEE, and Mr. FOX and Mr. DANA next, and the remainder of the party followed as near as possible in the order of their rank.

It was not long before the first soldiers met with on the road recognized the President, whose tall form and not very graceful appearance on horseback would attract attention under any circumstances. Immediately he received three hearty cheers, which he acknowledged by raising his bea-

ver [hat]. The hurrahing, thus initiated on the extreme right of the line was continued along its entire length of three miles and Mr. LINCOLN for the rest of the ride was compelled to remain uncovered, with his head exposed to the broiling heat of the sun. Such is the penalty of greatness! The cheering must, however, have been gratifying enough to make amends for the heat, dust and other physical discomforts which the President experienced. There was no mistaking the genuine, heartfelt enthusiasm of his reception by the troops in the ☞

field. Voluntarily forming in ranks in front of their earthworks, the men were unremitting in their compliments, and an evident smile of satisfaction lighted the President's sallow face, with its mingled expression of care and sadness, as he rode along. At one point of the line the unthinking enthusiasm of the soldiers might have got the President into trouble. It was where our men have been greatly annoyed by sharpshooters. They could not restrain themselves from shouting as the visitors passed; but as soon as their hurrahing ceased, they ran back into their bomb-proofs hurriedly — a movement suggestive enough to make some of the cavalcade wish for a quickening of the houses' paces; but neither the President nor Gen. BUTLER took the hint, riding along at the same jogging trot as before. Without presuming to criticise, I do not see that there was any necessity for either Mr. LINCOLN or Gen. BUTLER to take the risk of being shot by a sharpshooter. It may be very interesting, exciting and gratifying to curiosity, and all that sort of thing, to visit the picket line and catch some views of the enemy's works; but surely men whose lives seem to be now indispensable to the nation have no right to get into such dangerous positions. It is like tempting Providence.

The President expressed himself very hopefully regarding the military situation, and said that he did not know one-half of what had been accomplished here by the army before this opportunity of personal observation. Himself and the other gentlemen of the party returned with Gen. BUTLER to his camp, where they rested awhile and refreshed themselves with lunch. Later in the afternoon the President took passage on the steamer Baltimore for Washington.

H. J. W.[2] ✺

1. On June 21, the Confederates engaged in a long-range bombardment of the Union squadron in the James River near Trent's Reach.

2. Probably Times reporter Henry J. Wisner.

MR. CHASE'S RESIGNATION.

JULY 1

We have no reliable information as to the causes of Mr. CHASE'S resignation of the Treasury Department, though the fact itself seems to be sufficiently authenticated. We do not ascribe it to any anticipation of difficulty in carrying the financial department of the Government through the crisis which circumstances seem to have created for it, because Mr. CHASE is not the man to shrink from any duty or responsibility in which the honor and welfare of the nation are involved. The more threatening the aspect of affairs in his department, the more likely would he have been, other things being equal, to stand by the helm and do everything in his power to avert impending dangers. He has become involved, it is true, in a very embarrassing controversy with the State banks throughout the country, and has committed himself, perhaps too unreservedly, to certain theories of finance in connection with the war; and he may have thought that some other person could more gracefully introduce changes of policy, which experience has shown to be indispensable, than he could himself. But this is a very different thing, and has a very different motive, from abandoning the Ship of State because it seems to be threatened with danger.

We are inclined to attribute his resignation to another cause. It is very well known that, through the zealous and not always judicious efforts of his friends, Mr. CHASE had become deeply involved in the canvass for the Presidential nomination. Naturally enough, the great body of those who held office under his immediate appointment and oversight, were vehement advocates of his selection, and quite often lost sight of the proprieties of their position in their endeavors to promote his success. Mr. LINCOLN, it is notorious, made no attempt whatever to arrest this unusual and not very edifying demonstration, and his own nomination was made by a spontaneous popular movement, in opposition to the most strenuous efforts of the great body of persons holding office under the Treasury Department.... ✺

FROM SHERMAN'S ARMY.

THE ASSAULT ON THE KENNESAW MOUNTAIN.

JULY 4
CINCINNATI, SATURDAY, JULY 2

The Commercial has a special dispatch from Sherman's headquarters, dated June 27, which states that an unsuccessful assault was made on the positions of the rebels at Kenesaw Mountain on the morning of that day at 8 o'clock.

Selected portions of the Fourth, Fourteenth and ["Black Jack" John] LOGAN's Corps moved to the attack in three columns, striking the rebel intrenchments on the right, the left and the centre.

After a fierce fight, lasting between one and two hours, our troops were compelled to fall back everywhere, finding it impossible to carry the crest of the hill in the face of such a destructive fire.

Gen. HARKER fell in the assault on the right, and Col. DAN MCCOOK, both severely wounded.

Our position is now considerably in advance of that occupied before the assault.

Our loss is estimated at about two thousand.[1] ✺

1. Union losses in the assault at Kenesaw Mountain were 3,000; Confederate losses were 552.

Battle of Kennesaw Mountain.

THE PIRATE SUNK OFF CHERBOURG BY THE KEARSARGE.

DETAILS OF THE ENGAGEMENT.

JULY 6

By the [ship] City of Baltimore, the general details of whose news we give elsewhere, we have the highly important and gratifying intelligence that on Sunday, June 19, the rebel pirate Alabama was engaged off Cherbourg by the United States steamer Kearsarge, which sunk her after an engagement lasting an hour and a half.

The following is a brief statement of the battle as given by the English papers:

The report that the rebel cruiser Alabama gone out from Cherbourg to fight the United States steamer Kearsarge, which was hovering off that port, turned out to be true, and resulted in the sinking of the Alabama. The encounter was witnessed by the English steam yacht Deerhound, and that vessel picked up Capt. [Raphael] SEMMES and the crew of the Alabama, took them to Cowes, and furnished the following details of the affair:

On the morning of Sunday, the 19th, at 10:30, the Alabama was observed steaming out of Cherbourg harbor, toward the steamer Kearsarge. At 11:10 the Alabama commenced the action by firing with her starboard battery, at a distance of about a mile. The Kearsarge also opened fire immediately with her starboard guns, and a sharp engagement, with rapid firing from both ships, was kept up, both shot and shell being discharged. In the manoeuvring both vessels made seven complete circles, at a distance of from a quarter to half a mile.

At 12 o'clock the firing from the Alabama was observed to slacken, and she appeared to be making head sail and shaping her course for land, which was distant about nine miles.

At 12.30 the Confederate vessel was in a disabled and sinking state.

The Deerhound immediately made toward her, and in passing the Kearsarge was requested to assist in saving the crew of the Alabama. When the Deerhound was still at a distance or two hundred yards the Alabama sunk, and the Deerhound then lowered her boats and, with the assistance of those from the sinking vessel, succeeded in saving about forty men, including Capt. SEMMES and thirteen officers.... ◉

ENGLISH FEELING AT THE SINKING OF THE ALABAMA.

JULY 6

The sinking of the Alabama by the Kearsarge appears to have been a source of very great mortification among the foreign friends of the rebels. It is amusing to read the comments of the English papers which represent that class, and to see the misstatements which they make, the contradictions of each other, which they are not careful enough to avoid, and the shifts and excuses which they are fertile in, to lessen, if possible, the pain of the blow. They universally agreed at first that the Kearsarge was badly disabled in the fight. In fact, to read the accounts, one would think that her victory was quite accidental. They also were in one accord that the Alabama was entirely overmatched, and that the Kearsarge had "higher steam power and rate of speed, a crew nearly double that under Capt. SEMMES," and heavier guns.

Her guns were heavier no doubt, but her crew was only 180 in number to 150 on board the Alabama, and as to the superiority in speed, if there is anything which these same people have gloried over in reference to the Alabama, it has been that she could far outstrip any vessel that we had afloat. They have quite lamented over our inability to build a vessel that would steam so fast as she, in view of our claims to be able to accomplish something worth mentioning in building vessels. How does it come now, that all of a sudden we find such a superiority in speed admitted for the Kearsarge?

Of course, to read their account, all the glory was with the Alabama. They spread everywhere the picture of her crew firing their guns till their muzzles were under water and the vessel going down, without striking their flag, although SEMMES himself says that he hauled down his flag, at which time it is to be presumed his men ceased firing; and the log of the Deerhound says she did not strike till forty minutes after she fired her last shot.

They are very much puzzled to know why SEMMES went into a fight in which he was to be so badly beaten. The Liverpool correspondent of the Manchester Examiner explained it by saying that "SEMMES believed that WINSLOW, of the Kearsarge, a very young man, lacked experience and would rather run than fight." WINSLOW is about sixty,

Sinking of the CSS *Alabama* off the coast of France.

but would have certainly been as little likely to prefer running to fighting, if he had been younger than he is; and if SEMMES did calculate in that way, he did not know his man.

The [London] Times says, "It is not in our power to say why Capt. SEMMES, who had gained so much glory, and so unquestionable a reputation for courage, that he could afford to be prudent," came out to the fight. We doubt whether he would have done so if he could have avoided it; but if he did come out for the purpose of a fight, it seems to us quite probable that he was driven to it by the consciousness that his reputation for courage was very questionable. What he has ever done since he took command of the ship to show courage in is hard for us to see. His whole career has been one of running away from battle, with the sole exception of his attack upon the Hatteras, where he showed stratagem, but nothing else; and we are inclined to think that this feeling that to be always running after unarmed vessels, and flying from armed pursuers, was showing too much of the "better part of valor," that drove him at last into a fight which real discretion probably would have led him to avoid, if possible.

Charges of inhumanity on the part of the Kearsarge were also freely made. SEMMES himself says that she fired five guns after

he had struck his colors, and that there was no appearance of any boats coming from her after the ship went down. We should require very strong proof of this statement before we credited it for a moment, and as it is contradicted by all the other accounts, and as the Kearsarge took sixty-eight of the Alabama's crew, which her boats actually picked up, it is quite certain that there is not the shadow of a foundation for this charge.

We are not surprised at the state of feeling which led to such misstatements. The English feel in their hearts as if the conflict was their own. It was fought with an English-built vessel, with English guns and English powder, and an English crew. SEMMES openly declared that his best men were trained on board an English man-of-war, the Excellent — and to have a vessel thus built, and thus manned and equipped, so easily destroyed by an American vessel, with so little injury to herself, touches the old sore spot, the first blow upon which was struck when the flag of the Guerriere came down. We can well afford to let their vexation work itself off in ovations to SEMMES, and rejoicings over his escape in an English vessel. We doubt, however, whether it will amount to enough to procure him another ship. ⊛

GEORGIA.

JULY 6

The situation in Georgia is now of the deepest interest and importance. In the whole of our movements there during the past two months, the enemy has simply tried to retard our advance at such commanding positions as were found along the line of the railroad. Of course, in a mountainous region like that, it was very easy to make our advance difficult, and to delay us for a considerable time. But the enemy seem now to have got to the last defensive line of Atlanta outside of the city fortifications — the line of the Chattahoochee; and our army has followed him closely up to within a short distance of that line. If we can now force him to general battle, or if we can effect an investment of Atlanta, we shall soon see the breaking up of his army. If JOHNSTON evacuates Atlanta — which we do not believe he will do without a serious defence — he may still keep up the fight during the Summer in efforts to defend Milledgeville. ⊛

GEN. SHERMAN CONFIDENT OF SUCCESS.

JULY 26

Gen. SHERMAN's latest dispatches show an assured confidence in the capture of Atlanta, though the prize may not be won as speedily as the public had anticipated. …Gen. SHERMAN's dispatches also express the most profound grief at the death of MCPHERSON. That gallant soldier was killed about eleven in the forenoon, while riding in advance of his Staff to form a defensive line to meet the rebel attack.… ⊛

THE ADVANCE UPON ATLANTA.

JULY 27

EIGHT MILES FROM ATLANTA, GA., MONDAY MORNING, JULY 18

One of the most difficult jobs in the art of war is the successful crossing of a river in the face of the enemy, most especially when a structure has to be constructed under the fire of the opposing party. After considerable skirmishing, two pontoons were swung across the Chattahoochee, on the night of the 16th, and on the evening of the 17th the entire army and its baggage had been safely lodged on the south bank of the stream.

The successful passage of the Chattahoochee River was effected as follows: Early in the week, the Fifteenth, Sixteenth, Seventeenth, Twenty-third and Fourth Corps moved up the north bank of the river some fourteen miles, and crossed without opposition, leaving [Joseph] HOOKER and [John M.] PALMER on the opposite bank, with the railroad dividing their two corps. At a proper time, HOWARD moved down to the right, to be in readiness to form a junction with the two corps, and to protect them while crossing. At noon on the 17th inst., PALMER's corps commenced crossing — [Union Major General] JEFF. C. DAVIS' division in the advance. Before dark the Twentieth and Fourteenth were across, with their ammunition and baggage trains. At 9 o'clock that night, Gen. SHERMAN's whole force was upon the Atlanta side of the Chattahoochee, Gen.

REPORTS AND RUMORS.

JULY 27

A correspondent writes from Atlanta:

"The most interesting, and, perhaps, significant event of yesterday, was the arrival of Gen. BRAXTON BRAGG. Riding into the city yesterday, I saw the General and two or three other gentlemen — perhaps of his own personal staff — in a carriage, going out to Gen. JOHNSTON's headquarters."[1] ⊛

1. The purpose of Bragg's visit was to evaluate the situation, recommend to Jefferson Davis whether or not Johnston should be retained in command, and, if not, who should replace him. Based largely on Bragg's report, Davis dismissed Johnston on July 17 and appointed John Bell Hood in his place. Hood at once attacked.

PALMER's corps resting upon the river upon the right, near the mouth of Peachtree Creek, and in close proximity to where the railroad bridge (destroyed) spanned the stream, with HOOKER next on the left, then HOWARD and SCHOFIELD, while MCPHERSON's three corps formed the left wing, resting upon the river some fourteen miles from the extreme right.

The skirmishing was quite lively all day and until the first division had effected a crossing, when the enemy's sharpshooters retired, leaving us in full possession of the territory bordering upon the river....

From the river, of course, the direct route to Atlanta is by the railway and accompanying highway. Instead of advancing here, Gen. SHERMAN rests his extreme right at the crotchet formed by the river and the creek and extends his left northeast to a distance of more than fourteen miles, with the intention of cleaning out the enemy by swinging the left.

As soon as JEFF. C. DAVIS crossed, the rebels must have fled precipitately, as quite a considerable number of their dead and wounded were found upon the field. Our forces buried some twenty odd men, including two officers. The wounded included about the same number as the list of killed, and were the recipients of kind

attention and medical treatment. One of the officers found and buried by the Sixtyninth Ohio was labeled Major C. C. JAY, Thirteenth Mississippi. His pockets were turned inside out, and were bloody, giving one to understand that the surgeon had given him attention.

During this night (Sunday) the situation, at least for a non-combatant, was decidedly unpleasant. The lines were less than half a mile apart, our troops being engaged a portion of the night in erecting suitable defences.

Occasionally the rebels would salute us with a hissing shell or a cracking round shot, which made me feel duced restless, especially when they would strike (spud) in the dirt at a "respectable" distance, or lodge (chuck) in a tree in close proximity to my canvas-clad habitation. I felt on the whole, however, quite safe, as I was located nearly three-quarters of a mile from our own skirmish line.

The whole line moves this morning upon the enemy, and it is believed that if he is not too strong upon Peach-tree Creek, we shall have accomplished half the distance between this and Atlanta to-day.

We captured a half dozen prisoners in our advance yesterday, but they were all very sullen. They say that BRAGG is again in com-

mand, and that JOE JOHNSTON has been relieved for failing to cut up our rear.'....

MIDNIGHT.

I have just arrived from HOOKER's and HOWARD's headquarters, but learn nothing of interest. The ammunition and supply trains are coming up, and will park for the night in the rear of their respective corps.

The officers and soldiers of this army, although in ecstacies at their own successes, are much troubled in regard to the situation in the East, especially the raid [Jubal Early's raid on Washington]. They are troubled lest while we capture their queen we may lose our castle.

A difference of opinion exists as to whether we are to take Atlanta with or without a battle. For my part, I think that point will be decided to-morrow. There are many rebel "ditches" in this locality, and the deuce may be to pay ere Atlanta falls. We may have to encounter strong opposition at the eastern extremity of Peachtree Creek, yet; then there are two more ditches, and then, the defences of the city present themselves, and must be carried by flank or storm. ✸

1. The rumors were correct. Johnston had been relieved the day before (July 17).

A Kurz and Allison lithograph of the Battle of Atlanta.

THE BATTLE NEAR ATLANTA — NEWS TO THE 24TH.

AUGUST 1

TWO MILES FROM ATLANTA, SUNDAY, JULY 24
CORRESPONDENCE OF THE NEW-YORK TIMES.

After two of the severest conflicts of the campaign, Gen. SHERMAN has pushed his lines from the Chattahoochee River to within two miles of Atlanta, at whose gates he is now loudly knocking. On the 18th all the army had crossed to the south side of the river. On the 20th Gen. McPHERSON cut the railroad at Decatur, between Atlanta and Augusta. All communications by railroad from Atlanta are now severed, except the Macon route.

Gen. THOMAS' three corps, the Twentieth, Fourth and Fourteenth, occupied on the 20th the line of Peachtree Creek, running east and west about five miles north of the city. Gen. HOOKER, with his corps, effected a crossing with but little resistance. Gens. WARD and WILLIAMS' divisions occupied the right and left, and Gen. GEARY's division the centre, a few hundred yards in advance. The little opposition offered in crossing had allayed all apprehensions of attack, and but little preparation had been made toward intrenching or rendering the line secure. In fact, Gen. HOOKER was waiting for WARD and WILLIAMS to align themselves with GEARY in order to advance to a crest further in advance, where the position was to have been strengthened and maintained until better information of the enemy's whereabouts was obtained.

Before the lines were closed in upon GEARY his exposed right was assailed by an overwhelming force of the enemy, two corps strong.

The attack was made so suddenly that the men were many of them shot down before they could pick up their arms, which had been stacked while they rested waiting for the other divisions. The First Brigade was quickly demolished, and, leaving half its men dead and wounded on the ground, was driven in upon the second line, consisting of the Second and Third Brigades. These commands were made the centre of a cross-fire from the front and right flank, while several rebel regiments actually got in their rear and poured in from countless muskets a murderous fire. For an hour the contest was sanguinary and fearfully destroying to our men. Gen. GEARY, however, stood his ground, and though death and destruction were raining upon his devoted command from three sides, from foes as numerous, to all appearances, as the leaves on the trees, he would not yield or surrender, well knowing that soon the other divisions would come to his rescue. Gen. WILLIAMS was the first to charge the enemy's left, which he did in gallant style, forcing the rebels back from one side of GEARY. Gen. WARD followed, by making a most vigorous assault upon their right, while their whole attention was turned upon the other two divisions, and succeeded in throwing them into confusion, from which, though three times our number, they were not able to recover. All our killed and wounded were regained, and some hundreds of theirs, which they could not carry off. Gen. WARD captured several stand of colors. Their repulse was most complete.[1]

This occasion is the second of the campaign where Gen. GEARY, by his magnificent resolution and the unconquerable determination "never to yield" of his division, has wrested victory where defeat seemed certain. On this occasion he was assailed by an almost countless enemy. Those who saw the attack from the high grounds of Peachtree Creek say that the enemy's whole army appeared to be present — so numerous were the colors flying and so deep were their lines. The fight lasted from 3 o'clock until sunset. The loss of Gen. Hooker's corps was in the neighborhood of sixteen hundred.

It is no exaggeration of facts to say that one-half of the substantial results gained by Gen. SHERMAN in this Summer's campaign are due to the splendid fighting of Gen. HOOKER's corps. It has added a new chaplet to his brow already glittering with victories achieved during his connection with the Western Army. In his three Lieutenants — Gens. GEARY, WILLIAMS and WARD — he has three able and brave men, whose services in the hard-fought battles of the Army of the Potomac and elsewhere have won for them imperishable laurels.

The Confederate line on Peachtree Creek was evacuated by their army on the night of the 21st. Gen. THOMAS advanced his on the 22d, as far as its present location, which, as I before stated, is but two miles from Atlanta. We hold a high ridge confronting the northern side of the city, which is protected by a ridge higher than ours, and strongly fortified. Day before yesterday, the 22d, the enemy concentrated a heavy column upon Gen. MCPHERSON, who holds the left of the line resting on the Augusta road. The battle raged all day with great violence. Not less than a thousand were slain on both sides. While the battle was progressing in front, a force attacked the trains and batteries in Gen. MCPHERSON's rear. Report says that many of the batteries were captured, but afterwards retaken. Gen. MCPHERSON was killed, and his staff dispersed or captured. The loss in this army is terrible, but the fortunes of the day were retrieved. The enemy was repulsed with a loss of many prisoners, and a thousand killed. Prisoners report that the two repulses of the 20th and 22d, have almost destroyed HOOD's army.[2]

It has been definitely ascertained that HOOD is in command. JOHNSTON was relieved "for yielding too much territory." HOOD has manfully exerted himself to give up less, if we can judge of the matter by his desperate assaults. How he has succeeded may be judged from the fact that we can send our cannon shot into Atlanta.

Gen. SHERMAN's lines encircle the city on the north, east and west. Gen. [Lovell H.] ROUSSEAU arrived with his [cavalry] command to-day. He crossed the Tennessee River at Florence, Ala., and raided across the country, severing the lines of communication west and northwest of the city. The Montgomery road is destroyed.

In the fight of the 20th Gen. HOOKER's corps lost very heavily in officers. Among the slain are Col. GEORGE A. COBHAM, One Hundred and Eleventh Pennsylvania

Federal picket post shortly before the battle of July 22.

Volunteers; Lieut.-Col. [Charles B.] RAN-DALL, One Hundred and Forty-ninth New-York Volunteers, and Capt. THOMAS H. ELLIOTT, Assistant Adjutant-General to Gen. GEARY. The One Hundred and Forty-first New-York Volunteers lost all its field officers killed or wounded. In Col. [George A.] COBHAM the service lost one of its brightest ornaments. He was surrounded by the enemy and called upon by an officer to surrender. With a rare nobility of character he refused to yield, and for refusing was shot through the body by order of the rebel who made the demand, Mortally wounded, but not killed, COB-HAM turned, and, with the calm dignity that always characterized him, ordered a soldier who stood near him to "shoot that fellow." The order was promptly obeyed, and the murderer paid with his life the penalty of killing one of the noblest soldiers that the army ever contained....

While the losses of the army have been terrible during these battles, the enemy's losses are deemed much greater than ours. Gen. SHERMAN will, by severing the rebel General's communications, either force him out of Atlanta or destroy him inside of it. He is already weakened so much by his recent attacks that our lines are deemed impenetrable to his most determined efforts.

G.C. ✹

1. This was the Battle of Peachtree Creek (July 20, 1864). Union losses were 1,710, while Confederate losses were 4,796.

2. This was the Battle of Atlanta (July 22, 1864), also known as the Battle of Decatur or the Battle of Bald Hill. Hood sent Lieutenant General William J. Hardee on a long flank march around to the south to assail the corps of James B. McPherson, who was killed early in the fighting. Union losses in this battle were 3,641; Confederate losses were 8,499.

CHAPTER 21
"What These Old Heroes Do"

AUGUST–SEPTEMBER 1864

he relentless sieges of Richmond and Petersburg continued, as each side sought a solution that would break the stalemate.

Readers of The New York Times had long been treated to scoops about the latest developments in military technology: innovations like reconnaissance balloons and ironclad warships. But nothing could have prepared subscribers for the breathtaking news that arrived early in August: the explosion of arguably the largest and most devastating bomb ever detonated in any war. And nothing could have steeled readers for the almost unbearable news that the devastating innovation had failed to give Union troops the advantage they expected in their quest to take Petersburg, Virginia.

Generals Grant and Burnside had both been skeptical of the engineering proposal to dig a secret underground shaft all the way from Union positions before Petersburg to Confederate entrenchments guarding the city. The idea was to load explosives beneath rebel positions and then ignite them — opening a gaping hole through which Federal forces could break through. General Burnside approved the scheme.

The explosion itself succeeded (though it fizzled when the fuse was initially lit). The earthshaking predawn blast killed scores of soldiers and frightened away hundreds of others, leaving behind a scorched landscape that became known as "the Crater." But in the Union attack that followed, the Federals made the crucial mistake of leaping *into* the Crater, rather than surrounding it. With Union troops trapped inside, Confederate reinforcements returned to target confused and directionless Union soldiers inside the Crater. The

Detail of a woodcut depicting the Battle of Atlanta.

result was wholesale slaughter. The North further reeled from reports of atrocities — black soldiers executed on the spot even after laying down their arms and surrendering.

The disaster could not have come at a worse time for the Lincoln administration — with Election Day looming, only three months away. As The Times reported, often with barely concealed rage (editor Raymond, after all, was now serving as chairman of the Republican National Committee), Lincoln was being whipsawed by relentless criticism from both the left and the right. Democrats objected to the war's brutality, while liberal Republicans excoriated Lincoln for being too lenient in his plans for reconstruction.

It took an episode of good old-fashioned personal heroism — in the face of, instead of in sync with, modern technology — to begin turning the tide. On August 9, Admiral David Glasgow Farragut, lashed to the rigging of his wooden flagship, the USS *Hartford*, damned the torpedoes and steamed past the rebel forts guarding the entrance to Mobile, Alabama. Farragut held on even when the frightening Confederate ram *Tennessee* brushed past with guns blazing. Observing the duel between the ironclads *Monitor* and *Virginia* two years earlier, Herman Melville had cheered: "Hail to victory without the gaud of glory." Under Farragut, glory returned to the war at sea.

Still, most observers remained fully convinced that Lincoln would lose his bid for re-election — and lose badly. The war had simply raged for too long, and at much too high a cost, without victory. None of the skeptics were more despondent than Henry J. Raymond of The New York Times. On August 22, he wrote despairingly to Lincoln about "the political condition of the country as it strikes me." Reported the editor/campaign manager:

"The tide is turning strongly against us. Hon E. B. Washburne writes that 'were an election to be held now in Illinois we should be beaten.' Mr. Cameron writes that Pennsylvania is against us. Gov. Morton writes that nothing but the most strenuous efforts can carry Indiana…. And so of the rest. Nothing but the most resolute and decided action on the part of the government, and its friends, can save the country from falling into hostile hands."

Desperate, Raymond boldly proposed that Lincoln now send a delegation to Richmond to ask Jefferson Davis to cease hostilities by "*acknowledging the supremacy of the constitution,* — all other questions to be settled in a convention of the people of the States." In other words, Raymond was proposing, that Lincoln should renege on the promise of the Emancipation Proclamation if it would end the bloodshed and reunite the country. A few days later, Raymond called at the White House to renew his plea in person. Lincoln received him warmly, but bluntly told him that "to follow his plan of sending a commission to Richmond would be worse than losing the Presidential contest — it would be ignominiously surrendering it in advance." Raymond reportedly left Washington somewhat cheered by Lincoln's knowledge and determination. But Lincoln's good friend Leonard Swett arrived shortly thereafter in New York to find "the most alarming depression possessing the minds" of all the city's Republican editors. As he complained: "Raymond, the chairman of the National Committee, not only gave up, but would do nothing. Nobody would do anything." Indeed, Lincoln himself ended the month convinced of his defeat as well. He even asked the members of his Cabinet to sign, sight unseen, a memorandum pledging cooperation with the next administration.

Then, in the space of just a few days, the fate of both the Republican President and the entire Union shifted dramatically. On August 31, Democrats convening in Chicago as expected nominated George B. McClellan for president, but saddled him with a peace platform that gave The Times ammunition to attack him as a Copperhead bent on humiliating the country he had once served in uniform. Even McClellan's mild rebuke of the peace plank left him compromised.

Then, the very next day, on September 1, General Sherman captured Atlanta — the biggest prize yet in the Western Theater — after a campaign Lincoln cheered would remain forever "famous in the annals of war," and which The Times had covered intensely for many days. Two weeks later, the Richmond Dispatch noted bitterly that "Yankeedom" was "making precisely such a use of the capture of Atlanta that we foresaw … a continual support of Lincoln and the war."

Indeed, these victories altered the political landscape, and Lincoln reaped the harvest. In a Thanksgiving proclamation giving thanks for Farragut's and Sherman's triumphs, the President indelibly linked the Union cause — and his own political destiny — not only to the heroes of the day, but also to a God he now predicted would "continue to uphold the government of the United-States against all the efforts of public enemies and secret foes."

THE ASSAULT BY OUR TROOPS ON SATURDAY.

DESPERATE ATTEMPT TO CARRY THE ENEMY'S POSITION.

HEADQUARTERS OF THE ARMY OF THE
POTOMAC, Saturday, July 30

After the explosion at an early hour this morning,[1] everything betokened a brilliant victory, but soon after matters assumed a different aspect, part of the attacking force having given way, thus exposing the balance to an enfilading fire from both artillery, and infantry.

The programme was as follows:

The mine was to be exploded at 3 o'clock in the morning; the batteries to open at once along the entire line immediately after the explosion, and the Ninth Corps to make the charge, supported by the Eighteenth Corps, AYRE's division of the Fifth Corps, and the Third Division of the Second Corps.

The greater part of the arrangement was carried out as ordered, although the commencement was later than the hour designated, on account of the fuse going out twice.

August 2

sion, under the command of Brig.-Gen. WHITE,[2] was pushed forward and ordered to charge and carry the crest of the hill, which would have decided the contest.

The troops advanced in good order as far as the first line, where they received a galling fire, which checked them, and although quite a number kept on advancing, the greater portion seemed to become utterly demoralized, part of them taking refuge in the fort, and the balance running to the rear as fast as possible.

They were rallied, and again pushed forward, but without success, the greater part of their officers being killed or wounded.

During this time they seemed to be without any one to manage them, and finally they fell back to the rear and out of the range of the volleys of canister and musketry that were plowing through their ranks. ✸

Alfred Waud's sketch of the Battle of the Crater.

The explosion took place at precisely 4:40 o'clock.

The roar of artillery that immediately followed was almost deafening.

At 5 1/2 o'clock the charge was made, and the fort, with part of the line each side, was carried in the most brilliant style.

The Second Division, which was in the centre, advanced and carried, the second line, a short distance beyond the fort, and here rested, holding their ground with the utmost determination.

It was at this time the Colored Divi-

1. In June, Union engineers began digging a shaft nearly 600 feet long to a spot directly above Confederate entrenchments, filling it with four tons of gunpowder and igniting it on July 30. Nearly 300 Confederates perished in the explosion, and U.S. Colored Troops led the charge that followed. But Union officers foolishly ordered troops into the blackened trench, where they were surrounded and mowed down. The disaster cost the Union some 3,800 killed, wounded, and missing, with Confederate casualties at 1,500.
2. Julius White (1816–1890), who served as General Burnside's chief of staff.

THE WAR IN THE WEST.

HISTORY AND ACHIEVEMENTS OF THE ARTILLERY ARM OF THE SERVICE.

August 2

An officer in Gen. SHERMAN's army makes the following interesting statement regarding the progress and achievements of the artillery arm of the service in the Western armies:

"During the first years of the war the field artillery of the Eastern armies far excelled that of the West, and with good reason. Raised and equipped as were the former convenient to our best arsenals, they had the first pick of guns, obtained a uniform armament, and the choicest of ammunition to correspond. It was for them to test and adopt the latest inventions in projectiles and fuses. Schools of instruction were established for their benefit, and text books furnished in abundance; beside this, at the opening of the rebellion, nearly all the regular artillery batteries were incorporated in the Army of the Potomac. These batteries, during the months that that arm was organized under MCCLELLAN were made by Gen. BARRY,[1] then his Chief of Artillery, to serve as leaven for the whole lump of plastic volunteer material placed in his hands. That this leavening process might be thorough in its operation, he adopted the following plan: An average of four batteries was the complement of each division of the army. Of these, three were volunteers and one reguar. The four were brigaded under command of the officer commanding the regular battery. The result of example and instruction thus afforded was the most astonishing progress on the part of the new batteries. They soon became, both in appearance and practical efficiency, dangerous rivals of their exemplars.

The Western artillery, on the other hand, bad to struggle onward and upward without such helps. What it learned was often the result of dearly bought experience. Inferior and defective material injured its efficiency. Guns of odd calibre and pattern, long since rejected from the Eastern service, was thrust upon it with such an entire disregard to uniformity, that some batteries actually took the field with as many different calibres as they had pieces. You can readily imagine that the replenishment of the ammunition chests of such patchwork organizations, would become next to an impossibility amid the confusion of a general engagement. Super added to these embarrassments and disadvantages, the artillery of the West has suffered especially from another cause that has done much to cripple the artillery of all our armies in the field. I refer to the withdrawal from this branch of the service of officers of the old army of long standing and experience, who, after the inauguration of the present conflict, accepted, in volunteer and staff organizations, that promotion that was denied them in their own. While noting the fact and its ruinous consequences, I cannot blame these officers individually for adopting a course that has been fully justified by subsequent events. And, to prove this, I have only to instance the present status of those regular battery commanders who, at the opening of the war, preferred to remain identified with the artillery and share its fortunes. These are now, after three years' faithful service, battery commanders still, with no increased rank or pay, and no other prospect of direct promotion than the changes of the army list affords. In the meantime, the sense of justice and the professional pride of these men have been repeatedly outraged and wounded, by their having been compelled to serve subordinate to mere fledglings in both years and experience. Still, the service has suffered all the same, and the fault is due to imperfect legislation. By some strange oversight, every staff bill that has been passed by Congress has utterly ignored the claims and requirements of the artillery. While every corps and division staff is loaded down with officers of high rank on the Quartermaster's, Subsistence and Inspector-General's Departments, the poor devil of a Chief of Artillery, who has been selected for a position of equal importance and responsibility on such staff, must assume his extra duties with no increase of rank or pay, but, on the contrary, by relinquishing the immediate command of his battery, must drop certain perquisites which form a part of his remuneration as a battery commander. Is it any wonder that such injustice should have bred a spirit of dissatisfaction and revolt among its victims, and that, as a result, two-thirds of the best artillery officers we possess are to-day serving under volunteer appointments in the infantry and cavalry of the army? Aside from the pure injustice of the thing, the

course the Government has pursued in the matter has been very unwise and impolitic. Notwithstanding these many drawbacks, the artillery of the West has make for itself not only a creditable but an honorable record, has sustained heavy losses in all of the great battles, and when it has lost guns has done so with honor. Upon its labors and achievements in the present campaign under SHERMAN, too much praise cannot be bestowed. The character, both of the country and the campaign, has been such as to develop and tax to the utmost its good qualities. GRANT's artillery has been almost silent while the deadly infantry strife was raging among the tangled undergrowth of the Wilderness, but every hill side of Northern Georgia, from Tunnel Hill to the Chattahoochee, has echoed, by day and night, in thunder tones, the "deadly diapason" of our cannonade. I have never seen artillery employed so much at the very front as in this campaign. With a recklessness and audacity that have been quite at variance with all established laws, our batteries have always followed upon the very heels of our skirmishers. I have repeatedly seen a skirmishing line charge across a field and scarcely secure a precarious lodgment on a ridge beyond, before a section or battery has come rattling along to occupy and help to hold the same ground, its only immediate reliance and support the reserve of the skirmishers and the charges of canister in its guns. Again, where we have occupied for several days together, parallel lines of infantry parapet — two lines in reserve and the front line within eighty or one hundred yards of elaborate rebel works, as at New Hope Church. Dallas, and before Kenesaw, our artillery has always been found lining the foremost parapet — often in positions where our men could load their pieces only while lying at full length on their backs. Thus situated, it has, of course, shared the perils and the glory of repulsing the frequent attacks made by the rebels with the desperate purpose of breaking through our lines, and it is an equal credit to our infantry and artillery, to say that thus far not a gun has been lost.... ✹

1. William Farquhar Barry (1818–1879). In 1864, Barry became W. T. Sherman's chief of artillery and served in that capacity during the Atlanta campaign.

THE LATE ENGAGEMENT BEFORE ATLANTA.

AUGUST 5
FROM OUR SPECIAL CORRESPONDENT.
CAMP IN THE FIELD, BEFORE ATLANTA, GA.,
SUNDAY, JULY 24

The 20th and 22d inst. have been the two most eventful days in the campaign of SHERMAN's magnificent army in the Southwest. On those two days two great battles were fought, and two victories won. The former on the 20th, fought mainly by the Twentieth Army Corps, and the latter by the Army of the Tennessee, will each have its respective bearing on the total results of the war, and materially accelerate its felicitous termination. It cannot be but with a glow of self-satisfied thought and patriotic congratulation that every loyal citizen will review the events of those two days and raise his devout thanksgiving to the God of nations for the triumphs of the Union arms. The Twentieth Army Corps fought on Peachtree Creek, directly north of the city, and embraced in its line of battle many roads leading into it. The battle was fought against greatly superior numbers, and vastly more important strategic positions and developed itself as to time and situation where not very greatly expected. That the enemy, was not distant from us was patent to even unmilitary minds, but his purpose of making such a tremendous onset against us at the time and place he aid he had most profoundly concealed until, as he had doubtless flattered himself, the time for him to strike had come, when his whole design was unmasked and it was plain that the tug of war had commenced.

Peachtree Creek winds its course through a narrow valley, encompassed with innumerable bluffs, and entered by as many ravines. A place more opportune for a retreating array to take up his position of defence, it is difficult to conceive. The bluffs are in themselves superb military defences, while the dense forests that everywhere cover them cast the mantle of concealment over the presence and dispositions of the foe.

On the afternoon of the 19th inst., the Third Brigade of the Second Division of the Twentieth Army Corps, commanded by Col. IRLAND, crossed Peach-tree Creek, under cover of the fire of an infantry detachment of our troops detailed for that purpose. A temporary military bridge had been constructed without much trouble, and Col. IRLAND's brigade ☞

crossed with but few casualties. He at once deployed skirmishers, and drove the enemy from the first bluff which immediately commanded the crossing of the creek, and occupied it by his own brigade, thus securing it for the transit for the remainder of our troops. In less than an hour and a half after the occupation of the above bluff by IRLAND's brigade, the entire of Gen. GEARY's[1] command, two divisions of the Twentieth Corps, had crossed to support it. The men stacked arms and commenced throwing up intrenchments; sent out their pickets; and having put themselves in a tolerable posture of defence, rested for the remainder of the night. Nothing of interest occurred during the night but the occasional crack of the rifle, reminding us of our duty and making us vigilant.

The morning of the 20th was beautiful beyond description. The entire eastern horizon was mantled with a flame of golden light, and its softened atmosphere infused with the breath of immortality. Everything in nature was gay with an exuberance of joy, and her intelligent worshipers were led through her own inspiration to bow in devout adoration before Heaven. There was no augury in the character and associations of that morning of the carnage that evening would witness, no symptom of the coming storm, whose dire results were desolation and woe to many a home and heart, while it brought paeans of joy to the true and loyal throughout the land.

At early dawn, the First and Third Divi-

sions of our corps commenced crossing the Creek, and at nine o'clock A.M., they were all over and had begun to take their positions in line of battle. The Third Division, commanded by Maj.-Gen. BUTTERFIELD,[2] and at present, in his absence, by Brig.-Gen. WARD,[3] took the left, while the First, commanded by. Brig.-Gen. WILLIAMS, the right, leaving the entire of our cross line of battle to the Second Division, commanded by Brig.-Gen. J.W. GEARY. This was the disposition of our troops up to noon on the 20th inst. Gen. WARD's left flank was protected by the Second Division of the Fourth Army Corps, and Gen. WILLIAMS'[4] right by the Fourteenth Army Corps. Up to this hour little had been done more than the disposition of the troops, and a small advance of our picket line. About noon or shortly thereafter, Gen. GEARY sent forward two or three regiments of the First Brigade, commanded by Col. CANBY, together with Col. IRLAND's Third Brigade, to take up a new line of battle some 300 yards in advance of our then position. Accordingly they commenced feeling their way forward and up toward the enemy's hiding place, and posted themselves from three to five hundred yards in advance of the line occupied on the night of the 19th. Here they threw up a temporary and short line of breastworks, sufficiently extended from right to left only to admit eight guns. Maj.-Gen. HOOKER surveyed the position, and shortly after the two batteries of our division were in their places, confronting the foe. By the con-

tracted limits of the breastworks four guns of the two batteries were without cover. Two of them were thrown out on the right flank, and two on the left of the positions occupied by the other portions of the batteries. The two on the left in a corn-field, and the two on the right in the woods. In this position several discharges were fired, to elicit, if possible, a response from the enemy, and to determine his whereabouts. He, however, was too intent on his purpose to be provoked to utterance, and consequent betrayal. He had too much at stake. He observed a dogged silence.

Discovering no demonstrations nor even signs of the enemy near, Gen. GEARY in person went out some three hundred yards still further in advance and found no enemy nor sign of an enemy, more than in the capture of three prisoners, who stoutly affirmed there was no body of troops of any note in our front, guided partly by all he saw and partly by the reports of the captured men, he concluded to advance his batteries to another knoll and order Col. JONES, commanding the Second Brigade, to send out a regiment, his largest, to occupy the crest and throw up redoubts. Up to this period, for reasons unknown here, the right flank of the Second Division was left entirely uncovered, and exposed a deep ravine on his right, densely wooded, and affording an admirable cover for the enemy's unperceived advance was unoccupied by any force of our army. Gen. GEARY fully expected that his right was covered by the simulta-

Confederate attack on General John Logan's XV Corps during the Battle of Atlanta.

neous movement of the First Division with his own. This, however, proved not to be the case, and, minus this, the results we are about to relate followed. The Thirty-third New-Jersey, being the largest regiment in Col. JONES' brigade, was detailed to occupy the new line and prepare for the artillery, in obedience to orders. Lieut.-Col. FOURAT commanding Thirty-third New-Jersey, ordered his command forward. He led them out in front of the batteries by the right flank, up a road through the woods about a hundred, yards, formed them in line of battle on the south side of the road, and halted them until he had seen for himself the ground to be occupied. This done, he returned, put his regiment in order, and led them to the destined place.

The most undisturbed quiet reigned around while these movements were being made. Nothing occurred to break the wilderness of silence but the rustling tread of our advancing force, the orders of the commanding officer and the occasional thug of the rifle on our extreme right. But it was the silence that precedes the hurricane, the quiet that heralds the tornado.

Gen. NEWTON, of the Second Division, of the Fourth Corps, on the extreme left of our corps line-of-battle, had made, during the afternoon, similar advances with Gen. GEARY, and with a seeming equal success was making headway into Dixie. The advance up to this hour, 3:50 P.M., when the Thirty-third New-Jersey left the road before-named developed nothing of the Confederate leaders designs. When, however, they had gained the top of the hill, and began to prepare for their work, the rebel hordes began to precipitate themselves upon them in treble lines of battle. On they came, howling like the devil, and raining death on the little band of patriot soldiers, who had gone to their work, with a bravery that has characterized them in half a dozen desperate engagements. Flight, or certain capture, or probable death, was before them. They retired, defending their isolated situation as well as they could; but they felt their defence was feeble at best, yea, alarmingly so, when, having retired only one hundred and fifty yards, they beheld masses of the enemy closing on both their flanks. It now became a question of pedestrian skill and adroitness whether the rebels should possess this regiment, or be foiled in their sanguine hopes of conquest and booty. It proved, however, that Jersey boys, brave in fight and magnanimous in conquest, are also fleet of foot when visions of the Libby or Castle Thunder haunt their imaginations, or loom up before them, with all their horrors, when pressed hard by the rebels. Unfortunately for them, 15 of their brave boys were shot deed and 19 wounded, while 33 were taken prisoners. They also lost their State flag. The One Hundred and Thirty-fourth New-York Volunteers were marching out to the support of the New-Jersey Regiment by the flank, and suffered in an equal ratio with it. On, on, on they came, howling and screaming all along our extended line, and drove back in their impetuous sweep almost everything that opposed itself to them. They came down on our exposed flank, scattering confusion, dismay and death on every hand, and for a short time held in their own power the destiny of our whole division. It was broken and scattered. But with a surprising celerity, by the commanding officers, aided by the presence of Major-Gen. HOOKER, the troops were rallied, formed in line of battle, and hurled back with interest on the rebels heads the destruction they sought to inflict on us. Victory was wrenched from the band of the conqueror, and defeat was changed to conquest.... ❂

---

1. John White Geary (1819–1873), later a two-term governor of Pennsylvania.
2. Daniel Butterfield (1831–1901).
3. William Thomas Ward (1808–1878).
4. Alpheus S. Williams (1810–1878).

THE CRISIS IN GEORGIA.

AUGUST 5

FROM THE ATLANTA APPEAL, JULY 29.

The progress which the enemy has made toward the heart of the Confederacy, and the enterprise he has manifested by his raids upon our railroads and undefended points, ought to convince our people that there is no security from danger but in active, energetic self-defence. The people of the Gulf States have so long lived remote from the actual theatre of the war, that they have flattered themselves with the belief that their homes would never be visited by the relentless invader. The events of the last few weeks will serve to disabuse them of this fond delusion, and teach them that, if they would continue to live as freemen, they must arm and rally to the front in their own defence.

The guns of the tyrant foe are now thundering at their very doors, and supineness and inaction now are criminal; yea, suicidal. No one will for a moment deny but there are able-bodied men enough in the States of Georgia and Alabama either to annihilate SHERMAN and his army or to drive them howling back to the Ohio River. Will they not, at a crisis like this, come promptly to the rescue, and aid our veteran soldiers in the good and holy cause? If those living south of us would defend their homes, their property, their liberty and the rights they have inherited from a heroic ancestry, now is the time and Atlanta the place to make that defence. With them delay is not only dangerous, but fatal; for although our gallant army still stands between them and the foe, it may prove too weak to withstand the hosts that are being hurled against it. There is no safety to any one now living in the South but in the defeat of SHERMAN's army. With the united efforts and numbers of the people and the army this can be effectually done within the next two or three weeks. The Government now has arms to place in the hands of every man and boy who is ready and willing to defend his country and his home.

It is not now as it was in the earliest stages of the war, when men refused to enter the service because of the scarcity of arms, and when the Government had nothing to offer them but shot guns and Irish pikes. Arms are now plentiful, and what is now needed is men and boys to load and shoot them. Come up, then without hesitation or delay, to the rescue of your country and the defence of your own homes and firesides. A few weeks more and it may be too late. If, through the listless indifference and slothfulness of the people, Gen. HOOD is compelled to give up Atlanta, large districts of country now protected by his army will be exposed to the devastating raids of the enemy, thousands who now have homes they can call their own will have them no longer, and they themselves be driven outcast and beggars upon the world. Let us, then, hope that in view of the dangers that now threaten them so imminently, the people of Alabama and Georgia will think seriously and act wisely, and promptly in this matter. Let them cease praying to Hercules and put their own shoulders to the wheel. All will then be well. ❂

THE ARMY BEFORE ATLANTA.

AUGUST 6

CORRESPONDENCE OF THE CINCINNATI
GAZETTE.

NASHVILLE, TENN., SATURDAY, JULY 30

The battle of the 28th was but a passionate effort of the giant rebel to break the net in which he is fast being caught. It will be recorded in history as the episode of a siege, for the siege of Atlanta will date back from July 28. I believe the struggle of the 22d, in which MCPHERSON did not die until he had finished the investment and ran his rifle-pits through a part of the city, completed the investment and began the siege. At any rate, the siege is now begun, and the investment is complete. It is too late for HOOD to escape, if he wished to. Henceforth HOOD must sit and watch the meshes thickening around him from day to day, his only hope that a mistake on SHERMAN's part may give him a loophole out of which to crawl. What amiable feelings, despite their accompanying terror and despair, must be HOOD's as he sits watching his ruin and vainly striving to escape it. Next to those of the successful General, who watches the gradual tightening of his lines around a doomed city or army, the feelings of him who commands within must be most enviable.

Over the scene of HOOD's despair at Atlanta can you not see the figure of old BRAGG exulting in the defeat of the army and the ruin of the men who rejected him. BRAGG is one of the most vindictive men to whom the rebellion has given prominence, and I have no doubt in my own mind that he rejoices in the shelving of JOHNSTON and the ruin of the others who have succeeded him. Expelled from the Army of Tennessee, hated and despised, he has not forgotten the scorn which the men and prints showered upon him, and gloats over the chance that gave the ruin of that army into his hands. Of course you have heard the story, flow he came from Richmond, and met the retreating army of JOE JOHNSTON at Atlanta. At his command the retreat was slopped, and on July 15 and 16 a council of war was held in the Gate City. There is one here who knows that it was a stormy council of crimination and re-crimination, of bitter and rough criticism. BRAGG presided like Satan in the Council of the Fallen, and rejoiced over the troubles of each. His order first and last was fight. There were but three men in that council beside himself who cried "Bravo." HOOD, a brave, bold fellow, with little brains; STEWART, with more brains than HOOD, and not less brave, and CHEATHAM, with less of bravery and brains than either. JOHNSTON has played the part of FABIAN until he has won some character. He will not risk it in the new part of a fighter. He retires. HARDEE refuses to place himself in BRAGG's power, and declines to accept. Unfortunately for us, POLK had been killed in battle too soon, or we should have had a greater ass than HOOD in command. So HOOD gets the command, STEWART gets POLK's corps, CHEATHAM that of HOOD, and they cross swords in the air, swear to do or die, and old BRAGG, taxing the train for Macon and Richmond, laughs at the folly of the men he has ruined. SHERMAN does not object, and the casting of the net goes bravely on. ✪

A GREAT NAVAL BATTLE.

OUR FLEET PASSED FORT MORGAN AND CLOSE TO MOBILE.

DREADFUL HAVOC...

AUGUST 9

FROM HEADQUARTERS OF GEN. BUTLER,
MONDAY, AUG. 8 — 3 P.M.

To His Excellency, A. Lincoln, President:
The following is the official report, taken from the Richmond Sentinel of Aug. 8:

B. F. BUTLER, MAJOR-GENERAL[1].

"MOBILE, Aug. 5
Hon. J. A. Seddon,[2] Secretary of War:
Seventeen of the enemy's vessels, (fourteen ships and three iron-clads) passed Fort Morgan this morning. The Tecumseh, a monitor, was sunk by Fort Morgan. The Tennessee surrendered after a desperate engagement with the enemy's fleet. Admiral BUCHANAN[3] lost a leg, and is a prisoner. The Selma was captured. The Gaines was beached near the hospital. The Morgan is safe and will try to run up to-night. The enemy's fleet has approached the city. A monitor has been engaging Fort Powell all day.

(SIGNED) D.H. MAURY, MAJ.-GEN."[4] ✪

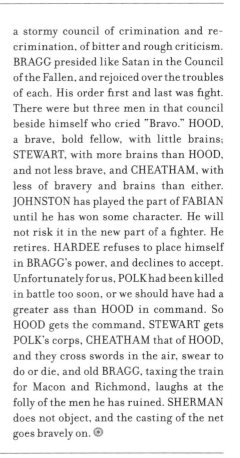

An 1886 Louis Prang chromolithograph of the Battle of Mobile Bay.

1. Admiral Farragut successfully led 14 wooden ships and four ironclads past Fort Gaines and Fort Morgan at the Battle of Mobile Bay. The Times quickly and proudly shared the first official reports from the defeated Confederates, which did not include the admiral's famous defiant cry about the mine-filled channel: "Damn the torpedoes, full speed ahead."
2. James A. Seddon (1815–1880), the last Confederate secretary of war.
3. Franklin Buchanan (1800–1874) had commanded the CSS Virginia. He remained a prisoner until February 1865, returning to formally surrender Mobile to the Union.
4. Dabney H. Maury (1822–1900) was Confederate commander of the Gulf.

WHAT SHERMAN HAS ACCOMPLISHED — WHAT THE REBELS HAVE LOST.

FROM THE ST. LOUIS UNION.

We are permitted to make the following extract from a private letter received in this city by a gentleman from his kinsman, a high officer in SHERMAN's army:

IN FRONT OF ATLANTA, MONDAY, JULY 25

We are in the immediate front of Atlanta, with the enemy well nigh shut up in its very defences. We occupy a curved line around the west, north and east sides of the city, about one to one and a half miles distant from it, and have the whole place under the

AUGUST 6

fire of our guns, to doses of which, anything but homeopathic, we have been treating it during the past forty-eight hours. We have fought some half dozen severe battles, and, with losses to ourselves (in all) of about 12,000 to 15,000, have placed of the enemy at least 30,000 hors de combat. We have captured twenty guns, twenty-five or thirty stand of colors, have destroyed two important railroads, occupying a third for our own uses; have burned a large number of cotton, woolen, rolling, paper and grist mills, near-

ly 4,000 bales of cotton, numerous railroad depots, and large quantities of subsistence and other military stores. We have captured thousands of horses, mules, beef cattle and sheep; and have sent to the rear nearly 10,000 prisoners. I place Jo. JOHNSTON's loss at 30,000, because, besides the above prisoners, we have either buried, or delivered up to him for burial, about 5,000 of his dead. Counting five wounded to one dead (which is a moderate proportion), and I think you will agree that I do not overestimate his entire loss. Unless some unforeseen accident or misfortune overtakes us, Atlanta will be ours very shortly. ✦

THE PRESIDENTIAL ELECTION.

AUGUST 10

The Democrats everywhere are very confident of victory in the pending. Presidential canvas. Their exultation may be premature, but it is sincere. They evidently believe they are going to win. And they base their expectations of success mainly, if not entirely, on the dissensions which prevail in the Union ranks. They point to the fact that whole classes of professed Union men feel under no obligation to support the Union ticket. One denounces Mr. LINCOLN because he did not abolish Slavery soon enough — another because he assumed to touch it at all. One refuses to vote for him because he keeps Mr. BLAIR in the Cabinet, another because he keeps somebody or anybody else. FREMONT runs against him because he disregards the Constitution, and WENDELL PHILLIPS[1] speaks against him because he recognizes that instrument at all. Some censure his lenient method of treating the people of the Southern States, — others his barbarous and inhuman mode of carrying on the war. One set of politicians vilify him for not admitting the Southern States at once into the Union, and WADE and DAVIS[2], with equal malignity, brand him as a usurper for proposing to admit them at all. Every unsuccessful applicant for office, — every volunteer adviser whose counsels have been rejected, — every wiseacre who fancies he was created to conduct the Government, and who finds Mr. LINCOLN indisposed to accept his dictation, — the whole of that countless brood of political seers

who knew from the beginning how "this thing" was coming out, and who found the President incredibly and idiotically deaf to their warnings and their threats, — are all now combined to vindicate their prescience and gratify their resentments by voting against him. And upon this concurrence of disappointed and underrated malignants, the Democrats base their hopes of a party success.

It may be that they are right. Possibly such a combination of selfishness and reckless passion may override the settled judgment and patriotism of the people. It would not be the first time in the history of Republics that private passion has proved too strong for devotion to the public good. It is by no means impossible that the people of this country may be betrayed by these base and selfish intrigues into putting power into hands which will use it for the division and destruction of the country.

We wish now merely to remind those who profess to be Union men that, if this catastrophe should happen, they alone will be responsible for the result. It will be due wholly and exclusively to their dissensions; to their paltry, personal bickerings; to their miserable, petty jealousies; to their intolerance of difference on minor points, and to the determination, cherished by many among them, to secure for their own personal views predominance in the public councils, at whatever sacrifice of the public good. If they see fit to persist in the indulgence of these selfish aspirations, they may possibly, by a combination of their forces, point to the ruin of their country as the monument of their victory.

The Democrats are quite right, in view of this state of things, to exult in the prospect of an easy triumph. They have good ground, in these dissensions among Union men, for exulting over their coming defeat. They do well, moreover, to take time by the forelock in these exultations, and to boast of victories which they expect to win; for it is possible that they may not win them after all. It is not wholly impossible that before the election comes round, Union men may see the folly of subjecting themselves to the rule of a common foe because each cannot establish his personal sway over all his associates. And our Democratic neighbors must excuse us for hinting, furthermore, that it is not yet quite certain that their harmony, after the Chicago Convention, will be any greater than that of the Union men seems to them at the present moment. ✦

1. Wendell Phillips (1811–1884), leading orator, reformer, and abolitionist.
2. A reference to a July bill aimed at toughening Lincoln's 10 percent reconstruction plan, which Lincoln pocket vetoed. On August 5, Massachusetts Senator Benjamin Franklin Wade (1800–1878) and Maryland Congressman Henry Winter Davis (1817–1865), both so-called Radical Republicans, responded by publishing a "Manifesto" in the New York Tribune charging Lincoln with "dictatorial usurpation" of Congressional power. The Times rallied to Lincoln's defense — no doubt inspired by the legislators' decision to publish their newsworthy declaration in a rival paper.

THE FAILURE BEFORE PETERSBURGH.

AUGUST 11
SPECIAL CORRESPONDENCE OF THE NEW-YORK TIMES.
IN FRONT OF PETERSBURGH

Since the recent unfortunate fiasco this army has settled down into its wonted quiet. Of course, the failure of the plans laid to capture Petersburgh by surprise, as it were, is the grand topic of conversation among both officers and men, and all feel that there was a serious mistake made by some one. Who shall be held responsible, is the subject under consideration by a competent tribunal. The result of the investigation, it is generally believed, will not be the stereotyped one usually found by coroners' juries upon investigating steamboat explosions and disasters upon railroads. The prevailing opinion is that in the present instance somebody should be held responsible for failing to accomplish such an important result as was reasonably anticipated.

Notwithstanding the croakers'[1] prediction as to the unhealthiness of this climate, the general health of the army remains good — much better indeed than one year ago when on the Rappahannock. When this can be said in truth just after so great a disappointment, no higher meed of praise can be conferred upon this army, nor can there be any stronger evidence of its morale....

As the war progresses, it would seem as though the desperation of the opposing forces in the heat of battle increases with the time of the contest. I do not know that the Union soldiers are less chivalrous, or show less humanity toward their enemies; but one thing is certain, — during the last three months more men have been killed in action than ever before under similar circumstances. This result may be, in part, owing to the fact that very generally our men have arrived at the conclusion that there can be no peace until a majority of the active and intelligent leaders opposing them are laid under the sod; and the sooner the Government and the people arrive at the same conclusion the better, I opine, it will be for all concerned. Fighting is a kind of pastime for the whites in the slave States, and their withdrawal from the usual walks of life does not seriously diminish the raising of all crops essential to sustain life, because the whites in these States never were a producing class; the negroes were and are to this day — in all districts where the Confederates hold full away — the real producers, and just so long as this is permitted to be the case, the rebels can hold out against the Government. Had a systematic effort been made to remove this producing class during the last three years, the rebellion would have fallen through from the mere want of supplies.

E.A. PAUL.

1. Period slang for chronic complainers and critics.

THE WADE AND DAVIS MANIFESTO.

AUGUST 11

The National Intelligencer finds much to commend in the manifesto of Senator WADE and H. W. DAVIS against President LINCOLN, which we published a day or two since. In styling it, however, a "Republican Manifesto," and in treating it as a Republican document, having the sanction or at least the toleration of the Republican party, that journal, it seems to us, somewhat transcends the facts of the case for the sake of giving a factitious weight to the document itself. We have seen nothing whatever to justify the assumption that either the Republican party, or the Union party, either indorse the sentiments of this extraordinary manifesto or regard the action of its authors in issuing it at the present crisis as anything but a treacher-

FROM MOBILE.
ADMIRAL FARRAGUT'S OFFICIAL REPORT.

AUGUST 16
WASHINGTON, MONDAY, AUG. 15.

The following official dispatches have been received by the Navy Department:

FLAGSHIP HARTFORD, MOBILE BAY, AUG. 5

SIR: I have the honor to report to the department, that this morning I entered Mobile Bay, passing between Forts Morgan and Gaines, and encountering the rebel ram Tennessee and gunboats of the enemy, viz., Selma, Morgan and Gaines.[1]

The attacking fleet was under way by 6:45 A.M., in the following order: The Brooklyn, with the Octoroon on her port side; Hartford, with the Metacomet; Richmond, with the Port Royal; Lackawana, with the Seminole; Monongahela, with the Tecumseh; Ossipee, with the Itasco; and the Oneida, with the Galena.

On the starboard of the fleet was the proper position of the monitors or iron-clads.

The wind was light from the Southwest, and the sky cloudy, with very little sun.

Fort Morgan opened upon us at ten min-

Taking a break during the siege at Petersburg, federal troops prepare to watch some cockfighting.

ous and malignant attempt to stab a President whom they profess to support.[1]

The [Washington National] Intelligencer concurs in the view taken by these gentlemen of the course of the President in not signing the bill of Congress, but avowing his purpose to act upon some of the principles embodied in it. That journal says:

"In our paper of the 21st ultimo was intimated our objections to this most anomalous proceeding on the part of the Executive. If the President had vetoed the act of Congress he would have simply exercised a right vested in him by the Constitution, and would have been answerable to Congress and the country only for the soundness of the reasons by which he might have justified his veto. If the President had simply withheld his signature from the bill, and had thus suffered it to fall to the ground, he would have still acted within the legitimate prerogatives of his office. But to attempt by proclamation to make

this bill a self-imposed rule for his guidance in some things, and to give reasons, not to Congress, but to the country, why he would not take it for his guidance in other things, seemed to us a solecism in politics, as much without defence in theory as it was without precedent in history."

A "solecism in politics" may be a very terrible thing; probably it is, else our venerable cotemporary would not terrible at its shadow. But really we see nothing very remarkable or very terrible in the President's action in this matter. He did not approve the bill as a whole, and, therefore, he did not sign it. This, says the Intelligencer, is all right. He acts "within the prerogatives of his office." But if there are some things in the bill which the President does approve, — if there are principles in it which he is quite willing to make his own, and to adopt as guides to his own official action, we do not see why he may not properly do so, — nor why he may

not, with equal propriety, tell the country or Congress, or both, his reasons for so doing. This is precisely what he has done, and it is all he has done. We see nothing in his action hostile to the Constitution or dangerous to the country, or necessarily fatal to anybody's peace of mind. Nor are we in the least degree enlightened on this point by the elaborate epigrams of Mr. DAVIS or the ponderous moanings of the Intelligencer. If Mr. LINCOLN has committed no political "solecisms" more formidable than this, the country will probably survive. ◉

1. Indeed, the Wade-Davis Manifesto backfired on its authors: Wade was condemned and Davis denied renomination to the House.

---

utes past 7 o'clock, and soon after this the action became lively.

As we steamed up the main ship channel, there was some difficulty ahead, and the Hartford passed on ahead of the Brooklyn.

At 7:40 the monitor Tecumseh was struck by a torpedo and sunk going down very rapidly, and carrying down with her all the officers and crew, with the exception of the pilot and eight or ten men, who were saved by a boat that I sent from the Metacomet, which was alongside of me.

The Hartford had passed the forts before 8 o'clock, and finding myself raked by the rebel gunboats, I ordered the Metacomet to cast off and go in pursuit of them, one of which, the Selma, she succeeded in capturing.

All the vessels had passed the forts by half past eight, but the rebel ram Tennessee was still apparently uninjured, in our rear.

A signal was at once made to all the fleet to turn again and attack the ram, not only with guns, but with orders to run her down at full speed.

The Monongahela was the first that struck her, and though she may have injured her badly, yet she did not succeed in disabling her.

The Lackawanna also struck her, but ineffectually.

The flagship gave her a severe shock with her bow, and as she passed poured into her a whole port broadside of solid 9-inch shot and thirteen pounds of powder, at a distance

of not more than twelve feet.

The iron-clads were closing upon her, and the Hartford and the rest of the fleet were bearing down, upon her, when, at 10 A.M., she surrendered.

The rest of the rebel fleet, namely, the Morgan and Gaines, succeeded in getting back under the protection of Fort Morgan.

This terminated the action of the day. Admiral BUCHANAN sent me his sword, being himself badly wounded with a compound fracture of the leg, which it is supposed will have to be amputated.

Having had many of my own men wounded, and the surgeon of the Tennessee being very desirous to have Admiral BUCHANAN removed to the hospital, I sent a flag of truce to the commanding officer of Fort Morgan, Brig.-Gen. RICHARD L. PAGE,[2] to say that if he would allow the wounded of the fleet, as well as their own, to be taken to Pensacola, where they could be better cared for than here, I would send out one of our vessels, provided she would be permitted to return, bringing back nothing she did not take out. ◉

A Louis Prang chromolithograph of Admiral David Glasgow Farragut aboard the USS Hartford.

1. Admiral Farragut's dispassionate report elevated his heroic status even further.
2. "Ramrod Page" (1807–1901), as he was known, remained a prisoner of war until June 1865.

WHAT IS AN HONORABLE PEACE?

AUGUST 19

"An honorable peace" is becoming a pet phrase of the Copperheads. It figures constantly in their party organs, and is finding a place in all their party platforms. The Copperhead State Convention of Maine just held, took pains to inlay it in three successive resolutions. They resolved that "the only hope of securing an honorable peace is by expelling the present corrupt, imbecile and revolutionary Administration;" that "the Administration is manifestly incapable of negotiating an honorable peace," and that they "are in favor of an honorable peace at the earliest practicable moment." It is high time to understand what this qualifying term honorable means.

The man would be accounted an imbecile who should talk of an honorable peace with the highwayman whose pistol was at his heart, or with the incendiary whose torch was at his roof. If he did not choose to fight he might parley, and induce his enemy to hold off by consenting to all demands. But it would be absurd to style a deliverance thus obtained an honorable peace. It might be a necessity, but it would be a humiliating one at best. In meeting the violence of outlaws, the question is not how to save your honor, but how to save your life. You may buy off the villains by a surrender of your property, if you do not like to play the man by self-defence; but the moment you begin to prate about your honor you make yourself not simply a coward but a fool. An honorable peace presupposes a respectable cause, or at least, a respectable color of a cause for the war, and a respectable standing in the parties to it. It may be a hard bargain for one of these parties, against whom the fortune of the war has turned; but it necessarily implies, if not equal power on both sides, at least an equal status.

The war with the self-styled "Southern Confederacy" has been prosecuted by our Government on the sole ground that this organization was a rebellion, pure and simple. President LINCOLN, as the head of the Government, has been fighting traitors banded to destroy the Government which he had sworn to defend and preserve. All the supporters of the Government have recognized that there could be no peace with these traitors but in their submission to the Government, or else in their absolute independence. That has been the only real issue in the war. The Government could know no other, for its first duty is the maintenance of its constitutional authority, which is its vital essence. It is this alone which has made its prosecution of the war right. It is this alone which has made the resistance of the rebels wrong. The Government is not fighting for its honor, but for its life. The rebels are not fighting for their honor, but to be "let alone" in their crime. The only truly "honorable peace" possible must come from a vindication of vital authority on the one side, and a submission to constitutional duty on the other.... ✪

MCCLELLAN NOMINATED FOR PRESIDENT.

SEPTEMBER 1
CHICAGO, WEDNESDAY, AUG. 31

The National Democratic Convention reassembled at 10 o'clock this morning.

The Wigwam is again densely packed, and the crowd outside is greater than ever ....

In announcing the vote of New-York Mr. SANFORD E. CHURCH said, that New-York regretted to pass by her favorite son,' but she stands now as she has ever stood, ready to sacrifice her dearest personal preferences for the public good, holding it her duty above all others to do all in her power to rescue the country from the tyranny that oppresses it. Having full confidence in the Democracy, ability and patriotism of Gen. GEORGE B. MCCLELLAN, New-York gives him her entire electoral vote.

Several delegations having cast their votes for HORATIO SEYMOUR when the call of the States had been gone through with, Gov. SEYMOUR remarked that some gentlemen had done him the honor to name him for the nomination. It would be affectation to say that their expressions of preference did not give him pleasure, but he owed it to himself to say that many months ago he advised his friends in New-York that, for various reasons, private and public, he could not be a candidate for the Chicago nomination. Having made that announcement, he would lack the honor of a man, be would do great injustice to those friends to permit his name to be used now. As a member of the New-York delegation, he

THE FALL OF ATLANTA.

SEPTEMBER 5

Five telegraphic words — "Gen. SHERMAN has taken Atlanta," on Saturday, thrilled the nation with a joy not lees heartfelt, if somewhat less demonstrative, than that of France, when through the streets of Paris ran the cry: Sebastopol est pris. Indeed, the Sebastopol of Georgia has fallen, and with this splendid achievement one-half of the great campaign of the Summer is finished, and the seal of success already set upon the military operations of the year 1864. With nothing more done, the sum of that which has been done is victory.

Four months of constant and vigorous

General Sherman, center on horse, at the Battle of Atlanta, an 1888 chromolithograp by Louis Prang.

personally thought it advisable to support an eminent jurist of that State for the nomination, but he was not actuated in this by any doubt of the ability or patriotism of the distinguished gentleman who has been placed in nomination. He knew that Gen. MC-CLELLAN did not seek the nomination. He knew that that able officer had declared that it would be more agreeable to him to resume his position in the army, but he will not honor any the less the high position assigned him by the great majority of the country, because he has not sought it. He desired to add a few words in reference to Maryland and her honored delegates here.... We are now appealing to the American people to unite and save our country. Let us not look back. It is with the present that we have to deal. Let by-gones be by-gones. He could say for our gallant nominee that no man's heart will grieve more than his will for any wrong done Maryland. As one who did not support him in my delegation, and as one who knows the man well, he felt bound to do him this justice. He (Gov. SEYMOUR)[1] would pledge his life that when Gen. MCCLELLAN is placed in the Presidential Chair, he will devote all his energies to the best interests of his country, and to securing, never again to be invaded, all the rights and privileges of the people under the laws and the Constitution.

The President [of the Convention] then announced the vote, which was received with deafening cheers, the delegates and the vast audience rising, the band playing, and the cheering lasting for several minutes.

Immediately after the nomination, a banner on which is painted a portrait of MCCLELLAN, and bearing as a motto, "If I cannot have command of my own men let me share their fate in the field of battle," was run up behind the President's platform, and was welcomed by the wild enthusiastic cheers of the multitude.

THE CONVENTION … A GREAT CROWD. VALLANDIGHAM WORSHIP.
CORRESPONDENCE OF THE NEW-YORK TIMES.

The convention is held in a large amphitheatre, located on the lake shore, about a mile south of the hotels. It has been erected by the Democrats of Chicago, at a cost of some $7,000, and is well adapted for the purpose, and capable of accommodating 15,000 people. A portion has been reserved for the delegates, and another section for their friends, for which tickets are necessary, in order to secure an admission. There is a ladies' gallery. These sections are seated. But the great presence chamber of the sovereigns is unseated, so that the people will have to stand "packed in a jam," while the leaders are hatching out a candidate and a set of principles for them to swear by.

Arrangements have been made on as extensive scale by the "Invincible Club," of this city, for a grand ratification demonstration on the evening of the day upon which the nomination is made. There is to be a torchlight procession, and every other kind of proceeding which will serve to make night hideous....

After the vote, VALLANDIGHAM made an appearance, and hats swung in the air, and lungs gave out their loudest notes. When this part of the programme had been gone through with, VALLANDIGHAM bowed and put himself on his blandest, and expressed his grateful emotions at this compliment from the people. He then exhorted to peace, harmony and union, everything for the cause, and told them that when the work of the convention was over, when a Democratic candidate, who was to rescue the Constitution and restore the liberties of the nation, was in the field, he should make it his business, in season and out of season, to address assemblages of his Democratic fellow-citizens in all parts of the country, until a glorious victory crowned their efforts.

OGDENSBURGH, WEDNESDAY, AUG. 31
The nomination of MCCLELLAN was received here with great rejoicing. Thirty-four guns were fired on the receipt of the news. This evening guns are firing, bands playing, bonfires blazing, rockets ascending, processions moving and people rejoicing. The Democrat office and many private residences are brilliantly illuminated. Prominent citizens are addressing the crowds.

POUGHKEEPSIE, WEDNESDAY, AUG. 31
A salute of one hundred guns was fired here this afternoon in honor of the nomination of MCCLELLAN and PENDLETON.

ALBANY, WEDNESDAY, AUG. 31
The nomination of MCCLELLAN caused great enthusiasm in this city. A hundred guns were fired at noon, and a hundred more at sunset. This evening a procession preceded by a band of music, and bearing torches and transparencies, is parading the streets. Banners bearing the name of MCCLELLAN, are displayed at different points.... ⊛

1. Governor Seymour.

campaigning, a contested march of full two hundred miles, ten pitched battles, and two score of lesser engagements by night and day, make up the price we paid for Atlanta. It is worth them all; for our highest estimate will not outreach the magnitude of the solid fact. Considering simply the military results of SHERMAN's campaign, in the first place, it has worsted and nearly destroyed the second army of the Confederacy. Fifty thousand men have dropped from the thinned ranks of that army since it lay encamped around Dalton on the first day of last May. Its riddled files have been partially supplied from the dregs of the Gulf States, the worst of fighting material — old men, boys, and such timorous conscripts as have hitherto, by many devices, eluded the clutch of the drafting officers. This motley array, whose cohesion was never of the strongest, has at length recoiled under a crushing and demoralizing defeat. Reeling back toward the coast, it parts at once with the city it was gathered to defend, and with that residue of hope under which this last effort has been made to hold the broad State of Georgia against the legions of the Union. Henceforth desertion will play a double part in the decimation of HOOD's army....

This is the place which, while rapidly approaching the fulfillment of CALHOUN's prediction, has been seized by the Union arms. At once the workshop, the granary, the storehouse, and the arsenal of the Confederacy, Atlanta and its environs were of incalculable value. The foundries, furnaces, rolling-mills, machine shops, laboratories and railroad repair-shops; the factories of cannon and small arms; of powder, cartridges and percussion caps; of gun carriages, wagons, ambulances, harnesses, shoes and clothing, which have been accumulated at Atlanta, are ours now. Much of the machinery and material has probably been destroyed or removed by the enemy; but that which is removed can never again be worked to such advantage as at Atlanta.

But the downfall of Atlanta does not mean the occupation of that city alone. It includes the assured possession of contiguous ☞

and valuable cities and regions — of Rome, Rossville and Marietta — where are manufactured guns, ammunition, cotton and woolen clothing in abundance. In one word, Atlanta is at the centre of a network of towns and villages, which have furnished forth half its war material to the entire Confederacy, from the Rappahannock to the Rio Grande. This valuable region is now all ours.

There is a geographical consideration also. Atlanta is the extremity of the vast grain-producing territory of northern Alabama and Georgia. Between it and the ocean lie the cotton lands. Atlanta ours, the great, rolling, fertile valleys at its back, teeming with food and forage, pass forever into our hands. Nor is even this all. A wide, mountainous region, comprising that portion of the Central Zone which is traversed by the manifold parallel ridges of the Alleghenies, is now surpassed, and the rest of SHERMAN's course lies over smoother ground, and through country less hostile to military operations. Should he direct his head of column away to the South, he would soon encounter the Pine Mountains, or, if to the Southwest, he would again skirt along the Alleghany chain. But toward the sea, which is the path most likely to be adopted, the land is less difficult.

From this time Atlanta will assume the role of a base of operations. The rugged region betwixt that point and Chattanooga, than which nothing could be more defensible, is surmounted once for all. It can hardly be appreciated what advantage has been gained in the elimination from future campaigns of 150 miles of hilly and wooded country, arduous and perilous, always interposed at the outset against every campaign whose base is Chattanooga. Now, in fine, SHERMAN marches against the cotton lands of the South. He has uncovered, in taking Atlanta, the entire series of railroads which form junction there, and threatens with imminent destruction every important city in Alabama and Georgia. On his right, Selma, Montgomery, Opelika, Columbus, lie at his mercy. Should his columns be directed toward the ocean, as is probable, cavalry would be dispatched to do all that is essential in the occupation of the former points.

UNCONDITIONAL SURRENDER.

SEPTEMBER 5

The Commander of Fort Morgan asked for terms. "The only terms we can make are unconditional surrender," was the reply. Thus FARRAGUT in the last stage of the war reiterates the words of GRANT in the first. These words make the rule of the war. There is no different policy known in either army or navy. The champions of our flag invariably refuse to accept anything short of an absolute yielding to it. They will have the rebel bunting lowered flat to the earth before making a single concession. They are too jealous of the authority and dignity of the nation to chaffer, in its name, with defiant treason.

What these old heroes do, the Union party means to do. It, too, insists upon an unconditional surrender to the national authority, as a preliminary to the consideration of any minor question. Precisely here lies the prime distinction between the Union party and that opposed to it. The Copperheads are for treating with the "Confederate" authorities without requiring from them any previous recognition of the supremacy of the old Constitutional Government. So far as there is any recognition at all, as a condition precedent to discussion, they are, in fact, the ones to make it. The Chicago platform is a recognition for the nonce — a recognition quoad hoc[1] — of Confederate independence, and, if fully carried out, would practically end in a recognition for all time. It carefully avoids the word rebellion, and every other implying that there is any allegiance due from the men who are fighting our Government. It asks that "immediate efforts be made for a cessation of hostilities, with a view to an ultimate convention of all the States." Such efforts would involve diplomatic intercourse with the Jeff. Davis "government." That in itself is recognizing that it has a certain civil status. That "government" has declared, again and again, that it will listen to nothing so long as what it calls the "invaders" are on its soil. If we withdraw our armies, it is a recognition on our part that they have been invaded, and that the "Confederate" soil is indeed independent

Fort Morgan shortly after its capture in the Battle of Mobile Bay.

In his front are the important cities of Macon and Milledgeville, and on his left the City of Athens. Against these towns, now, his operations will be directed, and even Augusta will not be safe. Three hundred miles away to the southeast, almost equidistant from Atlanta, lie Charleston and Savannah. In good time, even their distance from Atlanta will not preserve them from cooperative attack by land and sea. In effect, this successful General breaks the rebellious territory in twain, and has already severed the railroad communication of its eastern and western sections. The fall of Atlanta, and the southeasterly retreat of HOOD uncovers the Atlanta, West Point and Montgomery Railroad, which connects the former city and all the

region east and south of it with Mobile, with Montgomery and the great Mississippi Valley. The occupation of one little town will throw us effectually across this road between Macon and Montgomery — the town of Opelika, which the rebel General has now been forced to leave to its fate. Of the other three railroads which converge at Atlanta, the Western and Atlantic, which runs to Chattanooga and Memphis, is of course ours. Two roads remain to the enemy—the Georgia Central, running via Macon to Savannah, and the other road to Savannah and thence to Charleston via Augusta. But these two roads, forming an apex at Atlanta, thence constantly diverge. It follows that it will soon be impossible for the enemy to extend himself far enough to

occupy them both. One or the other will be surrendered, with the towns through which it takes its course.

Such, then, are the immediate military results which will flow from this crowning success of the Georgia campaign. But its effect on our arms in Virginia cannot fail to be most fortunate. The news has already spread throughout the camps along the Appomattox, and the enthusiasm of our cities upon its reception is tame and commonplace to that of the Army of the Potomac. That confidence in the future, based on past triumphs, which we call prestige, will surely spread its infection to the gallant army on the James, and ere long Virginia will echo the note of victory back to Georgia. ✹

---

soil.... Our Government could not more completely recognize the independence of the "Confederacy" for the time, than by suspending its military action in order that the "Confederate President," the "Confederate Congress," and a sovereign convention of the "Confederate States" should come to their respective decisions upon the question of "an ultimate convention" of all the States. It would be a practical acknowledgment that these authorities had discretion and authority in the premises....

Of course, there are many honest supporters of MCCLELLAN who think of no such application of his platform. But it is because they do not think at all....

JEFF. DAVIS could not possibly find any easier or cheaper road to reach what he has been so long in vain struggling for, than that which the Chicago Convention has designated.

But the loyal majority of the North do not intend that this road shall ever be opened. The path of peace these Confederates must travel begins at a different point altogether. It is Union ground from the start. The very first step involves submission, and a complete submission, to the old authority. Thus only can we have a clear and sure way to the adjustment of all the questions the war has generated; and thus only can our nationality be kept secure and inviolate. ✹

THE PRESIDENT AND OUR GENERALS — DIABOLISM IN HIGH PLACES.

SEPTEMBER 7

It is part of the plan of Copperhead operations against the Administration, whenever a General fails in the field, to declare, before anything whatever is known of the circumstances, that it was "LINCOLN" that was the cause of it; either by refusing reinforcements changing the plan of campaign, or performing some other knavish trick....

Occasionally, an attempt is made to lend a touch of solemnity to the farce by summoning LINCOLN and STANTON to answer to an imaginary indictment, for the failure of an assault in Georgia or the loss of a battle in Louisiana, before an imaginary tribunal, composed of the editor of the World or of the Daily News, or "any other man," where the two culprits receive a frightful "wigging," and are discharged with the assurance that if they are caught any more causing the loss of battles, of which they knew nothing until they were over, something still more dreadful will happen to them.

On the other hand, whenever a success is achieved, it is invariably assumed that for some time before the fight LINCOLN was maltreating the General who achieved it, and plotting for his overthrow, and the Democratic organs at once begin to pat him on the back, and stroke his head, and reassure the poor little fellow that naughty LINCOLN shall be made to let him alone. They always knew he was an able man, but LINCOLN, of course, put him in command

of a large army, and kept him fully supplied with men and provisions, solely with the diabolical design of ruining him. Any one whom LINCOLN fairly hates it appears he appoints to high commands, like GRANT's and SHERMAN's, and few of his victims would ever escape him if it were not for the interposition of the [New York] World, and the occasional remonstrances of Gov. SEYMOUR and Mr. VALLANDIGHAM.

An amusing illustration of these Copperhead dealings with the President was furnished by the World on Saturday, in an article discussing the news of SHERMAN's great victory. This news was a bitter pill, coming, as it did, just as the Copperheads were commencing their efforts for an "immediate cessation of hostilities;" but it had to be swallowed.

If there be one officer in the army, one of LINCOLN'S "dishonored subordinates," more thoroughly distasteful to a genuine Copperhead than another, it is SHERMAN. There was not a traitor or conspirator at the Chicago Convention in whose nostrils he does not stink. SHERMAN knows it, too, and is proud of it. He is a soldier of the Cromwellian type; believes that when a country has to be conquered it ought to be conquered in such fashion that the work need never be done over again; he believes in making war support war; in making rebels face the consequences of rebellion; he believes that Slavery has been the cause of this war, and he believes that there will be no real peace until it has disappeared; and on all these beliefs he has acted. He does not recognize Slavery; he car- ☞

---

1. Latin for "as far as it goes."

ries off negroes, chickens, bacon, corn, and everything he can lay hands on, wherever he goes, and uses them for the support of his own army. He gives all traitors and malcontents found within his lines the roughest and most summary justice. He does not allow negro recruiting in his lines because he wants to see able-bodied white Copper-heads in the army. There is not one of the Chicago leaders who dare give out any of his venom anywhere within fifty miles of his headquarters. In short, he is the antipodes of MCCLELLAN in every respect, the kind of men that "Conservatives" most dread to see at the head of our armies.... SHERMAN is only a soldier, and his victories would plunge President MCCLELLAN in a sea of trouble. ⊛

McCLELLAN ACCEPTS THE PLATFORM.

SEPTEMBER 18

The [New York] World has announced that Gen. McCLELLAN accepted the Chicago platform "of course, when he accepted the nomination." The News' of the same date declared that the Peace men would not now make a separate nomination. There may possibly be no connection between the two statements, but it is certainly "a coincidence" that we should have them both on the same day.

It is well that matters have taken this shape. We want the builders of that platform to come squarely before the people. We want the men who accept it, and who thereby declare that peace should be sought through an immediate cessation of hostilities, instead of through a steady and unwavering and more determined prosecution of the war, to come before the people of this country for their votes. And if the people do not sink that platform and its makers as speedily as Capt. Winslow sunk the Alabama, and with as utter and everlasting a destruction, then are the people not worthy of being saved from the ruin which its success will bring upon them. We suggest to some of McClellan's supporters that they had better now drop their talk of his having refused to accept the platform, kicked it over, made another platform of his own, etc. The World's statement is doubtless by authority, Let us have no more attempts to misstate the issue of the contest but meet it squarely on both sides. We have had shuffling enough.

The London Times very well says: "If the Democratic Party make a fight for power, they must do it substantially on principles of peace." The leaders of the party saw that this was so, and the platform which

WHAT NOW FOR SHERMAN?

SEPTEMBER 19

In the congratulatory order issued to his soldiers by Gen. SHERMAN when his army entered Atlanta, he says, after reciting the various steps in the triumphant campaign; the capture of Atlanta "completed the grand task which had been assigned us by our Government." What the entire scope and precise limitation of these words may be, it is difficult to say. We suppose the capture of Atlanta was the task assigned to our brave Western army when it set forth from Chattanooga in May last, and beyond that work it was impossible at that time to draw out any fixed line of military action. So far, it was definite, simple and essential; but, Atlanta once attained, our further progress would depend upon the condition of our army, upon the condition of the rebel army, upon its position and line of retreat, and upon the general aspect of the war. East and West. If the campaign had closed with the destruction of HOOD's force, the farther advance of Sherman's army, as a mass into Georgia, would have been unnecessary: if, on the other hand, the rebel force were borne away intact, SHERMAN's plans and movements would still remain to be dictated by great variety of circumstances.

In regard to the condition of HOOD's army, we judge the fact to be that, though not utterly destroyed, it was well-nigh broken after the retreat from Atlanta. Its long retreat, or series of retreats, continued without cessation for four months.... Were SHERMAN to advance directly upon it, it would doubtless retreat to Macon; were he to attempt to march in a southeasterly or southwesterly direction, it would try to bar his way, retard his progress or harass his line.

The easiest movement, and not the least effective, for SHERMAN to make with the bulk of his forces, after leaving a portion of them well fortified in Atlanta, would be to strike southwesterly for Montgomery, the old capital of the Southern Confederacy, and from there march upon and seize Mobile. He would thus not only capture these two important points, and dominate all the surrounding country, but he would establish a water-base for our Southwestern army. He could make a grand march like this even though Hood were to remain where he now is, or indeed without paying much regard to the line of communication....

That purpose is the capture of Richmond. On this one object the whole military power of the Federal Union will now be concentrated. Grant will no longer be distracted by two great enterprises. One of them is accomplished and well off his hands. He is at liberty now to give his whole force to the other. He commands all the armies of the United States, and his pride is up. The task which engaged his immediate personal supervision is yet unaccomplished; while that which was entrusted to a lieutenant has succeeded. Every brigade and regiment that can be spared from any other quarter of the compass will now certainly be ordered to Petersburg. The Northern people and their generalissimo concur in the conviction that they have the rebellion at last so circumstanced that one great blow must certainly destroy it; and they believe that blow is to be stricken in Virginia.

Petersburg is falsely esteemed the key to Richmond. The fall of one they erroneously suppose involves the other. But it cannot be denied that if they bring together a force large enough to overwhelm Lee's army, wheresoever the theatre of battle may be, they do imperil Richmond, and with it the Confederate cause itself. ⊛

An 1864 cartoon satirizing the Democratic national platform and presidential candidate, George McClellan.

they adopted placed their fight upon those principles. Frightened by the temper with which it was received by the people, they endeavored by the letter of acceptance to cover up their position. The only effect of the effort was to show them that what The Times says was true, and they now come back squarely up the platform of "cessation." Now let us have PENDLETON's[2] letter of acceptance, and then for a fair fight in a fair field, with no dodging. ✹

1. The anti-administration *New York Daily News*.
2. Antiwar Congressman George H. Pendleton (1825–1889) of Ohio, Democratic candidate for Vice President.

THE VICTORY IN THE SHENANDOAH VALLEY.

SEPTEMBER 21

The signal victory in the Shenandoah Valley on Monday[1] is one of that class which permits no cavil either as to its scope or its completeness. At the opening of the battle EARLY'S force, which, by Confederate accounts, has been positively put down at 27,000, was posted mainly at Bunker Hill, near Winchester, and at Darkesville. The Upequan [sic] creek was between our forces and the rebels and their works extended at some points on the centre and left to within three miles of the river. SHERIDAN's line extended, early in the engagement, over five miles in length, from Berryville towards Bunker Hill. The attack was made by our cavalry under AVERILL[2] by gray daylight on Monday, BRECKINRIDGE's division, posted near Darkesville, having been steadily driven a distance of seven miles, by one o'clock in the afternoon. The attack of our main army also commenced early in the morning at the point where the Opequan Creek is crossed by the Berryville turnpike. From this point our forces, by a series of stubborn and sanguinary engagements which lasted until 5 o'clock in the afternoon, compelled the rebels to fall back, completely defeated EARLY's main army, and drove it from one defended line of works to another, until what remained of the routed force, as Gen. STEVENSON tells us, was "sent whirling through Winchester;" all their dead, most of their wounded, and two thousand five hundred prisoners being left on our hands. The wounded in Winchester alone are found to number three thousand, and if the dead are counted in, the rebel loss will be found to exceed six thousand, or about one-fourth of the entire army under EARLY. In trophies and material our gain is also notable; fifteen army flags and five pieces of artillery having fallen into the possession of our army.

Our loss has been hastily computed at two thousand, and considering that the battle must have raged for nearly seven hours, the number will not be deemed excessive....

Never, probably, since he first set out from Lynchburgh at midsummer was EARLY so confident of his position as on this eventful morning, the 19th of September. Only one day previous the Southern reporter, who supplies military fictions for two of the McClellan organs here, writing professedly from the testimony of EARLY's confidants, had assured the sympathizing friends of that rebel that "Gen. SHERIDAN" main body remains where it has been for the last two weeks, strongly intrenched at Berryville. It is utterly powerless to do anything toward driving Early out of the Valley." The ink was barely dry upon the sheet which gave currency to these hollow pledges in behalf of EARLY when the thundering announcement rang through our streets, that this impregnable host of invaders, routed, beaten and all but cut in pieces, was using the last remnant of its strength in an inglorious and panic-stricken flight. Loyal men among us cheered lustily for the good cause. The craven-hearted peace-mongers went growling to their haunts. ✹

1. The Third Battle of Winchester (Opequon Creek), Virginia was a triumph for Union forces under General Philip H. Sheridan. The seizure of the town cost 4,018 Union casualties, and 3,921 Confederate.
2. William W. Averell (1832–1900), who later became an inventor.

CHAPTER 22

"The Very Life of the Nation is at Stake"

OCTOBER–DECEMBER 1864

I n the fall of 1864, as Grant continued to hold Lee in his defensive lines around Richmond and Petersburg, the opposing armies in the west headed off in opposite directions. Confederate General John Bell Hood, having failed to keep Sherman out of Atlanta, marched northward, hoping to draw the Yankees out of Georgia. Sherman followed him for a week, but then let him go and returned to Atlanta. As Hood continued first westward, then northward into Tennessee, Sherman prepared for his famous march to the sea.

Even as readers digested this important military news, most eyes turned by late autumn to an altogether different kind of American battleground: that of presidential politics. With Atlanta fairly won and Sherman advancing inexorably through Georgia, Lincoln's re-election fortunes seemed to be on the rise. But neither Confederates nor Democrats were ready to surrender without a fight.

Readers of the antiwar New York World, for example, were treated to relentless, racially tinged attacks on the administration, not limited to the pages of the daily paper. The World also masterminded an elaborate "dirty trick" meant to convince voters that Republicans secretly planned to move beyond emancipation and introduce full racial integration. The newspaper covertly issued an incendiary book titled *Miscegenation* — a new word derived from both Greek and Latin to mean "race mixing"— which trumpeted, in a concealed tongue-in-cheek style, a future society in which blacks could intermarry with whites. Then the publishers audaciously sent a copy to the President himself, seeking the era's equivalent of a blurb. Lincoln proved too clever to take the book seriously; sniffing out the hoax, he simply filed it away.

Republican 1864 presidential campaign poster featuring a portrait of Abraham Lincoln.

The World would not rest, however, and also financed a series of demagogic campaign lithographs charging, among other things, that the Union commander-in-chief had callously requested a comic song while touring an Antietam battlefield littered with dead soldiers. Lincoln was so infuriated by this particular calumny that he drafted an indignant reply, though in the end, as was often the case, he decided not to send it. Finally came a caricature called (like the book) *Miscegenation*, showing the President bowing to greet a mixed-race couple in a scene in which minstrel-like blacks assumed the superior position to whites. The race-baiting worked at least on one level: the World's nasty campaign managed to embroil most of the town's leading Republican dailies in an ugly internecine fight — with each accusing the other of being too soft on amalgamation of the races.

Regaining the offense by October, Republican newspapers countered with a string of pro-Lincoln, anti-McClellan editorials, none as vociferous as those in The Times. Its editor, Henry Raymond, was continuing his open second career as chairman of Lincoln's re-election campaign — a role that today would be regarded as an intolerable conflict of interest. In mid-century America, it seemed no more unnatural than the defiantly outspoken, undisguised partisan biases of the newspapers themselves.

Events helped Lincoln as much as Raymond did. In mid-October, the Union turned defeat into triumph at the Battle of Cedar Creek, capped by one of those instances of personal heroism that assumes the proportion of legend. General Philip B. Sheridan was returning to the Virginia front from a visit to Washington when he learned the news of an unexpected, nearly disastrous predawn attack on his distant army. He quickly began a dramatic gallop to the front at Winchester, rallying despondent troops all along his path. "On he rode," an eyewitness recalled admiringly, "his famous war-horse covered with foam and dirt, cheered at every stop by men in whom new courage was now kindled." The Heroism of "Little Phil" not only aroused his troops, it also inspired a famous poem and an equally renowned painting. Sheridan won the official thanks of Congress and a promotion to major general in the regular army, and the Union declared victory in the crucial Shenandoah Valley Campaign.

Around the same time, on October 11, early statewide elections in Ohio, Indiana, and Pennsylvania showed significant strength for the rebounding Republicans — a clear indicator of a comfortable victory in the national polling the following month. Just three days later, one of the most influential and enduring of Lincoln's Democratic critics died. Chief Justice Roger Brooke Taney, who had led the tribunal for nearly three decades, authored the infamous Dred Scott decision, and futilely attempted to block Lincoln's assumption of executive authority early in the war, finally expired at the age of 87. By the end of the year, after taking his time to fill the vacancy, Lincoln nominated another longtime nemesis, his former Treasury Secretary Salmon P. Chase, to be Taney's successor. In one deft move, Lincoln shrewdly silenced a long-irritable rival, while elevating a proven antislavery man to a court almost certain soon to hear vital test cases on emancipation.

Election Day proved a triumph for Abraham Lincoln. On November 8, the President easily won his once-hopeless campaign for a second term with nearly 56 percent of the popular vote and an overwhelming 212 electoral votes to George B. McClellan's mere 21 — with only Delaware, Kentucky, and New Jersey falling to the Democrats. In the separately tallied soldiers' vote, which the Republicans had worked assiduously to count, Lincoln won 116,887 to McClellan's 33,748 — as much an overwhelming vote of confidence in the war effort as a stinging rebuke of the general and his party's so-called peace platform. Two days later, McClellan officially resigned from the army and confided: "For my country's sake, I deplore the result."

Not surprisingly, Lincoln saw the mandate differently. Appearing at the White House to acknowledge a victory serenade the same day as McClellan shared his lament, he characteristically celebrated not his own victory, but the mere fact that the people had successfully carried off a free election. "It has long been a grave question whether any government, not *too* strong for the liberties of its people, can be strong *enough* to maintain its own existence, in great emergencies," he told the crowd. As he explained: "We can not have free government without elections; and if the rebellion could force us to forego, or postpone, a national election, it might fairly claim to have already conquered and ruined us."

For weeks, during the run-up to Election Day, rumors had abounded in New York that Confederate agents were about to strike against the city in order to disrupt the polling and throw Lincoln's expected victory into turmoil. Many dismissed these stories, arguing that local voters were disposed to vote *against* the President (which they did), and any attack would actually help the Republicans by curtailing turnout in the overwhelmingly Democratic metropolis. Election Day came and went without incident, but New York was not to be spared. Less than three weeks later, agents who today would be called "terrorists" tried to burn ☞

down hotels, theaters, and other public buildings in New York. The plot fizzled, but not without attracting headlines, analyses, editorials, letters, and a collective sigh of relief that the damage was so minimal.

Having won a ringing vote of confidence, Lincoln received yet another gift before year's end. After more than eight weeks of marching through Georgia — with only a scattering of reliable reports reaching a North collectively holding its breath — William T. Sherman's army reached the coast and occupied one of the great old cities of the South. In a dispatch to his commander-in-chief, Sherman grandly "presented" conquered and occupied Savannah, Georgia, to Lincoln as a Christmas gift.

"When you were about leaving Atlanta for the Atlantic coast, I was *anxious*, if not fearful," the President admitted in response to his triumphant general, "but feeling that you were the better judge, and remembering that 'nothing risked, nothing gained' I did not interfere. Now, the undertaking being a success, the honor is all yours... a great success."

And then, ever-impatient that the long war now might soon be drawn to a close, Lincoln added: "But what next?"

THE PRESIDENT AND GENERAL MCCLELLAN.

OCTOBER 10

The Copperhead press has been making a great deal of capital out of an alleged offer made by F. P. BLAIR, Esq.,' to Gen. Mc-CLELLAN. It has said that Mr. BLAIR had told the General that the President would give him a command in the field, provided he would decline being a candidate for the Presidency at the Chicago Convention. It was assumed and charged that in doing this Mr. BLAIR had acted for the President, and that the latter was therefore responsible for the offer.

In another column we publish a letter from Mr. BLAIR on this subject. He states, in the first place, that Mr. LINCOLN not only did not authorize him to make any such proposition to Gen. MCCLELLAN, but that he did not know of his intention to see him on that or any other subject, or of his purpose to visit New-York at all. He says, in the next place, that he never made any such offer to Gen. MCCLELLAN, or anything which could be construed into an offer of a command in the field on that or any other condition. And, in the third place, he states what he did say to Gen. MC-CLELLAN on that and other subjects. He advised him not to be a candidate for the Presidency, because he was certain to be defeated, and under such circumstances that he could never hope to rise again. He also advised him to apply to the President for a command in the field, because his military knowledge enabled him to be of service to the country in that capacity, and it was due to his friends, who believed he had talent, to evince a willingness to use it.

Now, in all this, we must say Mr. BLAIR showed his usual good sense. His advice was good, and the reasons which he gave for it were good also. Gen. MCCLELLAN will see the day when he will regret that he did not follow it. But Mr. BLAIR's positive and explicit statement, that the President had nothing to do with this conversation, that he knew nothing of it or of his interview with Gen. MCCLELLAN, ought to put a quietus on the story. There is little reason, however, to suppose that it will. The Opposition party and press are too short of material for carrying on the war against President LINCOLN, to afford to throw away so telling a fiction. And when we see the National Intelligencer willing to sacrifice its hitherto carefully-nursed reputation for candor and fair-dealing, and laboring through three columns of sophistry to fasten this imputation on the President in the face of Mr. BLAIR's distinct disavowal of all authority, there is not much reason to hope that the less scrupulous organs of that party will take a different course.... ❀

1. Francis Preston Blair (1791–1876) of Maryland was the father of a Union general and senator (Francis Jr., 1821–1875) and Lincoln's postmaster general (Montgomery, 1813–1883), and an influential political force since the Jacksonian era. The elder Blair later wrote a letter to The Times admitting he had met McClellan and openly predicted both his nomination and defeat at the polls, but adamantly insisted he had not been sent or authorized by President Lincoln.

A cartoon comparing the 1864 presidential campaign platforms of the Democratic and Republican parties.

THE OCTOBER ELECTIONS.

OCTOBER 10

Elections occur to-morrow in PENNSYL-VANIA, OHIO and INDIANA. They are watched with intense interest by men of all parties throughout the country. In themselves the results in these States are of comparatively little consequence; but the indications which those results will afford of the probable issue of the Presidential contest in November are of the utmost interest and importance.

In OHIO the contest has not been waged with any great degree of vigor or determination on the part of the so-called Democratic party. The canvass has been animated, but nothing more. The Copperheads do not seem to have had any great hope of success under any circumstances, and they have not, therefore, put forth any very strenuous exertions. There is very little doubt that the vote of Ohio will be cast for the Union ticket by a very handsome majority — we hope not less than 50,000.

In PENNSYLVANIA and INDIANA the contest has been more severe, and the result is consequently somewhat more doubtful. There is probably no loyal State in which sympathy with secession is more open and decided than in Indiana. Not content with endeavoring to overthrow the Administration, the Copperheads there have been hard at work in endeavoring to array the State openly and actively on the side of the rebels. The organization of the Sons of Liberty was intended to commence operations in that State. Secret importations of arms have been going on for months past, for the purpose of enabling the Copperheads of Indiana to take the field at home in armed opposition to the Government; and it was the action of that Government, in seizing these arms, that aroused the eloquent indignation of Gov. SEYMOUR in the Chicago Convention.

That party have been making the most desperate and determined efforts to defeat Gov. MORTON and throw the State into the ranks of the opposition. It has been thoroughly organized, abundantly supplied with money, and sustained by aid, in lavish profusion, from this City and other outside sources. Everything that desperate exertions can do to carry the State will be done to-morrow. Rebels expelled from Kentucky have been brought by thousands across the Ohio to give their votes against the Government. The whole power of the party will be put forth to carry the State. The soldiers in the field are not allowed to vote, and not less than 40,000 votes will thus be lost to the Union cause. Nevertheless, we have strong hopes of success. Gov. MORTON believes we shall succeed. The Chairman of the Union State Committee and other gentlemen of position actively engaged in the canvass, write that the chances are decidedly in our favor. COLFAX's reelection is reasonably certain, in spite of the most desperate efforts to defeat him; and we hope the Union State ticket will succeed by not less than from 5,000 to 7,500 majority.

PENNSYLVANIA is the battle-field. The Democrats have evidently made up their minds that unless they can carry that State now, it will be useless to hope for success in the November fight. They have accordingly put forth every possible effort to secure a show of victory. Their leading politicians from this State, Gov. SEYMOUR, JOHN VAN BUREN, DEAN RICHMOND, AUGUST BELMONT and others, have been giving Pennsylvania their special attention for some weeks past. Hundreds of thousands of dollars have been sent there within the last ten days. The Union men, meantime, have not been idle. They have been actively and carefully canvassing the State, holding large public meetings, discussing the issues involved, and striving to arouse and enlighten the public sentiment of the State in every possible way. Unless all the signs of the day prove deceptive, they will carry the State. No State ticket is in the field, and the election is only for members of Congress; — but it is confidently expected that we shall gain at least four members, and Gen. CAMERON, Chairman of the State Committee, thinks we may gain seven. With very many obstacles to contend against, peculiar to the present struggle, we believe the State will vote for the Union cause.

There is good reason, therefore, to expect substantial Union victories in each of these three great States. If all of them are thus carried, the Presidential contest will be substantially decided. If one or even two of them should vote against us, they will compel a sharper struggle and more strenuous efforts on our part; but even in that case they will not seriously jeopardize the result. ⊛

THE ELECTIONS — VICTORY!

OCTOBER 12

The great States of PENNSYLVANIA, OHIO and INDIANA, yesterday, gave their popular verdict in favor of the Union, the prosecution of the war against rebellion to its successful conclusion, and in favor of the present administration of the Government.

The verdict in all these States, as will be seen from our returns, is emphatic, even on the home vote in Pennsylvania, to which thousands, if not tens of thousands, will be added by the gallant soldiers of the proud old Commonwealth now in the field.

In Ohio the soldier's vote will not be needed to swell her triumphant majority to fifty or sixty thousand, though it may serve to sweep the last vestige of Peace Democracy from her Congressional Delegation. The city of Cincinnati, the home of GEORGE H. PENDLETON, the Peace colleague of Gen. MCCLELLAN on the Democratic ticket, has done nobly.

In the gallant Volunteer State of Indiana, where a Democratic Legislature has not permitted her soldiers to vote, the great civil victory of yesterday is truly astounding; at once inspiring to the Union hearts of the North, where, we confess, some doubt was felt of the reelection of Gov. MORTON, and crushing to the last hope of the Peace Democracy in the Northwest. ⊛

HOW THE SOLDIERS VOTE.

OCTOBER 13

To the Editor of the New-York Times:

Happening to notice an article in a New-York paper under date of Oct. 1, referring to the soldiers' politics of the One Hundred and Eighty-sixth Regiment N.Y.S.V., and to the manifestations by that regiment while passing through the City, we, the undersigned, would cheerfully say by the way of refutation, that the regiment from the time they took up their line of march at Battery Barracks until the time of their arrival at the foot of Canal-street, did not halt or in any manner stop, but did, while passing through Broadway upon coming up to the Lincoln and Johnson banner cheer roundly for the same, and that said cheering was cheerfully taken up by fully seven eighths of said regiment in favor of LINCOLN and JOHNSON; and further, that seven-eighths of the men in ☞

said One Hundred and Eighty-sixth Regiment are in favor of LINCOLN and JOHNSON, and if they were allowed to vote on the question to-day would so vote. That on the morning the regiment left Battery Barracks a vote was taken in said regiment, and that the vote showed the above statement to be true.

(SIGNED.) H.J. WELCH, CAPTAIN CO. A. 186 REGIMENT; JAMES W. WAYNE, CAPTAIN CO. B; EDWIN SWAN, CAPTAIN CO. C; LANSING SNELL, CAPTAIN CO. E; DAN'L B. ROOD, CAPTAIN CO. H; CHAS. D. SQUIRE, CAPTAIN CO. F; CHARLES S. MANNGS, CAPTAIN CO. G. HEADQUARTERS 186TH REGIMENT, N.Y.S.V., CITY POINT, VA., OCT. 9 ❂

DEATH OF CHIEF JUSTICE TANEY.

OCTOBER 14

ROGER BROOK TANEY, Chief Justice of the Supreme Court of the United States, died in Washington, at 11 o'clock Wednesday night, in the seventy-eighth year[1] of his age....

Mr. TANEY took his seat on the Supreme Bench in January, 1837. His name will be chiefly associated with the famous decision in the case of "DRED SCOTT,"which has gained special prominence from its bearings on some of the most important political issues of the age. The decision itself was in accordance with the opinion of the majority of the court, and was merely to the effect that the Circuit Court of the United States for Missouri had no jurisdiction in the suit brought by the plaintiff in error, but the Chief Justice went out of his way to indulge in a long and entirely irrelevant dissertation about the estimate which he claimed our ancestors placed upon the negro, and the rights to which he was entitled. In the course of his remarks the Chief Justice took occasion to assert, that for more than a century previous to the adoption of the Declaration of Independence, negroes, whether slave or free, had been regarded as "beings of an interior order, and altogether unfit to associate with the white race, either in social or political relations; and so far inferior that they had no rights which the white man was bound to respect;" that consequently such persons were not included "people"in the general words of that instrument, and could not in any respect be considered as citizens; that the inhibition of slavery in the territories of the United States lying north of the line of

30 degrees and 30 minutes, known as the Missouri Compromise, was unconstitutional; and that DRED SCOTT, the negro slave, who was removed by his master from Missouri to Illinois, lost whatever freedom he might have thus acquired by being subsequently removed into the territory of Wisconsin, and by his return to the State of Missouri. For the last two or three years Chief-Justice TANEY, on account of falling health, took very little part in public affairs; and he was by many suspected of leaning strongly in his sympathies toward the Southern side of the great issues which divide the nation. ❂

1. Taney was in fact 87.

Roger B. Taney, late chief justice of the Supreme Court.

THE DEATH OF ROGER B. TANEY.

OCTOBER 14

The demise of Chief-Justice TANEY comes almost like some strange visitation. For one full generation he has occupied the highest judicial position in the United States, and it almost seems identified with his name. The disturbance of old associations is all the greater, because it happens at the very height of the civil conflict which is linked indissolubly with the most important act of his judicial life. Judge TANEY was a man of pure moral character, and of great legal learning and acumen. Had it not been for his unfortunate Dred Scott decision, all would admit that he had, through all those years, nobly sustained his high office. That decision itself, wrong as it was, did not spring from a corrupt or malignant heart. It came, we have the charity to believe, from a sincere desire to compose, rather than exacerbate, sectional discord. But yet it was none the less an act of supreme folly, and its shadow will ever rest on his memory.

The original mistake was in gratuitously attempting to settle great party questions by judicial decision. The attempt was gratuitous, for the very decision of Judge TANEY, that the court had no jurisdiction in the case over the court below, was in itself sufficient reason for not undertaking a decision of all the constitutional questions incidentally connected with its merits. What Justice CURTIS declared in his very able opinion, that "on so grave a subject as this, such an exertion of judicial power transcends the limits of the authority of the court, as described by its repeated decisions," will unquestionably be the judgment of history.

The Supreme Court never from its first organization took faith which so much impaired the public action in its impartiality and wisdom. In view of the sides taken by the respective Judges, it was impossible for the body of the people not to believe that the court was influenced by party and sectional feeling. The court should have foreseen this invidious position, and have avoided it, by taking no further cognizance of the case than necessity absolutely demanded. It was useless for them to attempt to settle great political questions. Such attempts before made, even in the palmiest days of the court, and on questions of immeasurably less importance, had failed. The court is no oracle. It does not pronounce its decisions with a categorical Yea or Nay. It must, like a legislative body, stand on its rendered reasons; and these reasons must stand the test of criticism before they can be accepted as conclusive, and as authoritative law. If the reasoning of the court is no more cogent and luminous than the reasoning of the legislature, it is worth no more. No candid man who has read the decision of Judge TANEY will say that that opinion evinced more ability, more clearness of perception and strength of reasoning, than had been displayed by Mr. WEBSTER and Mr. CLAY in the Senate, in their maintenance of opposite opinions. Nor will any candid man who has read the dissenting opinions of Judges CURTIS and MCLEAN claim that their views were not as cogently put as those of the Chief Justice. It was a natural necessity that the final solution of these great civil questions could come only from continued public discussion, and the condition in which the public mind eventually reposes.

The Dred Scott decision was made public the very month that President BUCHANAN acceded to power, and it formed the basis of his whole policy in respect to Slavery through his entire administration. It shipwrecked both him and his party. It contributed, more than all other things combined, to the election of President LINCOLN. The people would not abide this attempt of the majority of the Supreme Court to foist upon the Constitution the extremest dogmas of JOHN C. CALHOUN. They would not tolerate the doctrine that the Constitution, by its own force, established Slavery in all the Territories of the United States, making Slavery a national instead of a local institution. That the Dred Scott decision was a complete yielding to the full desires and demands of Slavery, is made strikingly manifest by the fact that the Montgomery Constitution, which was shaped by slaveholders without the slightest let or hindrance, does not contain a syllable in the interest of Slavery which is not found precisely in this Dred Scott Decision of Chief-Justice TANEY. There is no shadow of a new guaranty for this institution except the section that in all newly acquired territory "Slavery shall be recognized and protected by Congress and by the territorial government, and the inhabitants of the several States shall have the right to take to such territory any slaves lawfully held by them;"and another section securing the right of "transit and sojourn in any State with slaves and other property."

Those are just the points on which would have been secured for Slavery under the Federal Constitution, had Judge TANEY's interpretation become established law.

His removal by death will make an epoch in the history of the Supreme Court. Unquestionably his place will be filled by some jurist who is in perfect accord with all the great Union principles and Anti-Slavery sentiments which will henceforth control the executive and legislative branches of the Government. It is true that the old Democratic Judges WAYNE, CATRON, NELSON, GRIER, and CLIFFORD will still constitute half of the court but even were they disposed to make another political decision in the interest of Slavery, their combined opinions would have no effect against the other half of the court, headed by the Chief-Justice. Whatever great questions may be forced upon the court in connection with the rehabilitation of the States whose people have been in rebellion we may now be confident, will be adjudicated in accordance with the fundamental principles of our Government, as recognized by its founders, and in harmony, too, with the great policies imposed upon the country by the necessity of destroying the present rebellion and every possibility of its recurrence in the future. ❂

THE SOLDIERS AND GEN. MCCLELLAN.

OCTOBER 15

What a rebuke of Major-Gen. Mc-CLELLAN is contained in the soldiers' votes now sweeping in! If there be one soldierly fibre in his bosom, how it must tingle with shame. His friends have always claimed that he had a peculiar power of inspiring his troops with personal devotion. All his addresses to them show that he made this a special object. Grant that he succeeded. Admit to the fullest extent all that his home admirers claim about his personal popularity with the soldiers. It makes their present rejection of him all the more dishonoring.

Soldiers naturally have a pride in their service. They believe in military men. Their very esprit du corps puts them in sympathy with their leaders. ☞

An 1864 cartoon questioning the military competence (and personal courage) of Democratic presidential candidate George McClellan.

And yet here is one who led them longer than any other, and who, it is claimed, had a peculiar hold upon their trust, repudiated almost unanimously in favor of a mere civilian — and that civilian too one whom the home supporters of MCCLELLAN have flouted at with every possible expression of contempt.

Surely it is a most extraordinary rebuff. How comes it? What has filled these hundreds of thousands of clear-headed American soldiers with all this distrust and aversion? Mainly, it is the consenting to be used for unsoldierly and unpatriotic purposes. The Major-General stands for office on a platform of concession to the rebels these patriot soldiers are fighting to subdue — and that is why they scorn him. His position, to their eyes, is a false one. He has drawn away from what they deem the line of duty. He is, as they consider, unfaithful to the flag. If there be any other reason more creditable to him that can account for this discarding by the soldiers, we should like to see it named.

It is a sad, shameful spectacle. He who was once the selected champion of the flag now leagued with those who would lower it to the dust He who prided himself in being at the head of our patriot armies, now hand in hand with their worst enemies — with the party leaders who have from the beginning done everything to hinder their reinforcement, who have decried their successes, have pronounced their war a failure, have given unceasing comfort and encouragement to their foes in the field, have used all conceivable means to render futile their heroism, have even denied that heroism and stigmatized them as "minions"and "hirelings."We don't wonder that the living soldiers are indignant at such a defection of him who once led them. It is enough to stir the bones of the dead. ⊛

THE LATE ELECTIONS.

October 15

Tuesday last[1] was an eventful day in the history of this continent. A battle was fought then whose results shall reach further than those of any engagement fought during this war. The simple farmer who, in the valleys of Pennsylvania and Ohio, or on the prairies of Indiana, deposited a vote that day, did his part in deciding a contest whose effects shall influence all future history. When we look down through the vista of coming time, and think what we so narrowly escaped and what we probably gained on that day, the mind is amazed at the immense results dependent on rival human actions.

Through the farmer's Union vote, so quietly given on that Tuesday, we behold the principles of Constitutional government reinstated over this continent; the right of the majority to rule, asserted for all coming time; the power of a base aristocracy, supported on oppression, broken for ever, and liberty made a possession of all classes and races in this Union. We see happy communities, millions after millions, from one age to another, growing up in such happiness, prosperity and enjoyment of equal rights on the rich fields of this virgin continent, as the world has never before witnessed; we behold the chains of slavery broken wherever the Union banner floats, and every corner of this land opened to the oppressed of Europe and to the free and intelligent laboring population. We can see freedom scattering its blessings where now slavery curses the soil and the people,

and peace reigning where now is havoc and war. All this we can picture to ourselves as the certain result through coming centuries, of that simple act of patriotism and duty, done by our farming population on Tuesday last.

Then, when we remember what we probably escaped on that eventful day; when we look down the future and imagine what would be the results of a Peace Democracy ruling at Washington and recognizing the Confederacy; when we fancy this proud Union broken into four or five jarring and hostile Confederations, all unity of administration and free intercourse on this broad continent barred up, the Border States become a "land of blood"for centuries, the chains riveted anew on the unhappy negroes, and fearful insurrections following, which should destroy both races and waste the soil to a desert, the growth of liberty, civilization, and even Christianity permanently checked on this Northern Hemisphere — our glorious Republic become a mockery and a by-word to all nations — we can see how tremendous a destiny may hang on the depositing of a single vote.

It is true that the success of the Peace Democracy in the State elections might not have defeated the Union candidates in the Presidential election. It is also true that MCCLELLAN and PENDLETON, even if elected, might not be able to bring about the armistice and peace which their party claims. The good genius of the Republic might preserve it, even under a Copperhead President. Still, the chances are, that if these State elections had gone against us, the Union party would have been discouraged, the rebels elated, and, possibly, our Presidential candidate defeated. With PENDLETON, VALLANDIGHAM and SEYMOUR as the advisers of the new Administration, there cannot be a doubt that vacillation of counsel, negotiation, then an armistice, and then peace, would have followed; and the only possible result of peace is the independence of the Confederacy, and the probable disintegration of our Union.

But, thank Providence! we have escaped all these dangers. Tuesday's silent battle of votes has decided the destiny of the Republic. Henceforth, "Union and Liberty"for all classes and races, are to reign over this continent forever. ⊛

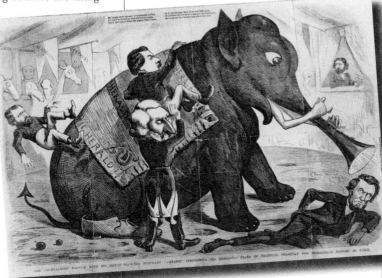

A cartoon satirizing the 1864 presidential campaigns.

1. Statewide elections in key Northern strongholds, including Pennsylvania and Indiana.

THE REBELS IN VERMONT.

OCTOBER 20

The rebels are making Canada their base of operations for both land and naval raids. It is only a few weeks since a body of Confederates, from the British side, made their rush upon our vessels in Lake Erie, and captured a couple of small steamboats, which they burned; and this morning we are startled with a telegraphic account of an invasion and raid upon St. Albans, Vermont, yesterday, by a band of a score or more of armed rebel desperadoes from Canada. These Confederated ruffians shot several citizens of the town, wounding two seriously, and it is feared fatally — assailed three banks, and plundered them of a very large sum of money — supplied themselves with horses, and threatened to burn the town, — after which they left in the direction of Canada. A body of citizens quickly started in pursuit; but as St. Albans is only about ten miles from the Canada line, there is little doubt that the rebel ruffians escaped.

This is a very serious matter, and demands immediate and decisive action on the part of the British authorities in Canada — action of a very different kind from that which they have lately taken in cases of violation of neutrality. If they look with unconcern on such attempts, or act in a feeble manner, and permit the Provinces to become not only a general rendezvous for rebels, but the region from which armed Confederates can most conveniently make forays upon our commerce and into our territory, it will assuredly lead to painful and most undesirable results. It will be impossible, after such affairs as that of yesterday, to prevent the outraged people from pursuing their enemies across the lines.

We have had occasion heretofore in two instances to compliment Lord MONCK for the promptitude with which he gave our Government information of the designs of rebels in Canada upon our territory. He has now something else to do. He must take measures to catch and punish these assassins, thieves and banditti. They violated British law as well as American rights, and it behooves the British authorities to see that there is no humbug about this matter. We see additional ground of hope for this in the reported seizure, by the British authorities at Bermuda, of Lieut. BRAINE, the rebel pirate who captured and destroyed the American steamship Roanoke. This BRAINE, it will be remembered, is the ruffian who seized the steamer Chesapeake on this coast, and who was permitted to go scot-free by the British courts at St. Johns.

We are earnestly anxious for peace and amity with Great Britain and her Provinces, and it becomes the authorities, both Provincial and Imperial, to see that no such outrages as that of yesterday are permitted to disturb that peace and amity. ✸

VICTORY!

ANOTHER GREAT BATTLE IN THE VALLEY.

LONGSTREET WHIPPED BY SHERIDAN.

VICTORY WRESTED FROM DEFEAT.

OCTOBER 21

WAR DEPARTMENT, THURSDAY, OCT. 20 — 10.45 A.M.

A great battle was fought, and a splendid victory won by SHERIDAN over LONGSTREET, yesterday, at Cedar Creek.

Forty-three pieces of artillery were captured and many prisoners, among them the rebel General RAMSUER.[1]

On our side Gens. WRIGHT and RICKETTS were wounded, and Gen. BIDWELL killed.[2]

Particulars, so far as received, will be forwarded as fast as the operator can transmit them.

EDWIN M. STANTON,
SECRETARY OF WAR.

SECOND DISPATCH. [OFFICIAL.] WAR DEPARTMENT, WASHINGTON, THURSDAY, OCT. 20 — 10:45 A.M.

Maj.-Gen. Dix:

Another great battle was fought yesterday at Cedar Creek, threatening at first a great disaster, but finally resulting in a victory for the Union forces under Gen. SHERIDAN, more splendid than any heretofore achieved. The Department was advised yesterday evening of the commencement of the battle by the following telegrams:

RECTERTOWN, VA., WEDNESDAY, OCT. 19 — 4 P.M.

Maj.-Gen. H.W. Halleck, Chief of Staff:

Heavy cannonading has recommenced in the valley, and is now going on.

(SIGNED,) C.C. AUGUR, MAJOR-GENERAL.

HARPER'S FERRY, VA., — 6:40 P.M., WEDNESDAY, OCT, 19

Hon. E.M. Stanton, Secretary of War:

Firing at the front has been continuous during the day. The direction seemed at intervals to be to the left of Winchester, as if at Berry's Ferry.

No news from the front.

(SIGNED,) JOHN D. STEVENSON, BRIGADIER-GENERAL.

HARPER'S FERRY, VA., — 8:45 P.M., WEDNESDAY, OCT. 19

Hon. Edwin M. Stanton, Secretary of War:

The enemy attacked our army with great impetuosity this morning at daylight.

The attack was made on the left of the Eighth Corps, and was at first successful, they capturing some guns, prisoners and wagons.

Our line was reformed and heavy fighting continued through the day.

SHERIDAN was reported at Winchester this morning, and went out to the front.

The particulars received are not official, and are not favorable, though no serious disaster could have occurred without direct news from SHERIDAN.

RESPECTFULLY,
JOHN D. STEVENSON,
BRIGADIER-GENERAL.

...A few minutes later the following official report of his victory was received from Maj. Gen. SHERIDAN:

CEDAR CREEK, WEDNESDAY, OCT. 19, 10 P.M.

To Lieut. Gen. Grant, City Point:

I have the honor to report that my army at Cedar Creek was attacked this morning before daylight and my left was turned and driven in confusion.

In fact most of the line was driven ☞

in confusion, with the loss of twenty pieces of artillery.

I hastened from Winchester, where I was, on my return from Washington, and found the armies between Middletown and Newtown, having been driven back about four miles.

I here took the affair in hand, and quickly united the corps, formed a compact line of battle just in time to repulse an attack of the enemy, which was handsomely done at about 1 P.M.

At 3 P.M., after some changes of the cavalry from the left to the right flank, I attacked with great rigor, driving and routing the enemy, capturing, according to the last report, forty-three pieces of artillery and very many prisoners.

I do not know yet the number of my casualties or the losses of the enemy.

Wagons, trains, ambulances and caissons in large numbers are in our possession.

They also burned some of their trains.

Gen. RAMSEUR is a prisoner in our hands, severely, and perhaps mortally wounded.

I have to regret the loss of Gen. BIDWELL killed, and Gens. WRIGHT, GROVER and RICKETTS wounded.

WRIGHT is slightly wounded.

Affairs, at times, looked badly, but by the gallantry of our brave officers and men disaster has been converted into a splendid victory.

Darkness again intervened to shut off greater results.

I now occupy Strasburgh.

As soon as obtained, I will send you further particulars.

(SIGNED,) P.A. SHERIDAN, MAJ. GEN. ✺

1. Stephen D. Ramseur (1837–1864) died a day after falling, with a bullet to the lungs, at Cedar Creek.
2. Horatio G. Wright (1830–1899), James B. Ricketts (1817–1887) survived the battle; Daniel D. Bidwell (1819–1864) was mortally wounded by a shell.

A Kurz and Allison lithograph of the Battle of Cedar Creek.

THE RESULT OF THE ELECTION — ITS CAUSE — THE DUTY OF THE DEFEATED.

NOVEMBER 10

ABRAHAM LINCOLN has two hundred and thirteen electoral votes against twenty-one for GEORGE B. McCLELLAN.[1] He has carried twenty-one States against three for GEORGE B. McCLELLAN. He has a popular majority of nearly, if not quite, 400,000, in round numbers.

This is the voice of the original loyal States, excluding the partially reclaimed States of Tennessee, Louisiana, and Arkansas, whose votes, so far as a Presidential vote was taken in them, was undoubtedly given Mr. LINCOLN, but on account of the still disorganized condition of these States, their vote will probably not be counted in the electoral college.

Such a preponderance of popular sentiment is unexampled since the reelection of JAMES MONROE, forty-four years ago, by an electoral vote of two hundred and twenty-eight votes to one. We accept it without surprise. It simply is a verification of what we have steadily declared from the outset, that the American people would stand by the Government as long as the Government stands by the flag. On that broad assumption we have rested our faith as on adamant. The man has been but a poor student of the Anglo-Saxon nature. Who has not learned that the national spirit is the strongest element in its blood. It is that quality of our race which has made England the foremost nation of Europe. War, instead of weakening it only intensifies it. Every new year of the twenty years' war against NAPOLEON, though bringing new burdens and new outpourings of blood, only set Saxon muscle all the firmer. Not one solitary instance can be found, either in English history or in American history, in which a party ever acquired power by working against a war in which the nation was once fairly embarked. It has been tried over and over again from the first existence of parties, but has uniformly failed. If this has been the uniform result where nothing but the pride or the material interest of the nation was concerned, the natural impulse must operate with vastly greater force when the life of the nation is at stake. It was downright infatuation in the leaders at Chicago to imagine that the American people would consent to give up the war as a failure, and trust to an "ultimate convention" to decide upon the national fate. It was a great weakness in Gen. McCLELLAN to fancy that he could stand on that Chicago platform and yet satisfy the national sentiment of the people by a few glittering generalities. Gen. McCLELLAN's strongest support has come from our adopted citizens — the very portion of our people who have none of that inborn sentiment. They cast a great multitude of votes, and in ordinary times hold the balance of power. But in a struggle like this they could accomplish nothing. When the life of the nation is concerned, the sovereign power is sure to be exercised by them who have sprung from the soil of the nation — and exercised, too, with the same resistless sweep we have just seen.

It is true that the native-born Americans of the Southern States have been deficient in this national sentiment. This is because the present generation of them have been vitiated by being bred in the false doctrines of the Calhoun school of State Rights. But that was rendered possible only by peculiar circumstances connected with a peculiar institution. That institution will soon disappear, and we shall then see the old national feeling again assert itself among the masses of the Southern people; and the recoil will dash forever from public life every Southern politician who has set it at naught.

ABRAHAM LINCOLN having been reelected President by this immense majority, through this national sentiment, the practical question for the supporters of Gen. McCLELLAN now is, in what spirit they will accept it. Their orators and their newspapers have done their utmost to destroy the confidence of the people in Mr. LINCOLN and the policy of his administration. They have exhausted argument, entreaty, denunciation, ridicule and defamation. They have subjected each and every official act to the most un-

A Harper's Weekly cartoon celebrating Abraham Lincoln's election: "Long Abraham Lincoln A Little Longer."

favorable criticism, and the worst misrepresentation, within their power. They have poured forth a ceaseless stream of abuse against all the more important members of his Cabinet. Whatever odium they could generate against him per se, or whatever by association, they have turned to account. Whatever political capital they could make for themselves by singleness of speech, and by doubleness of speech, they have realized. Whatever power there was in glittering promises to allure, or in dark warnings to intimidate, or in sordid appeals to corrupt, or in fierce tirades to inflame, or in big boasts to bamboozle, has been plied in this Presidential canvass to the uttermost limit. It has all miserably failed. Again we ask, what will these people do about it?

What they ought to do is plain enough. They should lay to heart the lesson that no public policy, in these times especially, has any chance, which is not thoroughly pervaded with an intense national spirit. They should understand that this spirit is utterly incompatible with faction in any form or measure; and that opposition to President LINCOLN's Administration on system, without a practical end is faction, pure and simple. By the sovereign decree of the people, Mr. LINCOLN will be again President of the United States for four years from the fourth of March next. It is now impossible to put another man in his place. He has in charge the most arduous work ever intrusted to mortal hands. He has a right to the sympathetic encouragement, the generous criticism, and the effective material and moral support of all the people, without distinction of party. We are not without the hope that the present opposition will recognize this and will now, for a time at least drop its character as an opposition; and, with a national spirit, will work with all national men in carrying this war through to its legitimate end, which, as the people have decided, alone can secure the true national destiny. ✸

1. Lincoln's final electoral vote count was 212.

THE VICTORY, AND HOW TO IMPROVE IT.

NOVEMBER 10

We doubt if in any one of President LINCOLN's memorable utterances, there is anything more indicative of a mind entirely great, than in that brief speech addressed by him, yesterday morning, to an appreciative, but most unseasonable, audience at the White House. It seems that the ardor of some of his Washington supporters called him from his room at 2 in the morning, to tell him in set phrase, what we have no doubt he knew very well before, that he had been reelected President of the United States.

In his own inimitable way, Mr. LINCOLN replied to his friends, thanking them genially for the particular mark of devotion they had shown by calling on him, but adding, at the same time, that "he always regretted to triumph over anybody."

We are satisfied that in this simple expression of feeling, uttered with no premeditation, may be found to lie the essence of that peculiar philosophy which the loyal people of America discovered in Mr. LINCOLN's character when they determined to intrust him anew with their suffrages. The vast intelligent body of electors who recorded their votes for Mr. LINCOLN on Tuesday, think precisely as Mr. LINCOLN thinks, that, unless this election is a triumph of principle, of right, of loyal honor, and not a mere triumph of party, it is no victory at all. Nay, it is the opening of a reign of faction, which will parallel in its dangers and disasters the terrible experience which sectionalism and secession have brought upon the revolted States. The victory of Tuesday derives its prime significance and its sole merits from the fact that it does not involve the supremacy of one party over another, but that it marks the triumph of the loyal opinion of the nation over a faction. The returns already received show that, apart from extemporized votes dragged out of the most ignorant and debased class of the foreign population, McCLELLAN's strength in 1864 — as far as the North was concerned — lay mainly where the strength of JOHN C. BRECKINRIDGE lay in 1861. To the support of both candidates many sincere and good citizens may have come from life-long party association. But even these, the best find purest of McCLELLAN's voters, must not complain if they are ranked for the time as sectionalists, unless their formal declaration of party faith was a carefully prepared lie.

Mr. LINCOLN's refusal to regard the contest as a struggle for mere party supremacy, we take, it, presents an open highway for many who have been deluded into supporting the sectional and disunion candidate to return to their allegiance — not to their allegiance to particular party leaders — but to that sense of obligation which in this fearful crisis they owe to the country. It cannot have been a pleasing association for the good and sound men of the Democratic party to find themselves, even for these few weeks of hot conflict, in the company of men who regarded, and regard now, every national victory won by our armies as a calamity, and who were prone to heap obloquy upon

HOOD AND SHERMAN — THE WESTERN CAMPAIGN.

NOVEMBER 16

We do not think that, in the whole course of the war, the rebels have ever made a military mistake as great as in the diversion of HOOD's army toward Tennessee. The soldiers of that army were publicly promised by their leaders a month ago that their feet would soon press the soil of that State, and JEFF. DAVIS himself, in his Columbia speech, spoke of their going as high northward as the Ohio River.

Now, when we reflect on the past course and present aspect of military affairs in the Southwest, the madness of such a project must be apparent. The war in that section was begun on the Ohio River, pushed up the Cumberland to Donelson, across Kentucky to Bowling Green and Mill Springs, down to Nashville and Memphis, onward to Corinth and Chattanooga, and still forward and southward till our army stood triumphant in Atlanta. As it marched, it destroyed or drove before it the armies of the rebels, defeating them in not less than twenty pitched battles of magnitude. The country we left behind us in our advance was very effectually conquered and subdued. The whole belligerent and able-bodied population was in the rebel armies that we whipped; and all the main strategic or otherwise important points we captured, fortified and garrisoned. In striking for Tennessee, HOOD struck for a region where the successful prosecution of offensive military operations was next to impossible. It was easy enough for FORREST and his horsemen to dash around and capture little towns or assault outposts. But when it came to the movement of a large army, the matter was altogether different. On every hand there were great fortresses; all around, there were minor but powerful works; the rivers were patrolled by gunboats; the railroads guarded by block-houses; the cities garrisoned; and beside all this, there was a large movable army (leaving SHERMAN altogether out of the count) ready at any point and at any moment to meet the rebels in front, to assail them in flank, to fall upon their rear, or to cut their communications and destroy their supplies. The rebels could not have selected a more hopeless region in which to campaign, with the prospect of any valuable or durable results, than the State of Tennessee. East, Centre and West, North and South, it is ours, and everywhere it is a field prepared for battle. Under these circumstances and conditions, what could HOOD possibly hope to effect? Sweep swiftly across Tennessee? — it might be done. Across Western Kentucky? — it were not altogether impossible. Up to the Ohio, and across the Ohio? — well, what then? Has he gained anything? — does he hold anything? — can he stay there? Has he got Chattanooga, or Murfreesboro, or Nashville? — has he got Knoxville or Memphis? Does he command the Cumberland, the Tennessee, or the Mississippi? Has he got the State of Tennessee? What has he done to forward the triumph or secure the independence of the Southern Confederacy? Well might the grim SHERMAN give vent to the most inexpressible contempt in regard to the northward movement of HOOD; well might he exclaim: "Let him go North, d--n him! If he will go to the Ohio River, I will give him rations."

Where HOOD's main body is stationed at this moment, is not given out; but the appearances are that he has not as yet pressed Tennessee; that he has not even yet got beyond North Alabama.

In the meantime, while HOOD's army, according to the programme set forth by himself and by JEFF. DAVIS, was to be moving into and through Tennessee, what was SHERMAN, at Atlanta, to be about? — what were the opportunities that this mad rebel movement afforded him? SHERMAN followed HOOD a considerable distance, but getting disgusted with the pursuit, and being determined, as he remarked, that the rebels should not plan

the illustrious dead of the national army, by proclaiming their labors a crime, and their sufferings and death a sacrifice in the cause of injustice, oppression, and wrong. No one will cast it up to the true Union-loving Democrat, that he found his party ties such as to temporarily estrange him from the path of political wisdom. The first to forget such estrangements, as Mr. Lincoln's timely words assure us, will be the President-Elect. When the very life of the nation is at stake, it can be no hour far prolonging party-fights among honest citizens, beyond the boundary which marks the issue of the contest. If victory tests with the supporters of the Administration, that victory can be made most perfect by disclaiming every disposition to turn it into any sectional channel, and by heartily, frankly, and in good faith, inviting the cooperation of loyal men of all classes in securing the victory which has yet to be won over armed treason, before the country is once more restored to Union and to peace. ✹

his campaigns or mark out his course for him, he turned back toward Atlanta, and prepared for the prosecution of a new campaign in rebeldom, upon his own plan. HOOD had not only gone where he himself could effect nothing; he had not only failed in drawing SHERMAN upon a wild-goose chase after him; but he had uncovered the whole of the important country between the Savannah and Alabama Rivers, and from the mountains to the sea. So that, whether SHERMAN desired to strike for Savannah, for Mobile, or for Lynchburgh, his work was simplified, and his path rendered comparatively clear, by the fact that HOOD was struggling deviously and wretchedly among the bristling strongholds of Tennessee.

The real purpose and direction of the new campaign which Gen. SHERMAN has embraced the opportunity of HOOD's absence to undertake, is still unknown. It has been a topic of the greatest public interest for the past week; but no man or journal is able, apparently, to give anything definite about it. Speculation runs over a thousand miles, from Lynchburgh to Mobile; but fortunately for SHERMAN, it can fix itself certainly nowhere. The rebels seem to be even more excited about the matter than we are; but they also fail to give us reliable news. ✹

SHERMAN'S MARCH.

THE ARMY REPORTED TO HAVE LEFT ATLANTA ON THE 12TH.

NOVEMBER 18

A dispatch was published in a Cincinnati paper of yesterday, giving some details of the departure of Gen. SHERMAN's columns from Atlanta, on the 9th or 12th, and their probable concentration at Augusta, which the War Department deems contraband, and we therefore refrain from publishing the report. —

ED. TIMES.

INTELLIGENCE FROM REBEL SOURCES.
SPECIAL DISPATCH TO THE NEW-YORK TIMES.
WASHINGTON, THURSDAY, NOV. 17

Richmond papers of Tuesday received here, furnish intelligence from Georgia up to the 14th inst. They state that SHERMAN left Atlanta on the 12th, moving northward, though they doubtless mean by that eastward on a northerly line.

REPORT FROM WASHINGTON.
WASHINGTON, THURSDAY, NOV. 17

No official intelligence has been received from Gen. SHERMAN for a week past.

Hood's Movements, Strength and Position....

SHERMAN'S MOVEMENT.

The Indianapolis Journal, of Tuesday last, says:

"We had a conversation yesterday with a gentleman who had just arrived in this city direct from Atlanta, having left there on Friday, Nov. 6.

Every arrangement had been made for a gigantic movement in some direction. One corps had already moved out of the city, and others were to follow, but had not done so up to the hour of his departure, in consequence of the illness of Gen. SHERMAN.

SHERMAN expresses the utmost indifference as to HOOD's movements, and says 'THOMAS has sufficient troops to attend to him and prevent his returning South.'

The officers and men of SHERMAN's army were never in better spirits or more confident of success. They regard this as the great movement of the war.

Most of our prisoners, heretofore confined at Anderson Ville, have been removed to Augusta, and as that place is directly in the line, SHERMAN will probably take it. They stand a good chance for a speedy release.

No private property in Atlanta had been burned or destroyed, nor was it expected that it would be. From Atlanta to Augusta is 171 miles; from Augusta to Charleston 121 miles; to Savannah 130 miles. But, as our cotemporary remarks, 'the country is not difficult; no mountain ranges lie in the way to make transportation laborious, such as ROSECRANS met in Tennessee in his campaign against Chattanooga; no passes or defiles present easily defensible positions to an opposing force; the whole region both to the south and east is rich in food, and has been untouched by the war.'

The Chicago Journal says: "A furloughed officer of SHERMAN's Staff states that he has been ordered, when his leave expires, to rejoin his command at Savannah. HOOD is said to be on the line of the Chattanooga and Atlanta Railroad. FORREST has not joined him, but is again moving toward Kentucky." ✹

Sherman's March to the Sea, a rendition by artist F.O.C. Darley.

GEN. SHERMAN'S MOVEMENT.

NOVEMBER 19
SPECIAL DISPATCH TO THE NEW-YORK TIMES.
WASHINGTON, D.C., FRIDAY, NOV. 18

The direction of Gen. SHERMAN'S grand counter-move in Georgia is not yet sufficiently indicated to authorize a determinate opinion as to his ultimate aim. Until we learn definitely the actual direction he has given his columns from Atlanta, we shall be left in doubt as to his real objective.

The rebels are equally mystified; for the two latest reports we have had from the Richmond papers make him march in diametrically opposite directions. Those of Tuesday state that SHERMAN left Atlanta on the 14th, moving northward — by which they mean eastward on a northerly line — and anticipate his striking Augusta, on route for Savannah. On the other hand, those of Wednesday, received here this morning, expressly report him as advancing on Selma and Montgomery, Ala., with, of course, Mobile as his goal; and they support this view by the announcement from Mobile of a large increase of the fleet, and especially of the transportation in the bay of Mobile.

There are almost equally good reasons for believing that he aims at the one point as at the other. It is almost equally probable that he will perform the military marvel of emerging on the Gulf of Mexico, or debouching his columns on the coast of the Atlantic. The results of every kind, military, material and moral, to be accomplished by either enterprise, are almost equally splendid; the damage to be inflicted on the enemy equally prodigious. It is a choice between two moves akin in their audacity, in difficulty of execution, and in the promise of their achievements. ⦾

SOUTHERN NEWS.
SHERMAN'S ARMY.

NOVEMBER 23

There no longer remains any doubt that SHERMAN has torn up the Atlanta and Chattanooga Railroad, boldly cut himself off from all connection with his base, and plunged headlong into the heart of Georgia, depending entirely upon the force he has with him, and the weakness of the country through which he designs to pass. His aim is, beyond all question, to secure a position upon the seaboard, where he may receive reinforcements and supplies at leisure, and having there established his base, to prosecute further operations next Spring or during the Winter. It is not known for what point his course is directed — whether he has selected Savannah or Charleston as his base, or whether he aims first at Selma and afterward at Mobile.

We are rather inclined to think that he will prefer the latter, being induced thereto, no doubt, by the refusal of the Alabama Legislature, when summoned by Gov. WATTS, to make any provision for the public defence: a refusal which the Yankee journals have not been slow to interpret into a desire on the part of that State to return to the "bosom of ABRAHAM," If we may be excused for adopting, for once, the profane expression of Secretary SEWARD, Such a movement on his part would, moreover, correspond with the design The NEW-YORK TIMES gave him credit for entertaining last Summer, when he made his famous march from Vicksburgh.

It may be, however, that he thinks it would redound more to his advantage to seize Augusta, the Importance of which has been grossly over-estimated, and thence match against Charleston, which, with the advantage of a water base, would allow free communication with all the ports of the United States. From Charleston he can lend a hand to GRANT. who he hopes will, by that time, be in possession of Richwood, in operations against Wilmington the result of which, he supposes, will entirely shut us out from the sea. The Yankee papers, several weeks ago, announced the determination to transfer the Winter campaign to the cotton States, and this, we presume, is the preliminary movement.

Whichever of the two movements SHERMAN has in view, it is evident that he calculates largely upon the weakness of the country through which he designs to march, or on its disloyalty to the Confederacy. In both calculations we are inclined to believe that he will be greatly mistaken. It will be the fault of the people it. habiting those countries if his army be not utterly destroyed long before it shall have reached either Mobile or Savannah.

The marches SHERMAN will be compelled to make in order to reach the several stages of his journey are great, considering that he must carry the greater part of his supplies with him. From Atlanta to Macon, the first stage, is somewhat more than one hundred miles, and here there is understood to be a strong garrison, defending powerful works. From Macon to Augusta, one hundred and seventy miles further, there is a railroad, the destruction of which will, of course, be attempted by our forces, and will be effected, at least, to the extent of retarding his progress until the portion broken down can be restored.

From Augusta to Savannah the distance is about twenty-five miles, and -at Savannah, whatever calculations he may now make, he will be pretty certain to meet with a stubborn resistance. Here, then. is a march before him of three hundred miles, through a country sparsely settled, and a cotton-growing country, where he will not find the necessaries of life so abundant that he can afford to dispense with magazines, or that he can replenish these so often as to be able at all times to have them close in his rear.

When he shall have reached Savannah, subdued the garrison and taken possession, he may think of Charleston, 100 miles further north. If SHERMAN can do all this with the force he has at command, which we are disposed to think does not exceed 40,000 men, then he is a much greater Commander than we take him to be, and the Georgians are much tamer people than they have credit for being. For our own part, we cannot see how the contemplated campaign is to advance the design of subjugation, let it terminate as it may.

It may serve us as an additional annoyance to the people, but it must be as destitute of results as the arrow is destitute of the power to wound the air through which it passes. It leaves absolutely open the entire country in the rear, from Chattanooga to the Gulf, wherever the Yankee army is not for the time encamped. ⦾

SHERMAN'S MARCH.

NOVEMBER 26

Gen. SHERMAN's army is making rapid progress in its great march through Georgia. Our advices are as late as Sunday last, at which time it was in the geographical centre of the State. The news of this morning will be found both important and exciting — though the excitement in the North can by no means approach the tremendous commotion it is producing in Georgia, and throughout the length and breadth of the whole Southern Confederacy.

From the various items of intelligence that have reached us within the week and up to this hour, mainly through rebel mediums, we are enabled to fix definitely two or three points which were for some time in doubt, to deduce some general results, and to draw some few inferences.

1. In the first place, as to the direction of SHERMAN's march. When the fact of a movement was originally announced to the public, it was a subject of distracting dispute, whither it was to tend. Speculators and journalists differed as widely and as variously as possible. The whole Confederacy lay before them where to choose their place of rest, with no guide but their own fancy. SHERMAN was marching upon Lynchburgh, in Virginia, to cooperate with GRANT on the James; he was marching upon Mobile, on the Gulf of Mexico; he was retreating into Tennessee; was moving upon HOOD's rear; was advancing into South or North Carolina; was striking for Pensacola. But the actual fact has turned out to be as foreshadowed in The Times of the 10th instant, that SHERMAN is marching through the State of Georgia to a base on the Atlantic coast.

2. SHERMAN is marching in two great columns, each of them two corps in strength, with cavalry — one column (HOWARD) striking southward for Macon, and the other (SLOCUM) eastward for Augusta — the whole of the four corps, it is supposed, to form a junction at Augusta, and thence advance to the sea.

3. By Sunday last, HOWARD's column had got as far as or beyond Macon, though it is not fixed that the place itself was taken. His advance had reached Gordon, sixty miles east of Macon, on the Savannah Railroad, and at the junction of the railroad to Milledgeville. This point is one hundred and forty-one miles from Savannah, and ninety miles from Augusta.

The main body was reported only twenty-three miles from Milledgeville, and the Legislature of Georgia had adjourned and left with precipitation. The other column (SLOCUM) had made about an equal distance along the railroad from Atlanta to Augusta. In other words, both columns had got about half way on their march to Augusta in six days, (14th to 20th.) SHERMAN's "Orders for the March" requires each of the columns to start habitually at 7 o'clock in the morning, and to make about fifteen miles per day. We judge that the six days' march to Macon was almost precisely up to orders.

4. In this hundred miles' march through the most densely populated section of Georgia, SHERMAN met with no serious obstruction from the rebels. COBB and his militia have popped up once or twice in the rebel newspapers, and it is not impossible that they took refuge in Macon, which is strongly fortified, and made such a show of defence, as to stop our forces, if not to cause them to pass by the place. Macon itself, indeed, may not have been, taken in HOWARD's line of March, as his troops passed to the northeast of it in the movement toward Milledgeville. Deserters from LEE's army, however, who came into our lines at City Point yesterday, report its occupation by our troops.

5. The march of our army seems to have been spread over a wide extent of country. According to the rebel reports, which are doubtless authentic, SHERMAN's two columns have already traversed eighteen of the most populous and wealthy counties in Central Georgia, viz.: Clay, Fayette, Fulton, De Kalb, Walton, Newton, Jasper, Morgan, Putnam, Jones, Butts, Henry, Spalding, Pike, Bibb, Twiggs and Baldwin; and either his infantry or cavalry have visited the following towns: Decatur, Jackson, Griffin, Forsyth, Monticello, Hillsboro, Covington, McDonough, Social Circle, and others. At a dozen different points he has touched both railroads, and the width of the strip of country over which his army moves is not less than seventy five miles covering both the railroad to Augusta and that to Savannah.

Thus far, then, the march, in whatever aspect viewed, has been a success. The compact columns have marched to time, and resistlessly. The rebels seem to be in de-

spair of stopping our army. BEAUREGARD has issued a highfalutin proclamation, announcing that he is flying to Georgia's relief; but more sober rebels than he are calling on the elements, the negroes, and all possible and impossible powers and weaknesses, to aid them. The whole Confederacy is evidently in a panic; and there is no doubt that JEFF. DAVIS will do all that is possible to thwart or overthrow SHERMAN during the last half of his extraordinary march. That they have not succeeded in doing anything from last Sunday until now, is evident enough from the fact that they have not informed us of it. ⊛

THE REBEL PLOT.

ATTEMPT TO BURN THE CITY.

NOVEMBER 26

The city was startled last evening by the loud and simultaneous clanging of fire-bells in every direction, and the alarming report soon spread from street to street that a pre-concerted attempt was being made by rebel emissaries, in accordance with the fiendish programme recently set forth by the Rich-mond papers, to burn New-York and other Northern cities, in retaliation for the dev-astation of rebel territory by Union armies. The facts gathered by our reporters appear to confirm the truth of these reports.

The plan adopted by the incendiaries was to set fire at once, or nearly at once, to the principal hotels and other public buildings in the city. At seventeen minutes of nine the St. James Hotel was discovered to be on fire in one of the rooms. On examination it was discovered that the bed and several other articles of furniture had been saturated with phosphorous and set on fire. A few minutes afterward Barnum's Museum was discov-ered to be on fire; but the flames were soon extinguished, and the building sustained very little damage. At five minutes of nine fire was discovered in rooms No. 138, 139, 140, and 174 of the St. Nicholas Hotel. The fire was got under without much difficulty by the fire department of the hotel, but not until the furniture and the rooms had been damaged to the amount of about $2,500. The beds in this case, also, were found to be saturated with inflammatory materials. At twenty minutes past nine the inmates of the Lafarge House were alarmed by the cry of fire; but the flames were extinguished without much difficulty, and the damage received was comparatively slight. Shortly after 10 o'clock the Metropolitan Hotel was discovered to be on fire; but by this time the police had given warning at all the hotels of the designs of the incendiaries, and the watchmen being on their guard, discovered the fire in time to put it out before it had done much damage. The Brandreth House, Frenche's Hotel, the Belmont House, Wal-lack's Theatre, and several other buildings were fired during the course of the evening, but none of them were seriously damaged.

About ten o'clock the Detective Police ar-rested a woman at the Metropolitan Hotel,

THE INCENDIARIES — FIRST FOREWARNINGS.

NOVEMBER 27

Regular and organized warfare outside of LEE's lines at Richmond, has become an absolute impossibility for the Confed-eracy, and we must be prepared to hear at intervals, for many months to come, that our larger cities are infested with incen-diaries in numbers heretofore altogether unknown to our experience of crime.

We must be prepared to find that our native thieves, burglars, forgers and mur-derers, who have only the purpose of in-dividual plunder to serve, are prepared to cooperate with the refugee class to the full measure of their vicious ability. The de-tective force of the city, therefore, should be doubled at once. We cannot afford to run any risk. Every respectable, law-abiding citizen should constitute himself, as far as his time and means will possibly admit, a volunteer watchman. Our hotels, such of them at least as have been known to be the resort of Southern skulkers, so aptly described by the Daily News, should be thoroughly scoured by judicious offi-cers of the police force and by detectives of well-established character. With only reasonable precaution, we can at once provide an effectual guarantee that this incendiary business shall not spread, and we can take most effectual steps to see that the city is shortly purged of the presence of hundreds and thousands of so-called Southerners. ✹

THE NEW APPOINTMENT TO THE CHIEF-JUSTICESHIP — HOW RECEIVED.

DECEMBER 8

The appointment of SALMON P. CHASE to the Chief-Justiceship of the Supreme Court gives very general satisfaction. Even his po-litical opponents — those of course excepted whose judgment is palsied by old prejudice — cheerfully concede that the President could have made no better selection. We can recall no Instance of one transferred from the political arena to the Supreme Bench with so little animadversion. It is a remarkable contrast to the storm of wrath raised by Gen. JACKSON's appointment of his immediate predecessor.

We consider this fact very significant. It is one of the most notable tokens we have had that the Republic has indeed entered upon a new era. There is no public man in the country whose anti-slavery record has been longer, or more consistent, or more decided than that of SALMON P. CHESE [sic]. Twenty-eight years ago, he was seen in the Ohio courts pleading with great power in behalf of fugitive slaves. He took the most determined ground against the entire system of fugitive slave sur-renders. The same intense anti-slavery spirit which always controlled him pro-fessionally attended his political life from the very first. One of the founders of the "Liberty party" in Ohio in 1841; an active member of the Buffalo Liberty Conven-tion in 1843; again an active member of the second Liberty National Convention in 1847; elected to the United States Sen-ate by the Democratic Legislature of Ohio in 1849, on distinctly avowed anti-slavery grounds; a most earnest opponent of Mr. CLAY's compromise measures of 1850; repudiating the Democratic party because it indorsed these measures in its Presi-dential platform of 1852; one of the fore-most advocates of the Kansas-Nebraska bill of 1854, adhering to his anti-slavery principles with the same tenacity as when Governor of Ohio in the slavery period of BUCHANAN's Administration; still un-compromising and unflinching as mem-ber of the Peace Convention which assem-bled in Washington on the eve of the great rebellion; known as the head of the radical wine of the radical wing of president LIN-COLN's Cabinet and the special favorite of the so-called radical portion of the Union party or the next Presidency, he yet is now made Chief Justice of the Supreme Court of the United States, with the almost uni-versal approval of both of the great par-ties. There are but one or two living public men in the country upon whom, in time past, the Democratic party has poured out contumely so bitter and so incessant, and yet now all this is either hushed into soft silence, or else positively converted into honeyed commendation.

This new leaning toward Mr. CHASE on the part of his old political opponents,

under circumstances that involve her in serious suspicion. She hails from Baltimore, and was noticed going from one hotel to another, leaving each hotel just previous to the breaking out of the fire. She strongly protests her entire innocence of the crime charged upon her; but the fact that the fires followed closely in her wake, as she passed from house to house, is a very suspicious circumstance, and justifies her arrest and detention.

The Police also made several other arrests; but in accordance with a request from Police Headquarters, we refrain from mentioning the names of the parties taken into custody.

The scenes at the various hotels, where the usual quiet of the evening was broken by the alarm of fire, and by startling rumors of extensive conflagrations through-out the city, were very exciting. At several of the hotels, the inmates of the rooms were requested to vacate their quarters and permit them to be carefully searched for incendiary materials. In several instances, beds in vacant rooms were found saturated with phosphorus and filled with matches. A box filled with inflammatory material was taken from the Metropolitan to the Police Headquarters, and after being exposed to the air for a short time, burst into flames.

To guard against the threatened conflagration, watchmen were put on at all the hotels, and a dozen pails of water were set on every floor, ready for instant use. Fire-Marshal BAKER is busy investigating the origin of the fires, and the Police are said to be on the track of several suspected persons. ❀

---

cannot be imputed to a satisfaction that he has quitted the political arena forever. Everybody knows that in his judicial capacity he will be required to pronounce upon many momentous questions affecting the interests of slaveholders, and intimately connected with old party issues. There is no danger that he will step out of his proper judicial province to do this, in imitation of the conduct of his predecessor in the Dred Scott case; but he cannot avoid these questions if he would. In conjunction with his brethren on the bench, he will have to settle most important points of constitutional law, growing out of the Emancipation Proclamation, the confiscation acts of Congress, and other enactments that have been passed, and are yet to be passed, for the suppression of the rebellion, and the reestablishment of constitutional rule. Yet for all that, almost everybody trusts him.

The simple truth is, that the terrible discipline of this war has wrought a complete change in the temper and sentiment of even the Democratic party, in respect to the South. This change has gone on in spite of even the fierce excitement of the late Presidential canvass. It asserted itself in the cheerful acquiescence, we may almost say the positive satisfaction, with which the reelection of Presi-dent LINCOLN was received by the great body of the party. It again asserts itself in this easy concurrence in the eminent fitness of the appointment of SALMON P. CHASE to be Chief-Justice. The Democratic party, in spite of all of its old habits, cannot help recognizing that the old order of things is at an end, and that the nation is passing into a new stage of being. It is more and more realizing the necessity of conforming to this transition; and submits, with a grace never felt before, not only to the transition itself, but to those public agents who guide it, however obnoxious these may have been in other days. This happy adaptation bespeaks an end of faction, and is a most propitious augury. ❀

DECEMBER 26
WAR DEPARTMENT, WASHINGTON, DEC. 25
— 8 P.M.

To Maj.-Gen, Dix, New-York:

A dispatch has been received this evening by the President from Gen. SHERMAN. It is dated at Savannah, on Thursday, the 22d inst., and announces his occupation of the city of Savannah and the capture of one hundred and fifty guns, plenty of ammunition, and about 25,000 bales of cotton. No other particulars are given.

An official dispatch from Gen. FOSTER to Gen. GRANT, dated on the 22d instant, at 7 P.M., states that the city of Savannah was occupied by Gen. SHERMAN on the morning of the 21st, and that on the preceding afternoon and night, HARDEE escaped with the main body of his infantry and light, artillery, blowing up the ironclads and the Navy-yard. He enumerates as captured 800 prisoners, 150 guns, 13 locomotives, in good order, 190 cars, a large lot of ammunition and materials of war, three steamers and 33,000 bales of cotton. No mention is made of the present position of HARDEE's force, which had been estimated at about 15,000.

The dispatches of Gen. SHERMAN and Gen. FOSTER are as follows:

SAVANNAH, Ga., Dec. 22

To His Excellency, President Lincoln:

I beg to present you as a Christmas gift, the city of Savannah, with one hundred and fifty heavy guns and plenty of ammunition, and also about twenty-five thousand bales of cotton.

(SIGNED,)
W.T. SHERMAN,
MAJOR-GENERAL. ❀

Alfred Waud's sketch of federal troops and fortifications for the Battle of Savannah.

TWO MONTHS OF WAR AND THEIR SIGNIFICANCE.

DECEMBER 26

The past two months' campaigning has taught the rebels a hard lesson. Each isolated event has an important lesson of its own, but taken together they open up startling revelations. It must be sufficiently distasteful to the rebels that an army of fifty thousand men can cut itself off from its base at Atlanta and at leisure establish another three hundred miles distant, on the Atlantic coast. This fact alone proves the helplessness of the Confederacy outside of its intrenched strongholds. The rebels may agree with DAVIS that Richmond, or any other fortified point, may be forced from them without their suffering vital loss, but this will not make them relish being pummeled everywhere else. Then, again, HOOD's defeat, taken by itself alone, conveys a scathing comment on DAVIS' policy of waging war. The same may be said of PRICE's defeat in Missouri, or of EARLY's in the Shenandoah. But in the summary, and considering the total result, there is conveyed to the minds of the rebels a still more disagreeable suggestion than is involved in simple defeat or indiscretion, and that is, that as their relative strength is diminished, the proportion of the waste attendant upon the war on their part is greatly increased.

During the last two months the rebels have lost forty thousand men, three fourths of whom have been taken prisoners on the battle field. Twenty-five officers of the rank of General have been placed hors du combat. More than three hundred and fifty pieces of artillery have been captured, (including those at Savannah,) and it is scarcely possible to estimate the number of small arms taken. These large captures of men and of guns appear almost incredible, when we consider that with the exception of Fort McAllister and Savannah, no fortress is included in the estimate; the captures were made on the battle field. Then look at the destruction of railroads, stores, and factories. Probably no country was ever more thoroughly devastated than the Shenandoah was by SHERIDAN after the battle of Winchester. SHERMAN, in his march through Georgia, entirely destroyed two hundred miles of railroad, besides large quantities of stores essential to the Confederate armies. All the great arsenals of the South outside of Richmond are within his grasp. CANBY's expeditions from Vicksburgh and Baton Rouge destroyed millions worth of stores which had been accumulating for HOOD, and long lines of railway. According to rebel reports STONEMAN and BURBRIDGE did equally efficient work in BRECKINRIDGE's rear on the Virginia and East Tennessee Railroad. WARREN's raid on the Weldon Railroad in the short space of three days destroyed twenty miles of the road — ties, rails and all — as effectually as if it had never been built.

In the meantime the rebels have so managed the Winter campaign that our losses during the last two month have been but trifling. HOOD's campaign in Tennessee has shortened this war by many months, not so much because he has been beaten by THOMAS, as because by taking himself away from SHERMAN's front, he

THE CLOSE OF SHERMAN'S GREAT CAMPAIGN — SAVANNAH OURS.

DECEMBER 26

SHERMAN'S resplendent campaign has had a logical termination, in the capture of Savannah, the chief city and seaport of the State of Georgia. This campaign, so unique and striking, is thus rounded and made complete. The military mystery, which for so long a time amazed and puzzled the country, is revealed, and is seen to be a thing whose character and object were fixed, definite and grand. The army, about which the rebels told so many falsehoods, from the hour of its "retreat" from Northern Georgia to the day they "ruined" it near Atlanta — from the time they had it "floundering through the bogs of Georgia" to the moment they brought it up in blank despair before the fortifications of Savannah — through all the defeats it suffered without knowing of them, and amid all the failures it enjoyed to read about — has marched onward to its destination with triumphant tread, has reaped fruits of victory as it went, and has grasped the prize when it reached the goal.

SHERMAN offers the President, as the head of the Republic and the representative of the people, the City of Savannah as a "Christmas gift."

The military and other spoils of the city are mentioned as one hundred and fifty cannon, much materiel of war, over two hundred cars and locomotives, twenty-five thousand (or according to FOSTER, thirty-three thousand) bales of cotton, and several steamers. The bulk of HARDEE's army escaped from the city on Tuesday last, the day before our army moved into it, and the prisoners are estimated at less than a thousand, but twenty thousand people were found in the city, "quiet and well-disposed." The rebel iron-clads have been destroyed and the navy-yard demolished, and FOSTER and DAHLGREN have opened up communications with the city through the Savannah River.

It would undoubtedly have been very gratifying to have taken captive all of HARDEE's army of fifteen thousand men. There was a break, however, in the line of SHERMAN's investment of the city. That break was on the eastern side of the place, and consisted in the space from the mouth of the Savannah River to a short distance above the city — a space of about seven miles. Had DAHLGREN's iron-clads been able to run up and cover this short line, HARDEE would have had no possible route of escape. We do not doubt that FARRAGUT, with wooden vessels would have accomplished this work. HARDEE may find some difficulty yet in getting his army on to the railroad or into Charleston; but the chances of success are in his favor.

The time covered by SHERMAN's campaign, from the day he left Rome until he planted his army within the defences of Savannah, was just about forty days. The campaign will stand as one of the most striking feats in military history, and will prove one of the heaviest blows at the vitality of the great Southern rebellion. ⊛

has enabled the latter in one short month to accomplish results which, in the ordinary course of military events would have required long delays. How different the Winter campaign would have looked now if HOOD had contented himself with simply resisting SHERMAN's further advance. Thousands of lives would have been lost, where, as the case now stands, SHERMAN has only had disabled about fifteen hundred men — a little more than LEE lost during the same thirty days by the shots of our pickets. Delay, too, would have been a great advantage to the rebels, as it would have given them several weeks of leisure in which to recuperate their armies. But that opportunity, thanks to rebel recklessness, is gone, and can never be recovered.

Never, we think, has it happened in any war that two months have been so decisive of grand results as the two which have just closed. It is only necessary that the people should hurry to the front every available soldier, in order to make the next few months completely decisive of this unhappy conflict. ⊛

Harper's Weekly illustration showing Sherman marching into Savannah.

CHAPTER 23

"No Such Thing as Compromise"

JANUARY–FEBRUARY 1865

he climactic year of the American Civil War began unfolding in a maelstrom of remarkable events that seemed concurrently to advance the conquest of the South, heighten the quest for an armistice, and widen the embrace of black freedom, all at the price of further bloodshed, devastation, and social upheaval.

In January, William T. Sherman, fresh from his long march from Atlanta to the sea, turned northward toward the Carolinas and resumed his destructive campaign through territory where the rebellion had begun four long years before. Many would observe that Sherman's army now included regiments of African-American troops, fully engaged in what seemed to be the final chapter of the fight for their own freedom.

In the respective capitals of Washington and Richmond, meanwhile, the Congresses of both the Union and the Confederacy went into session and focused attention on the question of black freedom. In the North, progressives labored to accomplish universally what the Emancipation Proclamation had begun. In the South, legislators considered offering the promise of freedom in exchange for military service, in a rather ironic and desperate attempt to replenish rebel forces. Though generations of Southern leaders had resolutely insisted on the inequality of black men, Confederate leaders now seriously considered conscripting the region's remaining slaves to fight to preserve the system that kept them in chains. The Confederate Congress did give a belated recognition to Robert E. Lee, making him general-in-chief almost in recognition of his resistance to a defeat that now seemed inevitable. It was a deliberate slight to President Jefferson Davis, who was the consti-

Detail of a print showing Major General Philip Sheridan after the Battle of Fisher's Hill.

tutional commander-in-chief, but Davis allowed it to stand since it boosted Southern morale at a time when the fortunes of the Southern confederacy were dire. Lee's great need, however, was not for increased authority but for more men, and there was nowhere else in the shrinking Confederacy to turn for them other than the South's black population. Indeed, the desperation of the dying Confederacy was nowhere more evident than in the decision by the rebel Congress to accede to Lee's request that he be allowed to arm some slaves.

Meanwhile, one of the South's great nemeses, Union general Benjamin F. Butler, lost his command after years of controversial field leadership and military administration. One thing could be said about the Massachusetts-born political general, however: he had consistently advocated for black freedom in all his posts.

When it came, Abraham Lincoln was so jubilant over passage of the Thirteenth Amendment to the Constitution, abolishing slavery everywhere, that he affixed his name to the Congressional resolution that formally sent the proposal to the states for ratification. The law did not require a Presidential signature on such a document, and in an apparent battle for glory and credit, Congress huffily passed an additional resolution criticizing the chief executive for his seeming impertinence. Lincoln hardly noticed the slap. The amendment, he told a throng gathered at the White House to celebrate on February 1, was "a King's cure for all the evils," adding: "It winds the whole thing up."

Not quite. Although Lincoln exulted that the Thirteenth amendment would be "the indispensable adjunct to the consummation of the great game we are playing," the game had not yet ended. Only a few weeks

earlier, in fact, the commander-in-chief had quietly asked General Grant to appoint the President's 21-year-old son, an officer on his personal staff. Robert had lobbied for years to be allowed to join the Union army, but his mother had opposed it. Now, in the last months of the war, Robert Lincoln got his wish. Like so many fathers in America, the President now had a son in the army.

And the fight did continue, notably under the command of William T. Sherman and his counterparts in the United States Navy. On January 13, with Admiral David Dixon Porter softening the resistance with a mighty fleet of 59 vessels packing more than 600 guns, the Union began an assault on Fort Fisher, which guarded the entrance to the Cape Fear River and access to Wilmington, North Carolina. The strategic Confederate port, the last with direct rail connections to Richmond, fell two days later. The Confederacy's Vice President, Alexander H. Stephens, called the demoralizing defeat "one of the greatest disasters which had befallen our Cause since the beginning of the war."

Three weeks afterward, Sherman himself was on the move, and by mid-February he had advanced well into the Carolinas. The relentless Union general captured the South Carolina state capital of Columbia on the 17th, and on the same day Confederate forces abandoned Charleston, the city where the war had begun with the firing on Fort Sumter in 1861. By now the fort, like Confederate dreams of independence, lay pounded into ruins — leveled by a bombardment from Union batteries on Morris Island and by Union vessels offshore.

With a Union victory on the horizon, Lincoln surprised many observers by agreeing to meet a Confederate peace delegation at Fortress Monroe, Virginia, early in February. The

conference, also attended by Secretary of State William H. Seward, marked the first, last, and only time Lincoln discussed peace directly with rebel leaders. The conference had been urged and arranged by Francis Preston Blair Sr., who had journeyed to Richmond to ask Jefferson Davis himself to agree to the attempt to end hostilities without further loss of life or property.

Leading the Confederate conferees was Vice President Stephens, Lincoln's old colleague from their days in the U.S. House of Representatives more than a decade before. Though he harbored few hopes for a negotiated settlement, Lincoln met with Stephens, former Senator Robert T. Hunter, and former Supreme Court Justice John A. Campbell for four hours on February 3 aboard his steamer, the *River Queen*. The conference went nowhere. The news that Congress had passed the Thirteenth Amendment abolishing slavery put a decisive chill on the discussion. Lincoln insisted that the only way to peace was for the Confederacy to lay down its arms, and Seward made clear that there was no chance of going back on the Emancipation Proclamation. The President did not foreclose the idea of compensating Southerners for lost slaves, but would not yield an inch on restoration of the union. The meetings ended with no resolution.

Once back in Washington, Lincoln acted to settle all lingering questions about whether he was now hoping for an armistice rather than unconditional surrender. At his instruction, Secretary of War Edwin M. Stanton wired Grant in the field: "Nothing transpired, or transpiring with the three gentlemen from Richmond, is to cause any change, hindrance or delay, of our military plans or operations."

The war would continue awhile longer.

PROGRESS OF THE WAR.

SHERMAN TO GO ON.

JANUARY 9

Events in the Southwest have justified my anticipations (frequently stated in the TIMES) of the important consequences to flow from the advance of our armies from the West. It would have rejoiced the nation to have taken Richmond at any time during the war; but at no time could it have been of half the importance of a continuous march from the West — cutting off the Southwestern States, destroying the lines of communication, practically annihilating the principal resources of the Confederacy, and reducing, not merely Richmond, but what Richmond holds, the rebel Government, to the last extremity. This process has been begun, and partly accomplished, by SHERMAN's victorious march through Georgia. But it will be far more apparent in what is to follow, if SHERMAN pursues his course, with the military sagacity which has heretofore guided him. His march on the single line of railroad through Branchville, (at any point on it which he may select,) his march on the railroads of North Carolina, and thence on the Roanoke, (at Danville,) utterly destroying all communication between LEE and his supports, are matters of course, unless the rebels can throw an army across his path stronger than that of LEE. How probable that is, we may know by reference to some obvious facts....

Now, in the absence of white men, what is left? Gen. LEE says, arm the slaves. Well, I don't doubt the slaves will make good soldiers, and with their masters for officers, will remain some time. But there are three things which will end that dream at an early day. First, half the slave country is in our possession, or cut off from the rebel Government; consequently they can get but a comparatively small number of able-bodied men slaves. They will not get as many as we do and it will require several months to discipline them. Secondly, as fast as their slaves are taken prisoners, or can get within our lines, they will never return. Thirdly, the arming of the slaves by the Confederacy will end the last doubt or question upon LINCOLN's Proclamation of freedom. Slavery is, by the confession and consent of the rebels, ended forever. Then, let them be armed by the South, that the jubilee of freedom may come, and this continent ring with the shouts of universal freedom! Let no man mistake this matter. If the rebels arm slaves, every negro on this continent is free. Nor is this all. We shall sweep the South with the besom of destruction. We shall put such an end to the war that slavery, and Southern rights, and State sovereignty shall be heard of no more in this land. And this was the end to which we were destined from the beginning. Liberty and Union, one and inseparable. A great country cannot be governed and sustained by the miserable dogma of State rights. The country must have a strong Government, founded on the representative principle, centralizing the power of a great nation, and extending its arm of protection to every individual within its vast embrace.

A VETERAN OBSERVER. ⊛

SHERMAN AND THOMAS — THE NEW CAMPAIGNS IN THE COTTON STATES.

JANUARY 9

The Richmond Examiner, of Friday last, says it is confirmed that SHERMAN'S troops have crossed the Savannah River and are believed to be marching toward Grahamsville, in the direction of Charleston. The rebels are now as much puzzled in regard to the nature and direction of the next campaign of SHERMAN as they were about his last campaign at the time of its inauguration and during its progress. They know that it must be eastward and northward, as there is no enemy in the whole region west of the Savannah worthy of his attention.

But is he going to strike first for Augusta, or for Branchville, or for Charleston? Or, will he adopt his Georgia policy and move his forces so as to appear to be striking for several places in one direction, while his real objective is another place in a different direction? It will be as hard for the rebels to find out as it would be for us to tell; but as the Unionist dispatches from Savannah a few days since announced that "SHERMAN's army was being rapidly reorganized and reequipped, preparatory to the commencement of a campaign as remarkable as its last," and, as the rebel dispatches are already beginning to report movements on SHERMAN's part, of a singularly incomprehensible character, we think it not unlikely that before the close of the present month, they will find out the whole secret of his puzzling plans. ⊛

MAJ.-GEN. B.F. BUTLER.

HIS REMOVAL FROM COMMAND.

JANUARY 11
CITY POINT, MONDAY, JAN. 9
SPECIAL DISPATCH TO THE NEW-YORK TIMES.

BUTLER is dethroned — ordered to report at Lowell, and Gen. ORD[1] takes his place. R.J.H.

DISPATCH TO THE HERALD.
CITY POINT, SUNDAY, JAN. 8

The news of the President's Order No. 1, series of 1865, removing Maj.-Gen. BENJAMIN F. BUTLER from the command of the Department of Virginia and North Carolina, is causing much comment, but, so far as I can learn, little or no animadversion.

The ostensible grounds for depriving him of his command are undoubtedly his recent fiascos of Wilmington and Dutch Gap. But a

LEE AS SOUTHERN DICTATOR — ITS EFFECT ON THE WAR — DRAFTING, VOLUNTEERING AND DODGING AN THE NORTH.

JANUARY 12
IN THE FIELD, BEFORE PETERSBURGH,
SUNDAY, JANUARY 1

To the Editor of the New-York Times:

From the straws that have been blown to the North in the blasts of Southern journals, we may infer that JEFFERSON DAVIS, the first President of that sinful conspiracy against human liberty — the Confederacy — may soon voluntarily yield the overwhelming responsibilities of his thankless and dangerous position to ROBERT E. LEE. The failing health of DAVIS, his still more rapidly failing popularity, the constant and increasing dissatisfaction at the unvarying current in the present tide of Southern affairs, may well induce him to pause — even to step aside, and permit his most able and successful General to take his place.

But it cannot be as President that LEE can assume this prominency; it must be by the consenting action of the rebel Congress; and we can well imagine that to some such step as this Mr. FOOTE[1] recently alluded in his disaffected speech before the rebel Senate. The South inau-

Major General Benjamin Butler, U.S.A.

mountain of dissatisfaction has been accumulating against him for months on account of alleged illegal and arbitrary arrests, imprisonments and punishments. It is said that many cases of glaring injustice have come to light, and many others are expected to be developed by his supersedure.

Maj.-Gen. BUTLER is ordered to turn over his command, all moneys and Government properly, and the civil fund in his possession, to the person named by Lieut.-Gen. GRANT as his temporary successor, and to proceed to Lowell. Mass., and to report to the War Department by letter.

Maj.-Gen. EDWARD OTHO CRESSUP ORD, commanding the Twenty-fourth Army Corps, has been named the temporary successor of Gen. BUTLER, and will at once take charge of the department.

To the Colored Troops of the Army of the James

In this army you have been treated, not as laborers, but as soldiers. You have shown yourselves worthy of the uniform you wear. The best officers of the Union seek to command you. Your bravery has won the admiration even of those who would be your masters. Your patriotism, fidelity, and courage have illustrated the best qualities of manhood. With the bayonet you have unlocked the iron-barred gates of prejudice, opening new fields of freedom, liberty, and equality of rights to yourselves and your race forever. Comrades of the Army of the James, I bid you farewell, farewell!

BENJAMIN F. BUTLER. MAJ.-GEN. ✺

1. E. O. C. Ord (1818-1883) assumed command this day of the Army of the James and the Department of North Carolina.

gurated this war, not more for separation from the North than to effect an entire change in the nature of its Government. We have often heretofore declared our conviction that republicanism was entirely hateful to the leaders of secession. Their aim was to change existing forms into monarchy, in some shape or other. They have succeeded perfectly in organizing the most complete military despotism the world ever saw. The Southern people are no longer their own masters, or they would long since have overthrown their oppressors; their very slaves are now more free than they. Yet Mr. DAVIS' despotism has not sufficed for the accomplishment of its avowed end — the procurement of Southern independence. It has not been able even to subdue entirely every expression of dissentient opinion, or to compel to its control every possible element of Southern strength. To effect these, constitutional rights must be put aside, and the fact must be practically enunciated that no dweller within the limits of rebel authority has any longer any rights whatever. This much Mr. FOOTE has foreseen and declared — and he has not been alone in these sentiments.

Hence the possible, if not probable, abandonment of the present form of the Confederate Government, in favor of still greater absolutism.

LEE is by far the most popular man now

before the Southern people; he has their perfect respect and confidence; they will look upon him whom their soldiery lovingly style "Uncle ROBERT," with an affection that will go far toward reconciling them to his extreme supremacy, no matter by what name it may be called.

In such an hypothesis we can see no reason to hope for an earlier peace. It is a measure looking rather to a more energetic prosecution of a game upon which the South has staked its all, and will be played until human passion and human folly shall have been exhausted from the Southern heart. Continually the declaration is reiterated that complete separation is the only and undying aim of the Southern people. Every hope of foreign aid, however slight, has passed away, and they have manfully supported the bitterness of their disappointment. Every prospect of active sympathy from Northern Secessionists has faded from the horizon; yet there is but little practical evidence of despair, and for all material purposes the South is just as resolute, at this moment, as on the day she opened her guns upon Fort Sumter.

There can, indeed, be no peace until the grand design of Providence that underlie all human agencies are fully effected. If this design is not that slavery shall be extirpated, root and branch, we have illy followed the indications of the Almighty will. Slavery is fast perishing from the land, as

much by the hands of its own supporters and worshippers as by those of its most bitter enemies. And it would appear that Providence is meeting out to the American nation, North and South, the severest plagues of war as a just punishment for ever having permitted the foul and accursed thing among them. So the war must go on until, in the Divine sight, the great end is attained. And we may safely infer that no such change in the Governmental status of the Confederacy, as is apprehended, can be for the purpose of bringing about a peace. The South is rather girding up her loins for another trial of strength. That strength will be better employed — certainly with the more cordial confidence and cooperation of the people — under LEE than any other leader of whom rebeldom can boast. A soldier is what the South wants. No State craft can do it service. Its best General should be at the head of its affairs, so long as its policy is purely warlike. ✺

1. Confederate Congressman Henry S. Foote (1804-1880) of Virginia, longtime foe of Davis.

WILMINGTON.
—
FORT FISHER CARRIED BY ASSAULT.

JANUARY 18

WASHINGTON, TUESDAY, JAN. 17 — 10:40 A.M.

Maj.-Gen. J.A. Dix:

The following official dispatches have just been received at this department:

HEADQUARTERS UNITED STATES FORCES ON FEDERAL POINT, N.C., JAN. 15, VIA FORTRESS MONROE, JAN. 17

Brig.-Gen. J.A. Rawlins:

GENERAL:

I have the honor to report that Fort Fisher was carried by assault, this afternoon and evening, by Gen. AMES' division and the Second Brigade of the First Division of the Twenty-fourth Army Corps, gallantly sided by a battalion of marines and seamen from the navy. The assault was preceded by a heavy bombardment from the Federal fleet, and was made at 3:30 P.M., when the First Brigade — CURTISS', of AMES' division-effected a lodgment upon the parapet, but full possession of the work was not obtained until 10 P.M. The behavior of both officers and men was most admirable. All the works south of Fort Fisher are now occupied by our troops. We have not less than 1,200 prisoners, including Gen. WHITING and Col. LAMB, the Commandant of the fort. I regret to say that our loss is severe, especially in officers. I am not yet able to form any estimate of the number of casualties.

(SIGNED,) ALFRED H. TERRY,
BREV. MAJ.-GEN., COMMANDING EXPEDITION.

The capture of Fort Fisher.

THE APPOINTMENT OF GENERAL-IN-CHIEF — JEFF. DAVIS VIEWS ON THE MATTER.

JANUARY 28

EXECUTIVE OFFICE, RICHMOND, JAN. 18.

Messrs. James F. Johnson, President pro tem, of Virginia Senate, and Hugh W. Sheffey, Speaker of Virginia House of Delegates.

GENTLEMEN:

I have the honor to acknowledge the receipt of your joint letter of the 17th inst., indorsing a resolution of the General Assembly of Virginia, passed on the 17th inst., and communicated to me in confidence, as directed by the Assembly.

This resolution informs me that, in the opinion of the General Assembly of Virginia, the appointment of Gen. ROBERT E. LEE to the command of all the armies of the Confederate States would promote their efficiency, and operate powerfully to reanimate the spirits of the armies, as well as of the people of the several States, and to inspire increased confidence in the final success of our cause. In your communication you kindly assure me that the General Assembly,

GEN. SHERMAN'S ORDER PROVIDING HOMES FOR THE FREED NEGROES.

JANUARY 29

HEADQUARTERS MILITARY DIVISION OF THE MISSISSIPPI, IN THE FIELD, SAVANNAH, GA., JAN. 16

SPECIAL FIELD ORDERS, No. 15.

I. The islands from Charleston south, the abandoned rice fields along the rivers for thirty miles back from the sea and the county bordering the St. John River. Florida, are reserved and set apart for the settlement of the negroes now made free by the acts of war and the proclamation of the President of the Untied States.

II. At Beaufort, Hilton Head, Savannah, Fernandina, St. Augustine and Jacksonville, the blacks may remain in their chosen or accustomed vocations; but on the Islands and in the settlements hereafter to be established, no white person whatever, unless military officers and soldiers detailed for duty, will be permitted to reside; and the sole and exclusive management of affairs will be left to the freed people themselves, subject only to the United States military authority and the acts of Congress. By the laws of war, and orders of the President of the United States, the negro is free, and must be dealt with as such. He cannot be subjected to conscription or forced military service, save by the written orders of the highest military authority of the department, under such regulations as the President or Congress may prescribe. Domestic servants, carpenters, blacksmiths and other mechanics will be free to select their own work and residence; but the young and able-bodied negroes must be encouraged to enlist as soldiers in the service of the United States, to contribute their share toward maintaining their own freedom and securing their rights as citizens of the United States. Negroes so enlisted will be organized into companies, battalions and regiments, under the orders of the United States military authorities, and will be paid, fed and clothed according to law. The bounties paid on enlistment may, with the consent of the recruit, go to assist his family and settlement in procuring agricultural implements, seed, tools, boats, clothing and other articles necessary for their livelihood.

III. Whenever three respectable negroes, heads of families, shall desire to settle on land, and shall have selected for that purpose an island or a locality clearly defined, within the limits above designated, the Inspector of Settlements and Plantations will himself, or by such subordinate officer as he may appoint, give them a license to settle such island or district, and afford them such assistance as

General Robert E. Lee, C.S.A.

with sincere confidence in my patriotic devotion to the welfare of the country, desire in this critical period of our affairs, by such suggestions as occur to them, and by dedication, if need be, of the entire resources of the Commonwealth to common cause, to strengthen my hand and to give success to our struggle for liberty and independence. This assurance is to me the source of the highest gratification, and while conveying to you my thanks for the expression of the confidence of the General Assembly in my sincere devotion to our country and its sacred cause, I must beg permission in return to bear witness to the uncalculating, unhesitating spirit

with which Virginia has, from the moment when she first drew the sword, consecrated the blood of her children and all her maternal resources for the achievement of the object of our struggles. The opinion expressed by the General Assembly in regard to Gen. R.E. LEE has my full concurrence. Virginia cannot have higher regard for him, or greater confidence in his character and ability, than is entertained by me. When Gen. LEE took command of the Army of Northern Virginia, he was in command of all the armies of the Confederate States by my order of assignment. He continued in this general command as well as in immediate command of the Army of Northern Virginia as long as I could resist his opinion that it was necessary to him to be relieved from one of these two duties. Ready as he has ever shown himself to be to perform any service that I desired him to render to his country, he left it for me to choose between his withdrawal from command of the army in the field, and relieving him of the general command of all the armies of the Confederate States. It was only when satisfied of the necessity that I came to the conclusion to relieve him from the general command, believing that the safety of the capital and the success of our cause depended in a great measure on their retaining him in command in the field — of the Army of Northern Virginia. On several subsequent occasions the de-

sire on my part to enlarge the sphere of Gen. LEE's usefulness had led to renewed consideration of the subject, and he has always expressed his inability to assume command of other armies than those now confided to him, unless relieved of the immediate command in the field of that now opposed to Gen. GRANT. In conclusion, I assure the General Assembly that whenever it shall be found practicable by Gen. LEE to assume command of all the armies of the Confederate States without withdrawing him from direct command of the Army of Northern Virginia, I will deem it promotive of the public interests to place him in such command, and will be happy to know that by so doing I am responding to their expressed desires. It will afford me great pleasure to see you, gentlemen, as proposed in your letter, whenever it may be convenient for you to visit me.

I am very respectfully and truly yours.

JEFFERSON DAVIS. ⊛

he can to enable them to establish a peaceable agricultural settlement, The three parties named will subdivide the land, under the supervision of the inspector, among themselves, and such others as may choose to settle near them, so that each family shall have a plot of not more than forty acres of tillable ground, and when it borders on some water channel, with not more than eight hundred feet front, in the possession of which land the military authorities will afford them protection until such time as they can protect themselves, or until Congress shall regulate their title. The Quartermaster may, on the requisition of the Inspector of Settlements and Plantations, place at the disposal of the Inspector one or more of the captured steamers, to ply between the settlements and one or more of the commercial points heretofore named in orders, to afford the settlers the opportunity to supply their

necessary wants, and to sell the products of their land and labor.

IV. Whenever a negro has enlisted in the military service of the United States he may locate his family in any one of the settlements at pleasure, and acquire a homestead and all other rights and privileges of a settler as though present in person. In like manner negroes may settle their families and engage on board the gunboats, or in fishing, or in the navigation of the inland waters, without losing any claim to land or other advantages derived from this system. But no one, unless an actual settler as above defined, or unless absent on Government service, will be entitled to claim any right to land or property in any settlement, by virtue of those orders.

V. In order to carry out this system of settlements a general officer will be detailed as Inspector of Settlements and Plantations, whose duty it shall be to visit the

settlements, to regulate their police and general management, and who will furnish personally to each head of a family, subject to the approval of the President of the United States, a possessory title in writing, giving as near as possible the description of boundaries, and who shall adjust all claims or conflicts that may arise under the same, subject to the like approval, treating such titles altogether as possessory. The same general officer will also be charged with the enlistment and organization of the negro recruits, and protecting their interests while so absent from their settlements, and will be governed by the rules and regulations prescribed by the War Department for such purpose....

BY ORDER OF MAJ.-GEN. W.T. SHERMAN. L.M. DAYTON, MAJOR AND ASSISTANT ADJT.-GENERAL. ⊛

THE ABOLITION OF SLAVERY.

FEBRUARY 1

Congress has decided to submit to the action of the several States an amendment of the Constitution prohibiting slavery forever within the limits or jurisdiction of the United States. The Senate adopted a resolution to this effect at its last session; and the House of Representatives concurred in its passage yesterday, by a vote of 119 ayes to 56 nays. Of those ordinarily and distinctively known as Democrats, there voted for it, Messrs. BAILEY, BALDWIN, COFFROTH, ENGLISH, GANSON, GRISWOLD, HERRICK, HUTCHINS, KING, MCALLISTER, NELSON, ODELL, RADFORD, ROLLINS, STEELE, WHEELER, YEAMAN. If this amendment is concurred in by the Legislatures in three-fourths of all the States, it will become part of the Constitution. The Union is composed of 36 States; the assent of 27 of these is therefore required for the ratification of this amendment. There is very little doubt that it will receive the prompt assent of the Legislatures of the following States:

Maine, Iowa, New-Hampshire, Wisconsin, Vermont, Minnesota, Massachusetts, Missouri, Connecticut, Kansas, Rhode Island, Nevada, New-York, Oregon, New-Jersey, California, Pennsylvania, Tennessee, Maryland, Arkansas, Ohio, Louisiana, Indiana, Virginia, Illinois, West Virginia, Michigan.

This is the full number required; but it is also probable that Delaware and Kentucky will also vote for the amendment within a year or two at furthest; and as no time is fixed by the Constitution within which the ratification must take place, their votes in its favor will be valid whenever cast.

It has already been objected to this action that it ought not to be taken while the States most directly interested are not in condition to vote upon it. They should have a voice, it is urged, in a measure designed to destroy an enormous interest peculiar to themselves. But it is their own fault that they do not vote, and they have no right to profit by their own wrong. Beside, a still more conclusive answer is found in the fact, that failing to vote is really equivalent to voting against the proposed amendment.

The adoption of this amendment is the most important step ever taken by Congress; and its ratification by the requisite number of States will complete the most important act of internal administration performed by any nation for a hundred years. It perfects the great work of the founders of our Republic. The national feeling was not strong enough to enable them to abolish slavery at the outset of our career; but although slavery has grown in power with gigantic strides since that time, the growth of the sentiment of nationality has outstripped it, and slavery is now abolished, not only without danger to the Union, but as the only means of preserving and making it perpetual. The rebellion, however, is the cause of its abolition. That act of madness and treason touched the very heart of the nation, and aroused to vigorous action the patriotism and national pride of the American people. But for the rebellion slavery would have lasted fifty years — perhaps twice as long — and its destruction, even if it had been achieved by peaceful means, would have cost as much in treasure and in human suffering as the war has involved.

With the passage of this amendment the Republic enters upon a new stage of its great career. It is hereafter to be, what it has never been hitherto, thoroughly democratic — resting on human rights as its basis, and aiming at the greatest good and the highest happiness of all its people. ✱

Celebration on the floor of the House of Representatives following the passage of the Thirteenth Amendment.

THE "SINGLE EYE" ON PRESIDENT LINCOLN.

FEBRUARY 2

The country will be glad to learn that Mr. FERNANDO WOOD, of this city, has introduced a resolution into the House of Representatives to the effect, that it is the duty of the President, under no circumstances, to proffer or accept negotiations which shall admit, by the remotest implication, the existence of any other Federal or Confederate Government within the territory of the United States. The friends of the Union will feel easy, now that they know that Mr. WOOD has his eye on Mr. LINCOLN. The well-known disposition of the President to acknowledge the Confederacy, renders the vigilance of a gentleman like Mr. WOOD, who has been from the outset the uncompromising foe of that institution, and the firm opponent of all attempts to tolerate its existence, peculiarly necessary at this juncture. We are glad to see, also, that Mr. WOOD is of opinion that it is "the duty of the President, in every legal and constitutional manner, to preserve the integrity of the Union." Should he get this resolution passed, it will then become Mr. LINCOLN's duty, if he retains a proper respect for Mr. WOOD and for the House, to try the only means of restoring the Union which, we believe, is, in Mr. WOOD's opinion, either "legal or constitutional," and that is, asking the revolted States, in a firm and decided manner, whether they are going to come back or not.

The question will probably suggest itself to most people, what will Mr. LINCOLN do, in case they decline to comply with his request. On this point, however, we need not give ourselves any uneasiness, as we believe Mr. WOOD's resources are not exhausted. He would doubtless, in case of the neglect or refusal of the leaders to heed Mr. LINCOLN's summons, have a commission appointed to proceed to Richmond and convince them of their mistake by reasoning with them. How long this process might last before it produced any results, it is impossible to say; but it is only the very shallow and flippant who will imagine that this uncertainty about its duration in any way lessens its value. It may last for years, or it may last forever. In the meantime, however, we should have an armistice, and should go on buying and selling, marrying and giving in marriage, as before the war. To the argument that the Confederacy would be all this time virtually independent, the answer is, that this would make no difference as long as we had not acknowledged its independence. If European Powers choose to disgrace themselves eternally by doing so, let them do it. We may rest satisfied that as long as we withhold our recognition, the Confederate leaders would never be able to pluck the rooted sorrow from their brains. DAVIS and STEPHENS are both said to be in delicate health, and there is little doubt that this want of courtesy on our part would kill them. Upon the more robust members of the Confederate Government, the effect of our coolness might not at first be so apparent, but it would surely do its work in the long run on the very healthiest of them. They would pine gradually away, their vitals eaten out by sorrow and disappointment. Neither cotton, nor "niggers," nor tobacco, would any longer afford them any delight, or change the sorrowful current of their thoughts; and when these things fail to cheer a drooping slaveholder, what is left for him but a premature grave? ⊛

THE CONSTITUTIONAL AMENDMENT.

REJOICINGS AND RATIFICATIONS — SERENADE TO THE PRESIDENT.

FEBRUARY 3
WASHINGTON, THURSDAY, FEB. 2

The serenading party, last night, having played several airs before the White House, the President appeared at the centre upper window, under the portico, and was greeted with loud cheers.

The President said he supposed the passage through Congress of the constitutional amendment for the abolishment of slavery throughout the United States, was the occasion to which he was indebted for the honor of this call. [Applause.] The occasion was one of congratulation to the country and to the whole world. But there is a task yet before us — to go forward and consummate by the votes of the States that which Congress so nobly began yesterday. [Applause, and cries, "They will do it," &c.] He had the honor to inform those present that Illinois had already done the work. [Applause.] Maryland was about half through; but he felt proud that Illinois was a little ahead. He thought this measure was a very fitting, if not an indispensable adjunct to the winding up of the great difficulty. [Applause.] He wished the reunion of all the States perfected and so effected as to remove all causes of disturbance in the future, and to attain this end it was necessary that the original disturbing cause should, if possible, be rooted out....

RATIFICATION BY RHODE ISLAND.
PROVIDENCE, R.I., THURSDAY, FEB. 2

The Rhode Island House of Representatives this morning passed a resolution, approving and adopting the proposed amendment to the United States Constitution. The vote stood 62 yeas against 4 nays.

The House also passed a resolution, requesting the Governor to make an application for the postponement of the draft.

RATIFICATION BY ILLINOIS.
CHICAGO, THURSDAY, FEB. 2

The General Assembly of Illinois yesterday ratified the Constitutional Amendment abolishing slavery. The vote in the Senate stood 18 yeas against 6 nays, and in the House, 48 against 28. Five Democratic Senators voted aye.

REJOICING IN CINCINNATI.
CINCINNATI, THURSDAY, FEB. 2

One hundred guns were fired at Columbus, Ohio, this evening, in honor of the passage of the Constitutional Amendment abolishing slavery.

MASSACHUSETTS REJOICING OVER THE CONSTITUTIONAL AMENDMENT.
BOSTON, THURSDAY, FEB. 2

National salutes were fired to-day in Boston and other cities; and there was also a general ringing of bells throughout the State in honor of the passage of the Constitutional Amendment abolishing slavery throughout the land. A bill was presented in the House this afternoon, ratifying the Constitutional Amendment abolishing slavery, and after a debate it was referred to the Committee on Federal Relations. At the proper time it is presumed the bill will be adopted nearly unanimously.

THE MICHIGAN LEGISLATURE.
DETROIT, MICH., THURSDAY, FEB. 2

The Constitutional Amendment abolishing slavery was ratified by the Legislature this morning. ⊛

THE PEACE CONFERENCE.

MOVEMENTS OF THE PRESIDENT.

FEBRUARY 3
SPECIAL DISPATCH TO THE NEW-YORK TIMES.
WASHINGTON, THURSDAY, FEB. 2

Secretary SEWARD, early this morning, telegraphed the President from Fortress Monroe, that his presence was needed immediately. Upon receipt of this dispatch, the President proceeded in a special car to Annapolis, where a Government vessel was awaiting to convey him to Fortress Monroe. Speculation is rife as to the meaning of this departure of the President to confer with the rebel Commissioners. Many infer that it is preliminary to peace; others, again, who are well informed, believe that the entire affair will end, for the present in no adjustment of our national difficulties.

WASHINGTON, THURSDAY, FEB. 2

At 11 o'clock this morning, President LINCOLN left Washington by a special train for Annapolis, at which place he arrived at 2 P.M., and embarked on the steamer Thomas Colyer for Fortress Monroe, which place he will reach at 1 to-morrow morning. Information received from Fortress Monroe to-night states that the Southern Commissioners on Tuesday morning were on board Gen. GRANT's dispatch-boat, the Mary Martin, awaiting the President's order as to whether they should proceed to Washington. ⊛

THE POPULARITY OF THE CONSTITUTIONAL AMENDMENT.

FEBRUARY 3

The Amendment obtained a majority in the House exceeding expectation. Its popularity, as now manifesting itself through the country, is more surprising yet. It is not only hailed with universal joy by the friends of the Administration, but it receives the willing acceptance, if not the positive favor, of the party which heretofore has stood firmly by every interest of slavery. The "Democracy," which always before the war rallied with peculiar spirit upon the slavery-protecting sections of the Constitution, and whose great watchword since the war, has been "the Constitution as it is," now move not a step in earnest, or lift a finger, to save slavery. A certain force of habit causes a portion of them to mouth a phrase or two of dissent, but there is no heart in it. They neither make, nor attempt to make, any serious fight. Whether or not they have the grace to welcome the right, they at least have the sense to recognize the inevitable.

The truth is, that this amendment is merely supplementary work — a form to close up what has already become essentially a finality. It is burying that from which the life has departed, and which stinks in the nostrils. The war had already given slavery its death-wound. What the amendment has to do is only to shovel it under, beyond resurrection.

FEBRUARY 3

The Southern people themselves, with all their errors and delusions, do not longer imagine that slavery can be saved. They have gradually come to a full understanding that the institution must come to an end without alternative. They realize that the armies of the "Confederacy" cannot be kept up to the fighting standard without enlisting such numbers of the slaves, and emancipating such numbers of their wives and children, as would make it objectless to try to keep the remainder in bondage. They also are as sensible that slavery could never enjoy peace and security again under a restored Union — that even at best, its existence would be a constant conflict, and an intolerable plague.

The change of feeling here in the North toward slavery since the war commenced is deemed wonderful. All the former charity which so largely prevailed has fallen into unqualified aversion, and all the former aversion has sunk into intensest detestation. All this has been the result of the tremendous attrition of the war — an attrition which has gradually ground to powder every pro-slavery bias here in the North. This effect here is patent to everybody; but we are too apt to make no account of any corresponding change in the South. We easily assume that the Southern people have yet the same intense attachment to slavery that so strongly characterized them at the beginning of the contest. The thing is morally impossible. To suppose it is to suppose the Southern people "stocks and stones," incapable of all reflection, insensible to all experience. The great fact has been brought home to them, as never before, that the moral sentiment of the world is irreconcilably opposed to slavery. Before the war they had deluded themselves into the belief that the civilized world might be converted to pro-slavery ideas; or, at least, that its interests in the staples produced by slavery would secure a general friendship toward their Government. The matter has been put to a test, and it is found that the European sentiment against slavery is as firmly planted as Gibraltar — that all considerations, whether material or political, in favor of breaking up the American Union, and securing success to the "Confederacy," are absolutely null before this moral intolerance of what

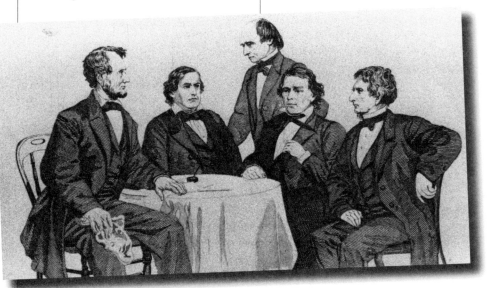

Hampton Roads peace conference members, from left: U.S. President Abraham Lincoln, Confederate Secretary of State Robert Hunter, Confederate Assistant Secretary of War John Campbell, Confederate Vice President Alexander Stephens, U.S. Secretary of State William Seward. This proof edition of a print was never completed and was never issued.

is deemed an outrage upon humanity.

How can it be supposed that a proud people can complacently cling to an institution which thus precludes every helping hand, even in their most trying hour, from those who would fain be their best friends? They may assume very independent tones about it; but it is not in civilized human nature to be insensible to such an alienation from the sympathies of the world. It is not possible for the Southern people to retain their old devotion to slavery, after such a practical realization that slavery puts them under the ban.

It is getting plain to the rebels that their attainment of independence is impossible. The South is daily becoming more and more shut up to the single question, whether to come back to the Union or to consent to foreign connections, which will be equivalent to a foreign protectorate. Slavery has no practical concern in either decision. In all Southern discussions, it is admitted or implied that both alike would involve its abandonment. And what is particularly observable is, that this necessity is nowhere urged as a reason for standing out against either course The great feeling appealed to against returning to the Union, is pride; and the great argument plied is the loss of State rights. The saving of slavery appears to be no longer an object of hope or thought. We have yet to see the first intimation in the Southern press that the prospective passage of the Constitutional amendment destroying slavery forever, is a new motive for remaining out of the Union. It is not recognized as having any bearing upon the question; and its adoption by the loyal States will not retard restoration one instant.

Our State Legislatures, twenty-two of which are now in session, are vieing with each other, in the promptness of their adoption of the Amendment. The ratification of the entire twenty-seven, necessary to give it effect, it is now quite certain, will be secured before the year closes. ✪

THE PEACE CONFERENCE.

FEBRUARY 4

For the first time since the war commenced we now have what may fairly be called a Peace Conference. Not a word has ever been directly exchanged between our Government and the rebel authorities concerning peace. The little communication which has taken place on the subject has all been the irresponsible work of private parties, officious not official, tolerated rather than sanctioned. It amounted, and in fact could amount, to no more than what was daily uttered by the public press of the two sections — simply restating the issues, and reprotesting a determination to fight it out on those issues to the last extremity. Furnished with no discretion, it could do nothing to adjust. Committing nobody who had any power in the premises, it could elicit nothing upon which official action could be ventured. The most it could do was to stir a little dust. It had no more real effect upon the mighty conflict than the frisking of the field mice in the track of our armies.

But this meeting of President LINCOLN and Secretary SEWARD, with the specially appointed agents of the "Confederate Government," though informal, and by no means plenipotentiary, has all the essential influence of a veritable Peace Conference. Our Government speaks through its highest embodiment; it is free to give the utmost possible latitude to its inducements in the interests of peace, and to deal directly with all possible apprehensions and objections. Whatever it promises it will make a part of its future policy, and doubtless will be able to carry through successfully, if accepted by the Southern people in good faith. The delegates from the rebel Government, we may take it for granted, are also at liberty to set forth its views without reserve, and to open the way for every practicable movement in the direction of peace. There are no men in the "Confederacy" of greater power, intellectual and moral, than the three who have been charged by JEFF. DAVIS with these responsibilities. There is no reason to believe that anything they recognize, or consent to, will be hereafter disavowed, or materially modified, by either the rebel President or the rebel Congress.

Peculiar interest, then, must attach to the conference now going on at Fortress Monroe. But it has been too quickly concluded that a speedy peace is likely to come from it. We have as yet seen nothing to justify any such belief. Certainly our own Government does not go into this conference with any design to concede one iota in respect to the great original requirement of the complete submission of the Southern States and people to the constitutional law of the land. On minor matters it may be prepared to make new advances toward conciliation, but here it must ever stand immovable. It can offer no terms or overtures; can enter into no negotiation, or parleying. Its only language must be that of authoritative demand; its only object unconditional submission. In considering the probabilities of peace, then, the great question is, whether the rebel Government is prepared to yield to this requirement. Will these commissioners assure President LINCOLN that, if he will facilitate, the authorities they represent will open the door for the return of the South, and that the South will use the privilege? Nowhere is there an inkling of any such intention or disposition. Not a syllable in that sense has been uttered, so far as is known, by either the rebel Executive or the rebel Congress, or the leaders of the rebel armies. Though, perhaps, the language in these quarters is not quite so imperious and defiant as it once was, it has not yet disclosed the least purpose, or even admitted the remotest possibility of resuming the old Constitutional relations. If we are to look to the press as an exponent of the spirit which prevails in the rebel capital from which these commissioners make their appearance, the articles which we daily reproduce from the Richmond prints, both friendly and unfriendly to JEFF. DAVIS, sufficiently testify that no purpose of submission is yet entertained. The Sentinel, which is accounted the special organ of DAVIS is as emphatic as the Examiner, his special adversary, in pronouncing all peace impossible which does not involve Confederate independence. It is easy to say that all this vehement language is bluster and buncombe, designed to hide actual wishes and designs. Even were that granted, the existence of a war spirit that must thus be dealt with, would be a fact not very auspicious for the speedy approach of a peace which we could welcome.

If it be asked why JEFF. DAVIS is so ready to send Peace Commissioners to our Government unless he deems peace practicable, it may be answered that this readiness is nothing new, that it is precisely ☞

what he has evinced from the beginning. One of the very first acts of the Confederate Government was to send commissioners to Washington to secure peace on the basis of Confederate independence; and again and again it has made attempts, direct and indirect, to accomplish the same thing. Though the rebel ruler must know that such efforts will not and cannot be responded to by our own Government in any way that will suit him, they yet go to silence his opponents, who complain that he trusts everything to arms, and nothing to diplomacy. There is every reason to suppose that this present action is meant by him as a political stroke against his home opponents, and a means of reuniting upon himself the popular favor which he has of late largely lost, rather than a bona fide essay to procure peace on any basis he deems practicable.

We again advise our readers not to be sanguine in anticipating that peace will be hastened by this conference. There is, indeed, a chance that it may be; and in view of the extreme desirableness of the end, President LINCOLN deserves commendation for making the most of that chance. Unquestionably, he will leave nothing unsaid or undone in this business that can contribute to any peace not inconsistent with the principles of the Constitution he has sworn to maintain. But it must not be forgotten that this is the very kind of peace JEFF. DAVIS and all his crew have sworn they will never accept; and that unless he has been converted by the progress of events and the steady advance of the Union armies, to more rational views, we have little to hope from his pacific inclination. ⊕

THE CONFERENCE PROBABLY ENDED.

SPECIAL DISPATCH TO THE NEW-YORK TIMES.
WASHINGTON, FRIDAY, FEB. 3

The extraordinary conference at Fortress Monroe, which for the past two days has fixed the attention of the whole country, has come to a close.

President LINCOLN and Secretary SEWARD are understood to be on their way to Washington, and, doubtless, by this time, Messrs. STEPHENS, HUNTER and CAMPBELL have returned to the rebel capital.

What transpired at this meeting remains, of course, a secret with the participants, and all speculation on the subject is the merest folly. Imagination has in this

PRESIDENT LINCOLN AND THE PEACE CONFERENCE.

FEBRUARY 7

We trust that Senator WADE will sleep better now that the attempt to negotiate a peace has utterly failed. His general temper, never, perhaps, too sweet and gentle, ought to be considerably mollified by the assurance that the war must still go on. In common with a good many other opponents of the Administration, he seems to have been greatly exasperated of late by the efforts of the President to ascertain whether peace was possible without sacrificing the object for which the war is waged — the integrity of the Union. We do not suppose that the result of these endeavors will soften his indignation against Mr. LINCOLN for having made them, but it may do something toward healing the wound which the possibility of peace was likely to make incurable. Mr. WADE, and those who sympathize with him, can rest easy in their minds. There is no immediate danger of peace. It is now quite certain that the rebels are not prepared to surrender. They are preparing to fight with new vigor and to make fresh sacrifices in the attempt to destroy the Union. We shall have more battles, more taxes, more drafts, — quite enough of all, we are sorry to believe, to satisfy the patriotic rapacity even of those who have come to love war for its own sake,

meeting, its circumstances, and results, ample scope and verge, and conjecture in regard thereto takes here probably much the same diverse directions it does with you. That the conference will result in an immediate cessation of hostilities, is certainly too much to believe; but it would certainly be unwarrantable to predict that it will have proved entirely fruitless. ⊕

because it gratifies certain resentments and hatreds in their natures, which have long since overborne their love of the Union and their regard for the Constitution of our common country.

We saw nothing to approve in the volunteer mission of Mr. BLAIR to Richmond. We objected to that on precisely the grounds which have led us to object to all the volunteer diplomacy which meddlesome busybodies have, from time to time, set on foot. All such negotiations, carried on without authority and involving no responsibility, are simply mischievous and discreditable. If there is ever any reason why our Government should make suggestions, invite conferences, or hint at negotiations with the rebel authorities, there is every reason why it should do so through its own agents, acting under its instructions, and saying precisely what it wishes said — nothing less, and nothing more. Any other mode of action subjects the Government to the chances of serious misconstruction, and may lead all parties into very damaging complications.

That we have escaped them in this case, is

Abraham Lincoln poses for Alexander Gardner at his final photographic sitting, Washington, February 5, 1865.

due far more to the practical good sense of President LINCOLN than to the intervention of Mr. BLAIR, who went to Richmond with full liberty apparently to talk just as he pleased, — to promise, solicit and assert whatever he might deem wise, — it being understood all the time that he could only talk for himself and not at all for the President. But the fact of his being in Richmond carried with it a certain presumption that whatever he might promise, the Government would feel, to a certain extent, bound in honor to fulfill. We had an instance of this at the very outset of the conference. The rebel commissioners insisted on going to Washington, — claiming the fulfillment of Mr. BLAIR's promise, that they should treat directly with the President. It is clear that one of the leading motives of JEFF. DAVIS in consenting to the appointment of commissioners at all was to secure what was really a tempting opportunity to do a little missionary work at the National Capital. The commissioners selected were precisely the men best fitted to impress favorably the men they counted on meeting. They were

men of ability, of large experience, personally acquainted from long residence at Washington with all the prominent politicians of the North, and quite certain to go back thoroughly advised upon all our weak points, and bearing with them renewed assurances of distinguished consideration from the whole brood of sympathizers with the rebel cause. But for Mr. BLAIR's promise on this point we should probably have had no commissioners from the rebel President, and we are indebted to the sagacity of Mr. LINCOLN for our deliverance from the manifold mischiefs which their appearance in Washington would have involved.

After Mr. BLAIR's volunteer diplomacy had, to a certain extent, committed the Government to a conference, nothing could be wiser, more patriotic, or more satisfactory, than the course pursued by President LINCOLN. He gave the strongest possible proof of his desire for peace, by meeting personally the rebel commissioners, and by giving the fullest and most liberal consideration to every proposition and suggestion they had to offer. Yet he did not permit

them for a single moment to believe, or even suppose, that peace was possible at cost of separation. The integrity of the Union must be preserved, the authority of the Government must be restored. Upon that point he was immovable and inflexible. And that was precisely the point upon which they were not authorized to make any concessions whatever. With them recognition of the independence of the Confederate States was indispensable as a preliminary condition to any negotiation for a close of hostilities.

The conference has had this good result: it has defined anew and made unmistakably clear the exact position of the contending parties. True, it has told us nothing new; but it has told us again, with fresh emphasis and authority, what special efforts at deception were leading many men to doubt, that the South is fighting for independence, and that only by successful war on our part can the Union be maintained. The demonstration thus afforded of this fact ought to unite all men, without distinction of party, in a cordial support of the Government and a vigorous prosecution of the war. ❂

THE PROPOSED FREEDMAN'S BUREAU.

FEBRUARY 7
WASHINGTON D.C., WEDNESDAY, FEB. 1
To the Editor of the New-York Times:

I look with extreme solicitude upon the propositions now being put forward in Congress to place the affairs of the freedmen in Treasury or civil hands.

The reason adduced for such control is startling. It is simply that if the plantations are put in civil control, so the freedman must follow. Was it not just that from which we supposed they were emancipated? They were the subordinates, the appendages of plantations — that was slavery. The interests of the man and of the plantation may be hay, in the nature of the case, are even opposite — just as the interest of buyer and seller are. One wants to buy cheap, the other to sell high. Just so with land and labor. The landed interest would cut off other avenues of labor for its own advantage, and would procure it at the lowest possible rates. Now, can it be safe to put the labor-owning freedmen by legislation into the hands of that landed interest? It does not matter where this interest is vested. Whether in agents of the Government or not, the principle is the same. The two in-

terests ought not, by any means, be put into the same set of hands — much less the men legislated under — into property hands.

Now this principle has full illustration in freed men's affairs already. For two years the plantation without legislation, has controlled the policy pursued toward the black to his hurt. The wages received by him have seldom done more then support him, while profitable labor was open to him on every hand. But the curse of the plantation system has been that it thrusts the people out of safe places where they could support themselves, and more, to utterly indefensible points along a line of a thousand miles. At these points they have been murdered by scores, captured and resold into slavery by the hundred, while hundreds more have saved themselves by flight and hiding, stripped of all things, and so cast themselves again upon the governmental care.

Aside from this disaster to the blacks, the plantations have furnished thousands of mules and vast supplies of food and clothing and money to the rebel armies. There can be no question of the disaster to the black, and the disgrace to the nation, of the plan hitherto. Beside these points, the plantations became the centre and heart of the whole speculative and trade interest, and of contraband traffic. They lie outside our mili-

tary lines, are open to the whole rebel country, while free ingress and egress across our lines for persons or supplies must be given. Estimate as best you can, the effect of such an open communication with the rebel territory, and that, too, when, by information of military movements, a man might save his plantation from plunder. There have been several cases of remarkable immunity from harm in most exposed localities.

This plantation reason for putting the blacks into civil hands is remarkable. Wherever the plantations go, there by all means do not let the blacks follow.

The results of such a civil control of the freedmen could not fail to be injurious in this respect. You are aware of the immense pressure of trade and speculative interest through all these regions. It has well nigh overborne military operations. There is to-day danger that we shall be swamped by them. Now these interests on the river make civil control of freedmen their central plan — their pet idea. If they can carry trade interests, control of lands, and control of the race of laborers into civil hands, the military ideas must succumb. You will notice that it is part of every congressional scheme of civil control of freedmen, that the military authorities shall lend their power to the execution of all the plans ☞

of the civil agents. When you have set such a scheme afoot, you will no longer have any simple, unadulterated military operation in any quarter. The civil speculative idea has a mortgage on everything — infects, taints — either controls or puts an injunction on every motion of military affairs. I think that these influences have had power enough without the alliance of Congress in this new league. Gentlemen do not appear to perceive it, but to us on the river it is perfectly clear that the question between a military and civil bureau of freedmen's affairs, as settled by Congress now, is really this: Whether war is our first and supreme work till honorable peace is achieved or not. It is a momentous question, and on it I believe that the fate of armies and campaigns yet depend.

Aside from these considerations which do appear to me weighty, is also this: None but the military arm can protect, control, or see justice done the freedmen while the war lasts. Civil courts either do not exist, or are of the old slave codes, and under them the black is whipped, fined double, convicted without evidence, debarred from the right to testify, has no redress for any wrong.

How shall civil agents help them? They are powerless over the old civil process. They are unknown to the military courts. Absolutely there is none but the military power to do anything for or with them. On it the civil agent must depend for the validity and force of every smallest act. What then is the use of such an insertion? If the military officer must do the thing, why not set him at it without putting a shadow between him and his work? Besides, when you have set a civil aged to do the thing, you cannot make the military officer responsible for doing it. You cannot make him do it. Such an attempt will end in conflict, failure, confusion.

Would it not be wiser to take your civil agent and put him in military authority and let him do his own work?

Civil agents, helpless during the war, will only begin to be efficient when the war is over. I suspect after all that this consideration of the hereafter is really the one that recommends to many the scheme. With me it is fatal to it. When the war is over we want no special control of black people. The war power will have to represent the Government until the old codes are rooted out — will have itself to root

them out; and when under its supervision the reconstruction is complete and civil affairs in loyal hands, the black man, a free man, with rights, the protection of the courts, and the worth of his labor and his vote, needs no special swaddling. No system of United States officials will need to interpenetrate the State system to take care of him. Indeed, it could not, however much needed. I know of no United States power, outside the courts, which can appear in a State except the military. So long as the freedman needs special protection, the military power will have it to do. The edict of emancipation was a military one, is made effective by military power. The freedmen are gathered in districts under martial law, protected by arms, supplied through army channels. Whatever the Government has done for them has been devised and done by the military authorities, on their own responsibility. Many mistakes have been made, doubtless, but all the experience in actual charge of these people is among military men. All the facts which can guide future operations wisely have been developed under their eyes. No set of men, theorists and lookers-on, are qualified as are they for the work. The most numerous

A PEACE POLICY NOW TREASON.

FEBRUARY 7

We have now a right to look for a consolidated support of this war by men of all parties in the North. The peace conference has confirmed beyond all question that there is no alternative to war but disunion. The commissioners of the rebel Government demanded the recognition of its independence as an indispensable preliminary to any negotiation for peace. President LINCOLN in vain exhausted every inducement to bring them to ground where compromise was possible. They would not swerve one hair's-breadth — in fact could not so move without violating their trust, and at once evoking a repudiation from Richmond. Their directness was honorable. They practiced no reserve or equivocation. They confronted us on their real position at the outset. So far from attempting to deceive, they, from the very beginning, made mistake impossible. No sine qua non was ever more sharply defined, or more positively claimed. It must be met in the same manly spirit. It cannot be yielded to without treason. It cannot be paltered with without imbecility.

From the time this war commenced, we

have never for an instant imagined that it could be ended by compromise. The issue was between the life and death of the Union, and between life and death there can be no such thing as compromise. Holding this absolute conviction, we have yet recognized that many good men have believed that the rebellion might be propitiated, and peace promoted, by liberal overtures. It was not difficult to see how such a belief could be honestly entertained. A large portion of our people had been educated to the idea that as the Union was originally created in compromise, and had worked habitually through compromise, the only possible mode of saving it must be by compromise. Within certain limits — as bearing on minor differences — this was all correct enough. Mutual concessions of sentiment and of interest always have been and always will be necessary to the successful working of our federal system. But the mistake of these peace men has lain in not recognizing that, while compromise may be ever so efficacious within its own range, there is an ultimate vital principle in Government to which it cannot apply. A Government, like a man, may give all that it hath for its life; but when the life itself is demanded, and no concession will be taken short of that, it must stop giving. There is no such thing as yield-

ing a part of the life, and reserving a part. The rebellion was an attack upon the life of the Government, and nothing else. From the beginning it has been simply and purely a disunion movement. Its essential nature, then, precluded the possibility of its being compromised with; and a peace policy, founded on the idea of compromise, could be nothing else than a mockery. But old associations had charmed many with the word compromise, and the delusion clung to them that somehow the rebel spirit could be laid by it. During the Presidential canvass, argument and evidence to the contrary were presented to an extent that should, we think, have convinced them, a hundred times over, of this error. All failed; yet in a vast number of cases, not because the spirit was essentially malignant and factious, but because the power of old association was too strong. But let all that past be forgotten. Whether or not the peace men ought to have been convinced long ago that their object could not be reached by compromise, it is enough that the proof of it now comes to them in a way that permits no doubt.

In the face of this attestation by the rebel Government itself, that it will not negotiate for peace except as an independent Power, every syllable henceforth uttered in favor of negotiation must be taken as a proclama-

and notable and devoted examples of labor and sacrifice for freedmen are to be found among the officers and men of the army. Witness the work of Gen. SAXTON and his officers, Col. EATON and his, and Gen. THOMAS' recent order in the Southwest. Is it wise to overset these men, with their practical experience and proven devotion, to put in their places men with theories and no experience, with plans and no power? We have had abundant experience of these theories and plans of lookers-on. Men write letters for information, run through the field, and up and down it for a month or so, and then publish their schemes and notions, get them adopted, and curse the black with them all. It was some such wisdom as that which, against the protest of every practical worker on the Mississippi, put the plantation plan at work last year, and unseated a plan of independent farming by the freedmen, which would have been safe, wise and profitable, and so honorable to the nation. I look with extreme dread upon the projected renewal of the reign of mere theory, especially when the theory is so contrary both to reason and experience as is this of civil control.

F.A.S. ⊛

tion of sympathy with treason, and its author should suffer the fullest force of public opinion. We hope now to see every peace man of the past, who has preserved one spark of loyalty, come squarely up to the support of the Government, in the most vigorous prosecution of a war, which shall crush what cannot be conciliated. Every loyal sentiment of every shade, throughout the length and breadth of the land, should be consolidated into one overwhelming determination to conquer the peace which baffles all other effort. The fact is patent to everybody that the war has already vastly reduced the strength of the rebellion. This the rebels themselves do not pretend to deny. It requires, then, but a perseverance in the war to exhaust the rebellion altogether. All military authority agrees that a few months, at most, will suffice for this, if the national armies are kept up to their proper standard. In fact, SHERMAN's last campaign has made it plain to all the world. Let it be honestly accepted, in conjunction with the result of the peace conference, and be resolutely followed up with a universal cooperation in meeting the last call of the Government for more soldiers. Even the most inveterate peace man of the past must admit that if the rebellion must be crushed, the sooner it is done the better. ⊛

ARMING SLAVES FOR THE REBEL SERVICE.

FEBRUARY 19

It seems to be more than probable that the rebels will make the experiment of arming at least a small number of their slaves. BENJAMIN[1] publicly confesses that the able-bodied white population is used up, and that Richmond must be evacuated unless the negroes be conscripted. Gen. LEE favors the measure the army calls for it, as we may see from the letters from the camps in the Richmond papers; DAVIS has long been an advocate of it. The strong aristocratic slaveholding caste must at length yield, and all its slaves, as well as its children, must be offered a sacrifice to the ambition of DAVIS and the pride of LEE. The so-called Congress, it is true, rejects any comprehensive measures for arming great numbers of slaves; but it allows twenty or thirty thousand to be employed as "pioneers and teamsters." How long will it take Gen. LEE to make passable soldiers of these pioneers and put them in garrison or on guard at bridges in his rear? Still time flies, and SHERMAN presses steadily on. Whatever regiments are to be drilled for the Spring and Summer campaign, must be drilled now. The area for conscripting the black population diminishes every day; the time for arming and exercising and organizing such a mass of raw troops grows continually shorter. It is not improbable that approaching ruin and the feeling of desperation will finally drive the rebel administration into the forcible conscription of masses of blacks, and the insurgent armies will be reinforced with these unwilling Sepoys.

It will need but this to be the crowning act in the providential drama of retribution on this accursed rebellion, made in the cause of human slavery — that its death-blow should at length be given by its own slaves, madly organized and armed in its defence. Divine justice can have no grander display, than a Slave Confederacy perishing by the hands of its bondmen. ⊛

1. Confederate Secretary of State Judah P. Benjamin (1811–1884).

African-American soldiers.

HIGHLY IMPORTANT.

CAPTURE OF COLUMBIA BY GEN. SHERMAN.

February 20

WAR DEPARTMENT, WASHINGTON, D.C., Feb. 18.

Major-Gen. Dix:

The announcement of the occupation of Columbia, S.C., by Gen. SHERMAN, and the probable evacuation of Charleston, has been communicated to the department in the following telegram just received from Lieut-Gen. GRANT.

EDWIN M. STANTON, Secretary of War.

FIRST DISPATCH FROM GEN. GRANT.
CITY POINT, 4:45 P.M., Feb. 18

Hon. Edwin M. Stanton, War Department:
The Richmond Dispatch of this morning says:

SHERMAN entered Columbia yesterday morning and its fall necessitates, it presumes, the fall of Charleston, which it thinks has already been evacuated.

U.S. GRANT, Lieut-General.

SECOND DISPATCH FROM GEN. GRANT.
CITY POINT, Va., Feb. 18

Hon. E.M. Stanton, War Department:
The following is taken from to-day's Richmond Dispatch:

THE FALL OF COLUMBIA.

Columbia has fallen. SHERMAN marched into and took possession of the city yesterday morning. The intelligence was communicated yesterday by Gen. BEAUREGARD in an official dispatch. Columbia is situated on the north bank of the Congaree River, just below the confluence of the Saluda and Broad Rivers.

From Gen. BEAUREGARD's dispatch it appears that on Thursday evening the enemy approached the south bank of the Congaree, and threw a number of shells into the city. During the night they moved up the river, and yesterday morning forded the Saluda and Broad Rivers. Whilst they were crossing these rivers our troops, under Gen. BEAUREGARD, evacuated Columbia. The enemy soon after took possession.

Through private sources we learn that two days ago. when it was decided not to attempt the defence of Columbia, a large quantity of medical stores, which it was thought it was impossible to remove, were destroyed. The female employees of the Treasury Department had been previously sent off to Charlotte, South Carolina, a hundred miles north; of Columbia. We presume the Treasury lithographic establishment was also removed, although as to this we have no positive information.

The fall of Columbia necessitates, we presume, the evacuation of Charleston, which, we think likely, is already on process of evacuation.

It is impossible to say where SHERMAN will next direct his columns. The general

General Sherman's troops watch and celebrate as Columbia, South Carolina, burns.

opinion is that he will go to Charleston and establish a base there; But we confess that we do not see what need he has of a base. It is to be presumed he is subsisting on the country, and he has had no battle to exhaust his ammunition. Before leaving Savannah he declared his intention to march to Columbia, thence to Augusta, and thence to Charleston. This was uttered as a boast, and to hide his designs. We are disposed to believe that he will next strike at Charlotte, which is a hundred miles north of Columbia, on the Charlotte and Columbia Railroad, or at Florence, S.C., the junction of the Columbia and Wilmington and the Charleston and Wilmington Railroads, some ninety miles east of Columbia.

There was a report yesterday that Augusta had been taken by the enemy. This we do not believe.

We have reason to feel assured that nearly the whole of SHERMAN's army is at Columbia, and that the report that SCHOFIELD was advancing on Augusta was untrue,

FROM THE RICHMOND WHIG, FEB. 18

The Charleston Mercury, of Saturday, announces a brief suspension of that paper, with a view to its temporary removal to another point. This is rendered necessary by the progress of military events, cutting it off from the mail facilities for distributing its paper to a large portion of its subscribers, while the lack of transportation renders its supply of paper precarious. ✦

THE FALL OF WILMINGTON.

FEBRUARY 25

Had any one, at the time of the Presidential election in November last, predicted the military achievements of the three months of Winter, he would have been looked on as a lunatic. The fall of the great rebel strongholds of Wilmington, Charleston and Savannah, the occupation of the Capitals of South Carolina and Georgia, the march of SHERMAN from Chattahoochee to the ocean, and from the ocean to the Great Pedee, the rout and demolition of HOOD's army, the scatteration of COBB's forces, the double hegira of HARDEE, the flight of BEAUREGARD, the flight of BRAGG or HOKE, the advance into North Carolina and toward LEE's rear the possibility of such a speedy achievement of such vast labors — the possibility of such a marvelous and unbroken series of successes, entered into no sane man's head. But this bold catalogue gives a faint idea of the greatness of the triumphs of the armies of the Union, and the staggering blows and irretrievable damage inflicted upon the rebellious South.

This morning it is Wilmington which we proudly record as being under our flag. Since the fall of Fort Fisher and the subsequent reinforcement of our army, operations have been steadily prosecuted by Gen. SCHOFIELD, looking to the capture of the city. The advance and success of our forces on the 11th, the movement of our troops to the west bank of the Cape Fear River, and the capture of the great earthwork called Fort Anderson on the 19th, rendered the city untenable; and it was almost immediately after the latter event that the rebel garrison decamped, and on Wednesday last — WASHINGTON's Birthday — our troops entered and took possession of the long-sought prize.

The various and vital bearings of the capture of Wilmington have often been shown. But now, it is of incalculably greater importance than ever it was before, from its relations to the present march and prospective advance of the army of Gen. SHERMAN. The large force of Gen. SCHOFIELD at Wilmington will now be relieved, and the Twenty-third Corps speedily effect a junction with their old comrades under Gen. SHERMAN, with whom they so long campaigned in the Southwest. (On this head, we may note, en passant, that the army of Gen. GILLMORE at Charleston, is now also released to co-operate or combine with SHERMAN.) Whether or not Gen. SHERMAN will now strike in the direction of Wilmington, is a matter about which nothing is known at present; but it is altogether likely that he will concentrate all the forces possible before he makes the grand and final advance, in cooperation with the Army of the Potomac, and under the orders of the Lieutenant-General, upon the rebel capital and LEE's rebel army. ✦

CHAPTER 24

"The Great Struggle Is Over"

MARCH–APRIL 1865

s spring arrived in New York, the news of the Confederacy's twin decisions to make Robert E. Lee the Southern commander-in-chief and to authorize the arming of black slaves for Confederate service provoked cynical responses in The Times. The news of Lee's new status triggered a lengthy editorial that inaccurately deprecated his wartime service, and the decision to arm slaves prompted another editorial (reprinted from the Louisville Courier) that dismissed entirely the notion that Southerners would ever find security by arming their chattels, since they could never "live in safety surrounded by millions of negroes accustomed to the use of arms, and the sight and smell of human blood."

On the battlefield, it was clear that Lee must somehow break the death-grip that Grant's armies had placed around Richmond and Petersburg, or lose the war. Lee tried to achieve this with an assault on Fort Steadman, one of the strong points on Grant's encircling lines, on March 25. When that failed, Grant at once launched a series of counterattacks, and a week later Union forces broke through south of Petersburg at a remote intersection called Five Forks, where five roads came together. Many of the reports from the front about these events came from George Forrester Williams, a daring and intrepid Times reporter who was so determined to get to the scene of action that when the clerk in charge of army transportation refused to honor his press pass that allowed him to use military transport, he borrowed a horse from another reporter and galloped the twelve miles to the front. Other reports to The Times came from Henry H. Young, who was one of the first reporters to enter the captured city of Petersburg after it fell.

President Abraham Lincoln and Major General William Sherman, detail of a lithograph depicting their final council of war.

The Battle of Five Forks on April 1 necessitated Lee's evacuation of Richmond, an event that took place the next day. Lincoln, who had come south by sea to visit the army, had waited so long for this moment that he now declared, "I want to see Richmond." It was a poignant tableau as the American president wandered the streets of the former Confederate capital accompanied only by a handful of sailors. The city's black population greeted him as a messiah, while the white population — those who had stayed — suspiciously peered out at him from behind shuttered windows. The Times was horrified by Lincoln's reckless behavior, and argued that the President had no right to put his own life at risk. "Mr. LINCOLN's life may be of no special value to himself," The Times proclaimed on April 4, the day of the President's visit, "but his official position makes it of special value to the country, and he has no right to put it at the mercy of any lingering desperado in Richmond."

Meanwhile, Grant pursued Lee's escaping army westward and caught up with it at Appomattox Court House. After Lee's surrender there on April 9, The Times' headline screamed "PEACE!" Not quite … for there were still other rebel armies in the field. The largest of them was Joseph E. Johnston's army in North Carolina. Having been dismissed by Davis the previous July for failing to stop Sherman's advance to Atlanta, Johnston was restored to command (despite Davis's misgivings) on February 22, 1865, after Lee requested it. After Lee's surrender, the question was, as The Times put it, "what will Jo. Johnston do?" Davis wanted him to fight on, but The Times suspected (correctly, as it proved) that he would "follow the example set for him by his chief and friend" and surrender his army, which he did on April 26. There

were still a few small Confederate forces in the field elsewhere, but for all practical purposes the war was over.

Lincoln had been developing a Reconstruction policy for years, and had already approved plans for Louisiana and Arkansas. Now, however, The Times and the rest of the North wondered how those policies might change with the war at an end. They would wonder a while longer, for Lincoln was reluctant to show his hand. The President was a practical politician who was unwilling to get too far ahead of public opinion. Just as he had disciplined generals like Fremont

and Hunter who got too far ahead of policy on the question of emancipation, so he would now step carefully on the question of black rights as citizens or voters. As The Times put it, "for the present, further developments in respect to this and many other important matters must be awaited. The President must exercise caution, the people patience."

Meanwhile, on April 12, three days after Lee's surrender, the President and Mrs. Lincoln attended a performance of the play *Our American Cousin* at Ford's Theatre.

ARMING THE SLAVES.
INGENIOUS COMPROMISE.

MARCH 4

FROM THE RICHMOND ENQUIRER, MARCH 1

We learn that the [Confederate] House of Representatives has recently passed in secret session, by a vote of forty to thirty seven, a bill which not only authorizes the arming of negroes tendered for military service by their owners, but also authorizes the President to call on each State, whenever he thinks it expedient, for her quota of three hundred thousand troops, in addition to those subject to military service under existing laws, or so many thereof as the President may deem necessary for purposes mentioned, to be raised from such classes; irrespective of the color of the population, in each State as the proper authorities thereof may deter-

mine. It is further provided that nothing in the act shall be construed to authorize a change in the relation which slaves shall bear toward their owners as property, except by the consent of the owners and of the States in which they may reside, and in pursuance of the laws thereof. The bill has not yet obtained the concurrence of the Senate; but it is said to have been framed with a view of obviating objections in that body to a proposition in another form of arming the slaves, and of obtaining a compromise of views on the subject.[1]

1. The Confederate House passed the bill on February 20, but the Senate tabled it, voting its approval only after the Virginia state legislature passed a similar bill. Then by a vote of 9–8, the Senate grudgingly concurred. Davis signed the bill into law on March 13. The legislation did not free any slaves, it only authorized them to fight for Confederate independence. The war ended before any of them saw military service.

COLORED TROOPS IN THE REBEL ARMY — WHAT THEY WILL DO.

MARCH 5

FROM THE LOUISVILLE JOURNAL, FEB. 25

It is now a settled matter that 200,000 slaves are to be put immediately into the Southern armies. Of course we do not know how this policy will work, but our present opinion is that it is extremely injudicious on the part of the South, and most likely to prove speedily fatal. In the first place, we do not believe that the South can ad-

equately arm 200,000 negroes; in the second place, we do not believe that she can feed her armies augmented by 200,000 negroes withdrawn from the pursuits of productive industry; in the third place, we do not believe that the negroes, as a general rule, will fight for the South; and, in the fourth place, we do not believe that the people of that section, even if their independence be achieved, will be able to live in safety surrounded by millions of negroes accustomed, to the use of arms, and the sight and smell of human blood.…

THE INAUGURAL ADDRESS.

MARCH 5

Fellow-Countrymen:

At this second appearing to take the oath of the Presidential office, there is less occasion for an extended address than there was at the first. Then a statement somewhat in detail of a course to be pursued seemed very fitting and proper. Now, at the expiration of four years, during which public declarations have been constantly called forth on every point and phase of the great contest which still absorbs the attention and engrosses the energies of the nation, little that is new could be presented.

The progress of our arms, upon which all else chiefly depends, is as well known to the public as to myself, and it is, I trust, reasonably satisfactory and encouraging to all. With high hope for the future, no prediction in regard to it is ventured.

On the occasion corresponding to this four years ago, all thoughts were anxiously directed to an impending civil war. All dreaded it; all sought to avoid it. While the inaugural address was being delivered from this place, devoted altogether to saving the Union without war, insurgent agents were in the city seeking to destroy it without war — seeking to dissolve the Union and divide the effects by negotiation. Both parties deprecated war, but one of them would make war rather than let the nation survive, and the other

The new Chief Justice of the Supreme Court, Salmon P. Chase, right, delivers the oath of office to President Abraham Lincoln.

would accept war rather than let it perish, and the war came.

One-eighth of the whole population were colored slaves, not distributed generally over the Union, but localized in the South-

ern part of it. These slaves constituted a peculiar and powerful interest. All knew that this interest was somehow the cause of the war. To strengthen, perpetuate and extend this interest, was the object for which the

FROM WASHINGTON.

THE INAUGURATION CEREMONIES.

MARCH 6

WASHINGTON, SATURDAY, MARCH 4

President LINCOLN was inaugurated for another term of four years at twelve o'clock, noon, to-day.

Overhead the weather was clear and beautiful, and on account of the recent rains the streets were filled with mud. Despite this fact the crowd that assembled was exceedingly large, and thousands proceeded to the capital to witness the inauguration ceremonies.

The procession moved from Sixteenth-street and Pennsylvania-avenue at about 11 o'clock.

President LINCOLN had been at the capital all day, and consequently did not

accompany the procession to the scene of the interesting ceremonies.

Several bands of music, two regiments of the Invalid Corps, a squadron of cavalry, a battery of artillery, and four companies of colored troops, formed the military escort.

The Mayor and Councilmen of Washington, visiting Councilmen from Baltimore, the firemen of this city and the visiting firemen from Philadelphia, the Good Will, Franklin and Perseverance companies, each company drawing its engine along, were also in the procession.

Among the benevolent societies present

were Lodges of Odd Fellows and Masons, including a colored Lodge of the latter fraternity. The public and principal private buildings along Pennsylvania-avenue were gaily decorated with flags, and every window was thronged with faces to catch a glimpse of the President elect.

The oath to protect and maintain the Constitution of the United States, was administered to Mr. LINCOLN by Chief-Justice CHASE, in the presence of thousands, who witnessed the interesting ceremony while standing in mud almost knee-deep.

The Inaugural was then read. ✹

insurgents would rend the Union by war, while the Government claimed no right to do more than to restrict the territorial enlargement of it.

Neither party expected for the war the magnitude or the duration which it has already attained. Neither anticipated that the cause of the conflict might cease, or even before the conflict itself should cease. Each looked for an easier triumph, and a result less fundamental and astounding.

Both read the same Bible and pray to the same God, and each invokes His aid against the other. It may seem strange that any men should dare to ask a just God's assistance in wringing their bread from the sweat of other men's faces, but let us judge not, that we be not judged. The prayers of both could not be answered. That of neither has been answered fully. The Almighty has his own purposes. Woe unto the world because of offences, for it must needs be that offences come, but woe to that man by whom the offence cometh. If we shall suppose that American slavery is one of these offences, which in the Providence of God must needs come, but which having continued through His appointed time, He now wills to remove, and that He gives to both North and South

this terrible war as the woe due to those by whom the offence came. Shall we discern there is any departure from those Divine attributes which the believers in a living God always ascribe to him? Fondly do we hope, fervently do we pray, that this mighty scourge of war may speedily pass away. Yet, if God wills that it continue until all the wealth piled by the bondman's two hundred and fifty years of unrequited toil shall be sunk, and until every drop of blood drawn with the lash shall be paid by another drawn with the sword, as was said three thousand years ago; so, still it must be said, that the judgments of the Lord are true and righteous altogether.

With malice toward none, with charity for all, with firmness in the right, as God gives us to see right, let us finish the work we are in, to bind up the nation's wounds, to care for him who shall have borne the battle and for his widow and his orphans, to do all which may achieve and cherish a just and a lasting peace among ourselves and with all nations. ✹

THE FIRST AND LAST TEST OF LEE'S GENERALSHIP.

MARCH 16

ROBERT E. LEE, just appointed to the supreme command of the rebel armies, has the name of being a military genius. The rebels, from the beginning of the war, have glorified him as such, and the North has never been much inclined to dispute it. Yet there is good reason to doubt whether, after all, his ability is not rather relative than absolute — whether he is not great as the one-eyed man in chief among the blind.

It is certain that at West Point he evinced no marked capacity.[1] The TIMES has published a communication from one of his old military instructors there, testifying explicitly to that effect. It is also certain that in his subsequent connection with the national army, though much engaged in active service in Mexico, he did nothing extraordinary.[2] Up to the period of the rebellion, he had the character of being simply a highly-intelligent officer and an accomplished gentleman. His first military service of the rebellion in Western Virginia was, as the rebel historian [Edward A.] POLLARD admits, a complete miscarriage. He owed his subsequent elevation to the command of the rebel army in Virginia to the dissatisfaction with BEAUREGARD's management at Bull Run, and to his high family position. So far as regards one of its great military objects, his management of that army has been an absolute failure. We mean the invasion of the North, and the capture of Washington. He undertook that thing twice, in two successive years, in full force, after months of preparation. On the first occasion he was met at South Mountain and Antietam, and, though as strong in numbers as the Union armies, and occupying positions of great natural advantage, was worsted and compelled to beat a precipitate retreat. On the second occasion, he was met at Gettysburgh, and suffered himself to be drawn into an attack upon a position whose natural advantages were in our favor; and the result was a defeat so damaging that he was again obliged to make all possible haste for the other side of the Potomac. Neither of the Federal commanders whom ☞

President Abraham Lincoln delivers his second inaugural address on March 4, 1865.

he had to cope with in these invasions ranks as our ablest. In his great aggressive movements LEE failed completely.

So far as regards the other great object of the rebel army of Virginia, the defence of the rebel capital, LEE has been more successful. Richmond still remains in rebel possession. But that, of itself, does not prove first-rate generalship. The direct defence of Richmond has been mainly a matter of mere engineering skill. In the present state of science, it requires no great genius to construct fortifications. When once constructed, it requires no great genius to keep an army behind them safely. When LEE abandoned the direct defensive, and assumed that style of warfare known as the offensive-defensive, he almost uniformly failed. His first attempts in this line were with MCCLELLAN, during the Peninsular campaign. But in no instance did he ever make a successful

Robert E. Lee after the war.

attack upon MCCLELLAN's army. Though often assailing at an advantage, he was, in the end, invariably repelled, and on three separate occasions — Williamsburgh, Fair Oaks, and Malvern Hill — with such damage that nothing but the over-caution of MCCLELLAN prevented our troops from pressing on and forthwith capturing Richmond itself. In the subsequent attempted campaign of BURNSIDE and HOOKER, he operated chiefly from behind his intrenched lines, and so used his advantages that our forces, after a bloody defeat, had to fall back to their original position, this side of the Rappahannock; but it is hard to see how first-rate Generalship would not have inflicted a far more terrible blow when our forces were in the act of recrossing that difficult stream, instead of letting them escape with no new loss. In our next and final campaign, under Lieut.-Gen. GRANT, LEE, notwithstanding his most extended and elaborate system of intrenchments, was driven back from the Rapidan to Richmond, and has since remained hemmed in there with an absolute incapacity to strike any serious blow at our army, and a certainty of capture unless he speedily takes to flight.

Thus, then, it stands. LEE failed completely in every purely aggressive effort. He never succeeded in keeping for a single month any foothold this side of the Potomac; while the leaders of our army planted themselves in Virginia at the very beginning of the war, and have not only foiled all attempts to dislodge them, but have been getting more and more of the State within their grasp. His defensive efforts have owed most of their success to good fortune, to the faults of the early leaders of the Army of the Potomac; have

cost him prodigious losses, and they result at last in the alternative of flight from the capital for which he has made so many sacrifices, or a surrender which will ruin the Confederate cause. It is not pretended that at any period of his career he has not controlled his army to suit himself. Though JEFF. DAVIS has always distrusted his military abilities, the Richmond Government has given him every discretion and every facility. To Gen. LEE alone belongs the responsibility of all that the rebel army in Virginia has failed to do.

Since LEE has been made General-in-Chief of all the rebel armies, he has not, so far as known here in the North, made a single combination or movement that has in the slightest degree retarded the progress of our arms. On the contrary, all the splendid strategy of SHERMAN, SCHOFIELD and SHERIDAN is working against him with crushing effect. To all appearance he is going to fail in his new capacity worse than ever. But we wait. He has declared that the military situation of the Confederacy presents no cause for discouragement. He has given it as his opinion that the national armies may yet be discomfited and driven back. Let us then accept the event of this as the decisive test of his military judgment and ability. If he succeeds, he will, with universal consent, in spite of the past, take rank as the great military genius of the age. If he fails, he will go into history as a man of small figure made conspicuous only by accidental position. ⚙

1. In fact, Lee graduated second in the West Point class of 1829, served as cadet first captain, and rather remarkably received not a single demerit during all four years there.

2. Once again, The Times is being not only uncharitable but also inaccurate. Lee acted as Winfield Scott's principal scout during the advance to Mexico City and twice found approaches that allowed the smaller U.S. army to outmaneuver and triumph over its more numerous foe.

GEN. GRANT'S ARMY.

HIGHLY IMPORTANT INTELLIGENCE.

MARCH 17

HEADQUARTERS ARMY POTOMAC,
WEDNESDAY, MARCH 15 — 8 A.M.

During the greater part of yesterday active operations on a most extensive scale could be discovered within the limits of the rebel army.

Camps were struck, and large and heavy masses of troops were seen in line of battle. Besides three columns of men were moving to and fro within their interior lines.

Nothing definite was or could be ascertained regarding the ultimate destination or meaning of these columns; but, as a matter of course, orders were at once issued for the different corps and other commands to be in instant readiness to move.

The movements of the enemy will govern our own, until something definite is learned regarding Gen. LEE's intentions.

In the centre of our line, near the Appomattox River, it is generally believed that the enemy has succeeded in mining our works, especially Fort Hell[1] and Fort Mor-

ton, and all last night our engineers were in busy search for any indication of the fact.

Nothing could be learned, at a late hour last night, as regarded the result of their search, as an unusual reticence was observable among the engineer officers.

During the best portion of last night, trains and other wagons were in active motion. The suttlers were also also ordered to the rear.

All along our front line of breastworks, the troops have been lying in position awaiting an attack, had any been made.

Suitable dispositions were likewise made along our flank. The army has been for the past eighteen hours in constant readiness, and kept well in hand for any hostile demonstration of the enemy.

As it stands at present, there is every indication of a speedy move, and appearances look very like a fight.

It is to be hoped that Gen. LEE will be induced, or compelled, to attack the Army of the Potomac in their intrenched positions, in

which case, the rebels will be met with firmness and decision. The Army of the Potomac are now stripping for the fight, and this gallant command were never in better trim or more courageous spirits for any approaching movements. Officers and men share alike in the feeling that the ensuing campaign, now about opening, will prove the last, provided they do the duty. This they are prepared to do. A slight picket fire was kept up in front of Petersburgh during last night. An informal review of the entire Fifth Corps took place yesterday before Gen. WARREN. Although not intended as a parade of strict ceremony the command appeared to great advantage.

GEO. F. WILLIAMS. ✪

1. The Union line around Petersburg was studded with 31 strong points or forts, most of them named for officers. Fort Sedgwick stood where the siege line crossed the Jerusalem Plank Road. It was nicknamed "Fort Hell" because it was closest to the rebel lines and drew a lot of hostile fie.

OUR ARMY BULLETIN.

DETAILS OF THE ATTACK — SUDDEN AND FURIOUS ONSLAUGHT.

MARCH 27

FROM OUR OWN CORRESPONDENT.
HEADQUARTERS, ARMY POTOMAC,
SATURDAY, MARCH 25 — 7 A.M.

At 4:30 o'clock this morning the enemy made a determined and energetic attack upon our right, near the Appomattox River, opening with a furious and prolonged bombardment of our whole line in front of Petersburgh, and by a powerful and sudden advance of their infantry, they succeeded in gaining possession of Fort Steadman.[1] The whole of the Ninth Corps were almost instantly under arms; and Gen. [Cadmus] WILCOX' division of that command speedily formed, and commenced a counter attack.

The cannonading at this moment was terrific. Soon after, the guns in the forts on the right and left of the captured fort opened with a very rapid fire, and several field batteries were also in position, playing with fierce energy upon the advancing columns.

Gen. WILCOX immediately pushed his

command forward, and at the moment at which I write the engagement is progressing with great fury. The awful roar of siege guns only for a moment relaxes its volume, when it recommences with almost redoubled vigor. Now and then, between intervals of heavy firing, the ear can distinguish the hoarse rattle of musketry, as the infantry become engaged. I think it is quite certain that for some time the enemy had possession of Fort Steadman, and about 260 rods of our main line of breastworks.

The Sixth Corps [Wright] are now under arms, and I doubt not the left wing of the army is also in a state of perfect readiness for any fresh demonstrations of the enemy.

Some expect a general attack on our whole line will be the result of this foolhardy attempt of the enemy to permanently break through our lines; but I consider our line too strong for the rebels to gain any tenable hold of any part of our extensive cordon of siege works.

The battle that is now progressing within five miles of these headquarters is evidently of the most determined character, and may result in very important movements before the day closes.

The mail train is just leaving for City Point, and I am unable to give you anything more than this very brief outline of the attack made this morning. I shall ride over as soon as this leaves my hands, and if possible reach the Point on horseback in time to give you the very latest news from the scene of engagement.

GEO. F. WILLIAMS. ✪

1. Lee sent a picked force of infantry under Major General John Gordon to seize Fort Steadman in the hope that this would compel Grant to withdraw some of the troops encircling Petersburg. Instead, the defeat of the assault weakened Lee further without any significant impact on Grant's siege.

SECOND DISPATCH.
TOTAL FAILURE OF THE ATTACK.

MARCH 27

CITY POINT, VA., SATURDAY MARCH 25 —
10 A.M.

I have just reached this place in time to send you the very latest and most reliable intelligence from the battle-field. The attack [on Fort Steadman], although for a time partially successful, has totally failed.[1] We have retaken all of our works and every gun. Although the enemy endeavored, by the most determined resistance, to maintain their hold on the fort, our batteries succeeded, by their enfilading fire, and by the brave and resistless onslaught of our infantry, in driving the rebels from their prize. You may rely upon this as reliable. I saw our advance line of infantry enter our old works as I rode away. The cannonading continued very heavy for some time after I left the field, but it almost entirely ceased before I reached the outskirts of City Point.

No alarm need be felt regarding the safety of our lines, for the Ninth Corps [Burnside] have established their front line without any assistance from any of the other corps.

There is no use speculating in regard to any ultimate result arising out of this aggressive movement on the part of Gen. LEE, for no one can tell what may come out of it.

GEO. F. WILLIAMS ◉

---

1. Casualties in the two days of fighting for Fort Steadman were: Union, 1,044; Confederate, 4,000.

Fort Stedman.

A Kurz and Allison lithograph of the Battle of Five Forks.

THE OPERATIONS OF THE FIFTH CORPS — SEVERE FIGHTING NEAR GRAVELLY RUN.

WASHINGTON, SUNDAY, APRIL 2

A letter from the Army of the Potomac, dated Friday evening [March 31], says there has been severe fighting on some parts of the line from morning till night, the result of which has been the extension of our lines still further westward, although at a considerable loss in killed and wounded.[1]

The Second Division of the Fifth Corps, supported by the Third, was thrown out toward the White Oak road, east of the Boydton plank road, and ordered to reach and take position there. After crossing a small branch of Gravelly Run, and while about forming in line, our troops were fired upon by a heavy force of the enemy, who were lying concealed in the woods, and also by the rebel artillery posted in favorable positions. Our men stood their ground for a while, but the enemy appearing to be moving to the left as if to turn their flank, the line was forced back to their first position where they were rallied and soon checked the enemy's advance.

About the same time another attack was made on our right flank of the Fifth Corps, but Gen. [Nelson A.] MILES' division of the Second Corps being posted here made a brilliant charge, and doubled up the enemy, driving them back a long distance, leaving hundreds of their dead and wounded on the field. This was a very handsome affair, and the division received the highest praise for the manner in which it was done. The loss on our side was about 400, as nearly as can be ascertained, mostly in the First Division.[2]

The Fifth Corps about noon again took the advance, and drove the enemy back about a mile and a half, and long before dark had reached the White Oak Road, for

APRIL 3

which they had started in the morning, and established their line across the same, driving the rebels into their strong works at Hatcher's Run. Their loss in the day's work will not be far from 1,200.

Among the casualties reported are Maj. MILLS, A.A.G. on Gen. HUMPHREYS' staff, killed by a shell; Col. SERGEANT, Two Hundred and Tenth Pennsylvania, severely wounded, and Gen. DENNISON, commanding a brigade in the Second Division, Fifth Corps, slightly wounded.

An attack was also made in front of the Sixth Corps, but it was not successful. After the rebels were driven back in front of the Fifth Corps, an attack was made with both infantry and cavalry on SHERIDAN's force, about three miles from the Southside road, near Sutherland Station, driving them back toward Dinwiddie, but subsequently they gained much more than they lost.

The roads are in a terrible condition, it being almost impossible to move the trains over them. The heavy rains have swollen the streams, and the engineers are busy day and night laying bridges and corduroys.

The loss of the enemy is not known, but judging from the number of dead lying in the woods and ravines where the fighting occurred, it must have been at least as heavy as our own. We took about one hundred and fifty prisoners during the day. ◉

---

1. This is a reference to the Battle of Dinwiddie Court House (March 31, 1865). Philip Sheridan, in command of the Union left, tried to outflank Lee's defenses south and west of Petersburg. Pickett counterattacked and drove back the probe.

2. Union losses in the battle were 354; Confederate losses were 760.

OUR SPECIAL ACCOUNTS.

—

DETAILS OF FRIDAY'S BATTLE.

HEADQUARTERS, ARMY POTOMAC,
SATURDAY, APRIL 1, — 7 A.M. VIA
WASHINGTON, SUNDAY, APRIL 2

After closing my dispatch yesterday morning and indulging in a brief sleep, I was again startled by the sound of cannon, and ascertained that the postponement of operations was not effective, except in regard to certain especial movements on the left. The fighting was resumed, and was apparently very severe. I immediately hastened to the scene of conflict, which I found to be on the extreme left of our line north of the Boydtown plank-road, on the Mrs. Butler farm. This was where the fighting commenced, but it extended down the line to the Spain farm, on the Second Corps' front, and later in the day about three miles north of the plank-road.[1]

THE FIFTH CORPS.

Early in the morning the extreme left of this corps, Gen. [Samuel W.] CRAWFORD's division, occupying a position north of the plank-road, which it had gained on the previous day without much fighting, was attacked by a large force of rebels, comprising all of [Richard H.] ANDERSON's and part of PICKETT's division, of LONGSTREET's corps, who had been sent over from north of the James since this movement on our side commenced, and massed on the enemy's right.[2] The skirmish line of the Third Division was not able to withstand the heavy force opposed to them, and fell back rapidly, but in tolerable order on the line of battle. The troops were at the time getting breakfast, and before they could get into line the enemy came upon them and compelled them to retire to the Boydtown road. Here they rallied and formed, and after severe fighting for four hours, drove the enemy back over the same ground, and about two miles further, being on the left of their own line, within about two miles of the Southside Railroad, and within a short distance of the enemy's main line of works south of the railroad.

In the beginning of the attack, PICKETT's division of the enemy sent a brigade around our left flank, and into the rear of our line. Our left was held by the First Brigade of the Third Division, known as the Iron Brigade. When it was discovered that the enemy had got into the rear, the bri-

gade faced about and, swinging its right back to connect with the next brigade in the line, threw its left around against the enemy's right, and succeeded in driving it back from the rear, so as to enable our line to fall back in order.

In executing this manoeuvre, the two opposing forces were brought into such close proximity that several hand to hand fights occurred. In one instance a rebel sergeant attempted to catch hold of one of the Sixth Wisconsin men to capture him, but the latter, stepping back, clubbed his musket and brained his foe. Capt. KEYWORTH, of the Seventh Wisconsin, was captured by the enemy and was being led away, when Sergeants ALBERT O'CONNOR and WM. JACKSON, of his company, rushed into the enemy's ranks rescued him and brought him back safely. He did not even lose his sword. Several similar instances occurred, but my time will not allow me to give them at present.

In this temporary repulse of the Fifth Corps it lost, perhaps one hundred prisoners, and suffered severely in killed and wounded. Subsequently, on entering the ground, it captured about four hundred of the enemy and two of their battle flags.[3]

I forgot to mention that the First Division, Gen. [Charles] GRIFFIN's, moved up to support the Third when the latter fell back, and rendered very important service in checking the enemy's progress, and holding them, until the Third Division was rallied and formed anew. It then moved up in line with the First. The Second Division, Gen. [Romeyn] AYRES, was also in the fight, and performed its portion of the day's labor with great gallantry and skill. It held its position of the line when the Third Division fell back, and, subsequently drove the enemy two miles and a half. The Third Division [Crawford's], however, deserves equal credit with the others, inasmuch as it was opposed to a much heavier force of the enemy, and occupied a more exposed position.

When I left the field, at about 5 o'clock, we were still driving the enemy slowly back on this portion of the front, and heavy firing, some four miles further on the left, indicated that SHERIDAN was engaged with the enemy on the line of the South-

APRIL 3

side Railroad. The firing appeared to be approaching slowly toward the position we occupied, and the general opinion was that it betokened his advance. The only report received from him was at about noon. He then sent word through that everything was progressing finely with him.[4]

It is impossible to conjecture the loss on either side in this part of the engagement. The country fought over is very rough, being a succession of hills and deep valleys, generally thickly wooded and very difficult of access. Large details were out bringing in the wounded and dead as rapidly as possible, but in the portion of the field I passed over I saw a great number still lying where they had fallen. A large proportion of those I saw were rebels, and I was told that the enemy had carried off a great many. The loss of the Fifth Corps will probably not exceed one thousand in the aggregate.[5]…

The results, which I must sum up in a very few words, as the mail is about to leave, are that we swung the left around three miles north of the Boydtown plank-road, and there is now between it and the Southside Railroad but a single line of breastworks, thrown up since Wednesday night. We have captured about a thousand prisoners, and our own loss is not over two thousand in the aggregate. The enemy have suffered much more heavily, and their forces were becoming demoralized very rapidly. Last evening they could not be induced to make another charge on the Fifth Corps' front, although they had fought desperately early in the day.

Our loss in officers is very severe, but there are no general officers killed, and the only one I hear of being wounded is Gen. A.W. DENNISON, of the Maryland Brigade. He was shot in the leg. He lost an arm in the Wilderness fight. Lieut.-Col. DENNIS B. DAILY, of the One Hundred and Forty-seventh New-York, and in command of the regiment, was wounded in the hand in the morning, but remained on the field all day.

I have many interesting incidents to relate, but am unable to give them now, for want of time.

Gens. GRANT and MEADE were both on the ground all day, and frequently under fire. They are very sanguine of success.

We shall probably have a severe ☞

battle to-day, if LEE does not retire, and attempt to get away, which is hardly likely, under existing circumstances. He has collected on our front all the troops he possibly can, and a large portion of the works are filled with citizens of Petersburgh and Richmond. These are, however, well drilled and organized, and will probably fight as well as many of the soldiers.

HENRY H. YOUNG. ⊛

1. This was the Battle of Five Forks, which took place early in the morning of April 1. Philip Sheridan, entrusted with command of the Union left wing, ordered Samuel Crawford's division to hold Pickett's Confederate division in place while the rest of Warren's Fifth Corps got around the rebel flank.

2. Young is in error here. The attack was initiated by the Union, and most of Lee's army remained north of the river.

3. Sheridan believed he was sending Warren against an open flank, but he misunderstood the battlefield and sent him instead against Pickett's entrenched division. Poor visibility and rough terrain slowed Warren's attack. Sheridan was so disappointed with Warren's initial repulse that he relieved him of command, wrecking Warren's career. Warren was exonerated by a special court in 1879.

4. While Warren engaged Pickett, Sheridan personally led an assault that broke through the rebel line. It was not immediately clear to Young or anyone else how badly Pickett's division had been mauled. Lee had ordered Pickett to "hold Five Forks at all hazards," but Pickett himself was not present, and the destruction of his division broke open the Confederate defensive line. Pickett's absence at a fish fry, or shad bake, became notorious and damaged his reputation. This loss threatened the South Side Railroad, Petersburg's last connection to the rest of the Confederacy. Lee began his evacuation of Richmond and Petersburg the next day.

5. Union casualties were 830; Confederate casualties 2,950, most of them taken prisoner.

THE PRESIDENT'S VISIT TO RICHMOND.

APRIL 4

If President LINCOLN has "gone to the front," or entered Richmond, he has departed widely from the discretion and good judgment which have hitherto marked his conduct. We can readily understand his personal eagerness to witness events of such transcendent importance as the defeat of the rebel army and the capture of the rebel capital; but we deem it his duty to have subordinated all such personal predilections to the higher considerations of public duty which the case involves. Mr. LINCOLN's life may be of no special value to himself, and of no more value to others, considered merely in his personal relations, than that of any other man. But his official position makes it of special value to the country, and he has no right to put it at the mercy of any lingering desperado in Richmond, or of any stray bullet in the field, unless some special service can be rendered by his personal presence. It seems to us he might have left to Gen. GRANT the closing up of the great campaign which he has so wisely planned and so ably executed, — and that his own share in the great transaction might have been as well performed at Washington as in front of Richmond. If nothing happens to him, this gratification of a very natural curiosity will be of little public consequence. But if he should happen to be singled out as a worthy mark for some reckless and desperate rebel sharpshooter, the country will scarcely approve the rashness which may have thrown its whole political organization into hopeless and needless confusion.[1] ⊛

1. Lincoln took a small boat from the Union fleet upriver to Richmond on April 4. Accompanied only by a small escort of sailors, he walked through the city, followed by an admiring throng of grateful blacks who knelt to him or tried to kiss the hem of his coat. "That is not right," Lincoln admonished them, "You must kneel to God only." He made his way to the Confederate White House and sat at Jefferson Davis's desk.

President Lincoln visiting Richmond.

THE FALL OF RICHMOND,
THE FALL OF THE CONFEDERACY.

APRIL 4

Illustration celebrating the federal capture of Richmond.

In the boastful message delivered by DAVIS to his Congress, at the close of last year, the chief of the rebel conspirators said there was no military success which could accomplish the destruction of the Southern Confederacy. "Not the fall," said he, "of Richmond, nor Wilmington, nor Charleston, nor Savannah, nor Mobile, nor of all combined, can affect the issue of the present contest."[1]

Words like these, uttered by a resolute and desperate man, controlling an armed and disciplined force on whose fealty he could thoroughly depend, ought to be of more account to-day, when the contingencies to which they point have arisen, than they were at the close of last year. But their significance is vastly lessened when we recall the important fact that while DAVIS was thus hectoring his recalcitrant legislators, and parading the invincibility of his dominion, the best informed and the most responsible representatives of the opinion of the South boldly pronounced his soothsayings a delusion, and his vain-glorious boastings a lie. Said the Richmond Examiner quoting DAVIS' words: "Let not this fatal error be harbored till it takes root in the

imagination. The evacuation of Richmond would be the loss of all respect and authority toward the Confederate Government, the disintegration of the army, and the abandonment of the scheme of an independent Southern Confederation." The outspoken journalist further declared that the war, carried on after the surrender of Richmond, would degenerate into an irregular contest, "which would have no other purpose than the mere defence or present safety of those immediately persisting in it."

We do not know, looking over the numerous points of the extraordinary picture presented in the article from which we quote, that it would be possible to present a more powerful array of arguments to sustain the theory that the overthrow of the rebel seat of power seals the final doom of the entire Confederacy. The article, which we quote in another column, is only less applicable to the situation now than it was a month ago, that every day intervening has seen the national army growing in strength, tightening its unyielding grasp, perfecting its combinations, and pressing irresistibly onward in its triumphant march. In all else the relative

condition of the opposing forces invites the application of the picture so forcibly drawn of the rebel government, driven from its local habitation, groping its way through uncertain latitudes in the wake of disjointed bands of guerrilla troopers, its separate members each bent exclusively on the safety of his individual self, with all that laid claim to the name of a Confederacy abandoned to accident, or to the clemency of the victors.

Since DAVIS last prophesied what should succeed the fall of Richmond, SHERIDAN has swept out of existence every line of supply — on the parallel of Richmond by which a rebel force could even be temporarily fed in the latitude of Richmond; SHERMAN has met and defeated the only force by which LEE could hope to defend his remaining channels of supply; THOMAS has barred the line of egress for the military relics of the Confederacy by South Western Virginia, and Eastern Tennessee; HANCOCK holds guard on the only possible northerly line of retreat; while GRANT having by a terrific and overwhelming succession of blows drawn his gigantic cordon of veteran troops around the rebel headquarters, has forced ☞

the evacuation at once of both Richmond and Petersburgh, and is to-day in search of the shattered remnants of what, but a few months ago, was the most formidable rebel force known to modern revolutionary epochs.

Such is the situation in which the inglorious flight of LEE from Richmond has left the "Confederacy" at home. What its situation will hereafter be abroad when this news reaches the political market of Europe, we may in part conjecture from the rapid decay of those "sympathizing" influences and agencies, which, under the varying guise of neutrality, belligerent immunities, and belligerent responsibility, have helped so much to prolong and embitter the conflict now closing. Three weeks ago the financial agencies of the rebellion were practically closed in England. In the keen-scented circles of Lombard-street these victories of GRANT and this midnight flight of LEE were all discounted in advance; and there the consternation and surprise will be less real and less visible than among those knavish political associations in England and France which have labored with unflagging zeal for the rebels, as promoters of forcible intervention. With these the intimation that the game is up will bring a sudden and surprising change of tone. Every hound in the pack that has barked, or set, or pointed for the rebel conspirators, will turn relentlessly upon his late masters, from the London leading oracle to the dirtiest of the Provincial touters. Cabinets and Princes will hasten to the conclusion that what they deemed a permanently established power, was after all but a rebellious outbreak whose existence it will be the part

of wisdom to forget. In all these regards the forecast of those Confederates who saw in the fall of Richmond, the fall of the Confederacy, promises to be fully justified.

To-day — wherever DAVIS and his Confederate Council may chance to be — they stand before their wretched victims, and before the world, henceforth, not in the character of a government, either de facto or de jure, but as political outcasts from a community they have aimed to ruin, and as outlaws from every immunity of citizenship. Hereafter, if the rebel leaders even should struggle to keep up for the time some armed organization, they can no longer assume the appearance of giving laws to any section of the Confederacy — either in civil or military affairs. The machinery — such as it was — of their political system, is wiped out of existence, and with it has gone every element of cohesion, every facility for political combination, for military recruitment, for provisioning, or attempting to pay the rank and file of their soldiery, and for making even the semblance of a figure in the world abroad, as a community having common purposes, or a common line of action. The fall of Richmond is practically the fall of the Confederacy. ⊛

1. The actual passage, contained in Davis's Message to Congress on November 7, 1864, was: "Not the fall of Richmond, nor Wilmington, nor Charleston, nor Savannah, nor Mobile, nor of all combined, can save the enemy from the constant and exhaustive drain of blood and treasure, which must continue until he shall discover that no peace is attainable unless based on the recognition of our indefeasible rights."

GRAPHIC ACCOUNT OF THE BRILLIANT OPERATIONS ON SUNDAY.

April 5
HEADQUARTERS ARMY OF THE POTOMAC, Monday, April 3 — 7 A.M. via WASHINGTON, April 4

As nearly as I can ascertain, while the combined forces of Gens. SHERIDAN and WARREN inflicted the most serious disasters upon the enemy, their own forces suffered comparatively little....

After capturing four heavy forts, all of which were well manned, and provided with powerful armaments, and seemed able to withstand a protracted siege, the Second Corps did not halt to give the enemy a breathing time, but followed them back, driving them from one position to another, until they were pressed around in front of the corps operating lower down the line. This corps was then set to work tearing up and destroying the Southside Railroad, from where it was struck by its left flank to the point where the Fifth Corps ceased the work of demolition on its right....

LATER.
PETERSBURGH, Monday, April 3

We entered the city [of Petersburg] at 3 o'clock this morning, the Ninth Corps being the first of this army to tread its streets, an honor they richly merited by their arduous labors and desperate bravery in their share of its capture.

H. H. YOUNG.

P.S. — At this hour the fighting has ceased, and the enemy has retired across the river. As for results, you will get them before this reaches you; and as the train is coming I will not attempt to give them.

H.H.Y. ⊛

DISPATCH TO THE ASSOCIATED PRESS.

April 5
HEADQUARTERS ARMY OF THE POTOMAC, April 2

The most important victory the Army of the Potomac has ever gained in Virginia was won to-day, and the outer line of works, which we have been trying in vain for months to overcome, has at last yielded to our victorious arms, and the greater portion of this army are to-night within a mile and a half of the city, on the southwest side.

The struggle made by the enemy to retain these works has been of the most

desperate character, and for the success obtained to-day we are indebted not only to the strategy exercised by the commanders, but to the overwhelming numbers and bravery of the troops that did the work ... .

Our captures will sum up about nine thousand prisoners and thirty-eight guns, including those taken by Gen. SHERIDAN yesterday.

The loss of the enemy in killed and wounded is not estimated, but in front of the Ninth Corps they lie on the ground very thick, for there they were mown down by the hundred, at each effort to regain their lost ground.

Gen. [Matthew W.] RANSOM is badly wounded, and a prisoner in our hands. He was found at a house on the Boydtown road, from which it was dangerous to move him.

Gen. A.P. HILL is reported killed, by prisoners.

MONDAY, April 3 — 5:30 A.M.
Petersburgh is ours. The Second Brigade, First Division, Ninth Corps, took possession this morning at daylight....

WASHINGTON, Tuesday, April 4.
Correspondents from City Point state that LEE has divided the remnant of his army, and is retreating in two small columns....

⊛

OFFICIAL FROM GENERAL GRANT.

APRIL 5

DISPATCH FROM GEN. GRANT.
WILSON STATION, VA., TUESDAY, APRIL 4

Hon. Edwin M. Stanton, Secretary of War:

The army is pushing forward in the hope of overtaking or dispersing the remainder of LEE's army, SHERIDAN with his cavalry and the Fifth Corps is between this and the Appomattox, Gen. MEADE, with the Second and Sixth, following.

Gen. [Edward O. C.] ORD is following the line of the Southside Railroad. All of the enemy that retains anything like organization have gone north of the Appomattox, and are apparently heading for Lynchburgh. Their losses have been very heavy. Houses through the country are nearly all used as hospitals for wounded men. In every direction I hear of rebel soldiers pushing for home — some in large, some in small squads, and generally without arms.

The cavalry have pursued so closely that the enemy have been forced to destroy probably the greater part of the transportation, caissons and munitions of war. The number of prisoners captured yesterday will exceed 2,000.

From the 20th of March to the present time our loss in killed, wounded and captured will not probably reach 7,000, of whom from 1,500 to 2,000 were captured, and many but slightly wounded.

I shall continue the pursuit as long as there appears to be any use in it.

(SIGNED) U.S. GRANT, LIEUT.-GEN. ✸

THE RETREAT AND ROUT OF LEE.

APRIL 7

Late on Wednesday night, the War Department was in communication, by telegraph, with a portion of the advance of our army at Burkesville Station, (the junction of the Southside and Danville Railroads) SHERIDAN, with the main body of his cavalry, at 3 P.M. of that day, was at Jetersville, on the Danville road, a station forty-three miles from Richmond. LEE, at the same date, with the remnants of his army, was at Amelia Court-house — a point thirty-six miles from Richmond, and seven miles north of SHERIDAN's advance. And on Wednesday evening, as appears from an intercepted letter of a rebel officer, LEE's army was drawn up in line of battle....

LEE by these reports, it will be seen, was so effectually headed off before the close of Wednesday night as to justify SHERIDAN's report to GRANT, that he felt confident, if his men properly exerted themselves, of capturing the entire army of Northern Virginia. By throwing out his cavalry in strong force toward the left on the fork between the Southside and Danville Roads, as he reports, SHERIDAN has got directly between the rebel army and Lynchburgh; and with the supports at his disposal on Thursday morning, and the aid of Gen. GRANT's presence, there is scarcely room to doubt that his anticipations of complete success have been fully justified. ✸

HANG OUT YOUR BANNERS

UNION VICTORY!

SURRENDER OF GENERAL LEE AND HIS WHOLE ARMY.

FINAL TRIUMPH OF THE ARMY OF THE POTOMAC.

OFFICIAL. THE PRELIMINARY CORRESPONDENCE. REJOICINGS.

APRIL 10

WAR DEPARTMENT, WASHINGTON
APRIL 9 – 9 O'CLOCK P.M.

This department has received the official report of the SURRENDER, THIS DAY, OF GEN. LEE AND HIS ARMY TO LIEUT.-GEN. GRANT, on the terms proposed by Gen. Grant.

Details will be given as speedily as possible.

EDWIN M. STANTON,
SECRETARY OF WAR. ✸

General Robert E. Lee, seated center left, surrenders to General Ulysses S. Grant, seated center right in the McLean House in Appomattox on April 9, 1865. Wilmer McLean, the owner of the home where the warring generals met, copyrighted this 1867 lithograph.

PEACE!

THE END OF THE GREAT REBELLION.

April 10

The great struggle is over. Gen. ROBERT E. LEE and the Army of Northern Virginia surrendered yesterday to Lieut. Gen. U.S. GRANT and the Army of the Potomac.

The thrilling word PEACE—the glorious fact of PEACE — are now once again to be realized by the American people.

The profound joy of the nation in this auspicious result, cannot be expressed in effervescent enthusiasm and noisy huzzahs; but will appear in the form in which it is so fitly and opportunely proclaimed by the Secretary of War — ascriptions of Praise to Almighty God and offerings of honor to the great leader of our armies, whom he has used as his instrument to save the nation.

The history of blood — the four years of war, are brought to a close. The fratricidal slaughter is all over. The gigantic battles have all been fought.

The last man, we trust, has been slain. The last shot has been fired. We have achieved, too, that for which the war was begun — that for which our soldiers have so long and grandly fought, and that for which so many thousands of brave men have laid down their lives.

We have achieved the great triumph, and we get with it the glorious Union. We get with it our country — a country now and forever rejoicing in Universal Freedom. The national courage and endurance have their full reward.

The event occurred on Palm Sunday — the day which commemorates the triumphal entry of Christ into Jerusalem. It will henceforth be a patriotic as well as a pious holiday in America.

Just four years almost to a day has the war lasted. It was on the 13th of April, 1861, that Sumter was surrendered to the rebels. It was on the 9th of April, 1865, that the great rebel army was surrendered to the power of the Union.

The surrender of the army of Gen. LEE solves a thousand difficulties that but lately threatened us in the future. It simplifies the work of pacification in the South. It gives hope for a speedy restoration of order and fraternity.

The correspondence between GRANT and LEE, which we give in full, is very direct and concise. GRANT proposed the surrender on Friday last, and in three days after LEE accepted the terms.

The terms proposed by GRANT are very simple, and doubtless had the approval of the President, who is at Richmond. We get all the rebel officers and soldiers, all the arms, artillery and public property; but the officers retain their side-arms, private baggage and horses. Each officer and man will be allowed to return to their homes, and will not be disturbed.

We have no idea that Jo. JOHNSTON's forces or any of the other rebel bodies will be of any trouble after this great event. LEE nominally only surrenders

Federal troops stationed at Appomattox Court House after the surrender.

his own immediate army; but he is commander of all the armed forces of the rebellion everywhere, and in one of his letters he speaks about negotiating with reference to the whole of the Confederate States forces under his command. This will undoubtedly be the upshot of the whole affair.

The great rebellion is crushed. The Republic is saved. PEACE comes again. To Heaven be the praise.

Beside the policy of concentration, which Gen. GRANT inaugurated, and to which, we have been indebted for the happy results of the last year's fighting, we owe him also that remarkable concert of feeling and action among the Generals, without which no plan of operations could have done us much good. The history of the Army of the Potomac before his day, was mainly made up of squabbles between Generals of corps and of divisions. After MCCLELLAN's removal, most of these whom he left behind in high commands were either so satisfied that he was the only person who was competent to command the army, or so determined that no one else should command it, that they made all active operations well nigh impossible. They hunted down POPE, who in spite of his bragging, proved himself an able and meritorious officer, and almost sacrificed the army and the nation to their desire to be rid of him. BURNSIDE's career in the chief command was one happily short struggle with their intrigues. They discussed his plans in the presence of officers and men, and openly predicted their failure; and at last gathering courage with impunity, some of them came up to Washington to get leave of the President to disobey his orders. And Gen. MEADE's operations, in the earlier period at least of his tenure of office, were marred by the timidity, growing out of the doubts which experience only too fully justified, of the hearty cooperation of those around him. In short, every division and every corps commander was a candidate for the highest place, and felt that the way to get it was to bring about the failure of the actual incumbent.

In such a state of things the wonder is not that we did not make more progress in Virginia, but that we got off so cheaply; not that LEE's army was not destroyed after three years of desperate fighting, but that it did not destroy ours. Since GRANT took the command in chief, however, we have heard no more of this. He has removed and retained whom he pleased,

and we have submitted without a murmur. There have been, undoubtedly, squabbles between Generals; for military officers, like other people, are human, but they have never been allowed to affect the course of events in the field. One or other of the disputants have been invariably packed off to settle his grievances at Washington or elsewhere, and the public has really known nothing of the matter, except that there has been a difference, and that somebody has retired, so that discipline has not been impaired nor the popular confidence weakened by the spectacle of "rows" between superior officers in the presence of the enemy. And we believe there has been but one — and that a very notorious — instance of wilful disobedience of GRANT's orders, or of the smallest disposition to doubt their wisdom, or even to criticise them.

He has from the outset exercised the power of removing officers from their commands, or transferring them to others, very lavishly without a whimper of complaint from any quarter. Some of the most conspicuous officers of the old Army of the Potomac have since his advance been sent to the West; some of the least known of the Western officers have, on the other hand, been brought to the East; and we doubt if history, except in NAPOLEON's case, contains a more remarkable example of judgment of character and skill in selection justified by events, than has been afforded during the last year by the career of GRANT's favorites — SHERIDAN, SHERMAN, THOMAS, MCPHERSON — have all proved themselves men worthy of the highest place in military annals, and yet though the war has lasted so long, it is only within little more than a year that they have been charged with any very important or conspicuous share in the conduct of it. Nothing short of their entire devotion to the cause, their implicit confidence in their great chief, and their hearty desire to carry out his plans, could have secured the success of the grand and extraordinary combination which has just culminated in the destruction of LEE's army and the overthrow of the

Drawing by Alfred R. Rudolph of Robert E. Lee leaving the McLean house after the surrender.

Confederacy. There has been through it all no blind striking, no marching hither and thither for want of anything better to do, or for the sake of making demonstrations. The smallest, as well as the greatest movements have been made to tell on the final result. SHERMAN was marching to Raleigh when he set out from Chattanooga; THOMAS was helping him along when he fought the battle of Nashville; SHERIDAN was helping GRANT when he defeated EARLY in the Valley, and so was [Alfred H.] TERRY when he stormed Fort Fisher; and all were working diligently for the destruction of LEE's army. ⊛

THE VICTORY.

—

THANKS TO GOD, THE GIVER OF VICTORY.

APRIL 10

The inspiration of the scene and the scope of this theme before us are beyond the feeble descriptive powers of the pen of your correspondent. No brilliant rhetoric, no vivid word-painting, no oratorical eloquence can portray the sublimity and the immensity of the great victory. It is almost beyond the power of the human mind to comprehend its extent, and when you begin to descend into detail, the task is simply appalling in its magnitude. Think of a line of operations, held defensively and operated from offensively with such success thirty-nine miles long from flank to flank, thoroughly fortified along its entire length! Think of the cities captured, of the fortifications stormed and taken with their hundreds of guns, great and small, of the material of war now in our hands, yet beyond the possibility of computation, of the terrible battles, and the and overwhelming defeat and rout of the chief army of the rebellion, of the prisoners captured counted by the tens of thousands; of the terrified flight of the arch-traitor and his few desperate minions; of the triumphant entry of ABRAHAM LINCOLN into treason's fallen capital. Let every lover of his country depict the vast scene in his own imagination for words to fitly describe it fail altogether....

L. L. CROUNSE ✦

GEN. JOHNSTON'S ARMY.

APRIL 11

The most interesting question now is, what will Jo. JOHNSTON do? He commands the only army of any magnitude now left in the Southern Confederacy. It is not a very formidable army in numbers, nor is it coherent in character. In every characteristic of an army, it is vastly inferior to that lately under LEE. It has never, as an army, fought a noteworthy battle. It has no traditions of success. It has no capable leaders. The troops of [William J.] HARDEE, who fled from Savannah and then from Charleston, form its nucleus, and to these have been added the tail of [John Bell] HOOD's old army, the Wilmington force of BRAGG, the picayune force of BEAUREGARD, various feeble forces and garrisons picked up around, and a cavalry force under WADE HAMPTON and [Joseph] WHEELER. It is a piebald collection. Since its organization — such organization as it has — it has been steadily on the retreat; and the last we hear of it is that it has fled from Raleigh, and it must be now somewhere near the Southern border of Virginia. It was supposed that, in the last resort, LEE would try and effect a junction with it; but JOHNSTON and his troops doubtless heard yesterday of the surrender of LEE and his whole army.

Opposed to JOHNSTON is the powerful and magnificent army of Gen. SHERMAN. It is utterly impossible that JOHNSTON should cope with it. He knows it would be ruin for him to try. He knows it would be madness.

In forming a judgment as to the possible course of JOHNSTON in this emergency, we must take into consideration JOHNSTON's hopeless prospect, as well as the great surrender of Sunday. We must take into account, too, the relations of Gen. JOHNSTON to JEFF. DAVIS, and also his relations to Gen. LEE. For nearly two years JOHNSTON and DAVIS have been in a state of bitter animosity with each other. They quarreled at the time of GRANT's operations against Vicksburgh; and the Richmond rebel papers have often given us accounts of the depth of their mutual hatred. Twice has DAVIS removed JOHNSTON from command; and on the last occasion, at Atlanta, it was under circumstances which stung JOHNSTON to the quick. The whole press and people of the South clamored loudly for his reinstatement; but DAVIS was implacable. On the other hand, the relations of JOHNSTON to LEE have always been those of mutual respect and friendliness. One of the first acts of Gen. LEE, when he received from the Confederate Congress the command of all the Confederate armies three months ago, was to put JOHNSTON in command of the only army beside his own that existed in the South.

Now, under these circumstances, leaving out of view the hopeless prospect, it may be doubted whether JOHNSTON will exhibit such devotion to the person and interests of DAVIS as to remain any longer in the field in his service. It is far more likely he will follow the example set film by his chief and friend, the Commander of the Confederate armies. If he does not do it quickly, SHERMAN will presently break him and his army to pieces. Then JEFF. DAVIS will be hardly able to get even a body-guard. This week will doubtless wind up JOHNSTON, one way or another.[1] ✦

1. Johnston met with Davis in a railroad car at Greensboro, North Carolina, on April 12, the day after this story appeared. Davis urged Johnston to continue the war, but Johnston declared that "our people are tied of the war, feel themselves whipped, and will not fight." Davis gave him permission to open negotiations "to terminate the existing war," but clearly there was no meeting of the minds. Johnston surrendered his army to Sherman on April 26, and Davis never forgave him.

THE PRESIDENT'S SPEECH — THE QUESTION OF RECONSTRUCTION.

APRIL 13

Those who expected from the President the statement of a settled reconstruction policy have been disappointed. His speech disclosed nothing new on that subject. It was made up chiefly of remarks upon the inherent difficulties of the general task, and upon the considerations that prompted the attempt to restore Louisiana to its old status on the basis of twelve thousand loyal voters. No pledge was given, or intention declared, to hold to this or any other particular plan for the future. The special characteristic of the speech was its reserve.[1]

Herein was wisdom. The time has not yet come for the establishment of any regular system of restoration. The simple reason is that one of the most important elements to be taken into account is yet to be developed. We mean the temper of the South. Upon this temper will depend the discretionary power that should be accorded. If the people lately in revolt choose to accept the result of the war like sensible men, if they exhibit a readiness to resume their relations to the Union in good faith, and to adapt themselves to the best of their ability to that free society which is indispensible to the national concord, every facility should be accorded them for their speedy repossession of every franchise and privilege existing under the constitution. But until time determines in what spirit the conciliatory spirit of the government will be met, it would be folly for the government to engage itself to any fixed line of action.

The Southern disposition hitherto manifested in the districts reduced to our control, is no test. So long as the Confederacy retained its capital and its great armies, almost every Southern mind was more or less under the delusion that it might still prevail, and was badly influenced. That delusion has now passed. The South now, for the first time, is in a condition to meet, with a clear judgment, the question of its future relations to the Union. Some little time must be allowed it to take the new bearings of the situation. Some little time must be allowed the Government, too, to learn what concurrence and cooperation a liberal policy would be likely to receive. Every day now is rapidly shedding light upon these points, and we may confidently expect that the government will soon be prepared to move in the most advantageous direction.

The practical sense which President LINCOLN brings to this momentous work of reconstruction is forcibly illustrated in the remark of his speech that the question whether the so-called seceded States are or are not yet in the Union, is a "pernicious abstraction."[2] A vast deal of controversy has been indulged in upon this subject, and sweeping conclusions have been drawn with a great deal of logical labor, from each hypothesis. The simple fact is that categories and formulas in a practical business of this kind are but an impertinence. They are fit only for that Hudibrastic[3] order of mind which must "tell the clock by algebra." Mr. LINCOLN spoke pat to the purpose when he said: "We all agree that the seceded States, so called, are out of their proper practical relation with the Union, and that the sole object of the government, civil and military, in regard to these States is again to get them into their proper practical relation." That covers the whole ground. Whether these States are out of the Union or not — though for our part we think it very plain that they are not — it is needless to dispute.

Of course, these "proper practical relations" mean equal relations. The great end is to get every Southern State back, so that it shall perform the same obligations, and exercise the same rights, identically that are performed and exercised by every Northern State. It would be ruinous to our Constitutional system to pervert it so as to keep one section of the country permanently subordinate to the rest. Every friend of the Constitution must desire to have this exceptional condition of the South terminated as soon as possible. Nobody, we believe, wishes to keep any Southern State under disabilities, simply as a punishment. Mr. [Charles] SUMNER himself, probably, does not want to transform the Southern States into territories for any such object. The real concern here is, whether the Southern States, if restored at once to their full State rights, would not abuse them by an oppression of the black race. This race has rendered an assistance to the government in the time of danger that entitles them to its benign care. The government cannot, without the worst dishonor, permit the bondage of the black man to be continued in any form. It is bound by every moral principle, as well as every prudential consideration, not to remit him to the tender mercies of any enemy. But it is to be hoped that the Southern people will understand that the interests of both races require a just relation between them, and that they will secure this by a prompt change of their State constitutions and laws. Every appearance, thus far, indicates such a disposition, and that in due time the government will be rid of this embarrassment. Yet for the present, further developments in respect to this and many other important matters must be awaited. The President must exercise caution, the people patience. ✸

1. Lincoln's last public speech, delivered on April 11, 1865, addressed the question of Reconstruction. To those who thought that the policy used in the case of Louisiana would become a model for the rest of the South, Lincoln replied, "What has been said of Louisiana will apply generally to other States. And yet so great peculiarities pertain to each state … that no exclusive, and inflexible plan can safely be prescribed as to details and collaterals." The speech can be found in Basler, Ed., *The Collected Works of Abraham Lincoln*, 8:399–405.

2. This abstraction was "pernicious" because if the seceded states remained in the Union, all that was necessary for them to resume their former status was to accept the national authority. If not, they would have to be readmitted by Congress.

3. This is a reference to Samuel Butler's 17th century poem "Hudibras," which employed a mock heroic verse structure.

CHAPTER 25

"This Hour of Mourning and of Gloom"

APRIL–MAY 1865

"**A**n eclipse," declared a Boston minister on Easter Sunday 1865, "seems to have come upon the brilliancy of the flag .... The sun is less bright than before .... It is manly to weep today."

The words spoke for untold hundreds of thousands of mourners throughout the North, suddenly plunged into profound shock by the assassination of Abraham Lincoln on Good Friday. The attack, and the vigil at the President's deathbed, tracked by the press in special bulletins and editions, doused the joyful public mood that had inspired wild celebrations in the week since Lee's surrender at Appomattox. "The bonfires of exultation which the night before lighted up the streets of many of our cities, as if in anticipation of the terrible event," another preacher observed, "left their ashes and blackened embers ... in readiness for the general sorrow." As one contemporary remembered: "Business stopped; hearts throbbed almost audibly; knots of men congregated on the streets; telegraph offices were thronged by anxious faces; and all were incredulous that such a stupendous, nefarious transaction had occurred in America."

But occur it did, and while Lincoln's murder was lamented as the gravest tragedy in the nation's history, it also became the century's biggest news story. The Times did not shrink from its journalistic responsibility during the crisis, whether events occurred in Washington, along the assassin's escape route, or outside its own headquarters in New York. The paper responded with an outburst of energetic, detailed reporting, wild but understandable speculation, and mournful editorials, never flagging in energy or attention to detail.

Nearly — but not quite — ignored in the wake of the immense tragedy

A Currier and Ives lithograph of the assassination of Abraham Lincoln.

were concurrent events that in fact did signal the closing chapters of the Civil War. On April 26, Confederate General Joseph E. Johnston surrendered his army at the Bennett House near Durham, North Carolina. Though for all intents and purposes Johnston's surrender ended the active fighting, it received far less attention in the press (and a far less venerated place in Civil War mythology) than Appomattox. Its relatively minor place in history was probably guaranteed when the two opposing generals required not one, but three meetings to iron out surrender terms, after the War Department rejected Sherman's original agreement because it embraced too many political issues outside his jurisdiction.

No story, however important, could possibly eclipse that of the President's sudden death, at the peak of his popularity and success, or the nation's unprecedented response. Not long before he ventured to Ford's Theatre that Good Friday evening, Lincoln had met with General James Van Alen, who offered what turned out to be a prophetic warning about his safety. The President promised to "guard his life," Van Alen remembered, and "not expose it to assassination as he had by going to Richmond" a few days before. In a written note — one of the last he ever wrote — Lincoln assured the general: "I intend to adopt the advice of my friends and use due precaution."

But he did not. That afternoon, he took a long carriage ride with his wife. "He was almost boyish, in his mirth," Mary Lincoln remembered. "I never saw him so surpassingly cheerful." They spoke of their shared hope for a happier future, visited an ironclad warship and crew recently returned to the Washington Navy Yard, then returned to the White House to dress for the theater. The Lincolns arrived after the play had begun, acknowledged the cheers of the audience, and bowed

to an impromptu rendition of "Hail to the Chief" by the orchestra. Then they took their seats in a special, patriotically decorated box directly above stage left, and held hands to watch an English comedy called *Our American Cousin*. Shortly after 10 p.m., John Wilkes Booth, an actor and Confederate sympathizer — a onetime Confederate agent of sorts, too — crept into the box and shot Lincoln point-blank in the back of the head. The President never regained consciousness, and died the following morning at 7:22 a.m.

Only three days before he attacked the President, Booth had joined a crowd on the White House lawn to hear Lincoln deliver what quickly became known as his final address — but, more to the point, was his *first* major speech since the end of the war, and the first on Reconstruction. As the racist Booth listened, the President suggested enfranchising African-Americans — if only the "very intelligent," and "those who serve our cause as soldiers." No American president had ever before spoken publicly of black voting rights, and hearing those words, Booth turned to a companion in a fury. "That means nigger citizenship," he growled. "Now, by God, I will put him through. That will be the last speech he will ever make." It was.

A celebrity in his own right, Booth was recognized by the theatergoers the night he killed Lincoln at Ford's, and though the ensuing manhunt was one of the largest ever undertaken to capture a criminal, the assassin eluded capture for days, transfixing the reading public. Newspapers overflowed with conjecture about whether Booth had been inspired or directed by the Confederate government, perhaps by Jefferson Davis himself.

As for Davis, his end was as inglorious as Lincoln's was sublime. Pursued by federal troops after escaping Richmond with his wife, the Confederacy's

first and only President was captured after attempting to flee captors while wearing Mrs. Davis's raglan-sleeved raincoat. For years, Varina Davis insisted she had thrown the garment on her husband only to assure he would be warm if he escaped. But the Northern press and cartoonists had a field day reporting that the starchy Southern gentleman had tried to flee wearing women's clothes — later exaggerated to include a petticoat! Four years earlier, The Times had published (and embellished) the report that Abraham Lincoln had *begun* his presidency by sneaking into his capital in disguise. Now it noted that his Confederate counterpart had *ended* his presidency by *fleeing his* capital in disguise. As Davis became a comic figure, the once-controversial Lincoln was transfigured into a revered one.

As Mary Lincoln was led from her husband's deathbed to a carriage waiting to take her back to the White House, she glanced at Ford's Theatre across the street and wailed: "That dreadful house! That dreadful house!" But the horror at the theatre had elevated its famous victim to martyrdom. Lincoln had become one of 620,000 casualties to die in the fight to preserve the *national* house. Back in 1858, he had invoked a biblical passage to warn: "A house divided against itself cannot stand." History had proven him right. Now, though "drenched . . . in blood and tears," as The Times put it, the house was again reunited.

AWFUL EVENT

PRESIDENT LINCOLN SHOT BY AN ASSASSIN.
THE DEED DONE AT FORD'S THEATRE LAST NIGHT.
THE ACT OF A DESPERATE REBEL.

APRIL 15

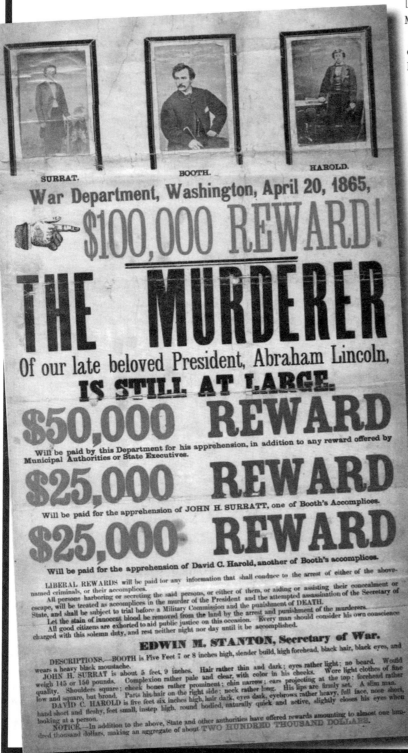

[OFFICIAL.] WAR DEPARTMENT, WASHINGTON, APRIL 15 — 1:30 A.M.
Maj.-Gen. Dix:

This evening at about 9:30 P.M., at Ford's Theatre, the President, while sitting in his private box with Mrs. LINCOLN, Mrs. HARRIS, and Major RATHBURN,[1] was shot by as assassin, who suddenly entered the box and approached behind the President.

The assassin then leaped upon the stage, brandishing a large dagger or knife, and made his escape in the rear of the theatre.

The pistol ball entered the back of the President's head and penetrated nearly through the head. The wound is mortal. The President has been insensible ever since it was inflicted, and is now dying.

About the same hour an assassin, whether the same or not, entered Mr. SEWARD's apartments, and under the pretence of having a prescription, was shown to the Secretary's sick chamber. The assassin immediately rushed to the bed, and inflicted two or three stabs on the throat and two on the face. It is hoped the wounds may not be mortal. My apprehension is that they will prove fatal.

The nurse alarmed Mr. FREDERICK SEWARD,[2] who was in an adjoining room, and hastened to the door of his father's room, when he met the assassin, who inflicted upon him one or more dangerous wounds. The recovery of FREDERICK SEWARD is doubtful.

It is not probable that the President will live throughout the night.

Gen. GRANT and wife were advertised to be at the theatre this evening, but he started to Burlington at 6 o'clock this evening.

At a Cabinet meeting at which Gen. GRANT was present, the subject of the state of the country and the prospect of a speedy peace was discussed. The President was very cheerful and hopeful, and spoke very kindly of Gen. LEE and others of the Confederacy, and of the establishment of government in Virginia.

All the members of the Cabinet except Mr. SEWARD, are now in attendance upon the President.

I have seen Mr. SEWARD, but he and FREDERICK were both unconscious.

EDWLN M. STANTON,
SECRETARY OF WAR. ⊛

1. The Lincolns' theater guests that fateful night were Clara Harris and her stepbrother and fiancé, Major Henry Rathbone. They were later married.
2. Seward's son had also served as his assistant secretary of state.

THE CONDITION OF THE PRESIDENT.

APRIL 15

WASHINGTON, APRIL 15 — 2:12 A.M.

The President is still alive; but he is growing weaker. The ball is lodged in his brain, three inches from where it entered the skull. He remains insensible, and his condition is utterly hopeless.

The Vice-President has been to see him; but all company, except the members of the Cabinet and of the family, is rigidly excluded.

Large crowds still continue in the street, as near to the house as the line of guards allows. ✹

THE SUCCESSION.

MR. JOHNSON INAUGURATED AS PRESIDENT.

APRIL 16

WASHINGTON, SATURDAY, APRIL 15 — 12 A.M.

ANDREW JOHNSON was sworn into office as President of the United States by Chief-Justice CHASE, to-day, at eleven o'clock.

Secretary MCCULLOUGH and Attorney-General SPEED[1], and others were present.

He remarked:

"The duties are mine. I will perform them, trusting in God." ✹

1. Hugh McCullough (1808–1895) had been Lincoln's third secretary of the treasury; James Speed (1812–1887) his second attorney general. Both continued in the Johnson administration.

The swearing-in of new President Andrew Johnson.

OUR GREAT LOSS.
DEATH OF PRESIDENT LINCOLN.
THE SONGS OF VICTORY DROWNED IN SORROW.

APRIL 16

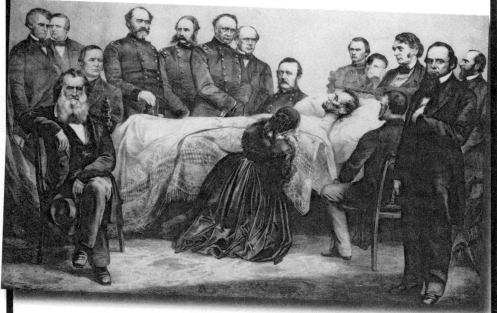

The deathbed of Abraham Lincoln, engraved by C.A. Asp, 1865.

WAR DEPARTMENT, WASHINGTON, APRIL 15 — 4:10 A.M.

To Major Gen. Dix:

The President continues insensible and is sinking.

Secretary SEWARD remains without change.

FREDERICK SEWARD'S Skull is fractured in two places, besides a severe cut upon the head.

The attendant is still alive, but hopeless. Maj. SEWARD's wound is not dangerous.

It is now ascertained with reasonable certainty that two assassins were engaged in the horrible crime, WILKES BOOTH being the one that shot the President, and the other companion of his whose name is not a known, but whose description is so clear that he can hardly escape. It appears from a letter found in BOOTH's trunk that the murder was planned before the 4th of March, but fell through then because the accomplice backed out until "Richmond could be heard from." BOOTH and his accomplice were at the livery stable at six o'clock last evening, and left there with their horses about ten o'clock, or shortly before that hour.

It would seem that they had for several days been seeking their chance, but for some unknown reason it was not carried into effect until last night.

One of them has evidently made his way to Baltimore—the other has not yet been traced.

EDWIN M. STANTON,
SECRETARY OF WAR.

WAR DEPARTMENT, WASHINGTON, APRIL 15
Major-Gen. Dix:

ABRAHAM LINCOLN died this morning at twenty-two minutes after seven o'clock.

EDWIN M. STANTON,
SECRETARY OF WAR. ✹

THE ASSASSINS.

CIRCUMSTANCES TENDING TO INCULPATE G. H. [*SIC*] BOOTH.

APRIL 16,
WASHINGTON, SATURDAY, APRIL 15

There is no confirmation of the report that the murderer of the President has been arrested.

Among the circumstances tending to fix a participation in the crime on BOOTH, were letters found in his trunk, one of which, apparently from a lady, supplicated him to desist from the perilous undertaking in which he was about to embark, as the time was inauspicious, the mine not yet being ready to be sprung.

The Extra Intelligencer says: "From the evidence obtained it is rendered highly probable that the man who stabbed Mr. SEWARD and his sons, is JOHN SURRATT,

of Prince George County, Maryland. The horse he rode was hired at NAYLOR's stable, on Fourteenth-street. SURRATT is a young man, with light hair and goatee. His father is said to have been postmaster of Prince George County."

About 11 o'clock last night two men crossed the Anacostia Bridge, one of whom gave his name as BOOTH, and the other as SMITH. The latter is believed to be JOHN SURRATT.

Last night a riderless horse was found,

Some of the Lincoln assassination coconspirators and their execution. Top row from left: George A. Atzerodt, Lewis Powell, Samuel Arnold, and Michael O'Laughlen. Middle: Mary Surratt. Bottom: David E. Herold. Large photograph: After a speedy military trial, Atzerodt, Herold, Powell, and Surratt, were executed by hanging on July 7, 1865.

THE NEW PRESIDENT.

THE POLITICAL HISTORY AND ANTECEDENTS OF ANDREW JOHNSON.

APRIL 17

ANDREW JOHNSON has been in continuous public life for thirty years. He entered the General Assembly of Tennessee as a member of the House of Representatives the first Monday in October, 1835, from the

County of Greene, in East Tennessee. He was reelected to the succeeding biennial Assembly in 1837, and again in 1839. In 1841 he was transferred to the State Senate by the Counties of Washington, Greene and Sullivan. In 1843 to a seat in Congress from the First Representative District, comprising the same counties and the new County of Johnson. He served the same district, by four successive reelections, until the new apportionment under the census of 1850, in all ten years, when, in

1853, he was made Governor of Tennessee, and was subsequently reelected in 1855. At the end of his second term, in 1857, he was made United States Senator, his term expiring on the 4th of March, 1863, since when, and until his recent election as Vice-President of the United States, he was Military Governor of Tennessee....

Above all, Mr. JOHNSON is a true, as well as a brave man; faithful four years ago among the faithless of his old rivals of the Whig party, and his old colleagues of

which has been identified by the proprietor of one of the stables previously mentioned as having been hired from his establishment. Accounts are conflicting as to whether BOOTH crossed the bridge on horseback or on foot; but as it is believed that be rode across it, it is presumed that he had exchanged his horse.

From information in the possession of the authorities it is evident that the scope of the plot was intended to be much more comprehensive.

The Vice-President and other prominent members of the Administration were particularly inquired for by suspected parties, and their precise localities accurately obtained; but providentially, in their cases, the scheme miscarried.

A boat was at once sent down the Potomac to notify the gunboats on the river of the awful crime, in order that all possible means should be taken for the arrest of the perpetrators.

The most ample precautions have been taken, and it is not believed the culprits will long succeed in evading the overtaking arm of justice....

At the Cabinet meeting yesterday, which lasted over two hours, the future policy of the government toward Virginia was discussed, and the best feeling prevailed. It is stated that it was, determined to adopt a very liberal policy, as was recommended by the President. It is said that this meeting was the most harmonious held for over two years, the President exhibiting throughout that magnanimity and kindness of heart which has ever characterized his treatment of the rebellious States, and which has been so illy requited on their part.

One of the members of the Cabinet remarked to a friend he met at the door, that "The government was to-day stronger than it had been for three years past." ✺

the Democratic party of Tennessee; true to the Union, when it cost something to be true; to the government in its life struggle against rebellion and insurrection; to free labor and its disenthralment from the incubus of slavery, and to that unswerving line of duty and devotion to hard study, progressive statesmanship and ripening experience which have carried him from the humblest to the top-most round of human ambition. ✺

THE MURDER OF PRESIDENT LINCOLN.

APRIL 16

The heart of this nation was stirred yesterday as it has never been stirred before. The news of the assassination of ABRAHAM LINCOLN carried with it a sensation of horror and of agony which no other event in our history has ever excited. In this city the demonstrations of grief and consternation were without a parallel. Business was suspended. Crowds of people thronged the streets — great gatherings sprung up spontaneously everywhere seeking to give expression, by speeches, resolutions, &c., &c., to the universal sense of dismay and indignation which pervaded the public mind.

Perhaps the paramount element in this public feeling was evoked by personal regard for ABRAHAM LINCOLN. That a man so gentle, so kind, so free from every particle of malice or unkindness, every act of whose life has been so marked by benevolence and goodwill, should become the victim of a cold-blooded assassination, shocked the public heart beyond expression. That the very moment, too, when he was closing the rebellion which had drenched our land in blood and tears — by acts of magnanimity so signal as even to excite the reluctant distrust and apprehensions of his own friends — should be chosen for his murder, adds a new element of horror to the dreadful tragedy.

But a powerful element of the general feeling which the news aroused was a profound concern for the public welfare. The

President Andrew Johnson.

whole nation had come to lean on ABRAHAM LINCOLN in this dread crisis of its fate with a degree of confidence never accorded to any President since GEORGE WASHINGTON. His love of his country ardent and all-pervading, — swaying every act and prompting every word, — his unsuspected uprightness and personal integrity, — his plain, simple common sense, conspicuous in everything he did or said, commending itself irresistibly to the judgment and approval of the great body of the people, had won for him a solid and immovable hold upon the regard and confidence even of his political opponents. The whole people mourn his death with profound and sincere appreciation of his character and his worth.

ANDREW JOHNSON, of Tennessee, is now the President of the United States. We have no doubts and no misgivings in regard to the manner in which he will discharge the duties which devolve so suddenly upon him. This country has no more patriotic citizen than he — no one among all her public men who will bring to her service a higher sense of his responsibilities, a sounder judgment in regard to her interests, or a firmer purpose in the maintenance of her honor and the promotion of her welfare. He has suffered, in his person, his property and his family relations, terribly from the wicked rebellion which has desolated the land; but he is not the man to allow a sense of personal wrong to sway his judgment or control his action in a great national emergency. Traitors and rebels have nothing to expect at his hands, but strict justice, tempered with such mercy only as the welfare of the nation may require.

In this hour of mourning and of gloom, while the shadow of an awful and unparalleled calamity hangs over the land, it is well to remember that the stability of our government and the welfare of our country do not depend upon the life of any individual, and that the great current of affairs is not to be changed or checked by the loss of any man however high or however honored. In nations where all power is vested in single hands, and assassin's knife may overthrow governments and wrap a continent in the flames of war. But here the PEOPLE rule, and events inevitably follow the course which they prescribe. ABRAHAM LINCOLN has been their agent and instrument for the four years past; ANDREW JOHNSON is to be their agent for the four years that are now to come. If the people have faith, courage and wisdom, the result will be the same. ✺

NEWS FROM WASHINGTON.

THE INVESTIGATION OF THE MURDER.

APRIL 17

The city and military authorities have been quietly pursuing investigations since yesterday morning, and persons conversant to some extent with the results thereof, are very confident that the murder of Mr. LINCOLN and the attempted murder of Mr. SEWARD, are only part of a carefully planned conspiracy that intended the murder also of other members of the Cabinet, and the destruction of some of the public buildings, and perhaps certain sections of the city.[1] Nothing has yet been brought to light calculated to fix the identity of the assassin of Mr. SEWARD,[2] though various parties have been arrested and examined, and two or three are held for further examination.

RUMORS OF BOOTH'S ARREST.

Rumor has arrested BOOTH a dozen times already, and many persons will retire to-night in the confident belief that he is confined ion a gunboat t the Navy-yard, but so far as can be learned from the authorities he has not been arrested, but very little is known of the route he took in escaping. The aggregate reward now offered here for the arrest of these men is thirty thousand dollars.

MRS. LINCOLN

Mrs. LINCOLN is yet much depressed, though less so than yesterday. She remains at the White House....

THE BODY OF MR. LINCOLN.

The body of Mr. LINCOLN, dressed in the plain black suit he wore on inauguration day, is lying in the northwest corner of the second floor of the White House, The head lies amidst white flowers, and the features wear the calm peaceful expression of deep sleep. The corpse will be laid in state in the east room on Tuesday, and the funeral will be held on Wednesday.... ⊛

1. In fact, Booth intended for coconspirator George Atzerodt to murder Vice President Andrew Johnston, but Atzerodt lost his nerve.
2. Seward was viciously knifed by Lewis Powell, alias Paine, a hulking former Confederate soldier. He was later captured and hanged.

John Wilkes Booth.

THE LAST ADDRESS OF THE PRESIDENT TO THE COUNTRY.

APRIL 17

Probably all men in all quarters of the world, who read President LINCOLN'S last Inaugural Address, were impressed by the evident tone of solemnity in it, and the want of any expression of personal exultation. There he stood, after four years of such trial, and exposed to such hate and obloquy as no other great leader in modern history has experienced, successful, reelected, his policy approved by the people and by the greater test of events, the terrible rebellion evidently coming to its end, and he himself now certain of his grand position in the eyes of history — and yet not a word escaped him of triumph, or personal glory, or even of much hopefulness. We all expected more confidence — words promising the close of the war and speaking of the end of our difficulties. Many hoped for some definite line of policy to be laid out in this address. But instead, we heard a voice as if from some prophet, looking with solemn gaze down over the centuries, seeing that both sides in the great contest had their errors and sins, that no speedy victory could be looked for, and yet that the great Judge of the world would certainly give success to right and justice. The feeling for the bondmen and the sense of the great wrong done to them, with its inevitable punishment, seemed to rest with such solemn earnestness on his soul, that to the surprise of all and the derision of the flippant, an official speech became clothed in the language of the Bible. The English and French critics all observed this peculiar religious tone of the Inaugural, and nearly all sensible persons felt it not unsuited to the grandeur and momentous character of the events accompanying it. Many pronounced it a Cromwellian speech; but it had one peculiarity, which CROMWELL's speeches never possessed — a tone of perfect kindness and good-will to all, whether enemies or political opponents.

"With charity to all and malice for none," President LINCOLN made his last speech to the world. Men will reperuse that solemn address with ever increasing interest and emotion, as if the shadow of his own tragic fate and the near and unseen dangers to the country, rested unconsciously on its words. It will seem natural that no expression of exultation or personal triumph escaped the great leader of this revolution, but that his mind was filled with the impressive religious lessons of the times. It will be thought characteristic of his sense of justice and his sincere humanity, that his last public address to the country was most of all occupied by the wrongs done to the helpless race, whose friend and emancipator he had been. And it will seem but a part of his wonderful spirit of good-will to all, that not a syllable of bitterness toward the enemies of his country, to the traitors at home, or his personal revilers, passed his lips. ⊛

THE NATION'S BEREAVEMENT.

APRIL 17

Death, as the Northmen imaged him, is no dart-brandishing skeleton, but a gigantic shape, that in wraps mortals within the massive folds of its dark garment. Long has it been since those dread robes closed upon a mightier victim than President LINCOLN. It is like the earth's opening and swallowing up a city. The public loss is so great, the chasm made in our national councils so tremendous, that the mind, not knowing how to adjust itself to such a change, shrinks back appalled. It comes home to every bosom with the force of a personal affliction. There is not a loyal family in the land that does not mourn. It is as when there "was a great cry in Egypt, for there was not a house where there was not one dead."

No public man has ever died in America invested with such responsibilities, and the mark of so much attention, as ABRAHAM LINCOLN. The unprecedented manner of his death has shocked inexpressibly; but it is not that which most harrows with anguish. It is the loss of the man himself—the privation of him when he seemed peculiarly necessary to the country, and when the heart of the people was bound to him more than ever. Had he been taken by a natural death, the public grief would have been just as profound, though unaccompanied with the other emotions which his assassination has excited. All true men feel that they have lost a man of wondrous fitness for the task he had to execute. Few Americans have lived who had such a faculty of discovering the real relations of things, and shaping his thoughts and actions strictly upon them without external bias. In his own independent, and perhaps we may say very peculiar way, he invariably got at the needed truths of the time. Without anything like brilliancy of genius, without any great breadth of information or literary accomplishment, he still had that perfect balance of thoroughly sound faculties which gives an almost infallible judgment. This, combined with great calmness of temper, great firmness of purpose, supreme moral principle, and intense patriotism, made up just that character which fitted him, as the same qualities fitted WASHINGTON, for a wise and safe conduct of public affairs in a season of great peril.

Political opponents have sometimes denied that Mr. LINCOLN was a great man.

But if he had not great faculties and great qualities, how happens it that he has met the greatest emergencies that ever befell a nation in a manner that so gained for him the confidence of the people? No man ever had greater responsibilities, and yet never were responsibilities discharged with greater acceptance. All disparagement sinks powerless before this one fact, that the more ABRAHAM LINCOLN was tried, the more he was trusted. Nobody can be so foolish as to impute this to the arts and delusions which sometimes give success to the intriguer and demagogue of the hour. It would be the worst insult to the American people to suppose them capable of being so cajoled when the very life of their country was at stake. Nor was it in the nature of Mr. LINCOLN to act a part. He was the least pretentious of men. He never sought to win confidence by any high professions. He never even protested his determination to do his duty. Nor, after he had done his duty, did he go about seeking glory for his exploits, or asking thanks by his presence for the great benefits he had conferred. Sampson-like, he could rend a lion and tell neither father nor mother of it. He was a true hero of the silent sort, who spoke mostly by his actions, and whose action-speech was altogether of the highest kind, and best of its kind. He was not an adventurer, aiming at great things for himself and courting the chances of fortune; nor was he a great artist in any sense, undergoing passions and reflecting them; but he was a great power, fulfilling his way independently of art and passion, and simple, as all great powers are. No thought of self — no concern for his own repute — none of the prudish sensitiveness for his own good name, which is the form selfishness often assumes in able and honorable men, ever seemed to enter his mind. To him it was but the ordinary course of life to do that which has made him illustrious. He had a habit of greatness. An intense, all-comprehensive patriotism, was a constant stimulus of all his public exertions. It grew into the very constitution of his soul, and operated, like a natural function, continuously, spontaneously and almost as it were unconsciously. It pervaded and vivified all that he said, and formed the prime incentive of all that he did. If he had ambition, it was to serve his country, and in that sphere where he might do it most effectually. In no way did he ever fail his country in the time of need. He was independent, self-

The last photograph of President Abraham Lincoln. It was taken on the balcony of the White House by photographer Henry F. Warren on March 6, 1865.

poised, steadfast. You always knew where to find him; you could calculate him like a planet. A public trust was to him a sacred thing. Sublimer moral courage, more resolute devotion to duty, cannot be found in the history of man than he has displayed for the salvation of the American Union. It was the sublime performance of sublime duties that made him so trusted, and which has given him a fame as solid as justice, and as genuine as truth....

No public power, no public care, no public applause could spoil him; he remained ever the same plain man of the people. It was this which peculiarly endeared him to the people, and makes the sorrow for him so tender as a personal feeling, apart from the sense of a national calamity. It is not simply because "he hath been so clear in his great office," but because "he hath borne his faculties so meek."

"That his virtues Will plead like angels, trumpet-tongued, against The deep damnation of his taking off."[1] ✴

1. A quote from *Macbeth*, Lincoln's favorite Shakespearian tragedy, invoked often in the days of mourning for the late President.

THE PROCESSION.

EIGHT GRAND DIVISIONS. THE SPECTATORS.

APRIL 26

Even during all the night before yesterday, preliminaries for the great funeral procession had been going forward at many points in the city. Before dawn, the stir increased. Almost as soon as it was light, the vast mass of our great metropolitan population began to move perceptibly toward the sadly magnificent ceremony of the day. At first, solitary soldiers, uniformed and armed, or single civilians, in decent black, were gathering to a thousand rendezvous of regiment, society, club or association, as to centres of crystallization sprinkled over the extensive city map. And while uniform and civic costume varied in their respective many ways, two universal marks, distinguishable, indeed, in almost every citizen, whether to be participant or spectator of the sombre pageant — the crape badge on the arm, and the countenance serious and often sad — silently witnessed that the vast city arose in oneness of heart to offer a last testimony of grief and love at the death of the liberator, the patriot, the honest man and the wise ruler....

As the time of starting approached, a tremendous crowd of spectators lined the whole of the appointed route, standing often in a dense human hedge twelve or fifteen feet deep along the curb-stones.

Another almost equally numerous body occupied the steps, gratings and inner border of the walk; while all windows were filled with men, women and children — occupancy being often sold for money, and advertised by handbills posted up outside, thousands and thousands of these lookers-on were too young to know their right hands from their left — and were doubtless brought in order that, in old age, they might say they saw the funeral procession of ABRAHAM LINCOLN. Eaves, roofs, trees, posts, were edged or tint or fructified with men or women. Along the middle of each sidewalk crept in either direction a sluggish, narrow stream of passengers, like the slow snow-broth of a half-frozen stream creeping between wide edgings of fixed ice. And

between two such triple living borders, the watchful and peremptory policemen — their active efforts seconded by the desire of all to comply with the regulations of the day — easily secured an empty roadway, perfectly clear from curbstone to curbstone.

It is 1 o'clock, and with prompt good faith the great procession gets forward. The right of the first or military division resting on Fourteenth-street, it was of course at that point that the actual movement began....

Down the whole long line of the great thoroughfare, clear to the Park, the regiments are standing at ease, facing eastward. One after another, in quick succession, they now break into column of sections, and now a bird's eye view would show the whole distance from Union Park to the City Hall, one long track of stoney gray, bordered with the heavy black masses along each sidewalk, and from end to end, transversely striated with the sections, deliberately gliding northward in common time, the swords and bayonets sparkling and glinting in the perfect sunlight. But to us on the earth, this impressive effect is invisible except in imagination; we count the soldiers and the guns; we can scarcely perfectly apprehend at one glance the twenty sections of one full

Abraham Lincoln's funeral procession passing Union Square in New York City, a lithograph by Currier and Ives.

regiment As we look, however, section after section, regiment after regiment, brigade after brigade, marches steadily by. They may be called our household troops. They are our own city regiments, and though most of their members have the pale face that tells of recent indoor life, yet many of them have once, at least, been embrowned by the Southern sun in actual service. In close lines, marching true and even, they pass and pass, until seemingly a whole army has gone by already, and still the long vista of the street is blue with the troops coming up from the South, nor can any sign of the funeral car yet be seen....

The car itself rolls slowly and gloomily before us. Its sixteen gray horses are shrouded in black, and led each by a colored groom. Immediately about it march the faithful squad of soldiers of the Veteran Reserves who have accompanied the remains from Washington. The car itself consists of a broad platform fourteen feet by eight, on which is a stage or dais where the coffin lies. Over this is a rich canopy upon four columns, having planted at the foot of each column three national flags festooned and craped. Above the four corners of the canopy are four great shadowing and waving masses of sable plumes, and at the top is a smell model of a circular temple, unwalled, open, empty. Thus — so would teach this little emblem — was the nation, the home of freedom, bereft of its representative man. Or, perhaps — thus

empty of its former tenant, is the body of the dead, the temple of life, within, the car is lined with white satin, and above the coffin hangs a large eagle, his wings outspread as if he hovered there, and carrying in his talons a wreath of laurel....

The immense number of organizations, political, benevolent, municipal and others, renders it impossible to give details in full and connectedly, of its parts. It was, moreover, a very interesting observation, that of all the high dignitaries national, State and city, only a very small number could possibly have been distinguished from their companions, except by a knowledge of their persons. Governors, Judges, officials of every grade and kind, walked quietly by, in the same ranks of twenty each, with private citizens, and the utter absence of signs of rank was even an inconvenience to the inquisitive beholder....

The numerical strength and watchful nationality of the Irish among us was once more shown by the fact that one whole division, the Fifth, consisted entirely of Irish associations — and a large division it was. Among them marched, as in the inauguration procession, a number of companies of boys, in green blouses, and hand in hand. The little fellows looked well and marched finely.

The athletic German turners, in their plain linen coats, looked strong, ready and sensible.

A long array of mechanics' protective

and provident associations constituted the latter part of the civilians' procession, a very few among them here and there, disgracefully enough, showing the influence of liquor.

The Brooklyn delegation constituted the Eighth Division, and after it, bringing up the rear, with a strong double rank of policemen before and behind, came a body of about two hundred colored men. Part of them were freedmen recently from slavery, and these bore a banner with two inscriptions: "ABRAHAM LINCOLN our Emancipator," and "To Millions of Freemen he Liberty gave." This was the only portion of the procession which was received with any demonstrations of applause. For them, a just and kindly enthusiasm overrode the strict proprieties of the occasion, and handkerchiefs waved and voices cheered all along as they marched....

The deep sobriety of this ceremony gave it a profound and weighty character, far more impressive than the festal pomp of most pageants. And the walling notes of the dirges played by the bands greatly increased this effect. The streets were in remarkably good condition. The air and sky were perfect; the arrangements for the occasion very good indeed; and in grandeur of form, as well as in ethical and political meaning, the great funeral pageant given by the City of New-York to the remains of President LINCOLN was entirely successful. ◉

THE LAST TRIBUTE OF THE METROPOLIS TO THE DEAD PRESIDENT.

APRIL 26

The partial loss of decorum which attended the overcrowding of the spectators at night in the first day's observances, was amply atoned for in the marked order and seemliness of the unparalleled funeral demonstration yesterday. As a mere pageant, the vast outpouring of the people, the superb military display, the solemn grandeur and variety thrown into the procession by the numberless national, friendly, trade and other civic societies; the grand accompaniment of music; and, above all, the subdued demeanor of the countless multitude of onlookers, made the day memorable beyond the experience of the living generation. The first thought

with those who found the occasion one favorable to quiet contemplation, must have taken form in a reflection upon the continuity of those feelings of anguish, sorrow and poignant regret (among the vast body of the people,) which had their first sudden impulsive outburst twelve days ago. Twelve days of human sorrowing — even when the affliction, or bereavement comes closely home to the household affections, represent a longer period than many would at first be ready to admit. Twelve days, voluntarily devoted to the expression of a grief which arises from a public loss, measured by comparison with all our past experience, or even with all our historical acquaintance, seem to expand almost into an age. And when these days of relaxation from secular thought and occupation are measured by the value of time in a vast industrial community, we stand almost amazed at the self-sacrifice of the people....

The tribute, then, unparalleled as it has been in its character and costliness, becomes, in this light, not the heedless offerings of prodigality, but primarily a prompt, spontaneous and deliberate sacrifice by the industrious, the frugal, the pecuniarily responsible body of the people. Viewed as such, it forms not only the grandest oblation ever made on the altar of departed worth, as embodied in Statesman, President or Monarch, but it raises the character of the whole nation far above the imputation of sordidness, of persistent and unchangeable devotion to Mammon, so falsely urged against it by outside commentators, whose pleasure and privilege is uniform destruction. And we may also say that, in the presence of the ready self-sacrifice which out present bereavement has illustrated, the theory that republics are ungrateful may at least bear revision. ◉

THE MOURNING CROWDS.
AT THE CITY HALL.

APRIL 26

Yesterday will be a day long to be remembered as one marked by the most tremendous crowds ever seen in this city, celebrated as it is for its crowds and gatherings. To say that New-York was full of people would convey a very faint idea of the actual state of our streets during the whole of yesterday. New-York is always full of people, too much so for the comfort of the actual inhabitants, but yesterday the city simply overflowed with humanity. There was not room for all the visitors who wished to see the funeral cortege doing honor to our beloved and martyred President. The streets along the route of the procession were filled in most cases with a compact mass of human beings, who were unable to see anything for themselves, nor could they give way for a still more unfortunate class, those who wanted to gain a foothold. In the streets, on the housetops and in the windows the people swarmed and struggled. Everywhere and anywhere the eager citizens endeavored to gain some position that would afford a sight of the ceremonies of the day.

The weather was warm and fine, the event was an interesting and important one, and all Manhattan was about to participate in the ceremonies of the day. Every condition in life and every age and class of society went forth. Here you could see the velvets and rustling silks of the rich, and there the humbler garments of the honest poor; now a fair and haughty damsel moved past, leaning upon the arm of one who sported the latest hat and fashion, whose bonnet is a study, and whose gloves are a surprise in their way. Again, you see the hard-handed laborer, attending the partner of his humble joys, and who shall say which has the greatest interest in the proceedings. Young boys, who will live to tell of this great day to their children when this century has passed away. Old men, who have seen the wars of 1812 and of 1861-5, and now come out into the genial sunshine to see our second WASHINGTON carried to his tomb, their aged and tear-dimmed eyes have beheld the country twice convulsed by war, and are now preparing to go to that bright abode to which our heroic LINCOLN has gone before.

Notwithstanding that the body of the President was kept on view all night, the morning's sun of yesterday saw large crowns still standing in patient waiting for a chance to see the face of the Great Emancipator. The lines were better kept than on Monday, but there were more of them, and they usually lead nowhere in particular, and anywhere in general. Down Centre-street the actual line of visitors were stationed, and in the hot sun they stood for hours together, boiling and sweating and suffering. Moving slowly and painfully this large line of jammed humanity remained in patient endeavor to reach the coveted space inside the Hall, where lay in State the remains of the President.

In Broadway several lines of people could be seen, extending for whole blocks in various directions, the heads of each devoted column converging to one common centre — the dense crowd near the entrance of the Park. These ill-fated people were doomed to certain disappointment, and in no case did these impromptu lines come to any realization of their fallacious hopes.

To endeavor to reach the TIMES Office from up Broadway, by any of the accustomed thoroughfares, was to attempt impossibility. For blocks round the City Hall the people surged and crammed themselves into the most compact of all masses. Hoping against hope this immense crowd kept its position during the entire morning. Viewed from

A Currier and Ives print depicting Abraham Lincoln's coffin, lying in state at the City Hall in New York City, April 24-25,1865.

the windows of the TIMES office the scene was one of peculiar interest. The clear space in front of the hall hedged by a large force of police and military, outside of which the tumultuous and surging crowd heaved with a mighty motion. Within all was quiet and orderly, outside all was confusion and noise. The Twenty-sixth Precinct Police picked up in the City Hall Park several ladies' veils, furs and shawls, at which Station-house they will remain for identification.

Going up town the spectator found it almost beyond the power of man to progress by the sidewalk. In the middle of the street one could get along slowly. When the military made their appearance and formed in line, the crowd, from a moving body, became a rigid and fixed object. Passage was then perfectly impossible, and it required an immense amount of labor on the part of the police to keep any more people from wedging themselves into the street. In the windows of the buildings along the street could be observed a great number of spectators — the cornices and other projections on the buildings were studded with little knots of people. Ladies ventured on the most dangerous ground, and boys hung on to the awning-posts, and clambered up telegraph and flag poles. In a number of instances windows were advertised to let, and seats were obtainable all along the route. Impromptu stands were frequently erected in front of stores and places of public resort. The most fabulous prices were asked and obtained for priveliges of this kind, forty dollars for a single window being often given by those desirous of seeing the procession from a favorable and comfortable stand-point. At each cross street huge vans and numerous carts stood loaded down with a swarming crowd of women and children, thus making a complete barrier against any progress down those streets. Down each of these streets more crowds could be seen, constant to catch a glimpse even of the most salient points in the procession. From the windows of the houses in these streets for several blocks eager heads and straining eyes gazed feverishly toward Broadway, waiting for the cortege to move. On the house-tops peered down upon the crowd below adventurous spirits who had gained their dizzy and dangerous heights for a better, though not very secure view of the spectacle spread out at their feet. Everywhere the eye ranged black and serried masses of men, women and children appalled the vision, and astonished the spectator. ✹

THE OBSEQUIES.

DEPARTURE OF THE FUNERAL TRAIN.

APRIL 26

The coffin in which was deposited the dead body of our deceased President was kept open from 12 o'clock Monday noon, until 12 o'clock Tuesday noon. From the earliest moment to the latest, every facility compatible with the narrow arrangements of the committees, was afforded the public for viewing the remains. The Guard of Honor, divided into twelve watches, did duty until the lid was fastened on the casket, relieving each other every two hours....

During these hours the pressure very sensibly diminished — the successful people had gone home disappointed, and the unsuccessful had gone provoked. Their places, in the main vacant, were filled partially by new comers, men who had slept all night, risen early, taken breakfast, and were prepared with vigor for the race set before them. These were gradually reinforced by crowds from the adjoining cities and the country round about. The Fulton and other ferries, more particularly the former, had been patronized to an incredible extent all day, but their receipts at night doubtless exceeded those of any other occasion. The boats were loaded to the very edge. Gentlemen with ladies, thinking the early morning hours the best, had gone over at 1 or 2 o'clock, only to find the streets blockaded and the passage to the Hall impossibility. Disliking to give it up so, they would hang about the place for an hour or two and then retrace their steps, meeting on their homeward route as many more, who preferred the experience of the moment to the wisdom of its predecessors....

At a little after 12 1/2 o'clock a stir was made at the west end of the Park, and there, drawn by sixteen magnificent gray horses, led each by a colored groom, came.

It was drawn slowly down the line to the east gate, then turned back and nearly up to the centre of the esplanade, leaving a line of march of, perhaps, forty feet from the precise centre, to the car. The reader will picture it thus; imagine a box twelve or fifteen feet long, by six feet wide, on wheels; the box covered with black broadcloth, which falls to the ground, entirely concealing the wheels; on this, silver lace and fringe are elaborately and effectively displayed, embroidered in the shape of shields and stars, and fringing

delicately yet richly the entire crape; above this box is reared a pavilion, American flags decorating each pillar, and it in turn covered with cloth ornamented like the other, and surmounted by a temple of liberty with a guided dome, from which floats the national colors; heavy mourning plumes from every available point, and the elegance and costliness of the arrangement are only equaled by the entire beauty and symmetry of its shape and its perfect adaptation to the service for which it was intended....

On the sturdy shoulders of the Veteran Reserves the casket was tenderly taken from the dusty catafalque, borne down the winding stairs end brought to the City Hall steps. Here a hall of a few minutes occurred, when the procession moved forward to the car, the troops presented arms, the drums rolled, the colors drooped, and the thirty thousand men in front bared every one his head. It was a memorable scene. ✹

BOOTH KILLED.

APRIL 28

WASHINGTON, April 27 — 9:20 A.M.

Maj.-Gen. John A. Dix, New-York:

J. WILKES BOOTH and HARROLD[1] were chased from the swamp in St, Mary's County, Maryland, to Garrett's farm, near Port Royal, on the Rappahannock, by Col. BAKER'S force.

The barn in which they took refuge was fired.

BOOTH, in making his escape, was shot through the head[2] and killed, lingering about three hours, and HARROLD was captured. BOOTH's body and HARROLD are now here.

EDIWN M. STANTON,
SECRETARY OF WAR. ✹

1. Booth coconspirator Davy Herold.
2. In fact, he was shot through the top of his spine.

ACCURATE ACCOUNT OF THE PURSUIT AND CAPTURE OF BOOTH.

APRIL 28

Special Dispatch to the New-York Times.
WASHINGTON, Thursday, April 27

Without recurring to the circumstances that brought together and put to work a large body of detectives in pursuit of the assassin BOOTH and his accessories in crime, I propose to state briefly and consecutively the incidents in the pursuit from the time the detachment started from this city until their arrival here this morning with the corpse of BOOTH and the body of HARROLD The following facts I obtained from Col. BAKER' and the other persons engaged with him.

From the time the Secretary of War telegraphed Col. L.C. BAKER at New-York, twelve days ago, to come here immediately and take charge of the matter of ferreting out the facts, and arresting the criminals in the assassination, up to last Sunday, but little progress was made in the right direction. All the lower counties of Maryland were scoured by a large force consisting of 1,600 cavalry and 500 detectives and citizens. On Sunday last Col. BAKER learned of a little boy in Maryland some facts which satisfied him that BOOTH and HARROLD had crossed the river about 11 o'clock A.M. and had gone into Virginia. A telegraph operator with a small body of soldiers was sent down the river to tap the wires at a given place and make certain inquiries. This party returned on Monday morning last, bringing with them a negro man whom they picked up at Swan Point, who, on being closely interrogated, disclosed that he had seen parties cross in a boat, and the description of these parties assured Col. BAKER that BOOTH and HARROLD were the men. No examination or search had yet been made by official authority in Virginia. Demand was made upon Gen. HANCOCK for a detachment of cavalry, and twenty-eight of the Sixteenth New-York were immediately sent to Col. BAKER, under command of Lieut. DOHERTY, one of this detachment being BOSTON CORBETT. The whole party were put in charge of Lieut. L.B. BAKER and Lieut.-Col. E.J. CONGOR. They were instructed to go immediately to Port Royal; that BOOTH had crossed the river, and had had about time to reach that point; that he could not ride on horseback, and must therefore have traveled slowly.

At twenty-five minutes past four o'clock on Monday afternoon, this force left the Sixth-street wharf in the steamer Ida. They were directed that when they arrived at the landing place — Belle Plain — they should shove or swim their horses to the shore, if they could not make a landing, for they must have the horses on land. That night the party went down the river four miles, but heard nothing satisfactory. They finally, at daylight, brought up below Port Royal some miles. They returned, finding no trace of the criminals till they got to Fort Royal Ferry. Lieut. BAKER rode up, found the ferryman, and made inquiries. The ferryman stoutly denied having seen any such persons as those described. Lieut. BAKER throttled him and threatened him, yet he denied any knowledge of the persons sought. By the side of the ferryman a negro was sitting. Lieut. BAKER presented a likeness of BOOTH and HARROLD. The negro upon looking at these exclaimed. "Why, Massa, them's the gentlemen we brought cross the river yesterday." The ferryman then admitted that he had brought BOOTH and HARROLD over the river in his boat. The cavalry was started off and went fourteen miles beyond Garrett's place. There they met a negro who said he saw two men sitting on Garrett's porch that afternoon. The description of one accorded with that of BOOTH. Lieut. BAKER and his party returned to GARRETT's house. GARRETT denied that the two men had been there. BAKER threatened to shoot him if he did not tell the truth. GARRETT's son thereupon came out of the house and said the two men were in the barn. The barn was at once surrounded. This was about 2 A.M. BAKER went up and rapped at the door. BOOTH asked "Who are you, friends or foes? Are you Confederates? I have got five men in here, and we can protect ourselves." Col. BAKER replied, "I have fifty men out here; you are surrounded, and you may as well come out and surrender." BOOTH answered, "I shall never give up; I'll not be taken alive." The instructions were that every means possible must be taken to arrest BOOTH alive, and BAKER, CONGER and DOHERTY held a consultation a few feet from the barn. In the meantime BOOTH was cursing HARROLD for his cowardice, charging him with a desire to meanly surrender, etc.

Col. BAKER and his party returned and held a parley with BOOTH, thus consuming about an hour and a quarter. Another consultation of officers was held, and it was determined that, in view of the probability of an attack from a tolerably large force of rebel cavalry, which they had learned were in the neighborhood, the barn should be fired, and BOOTH thus forced to come out.

CONGER gathered a lot of brush, and placed it against and under the barn, and pulled some hay out of the cracks, in the mean time holding a lighted candle in his hand. BOOTH could now see through the openings of the barn all their movements. The lighted candle was applied to the hay and brush, and directly the flames caught the hay inside the barn. BOOTH rushed towards the burning hay and tried to put out the fire. Failing in this, he ran back to the middle of the floor, gathered up his arms and stood still pondering for a moment. Whilst BOOTH was standing in this position Sergt. BOSTON CORBETT ran up to the barn door and fired. Col. BAKER, not perceiving where the shot came from, exclaimed "he has shot himself," and rushed into the barn and found BOOTH yet standing with a carbine in hand. BAKER clasped BOOTH around the arms and breast; the balance of the party had also, in the mean time, got inside. CORBETT then exclaimed "I shot him." BOOTH fell upon the floor apparently paralized. Water was sent for and the wound bathed. It was now just 3:15 o'clock. The ball had apparently passed through the neck and the spine. In a few moments BOOTH revived. He made an effort to lift his hands up before his eyes. In this he was assisted, and upon seeing them he exclaimed somewhat incoherently. "Useless! — useless! — blood! blood!! and swooned away. He revived from time to time, and expressed himself entirely satisfied with what he had done. He expired at 7:10 yesterday morning.

The body was placed in a cart and conveyed to the steamer Ide, and brought upon that vessel to the navy-yard, where the boat arrived at 5:20 o'clock this morning.

While the barn was burning, HARROLD rushed out and was grappled by Lieut. BAKER, thrown to the ground and secured.

CORBETT says he fired with the intention of wounding BOOTH in the shoulder, and did not intend to kill him.

BOOTH had in his possession a diary, in which he had noted events of each day since the assassination of Mr. LINCOLN. This diary is in possession of the War Department. He had also a Spencer carbine, a seven-shooter, a revolver, a pocket pistol and a knife. The latter is supposed to be the one with which he stabbed Mayor RATH-BURNE. His clothing was of dark blue, not Confederate gray, as has been stated.

[Sergeant Boston] CORBETT, who shot BOOTH, was born in England, and is about 33 years old. He came to this country some years since, and resided for several years in Troy, N.Y. He resided for a time in Boston, where he became a member of a Methodist Church, and took in baptism the name of "Boston." He is a man of small stature, slight form, mild countenance and quiet deportment.[2]

Surgeon-Gen. BARNES says the ball did not enter the brain. The body, when he examined it this afternoon, was not in a rapid state of decomposition, but was considerably bruised by jolting about in the cart. It is placed in charge of Col. BAKER, in the attire in which he died, with instructions not to allow any one to approach it, nor to take from it any part of apparel, or thing for exhibition hereafter; in brief, it is necessary for the satisfaction of the people that two points shall be positively ascertained; first, that the person killed in GARRAT's barn, and whose body was brought to this city, was J. WILKES BOOTH; secondly, that the said J. WILKES BOOTH was positively killed. The first point was to-day confirmed by overwhelming testimony, such as no jury would hesitate to accept. The substantial one of the second point is shown in the report of Surgeon-General BARNES, which will be officially announced.

BOOTH's leg was not broken by falling from his horse, but the bone was injured by the fall upon the stage at the theatre.

Besides the articles heretofore mentioned, BOOTH had on his person a draft for sixty pounds drawn by the Ontario Bank of Canada on a London banker. The draft was dated in October last. ⊛

1. Colonel Lafayette C. Baker (1826–1868) organized the pursuit of John Wilkes Booth.
2. Corbett was later lionized as a hero.

BOOTH'S BODY IN WASHINGTON.

APRIL 28
WASHINGTON, THURSDAY, APRIL 27

The greatest curiosity is manifested here to view the body of the murderer, BOOTH, which yet remains on the gunboat, in the stream off the Navy Yard. Thousands of persons visited the yard, today, in the hope of getting a glimpse at the murderer's remains, but none not connected with the yard were allowed to enter.

The wildest excitement has existed here all day and the greatest regrets are expressed that BOOTH, was not taken alive. The news of BOOTH's death reached the ears of his mistress while she was in a street car, which caused her to weep aloud, and drawing a photograph likeness of BOOTH from her pocket, kissed it fondly several times.

HARROLD, thus far, has evaded every effort to be drawn into a conversation by those who have necessarily come in contact with him since his capture; but outward appearances indicate that he begins to realize the position in which he is placed. There is no hope for his escape from the awful doom that certainly awaits him. His relatives and friends in this city are in the greatest distress over the disgrace that he has brought upon themselves. ⊛

JOHNSTON'S SURRENDER.

APRIL 29

The dilemma in reference to the rebel army of Gen. JOHNSTON is satisfactorily solved. The Lieutenant-General has sent official information to the War Department from North Carolina that JOHN-STON has surrendered the forces of his command on the basis agreed upon, on the 9th instant, for the surrender of the army of Gen. LEE. We need not say that this will be perfectly satisfactory to the country, as it assuredly is to the government.

The rebel forces embraced in this surrender include all that are in arms between the Southern border of Virginia and the Chattahoochee River. The Chattahoochee forms for a great distance the Western boundary of the State of Georgia; so that the territory covered, or rather uncovered, by this great surrender, embraces the States of North Carolina, South Carolina, Georgia and Florida, or a distance of over five hundred miles from east to west. The reason, we suppose, that it did not extend an indefinite distance further, is that the Chattahoochee is the western boundary of Gen. JOHNSTON's command. This shows that, unlike the Sherman negotiation of April 18, the present is strictly a military surrender, and that neither JEFF. DAVIS, BRECKINRIDGE, nor any of the civil rebel leaders had anything to do with it. The negotiation of the 18th, of which DAVIS was the dictator, covered the entire Confederate territory and secured his own safety.

The region between the Chattahoochee and the Mississippi includes the States of Alabama and Mississippi. Every important position in both these States is in our hands, and the only rebel troops in them are the few thousand fugitives who escaped from Mobile recently on its surrender, and who have probably been chased into chaos before this time by the cavalry of Gen. WILSON.

Thus, it can now be said that peace reigns over the entire South — if we except the single State of Texas. The great armies of the rebels are now all broken up, and every man of them is sworn to keep the peace. All the rebel arms, artillery, and munitions of war are in our keeping. Under these circumstances, there will be little difficulty in maintaining order and the national authority all over the South.

Secretary STANTON's important order, issued on the 13th inst., providing for the reduction of the army, the curtailment of expenses, and the opening up of trade and commerce, can now very soon take actual effect. ⊛

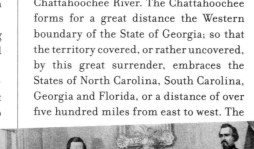

A Currier and Ives depiction of Confederate General Joseph Johnston, seated left, surrendering to General William Sherman, seated right.

RETURN OF GENERAL GRANT TO WASHINGTON.

APRIL 30

SPECIAL DISPATCH TO THE NEW-YORK TIMES.
WASHINGTON, SATURDAY, APRIL 29

Gen. GRANT arrived here, to-day, direct from SHERMAN's headquarters. From one who was present when Gen. GRANT arrived there, we learn that the latter immediately on his arrival, sent a message to JOHNSTON that the Sherman-Johnston agreement had been disapproved, and that hostilities would recommence within forty-eight hours from the time the messenger passed within the rebel picket line. On the same day SHERMAN made a demand upon JOHNSTON to surrender. JOHNSTON requested a further armistice, and an interview, which was appointed for noon of the 26th. Gen. SHERMAN was at the appointed rendezvous at the time named, and JOHNSTON arrived in about an hour after, he having been detained by some accident. After a short conference, it was agreed that JOHNSTON should surrender on terms substantially the same as those agreed upon by Gen. LEE, when he surrendered to Gen. GRANT. From the best information at that time obtainable, Gen. JOHNSTON's command embraced nearly thirty thousand troops. ✸

A GRAND REVIEW OF OUR ARMIES — PROPOSITION FOR A CROWNING HONOR BY THE NATION TO OUR TRIUMPHANT SOLDIERS

MAY 4

We cannot help hoping that before SHERMAN'S and MEADE'S armies are broken up, arrangements will be made for a great military display, at which the larger portion at least of both may be present, and at which an opportunity would be afforded to the public to express in some striking and worthy manner the general sense of our obligations to these great and famous corps.

This war has been singularly wanting in "pomp and pride and circumstance." Most of the great military movements — the battles, sieges and marches, have taken place in a sparsely settled, forest-covered, and semi-barbarous country. The service has been one of unusual hardship too, and it has never, or only rarely been lighted up, by those seasons of repose in great cities, or thickly settled or fertile districts, which makes holiday work of much of the campaigning in European countries. Our men have only known war in its hardest, sternest and most repulsive aspect. They have toiled through swamps, and forests, and pine barrens, forded rivers, trudged thousands of miles over muddy roads, fought day after day, and filled every lonely thicket with their dead, without other actual lookers on than contrabands or poor whites; and when they have marched through a city, it has been between closed blinds, and under the scowling looks of the remnant of the population.... ✸

JEFF. DAVIS THE ASSASSIN — REWARD FOR HIS CAPTURE.

MAY 4

President JOHNSON, as will be seen, has issued a proclamation announcing that, as appears from evidence in the Bureau of Military Justice, the atrocious murder of the late President, and the attempted assassination of the Secretary of State, were incited, concerted and procured by and between Jefferson Davis, late of Richmond, Jacob Thompson, Clement C. Clay, Beverly Tucker, Geo. N. Sanders, W.C. Cleary and other rebels and traitors harbored in Canada; therefore, to the end that justice may be done, the following rewards are offered and promised for the arrest of said persons, or either of them, within the limits of the United States, so that they can be brought to trial, to wit: For the arrest of Jefferson Davis, one hundred thousand dollars; for the arrest of Clay, Thompson, Sanders and Tucker, twenty-five thousand dollars each; and for the arrest of Cleary, ten thousand dollars. The Provost-Marshal-General of the United States is directed to cause a description of said persons to be published, with the notice of the above rewards.

Thus ignominiously passes out of history, and thus passes into history, the rebel President, who for the last four years has been patronized and encouraged by half the Kings of Europe, and nearly the whole of its aristocracy. His last act was worthy of himself and of his whole career.

JEFFERSON DAVIS is still on our soil, and at last accounts was in full flight and closely pursued through the Carolinas and Georgia. He is probably the only one of the conspirators mentioned who is in the South, though the Canadian organ of the rebels lately said JACOB THOMPSON was in Virginia, and that CLEARY also might be there; while we know that SANDERS was close to our Northern lines a few days ago. The precise whereabouts of the others is not positively known. ✸

THE ARREST OF JEFF. DAVIS.

MAY 15

The arrest of DAVIS, while it gratifies the sentiment of justice in every loyal heart, imposes new duties and responsibilities upon the government. He has been guilty of the highest crime known to the laws of any nation, one which involves the accumulated guilt of many murders, and upon

A cartoon lampooning Confederate President Jefferson Davis's alleged attempt to escape Union troops in Georgia by wearing women's clothes.

THE BURIAL.

PRESIDENT LINCOLN AGAIN AT HIS WESTERN HOME.

THE MORTAL, FOUR YEARS ABSENT, RETURNS IMMORTAL.

MAY 5

SPRINGFIELD, ILL., THURSDAY, MAY 4

Never before was there so large a military and civic display in Springfield. There were immense crowds of people in the immediate vicinity of the Capitol to see the procession as it passed, and the people for several miles occupied the sidewalks....

Thousands of persons were assembled at the cemetery before the arrival of the procession, occupying the succession of green hills. The scene was one of solemnly intense interest. The landscape was beautiful in the light of an unclouded sun.

The religious exercises were commenced by the singing of a dirge. Then followed the reading of appropriate portions of the Scriptures and a prayer. After a hymn by the choir, Rev. Mr. HUBBARD read the last inaugural of President LINCOLN. Next a dirge was sung by the choir, when Bishop [Matthew] SIMPSON delivered the funeral oration. It was in the highest degree eloquent, and the patriotic portions of it was applauded. Then followed another hymn, when benediction was pronounced by Rev. Dr. [Phineas] GURLEY. The procession then returned to the city.

We have followed the remains of President LINCOLN from Washington, the scene of his assassination, to Springfield, his former home, and now to be his final resting-place. He had been absent from this city ever since he left it in February, 1861, for the national Capital, to be inaugurated as President of the United States. We have seen him lying in state in the executive mansion, where the obsequies were attended by numerous mourners, some of them clothed with the highest public honors and responsibilities which our republican institutions can bestow, and by the diplomatic representatives of foreign governments. We have followed the remains from Washington through Baltimore, Harrisburgh, Philadelphia, New-York, Albany, Buffalo, Cleveland, Columbus, Indianapolis and Chicago to Springfield, a distance in circuit of 1,500 or 1,800 miles. On the route millions of people have appeared to manifest by every means of which they are capable, their deep sense of the public loss, and their appreciation of the many virtues which adorned the life of ABRAHAM LINCOLN. All classes, without distinction of politics or creeds, spontaneously united in the posthumous honors. All hearts seemed to beat as one at the bereavement, and, now funeral processions are ended, our mournful duty of escorting the mortal remains of ABRAHAM LINCOLN hither is performed. We have seen them deposited in the tomb. The bereaved friends, with subdued and grief-stricken hearts, have taken their adieu and turn their faces homeward, ever to remember the affecting and impressive scenes which they have witnessed. The injunction, so often repeated on the way, "Bear him gently to his rest," has been obeyed, and the great heart of the nation throbs heavily at the portals of the tomb. ✸

---

which the laws of every nation impose the most awful penalties which it is possible for human laws to pronounce. It is true, he has not been alone in his crime. He has but shared the treason of thousands of others, and made himself the representative and the executor of their treasonable designs. But he stands before the world as the foremost figure in this great rebellion. He has wielded all its power and put in execution all its decrees. It was the weight of his example, far more than all other influences, which banded the rebel States so long together in their determined hostility against the Government of the United States. It has been his voice, his will, his ability, his determination, to overthrow that government, which has rallied to the rebel standard the whole strength of the Southern States, and plunged this whole country into the dreadful carnage of the last four years.

DAVIS will unquestionably be tried for treason, and that trial must be in the civil courts and in the presence of the public. He is charged with complicity in the assassination of President LINCOLN, and may, if the government so decide, be tried by court-martial for that offence. It is probable, however, that he will be tried for the greater crime first; and of his conviction there can be no doubt. There is no possible definition of the crime of treason which can relieve him from its guilt. He has "levied war" — openly, ostentatiously, avowedly — "against the United States." The whole world has been cognizant of his treason, and more than half a million of the bravest and noblest of the land, sleep in their graves as the consequence of his crime. If that crime should not be punished, what crime should? In the strong, direct phrase of President JOHNSON, if treason such as his may go unwhipt of justice, why should laws longer remain on the statute book to punish the murderer or the robber?

We shall have vehement appeals from foreign nations on behalf of DAVIS. His anticipated punishment is denounced already as barbarous and blood-thirsty. Foreign journalists affect to be profoundly impressed by the courage and persistency which he has evinced, and deplore the "madness" which may prompt our government to overlook these qualities and regard him only as a traitor and a rebel. Fortunately, we are under no necessity of paying any heed to their remonstrances, and their course hitherto has rendered it impossible to attach any moral weight to their advice. They have given their support to the rebellion, not because they admired the courage of its leaders or approved the principles on which it rested, but because it threatened to divide and destroy the power of this republic. It is natural, now that the rebellion has failed, that they should try to screen the leaders who have sacrificed everything on their behalf.

Our latest advices show that the behaviour of DAVIS at the moment of his arrest was well calculated to strip him of whatever romance anybody may have been inclined to surround him with. A great leader, —the hero of a grand and noble revolution, would scarcely try to evade the consequences of defeat by disguising himself in his wife's dress, nor would he claim immunity because he had surrounded himself with the women and children of his family. DAVIS proves to have been a very paltry character after all. ✸

REVIEW OF THE ARMIES.

PROPITIOUS WEATHER AND A SPLENDID SPECTACLE.

NEARLY A HUNDRED THOUSAND VETERANS IN THE LINES.

MAY 24

SPECIAL DISPATCH TO THE NEW-YORK TIMES.
WASHINGTON, TUESDAY, MAY 23

The Army of the Potomac has passed in review. The first day's pageant is over, and to the correspondent falls the duty of depicting a scene almost devoid of incident, save in its grand aspiration. Every circumstance has combined to make it a complete success. The weather has been magnificent; the air, delightfully tempered by the rains of the past week, is cool and fragrant, and dust is for the time subdued.

Washington has been filled as it never was filled before; the hotel-keepers assert that the pressure upon their resources never was so great, and thousands of people have been nightly turned away to seek a place of rest where best they might. The train which left New-York on Monday evening consisted of twenty-one overcrowded cars, and only reached Washington at ten o'clock this morning, an hour after the grand column had begun to move. Still are the crowds pouring in, particularly from the West, with the friends and admirers of SHERMAN's great armies, which pass in review to-morrow.

Though the city is so crowded, it is yet gay and jovial with the good feeling that prevails, for the occasion is one of such grand import and true rejoicing, that small vexations sink out of sight. With many it is the greatest epoch of their lives; with the soldier it is the last act in the drama; with the nation it is the triumphant exhibition of the resources and valor which have saved it from disruption and placed it first upon earth.

So the scene of to-day (and that of to-morrow) will never be forgotten, and he who is privileged to be a witness will mark it as a white day in the calendar, from which to gather hope and courage for the future.

As you are already informed, the troops participating in this most interesting pageant that has ever been known in the history of the country, left their camps yesterday and marched to positions convenient to the city. The Ninth Corps, which was encamped near Alexandria, left their camp at an early hour yesterday morning, and marched through Alexandria, along the turnpike, thence to Long Bridge, across the bridge, and through Maryland-avenue to a field about one and a half miles east of the Capitol, where they encamped for the night....

The President arrives in his carriage. Directly after, however, almost at the same moment, Gen. GRANT and Staff walk briskly from their headquarters and assume their designated positions. Gen. MEADE and Staff having passed, they now return dismounted, and soon the sharply-defined head of the Commander of the Army of the Potomac adds another to the group of distinguished persons, on whom the eyes, the opera-glasses, and even the photographers' lenses are resting. And now begins the review proper, the re-

Grand review of the Army of the Potomac in Washington, D.C.

nowned Cavalry Corps, first mobilized by HOOKER, first successfully fought by PLEASONTON, and which has gained such great renown under SHERIDAN, and now led by MERRITT, begins to pass by in platoons of sixteen horsemen each, with sabres drawn. The drum corps opposite the reviewing-officer peals out a salute, and the march commences.

Just here is the most exciting little incident of the day. CUSTER leads his famous division around the corner of Fifteenth-street when some fair hand throws out a beautiful wreath; the General catches it upon his arm, but the movement so frightens the magnificent stallion which the General rides, that he becomes unmanagable and dashes up the avenue at a frightful speed; but CUSTER is too good a horseman to be so easily unseated; minus hat and sabre, holding on to the wreath with one hand, he brings his steed down with the other, and curbing him severely, brings him back to his good behavior and in his place at the head of the division, and horse and rider, with superb spirit, have afforded the spectators the finest equestrian exhibition of the day....

The whole army, numbering in the aggregate over eighty thousand men, thus passed a given point in just five hours and a half, marching by company front of twenty miles. This is a very remarkable feat.

During the entire march along Pennsylvania-avenue no unpleasant incident occurred to mar the general harmony. The street was kept entirely clear of pedestrians not belonging to the army, and by this careful management no opportunity for accident or disorderly proceedings occurred. All the liquor establishments were closed by order yesterday, and will remain so until Thursday morning.

The day has been memorable and enjoyable beyond expectation or precedent. ⊛

REVIEW OF THE ARMIES.
THE SECOND AND LAST DAY OF THE GREAT PAGEANT.

—

WHOLE-SOULED WELCOME TO THE GLORIOUS VETERANS OF THE WEST.

MAY 25
SPECIAL DISPATCHES TO THE NEW-YORK TIMES.
WASHINGTON, WEDNESDAY, MAY 24 — 8 P.M.

The great display is over. SHERMAN's two armies — the most superb material over molded into soldiers — has passed in review through the streets of the capital, of which they have heard so much, and toward the safety of which they have done so much, and yet had never seen.

The men who marched from the Ohio to the Tennessee under BUELL, only to march back again; who first penetrated down into Alabama under the daring and nervous MITCHELL; who fought at Perrysville under MCCOOK, and checked the advancing tide of the rebellion to again send it reeling southward, at Stone River, under the chivalrous ROSECKANS; who toiled over the rugged passes of the Cumberland Mountains and seized the great natural fortress of Chattanooga; who held the left with a tenacity that saved them from defeat at Chickamauga, under the ever-victorious THOMAS; who stormed Lookout Mountain, and fought above the clouds with HOOKER; who cut their way from Chattanooga to Atlanta, and from Atlanta to the sea; who swept the Carolinas as with a besom of destruction, and who gave the finishing blow to the great rebellion, in following the lead of SHERMAN, and HOWARD, and SLOCUM — these were the men who received to-day the enthusiastic plaudits of a hundred thousand spectators.

The interest of to-day has exceeded that of yesterday. The Army of the Potomac is our old acquaintance, but the Armies of Georgia and Tennessee few people here had ever seen. The most eager interest was therefore exhibited to view the Veterans of the West, whose marches can only be counted by thousands of miles.

The weather was even more propitious than yesterday, the temperature being several degrees cooler, and the streets comparatively free from dust. The army of spectators was, therefore, greater, especially in the vicinity of the stands, to which tickets were issued adlibitum.... ⊛

"What Is To Be Done With the Negro?"

THE ERA OF RECONSTRUCTION 1865–1877

Appomattox marked an ending, but also a beginning. What had been resolved by the war was clear: the United States was whole again — the Union was inviolate, and slavery was dead. What remained unclear, however, were the relationship of the former Confederate States to the Union they had tried to dissolve, and — most important — the new legal status of the former slaves. That they would not be slaves was manifest, but what they would be remained uncertain. Many of those who abhorred slavery objected nearly as much to the notion that the former slaves should now be their fellow citizens with equal rights under the law. Most simply assumed that the freed slaves would stay in the South, continue to labor on the plantations, and remain socially subordinate to whites, the principal difference being that they would now be paid something for their labor and could no longer be sold. The former chattels themselves had other ideas. They saw what freedom was for whites, and aspired to the same freedom for themselves: the right to own land, the right to go where they pleased, and the right to the full protection of the law. Would they be citizens? Serve on juries? Vote? Lincoln had deliberately postponed making any final decisions about these crucial questions for fear of fracturing his political coalition, though just three days before his assassination he became the first President to propose voting rights for at least some African-Americans. Once the shooting stopped, however, those decisions could be postponed no longer. As Henry Ward Beecher put it in a letter to The Times: "What is to be done with the Negro?"

The question was even more problematical after Lincoln's death

Detail from J.L. Giles' allegorical 1867 lithograph, *Reconstruction*, promoting sectional reconciliation between Northern and Southern whites, but pointedly excluding African-Americans.

put Andrew Johnson in the White House, for Johnson, after all, was a Southern Democrat. A self-made man (his critics called him the "Tennessee tailor"), he had opposed slavery mainly because it gave advantages to the Southern aristocrats, and unlike Lincoln, he had little empathy for the slaves themselves. He was perfectly willing for their new status to be defined by those who had supervised them in the years before the war. This was unacceptable to the Republican progressives in Congress — the so-called Radicals — who wanted to enact new laws, even Constitutional amendments if necessary, to protect the newly emancipated blacks in their freedom, and ensure compliance by white Southerners. Johnson did not think any of that was necessary, and the dispute split the Republican Party. Henry Raymond sided with the new President. He argued that the freed blacks could take care of themselves without assistance or protection — even (in his words) "the primitive African type." He concluded that the effort by the Radicals to add Constitutional amendments to ensure citizenship and civil rights for the freedmen was unnecessary and dangerous.

In the last year of the war, Congress had established a Freedmen's Bureau with oversight responsibility to help smooth the slaves' transition to freedom. Major General Oliver O. Howard, who had commanded the Army of the Tennessee and was a devout Christian, became its commissioner. That initial legislation had established the agency for one year, but when Congress renewed it for another year in February 1866, Johnson vetoed the bill, declaring that the bureau was no longer necessary since "the ordinary course of judicial proceedings" was sufficient to the task. The Radicals saw that relying on existing processes would put all questions regarding the status of the freedmen in the care of Southern courts, a prospect they found appalling.

Raymond and The Times supported Johnson's veto. Raymond insisted it "implies no essential difference of opinion between the Executive and the majority in congress in the primary object of the bill." But in that he was wrong, for there was an "essential difference of opinion" between the White House and Congress. Radicals in Congress believed the freedmen were under threat from their former masters, while Johnson denied that "the position of the freedmen is one so exposed as has been represented."

By now Raymond was not only the owner and editor of The New York Times, but also a Republican member of Congress. He voted with the majority in March 1866 to pass a Civil Rights Bill, the first in American history, but even after Johnson vetoed that, too, Raymond continued to defend the President, insisting that Johnson's opposition derived from his fear of "undermining the independence of the judiciary." This time, however, Johnson's veto angered even moderate Republicans, and Congress passed the Civil Rights Bill over Johnson's veto, at the same time passing the Freedmen's Bureau Bill as well. Raymond continued to stick by the President, backing Johnson's unsuccessful effort to create a separate party of "National Unionists" in competition with the Republicans, in consequence of which Raymond lost his position as chairman of the Republican Party. Johnson rewarded Raymond's loyalty by naming him ambassador to Austria, though the Republican Senate refused to confirm him.

During 1866, Johnson's laissez-faire policy toward the South was discredited in the public mind by a terror program directed at the freedmen by organizations like the Ku Klux Klan. Some Southern states passed laws making it illegal for freedmen to own land; others decreed that it was unlawful for them not to be employed by a white man. These circumstances inflamed Northern voters and fueled a Republican triumph in the 1866 elections that gave the Radicals a veto-proof majority. When this new majority took office in March 1867, it instituted a new Reconstruction program that re-established a military occupation of the South and enacted programs to protect the civil rights of the freedmen. The Radicals passed the Fourteenth (black citizenship) and Fifteenth (black suffrage) Amendments to the Constitution, and required their ratification by Southern states as a condition of re-admission. They passed the Tenure of Office Act, designed to force Johnson to keep the Cabinet he had inherited, and when the President intentionally violated it to test its constitutionality, they impeached him.

By 1870 there was a new editor at The Times. Henry Raymond died in 1869 at the age of 49, and his erstwhile business partner, George F. Jones, took over editorial management. Jones proved to be something of a crusader, authorizing a series of articles exposing the power and influence of the political organization in New York run by William Marcy Tweed, known as the Tweed Ring, and others that revealed the horror of Klan violence in the South. It reported the findings of Congressional investigators who went to South Carolina to look into Klan activities, and covered Benjamin Butler's attempt to make Klan-like terrorism illegal. It covered the so-called Colfax Riot in Louisiana in April 1873, when members of "The White League," a Klan-like paramilitary group, attacked an element of Louisiana's nearly all-black state militia, killing more than a hundred men, most of them burned alive in the town courthouse. ☞

In spite of such articles, however, the Northern public was growing weary of endless tales of brutality against former slaves. The Fifteenth Amendment (ratified on February 3, 1870) completed the Constitutional changes wrought by the Civil War. Blacks had been given their freedom, citizenship, and the ballot. Most Northerners seemed to think that it was now up to them to make a go of it. How long, after all, could the North be expected to watch over them? A Union veteran who had come South to settle after the war (a carpetbagger in the local parlance) wrote a memoir/novel in 1879 called *A Fool's Errand*. In it, he suggested that the attitude of most Northerners toward the black population of the South was "root hog, or die." The Times did not formally adopt this view, but the declining number of stories of both official and clandestine abuse testified to the Northern public's slipping interest in the issue.

The period of "Radical Reconstruction" lasted only a few years. Tennessee was readmitted in 1867, and other states followed one by one. In 1876, Jones and The Times backed the Republican candidate, Rutherford B. Hayes, against New York's governor, Democrat Samuel Tilden. Initial returns appeared to make Tilden the winner, and in a foreshadowing of the famous "DEWEY DEFEATS TRUMAN" headline, Jones telegraphed Hayes the news that he had been beaten. But then, in a prolonged and bitter postelection fight, a deal was struck in which conservatives agreed to award all the electoral votes from the still-occupied Southern states of South Carolina, Louisiana, and Florida, plus one vote from Oregon, to Hayes if he pledged to remove all military forces from the South. This return to "home rule" doomed the freedmen for several generations, because each "redeemed" Southern state at once passed laws restricting the rights of blacks and limiting their opportunities. The result was an era of segregation and Jim Crow laws that lasted through the rest of the 19th and into the 20th century.

It was an ignoble legacy for so costly and heroic a struggle.

THE ELEVATION OF THE FREEDMEN — AN INDISPENSABLE CONDITION.

SEPTEMBER 2, 1865

Our South Carolina correspondent, after a constant and close observation of over two years, testified with great emphasis to the capacity of the freedmen to make rapid improvement physically and morally, under friendly and wise management. If this is true of South Carolina negroes, it established the fact in respect to all those of the rest of the South; for the slaves of South Carolina remained the nearest of any to the primitive African type. Their ancestors immediately after being landed at Charleston have settled upon the large cotton and rice plantations of the State, and the succeeding generations have lived almost entirely secluded from contact with white men, excepting overseers, and consequently they have made very little advance. The experiment with the freedmen upon the Carolina coast we have always regarded as the crucial test.' What can be made of the African race there, can surely be made of them anywhere in the South.

This question of the capacity of the freedmen to become honest, industrious, and self-supporting, without any external constraint, is a question of immense import in the renovation of the South. The chief justification of Southern Slavery has always been the natural inability of the African to enjoy freedom without becoming a curse to himself and to all about him. It was claimed that his mental and moral capacities were too small, and his animal propensities to sloth and self-indulgence too stubborn, for him to be kept at work and in order by any incentive short of physical compulsion. Had that been actually the fact, slavery in some form, milder than that which existed, might perhaps have been as justifiable as the laws against vagrancy and the work-house system in any civilized country. Every society has a natural right to protect itself from vagabondism and disorder, whether coming from imbecility or wickedness. But that plea for the necessity of slavery has been brought to naught by the general good conduct of the freedmen. What can be made of these people does not yet fully appear; but it is settled beyond all controversy that at least it does not require a system of chattel slavery to control thorn and make them useful. It is no longer a question whether the liberty of the black race is a social necessity for the South. That question has been reduced to the milder shape — whether a repressive and regulative system of any kind is necessary for them, apart from the general laws to which all people must be subject.

A Reconstruction-era cartoon comments on white Southern threats to freed African-Americans.

This question has been, and still is, a more doubtful and serious one than some of the familiar friends of the race imagine. Whether the races of Africa are naturally inferior to the races of Europe or not, the fact is indisputable that the actual development of the African race in our Southern States at the present time, is very far below that of the white man. Can it be brought up to that of the white man, or near enough to make it practicable to leave the race subject to no laws or regulations not binding upon the whites? If this is possible, how long will it take to accomplish it? Can it be realized in this generation? Can it be attained from

FROM MISSISSIPPI.

PROCLAMATION BY GOV. SHARKEY — THE RIGHTS OF FREEDMEN.

OCTOBER 1, 1865

JACKSON, MISS., FRIDAY, SEPT. 29

Gov. [William L.] SHARKEY[1] to-day issued a proclamation accepting the proposition of Col. [Samuel] THOMAS, Assistant Commissioner of the Freedmans' Bureau of Mississippi, transferring the right of trying all cases in which the rights of freedmen are involved, from the Freedmens' Bureau to the civil authority, upon condition that the Provisional Government of that State will take for their mode of procedure the laws now in force, except so far as these laws make distinction on account of color. The negroes are also to be protected in person and property. They can be sued and are to have the right to sue. They are also to be competent witnesses according to the laws of evidence.

The News, in an editorial, denounces the act as an encroachment upon the rights of the whites, and says it will be repudiated by the people. ⊛

1. William L. Sharkey (1798–1873) was that rare thing, a Mississippi Unionist. President Johnson appointed him provisional governor in 1865, though he was superseded by Benjamin Humphreys after elections in October.

A racist poster condemning the Freedmen's Bureau and African-American suffrage.

the adult portion of this generation, or only years hence from those who are now the rising generation? These are important questions, as affecting the civil and social reorganization of the South, which cannot be long delayed....

One thing is certain: the freedmen will never be elevated by the mere laws of political economy. The operation of human selfishness will have no more effect in advancing the freedmen of the South than they had in knocking off his bonds. If the stronger race has no principle in its treatment of the weaker race but that supplied by self-interest, the weaker will still remain in ignorance and degradation. The promotion of their good must be the primary object in any system designed for them. The leading question must be, not how to get the most work from them, but how to improve them mentally and morally. We may not be able to say just when the ends proposed will be completely realized, but it is a great point gained that the capacity of the race for improvement has already been so clearly demonstrated. ⊛

1. During the war, runaway slaves (contrabands) had settled in a series of colonies on the coastal islands off South Carolina and Georgia. They raised their own crops on small farms and were virtually self-sufficient, proving that the slaves could, in fact, manage their own affairs and raise a cash crop. After the war, however, all the land on which they had settled was returned to its white owners.

THE RESTORATION PROBLEM.

SPECIAL DISPATCH TO THE NEW-YORK TIMES.
MONTGOMERY, ALA., FRIDAY, SEPT. 29

The convention to-day passed an ordinance by a vote of 59 to 16, which practically abolishes the right of admission of negro testimony in courts of justice in

OCTOBER 1, 1865

all difficulties arising between negroes themselves, or between whites and negroes. This is to continue until the adjournment of the next Legislature, giving that body the privilege of making the organic law of Alabama. ⊛

THE TWO RACES IN THE SOUTH.

OCTOBER 5, 1865

The future happiness of the Southern negroes depends so largely upon their being able to maintain amicable and profitable relations with those who formerly stood in the relationship of masters to them, and who yet are, and for a long time will remain, the principal holders of real estate and owners of capital, that we have frequently taken occasion to deprecate every scheme which had a tendency to stir up animosities of race or collisions of interest. The Southern whites will inevitably control the labor and the fortunes of the blacks for many years to come, and in all the daily affairs of life, will exercise an immediate and controlling power. The blacks will constitute a great population of subordinate laborers, making continual advances in well-being and intelligence, or else will retrograde into a condition worse in many respects than the bondage from which they have been emancipated. Which of these fortunes is in store for the Southern negro, depends more upon the whites of the South than upon anything that can be said or done in the North.

We have chronicled in our columns many instances in which the most desirable relations, in every respect, have been established between bodies of freedmen and their former masters. One of our correspondents in West Tennessee mentions a case which we are glad to believe is not an isolated one in that section of country, but which offers an example worthy of being widely followed:

"Col. [William E.] TRAVIS was a prominent politician and lawyer. He had a fine farm, with thirty slaves. When the rebellion commenced, he raised a regiment, and served till the close of the war. ☞

He is a ruined man, excepting his lands. With a trunk-full of rights, in the shape of $65,000 worth of Confederate bonds, he says he is satisfied for the balance of his days. His slaves all stayed at home but two young men, who entered our army. On his return (he surrendered with JOHNSTON) he called the negroes together and told them they were all free; that they became so as the result of the defeat of the South; that they were as free as himself; that as they had stayed at home and helped to take care of his family, he proposed to do the best he could by them, if they wished to stay. This year they were all poor together, and all would share alike. Next year he proposed to rent his farm to them on shares.

This plan the Colonel is carrying out in good faith. The first step he took shows his knowledge of the difference under the slave system. The negroes lived in quarters, near the "big house," and under the master's eye. Col. TRAVIS says this must be discontinued. He has seven hundred acres in his home farm. About six families of negroes live in quarters. He is building cabins at convenient points on the place, and allotting them to the family he thinks can conveniently cultivate the unit of land to which he is contiguous. He is doing this on the principle that the freed people must be isolated and made self-reliant. He lets his land on shares. One-third of the crop is rent for land, one-third for tools, subsistence, stock and forage, and one-third for labor. If the laborer furnished himself, and the tools, &c., he gets two-thirds. If part of these necessaries, one-half. Some of Col. TRAVIS' people have stock of their own, and between the landlord and tenant, enough will be had to cultivate the farm effectually. Col. TRAVIS is confident that, so far as he is concerned, he will get a good return from his land without so much labor as formerly; he believes the people will do well for themselves, for he says they have always been faithful to him." ⊛

THE GULF FREEDMEN.

NOVEMBER 10, 1865

There is a curious lot of items about the Southern negroes in the New-Orleans dispatches of this morning:

"Gen. [Joseph S.] FULLERTON has issued a circular reminding the freedmen that the time is approaching to make contracts for labor for another year.[1]

"The planters have adopted a plan to get the freedmen to pick their cotton, and it is meeting with success. When the day's work is done, the cotton picked by each freedman is measured, and he is paid according to the amount of cotton he has picked.

"The cotton-fields of Texas continue unpicked, the freedmen refusing to work.

"The total vote of the city is two-thirds of that before the war. The negroes had nine polls open in this city, and two or three in the Platte District, opposite the city.

"Gov. HUMPHREYS,[2] of Mississippi, calls upon the people of that State to organize companies to aid the civil authorities in maintaining law and order, and cautions them against oppressing the negroes in any way."

The first of these five items is easily comprehended, and seems to indicate that the strange plan of operations mentioned in the second is likely to be changed for something better. We fancy that the circumstance of negro idleness in Texas is not by any means applicable to the entire race in that State. The negroes, we suppose, were playing at voting in the Louisiana election, for they have not been admitted to the franchise there. The last item, giving the advice offered to the people of Mississippi by the Governor as to their treatment of the negroes, is very good; but we should prefer to hear that the Legislature of that State had made suitable legal provision for the securing to them of justice. ⊛

1. Joseph S. Fullerton (1834–1907), a conservative, replaced the antislavery Thomas W. Conway as assistant commissioner of the Freedmen's Bureau for South Carolina and Louisiana in October 1865.
2. Benjamin Grubb Humphreys (1808–1882) replaced William Sharkey as governor of Mississippi on October 16, 1865.

THE DANGER TO THE SOUTH.

NOVEMBER 12, 1865

It is a matter of congratulation to this journal that the two most thorough and scientific works on the economics of slavery, appeared first in its columns. We refer to the letters of Mr. [William G.] SEWELL on "Emancipation in the West Indies," and of Mr. [Frederick Law] OLMSTED on the "Cotton and Seaboard States."[1] In the former, it will be remembered that Mr. SEWELL showed conclusively that the so-called "failure of Jamaica emancipation" was merely a diminished production, resulting not from the idleness of the negro, but from the entanglements of the estates, and especially from the prejudices and rancor of the planters against the freed blacks, showing itself especially in efforts to continue a kind of serfdom, and to cheat the negroes of their wages or to under pay them. The result was, that a great gulf was created between capital and labor, which has not, to this day, been fairly bridged over in Jamaica. The freedmen abandoned their old masters' estates in distrust and with hostility, and squatted on unoccupied lands, raising enough for their own wants, but letting the large estates go to ruin, and causing the production of sugar, which depends much on a combination of labor and capital, very largely to fall off.

There is some reason to fear a similar result in parts of our cotton States. The planters are naturally bitter and hostile both toward "Yankees and niggers." They dislike the sight of a freed slave; they are galled at the idea of his being at liberty to choose his work and his employer; they hate his new airs of independence; and often with the ill-blood which unsuccessful war leaves behind, they wreak their chagrin at defeat on the inoffensive freedman.

The freedmen are naturally distrustful of their ancient masters; in some cases they believe (much as Anglo-Saxons would in their places) that freedom, after such a long period of forced labor, means idleness; others find that the masters only pay them one-half or one-quarter of what they used to earn as hired slaves for these very masters. They have no means of redress; they cannot sue or try to relieve the value of their labor, and they emigrate or refuse to work on the plantations. The effect is gradually to make a Jamaica gap between capital and labor, which will be most disastrous for the future interests of the South. For it is all very well to talk of free white labor flowing in and filling the space left by black, yet every Southern man knows that for a good cotton crop the next four years, an old field hand, accustomed to a cotton plantation, is worth far more to him than any white laborer that could be introduced. He understands the negro, the negro knows him and his ways, is used to the climate and the business, and will work for lower wages than a white foreigner. The immigration of a large population is a slow matter, while the South have at hand an excellent hard-working laboring class, who will do well if they are only treated well. To hope to get rid of four millions of a tough race who have furnished two hundred thousand fighting men for the war, and to banish them, is a delusion.[2] The whole remaining power of the South could not accomplish it. And if it could it would be a disaster to the Cotton States, to which the banishment of the Moors from Spain, or the Huguenots from France, would only be a feeble parallel.

Why should the South desire it? Why not take the rational and wise course — the one most advantageous for their own interests, and accept calmly emancipation with all its consequences? The freedmen could now, by firmness and justice, be won over to be a most profitable agricultural class. Let each employer treat them precisely as a Northerner would treat his laborers, with justice and nothing more; protecting them by law, admitting their

testimony, paying them the market rate of wages, and requiring a full day's work — being prompt, exact and fair with them.

The Southern planters who have tried this humane and just method are now making large profits, as we know — heavier than under slavery. If the other plan be followed — if the country be "made too hot "for the freedmen, if the planters expect work without fair pay, if they will personally abuse the negroes and suffer abuses to be practiced, if they refuse to allow the negro the ordinary rights of a citizen of the United States — they are laying up for themselves a harvest of retribution, in the disturbance of labor, internal quarrels, and the distrust and dislike of the civilized world, which it would be much better for them to avoid, We understand perfectly the influences against which they have to contend; but we are quite sure they will learn ere long to appreciate the friendly motive of those who urge them to follow the dictates of wisdom and justice rather than those of passion and resentment. ✸

---

1. William G. Sewall (1829–1862) wrote *The Ordeal of Free Labor in the British West Indies* (1861), and Frederick Law Olmsted (1822–1903), who was the former head of the Sanitary Commission and the designer of New York's Central Park, among other sites, wrote *The Cotton Kingdom: A Traveller's Observations on Cotton and Slavery in the American Slave States* (1862).
2. This is a reference to a variety of proposals that would require the forced emigration of the freed slaves to Africa, Haiti, or Central America.

SOUTHERN ITEMS.
TROUBLE IN [VIRGINIA AND] MISSISSIPPI.

NOVEMBER 12, 1865

There is some uneasiness in Richmond about alleged preparations for an insurrection making by the 25,000 or 30,000 negroes huddled in tents on the York River Peninsula, between the towns of Hampton and Williamsburgh. These negroes have been notified that on Jan. 1 the lands they now occupy will be turned over to their former owners, and if the reports are true, the dissatisfaction caused by a knowledge of this fact has been increased by the presence among them of free negroes from the North, who incite also a spirit of insurrection and revenge. The proposed plan is said to be to cross York River and sweep through the counties of Gloucester, King and Queen, and those adjacent, increasing their ranks as they move onward by the volunteer or forced addition of such negroes as may be laboring or idling in the section of the country through which they pass.

The colored people of Selma held a meeting on the 19th ult., and passed a series of resolutions, in which they complain that they are every day robbed and beaten by men wearing the Federal uniform, and that they had appealed in vain to the police and military guard for protection. A committee of three was appointed to wait upon the Mayor and commanding officer of the district, to invoke their authority to suppress the outrages complained of. The resolutions conclude with the expression of a sincere desire to live on terms of peace and quietness with the Southern people, and earn an honest living. The paper which prints these "resolutions," unfortunately neglects to state who drew them up. ✸

An allegorical tribute to the Freedmen's Bureau, represented by the man in the middle, standing between armed groups of whites and African-Americans.

AFFAIRS IN THE SOUTH.

TROUBLESOME TIMES AND DISMAL PROSPECTS.

NOVEMBER 13, 1865

CORRESPONDENCE OF THE NEW-YORK TIMES:
NEW ORLEANS, LA., FRIDAY, OCTOBER 27

Mr. [Thomas W.] CONWAY [Commissioner of Freedman's Affairs in Louisiana] was about to lease sixty thousand acres of land, which was either abandoned or confiscated, to the freedmen and refugees of the State, who were able to cultivate it, when the President sent Gen. [Joseph S.] FULLERTON to relieve him, and to suspend his arrangements for that purpose.

Instead of leasing lands, as provided by the law of Congress, Act of March 3, 1864, the President has directed that all such lands as are alluded to in the act, be restored to their former owners, excepting the classes specified as "exceptions" in his proclamation, who of course get his special pardon. The land aristocracy is continued, and it is no fault of the present policy, if it be not fully revived, with all its dangers and power. Under the law of Congress, there was a prospect that poor men could procure small tracts of land, and work them. The arrangements were made under the order of Gen. [Oliver Otis] HOWARD, and if not hindered, would have been soon completed.[1]

Gen. FULLERTON, who relieved Mr. CONWAY as Commissioner of the Bureau, proclaimed, in his first address to the freedmen, that they could have no land. Mr. CONWAY, two weeks before, in accordance with the law, and in compliance with its requirements, proclaimed to all freedmen and refugees who had the necessary means to cultivate the lots of land allowed by law, that they could have as much land as they were allowed. Four or five hundred industrious freedmen, who had saved their money, accepted the invitation, and applied for the land. The result of the "no-land" policy is, that the freedmen are expecting to be compelled to spend their lives as formerly, toiling for others, and having nothing like an equal chance to rise in the world, and do for themselves.

Gen. FULLERTON had not been at work one week before he issued an order for the discontinuance of the two orphan asylums in this city for the children of deceased freedmen.

This order fell upon the community like the land order, giving delight to the rebels and sadness to the few loyal white people and all the colored people in the city. The orphans themselves, learning that Gen. FULLERTON had ordered that they be apprenticed to citizens, ran away from the asylums, so that the matrons of the establishments found, on the following morning, about one-half of them missing. Even the children of the freedmen would rather die than be bound again by any chains. Under the apprenticeship order some of the former slaveholders went to the asylums asking for "nice fat nigger girls," others for "little niggers fit to black boots and do a little dirty work around the yards." ✳

1. Oliver Otis Howard (1830–1909), the former commander of the XI Corps in the Army of the Potomac in Virginia, and afterward the Army of the Tennessee in the Western Campaigns of 1864–1865, was the commissioner of the Bureau of Refugees, Freedmen, and Abandoned Lands.

NEGRO LABOR IN SOUTH CAROLINA.

DECEMBER 5, 1865
FROM THE CHARLESTON NEWS.
SUMMERVILLE, S.C., OCT 7, 1865

MR. EDITOR: In your issue of to-day (Saturday) is a most seasonable article over the signature of "Planter." He expresses, I am convinced, the sentiments of the planting community of South Carolina, if not of the whole South. It is a question, however, whether Northern philanthropy and red republicanism will not defeat any efforts looking to the effectual reorganization of the labor of the South .... In a letter addressed since the meeting of the convention to Hon. D. L. WARDLAW, I endeavored to call his attention to a plan said to have been originated by the Emperor LOUIS NAPOLEON, and to have proved effectual in restoring the ruined estates of the planters of French Guiana, and has rendered the labor of the freedmen there as effective as when they were slaves. It has been quietly put in execution by the French Government, and estates that were abandoned by the planters in that colony are again in successful operation. It will be seen that this plan avoids the infliction of chastisement by the employer, yet has proved effective in preventing vagabondage and pauperism among a race who, if left to themselves, will not voluntarily labor, a fact conceded by everyone who is guided by observation and common sense, and not by "higher laws" and "inner lights." The plan is as follows: Every freedman dependent upon his daily labor for his daily bread, is compelled by law to hire himself to some employer for the year. The whole State is laid out into districts; each district has its house of industry, its magistrate and police, whose sole attention is given to the affairs of the freedmen and their employers. As I have said above, every freedman is compelled by law to contract with an employer. There are three parties to the contract — the employer, employe, and the State; the last, represented by the magistrate, enters as one of the parties to enforce the contract, and to receive a stipulated sum to be set aside for times of sickness or old age of the employe. In case of disagreement between the employer and employe, the magistrate or police are appealed to. If the matter cannot be settled by them to the satisfaction of the parties, then the employer gives notice to the police of his intention to discharge the employe, who is forthwith taken in charge by the police, and conveyed to the House of Industry, where he works for his support until hired by some other party. If the employer discharges the employe, or the employe leaves his place, without due notice to the police, then the party so offending is subject to a penalty fixed by law. No freedman can leave his district and go into another without a written sanction or transfer from the magistrate of one district to the magistrate of another. Thus it will be seen that the above system prevents oppression on the one hand and license on the other; checks vagabondage by providing employment for the year; removing these great inducements to forsake his employer, idleness and vagabondizing, by confining his choice to his removal from one scene of labor to another — from his employer to the House of Industry. It prevents pauperism, by the State keeping a reserve fund out of the freedmen's wages for times of sickness and old age. Frenchmen who have tried the system assured Col. ROMAN that it had proved equally effective and far more agreeable than slavery. The above sketch is given from memory, and may not be entirely correct. Whether this or any other effectual system will exempt us from

TEXAS AND THE CONSTITUTIONAL AMENDMENT.

DECEMBER 10, 1865
THE GALVESTON NEWS OF THE 29TH ULT.
SAYS:

"It has been said that the Constitutional Amendment requires nothing more of us than we are willing to admit in our State Constitution. We think differently. Admitting that we are willing to agree that slavery shall never again exist in Texas, we certainly cannot be willing to permit Congress to have power to carry the provision into effect. What Congress might consider carrying such a provision into effect, we can have no means of knowing; and, besides, it is contrary to all precedent and the whole spirit of our history to give Congress the right to interfere in the domestic concerns of the States. No! Texas will never adopt that Amendment, unless she is forced to do it." ✲

A lithograph commemorating the passage of the Fifteenth Amendment.

that pestilent, intermeddling philanthropy which, however excellent in spirit, has proved so destructive to white and black in practice, is problematical. I have my doubts if even LOUIS NAPOLEON's or French philanthropy and humanitarianism will prove acceptable to the spotless descendants of the Plymouth Rock Pilgrim Fathers, whose garments are so clean that they never require inspection, and as a natural sequence, they are always searching for spots on their neighbors' coats. It is true the above system is different from and inferior to slavery in this respect — that it does not provide for the increase of the colored race. That property in the negro which made the planter so carefully nurture the children upon his plantation is gone with the institution of slavery. Already the havoc among the colored innocents has been fearful, more so than the terrible destruction to the older negroes, which has been frightful enough to have satisfied the vengeance of their worst enemies.

BENJAMIN RHETT.[1] ✲

1. Dr. Benjamin Rhett (1826–1884) served in the Confederate army as a surgeon and was a political leader in South Carolina.

MISSISSIPPI.

THE REJECTION OF THE PROPOSED CONSTITUTIONAL AMENDMENT.

DECEMBER 11, 1865

The New-Orleans Picayune of the 2d inst. has the following:

On Monday the House of representatives of the State of Mississippi adopted the report made by a joint committee of the two Houses on the Constitutional Amendment prohibiting slavery.

The report, which is the production of Hon. Mr. SIMRALL,[1] of Wikinson County, closes in the following terms:

"They (the committee) therefore think the Legislature ought not to accede to said Amendment."

The reasoning of the report is that the amendment is unnecessary. Slavery is abolished forever, and it is positively impossible to reestablish or reintroduce it anywhere in the South. The new Mississippi constitution has incorporated the freedom of the African race into the organic law. The people accept and will abide by it. But they see in the power conferred on Congress by the second clause to enforce the first by "appropriate" legislation, a superfluous grant of authority which may be used to expand the power of the General Government over the social affairs of the States to a dangerous extent; and they express the apprehension that it will be used to legislate the negroes in the South into social and political equality with the whites. ✲

1. Horatio F. Simrall (1818–1901) became chief justice of the Mississippi Supreme Court.

MISSISSIPPI AND THE CONSTITUTIONAL AMENDMENT.

DECEMBER 17, 1865

The Mississippi Legislature, it appears, has reconsidered the vote rejecting the Constitutional Amendment, and ratified it in the following form:

Resolved by the Legislature of the State of Mississippi, That the proposed Amendment of the Constitution of the United States be and the same is hereby ratified.

Resolved further, That the ratification is expressly made and adopted upon the conditions and with the reservations following:

1. It shall not be construed into an approval or indorsement of the political principles or doctrines that the reserved rights of a State can, without the consent of such State, be usurped or abridged by the Federal Government, through the instrumentality of a Constitutional Amendment.

2. It shall not be construed into expressed or complied consent on the part of the Legislature that Congress shall abolish slavery where it lawfully exists in any State that may refuse to ratify said amendment.

3. The emancipation of slavery in this State being a fixed fact, distinctly recognized by her condition, and by recent legislative enactments, is designed in good faith to maintain and protect the civil rights of the freedmen appertaining to their new condition of freedom.

The second section of said amendment shall not be construed as a grant of power to Congress to legislate in regard to the freedmen of this State; but so far as relates to this State it shall be construed simply as a grant of power to Congress by appropriate legislation to prohibit and prevent the reestablishment of slavery therein. ✹

TEXAS.

GOV. HAMILTON TO THE FREEDMEN OF TEXAS.

DECEMBER 17, 1865

Gov. HAMILTON,[1] of Texas, recently addressed the freedmen, to remove from their minds the present impression that Christmas will bring to them great gifts and privileges. We extract the following:

I have been informed, from many sources, that you have been told that about Christmas something would be done for you by government. That there would be a division of property for your benefit — that homes would be furnished to you by the government, and other things given to you without price. I tell you, in the name of the President and the government, whose servant I am, that all this is false — whoever has told you this has lied to you. The government has given you all that it can give you — that is your freedom. If you are not willing to work for your living you do not deserve to be free. The great mass of men, white as well as black, have to work for a living, and those who refuse to do so are not friends but enemies of the government. If, then, you are friends to the government, you will work for a living — you will obey the laws — you will not be idle and vicious — you will do your duty, and try to preserve the good name which you have won by your good conduct in the past. You can only do this by labor.

The United States Government has no land in Texas to give you; it owns no land in Texas, and none will be taken from white people to give to you. The government will do no wrong. Every man who is idle, and not engaged in making an honest living, is an enemy to the government. The government cannot protect its enemies, and every one is its enemy who does not obey the laws. The laws require everyone to respect the property of others. If you disturb the property of others, you are enemies of the laws and of the government, and will be treated accordingly. The laws must be preserved — they shall be preserved — against every enemy, white or black. You are without homes, and you have no means of living by your labor but by hiring to labor for others. This is not hard — it is right. I know it is not hard, for in early life I tried it myself. When you have labored long enough to lay up some money, you can then buy homes of your own. Now, if you are relying upon what some fool has told you the government would do for you, bitter disappointment will be your lot. The government has given you all that it has to give you, and that is your freedom. That is enough; if you deserve freedom, you can do the rest. ✹

1. Lincoln had appointed Andrew Jackson Hamilton (1815–1875) as military governor of Texas in 1862; in 1865, Johnson named him the provisional civilian governor.

GEN. HOWARD'S REPORT ON THE FREEDMEN'S BUREAU.

DECEMBER 25, 1865

The most important interest in the economical reconstruction of the South, is the relation of Labor to Capital of the freedmen to their former masters. If the former become permanently averse to or suspicious of their employers, if they find that the local juries of white men will not do them justice, if they cannot recover their wages, or even suppose that they cannot or if on the other hand the old masters cannot hold the negroes to their contracts, or are disposed to press hard upon them and pass oppressive laws, and neglect their education and welfare, a gap will be formed between the two races, between Labor and Capital like that in Jamaica, with most disastrous and dangerous results to the future prosperity of the South.

The negroes will leave the large plantations for their little farms and gardens, they will become more ignorant and degraded every year, as well as poorer. Cotton-growing will diminish, the South will become impoverished, and at length fearful collisions occur between the ignorant freedmen and the governing race, bringing calamity and disorganization to the land. This is the inevitable course of things, unless the government stretches

THE FREEDMEN AND THE RIGHT TO OWN LAND.

JANUARY 4, 1866

It is reported on good authority that some of the Legislatures of the lately insurgent States have passed laws to prevent the freed blacks from holding real estate. We can not well conceive a measure more disastrous to the future productive interest of these States, or more unjust in itself. All economists agree that the holding of land has a remarkable moral and therefore industrial effect on the peasantry of a country — especially if the land be not too much subdivided, so that each person can secure a fair livelihood from his little plot.

The hope of possessing land is one of the most powerful motives acting on the human mind. It is often this hope and desire which bring over such crowds of emi-

out a protecting hand to this unfortunate peasantry, who are in fact, through our act of emancipation, in a limited sense the wards of the nation. They are intrusted to the honor of the republic. With these dangers in view and this implied pledge, Congress have founded one of the most remarkable departments originated during this war — the Freedmen's Bureau. We published a few days since Gen. HOWARD's first report of its operations.

This new department of the government (as it might almost be called) has had charge since March last of all lands abandoned by the rebels, and of their rental and sale to freedmen, of the education, labor, and moral and industrial condition of some millions of persons just freed from slavery.... The law founding the bureau undoubtedly gave the impression that the lands of disloyal owners would be divided among the freedmen. The impression was strengthened by our own soldiers and officers, and often by speculators, so that the negroes have come confidently to believe in a general partition of lands among them, to take place on Christmas. The bureau are doing their best to correct this dangerous notion.

With regard to labor, Gen. HOWARD required that the freedmen should be free to choose their own employers, and be paid for their labor. He demanded that agreements should be voluntary acts, approved by proper officials, and obligatory on both parties. He very wisely did not attempt to fix the price of labor. In order to drain off the superfluous freedmen who were crowding the cities, he established intelligence offices; for others, he permitted industrial schools to be established by private persons, and aided them with means; for still others, he opened government farms, in order to employ idle hands, and prepare them for a more skillful agriculture by and by. Common schools were founded or aided by the bureau to advance this great mass of ignorant people, and but for the protection and encouragement of this department, few of the schools which have already done such vast good at the South could have been continued.

In the great matter of charity the bureau has done a most beneficent work, and apparently with an earnest purpose, everywhere to discourage idleness and pauperism....

The bureau has been the great dispenser of justice to the freedmen in their state of transition. These people had full confidence in its officers, and abode faithfully by its decisions; so that often a planter secured a willing laborer, when a similar decision from a jury of his own class, would have only inspired distrust. The negro, too, was thus protected from oppressive local legislation, or from violence and fraud. The freedmen's courts were frequently constituted in favor of resident civilians, and in some of the states the civil courts were changed by the Provisional Governors into freedmen's courts, the agents of the bureau acting as the advocates of the negro.

Gen. HOWARD states as his careful conclusion that free labor will prove successful, provided confidence be restored between the holders of property and the freedmen. He holds that the bureau should be continued especially for this object, as the negroes now have confidence in it. Then he thinks justly that these people being emancipated by the government, ought not to be left to any chance of oppression or injustice by local law, and that their poor and sick and orphans must for a time be chargeable on the nation. Their protection and their relief, as well as the charge of their education, and the distribution of their labor, would be best undertaken by this or a similar department for a few years, till mutual confidence was restored between all the classes at the South, and emancipation, with all its consequences, was entirely accepted.

He recommends also that education be placed on a firmer footing for these wards of the government, by securing sites and buildings for school purposes in the different States, to be held as United States property, until the same people shall be able to repurchase the same.

The report is an exceedingly important one, and we trust that its suggestions will be carefully discussed by Congress. ✸

grants from Europe. They push on toward the West, with the prospect each of satisfying his passion for owning some portion of the mother earth....

The negro is peculiarly affected by it. He is especially a localizing producer. He sticks his ground. If this be held on a bad tenure, if he is liable at any time to be turned out, and especially if he is not permitted to hope for or to own real estate he naturally loses his greatest impulse to labor. ✸

THE PRESIDENT SPEAKS.

SPECIAL DISPATCHES TO THE NEW-YORK TIMES. WASHINGTON, SUNDAY, JAN. 28

The following is the substance of a conversation which took place to-day between the President and a distinguished Senator. The President said that he doubted the propriety at this time of making any further amendments to the constitution. One great amendment had already been made, by which slavery had forever been abolished within the limits of the United States, and a natural guarantee thus given that the institution should never again exist in the land. Propositions to amend the constitution were becoming as numerous as preambles and resolutions at town meetings called to consider the most ordinary questions connected with the administration of local affairs. All this, in his opinion, had a tendency to diminish the dignity

JANUARY 29, 1866

and prestige attached to the constitution of the country, and to lessen the respect and confidence of the people in their great charter of freedom. If, however, amendments are to be made to the constitution changing the basis of representation and taxation, (and he did not deem them at all necessary at the present time), he knew of none better than a simple proposition embraced in a few lines making in each State the number of qualified voters the basis of representation, and the value of property the basis of direct taxation. Such a proposition could be embraced in the following terms: "Representatives shall be apportioned among the several States which may be included within the Union according to the number of qualified voters in each State. Direct taxes shall ☞

be apportioned among the several States which may be included within the Union according to the value of all taxable property in each State." An amendment of this kind would, in his opinion, place the basis of representation and direct taxation upon correct principles.... It would leave the States to determine absolutely the qualifications of their own voters, with regard to color, and thus the number of representatives to which they would be entitled in Congress would depend upon the number upon which they conferred the right of suffrage. The President in this connection, expressed the opinion that the agitation of the negro franchise question in the District of Columbia at this time was the mere entering wedge to the agitation of the question throughout the States, and was ill-timed, uncalled for, and calculated to do great harm. He believed that it would engender enmity, contention and strife between the two races, and lead to a war between them, which would result in great injury to both and the certain extermination of the negro population.... ⊛

THE FREEDMEN'S BUREAU BILL — THE PRESIDENT'S VETO.

FEBRUARY 20, 1866

The country will not be taken by surprise in reading the announcement of the President's veto of the Freedmen's Bureau bill. That veto implies no essential difference of opinion between the Executive and the majority in congress in the primary object of the bill.

The promoters of the measure regarded it as a necessary corollary of the enactments under which the slaves of the South acquired their freedom. But of these promoters a large proportion, we venture to think, were prepared to accept any modification in the proposed organization which, without imperiling the main object sought for, should better affirm a faith in the returning loyalty and good sense of the governing class at the South.

The President has not for one moment concealed, either from party friends or party opponents, that he cherishes this faith, and that he cherishes it in the face of an experience more bitter than fell to the lot of any public man of his rank who dared

to stand by the Union in its hour of extreme peril. Just in proportion as he was prepared to make sacrifices for the integrity of the Union, when that integrity was most endangered, to the same extent to-day would he forego the éclat of a sectional popularity where his judgment refuses its assent. In the former case the severe test of experience have shown him to have been right. In the present instance he does not claim — and only the most indiscreet of those who call themselves his friends will claim on his behalf — any infallibility of judgment.

What must chiefly concern the President now, and what will most materially affect the position he is destined to hold in the judgment of his countrymen hereafter, lie in the assurance which the temper and bearing of his policy gives to all classes and sections that he has the permanent welfare and unity of the country at heart, above and beyond all other considerations. To dispute his right to recall the attention of Congress to considerations which may have escaped its attention in the enactment of specific measures, for the benefit of the freedmen or any other class, is to dispute the Executive authority as a coordinate branch of the National Legisla-

THE CIVIL RIGHTS BILL AND THE PRESIDENT'S VETO.

MARCH 28, 1866

The Message of the President announcing his veto of the Civil rights Bill, which we publish in full in other columns, may not command universal assent. But we venture to think that few state papers have ever been given to the world that will so thoroughly compel the attention of thinking men of whatever creed, or kindred, or party.

The President deals almost exclusively with the details of the bill as it passed through Congress, reserving his comments upon its policy to a few sentences at the close of the message. The analysis of the details, however, is of so keen and searching a character, the logic is so irresistible, that we should hope even the strongest advocates of the measure will see how vastly important it is that the constitutional power of the veto should exist, and how important, also, in a higher sense, it is that such a constitutional power should be intrusted to a President endowed with judgment, discretion and most uncommon courage.

The point in the President's argument

which stands out in boldest relief is that which portrays with almost startling vividness the danger — not only possible, but certain — of undermining the independence of the judiciary. If Federal District-Attorneys, Marshalls, Deputy Marshall, Agents of the Freedmen's Bureau, and other officials are to be entrusted with the power of arraigning any State Judge who may interpret a State law in a way which a claimant of justice may disapprove, of what possible use can be State laws, and of what conceivable use can be State judges? Better abolish both at once. But not only are these petty Federal officials empowered, under this Civil Rights Bill, to appear as accusers of the State Judiciary; they have a premium held out to them to prefer charges. For every case of alleged injustice to freedmen, they get a fee. The accused may be innocent; if so, the fee comes out of the United States Treasury. If the accused is guilty, he has to pay his share of the perquisites accruing to the Federal official.

The strictly legal interpretation which the President applies to particular sections of the act is so overwhelmingly strong, that the members "learned the law" who voted for it, can hardly help blushing to find themselves so entirely at fault, under the sharp logic of a layman. So far as we can learn the sentiment of the more discreet portion of the majority that voted for the bill, they are ready to confess that the President's reasons are too strong for them, and they are fain to fall back on what they call his political *animus* to excuse their non-acceptance of his arguments. Those who have throughout doubted the expediency of multiplying discriminating laws in favor of a class which has achieved an enfranchisement and social elevation unexampled in its suddenness and completeness in the history of the human race, must necessarily be pleased that the President goes even further in his veto than to interpret the mere technicalities of the law. To moderate and rational reformers the few simple but pregnant words which Mr. JOHNSON utters on the policies of enforcing the laws of *political economy* through the agency of a countless army of stipendiaries, have a

ture. To interpret his veto of this particular measure as an act at variance with the scope and direction of the national policy, would be a declaration of non-confidence more fatal to complete and cordial restoration, than all the acts of secession that were ever passed or conceived in the rebel States. The President abates nothing of his oft-expressed desire to see full and ample protection extended to the freedmen of the South. He is now, as he has been through the most trying crisis of the rebellion, profoundly and solemnly impressed with the belief that the question of Union is paramount to all others. And we are bound to believe him when he tells us in the opening sentence of this veto message, that it is, "with profound regret" he has come to the conclusion that "it would not be consistent with the public welfare" to give his approval to the measure. We are also bound to believe, that a measure which should assure to the freedmen the same protection which the present was designed to provide, and which should offer fewer points open to objection in its details, would meet with a ready assent.... ❋

value far beyond the mere enforcement of the immediate argument. They are words which have a scope and a bearing aside from the provisions of this or any other negro protection bill. And they show how far above the majority which desires to control his action, are the views of the Executive in all that appertains to the maintenance of constitutional freedom.... ❋

THE SENATE AND THE PRESIDENT.

The President in the exercise of his constitutional power, returned to the Senate, without his approval, a measure called the Civil rights Bill. The Senate in turn, yesterday exercised its constitutional prerogative in voting by the requisite majority that the measure should become law, independently of the Executive Veto.

We trust no true and leal supporter of the President's policy will imitate the radical extremists, and question the loyalty and honesty of the Senators who went with the majority. No doubt a large proportion of those who voted to overrule the veto were Senators who have great confidence in the discretion, the judgment, and the loyal devotion to the Constitution by which ANDREW JOHNSON will be guided, hereafter, as he has been guided heretofore, no matter how vast may be the power put into his hands. This rational section of the Senate majority see that under no conditions can the President be tempted to assume dictatorial powers; that he deprecates becoming the dispenser of a vast and almost illimitable patronage that he dreads — with the instinct of a true Republican — large standing armies; and that he has no schemes of personal aggrandizement reserved for future Presidential contests.

APRIL 7, 1866

The moderate men, therefore, who yesterday voted to override the Veto, pay a tribute — which we are willing to believe is not altogether censorious — to the inflexible integrity and the profound regard for constitutional obligations which they know will mark the President's course, let the power and patronage placed at his disposal be ever so great.

In voting as they have done, the majority ostensibly declare that they regard all existing laws as insufficient to protect the freed negroes of the South in their newly-acquired rights. The President takes a more complaisant view of the matter. And it is fortunate alike for North and South that he does so. A sectionalist and a partisan in the President's position at this crisis, entrusted with such powers as a majority in Congress desire to confer upon ANDREW JOHNSON, would become a vile and intolerable usurper and tyrant. There is no danger, in the actual circumstances, of such a result. The honest and common sense of the Executive will prove the salvation of the country in these first years of restored peace, as the honesty and common sense of his predecessor carried the nation safely through the terrible perils of the war. ❋

THE ELECTION.
LARGE REPUBLICAN GAINS EVERYWHERE.

One thing to be steadily kept in view by the party which has been victorious in this election is their responsibility for the good government of the country.[1] They do not stand in the position of an ordinary legislative majority. In all that appertains to national affairs, their will is supreme. They can override the vetoes of the Executive in nearly every one of the northern States. They have equally shown their power in Congress to give effect to great measures of national concern, despite the President's constitutional right of dissent. They enjoy, to-day, and are likely to enjoy in the next Congress, a power of control over all that belongs to the government of the country, to which there is neither check nor limit, to say nothing of precedent. It is scarcely possible to measure the scope of

NOVEMBER 8, 1866

the authority now vested in the Legislative branch of the Government. The temporary deposit of supreme power in that branch may be a necessity growing out of the insurrection; and regarded in that light, the exercise of such power will not be held to be intolerable by loyal men. But those who have the greatest dread of the dominance of sectionalism, let it come from what quarter it may, most sincerely pray that compromise ground may be speedily found so that the functions of government may be performed as they were before the insurrectionary epoch, and that each department of the Administration may repossess its constitutional force.

Until that result is obtained, there surely rests upon the Legislative majorities in the States recently heard from, a heavy ☞

responsibility to use their power with the utmost discretion. He must be a very confident man who will affirm that the anxieties and difficulties which affect our Government centre alone upon the question of admitting or refusing to admit certain States upon their individual conformity to given Congressional enactments. Outside of, and beyond all that bears directly upon restoration, are issues of a far-reaching character, involving the maintenance of the national influence, the national credit and the national dignity abroad. It can hardly be wise to put forward strong pretentions to a potential authority in the concerns of other communities, until we show that we have compassed a solution of the difficulties which have so long beset ourselves. ✸

1. The Republicans gained 37 seats in the election. That gave them 173 seats in the 40th Congress, to the Democrats' 47 (plus 2 others). As a result, Republicans could easily override Johnson's vetoes.

Congressman Thaddeus Stevens of Pennsylvania.

VETO OF THE MILITARY GOVERNMENT RECONSTRUCTION BILL — THE BILL PASSED OVER THE VETO.

MARCH 3, 1867
SPECIAL DISPATCHES TO THE NEW-YORK TIMES.
WASHINGTON, SATURDAY, MARCH 2

If Congress was dull and uninteresting yesterday, it has made abundant amends therefore to-day, and the prospect is that the current legislative day will go into the journal as having commenced Saturday, March 2, at 11 A.M., and ended Monday, March 4, at 12 M. The fact was soon demonstrated that the vetoes were certainly coming to-day, as certain persons had seen one of the documents in print, and during the call of the roll on a motion to pay Mr. [Turner M.] MARQUETTE, the new member from Nebraska, full pay and mileage since his election, Col. [W. G.] MOORE of the President's staff, entered the House chamber, bringing with him the veto of the Reconstruction Bill, and at 1:35 it was presented. Mr. [Thaddeus] STEVENS[1] was absent from his seat at the time, and several frightened members interrupted the breathless silence which prevailed with energetic inquiries, such as "Where's STEVENS?" "Where is he?" "Go, bring him in," &c. The pending business having been disposed of, the message was read by Mr. McPHERSON, the clerk of the House. Mr. STEVENS came in just before he commenced, and after seating himself, began writing. He was about the only member who did not listen attentively. The result of this writing was submitted to the inspection of the Speaker by Mr. STEVENS himself, during the progress of the reading, also to Messrs. [James G.] BLAINE, [James] GARFIELD, and others, in a very quiet manner. Mr. BLAINE amended

it somewhat. A few members had been furnished with copies of the message and occupied themselves in reading it, line for line, with the Clerk. Gen. [Robert C.] SCHENCK and Mr. [John A.] KASSON being engaged in caucusing the mysterious paper prepared by Mr. STEVENS, a point of order was raised, and they adjourned to the cloak-room to continue their consultation. The floor was filled with members elect and privileged persons, and during the entire reading the decorum of the House was preserved in a manner worthy of the importance of the occasion. The galleries were crowded to suffocation, and maintained excellent order, with the exception of a baby in the diplomatic box. At 2:35 o'clock the reading was ended, and, amid great confusion, Mr. STEVENS obtained the floor, but yielded to Mr. [Charles A.] ELDRIDGE, who stated that he knew that it was physically impossible to attempt to delay the passage of the bill, although the minority felt that course to be their duty, in order that they might prevent the majority from dissolving the Union. [Francis C.] LABLOND echoed the same sentiment, using the phrase, "death knell of Republican institutions." Mr. [Markley] BOYER followed, denying the authority of Mr. ELDRIDGE to speak for the minority, whereupon that gentleman announced that he had been informed that the Speaker would overrule all attempts at filibustering. Mr. [Sydenham Elnathan] ANCONA, evidently bewildered with the responsibility of the subject, denounced ELDRIDGE as a usurper, and proposed to fight as long as he had breath, and was supported in this determination by Mr. [William E.] FINCK. The Speaker then announced that the anticipated decision was not a new thing, but its history was as old as the House itself, and stated that it was competent to suspend all rules by a two-thirds vote, on Mondays after the morning hour, and during the last ten days of the session. Mr. STEVENS resumed the floor for the purpose of allowing Mr. BLAINE to present the mysterious paper which he had prepared, and which turned out to be a resolution to suspend the rules, in accordance with the decision just rendered, for the passage of the bill over the veto. In a few words he adverted to the melancholy feelings which must have filled the breast of the minority, and ironically invited them to attend the funeral of the Republic. Mr. ELDRIDGE then moved to lay the bill on the table, FINCK to lay the resolution on the table, LEBLOND to adjourn. The first two motions were decided out of order, as the resolution pending would deprive him of the liberty of making such a motion, if adopted. An appeal was taken from the decision of the Chair, and Mr. ANCONA moved to lay the appeal on the table. As this latter motion was in effect playing into the hands of the minority, it created great laughter, and Mr. ANCONA's earnestness, exhibited in pledging his word of honor that he had been on his feet previous to the calling of the first name on the roll, added to the ridiculous aspect of his attempt to filibuster. He finally withdrew his motion, but not until after its effect had been explained to him by some of this Democratic friends, and the roll call proceeded, resulting in one hundred and seventy-two ayes, sustaining the Chair, and four noes. The question then recurred on the passage of the resolution, on which the result was one hundred and thirty-five ayes and forty-three noes. Mr. ELDRIDGE then very innocently asked the Chair if a motion to adjourn was in order, and received a negative reply, after which the Speaker announced the question, "Shall the bill pass, the objections of the President to the contrary notwithstanding?" on which the Constitution demands the yeas and nays, which were called, resulting, yeas 135, nays, 47.

THE TENURE OF OFFICE BILL VETO MESSAGE[2]

The vote of the Tenure of Office Bill was received in the Senate simultaneously with that of the Reconstruction Bill in the House. The Senate was engaged on items of appropriation, conference reports, &c., but at three o'clock the bill was taken up, and with very brief debate, including a speech against it by REVERDY JOHNSON, it was passed by yeas 35 and nays 11. It was at once sent to the House. The Reconstruction bill and veto were received from the House, when the Senate went into executive session and soon after adjourned for the recess. ✹

---

1. Thaddeus Stevens of Pennsylvania (1792–1868) was the leader of the Radical Republican contingent in the House of Representatives.

2. The Tenure of Office Act denied the President of the United States the power to remove from office anyone who had been appointed by a previous President without the advice and consent of the Senate. Johnson's deliberate violation of the act — his firing of Secretary of War Stanton — is what led to his impeachment by the House.

THE IMPEACHMENT.

FEBRUARY 24, 1868

The Republican Party in Congress seems at last to be unanimous in favor of impeachment. Those who have hitherto been most conservative in this matter, seem now most zealous and demonstrative on the other side. There can be very little doubt that the President will be impeached by the House and sent before the Senate for trial — the specific misdemeanor for which he is arraigned being the violation of the Tenure of Office Law, in the removal of Secretary STANTON and the appointment of Gen. [Lorenzo] THOMAS in his place ad interim.

There can be no doubt, we presume, that the President's action is in violation of the law. The first section declares that "every person holding any civil office to which he has been appointed by and with the advice and consent of the Senate, is and shall be entitled to hold such office until a successor shall have been *in like manner* appointed and duly qualified." This clause deprives the President of the power to remove any such officer without the consent of the Senate. The second section gives him the power to suspend officers "during the recess of the Senate" until its next meeting and for one month thereafter, under certain specified circumstances, and to fill vacancies in the same way and upon the same conditions....

The President's removal of Mr. STANTON and his appointment of Gen. THOMAS were in distinct and unmistakable defiance of these provisions of that law. It is also clear that this violation of the law has been *intentional* on the President's part — not with a view, as the heated zealots of Congress assume, of usurping power and overthrowing the institutions of the country, but for the purpose of *testing the constitutionality of the law*, and of procuring a judicial definition of the limits and prerogatives of the Executive Department of the Government under the Constitution of the United States....

He is not only entitled to such a decision, but the whole country is interested in having it given. Under our form of government, as under every form of government which has been or can be devised, doubts will arise as to the proper distribution of authority and power. We have, unlike Governments of a different form, a written Constitution by which the limits of official authority are defined, and the powers and prerogatives of the several departments of the Government are described and conferred; and, consequently, the only controversies that can arise out of attempts on the part of one department to encroach on the jurisdiction of another, become questions of construction....

There can be no doubt, we presume, in any one's mind, that the Supreme Court is the proper tribunal for the decision of the question involved in this particular conflict between the President and Congress....

The impeachment of the President, if pushed to trial in advance of such a decision by the Supreme Court, is in violation of this principle. ✹

Congressman Thaddeus Stevens delivering his closing speech for President Johnson's impeachment in the House chamber.

IMPEACHMENT.

FINAL VOTE IN THE SENATE.

MAY 17, 1868
SPECIAL DISPATCH TO THE NEW-YORK TIMES.
WASHINGTON, SATURDAY, MAY 16

The great impeachment drama is practically at an end, and the President stands acquitted of the principal charge. Nineteen votes against thirty-five — just enough, and no more, to turn the scale of the verdict. Twelve Democrats and seven Republicans — that magical number of seven — against thirty-five Republicans! My calculations since Tuesday are fully verified. Thirty six was the best vote the friends of conviction could possibly count upon after Tuesday, and even since then the fight has been to get the one necessary vote for acquittal on the one side and to keep the one necessary vote for conviction on the other. The debate of Monday developed the fact that the President had five Republican votes sure.

Congressman Thaddeus Stevens delivers the formal notice of impeachment of President Andrew Johnson in the Senate chamber.

Senator [Joseph Smith] FOWLER's course developed the fact on Tuesday that he had six. It has been the work of the week to get the seventh man, and EDMUND G. ROSS, of Kansas, was secured. When Gen. THOS.

EWING, Jr., said yesterday that ROSS would vote for acquittal if necessary to secure it, he knew whereof he spoke. ⊕

CONGRESS DEALING WITH THE QUESTION OF SOUTHERN OUTRAGES.

MARCH 16, 1871
SPECIAL DISPATCH TO THE NEW-YORK TIMES.
WASHINGTON, MARCH 15

The House finally decided the question of legislation for Southern disorders in a summary manner. It threw overboard, this afternoon, all propositions for legislation,

President Ulysses S. Grant, seated left, signs the Ku Klux Klan Act into law.

appointed a committee to inquire into the cause and effect of disorder at the South, and then voted very decidedly that it was proper Congress should adjourn next Monday and go home. It was, in several respects, a very remarkable day in the House. The Democrats, under the inspiriting effect of the New-Hampshire election,[1] were like "steers in the corn." They felt decidedly jolly, and pending the efforts of [Benjamin] BUTLER to get in his Kuklux bill,[2] ELDRIDGE gravely proposed a bill for the suppression

of the Kuklux in New-Hampshire. From the reading of the journal the Democrats showed a determination to resist even the introduction of a bill by every species of parliamentary tactics, including organized and determined filibustering. This was discovered subsequently to have been the Democratic programme resolved upon in caucus. Mr. [James F.] BECK disclosed that in a little colloquy between himself, the Speaker and Gen. BUTLER, in which he said it had been resolved upon to permit no more business to be done except in the way provided by the rules, to wit, by the appointment of the regular committees and the regular reference of all measures to be considered and reported back in regular order. With their increased numerical strength the Democrats feel equal to almost anything, and so they filibustered very defiantly for two hours or more, and BUTLER's bill didn't get in, but three were a great many Republicans not sorry for that. While the yeas and nays were being called a number of the leading men on the Republican side consulted with the Speaker, and the result was that the latter prepared a simple resolution which settled the Kuklux business very unceremoniously. It was sent down to Mr. [John A.] PETERS [of Maine], who offered it, and was agreed to by 126 yeas to 64 nays. Of the yeas 58 were Republicans

DOMESTIC NEWS. RETURN OF THE KUKLUX COMMITTEE FROM SOUTH CAROLINA.

JULY 30, 1871
WASHINGTON, JULY 29

The Sub Ku-Klux Committee, consisting of Senator [John] SCOTT [R-Penn.] and Representatives [Job E.] STEVENSON [R-Ohio] and [Philadelph] VAN TRUMP [D-Ohio], reached Washington today, returning from a sojourn of four weeks in various parts of South Carolina, where they have been investigating Kuklux outrages on the spots where they occurred. They first visited the capital, Columbia. More than a hundred refugees, who had fled from violence in various counties were there, but after examining witnesses for two days, the Committee determined to go closer to the scenes of alleged violence and went to Spartanburg. They expected to

and 14 Democrats. So a majority if each party present voted for the resolution. The resolution provides for the appointment of a committee of thirteen to investigate the whole subject, to have power to send for persons and papers, to go South by subcommittee for the purpose of taking testimony, and to report next December. When this was proposed, Gen. BUTLER grew very angry. He denounced those Republicans who favored it as guilty of selling out to the Democrats, and stormed considerably to no purpose. The effect is to render all legislation on this subject impossible at this session. ✸

1. Ellery A. Hibbard, a Democrat, won election to the House of Representatives from New Hampshire in 1871.
2. This was a bill introduced by Benjamin Butler aimed at suppressing the violence of the Ku Klux Klan and other such organizations in the South. Though it was delayed here, it passed on April 20. It was designed to prevent state and local courts from excusing violence against freedmen, and read, in part: "any person who, under color of any law, statute, ordinance, regulation, custom, or usage of any State, shall subject, or cause to be subjected any person within the jurisdiction of the United States to the deprivation of any rights, privileges, or immunities secured by the Constitution of the United States, shall, any such law, statute, ordinance, regulation, custom or usage of the State to the contrary notwithstanding, be liable to the party injured in any action at law...."

remain there three or four days, but stayed eleven. When word got out through Spartanburg County that they were there, the whites and negroes, victims of violence, came in by scores every day, from all directions. Murders and cruel whippings by the Kuklux bands had so terrified them that in many neighborhoods nearly every negro man and Republican white man had slept in the woods for months every night. They showed scarified backs, gunshot wounds, maimed ears, and other proofs of violence they had suffered.

In Limestone Springs township, 118 cases of whipping were proved. The Committee awoke every morning to find, in the yard by the hotel, a new crowd of victims of Kuklux, some including whites, who had suffered outrages which cannot be described with decency. After being whipped, the victims, if well-known persons, were often commanded, under pain of death, to publish a card renouncing the Republican Party. In a file of the South Carolina Spartan, the Democratic newspaper, forty-two such cards were found recently published.

At Unionville the committee remained two days. Not an avowed white Republican was heard in the place, though privately assured by a few that they would avow themselves if protected. The terror of the negroes here is complete. The last election was carried by a Republican majority, but the Republican County officers received Kuklux notices, and all resigned or fled. The policy there has been more toward murder and less toward whipping. The killing of ten negroes, taken from the jail by several hundred Kuklux, acting under military organization, was investigated. A prominent lawyer of the place, Mr. SHARD, a Democrat, on cross-examination, startled the Committee by stating that he believed almost every respectable unmarried man in the community belonged to this Kuklux, and he believed a thousand Kuklux were within a days' march of that village. A negro Methodist preacher named LOUIS THOMPSON, who had an appointment June 11 at Goshen Hall Church, in Union County, received a Kuklux notice in the usual form not to preach. He preached, notwithstanding, to a very few, most of the congregation fleeing when they saw the notice. In the evening a clan of twenty mounted Kuklux came, tied him and whipped him, led his off several miles, dragging him part of the way tied to horses, whipped him again until death, muti-

lated him in a way that cannot with propriety be described, hung him, and threw the body into the Tiger River, bearing a notice forbidding anyone to bury him.

Before the committee returned, Senator SCOTT sent THOMPSON's brother, now a refugee from Columbia, to Union County, with a letter to provide him a strong guard of United States cavalry, to go to the body, which was reported to be still lying half decomposed on the water's edge.

Two more days were spent in examining witnesses in Columbia. On returning from Spartanburg, one day was occupied in hearing the statements and general views of Gen. WADE HAMPTON and Gen. BUTLER, the Democratic candidate for Governor last Fall.[1]

The Committee then visited York County, where they remained nearly a week. They discovered at Yorkville a bitter spirit among the white citizens. At supper at the hotel on the evening of their arrival, Major JAMES BERRY threw a pitcher of milk over Hon. A. T. WALLACE, the Representative of the District, and Hon. J. E. STEVENSON of the Committee. They were just seating themselves at the table, and not a word had been spoken. Mr. WALLACE jerked out a revolver and raised it to shoot BERRY—the ladies screaming—but the landlord threw himself before BERRY and Mr. STEVENSON coolly caught WALLACE's hand, and ordered the landlord to take that man out of the room. Half a dozen friends gathered around BERRY, and he went out. In the course of an hour several citizens of prominence called to apologize in the amplest manner on behalf of BERRY, who was willing to go on his knees if required for what he alleged was an unintentional affront to Mr. STEVENSON. It was subsequently ascertained that the business had been discussed by BERRY and his friends during the afternoon it was to be carried out, and that BERRY had proposed to use hot coffee, but had finally concluded on milk. The colored band serenaded the Committee later in the morning. A crowd of young white men filled the porch of the hotel and were about the band frequently, cursing the negroes and the Yankees in an insulting manner. As the band went away the crowd followed and nearly filled the sidewalk. One negro was thrust off by a policeman, who says the negro resisted and struck him. The negro and two men who were close by say the negro struggled to get away from the grip of the policeman, ☞

who seized, cursed, and struck him, but that the negro did not strike. As he pulled away the policeman fired at the negro, and continued firing until he had inflicted five wounds. The man was still living when the Committee left. The testimony taken showed that both policeman and Mayor were members of the Kuklux. No one was arrested. The community on York County was found to be in almost utter [unintel.], the civil authorities being a useless farce, and a mockery of the victims of the Kuklux Klan. Col. [Lewis] MERRILL, in command of a small force stationed there, an officer of high character and great energy, laid before the Committee the details of sixty-eight cases of outrages which he had investigated, some of them most revolting and horrible. It was found impossible for the Committee to examine more than a small part of the crowds of whipped, maimed, or terror-stricken wretches who flocked in upon hearing of their coming. When the Committee adjourned, the building in which they had sat was filled, stairs, halls, and porches, with those waiting to be heard.... ❖

1. Wade Hampton (1818–1896), reputedly the richest man in South Carolina, was a former Confederate cavalry commander and post-war political leader who would be elected governor in 1876 and U.S. Senator in 1879. In the 1876 campaign, his followers, known as the Red Shirts, practiced political intimidation. Mathew Calbraith Butler (1836–1909) was a former Confederate major general who had run unsuccessfully for lieutenant governor (not governor) in 1870. He was subsequently elected to the U.S. Senate by the State legislature.

THE WAR OF RACES.

APRIL 16, 1873

SPECIAL DISPATCH TO THE NEW-YORK TIMES.
NEW-ORLEANS, APRIL 15

Intelligence has just reached this city to the effect that a terrible and sanguinary riot occurred on Sunday last in Grant Parish [Louisiana], in the county of that name. The disturbance grew out of the increasing animosity which has existed between the negroes of Grant Parish and the whites of Rapides Parish, each color predominating in their respective localities.

All day Sunday the two factions quarrels at the Court house in the village town of Colfax, and the riot finally culminated in the Court house being set on fire by the whites and burned to the ground, together with from two to three hundred negroes who were unable to escape from the burning building. The unfortunate colored men were literally roasted alive in the sight of their enemies.

Of all the whites who were engaged in the fight, there were only two or three who were killed or wounded, owing to the fact that very few of the negroes were in possession of arms or weapons.

The details of this sanguinary riot are quite shocking, and the news has created intense excitement throughout the city. It is understood that the United States authorities intend making a thorough investigation into the affair for the purpose of securing the punishment of the guilty parties, whoever they may be.

The war between the races, so constantly carried on in this distracted State, has seldom presented such a horrifying instance as this burning of a court-house filled with human beings. It is scarcely credible, but the news is unfortunately too true for the reputation of our people. ❖

THE PRESIDENTIAL VOTE.
ASSURANCE OF THE REPUBLICAN VICTORY.

NOVEMBER 13, 1876

Every day accumulates the proof that Gov. Hayes has been elected President.[1] To elect Mr. Tilden it would be necessary for him to have carried either one of the States of Florida, Louisiana, and South Carolina; and our dispatches from those States confirm the previous reports that they have all been carried by the Republicans. Our information, coming from the most trustworthy sources, make it certain that South Carolina will show a Republican majority of between two and five thousand; that the majority in Louisiana will be decisive, and that on a fair count in Florida that State will show a Republican majority of over one thousand. The official count is now proceeding in South Carolina; it will commence on Friday in New Orleans; but in Florida the Board of Canvassers will not complete their work for probably two weeks. Desperate attempts are being made by the more violent and lawless element of the Democracy in these States, to overturn by force the result of the election; but the timely presence of troops there will render these attempts futile.... ❖

1. Rutherford B. Hayes, the Republican candidate from Ohio, won 4,034,311 votes while Democrat Samuel J. Tilden of New York won 4,288,546 votes and a plurality of more than 250,000 votes. Disputed returns from the three Southern states still occupied by Federal troops (South Carolina, Louisiana, and Florida), plus one elector in Oregon, left the Electoral College outcome in doubt. In the end, it was agreed that Hayes would get the disputed votes in return for his pledge to remove the troops.

RETURNS FROM FLORIDA.

NOVEMBER 13, 1876

Returns from Florida are still incomplete. So far as they have been received, however, they confirm the belief that the State has not only given HAYES a fair majority, but that he would have carried it by at least 3,000 if intimidation and fraud had not been freely resorted to by his opponents. Meantime, the Democrats are industriously making up "returns" on no basis whatever. These are ingeniously fixed up into positive and genuine-looking figures, and sent North for party uses. In this way so called official returns are sent from counties which have given no report whatever. It is expected that this ingenious dodge will be used for a day or two longer. The plain facts are against all such falsified statements, as the official figures will undoubtedly show. ❀

THE WORK OF THE TRIBUNAL.
THE PREPARATIONS FOR COUNTING THE VOTES.

JANUARY 31, 1877
SPECIAL DISPATCH TO THE NEW-YORK TIMES.
WASHINGTON, JAN. 30.

The two houses having formally elected their members of the Electoral Commission and provided for appointing tellers, and the four Justices having chosen a fifth, the entire commission is now formed and the preparations for beginning the counting of the votes on the day after to-morrow are complete, so far as preparations are required by law. The two Houses will meet together at one o'clock on Thursday [February 3], and the president of the Senate will immediately begin opening the certificates. ❀

MR. HAYES LEAVES OHIO.

MARCH 2, 1877

SPECIAL DISPATCH TO THE NEW-YORK TIMES.
PITTSBURG EN ROUTE TO WASHINGTON,
MARCH 1.

Gov. Hayes and party left Columbus at 1:10 P.M. to-day for Washington via Pittsburg and Harrisburg. The Governor was escorted from the executive mansion to the depot, half a mile distant, by the Columbus cadets, preceded by a military band and followed by a large concourse of citizens. He rode to the depot in an open carriage and on his arrival was greeted with prolonged cheers by a crowd numbering many thousands, who had gathered to witness his departure. Two special cars had been provided for the Governor and family with their friends, and the intervening time between their arrival at the depot and the starting of the train was occupied in cheers for "Gov. Hayes," "President Hayes," and "Our Next President" &c. the band meantime playing "Auld Lang Syne." ❀

Incoming President Rutherford B. Hayes was a wounded Civil War veteran who rose to the rank of Major General of his Ohio Regiment and took part in 50 engagements—a record he rode all the way to the White House.

The New York Times Chronology of the Civil War

At the end of each of the first four years of the Civil War, from 1861 through 1864, The New York Times amassed and published a dense and thorough "chronology" of important military and political events of the preceding twelve months. This long and exhaustive annual summary provided not only a kind of index to the coverage the paper had provided all year long, but a historically important review of the progress of the war itself. The following pages contain a long-needed reprint of those original summaries. Full articles detailing the events can be found on the enclosed DVD-ROM. The 1865 chronology, which the paper did not publish even though the war continued through the spring of that final year of fighting, has been provided, with an attempt at recreating the original New York Times style, by the editors.

1861

HISTORY OF THE REBELLION.
CHRONOLOGICAL RECORD OF THE
LEADING INCIDENTS OF THE WAR.

DECEMBER 31, 1861

At this season — the close of the year — a resume of the principal events that have occurred during the past twelve months will be read with interest. No one can say that the record is dull or uninstructive. For the convenience of the reader we have prepared two chronological tables — one giving the history of the rebellion, and of the operations, on land, the other detailing more particularly the operations at sea. Both are convenient for future reference, and give, almost at a glance, a correct and concise account of the rise and progress of this great Southern rebellion — of the efforts that have been made to suppress it — and of the naval and military engagements that the war has engendered.

CHRONOLOGY OF THE WAR

DECEMBER 1860.

December 20.
· Secession of South Carolina.

December 24.
· Withdrawal of the South Carolina delegation from Congress.

December 26.
· Evacuation of Fort Moultrie by Major ANDERSON.

December 27
· The Palmetto flag raised in Charleston.
· Forts Pinckney and Moultrie occupied by State troops.

December 29.
· Mr. FLOYD tenders his resignation as Secretary of War.
· President BUCHANAN accepts it.

December 30.
· Arsenals in South Carolina seized by State troops.

December 31.
· Exciting session of the Senate.
· Mr. BENJAMIN, of Louisiana, delivers a violent secession speech. 1861.

JANUARY 1861.

January 1.
· First symptoms of life in the Buchanan Administration.
· The frigate Brooklyn and another war-vessel ordered to Charleston.

January 2.
· Fort Pulaski. at Savannah, taken by order of the Governor of Georgia.

January 3.
· The President, having sent back the last communication of the South Carolina Commissioners unopened, they return to Charleston.

January 4.
· National Fast.
· The United States arsenal at Mobile taken by the local troops.

January 5.
· South Carolina Convention adjourned.
· The Star of the West leaves New-York with reinforcements for Fort Sumter.

January 6.
· Gov. HICKS refuses to convene the Maryland Legislature.

January 7
· TOOMBS delivers a violent secession speech in the Senate.
· Maj. ANDERSON's course in evacuating Fort Moultrie sustained by the House of Representatives.

January 8.
· Resignation of Secretary THOMPSON.
· North Carolina forts seized by the State Government.

January 9.
· The Star of the West, endeavoring to enter Charleston Harbor, was fired upon from Morris Island and Fort Moultrie, and compelled to return.
· The President sends a special message to Congress.

January 10.
· Arsenals and forts of Louisiana seized by the State Government.
· Secession of Mississippi.
· Secession of Florida.

January 11.
· Secession of Alabama.
· Resignation of Secretary THOMAS.
· Appointment of Gen. DIX as Secretary of the Treasury.

January 12.
· Mr. SEWARD speaks in the Senate on the National troubles.

January 13.
· Pensacola Navy-yard seized by Secessionists.

January 15.
· Secession Meeting in New-York.

January 17
· Mr. HOLT nominated Secretary of War.

January 18.
· Close of the Debate on the Crisis in the House of Representatives.

January 19.
· Secession of Georgia.

January 21.
· Withdrawal of the Alabama, Mississippi and Florida Delegations from Washington.

January 22.
· Arms destined for Alabama seized in New-York.

January 23.
· Second seizure of arms in New-York.

January 25.
· Ex-Secretary FLOYD presented by the Grand Jury for malfeasance in office.
· Secession of Louisiana.

January 28.
· Withdrawal of the Georgia Delegation from Congress.
· The Legislature of South Carolina resolve to demand the surrender of Sumter.

January 29.
· President Buchanan again evinces an unsteadiness of purpose, and an indisposition to deal vigorously with the rebellion.

FEBRUARY.

February 1.
· Warlike preparations at Charleston.
· Secession of Texas.

February 2.
· The cutter Lewis Cass surrendered to the State of Alabama.

February 4.
· Assembling of the Peace Convention at Washington.
· Organization of the Southern Convention at Montgomery.

February 5.
· Withdrawal of the Louisiana Delegation from Congress.

February 6.
· Important speech in the Senate of Senator JOHNSON, of Tennessee.

February 8.
· The Montgomery Convention adopt the Constitution of the United States for the Provisional Government of the "Confederate States of America."

February 9.
· JEFFERSON DAVIS, of Mississippi, elected President, and A.H. STEPHENS, of Georgia, Vice-President of the Southern Confederacy, by a unanimous vote.
· Arkansas arsenals seized by the State Government.

February 11.
· Mr. LINCOLN, President elect, leaves Springfield, Ill., and commences his journey to Washington.

February 12.
· The Confederate States Government takes charge of all questions pending between the Southern States and the United States Government.

February 17
· First speech of JEFFERSON DAVIS after his election.

February 18.
· Inauguration of the President of the Confederate States at Montgomery
· Defeat of secession in Missouri.

February 19.
· The President elect in New-York.

February 21.
· The President elect in Philadelphia.
· He learns of a plot to take his life.

February 23.
· The President elect passes through Baltimore secretly, and arrives in Washington.

February 25.
· Information received of the treason of Gen. TWIGGS in Texas, of the surrender of forts in Texas to the State Government, and also of a large body of United States troops.
· The Peace Conference agree upon FRANKLIN's Territorial Proposition for a division of the Territory on the line of 36° 30'.

February 28.
· President DAVIS vetoes the bill legalizing the African Slave-trade.

MARCH.

March 2.
· Revenue cutter Dodge seized by the Texan authorities.

March 4.
· Inauguration of President LINCOLN.

March 16.
· Adjournment of the Southern Congress.

March 18.
· Important Diplomatic appointments by President LINCOLN.

March 20.
· Secession of Arkansas.

March 21.
· A vessel with supplies for the United States fleet seized by rebels off Pensacola.

APRIL.

April 3.
· Great preparations commenced in the Northern Navy Yards.

April 4.
· Excitement at Charleston.

April 5.
· Preparations of BEAUREGARD to bombard Sumter.

April 9.

· JEFFERSON DAVIS makes a requisition for troops.

April 11.
· Demand made by BEAUREGARD for the unconditional surrender of Fort Sumter.

April 12.
· The Charleston batteries open on Sumter.

April 13.
· Surrender of Sumter.

April 15.
· The President issues his Proclamation for 75,000 volunteers.
· Tremendous excitement in the North.

April 16.
· The Confederate Government call for 32,000 more troops.
· Fort Pickens reinforced by Col. BROWN's command.

April 17
· Gov. LETCHER, of Virginia, issues a Proclamation hostile to the National Government.

April 18.
· Arrival in New-York of the Sixth Massachusetts Regiment en route to Washington.
· Fears begin to prevail for the safety of the capital.

April 19.
· The Massachusetts Sixth Regiment attacked in Baltimore by a mob and several of its members killed.
· The Seventh New-York Regiment leave for Washington.

April 20.
· Immense Union demonstration in New-York.
· Burning of the Gosport Navy-yard, including three ships of the line, three frigates, two sloops and a brig, mounting over 400 guns.

April 25.
· Virginia joins the Confederate States.

April 27
· Twenty-one thousand National troops in Washington.

MAY.

May 3.
· President issues a proclamation calling for more troops to serve for three years, and directing the increase of the Regular army and the enlistment of addition seamen.

May 13.
· Resumption of the interrupted communication with Washington via Baltimore.
· Baltimore occupied by Federal troops.
· Anti-Secession Convention in Western Virginia.

May 17.
· Union triumph in Kentucky.
· The Confederate Congress authorize the issue of $50,000,000 in bonds, payable in twenty years.

May 21.
· Seizure of telegrams by the Government.

May 22.
· The seat of the rebel Government transferred to Richmond.

May 24.
· Advance of the Union Army into Virginia. Assassination of Col. ELLSWORTH.

May 27
· Occupation of Newport's News by Gen. BUTLER.

May 28.
· BANKS and FREMONT appointed Major-Generals.

May 31.
· Cavalry skirmish at Fairfax Court-House.

JUNE.

June 2.
· Union victory at Phillippa, Western Virginia.

June 3.
· BEAUREGARD arrives at Manassas Junction and takes command of the Confederate army. Border State Convention meet at Frankfort, Ky.

June 10.
· Affair at Big Bethel.

June 11.
· Skirmish at Romney, Western Virginia.

June 13.
· Evacuation of Harper's Ferry by the rebels.

June 17.
· Successful engagement with the rebels at Booneville, Mo.

June 28.
· Arrest of Marshal KANE in Baltimore.

JULY.

July 1.
· Arrest of the Baltimore Board of Police Commissioners.

July 2.
· Successful engagement of Gen. PATTERSON's column near Martinsborgh.

July 4.
· Meeting of Congress.

July 5.
· Successful engagement at Brier Forks, Mo., between the troops under SIEGEL and the rebels under Gov. JACKSON and RAINS.

July 11.
· Defeat of PEGRAM by MCCLELLAN at Rich Mountain, Va.
· Surrender of the entire rebel force.

July 13.
· Engagement at Carrick's Ford. Defeat and death of the rebel Gen. GARNETT.

July 16.
· Advance of the army of the Potomac.

July 21.
- Battle of Bull Run.
- Arrival of Gen. MCCLELLAN in Washington, to take command of the army of the Potomac.

July 25.
- Gov. MORGAN, of New-York, calls for 25,000 more troops from the State.

July 27.
- Return of the Sixty-ninth and other New-York regiments from Washington.

July 28.
- The command under Gen. BANKS, at Harper's Ferry, is withdrawn to the Maryland side of the Potomac.

AUGUST.
August 6.
- Adjournment of Congress.

August 7.
- Hampton burnt by the rebels.

August 10.
- Battle of Wilson's Creek, near Springfield. Death of Gen. LYON.

August 12.
- Arrest of Hon. C.J. FAULKNER, late United States Minister to France.

August 16.
- Proclamation of the President declaring the States of Virginia, North Carolina, Tennessee and Arkansas in insurrection.

August 24.
- The transmission of secession journals through the mails prohibited.

August 26.
- Skirmish at Summersville.

August 28.
- Capture of the Hatteras Inlet forts by the expedition under Commodore STRINGHAM and Gen. BUTLER.

August 30.
- Gen. FREMONT issues a proclamation confiscating the slaves of rebels.

SEPTEMBER.
September 4.
- False reports of the death of JEFFERSON DAVIS gain circulation and credit.

September 6.
- The Confederates advance into Kentucky.
- Gen. GRANT, with National troops, takes possession of Paducah, Kentucky.

September 10.
- Defeat of FLOYD, near Gauley River.

September 11.
- The Kentucky Legislature pass a resolution ordering rebel troops to leave the State.
- The President, in a letter to Gen. FREMONT, directs him to modify the confiscation clause of his proclamation of August 30.

September 16.
- Wholesale arrest of members of the Maryland regiment.

September 20.
- Surrender of Col. MULLIGAN, at Lexington.

September 25.
- Occupation of Romney, Western Virginia, by National troops.

September 28.
- Occupation of Munson's Hill by National troops.

OCTOBER.
October 5.
- Unsuccessful effort of rebels to retake the Hatteras Inlet forts.

October 7.
- Gen. FREMONT and his army leave Jefferson City in pursuit of PRICE.

October 8.
- Attack of rebels on Santa Rosa Island, and repulse by regulars and WILSON's Zouaves.

October 11.
- Naval collision between rebel gunboats and National vessels at the head of the Mississippi passes. Unsuccessful attempt of the steam ram "Turtle" to sink one of the National ships.

October 16.
- Successful skirmish near Harper's Ferry. Capture of a rebel cannon by troops under Col. GEARY.

October 20.
- Partial blockade of the Potomac by rebel batteries.

October 21.
- Part of Gen. STONE's Division cross the Potomac at Ball's Bluff, and after severe fighting are driven back, with great loss, by the enemy. On this occasion Gen. BAKER fell.
- Engagement near Frederickstown, Mo., and defeat of rebels under JEFF. THOMPSON.

October 25.
- Gallant charge of the Frement Guard, under Maj. ZAGONYI, against a superior body of rebels at Springfield.

October 26.
- Brilliant success of National troops under Gen. KELLEY at Romney.

October 31.
- Retirement of Gen. SCOTT.
- Gen. MCCLELLAN appointed Commander-in-Chief.

NOVEMBER.
November 2.
- Removal of Gen. FREMONT from command in the West.

November 7.
- Engagement at Belmont, Mo.
- Bombardment and capture of the forts at Port Royal Entrance by United States squadron.

November 8.
- Capture of the rebel Commissioners SLIDELL and MASON, on the British mail steamer Trent, by the United States war sloop San Jacinto.

November 18.
- Message of JEFF. DAVIS to the rebel Congress.

November 20.
- Disbanding of rebel troops in Accomac and Northampton Counties, Va. Return of the population to their allegiance.

November 23.
- Bombardment of the rebel batteries by Fort Pickens and the ships-of-war Niagara and Richmond.

DECEMBER
December 2.
- Meeting of Congress.

December 4.
- Occupation of Ship Island by National troops.

December 6.
- Occupation of Beaufort, S.C., by the National troops.

December 11.
- Great fire in Charleston.
- Loss estimated at $7,000,000.

December 12.
- Occupation of Tybee Island by National troops.

December 13.
- Engagement at Alleghany Camp, Pocahontas County, Va.

December 16.
- Threatened War between the United States and Great Britain.

December 18.
- Large bodies of rebels dispersed by Gen. POPE in Missouri.
- Capture of a rebel camp with 1,300 prisoners.
- Gallant affair at Drainesville.
- Retreat of the enemy.

December 20.
- Sixteen old whalers sunk by the National forces at the mouth of Charleston Harbor.

December 22.
- Skirmish near Fortress Munroe.

December 25.
- Retreat of the rebel Gen. PRICE to Arkansas.

December 28.
- Adjustment of the Mason-Slidell difficulty.
- Suspension of specie payments in New-York.

December 30.
- Delivery of the rebel Commissioners, MASON and SLIDELL, to the British.

CHRONOLOGY OF THE BLOCKADE

APRIL 1861.

April 19.
· Presidential proclamation authorizing the blockade.

April 27.
· Supplementary proclamation announcing the blockade of North Carolina and Virginia ports.

MAY.

May 4.
· The British ship Hiawatha, twice fired at by the Cumberland, escapes and gets into Norfolk.

May 6.
· The Monticello is blockading the mouth of the Elizabeth River, and the Quaker City is off the Virginia capes.

May 8.
· Shipment of arms via the Mississippi prohibited.

May 9.
· Blockade of Charleston by the Niagara.

May 11.
· Pensacola blockaded. The Pawnee. Monticello, Harriet Lane and Yankee are off Fortress Monroe.

May 18.
· Prizes arrive at Philadelphia.
· Savannah blockaded.

May 20.
· At this date six American flag-ships, with full rank Commodores attached, belong to the blockading squadron.

May 22.
· Complaints of the inefficiency of the blockade, particularly of Charleston.
· The Niagara captures the ship Gen. Parkhill off Charleston.

May 25.
· Blockade of the Mississippi established.

May 27.
· Mobile blockade.

May 28.
· Blockade of Pensacola considered thorough and effective.
· The Brooklyn blockading off the mouths of the Mississippi.

JUNE.

June 1.
· At this date twelve ships, two barks, one brig and five schooners had been captured by the blockading squadron.
· We have at this date our first intimation of an attempt to raise a Confederate navy. Reports received from New-Orleans, state that a flotilla of gunboats and a floating battery are being constructed there.

June 4.
· Engagement between the Harriet Lane and a rebel battery, at the mouth of the Nansemund River.

June 5.
· At this date the Massachusetts had captured twenty-five prizes at the Passes of the Mississippi.

June 11.
· Blockade of Apalachicola by the Montgomery.

June 25.
· Blockade of Mississippi Sound.

JULY.

July 1.
· The Sumter privateer runs the blockade at New-Orleans.

July 4.
· It is announced that thirty-seven men-of-war and thirty-nine steam gunboats are engaged in the blockading service.
· Blockade of Galveston established.
· Seven prizes taken there by the South Carolina between the 4th and 7th of July.

July 17.
· The pirate Sumter is supplied with coal at Curacoa.

July 20.
· Reinforcement of the blockading squadron at the mouths of the Mississippi.

July 30.
· The pirate Sumter supplied with coal at Trinidad.

AUGUST.

August 4.
· Destruction of the rebel privateer Petrel by the St. Lawrence.

August 9.
· A steamer runs the blockade of Charleston.
· Great complaints of the inefficiency of the blockade at that port.

August 16.
· Reports of privateers abound.
· Inefficiency of the blockade of North Carolina ports.
· Vessels from Wilmington and Beaufort arrive at Halifax and other British ports.

August 17.
· Charleston blockading squadron increased.
· It consists now of the Roanoke, Vandalia, Seminole and Iroquois.
· Fernandina strictly blockaded.
· Vessels arrive at Havana from Savannah and New-Orleans.

August 26.
· The ship Finland burnt by the R.R. Cuyler off Apalachicola.

August 28.
· Capture of the Hatteras forts by the United States squadron.

SEPTEMBER.

September 6.
· Charleston is blockaded by the Wabash and Vandalia.

September 14.
· Destruction of the privateer Judah by the United States frigate Colorado off Pensacola harbor.

OCTOBER.

October 5.
· Great slaughter among the enemy at Hatteras by the Monticello's guns.

October 7.
· Unsuccessful attempt to cut out a privateer at Beaufort, S.C.

October 8.
· Mobile is said to be thoroughly blockaded.

October 11.
· Escape of the Theodora from Charleston harbor with MASON and SLIDELL on board.
· A rebel squadron, under HOLLINS, engages the National fleet at the head of the Mississippi passes, and is driven off.

October 15.
· The ship Thomas Watson, attempting to get into Charleston, is burnt to the water's edge by the blockading squadron.
· The schooner Emily Tenbrook runs the blockade at Savannah, and gets into St. Thomas.
· Engagement between the Seminole and rebel batteries at Quantico.

October 17.
· The Nashville runs the blockade at Charleston.

October 19.
· Engagement between the Massachusetts and a rebel steamboat at the mouth of the Mississippi.

NOVEMBER.

November 2.
· The rebel steamer Bermuda, laden with cotton for Liverpool, runs the blockade at Savannah.

November 7.
· Capture by the United States squadron of the forts at Port Royal entrance — Destruction off Galveston of the privateer Royal Yacht by the Santee frigate.

November 9.
· Capture of MASON and SLIDELL by the San Jacinto.

November 19.
· American ship Harvey Birch burnt at sea by the pirate Nashville.

November 20.
· Twenty-five vessels, laden with stone, sail from New-Bedford, to be sunk at the mouth of Charleston Harbor.

November 21.
· The pirate Nashville enters the British port of Southampton.

November 25.
· Capture by the Penguin of the schooner Albion, of Nassau, N.P., with a cargo valued at $100,000.
· The privateer Sumter escapes the Iroquois, which was watching for her off Martinique.

DECEMBER.

December 1.
· The Secretary of the Navy reports that 160 prizes have been captured since the commencement of the blockade, by 43 vessels of the squadron.

December 20.
· Sixteen vessels sunk at the mouth of Charleston Harbor.

1862

A Year Of War.

Diary of Military and Naval
Events of 1862.

Victories and Defeats, Triumphs
and Disasters, Successes and
Reverses of the Army and Navy
of the Union.

December 31, 1862

JANUARY.

January 1.
- MASON AND SLIDELL LEFT FORT WARREN, having been transferred to a British gunboat.
- Battle between Fort Pickens and the rebel batteries.
- The Union prisoners transferred from Charleston to Columbia, S.C.

January 2.
- Steamer Ella Warley ran the blockade into Charleston, S.C.

January 3.
- Reconnaissance to Big Bethel, Va.

January 4.
- Huntersville, Va., attacked by Union troops, and the rebel stores there captured or destroyed.

January 5.
- Slight skirmish near Port Royal, S.C.

January 7.
- Ex-Gov. MOREHEAD, of Kentucky, releases from Fort Warren
- Gunboat reconnaissance to within two miles of Columbus, Ky.

January 8.
- Rebels in Randolph County, Mo., routed.

January 10.
- Expedition bound down the Mississippi left Cairo.
- HUMPHREY MARSHALL defeated near Preston-burgh, Ky.

January 11.
- Gunboat action near Columbus, Ky.
- Bridges on the Louisville and Nashville Railroad burned by the rebels.

January 12.
- Sloop-of-war Pensacola ran past the rebel batteries on the Potomac.
- Gen. BURNSIDE's advance sailed from Fort Monroe.
- A nephew of Gen. POLK (rebel) captured, bearing dispatches.

January 13.
- RESIGNATION OF SECRETARY CAMERON.
- EDWIN M. STANTON was appointed Secretary of War.

January 14.
- Gunboat reconnaissance to within a mile and a half of Columbus, Ky.

January 15.
- Rebel schooner burned by the men on vessels blockading the Rappahannock.

January 16.
- Reconnaissance from Lexington, Mo.

January 17.
- Gen. BURNSIDE's expedition arrived at Hatteras, N.C., after meeting with heavy gales.

January 18.
- Death of Ex-President JOHN TYLER, at Richmond, Va.
- Reconnaissance of the gunboat Conesloga, up the Tennessee River.

January 19.
- BATTLE OF MILL SPRINGS, KY., in which the rebel Gen. ZOLLICOFFER was killed Rebel schooner Lizzie Weston captured.

January 20.
- Order issued for the appointment of Commissioners to visit Richmond, to provide for the welfare of our troops imprisoned there.
- Rebel schooner Wilder captured, in Mobile Bay.

January 21.
- Gen. MCCLERNAND's expedition returned to Cairo, from reconnoitering in the vicinity of Columbus, Ky.

January 23.
- A second fleet of stone-laden vessels sunk in Charleston, S.C., harbor.
- Rebel steamer Calhoun captured off Southwest Pass, month of the Mississippi.

January 24.
- Two rebel vessels grounded, in attempting to run the blockade at the mouth of the Mississippi. They were burned.

January 26.
- Anniversary of the secession of Louisiana. The day celebrated in New-Orleans.
- Reconnaissance toward Munfordsville, Ky.

January 27.
- Bishop AMES and Hon. HAMILTON FISH appointed Commissioners to visit Richmond under the order of the 20th.

January 28.
- Gunboat expedition to reconnoitre in the neighborhood of Fort Pulaski, below Savannah. Engagement between our boats and those of rebel Commodore TATNALL.

January 30.
- THE MONITOR LAUNCHED.

January 31.
- Secretary SEWARD ordered the release of the prisoners in Fort Lafayette who were taken on vessels which had violated the blockade.
- The President was authorized by Congress to take possession of the railroad and telegraph lines of the United States.
- Queen VICTORIA declared anew her intention to observe neutrality in the American war.

FEBRUARY.

February 1.
- Skirmish near Bowling Green, Ky.

February 2.
- Cavalry charge of the rebels on a small force of Union infantry in Morgan County, Tenn.

February 3.
- The privateersmen who, up to this date, were confined in the city jails were released there from and imprisoned in Fort Lafayette.
- Rebel steamer Nashville sent from Southampton, Eng.
- The Union gunboat Tuscarora, starting in pursuit, was stopped by British frigate Shannon.

February 4.
- Brisk skirmish on the Potomac, near the Occoquan.
- Discussion in the rebel Virginia House of Delegates on the subject of enrolling free negroes.

February 5.
- Gen. THOS. FRANCIS MEAGHER took command of the Irish Brigade in MCCLELLAN's army.
- British schooner Mars captured off Florida.

February 6.
- FORT HENRY, ON THE TENNESSEE RIVER, TAKEN BY OUR WESTERN GUNBOAT FLEET under command of Flag-Officer A.H. FOOTE. Gunboat expedition left Fort Henry.

February 7.
- BATTLE OF ROANOKE ISLAND, N.C. Harper's Ferry, Va., shelled by our batteries by order of Col. GEARY, on account of the rebels firing on a boat under flag of truce.
- Romney, Va., occupied by our troops under Gen. LANDER.
- Rebel picket guard surprised at Germantown, Va.
- Two rebel transports on the Tennessee River destroyed.

February 8.
- BATTLE OF ROANOKE ISLAND continued. The Island, with all its fortifications, captured, 3,000 stand of small arms, 3,000 prisoners, 6 forts and large quantities of military supplies taken by Gen. BURNSIDE's force. Capt. O. JENNINGS WISE mortally wounded.
- Rebel boats, the Sallie Wood and Muscle, captured at Chickasaw, Miss.; also, three steamboats burned at Florence, Ala.

February 9.
- Arrest of Gen. C.P. STONE. He was sent to Fort Lafayette.

February 10.
- The rebel squadron from Roanoke Island attacked and destroyed.
- Elizabeth City, N.C., surrendered.
- Martial law proclaimed in Kansas.

February 11.
- Bursting of the Sawyer gun at Newport's News, Va.

February 12.
- Edenton, N.C., taken by Lieut. MAURY, U.S.N.
- Retreat of rebel Gen. PRICE from Springfield, Mo.

February 13.
- Springfield, Mo., occupied by the Union troops under Gen. CURTIS
- The rebel Gen. PRICE hastily evacuated the place in the morning.
- Expedition for the destruction of the Chesapeake and Albemarle Canal, N.C., accomplished the work.

February 14.
- The Secretary of War ordered the release of all political prisoners, on condition of their taking an oath not to aid the rebellion.
- Amnesty granted to such by the President.
- Return of Messrs. AMES and FISH from Fort Monroe. The rebels refused to allow them within their lines for the object on which they went, but agreed to exchange all the prisoners, releasing 300 Union prisoners more than we released rebels, on condition of the release of the next 300 falling into our hands.
- Cavalry reconnaisance to Blooming Gap, Va.

February 15.
- Bowling Green, Ky., evacuated by the rebels and occupied by Gen. BUELL's army.
- Engagement between rebel gunboats and our batteries near Fort Pulaski, Georgia.

February 16.
- SURRENDER OF FORT DONELSON to Gen. GRANT. We captured from 12,000 to 15,000 prisoners and large quantities of stores and artillery. Gens. FLOYD and PILLOW, (rebels), escaped. Gens. BUCKNER and TILGHMAN captured.

February 17.
- Two rebel regiments, marching to reinforce Fort Donelson, captured.
- Battle at Sugar Creek, Arkansas.

February 18.
- Proclamation of Gen. BURNSIDE and Flag-Officer GOLDSBOROUGH in North Carolina issued.
- Skirmish at Independence, Mo.
- Rebel Congress met at Richmond.

February 19.
- Com. FOOTE took possession of Clarksville, Tenn.

February 20.
- Winton, N.C., burned by Gen. BURNSIDE's troops.
- Gunboat Reconnaissance up the Occoquan Creek, Va.

February 21.
- Execution of Capt. NATHANIEL P. GORDON, a slave-trader, at New-York.
- National troops defeated on the Rio Grande, New-Mexico.

February 22.
- JEFF. DAVIS INAUGURATED AT RICHMOND, Va.
- Martial law proclaimed over West Tennessee.
- The day appointed by the President for a general movement of the land and naval forces.

February 23.
- The rebels evacuated Nashville, Tenn.
- Gen. CURTIS captured Fayetteville, Ark., the rebels fleeing in contusion.
- Gallatin, Tenn., occupied by Gen. BUELL.

February 24.
- Harper's Ferry occupied by Gen. BANKS' troops.

February 25.
- NASHVILLE, TENN., OCCUPIED BY THE UNION ARMY.
- Order issued by the War Department forbidding the publication of war news not authorized by the Government. The telegraph lines taken possession of the Government.

February 26.
- The Loan and Treasury Bill (legal tender) approved by the President.

February 27.
- The rebels began to evacuate Columbus, Ky.
- The Monitor sailed from New-York.

February 28.
- The steamer Nashville ran the blockade at Beaufort, N.C.
- Fast Day in the "Confederate" States.
- Skirmish at Sikeston, Mo.
- Charlestown, Va., occupied by the Union troops.

MARCH.

March 1.
- JOHN MINOR BOTTS arrested in Richmond, Va., for treason to the Confederacy.
- Schooner British Queen captured endeavoring to run the blockade at Wilmington, N.C.

March 2.
- Death of Gen. F.W. LANDER.
- Gunboat engagement with rebel batteries at Pittsburgh, Tenn.

March 3.
- COLUMBUS, KY., OCCUPIED BY OUR FORCES, the city having been deserted by the rebels.
- Martinsburgh, Va., occupied by Gen. BANKS' forces.
- Gen. POPE's forces engaged with the enemy near New-Madrid, Mo.
- Fernandina, Fla., surrendered to Com. DUPONT and Gen. WRIGHT, (Union.)

March 5.
- Our pickets at Columbus, Ky., driven in.
- Bunker Hill, Va., occupied by Union forces.
- Rebel schooner Wm. Mallory captured.
- BEAUREGARD assumed command of the rebel army of the Mississippi.

March 6.
- PRESIDENT LINCOLN'S EMANCIPATION MESSAGE sent to Congress.
- Smithfield, Va., occupied by our troops.
- Battle of Pea Ridge, Ark., commenced.

March 7.
- Battle of Pea Ridge continued. The rebels were under command of BEN MCCULLOCH, and our troops of Gen. CURTIS.
- The rebels commenced their retreat from Centreville, Va.

March 8.
- BATTLE OF PEA RIDGE ENDED, by the defeat and rout of the rebels.
- BEAUREGARD called on the planters to send their bells to depots, for conversion into cannon.
- The Army of the Potomac divided into five Corps d'Armee.
- THE MERRIMAC, FROM NORFOLK, ATTACKED OUR FLEET IN HAMPTON ROADS. She sunk the Cumberland. The Congress surrendered and was burned. The Minnesota grounded. The St. Lawrence was engaged. The gunboats Oregon and Zouave were badly damaged.

March 9.
- The Battle between the Merrimac and our Vessels continued. The Monitor, having arrived on the evening of the 8th, entered into the contest and fought the Merrimac, the two vessels touching each other part of the time. The Merrimac retired, the Monitor being undamaged. Lieut.-Commanding WORDEN, of the Monitor was injured. Cockpit Point, Va., occupied by our troops.
- The rebel steamer Geo. Page burned by the rebels.
- Point Pleasant, Mo., taken by a brigade of Union troops.

March 10.

- CENTREVILLE, Va., occupied by our forces.
- Gunboat Whitehall destroyed by fire in Hampton Roads.
- The last of the rebels left Manassas and our scouts approached the place.

March 11.

- Our troops entered the works at Manassas Junction.
- Gen. MCCLELLAN having taken the field with the Army of the Potomac, the President relieved him of the command of the other military Departments.
- Gen. HALLECK assigned to the command of the Department of the Mississippi.
- Gen. FREMONT placed in command of Mountain Department.

March 12.

- JACKSONVILLE, Fla., occupied by our troops.
- Winchester, Va., reached by BANKS' forces.
- Forts in New York harbor garrisoned.
- Schooner Fair Play captured off South Carolina.

March 13.

- JOS. HOLT and ROBT. DALE OWEN appointed to audit claims against the United States.

March 14.

- BATTLE OF NEWBERN, N.C.
- The rebels evacuated New Madrid, Mo., leaving immense stores, &c., in our hands.
- Gen. MCCLELLAN issued an address to his army.
- Reconnaissance to Cedar Run. Va.

March 15.

- Naval expedition left Cairo for Hickman, Ky.

March 16.

- Rebels defeated by Gen. GARFIELD in the Cumberland Mountains, East Tenn.

March 17.

- Gunboat Cimerone launched.

March 18.

- Ship Emily St. Pierre captured near Charleston S.C.
- Steamer Nashville escaped from Beaufort N.C.
- Rebel gunboat sunk near New Madrid by a masked battery.
- Gen. DIX assigned to the command of the "Middle" Department.
- Aquia Creek, Va., evacuated by the rebels.

March 20.

- An expedition of engineers from Gen. POPE's army, having reached Commodore FOOTE above Island No. 10, started on its return and commenced cutting the famous canal for the passage of gunboats to New Madrid.

March 21.

- Gen. BUTLER arrived at Ship Island.
- Washington, N.C., occupied by Gen. BURNSIDE's troops.
- Departments of the Gulf and of the South constituted. Gen. BUTLER assigned to the former, and Gen. T.W. SHERMAN to the latter.

March 22.

- Reconnaissance in force to Cumberland Gap.

March 23.

- BATTLE OF WINCHESTER, VA. Rebels defeated, with a loss of 869 killed, wounded and missing. Union loss 115 killed, 450 wounded.
- Surrender of Fort Macon, North Carolina, demanded by our forces, which being refused, the fort was invested.

March 24.

- Engagement between the gunboats Tyler and Lexington and a rebel masked battery near Eastport, Tenn.

March 27.

- Schooner Julia Warden captured near Charleston, S.C.

March 28.

- Shipping Point, Va., occupied by Union troops.
- Reconnaissance beyond Warrenton, Va.
- Battle 20 miles from Santa Fe. New-Mexico.

March 29.

- "Middle" Department constituted.
- Charge through Middleburgh, Va., in pursuit of rebels fleeing from the place.
- Schooner Lydia and Mary captured.

March 31.

- Gen. HUNTER assumed command of the Department of the South.

APRIL.

April 2.

- Gen. BANKS' force proceeded from Strasburgh to Woodstock, Va., and were engaged with the enemy at the latter place.
- The President's Emancipation and Compensation resolutions passed the Senate.
- Thoroughfare Gap, Va., occupied by Gen. GEARY's Union army.
- Early in the morning, Col. ROBERTS spiked the guns of the upper rebel battery at Island No. 10.
- The pioneer steamer passed through the newly-constructed canal from above Island No. 10 to New-Madrid.

April 3.

- Bill for the abolition of Slavery in the District of Columbia passed the Senate.
- Apalachicola, Fla., surrendered to our seamen.

April 4.

- Departments of the Shenandoah and of the Rappahannock constituted.
- The rebel floating battery at Island No. 10 again shelled.
- Our forces at Pittsburgh Landing, Tenn., attacked.

April 5.

- THE ARMY OF THE POTOMAC ARRIVED IN FRONT OF THE ENEMY's WORKS AT YORKTOWN. The rebels fired the first shot, after which the cannonading continued with but slight intermission until dark.
- The gunboat Carondelet arrived at New Madrid, Missouri, having run the rebel batteries in a terrible thunder storm.

April 6.

- BATTLE OF SHILOH, OR PITTSBURG LANDING, COMMENCED. The rebels outnumbered us, and on this day succeeded in driving our troops back to the protection of the gunboats.
- Gunboat Pittsburgh ran the batteries a Island No. 10 under a terrific fire from the rebel batteries.
- The Carondelet engaged with rebel batteries all day.
- Gen. MITCHEL reached Shelbyville, Tennessee.

April 7.

- SURRENDER OF ISLAND No. 10.
- Gen. POPE having crossed his army to the Tennessee shore below the Island.
- Battle of Pittsburgh Landing continued.
- Our troops, reinforced, retook the camp and batteries captured by the rebels on the 6th, and captured a large number of prisoners. The enemy put to a full retreat, and Gen. A.S. JOHNSTON (rebel) killed.
- The rebels were commanded by POLK and BEAUREGARD.

April 9.

- Great rejoicing throughout the loyal State over the Union victories. Congratulatory orders issued by Secretaries STANTON and WELLES.
- Gen. HALLECK left St. Louis to assume command of his department in the field.

April 10.

- Bombardment of Fort Pulaski commenced.

April 11.

- BOMBARDMENT OF FORT PULASKI CONTINUED. THE FORT SURRENDERED.
- The District of Columbia Emancipation Bill passed by the House of Representatives.
- Huntsville Ala., occupied by Gen. MITCHEL's forces.
- SECOND APPEARANCE OF THE MERRIMAC and her consorts in Hampton Roads. She captured three small vessels and then returned.
- Gen. HALLECK arrived at Pittsburgh Landing.

April 12.

- Gen. HUNTER, at Fort Pulaski, declared free all slaves in the Fort and on Cockspur Island.
- Engagement at Monterey, Va.
- Expedition from Huntsville, Ala., seized the junction of the Memphis and Charleston Railroad.
- Another expedition from Huntsville arrived at Decatur in time to save the railroad bridge, which they found in flames.

April 13.

- Two bridges on the Mobile and Ohio Railroad destroyed by an expedition from Pittsburgh Landing.

April 14.

- Bombardment of Fort Pillow commenced.
- Gunboat expedition from the Potomac flotilla up the Rappahannock. The batteries at Lowry's Point shelled out.

April 15.

- Our gunboats shelled the neighborhood of Gloucester, Va., near Yorktown.
- The rebels cut the levee on the Arkansas side of the Mississippi near Fort Wright. Immense destruction of property in consequence.
- Ex-Secretary CAMERON arrested on charge of falsely imprisoning PIERCE BUTLER.

April 16.
- THE PRESIDENT SIGNED THE BILL ABOLISH-ING SLAVERY IN THE DISTRICT OF COLUMBIA.
- M. MERCIER, French Minister, arrived in Richmond.
- Troops left Ship Island for New-Orleans.
- Spirited engagement at Lee's Mills, near Yorktown.

April 17.
- Mount Jackson and Newmarket, Va., occupied by BANKS' troops.
- A part of MCDOWELL's force marched from Warrenton on Fredericksburgh.
- An expedition, under Gen. RENO, left Newbern, N.C., to attack a body of rebels near Elizabeth City.

April 18.
- BOMBARDMENT OF FORTS JACKSON AND ST. PHILIP, BELOW NEW-ORLEANS, COMMENCED.
- Gen. RENO's expedition landed above Elizabeth City.
- The rebels at Yorktown repulsed in a night attack on our troops.
- Falmouth, opposite Fredericksburgh, Va., occupied by our troops.

April 19.
- BATTLE OF CAMDEN, (or South Mills,) N.C.
- Gen. BANKS' advance occupied Sparta, Va.
- Gen. MITCHEL at Iuka, Miss.
- Bombardment of Fort Wright continued.

April 21.
- Ship R.C. Files captured at Mobile.

April 22.
- Gen. BANKS' advance reached Harrisonburgh, Va.
- Bombardment of Fort Jackson continued.
- Rebel Congress at Richmond suddenly dispersed.

April 23.
- Gunboat Santiago de Cuba chased the Nashville unsuccessfully.

April 24.
- Destruction of the Dismal Swamp Canal, North Carolina, completed.
- Our fleet passed Forts Jackson and St. Philip below New-Orleans.
- United States Steamer Varuna sunk, after a most gallant action.
- Great destruction of property in New-Orleans, in anticipation of the approach of our forces.
- Rebels near Corinth attacked and driven back.

April 25.
- ARRIVAL OF OUR SQUADRON OFF NEW-ORLEANS.
- Surrender of Fort Macon, North Carolina, after a bombardment of ten and a half hours by our fleet and batteries.
- Death of Gen. C.F. SMITH.

April 26.
- Com. FARRAGUT demanded the surrender of New-Orleans. The Mayor replied that the city was at the mercy of our gunboats.
- Capture of a rebel outwork at Yorktown.
- Fort Macon occupied by our forces.

April 27.
- AMERICAN FLAG RAISED OVER THE MINT IN NEW-ORLEANS.
- Severe skirmish near Newbern, N.C.
- Gen. BUTLER landed his troops above Fort St. Philip.

April 28.
- Surrender of Forts Jackson and St. Philip.
- Rebel gunboats on the Warwick River shelled our encampments.
- Skirmish at Monterey, Tenn.
- Captured steamer Ella Warley arrived at Port Royal, S.C.

April 29.
- Gen. MITCHEL routed the rebels at Bridgeport, Ala.
- Successful skirmish near Corinth.
- Rebel battery near Port Royal captured.

April 30.
- Cannonading at Yorktown.
- The rebels cut the telegraph wire near Huntsville, Ala., and attacked one of our brigades.

MAY.

May 1.
- Huntsville, Ala., in possession of Gen. MITCHEL.
- Great rise in the Mississippi.
- Rebel battery at White Point, North Edisto Island, captured.
- Schooner Magnolia captured.

May 2.
- Rebel Gen. MORGAN captured some of our troops at Pulaski, Tenn.
- Gen. BUTLER took possession of the True Delta in New-Orleans.

May 3.
- Rebels near Farmington, Miss., attacked. The position carried and two bridges destroyed.

May 4.
- YORKTOWN EVACUATED BY THE REBELS early in the morning, and our troops occupied the works.
- Brisk fight between our cavalry and artillery and the rebels, from Yorktown near Williamsburgh.
- Gen. MCCLELLAN reported the capture of 71 heavy guns and large amount of ammunition, tents, & c.
- Gloucester taken.
- MORGAN's rebel cavalry attacked at Lebanon, Tenn.
- English steamer Circassian captured near Havana.

May 5.
- BATTLE OF WILLIAMSBURGH, VA. After a hard-fought battle in which we came near being defeated, our forces were victorious, and the enemy abandoned their position in the night, leaving sick and wounded in our hands.

May 6.
- Williamsburgh occupied by our troops.
- The Merrimac moving and the Monitor and other vessels prepared for action.
- The rebels burned their gunboats on the York River.

May 7.
- BATTLE OF WEST POINT, VA. Gen. FRANKLIN's division was engaged in a terrible conflict with the rebels under LEE, but succeeded in driving them back in the Chickahominy.
- The President visited Fort Monroe, the Galena, Monitor and Minnesota.
- The Merrimac appeared off Craney Island and returned to Norfolk.
- Gen. MILROY, in the Mountain Department, fell back after some skirmishing.

May 8.
- The iron clad Galena and gunboats Aroostook and Port Royal started up James River.
- Monitor, Naugatuck and several gunboats left for Sewell's Point which place they attacked.
- Merrimac appeared but refused to fight.

May 9.
- Gen. MCCLELLAN effected a junction with FRANKLIN's Corps at West Point.
- Monitor fired on the batteries at Sewell's Point.
- Battle at Farmington, near Corinth, Miss. The rebels attacked our position, and though our forces were at first compelled to fall back, the fight resulted in a victory for our arms.
- Gen. HUNTER issued his order declaring free the slaves in Georgia, Florida and South Carolina.
- Evacuation of Pensacola by the rebels completed.
- Engagement at Slater's Mills, Va.
- Gunboat fight at Fort Darling, on the James River.

May 10.
- SURRENDER OF NORFOLK.
- Gosport Navy-yard burned by the rebels.
- Victory on the Mississippi, near Fort Pillow, in a gunboat engagement between eight rebel iron-clads and six Union boats. Two of the rebel gunboats blown up and one sunk.
- Craney Island abandoned by the rebels.
- Gen. BUTLER seized $800,000 in the office of the Consul of the Netherlands, New-Orleans.

May 11.
- THE REBELS SET FIRE TO THE MERRIMAC. She blew up at 5 A.M.
- Monitor and other gunboats proceeded toward Norfolk.

May 12.
- Great destruction of tobacco on the Elizabeth River.
- Rebel steamer Gov. Morton captured.

May 13.
- MCCLELLAN's advance guard at White House, Va.; Gen. MCCLELLAN's Headquarters at Cumberland, near which was skirmishing with the enemy.

May 15.
- Dash of mounted guerrillas on our railroad guard beyond Front Royal, Va.

May 16.
- United States transport Oriental wrecked near Cape Hatteras.

May 17.
- The rebels driven across the Chickahominy at Bottom's Bridge. The rebels burned the bridge, and obstructed the march of our troops.

May 19.
- The rebels attacked, killed and took prisoners a party of our men on the James River, landing under flag of truce.
- The President, by proclamation, repudiated the order of Gen. HUNTER liberating the slaves in his department.

May 20.
- Gen. MCCLELLAN's advance reached New Bridge, 8 miles from Richmond.
- Advance of all his army.

May 23.
- TERRIFIC, FIGHTING BETWEEN GEN. BANKS' ADVANCE UNDER COL. KENLEY AND THE REBELS AT FRONT ROYAL, VA.
- A portion of Gen. MCCLELLAN's army crossed the Chickahominy.
- MCCLELLAN's army engaged in three skirmishes the rebels driven from Mechanicsville.
- The rebels defeated at Lewisburgh, Va., in the Mountain Department.

May 24.
- Gen. BANKS' column retreated from Strasburgh to Winchester, Va., fighting the rebels gallantly.

May 25.
- Gen. BANKS retreated from Winchester to Martinsburgh, Va., fighting as he went. Our troops were attacked early in the morning, and fought during most of the dry. Our baggage trains reached the Potomac.

May 26.
- THE CAPITAL SUPPOSED TO BE IN DANGER.
- Hanover, Courthouse, Va., captured by Gen. MCCLELLAN. The rebels completely routed.
- Gen. MORGAN ordered the Seventh Regiment to Washington. Other regiments to follow.

May 27.
- President LINCOLN delivers to Congress a message relative to Secretary CAMERON's transactions.
- Steamer Patras captured.

May 28.
- RETREAT OF THE REBELS FROM CORINTH, Miss., COMMENCED.
- An expedition under Col. ELLIOTT, sent from Camp near Corinth to the Sashville and Ohio Railroad, was successful.

May 29.
- Evacuation of Corinth, by the rebels completed in the night.
- Bridge 500 feet long across South Anna Creek, Va., burned by our cavalry, who also captured Ashland, Va.

May 30.
- Front Royal occupied by our troops.

May 31.
- BATTLE OF FAIR OAKS, before Richmond, commenced. The result of the day's fighting was unfavorable.

JUNE.

June 1.
- The battle of Fair Oaks continued. This day's fight was very severe, and we regained our position of the day before. The Union loss in two days' battles was, in killed, wounded and missing, 5,739
- The rebels driven out of Strasburgh, Va., and the town occupied by FREMONT's army.

June 3.
- Landing of Union troops on James Island, S.C.

June 4.
- Gen. POPE 30 miles south of Corinth, pushing the enemy.
- Skirmish on James Island, S.C.
- The rebels burned their works near Fort Pillow.

June 5.
- Artillery battle at New Bridge, near Richmond.
- Fort Pillow evacuated after a siege of 52 days.

June 6.
- Memphis, Tenn., occupied by the Union army.
- Great gunboat battle opposite Memphis; 7 of the enemy's gunboats and rams destroyed.
- Gen. FREMONT attacked the rebel rear guard near Harrisonburgh, Va.

June 7.
- Battle at Union Church near Harrisonburgh, Va. The rebels routed.
- Rebel batteries at Chattanooga silenced.
- WM. B. MUMFORD executed for tearing down the American flag from the mint at New-Orleans.

June 8.
- Battle of Cross Keys, Va. FREMONT's army engaged.

June 9.
- Battle of Port Republic, Va., between SHIELDS' and JACKSON's forces.

June 10.
- Skirmish near James Island.

June 13.
- Our pickets driven in from Old Church before Richmond.
- The railroad behind MCCLELLAN's army, four miles from White House, cut by the rebel cavalry.

June 15.
- Gen. WOOL visited Harper's Ferry.

June 16.
- Battle of James Island, S.C.; our forces repulsed.

June 17.
- Battle between our gunboats and rebel batteries at St. Charles, Ark., on the White River.

June 18.
- Cumberland Gap occupied by Union Gen. MORGAN's force.

June 20.
- Commodore PORTER arrived off Vicksburgh with ten mortar-boats.
- Free Territory act signed by the President.
- Holly Springs occupied by our forces.

June 21.
- Death of Col. ELLET, of the Mississippi ram fleet.

June 24.
- EVACUATION OF WHITE HOUSE LANDING by MCCLELLAN commenced. Gen. HOOKER's Division attacked by the rebels, who were repulsed at the point of the bayonet.
- President LINCOLN at West Point, N.Y.

June 25.
- SEVERE AND SUCCESSFUL FIGHTING BEFORE RICHMOND. Reconnoitering expedition left Newbern, N.C.
- Gen. BUTLER ordered the seizure of the property of the traitor TWIGGS.

June 26.
- TERRIFIC FIGHTING BEFORE RICHMOND, the rebels having attacked our right wing when engaged in changing base from the Pamunkey to the James Rivers.
- The rebels destroyed their gunboats the Van Dorn, Polk and Livingston, on the Yazoo River.
- Gen. POPE assigned to the command of the Army of Virginia.

June 27.
- BATTLE OF GAINES' HILL, near Richmond. Stonewall JACKSON and EWELL attempted to turn our right flank and were repulsed. The entire right wing of our army crossed the Chickahominy in the night in perfect order.
- Shelling of Vicksburgh.
- Gen. FREMONT relieved of the command of the Mountain Department.

June 28.
- BATTLES BEFORE RICHMOND CONTINUED.
- Evacuation of White House Landing completed.

June 29.
- BATTLE FOUGHT 1 1/2 MILES FROM SAVAGE's STATION, near Richmond. At dark the rebels were repulsed, and forced to abandon their position.
- The crew of the steamer Kanawha cut out the English steamer Ann from under the guns of Fort Morgan, Mobile.

June 30.
- BATTLE OF CHARLES CITY CROSS ROADS, or White Oak Swamp, near Richmond. The rebels still held at bay. Loss very heavy on both sides.

JULY.

July 1.
- BATTLE OF MALVERN HILL, before Richmond. Our troops were more successful this day than on those preceding, having been victorious in every action.
- Brilliant cavalry engagement near Boonsville, Miss. The rebels attacked our forces, but were repulsed after seven hours' hard fighting.
- The President announced his decision to call for 300,000 more volunteers.
- Tax Bill approved.

July 2.
- Gov. MORGAN appealed to the people of New-York to volunteer.

July 4.
- Gen. MCCLELLAN issued a congratulatory address to his army, in which he declared that it should enter Richmond.

July 5.
- Vigorous bombardment of Vicksburgh.

July 7.
- Gen. CURTIS' advance in Arkansas attacked by the rebels, near Bayou Cache. The rebels repulsed and put to flight.
- Gen. BURNSIDE's flagboat arrived at Fort Monroe.

July 8.
- President LINCOLN and Gen. BURNSIDE arrived at Fort Monroe. The President proceeded up the James River.
- An expedition up the Roanoke River started from Plymouth, N.C.

July 10.
- BURNSIDE's force encamped at Newport's News.

July 11.
- Gen. HALLECK assigned by the President to the command of the whole land forces of the United States, as General-in-Chief.

July 12.
- Gen. ALBERT PIKE resigned his command in the rebel army.
- Gen. CURTIS' command arrived at Helena, Ark.

July 14.
- Gen. POPE assumed command of the Army of Virginia, and issued his famous order, discarding the idea of maintaining lines of retreat and bases of support.
- Battle at Fayetteville, Ark.

July 15.
- Gen. STEVENS' division from South Carolina arrived in Hampton Roads to reinforce MCCLELLAN .
- Rebel iron-clad gunboat Arkansas run past our vessels and succeeded in reaching the rebel batteries at Vicksburgh, before reaching which she had a desperate fight with the Union iron-clad Carondelet.

July 17.
- Congress adjourned.
- CYNTHIANA, KY., taken by the rebels.

July 18.
- Death of the rebel Gen. D.E. TWIGGS.

July 19.
- Gen. BUTLER issued an order emancipating certain negroes.

July 20.
- The expedition from Fredericksburgh made a descent on the Virginia Central Railroad at Beaver Dam Creek; the railroad and telegraph lines for several miles were destroyed.

July 22.
- The President issued an order for the seizure of supplies needed by our armies; directing that negroes should be employed as laborers, giving them wages for their labor.
- The President ordered that foreigners should not be required by military commanders to take the oath of allegiance.

July 23.
- Gen. POPE ordered the arrest of all disloyal male citizens in the lines of his army.
- A cavalry expedition from Fredericksburgh met and defeated two bodies of rebel cavalry.

July 24.
- Gen. HALLECK left Washington for Fortress Monroe.
- British steamer Tubal Cain captured.

July 25.
- Steamer Cuba ran the blockade into Mobile.
- President issued a proclamation warning rebels of the provisions of the Confiscation act.

July 27.
- British steamer Memphis ran out of Charleston.
- Reconnaissance in force in direction of Kinston, N.C.
- Gen. POPE left Washington for his army.

July 30.
- A part of Com. PORTER's mortar fleet arrived in Hampton Roads.

AUGUST.

August 1.
- Severe fight at Newark, Mo.
- Retaliatory order issued by the rebel Government. Gen. POPE and his officers declared not to be entitled to the privileges of prisoners of war.

August 2.
- Reconnoitering column from POPE's army crossed the Rapidan and took Orange Courthouse, Va.
- Railroad and telegraph lines between Orange Court-house and Gordonsville destroyed.
- Brush with the rebels at Ozark, Mo.

August 3.
- Reconnoitering party from the Army of the Potomac advanced to within 14 miles of Petersburgh, Va.
- Steamer Columbia captured with a valuable cargo.

August 4.
- A DRAFT FOR 300,000 MEN FOR NINE MONTHS ORDERED.

August 5.
- BATTLE OF BATON ROUGE.
- Malvern Hill occupied by our troops after a right of 1 1/2 hours, our gunboats shelled a rebel encampment beyond Malvern Hill.
- Gen. ROBERT MCCOOK, assassinated by the rebels, near Salem, Tenn.

August 6.
- REBEL RAM ARKANSAS BLOWN UP.
- 3000 prisoners exchanged.
- Gen. HOOKER retired in the night from Malvern Hill.
- Death of Gen. ROBERT MCCOOK.

August 7.
- Guerrilla fight near Kirksville, Mo., the rebels defeated.
- English steamer Ladona captured. The rebels grossed the Ranidac and advanced toward Culpepper Court-house and Madison Court-house, Va.

August 8.
- POPE's advance fell slowly back, our forces concentrating at Culpepper Court-house.

August 9.
- BATTLE OF CEDAR MOUNTAIN.
- Guerrilas at Stockton, Mo., defeated.
- Regulations for the enrollment and draft issued.

August 10.
- Slight skirmishing at Cedar Mountain, Va. The enemy fell back two miles from our front.

August 11.
- The enemy sent a flag of truce to Culpepper Court-house, asking permission to bury their dead of the battle of Cedar Mountain. The day spent in burying the dead.
- Independence, Mo., captured by the rebels.
- Guerrilla fight near Williamsport, Tenn.

August 12.
- Reconnaissance in force from POPE's army in the neighborhood of Slaughter Mountain.

August 13.
- Collision between the steamers Peabody and West Point on the Potomac; about 80 lives of convalescent soldiers lost.

August 14.
- Gen. BURNSIDE's corps d'armee arrived at Fredericksburgh.
- The draft ordered to take place Sept. 1.

August 16.
- UNION TROOPS EVACUATED HARRISON's LANDING, Va. The rebels made a feint of an attempt to cross the Rapidan but were driven back.
- Fight in Charlton County, Mo.
- Gen. MCCLELLAN's advance arrived at Williamsburgh.

August 17.
- Gen. MCCLELLAN's advance from Harrison's Landing reached Hampton.

August 18.
- The rear guard of MCCLELLAN's army crossed the Chickahominy on its way toward Fort Monroe.
- Gen. POPE's retreat commenced.
- The rebel Congress met.

August 20.
- The Sioux Indians attacked Fort Ridgely, Minn., and were repulsed.
- The rebels drove in our pickets between Culpepper Court-house and the Rappahannock.

August 21.
- Two rebel regiments crossed the Rappahannock in face of Gen. SIGEL's batteries, which opened on them, killing many and driving the rest back in confusion.

August 22.
- STUART's Cavalry attacked a train of sick and wounded at Catlett's Station, Va.
- Reception of Gen. CORCORAN in New-York.

August 23.
- Early in the morning our artillery all along the line opened on the enemy from this side of the Rappahannock. For several hours a terrific artillery duel was kept up. Rappahannock Bridge blown up.

August 25.
- Sharp skirmish at Waterloo Bridge, Va.
- "Stonewall" JACKSON left the rebel army with his force, and took the direction of Manassas, which he approached through Thoroughfare Gap.
- The rebels were repulsed in an attack on Fort Donelson.

August 26.
- The rebel cavalry reached Manassas, having marched sixty-two miles in less than two days. From Manassas they advanced nearly to within cannon-shot of Washington.

August 28.

- Gen. POPE found Manassas Junction evacuated by the rebels.

- MCDOWELL's column reached the rebels near Haymarket, and after a prolonged fight drove the entire force of JACKSON back.

- City Point, Va., entirely demolished by the Union gunboats.

August 29.

- BATTLE AT GROVETON, NEAR BULL RUN. The Corps of Gen. SIGEL engaged. The battle of this day ended in a victory for our arms, and at night our army rested near its dead and wounded. The engagement was furious, and the rebels were everywhere repulsed. Col. FLETCHER WEBSTER killed.

- Return of the Seventh Regiment to New-York.

August 30.

- SECOND BATTLE OF BULL RUN. Though our position was maintained during the day, Gen. POPE ordered, in the night, a general retreat. Our army fell back toward Centreville.

- Severe battle near Richmond. Ky. Our forces were outnumbered and fell back to Lexington.

- Fight at Bolivar, Tenn. Enemy repulsed.

SEPTEMBER.

September 1.

- Gens. KEARNY and I.S. STEVENS killed in a severe engagement near Chantilly, two miles from Fairfax Court-house, Va.

- Fredericksburgh evacuated by Gen. BURNSIDE's army.

- Lexington, Ky., evacuated by our troops, who fell back on Covington. Great excitement in Louisville in anticipation of an attack.

- Battle of Button's Lane, Tenn. The rebels, estimated to be 5,000 strong, were opposed to a Union force of only 800, under Col. DENNIS. After a fight of four hours, the rebels left Col. DENNIS in possession of the field.

September 2.

- Gen. MCCLELLAN assigned to the command of the fortifications of Washington and of the troops for the defence of the Capital.

- Business entirely suspended at Cincinnati and martial law proclaimed.

- Considerable fighting between Fairfax Courthouse and Washington; the rebels being held in check by Gens. HOOKER and FITZJOHN PORTER.

- Engagement at Plymouth, N.C., in which the rebels were thoroughly routed.

September 3.

- Gen. WHITE entered Harper's Ferry with his force from Winchester, Va.

September 4.

- The rebel steamer Oreto ran the blockade into Mobile Bay, escaping the steamer Oneida in pursuit.

September 5.

- REBELS CROSSED THE POTOMAC INTO MARYLAND, near Point of Rocks, in the night, and marched to White Oak Springs, Md. Col. THOS. H. FORD took command of the forces on Maryland Heights. Forces were stationed at Solomon's Gap and Sandy Hook, near Harper's Ferry.

September 6.

- The rebels in Maryland. A force under Gen. HILL occupied Frederick City. BRADLEY T. JOHNSON was made rebel Provost-Marshal.

- Battle at Washington, N.C. Our troops captured four guns and many prisoners.

- The pirate Alabama captured and destroyed the whaler Ocmulgee.

September 7.

- Gen. MCCLELLAN left Washington, under orders to drive the enemy from Maryland, most of his force having preceded him. He established his headquarters at Rockville, Md.

- Schooner Starlight captured by the Alabama, near Flores.

- Bowling Green, Ky., occupied by our advance force under Gen. NEGLEY.

- Gen. POPE relieved of the command of the Army of Virginia. and assigned to that of the Northwest.

September 8.

- Gen. MCCLELLAN passed through Rockville. His main army followed him, his advance having preceded him some days.

- Fight at Poolesville, Md.

- Gen. LEE issued his celebrated proclamation to the people of Maryland.

- Gen. ROUSSEAU crossed the Cumberland River, moving North.

- Restrictions on travel rescinded, and arrests for disloyalty, &c., forbidden, except by direction of the Judge-Advocate at Washington.

September 9.

- Rebel cavalry attacked our force stationed at Williamsburgh, Va. We succeeded in holding the place.

- Evacuation of Fredericksburgh by the rebels commenced.

- The pirate Alabama captured the bark Ocean Rover and the schooner Weather Gauge, which, seeing the Ocean Rover in flames, had come to her assistance. She also captured and burned the bark Alert.

September 10.

- Gov. CURTIN issued an order calling on all able-bodied men in Pennsylvania to organize immediately for the defense of the State.

- Cavalry Reconnaissance in the direction of Sugar Loaf Mountain, Md.

- Large force of rebels at New-market, eight miles from Frederick, Md.

- Great excitement in Cincinnati; 3,000 laborers ordered to the trenches. The rebels, 10,000 strong, believed to be approaching the city.

- Attack by a rebel column on our troops near Gauley, Western Virginia.

- Stringent order against straggling issued.

- Skirmish near Covington, Ky.

September 11.

- Union troops occupied Newmarket, Md.

- Hagerstown occupied by the rebel troops, who capture a large quantity of flour and commence to tear up the railroad track.

- Gen. PLEASANTON's Cavalry crossed the Monocacy near the Potomac, and found no enemy in force.

- Sugar-Loaf Mountain, Md., occupied by our forces.

- Rebels made a cavalry raid into Westminster.

- Gen. BUELL's army hastening to the support of Nashville. The city being fortified.

- Bloomfield, Mo., captured by the rebels.

- Skirmishing along the entire line of the West Licking River.

- Maysville, Ky., taken by the rebel MORGAN.

- Gen. MCCLELLAN telegraphed from Rockville, Md., to Gen. HALLECK to have Col. MILES (at Harper's Ferry) join him at once. Our forces stationed at Solomon's Gap, near Harper's Ferry, were driven in by the enemy. Col. FORD called on Col. MILES for reinforcements.

September 12.

- Gen. HOOKER's forces arrived in Frederick, Md. They were received with the greatest enthusiasm by the inhabitants of the city.

- Gen. WHITE returned to Harper's Ferry, where he remained till the surrender without taking command. Reinforcements sent to Col. FORD. Skirmishing commenced at Maryland Heights.

- Reconnaissances in force from Cincinnati found that the enemy had fallen back.

- Desperate fight on Elk River, Western Virginia.

September 13.

- Gen. MCCLELLAN reached Frederick.

- Further reinforcements sent to Col. FORD. The enemy made an attack on the crest of the hill (Maryland Heights.) Our troops retired to the breastworks. The One Hundred and Twenty-sixth Regiment N.Y.V. fled in confusion at the second attack. Col. MILES ordered Col. FORD to spike his guns and throw the heavy ones down the mountain in case he should be compelled to evacuate Maryland Heights. Gen. MCCLELLAN established his headquarters at Frederick City in the morning. Col. MILES sent to him informing him that he could not hold Harper's Ferry more than forty-eight hours unless reinforced.

- The pirate Alabama captured and burned the whaler Benj. Tucker.

- Cavalry charge on the rebels near Middletown, Md. The rebel wagon train was so pushed that a large number were burned, to prevent their falling into our hands The rebel army threatening Cincinnati fell back beyond Florence.

September 14.

- BATTLE OF SOUTH MOUNTAIN, MD. After a very severe engagement, the corps of Gens. HOOKER and RENO carried Hagerstown Heights by storm. Gen. FRANKLIN's Division engaged the enemy at Crampton's Gap, and, after a hot contest, gained a complete success. Gen. RENO was killed. The rebels retreated in the night toward the Potomac, our army pressing them closely. Our loss in the battle of South Mountain was, in killed, wounded and missing, 2,325.

- Attack on Harper's Ferry. At 2 o'clock A.M. Maryland Heights were abandoned. Col. D'UTASSY sent four companies to the Heights, who brought off four brass twelve-Sounders and a wagon-load of ammunition. Col. MILES' message reached Gen. MCCLELLAN. The rebels attacked our extreme left on Bolivar Heights, and were repulsed by Gen. WHITE. In the night our cavalry escaped from Harper's Ferry.

- At light the rebels attacked our forces at Munfordsville, Ky., with artillery. After a hard artillery fight, the rebel infantry attacked our troops, and were repulsed five successive times.

September 15.

- HARPER's FERRY SURRENDERED by Col. MILES. The cavalry from Harper's Ferry reached Greencastle, Penn., having captured an ammunition train belonging to the rebel Gen. LONGSTREET. Gen. PLEASANTON, of MCCLELLAN's army, started after the enemy, and captured two of their guns. Gen. RICHARDSON's Division came up with the enemy in large force near Sharpsburgh. During the night the greater part of our army arrived on the ground.

- Business in Cincinnati resumed.

September 16.

- BATTLE AT MUNFORDSVILLE, Ky., renewed; desperate fighting throughout the day.

- Terrific fighting near Sharpsburgh and Antietam Creek, Md. The day closed without any definite result.

September 17.

- BATTLE OF ANTIETAM. The fight of the previous day was renewed in the morning, and raged with the greatest fury. The battles of the 16th and 17th were the most furious and obstinate of the war, and the carnage on both sides was terrible. The rebels were defeated and our army left in possession of the field. Gen. MANSFIELD was killed and Gens. HOOKER and RICHARDSON (the latter mortally) wounded. Surgeon-Gen. HAMMOND telegraphed North for volunteer surgeons for the battle-field of Antietam. Our loss in the battle of Antietam was 12,469; estimated rebel loss in the battles of South Mountain and Antietam 25,542.

- Reconnaissance toward Leesburgh, Va. The rebel force driven back at the point of the bayonet.

- Cumberland Gap, Ky., evacuated by the Union forces under Gen. GEO. W. MORGAN, though almost completely surrounded by the enemy, he succeeded in saving his command, which reached Greenupsburgh, Oct. 3.

- At the time of the evacuation, the rebel Gen. STEVENSON was three miles in his rear; Gen. BRAGG on his left; MARSHALL on his right, and KIRBY SMITH in his front. Before leaving, MORGAN exploded the mines and magazines, and burned the store-houses at the Gap.

- A strong column of Gen. BRAGG's force reinforced the rebels before Munfordsville, and the combined forces completely surrounded our troops. The latter, to the number of 4,600, were compelled to surrender at 6 A.M.

- Gen. MITCHEL took command of the Department of the South.

September 18.

- The rebels in front of Gen. MCCLELLAN abandoned their position in the night, leaving many of their dead and wounded on the field An expedition left Pensacola for Sabine Pass and Galveston.

- The rebel army from Maryland passed hastily through Sharpsburgh.

September 19.

- BATTLE OF IUKA, MISS. Gen. ROSENCRANS' army marched 20 miles, driving in the rebel outposts for the last eight miles. He reached the front of Gen. PRICE's army, advantageously posted in unknown woods, and opened the action at 4 P.M. The battle raged furiously till night closed in, when our army rested on the field from which the enemy retired during the night.

- A reconnoitering force from our army crossed the Potomac at Shepardstown, after a stout resistance on the part of the rebels. Four pieces of artillery were captured by our troops. By daylight the main body of rebels, with their artillery, had crossed the Potomac. Our cavalry entered Sharps burgh. The last of the rebels left Harper's Ferry.

- Gen. MCCLELLAN reported that Gen. PLEASANTON was driving the enemy across the Potomac, and that our victory was complete.

September 20.

- A Reconnaissance in force across the Potomac, and though our forces were supported by artillery they were compelled to recross the Potomac after a stubborn resistance.

- The enemy crossed at Williamsport, but were driven back by the advance of our army and the town was afterwards occupied by us in strong force.

- Reconnaissance to Ashby's Gap.

- Gov. CURTIN withdrew the Pennsylvania militia.

- Commander GEO. H. PREBLE, U.S.N., dismissed from the service for allowing the steamer Oreto to escape him at Mobile.

September 21.

- The armies of Gen. BUELL and Gen. BRAGG left Lebanon, Tenn., and Carthage respectively on their way toward Louisville. Our army traveled 361 miles; BRAGG's army 206.

- BUELL's army reached Northern Kentucky one day ahead of BRAGG's.

- Arrival of the advance boats of of the expedition to Galveston off the bar of that city.

- The rebels driven out of Munfordsville, Ky.

- Raid of STEWART's Cavalry in the direction of Williamsport.

- Reconnaissance beyond Chantilly, Va.

September 22.

- PRESIDENT LINCOLN'S EMANCIPATION PROCLAMATION issued, declaring the slaves in any State in rebellion on Jan. 1, 1863, thenceforward and forever free.

- Battle of Wood Lake, Minnesota, with the Indians.

September 24.

- The Governors of the loyal States met in Convention at Altoona, Penn., seventeen States being represented.

- Great excitement in Louisville, Ky.; business suspended and all required to labor on the fortifications.

- Gen. BUELL arrived there at midnight.

- Engagement between the forces sent from New-Orleans and the rebels at Donaldsonville.

September 25.

- A portion of Commodore WILKES' fleet arrived at St. George, Bermuda, and was notified to leave in twenty-four hours, which notice he disregarded, not leaving the port until Oct. 2.

- Reconnaissance to Warrenton Junction.

September 27.

- Augusta, Ky., 40 miles from Cincinnati, on the Ohio River, taken by rebel cavalry, who destroyed the place.

September 28.

- English steamer Sunbeam captured by the gunboats Stale of Georgia and Mystic while attempting to run the blockade at Wilmington, N.C.

September 29.

- Gen. BUELL ordered to turn over the command of his army to Maj. Gen. THOMAS.

- Maj. Gen. NELSON killed by Brig. Gen. JEFF. C. DAVIS, at the Galt House, Louisville, for an assault offered by the former.

- Gen. STAHL's advance took Warrenton, Va.

- Death of Gen. I.P. RODMAN, wounded at Antietam.

- Retaliatory resolutions introduced in the rebel Congress, on account of the Emancipation Proclamation.

OCTOBER.

October 1.

- President LINCOLN arrived at Harper's Ferry.

- Gen. HALLECK sent to Gen. MCCLELLAN, urging him to cross the Potomac at once, and give battle to the enemy.

- Gen. PLEASANTON crossed the Potomac on a Reconnaissance, near Shepherdstown. He met the rebels there, and drove them to Martinsburgh.

- Secretary STANTON transferred the Western gunboat fleet to the Navy Department.

- Gen. BUELL's army left Louisville, Ky.

October 3.

- THE REBELS ATTACKED OUR ARMY NEAR CORINTH, MISS., early in the morning. The fight continued during the day, the rebels succeeding in capturing some of our guns, and driving our forces back three or four miles to the fortifications of the town.

- President LINCOLN reviewed the Army of the Potomac.

- Ship Brilliant, from New-York to London, burned by the pirate Alabama.

- Union Gen. GEO. W. MORGAN reached Greenupsburgh, Ky., 15 miles from Portsmouth, Ohio, with his forces from Cumberland Gap, having marched 219 miles in 16 days.

- Rebel Gen. JOHN MORGAN repulsed near Olive Hill, Ky.

October 4.

- After a quiet night, the attack on our troops at Corinth, Miss., was resumed early in the morning. The battle ended by a retreat of the whole rebel army. It was won with great loss on both sides.

- Gen. BUELL's troops reached Bardstown, Ky., driving out the enemy's rear guard of cavalry and artillery. The pursuit was continued toward Springfield.

October 5.

- Galveston, Texas, occupied by the Union forces.

- The rebels, retreating from Corinth, reached the Hatchee River, where they were attached and lost two batteries and some prisoners.

October 6.

- Gen. HALLECK peremptorily ordered Gen. MCCLELLAN "to cross the Potomac and give battle to the enemy, or drive him south. Your army must move now, while the roads are good."

- English mail steamer Merlin brought to off the harbor of St. George, by a shot from one of Commodore WILKES' fleet. Gunboat Tascarora sailed from Fayal, in search of the Alabama.

- Expedition to destroy the salt works of the rebels, on the coast of Florida.

October 7.

- Gen. BUELL's army arrived within two miles of Perryville, Ky., where the enemy were found to be in force.

- Gen. MCCLELLAN's order, calling attention to the President's emancipation proclamation, and explaining the duties of the officers and soldiers.

- Reconnaissance to the Rappahannock, through Centreville and Manassas Junction.

October 8.

- BATTLE OF PERRYVILLE, KY. The battle was severe, commencing at 12 1/2 P.M. and continuing furiously until dark. The rebel army was under command of Gen. BRAGG, the different divisions being commanded by Gens. POLK, CHEATHAM, BUCKNER and ANDERSON. The battle was commenced by the rebels furiously assaulting our army. Gen. BRAGG styled it in his report the severest and most desperately contested engagement within his knowledge. He acknowledged a loss in killed, wounded and missing, of 2,500.

- Among his wounded were Brig.-Gens. WOOD, CLEBURN and BROWN. Gen. HARDEE was engaged in the battle, commanding the rebel left wing. The rebels were everywhere repulsed, but not without some momentary advantages on the left. The Union Gens. JACKSON and TERRELL were killed. Gen. ROUSSEAU was in the thickest of the fight and covered himself with glory. The battle did not accomplish what was hoped, as the enemy had escaped by the morning after the fight.

October 9.

- Gen. GRANT recalled Gen. ROSECRANS from the pursuit of the rebels defeated at Corinth.

- The rebel army under Gen. BRAGG, was attacked at Chaplin Creek on its retreat. A short but sharp fight ensued, when the rebels broke and fled.

- STUART's cavalry started on their expedition to Pennsylvania. The force consisted of 1,800 cavalry, 4 pieces of horse artillery, under command of Gen. HAMPTON and Cols. W.H. LEE and JONES. The troops rendezvoused at Darksville at 12 M., marched thence to the vicinity of Hedgeville, where they encamped for the night.

October 10.

- REBEL INVASION OF PENNSYLVANIA. STUART's rebel cavalry reached Chambersburgh Penn., about 6 P.M., having crossed the Potomac at McCoy's, between Hancock and Williamsport.

- Gen. ROSECRANS returned from the pursuit of PRICE's army, reporting it dispersed, demoralized, and incapable of further mischief.

- Ship Tonawanda captured by the pirate Alabama, and released on giving bonds for $80,000, payable to the President of the Confederate States thirty days after the declaration of peace. Ship Manchester and brig Dunkirk also captured.

October 11.

- The rebel STUART's cavalry destroyed two warehouses at Chambersburgh, containing military stores; also the buildings of the Cumberland Valley Railroad, including the machine shops; the rolling stock collected there was also destroyed. They also burned the railroad bridge at Scotland, five miles from Chambersburgh.

- Gen. WOOL and staff arrived at Harrisburgh, Penn., and assumed the command and direction of the troops for the defence of the State.

- Rebels in large force near Nashville, Tenn. They sent a flag of truce, demanding the surrender of the city, which was refused by Gen. NEGLEY, in command of the post.

- Great battle between Harrisburgh and Danville, Ky., in which the rebels were defeated, after which they retreated to Camp Dick Robinson.

- The whole rebel army engaged in the battle of Perryville, reached Bryantsville, Ky., our army slowly following.

- Skirmish near Lagrange, Ark., the rebels defeated.

October 12.

- STUART's rebel cavalry occupied Leesburgh, Va., returning from their raid into Pennsylvania. Gen. PLEASANTON passed through Frederick City, Md., in pursuit. The rebels passed a few miles from Frederick, and effected their escape by crossing the Potomac at White's Ferry. Here the chase ended, our troops having met the rebels near the mouth of the Monocacy. The rebels were clothed in captured National uniforms, which misled our soldiers, who were received, when in close proximity, by a fire of carbines and pistols. Gen. PLEASANTON's cavalry marched 90 miles in 24 hours.

October 13.

- Gen. BRAGG's army evacuated Camp Dick Robinson, Ky.

October 14.

- Our whole force moved in pursuit of BRAGG's army early in the morning. During the day some skirmishing took place.

- The first donation of $100,000 by San Francisco, received by the Sanitary Commission.

October 15.

- Gen. STAHL left Centreville, with cavalry and artillery, to find the rebel Gen. STUART. He had some skirmishes, but nothing decisive resulted there from.

- Heavy fight between Lexington and Richmond, Ky., in which the rebels were repulsed.

- Our army reached Crab Orchard, Ky., after severe skirmishing.

- Bark Lamplighter, of Boston, captured and burned by the pirate Alabama.

October 16.

- Advance of Gen. MCCLELLAN's army from Harper's Ferry.

- Pursuit of BRAGG's army in Kentucky virtually abandoned.

- British steamer Wachuta captured, after an all-day's chase, of the coast of North Carolina.

- A Reconnaissance up the Apalachicola River, Fla. The expedition captured a sloop laden with cotton.

October 17.

- Return of Gen. HANCOCK's expedition to Boliver Heights. They found the enemy in force at Bruce-town, 5 miles from Winchester, Va., and captured 1,500 bushels of wheat.

- HUMPHREY's division, which crossed near Shepherdstown, returned after finding the enemy in considerable force and after some artillery skirmishing.

October 18.

- The guerrilla Chief MORGAN dashed into Lexington, Ky., at the head of 1,500 troops and took 125 prisoners, killing six of our men.

- Federal steamer fired into by the rebels thirty miles below Memphis.

- Steamer Gladiator also attacked 25 miles below and set on fire by the rebels; the flames were extinguished.

October 19.

- The rebel JOHN MORGAN, left Lawrenceburgh, Ky., with about 1,200 men, closely pursued by Gen. DUMONT.

- Col. MILLER, of Gen. NEGLEY's army, had a brush with the enemy, near Nashville, Tenn., and captured several.

- On the 18th and 19th, a lage force of rebels under EWELL and JACKSON entered Martinsburgh, and completed the destruction of the railroad property there, including the depot and workshops.

- A powerful iron steamer ran the blockade at Charleston, S.C., (on the night of the 18th).

October 20.

- At 3 o'clock in the morning, 300 or 400 of MORGAN's men, captured a Union train of 81 wagons, (51 of which were loaded,) near Bardstown, Ky. MORGAN then went toward Bardstown and captured another train at daylight.

October 21.

· Expedition from MCCLELLAN's Army to intercept a force of rebel cavalry foraging in London County, Va. The Expedition was successful.

· Dashing Reconnaissance in the direction of Leesburgh, Va. Skirmishing with the rebel cavalry.

· Gen. JEFF. C. DAVIS released from arrest, and ordered to report for duty at Cincinnati.

· An expedition, consisting of 4,000 or 5,000 men, with artillery, and fifteen transports and gunboats, left Hilton Head for a Reconnaissance along the Charleston and Savannah Railroad.

· Successful attack on a rebel force near Nashville, Tenn.

October 22.

· The Governor of Kentucky called on the people of Louisville to rally for the defense of the city.

· HUMPHREY MARSHALL's force retreated from Mount Stirling toward East Tennessee.

· Gen. BRAGG's rebel army moved through Cumberland Gap.

· Our forces attacked Pocotaligo and Coosawhatchie, S.C. They succeeded in reaching the Charleston and Savannah Railroad, and did it some damage. The force was engaged in desperate fight with the rebels. The expedition was not entirely successful in accomplishing its mission.

· A force sent on a Reconnaissance in the neighborhood of Martinsburgh had some skirmishing with the enemy, and captured a few prisoners. Return of GEARY's expedition, which left on the 21st, to Harper's Ferry.

· Battle at Maysville, in the northwest corner of Arkansas, (second battle of Pea Ridge). Our forces, under Gen. BLUNT, attacked the enemy, supposed to be 6,000 to 7,000 strong, end after an hour of fighting totally routed them, with a loss on the part of the rebels of all their artillery, a battery of six pounders, a large number of horses and their equipments. By this battle all the organized forces of the enemy were driven back to the Valley of the Arkansas.

October 23.

· Dashing fight at Waverley, Tenn., between a small force of rebels and Union soldiers, in which the rebels were defeated and lost many more than we did.

· Skirmishing in Kentucky with MORGAN's guerrillas.

· Ship Lafayette, of New-Haven, captured and burned by the pirate Alabama.

· English schooner Francis captured.

October 24.

· GEN. BUELL REMOVED FROM THE COMMAND OF THE ARMY IN KENTUCKY, and Gen. ROSECRANS assigned to the command.

· Gen. H.S. GRANT reported a skirmish at Brownsville, Tenn., in which the rebels were defeated with a loss of 40 prisoners and some property.

· Difficulty with the coal miners, in Pennsylvania, relative to the draft, adjusted.

· Skirmish with MORGAN's guerrillas at Morgantown, Ky.; 16 rebels captured.

· English steamer Scolia, loaded with arms, powder, & c., captured at Bull's Bay, S.C.

· Gen. WEITZEL's Brigade, 5,000 strong, left Carrollton above New-Orleans. The expedition was made up of transports and gunboats.

October 25.

· Slight cavalry skirmishing at Manassas Junction and Bristol Station.

· Our forces routed the rebels at Greenville, Mo.

· Gen. SHERMAN issued a stringent order for the Government of Memphis.

October 26.

· Heavy rain, and rise in the Potomac.

· Advance of MCCLELLAN's army commenced.

· Gen BURNSIDE's Division crossed into Virginia.

· Gen. PLEASANTON's cavalry reached Purcellsville.

· MCCLELLAN established his Headquarters in Virginia.

· Schooner Crenshaw, of New-York, captured and burned by the pirate Alabama.

· Gen. WEITZEL's Expedition from New-Orleans landed at Donaldsonville, and his troops took up the line of march. A sharp engagement ensued, in which we took 268 prisoners and I piece of artillery.

October 27.

· Gen. JEFF. C. DAVIS indicted for killing Gen. NELSON.

· 1,500 rebels attacked and defeated at Putnam's Ferry, Mo.

· English steamer Anglia, of Liverpool, captured four miles inside of Bull's Bay, S.C. She was loaded with arms, ammunition' and other contraband goods.

· Rebel army under Gens. ECHOLS, FLOYD and JENKINS retreated from Charlestown, Va.

· Battle at Labadieville, on Bayou La Fourohe, La. The rebels were put to flight after a short resistance.

October 28.

· Our troops occupied Halltown, Va., and our pickets extended beyond there.

· Gen. PRICE's, pickets driven from Grand Junction.

· The Union troops, under Brig.-Gen. HERRON, attacked a rebel camp four miles, from Fayetteville, Ark. After a sharp engagement of an hour the enemy were completely routed, leaving all their camp equipage and a few wagons. Gen. HERRON pursued the rebels several miles into the Boston Mountains.

· Skirmish at Snicker's Gap, Va.

· Bark Laurietta captured and burned by the pirate Alabama.

October 29.

· Skirmish between Gen. WALKER's (rebel) force and Gen. BAYARD's Cavalry, at Upperville and Paris, Va.

· Great fire at Harper's Ferry; twenty-six cars loaded with hay were simultaneously in flames. A part of the railroad bridge was destroyed.

· Gen. U.S. GRANT reported that the guerrillas at Clarkson, Mo., had been attacked, routed, and utterly dispersed.

· Rebels at Snicker's Gap, Va., in force.

· Gen. RICHARDSON's Division, of MCCLELLAN's army, passes Snicker's Gap to Paris, Va.

· Brig Baron de Castine captured by the pirate Alabama, and released on giving bonds for $6,000, payable to the President of the Confederate States thirty days after peace shall be declared.

· The corps d'armee under Brig.-Gen. Cox reached Charlestown, Va. On their entrance they were greeted with cheers and other demonstrations of favor.

October 30.

· Gen. ROSECRANS and staff arrived at Louisville, Ky.

· Gen. O.M. MITCHELL, Commander of the Department of the South, died of yellow fever at Beaufort, S.C.

· English brig Hermasa captured.

October 31.

· Skirmish with STUART's cavalry at Marysville, Va.

· The advance guard of the column for the relief of Nashville passed through Bowling Green, Ky.

NOVEMBER.

November 1.

· Artillery fight between Gen. PLEASONTON's force and the rebels at Phillimont, Va., lasting five hours.

· Grand ovation to Gen. FREMONT in St. Louis.

· Rebel steamboat A.B. Ligur captured near New-Orleans.

November 2.

· The artillery fight at Phillimont renewed and the rebels fell back.

· Additional force of our troops took possession of Snicker's Gap, Va.

· Gen. FOSTER's expedition from Newbern took up its line of march.

· Schooner Alice captured by the Alabama.

November 3.

· Gen. PLEASONTON's Cavalry occupied Upperville, Va., after a spirited engagement with the enemy of about four hours.

· Gen. STAHL's Cavalry drove the enemy from Thoroughfare Gap, Va., which was afterward occupied by Gen. SCHURZ.

· Maj.-Gen. J.B. RICHARDSON died at Sharpsburgh, Md., from wounds received in the battle of Antietam.

· Commodore W.D. PORTER offered the merchants of New-York to take the clipper ship Dreadnought and pursue the pirate Alabama.

· Piedmont, Va., occupied by our cavalry, under Gens. PLEASANTON and AVERILL.

· Maj. REID SANDERS, C.S.A., captured on the coast of Virginia, endeavoring to escape with rebel dispatches.

· Reconnaissances through Snicker's Gap, Va. The object fully accomplished, after some severe skirmishing and brave charges made by our troops.

November 4.

· Ashby's Gap taken possession of by Union troops.

· Gen. MCCLELLAN's headquarters at Upperville, Va.

· Gen. GRANT, with several divisions of the army from Bolivar, Tenn., and Corinth, Miss., marched into Lagrange, Miss., the rebels, under Gen. EARL VAN DORN, being in large force at Holly Springs, Miss.

· Spirited engagement, at Markham, Va.

· Salt works at Kingsbury, Ga. destroyed, in effecting which our forces were attacked.

November 5.
· Gen. PLEASANTON reached a point near Chester Gap, Va., before reaching which he routed STUART's cavalry.

· Engagement at New-Baltimore, Va.

· Two vessels laden with cotton captured in Nassau River.

· Skirmishing near Nashville, Tenn.

November 6.
· Death of Brig.-Gen. CHAS. D. JAMESON.

· Warrenton, Va., occupied by advance of the Army of the Potomac.

· Death of Commodore G.J. PENDERGRAST, U.S.N.

· Advance of Gen. MCCOOK's corps arrived at Nashville.

· English schooner Dart captured.

November 7.
· GEN. MCCLELLAN REMOVED FROM THE COMMAND OF THE ARMY OF THE POTOMAC, AND THE COMMAND TURNED OVER TO GEN. BURNSIDE.

· Gen. BAYARD attacked at Rappahannock Station, Va.

· Expedition up Sapelo Sound, Ga., partly made up of negro troops.

November 8.
· Gen. PLEASANTON engaged in a skirmish near Little Washington, Va.

· Gen. BAYARD held the railroad bridge across the Rappahannock.

· Cavalry charge on the rebels near Gaines' Cross Roads.

· Ship T.B. Wales captured by the Alabama.

November 9.
· Gen. BUTLER sequestered the property in the district of La Fourche, La., and declared all sales made by disloyal persons, since Sept. 18, void.

· Brilliant cavalry dash of BAYARD's men at Fredericksburgh.

November 10.
· Gen. ROSECRANS arrived at Nashville.

· Gen. HALLECK ordered to their regiments all absent officers.

· Gen. PLEASANTON's pickets attacked near Amosville, Va.

· Great Union demonstration in Memphis.

November 11.
· Gen. GRANT reported a victory at Garrettsburgh, Ky.

· Gen. ROSECRANS' command arrived at Fort Donelson.

November 12.
· Gen. HALLECK visited the Army of the Potomac.

· Gen. GRANT's advance reached Holly Springs.

November 13.
· Skirmish near White Sulphur Springs, Va.

· Holly Springs occupied by the Union troops, after a slight skirmish.

November 15.
· A.J. HAMILTON appointed Military Governor of Texas.

· Artillery fight near Fayetteville, Va.

· Warrenton, Va., evacuated by our troops.

November 16.
· Gen. BURNSIDE's headquarters moved to Catlett's Station, Va.

November 17.
· Artillery engagement near Fredericksburgh, Va.

· JEFF. DAVIS ordered retaliation for the execution of 10 rebels in Missouri.

· The Alabama arrived at Martinique. The United States frigate San Jacinto arrived at the same place, but immediately went outside the harbor, to await the appearance of the Alabama.

November 18.
· The Army of the Potomac reached Falmouth, opposite Fredericksburg, Va.

· Skirmish at Rural Hill, Va.

· Escape of the Alabama from Martinique.

November 19.
· Stuart's rebel cavalry near Warrenton Junction.

· Our pickets driven in at Suffolk, Va.

November 20.
· Skirmish at Charlestown, Va.

November 21.
· Gen. SUMNER demands the surrender of Fredericksburgh.

November 22.
· The War Department issued an order releasing persons who had been imprisoned for resisting the draft, discouraging enlistments, & c., and also paroling persons who had been sent from the rebel States by the Military Commanders or Governors.

· Suicide of Brig.-Gen. FRANCIS E. PATTERSON.

November 24.
· Scouting parties left camp near Charlestown, Va., and marched 210 miles in 70 hours.

November 25.
· Rebel raid into Poolesville, Md.

· Attack of the rebels on Newbern, N.C.

November 26.
· The President visited Gen. BURNSIDE at Belleplaine, Va. Successful Reconnaissance from Bolivar Heights.

· Gen. SHERMAN's force left Memphis.

· The rebel camp at Cold Knob, Va., surprised.

November 27.
· Skirmish near Nashville, Tenn.

· Railroad from Aquia Creek to Falmouth, Va., completed.

· Reconnaissance in force by General STAHL's troops.

November 28.
· BATTLE OF CANE HILL, ARKANSAS. Gen. STAHL's force drove in the rebel pickets at Ashby's Gap.

· Gen. BURNSIDE arrived in Washington from the Army of the Potomac.

· General GRANT's army struck their tents and marched in in the direction of Holly Springs.

November 29.
· Gen. STAHL's force reached Perryville, Va., via Snicker's Gap, where they had a skirmish with the enemy, whom they completely routed.

November 30.
· Steamer Vanderbilt returned from a cruise after the Alabama.

DECEMBER.

December 1.
· Tallahatchie, Miss., evacuated by the rebels.

December 2.
· Party of Union cavalry surprised and captured at King George Court-house, Va.

· Fight at Suffolk, Va.

· The rebels desert their fortifications at Abbeville, Miss., and the place was occupied by the cavalry of Gen. GRANT's army.

December 3.
· Surrender, of Winchester, Va., to Gen. GEARY; the place occupied.

December 4.
· Gen. BANKS and part of his expedition sailed from New-York.

December 5.
· Cavalry engagement near Coffeeville, Miss.

December 6.
· Attack on our force at Cane Hill, Ark. the rebels repulsed.

December 7.
· BATTLE OF FAYETTESVILLE OR PRAIRIE GROVE, ARK., Union victory.

· Battle with MORGAN's force at Hartsville, Tenn. A Union brigade captured by the rebels, who were afterward put to flight.

· Capture of the California steamer Ariel by the pirate Alabama. The Ariel was released on giving bonds for $228,000, payable 30 days after the recognition of the Southern Confederacy.

December 8.
· The President ordered the execution of thirty-nine Indians in Minnesota, to take place of Dec. 19.

· Steamer Lake City destroyed by the rebels at Concordia, Ark.

December 9.
· Sharp fight at Lavergne, Tenn.

December 10.
· The rebels appeared in force near Nashville, driving in our pickets.

· Gunboat fight at Port Royal, Va.

· Plymouth, N.C. destroyed by the rebels.

December 11.
· SHELLING OF FREDERICKSBURGH. The place occupied by our troops, who crossed in the face of a terrible fire. The city partially destroyed.

· Successful Reconnaissance from Nashville.

· Arrival of two of Gen. BANKS' vessels, disabled, at Port Royal, S.C.

December 12.
· Crossing of our army at Fredericksburgh continued. Artillery duel between the two forces.

· Skirmish near Suffolk, Va.

· Destruction of the gunboat Cuiro on the Yazoo River by a rebel torpedo.

December 13.
· BATTLE OF FREDERICKSBURGH, fought back of the town. Gen. BAYARD killed.

· Battle of Zuni, N.C.

· Gen. FOSTER attacked Kinston, N.C.

December 14.
- Another raid of rebel cavalry into Poolesville, Md.
- Firing on the rebel pickets or James Island, N.C.
- Kinston, N.C., occupied by Gen. FOSTER's Army.
- Rebel Saltworks at Yellville, Ark., destroyed by Capt. BIRCH.
- Gen. N.P. BANKS arrived at New-Orleans with his Expedition.

December 15.
- FREDERICKSBURGH EVACUATED BY OUR ARMY in the night. BURNSIDE's Army crossed to Falmouth.
- Gen, BUTLER issued his farewell address to his army.

December 16.
- Letter of Gen. BURNSIDE, assuming the responsibility of the defeat at Fredericksburgh, written.
- Rebel raid on Occoquan, Va.
- Gen. BUTLER transferred the command of the Department of the Gulf to Gen. BANKS. Gen. BANKS issued his General Order assuming command of the Department of the Gulf, including Texas.
- An expedition left New-Orleans for Baton Rouge, La.

December 17.
- Baton Rouge recaptured.

December 22.
- Address of the President to the Army of the Potomac in regard to the occurrences at Fredericksburgh.

December 23.
- Report of the Congressional Committee, on the battle of Fredericksburgh.
- Gen. BURNSIDE returned to his army, from Washington.
- Winchester, Va., reoccupied by Union forces under Col. KEYES.
- JEFF. DAVIS issued a Retaliatory Proclamation, especially directed against Gen. BUTLER and his officers.

December 24.
- Severe skirmish on the Blackwater.

December 25.
- The Rebels, under Gens. FLOYD and MARSHALL, reported to have reentered Eastern Kentucky through Pound Gap.
- Glasgow, Ky., captured by the rebel MORGAN.

December 26.
- Execution of 38 Indians in Minnesota.

December 27.
- A party of rebel cavalry repulsed at Dumfries, Va.
- JOHN MORGAN and his guerrillas attacked a Union force at Elizabethtown, Ky.

December 28.
- Bridge on the Louisville and Nashville Railroad destroyed by MORGAN.
- New-Madrid evacuated.
- Unsuccessful attempt of the rebel Gen. STUART to capture the depot of stores at Fairfax Station, Va.
- Van Buren, Ark., captured and the rebels put to flight.

1863

BATTLE RECORD FOR 1863.

CHRONOLOGICAL TABLE OF THE EVENTS OF THE YEAR.

OUR VICTORIES AND DEFEATS BY LAND AND SEA.

THE GREAT BATTLES AND EVENTS OF THE YEAR.

DECEMBER 31, 1863

JANUARY.

January 1.
- THE EMANCIPATION PROCLAMATION OF PRESDENT LINCOLN, DECLARING SLAVES IN THE INSURRECTIONARY STATES AND DISTRICTS FOREVER AND HENCEFORWARD FREE, issued.
- The battle of Murfreesboro, Tenn., commenced Dec. 31, 1862, continued. The engagement opened at dawn by Gen. ROSECRANS. The battle was hotly contested, and the losses great on both sides.
- The rebel guerrilla MORGAN defeated in Kentucky.
- Emancipation Jubilee of the negroes at Hilton Head, S.C.
- The rebel Gen. FORREST defeated at Hunt's Cross Roads, Tenn., by Gen. SULLIVAN.
- Galveston, Texas, recaptured by the rebels, who also took the steamer Harriet Lane. The steamer Westfield was blown up by its commander to prevent it from falling into the hands of the rebels.
- Gen. BUTLER and Staff arrived in New-York City from New-Orleans.
- Charges preferred against the New-York Police Commissioners for illegal action in making arrests for treason, & c.

January 2.
- Battle of Murfreesboro, Tenn., continued, the rebels being repulsed in an attack on our left wing.
- Gen. SHERMAN's force, operating against Vicksburgh, was withdrawn from the Yazoo River.
- Dumfries entered by STUART's cavalry, who captured some public stores, & c.
- Gen. BURNSIDE returned to the Army of the Potomac from Washington.

January 3.
- The rebels retreated from the battle-field of Murfreesboro.
- Gov. SEYMOUR, of New-York, appointed this day for the trial of the New-York Police Commissioners.
- Arrest of ISAAC N. COOK, in Cincinnati, as a defaulting Paymaster.
- Arrival in New-York of a cavalry company from California.
- Our forces at Moorefield, West Va., attacked.
- The boat containing a missing portion of the Monitor's crew picked up on Hatteras Shoals.
- Department of the East, including the New-England States and the State of New-York, created, and Gen. JOHN E. WOOL assigned to its command.

January 5.
- Murfreesboro, Tenn., occupied by a National force.
- J.P. USHER, of Indiana, nominated as Secretary of the Interior.
- Gen. MILROY, in Western Virginia, issued a proclamation notifying the people of Winchester and neighborhood of the provisions of the President's Emancipation Proclamation.

January 6.
- Gen. CARTER's Union force reached Manchester, Ky., on its return from a raid into East Tennessee, where they destroyed bridges and took a number of prisoners.

January 7.
- Successful reconnaissance of Union troops from Yorktown in the neighborhood of West Point, Va.

January 8.
- Springfield, Mo., attacked by the rebels.
- Rebel camp at Huntoon's Mills, near Fort Pillow, surprised.
- Steamer Mussulman burned by guerrillas near Memphis, Tenn.

January 9.
- Order issued by Gen. HALLECK, thanking Gen. ROSECRANS and his army for the victory of Murfreesboro.
- Return of the reconnoitering expedition from West Point, Va., to Fort Monroe.
- The rebels repulsed at Providence Church, on the Blackwater, Va.

January 10.
- Cavalry skirmish at Catlett's Station, Va.
- Battle at Arkansas Post commenced.
- English steamer Rising Dawn captured.
- Brig J.P. Ellicott captured by the privateer Retribution.

January 11.
- Fort Hindman and Arkansas, forts on the Arkansas River, surrendered by the rebels.
- Fight at Huntsville, Mo.
- Union gunboat Hatteras sunk by the Alabama, on the coast of Texas.
- Gen. WEITZEL crossed Berwick Bay and attacked the rebel gunboat Cotton in the Bayou Teche.

January 12.
- Gen. JOHN E. WOOL assumed command of the Department of the East headquarters at New-York City.
- JEFF. DAVIS' Message sent to the rebel Congress.
- Gen. JOHN A. MCCLERNAND congratulated his army on the capture of Arkansas Post.

January 13.
- Peace resolutions introduced into the New-Jersey Legislature.

January 14.
- Col. JAMES W. WALL elected United States Senator from New-Jersey.
- Engagement at the Bayou Teche, La.
- Lieut.-Commander (Union) THOS. MCKEON BUCHANAN killed.

January 15.
- Union gunboat Columbia destroyed by rebels near Wilmington, N.C.

January 16.
- Rebel privateer Oreto ran the blockade out of Mobile.

January 17.
- Steamer Vanderbilt arrived at Fortress Monroe after an unsuccessful cruise after the Alabama.
- Rebel privateer Oreto destroyed the brig Estelle.

January 18.
- Gen. HUNTER arrived at Hilton Head to take command of the Department of the South .
- A large fleet sailed from Napoleon and Memphis for Young's Point and Milliken's Bend, near Vicksburgh, on this and the following days.

January 20.
- Gen. BURNSIDE announced to the Army of the Potomac that it was about to meet the enemy again.
- Gen. HUNTER assumed command of the Department of the South.
- The rebel privateer Alabama arrived at Jamaica.

January 21.
- The expedition under Gen. GRANT, from Napoleon, arrived at Young's Point, nine miles from Vicksburgh.
- Engagement near Sabine Pass, Galveston, Texas.
- Gunboat Morning Light and the bark Velocity, captured by the rebels off Sabine Pass, Texas.

January 24.
- Gen. BURNSIDE relieved of the command of the Army of the Potomac, and the command assigned to Gen. HOOKER.

January 25.
- Cars on the railroad, between Nashville and Franklin, Tenn., destroyed by rebels.
- The iron-clad Montauk arrived off Fort McAllister, Ga.

January 26.
- Gen. BURNSIDE turned over the command of the Army of the Potomac to Gen. HOOKER.
- Gen. HOOKER, in general orders, assumed command.
- Gen. W.B. FRANKLIN, having been relieved of his command in the Army of the Potomac, took leave of his division.
- Gen. SUMNER relieved of his command.
- Bark Golden Rule burned by the Alabama.
- Ship Washington captured by the Alabama.

January 27.
- Gen. HOOKER visited Washington.
- THURLOW WEED took leave of the Albany Evening Journal.
- Cavalry skirmish at Middleburgh, Va.
- Gen. BURNSIDE arrived in New-York.
- A.D. BOILEAU, proprietor of the Philadelphia Evening Journal, arrested by order of the Government.
- Bombardment of Fort McAllister, on the Ogeechee River, Ga., by the Montauk.
- Brig Chastelaine burned by the Alabama.

January 29.
- Excitement in Philadelphia over the arrest of the editor of the Evening Journal.
- Charge of Judge LUDLOW to the Grand Jury on the subject.
- English steamer Princess Royal captured off Charleston, S.C.

January 30.
- Victory of Gen. CORCORAN over the rebel Gen. ROGER A. PRYOR's force near the Blackwater, the engagement being called the Battle of the Deserted House.
- Union gunboat Isaac Smith, captured by the rebels in the Stono River, S.C.

January 31.
- The fleet blockading Charleston, S.C., attacked by the rebel iron-clads Chicora and Palmetto State.
- Gen. BEAUREGARD and Flag-Officer D.N. INGRAHAM (rebel), formally declared by proclamation that the blockade of Charleston, S.C., was raised.
- Union gunboat Mercedita surrendered.
- J.P. BENJAMIN, Secretary of State of the Confederate States, gave official notice that the blockade was broken.
- Schooner Hanover destroyed by the Retribution.

FEBRUARY.

February 1.
- Franklin, Tenn., occupied by Federal forces.
- A.J. BOILEAU, editor of the Philadelphia Evening Journal, released from Fort McHenry.
- Fort McAllister, Ga., again attacked.
- Gunboat New Era attacked Island No. 10.

February 2.
- A bill providing for the employment of negro soldiers passed the United States House of Representatives.
- Rebel camp at Middletown, Tenn., surprised.
- Department of Washington, under command of Gen. HEINTZELMAN, constituted.
- The Union ram Queen of the West ran past the rebel batteries at Vicksburgh, and attacked the rebel steamer City of Vicksburgh.

February 3.
- The rebels repulsed in an attack on our forces at Dover, Tenn., by Union gunboats.
- Fort Donelson, Tenn., invested by the rebels.

February 4.
- Engagement at Fort McAllister, Ga.

February 5.
- Our forces repulsed a rebel attack on Fort Donelson, Tenn.
- Union ram Queen of the West returned from her expedition past the batteries of Vicksburgh, having destroyed three rebel transports and an immense quantity of rebel stores.

February 6.
- Raid of Union cavalry to Middleburgh and Aldie, Va.

February 7.
- Reconnaissance from the right wing of the Army of the Potomac.
- Engagement near Williamsburgh, Va.

February 8.
- Our forces entered Lebanon, Tenn., capturing a number of rebels.

February 9.
- Collision between the transport North Star and the steamer Ella Warley near Sandy Hook.
- Reconnoitering expedition, under Col. WYNDHAM, left Centreville, Va.

February 10.
- Gen. ROSECRANS issued an order declaring that all rebel soldiers found in National uniforms should not be treated as prisoners of war, or receive quarter in battle.
- Official denial that the blockade at Charleston, S.C., had been raised.

February 11.
- Secretary SEWARD transmitted to the Senate a communication relative to the visit of the French Minister to Richmond.

February 12.
- Passage of the National Currency bill by the Senate.
- Slight skirmish near Smithfield, Va.
- Great fire at Norfolk, Va.
- Ship Jacob Bell, from China, captured and burned by the Florida.
- Rebel fort on Pelican Island, near Galveston, Texas, shelled by the Brooklyn.

February 13.
- A Court of Inquiry, relative to cotton and other traffic on the Mississippi River, instituted.
- Skirmish near Bolivar, Tenn.
- Gunboat Indianola ran the blockade at Vicksburgh.

February 15.
- Slight skirmish near Nolinsville, Ky.

February 16.
- The Conscription bill passed by the United States Senate.
- Brig.-Gen. THOS. G. STEVENSON placed in arrest by Gen. HUNTER, at Port Royal, for objecting to fight in company with negroes.

February 18.
- Gen. BEAUREGARD issued a proclamation announcing that an attack on Charleston and Savannah would probably soon be made.
- Bombardment of Vicksburgh, Miss.

February 19.
- Brig Emily Fisher captured and bonded by the privateer Retribution.

February 20.
- The National Currency Bill passed the House of Representatives.
- United States steamer Alabama left St. Thomas in search of the Florida.
- The Vanderbilt left St. Thomas on a cruise for privateers.

February 21.
- The pirate Alabama burned the bark Olive Jane.

February 22.
- Richmond, Ky., occupied by rebel cavalry.
- Tuscumbia, Ala., reached by a Union cavalry force.
- Ship Golden Eagle destroyed by the Alabama.

February 23.
- Bill authorizing the suspension of the writ of habeas corpus passed by the United States Senate.

February 24.
- The iron-clad gunboat Indianola captured by the rebels near Vicksburgh.
- Some shells thrown into Galveston, Texas, by the Brooklyn.

February 25.
- Cavalry skirmish at Piedants Farm, Va.
- Cavalry fight near Strasburgh, Va. Our forces defeated.
- Privateer Retribution arrived at Nassau.
- Capture of the Anglo-rebel steamer Peterhoff by the Vanderbilt, near St. Thomas.
- An expedition through Yazoo Pass, near Vicksburgh, left Moon Lake.

February 26.
- Death of Col. D.D. TOMPKINS.

February 27.
- Col. WYNDHAM's cavalry left Centreville, Va., on a reconnaissance, afterward reaching Falmouth, Va.
- Brig.-Gen. JOHN COCHRANE, having resigned his commission, took leave of his corps of the Army of the Potomac.
- JEFF. DAVIS issued a proclamation appointing March 27 as Fast Day in the Confederate States.
- Gen. STEVENSON released from arrest by Gen. HUNTER.
- Three Anglo-rebel steamers, the Georgiana, the Britinnia and the Gertrude, arrived at Nassau.
- A sham monitor sent by Admiral PORTER past the rebel batteries at Vicksburgh.
- Schooner Palmetto captured by the Alabama.

February 28.
- President LINCOLN called an extra session of the Senate.
- Col. WYNDHAM's cavalry arrived at Falmouth, Va.
- The rebel steamer Nashville destroyed by the Montauk in Ogeechee River, Ga.
- The Yazoo Pass expedition reached the Coldwater River, twelve miles from Moon Lake, through Yazoo Pass.

MARCH.

March 1.
- Rebels defeated at Bradyville, Tenn.

March 2.
- Ship John A. Park captured and burned by the Alabama.

March 3.
- Act amendatory to the Tax Law passed both Houses of Congress, as amended by a Conference Committee.
- An expedition left Belle Blain, Va., for Northumberland County, Va.
- Gunboat Indianola destroyed by the rebels.

March 4.
- Congress adjourned.
- Skirmish near Franklin, Tenn.
- Skirmish at "Skeet," N.C.

March 5.
- Severe engagement near Springville, Tenn.
- Brig.-Gen. H.M. NAGLEE relieved of his command by Gen. HUNTER.
- Gen. HALLECK addressed a letter to Gen. ROSE-CRANS, relative to the treatment of disloyal persons.
- Col. COLBURN's force (Union) captured at Thompson's Station, Tenn.

March 7.
- The Union expedition into Northumberland County, Va., returned to the headquarters of the Army of the Potomac from a very successful recon-noitering expedition, during which large captures of provisions, & c., were made.
- Cavalry engagement at Unionville, Tenn., near Murfreesboro.
- The Yazoo Pass expedition arrived in the Tallahatchie.

March 8.
- Schooner Enterprise captured off the coast of Florida.

March 9.
- The rebels entered Fairfax Court House, Va., and captured Brig.-Gen. E.H. STOUGHTON and his guard.
- Anglo-rebel steamer Douro captured by the Quaker City.

March 10.
- President LINCOLN issued a Proclamation ordering soldiers absent from their regiments to return immediately.
- Skirmishing at Rutherford's Creek, near Columbia, Tenn.
- Gen. VAN DORN's force retreated toward Shelbyville, Tenn.
- Rebel steamer Parallel burned on the Tallahatchie.

March 12.
- Successful rebel raid to Hilton Head Island, S.C., in the night.
- Gunboat Chilticothe attacked at the town of Greenwood, near Vicksburgh.

March 13.
- The rebels attacked Newbern, N.C.
- Fight between the Union gunboat Chillicothe and the rebel Fort Pemberton, near Vicksburgh, at the mouth of the Tallahatchie River.
- Affair at Deep Gully, N.C., between Union and rebel forces.
- VAN DORN's forces escape from before Gen. ROSECRANS at Duck River, Tenn.

March 14.
- Port Hudson attacked by Admiral FARRAGUT.
- The steamer Mississippi ran aground, and was burned.
- Gen. FITZHUGH LEE made an advance on our lines at Gloucester, Va., but retired on learning that we had been reinforced.
- Engagement at Deep Gully, N.C., continued.
- Ship Punjaub captured Tay the Alabama.

March 15.
- Schooner Chapman taken possession of at San Francisco as privateer.
- The Jefferson newspaper office destroyed at Richmond, Ind.

March 16.
- Great Union meeting in Brooklyn.
- Gen. ROSECRANS reported the exploits of his cavalry .
- Water admitted into the canal at Lake Providence, near Vicksburgh.

March 17.
- Col. JAMES B. FRY appointed Provost-Marshal General.
- Spirited fighting on the Blackwater.
- Unsuccessful attempt to carry the rebel breastworks.
- Brilliant cavalry fight at Kelly's Ford on the Rappahannock.
- Steamer Calypso arrived at Charleston, S.C., having run the blockade.

March 19.
- The rebel cavalry crossed Duck River, advancing toward Franklin, Tenn., but were driven back by Union cavalry.
- Rebel guerrillas attacked a railroad train near Richland, Ky.
- Anglo rebel steamer Georgiana ran ashore near Charleston.

March 20.
- Engagement at Milton, Tenn.
- Two of Commodore FARRAGUT's vessels arrived at the mouth of the canal opposite Vicksburgh.
- Fight at Auburn, Tenn.

March 21.
- Steamer Nicholas I. captured off Wilmington, N.C.
- Steamer Aries captured off Charleston .
- Death of Gen. E.V. SUMNER.

March 22.
- Gen. WOOL, commanding the Department of the East, issued an order relative to deserters.
- Capture of Mount Sterling, Ky., by rebels, who burned the town.
- Steamer Granite City captured off the Bahamas.
- Steamer Bio Bio burned at New-Orleans.

March 23.
- Our pickets at Chantilly attacked.
- A portion of Pensacola, Fla., destroyed by Union troops.

March 24.
- Capture of a guerrilla party near Stafford Court-house, Va.
- Our fleet commenced entering the Yazoo Pass near Vicksburgh.

March 25.
- Capture of Union troops at Brentwood, Tenn.
- Union rams Lancaster and Switzerland attempted to run past the batteries at Vicksburgh, the former being sunk and the latter captured.
- JEFF. DAVIS signed a bill for the impressment of property.

March 26.
- Skirmish near Camp Dick Robinson, Ky .
- Orange Grove, Fla., Occupied by a Union regiment of colored soldiers.

March 27.
- Fast day in the Confederate States.
- Deserter shot at Indianapolis, Ind.
- Arrest of the rebel Col. TALCOTT in New-York.
- Palatka, Fla., occupied by a Union regiment of colored troops.
- Admiral FARRAGUT engaged the rebel batteries at Warrenton, three miles below Vicksburgh.

- Bark Lapwing and M.J. Colcord taken by the Florida.
- United States troops landed at Cole's Island near Charleston, S.C.
- Bombardment of Fort Pemberton, Vicksburgh, commenced.

March 28.
- Danville, Ky., recaptured by Union troops.
- A Union train captured between Memphis, Tenn., and Grand Junction.
- Cole's Island, nine miles from Charleston, S.C., taken possession of by Union troops.
- Steamer Aries captured running the blockade at Charleston, S.C.
- Union gunboat Diana captured by rebels in Louisiana.
- Our pickets at Washington, N.C., driven in.
- Our fleet reached the Coldwater River, near Vicksburgh, by the Yazoo Pass.

March 29.
- Williamsburgh, Va., attacked by the rebels.

March 30.
- Point Pleasant, Va., captured by rebels, but subsequently recaptured.
- Commencement of the investment of Washington, N.C.
- Richmond, near Vicksburgh, taken possession of by our forces.

March 31.
- Great Union meeting in Washington.
- Sharp battle near Somerset, Ky.
- The rebels defeated.
- Jacksonville, Fla., evacuated by Union troops, the town having been burned by them.
- Union gunboat St. Clair attacked by the rebels on the Cumberland.
- Woods near Washington, N.C., shelled by Union gunboats.
- The rebels opened fire on the fort back of Washington, N.C., the place being closely invested by the rebels.
- The rebel batteries at Grand Gulf on the Mississippi attacked.
- Schooner Antelope captured off Charleston, S.C.

APRIL.

April 1.
- Sharp cavalry fight at Broad Run, Va., near Drainesville, Va.

April 2.
- Grand reception of Gen. BUTLER at the New-York Academy of Music.
- Rebel attack on our iron-clads at Tuscumbia, Ala.
- Serious bread riot in Richmond, Va. A large number of women attacked the storehouses.

April 3.
- The rebel Gen. MORGAN defeated at Liberty, Tenn.

April 4.
- Gen. MCCLELLAN's report of his campaign, dated Oct. 15, 1862, made public.
- Town of Palmyra, on the Cumberland, destroyed by our forces, in retaliation for the attack on the gunboat St. Clair.
- The rebels repulsed at Woodbury, Tenn.
- The Yazoo Pass expedition operating against Vicksburgh, returning, left Fort Greenwood.

April 5.
- A force left Newbern, N.C., to rescue Gen. FOSTER's army besieged at Washington, N.C.
- Iron-clad fleet armed at Charleston Bar.

April 6.
- Report of the Committee on the Conduct of the War made public.
- Gen. MITCHELL dashed into a rebel camp at Green Hill, Tenn.
- Visit of the President and his family to the Army of the Potomac.
- The expedition against Charleston, S.C. started for that city.

April 7.
- ATTACK ON FORT SUMTER, CHARLESON HARBOR, BY OUR MONITORS, AND OUR FORCES REPULSED.
- An additional force left Newbern, N.C., to aid Gen. FOSTER at Washington, N.C.

April 8.
- The Army of the Potomac, reviewed by the President.
- The Keokuk, monitor, sank in Charleston harbor from the shots received in bombarding Fort Sumter.
- Arrival of the Yazoo Pass expedition, operating against Vicksburgh, at Helena, Ark.
- Ship Morning Star captured by the Alabama.

April 9.
- Fight at Blount's Bridge, N.C. and at Kuff's Mills, N.C.

April 10.
- Gen. GRANGER attacked by the rebel VAN DORN's army at Franklin, Tenn.
- A passenger train near Lavergne, Tenn., attacked by a rebel force.
- Address of JEFF. DAVIS to the rebel States issued.

April 11.
- Great meeting in New-York in commemoration of the attack on Fort Sumter in 1864.
- Skirmishing at Williamsburgh, Va.

April 12.
- Col. E.A. KIMBALL killed by Gen. CORCORAN.
- Battle between Gen. BANKS' army and the rebels in the Teche country, La.
- Steamer Stonewall Jackson destroyed off Charleston. Our iron-clads left Charleston Harbor.

April 13.
- Riot between black and white laborers in South street, N.Y.
- The rebels evacuated their works at Centreville, La., in the night.
- The fighting in the Teche country, Louisiana, continued.

April 14.
- Fight near Suffolk, Va.
- Aid reached Gen. FOSTER, at Washington, N.C.
- Repulse of the rebels in the Nansemond River, Va.
- The ram Queen of the West recaptured from the rebels in Grand Lake, La.
- The final action between Gen. BANKS' army and the rebels in the Teche country.
- Fight at Kelly's Ford, near Fredericksburgh.

April 15.
- A rebel battery near Suffolk, Va., silenced.
- Gen. FOSTER arrived at Newbern, N.C., from Washington, N.C., where his army was besieged.

April 16.
- FEDERAL GUNBOATS BENTON, TUSCUMBIA, LAFAYETTE, PITTSBURGH, CARONDELET, GEN. PRICE AND THREE TRANSPORTS RAN PAST THE REBEL BATTERIES AT VICKSBURGH IN THE NIGHT.

April 17.
- Engagement at Vermillion Bayou, La., resulting in success for our troops.
- Col. GRIERSON started on his great cavalry expedition for Baton Rouge, La.

April 18.
- Fayetteville, Ark., attacked by the rebels, who were repulsed.
- Skirmish near Ceclina, Tenn.
- Fighting near Memphis, Tenn.
- Steamer St. John's captured off Charleston, S.C.

April 19.
- Rebel battery at the West Branch, Nansemond River, near Suffolk, Va., captured.
- Our forces landed at Eastport.
- Sloop Neptune captured off Charleston, S.C.
- Steamer Norseman destroyed off Charleston.

April 20.
- Great mass meeting in New-York in commemoration of the grand, uprising of the people in 1861.
- Opelousas and Washington, La., occupied by Gen. BANKS.
- Rebel fort at Butte a la Rose, La., captured.

April 21.
- Visit of Gen. HALLECK to Suffolk, Va.

April 22.
- McMinnville, Tenn., taken by our troops, and the rebel stores there destroy ed.
- Tompkinsville, Ky., destroyed by our troops.
- A LARGE FORCE WITH GUNBOATS RAN PAST THE REBEL BATTERIES AT VICKSBURGH.
- Union raid on Middleton, Tenn.

April 23.
- Gen. HUNTER addressed a letter to JEFF. DAVIS, threatening retaliation for the execution of negro soldiers and their officers.

April 25.
- Tuscumbia, Ala., occupied by our cavalry.
- Ship Dictator destroyed by the Georgia.

April 26.
- The rebels at Cape Girardeau, Mo., routed.
- Schooner Clarinda, blockade runner, captured.

April 27.
- Scouting expedition under Gen. STAHL left Fairfax Court-house, Va.
- Fighting near Kinston, N.C.s
- STONEMAN's cavalry expedition left Warrenton Junction, Va.
- U.S. sloop-of-war Preble destroyed by fire.

April 28.
- Skirmish near Kinston, N.C., continued.
- STONEMAN's cavalry crossed the Rappahannock at Kelley's Ford.

April 29.
- The Rappahannock crossed by Gen. HOOKER at Kelley's Ford in the advance upon Fredericksburgh.
- Attack on the rebel batteries at Grand Gulf, Miss. Haines' Bluff near Vicksburgh, bombarded.
- Orange Springs reached by, Gen. STONEMAN's cavalry.
- Louisa Court-House, Va., reached by STONEMAN's cavalry in the light.
- Ship Oneida destroyed by the. Florida. The bark Henrietta also destroyed.

April 30.
- Fast day in the United States.
- Chancellorsville, Va., occupied by Gen. HOOK-ER's army.
- Withdrawal of the rebel Gen. LONGSTREET's army from the south side of the James River commenced.
- Cavalry fight at Dayton's Gap, Ala.
- Gen. GRANT's army landed at Bruinsburg, Miss.

MAY.

May 1.
- BATTLE OF CHANCELLORSVILLE COMMENCED.
- Cavalry engagement at Blountsville; Ala.
- Battle of Thompson's Hills, Miss., or Port Gibson.
- Port Gibson occupied.

May 2.
- Battle of Chancellorsville continued.
- Culpepper Court-house, Va., fell in our hands .
- BIG BLACK RIVER, MISS., REACHED BY OUR FORCES.
- COL. GRIERSON's CAVALRY FORCE reached BATON ROUGE, LA., FROM TENNESSEE.

May 3.
- BATTLE OF CHANCELLORSVILLE, VA., CONTINUED. TERRIFIC FIGHTING. The Chancellor mansion shelled and burned by the rebels. Gen. BERRY killed. "Stonewall" JACKSON mortally wounded. Attack on Fredericksburg by Gen. SEDGWICK. Storming of Mary's Hill.
- Great panic in Richmond, Va., on the approach of STONEMAN's cavalry.
- Columbia, Va., on the James River, reached by our cavalry, who destroyed the canal there. Goochland, Va., visited by our cavalry.
- Fight near Suffolk, Va.
- Fighting near Warrenton Junction, Va.
- Capture of Grand Gulf, Miss., by Admiral PORTER's fleet.
- Battle of Salem Heights, near Fredericksburgh, Va.

- Beaver Dam, Ashland and Hanover Court-house, Va., reached by Gen. STONEHAN's cavalry.
- Capture of newspaper correspondents running past the rebel batteries at Vicksburgh.
- Col. KILPATRICK's cavalry left Louisa Court-house, Va.
- Capture of Col. STREIGHT's Union cavalry, near Rome, Ga.

May 4.
- Panic in Richmond, Va., on the approach of STONEMAN's cavalry.
- STONEMAN's cavalry within two miles of Richmond, Va.
- He reached Chickahominy Bridge.
- Hungary, Va., reached by Col. KILPATRICK.
- Meadow Bridge, on the Chickahominy, destroyed by Col. KILPATRICK.
- Schooner Juniper, blockade-runner, captured.

May 5.
- HON. C.L. VALLANDIGHAM ARRESTED AT DAYTON, OHIO, FOR TREASON.
- Riot and attempt to rescue him at Dayton.
- RETURN OF THE ARMY OF THE POTOMAC FROM CHANCELLORSVILLE, ACROSS THE RAPPAHANNOCK, COMMENCED.
- Col. KILPATRICK surprised some rebel cavalry at Aylett's, Va.
- The Governor of Mississippi called on the people of the State to arouse for its defence.

May 6.
- Trial of VALLANDIGHAM at Cincinnati commenced.
- Return of the Army of the Potomac across the Rappahannock continued.
- Gen. HOOKER issued an address to his army in respect to the battles at Chancellorsville.
- Severe battle at Clinton, Miss.
- Steamer Eugenie captured off Mobile Bay, by a Union gunboat.
- Battle of Fourteen-Mile Creek, near Vicksburgh.

May 7.
- President LINCOLN and Gen. HALLECK visited the Army of the Potomac at Falmouth, Va.
- Arrival of Col. KILPATRICK, with a force of cavalry, at Gloucester Point, Va.
- Death of Gen. WHIPPLE.
- Trial of C.L. VALLANDIGHAM concluded.
- West Point, Va., occupied by our forces.
- Bridges, & c., near White House, Va., destroyed by our troops.
- Gen. LEE issued a congratulatory address to his army.
- Steamer Cherokee captured off Charleston, S.C.

May 8.
- Proclamation of President LINCOLN in relation to the draft, defining, the duties, of persons of foreign birth.
- Gen. T.F. MEAGHER resigned his commission.
- Gen. BANKS reached Alexandria, La., having captured in his expedition 2,000 prisoners, 20 pieces of artillery, 2 transports, and a large amount of property.

May 9.
- Rebel guerrillas attacked at Horseshoe Bend, on the Cumberland River, Tenn.
- Schooner Sea Lion captured off Mobile Bay.

May 10.
- Death of Stonewall JACKSON.

May 12.
- Union victory at Raymond, Miss.

May 13.
- The rebels defeated at Mississippi Spring, Miss.
- Gen. JOE JOHNSTON arrived at Jackson, Miss.
- A large amount of rebel property destroyed at Yazoo City.
- Schooner A.J. Hodge captured.
- Ship Crown Point burned by the Florida.

May 14.
- JACKSON, MISS., TAKEN BY GEN. GRANT.
- Resignation of Gen. THOS. F. MEAGHER accepted.
- Schooner Sea Bird captured.
- Clinton, Miss., occupied by our troops.

May 15.
- Capture of a company of United States cavalry at Charlestown, Md.
- Destruction of rebel stores at York River, Va.
- Fight at Carrsville, Va.
- Jackson, Miss.
- Evacuation of by Union troops commenced.
- British brigantine Cornet captured.
- Ship Byzantium burned by the Tacony.

May 16.
- Recapture of the cavalry taken by the rebels at Charlestown, Md.
- Rebels under Gen. PEMBERTON defeated at Edward's Station, Miss.
- GREAT BATTLE AT BAKER's CREEK, NEAR VICKSBURGH, CALLED THE BATTLE OF CHAMPION's HILL.
- Engagement at Berry's Ferry, Va.

May 17.
- Steamer Cuba pursued and destroyed, and schooner Hunter captured.
- Battle of Big Black River Bridge, Miss.

May 18.
- Meeting to express sympathy with VALLANDIGHAM held in New-York.
- VALLANDIGHAM sentenced to confinement in Fort Warren.
- Union victory on the Big Black River, Miss.
- Capture of Haines' Bluff, near Vicksburgh, by Admiral PORTER.
- Schooner Isabel destroyed off Mobile Bay.
- Schooner Ripple captured off Mobile Bay.

May 19.
- Gen. MEAGHER took leave of his troops.
- Richmond, Mo., sacked by guerrillas.
- Vicksburgh fortifications assaulted.
- Blockade runner steamer Union captured.

May 20.
- Steamer Stono, late United States gunboat Isaac Smith, destroyed off Charleston.
- Bark Goodspeed destroyed by the Tacony.
- VICKSBURGH INVESTED.

May 21.
- Assault on the rebel works at Vicksburgh, Miss. Our forces repulsed with severe loss.

May 22.
- The sentence of VALLANDIGHAM changed to banishment.
- Blockade runner Eagle captured.
- Assault on Vicksburgh continued.
- Battle at Gum Swamp, N.C.
- Engagement at Port Hudson Plains.

May 23.
- Battle at Gum Swamp, N.C., continued.
- Junction of Gen. BANKS' forces with those of Gen. AUGUR at Bayou Sara.

May 24.
- Capture of schooners Gen. Prim and Rapid and sloops Jane, Adelie and Bright.

May 27.
- Presentation of Kearney medals to the Third army corps.
- Rebels defeated at Florence, Ala.
- Attack on Port Hudson commenced.
- Union gunboat Cincinnati sunk by rebel batteries at Vicksburgh.

May 28.
- Attack on Port Hudson continued. Our forces repulsed.
- Blockade runner Victoria captured.

May 29.
- Skirmish near Thoroughfare Gap, Va.
- Gen. KILPATRICK left Yorktown on a raid up the Peninsula, which resulted very successfully.

May 30.
- Attack on a train of cars near Catlett's Station, Va., by MOSEBY's rebel cavalry.
- MOSEBY's force defeated near Greenwich, Va.
- Train of cars destroyed near Kettle Run, Va.

May 31.
- Skirmishing near Monticelio, Ky.
- Schooner Echo captured.

JUNE.

June 1.
- Meeting of sympathizers with VALLANDIGHAM at Philadelphia.
- James Island evacuated by the Union troops.

June 2.
- Gen. BURNSIDE suppressed the circulation of the New-York World and Chicago Times in his department.

June 3.
- Great Peace meeting in New-York.
- Gen. LEE broke up camp at Fredericksburgh, Va.

June 4.
- Our force at Franklin, Tenn., attacked.
- Gen. BURNSIDE revoked his order suppressing the New-York World and Chicago Times, by order of the President.
- Departure of an expedition into King William County, Va. from Yorktown, which was highly successful in its results.
- Brisk fight at Sataria, on the Yazoo.

June 6.
- Bark Whistling Wind destroyed by a privateer.
- Rebels attacked Milliken's Bend and Young's Point, near Vicksburgh, but were repulsed.
- Shawneetown, Kan., destroyed by guerrillas.

June 7.
- Battle of Milliken's Bend concluded.

June 9.
- Severe cavalry engagement at Brandy Station or Beverly's Ford, Va., on the Rappahannock.
- The rebels driven from Monticelio, Ky.
- Departments of the Monongahela and Susquehanna created.
- Execution of two spies by Gen. ROSECRANS.

June 10.
- The draft in Indiana resisted.
- Engagement near Monticelio, Ky.
- Lake Providence attacked by rebels and successfully defended by negro troops.
- The Havelock sunk off Charleston bar.

June 11.
- C.L. VALLANDIGHAM nominated for Governor of Ohio.
- Darien, Ga., destroyed by our forces.
- The Herald destroyed by Union gunboats, Charleston Harbor.
- Steamer Calypso captured.
- Gen. HALLECK directed the Garrtsons at Martinsburgh and Winchester, Va., to retire to Harper's Ferry.s
- Triune, Tenn., attacked by the rebels.

June 12.
- Gov. CURTIN, of Pennsylvania issued a proclamation calling for volunteers to repel the anticipated invasion of that State by the rebels.
- Gen. COUCH assumed command of the Department of the Susquehanna.
- President LINCOLN addressed a letter to ERASTUS CORNING and others, in relation to the arrest of VALLANDIGHAM, & c.
- Gen. HUNTER left the Department of the South.
- Gen. Q.A. GILLMORE assumed command.
- Brisk engagement, between Union batteries on Folly Island and the rebel batteries on Morris Island, Charleston Harbor.

June 13.
- Town of Eunice, near Vicksburgh, destroyed by our gunboats.s
- Winchester, Va., attacked and its armament and a part, of its garrison captured.

June 14.
- Skirmish at State Creek, Ky.
- Berryville and Martinsburgh occupied by the rebels.
- THE ARMY OF THE POTOMAC LEFT FALMOUTH FOR PENNSYLVANIA IN PURSUIT OF LEE.
- Port Hudson assaulted.
- Our forces repulsed with heavy loss.
- Gen. ROSECRANS commenced a forward movement.

June 15.
- The President called for 100,000 volunteers to repel the invasion of Pennsylvania.
- Gov. CURTIN, of Pennsylvania, called on the people of the State to enroll themselves for its defence .
- Chambersburgh, Penn., occupied by the rebels.
- Winchester, Va., evacuated by Gen. MILROY, at 1 o'clock, A.M., after which he was pursued and engaged in a severe battle.

June 16.
- Harper's Ferry reached by MILROY's army.
- Gov. CURTIN appealed to the people of Philadelphia to rise.
- Gov. PARKER, of New-Jersey, called for volunteers to repel the invasion of Pennsylvania.
- Harper's Ferry invested and attacked. Our forces retired to Maryland Heights and shelled the rebels out.
- Brig Umpire captured by the Tacony.
- Gen. MEAGHER tendered the hospitalities of New-York City.

June 17.
- Great excitement over the invasion of Pennsylvania.
- Spirited cavalry engagement at Aldie, Va.
- Draft in Ohio resisted.
- Capture of the rebel steamer Atlanta, late the Fingal, near Savannah, Ga.

June 19.
- The rebels crossed the Ohio River into Indiana.
- Skirmish at Orleans, Ind.

June 20.
- Ship Isaac Webb captured and bonded by the Tacony.
- Frederick, Md., occupied by the rebels.

June 21.
- Great cavalry engagement near Middleburgh and Upperville, Va.
- The rebels driven from Frederick, Md.

June 22.
- Millerstown, eight miles from Gettysburgh, Penn., occupied by the rebels.
- Greencastle reoccupied by the rebels. The portion of EWELL's corps which had not yet arrived in Pennsylvania crossed the Potomac and moved up the valley.
- The rebels driven from Cumberland, Md.
- Brashear City, La., captured by the rebels.

June 23.
- Chambersburgh, Penn., reoccupied by the rebels.

June 24.

- Shippensburgh, Penn., reached by a portion of the rebel army.

- Severe skirmish of Gen. ROSECRANS' army at Hoover's Gap, Tenn., successful to our arms in its results.

- The rebels driven from Liberty Gap, near Murfreesboro.

- Heavy skirmishing near Murfreesboro, Tenn.

- The main body of LEE's army entered Maryland, crossing the Potomac at Shepperdstown and Williamsport, instead of east of the Blue Ridge, as had been the intention.

June 25.

- Fairfax Court-house, Va., occupied by the rebels.

- Skirmish at Marysrille, Penn., near Harrisburgh.

- Another engagement at Liberty Gap, Tenn.

- An expedition left West Point, Va., for the interior.

- Destruction of one of the rebel forts at Vicksburgh by the explosion of one of our mines.

- Ship Constitution captured by the privateer Georgia.

- The Union army crossed the Potomac at Edwards' Ferry.

- Gen. ROSECRANS resumed his march.

June 26.

- Gettysburgh, Penn., occupied by the rebels.

- Gov. CURTIN issued another proclamation to the people of Pennsylvania.

- Rebel privateer Archer (with the crew of the Tacony) entered Portland harbor, and captured the revenue cutter Caleb Cushing, which enterprise resulted in the capture of the Archer.

- White House, Va., occupied by our troops.

June 27.

- The advance of Gen. ROSECRANS' army arrived at Manchester, Tenn.

- Kingston, Penn., occupied by the rebels.

- York, Penn., also occupied.

- Chambersburgh, Penn., occupied by the divisions of the rebel army under Gens. LONGSTREET and HILL.

- The whole rebel army consisting of 90,000 infantry, upward of 10,000 cavalry and 4,000 or 5,000 artillery.

June 28.

- Gen. HOOKER relieved of the command of the Army of the Potomac and Gen. MEADE appointed in his place.

- The rebels within four miles of Harrisburgh, Penn.

- Bridge over the Susquehanna at Columbia, Penn., burned.

- Mechanicsburgh surrendered to the rebels.

- Brookville, Md., occupied by the rebels.

- Attempt of the rebels to take our fort at Donald-sonville, La.

June 29.

- Wrightsville, Penn., evacuated by the rebels.

- Fight at McConnellsburgh, Penn.

- Gen. MEADE's army put in motion and at night was put in position, its left at Emmettsburgh and its right at New-Windsor.

June 30.

- York, Penn., evacuated by the rebels.

- Martial law proclaimed in Baltimore.

- Skirmish at Sporting Hill, Penn., near Oyster Point.

- Cavalry battle at Hanover Junction, Penn.

- Skirmish near Mechanicsburgh, Penn.

- Gen. BUFORD passed through Gettysburgh on a reconnaissance in force.

- At nightfall the greater part of the rebel force was concentrated in the immediate vicinity of two corps of the Union army.

JULY.

July 1.

- FIRST DAY OF THE BATTLE OF GETTYSBURGH.

- The First and Eleventh army corps engaged. Gen. REYNOLDS killed.

- Large losses on both sides.

- Brilliant fight at Carlisle between the rebel cavalry and artillery of Gen. FITZHUGH LEE, and our forces, under Gen. W.F. SMITH.

July 2.

- SECOND DAY OF THE BATTLE OF GETTYS-BURGH. The rebels attacked our forces in large numbers, but were repulsed. Gens. WEED and ZOOK killed, and Gen. SICKLES wounded. The rebel Gen. BARKSDALE, of Mississippi, killed. Chambersburgh and Shippensburgh, Penn., evacuated by the rebels.

- Skirmish near Bottom's Bridge, Va.

- Tullahoma, Tenn., occupied by our forces.

July 3.

- THE BATTLE OF GETTYSBURGH CONCLUDED. Heavy losses on both sides. A great victory gained by the Union army, and the rebels compelled to retreat.

- Rebel pontoon bridge over the Potomac near Williamsport, Md., destroyed.

- Departure of a cavalry expedition from Newbern, N.C., into the interior.

- Conference of Union and rebel commanders at Vicksburgh, Miss., relative to the surrender of the city to our forces.

July 4.

- SURRENDER OF VICKSBURGH, MISS., WITH 31,000 TROOPS, 220 GUNS AND 70,009 SMALL ARMS, TO Gen. U.S. GRANT.

- Union victory at Helena, Ark.

- The retreat of the rebels from the battle-field of Gettysburgh, Penn., commenced.

- Proclamation of President LINCOLN announcing a victory at Gettysburgh.

- Gen. MEADE issued a congratulatory address to his army on the victory at Gettysburgh.

- ALEXANDER H. STEPHENS, Vice-President of the Confederate States, applied for permission to visit Washington as bearer of a letter from JEFF. DAVIS to President LINCOLN. He was refused.

July 5.

- The day occupied by Gen. MEADE in succoring the wounded and burying the dead left on the field of Gettysburgh.

July 6.

- Defeat of the rebel Gen. JOHNSTON on the Big Black. His rear-guard captured at Bolton.

- The rebel army from Gettysburgh arrived at Hagerstown, Md.

- Defeat of STUART by BUFORD, at Hanover.

July 7.

- Battle at Williamsport, Md.

- The rebel Gen. MORGAN's force at Bardstown, Ky.

- RETREAT OF BRAGG's ARMY ACROSS THE TENNESSEE RIVER.

- Gen. MEADE started in pursuit of LEE, by a flank movement on Middletown.

July 8.

- SURRENDER OF PORT HUDSON, with 7,000 prisoners, and a large number of cannon and small arms, to Gen. BANKS.

- The rebel Gen. MORGAN crossed into Indiana, and captured the town of Corydon.

- Gen. GILLMORE issued orders for an attack on Morris Island, Charleston harbor.

July 9.

- Port Hudson taken possession of by our army.

- Victory of our cavalry under BUFORD and KILPATRICK at Boonsboro.

July 10.

- Gen. GILLMORE commenced operations against the rebel batteries on Morris Island, Charleston harbor.

- Gen. STRONG took possession of several of the rebel works.

- Martial law declared in Louisville, Ky.

- Engagement at Jackson, Miss.

- Engagement at Sharpsburgh, Md.

- Skirmish near Funkstown.

July 11.

- BRILLIANT Engagement on MORRIS ISLAND. All the batteries evacuated by the rebels, who defended themselves in Fort Wagner.

- Commencement of the Draft in New-York City.

July 12.

- Our forces entered Hagerstown, Md., the rebels having evacuated the town in the night.

- Our forces having passed through South Mountain, came up with the rebel army of Gen. LEE, securely posted on the heights of Marsh's Run.

July 13.

- COMMENCEMENT OF THE GREAT DRAFT RIOT IN NEW-YORK CITY.

- The drafting office in Third-avenue destroyed; a negro hung, and public and private property destroyed.

- Gen. LEE's army escaped across the Potomac River in the night.

- Gen. MEADE reconnoitered the rebel position, and made preparations for an attack.

- Engagement at Jackson, Tenn.

- Capture of Yazoo City by our troops.

July 14.
- The Draft Riot in New-York City continued; business, suspended; negroes hung; Col. O'BRIEN killed; conflict between the mob and soldiers; Proclamation of Gov. SEYMOUR; Postmaster WAKEMAN's house destroyed; speech of GOV. SEYMOUR to "his friends."
- Riot in Boston.
- Advance of Gen. MEADE.
- Our cavalry occupied Falling Waters, on the Potomac, and captured a brigade of rebels.
- Williamsport, Md., occupied by our forces.
- Admiral LEE captured Fort Powhattan, on the James River.

July 15.
- The Draft Riot in New-York continued; the military routed! more negroes hung; terrible excitement in New-York and neighborhood; Proclamation of Mayor OPDYKE.
- Gen. DIX ordered to New-York, and Gen. J.G. FOSTER to Fort Monroe.
- Proclamation of the President issued appointing Aug. 6 for a National Thanksgiving for our great victories.
- A mob in Troy destroyed the Times office and other property.
- Arrival of VALLANDIGHAM at Niagara Falls, Canada, from his journey through the Southern States.
- Jackson, Miss., shelled by our forces.
- JEFF. DAVIS ISSUED A PROCLAMATION IMMEDIATELY CONSCRIPTING EVERY ABLE-BODIED MAN between the ages of 18 and 45.
- Gen. BLUNT crossed the Arkansas River.

July 16.
- The draft riot in New-York continued; Archbishop HUGHES invited the mob to visit him at his residence on the following day.
- Arrival of Seventh regiment in New-York.
- Gen. JOE JOHNSTON evacuated Jackson, Miss., in the night.
- The rebels routed in the Indian Country.
- Brisk engagement on James Island, S.C.
- Victory of Gen. BLUNT at Elk Creek over 5,000 rebels.
- Jackson, Miss., taken by our army.

July 17.
- Quiet restored in New-York; the Draft Riot suppressed; Gen. BROWN succeeded by Gen. CANBY in command of the troops in New-York; speech of Archbishop HUGHES to the mob.
- Battle with the rebel Gen. MORGAN at Berlin, Ohio.
- Two expeditions — one up the Red River and one to Natchez — made large captures of arms, ammunition and cattle.

July 18.
- STORMING OF FORT WAGNER, CHARLESTON HARBOR.
- Arrival of Gen. FOSTER at Fort Monroe.
- Gen. LEE's rear-guard left Martinsburgh. Va.

- MORGAN's force dispersed and a large number of his men captured.
- Fight with MORGAN's men at Buffington, Ohio.
- Admiral PORTER reported the complete success of the Red River expedition.
- Bombardment of Fort Wagner, Charleston Harbor; the fort stormed and our troops repulsed.

July 19.
- The rebel MORGAN made an unsuccessful attempt to cross the Ohio River; more of his men captured.
- Two companies of rebels and an ammunition train captured at Jackson, Tenn.

July 20.
- Gov. SEYMOUR ordered the return of the State arms used against the rioters in New-York City.
- Cavalry reconnaissance to Front Royal, Va..
- Sharp fight with the rebel guerrilla MORGAN, and capture of a large portion of his force at George's Creek.
- Destruction of railroad and other property at Rocky Mount, N.C., by an expedition of Union troops.

July 22.
- Railroad bridge, 350 feet long, over Tar River, at Rocky Mount, N.C., destroyed by a cavalry expedition from Newbern, which also destroyed a large amount of property.
- Recapture of Brashear City, La., by our troops.

July 23.
- Sharp fight near Front Royal, Va.

July 24.
- Col. TOLAND attacked the enemy at Wytheville, on the East Tennessee and Virginia Railroad, capturing two pieces of artillery, 700 muskets and 125 prisoners.

July 25.
- Steamer Merrimac captured, running the blockade at Wilmington, N.C.

July 26.
- Death of Hon. JOHN J. CRITTENDEN.
- MORGAN AND THE REMAINDER OF HIS BAND CAPTURED NEAR NEW-LISBON, OHIO.

July 27.
- The rebel pirate Alabama arrived off the coast of Africa near Cape of Good Hope.

July 28.
- Death of WILLIAM L. YANCEY, of Alabama.
- The rebels defeated at Lexington, Tenn.

July 29.
- Repulse of the rebels at Paris, Ky.

July 30.
- Proclamation of President LINCOLN in regard to rebel treatment of colored troops, issued.
- Cummings Point rebel battery, Charleston harbor bombarded.
- Rebels defeated at Winchester, Ky.

July 31.
- Heavy bombardment of our works on Morris Island, Charleston harbor, from Fort Wagner.
- Successful attack on the rebels at Lancaster, Ky.
- Reconnaissance to Sperryville, Va.

AUGUST.

August 1.
- Battle between the cavalry of the two armies near Culpepper, Va.
- JEFF. DAVIS appealed to the deserters from the rebel army to return, offering them pardon and amnesty.

August 3.
- Gov. SEYMOUR indited a letter, to the President, remonstrating against the enforcement of the draft in New-York City because of unfair enrollment, & c.

August 4.
- Engagement neat Brandy Station, Va.
- Steamer Ruth, with $2,500,000 in Government funds, burned on the Mississippi River.
- Reconnaissance of Fort Darling on the James River.

August 6.
- Ship Francis B. Cutting captured and bonded by the Florida.
- National Thanksgiving Day.

August 7.
- Reply of President LINCOLN to Gov. SEYMOUR's letter of remonstrance against the draft, in which he asserted that the draft should proceed.

August 8.
- Gov. SEYMOUR replied to President LINCOLN's letter relative to the draft.

August 11.
- President LINCOLN ended the correspondence with Gov. SEYMOUR relative to the draft.

August 12.
- Fort Sumter, Charleston harbor, battered by our shot.
- The rebels opened on our works near Charleston with grape and canister.

August 13.
- An expedition left Lagrange, Tenn., for Central Mississippi.

August 14.
- Death of Commodore MORRIS.

August 15.
- The authorities of the City of New-York appropriated $3,000,000 to pay for substitutes.

August 16.
- Steamer Alice Vivian captured running out of Mobile.
- GEN. ROSECRANS COMMENCED HIS ADVANCE ACROSS THE CUMBERLAND MOUNTAINS.

August 17.
- Great distruction of rebel property at Grenada by our troops from Tennessee.
- COMMENCEMENT OF THE GRAND ATTACK ON FORT SUMTER, CHARLESTON HARBOR. The iron-clad fleet and the land batteries attacked the fort.
- Explosion of the steamer City of Madison on the Mississippi.
- Address of Gen. DIX to the citizens of New-York relative to the draft.
- Reconnaissance in force from the rebel army in Virginia.
- Steamer Nita captured running out of Mobile.

August 18.
- Bombardment of Fort Sumter continued.

August 19.
- Draft in New-York City recommenced.
- Bombardment of Fort Sumter continued.

August 20.
- Bombardment of Fort Sumter continued.
- The Tennessee River reached by Gen. ROSECRANS.

August 21.
- Lawrence, Kan., pillaged and burned by guerrillas.
- Gen. GILLMORE demanded the surrender of Morris Island and Fort Sumter, and threatened to shell Charleston in case of non-compliance with his demand.
- Our batteries opened on Charleston, S.C., in the night.
- The advance of the Army of the Cumberland appeared before Chattanooga, Tenn., and opened fire on the city.

August 22.
- Gen. BEAUREGARD protested against the shelling of the City of Charleston.

August 23.
- Fort Fisher, near Wilmington, N.C., bombarded by the frigate Minnesota.
- Capture of JEFF. THOMPSON.

August 24.
- Charleston, S.C., again shelled by Gen. GILLMORE.

August 26.
- An expedition left Williamsburgh, Va., for Bottom's Bridge, Va.
- Attack on the rebel riflepits near Fort Wagner.

August 27.
- Death of the rebel JOHN B. FLOYD.

August 28.
- The rebels driven across Bayou Metairie Bridge, Ark., with considerable loss.

August 30.
- The Army of the Cumberland crossed the Tennessee River.

August 31.
- Fourt Moultrie, Charleston harbor, attacked.

SEPTEMBER.

September 1.
- Fierce artillery fight at Port Royal, Va.
- KNOXVILLE, TENN., CAPTURED by Gen. FOSTER, of BURNSIDE's army.
- Fort Smith, Ark., occupied by our forces.

September 2.
- Kingston, Tenn., captured by Gen. BURNSIDE.

September 3.
- Battle with the Indians at Whitestone Hall.

September 4.
- Bread riot in Mobile, Ala.
- An expedition left New-Orleans, La., for Texas, under Gen. FRANKLIN.

September 5.
- Furious bombardment of Forts Wagner and Gregg, Charleston harbor.

September 6.
- THE REBELS EVACUATED FORTS WAGNER AND GREGG, CHARLESTON HARBOR, AT NIGHT.

September 7.
- Gen. GILLMORE took possession of Fort Wagner and Battery Gregg in the morning, having captured 36 pieces of artillery and a large amount of ammunition.

September 8.
- Our forces at Bath, Va., attacked.
- Unsuccessful naval assault on Fort Sumter.
- Bombardment of Fort Moultrie. One of its magazines exploded.
- Unsuccessful attack on the rebel fortifications at Sabine Pass, Texas.

September 9.
- Gen. CRITTENDEN took possession of Chattanooga, Tenn.
- Cumberland Gap taken by our army.
- Bombardment of Fort Moultrie continued.
- Skirmish at Telford, East Tennessee.

September 10.
- Little Rock, Ark., occupied by our forces.

September 11.
- Arrival at New-York of the first vessel of the Russian fleet.
- IMBODEN attacked a small force of our troops at Moorefield, wounding 15 and capturing about 150.

September 13.
- Brilliant cavalry fight at Culpepper, Va. .
- Gen. ROSECRANS' army attacked at Bird's Gap.

September 15.
- Proclamation of the President, suspending the writ of habeas corpus in certain cases.
- Order of Gen. GILLMORE congratulating his troops on their success in Charleston Harbor.

September 16.
- Skirmish at Raccoon Ford on the Rapidan.

September 19.
- COMMENCEMENT OF THE GREAT BATTLE OF CHICKAMAUGA. Our army attacked in large force by the rebels under Gen. BRAGG, who had been reinforced by Gen. LONGSTREET's corps from Virginia.
- Defeat of the rebels in the Indian Country.

September 20.
- The great battle at Chickamauga, Ga., continued.
- Union attack on Zollicoffer, Tenn.

September 21.
- Gen. THOMAS repelled the assault of the rebels on his corps at Rossville.
- Conclusion of the great battte, which resulted in our forces falling back to Chattanooga after a gallant fight by Gen. THOMAS' corps. The battle commenced on the Chickamauga Creek, and was waged from that point to Chattanooga. Gen. THOMAS' corps displayed great gallantry, and by its bravery saved the army from great disaster. The rebels acknowledged very heavy loss in officers and men.

September 22.
- Gallant cavalry action near Madison Court-house, Va.
- Skirmish near Rockville, Md.

September 24.
- Alexandria, Va., opened to trade by Proclamation of the President.

September 28.
- The Army of the Potomac reviewed by Gen. CORTEZ.

September 29.
- Engagement near Morganzia, La.

OCTOBER

October 1.
- Reception of the officers of the Russian fleet by the military and civil authorities of New-York.

October 2.
- Successful cavalry engagement at Anderson's Cross-roads, Ky.

October 3.
- Proclamation of the President issued, appointing Nov. 26 as Thanksgiving Day.
- McMinnville attacked by rebels.

October 5.
- Railroad bridge south of Murfreesboro', Tenn., destroyed by the rebels.
- The rebel batteries opened on ROSECRANS at Chattanooga.
- Frigate Ironsides attacked by a rebel vessel and torpedo in Charleston Harbor in the night.
- Engagement at Blue Springs, Tenn.

October 8.
- The rebel rams in the Mersey placed under the supervision of English officials.

October 10.
- Sharp fight with the rebel STUART's cavalry at Robertson's River.
- Skirmish between the rebels and Gen. BURNSIDE's forces at Blue Springs, Tenn.
- Engagement at James City, Va. .
- Commencement of the strategical movements of the Army of the Potomac and that of Gen. LEE.
- JEFF. DAVIS reviewed the rebel army before Chattanooga.

October 11.
- The Army of the Potomac withdrew to the north side of the Rappahannock.
- Attack on the Memphis and Charleston Railroad, near Germantown, Tenn.

October 12.
- The rebels driven to Brandy Station, Va.

October 13.
- Defeat of VALLANDIGHAM, the Copperhead candidate for Governor of Ohio.
- Reelection of Gov. CURTIN of Pennsylvania.

October 14.
- Battle of Broad River or Bristoe Station, Va.

October 16.
- Gen. GRANT ordered to the command of the Departments of the Ohio, the Cumberland, and the Tennessee.
- Rebel raid into Brownsville, Mo.

October 17.
- Spirited engagement at Manassas Junction.
- The President called for 300,000 volunteers to be raised before the 5th of January, stating that a draft would then take place for any deficiency in the quotas of the States existing at that time.

October 18.
- Gen. GRANT ASSUMED COMMAND OF THE DEPARTMENTS OF THE OHIO, CUMBERLAND, AND TENNESSEE.
- Charlestown, Va., attacked by the rebels.
- Arrival of Secretary STANTON in Louisville, Ky.

October 19.
- Gen. ROSECRANS relinquishes the command of the Army of the Cumberland.

October 20.
- Gen. GEORGE H. THOMAS assumed command of the Army of the Cumberland.
- Gov. SEYMOUR issued a Proclamation in response to that of the President calling for troops.

October 21.
- Battle near Tuscumbia, Ala.
- Fight near Philadelphia, Tenn.
- Cavalry skirmish near Sulphur Springs, Va.

October 22.
- Cavalry skirmish near Fayetteville, Va.

October 23.
- Execution of Dr. WRIGHT at Norfolk, Va.

October 26.
- Skirmishing along the lines of the Army of the Potomac.
- Bombardment of Fort Sumter renewed.
- Gen. HOOKER moved from Bridgeport, Tenn.

October 27.
- Shells thrown into Charleston, S.C., by Gen. GILLMORE.

October 28.
- Gen. HOOKER's division of the army at Chattanooga repulsed an attack of the enemy.
- Battle near Lookout Mountain, important in its result of reestablishing our communications with the army at Chattanooga.
- The rebels repulsed at Pine Bluff, Ark.
- Our troops occupied Arkadelphia.

October 29.
- Furious bombardment of Fort Sumter.

October 30.
- Union meeting at Little Rock, Ark.

NOVEMBER.

November 1.
- Discovery of a plot to liberate the rebel prisoners in Ohio.

November 2.
- OCCUPATION OF BRAZOS ISLAND, TEXAS, and capture of Boca Chica by Gen. BANKS' army.

November 3.
- ELECTION IN NEW-YORK, NEW-JERSEY, MASSACHUSETTS, MINNESOTA, MISSOURI and WISCONSIN.
- Success of the Union ticket in all the States but one.
- Reconnaissance to Falmouth, Va.
- Repulse of the rebels at Colliersville, Tenn.
- Battle of Bayou Coteau in the Teche country, La.

November 4.
- Capture of Brownsville, Texas, by Gen. BANKS' army.

November 5.
- Ball in New-York in honor of the Russians.
- Skirmish at Metley's Ford, Tenn.
- Capture of the steamer Margaret and Jessie by the Fulton .
- Gen. AVERILL attacked and defeated the enemy near Lewisburgh, capturing three pieces of artillery, 100 prisoners, and a large number of small arms, wagons, and a large quantity of camp equipage. The enemy's loss in killed and wounded estimated at 300.

November 6.
- Engagement in West Virginia.
- Reconnaissance of the Chowan River, N.C., to near the mouth of the Blackwater.

November 7.
- Battle on the banks of the Rappahannock, near Rappahannock Station; our army very successful; rebel redoubts and 2,000 prisoners taken in West Virginia.
- Continuation of the reconnaissance of the Chowan River, N.C.

November 8.
- Cavalry, fight at Hazel Run, Va.
- Gen. MEADE reported that on advancing from Kelly's Ford, in the morning, it was discovered that the rebels had evacuated their position on the Rappahannock. Our army was put in motion and the pursuit of the rebels continued by the infantry to Brandy Station, and by the cavalry beyond. Our captures in the fight at Rappahannock were four guns, eight battle-flags, and over 1,900 prisoners.
- Capture of the rebel steamer Cornubia at Wilmington, N.C.

November 9.
- Reconnaissance to Culpepper, Va.
- Gen. MEADE issued a congratulatory order to his troops on their successful passage of the Rappahannock.

November 11.
- Formal presentation to Gen. MEADE of the battle-flags captured in the battle on the evening of the 7th.
- Lord LYONS officially informed the Government at Washington that he had received information from the Governor-General of Canada of a plot to invade the United States from Canada, destroy the City of Buffalo and liberate the rebel prisoners on Johnson's Island in Lake Erie.
- Gen. BUTLER assumed command of the Departments of Eastern Virginia and North Carolina, headquarters at Fortress Monroe
- Gen. FOSTER took leave of his command at Fort Monroe.

November 12.
- Strikes of the laborers, car-drivers and conductors in New-York City-stoppage of the cars on some of the City railroads.
- Gen. KILPATRICK's camp, near Stevensburgh, Va., shelled by the rebels.
- A body of rebel cavalry crossed the Tennessee River and destroyed two railroad bridges near Lynnville.

November 14.
- Gen. LONGSTREET crossed the Tennessee River in his march against Knoxville, Tenn.

November 15.
- Reconnaissance of our forces along the Rapidan at Raccoon Ford.
- Advance in force of Gen. LONGSTREET on BURNSIDE's ' force. Commencement of the retreat of our forces to Knoxville, Tenn.
- Capture of Corpus Christi, Texas, by Gen. BANKS' troops.

November 16.
- The rebel battery on Lookout Mountain, near Chattanooga, was quite, vigorously worked, and HOOKER's camp, Mocassin Point, and the Chattanooga camps shelted.
- Gen. BURNSIDE evacuated Lenoir.
- Our outposts near Knoxville attacked by the rebel advanced guard.

November 17.
- Enthusiastic reception of HENRY WARD BEECHER at his church in Brooklyn on his return from Europe.
- One of our camps near Chattanooga shelled by a rebel battery.
- Our troops, falling back before Gen. LONGSTREET's army, reached Knoxville, Tenn.
- Attack of the rebels on our forces.
- COMMENCEMENT OF THE SIEGE OF KNOXVILLE, TENN., BY LONGSTREET's ARMY.
- Shell thrown into Charleston from Fort Gregg.
- Schooner Jas. L. Gerety, from Matamoras, seized by rebel passengers.
- Cavalry fight near Strausburgh, Va..
- Capture of Aranzas, Texas, by Gen. BANKS' troops.

November 19.
- The Gettysburgh battle-field consecrated as a National Cemetery for the Union soldiers who fell in the July battles at that place. Addresses by President LINCOLN and EDWARD EVERETT.
- Attack on a rebel camp at New Iberia, La.

November 23.
- THE BATTLE OF CHATTANOOGA COMMENCED.
- Our forces advanced directly in front of the fortifications, drove in the enemy's pickets, and carried his first line of rifle-pits. Gen. HOOKER carried the northern slope of Lookout Mountain.

November 24.
- Gen. SHERMAN crossed the Tennessee River before daylight, at the mouth of the South Chickamauga, and carried the northern extremity of Missionary Ridge.
- Battle of Lookout Mountain.

November 25.
- Brisk engagement near Chattanooga. The rebels driven entirely off Lookout Mountain. Missionary Ridge taken from the rebels. Battle of Tunnel Hill. Gen. GRANT announced a complete victory over BRAGG.
- The rebels repulsed at Kingston, Tenn.

November 26.
- Thanksgiving Day. Advance of the Army of the Potomac. Crossing of the Rapidan .
- Severe cavalry battle near the Rapidan, in which the rebels were driven back.
- Our forces left their camps near Missionary Rhine, and marched toward Chickamauga, which they reached at 10 A.M., finding that the rebels had left the place, after destroying a large quantity of stores, & c. HOOKER's column engaged in skirmishing.

November 27.
- Gen. GRANT reported, that the route of the rebels was most complete, and that BRAGG's loss would fully reach 60 pieces of artillery.
- Gen. HOOKER's, PALMER's and SHERMAN's commands reported ten miles beyond Chickamauga Creek, in pursuit of the rebels.
- Fight near Germanna Ford, on the south side of the Rapidan. The rebels fell back to a stronger position.
- HOOKER's corps engaged near Ringgold, Ga.
- Battle of Ringgold.
- Escape of the rebel Gen. JOHN MORGAN and six of his officers, from the Ohio Penitentiary, in the night.

November 28.
- The rebels made an attack in force upon a large portion of our line, at Knoxville, Tenn., the attack being a feint to cover the real point of attack.

November 29.
- THE REBELS IN FRONT OF KNOXVILLE REPULSED WITH HEAVY LOSS.

November 30.
- The rebels blew up the magazines of Fort Esperanza, Matagorda Bay, Texas.

DECEMBER.

December 1.
- The Army of the Potomac commenced falling back, and at night crossed the Rapidan in safety.

December 2.
- The rebel cavalry repulsed at Clinch River, Tenn.

December 4.
- Rebel cavalry attack on our forage wagons near Harrison, twelve miles from Chattanooga.

December 5.
- Destruction of the steamer Isaac Newton .
- The rebels threatened our forces near the Rapidan.
- Gen. BUTLER issued an important order relative to colored troops.

December 6.
- The advance-guard of Gen. SHERMAN's force, sent to the relief of BURNSIDE, arrived at Knoxville.
- Steamer Chesapeake taken possession of, in the night, by sixteen rebel passengers, near Cape Cod.
- The monitor Weehawken foundered at her anchors inside Charleston (S.C.) harbor.
- Rebel attack on Union troops garrisoning Natchez, Miss.

December 7.
- Meeting of Congress. Election of SCHUYLER COLFAX, Speaker of the House of Representatives. President LINCOLN issued a proclamation, recommending that all loyal people assemble at their places of worship and give thanks for our great victories.
- Gen. FOSTER reported LONGSTREET in full retreat.
- A division of Gen. KELLY's troops moved from Beverly, Va., to cooperate with Gen. AVERILL'a expedition.

December 8.
- The House of Representatives unanimously passed a vote of thanks to Gen. U.S. GRANT and his army, and ordered that a medal be struck in his honor, in the name of the people of the United States.
- PROCLAMATION OF AMNESTY ISSUED BY THE PRESIDENT.
- Gen. AVERILL's expedition moved to cut the Virginia and Tennessee Railroad.

December 9.
- The President's Message transmitted to Congress.
- The Captain and crew of the Chesapeake landed at St. John.

December 10.
- Shells thrown into Charleston, S.C., in the night.

December 11.
- Fort Sumter on fire.

December 12.
- Gen. BUTLER gave notice that the rebel authorities had refused to receive more supplies for the Union prisoners in Richmond.
- The rebel General JOHN MORGAN escaped across the Tennessee River at Gillespie's Landing, 60 miles from Chattanooga.

December 14.
- A portion of Gen. LONGSTREET's army made a descent from Rogersville and engaged the advance of our forces near Bean's Station.
- Gen. LONGSTREET divided his army and made, with one portion, an attack on Bean's Station, and with the other an attack on Kelly's Ford.

December 16.
- The Virginia and Tennessee Railroad cut at Salem by Gen. AVERILL's cavalry expedition. Three depots were destroyed, containing 2,000 barrels of flour, 10,000 bushels of wheat, 100,000 bushels of shelled corn, 50,000 bushels of oats, 2,000 barrels of meat, and many other articles.

December 17.
- The steamer Chesapeake, captured by rebel passengers on Dec. 6, retaken by the Elia and Annie in Sambro Harbor, near Halifax.
- Raid of STUART's rebel cavalry on the Orange and Alexandria Railroad.

December 18.
- Explanations made between Lord LYONS and Secretary SEWARD relative to the capture of the Chesapeake.

December 19.
- The Chesapeake delivered over to British authorities at Halifax. The prisoners, on landing, were rescued by the citizens.

December 22.
- Death of Gen. MICHAEL CORCORAN.

December 24.
- Vigorous bombardment of the city of Charleston, S.C. in the night.

December 25.
- The shelling of Charleston, S.C., continued; ten or twelve buildings destroyed by fire.

December 27.
- Obsequies of Gen. CORCORAN.

December 29.
- Return to Harper's Ferry of an expedition sent to cooperate with that of Gen. AVERILL.

1864

CHRONOLOGICAL RECORD OF THE
MILITARY, NAVAL AND POLITICAL
EVENTS OF THE YEAR.

A YEAR OF GREAT EVENTS, GREAT
BATTLES, GREAT TRIUMPHS AND
GREAT RESULTS.

DECEMBER 31, 1864

JANUARY

January 1.

· Discovery in New-York of a portion of the machinery, consisting of a geometrical lathe and a large number of dies and plates, used by a contractor with the Confederate States in making Confederate bonds and Treasury Notes. Arrest of the contractor, and seizure of about $6,000,000 in Confederate bonds and $1,000,000 in Confederate Treasury Notes.

· Emancipation jubilee of the colored inhabitants of Norfolk, Va., and vicinity, on the anniversary of the issuing of the President's Proclamation of Freedom.

· The State officers of New-York, elected in November, sworn in at Albany.

· Departure of a cavalry reconnaissance to Front Royal, Va.

January 2.

· Seizure of more machinery used by the contractors with the rebels in making Confederate bonds and Treasury Notes.

· The Police Commissioners of New-York, who had been removed from office by Gov. SEYMOUR, on Dec. 31, replied to the Governor's communication, declining to relinquish their offices until they had been accorded a trial on the charges preferred against them.

January 3.

· Death of Archbishop HUGHES.

· Three hundred of our troops at Jonesville, Va., attacked by an overwhelming force of rebels. After a desperate resistance, our forces surrendered, losing thirty killed, thirty wounded, one gun, and two small howitzers.

January 4.

· Inauguration of C. GODFREY GUNTHER, Mayor of New-York.

· Return to the Army of the Potomac of the cavalry reconnaissance sent on the 1st to Front Royal, Va.

January 6.

· Skirmish at Newtown, West Virginia.

January 7.

· Obsequies of Archbishop HUGHES.

· Arrest of A.M. PALMER, Private Secretary of Collector BARNEY, for complicity in shipping goods to the rebels. He was sent to Fort Lafayette.

· Death of Judge CALEB B. SMITH, late Secretary of the Interior.

January 8.

· Our garrison at Petersburgh, West Virginia, surrounded by the rebels.

· Chase and destruction of the Anglo-rebel steamer Dare.

January 10.

· A heavy fight occurred near Strawberry Plains, East Tennessee. The rebels repulsed with heavy loss.

· A battalion of Maryland cavalry attacked by the rebel guerrilla MOSBY, in London County, Va.

January 12.

· An expedition left Point Lookout on a raid through Westmoreland, Northumberland and Richmond Counties, Va. The force succeeded in destroying a large amount of property.

January 14.

· Our pickets at Three Mile Station, Va., attacked by rebel cavalry.

· Return to Point Lookout of a force of Union troops from a raid in Virginia.

· The rebels under Gen. VANCE made a raid toward Tenisville, Tenn., and captured a train of 23 wagons. He was promptly pursued by Col. PALMER, who recaptured the wagons and took an ambulance loaded with medicines, 150 saddle-horses, and 100 stand of arms. Gen. VANCE, together with his Adjutant-General and Inspector-General, was captured.

· The rebel steamer Mayflower captured in Sarasote Pass, Fla.

January 19.

· An unsuccessful attempt was made to burn JEFF. DAVIS' house at Richmond.

January 21.

· Extensive conflagration of hospital buildings at Camp Winder, near Richmond.

January 23.

· Two Mississippi regiments attempted to fight their way out of the rebel lines, for the purpose of taking the oath of allegiance to the United States.

January 24.

· Gen. BUTLER issued an order forbidding the passage through our lines of white women and children from the South.

January 26.

· Senator BAYARD, of Delaware, announced his determination to resign his office, and delivered his valedictory.

· Athens, Ala., taken by the rebels.

· Gen. PALMER sent an expedition into Jones and Ouslow Counties, N.C., which succeeded in destroying large quantities of stores.

January 28.

· The resolution in the Senate, to expel Senator DAVIS withdrawn.

· Gen. PALMER made a reconnaissance to Tunnel Hill, Ga. The rebels retreated in the night.

January 29.

· Three brigades of a cavalry corps, about 1,600 strong, skirmished with the rebels under Gen. JONES on the Virginia road, 13 miles from Cumberland Gap. The skirmishing lasted three hours. Our forces held their position until dark, though they were attacked by a superior force, when they withdrew to their camps, three miles in the rear.

January 30.

· A supply train captured by the rebels near Petersburgh, West Virginia. The garrison of Petersburgh, West Virginia, evacuated the place in the night.

· The engagement with the rebels endeavoring to retake Cumberland Gap, continued.

January 31.

· An expedition went up the James River to Smith-field to destroy provisions, &c., of the rebels.

· Engagement at Smithfield, Va.

· Final repulse of the rebels endeavoring to retake Cumberland Gap.

FEBRUARY

February 1.

- Advance of the rebels in Western Virginia, Burlington occupied by them.

- Fighting in the New Creek, Va., valley.

- Engagement at Smithfield, Va., continued.

- Our outposts at Bachelor's Creek driven in by a strong force of rebels threatening Newbern, N.C.

- The President ordered that a draft for 500,000 men, to serve for three years or during the war, be made on the 10th day of March, for military service of the United States, crediting and deducting therefrom so many as may have been enlisted or drafted into the service prior to the first day of March, and not heretofore credited.

- Our outposts at Bachelor's Creek driven in by a strong force of rebels threatening Newbern, N.C.

- Engagement at Smithfield, Va., continued.

February 2.

- A portion of our forces encountered a large force of rebels in Mechanicsburgh Gap, near Romney, West Va. We succeeded in forcing the rebels to retreat.

- A guard posted at Patterson's Creek bridge, on the Baltimore and Ohio Railroad, attacked by rebel cavalry. The rebels fired the bridge, which was not consumed. The rebels were driven back from the railroad at all points.

- A vessel which had run into Charleston Harbor was destroyed by shot from our vessels.

February 3.

- Gen. SHERMAN's expedition left Vickburgh, Miss.

- The rebels threatening Newbern, N.C., retired to Kingston, and Newbern was relieved from danger of attack.

- An expedition left Newport for White Oak River on a reconnaissance.

February 4.

- Col. MULLIGAN drove the rebels from Morefield, West Va., after six hours' hard fighting.

- The expedition to White Oak River came on a body of rebel cavalry about five miles from Young's Cross Roads, capturing the entire party.

- Skirmishing of Gen. SHERMAN's forces near Champion Hill.

February 5.

- A formidable expedition left Port Royal, S.C., under command of Gen. SEYMOUR, for Jacksonville, Fla.

- Gen. SHERMAN entered Jackson, Miss., the rebels offering but little resistance.

- Engagement between Gen. SHERMAN's forces and the rebels at Bear Creek, near Clinton, Miss.

February 6.

- The expedition sent out by Gen. BUTLER with the object of liberating our troops held as prisoners at Richmond, made a demonstration at Bottom's Bridge and drove in the rebel pickets. Great excitement in Richmond.

- A portion of the Army of the Potomac engaged.

February 7

- The portion of the Army of the Potomac which had been sent out on a reconnaissance, returned to its old quarters.

- The rebels driven across the Rapidan.

- Great excitement in Richmond in expectation of the approach of Gen. BUTLER's force.

- An expedition sent from Knoxville, Tenn., returned, having surprised a body of rebels, killed and wounded 215, taken 50 prisoners, and dispersed the remainder of the band.

February 8.

- A band of rebel guerrillas crossed from Missouri into Kansas, near Aubrey.

- The Florida expedition reached Jacksonville, Fla.

February 9.

- The rebel MOSBY appeared with 300 men on the old Bull Run battle-field.

February 11.

- Gen. W.L. SMITH's cavalry expedition started in the direction of Collersville, Tenn.

February 12.

- Passage of the Enrollment Bill by the House of Representatives.

February 13.

- The entire line of the Memphis and Charleston Railroad evacuated by our forces.

February 14.

- Meridian evacuated by the rebels.

- Guerrilla attack at Tecumseh Landing, Miss.

February 16.

- The Governor of Alabama issued a proclamation to the citizens of Mobile, informing them that the city was about to be attacked, and exhorting non-combatants to leave.

- Gen. SHERMAN's expedition reached Meridian.

February 18.

- Gen. SEYMOUR left Jacksonville, Fla., and established a depot of supplies at Baldwin.

- Gen. SMITH's Union expedition reached Okolona, 75 miles south of Corinth, Miss.

February 19.

- Gen. SEYMOUR's forces advanced to Barber's Station, a distance of 12 miles.

February 20.

- Skirmish with MOSBY's cavalry at Piedmont Station, Va.

- BATTLE of OLUSTEE, FLA. Our troops under Gen. SEYMOUR met 15,000 rebels, 55 miles beyond Jacksonville. The battle was desperately fought during three hours, and at sunset our forces retired, overpowered, to Sanderson.

February 21.

- A force of troops left Hilton Head and proceeded up the Savannah River.

- Heavy fighting at Pontotoc, Miss.

February 22.

- Gen. PALMER's forces occupied Ringgold, Ga.

- The expedition up the Savannah River withdrew.

- Loss of the steamer Bohemian off Cape Elizabeth.

- Opening of the great Sanitary Fair in Brooklyn.

- Call of the Republican National Committee, appointing June 17, as the day for the convention to meet at Baltimore.

February 23.

- Bombardment of Fort Powell, Mobile Bay, by our mortars.

- Desperate charge on the rear-guard of Gen. SMITH's cavalry force.

- Skirmish near Tunnel Hill, Ga. In the afternoon a contest for its possession commenced.

February 24.

- Engagement at Tunnel Hill, Ga.

- Passage by the Senate of a bill authorizing the appointment of a Lieutenant-General.

February 25.

- Gen. KILPATRICK's FORCES COMMENCED MOVING ON AN EXPEDITION TO RICHMOND.

- Skirmish at Bean Station.

- Our army in front of Dalton, Ga. TUNNEL HILL CARRIED BY OUR FORCES AFTER CONSIDERABLE FIGHTING.

- Rebel raid on Maysville, Ky.

February 26.

- Gen. SMITH's expedition arrived in the vicinity of Memphis, Tenn.

February 27

- General movement of KILPATRICK's forces on the expedition toward Richmond. They left camp near Culpepper Court-house and encamped eight miles south of the Rapidan.

February 28.

- Gen. KILPATRICK's forces made demonstrations in front of the rebel works at Mine Run. Gen. CUSTER started on a reconnaissance toward Gordonsville, in cooperation with Gen. KILPATRICK.

- Arrival of Gen. SHERMAN at Vicksburgh, Miss., on his return from his great raid through Mississippi.

February 29.

- At 8 o'clock A.M., Gen. KILPATRICK's forces took up their line of march along the road to Spottsylvania Court-house, Va., en route for the junction of the Virginia Central and the Richmond and Fredericksburgh Railroad. The command arrived at Spottsylvania Court-house. Col. DAHLGREN's command attacked. Great destruction of bridges, railroad track, & c., KILPATRICK reached and destroyed a portion of the Richmond and Fredericksburgh Railroad. His forces left Frederickshall for Richmond.

- Gen. BUTLER ordered to send out a force to meet KILPATRICK.

MARCH

March 1.

- KILPATRICK's EXPEDITION REACHED THE OUTER FORTIFICATIONS OF RICHMOND early in the morning; carried the outer line of works, but was repulsed from the next.

- KILPATRICK's and BUTLER's forces met in the night.

- Arrival of Gen. SHERMAN and his Staff in New-Orleans.

- Return of Gen. CUSTER's cavalry expedition to Culpepper.

- Election in Louisiana.

March 2.

- Uniting of KILPATRICK's and BUTLER's forces.

- Provost-Marshal-General FRY ordered the draft to take place on the 10th inst. in all sub-districts which had not filled their quotas on the 1st inst.

March 3.

- Gen. KILPATRICK arrived within the lines of BUTLER's army.

March 4.

- Gen. CUSTER made a reconnoissance to Ely's Ford on the Rapidan.

- SHERMAN's army reached Vicksburgh, returning from their raid through Mississippi.

- Inauguration of Gov. HAHN, of Louisiana.

- Death of THOS. STARR KING.

March 5.

- Secretary CHASE, in a letter to Hon. JAS. C. HULL, of Ohio, withdrew his name as a Presidential candidate.

March 8.

- Special election in New-York State, resulting in allowing soldiers to vote.

- Election in New-Hampshire.

- Gen. GRANT visited Washington.

March 9.

- Formal presentation of the Lieutenant-General's commission to Gen. GRANT by the President.

- A skirmish took place near Suffolk, Va., in which colored troops were engaged.

- An expedition from Yorktown, Va., to the vicinity of Kings and Queens Court-house met and dispersed a body of rebels.

March 10.

- Gen. GRANT arrived at the headquarters of the Army of the Potomac.

- Pilatka, Fla., occupied by our troops.

- An expedition left Vicksburgh, Miss., for Fort De Russey, La.

- Emancipation Report adopted by the Virginia Constitutional Convention at Alexandria.

March 11.

- Fight with guerrillas on the Atchafalaya River, La.

March 13.

- A portion of our fleet arrived before Alexandria, La., and demanded its surrender, which was complied with.

March 14.

- FORT DE RUSSEY, ON THE RED RIVER, LA., ATTACKED AND CAPTURED by Union forces under Gen. SMITH.

March 15.

- Official order issued, promulgating the President's call for 200,000 more troops and ordering a draft for any deficiency, on the 15th of April.

- Gov. SEYMOUR signed the Police Bill and the Commissioners were sworn in.

March 16.

- Rebel guerrillas attacked a train from Nashville, near Estelle Springs, Tenn.

- The rebels shelled from a camp, near Bennett's Ferry, on the Cumberland.

- Rebel attack on our forces at Skull Creek, near Hilton Head, frustrated.

March 17

- Rebel night raid on Magnolia, Fla.

March 19.

- Attempt of a body of rebels to land near Port Royal Ferry, S.C.

March 20.

- Rebel attack on Jenkins' Island and Spanish Wells, Hilton Head, S.C. frustrated.

March 21.

- Engagement near Teachoes, La .

- The rebels defeated at Nachitoches, on the Red River, La.

March 22.

- Gen. THAYER, with an army of 5,500 men, left Fort Smith, Arkansas, to cooperate with Gen. STEELE's army.

March 23.

- Gen. STEELE's army left Little Rock, Arkansas.

- Order reorganizing the Army of the Potomac.

March 24.

- Surrender of the Union garrison at Union City, East Tennessee, after repulsing the rebels, 2,000 strong, three times.

March 25.

- Attack on Paducah, Ky., by the rebels. The city partially fired.

- Death of Hon. OWEN LOVEJOY.

March 26.

- President LINCOLN issued a proclamation defining the Amnesty Proclamation. Gen. FRANKLIN's forces reached Alexandria, La.

March 28.

- The advance of Gen. BANKS' army left Alexandria, La.

- Copperhead riot at Charleston, Ill.

- Battle on Cane River, La., thirty-five miles above Alexandria. The rebels defeated.

March 29.

- A rebel force crossed the Cumberland River at Eddyville.

March 30.

- Engagement in Arkansas with 1,200 rebels, who were routed and pursued ten miles.

March 31.

- An expedition to Mount Elba and Longview, Ark., returned to Pine Bluff, having destroyed a large amount of rebel property.

APRIL.

April 1.

- Gen. GRANT visited Fort Monroe.

- Fight near Snyder's Bluff, on the Yazoo.

April 2.

- Fight between GRIERSON's and the rebel FORREST's cavalry, near Summerville, Tenn.

April 4.

- Fight at Roseville, Ark.

- Gunboat expedition up the Chickahominy.

- Gen. GRANT returned to Washington.

- Opening of the great Sanitary Fair in New-York.

April 5.

- Fight between gunboats and guerrillas at Hickman, Ky.

- Gen. GRANT left Washington for the Army of the Potomac.

April 7

- Brisk fighting in Louisiana.

April 8.

- The Senate passed a resolution to submit to the Legislatures of the States an amendment of the Constitution, abolishing slavery.

- BATTLE NEAR MANSFIELD, LA. The rebel Gen. TAYLOR attacked. Our army, unexpectedly, came on the rebels in full force. Our troops were entrapped, surrounded and flanked. They fell back, but their retreat was impeded by wagons, and the retreat became a rout.

April 9.

- BATTLE OF PLEASANT HILL, LA. A severe battle, our troops falling back in the night.

- The rebels attempted to blow up the United States steam frigate Minnesota before light in the morning.

April 10.

- Death of Hon. W.S. THAYER, Consul-General to Egypt.

April 11.

- Gen. BANKS' army all reached Grand Ecore, La.

- The rebels repulsed in an attack on Roseville, Ark.

April 12.

- MASSACRE OF NEGRO SOLDIERS AT FORT PILLOW, TENN. The rebels drove in our pickets just before sunrise. In the afternoon, a flag of truce was sent by the rebels, with a demand to surrender in twenty minutes. This being refused, the rebels rushed from positions treacherously gained, and carried the fort, after which they slaughtered, indiscriminately, men and women, white and black.

April 13.

- Rebel Gen. BUFORD appeared before Columbus, Ky., and demanded its unconditional surrender, threatening, in case of refusal, to give no quarter to negro soldiers. The enemy retired without an attack.

- A portion of BANKS' army attacked near Blair's Landing, La. The rebels repulsed with slaughter.

April 14.

- The surrender of Paducah, Ky., again demanded by the rebels.

- Skirmish and defeat of the rebels in Kentucky.

April 15.

- Gen. MOSBY's force suddenly appeared near Bristow Station, Ga.

April 16.

- Gen. THAYER's force from Fort Smith, Ark., joined the main army at Prairie d'Anne.

April 17

- Bread riot by females in Savannan, Ga.

- The rebels in force assaulted Plymouth, N.C., but were repulsed with considerable loss.

April 18.

- A rebel ram came to within a few miles of Plymouth, N.C., and attacked our fleet, sinking the Smithfield and another gunboat.

- The rebels attempted to blow up the frigate Wabash, blockading Charleston, N.C.

April 19.

- Fort Wessels, Plymouth, N.C., evacuated by our troops.

April 20.

- Gen. STEELE's army entered Camden, Ark.

- The rebels stormed Fort Williams, Plymouth, N.C., carrying it, and capturing Gen. WESSELS and 2,500 men. Massacre of negro troops.

- PLYMOUTH SURRENDERED TO THE REBELS.

April 21.

- Successful expedition to Hasonborough, N.C.

April 22.

- The rebels captured the gunboat Petrel on the Zazoo River.

- Our troops left Nachitoches and Grand Ecore for Alexandria, by land.

April 23.

- Sharp fight on Cane River, La., near Chetersville.

- BRISK ENGAGEMENT NEAR CAMDEN, ARK.

- The rebels were several times repulsed, but carried the day.

April 24.

- The rebels made an impetuous charge on the rear of BANKS' army in Louisiana. They were repulsed, but made another charge, and, after a two hours' battle, were driven back at all points.

April 25.

- A train of 240 wagons, of Gen. STEELE's army, captured by the rebels while on its way to Pine Bluff, Ark.

- Gen. BANKS' army reached Alexandria on its retreat.

April 26.

- Gen. STEELE left Camden for Little Rock, Ark.

- The rebels in strong force attacked our gunboats in Louisiana.

April 28.

- Little Washington, N.C., evacuated by our troops.

April 30.

- The President approved a joint resolution raising duties on imports 50 per cent.

- Gen. STEELE's army in Arkansas crossed the Saline River, after a fight with the rebels.

MAY

May 1.

- Death of Commodore W.D. PORTER.

- A cavalry expedition returned to Vienna, Virginia, after having an encounter with MOSBY's guerrillas, and after destroying Madison Court-house, Virginia.

- Gen. STEELE's army forty miles from Little Rock, Arkansas. His cavalry reached that city.

May 2.

- ADVANCE OF THE ARMY OF THE POTOMAC COMMENCED.

- Gen. MEADE issued an order regarding soldiers who claimed that their time of enlistment had expired, announcing the penalty of mutiny as instant death.

- WEST POINT, VIRGINIA, OCCUPIED BY OUR FORCES. Gen. STURGIS' cavalry encountered a band of the rebel FORREST's men near Bolivar, Tennessee, and after a severe fight defeated them.

May 3.

- THE CROSSING OF THE RAPIDAN OF THE ARMY OF THE POTOMAC EFFECTED, without opposition, at Culpepper, Germania and Ely's fords.

- The Secretary of the Navy sentenced Admiral WILKES to be reprimanded and suspended for three years for insubordination, & c.

May 4.

- The crossing of the Rapidan by the Army of the Potomac continued.

- Gen. MEADE issued an address to the Army of the Potomac on the commencement of their march. Gen. WARREN's headquarters at the Wilderness.

- A fleet of transports on Hampton Roads commenced embarking troops.

- Rebel raid into Princeton, Kentucky.

May 5.

- BATTLE OF THE WILDERNESS COMMENCED.

- A day of terrific fighting on most difficult ground in the Wilderness, near Chancellorsville, Va. Night closed in without any definite result. Gen. HAYS killed.

- Gen. BUTLER's army passed Fortress Monroe in transports on their way up the James River.

- Gen. KAUTZ forced the Blackwater, burnt the railroad bridge at Stony Creek, cutting BEAURE-GARD's forces in two.

- Naval engagement between the rebel ram Albermarle and our fleet near the mouth of the Roanoke River.

- Skirmish at Thoroughfare Gap, Va. BURNSIDE's cavalry attacked the enemy on their passage through the Gap.

May 6.

- BATTLE OF THE WILDERNESS CONTINUED.

- Another day of terrible fighting, resulting in the falling back of LEE's army. Gen. WADSWORTH killed. The rebel Gen. LONGSTREET wounded. Our wounded, who had been removed to Fredericksburgh, fired on by citizens.

- Gen. BUTLER's forces effected a successful landing without resistance.

May 7

- GEN. GRANT's ARMY IN PURSUIT OF LEE.

- Having marched fifteen miles in the night of the 6th, it was, in the morning, in position at Todd's Tavern.

- Battle near Petersburgh, Va., between Gen. BUTLER's army and the rebels.

- GEN. SHERMAN REPORTED THAT GEN. THOMAS HAD OCCUPIED TUNNEL HILL, GA., and that the rebels had taken position at Buzzards' Roost Pass, north of Dalton, Ga.

May 8.

- Gen. HANCOCK's corps passed through Spottsylvania Court-house at daylight, and at noon our headquarters were twenty miles south of the battlefield of the 6th.

- BATTLE OF SPOTTSYLVANIA COURT-HOUSE, VA., COMMENCED. The armies near Spottsylvania Court-House, engaged from 8 to 12 M., at which time our forces gained the point for which they contended. At 6 P.M., two fresh divisions were thrown in, and after a severe engagement of an hour and a-half, the rebel position was carried and their first line of breastworks occupied.

- General engagement at Mill Creek Gap, Ga.

- Our troops held possession of Fredericksburgh, Va.

May 9.

- BATTLE OF SPOTTSYLVANIA COURT-HOUSE, VA., CONTINUED.

- LEE's army made a stand, but no general engagement occurred in the morning. Maj.-Gen. SEDG-WICK killed. The fight in the evening was brought on by HANCOCK, who crossed the River Po, and established himself on the south bank. President LINCOLN issued a proclamation, announcing that enough was known respecting the success of GRANT's army to claim especial gratitude to God, and recommending that all patriots unite in thanksgiving and prayer. Gen. BUTLER reported that his army had landed at Bermuda Landing, and was in a strong position. HIS FORCES DEFEATED A PORTION OF BEAUREGARD's ARMY UNDER GEN. HILL. The fight commenced at noon and continued till night. The rebels driven back three miles.

- The railroad between Richmond and Petersburgh in our possession.

- Night attack on Gen. BUTLER's lines. The rebels repulsed.

- Gen. SHERIDAN marched around the rebel right flank, and reached the North Anna River in safety in the evening. In the night he destroyed a great quantity of rebel stores, & c.

May 10.

- BATTLE OF SPOTTSYLVANIA COURT-HOUSE CONTINUED. A general advance of our army ordered at 5 A.M. A tremendous conflict ensued. In the afternoon an attack was made on the rebel batteries. After the assault had continued some time it was found that the rebel batteries could not be carried without great loss, and the effort for the time was abandoned. The battle ceased about 9 P.M., and was one of the most terrible and bloody of the war.

- Gen. SHERIDAN reported that he had turned the rebel right, reached their rear, and destroyed from eight to ten miles of railroad, and other property.

- Gen. SHERIDAN crossed the South Anna River.

- Gen. AVERILL's force fought a battle near Wytheville, Va.

- Secretary STANTON reported that Gen. MCPHERSON was within seven miles of Resaca, Ga.

- Gen. SHERMAN in front of Buzzard Roost Gap, Ga.

May 11.

- The armies under GRANT and LEE engaged with varied success until 11 A.M., when our line was somewhat advanced. Gen. LEE proposed a cessation of hostilities for 48 hours, to bury the dead, which Gen. GRANT refused. Gen. GRANT reported to the War Department, that after six days' fighting the result was much in our favor, declaring that he intended "to fight it out on this line if it took all Summer".

- After three days of skirmishing we drove the rebels back to Rocky Ridge and Buzzard Roost Mountain, Ga.

- Gen. SHERIDAN captured Ashland Station, destroying a large amount of stores. HE ATTACKED GEN. STEWART AT YELLOW TAVERN, NEAR RICHMOND AND PENETRATED THE FIRST AND SECOND LINES OF THE REBEL DEFENCES.

May 12.
- THE BATTLE BETWEEN GRANT's AND LEE's ARMY RENEWED FIVE MILES BELOW SPOTT-SYLVANIA COURT-HOUSE, VA. Gen. HANCOCK opened the battle and made a brilliant assault on A.P. HILL's division, which he routed. Gen. GRANT reported that the day closed leaving between 3,000 and 4,000 prisoners in our hands for the day's work, including two general officers and over thirty pieces of artillery. This day's battle was a decided Union success. In the night LEE abandoned his position.
- Gen. SHERIDAN's army encamped at Walnut Grove and Gaine's Mills.
- Gen. BUTLER's army engaged.

May 13.
- GEN. BUTLER's ARMY ADVANCED TOWARD PETERSBURGH, VA.
- Skirmishing with the rebels in the afternoon.
- Gen. MEADE issued a congratulatory address to his army. The rebels in his front fell back early in the morning, our troops following.
- Gen. SHERIDAN's forces encamped at Bottom's Bridge.
- Gen. SHERMAN's army in line of battle in Sugar Valley.

May 14.
- GEN. "Baldy" SMITH CARRIED THE FIRST LINE OF REBEL WORKS AT PETERSBURGH, VA. The rebels attacked the Fifth Corps, Army of the Potomac, but were finally driven back with severe loss, after a furious cannonade. Our forces then charged the rebel lines.
- Gen. SHERMAN's FORCES ACTIVELY ENGAGED. Gen. HOOKER's corps attacked by the rebel Gen. HOOD's division. The rebels repulsed. General battle, which lasted till midnight, each party holding its respective position.

May 15.
- BATTLE OF RESACA, GA. An all-day battle, in which we were successful. The rebels forced to evacuate Resaca. Gen. JOHNSTON retreated from our front in the night.
- Gen. SIGEL fought a battle at Newmarket, Va. The rebels successful. Our forces fell back to Strasburgh, Va. Gen. BANKS' gunboats arrived at Fort de Russey, La.

May 16.
- The rebel army encamped around Spottsylvania Court-house, Va.
- The rebels in force attacked Gen. "Baldy" SMITH's lines, and forced them back with considerable loss.
- GEN. BUTLER's FORCE ATTACKED BY TROOPS FROM PETERSBURGH. Furious fighting. The rebels made a desperate onslaught in a fog, but were repulsed.
- Resaca, Ga., occupied by Gen. SHERMAN.

May 17
- Gen. KAUTZ reached City Point, Va., returning from his raid on the Danville Railroad.
- Gen. SHERMAN's army at Colburn, Ga.
- Gen. BANKS' forces reached Semmesport, La.

May 18.
- HEAVY ENGAGEMENT BETWEEN THE ARMIES IN VIRGINIA. Gen. HANCOCK charged the enemy and carried the first line of rebel intrenchments.
- Gen. SHERMAN reached Adairsville, Ga., where he was engaged in skirmishes.

- Secretary STANTON announced that a draft would be ordered to take place July 1.
- A pretended proclamation of the President, calling for 400,000 men, and announcing the Spring campaign closed, published in the Journal of Commerce and the World.
- The two papers suppressed.
- Gen. A.J. SMITH's army had a spirited engagement.

May 19.
- Gen. EWELL attempted to turn GRANT's right, but was repulsed.
- Gen. SHERMAN advanced on the enemy, who retreated.
- Kingston, Ga., reached.
- Gen. SHERMAN pushed a column as far as Casville, Ga.

May 20.
- Gen. BUTLER's forces engaged.
- Gen. GRANT commenced a new flank movement.
- Gen. HUNTER placed in command of the Department of West Virginia.
- Arrest of HOWARD, the forger of the bogus proclamation.

May 21.
- Gen. HANCOCK's forces entered Bowling Green, Va. Milford reached by our troops.

May 22.
- ROME, GA., OCCUPIED BY GEN. SHERMAN without opposition.

May 23.
- Gen. GRANT's army moved to the North Anna, closely following LEE's army. The rebels attacked but were repulsed.

May 24.
- Gen. GRANT's army at Mount Carmel Church, Va. Our army engaged, and 1,000 prisoners taken. Gen. BUTLER's position at Wilson's Wharf attacked, but the rebels repulsed. Gen. SHERMAN resumed his march from Kingston, Ga.

May 25.
- BATTLE OF DALLAS, GA., COMMENCED.
- A sharp a bloody fight between HOOKER's corps of SHERMAN's army and HOOD's rebel division. Our army gained two miles and a favorable position. A reconnoissance up the Ashepoo River. Department of the South.

May 26.
- BATTLE OF DALLAS, GA., CONTINUED. Our army withdrawn to the north side of the North Anna River, Va., in the night, and moved toward Hanovertown. Secretary STANTON reported that the rebels held a strong position between the North and South Anna Rivers. Gen. J.G. FOSTER assumed command of the Department of the South.

May 27
- Gen. GRANT's army all in motion. THE BATTLE OF DALLAS, GA., CONTINUED. Severe fighting on SHERMAN's left. SHERMAN's headquarters at Dallas.
- Gen. SHERIDAN took possession of Hanover Ferry and Hanoverton, Va.

May 28.
- BATTLE OF DALLAS, GA., CONCLUDED. The rebels suffered severely, leaving 2,000 dead and wounded in our hands. Gen. MCPHERSON's corps drove back the rebels with great loss.

- TWO DIVISIONS OF GEN. GRANT's ARMY HAD A SEVERE ENGAGEMENT.

May 29.
- The rebels made a night attack on SHERMAN, but were repulsed.
- Gen. "Baldy" SMITH's command arrived at Fortress Monroe from Bermuda Hundreds on its way to join Gen. GRANT.

May 30.
- The rebels attacked the left wing of GRANT's army but were easily repulsed with considerable slaughter. Gen. HANCOCK's division attacked the rebels and drove them from their intrenched skirmish line. At midnight, the rebels attacked HANCOCK, but were repulsed. Gen. WARREN's corps engaged, near Bethesda Church, Va. Gen. GRANT reported that his army had successfully crossed the Pamunkey River.
- The rebels repulsed in an attack on Gen. BUTLER's line. Gen. SMITH's corps occupied White House, Va.
- Heavy skirmishing with SHERMAN's army.

May 31.
- The rebels attacked Gen. SHERMAN's army, but were repulsed after a three hours' flight. Our left reached the railroad near Marietta, Ga.
- A hard fight near Hanover Court-house, Va.
- Battle between SHERIDAN's and FITZ-HUGH LEE's cavalry at Cold Harbor, Va. The rebels defeated, and SHERIDAN retained possession of the place.
- Another artillery attack on BUTLER's forces.
- Nomination of JOHN C. FREMONT and JOHN COCHRANE for President and Vice-President, by the Cleveland Convention.

JUNE

June 1.
- BATTLE OF COLD HARBOR, VA.
- Our corps at Cold Harbor attacked the rebels at 5 P.M., and carried the enemy's works on the right. The rebels attacked the corps not engaged in the assault, but were repulsed.
- BURNSIDE's advance a mile and a half from Mechanicsville, Va.
- Gen. MCPHERSON's corps of SHERMAN's army moved to the front of the rebels at New Hope Church. The rebels shelled our hospitals.
- Gen. BUTLER's left wing attacked. Spirited fight resulting in a rebel repulse.
- Steamer Pocahontas sunk at sea by collision, and 40 lives lost.

June 2.
- Gen. SCHOFIELD's and HOOKER's corps of SHERMAN's army pushed forward toward Marietta, Ga.
- Our cavalry took possession of Allatoona Pass, Ga.

June 3.
- BATTLE OF THE CHICAHOMINY.
- A short but terrible battle. Gen. GRANT assaulted the rebels at 4:30 A.M., driving them from their intrenchments at all points, but without gaining any decisive advantage. At 7 P.M. the rebels attacked. The battle lasted with great fury half an hour, at the expiration of which the rebels were repulsed. The blockader Water Witch captured by the rebels in Warsaw Sound.

June 4.

- Gen. SHERMAN thirteen miles from Marietta, Ga. The rebels, discovering our forces moving around their right flank, abandoned their position. Considerable skirmishing.

June 5.

- The rebels attacked our forces after dark, near Coal Harbor, in a fog, but were disastrously repulsed.

- BATTLE OF PIEDMONT, WEST VIRGINIA. Our forces under Gen. HUNTER came on the rebels in force at Piedmont, 15 miles north of Staunton, Va., and after a brief and spirited fight, whipped them.

- The rebels before SHERMAN evacuated their position.

June 6.

- An assault at midnight on BURNSIDE's corps repulsed.

- Gen. SHERMAN's army moved toward Marietta, Ga.

- Gen. HUNTER pursued the rebels through Staunton, West Virginia.

June 7

- Gen. SHERIDAN crossed the Pamunkey.

- Engagement between our torts and the rebel batteries on Sullivan and James Islands, S.C.

- Assembling of the National Union Convention at Baltimore.

June 8.

- Nomination of ABRAHAM LINCOLN and ANDREW JOHNSON by the Union Convention for President and Vice President of the United States.

- Capture of Mount Stirling, Ky., by the rebel JOHN MORGAN. MORGAN entered Paris, Ky.

- Burning of the steamer Berkshire on the Hudson.

June 9.

- Gen. SHERMAN's cavalry developed the position of the enemy in a line along the hills from Kenesaw to Lost Mountain.

- SHERIDAN's cavalry started on a raid.

- MORGAN's guerrillas whipped at Mt. Stirling, Ky.

- President LINCOLN informally accepted a renomination.

June 10.

- Lexington, Ky., entered by Morgan's forces.

- Attack on Cynthiana, Ky., commenced.

- Gen. STURGIS' expedition defeated by the rebels at Guntown, south of Corinth, Miss.

- Gen. HUNTER's army advanced from Staunton, Va.

- GEN. KAUTZ CHARGED THE REBEL WORKS AT PE-TERSBURGH and carried them, penetrating to near the town, but, supporters not coming up, withdrew.

June 11.

- Cynthiana, Ky., captured by the rebel Gen. JOHN MORGAN, after a pretty severe fight. Gen. BUR-BRIDGE attacked and totally defeated the rebels.

- THE MOVEMENT OF GRANT's ARMY TO THE SOUTH SIDE OF RICHMOND COMMENCED.

- Gen. SMITH's corps marched to White House and embarked for Bermuda Hundreds. The other corps crossed the Chickahominy.

- Gen. SHERIDAN's forces had an obstinate engagement at Trevilian Station near Richmond.

- They drove the rebels from successive lines of earthworks.

- Gen. HUNTER's army reached Lexington, Va.

June 12.

- Gov. LETCHER's house burned by HUNTER's troops.

June 13.

- Gen. SHERIDAN destroyed the railroad from Trevillon Station to Lorraine Court-house, near Richmond.

June 14.

- Very heavy skirmishing between SHERMAN's army and the rebels; the position of our army changed in the night.

June 15.

- GEN. SMITH ASSAULTED AND CARRIED THE PRINCIPAL LINE OF THE ENEMY BEFORE PETERSBURGH.

- Gen. FOSTER reported that five general officers of the United States had been placed under fire at Charleston, S.C., by the rebels, asking an equal number of rebel officers to place under fire in retaliation.

- Gen. SHERMAN's army engaged all day in skirmishing.

June 16.

- CANNONADING ALONG THE WHOLE OF SHERMAN's LINE.

- The greater portion of both armies were engaged before noon. The rebels compelled to evacuate a splendid position near the base of Lost Mountain.

- Heavy firing at night, between GRANT's and LEE's armies.

- Gen. HUNTER's army entered Liberty.

- The Cummings' Point, S.C., (Union) batteries shelled by rebel batteries.

June 17

- THE NINTH CORPS CARRIED TWO MORE RE-DOUBTS AT PETERSBURGH, VA.

- Gen. HUNTER's forces engaged at Quaker Church, Va.

June 18.

- SEVERE BATTLE NEAR LYNCHBURGH, VA.

- Our forces charged, were repulsed, and charged again. Finding the enemy's position too strong, and numbers too great, our forces commenced falling back. Our forces advanced close to Petersburg Va.

- The rebels before Gen. SHERMAN gave way at night, abandoning their works in front of Kenesaw Mt.

June 19.

- GREAT NAVAL BATTLE BETWEEN THE ALA-BAMA AND KEARSARGE, OFF THE HARBOR OF CHERBOURG, FRANCE. The Alabama sunk and Capt. SEMMES saved by an English yacht.

June 20.

- THE REBELS MADE SEVEN DISTINCT ASSAULTS ON SHERMAN's LINES in a desperate attempt to take the position at Kenesaw Mountain, which they had lost the day before.

- A rebel force attacked our troops at White House, Va., but were repulsed.

- Gen. SHERIDAN's advance arrived at White House, Va.

June 21.

- THE REBELS MADE A FIERCE ATTACK ON GEN. HUNTER's REAR.

- SKIRMISHING near White House, Va.

- Manoeuvring of GRANT's army.

- Lively skirmishing. Our advance interrupted.

- A cavalry expedition under Gen. WILSON, left Bermuda Hundreds.

June 22.

- THE SECOND CORPS ATTACKED NEAR THE WELDON RAILROAD. A severe engagement. The rebels forced back in a charge by the Sixth Corps. Our forces not successful in the day's battle.

- Gen. WILSON's cavalry crossed the Weldon Railroad at Ream's Station, and commenced destroying the track and other property there.

- SEVERE ENGAGEMENT IN SHERMAN's ADVANCE. A victory won by his army.

- Arrest of ISAAC HENDERSON, Navy Agent at New-York.

June 23.

- At daylight an advance of our whole line near the track of the Petersburgh and Weldon Railroad, was ordered.

- A part of our cavalry reached the junction of the Lynchburgh and Danville Railroad, and destroyed the track.

- The rebels assaulted Gens. SCHOFIELD's and HOOKER's Corps of SHERMAN's army. Our advance pressed forward. NIGHT ATTACK ON THE REBEL WORKS AT KENESAW MOUNTAIN, GA.

June 24.

- Batteries of the Eighteenth, Fifth and Second Corps opened on Petersburg, Va. Gen. BURNSIDE's Corps attacked. The attack a failure. Our lines advanced half a mile. TERRIBLE ARTILLERY ATTACK ON THE RIGHT FLANK OF THE ARMY OF THE POTOMAC.

- Gen. PILLOW demanded the surrender of Lafayette, which was refused and the rebels repulsed.

- Severe skirmishing before Kenesaw Mountain, Ga.

June 25.

- An attack on BURNSIDE's line at 11 P.M. Pretty severe engagement between our cavalry and the rebels at the Chickahominy River. Raid on SHERMAN's rear by 2,000 rebels.

- Destruction of railroad by WILSON's cavalry continued at Drake's Station.

- Engagement at Roanoke Station.

June 27

- BATTLE OF KENESAW MOUNTAIN, GA. An unsuccessful attack made by our forces on the rebels. Gen. MCPHERSON's corps attacked the rebels at the southwest end of Kenesaw Mountain. Gen. THOMAS also attacked further south. Firing along the whole line. Neither attack succeeded. Formal acceptance of a renomination by President LINCOLN.

June 30.

- Hon. SALMON P. CHASE resigned his position as Secretary of the Treasury. President LINCOLN sent to the Senate the nomination of DAVID TOD, of Ohio, as Secretary of the Treasury.

- Gen. KAUTZ's division of WILSON's cavalry force re-entered our lines, returning from their great raid.

JULY

July 1.

- Gov. TOD having declined the appointment as Secretary of the Treasury, his nomination was withdrawn, and that of WM. PITT FESSENDEN substituted.

- An expedition left Hilton Head, S.C., in the direction of North Edisto River.

- The southern end of James Island, S.C., occupied by our forces.

July 2.
- The expedition from Hilton Head disembarked at Seabrook Island.
- An unsuccessful attempt to take the rebel Fort Johnson on the north end of James Island.

July 3.
- Our army entered Marietta, Ga.
- A rebel force appeared near Martinsburgh, Va.
- A part of the expedition from Hilton Head repulsed.
- The rebels overtaken by SHERMAN, two miles south of Marietta, Ga.

July 4.
- The rebels took possession of Bolivar City, half a mile from Harper's Ferry, on their advance into Maryland, where they were attacked. Gen. SIGEL arrived at Sandy Hook. Gen. MULLIGAN evacuated Bolivar Heights.
- The rebels made a raid on Point of Rocks, Md.
- Naval operations in Stono River.

July 5.
- The President issued a proclamation declaring martial law in Kentucky and suspending the action of the writ of habeas corpus.
- Secretary FESSENDEN sworn in.
- An expedition started from Lagrange, Tenn., in pursuit of the rebel FORREST.

July 6.
- Secretary WELLES addressed a dispatch to Capt. WINSLOW, of the Kearsarge, in recognition of his services in the destruction of the pirate Alabama.

July 7
- Our forces ordered to evacuate Harper's Ferry by Gen. SIGEL. Rebel raiders near Frederick, Md. The rebels checked at Monocacy Bridge.
- Proclamation issued by President Lincoln appointing the first Thursday in August as a Fast Day.

July 8.
- Harper's Ferry reoccupied by our forces.
- The rebel pirate Florida, on our coast, captured the bark Golconda.
- Capture of Platte City, Mo., by guerrillas.

July 9.
- BATTLE AT MONOCACY, Md., lasting from 9 A.M. to 5 P.M. Our forces overpowered and forced to retreat in disorder.
- Proclamation issued by President LINCOLN giving his views on reconstruction and his reasons for not signing a bill passed by Congress providing for the same.
- The Florida, continued her depredations on our coast.
- Our forces on John's Island, S.C., twice repelled a rebel assault.
- Gen. SHERMAN reached the Chattahoochee.
- Gov. BROWN, of Georgia, ordered all the militia of the State into active service.

July 10.
- A portion of the rebels encamped at Rockville, Md.
- A Union cavalry expedition left Decatur.

July 11.
- THE REBELS NEAR WASHINGTON, D.C. Capture by the rebels of a railroad train at Magnolia Station, between Philadelphia and Baltimore. The rebels captured Maj.-Gen. FRANKLIN, who was on the train. Burning of Gunpowder Bridge by the rebels.

- Mayor GUNTHER protested against sending the militia from New-York City, in response to a call from the President.

July 12.
- ENGAGEMENT NEAR FORT STEVENS, ONE OF THE DEFENCES OF WASHINGTON. The rebels driven off.
- Gov. SEYMOUR issued a general order, directing the Commanders of regiments of the National Guards to hold themselves in readiness for immediate service.
- Gov. PARKER, of New-Jersey, issued a proclamation calling on the people of his State to organize for 30 days' service.

July 13.
- Battle at Tapaluci, Tenn.

July 14.
- Arrival of Maj.-Gen. FRANKLIN in Baltimore, having escaped from the rebel raiders.

July 15.
- Engagement with the rebel FORREST in Tennessee.

July 16.
- A rebel force captured the Federal stockade at Brownsboro, on the Memphis and Charleston Railroad.

July 17
- Gen. SHERMAN's command moved forward to within five miles of Atlanta, Ga. His advance crossed the Chattahoochie River.
- Gen. JOS. E. JOHNSTON turned over the command of the rebel army at Atlanta to Gen. J.B. HOOD.
- Severe fight near Grand Gulf.
- Indian raid on our post at Fort Larned.

July 18.
- Gen. J.B. HOOD assumed command of the rebel army at Atlanta, Ga.
- Decatur, Ga., occupied by our forces.
- President LINCOLN issued an order for a draft of 500,000 men to take place immediately after Sept. 5, the term of service to be one year, volunteers to be credited till Sept. 5.
- HORACE GREELEY reached Niagara Falls to hold a conference with some self-constituted Confederate Commissioners in Canada. The President sent his famous "To whom it may concern" dispatch.
- Fights at Snicker's Gap.
- Attack by Indians on a train near Fort Larned.

July 19.
- Our forces reached Peachtree Creek, four miles north of Atlanta, Ga. They were attacked by HOOD's troops.

July 20.
- THE REBELS ASSAULTED SHERMAN's ARMY THREE TIMES — each time being repulsed. Our army was engaged all day and drove the rebels steady on into their intrenchments.
- Gen. SMITH's forces reached La Grange, Tenn.
- Gen. "Baldy" SMITH took leave of his command before Petersburgh, Va., and Gen. MARTINDALE assumed command.
- Gen. AVERILL attacked and defeated the rebel EARLY in front of Winchester, Va.

July 21.
- The rebel lines contracted close to Atlanta.
- Skirmishing on the James River.

July 22.
- GREAT BATTLE BEFORE ATLANTA.

- The rebels assaulted our lines near Atlanta with great fury seven times, and were as often repulsed after a terrible struggle. Our loss was 3,521; the rebel loss estimated at 10,000.
- Gen. MCPHERSON was killed.
- Skirmishing in front of BURNSIDE's corps of the Army of the Potomac.

July 23.
- Burial of the dead before Atlanta.
- Atlanta shelled.
- Heavy fighting in the Shenandoah Valley.

July 24.
- The cavalry expedition which left Decatur July 10, arrived at Marietta, Ga., having been completely successful in a raid on the Montgomery and West Point Railroad.
- Fighting in the Shenandoah Valley.

July 25.
- The rebels again occupied Martinsburgh, Va.
- A reconnaissance of our forces near Helena, Ark.

July 26.
- BATTLE NEAR HELENA, ARK.
- Our forces at first were unsuccessful, but afterward repulsed the enemy and charged through their lines.
- Engagement at Point of Rocks, Md.
- The rebels made an attempt to flank Gen. BUTLER's position.
- Gen. THOMAS issued a congratulatory address to his army.
- Gen. STONEMAN dispatched a cavalry force to destroy the Macon and Western Railroad. They succeeded in destroying 18 miles of track, and in inflicting other damage.
- Our gunboats went on an expedition up Grand Lake, La., and destroyed a number of rebel flatboats.

July 27
- Our army attacked while crossing James River.
- A spirited engagement, in which the rebels were driven back. Our troops attacked and carried their position.
- Gen. O.O. HOWARD assumed command of the Department and Army of the Tennessee, lately commanded by Gen. MCPHERSON.
- Our cavalry, under Gens. STONEMAN and MCCOOK, started on a raid on the communications of the rebel army in Georgia.

July 28.
- THE SIEGE OF ATLANTA COMMENCED.
- The Fifteenth Corps of SHERMAN's army assaulted the rebels in force and defeated them. The rebel army under HOOD was repeatedly hurled against SHERMAN's army. The rebels suffered severely without gaining any advantage.
- An expedition sent into North Carolina.
- Gen. HOOKER relieved of his command at his own request.
- Our gunboats in Louisiana destroyed a large amount of rebel lumber and two saw-mills.

July 29.
- The rebels crossed the Potomac on their raid into Maryland and Pennsylvania.
- Our cavalry occupied Fayetteville, Ga.
- They cut the Atlanta and Macon Railroad.
- Fights with the rebels near Morganzia, La.

July 30.
- EXPLOSION OF AN IMMENSE MINE BY OUR TROOPS IN FRONT OF BURNSIDE's POSITION BEFORE PETERSBURGH. Its explosion was the signal for the discharge of every piece of artillery on our line from the Appomatox to the extreme left. After the discharge of the artillery our army advanced and assaulted the rebel works, but after a desperate attempt to carry them was repulsed.
- THE REBELS ENTERED CHAMBERSBURGH, PENN., where the rebel Commander demanded $500,000 under threat of burning the city. His demand not being complied with, the city was burned.
- Our cavalry cut off, 40 miles from Atlanta.
- Gen. SHERMAN's celebrated letter on the recruiting of negroes in rebel States.

July 31.
- Gen. STONEMAN and part of his command captured by the rebels.
- The rebels occupied Frederick, Md.

AUGUST

August 2.
- Gen. BANKS issued an order enlisting all able-bodied colored men between 18 and 40 years of age.

August 3.
- Return to Norfolk, Va., of a cavalry expedition sent into North Carolina, July 28, after having visited five counties and captured considerable property.
- Gov. SEYMOUR addressed Secretary STANTON, complaining of an excessive quota for New-York City.

August 4.
- Fast Day.
- A Government transport fired on by rebel batteries on the James River.
- Exchange of the Union and rebel officers under fire at Charleston, S.C.
- Gen. KELLY repulsed the rebels at New-Creek, Md. The fight continued until after dark, the rebels retiring in the night.

August 5.
- GREAT BATTLE AT THE ENTRANCE OF MOBILE BAY. Fort Gaines opened on our fleet at about 7 A.M., the monitor Tecumseh having opened the attack a short time before. The rebel ram Tennessee captured after one of the fiercest naval battles on record. In the night the rebels evacuated and blew up Fort Powell. The monitor Tecumseh was blown up by a rebel torpedo.
- Explosion of a rebel mine near Petersburgh, Va.; but little damage done. A TERRIFIC FIGHT IN FRONT OF PETERSBURGH, lasting from 5:30 to 7:30 P.M. It commenced by a charge of the enemy, which was repulsed with slaughter.
- Gov. CURTIN, of Pennsylvania, issued a proclamation, announcing that the rebel army had again crossed the Potomac, and occupied Hagerstown, Md.

August 6.
- COMMODORE FARRAGUT SHELLED FORT GAINES, MOBILE HARBOR. He issued a congratulatory order to his command.
- Battle of Atlanta. The rebels made a demonstration on the Sixteenth Corps, and were heavily punished, and driven back.
- Indian massacre near Beaver Creek.

August 7
- BOMBARDMENT OF FORT GAINES CONTINUED. The rebels proposed to surrender.
- Gen. AVERILL overtook the rebels near Moorefield, in the Shenandoah Valley, and attacked them with great success, routing the rebels, capturing their artillery, a large number of prisoners, horses and arms.

August 8.
- SURRENDER OF FORT GAINES TO COMMODORE FARRAGUT.
- Gen. SHERIDAN assigned to the command of the troops in the Shenandoah Valley.
- Steamboat Vanderbilt sunk in the Hudson.

August 9.
- Terrible explosion of a boat loaded with ammunition at City Point, Va.
- Heavy shelling of Atlanta.

August 10.
- Gen. SHERIDAN's army skirmishing near Winchester, Va. Sharp fight near Martinsburgh.
- Steamer Empress fired into by rebel batteries on the banks of the Mississippi.
- Sharp skirmish near Abbeyville, Miss.

August 11.
- Secretary STANTON replied to Gov. SEYMOUR alleging that his claim of an excessive enrollment in New-York was not well founded.

August 12.
- The Tallahassee bonded the bark Fuliote, burnt the schooner Spokelane and ship Adriatic, scuttled the brig Billow, bonded for $30,000 the schooner Robert E Pecker.
- Attack of guerrillas on the gunboat Reliance, in Northumberland County, Va.

August 13.
- Gen. GRANT threw a powerful force, under Gen. HANCOCK, across the river at Deep Bottom. HANCOCK took position 10 miles from Richmond. Gen. BIRNEY assaulted the rebel was works in his front.
- Gen. BURNSIDE relieved.
- Guerrillas attacked Selma, Ky.
- Gen. SMITH attacked the rebels at Hurricane Creek, Miss., and defeated them.
- The Tallahassee scuttled the bark Glavomore, and burned the schooner Lamot Dupont.

August 14.
- Fighting near Richmond.
- The rebel Gen. WHEELER demanded the surrender of Dalton, Ga. which was refused. The rebels entered the town, but were kept at bay by the garrison.
- The Tallahassee scuttled the ship James Littlefield.

August 15.
- Fighting near Richmond.
- Our garrison at Dalton, Ga., was reinforced, and the rebels driven off in confusion.
- The Tallahassee scuttled schooners M.A. Howe, Howard, Floral Wreath, Restless, Etta Caroline, and bonded schooner S.K. Harris.

August 16.
- Fighting on the north bank of the James. The engagement resulted favorably, though not decisively, for us. The enemy somewhat driven back from their position.
- Cavalry fight between a division of SHERIDAN's army and the rebels, near Front Royal, Va.
- Fight near Chattanooga.
- The Tallahassee scuttled the bark P.C. Alexander, and burned the schooners Leopold, Pearl, Sarah Louisa and Magnolia.

August 17
- The Tallahassee scuttled the schooner North American, and bonded the brig Neva for $17,500.

August 18.
- A FURIOUS ATTACK ON BURNSIDE's CORPS, NEAR PETERSBURGH, which was repulsed with great loss to the rebels.
- Gen. WARREN moved his corps across the Weldon Railroad, in doing which he was engaged in considerable fighting.
- The Tallahassee arrived at Halifax after having burned the schooners Josiah Acorn, Diadem, Sea Flower and brig Roan.

August 19.
- THE REBELS DROVE IN WARREN's PICKETS AND FORCED BACK TWO DIVISIONS OF OUR ARMY. A heavy fight took place, resulting in reestablishing our lines and capturing many prisoners. Our troops were surprised, but recovered their lost ground.

August 20.
- The Tallahassee sailed from Halifax.
- Surg.-Gen. HAMMOND dismissed from the service and disqualified from holding office.

August 21.
- THE REBELS MADE THREE DESPERATE CHARGES ON OUR LINES ON THE WELDON RAILROAD, but were repulsed with heavy loss.
- Brisk engagement near Charlestown, Va. The rebels charged on our lines, and after a sharp struggle our skirmishers gave way.
- ATTACK ON MEMPHIS, TENN. The city entered by rebel cavalry.

August 22.
- CANNONADE OF OUR WORKS NEAR PETERSBURGH. The rebels charged, but finding themselves in a trap, retreated in confusion. The rebels disappeared from our front on the Weldon Railroad.
- Return of KILPATRICK to SHERMAN's lines from a successful raid.

August 23.
- Gen. WARREN advanced his line one mile toward Petersburgh.
- FORT MORGAN, MOBILE BAY, SURRENDERED UNCONDITIONALLY. By its surrender we captured 200 prisoners, 60 pieces of artillery and a large quantity of material.

August 24.

- Skirmish on SHERIDAN's left.

- Reconnaissance of Gen. CROOK's command in the Shenandoah Valley.

August 25.

- SEVERE BATTLE ON THE WELDON RAILROAD, NEAR REAM's STATION. A desperate attempt of the rebels to retake the road. HANCOCK's corps was several times attacked, the enemy being each time repulsed. At 5:30 P.M. a combined attack on his centre and left was repulsed after one of the most desperate battles of the war, the enemy withdrawing, leaving their dead and wounded on the field. Our forces afterward fell back.

- Gen. BUTLER's picket-line driven in, but re-established.

- Severe battle with SHERIDAN's army.

August 26.

- The rebel Gen. EARLY attempted to cross the Potomac, but was driven back by AVERILL.

- The rebels in SHERIDAN's front fall back.

August 27

- Guerrillas defeated at Shelbyville, Ky.

August 28.

- Gen. SHERMAN's army reached the West Point Railroad at Red Oak, thirteen miles from Atlanta, and began the destruction of the road from that point.

- Advance of our army in pursuit of EARLY.

August 29.

- Meeting of the Democratic Nominating Convention at Chicago.

August 30.

- The Army of the Tennessee skirmished considerably with rebel cavalry.

August 31.

- GREAT BATTLE NEAR ATLANTA.

- During the forenoon, our artillery kept up a cannonade to provoke the rebels to an assault. In the afternoon the rebels assaulted our lines, but were repulsed with great loss. The rebel loss in the attack on RAMSOM's and LOGAN's lines estimated at 3,000.

- In the evening the Fourteenth Corps struck the railroad, five miles south of Jonesboro. The work of destruction commenced immediately.

- GEORGE B. MCCLELLAN and GEORGE H. PENDLETON nominated by the Chicago Convention for President and Vice President.

SEPTEMBER

September 1.

- THE BATTLE OF ATLANTA CONTINUED.

- A brilliant charge was made at 5 P.M. by Gen. DAVIS' force, resulting in the discomfiture of the rebels and surrender of a large number. Great destruction by the rebels of large magazines of stores accumulated at Atlanta. They blew up, in addition to other things, 80 car-loads of ammunition. Gen. SLOCUM's corps assaulted the enemy's works around the city in the afternoon. Panic and evacuation of the city.

September 2.

- ATLANTA, GA., OCCUPIED BY SHERMAN's ARMY AT 11 A.M.

- Sharp fighting near Martinsburg, Va.

September 3.

- Gen. SHERMAN issued a congratulatory order on the occupation of Atlanta.

- The rebels handsomely beaten near Berryville, Va.

- Rebel cavalry attacked by Gen. MILROY near Murfreesboro, Tenn.

September 4.

- Gen. GILLEM SURPRISED JNO. MORGAN's BAND, AND KILLED MORGAN AT GREENVILLE, TENN.

- The rebels near Murfreesboro retreated.

September 5.

- Steamer Elsie captured in running the blockade at Wilmington.

- The President issued a proclamation, recommending that Sunday, Sept. 11, be observed as a day of Thanksgiving.

September 6.

- During a battle between the French and CORTINAS and Mexican forces, near Brownsville, Texas, Col. FORD, the rebel Commander at that point, came down from Texas, on the Rio Grande, with a large drove of cattle for the French, and seeing that they were engaged with CORTINAS, opened on the Mexican rear.

- The rebels and French repulsed CORTINAS. CORTINAS afterward crossed the Rio Grande, into Texas, and raised the American flag.

September 7

- The rebels routed at Readyville, Tenn.

- Hon. REUBEN E. FENTON nominated for Governor of New-York.

September 8.

- Brownsville, Texas, attacked by CORTINAS, and the rebels driven from the town.

- Gen. MCCLELLAN accepted the nomination for the Presidency.

- Gen. SHERMAN ordered the removal of the inhabitants of Atlanta, and proposed a truce of ten days.

September 9.

- Spirited attack on the rebel pickets near Petersburgh, in the night.

September 10.

- Gen. SHERIDAN's forces in the Shenandoah Valley attacked at Darksville, Va.

- Gov. BROWN, of Georgia, recalled the militia of the State from HOOD's army.

- Gen. SHERMAN replied to a communication from HOOD, charging him with "studied and ungenerous cruelty" in ordering the evacuation of the city by its inhabitants. A truce for ten days declared by Gen. SHERMAN.

September 11.

- An expedition left Fort Morgan, near Mobile, and proceeded up White River, destroying a large amount of lumber at Smith's Mills.

September 12.

- Gen. SHERMAN replied to a remonstrance of the Mayor of Atlanta against removing all the inhabitants of the city.

September 13.

- Attack on the rebels near Occoquan Creek by some of SHERIDAN's forces. A South Carolina regiment captured.

September 14.

- Secretary STANTON ordered the draft to be commenced Sept. 19.

- Gen. SHERMAN ordered the people of Atlanta to evacuate the city.

September 16.

- A large body of rebel cavalry made a raid on our reserve cattle herd, opposite Harrison's Landing, and succeeded in carrying off the entire herd.

- Departure of an expedition under Gen. ASBOTH on a raid into Western Virginia.

September 19.

- BATTLE OF BUNKER HILL, VA. A great battle fought by SHERIDAN in the Shenandoah Valley. SHERIDAN made the attack and won a splendid victory, capturing over 2,500 prisoners, together with nine battle-flags, and five pieces of artillery. The rebel Gens. GORDON and RHODES were killed, and three other general officers wounded. All of the rebel killed and most of the wounded fell into our hands.

- The steamers Philo Parsons and Island Queen seized by a band of rebels on the Canadian frontier.

September 20.

- Gen. SHERIDAN crossed Cedar Creek, having pursued the rebels thirty miles.

September 21.

- Gen. SHERIDAN attacked the rebels beyond Strasburgh, Va., and carried and held the crest of the hill occupied by them.

- FREMONT and COCHRANE withdrew their names as candidates for President and Vice-President.

September 22.

- BATTLE OF FISHER's HILL, VA., in the Shenandoah Valley. Gen. SHERIDAN found the rebel army occupying a position which appeared almost impregnable. His forces, however, attacked and drove the rebels in the utmost confusion, capturing twenty pieces of artillery and a large number of caissons, artillery, horses, & c.

September 23.

- MONTGOMERY BLAIR resigned his office of Postmaster-General.

- A part of the rebel Gen. FORREST's force, about four hundred strong, crossed the Tennessee River at Bates' Landing.

- Our garrison at Athens, Ala., compelled to surrender.

September 25.

- Gen. SHERIDAN's advance passed beyond New-Market. His forces drove the enemy from Mount Jackson.

- The rebels at Luray, attacked.

- A force of rebel cavalry occupied Frederickstown, Mo., twenty miles east of Pilot Knob.

- Athens, Ala., occupied by the rebel Gen. FORREST's troops.

September 26.

- Gen. SHERIDAN's headquarters at Harrisonburgh, Va.

- Our cavalry entered Stanton, Va., and destroyed a large quantity of rebel government property. They then proceeded to Waynesboro', destroying an iron bridge over the Shenandoah and a large amount of property. Gen. EARLY's rebel army routed and demoralized, fled through Brown's Gap toward Gordonsville.

September 27
- Skirmish with FORREST's troops in Tennessee.
- The rebels attacked our forces at Mineral Point, Mo.

September 28.
- The rebel Gen. FORREST at Fayetteville, on his way to intercept SHERMAN's communications.
- Admiral PORTER issued his farewell order to the Mississippi Squadron.

September 29.
- Gen. ORD's CORPS OF GRANT's ARMY ADVANCED AND CARRIED A VERY STRONG FORTIFICATION AND LINE OF INTOENCHMENER BELOW CHAPIN's FARM, taking fifteen pieces of artillery and 200 or 300 prisoners.
- Gen. BARNEY advanced from Deep Bottom and carried the New-Market Road.
- Mayor GUNTHER vetoed a resolution of the Common Council, to illuminate the city in celebration of our victories.

September 30.
- Gen. WARREN attacked and carried the rebel line on their extreme right, capturing a number of prisoners.
- Gen. MEADE moved from his left and carried the enemy's line near Poplin Grove Church.

OCTOBER
- Gen. BUTLER's forces assaulted the rebels in three columns near Chapin's Farm.

October 2.
- The rebels attacked at Saltville, Va.

October 6.
- Gen. SHERMAN commenced moving back from Port Republic, Mount Crawford and Harrisonburgh, Va....the whole country from the Blue Ridge to the North Mountain was made untenable for the rebel army by destroying an immense quantity of stores, grain, & c.
- Clinton, La., taken by our troops.

October 7
- Gen. KAUTZ' cavalry attacked by the rebels who suffered considerably. They afterward attacked BIRNEY's division, who also repulsed them with very heavy loss. In the afternoon, Gen. BUTLER took the offensive and recaptured some intrenchments which had been taken from KAUTZ.
- The rebels appeared before Jefferson City, Mo.
- The advance of the rebels from the Osage River, Mo., spiritedly contested by our cavalry.
- Gen. SHERIDAN's forces reached Woodstock, Va.
- CAPTURE OF THE PIRATE FLORIDA BY THE STEAMER WACHUSETT, in the Bay of St. Salvador, Brazil.
- A band of 200 rebels captured a steamboat and crossed into Kentucky.

October 8.
- The Fifth and Ninth Corps, Army of the Potomac, advanced their lines half a mile, driving the rebel skirmishers into their breastworks.
- The rebels drew up in line of battle near Jefferson City, Mo., but afterward moved off toward the west.

October 9.
- An engagement took place near Fisher's Hill, Va., in which the rebels were defeated, leaving eleven pieces of artillery and other munitions of war.

October 10.
- Engagement with the rebel Gen. FORREST at East Point, Tenn.
- Reconnaissance to within three miles of Mobile.

October 11.
- Gen. CURTIS drove the rebels out of Independence, Mo.
- Skirmish near Fort Wilson, Tenn.
- The rebel Gen. BUFORD crossed the Cumberland River with 1,200 mounted men.
- Bloody fight with guerrillas near Winchester, Va.
- Successful reconnaissance from the Army of the Potomac to Stony Creek.

October 12.
- Death of Chief-Justice ROGER B. TANEY.
- Gen. HOOD demanded the surrender of Resaca, Ga., threatening, in case of resistance, to take no prisoners.

October 13.
- Reconnaissance in force from the Army of the James.
- Attack on Resaca, Ga. The rebels repulsed.
- Engagement at Greenville, East Tennessee.

October 15.
- The rebel army under LONGSTREET having appeared near Strasburgh, Va., Gen. SHERIDAN advanced and found them drawn up in four lines of battle, but, on charging, the rebels fled.

October 16.
- HOOD's army at Lafayette.
- Gen. SHERMAN took Ship's Gap.

October 17
- The rear of Gen. HOOD's army left Lafayette, going South. The Secretary of War telegraphed that Gen. HOOD, after striking the railroad near Dalton and Resaca, had fallen back before SHERMAN without fighting, abandoning his movement on our line of communication.
- Arrest in Baltimore of a number of merchants, charged with contraband trade with the rebels.

October 18.
- Gen. BLUNT, with 2,000 cavalry and four howitzers, entered Lexington, Mo.
- Death of Major-Gen. D.B. BIRNEY.

October 19.
- BATTLE OF CEDAR CREEK, SHENANDOAH VALLEY. Gen. SHERIDAN's army was attacked before daylight and its left turned and driven in confusion, with a loss of twenty pieces of artillery. Gen. SHERIDAN afterward arrived on the field and drove the rebels, taking 48 pieces of artillery and many prisoners, gaining a great victory. SHERIDAN pursued the rebels to Mount Jackson, which he reached in the night.
- The rebel Gen. PRICE attacked Gen. BLUNT at Lexington, Mo., with an overwhelming force, and after a sharp fight drove him from the city. Gen. BLUNT fell back to the Little Blue River, fighting desperately, and retarding the advance of the enemy.
- The rebels entered Mayfield, Ky.

October 20.
- Capture of the St. Albans robbers.
- Skirmishing between the Little and Big Blue River, Mo.

October 21.
- A very gallant fight between Little Blue River and Independence, Mo. Our troops fought PRICE's entire army five hours. The Union forces evacuated Independence, falling back on the Big Blue.

October 22.
- Gen. CURTIS telegraphed from Kansas, Mo., that he had been pressed all day, and that in the afternoon the rebels passed around his flank, when CURTIS gave him heavy blows for several hours.
- Col. JAMIESON was attacked at Bryan Ford, Mo., by a heavy column of rebels, at 10 A.M. At 3 P.M., the rebels forced the ford. Our troops fought the rebels until after dark, driving them four miles. Gen. PLEASONTON pursued PRICE, with 2,000 men, fought him on the battle-field of the day before, drove him from Independence, and pursued him sharply. PLEASONTON captured a large number of prisoners and three pieces of artillery.
- The President issued an order thanking Gen. SHERIDAN for gaining the victories in the Shenandoah.

October 25.
- Fighting in Missouri. The rebels badly whipped.

October 26.
- Gen. DOUBLEDAY's Court-martial ordered to Baltimore to try the soldiers' voting fraud cases.

October 27.
- An advance in force, on a reconnaissance, made by WARREN's Corps of GRANT's army. In the evening the enemy attacked HANCOCK's Corps vigorously, but were repulsed. The purpose being accomplished, our troops were withdrawn to nearer their former lines.
- The rebel ram Albemarle sunk by Lieut. CUSHING, in the Roanoke River.
- Arrest of Col. NORTH on charges of fraud in the matter of soldiers' votes.

October 28.
- Gen. DIX issued an order requiring all refugees from the South to register their names, declaring that those who refused or neglected to obey the order, should be treated as spies.
- Gen. GILLEM had a fight with the rebels at Norristown, East Tenn., completely routing them, and capturing a number of prisoners and pieces of artillery.
- Gen. GRANT's army returned to its old quarters.
- Fight with the rebel Gen. PRICE at Newtonia, Mo.
- A rebel force of 2,500 attacked Fayetteville, Ark., but was repulsed with heavy loss.

October 29.
- Maryland proclaimed a Free State by Gov. BRADFORD.

October 30.
- Our fleet shelled Plymouth, N.C.

October 31.
- Nevada admitted as a State by proclamation of the President.
- The commissioners appointed by Gov. SEYMOUR to investigate the soldier voting frauds, had an interview with the President and Secretary of War.
- Capture of the rebel batteries, and their ordnance and ordnance stores, at Plymouth, N.C.

NOVEMBER

November 2.
- Gov. SEYMOUR issued a proclamation relative to the election.
- Gen. DIX issued an order concerning fraudulent voting.

November 3.
- The rebel army under HOOD attempted to cross the Tennessee, near the mouth of the Blue Water, and were repulsed by Gen. SHERMAN.
- The rebels bombarded Fayetteville, Ark.
- Commencement of Col. NORTH's trial.

November 4.
- Engagement on the Tennessee River.
- The siege of Fayetteville, Ark., by the rebels, raised.
- Revelation by one of the conspirators of a plot to overthrow the Government, release and arm the rebel prisoners, and kill Gov. MORTON, of Indiana.

November 5.
- A midnight attack by the rebels on our works southeast of Petersburgh, Va. A brisk fight and temporary success on the part of the rebels.
- Gen. BUTLER assumed command of the troops arrived and to arrive in New-York City to protect the city during election.

November 6.
- Attack on our pickets before Richmond.
- Gen. CANBY wounded in Louisiana.

November 7
- A rebel attack on our pickets south of Atlanta.

November 8.
- Presidential election. RE-ELECTION OF ABRAHAM LINCOLN AS PRESIDENT, AND ELECTION OF ANDREW JOHNSON AS VICE-PRESIDENT.
- Gen. MCCLELLAN resigned his commission in the United States Army.
- Atlanta attacked by the rebels under Gen. IVERSON.

November 9.
- Gen. SHERMAN issued his orders regulating the march of his army through Georgia, commanding his troops to forage on the country, to abstain from trespassing except when molested by guerrillas, & c., when corps commanders were authorized to devastate the surrounding country.
- Advance and repulse of a small rebel force near Fort Steadman, army of the Potomac.

November 10.
- Arrest on board of the vessel, of a party of rebels, conspiring to seize the Panama Railroad Co.'s steamship Salvador, on the Pacific.

November 11.
- Reconnaissance by the rebels in the Shenandoah Valley.
- Commencement of the burning of Atlanta, Ga.

November 12.
- The rebels in the Shenandoah Valley attacked our forces but were disastrously repulsed.
- Burning of Atlanta continued. The public buildings destroyed.

November 13.
- Gen. SHERMAN's right wing, under Gen. HOWARD, moved out of Atlanta and began its march through Georgia.

November 14.
- Gen. SHERMAN's left wing left Atlanta.
- Union reverse at Bull's Gap.
- A division of PRICE's rebel army assaulted the works at Fayetteville, Ark., but were repulsed.

November 15.
- The last of SHERMAN's forces left Atlanta.

November 16.
- Gen. SHERMAN's right wing passed through Jonesboro, Ga.
- The rebel cavalry, under WHEELER, engaged our cavalry at Bear Creek Station.
- Jackson, Ga., reached by SHERMAN's right wing.

November 17
- A night attack on our lines near Richmond.
- A column of SHERMAN's army occupied McDonough, Ga.
- Our cavalry occupied Griffin, Ga.
- SHERMAN's left wing reached Covington, Ga., the cavalry pushing on to Social Circle.

November 18.
- SHERMAN's cavalry drove WHEELER out of Barnesville, Ga.
- Gov. BROWN and the Georgia Legislature fled from Milledgeville, Ga.
- Gen. BUTLER rejoined the Army of the James.
- Exchange of prisoners at Savannah; commencement of the reception of our men.

November 19.
- Gov. BROWN, of Georgia, issued a proclamation, ordering a levy en masse to oppose SHERMAN.
- The advance of BEAUREGARD's army at Waynesboro, Tenn. BEAUREGARD's headquarters at Corinth, Miss., and HOOD's at Florence.
- MOSBY's force captured a party of Union cavalry.

November 20.
- Gen. SHERMAN ATTACKED EAST MACON, Ga. His troops crossed the Ocmulgee River, and his cavalry advanced to Griswoldville, eight miles east of Macon, Ga.

November 21.
- Heavy skirmishing near Cumberland Gap.
- Gen. SHERMAN's RIGHT WING CAPTURED MILLEDGEVILLE, Ga. Gordon, Ga., occupied. SLOCUM's column reached Etonville, Ga.

November 22.
- BATTLE OF ROOD's HILL, Va., between SHERIDAN's and EARLY's forces. The rebels being found in superior force, our troops retired.
- The rebel armies under HOOD and BEAUREGARD, having been reinforced by 9,000 men, advanced and encamped 20 miles from Pulaski, Tenn.
- SHERMAN's rear guard at Griswoldville attacked. Gen. SLOCUM's column reached Milledgeville, Ga., where both wings united.

November 23.
- Our forces withdrew from Pulaski, Tenn.
- SHERMAN's cavalry occupied Toomsboro, on the Georgia Central Railroad.
- Fight near Griswoldville, Ga.
- HOOD's infantry at Waynesboro and Lawrenceburgh.
- Fight at the Oconee River, Ga.

November 24.
- Second day of fighting up the Oconee River, Ga.
- Severe skirmishing near Columbia, Tenn.
- SHERMAN's rear guard left Milledgeville, Ga.
- SLOCUM's column at Devereaux, Ga.
- Our troops made a flank Movement on Jackson, Miss.

Thanksgiving Day. November 25.
- ATTEMPTED BURNING OF A LARGE NUMBER OF HOTELS IN NEW-YORK CITY, BY REBEL SPIES.
- Severe fighting west of Columbia, Tenn., between HOOD's and THOMAS' armies.
- A large number of Federal prisoners continued at Saulsbury, N.C., attempted to escape, but were overpowered by the guard, who opened upon them with grape and canister.
- Cavalry battle at Sandersville, Ga.
- The Mayor of Milledgeville, Ga., sent a dispatch to Macon for provisions, as the citizens were utterly destitute.

November 26.
- Columbia, Tenn., evacuated by Gen. THOMAS' army.
- Gen. SLOCUM's column of SHERMAN's army at Warrenton, Ga.
- Gen. HOWARD's column reached Sandersville, Ga., and cut the railroad.
- Gen. DIX issues an order, declaring those engaged in the attempt to burn New-York spies, and that in case of capture they should be tried by court-martial, and on conviction be executed "without the delay of a single day."

November 27
- Our stores and sick and wounded removed from Columbia, Tenn., to Nashville.
- Capture of ROGER A. PEYOR near Petersburg, Va.
- Gen. CANBY's troops reached and destroyed Big Black Bridge on the Mississippi Central Railroad.

November 28.
- Our forces evacuated Columbia, Tenn.
- The rebels surprised and captured Fort Kelly on New-Creek, Va.

November 29.
- Sharp fight at Spring Hill, 12 miles south of Franklin, Tenn.
- Our cavalry were driven back on the infantry, who checked the progress of the rebels.
- Gen. FOSTER's expedition, cooperating with SHERMAN, landed at Broad River.

November 30.
- BATTLE OF FRANKLIN, TENN.
- The rebels attacked THOMAS' army at Franklin, but were repulsed at all points with heavy loss. The rebels commenced advancing on our lines at 4 P.M. They charged furiously on our lines, but were driven back and a great victory gained. Gen. A.J. SMITH's army passed through Nashville and reinforced THOMAS.
- Battle of Grahamsville, on the Charleston and Savannah Railroad.
- HOWARD's column of SHERMAN's army passed through Louisville, Ga.
- A cavalry expedition arrived at Tangipahoe, La.
- Hon. JOS. HOLT appointed Attorney-General.

DECEMBER

December 1.

- The armies near Nashville engaged in heavy skirmishing.

- Reconnaissance by Gen. GREGG from the Army of the Potomac. He captured Stony Creek Station and destroyed a considerable amount of stores.

- Rebel pickets attacked our lines at Bermuda Hundreds.

- Death of Hon. WM.L. DAYTON, United States Minister to France.

December 2.

- Gen. BRECKINRIDGE issued an order to husband arms, & c., and to glean lead from battle-fields.

- Gen. SHERMAN's army passed through Millen, Ga., and encamped in its vicinity.

December 3.

- WHEELER's cavalry attacked SHERMAN's force on the Savannah Railroad, a few miles below Haynesboro.

- An expedition sent from Roanoke Island, N.C., which met with perfect success in destroying rebel property.

- Heavy skirmishing before Nashville, Tenn.

December 4.

- Lieut.-Com. FITCH defeated and drove the left wing of HOOD's army on the Cumberland River, with heavy loss to the rebels. He also recaptured two transports.

- Capture of rebel works and cannon near Pocotaligo, S.C., by Gen. FOSTER's troops.

- Cavalry battle in Georgia. SHERMAN's army started for Savannah.

- Gen. DIX caused the arrest of sixty persons who were under suspicion of being connected with the attempt to burn New-York.

December 5.

- Meeting of Congress.

December 6.

- Heavy skirmishing near Nashville, Tenn.

- Rebels defeated near the Charleston and Savannah Railroad.

- Destruction of Pocotaligo Bridge on the same road.

December 7

- A cavalry expedition started South from the Army of the Potomac.

- Engagement near Murfreesboro, Tenn.

December 8.

- A cavalry force sent out on the left of the Army of the Potomac engaged in skirmishing.

December 9.

- Gen. HOWARD, of SHERMAN's army, reported that the army had met with perfect success.

- Reconnaissance from the Army of the Potomac toward Hatcher's Run.

- Charge on the rebel works at Jarrett's Station, Va.

December 10.

- Gen. SHERMAN's troops five miles from Savannah.

- Rebel reconnaissance toward the Army of the Potomac.

December 11.

- A messenger from SHERMAN's army reached our fleet.

December 12.

- Arrival of Gen. HOWARD's messengers at Hilton Head, S.C.

- Sailing from Fortress Monroe, in the night, of the transports of PORTER's and BUTLER's expedition for North Carolina.

December 13.

- DEPARTURE OF THE GREAT NAVAL EXPEDITION FROM FORTRESS MONROE.

- Fort McAllister, Savannah, carried by assault, with its garrison and stores.

- Sharp skirmishing near Nashville.

- The St. Albans robbers released by the Canadian Judge COURSOL.

- The rebels routed at Kingsport, Tenn.

- Gen. SHERMAN reported his arrived before Savannah without the loss of a wagon.

December 14.

- Gen. DIX issued an order on the occasion of the release of the St. Albans robbers, directing military commanders on the frontier to shoot down rebel marauders, and, if necessary, to pursue them into Canada.

- Interview between Gens. FOSTER and SHERMAN.

- An expedition threatening Mobile reached Pascagoula.

December 15.

- BATTLE OF NASHVILLE COMMENCED. General THOMAS attacked HOOD's army at 9 A.M. Our lines advanced on the right five miles. The rebels were driven from the river, from their intrench-ments, from a range of hills, on which their left rested, and forced back upon the right and centre. The rebels lost much artillery, many prison-ers, and a whole line of earth works. In the night HOOD withdrew his right from the river.

- The rebel Gen. FORREST attacked Murfreesboro, Tenn.

- Our forces surprised the rebels at Glades' Spring, Va., in BRECKINRIDGE's rear.

December 16.

- BATTLE OF NASHVILLE CONTINUED. Our army again gained a brilliant victory, and put HOOD's army to flight, with a loss in the two days estimated at 17,000 men and 51 cannon.

- A Union force occupied Pollard, 70 miles north of Mobile, and burned the Government and railroad buildings.

- Secretary STANTON announced that Gen. CANBY's two expeditions cooperating with SHERMAN, had met with perfect success.

- The rebels attacked and defeated 16 miles from Wytheville, Southwestern Virginia.

December 17

- Gen. MCCOOK defeated the rebel Gen. LYON in a sharp fight at Ashbvville, Ky.

- Gen. THOMAS reported continued success in the pursuit of HOOD. An engagement six miles beyond Franklin, Tenn.

- Our troops entered Wytheville, Southwestern Virginia, destroyed the depot and other build-ings, and injured the lead mines in the vicinity.

- A detachment of Union artillery cut up near Millwood, Va.

December 18.

- Gen. THOMAS reported that the enemy had been vigorously pursued, but had studiously avoided attack. A few additional prisoners captured.

- Gen. E.D. MCCOOK defeated a part of the rebel Gen. LYON's force at Hopkinsville, Ky.

December 19.

- Gen. THOMAS reported that little additional progress had been made, on account of stormy weather. Cavalry skirmish and capture of three guns at Spring Hill.

- The President issued a proclamation calling for 300,000 troops to fill deficiencies in the last draft, and ordering a draft in all districts which had not filled their quotas on February 15.

- Gen. CUSTER's Cavalry started on an expedition up the Shenandoah Valley.

December 20.

- Rearrest of one of the St. Albans robbers.

- Gen. SHERMAN demanded the surrender of Savannah. The city was evacuated by HARDEE's army in the night. The rebels blew up their rams at Savannah.

- Capture of rebel salt works at Saltville, Va.

December 21.

- CAPTURE OF SAVANNAH, GA., BY GEN. SHER-MAN, with 25,000 bales of cotton, a large amount of stores, and 150 cannon.

- Recapture of two of the St. Albans robbers.

- Admiral FARRAGUT appointed Vice-Admiral.

- Admiral PORTER's fleet appeared before Wilmington.

- Gen. CUSTER's force in the Shenandoah Valley engaged with rebel cavalry. The rebels drove in our men, but were afterward defeated.

December 22.

- Fighting near Gordonsville, Va.

- Loss of the United States transport North Ameri-can, by foundering at sea. 194 lives lost.

December 23.

- Fight near Gordonsville, Va.

December 24.

- ATTACK ON FORT FISHER, WILMINGTON, BY PORTER's FLEET. The bombardment lasted from 1 P.M. till night. A furious cannonade.

December 25.

- ATTACK ON FORT FISHER CONTINUED. Our troops landed under cover of the fire from the fleet, and were immediately engaged. In the night our infantry attacked the fort, but were repulsed. The land force reembarked.

- Gen. THOMAS' army 21 miles south of Columbia.

December 26.

- Heavy cannonading on Broad River, between SHERMAN's and HARDEE's forces.

December 27

- Destruction of a fort and artillery at Chicasaw, Ala. The means of crossing the Tennessee River, below Florence, by Gen. HOOD, destroyed.

1865

CHRONOLOGICAL RECORD OF THE
MILITARY, NAVAL AND POLITICAL
EVENTS OF THE YEAR.

A YEAR OF VICTORY AND MOURNING.

JANUARY.

January 1.
- The City of New York awarded DAVID G. FARRAGUT a $50,000 gift in thanks for his victory at Mobile.

January 2.
- ABRAHAM LINCOLN held his annual reception for government workers and members of the diplomatic corps.

January 4.
- Federal troops under Major General ALFRED H. TERRY embarked on transports for a second attempt to capture Fort Fisher at the mouth of the Cape Fear River below Wilmington, N.C.
- REUBEN E. FENTON was inaugurated governor of New York.
- G. G. HASKINS was elected Speaker of the New York Legislature.

January 6.
- The House of Representatives opened debate on the passage of the Thirteenth Amending to the Constitution abolishing slavery. It had previously passed the Senate.

January 7.
- Navy Secretary GIDEON WELLES and Admiral FARRAGUT met with President LINCOLN in the White House to discuss the Battle of Mobile Bay.
- ULYSSES S. GRANT relieved BENJAMIN BUTLER of his command of the Army of the James. GRANT was concerned because BUTLER is the most senior Major General in the army, he would assume command in GRANT's absence.

January 9.
- A Constitutional Convention in Tennessee adopted an amendment abolishing slavery in the State pending a vote by the citizens.

January 10.
- Debate over the Thirteenth Amendment continued in House of Representatives.

January 11.
- The Missouri Constitutional Convention accepted the abolition of slavery.

January 12.
- The "great armada" of DAVID DIXON PORTER with eight thousand soldiers under Major General TERRY got underway from Beaufort, North Carolina and arrived off the mouth of the Cape Fear River for a second attempt to capture Fort Fisher.
- FRANCIS P. BLAIR, Sr. met with JEFFERSON DAVIS in Richmond on a peace mission.

January 13.
- The second attack on Fort Fisher below Wilmington, N.C. began. Fifty nine ships in the fleet commanded by DAVID DIXON PORTER fired some 20,000 shells into the fort.
- Following his disastrous invasion of Tennessee and repulse from Nashville, Confederate Lieutenant General JOHN BELL HOOD offered his resignation, which was accepted.

January 15.
- Federal troops under TERRY captured Fort Fisher. Following a lengthy bombardment by the ships of Rear Admiral PORTER's fleet, TERRY's soldiers attacked the northwest salient while a party of sailors and Marines attacked the northeast corner. The sailors and Marines were repulsed, but they allowed the soldiers to get inside the fort where, after severe hand-to-hand fighting, the Union prevailed.

January 16.
- BRAXTON BRAGG ordered the evacuation of the river forts below Wilmington.
- FRANCIS P. BLAIR, Sr. reported to Lincoln the results of his mission to Richmond, and gave LINCOLN a letter from DAVIS suggesting negotiations but which made a pointed reference to securing peace "to the two countries."
- The Confederate Congress made ROBERT E. LEE commander-in-chief of all Confederate armies.

January 18.
- LINCOLN replied to DAVIS's letter with one of his own in which he conspicuously referred to "our one common country" making it clear that negotiations for a separation are unacceptable.

January 19.
- WILLIAM T. SHERMAN ordered his army to march northward from Savannah, Georgia, into South Carolina.
- LINCOLN asked GRANT if he could find a place for ROBERT LINCOLN as a volunteer officer in his "military family." Robert subsequently became a captain on Grant's staff.

January 23.
- The Confederate James River Squadron under Flag Officer JOHN K. MITCHELL got underway in an effort to drive Union forces away from Richmond.

January 25.
- The CSS SHENANDOAH under the command of Confederate Navy Captain JAMES I. WADDELL put into Melbourne, Australia en route to its cruising ground in the North Pacific. It was received with great enthusiasm.

January 28.
- LINCOLN met with GRANT, SHERMAN, AND PORTER on board the steamer RIVER QUEEN on the James River. They discussed the war, and LINCOLN expressed his desire to shed as little blood as possible.
- In consequence of FRANCIS P. BLAIR's mission, JEFFERSON DAVIS named commissioners to meet with Federal representatives for informal talks.

January 30.
- LINCOLN approved giving a pass to the Confederate commissioners to allow them to go to Fort Monroe for negotiations.

January 31.
- House of Representatives passed the Thirteenth Amendment. Having previously been passed by the Senate, it still had to be ratified by the States.
- ROBERT E. LEE was formally named commander-in-chief of the Confederate armies.

FEBRUARY.

February 1.
- Illinois was the first State to ratify the Thirteenth Amendment.
- SHERMAN's army continued its campaign in South Carolina.

February 2.
- LINCOLN left Washington for a trip by sea to the front in Virginia.

February 3.
- In Hampton Roads, LINCOLN met with the Confederate commissioners on board the RIVER QUEEN. As the diminutive Confederate Vice President ALEXANDER STEPHENS took off one heavy coat after another, LINCOLN quipped that he had never seen so small a cob emerge from so large a husk. The Confederate emissaries ask for an armistice, but LINCOLN told them that all that is necessary to achieve peace is for the rebel armies to stop fighting.
- Three more States (Maryland, New York, and West Virginia) ratified the Thirteenth Amendment.
- SHERMAN's army crossed the Salkahatchie River in South Carolina.

February 4.
- LINCOLN returned to Washington after the Hampton Roads Conference.

February 5.
- Outside Petersburg, Virginia, Union forces of the II and V Corps assailed Confederate positions near Hatcher's Run.

February 6.
- President DAVIS appointed former U.S. Vice President JOHN C. BRECKINRIDGE as Secretary of War to replace JAMES SEDDON.
- Fighting continues near Hatcher's Run.

February 7.
- Maine and Kansas ratified the Thirteenth Amendment.
- The fighting near Hatcher's Run ended with Federals digging in at a new position. Active operations on the Richmond-Petersburg front ended for the winter.

February 8.
- In South Carolina, there was fighting along the Edisto River.
- Massachusetts and Pennsylvania ratified the Thirteenth Amendment.

February 9.
- The unionist Virginia State government (in northern Virginia) ratified the Thirteenth Amendment.

February 10.
- LINCOLN reported to Congress on the failure of the Hampton Roads peace conference.
- Confederate Navy Captain RAPHAEL SEMMES was promoted to Rear Admiral and put in charge of the James River flotilla.
- Ohio and Missouri ratified the Thirteenth Amendment.

February 12.
- The official Electoral College vote gave LINCOLN 212 votes to GEORGE B. MCCLELLAN's 21, and LINCOLN was re-elected President for a second term.
- Skirmishing continued in South Carolina as SHERMAN's troops, moving on a wide front, continued their march northward.

February 14.
- SHERMAN's troops crossed the Congaree River in South Carolina and moved toward the State capital at Columbia.

February 17.
- SHERMAN's army occupied Columbia. That night, stockpiled cotton that had been set afire by evacuating Confederate cavalry under JOSEPH WHEELER, flamed up and started a conflagration that left much of the city in ashes. Confederates blamed Sherman; Sherman blamed the Confederate cavalry that initially set the fire. Some Union troops tried to put out the fires; others hindered their efforts. Some Union troops found liquor and become drunk. The entire episode became controversial on both sides.

February 18.
- SHERMAN added to the destruction of Columbia, S.C. by deliberately destroying the railroads, supply dumps, machine shops, and public buildings used by the Confederate government.
- The Confederates evacuated Charleston, South Carolina.

February 20.
- Union forces closed in on Wilmington, North Carolina after working their way up the Cape Fear River from Fort Fisher.
- The Confederate House of Representatives approved the enlistment of slaves in the army. They would earn their freedom only after the war, assuming a Confederate victory. The bill then went to the Senate.

February 22.
- Union soldiers captured the city of Wilmington, N.C.
- ROBERT E. LEE named JOSEPH E. JOHNSTON to command the Department of South Carolina, Georgia, and Florida as well as Tennessee and Georgia, effectively giving him command of all units east of the Mississippi that were not in LEE's army. JOHNSTON's orders were to unify his troops and "drive back Sherman."
- Tennessee voters approved a new State constitution abolishing slavery.

February 25.
- JOSEPH E. JOHNSTON assumed command of the remnants of the Army of Tennessee at Charlotte, N.C. His force numbered some 20,000 men, but they were scattered over a wide area. JOHNSTON wrote, "it would scarcely have been possible to disperse a force more effectually."

February 26.
- SHERMAN's army reached Hanging Rock, N.C.

February 27.
- In Virginia, Major General PHILIP SHERIDAN began his campaign to render the Shenandoah Valley incapable of providing support to Lee's army.
- There was nearly constant skirmishing as SHERMAN's army continued its northward march; JOHNSTON tried to unify his scattered forces.

MARCH.

March 1.
- SHERIDAN skirmished with Confederate forces under JUBAL EARLY in the Shenandoah Valley.
- SHERMAN's forces skirmished with Confederates near Wilson's Store, N.C.
- Wisconsin ratified the Thirteenth Amendment.

March 2.
- SHERIDAN's army won a skirmish at Waynesborough, Virginia. EARLY's army was nearly destroyed.

March 3.
- On the last day of the lame duck Congress, the House passed the Freedman's Bureau Bill.
- LINCOLN wrote GRANT telling him "to have no conference with General Lee unless it be for the capitulation of Gen. Lee's army."

March 4.
- LINCOLN was inaugurated for a second term as President. In his inaugural address, he closed with the stirring lines: "With malice toward none, with charity toward all, with firmness in the right as God gives us to see the right, let us strive on to finish the work we are in; to bind up the nation's wounds; to care for him who shall have borne the battle, and for his widow, and his orphan—to do all which may achieve a just and lasting peace, among ourselves, and with all nations."
- ANDREW JOHNSON was inaugurated Vice President.

March 7.
- SHERMAN's army entered North Carolina.
- Union forces under JACOB D. COX took control of New Berne, North Carolina to use it as a base to supply SHERMAN's army.

March 8.
- A Confederate force under BRAXTON BRAGG that had evacuated Wilmington, N.C., attacked JACOB COX's force at Kinston, N. C. Though BRAGG's force achieved some initial success, it failed to halt or slow the Federal advance.
- The Confederate Senate approved the enlistment of slaves in the Confederate army.

March 9.
- Fighting continued in the Battle of Kinston.
- Confederate cavalry under WADE HAMPTON and JOE WHEELER surprised Federal cavalry under JUDSON KILPATRICK near Monroe's Cross Roads, and KILPATRICK had to escape in his underwear.
- Vermont ratified the Thirteenth Amendment.

March 10.
- LEE writes DAVIS that he intended to implement the new law authorizing the enlistment of slaves as soon as possible.

March 11.
- SHERMAN's army occupied Fayetteville, North Carolina, where it remained until March 14.
- Aware that JOHNSTON was in command of the Confederate troops in North Carolina, and anticipating greater resistance, he moved to bring his own scattered columns together.

March 13.
- JEFFERSON DAVIS signed the law authorizing black soldiers.

March 15.
- SHERMAN's army moved from Fayetteville toward Averasboro, N.C.

March 16.
- In the Battle of Averasboro, SHERMAN's left wing under Major General HENRY W. SLOCUM attacked the army of Confederate Lieutenant General WILLIAM HARDEE. HARDEE fell back toward Smithfield; his assignment had been to slow the Federal advance, and he moved to rejoin JOHNSTON's main force.

March 18.
- The Confederate Congress adjourned its session, despite a plea from JEFFERSON DAVIS to remain in session.
- Elements of JOHNSTON's army skirmished with SHERMAN's forces as they approached Bentonville, N.C.

March 19.
- The Battle of Bentonville was the last major engagement between armies during the Civil War. JOHNSTON's plan was to ambush the column commanded by HENRY SLOCUM. He blocked the road with BRAXTON BRAGG's small army, and when SLOCUM's men deployed to attack it, the forces of HARDEE and ALEXANDER STEWART assailed them in the flank. Though the Confederates achieved some initial success, Federal reinforcements soon turned the tide, and it was the Confederate army that had to give way. JOHNSTON himself called it a southern victory, but it had little impact on collapsing Confederate fortunes.

March 20.
- Federal cavalry commander GEORGE STONEMAN left with four thousand troopers on an extended raid through Tennessee, Virginia, and the Carolinas.

March 21.
- JOHNSTON, hemmed in on three sides by the growing Federal army, retreated northward from the Battlefield at Bentonville.

March 22.
- Union Major General JAMES HENRY WILSON began a cavalry raid through Alabama and Georgia, that included the capture of Selma, Alabama.
- SHERMAN ordered his army to concentrate on Goldsboro, N. C.

March 24.
- LEE prepared to try to break the Federal grip on Richmond and Petersburg by attacking a Federal strong point in the encircling line at Fort Stedman.
- LINCOLN, accompanied by his wife and son TAD, arrived by sea at Fort Monroe near Hampton Roads on another trip to the front. They then ascended the James River to Grant's supply base at City Point, Virginia.

March 25.
- Lee launched an all-out assault on Fort Stedman, one of the strong points in the Federal line, in the hope of breaking the siege. The attack was led by Major General JOHN B. GORDON and though it was successful in taking the fort, GORDON's outnumbered men could not hold it against a strong Federal counterattack. Worse, the Confederates lost four thousand men they could not afford, against Federal casualties of only 1,500.
- The failure of the assault exposed the weakness of Lee's army, and GRANT determined to apply pressure all along the line.

- In Alabama, a Federal army under EDWARD CANBY, closed in on the forts defending the city of Mobile.
- LINCOLN visited GRANT's headquarters, and Fort Stedman.

March 26.
- PHIL SHERIDAN's army crossed the James River and achieved a junction with GRANT.

March 27.
- LINCOLN met with GRANT and SHERMAN on board the RIVER QUEEN in Hampton Roads, Virginia. They talked for two days, planning the final phase of the war.

March 28.
- DAVID DIXON PORTER joined the conference on board the RIVER QUEEN.

March 29.
- There was heavy skirmishing south of Richmond as GRANT tried to move around LEE's right. A fight near Gravelly Run again exposed the weakness of LEE's lines.
- STONEMAN's cavalry raid continued; his troopers fought a skirmish near Wilkesboro, N.C.
- The USS OSAGE hits a "torpedo" or mine in the Blakely River, Alabama, and is sunk.
- LINCOLN remains at City Point, Virginia.

March 30.
- More skirmishing south of Petersburg at Gravelly Run and Hatcher's Run near Dinwiddie Court House. LEE sent GEORGE PICKETT and his own nephew FITZHUGH LEE to a crossroads called Five Forks to halt the Federal advance.
- The cavalry raid of JAMES WILSON continued in Alabama.

March 31.
- More battles occurred south of Petersburg: At Dinwiddie Court House, fifty thousand Union soldiers under SHERIDAN assailed ten thousand Confederates. The Confederate line held, but that night, PICKETT pulled back toward Five Forks.
- WILSON's cavalry wrecked the iron foundry at Montevallo, Alabama.

APRIL.

April 1.
- In the Battle of Five Forks, Federal infantry finally broke through the Confederate lines south of Petersburg. SHERIDAN believed that WARREN's V Corps had been tardy in the attack and relieved him of his command (WARREN was subsequently exonerated). Nevertheless, the assault was successful and forced LEE to plan an immediate evacuation of Richmond and Petersburg.
- SHERMAN continued his advance northward in North Carolina.
- In Alabama, WILSON pursued NATHAN BEDFORD FORREST's cavalry toward Selma.

April 2.
- The Confederate government evacuated Richmond.
- LEE's army evacuated the city, too, with the men marching westward toward Lynchburg.
- Confederate Secretary of the Navy STEPHEN MALLORY ordered the destruction of the James River Squadron and directed its men to join General LEE's army. The sailors were formed into a "naval brigade" commanded by Rear Admiral RAPHAEL SEMMES.

- In Alabama, WILSON's cavalry defeated FORREST's men in a series of small skirmishes and the Federals captured Selma.

April 3.
- Union troops entered Richmond. Regimental bands competed with one another to play various patriotic airs. The black residents of the city "danced and shouted" and hugged one another; the while citizens mostly stayed indoors.
- LEE's army continued to march westward, with elements of GRANT's army in pursuit.
- JEFFERSON DAVIS and his party headed south by rail to Danville, Virginia.

April 4.
- LINCOLN entered Richmond, walked its streets, and visited the Confederate White House where he briefly sat at JEFFERSON DAVIS's desk. During the visit, the former slaves joyfully welcomed him and they fell to their kneews. The President told them "That is not right. You must kneel to God only."
- LEE's retreating army skirmished with its pursuers at Amelia Court House.
- In Alabama, WILSON's cavalry occupied Tuscaloosa.

April 5.
- After a short rest, LEE's army continued west toward Appomattox.

April 6.
- In an engagement at Saylor's Creek, LEE's army demonstrated confusion and perhaps a collapse of morale as some eight thousand men surrendered. With perhaps sixteen thousand men left, LEE continued his westward retreat.

April 7.
- GRANT wrote to LEE inviting him to consider a capitulation. LEE was cautious in his reply asking GRANT what terms he would consider on the "occasion of its surrender."
- WILSON's cavalry skirmished with FORREST in Alabama.
- Tennessee ratified the Thirteenth Amendment.

April 8.
- LEE found Federal forces blocking the road west to Lynchburg. Surrounded on both flanks with a large army in close pursuit, LEE held a council of war. It was agreed that they would test the strength of the enemy line to the west to see if they could break out of the encirclement. If it was only cavalry to their front, they might still escape.

April 9.
- A force of Confederates attacked the Federal position west of Appomattox Court House, and were repulsed by Union infantry. LEE wrote to GRANT to request "a suspension of hostilities pending adjustment of the terms of the surrender of this army."
- GRANT and LEE met in the parlor of WILMER McLEAN's house at Appomattox and agreed to terms of surrender.

April 10.
- LINCOLN was serenaded by crowds of citizens in Washington. When a band asked him for his choice of music, he requested "Dixie."

April 11.
- JEFFERSON DAVIS arrived in Greensboro, North Carolina by rail.

- In Washington, LINCOLN addressed a cheering crowd, and suggested that the elective franchise might be extended to some Negroes, "the very intelligent" and those who had served in the army. Listening to him was the actor John Wilkes Booth, who was horrified by the thought of black voters, and vowed to "put him through."

April 12.

- Mobile, Alabama surrendered.

- WILSON's cavalry occupied Montgomery, Alabama.

- At Appomattox, there was a formal surrender ceremony as the Confederate troops lay down their arms.

- In Greensboro, DAVIS met with JOSEPH E. JOHNSTON and urged him to fight on, but JOHNSTON pressed him for authority to begin negotiations, and DAVIS agreed.

April 14.

- The same flag that Major ROBERT ANDERSON had lowered when he surrendered Fort Sumter four years earlier, was re-hoisted there during a formal ceremony in Charleston Harbor.

- ABRAHAM LINCOLN was fatally shot by John Wilkes Booth in Ford's Theater.

April 15.

- LINCOLN died at 7:20 A.M.

- ANDREW JOHNSON was sworn in as President.

- JEFFERSON DAVIS headed south from Greensboro on horseback with a small cavalry escort.

April 17.

- SHERMAN and JOHNSTON met at the Bennett House near Durham, N. C. to begin negotiations. SHERMAN informed JOHNSTON of LINCOLN's assassination. They discussed a surrender not merely of JOHNSTON's army, but of all Confederate armies.

- JEFFERSON DAVIS arrived at Salisbury, N.C.

April 18.

- SHERMAN and JOHNSTON sign an agreement ending the war; it was subsequently disavowed by the national government in Washington, which was still reeling from the news of LINCOLN's assassination.

April 21.

- LINCOLN's body began its journey from Washington to Springfield for burial. En route, there were mourning ceremonies in most northern cities.

April 24.

- SHERMAN learned that the government had disavowed his initial agreement and informed JOHNSTON that he will resume hostilities. JOHNSTON asked for another meeting at the Bennett House.

April 25.

- JOHN WILKES BOOTH, fleeing southward, stops at the farm of RICHARD H. GARRETT near Port Royal, Virginia.

April 26.

- SHERMAN and JOHNSTON met for the second time at the Bennett House, and this time JOHNSTON surrendered his army, which, in the interim, had all but evaporated.

- Federal cavalry find JOHN WILKES BOOTH hiding in the barn at the Garrett Farm. When he refused to surrender, Sergeant BOSTON CORBETT shot him. BOOTH died a few hours later.

MAY.

May 10.

- JEFFERSON DAVIS was captured by Federal cavalry near Irwinville, Georgia. Surprised in the middle of the night, he threw on a cloak in the dark as he ran from his tent. It turned out to be his wife's cloak, which led to stories later that he was caught wearing women's clothes.

May 23-24.

- Washington D.C. hosted a huge parade honoring the Grand Army of the Republic: soldiers from both the eastern and western armies who paraded through the streets of the national capital in a celebration of victory and peace.

May 26.

- General EDMUND KIRBY SMITH formally surrendered all Confederate armies west of the Mississippi River.

JULY.

July 7.

- The surviving convicted conspirators of the LINCOLN assassination, MARY SURRATT, LEWIS POWELL, DAVID HEROLD, and GEORGE ATZERODT were hanged in the Old Arsenal Penitentiary in Washington D.C.

NOVEMBER.

November 6.

- The CSS SHENANDOAH dropped anchor in Liverpool, England, after a round-the-world cruise and hauled down its flag. It was the last Confederate surrender of the war.

Index

Illustrations are indicated in bold.